T0179261

French Dictionary of
Information Technology

French Dictionary of Information Technology

T. R. Pyper

FRENCH/ENGLISH
ENGLISH/FRENCH

London and New York

First published 1989
by Routledge
2 Park Square, Milton Park, Abingdon, Oxon, OX14 4RN
270 Madison Ave, New York NY 10016

Reprinted 2002

Transferred to Digital Printing 2007

Routledge is an imprint of the Taylor & Francis Group

British Library Cataloguing in Publication Data

Pyper, T. R. (Terence Richard), 1939–
    French dictionary of information
    technology : French/English, English/French
    1. Information systems
    I. Title
    001.5

Library of Congress Cataloging in Publication Data

Pyper, T. R. (Terry L.), 1939–
    French dictionary of information technology,
French/English, English/French.

    1. Information technology—Dictionaries—French.
2. French language—Dictionaries—English.
3. Information technology—Dictionaries. 4. English
language—Dictionaries—French. I. Title.
TK5102.P97 1988 621.38   88–26366
ISBN 0–415–00244–3

Publisher's Note
The publisher has gone to great lengths to ensure the quality of this
reprint but points out that some imperfections in the original
may be apparent

CONTENTS

PREFACE

This dictionary grew out of the recent prodigious advances in telecommunications, largely made possible by the astonishing development of computer science and electronics over the past decade. The convergence of these disciplines under the banner of Information Technology has brought a vast stock of new vocabulary, whilst reviving much of the day-to-day vernacular from communications procedures of a less sophisticated age.

Yet the terminology of today is not always clearly defined, since the systems themselves are still evolving and there remains an overlapping vagueness between the various specialist fields. For instance, the French 'défaut' might be an engineering defect, a software error, or a hardware fault/failure/malfunction (even a 'bug' or a 'glitch' in the jargon of the initiated). The English 'pad' may be a digitizing tablet, an attenuator, a capacitor, a terminal on a printed circuit, a cluster of pushbuttons, a temporary storage area, a filler character, a satellite launch platform, or the acronym for a packet assembly-disassembly software routine.

For these reasons, the dictionary was originally designed to serve more as a thesaurus – a bran tub of diverse interpretive ideas – rather than a pure lexicon. Hence, no single entry should be regarded as exclusive or even necessarily correct in every context. Parsimony and preference were never guiding principles in its compilation (over 40 alternatives – note our avoidance of the word synonym – are given for the ubiquitous 'blocage' and a comparable number are offered for the versatile 'reprise'). The aim instead was to steer the translator's attention away from strict etymology and academic rigour in order to suggest fresh ways of looking at new or familiar words and constructions in a singularly articulate technical environment, rich in colloquialisms. (Consider, for instance, the 'hot potato network', 'all-seems-well bus', 'round robin hunting', 'robber bar', 'cycle stealing', 'don't-care gate', 'purple plague', 'number cruncher', 'crippled leapfrog test', 'hot slide-in', 'piggyback board', 'thin-route telephony' and so forth.)

Our only serious restriction was physical space. It was impossible, for example, to repeat entries for compound expressions under each of the key components. 'Marquage centralisé', rendered as 'end-to-end pathfinding', offers interesting variants for both elements; if it were possible to include all compound expressions with each significant element as the headword, this might greatly simplify the translator's burden. Fortunately, in this case the adjective merited an entry of its own but, generally speaking, it was impractical to allow a compound expression to appear more than once. Nor was it possible, with sufficient accuracy, to specify usage in particular fields (transmission, switching, programming, circuit tests, etc), except by giving examples to enable users to compare their own contextual setting.

At the outset, it was thought that the inclusion of parts of speech might further clutter the layout since it was assumed that the average user would certainly have more than an elementary knowledge of grammar; thus we preferred to illustrate gender by means of the adjectival form in compound expressions. However, adjectives such as 'électronique' do nothing to clarify the situation; in addition, more and more substantives are today used indiscriminately as both noun and adjective. Finally, it was decided that the annoyance of needing to refer to secondary sources for parts of speech might usefully be avoided.

Hyphens are inserted liberally in many English terms, partly to assist in pronunciation (re-entrant, anti-dazzle, de-icing and, in particular, 're-storing', i.e. storing again) but also to show the adjectival construction: call-forwarding tone, time-delay relay, log-on menu, etc. In practice, however, the hyphen is increasingly omitted today; indeed, artificially fused terms, such as 'timebase', 'speechpath' and 'multi-tasking', are now commonly accepted.

We have, in general, deprecated the use of anglicized French hybrids ('spouling' where 'impression différée' is quite adequate, or 'débogueur' where 'aide à la mise au point' – albeit protracted – explains the situation fully). Lately, though, certain expressions have imposed themselves ('bufférisation' instead of 'tamponnage'), whereas others simply cannot be divined ('taux de PIP' for 'plug-in-and-play') and, regrettably, these have had to be included. Similarly, we felt bound to highlight common French spelling errors based on pronunciation: 'papier cadrié' rather than ' . . . quadrillé', or 'cimblot' in mistake for 'simbleau' (a wholly forgivable error since the first seems more plausible).

Despite attempts to introduce a measure of consistency with regard to the orthography of proper nouns and their adjectival forms (Gaussian noise, Brownian motion of electrons, Boolean algebra, Morse code – but 'erlang' and 'baud'), contemporary usage would normally disregard such distinctions and the initial capital is frequently abandoned. This does, however, pose severe problems with respect to the use of registered trade marks, since in many cases the ostensible legal ownership is either not known or the trade mark is not actually protected. Otherwise they have passed into everyday language and therefore tend to lose the initial capital. We have indicated possible legal protection by assigning the expression [T.N.] for 'trade name', or its French equivalent [A.C.] for 'appellation commerciale'. Needless to say, the presence or absence of such designations in no way affects the legal status of registered trade marks.

English spelling throughout tends toward the mid-Atlantic persuasion, thus: '-ize' rather than '-ise' (allowing for the few exceptions, such as 'comprise' or 'televise', but without yielding to 'analyze'). 'Disk' is preferred to 'disc' – in fact, this is also the first choice of the authoritative English dictionaries; 'adaptor' instead of 'adapter', but 'multiplexer' rather than the American 'multiplexor'; 'program' when referring to computers – otherwise 'programme' for a radio or television broadcast, a schedule, time-table, plan or prospectus.

All abbreviations appear as separate headwords referring the user to the original expanded entry and are indicated in round brackets with the symbol v. (refer to). We have resisted the temptation to generate abbreviations in the target language where the source expression is often better known by its short form (PABX, EPROM, LSI, etc), although in certain cases the individual abbreviations are commonly encountered in both languages (for example, PCM in English and MIC in French). In most cases, abbreviations appear in upper case without full stops, although some which are not usually seen other than in lower case (c.c. for 'courant continu') or as a combination of upper and lower case (Ah for 'ampere-hour') are reproduced in the conventional form.

The entry structure has been kept as simple as possible. The first element, or headword, is emboldened ('**appel**') or, if the entry consists of more than one word, all of the elements are in bold type ('**appels en chaîne**'). The first element is followed immediately by an italicized abbreviation for the part of speech – see the list given on p. xii – which appears on the source side only (*n* for a noun in the English-French section, for example, or *m* for a noun of masculine gender in the reverse section: *f* for a feminine noun and so forth).

Parentheses (round brackets) are used to indicate: a) the context or an explanation: for example, under 'gravure' . . . 'printing (of film)'; b) usage: (math.) for 'mathematics', or (vern.) for 'vernacular'; c) an optional or alternative element of a compound expression: for example, 'modulation (d'amplitude) par variation de charge' means that the element in brackets may be omitted without changing the English translation 'pulse amplitude modulation'. Square brackets introduce a comment, such as [T.N.] for 'trade name', or [deprecated/déconseillé] for terms which, ideally, should be avoided. The abbreviation cf. (compare) is used occasionally to suggest a contrasting cross-reference. Reflexive verbs are simply indicated by (s') *after* the headword, in order to retain strict alphabetical sequence.

In multiple (nested) entries, the swung dash (~) indicates repetition of the headword, together with the following element or elements: for example, within the 'appel' cluster . . . '~ permanent false-start call'. The dotted swung dash ≐ stands for repetition of a common abbreviation (such as 'BA', 'PM', etc). Less frequently, the swung dash is followed by a vertical stroke to indicate a different part of speech for the headword: for example, '~| adj' to point out the adjectival usage of the noun 'aérien'.

Double quotation marks represent a word that may cause confusion in isolation, such as "over" (the 'ready-to-receive' cue during a voice transmission), or "handle" (the callsign of a citizen's band radio operator).

ACKNOWLEDGEMENTS

Very many people contributed, directly or indirectly, to the compilation of this dictionary and I would like to express my gratitude to those whose work or influence has been of outstanding importance.

Publisher Wendy Morris, of Routledge, has supported this venture with fortitude and extreme kindness from submission of the original manuscript. Her suggestions for improving the presentation and her experience in the field of lexicography have together helped to produce a far more authoritative work than would otherwise have been possible. Otto Vollnhals, of Siemens A.G. in Munich, has also played a major role in the preparation: his TEAM system – a highly versatile computer data bank – was used for the French-English reversal and sorting process, through to typesetting of the finished product. I am indebted to him for his willing collaboration throughout the lengthy proof-reading stage, his expertise and carefully reasoned approach to thorny linguistic problems and his friendship and generosity as a host.

I am fortunate to have enjoyed further intellectual, professional and personal support over many years in the form of stimulating discussions, guidance and direct assistance. My thanks go, in particular, to Gérald Gros, a close friend from my formative years and an important influence in nurturing my high esteem for the French people and their language. Olga Samilova, Bert Pockney, Lydia Saharova and Robert Lord of Surrey University were largely responsible for my enthusiasm and respect for the intricacies of linguistics and regional culture. Peter Frank and Mary McAuley of Essex University taught me the benefits and skills of research.

It is impossible to express adequate appreciation for the contribution made by many of my present and former colleagues and friends, therefore I shall simply record the names of some in the hope that they will understand: George Klokkos, J. T. Carter, Anastasios Malakis, François and Françoise Simonot, Malcolm Wirth and naval associates Jeffrey Binns, Malcolm Brightmore and Michael Hodgkiss. I also acknowledge the participation of Ian and Susan McDonald, who kindly allowed me free access to their word processing equipment during the early input stage of the dictionary, and the inspiration derived from my work as a translator with J. H. Goundry, Nat Minzly, Steven Simmons and John Flood-Paddock.

Probably one of the most exacting tasks in a project of this kind is that of typing, sorting and printing the original manuscript. This feat was performed with great accuracy, speed and patience by Elizabeth Barley. Without her assistance, this huge undertaking might not have been ready for publication for several more years. Teresa Burrell produced many pages of the first drafts and, again, this enabled me to hasten the progress of the final manuscript. I received much valuable help from Pat Hobby, whose knowledge of word processors (and the short cuts to a more efficient presentation) also served to lighten the chore.

Finally, I shall record my gratitude for the affectionate forbearance and encouragement of my wife, daughter and sons and, of course, my wider family. This book is dedicated to my granddaughter Lydie Méot.

ABBREVIATIONS

[A.C.]	appellation commerciale
adj	adjective/adjectif
adv	adverb/adverbe
cf.	compare/comparez
f	feminine/féminin
f ou adj	feminine noun or adjective/nom féminin ou adjectif
f pl	feminine plural noun/nom féminin pluriel
m	masculine/masculin
m ou adj	masculine noun or adjective/nom masculin ou adjectif
m ou f	masculine or feminine noun/noun masculin ou féminin
m pl	masculine plural noun/nom masculin pluriel
(math.)	mathematics/mathématique
n	noun/nom
n pl	noun plural/nom pluriel
s.	see (voir)
[T.N.]	trade name (proprietary mark)
(U.K.)	British/anglais britannique
(U.S.)	American/anglais américain
v	verb/verbe
v.	voir (see)
(vern.)	vernacular/vernaculaire

FRENCH/ENGLISH

A

à **vous** ready cue; "over"

abaissement *m* dip; drop; decrease; deceleration; diminution; lull; attenuation; sinking; depression; lowering; abatement; step-down

abandonner *v* abort; abandon; exit; quit; discard; renounce; drop; shelve; dump; clear

abaque *m* abacus; chart; nomogram; alignment chart

abat-son *m* acoustic chamber

aberrant *adj* spurious; deviant; runaway

aberration *f* aberration; drift; wander; ~ **chromatique** chromatic aberration; colour aberration; ~ **d'ouverture** aperture aberration; ~ **en coma** coma aberration; plumed/pear-shaped distortion (of CRT spot); ~ **optique** optical aberration; ~ **sphérique** spherical aberration; loss of definition

aberré *adj* runaway

abonné *m f* party; subscriber (line); station; user; extension (of PABX system); customer; member; consumer (of electricity); ~ **absent** (service d'a.) absent subscriber service; answering service; ~ **analogique** VF subscriber line; ~ **appelant** calling subscriber; caller; calling party; A-subscriber; source; ~ **appelant** source; calling party; caller; ~ **appelé** called party; B-subscriber; wanted party; ~ **avec priorité** subscriber (line) with priority; ~ **d'affaires** business (rate) subscriber; ~ **défaillant** bad payer; defaulter (subscriber account); ~ **demandé (DE)** called party; wanted party; B-subscriber; called/wanted subscriber; ~ **demandeur (DR)** caller; calling party; A-subscriber; ~ **discriminé** subscriber with special class of service; restricted access subscriber; special subscriber line; ~ **en faux appel** subscriber line with permanent line condition; ~ **essentiel** priority subscriber line; always-open (subscriber) line; ~ **isolé** disconnected subscriber; ~ **itinérant** roamer; roaming subscriber; ~ **libre** subscriber free; free subsriber; ~ **lointain** remote subscriber; distant(-end) subscriber; ~ **mobile** roaming subscriber; roamer; ~ **non sonné** no-bell station; ~ **numérique** digital line; PCM subscriber line; ~ **observé à l'arrivée (OBA)** terminating observed subscriber (line); ~ **observé par sondage (OBS)** subscriber (line) observed by sampling; ~ **occupé** subscriber busy; busy subscriber; ~ **ordinaire** residential subscriber; ~ **privilégié** (VIP) executive station; priority subscriber line; ~ **réclamant** faulty subscriber line; ~ **renvoyé temporaire** follow-me call forwarding service; ~ **résidentiel** residential (rate) subscriber; ~ **résilié** cancelled subscriber; ceased line; ~ **rural** rural subscriber; ~ **sans priorité** subscriber (line) without priority; ~ **sans taxe** charge-free subscriber; ~ **simple** individual subscriber; ordinary subscriber line; residential subscriber; ~ **spécialisé en arrivé (SPB)** denied-origination subscriber; ~ **spécialisé en départ (SPA)** denied-termination subscriber; ~ **sur circuit** trunk (circuit) subscriber; ~ **suspendu** temporarily-disconnected subscriber; ~ **télétaxé** subscriber with private meter; ~ **télex** telex subscriber; ~ **transféré** transferred subscriber; changed number intercept; ~ **utilisateur** party; subscriber; user

abonnement *m* subscriber account; subscription; standing charge; connection (fee); ~ **de nuit** midnight-line service; ~ **résilié** ceased line; withdrawn line; ~ **suspendu** line out of service; ~ **transféré** changed subscriber

abordable *adj* accessible

aboutir *v* (à) arrive (at); reach; terminate (at)

aboutissement *m* connect-through; termination; arrival; end-point; node

abrégé *adj* abbreviated; short

abréger *v* abbreviate; abstract; curtail; abridge

abréviation mnémotechnique mnemonic (code); key word

abri *m* container; housing; shelter

abrité à ventilation forcée totally enclosed; screened

abscisses et ordonnées coordinates

absence de blocage non-blocking; ~ **de terre** absence of ground; ~ **totale** completely devoid of

absorbeur d'ondes surge modifier; surge absorber

absorption *f* absorption; ~ **acoustique** acoustic absorption; ~ **atmosphérique** atmospheric absorption; ~ **aurorale** auroral absorption; ~ **avec déviation** deviation absorption; ~ **complète** black-out; ~ **de porteurs électrisés** absorption of charged particles; ~ **de résonance** resonance scattering; ~ **des aigus** high-frequency absorption; ~ **d'ondes électromagnétiques** electromagnetic wave absorption; ~ **extrinsèque** extrinsic absorption; ~ **intrinsèque** intrinsic absorption; ~ **ionosphérique** ionospheric absorption; ~ **ionosphérique à déviation de vitesse de groupe** deviation absorption; ~ **ionosphérique sans déviation de vitesse de groupe** non-deviation absorption; ~ **optique** optical absorption; ~ **par le sol** ground absorption; ~ **sans déviation** non-deviation absorption; ~ **troposphérique** atmospheric absorption; tropospheric absorption
ACC (v. amplificateur à champs croisés)
accéder (à) access; gain/obtain access (to); GET (op code)
accélérateur *m* accelerator; activator; throttle
accélération *f* acceleration; ~ **automatique** automatic speed control; ~ **de la retenue** high-speed carry; ~ **linéaire** acceleration
accélérer *v* expedite; hasten
accéléromètre *m* accelerometer
accentuation *f* boosting; emphasizing; peaking; heightening; pre-emphasis; accentuation; ~ **des hautes fréquences** high-frequency emphasis
acceptance optique optical acceptance
acceptation d'appel call accepted; ~ **de la sélection rapide** fast-select acceptance; ~ **de manœuvre** facility acceptance (tone)
accepteur *m* acceptor
accès *m* access; I/O port; availability; lead-in; terminal; dialling; approach; entry; accessibility; polling; interface; log-in; exchange termination; gateway; path; inlet; right-of-way; reading; opening (of file); ~ **à interurbain** direct distance dialling (DDD); standard trunk dialling (STD); ~ **à l'international automatique** direct outward dialling (DOD) on international calls; ~ **à un service de dictée centralisé** dial-dictation access; ~ **aléatoire** random access; ~ **aléatoire par clé** keyed random access; ~ **au faisceau réseau** trunk access; ~ **au réseau contrôlé** (par l'opérateur) controlled outward dialling; controlled trunk group access; trunk reservation; ~ **au réseau contrôlé par le PO** controlled outward dialling; ~ **automatique au réseau** pre-selection; ~ **aux accents et aux symboles spéciaux** single shift 2

(SS2); ~ **aux caractères** shift in (SI); ~ **aux symboles graphiques** shift out (SO); ~ **avec file d'attente** queued access; ~ **bidirectionnel** transceiver; ~ **commun** joint access; shared access; ~ **commuté** switched access; dial-up access; ~ **de sortie** output port; ~ **d'entrée** input port; inlet; entry point; ~ **direct** immediate access; direct access; random access; ~ **direct aux postes supplémentaires** direct inward dialling (DID); ~ **direct en mémoire** direct memory access (DMA); data break; cycle stealing; ~ **d'un réseau** one-port network; two-terminal network; ~ **en parallèle** parallel interface; ~ **en série** serial interface; ~ **imparfait** limited availability; restricted access; ~ **instantané** direct access; immediate access; random access; ~ **intempestif** unauthorized access; ~ **mémoire simultané** interleaving; ~ **mode canal (AMC)** channel mode access (CMA); ~ **multicritères** multi-aspect search; ~ **multiple** multiple access; ~ **multiple à répartition dans le temps (AMRT)** time-division multiple access (TDMA); ~ **multiple avec adresse par impulsions (AMAI)** pulse-address multiple access (PAMA); ~ **multiple avec assignation en fonction de la demande (AMAD)** demand-assignment multiple access (DAMA); ~ **multiple par différence de code** code-division multiple access (CDMA); ~ **multiple par étalement du spectre (AMES)** spread-spectrum multiple access (SSMA); ~ **multiple par répartition en fréquence (AMRF)** frequency-division multiple access (FDMA); ~ **par file d'attente** queued access; ~ **parfait** full availability; unrestricted access; ~ **pupitre manuel** manual console I/O port; ~ **rapide** fast access; ~ **sélectif** random access; polling; ~ **séquentiel** batch processing; serial access; ~ **séquentiel par clé** keyed sequential access; ~ **simple** single access; ~ **unilatéral** barred access
accesseur *m* link program; interface module
accessibilité partielle limited availability; restricted access; ~ **restreinte** limited availability; ~ **totale** full availability; unrestricted access
accessible *adj* accessible; retrievable; interfaceable; open; adj.; unencumbered; readily reached
accessoire *m* accessory; attachment
accidentel *adj* fortuitous; chance; occasional; random
accolade *f* brace; bracket
accompagnement *m* contact follow; ~ **moteur (aM)** motor protection (fuse type)

accord *m* resonance; matching; harmony; agreement; tuning; alignment; syntony; settlement; response; ~ **aigu** sharp tuning; ~ **aplati** broad tuning; ~ **approximatif** flat tuning; ~ **automatique** automatic tuning; ~ **commun** mutual consent; ~ **d'antenne** alignment input; aerial tuning; ~ **décalé** stagger tuning; ~ **d'émetteur** transmitter tuning; ~ **électronique** electronic tuning; ~ **fin** fine tuning; ~ **par réluctance permeability tuning; reluctance tuning;** ~ **parasite** stray resonance; spurious response; ~ **pointu** sharp tuning; ~ **précis** fine tuning; ~ **silencieux** aural null; dead space; squelch; ~ **thermique** thermal tuning

accordé *adj* tuned

accorder *v* tune; match; balance; set; select; coordinate; correlate

accordeur *m* tuner

accouplé *adj* coupled; ganged; mated

accouplement *m* clutch; coupling; ganging; ~ **mécanique** ganging

accoutumance *f* familiarity

accrochage *m* synchronization; latching; oscillation; ~ **bas** down-locking; ~ **de la tête** head crash; ~ **de phase** phase locking; phase sync; ~ **rentré** up-locking

accrocheur *m* latch (of connector); locking lever

accroissement *m* increment; increase; multiplication; ~ **du parc de lignes principales** increase in (number of) main subscriber lines

accroître *v* maximize

accueil *m* reception; host(ing); log-in; sign-on

accumètre *m* battery capacity indicator

accumulateur *m* arithmetic module; storage battery; secondary cell; register; ~ **à décalage** shift register; ~ **alcalin** alkaline accumulator; ~ **au plomb** lead-acid battery; ~ **cadmium-nickel** nickel-cadmium battery; ~ **déchargé** run-down battery; ~ **inversible** non-spill battery; ~ **stationnaire** (au plomb) stationary (lead acid) battery; ~ **tampon** buffer register

accusation *f* implication; diagnosis; potential malfunction; troubleshooting

accusé *m* (de réception) acknowledge signal; ~ **de réception (AR)** acknowledgement (ACK); advice note; ~ **de réception automatique** automatic acknowledgement; ~ **de réception de blocage** blocking acknowlegement; ~ **de réception de liaison de déblocage** unblocking acknowledgement; ~ **de réception de liaison de réserve prête** standby-ready acknowledgement; ~ **de réception négatif (NAK)** negative acknowledgement (NAK)

accuser réception acknowledge

acheminement *m* wiring; transport; forwarding; handling; conveyance; routing; traffic route; trunking; ~ (chemin logique) traffic routing (logical path); ~ **alternatif** alternate/overflow (least-cost) routing; ~ **avec débordement** alternative routing; least-cost routing; overflow routing; ~ **avec offre sur poste occupé** busy station override; ~ **de débordement** alternate/overflow (least-cost) routing; ~ **de messages** data routing; ~ **de secours** alternative routing; least-cost routing; back-up route; ~ **de transit** transit routing; tandem trunking; ~ **départ** outgoing routing (O/G); ~ **détourné** alternate routing; least-cost routing; ~ **direct** direct routing; ~ **du signal** signal routing; ~ **du trafic** traffic routing; ~ **erroné** mis-routing; ~ **hors hiérarchie** skip routing; ~ **immédiat** hot line; ~ **normal** normal routing; ~ **par voie détournée** alternate/overflow (least-cost) routing; ~ **premier choix** first-choice routing; ~ **sur abonné libre** call-forwarding to free subscriber; ~ **sur abonné occupé** call-forwarding to busy subscriber; ~ **sur voie de débordement** alternative routing; least-cost routing; ~ **sur voie secondaire** alternative routing; least-cost routing

acheminer *v* route; forward; carry

acheteur *m* buyer; vendee; end-user; purchaser

achever *v* complete

acier de décolletage free-cutting steel; ~ **doux** mild steel; ~ **dur** high-carbon steel; tough steel; ~ **galvanisé** (zinc-)electroplated steel; ~ **inoxydable** stainless steel; ~ **mécano-soudé** welded steel

acompte *m* instalment; prepayment; credit; advance

acoustique *adj* acoustic; sonic; aural; audio; sound

acquéreur *m* customer; vendee; purchaser; end-user; buyer

acquérir *v* acquire; gather; get; obtain; capture; retrieve; collect; establish

acquis *m* experience; expertise; background; track record

acquisition *f* input; entry; capture; collection; GET (function); pick-up; ~ **de données** data acquisition; logging; ~ **de la cible** target acquisition/pick-up; ~ **de satellite** satellite acquisition; satellite tracking; ~ **tout ou rien (TOR)** digital data capture; binary data capture

acquittement *m* cancel(lation); clear; clearance; discharge; acknowledgement; acquittal; time-out; ~ (des messages) message processing; ~ **d'interruption** interrupt timed-out

actif à l'état bas negative logic; low-level active; ~ **à l'état haut** positive logic; high-level active; ~ **(en) état bas** low-level active; active when low (negative logic)

actinique *adj* ultra-violet (UV)

action *f* action; motion; activity; response; step; function; service; operation; measure; ~ **dérivée** derivative action; ~ **différée** deferred action; delayed action; time lag; offset; ~ **directe** forward-acting; ~ **instantanée** non-delayed action; immediate response; ~ **tout ou rien** on-off action

actionné *adj* clocked

actionnement *m* activation; actuation

actionner *v* activate; actuate; trigger; trip; throw; press; depress; ~ **une boucle** instigate a loop

actionneur *m* actuator

activable *adj* on standby; ready; set; armed

activateur *m* accelerator (catalyst)

activation *f* initiation; enabling; ~ **de la porteuse par la parole** voice-activated carrier; ~ **d'une interruption** setting an interrupt; ~ **d'une partition** select current partition (SCP)

activer *v* enable

activité *f* activity; movement; operation; pursuit; business; affair; pre-occupation; ~ **du cristal** crystal activity

actualiser *v* up-date; streamline; up-grade

actualités *f pl* current affairs

actuel *adj* prevailing; existing; current; present

acuimètre *m* Q-meter

acuité auditive aural acuity

acyclique *adj* acyclic; aperiodic

adaptable *adj* (à) interfaceable; compatible; open-ended

adaptateur *m* adaptor; adapter; stub (of waveguide); extension; coupling; interface; ~ **à bande latérale unique** single-sideband adaptor; ~ **de données local (ADL)** local data adaptor (LDA); ~ **de jonction** interface adaptor; ~ **de ligne** line adaptor unit; matching stub; ~ **de signalisation** signalling adaptor; ~ **d'entrée-sortie** peripheral interface channel; I/O adaptor; ~ **d'impédance** impedance-matching transformer; ~ **d'indice** index-matching material; ~ **d'interface** data adaptor unit; ~ **mâle-femelle** gender changer; ~ **pour ligne longue** loop extender; long-line adaptor

adaptation *f* tuning; matching; interfacing; mating; integration; customizing; tailoring; coupling; accommodating; retrofit;

~ **d'antenne** aerial matching device; ~ **de la vitesse** buffering; ~ **de liaison série RS 232** serial interface (RS 232); ~ **de phase** phase matching; ~ **d'impédance** impedance matching; ~ **en delta** delta matching; ~ **incorrecte** mismatching; ~ **mémoire** memory interface; ~ **métamérique** metameric matching; ~ **sur la longueur de bande** bandwidth conditioning

adapté *adj* (à) oriented; terminated (in); bespoke

adapter *v* (à) cater for; match; suit

addeur *m* (= additionneur) adder

additif *m ou adj* add-on (equipment); top-up; admixture; ~ **aveugle** equipment for blind operator

addition *f* addition; add; logical sum; disjunction; union; ~ **accélérée** by-passed addition; ~ **d'amplification** amplification addition; ~ **destructive** destructive addition; ~ **en double longueur** double-length add; ~ **en double précision** double-length add; ~ **en puissance** power addition; ~ **en tension** voltage addition; ~ **horizontale** crossfooting; ~ **sans report** false add; ~ **sans retenue** Exclusive-Or (operation); symmetric difference

additionneur *m* (full) adder; three-input adder; digital adder; ~ **à deux entrées** two-input adder; ~ **à trois entrées** three-input adder; full adder; digital adder; ~ **complet** full (three-input) adder; digital adder; ~ **deux mots de 4 digits** four-bit binary full adder; ~ **élémentaire à deux entrées** half-adder; one-digit adder; ~ **en série** serial adder; ~ **parallèle/série** parallel-serial full adder; ~ **sans retenue** half-adder; one-digit adder

additionneur-soustracteur adder-subtractor

adduction directe direct connection

adhérence *f* key; grip; ~ **du revêtement** surface coating adhesion

adiabatique *adj* adiabatic

adjacent *adj* flanking; contiguous; adjacent; near; adjoining; neighbouring

adjonction *f* attachment; extra; addition; ~ **de lignes** addition of lines

adjudicataire *m ou f* successful tendering party

adjudication *f* award (of contract)

ADL (v. adaptateur de données local)

administrateur de base de données data base manager

administratif *adj* office

Administration (PTT) Administration; operating authority

admissible *adj* rated; allowable; permitted; acceptable; safe

admission *f* inlet
admittance *f* admittance; ~ **acoustique** acoustic admittance; ~ **caractéristique** characteristic admittance; surge admittance; ~ **de l'espace d'interaction** circuit-gap admittance; ~ **de réaction** feedback admittance; ~ **de transfert** transfer admittance; ~ **d'électrode** electrode admittance; ~ **d'entrée** driving-point admittance; ~ **d'ouverture** aperture admittance; ~ **effective de sortie** effective output admittance; ~ **effective d'entrée** effective input admittance; ~ **électronique de l'espace d'interaction** electronic gap admittance; ~ **en circuit ouvert** open-circuit admittance; ~ **en court circuit** short-circuit admittance; ~ **en espace libre** free-space admittance; ~ **mécanique** mechanical admittance
adopter *v* assume; acquire; adopt
adoucissage *m* deburring; buffing
adressage *m* addressing; selection; handshaking; ~ **à progression automatique** one-ahead addressing; ~ **absolu** absolute addressing; ~ **auto-relatif** self-relative addressing; ~ **différé** deferred addressing; ~ **direct** direct addressing; immediate addressing; ~ **en XY** X-Y addressing; ~ **implicite** default addressing; implied addressing; ~ **indirect** indirect addressing; deferred addressing; multi-level addressing; ~ **inhérent** inherent (hardware) addressing; ~ **multiple** multiple addressing; ~ **optimal** optimum addressing; ~ **par coordonnées** coordinate addressing; ~ **par indirection** indirect addressing; ~ **rapide** high-speed addressing; ~ **réel** absolute addressing; ~ **répétitif** repetitive addressing; ~ **virtuel** virtual addressing
adresse *f* address; address wire; bucket; location; address code; load point; entry point; ~ **de branchement** branch address; branchpoint; ~ **absolue** absolute address; actual address; direct address; first-level address; machine address; one-level address; specific address; ~ **auto-relative** self-relative address; ~ **blocage** halt address; ~ **calculée** synthetic address; generated address; ~ **complémentaire** second-level address; indirect address; ~ **d'aiguillage** branch address; ~ **d'appel** call address; station address; ~ **de base** home address; presumptive address; base address; start address; reference address; bias; ~ **de chaînage** link; return address; pointer; ~ **(de) début** base address; home address; start address; ~ **de début** base address; home (position); ~ **de décalage** offset (base) address; ~ **de destination**

destination address; ~ **de distribution** scanning address; ~ **de fin (de fichier)** end-of-file (EOF); ~ **de lancement** start address; entry point; ~ **de lecture** read address; ~ **de phase** instruction address; ~ **de rangement** home address; ~ **de réacheminement** redirection address; ~ **de recherche** seek address; ~ **de retour** return address; link address; ~ **d'écriture** write address; ~ **d'entrée** entry (point); entrance; ~ **d'espacement** relative address; displacement address; ~ **différée** deferred address; indirect address; ~ **d'implantation** loading address; memory location; base address; memory address; ~ **d'instruction** instruction address; ~ **directe** absolute address; direct address; first-level address; immediate address; zero-level address; home address; one-level address; ~ **domiciliaire** home address; absolute address; ~ **d'opérande** operand address; ~ **d'origine** base address; presumptive address; initial address; program origin; source; ~ **doublement indexée** double-indexed address; ~ **effective** effective address; absolute address; ~ **électrique** absolute address; ~ **fictive** dummy address; ~ **flottante** floating address; relative address; symbolic address; ~ **fonctionnelle (AF)** hardware address; absolute address; ~ **gauche** high-order address; ~ **géographique** physical address (NOT hardware address); ~ **immédiate** immediate (zero-level) address; ~ **implicite** implicit address; default address; ~ **indexée** indexed address; variable address; ~ **indirecte** multi-level address; indirect address; N-level address; second-level address; ~ **logicielle** software address; ~ **logicielle** software address; ~ **logique** program address; base address; pointer; file name and record; ~ **modifiée** effective address; absolute address; ~ **ouverte** open address; ~ **physique** track (of disk); sector; side and volume; ~ **primitive** origin; presumptive address; float factor; base address; absolute address; reference address; ~ **provisoire** tentative address; ~ **réelle** absolute address; effective address; ~ **relative** relative address; floating address; ~ **secteur** half-word address; ~ **source** source address; ~ **spécifique** absolute address; ~ **symbolique** floating address; relative address; symbolic address; ~ **synthétique** generated address; ~ **translatable** relocatable address; ~ **virtuelle** virtual address; immediate address; real-time address
adresse-base reference address; home address

adresse-machine absolute address; hardware address
adresse-mémoire store address; memory address
adresser *v* address; select; ~ (s') handshake
adresses multiples multi-address calling
adverse *adj* inclement; deleterious
AEN (v. affaiblissement équivalent pour la netteté)
aérer *v* fan; ventilate; space out; cool
aérien *m* aerial (array); ~ *adj* aerial; overhead
aérolique *adj* aerodynamic
aérotransportable *adj* air-lifted
AF (v. adresse fonctionnelle)
affaiblir *v* (s') fade; attenuate; decay
affaiblissement *m* attenuation; loss; weakening; decay; de-emphasis; muting; fading; ~ **à la réception** receive loss; ~ **à travers d'un relais hertzien** attenuation over a section of radio link; ~ **actif d'équilibrage** active balance return loss; ~ **aller-retour** loop echo path loss; ~ **apériodique** aperiodic damping; ~ **apparent** apparent attenuation; ~ **atmosphérique** atmospheric loss; ~ **au niveau des échos fixes** clutter attenuation; ~ **composite** effective attenuation; overall loss; composite loss; ~ **copolaire** co-polar loss; ~ **d'absorption** absorption loss; absorption fading; ~ **d'adaptation** balance return loss; return loss; ~ **d'adaptation pour la stabilité** stability return loss (SRL); ~ **d'adaptation pour l'écho** echo return loss (ERL); ~ **dans la bande** in-band attenuation; ~ **dans le mode commun** common mode rejection ratio (CMRR); ~ **de blocage** blocking attenuation; stop-band attenuation; suppression loss; ~ **de boucle** loop attenuation; ~ **de branchement** branch-off attenuation; ~ **de canaux adjacents** adjacent channel attenuation; ~ **de coordination** co-ordination loss; ~ **de diffraction** diffraction attenuation; ~ **de distorsion harmonique d'ordre n** n^{th} order harmonic distortion; ~ **de distorsion harmonique totale** total harmonic ratio; ~ **de la bande latérale** sideband attenuation; ~ **de la bande passante** band-pass attenuation; band-pass loss; ~ **de l'écho** echo attenuation; active return loss; ~ **de ligne** line attenuation; ~ **de l'onde réfléchie sur les irrégularités** regularity return loss; ~ **de propagation** propagation loss; path attenuation; ~ **de référence** reference loss; ~ **de référence par unité de longueur** volume loss per unit length; ~ **de régularité** structural return loss (SRL); regularity return loss; ~ **de résistance** resistance attenuation; ~ **de symétrie** balance return

loss; longitudinal conversion loss (LCL); ~ **de transmission** transmission loss; ~ **de traversée** (end-to-end) insertion loss; ~ **d'écho de l'impulsion de mesure** pulse echo attenuation; ~ **d'élimination de bande** stopband attenuation; balance; ~ **d'équilibrage** return loss (RL); balance return loss; ~ **des courants d'écho** active (balance) return loss; ~ **des courants réfléchis** return loss; ~ **diaphonique** crosstalk attenuation; ~ **différentiel** differential attenuation; ~ **d'insertion** insertion loss; ~ **d'interaction** interaction loss; ~ **dû à la chute de neige** snowfall attenuation; ~ **dû à la pluie** rainfall attenuation; ~ **dû à l'absorption** absorption loss; absorption fading; ~ **dû à une dérivation** bridging loss; ~ **dû aux hydrométéores** hydrometeor fading; ~ **dû aux scintillations** scintillation fading; ~ **du câble** cable attenuation; ~ **du récepteur** receiver attenuation; ~ **du signal** signal loss; signal attenuation; ~ **du suppresseur d'écho** blocking attenuation; ~ **d'un termineur** term-set attenuation; ~ **d'une impulsion** pulse decay; ~ **effectif** effective loss; overall loss; ~ **en espace libre** free-space loss; free-space attenuation; ~ **équivalent** equivalent attenuation; ~ **équivalent pour la netteté (AEN)** equivalent articulation loss; articulation reference equivalent; ~ **évalué** ascertained attenuation; ~ **idéal de propagation** basic path attenuation; ~ **itératif** iterative attenuation coefficient; ~ **linéique** attenuation coefficient; attenuation per unit length; ~ **maximal** attenuation peak; ~ **net** overall loss; net loss; ~ **net de commutation** net switching loss (NSL); ~ **nominal entre extrémités virtuelles du circuit à quatre fils** nominal transmission loss of the four-wire circuit between virtual switching points; ~ **non sélectif** non-selective attenuation; ~ **non uniforme** shaped loss; ~ **par couplage de polarisation** polarization-coupling loss; ~ **par couplage entre sites** inter-site coupling loss; ~ **par défaut d'adaptation** mismatch loss; ~ **par diffraction** diffraction loss; ~ **par dissipation** dissipative attenuation; ~ **paradiaphonique** near-end crosstalk attenuation; ~ **passif d'équilibrage** passive (balance) return loss; ~ **réel** true attenuation; actual measured loss (AML); ~ **relatif en émission** transmission reference equivalent; ~ **résultant** composite attenuation; overall (net) loss; ~ **secret** hidden loss; ~ **sélectif** selective attenuation; selective fading; differential gain control; ~ **sélectif en fréquence** frequency selective attenuation; ~ **sur image** image attenuation coefficient; image attenuation constant; ~ **sur impédances conjuguées** conjugate attenuation coefficient; ~ **sur le trajet** path loss; ~ **télédiaphonique** far-end crosstalk attenuation; ~ **transductique** transducer loss; ~ **uniforme** flat loss

affaiblisseur *m* pad; attenuation pad; attenuator; de-emphasizer; ~ **à absorption** absorptive attenuator; resistive attenuator; ~ **à cloison longitudinale** vane attenuator; ~ **à coupure** cut-off attenuator; ~ **à disque** disk attenuator; ~ **à guillotine** flap attenuator; ~ **à lame tournante** flap/guillotine attenuator; ~ **à lamelle** strip attenuator; ~ **à piston** piston attenuator; plunger attenuator; ~ **d'antenne** aerial attenuator; ~ **de sortie** output attenuator; ~ **fixe** fixed attenuator; pad; ~ **non réciproque** isolator; ~ **réactif** reactive attenuator; ~ **réglable** variable attenuator; ~ **résistif** absorptive attenuator; resistive attenuator; ~ **rotatif** rotary attenuator; ~ **variable** variable attenuator

affaire *f* contract; business; undertaking; ~ **en participation** joint venture

affectable *adj* assignable

affectation *f* allocation; assignment; allotment; mapping; ~ **adaptable de voies** adaptive channel allocation; ~ **de mémoire** storage allocation; memory mapping; ~ **des fenêtres aux partitions** map partition onto window (MPW); ~ **des résultats** attribution of profits; ~ **des voies** channel allocation; bus grant; ~ **directe** direct allocation; ~ **dynamique** dynamic allocation; ~ **dynamique adaptable des voies** adaptive channel allocation; ~ **dynamique de mémoire** dynamic storage allocation; ~ **facultative** optional assignment; ~ **fixe** direct allocation

affecter *v* allocate; assign; allot; ascribe; deploy; detail; distribute; confer; grant; map

affichable *adj* printable; display

affichage *m* display; readout; input; loading; tracking; soft copy; selection; setting; stimulus; ~ **à diodes (électroluminescentes)** LED display; ~ **de paramètres** control message display; ~ **d'un menu** menu display; ~ **dynamique** moving display; ~ **écran** screen display; ~ **écran** menu display; soft copy; ~ **en attente** conceal display; ~ **non rémanent** volatile display; ~ **numérique** digital display; ~ **superposé** head-up display

affiche murale wall chart

affiché *adj* **en complément à deux** twos complemented

afficher *v* display; enter; set; preset; post; show; load; dial; indicate; rotate; map

afficheur *m* display panel; thumbwheel switch; LED display; lamp panel; ~ **à cristaux liquides** liquid crystal display (LCD); ~ **de consigne** set value adjuster; ~ **électroluminescent** light-emitting diode (LED); ~ **monté** indicator on

afficheurs numériques digital indicators; display panel

affiné *adj* enhanced; refined

affirme *adj* true

affleurant *adj* inset; flush-mounted; recessed

affleuré *adj* levelled off; flush; recessed

affluent *m ou adj* tributary; feeder

afflux *m* surge (of current)

affolement *m* thrashing

affût *m* turret

affûtage du minimum du relèvement sharpening of the minimum

agence commerciale (telephone) sales

agencé *adj* fitted

agencement *m* organization; layout; configuration

agenda *m* schedule; agenda; diary; repertory dialler

agent *m* operative; representative; official; engineer; agent; craftsperson; ~ **commercial** sales representative; salesman; ~ **de gravure** etchant; ~ **de maîtrise** foreman; ~ **de service** duty engineer; ~ **réfrigérant** coolant; heat-transfer agent; ~ **refroidissant** heat-carrying agent; ~ **technique** laboratory technician

aggloméré *m* chipboard; *adj* compact; sintered

aggravation *f* upgrading (of alarm condition)

agio m. finance charge (rate)

AGL (v. atelier de génie logiciel)

agrafe *f* clip; staple; fastener; clasp; jumper

agrandissement cathodique blowback

agréé *adj* approved; licensed

agrégat de scalaires scalar group

agréger *v* collate

agrément *m* (type) approval; authorization; licence; convenience

agressif *adj* hostile

agression visuelle eyestrain

agressivité *f* degree of attack (of cables); corrosion

AHC (v. appel à l'heure chargée)

aide *f* back-up; facility; tool; help function; support; aid

AIDE HELP (key)

aide à la navigation navigation aid; ~ **à l'opérateur** help function

aides de programmation software

aigrette *f* brush discharge; light beam; corona

aigu *adj* high-pitched; treble; sharp

aiguillage *m* branch; switchpoint; switching; logging; direction; routing; segregation; jump; gating; forwarding; splitting; multiplexing; program switching; referring; device configuration; **~ (de paquets)** switch (of packet switching system); **~ des appels** call forwarding; **~ des messages système** set log; **~ spatial** space(-division) switching; **~ sur groupements** split groups

aiguille *f* stylus; pointer; indicator; needle; pin; marker; cursor; index; rod; **~ astatique** astatic needle; **~ de tri** picker; sorter

aiguillé *adj* forwarded; gated; channelled; referred

aiguiller *v* route; control; switch; direct; forward; despatch; connect; gate; multiplex; channel; refer; **~ sur le bus de lecture** gate onto read bus

aiguilleur *m* alteration switch; selector; sampler; sense switch; **~ du ciel** air-traffic controller

ailette *f* fin; tab (of heat sink); **~ de refroidissement** heat sink; cooling vane

aimant *m* magnet; **~ de cadrage** scanning coil; **~ de concentration** focussing magnet; **~ de progression** stepping magnet; **~ d'entraînement** feed magnet; **~ interrupteur d'entraînement** feed suppression magnet; **~ naturel** natural magnet; **~ permanent** permanent magnet; **~ torique** annular magnet

aimantation *f* magnetization

ainsi *adv* indeed; consequently; hence; thus

air insufflé drawn-in air; blown-in air

aire *f* **de confusion** confusion area; **~ de fonctionnement de sécurité** safe operating area (S.O.A.); **~ de lecture** reading band; (scanned) coverage; **~ de réception** parking area; **~ de rerayonnement** scattering cross-section; **~ de transit** overlay area; overlay zone; **~ d'ouverture** aperture area; **~ exploré** scanned area; **~ plane** hard standing; apron

aisé *adj* smooth; comfortable; trouble-free

ajour *m* hole; aperture; orifice; slot; cut-out

ajouré *adj* pierced; drilled; perforated; punched; louvred

ajourement *m* cut-out

ajourner *v* defer; postpone

ajouter *v* append

ajustage *m* machining; tailoring; trimming; fit; calibration; correction; **~ d'amplitude** amplitude adjustment; **~ de la linéarité** linearity correction; **~ de niveau** level adjustment; **~ de phase** phase adjustment; **~ de résistance** trimming; **~ serré** shrink fit

ajustement *m* adjustment; fitting; further

elaboration (of data); setting; fit; **~ glissant** sliding fit; **~ immobile** interference fit; **~ mobile** clearence fit; **~ serré** tight fit; close fit; shrink fit

alarme *f* alarm; **~ de groupe** group alarm; minor carrier alarm; **~ différée** non-urgent alarm; delayed alarm; **~ effraction** intruder alarm; burglar alarm; **~ immédiate** prompt alarm; urgent alarm; **~ intervention différée** non-urgent alarm; delayed action alarm; **~ intervention immédiate** urgent alarm; prompt alarm; immediate action alarm; **~ sans intervention** non-urgent alarm; **~ sonore** audible alarm; klaxon; tone burst; buzzer; hoot stop; **~ temporisée** delayed-action alarm; **~ urgente** major alarm; urgent alarm; **~ visuelle** hashing alarm; visual alarm

albédo *m* albedo; directional reflectance; **~ de la terre** earth's albedo

album *m* specifications

alcool *m* spirit; **~ dénaturé** methylated spirits; denatured alcohol; **~ méthylique** methanol; methylated spirits; methyl alcohol; **~ méthylique dioxane** methanol dioxane

aléa *m* unusual circumstance; fault; discrepancy; **~ de fonctionnement** malfunction; technical hitch; discrepancy; failure

aléatoire *adj* random; arbitrary; ad lib; spontaneous; stochastic; haphazard

alerte *f* **avancée** distant early warning; **~ avancée à microondes** microwave early warning (MEW)

algèbre *f* **booléenne** Boolean algebra; Boolean calculus/logic; **~ de Boole** (v. algèbre booléenne); **~ des circuits** switching algebra

algébrique *adj* algebraic

algorithme *m* algorithm; model; **~ complexe** complex algorithm; **~ DAMIER-DAMIER** checkerboard algorithm; chessboard configuration; **~ d'assignation** assignment algorithm; **~ de conversion** hashing; hash addressing

algorithmique *adj* algorithmic; procedural; step-by-step problem-solving

alibiphone *m* telephone-answering machine

aligné *adj* bounded; aligned

alignement *m* array; alignment; registration; line-up; clamping; collimation; compliance; conformity; boundary definition; **~ de caractères** character alignment; **~ de crête** peaking; **~ de message** message alignment; **~ de trame** frame alignment; **~ des trames sémaphores** signal unit alignment; **~ d'octet** byte alignment; **~ du faisceau** beam alignment; **~ du niveau du noir** black level clamping; **~ d'un circuit**

clamping; alignment; ~ **initial** initial alignment; ~ **sur les fonds** amplitude clipping (of sync pulse separation); ~ **sur l'octet** byte alignment; ~ **sur norme** compliance with standard; ~ **vidéo** video clamp

aligneur *m* aligner (digroup terminal); tracking device

alimentation *f* power supply (unit); power feed; power distribution; power pack; ~ **à découpage** switch-mode power supply; ~ **à la base de l'antenne** end feed; ~ **anodique** anode supply; ~ **axiale** vertex feed; ~ **colonne par colonne** end-wise feed; face-down feed; serial feed; ~ **de la ligne** power feed; ~ **de référence** reference supply; ~ **de secteur** mains supply; ~ **double** split power supply; ~ **en cartes perforées** card feed; ~ **en courant** current source; ~ **en énergie** power supply; power feed; ~ **en extrémité** end-feed; ~ **en haute tension** HT supply; high-voltage supply; ~ **en papier** form feed (FF); ~ **en parallèle** parallel feed; shunt feed; ~ **en polarisation circulaire** circularly-polarized feed; ~ **en tonalités** tone feed; ~ **excentrée** offset-fed; ~ **feuille à feuille** automatic sheet feed (ASF); ~ **focale** focal-fed; ~ **frontale** front-fed; ~ **latérale** side-fed; ~ **médiane** centre-fed; ~ **microphonique** microphone current; ~ **par fentes** Cutler feed; ~ **par le secteur** mains-powered; ~ **par pile** battery-powered; ~ **plaque** anode feed; anode supply; ~ **secourue** uninterruptible power supply (UPS); ~ **secteur** mains (power) supply; ~ **séparée** separately supplied; self-sufficient; ~ **siamoise** split power supply; symmetrical power supply; ~ **stabilisée** regulated power supply; stabilized supply; ~ **symétrique** (v. alimentation siamoise); ~ **symétrique d'antenne** balanced feed; ~ **traversière** rear-fed

alimenter *v* drive; feed; supply; energize; load; ~ **en énergie** power (up)

alimenteur *m* feed junctor

alinéa *m* subsection; clause; paragraph; indent

allège *f* daïs; parapet

allégé *adj* reduced; partial; limited; short

allègement *m* relief

aller-retour reciprocating (motion); to-and-fro; trade-off; give-and-take; round trip; turnaround

alliage corroyé wrought alloy; ~ **de transformation** wrought alloy

allocateur *m* bus controller

allocation de temps time slicing; ~ **dynamique** dynamic allocation

allocution du président chairman's address

allongement *m* extension (of file); stretching; ~ **à la rupture** elongation at rupture; ductility; ~ **à la traction** stretch

allotissement *m* allotment; ~ **de fréquences** frequency allotment

allouer *v* assign

allumage *m* image; illumination; firing; ignition; ~ **en retour** arc-back; backfire

allumé fixe 'on' steady (lamp)

allumer *v* light (up); turn on; switch on; ignite; fire; start; ~ **(s')** come on; glow; light (up); ignite

allumeur *m* starter

allure *f* trend; rate; speed; pace; tempo; state; characteristic

alphabet *m* alphabet; code; ~ **à cinq éléments** five-unit code; five-unit alphabet; ~ **à cinq unités** (v. alphabet à cinq éléments); ~ **à sept moments** seven-unit code/alphabet; ~ **télégraphique** telegraph alphabet/code; ~ **télégraphique international** international telegraph alphabet

alphabétique *adj* alphabetic(al)

alphanumérique *adj* alphanumeric; alphameric

altérable *adj* volatile

altération *f* garbling; scrambling; mutilation

altérer *v* deform; impair; corrupt; mutilate; adversely affect; garble; scramble; destroy; damage

alternance *f* (half)cycle; flip-flop; toggling; half-wave; ping-pong; ~ **de conduction** forward-biasing pulse (cycle); ~ **des 0 et 1** marching ones and zeros

alternat *m* indicator; ~ **unidirectionnel** simplex (operation)

alternateur *m* alternator; AC generator; ~ **à haute fréquence** high-frequency alternator; ~ **de parc** ground supply (alternator); ~ **hétéropolaire** heteropolar alternator; ~ **homopolaire** homopolar alternator; ~ **synchrone** synchronous alternator; ~ **tachymétrique** tachogenerator

alternatif *adj* reciprocating; alternating; pulsed

alterné *adj* staggered; varying; interspersed; reverse

alternistor *m* thyristor communicating circuit

alternostat *m* variable autotransformer; compensator

altimètre *m* **radioélectrique** terrain clearance indicator; altimeter

altitude *f* **d'orbite** orbital altitude; orbital height

alumine *f* alumina (aluminium oxide)

aluminium brossé spun aluminium; brushed aluminium; satinized; ~ **satinisé** satin-ano-

dized aluminium
alvéolaire adj cellular
alvéole m ou f shelf; subrack; crate; cage; bush; well; recess; plug; inset; receptacle; hole; cavity; socket; compartment; drawer; partition; nest; (cable) duct; ~ **nu** unwired subrack
aM (v. accompagnement moteur)
AMAD (v. accès multiple avec assignation en fonction de la demande)
AMAI (v. accès multiple avec adresse par impulsions)
amateur de radio radio ham; home amateur
ambiance f format; ~ **du laboratoire** laboratory ambient temperature
AMC (v. accès mode canal)
âme f core; conductor; ~ **centrale** central strength member
amélioration du minimum zero clearing; minimum clearing; ~ **du zéro** (v. amélioration du minimum)
améliorer v enhance; upgrade; improve; intensify
amenage m feed; transport; conveyance
aménagement m format; housekeeping; layout; disposition; refurbishment
aménagements futurs future expansion; development
amenée f source; duct; lead; inlet; supply
amener v (dans) feed (into)
AMES (v. accès multiple par étalement du spectre)
amiante m asbestos
amont (en ~) backward; upward; up-line; above; tail; upstream; input side; source side; upside; called end; incoming side/end; before; mains end; inlet side; astern; line (side); driving; preceding; GO side
amorçage m singing; firing; triggering; turn-on; ignition; arc-over; spark-over; ~ **basse fréquence** motorboating; ~ **BF** (v. amorçage basse fréquence); ~ **d'oscillations** singing; ~ **d'un parafoudre** sparkover of a lightning conductor; ~ **dynamique** dynamic firing; ~ **statique** static firing
amorce f bootstrap; (tape) leader; fuse; mark; ~ **de** incipient; ~ **de rupture** incision
amorcer v initiate; prime; energize; arc; strike; kick; start; fire; engage; whistle (of circuit); sing; build up (of charge)
amorti adj damped; decayed; choked; cushioned; quenched; muffled
amortir les investisssements recoup investments
amortissement m damping; quenching; depreciation; decay; ~ **acoustique** acoustic damping; ~ **critique** critical damping
amortisseur m resilient mounting; damper;

baffle; arrester; absorber; ~ **de chocs acoustiques** acoustic shock absorber
amovible adj removable; non-resident; detachable; disk-resident; overlay; relocatable; portable; plug-in; erasable; computer-compatible
ampère-heure m ampere-hour (Ah)
ampèreheuremètre m ampere-hour meter
ampèremètre m ammeter; ~ **à cadre mobile** moving-coil ammeter; ~ **à thermocouple** thermocouple ammeter; ~ **d'induction** induction ammeter; ~ **enregistreur** recording ammeter; ~ **thermique** hot-wire ammeter
ampère-tour m ampere-turn (a.t.)
amplificateur m amplifier; driver; booster; repeater; emphasizer; magnifier; ~ **à accords décalés** stagger-tuned amplifier; ~ **à amplification constante** stabilized amplifier; ~ **à anode à la masse** grounded-anode amplifier; ~ **à atténuation décalée** stagger-damped amplifier; ~ **à bande étroite** narrow-band amplifier; ~ **à bande large** broadband amplifier; ~ **à basse fréquence** audio(-frequency) amplifier; ~ **à bruit** noise amplifier; ~ **à chaîne** cascade amplifier; ~ **à champs croisés (ACC)** crossed-field amplifier (CFA); ~ **à charge cathodique** cathode amplifier; ~ **à compensation de dérive** drift-corrected amplifier; ~ **à condensateur vibrant** vibrating reed amplifier; contact-modulated amplifier; ~ **à contre-réaction** bootstrap amplifier; degenerative (negative-feedback) amplifier; ~ **à correction de dérive** (v. amplificateur à compensation de dérive); ~ **à couplage direct** direct-coupled amplifier; ~ **à découpage** chopper-stabilized amplifier; ~ **à deux accords** double-tuned amplifier; ~ **à deux étages** two-stage amplifier; ~ **à deux faisceaux** double-stream amplifier (of TWT); ~ **à deux voies** two-channel amplifier; ~ **à élément ferro-électrique** dielectric amplifier; ~ **à faible bruit** low-noise amplifier (LNA); ~ **à grille à la masse** grounded-grid amplifier; ~ **à haute fréquence** radio-frequency amplifier; ~ **à haute impédance d'entrée** high-input impedance amplifier; ~ **à impédance** choke-coupled amplifier; ~ **à interrupteur** contact-modulated amplifier; chopper amplifier; ~ **à large bande** broadband amplifier; wideband amplifier; ~ **à l'émission** amplifying telephone handset; faint speech amplifier; ~ **à modulation de vitesse** velocity-modulated amplifier; ~ **à ondes progressives** travelling-wave amplifier; ~ **à paroi ondulée** rippled-wall amplifier; ~ **à**

réaction stabilized-feedback amplifier; ~ à **répartition** distributed amplifier; transmission-line amplifier; ~ à **transformateur** transformer-coupled amplifier; ~ à **transistor bipolaire** bipolar-transistor amplifier; ~ à **trois états, huit bascules** octal tri-state buffer/latches; ~ à **tube** vaccum-tube amplifier; ~ **accordable** tuned amplifier; ~ **aiguillage d'adresses** buffer/address multiplexer; ~ **asymétrique** single-ended amplifier; ~ **avec cathode à la masse** grounded-cathode amplifier; ~ **avec grille à la masse** grounded-grid amplifier; ~ **basse fréquence** (v. amplificateur à basse fréquence); ~ **batterie** battery amplifier; ~ **BF** (v. amplificateur à basse fréquence); ~ **cathodique** cathode follower; ~ **chaîne** cascade amplifier; ~ **compensé** push-pull (balanced) amplifier; ~ **conformateur de signaux** signal-shaping amplifier; ~ **contre-réactionné** feedback-stabilized amplifier; ~ **correcteur** correcting amplifier; equalizing amplifier; ~ **d'antenne** aerial amplifier; ~ **d'asservissement** servo-amplifier circuit; ~ **de bande** band amplifier; ~ **de bande de base** baseband amplifier; ~ **de boucle** null circuit; ~ **de bus** bus driver; ~ **de canal** channel amplifier; ~ **de courant continu** DC amplifier; direct current amplifier; ~ **de déviation** deflection amplifier; ~ **de distribution** distribution amplifier; ~ **de groupe** group amplifier; ~ **de lecture** read amplifier; ~ **de l'électromètre** electrometer amplifier; ~ **de ligne** line amplifier; line driver; bus driver; ~ **de mesure** instrumentation amplifier; ~ **de modulation** speech amplifier; ~ **de puissance** high power amplifier (HPA); booster amplifier; ~ **de puissance à klystron** klystron power amplifier; ~ **de puissance à TOP** TWT power amplifier; ~ **de puissance de l'oscillateur pilote** master oscillator power amplifier (MOPA); ~ **de rapport** ratio amplifier; ~ **de réception** receiving amplifier; receive amplifier; ~ **de seuil** step-down (inverted) amplifier; ~ **de signal** signal amplifier; ~ **de sonorisation** public-address amplifier; ~ **de sortie** output amplifier; final amplifier; ~ **décalé** stagger-tuned amplifier; ~ **d'écart** dual op amp; ~ **d'écoute** monitoring amplifier; ~ **d'écriture** digit driver; write buffer; ~ **d'émission** send(ing)/transmitting amplifier; ~ **d'entrée** input amplifier; ~ **déphaseur** seesaw (paraphase) amplifier; ~ **d'erreur** error amplifier; ~ **d'exploration** scanning amplifier; ~ **différentiel** differential amplifier; ~ **d'impulsions** pulse amplifier; ~ **d'isole-**

ment isolation amplifier; buffer; ~ **du courant différentiel** differential-current amplifier; ~ **du signal d'appel** call amplifier; ~ **écrêteur** chopper-stabilized amplifier; ~ **en bande X** X-band amplifier; ~ **en cascade** cascade amplifier; multi-stage amplifier; ~ **final** output/final amplifier; ~ **fonctionnel** operational amplifier; ~ **intermédiaire** buffer amplifier; ~ **inverseur** inverting amplifier; ~ **limiteur** clipper amplifier; ~ **limiteur de crêtes** peak-limiting amplifier; ~ **linéaire** linear amplifier; ~ **logarithmique** logarithmic amplifier; ~ **logique** logic amplifier; ~ **modulé** modulated amplifier; ~ **non inverseur** non-inverting amplifier; ~ **normaliseur** pulse shaper; ~ **paramétrique** parametric amplifier (paramp); variable reactance amplifier; mavar (mixed/modulated amplification by variable reactance); ~ **passe-bande** band-pass amplifier; ~ **push-pull** push-pull amplifier; balanced amplifier; ~ **sélectif** emphasizer; ~ **séparateur** buffer amplifier; multicoupler; ~ **stabilisateur** stabilizing amplifier; ~ **stéréophonique** stereo amplifier; ~ **suiveur** (v. amplificateur non inverseur); ~ **symétrique** push-pull amplifier; ~ **symétrique série** single-ended amplifier; ~ **symétriseur** balanced amplifier; push-pull amplifier; ~ **synchronisé** lock-in amplifier; ~ **syntoniseur** tuned amplifier; ~ **tampon** buffer; ~ **tampon stabilisé** buffer amplifier; isolation amplifier; ~ **télégraphique** telegraph magnifier; ~ **tube à ondes progressives (ATOP)** travelling-wave tube amplifier (TWTA); ~ **ultralinéaire** ultralinear amplifier; ~ **universel** universal amplifier; ~ **vidéo** video amplifier

amplification *f* amplification; gain; repeating; boosting; ~ **de courant** current gain; ~ **de puissance** power amplification; ~ **des graves** bass boosting; ~ **en phase** in-phase amplification; ~ **linéaire** linear gain; ~ **non linéaire** non-linear gain

amplifier *v* amplify; boost; enhance; magnify; repeat; expand; enlarge; broaden; ~ **en courant** amplify current component

ampli-op bipolaire bipolar op-amp

Amplistat A.C. magnetic amplifier

amplitude *f* amplitude; pulse height; crest/peak value; vertical deflection coefficient; ~ **crête-à-crête** peak-to-peak amplitude; ~ **de battement** beat amplitude; ~ **de crête** peak amplitude; ~ **de crête d'un écho élémentaire** peak amplitude of an elementary echo; ~ **de décision** decision value; ~ **de décision centrale** centre decision value; ~ **de l'œil** eye amplitude; ~ **de signal** signal amplitude; ~ **d'échantillon** sample size; ~ **efficace** r.m.s. amplitude; ~ **en régime permanent** steady state amplitude; ~ **positive** positive voltage; ~ **quadratique moyenne** r.m.s. amplitude; ~ **spectrale** spectral amplitude; ~ **verticale** vertical scan (of oscilloscope); ~ **virtuelle de décision** virtual decision value

ampoule *f* envelope; blister; bulb; ~ **à filament rectiligne** linear filament lamp; ~ **électrique** (electric) light bulb

amputé de deprived of; without

AMRF (v. accès multiple par répartition en fréquence)

AMRT (v. accès multiple à répartition dans le temps)

analogique *adj* analogue; analog; linear (of IC)

analyse *f* analysis; dump; parsing; trace; scanning; research; study; scrutiny; sensing; diagnostic routine; abstract; ~ **à spot lumineux** flying spot scanning; ~ **compartimentale** black-box approach; ~ **d'amplitude** amplitude analysis; pulse-height analysis; ~ **dans le domaine fréquentiel** frequency-domain analysis; ~ **de la numérotation** dialling analysis; address digit analysis; ~ **de marché** marketing; market research; market survey; ~ **de message** message analysis; ~ **de point mort** break-even analysis; ~ **de sensibilité** sensitivity analysis; ~ **de signaux** signal analysis; ~ **du volume de trafic** traffic volume analysis; ~ **(d'une) image** scanning; ~ **en spirale** spiral scanning; ~ **fonctionelle de systèmes** systems analysis; ~ **globale** feasibility study; ~ **harmonique** frequency analysis; harmonic analysis; ~ **ligne par ligne** line-by-line scanning; ~ **(ligne par ligne) entrelacé** interlaced scanning; ~ **non entrelacée** sequential scanning; ~ **organique** detailed analysis; ~ **par points (successifs)** dot (interlace) scanning; ~ **par régression linéaire** linear regression analysis; ~ **(point par point) entrelacée** dot interlace scanning; ~ **préalable** feasibility study; ~ **rétrospective** audit trail; ~ **spectrale** spectrum analysis

analyse-mémoire dump

analyser *v* scan; monitor; sense; scrutinize; parse

analyseur *m* analyser; scanner; ~ **de couleur** colour analyser; ~ **de débordement** traffic scanner; ~ **de distorsion** distortion analyser; ~ **de distorsion non linéaire** distortion analyser; ~ **de formes en relief** shape analyser; ~ **de lampes** valve tester; ~ **de**

parole speech analyser; ~ **de polarisation** polarization analyser; ~ **de réseaux** network analyser; ~ **de son** sound analyser; ~ **de spectre** spectrum analyser; ~ **d'harmoniques** harmonic analyser; ~ **différentiel électronique** electronic differential analyser; ~ **d'impulsions** pulse analyser; ~ **d'onde carrée** square-wave analyser; ~ **d'ondes** wave analyser; ~ **monocanal** single-channel analyser; ~ **multicanaux** multiple-channel analyser; kicksorter; ~ **multispectre** multi-spectral scanner; ~ **optique** image analyser; ~ **voltmètre sélectif** selective level synthesizer

analyste *m ou f* analyst; abstractor; designer; ~ **de systèmes** systems analyst

analytique *adj* probing; forensic

anarchique *adj* haphazard; chaotic

ancien *adj* earlier; former; previous; back

ancienneté *f* seniority; backlog; maturity; ~ **de la demande** length of time on waiting list

ancrage *m* purchase; grip; base plate

anémomètre à fil chaud hot wire anemometer

angle *m* bend; corner; angle; degree; slope; dip; tilt; edge; ~ **abattu** rounded edge; rounded tip; ~ **aigu** acute angle; ~ **apparent d'arrivée** apparent angle of approach; ~ **cassé** chamfer; ~ **critique** stalling angle; critical angle; ~ **d'arrivée** angle of approach; angle of arrival; ~ **d'attaque** rake angle; incident angle; ~ **d'azimut** azimuth angle; ~ **de Brewster** Brewster angle; ~ **de calage** blade angle; angle of incidence; electrical degree; ~ **de conduction** conduction angle (of rectifier); ~ **de convergence** convergence angle; ~ **de coupe** lip angle; ~ **de courbure** bending angle; ~ **de décalage de phase** phase displacement angle; ~ **de décalage en arrière** lag angle; ~ **de décalage en avant** lead angle; ~ **de décrochage** stall(ing) angle; ~ **de dégagement** rake angle; ~ **de déphasage** phase (displacement) angle; ~ **de déviation** deflection angle; lateral shift; ~ **de diffraction** angle of diffraction; ~ **de diffusion** scattering angle; ~ **de directivité** direction angle; ~ **de discrimination** angle of discrimination; ~ **de distribution** viewing angle (of LED); ~ **de faisceau** beam angle; ~ **de flèche** sweep angle; ~ **de garde** clearance; ~ **de groupement** bunching angle; ~ **de lacet** yaw angle; ~ **de passage** angle of flow; ~ **de perte** loss angle; ~ **de phase** phase angle; ~ **de phase de la modulation** modulation phase angle; ~ **de phase de la porteuse** carrier phase angle; ~ **de pivotement** gimbal angle; ~ **de**

pointage pointing angle; ~ **de polarisation** Brewster angle; ~ **de rabattement** clinch angle; ~ **de rayonnement** beam direction; radiation angle; ~ **de recouvrement** overlap angle; ~ **de réflexion** reflection angle; ~ **de réfraction** refraction angle; ~ **de relèvement** observed bearing; ~ **de relèvement corrigé** corrected bearing; ~ **de rotation électrique** electrical rotation (of potentiometer); ~ **de rotation totale** mechanical rotation (sweep of potentiometer); ~ **de site** angle of site; elevation angle; ~ **de site au sol** ground elevation angle; ~ **de site de l'horizon** horizon elevation angle; ~ **de strabisme** squint angle; ~ **de tangage** pitch angle; ~ **de tir** quadrantal elevation; angle of departure; ~ **de transit** transit phase angle; ~ **de tressage** angle of weave; braiding angle; stranding angle; ~ **de visée** aiming angle; ~ **de vision** viewing angle; ~ **de vision latérale** side-viewing angle; ~ **d'élévation** elevation angle; ~ **d'empiètement** overlap angle; ~ **d'espacement** angular spacing; ~ **d'illumination** illumination angle; acceptance angle; ~ **d'incidence** angle of incidence; incident angle; angle of dip; relief angle; ~ **d'inclinaison** tilt (angle); pitch attitude; slope; ~ **d'inclinaison latérale** bank angle; ~ **d'inclinaison longitudinale** pitch attitude; ~ **d'obliquité** canting angle; ~ **d'orientation** orientation angle; steering angle; ~ **d'ouverture** firing angle; gate angle (of thyristor); angle of flow; ~ **d'ouverture d'un sillon** groove angle; ~ **droit** right angle; ~ **effectif de transit** effective bunching angle; ~ **électrique** phase angle; ~ **mort** blind angle; ~ **oblique** mitre; bevel; ~ **par rapport à l'axe** off-axis angle; ~ **par rapport à l'axe de visée** off-boresight angle; ~ **plan** plane angle (in radians); ~ **rasant** grazing angle; ~ **rentrant** concave angle; ~ **saillant** convex angle; ~ **solide** solid angle; ~ **topocentrique** topocentric angle; ~ **total d'ouverture à mi-intensité** half-power firing angle; ~ **vif** acute angle; sharp edge; ~ **zénithal** zenithal angle
angles vifs abattus sharp edges to be rounded off
anhydride carbonique carbon dioxide (CO_2)
animer v organize; conduct; promote
anisochrone adj anisochronous; asynchronous
anisotropie f anisotropy
anneau m colour coding band (of resistor); annulus; ring; circlip; link list; core; ~ **collecteur** commutator ring; ~ **d'autorisation d'écriture** write-permit ring; write-enable ring; file-protect(ion) ring; ~ **(de ferrite)** core; ~ **de garde** guard ring; lip ring; ~ **de Gramme** ring armature; ~ **de marquage** colour-coding band (of resistor); ~ **de mesure de distance** variable range ring; ~ **de protection** file-protect(ion) ring; ~ **de stockage** storage ring; ~ **d'écriture** write-permit ring; write-enable ring; ~ **extérieur** external retaining ring (circlip); ~ **hybride** rat-race; hybrid ring; ~ **intérieur** internal retaining ring (circlip); ~ **stoppeur** stopper ring; ~ **Truarc** circlip; retaining ring
annexe f ou adj standby; ancillary; attached; supporting document; annex; appendix; back-up; backmatter; collateral; enclosure
annonce de patience recorded delay announcement; ~ **parlée** recorded announcement
annonciateur m annunciator; drop; ~ **d'appel** drop (indicator); ~ **de fin de conversation** clearing drop indicator; ~ **d'occupation** busy drop indicator
annotateur m number receiver; ~ **ordonnanceur** register-translator; director
annotation f recording; (call) booking
annotatrice f toll operator; trunk operator
annoter v mark; post; annotate; flag
annuaire m directory; ~ **électronique** electronic directory
annulation f cancel (CAN); undo (function); ~ **de la réflexion** echo cancelling; hybrid separation; ~ **de la tension de décalage** offset null
annule et remplace supersedes
annuler v cancel; invalidate; delete; override; dismiss; scrub
annuleur d'écho echo canceller
anode f anode; plate; ~ **active** sacrificial anode; ~ **collectrice** signal plate; ~ **d'entretien** keep-alive electrode; excitation anode; ~ **d'excitation** keep-alive electrode; excitation anode; ~ **divisée** split anode; ~ **enterrée** sacrificial anode; ~ **fendue** split anode; ~ **frittée** sintered anode; ~ **poreuse** porous anode; ~ **sur la paroi** wall anode
anomalie f out-of-limits parameter; discrepancy; fault; malfunction; defect; flaw; disorder; abnormality; error; ~ **câblée** hard error; ~ **(de fonctionnement)** fault condition; error; malfunction; abnormality; disorder; ~ **de l'ionisation** ionization anomaly; ~ **permanente** non-transient fault
anormal adj freak; out-of-the-ordinary; off-normal
antagoniste adj contentious; restraining
antémémoire f cache; (high-speed) buffer; scratch-pad memory; ~ **d'écriture** write-through cache
antenne f aerial; antenna; radiator; array; loop; stub; dipole; rig; ~ **à accord multiple**

multi-tuned aerial; ~ à **adaptateur d'impé-dance** stub-matched aerial; Q-aerial; ~ à **ailettes** fin aerial; ~ à **alimentation Cassegrain** Cassegrain aerial; ~ à **alimentation en parallèle** shunt-fed aerial; ~ à **alimentation focale** focal-fed aerial; ~ à **alimentation terminale** top-fed aerial; ~ à **balayage** scanning aerial; ~ à **cadre** frame aerial; coil aerial; loop aerial; ~ à **cadres croisés** crossed-loop aerial; coil aerial; turnstile aerial; Bellini-Tosi aerial; ~ à **capacité terminale** top-loaded aerial; ~ à **champ tournant** rotating-field aerial; turnstile aerial; Bellini-Tosi (crossed-loop) aerial; ~ à **charge série** series-loaded aerial; ~ à **cornet** horn aerial; cheese; ~ à **cylindre fendu** slotted cylinder aerial; ~ à **cylindre parabolique** parabolic (dish) aerial; ~ à **demi-cornet** half-cheese aerial; ~ à**deux réflecteurs** dual-reflector aerial; ~ à **diagramme directionnel spécifique** shaped-beam aerial; à **disque** disk aerial; ~ à**double cône** double-cone aerial; ~ à **doublet** dipole aerial; ~ à **effet directif** directional aerial; Beverage aerial; ~ à **excitation par choc** pulse-excited aerial; ~ à **faisceau** beam aerial; ~ à **faisceau en pinceau** spot-beam aerial; ~ à **faisceau étalé** fan-beam aerial; beaver-tail aerial; ~ à **faisceau étroit** narrow-beam aerial; spot-beam aerial; ~ à **faisceau (con)formé** shaped-beam aerial; ~ à **faisceau ponctuel** spot-beam aerial; ~ à **faisceau rotatif** rotary beam aerial; ~ à **faisceau très étroit** pencil-beam aerial; ~ à **faisceaux multiples** multiple-beam aerial; multi-beam aerial; ~ à **fente(s)** slot aerial; ~ à **fentes axiales** axial slot aerial; ~ à **fentes croisées** crossed-slot aerial; ~ à **ferrites** ferrite rod aerial; loopstick aerial; ~ à **fil unique** single-wire aerial; ~ à **fil vertical** vertical-wire aerial; ~ à **fils inclinés** sloping-wire aerial; ~ à **fouet** whip aerial; ~ à **gain élevé** high-gain aerial; ~ à **grande ouverture** large-aperture aerial; broadside array; ~ à **haute pureté de polarisation** high polarization discrimination aerial; ~ à **hyperfré-quences** microwave aerial; ~ à **impédance élevée** quarter-wave stub; ~ à **jupe** quarter-wave skirt dipole; sleeve dipole; coaxial aerial; ~ à **large bande** broadband aerial; wideband aerial; ~ à **large ouverture** wide-aperture aerial; ~ à **long fil** long-wire aerial; ~ à **noyau magnétique** ferrite rod aerial; magnetic rod aerial; loopstick; ~ à **onde progressive** travelling-wave aerial; ~ à **ondes stationnaires** standing-wave aerial; ~ à **ouverture** aperture aerial; ~ à **plan de sol** ground-plane aerial; omnidirectional aerial; ~ à **polarisation circulaire** circular-ly-polarized aerial; circular polarization aerial; ~ à **polarisation circulaire sinistror-sum** left-hand circularly-polarized aerial; ~ à **polarisation horizontale** horizontally-polarized aerial; ground-plane aerial; om-nidirectional aerial; ~ à **polarisation verticale** vertically-polarized aerial; Adcock aerial; ~ à **quatre hélices** quad helix aerial; ~ à **rayonnement latéral** low side-lobe aerial; ~ à **rayonnement longitudinal** end-fire array; yagi array; ~ à **rayonnement transversal** broadside array; Chireix-Mesny aerial; ~ à **rayonnement zénithal réduit** anti-fading aerial; ~ à **réflecteur** reflecting aerial; reflector aerial; ~ à **réflecteur dièdre** corner-reflector aerial; ~ à **réflecteur échelonné** stepped-reflector aerial; ~ à **réflecteur en cornet** horn-reflector aerial; ~ à **réflecteur excentré** offset-reflector aerial; ~ à **réflecteur parabolique** dish-re-flector aerial; ~ à **réflecteur plan** plane-re-flector aerial; ~ à **tige de ferrite** ferrite-rod aerial; ~ **accordée** resonant aerial; tuned aerial; directional aerial; ~ **accordée à impédance élevée** stub-matched aerial; ~ **achromatique** achromatic aerial; ~' **adaptée en delta** delta aerial; ~ **alimenté par un guide d'ondes** waveguide-fed aerial; ~ **apériodique** Beverage aerial; non-reso-nant aerial; beam aerial; rhombic aerial; untuned aerial; wave aerial; directional aerial; aperiodic aerial; ~ **artificielle** dummy load; dumb aerial; phantom aerial; ~ **autoguidage** homing aerial; ~ **Bellini-Tosi** crossed-loop aerial; turnstile aerial; ~ **Beverage** wave aerial; rhombic aerial; directional aerial; non-resonant aerial; ~ **biconique** biconical aerial; ~ **bidirection-nelle** bilateral aerial; ~ **bipolarisée** dual-polarized aerial; ~ **cadre** loop aerial; frame aerial; coil aerial; ~ **Cassegrain** Cassegrain aerial; dish aerial; ~ **Cassegrain à haut rendement** high-efficiency Cassegrain aeri-al; ~ **chargée** loaded aerial; ~ **colinéaire** Kooman's aerial; end-fire array; pinetree aerial; ~ **collective** community (TV) aerial; ~ **commune** common aerial; community aerial; ~ **compensée** cosecant-squared aerial; ~ **contre-rotative** (mechanically/electronically) de-spun aerial; ~ **courte** stub aerial; ~ **croisée** Bellini-Tosi (crossed-loop) aerial; turnstile aerial; ~ **croisée multiple** bat-wing aerial; ~ **de balise** marker aerial; ~ **de Beverage** wave aerial; non-resonant aerial; directional aerial; rhombic aerial; ~ **de contrôle** monitoring aerial; ~ **de couplage** straight-wire probe; ~ **de fortune** jury aerial; makeshift rig; ~ **de poursuite** tracking aerial; ~ **de radio-guidage** homing aerial; ~ **de radiotéléphone** radiotelephone aerial; ~ **de réception** receiving aerial; receiver aerial; ~ **de réflexion à trois angles** trigonal reflector aerial; trihedral aerial; ~ **de satellite** satellite aerial; ~ **de secours** jury aerial; emergency aerial; ~ **de télévision** television aerial; ~ **de toit** roof aerial; ~ **décalée** slewed aerial; ~ **demi-onde** half-wave aerial; ~ **d'émission** transmit(ting) aerial; radiating aerial; ~ **d'émission-réception** transmit-receive aerial; ~ **déployable** unfurlable aerial; ~ **déployable dans l'espace** space-erectable aerial; ~ **déroulée** paid-out aerial; reeled-out aerial; ~ **d'essai** test aerial; ~ **dièdre** corner reflector aerial; ~ **diélectrique** dielectric radiator; polyrod; ~ **dipôle** dipole aerial; ~ **dipôle magnétique** magnetic dipole aerial; ~ **directionnelle** beam aerial; ~ **directive** (v. antenne directionnelle); ~ **directrice** (v. antenne directionnelle); ~ **dirigée** (v. antenne directionnelle); ~ **discône** discone (aerial); ~ **disque-cône** discone (aerial); ~ **doublet** dipole aerial; ~ **du moniteur de réception** monitoring aerial; ~ **émettrice** transmitting aerial; ~ **en anneau** ring aerial; ~ **en arête de poisson** fish-bone aerial; pine-tree aerial; end-fire array; Kooman's array; ~ **en boucle** loop aerial; ~ **en cage** cage aerial; ~ **en cierge** dielectric rod radiator; polyrod; ~ **en cône** cone aerial; ~ **en cône renversé** inverted cone aerial; ~ **en cornet** horn aerial; ~ **en D** cheese aerial; pill-box aerial; ~ **en demi-onde** half-wave aerial; ~ **en dents de scie** zigzag aerial; broadside array; ~ **en dièdre** corner reflector; ~ **en espace libre** free-space aerial; ~ **en étoile** star aerial; ~ **en éventail** fan aerial; ~ **en éventail double** di-fan aerial; ~ **en fil horizontal** horizontal-wire aerial; ~ **en H** H-aerial; ~ **en hélice** corkscrew aerial; ~ **en J** J-aerial; end-fed aerial; ~ **en L** L-aerial; ~ **en losange** rhombic aerial; diamond-shaped aerial; non-resonant (Beverage) aerial; ~ **en nappe** flat-top aerial; ~ **en papillon** bat-wing aerial; ~ **en parapluie** umbrella-loaded aerial; ~ **en pelure d'orange** laminated aerial; ~ **en pyramide renversée** horn aerial; ~ **en réseau** aerial array; ~ **en réseau de doublets** dipole array; ~ **en sapin** pine-tree aerial; fishbone aerial; end-fire array; Kooman's array; ~ **en spirale** spiral aerial; ~ **en spirale conique** conical spiral aerial; ~ **en super-**

tourniquet super-turnstile aerial; ~ **en tige** rod aerial; ~ **en tourniquet** turnstile aerial; crossed-loop aerial; Bellini-Tosi aerial; ~ **en trèfle** clover-leaf aerial; ~ **en triangle** triangle aerial; trihedral aerial; ~ **en V** V-aerial; ~ **en V incliné** inclined V-aerial; ~ **en V renversé** inverted V-aerial; ~ **encastrée** suppressed aerial; ~ **enterrée** buried aerial; earth aerial; ~ **équidirective** omnidirectional aerial; isotropic radiator; ~ **excentrée** offset aerial; ~ **extérieure** elevated aerial; outdoor aerial; ~ **fictive** dummy aerial; dummy load; artificial aerial; phantom aerial; ~ **fixe** base aerial; ~ **fromage** cheese aerial; ~ **Gouriaud** Alford loop (aerial); ~ **guide à fente** slotted guide aerial; ~ **hélicoïdale** corkscrew aerial; ~ **illuminée du foyer** focal-fed aerial; ~ **illuminée par le foyer** focal-fed aerial; ~ **incorporée** built-in aerial; ~ **isotrope** isotropic radiator; omnidirectional aerial; ~ **lame** blade aerial; ~ **lentille** lens aerial; ~ **lentille à lacets de chaussure** bootlace-lens aerial; ~ **lentille à zones** zoned-lens aerial; ~ **libre** open aerial; ~ **linéaire** linear aerial; ~ **microondes lenticulaire** microwave lens aerial; ~ **moyenne** medium-sized aerial; ~ **multibande** multi-band aerial; ~ **musa** multiple-unit steerable aerial (MUSA); ~ **non directionnelle** non-directional aerial; ~ **non directive** non-directional aerial; ~ **omnidirectionnelle** omnidirectional aerial; non-directional aerial; all-round aerial; equiradial aerial; isotropic radiator; ~ **omnidirective** (v. antenne omnidirectionnelle); ~ **optique** optical aerial; ~ **orientable** directional aerial; multiple-unit steerable aerial (MUSA); ~ **orientée vers la terre** ground-plane aerial; ~ **papillon** bat-wing aerial; bow-tie aerial; ~ **parabolique** parabolic aerial; dish aerial; Cassegrain aerial; ~ **périodique à accord logarithmique** log-periodic aerial; ~ **périscope** periscope aerial; ~ **plaquée** suppressed aerial; ~ **polarisée** polarized aerial; ~ **polarisée verticalement** vertically-polarized aerial; Adcock aerial; ~ **projecteur** beam aerial; high-directional aerial; ~ **provisoire** jury aerial; makeshift rig; ~ **pylône** tower aerial; ~ **pylône diélectrique** dielectric rod radiator; polyrod; ~ **pyramidale** sausage aerial; prism aerial; ~ **Q** stub-matched aerial; Q-aerial; ~ **quadrant** quadrant aerial; ~ **quart d'onde** quarter-wave (-length) stub/aerial (QWA); ~ **quasi-équidirective** quasi-omnidirectional aerial; ~ **radiogoniométrique** direction-finding aerial; ~ **réflecteur** reflector aerial; ~ **re-**

pliée folded (dipole) aerial; bow-tie aerial; ~ réseau aerial array; stacked array; tiered array; ~ rideau aerial array; stacked array; tiered array; ~ rotative scanning aerial; ~ rotative de radar à grande vitesse high-speed scanning aerial; ~ sans charge dumb aerial; dummy load; phantom aerial; artificial aerial; ~ sans effet directif non-directional aerial; omnidirectional aerial; isotropic/equiradial aerial; ~ sousmarine submerged aerial; ~ souterraine underground aerial; ~ stabilisée par contre-rotation mécanique mechanically-despun aerial; ~ stable dans l'espace de-spun aerial; ~ téléscopique telescopic aerial; ~ terrestre terrestrial aerial; ~ théorique ideal aerial; ~ tige rod aerial; ~ totalement orientable fully-steerable aerial; ~ tournant embarquée ship radar scanner; ~ traînante drag aerial; trailing aerial; ~ transhorizon over-the-horizon aerial; ~ transportable mobile aerial; ~ trombone folded dipole; bow-tie aerial; ~ unidirectionnelle unidirectional aerial; ~ unifilaire single-wire aerial; ~ unipolaire monopole aerial; unipole aerial; ~ unipolaire de radiop re monopole beacon aerial; ~ verticale vertically-polarized aerial; ~ verticale au sol vertical unipole aerial; ~ verticale isolée à la base series-fed vertical aerial; ~ Yagi Yagi aerial; end-fire array

antérieur adj previous; earlier

antérieurement adv hitherto; formerly

antéserveur m subordinate computer centre; front-end processor (FEP)

antibourrage m anti-blocking

antibrouillage m anti-jamming (AJ)

anticathode f anode

anticipation f look-ahead

antidéflagrant adj explosion-proof

antidictionnaire m stop-words list

anti-éblouissant adj anti-dazzle; glare-free; anti-flare

anti-évanouissement m anti-fading; automatic gain control (AGC)

antifading m automatic gain control (AGC); ~ à réglage silencieux quiet automatic volume control (QAVC); squelch

antimaculage m smudge-proof

antiparasitage m interference suppression

antipompage m anti-hunting

antirebondissement bounce-free

antireflet adj anti-dazzle; non-reflective; glare-free

anti-tintement m anti-tinkle circuit (of ringer)

antivibratile adj vibration-resistant

antivibratoire adj anti-hunting

apercevoir v discern

aperçu m outline

apériodique adj aperiodic; transient; overdamped; untuned

aplomb m indent(-ion)

apogée m apogee

appairage m match

appareil m apparatus; device; unit; assembly; set; appliance; equipment; stage; meter; component; network; instrument; ~ à aiguille indicating instrument; ~ à prépaiement coin box; ~ arythmique start-stop apparatus; ~ automatique de mesure de la transmission automatic transmission measuring set; ~ automatique de réponse answer-only set; ~ automatique d'identification de stations automatic station identification device; ~ Baudot Baudot apparatus; ~ d'abonné subset; ~ d'acquisition de la cible et de contrôle du tir target acquisition and fire control; ~ d'asservissement servo-mechanism; ~ de commande pilot device; ~ de commutation switching apparatus; ~ de détection de petits objets small-object detector; ~ de détente pressure regulator; ~ de déviation télégraphique telegraph by-pass set; ~ de fac-similé facsimile equipment; ~ de levage lifting tackle; hoisting gear; ~ de localisation de cibles target locating set; ~ de manipulation keying unit; ~ de manœuvre scratch device; ~ de mesure measuring set; measuring apparatus; tester; ~ de mesure à aiguille moving-coil meter; ~ de mesure de bruit noise measuring apparatus; ~ de mesure de la distorsion télégraphique telegraph distortion measuring set (TDMS); ~ de mesure de la tension de crête de bruit peak noise meter; ~ de mesure de niveau level measuring set; ~ de mesure de transmission measuring set; ~ de mesure du niveau de modulation modulation level meter; ~ de mesure du retour d'impulsions pulse echo meter; ~ de mesure subjective du bruit subjective noise meter; ~ de péritéléphonie telephone support equipment; telephone peripheral accessory; ~ de pointage radioélectrique radio aiming device; ~ de poursuite infrarouge infra-red tracker; ~ de référence pour la détermination des affaiblissements équivalents de référence reference system for the determination of the articulation reference equivalents; ~ de repérage acoustique sound locator; ~ de rétrodiffusion reflectometer; ~ de rigidité voltage proof tester; ~ de surveillance monitor; ~ de surveillance du taux d'erreur error rate monitor; ~ de télégraphie fac-similé facsimile apparatus; ~ d'enregistrement sound recorder; ~ **d'enregistrement direct** keytape; ~ **d'essai** test apparatus; test instrument; ~ **d'essai du modulateur** modulator load; ~ **d'interception** intercept receiver; ~ **émission-réception** transceiver (XCVR); ~ **envoyeur automatique** automatic repeat dialling device; ~ **explorateur de bande** tape sensing device; ~ **imprimeur** type printer; ~ **périphérique** peripheral unit; ~ **phototélégraphique** phototelegraphic apparatus; ~ **pour annoncer** answeronly machine; ~ **télégraphique** telegraph apparatus; ~ **télégraphique arythmique** teleprinter (start-stop); ~ **télégraphique multiple à courants alternatifs accordés** harmonic multiple telegraph; ~ **téléphonique** telephone set; ~ **téléphonique à amplificateur du son** faint-speech amplifying telephone; ~ **téléphonique à appel magnétique** magneto telephone set; ~ **téléphonique à batterie locale** local-battery telephone set; ~ **téléphonique à batterie centrale** common-battery telephone set; ~ **téléphonique à cadran** (rotary) dial telephone set; ~ **téléphonique à clavier** pushbutton telephone set; ~ **téléphonique à prépaiement** pay-phone; public callbox; coinbox telephone; ~ **téléphonique de table** desk set; ~ **terminal** terminal apparatus

appareillage *m* instruments; equipment; control and switchgear

apparent *adj* exposed; visible

apparentés *adj* related; associated; cognate

apparié *adj* matched; paired

apparition affichage écran complet full-screen reveal

appartements de fonction ancillary services

appartenance *f* membership

appel *m* log-in; log-on; call(-up); calling (sequence); signal(ing); dialling; ringing; attraction; entry code; cue; call-up; polling; address(ing); transfer of control; paging; look-up; ~ (caractère) bell character (BEL); ~ **à batterie centrale** common-battery signalling; ~ **à fréquence vocale** VF ringing; ~ **à l'heure chargée** busy hour call attempt (BHCA); ~ **à l'heure chargée (AHC)** busy hour call attempt (BHCA); ~ **à trois** three-way call; ~ **abandonné** aborted call; ~ **aboutissant à un faux numéro** completion to wrong number; ~ **abusif** mischief call; nuisance call; ~ **au cadran d'un centre manuel distant** dialling-out; ~ **au clavier** touch(-tone) dialling; ~ **au décrocher/décroché** hot line; ~ **automatique** autodialling; automatic dialling; automatic call; keyless ringing; ~ **automatique-service libre** automatic free-phone

service; ~ **avec attente** delay call; delay working; ~ **avec indication de durée et de taxe** advise-duration-and-charge call (ADC); ~ **avec préavis (PAV)** personal call; person-to-person call; ~ **bi-courants** AC/DC ringing; superposed ringing current; ~ **cadencé** interrupted ringing (tone); ~ **collectif** multi-party call; conference call; ~ **conférence** conference call; ~ **coupé** interrupted call; ~ **de courant** inrush current; ~ **de courant d'entrée** inrush current; ~ **de dérangement** signalling fault; ~ **de détresse** distress signal; ~ **de données** data call; ~ **de l'abonné** call to subscriber; ~ **de macro(-programme)** macro call; ~ **de pages** paging; ~ **de sécurité** safety call; ~ **de zone** local (area) call; ~ **défectueux** defective ringing; ~ **départ** originating call; ~ **d'essai** test call; ~ **détourné** diverted call; ~ **différé** delay working; delayed call; ~ **direct** direct signalling (hotline); ~ **direct (de l'opératrice)** direct signalling (hot line); direct (operator) call; speed dialling; ~ **direct en connexion simultanée avec retour par la terre** differential earth ringing; ~ **dirigé** directed call; automatic ringing; ~ **d'offre** offering call; ~ **d'offres** invitation to tender; call-for-bids; request for proposal; ~ **d'ordres** order-wire call; direct operator call; ~ **double** consultation call with hold; call-back; ~ **du central** exchange call; ~ **du distant** call to distant end; ~ **d'une application** call; sign-on; log-on; ~ **d'une instruction** fetching (of instruction); ~ **d'urgence** emergency call; ~ **écoulé** trunk-routed call; ~ **efficace** completed call; ~ **en conférence automatique** dial-up conference call; ~ **en conférence établi par l'opérateur** operator-assisted conference call; ~ **en cours de traitement** call awaiting completion; ~ **en diffusion** broadcast call; general call; public-address call; paging call; ~ **en franchise** free-phone call; ~ **en instance** call camped-on; call waiting; ~ **en interphonie** intercom call; ~ **en PCV** reverse charge call; transfer charge call; collect call; ~ **en série** serial call; chain call; serial poll; ~ **en transit** tandem call; transit (test) call; ~ **enregistré** stored call facility; automatic call-back; last-number redial; recorded number call; hot-line call; ~ **entrant** incoming call; ~ **établi** completed call; connected call; ~ **extérieur** incoming call; outside call; ~ **général** common alerting system; night service (general ringer); ~ **immédiat** immediate ringing; ~ **importun** abusive call; mischief call; nuisance call; ~ **incomplet** incomplete call; ~ **individuel** direct operator signalling; ~ **inefficace** uncompleted call; abortive call; ~ **infructueux** uncompleted call; unsuccessful call; abortive call; ~ **instable** uncompleted call; abortive call; ~ **interdit** call barred; ~ **intérieur** local call; ~ **interne** station-to-station call; intra-office call; local call; ~ **interurbain** trunk call; trunk dialling; toll call; long-distance dialling; ~ **libre** free-phone; toll-free call; ~ **local** intra-office call; local call; station-to-station call; ~ **local banalisé** (LB) bothway local call; ~ **longue-distance** long distance call; ~ **magnétique** generator ringing; ~ **malveillant** malicious call; nuisance call; mischief call; abusive call; ~ **manuel** manual call; manual calling; manual ringing; ~ **manuel par clé** manual ringing; ~ **marqueur** call to marker; ~ **multi-adresses** multi-address call; ~ **n'ayant pas abouti** unsuccessful (uncompleted) call; ~ **non desservi** unconnected call; ~ **non établi** uncompleted call; ~ **non taxé** free call; non-chargeable call; ~ **non valable** invalid call; ~ **nouvel** new call; ~ **offert** call presented to circuit group; routed call; ~ **par courant alternatif** power ringing; ~ **par courant superposé** superposed ringing; AC/DC ringing; ~ **payable à l'arrivée** collect call; transfer-charge call; ~ **PCV** collect call; transfer charge call; ~ **perdu** lost call; ~ **permanent** false-start call; ~ **personne à personne** person-to-person call; ~ **phonique** buzzer call; ~ **présenté** seizure request; call offered; ~ **privilégié du pupitre opérateur** direct operator signalling; ~ **récursif** recursive call; re-entrant procedure call; ~ **réduit** centum call second (CCS); ~ **relâché** released call; ~ **sans aboutissement** uncompleted call; abortive call; ~ **sans numérotation** hot-line call; direct call; no-dialling call; ~ **sans réponse** unanswered call; no-answer call; ~ **sélectif** selective ringing; coded ringing; (group) poll; polling; ~ **semi-automatique** machine ringing; ~ **semi-dirigé** semi-automatic call; ~ **sortant** outgoing (O/G) call; ~ **systématique** polling; ~ **tandem** link-by-link signalling call; ~ **taxé** billable call; chargeable call; ~ **traité** processed call; route analysis completed; ~ **transit** tandem call; transit call; end-to-end signalling call; ~ **urbain** local area call

appelant *m adj* calling; signalling; calling program; source

appelé *m ou adj* energized; fetched (of instruction); called; dialled; rung; signalled (station); addressed (subscriber); destination

appeler *v* call; ring; fetch; retrieve; poll; dial; page; log-on; invoke; address; cue; call up; signal (to); pick up; elicit; energize; attract

appeleur *m ou adj* caller; calling; ~ **de robots** call-through test set

appels en chaîne serial call; serial poll

applicable *adj* in force

application *f* application; dedicated tasks; user programs; ~ **des critères de reconnaissance** decoding; ~ **des valeurs limites** limiting conditions of use

applique *f* strip-light holder

appliquer *v* map; apply; ~ **le courant de signe** mark

appontage *m* bridging

apport *m* filler; contribution; ~ **d'alliage** filler

apposé *v* (sur) affixed; attached (to)

apposer *v* superimpose; apply; affix

apprendre *v* glean; ascertain

apprentissage automatique machine learning; computer-assisted learning; ~ **proprioceptif** self-teaching

apprêter *v* prime; set up; ready

approche *f* advance; feed; homing; approximation; ~ **ascendante** bottom-up method; ~ **descendante** top-down method; ~ **d'un radiophare** homing

approché *adj* approximate(d)

approfondi *adj* intensive; in-depth; knowledgeable; complex

approfondissement *m* elaboration

approvisionnement *m* supply; procurement; replenishment; loading; acquisition; stock (up); buying-in; requisitioning; purchasing; inventory control; ~ **en papier** loading paper (in printer)

approximation *f* rule-of-thumb; ~ **de portée zéro** zero-range approximation; ~ **de Tchebychev** Chebyshev approximation

approximations successives trial and error; successive approximation

appui *m* hitting (of key); depression; support; rest; prop; stay

appuyer *v* press; depress

aptitude *f* suitability; qualification; hands-on experience; flair; ~ **au service** serviceability

apurement du dossier douanier customs clearance

AR (v. accusé de réception); ~ (v. arrière); ~ (v. avis de réception)

arabesque *f* 'at' sign (@)

araser *v* trim; smooth off; crop (of component leads)

arborescence *f* directed tree; (multilevel) tree

structure; (detailed) breakdown; reduction/expansion cascading

arbre *m* tree (of data base); spanning tree; axle; spindle; transmission unit; shaft; arbor; mandrel; ~ **binaire** binary tree; B-tree; ~ **creux** hollow shaft; ~ **de couche** drive shaft; main shaft; ~ **de dépannage** troubleshooting chart; ~ **de fusion optimum** optimal merge tree; ~ **de recouvrement** overlay tree; ~ **d'entraînement** drive shaft; ~ **d'implication** relevance tree; ~ **électrique** synchro (generator/transmitter); autosyn; selsyn; ~ **optimum** minimal tree; ~ **ordonné** ordered tree; ~ **sorti** solid shaft

arc *m* directed link (of graph); bank multiple; bank (of contacts); ~ **à chauffage externe** externally-heated arc; ~ **à effet de champ** high-field emission arc; ~ **de service** service arc; ~ **d'orbite** orbital arc; ~ **en retour** flash-back; backfire; ~ **encombré** congested arc; ~ **thermoélectronique** thermionic arc

architecture *f* architecture; ~ **à cœur réparti spécialisé** dedicated distributed core; ~ **à cœur réparti universel** non-dedicated distributed core; ~ **d'association** control unit coupling; ~ **déconcentrée** deconcentrated core; ~ **du système** system architecture; ~ **éclatée** fully-distributed core; ~ **moderne** state-of-the-art architecture

archivage *m* filing; storage; dump storage; permanent storage; bulk storage; secondary storage; master copy; import (of files)

archive *f* storage; dump storage file; registry

aréomètre *m* hydrometer

arête *f* main trunk route; link; edge; branch; ~ **de diffraction** diffraction edge; diffracting edge; ~ **en lame de couteau** knife edge

argenté *adj* silver-plated

argument *m* argument; control field; code; message field; ~ **de paramètre composé** compound parameter argument; ~ **de tri** control field

argumentaire *m* (persuasive) message

arithmétique en virgule fixe fixed-point arithmetic; ~ **en virgule flottante** floating-point arithmetic

armature *f* armature; shield; armour; reinforcement; sheath; keeper; ~ **de câble** cable armour; ~ **de relais** relay armature; ~ **d'un condensateur** armature; plate; disk; vane; foil; ~ **en anneau** ring armature; ~ **extérieure** external foil

armement *m* setting; initialization; enabling; ~ **temporisation** time-delay initiation

armer *v* arm; set; prime; load; activate

armoire *f* cubicle; cabinet; enclosure; rack; closet; ~ **alimentation** (power) supply cabinet; ~ **de distribution** distribution cabinet; ~ **de relayage** relay cabinet; ~ **équipée** fitted cabinet

armure *f* armour (of cable); pole-piece

arobas ('a' commercial) 'at' sign (@)

arrangement *m* array; configuration; structure; layout; organization

arrêt *m ou adj* off; immobilized; stopped; end; cut-off; de-energized; shutdown; suspension; interrupt; termination; pause; disabled; crippled; terminated; aborted; disruption; clamping; cessation; trip; standstill; closedown; break(point); inhibited; crashed; halted; ~ **anormal** abnormal termination; abend; ~ **automatique** automatic stop; ~ **automatique d'appel** automatic ringing (current) trip; ~ **bip** mute; ~ **calculateur** processor crash; ~ **d'appel** ring-trip; ~ **de la transmission** transmitter off (X-OFF); ~ **de papier** form stop; ~ **de rebouclage** dynamic stop; hang-up; ~ **différé** delayed stop; time lag; deferred stop; ~ **du courant d'appel** ringing (current) trip; ~ **du courant de sonnerie** ringing current trip; ~ **d'urgence** emergency stop; ~ **dynamique** breakpoint instruction; breakpoint halt; ~ **dynamique conditionnel** conditional breakpoint instruction; ~ **forcé** deadlock; deadly embrace; ~ **grappe** disable cluster; ~ **immédiat** drop-dead halt; dead halt; ~ **imprévu** hang-up; crash; ~ **inopiné** crash; ~ **intempestif** premature stoppage; crash; ~ **inversion de batterie** end-of-battery-reversal signal; ~ **involontaire** system crash; hang-up; ~ **momentané** temporary stop; pause; ~ **normal** orderly closedown; ~ **programmé** coded stop; programmed halt; ~ **refus** stop-on-fail; ~ **sur adresse** halt on address; stop on address; ~ **sur boucle** dynamic stop; hang-up; ~ **sur code** coded stop; ~ **sur faute** halt on error; stop on fault; ~ **sur image** pause (of video recorder); freeze frame

arrêté ministériel statutory instrument; ruling; regulation

arrêter *v* de-activate; terminate; cripple; halt; inhibit; abort; disable; turn off

arrêtoir *m* catch; stopper; keeper; buffer

arrière (AR) rear; lagging

arriéré *m* backlog

arrière-plan *m* background

arrivée *f* terminating; feed(er); incoming; lead-in; inward; completing; inbound; front-end; ~ **d'air** air inlet; ~ **extérieure** incoming trunk call; ~ **intérieure** extension call

arrondi *m* radius; fillet

arrondir *v* round (off); half-adjust; ~ **par**

défaut round down; ~ **par excès** round up
arsenal *m* dockyard; ammunition dump; ammunition depot
arséniure *m* **de gallium (AsGa)** gallium arsenide (GaAs)
art de fabrication manufacturing technology
artère *f* artery; highway; route; link; wire; conductor; lead; core; feeder; bus; pipe; ~ **à fort trafic** high-usage route; ~ **à grande distance** long-haul link; ~ **de transmission** transmission link; ~ **hertzienne** radio-relay route; microwave link; ~ **multiplex** carrier route; ~ **principale** backbone route
article *m* article; item; record; element; logical record; data record; clause; ~ **complémentaire de fin** trailer record; ~ **de longueur fixe** fixed-length record; ~ **détail** member; ~ **du fichier permanent** master record; ~ **éliminé** deletion record; ~ **fin de fichier** end-of-file record; ~ **fini** end item; finished product; ~ **logique** logical record; ~ **maître** owner; ~ **mouvement** transaction record; detail file; ~ **supplémentaire** addition record
article-label *m* label record
articulation *f* coupling; connection; contents (of file); deployment; interlocking; chain of command; structure; control sequence; ~ **aval** linkage data (called side); ~ **de syllabes** syllable articulation; ~ **des mots** word articulation; word chaining; intelligibility; ~ **idéale** ideal articulation
articulé *adj* linked
artificiel *adj* man-made; synthetic; dummy; false; phantom
artisanal *adj* unsophisticated
arythmique *adj* start-stop; asynchronous
ascendant *adj* incrementing (order); upward; forward; rising; climbing; bottom-up
ascenseur *m* dumb-waiter; lift; hoist; elevator
aselfique *adj* non-inductive
AsGa (v. arséniure de gallium)
aspect *m* visual examination; review; survey
aspérité *f* roughness; unevenness
aspirateur *m* vacuum drier
aspiration *f* down-draught; intake
assemblable *adj* compilable
assemblage *m* assembly; stack; building blocks; ~ **(de câbles)** (cable) assembly; form; harness; ~ **conditionnel** conditional assembly; ~ **de 15 groupes secondaires** fifteen-supergroup assembly; ~ **de 15 groupes secondaires point de transfert d'assemblage** through 15-supergroup assembly connection point; ~ **de base de 15 groupes secondaires** basic 15 supergroup assembly; ~ **de paquets** packet assembly;

~ **symétrique** mount reverse
assemblage-désassemblage des paquets packet assembly-disassembly (PAD)
assembler *v* assemble; stack; link; collate
assemblés en hélice twisted (together)
assembleur *m* assembly program; assembler; symbolic machine language; ~ **de paquets** packet assembler
assembleur-désassembleur de paquets packet assembler and disassembler
assembleuse *f* collator
asservi *adj* slaved; compelled; locked; dependent; oriented; controlled; synchronized; remote; ~ **à la vitesse de calcul** compute-limited; ~ **avec chevauchement** overlap-compelled
asservir (s') be synchronized
asservissement *m* feedback; control; locking; compelled (signalling); phase-locked loop (PLL); ancillary system; ~ **extérieur** external slaving; ~ **intérieur** internal slaving; ~ **numérique** digital feedback
asservisseur *m* controller; drive operation; ~ **commandes** drive operation controller
assignation *f* assignment; ~ **à la demande** demand assignment; ~ **de fréquence** frequency assignment; ~ **en fonction de la demande** demand assignment; ~ **en fonction de la demande pour accès multiple** demand assignment multiple access (DAMA); ~ **permanente** permanent assignment
assigner *v* assign; allocate
assimilable à comparable to
assimilation *f* familiarization; learning
assimiler *v* digest; take on board; grasp
assistance *f* assistance; aid; operator recall; ~ **d'un opérateur** operator assistance; ~ **technico-commerciale** systems engineering; ~ **technique** technical assistance
assisté *adj* (power-)assisted
association *f* inter-working; association (of chained structure); synergistic association; combination
associé *adj* (à) (used) in conjunction (with); related to; structurally similar; companion; uniform (with); combined (with)
assortiment *m* match; mix; variety; range
assortir *v* match (of resistors)
assurance *f* **(de la) qualité** quality assurance; quality conformance; assessed quality
assuré *adj* (par) handled (by)
assurer *v* provide; implement; endorse; secure; achieve; accomplish; afford; endow (with)
astable *adj* astable; free-running
astreintes *f pl* state of readiness
astuce *f* gimmick; trick-of-the-trade; contrivance; artifice; stratagem; ploy

astucieux *adj* shrewd

asymétrie *f* asymmetry; mismatch; imbalance; ~ **de la voie de conversation** speech path asymmetry

asymétrique *adj* asymmetric(al); unbalanced; single-ended (of amplifier)

asynchrone *adj* asynchronous; start-stop; time-uncoordinated; time-invariant

asynchronisme *m* loss of sync

asyndétique *adj* asyndetic (devoid of connectives)

atelier *m* **de dépannage** repair shop; ~ **de génie logiciel (AGL)** software engineeering workshop; ~ **d'énergie** power plant; ~ **mécanographique** electrical accounting machine department

atmosphère *f* atmosphere; ~ **de référence** reference atmosphere; ~ **exponentiel** exponential atmosphere; ~ **fondamentale de référence** basic reference atmosphere; ~ **ionisée** ionized atmosphere; ~ **linéaire** linear atmosphere; ~ **neutre** inert atmosphere; ~ **radioélectrique** radio atmosphere; ~ **radioélectrique normale** standard radio atmosphere

atmosphérique *adj* atmospheric; ambient; free-air; static

atome-gramme *m* gram-atom

ATOP (v. amplificateur tube à ondes progressives)

atout *m* feature; advantage; benefit; asset; stock-in-trade; nest-egg; refinement; ~ **supplémentaire** bonus

attache *f* **rapide** snap fastener; clip; clasp

attacher *v* attach; tie; secure; bind

attaque *f* actuation; operation; activation; drive; firing; input; control; ~ **chimique** etch; ~ **de grille** drive; excitation; ~ **directe** direct drive; ~ **d'un récepteur** gating; ~ **électrolytique** electrolytic corrosion

atteindre *v* access; reach; attain; achieve

attendre le mot take one's cue

attente *f* delay; wait(ing); latency; queuing; camp-on; clamp-on; ~ **active** hot standby; ~ **après numérotation** post-dialling delay; ~ **de l'entrée** prompt; ~ **de tonalité** dial-tone delay; incoming response delay; ~ **d'horloge** clock wait; ~ **d'interruption** halt; ~ **musicale** music-on-hold; ~ **signalé sur abonné occupé** camp-on busy subscriber; ~ **signalée** camp-on warning tone; ~ **sur occupation** camp-on busy; ~ **sur poste occupé** camp-on; camp-on busy station

atténuateur *m* attenuator; pad; de-emphasizer; ~ **d'entrée** input attenuator; ~ **d'équilibrage** balance attenuator; ~ **différentiel** differential attenuator; ~ **rectiligne** slide attenuator; ~ **réglable** variable attenuator; ~ **rotatif** rotary attenuator

atténuation *f* attenuation; damping; muting; loss; ~ **différentielle** differential loss; ~ **effective** effective attenuation; ~ **linéique** attenuation per unit length

attestation *f* certificate; affidavit

attester *v* certify

attraction *f* **universelle** universal attraction

attribuer *v* award (of contract); allocate; assign; v.; ascribe

attribut *m* attribute; data attribute; ~ **de définition** qualification attribute; ~ **de définition de zone** define area qualification (DAQ); ~ **de définition de zone** define area qualification (DAQ); ~ **italisé** italics (font); ~ **par défaut** default attribute

attribution *f* allocation; posting; duty; assignment; ~ **de fréquence** frequency allocation; ~ **des voies de transmission** channel allocation; ~ **d'orbite** orbit assignment; ~ **du bruit** noise allotment; noise allocation; ~ **fixe** direct allocation

attributs complets d'appareil complete terminal attributes (CTA); ~ **d'écran complet** full-screen attributes; ~ **par défaut d'écran complet** default full-screen attributes; ~ **par défaut pour ligne complète** default full-row attributes

au large at sea; in the open sea

audibilité *f* audibility

audible *adj* audible

audioconférence *f* audioconference

audiofréquence *f* audio; audio-frequency

audiogramme *m* hearing-loss plot; audiogram

audiographie *f* audiography

audiomatique *f* audiomatics

audiomètre *m* audiometer

auditeur *m* listener

audition *f* audibility; hearing; playback; aural acuity

augmentation *f* increment; gain; increase; growth; hike; expand; rise; extension; prolongation; ~ **de l'affaiblissement** attenuation increase

augmenté *adj* protracted; incremented; stepped up

autant *adj* proportionately

auto- *adj* spontaneous; self-; auto-; unassisted; automatic; independent; unattended; stand-alone; unmanned; free-acting; self-contained

auto-adaptatif *adj* self-adapting

autobrouillage *m* self-interference; self-jamming

autocicatrisation *f* self-healing

autoclave *m* autoclave (test chamber)

autocode *m* assembler; assembly language

autocommutateur *m* dial office; dial exchange; automatic switching centre; automatic exchange; switching unit; switchgear; switching node; switch module; ~ **d'abonnés** central dial office; local subscriber exchange; ~ **d'arrivée** terminating exchange; ~ **de départ** originating exchange; ~ **de position(s) de réponse** automatic call distribution system; ~ **de rattachement** local exchange; subscriber exchange; ~ **de transit** transit exchange; ~ **électronique** electronic exchange; ~ **mixte** ordinary and multiline extension PABX; ~ **privé** private automatic exchange (PAX); ~ **privé à prise directe du réseau** private automatic branch exchange (PABX); ~ **rural** rural automatic exchange; ~ **temporel** time-division exchange; ~ **universel** general-purpose exchange

autocomplémenteur *adj* self-complementing
autoconfigurer *v* (s') self-reset
autocontrôle *m* self-testing
autocopie *f* single-copy shot
autocorrecteur *adj* error-correcting; error-correction; self-correcting
autocorrélation *f* autocorrelation
autodégrader *v* (s') self-destruct
autodidacte *adj* self-learning; self-taught
autodyne *f* autodyne; endodyne
auto-excitation *f* self-excitation
auto-excité *adj* self-starting
autographique *adj* facsimile
autoguidage *m* homing
auto-induction *f* self-induction
automate *m* link sequencer; automatic controller; robot; automaton; black box; front-end controller; programmed algorithm; handler; Turing machine; microprogram; ~ **câblé** (hard-)wired logic; firmware; ~ **central** inter-processor link access; ~ **de gestion** bus controller; single-board computer (SBC); ~ **détaillé** software routine; ~ **industriel à relais** automatic controller; ~ **mémoire** memory access interface; ~ **programmé** stored program (control) system
automaticien *m* control engineer
automatique *adj* self-service; customer-operated; dial-up; spontaneous; hands-free
automatisation *f* automation; ~ **des dossiers d'étude** automatic design engineering
automatisé *adj* computerized; automated; computer-based; computer-oriented; computer-assisted
automatisme *m* process control; robotics; ~ **industriel** process control
automodulation *f* self-modulation

autonome *adj* stand-alone; off-line; free-standing; self-contained; integral; isolated; unmanned; independent; free-acting; discrete; spontaneous; self-maintained; self-sufficient; detached; separate; hands-free
autonomie *f* autonomy; discretionary powers; out-of-traffic mode; self-sufficiency; discharge time (of battery); reserve; freedom of action; cruising range; radius of action; ~ **d'acheminement** multi-routing capability; ~ **d'acheminement au départ** multi-routing of outgoing calls; ~ **de batterie** battery discharge time; reserve time; ~ **de fonctionnement** working life
auto-oscillateur *adj* free-running (circuit); self-oscillator
autopolarisé *adj* self-biased
autoporteur *adj* self-supporting; free-standing
autopostage **générique** generic posting; up-posting; ~ *m* **spécifique** down-posting
autoprogrammeur *m* compiler
autopsie *f* post-mortem (routine); dump
autoréaction mutuelle bootstrap feedback
autorégénération *f* self-healing
autorisation *f* enable (code); enabling; clearance; permission; authorization; ~ **de lecture** read enable; clear-to-send (signal); ~ **de transfert** transfer allowed; ~ **d'émission** clear-to-send (CTS); ~ **partielle** class-of-service (COS)
autoriser *v* enable
autoroute *f* **électronique** PCM highway
autoscopie *f* personal insight; self-revelation; self-analysis
autosifflement *m* self-whistling
autosurveillé *adj* fail-safe
autotest *m* self-test(ing)
autotransformateur *m* autotransformer; compensator; ~ **de réduction** step-down transformer; ~ **élévateur** step-up transformer; ~ **réducteur** step-down transformer; ~ **survolteur** step-up transformer
autotranslatable *adj* self-relocating
auxiliaire *m ou adj* standby; auxiliary; ancillary; relief; back-up; service circuit; tones and announcements system; ~ **de commande** pilot device; ~ **de numérotation** (address) digit receiver
AV (v. avant)
aval *m* (en) forward; destination side; ahead; down-stream; onward; output side; below; downside; load end/side; calling end/side; outgoing side; after; following; endorsement; driven; subsequent; decentralized; remote; return side; front-end
avalanche *f* inrush; deluge; crash; ~ **électronique** electron (ion) avalanche
avance *f* proceeding; forward transfer; feed;

step; advance; advancement; movement; drive; lead; stepping; slewing; incrementing; step-mode execution; ~ **de ligne** line feed; ~ **de phase** phase lead; ~ **du curseur** cursor forward (CUF); ~ **papier** paper feed; ~ **pas à pas** inching; stepping; pulse-controlled

avancé *adj* offset

avancement de la bande tape feed

avant (AV) front; leading; ~ **garde** advanced; leading

avant-coureur *m* symptom; precursor; forerunner

avant-plan *m* foreground

avant-projet *m* prototype; preliminary; breadboard; trial model; design; draft

avant-trou *m* lead-in; pilot hole

avarie *f* failure; fault; malfunction

avertissement *m* de collision collision warning; ~ **par ronfleur** tone buzzing; ~ **radioélectrique** radio warning; ~ **téléphonique d'incendie** fire flash call

avertisseur *m* warning device; indicator; detector; alarm annunciator; ~ **de hauteur** terrain clearance warning indicator; ~ **public** street alarm box; street fire alarm; ~ **sonore** audible alarm; hoot stop

avis *m* notice; recommendation; appraisal; circular; notification; warning; advice note; opinion; ~ **d'attente enregistré** recorded delay announcement; ~ **de réception (AR)** goods inward inspection voucher; ~ **d'occupation** busy response

avivage *m* etching; pickling (in acid)

avocat *m* **de brevets d'invention** patent counsellor

avoir *m* credit note

AVP (v. conversation avec avis d'appel)

axe *m* plane; centre-pin; hinge-pin; axle; stud; pin; shaft; centre-line; spindle; hub; pintle; pivot; arbor; coordinate; rivet; bolt; axis; mounting (direction); ~ **articulé par cardan** gimbal axis; ~ **balisé** radio beam; ~ **d'articulation** trunnion axis; hinge-pin; ~ **de codeur** encoder shaft; ~ **de commande** control axis; ~ **de cotation** X-Y plane (of numerical control); ~ **de lacet** yaw axis; ~ **de l'ordonnée** Y-axis (line); vertical coordinate; lateral axis; ~ **de propagation** propagation axis; ~ **de rotation propre** spin axis; ~ **de roulement** bearing pin; ~ **de roulis** roll axis; ~ **de symétrie** axis of symmetrie; ~ **de tangage** pitch axis; ~ **de visée** boresight (direction); ~ **des X** X-axis; ~ **des Y** Y-axis; vertical coordinate; ordinate; ~ **du faisceau** beam axis; ~ **d'un faisceau électromagnétique** beam axis; ~ **d'une antenne** antenna axis; ~ **fileté** threaded cotter pin; ~ **focal** focal axis; ~ **goupillé** clevis pin; ~ **optique** optical axis

azimut *m* azimuth; true bearing; ~ (direct) true bearing; azimuth; ~ **du grand arc** long-path bearing; ~ **du petit arc** short-path bearing; ~ **inverse** reciprocal bearing; ~ **magnétique** magnetic bearing

B

BA (v. béton armé); ≃ (v. barre d'aluminium); ≃ (v. barre d'alimentation)

bac *m* tray; tub; recess; well; trough; pan; magazine; storage bin; tote box; (paper) hopper; ~ **à cartes** card frame; subrack; cage; crate; ~ **à fils** wiring panel; bin; backplane

badge *m* badge

bagottement *m* activation (of alarm)

bague *f* spacer; ring; collar; coupling; (relay) coil circuit; transformer coupling bush; sleeve; slug; ~ **collectrice** slip ring; ~ **d'autorisation d'écriture** write-permit ring; write-enable ring; ~ **d'interdiction d'écriture** write-inhibit ring; file-protect ring

baguette *f* beading; wand; rod; ~ **de soudure** welding rod; solder stick

baie *f* bay; section (of assembly); rack; bank; cubicle; frame; ~ **à multiplage partiel** graded rack; ~ **de relais** relay rack; ~ **de répéteurs** repeater rack; ~ **d'équipements de voie** channel bank; ~ **d'équipements d'extrémité** channel bank (bay); ~ **des lignes d'abonnés et des sélecteurs** subscriber line and final selector unit

bain de soudure *m* dip solder bath; ~ **de Watt** (mat) (matt) Watts bath; ~ **fluidisé** fluidizing bath; ~ **marie** water bath; steamer; steam bath; ~ **mort** still bath; static pool (of molten solder)

baïonette *f* bayonet coupling; socket

baisse *f* drop; decline; diminution; abatement; ~ **accidentelle de la tension** brownout

baissé *adj* down; faulty; failed

baisser *v* set down (of switch); throw

baladeuse (lampe b.) wander lamp; (portable) inspection lamp

balai *m* brush; wiper; ~ **à contact** brush; ~ **à franges** mop; ~ **collecteur** wiper; ~ **de charbon** carbon brush; ~ **de lecture** brush (card reader); ~ **d'exploration** pick-off brush; ~ **métallographique** graphite-metal brush (phosphor bronze)

balance commerciale excédentaire *f* trade surplus; ~ **compteuse** counting scales; ~ **électrodynamique** Cotton balance; electromagnetic balancer; current weigher; current balance; ~ **magnétique** magnetic balance; ~ **voltmétrique** voltage balancer

balancelle *f* suspended cage

balancement *m* swinging; oscillation; ~ **du chercheur** swinging; ~ **du relèvement** bearing oscillation

balancer balance; compensate

balancier *m* fly press; rocker arm; crimp press; ~ **d'accompagnement** swinging cable link; cable support

balayage *m* scanning; sweeping; tracking; browsing; polling; slewing; ~ **à faisceau laser** laser beam scanning; ~ **alterné** alternating sweep; ~ **approximatif** coarse scanning; ~ **cathodique entrelacé** interlaced scanning; ~ **circulaire** circular scanning; ~ **de fréquence** frequency excursion; ~ **de ligne** line sweep; ~ **de rangées** row scanning; ~ **de trame** field sweep; ~ **dent de scie** ratchet time base; ~ **des rangées** row scanning; ~ **entrelacé** interlaced scanning; line-jump scanning; ~ **horizontal** line sweep; ~ **intercalaire** interleaved scan; ~ **vertical** field sweep; vertical deflection

balise *f* beacon; light; marker; indicator; cone; reflector; ~ **de radiodétection** radar beacon; ~ **passive** radar reflector

baliser *v* flag

ballast *m* regulating transistor; pass transistor; starter (of fluorescent tube); series ballast; voltage sensing

ballon *m* envelope (of lamp bulb); flask

ballottement *m* fluctuation (of pointer)

balourd *m* unbalance; imbalance; ballooning

banal *adj* general-purpose

banalisation *f* standardization; ~ **progressive** expansion cascading

banalisé *adj* non-dedicated; standardized; diversified; open-systems; unified; bothway; common; shared; combined; scratch; standard

banaliser *v* scratch; float (of channel); common

banane *f* separator

banc *m* bank (of resistors); (memory) bank; pool (of machines); fixed contact; console; cluster; bench; station; stack; pile-up (of contacts); ~ **à bobiner** winding bench; ~ **aligné** straight bank; ~ **de broches** contact bank; bank of contacts; level; ~ **de contacts de lignes** line (contact) bank;

multiple; ~ **de maintenance** maintenance console; portable maintenance kit; tester; ~ **de mémoire** memory bank; storage bank; ~ **de mesure** slotted measuring section; slotted line; ~ **de mesure d'abonnés** routiner; subscriber loop tester; ~ **de mise en chauffe** heater; hot-plate; ~ **de montage** assembly line; work-bench; ~ **de sélecteurs** bank of selectors; selector bank; ~ **de test** tester; ~ **de voies** channel bank; ~ **décalé** slipped bank; ~ **d'épissurage** splicing station; ~ **d'essai(s)** test(ing) bench; test rig/bed; jig; test position; tester; test console; test machine; ~ **d'étalonnage** calibration bench; ~ **final** final inspection bench; ~ **(mémoire) d'octets** memory bank
bande *f* tape; band; channel; strip; ribbon; rail; track; roll; web (of paper); loop; file; sweep range; strap; tape roll; ~ **à fréquences vocales** voice-band; VF band; ~ **à perforation complète** chadded tape; ~ **à perforation partielle** chadless tape; ~ **adhésive** splicing tape; adhesive tape; ~ **aller** go band; ~ **atténuée** attenuated band; ~ **attribuée** service band; ~ **audionumérique** digital audio tape (DAT); ~ **banalisée** citizen's band (CB); ~ **bibliothèque** library tape; ~ **caractéristique** characteristic band; ~ **Caroll** sprocket holes (of continuous form stationery); ~ **commune** shared band; ~ **d'absorption** absorption band; ~ **d'alimentation** power rail; ~ **d'alu(minium)** aluminium strip; ~ **d'amateur** amateur (radio) band; ~ **de base** baseband; ~ **de cerclage** banding strip; hoop; binder; ~ **de conduction** conduction band; ~ **de conversation** speech band; ~ **de cuivre** copper strap; ~ **de fréquence commune supprimée** common suppressed frequency band; ~ **de fréquence du bruit** noise band; ~ **de fréquence pour le radar** radar (R) band; ~ **de fréquence supprimée** suppressed frequency band; ~ **de fréquences** frequency band; ~ **de fréquences d'amateur** amateur (radio) frequency band; ~ **de fréquences moyennes** medium frequency (MF) band; ~ **de fréquences pour ligne dérivée** spur band; ~ **(de fréquences) publique** citizen's band (CB); ~ **de garde** guard band; ~ **de jacks** jack strip; ~ **de manœuvre** scratch tape; working tape; ~ **de papier** paper tape; ~ **de papier perforée** punched tape; chadded tape; ~ **de radiodiffusion** broadcast band; ~ **de réjection** rejection band; ~ **de sécurité** clear area; clear band; ~ **de spectre** spectral band; ~ **de stockage des erreurs** error tape; ~ **de télévision** television band;

~ **de transmission** transmission band; ~ **de valence** valence band; ~ **de vidéofréquences** video-frequency band; ~ **d'énergie** (de F. Bloch) (Bloch) energy band; ~ **d'enregistrement** recording tape; ~ **d'excitation** excitation band; ~ **d'exploration** scanning strip; sweep range; ~ **d'impression** tally roll; printer tape; ~ **d'octave** octave; ~ **d'ondes** waveband; ~ **étalon** calibration tape; reference tape; ~ **interdite** forbidden band; band gap; ~ **large** broadband; wideband; ~ **latérale** sideband; ~ **latérale de la sousporteuse** subcarrier sideband; ~ **latérale directe** erect sideband; ~ **latérale inférieure** lower sideband; ~ **latérale parasite** spurious sideband; ~ **latérale résiduelle (BLR)** vestigial sideband; ~ **latérale restante** vestigial sideband; ~ **latérale supérieure** upper sideband; ~ **latérale supprimée** suppressed sideband; ~ **latérale unique (BLU)** single sideband (SSB); sideband only (SBO); ~ **magnétique** magtape; magnetic tape; ~ **mouvement(s)** change tape; transaction tape; ~ **Nyquist** Nyquist interval; ~ **optique** film strip; ~ **passante** pass-band; bandwidth; bandpass; ~ **perforée** punched tape; chadded tape; ~ **permise** authorized band; allowed band; ~ **pilote** control loop; control tape; (paper) tape loop; carriage tape; format tape; vertical format unit; ~ **porteuse** tape roll; ~ **première génération** grandfather tape; ~ **principale** transmitted sideband; main sideband; ~ **programme d'exploitation** master library tape; master program file; ~ **proportionnelle** proportional band; ~ **publique** citizen's band; ~ **résiduelle** vestigial (asymmetric) sideband; ~ **retour** return band; ~ **sans fin** endless loop; ~ **semi-perforée** chadless tape; ~ **sonore topée** audio sync pulse tape; ~ **système** operational software magnetic tape; system (loading) tape; ~ **télégraphique** ticker tape; ~ **téléphonique** voice-band; VF band; ~ **transmise** transmitted band; ~ **utile** passband; bandwidth; ~ **utilisée en alternance** overflow tape; ~ **vide** empty band; dead band; ~ **vocale** voice band; speech band
bandeau *m* edge strip (of PCB); overlay (of keyboard); ~ **avant** front panel; edge strip; ~ **lumineux** strip light; lamp field; lamp panel
bandothèque *f* tape library
bannière *f* list heading; flag; sign-on; banner (page)
banque *f* bank; ~ **d'affaires** merchant bank; ~ **de compensation** clearing bank; ~ **de**

B

données data bank; ~ **d'images** picture bank

banquette f console

BAR (v. boîtier d'adaptation réseau)

barème m scale; scheme; schedule; list; chart; table; rate; ~ **de temps** time scale

barge f **de forage** drilling rig; oil exploration platform

barillet m barrel; drum; cylinder; lock; index

barre f tag; strip; bar; rod; reed (of relay); bus; switchpath; busbar; fraction sign; oblique stroke; slash; slant; rail (of busbar); socket strip; ~ **à caractères** type bar; ~ **adoucie** smoothed bar; tempered steel bar; ~ **antimaculage** paper bail (of printer); ~ **bus** (barre omnibus) busbar; ~ **collective** busbar; ~ **d'alimentation (BA)** busbar; supply busbar; power rail; ~ **d'alimentation horizontale** horizontal busbar; ~ **d'aluminium (BA)** aluminium bar; ~ **de commutation** commutating bar; ~ **de masse** earth rail; ~ **de raccordement** connecting bar; ~ **de sécurité** standby battery bar; ~ **de sélecteurs** combination bar; ~ **de sinus** sine bar; ~ **délestable** load-shedding busbar; load relief busbar; ~ **d'espacement** space bar; ~ **génératrice** generator busbar; ~ **horizontale de commutateur** crossbar switch horizontal; ~ **inversée** backslash; inverted solidus; ~ **oblique** slant; slash; stroke; solidus; diagonal; ~ **omnibus** busbar; ~ **presse-papier** paper bail; ~ **sélectrice** code bar; ~ **zéro** (0B) earth plane; reference voltage busbar; ground bus

barré strike-through (screen attribute)

barreau de coeur core material rod; ~ m **support** mounting bar; ~ **tube** rod-in-tube (method)

barrette f strip; bar; rod; jumper; strap; link; terminal block; stalk; stub; ~ **à bornes** terminal strip; ~ **à visser** barrier strip; ~ **de connexion** connecting strip; ~ **de continuité** shorting strip; ~ **de fixation** securing strip; mounting bar; rod; ~ **de masse** earthing strip; ~ **de raccordement** connecting strip; terminal strip; ~ **de sectionnement** isolating strip; ~ **de terre** earthing strip

barrière f **de potentiel** potential barrier; dipole layer; charge region; depletion region; junction barrier

bas adj low-profile; down; bottom; ~ **de casse (bdc)** lower case (lc); ~ **de gamme** bottom of range; ~ **de page** footer

basculant tilting

bascule f trigger; flip-flop; tilt; bistable circuit; latch; switchover; switch; swap; alternation; staticizer; stage (of shift register); two-state device; see-saw; Eccles-Jor-

dan circuit; gate; half-shift register; condition code (cc); ~ **à commande dissymétrique** RS (reset-set) flip-flop; positive edge-triggered latch; ~ **à commande symétrique** T flip-flop; ~ **à couplage** direct-coupled flip-flop; ~ **adressable** addressable latch; ~ **antirebond** bounce-eliminator flip-flop; non-toggling flip-flop; ~ **astable** free-running circuit; ~ **binaire** binary pair (flip-flop); ~ **bistable** bistable trigger circuit; Eccles-Jordan circuit; half-shift register; ~ **bistable à une entrée** single-control bistable trigger circuit; ~ **de distribution rapide** fast-driving flip-flop; ~ **de prise** arbiter; ~ **de retenue** latch; memory flip-flop; ~ **dédoubleuse** binary divider; scale-of-two counter; ~ **d'événement (BEV)** event flip-flop; ~ **instable** multivibrator; ~ **monostable** monostable trigger circuit; one-shot trigger circuit; gated multivibrator; Kipp relay; ~ **type DTRS** positive edge-triggered D-type flip-flop; ~ **(type) SR** set/reset latch; negative edge-triggered latch

basculement m switchover; transfer; cutover; throwing; turning-on; stepping; triggering; flip (of switch or core); latch; toggling (of switch); changing (of polarity); gating; ~ **du traffic** traffic transfer

basculer switch; change; transfer; toggle; trip; throw; step; flip; latch; swing; tilt; cut over; trigger; change state; gate

basculeur m toggle switch; ~ **bistable** (scale-of-two) multivibrator; stable trigger circuit; trigger pair circuit; ~ **bistable à deux entrées** dual-control bistable trigger circuit; ~ **électronique** electronic two-state device; ~ **monostable** monostable trigger circuit

base f derivative; base; radix; root; host; matrix; footing; bias (base address); rudiment(s); substrate; ~ **arrière** off-site; back-up; ~ **commune** common base (of semiconductor); ~ **d'accrochage** primer; conversion film; conversion layer; ~ **de données** data base; ~ **de données textuelle** documentary data base; ~ **de la caractéristique** floating point radix; ~ **de numération** base notation; radix; ~ **de numération 2** modulo 2 sum; inclusive-OR; ~ **de temps (BT)** timebase; clock; sweep speed; ~ **de temps générale (BTG)** exchange time base; ~ **de temps mobile** local time base (independent of exchange time base); ~ **de temps pour les caractères reçus** received character timing; ~ **de temps pour les éléments de signal à l'émission/réception** transmitter/receiver signal element timing

(DTE/DCE); ~ **TVA** value-added tax (VAT) threshold; ~ **volumique** bulk; mass; density

basse fréquence voice frequency; ~ **fréquence (BF)** low frequency (LF); audio-frequency (AF); voice frequency (VF); ~ **pression atmosphérique** low air pressure; ~ **tension** low voltage; low tension (LT); ~ **vitesse** low speed

bassin *m* **d'emploi** labour catchment

bâti *m* rack; frame; assembly; jig; bank; chassis; plinth; ~ **d'amplificateurs** amplifier rack; ~ **de préselecteurs** line switchboard; ~ **de test** test jig; ~ **d'équipements de voie** channel bank; ~ **étroit** terminal rack; ~ **mécanique** frame; framework; ~ **mécano-soudé** welded rack

bâtiment *m* vessel; ship; craft; surface vessel; ~ **atelier** depot ship

bâton *m* legend; ~ **de ferrite** ferrite rod (of aerial)

bâtonnet *m* bar; (magnetic) stroke; ferrite rod; segment (of display character); prod; stylo

battage *m* joggling (of cards)

battement *m* beat; beating; surge; float; tick; pulsing; fluctuation; chatter (of relay contacts); bounce; flutter; waiting, time; operation; oscillation; ~ **nul** zero beat; ~ **zéro** zero beat

batterie *f* battery; bank; cluster; pool; accumulator; suite; ~ **à plomb** lead-acid battery; ~ **centrale (BC)** common battery (CB); ~ **centrale pour la signalisation** common signal battery; ~ **commune (BC)** common battery (CB); ~ **d'accumulateurs** storage battery; ~ **d'anode** anode battery; plate battery (B); ~ **de chauffage** heater battery; filament battery (A); ~ **de démarrage** starter battery; ~ **de filament** filament battery (A); heater battery; ~ **de grille** grid battery; ~ **de plaque** anode battery; plate battery (B); ~ **de polarisation de grille** biasing battery; ~ **de résistances** bank of resistors; impedance; ~ **de signalisation** signalling battery; ~ **en tampon** floating battery; divided-float battery; equalizing battery; ~ **équilibrée** divided-float battery; floating battery; buffer battery; equalizing battery; ~ **flottante** floating battery; ~ **locale (BL)** local battery (LB); ~ **tampon** booster battery; floating accumulator

batteur de cartes joggler

battre *v* joggle; beat; oscillate

baud baud

bavard *adj* responsive; on a conversational footing; interactive

bavure *f* burr; rough edge; swarf; seam; flash

BC (v. batterie centrale); ~ (v. batterie commune)

bdc (v. bas de casse)

bec usiné machined nozzle

bécane *f* machine (jargon)

becquet (béquet) blade; tab (of connector tine); lug

bélinogramme *m* photo-telegram; facsimile telegraphy; video transmission

bénéfices *m pl* income; revenue; profit; ~ **non distribués** retained earnings

bénéficiaire creditor

bénéficier flourish

béquille de réglage d'inclinaison (keyboard) tilting arm

berceau *m* cradle; rest; bed; carriage; mounting; support; rack; hook; saddle

besoin de page page fault; missing page interruption; page translation exception

béton armé (BA) reinforced concrete

BEV (v. bascule d'événement)

BF (v. basse fréquence); ~ (v. générateur basse fréquence)

biais (mettre en) bias; askew; (to) skew; comparison (of check sums)

biaisage *m* biasing

biaiser *v* bias; skew

biannuel twice yearly

bibliothécaire *m/f* librarian

bibliothèque *f* **de données** data library; ~ **de liaison** link library; ~ **de programmes** software library; ~ **d'entrée/sortie** input/output library; ~ **exécutable** run file library; core image library; load module library; ~ **image-mémoire** core image library; load-module library

bi-canal dual highway; two-channel

bicarré *adj* biquadratic

bidirectionnel *adj* bidirectional; bothway; duplex; two-way; ~ **non simultané** half-duplex; ~ **simultané** full-duplex

bidon *m* canister; ~ *adj* dummy

bielle *f* rod; strut; brace; truss; link

biellette *f* hinge bar; link

bien *m* commodity; property; ~ *adv* securely; firmly; thoroughly; correctly

bifilaire *adj* two-core; dual-conductor; twin-wire; pair

bifréquence *adj* dual frequency; multifrequency

bifurcation *f* branchpoint; fork; branch

bigramme *m* two-letter code (digraph); directed graph

bijection *f* one-to-one correspondence

bijoncteur *m* dual-input bus

bilame *f* bimetallic strip; twin blade; thermal switch

bilan *m* inventory; evaluation; assessment;

tally; results; record; schedule; checklist; index; ~ **de consommation** power budget; ~ **de liaison** link budget; ~ **typique** gross power budget (in dB)

bille f ball; bead

bimensuel adj fortnightly

bimestriel adj two-monthly

bimétallique adj bimetallic

bimoteur m ou adj twin-engined

binaire adj binary; dyadic; bivalent; two-valued; scale-of-two; bipolar; ~ **absolu** absolute binary; ~ **codé décimal** binary-coded decimal (BCD); ~ **décalage** binary shift; ~ **exécutable** object code; executable machine language; ~ **exécutable** object code; machine code; ~ **naturel** straight binary; ~ **(par) colonne** Chinese binary; column binary; ~ **par ligne** row binary; ~ **translatable (BT)** relocatable binary

binoculaire adj binocular eyepiece; stereo (of microscope)

binode f double diode; binode (epitaxial rectifier)

binôme m two-part; binomial

binon m bit; begit

binoquet m zero print key (jargon)

biométrie f biometry (biological statistics)

biotechnique f ergonomics; biotechnology; work study

bip m brief tone burst; bleep; beep; tone alert (of pager)

BIP (v. boîte aux lettres inter-processeur)

biphase two-phase; full-wave

biplex adj duplex

bipolaire adj bipolar; double-pole; ~ **à deux directions** double-pole double-throw (DPDT); ~ **double course** double-pole double-throw (DPDT)

bipolarité f alternate mark inversion

biprocesseur m dual processor; tandem (processor) system; duplex computer

biprogrammation f dual programming (mode)

biquinaire adj biquinary (code)

bis (fonction ~) last number repetition

bisaïeul m ou adj third generation

biseau m bevel

bissé adj emboldened; bold (print); double strike

bissextile adj leap year

bistable m bistable circuit; flip-flop; lock-over circuit; scale-of-two circuit; toggle circuit

bit m binary digit; bit; element; ~ **baladeur** marching bit; scanning test bit; ~ **bien reçu (BR)** acknowledge(ment) bit; ~ **clé** check bit; check digit; check number; ~ **clé de parité** parity bit; ~ **d'appel** call bit; ~ **d'arrêt** stop bit; ~ **de bonne réception** acknowledge bit; ~ **de commande** control

bit; ~ **de contrôle** check bit; check digit; check number; redundant bit; ~ **de contrôle d'erreur** error control bit; ~ **de contrôle transversal** lateral parity bit; ~ **de départ** start bit; ~ **de données appliqué** applied data bit; ~ **de droite** low-order bit; LSB; ~ **de gauche** high-order bit; MSB; ~ **de message** decoded chip; ~ **de parité** parity bit; ~ **de pas** (quantizing) step bit; ~ **de poids faible** low-order bit; least significant bit (LSB); ~ **de poids fort** high-order bit; most significant bit (MSB); ~ **de présence** flag; ~ **de rang inférieur/supérieur** low-/high-order bit; LSB/MSB; ~ **de redondance** redundancy bit; check bit; ~ **de réponse** answer bit; ~ **de reprise** restart bit; ~ **de réserve** spare bit; ~ **de service** service bit; housekeeping bit; ~ **de signe** sign bit; ~ **de synchronisation de trame** frame synchronizing bit; ~ **de télétaxe** own-premises metering bit; ~ **de verrouillage de trame** frame bit; alignment bit; framing bit; ~ **d'état** status bit; ~ **d'exclusivité** exclusion bit; ~ **d'imparité** parity bit; ~ **drapeau** tag bit; flag bit; ~ **erroné** corrupt bit; erroneous bit; ~ **hors texte** zone bit; ~ **indicateur** flag; designator; ~ **indicateur vers l'arrière** backward indicator bit; ~ **significatif** data bit; ~ **suivant transmis** next transmitted bit; ~ **supplémentaire** overhead bit; added bit; extra bit; ~ **utile** data bit

bi-tension f dual voltage

bi-univoque one-to-one (correspondence)

bivalent adj binary; bivalent; dual mode; divalent

bivocal bivocal

BL (v. batterie locale); ≁ (v. bordereau de livraison)

blanc m ou adj blank; white; empty; clear; space; void; virgin; ~ (caractère b.) blank; space; ~ **artificiel** artificial white; nominal white; ~ **cassé** off-white; ~ **de chiffres** figures blank; ~ **de lettres** letters blank; space; ~ **des lettres** (automatique) unshift-on-space; ~ **d'image** picture white; ~ **maximum** peak white; ~ **parfait** peak white

blindage m shield; screening; armour; cladding; ~ **magnétique** magnetic screen; ~ **magnétique** magnetic screening

blindé adj screened; shielded; encased; armour-plated; clad

bloc m (physical) record; block; record; subset; module; unit; pack; board; yoke (of printer); increment; section; cluster; pad; drive(r); subsystem; bin (of data on tape); ~ **afficheur de quatre chiffres** four-digit multiplexed display; ~ **amortisseur** resilient mounting; ~ **amovible** plug-in unit; ~ **d'accord** tuner; ~ **d'adaptation** matching unit; adaptor; interface; ~ **d'adresse initiale** initial address block; ~ **d'alimentation** power supply; power pack; ~ **de base (de volume)** (volume) home block; ~ **de calcul** arithmetic module (ALU); processor; ~ **de circuit imprimé** printed circuit board (PCB); ~ **de combinaisons** strapping block; ~ **de commande** control unit; driver; control keypad; ~ **de commande générale** main control unit; ~ **de commutation enfichable** plug-in unit; ~ **de construction** strapping block; ~ **de déflexion** deflection coils; ~ **de déviation** deflection coils; ~ **de données** block of data; data block; bin (of data on tape); ~ **de fonctions** stunt box; ~ **de gestion de lignes** line control block; ~ **de paramètres** parameter block; ~ **de puissance** power pack; driver; contactor unit; drive; reverser/contactor block; ~ **de raccordement** terminal block; ~ **de sous-répartition** cross-connect terminal block; ~ **de touches** keypad; pad; ~ **de transmission** transmission block (X-block); ~ **de ventilation** blower unit; ~ **début d'en-tête** block header; ~ **d'échange** data transfer unit; ~ **d'entrée** entry block; input block; ~ **d'informations** data block; ~ **du curseur** cursor control keys; ~ **échangeur** interchange unit; ~ **émetteur** source; ~ **en-tête de fichier** file header block (FHB); ~ **erroné** erroneous block; corrupt (data) block; ~ **étalon** calibration block; ~ **fin** trailer block; ~ **fonctionnel** functional block; functional unit; ~ **individuel** rack-mounting unit; ~ **isolé** stand-alone unit; ~ **machine à écrire** typewriter pad; printer keyboard; ~ **mémoire** storage block; ~ **numérique** numeric keypad; digital block; ~ **opérateur** arithmetic and logic unit (ALU); ~ **primaire** digroup; primary block; ~ **programme** program subset; ~ **récepteur** sink; ~ **reporteur** (offset) blanket; ~ **source** source; ~ **supplémentaire** overhead block; added block; extra block; ~ **temporisé** timer unit

blocage *m* barring; binding; blanking; blocking; busying; caging; choking; clamping; congestion; cut-off; denial; drop-out; freezing; gating; halt; hang-up; hold-up; inhibiting; interlock(ing); interrupt(ion); jamming; knock-off (of armature); latching; locking; lock-on (to target); lock-out; muting; override; retaining; screen(ing); securing; seizing; seizure; squelch; stalling; sticking; stopping; stoppage; suspension; turn-off; write mode (of file records); deadlock; ~ (d'un récepteur) muting circuit; ~ **automatique** muting; squelch; ~ **brutal** instant blocking (forced call release); ~ **cames** time delay disable; ~ **de chaîne** holdover; ~ **de la composante continue** direct-current (DC) blocking; ~ **de liaison** link isolation; ~ **doux** soft fail; graceful degradation; delayed blocking; ~ **d'un canal sémaphore** signalling link blocking (common channel); ~ **en arrière d'un groupe** group control; group backward busying; ~ **externe** external blocking; ~ **interne** internal blocking; congestion; ~ **nul** zero-blocking; ~ **programme** program halt; ~ **sur phase** halt on instruction; ~ **sur une phase** halt on instruction; stop at address; ~ **système** access denial; system blocking; ~ **vers l'arrière** backward busying

bloc-notes jotter; scratchpad

bloqué *adj* biased beyond cut-off (of transistor); isolated; back-biased; busied-out; stuck; jammed; frozen; stopped; disabled; barred; inhibited; ~ **à l'état actif** jammed active; ~ **à l'état inactif** jammed inactive

bloque-cartes compressor

bloquer *v* inhibit; latch; block; interlock; halt

bloqueur *m* lock-out; holding circuit; interlock; static relay; static modulator

BLR (v. bande latérale résiduelle)

BLU (v. bande latérale unique)

bobinage *m* coil; winding(s); inductance; ~ **à trois encoches** three-slot winding; ~ **avant** fast forward (recorder control); ~ **de champ** field winding; ~ **d'excitation** field coil; ~ **en galette** pie winding; ~ **primaire** primary winding; ~ **rapide** cue (recorder control)

bobine *f* coil; reel; spool; reactor; choke; drum; bobbin; inductance; winding; shaft; ~ **à air** air-core coil; ~ **à couches multiples** multilayer coil; ~ **à noyau de fer** iron-core coil; ~ **à noyau mobile** ferrite coil; slugged coil; ~ **à ruban** tape reel; spool; ~ **à une couche** single-layer coil; ~ **cylindrique** cylindrical spool; ~ **d'accord** tuning coil; ~ **d'allumage** ignition coil; ~ **d'amortissement** damping coil; choke; ~ **d'antenne** aerial coil; ~ **d'arrêt** choke; ~ **de balayage** deflecting coil; ~ **de blocage** choke; ~ **de charge** load coil; loading coil; ~ **de charge de circuit fantôme** phantom loading coil; ~ **de choc** choke; ~ **de concentration** focussing coil; ~ **de couplage** coupling coil; jigger; ~ **de courant** current coil; ~ **de déviation** yoke; deflector coil; ~ **de filtrage** smoothing choke; ~ **de focalisation** focuss-

B

ing coil; ~ **de limitation** limiting coil; ~ **de modulation** modulating choke; ~ **de pupinisation** loading coil; ~ **de réactance** reactance coil; ~ **de réaction** feedback coil; reaction coil; ~ **de réception** take-up spool; ~ **de relais** relay coil; trip coil; ~ **débitrice** feed spool; ~ **d'équilibrage** arc-suppressor coil; ~ **d'excitation** exciter coil; ~ **d'extinction** arc-suppressor coil; ~ **d'inductance** inductance coil; inductor; ~ **d'induction** induction coil; ~ **d'induit** armature coil; ~ **égalisatrice** compensating coil; ~ **en nid d'abeille** honeycomb coil; lattice coil; ~ **enrouleuse** take-up spool; ~ **exploratrice** search coil; probe coil; ~ **magnétique** magnet coil; ~ **mobile** moving coil; ~ **primaire** primary coil; ~ **pupin** loading coil; ~ **réceptrice** take-up spool; ~ **secondaire** secondary coil; ~ **self-induction** self-induction coil; choke; ~ **selfique** choke; ~ **thermique** heat coil; ~ **translatrice** repeater; repeating coil; ~ **translatrice de circuit** phantom repeating coil
bobiné *adj* wirewound
bobineau *m* reel; printer tape; bobbin
bobineuse *f* manual coil winder
bocage *m* scrap; flash
bois résinifié resin-bonded plywood
boisseau *m* gate valve
boîte *f* box; case; casing; kit; unit; container; carton; enclosure; canister; ~ **à décades** decade (resistance) box; ~ **à lettres** mailbox; ~ **américaine** cardboard packing case; carton; ~ **aux lettres inter-processeur (BIP)** inter-processor mailbox; ~ **composée (de) douilles américaines** A/F socket set; ~ **d'accus** (storage) battery; ~ **d'antenne** aerial bay; ~ **de branchement** branching box; splitter; junction box; ~ **de contrôle de jonction** break-out box; ~ **de contrôle d'interface** break-out box; ~ **de décades** decade resistance box; ~ **de dérivation** junction box; branch(ing) box; splitter; ~ **de distribution** junction box; splitter; branching box; terminal box; ~ **de jonction** junction box; splitter; splicing chamber; ~ **de lovage** cable slack compartment; ~ **de piges** box of measuring rods; ~ **de raccordement** junction box; cable terminal; connection box; coupling box; ~ **de résistance** resistance (decade) box; ~ **d'écho** echo box; ~ **d'éclatement** junction box; break-out box; drop terminal; ~ **d'écoute** audio control panel; ~ **d'emballage** packing case; crate; ~ **d'encastrement** pattress; ~ **d'entrée de poste d'abonné à protection** subscriber station protector; ~ **d'extrémité** terminal box

boîtier *m* package; module; chip; case; casket; box; casing; housing; shell; integrated circuit; panel; pack; unit; container; enclosure; capsule; device; ~ **à cavité** cavity package; ~ **à la masse** can earthed; package earthed; ~ **à sorties bilatérales** dual-in-line package (DIL); ~ **céramique** ceramic encapsulation; ~ **d'adaptation réseau (BAR)** network interface module (NIM); line driver; ~ **de circuit intégré** integrated circuit package; ~ **de compoundage** commoning block; ~ **de piquage** drop terminal; ~ **de puissance** driver; ~ **de résistances** resistance network; ~ **de test** test module; ~ **d'inducteur** generator box; ~ **enfichable (à sorties bilatérales)** dual-in-line package (DIP); DIL package; ~ **étanche** dust-and-damp-proof enclosure; fully-enclosed container; ~ **étanche aux poussières** dustproof enclosure; ~ **mémoire** memory chip; ~ **métallique** can; ~ **plastique diffusant** diffused lens package; ~ **plat (à sorties unilatérales)** single-in-line package (SIP); SIL package; flat pack; ~ **rond** (metal) can; metal package; ~ **temporisateur** programmable interval timer (PIT); ~ **test** test module
bolomètre *m* bolometer
bombement *m* swell; bulge; dome
bon *m* voucher; slip; chit; note; schedule; docket; ~ *adj* satisfactory; correct; permitted; passed; approved; fit; suitable; OK; proper; proven; up-to-standard; sound; ~ **aux essais** test OK; ~ **marché** economic; inexpensive; bargain; ~ **renom** corporate image
bond *m* hop; increment; step; section; leap; stride
bonne réception (BR) acknowledgement (bit)
bonnet à trèfle dimmer cap; slotted light shield
bord *m* edge; boundary; side; ~ **arrière** trailing edge; ~ **d'attaque** leading edge; ~ **de référence** reference edge; guide edge
bordereau *m* schedule; source document; job sheet; programming sheet; summary; ~ **de livraison (BL)** shipping note; delivery docket; delivery schedule; ~ **de mise à jour** document release bulletin (updates); ~ **de perforation** coding sheet; source document; ~ **d'envoi** despatch note; consignment note; ~ **d'expédition** despatch note; consignment note
bordure *f* trim; edging; margin
borne *f* bound; boundary; terminal; stud; port; tag; fence; delimiter; post; pin; definition parameter; ~ **à étriers** bridge terminal; ~ **à vis** binding post; ~ **d'antenne**

aerial terminal; aerial connection; ~ **de base** base terminal; ~ **de collecteur** collector terminal; ~ **de connexion** connecting terminal; binding post; ~ **de l'émetteur** emitter terminal; ~ **de reprise** return terminal; ~ **de sortie** output terminal; ~ **d'entrée** input terminal; entrance terminal; ~ **multipolaire** multi-way terminal; ~ **négative** negative terminal; ~ **positive** positive terminal

borné *adj* limited; bounded; restricted; confined

bornes d'entrée et de sortie input and output ports

bornier *m* terminal board; tag strip

bossage *m* projection; boss; relief; shoulder (of IDC terminal)

bosse *f* peak

bosselure *f* dent

botte *f* coil (of cable)

bouche à oreille word of mouth; ~ **artificielle** artificial mouth

bouchée *f* bung; stopper

boucher *v* obstruct; block

Boucherot *m* double squirrel-cage motor

bouchet hole

bouchon *m* program connector; plug; cap; stopper; bung; ~ **d'absorption** acceptor; ~ **fusible** fuse plug; ~ **obturateur** blanking plug; ~ **résistif** programmable connector; resistance plug

bouclage *m* clinch (of component leads); loop(-back); wraparound; op-code DO; iteration; re-entry; tromboning (of calls); busback; recursion; double-check; cross-check; ~ **local** local loopback

boucle *f* loop; line loop; ring(-main); wraparound; mesh; cycle; go-and-return circuit; iteration; antinode; clasp; lug; ear; recursion; ~ **à accès rapide** rapid-access loop; revolver; ~ **à asservissement de phase** phase-locked loop (PLL); ~ **à verrouillage de phase** phase-locked loop (PLL); ~ **analogique** analogue loop(-back); ~ **auto-restaurée** self-resetting loop; ~ **auxiliaire** inner loop; minor loop; ~ **bloquée** closed loop (of control system); ~ **confirmée** confirmed loop condition; ~ **d'adaptation** balun; 'bazooka'; ~ **d'alarme** alarm loop; hoot stop; ~ **d'appel** calling loop; ~ **d'asservissement** control loop; control tape; paper tape loop; carriage tape; ~ **d'attente** busy loop; ~ **de commande** control loop; ~ **de compensation** correcting loop; clearing loop; ~ **de compensation de l'erreur quadrantale** quadrantal error clearing loop; ~ **de couplage** coupling loop; ~ **de phase** phase-locked loop; ~ **de protection contre**

les erreurs error control loop; ~ **de réaction** feedback loop; ~ **de réaction à accrochage de phase** phase-locked loop (PLL); ~ **de régulation** control loop; ~ **de scrutation** scanning loop; ~ **d'équilibrage** balancing loop; ~ **d'hystérésis** hysteresis loop; ~ **d'itération** iterative loop; ~ **emboîtée** nested loop; ~ **en transit** transit loop; ~ **faible** low-resistance loop; ~ **fermée** closed loop; ~ **forte** high-resistence loop; ~ **franche** non-reactive loop; ~ **imbriquée** nested loop; ~ **inactive** idle loop; ~ **ouverte** open(-wire) loop; ~ **permanente** permanent loop; ring-around-the-rosy; ~ **pour contrôle de continuité** check loop; ~ **pour essais de continuité** check loop; ~ **principale** outer loop; major loop; ~ **sèche** dry loop; ~ **secondaire** inner loop; minor loop; ~ **selfique** inductive loop; non-reactive loop

boucler *v* loop; iterate; wrap-around; busback; re-enter; cycle; DO (instruction); ~ **sur une charge** terminate in a load; ~ **un cycle** cycle

bouclette *f* short cycle

bouclier thermique heat shield

boudinette *f* coil; filament

bouée *f* buoy; ~ **à balise passive** radar reflector buoy; ~ **de radar** radar (reflector) buoy

bougie poreuse porous stone (of foam fluxer)

boule *f* sphere; golfball; typing element; ~ **courte** stubby screwdriver; chubby screwdriver

boulier *m* abacus

boulisterie automatique automatic messaging

boulonnerie *f* securing components (nuts and bolts); fasteners

bourdonnement *m* hum

bourrage *m* stuffing bit(s); padding; jamming; filler; ~ **de cartes** card jam; wreck; crash; ~ **d'impulsions** justification; pulse stuffing; bit packing

bourre *f* wadding

bourrelet *m* weld; bulge; blob; shoulder; land; fillet

boursoufflure *f* swelling; blister

boussole *f* galvanometer; compass; ~ **de sinus** sine galvonometer; ~ **de tangentes** tangent galvanometer; ~ **répétrice de radiogoniomètre** direction-finder (DF) repeater compass

bout *m* termination; end; extremity; tip

bouteille *f* cylinder; bottle; canister; ~ **anti-coup de liquide** suction accumulator

bouterolle *f* rivet snap; rivetting bar; dolly

bouton *m* button; key; knob; ~ **à double effet** alternate-action switch; ~ **à enclenchement**

B

self-locking button; locking button; latching pushbutton; ~ **à impulsion calibrée** flash button; ~ **à levier** lever-action DIL switch; ~ **à retour** non-locking button; self-return button; ~ **calibré** loopbreak button; ~ **coup par coup** frequency switch; ~ **d'accord** tuning knob; ~ **d'alternat** press-to-talk switch (PTT); ~ **d'annulation** cancel key; ~ **d'appel** ringing key; call button; ~ **de commande** control knob; ~ **de libération** release button; clear button; ~ **de manœuvre** earth button; loop-break button; ~ **de rappel** recall key; flashing button; ~ **de reprise** earth button; loop-break button; ~ **de signalisation** signalling button; ~ **de terre** service earth; ground button; loopbreak button; service button; call-transfer button; ~ **d'espacement** spacer key; spacing key; ~ **d'isolement** disconnect key; ~ **d'occupation** busy key; ~ **éclairé** illuminated pushbutton; ~ **flashing** register recall button; ~ **moleté** knurled thumbscrew; milled knob; ~ **poussoir (BP)** pushbutton; bell button; plunger key; ~ **poussoir (à tête) à impulsion** momentary-action pushbutton; ~ **poussoir (à tête) pas à pas** alternate-action pushbutton; ~ **poussoir à retour** non-(self-)locking key/pushbutton; ~ **repos (R)** NC push-button (break); ~ **test** push-to-test button

BP (v. bouton poussoir)

BR (v. bit bien reçu); ≈ (v. bonne réception)

bracelet *m* earthing strap

brancard *m* sliding fixture

branche *f* leg; wing; spur; branch; path; arm; section; stroke; lead (of wire)

branchement *m* branch; branching; control transfer; wiring; connection; jump; routing; spur; drop; tap(ping); leg (of cable); termination; ~ **à quatre fils** four-wire termination; ~ **adresse démarrage** jump to start address; ~ **conditionnel** arithmetic I F; computed GO TO; conditional jump; ~ **conditionnel à une adresse réelle** absolute conditional branch; ~ **d'abonné** drop wire; ~ **en dérivation** bridged tap; shunt-connect; ~ **E/S** proceed I/O (input/output); ~ **inconditionnel** unconditional jump; GO-TO function; ~ **systématique** unconditional jump

branchement-débranchement make-and-break

brancher *v* (sur) plug in; connect; lead (to); trap (to); wire (to); switch on; ~ **sur une adresse** trap to an address

branle *m* oscillation

bras *m* spur; wing; arm; dolly; bank; ~ **amortisseur** tension arm; ~ **d'accès** access arm; ~ **de chargement** loading arm;

~ **de lecture** access arm; pick-up arm; ~ **de réactance** non-dissipative stub; ~ **d'écriture** access arm; ~ **d'interrupteur** dolly

brasabilité *f* solderability

brasage *m* (hard) soldering; brazing; ~ **par flux d'air chaud** reflow soldering

brassage *m* cross-connection; mixing; jumper layout; strapping; strap configuration; grading; concentration terminal circuit connections; patching; ~ **de maille** path mixing stage

brassages et interconnections terminal circuit connections; cross-connect (panel)

brasseur *m* cross-connect panel; jumper field; patch panel; ~ **(de voies numériques)** digital distributor

brasure *f* hard-soldered joint; brazing

brevet *m* patent

bricoleur *m* hobbyist; D-I-Y enthusiast; dabbler; amateur inventor

bridage *m* **sur barreau** fixing centre

bride *f* paired operator connection; coupling; circuit; strap; tie; interface; ~ **à capote** G-cramp; clamp; ~ **à piège** choke coupling; choke connector; ~ **de fixation** coupling; connector; ~ **de serrage** clamp; G-cramp; ~ **lisse** plain coupling

bridé *adj* curbed

bride-ressort spring clip; retaining clip (of pot core)

brillance *f* brightness; gloss; sheen

brillant *adj* glossy; bright; brilliant

brin *m* strand; thread; ~ **toronné** twisted strand

brique (de logiciel) *f* software module

brise jet spray shield

brochage *m* pin configuration; pin-out(s); lead-out; pin identification; pin assignment; ~ **compatible avec** pin-to-pin compatible with

broche *f* pin; tag; spigot; stud; link; shaft; spindle; arbor; axis; lug; ~ **à insertion sans soudure** force-fit pin; solderless pin; Press-Fit pin; ~ **affichée** selected pin; ~ **de culot** base pin; ~ **de sectionnement** isolating link; ~ **logique** logic pin

brochette *f* quintuplet (five-coil) relay

bromure de méthyle bromomethane; methyl bromide

bronze *m* gun metal

brosse de lecture *f* brush; wiper; ~ **de masse** grounding brush; ~ **métallique** wire brush

brouillage *m* interference; jamming; scrambling; mush; spurious condition; atmospherics; ~ **à bande étroite** spot jamming; ~ **accidentel** passive jamming; inadvertent jamming; ~ **dû à une bande latérale** sideband interference; ~ **électromagnéti-**

que electromagnetic interference (EMI); ~ **intentionnel** active jamming; ~ **radioélectrique** radio interference; ~ **volontaire à large bande** barrage jamming
brouillard salin salt mist (test); salt spray
brouiller *v* (intentionellement) scramble; jam
brouilleur *m* interfering transmitter; scrambler; jammer; ~ **à antenne en tourniquet** turnstile jammer; ~ **à bande étroite** spot jammer; ~ **à grande puissance** disruptive jammer; ~ **à large bande** barrage jammer; ~ **à modulation par courant** modulated CW jammer; ~ **à polarisation croisée** cross-polarisation jammer; ~ **accordable** concurrently-tuned jammer; ~ **automatique d'exploration** automatic search jammer; ~ **de radar** radar jammer; ~ **intentionnel** active jammer; ~ **intentionnel à impulsions retardées** locked pulse jammer; ~ **préréglé** preset jammer; ~ **répéteur à rayonnement double en contrephase** dual-source repeater jammer; ~ **terrestre** ground-based jammer; ~ **wobulateur** sweep-through jammer
brouillon *m* scratch-pad
broutage *m* scanning; judder; chatter; browsing; ~ **longitudinal** longitudinal judder
broutement *m* chattering
broutille *f* doodle (of graphics package)
broyeur *m* crusher
brucelles *f pl* tweezers
bruit *m* noise; interference; discrepancy; glitch; hiss; jitter; hum; howl; babble; din; ripple; click; false retrieval; false drop; distortion; ~ **à spectre continu et uniforme** uniform random noise; white noise; ~ **à spectre de Hoth** Hoth noise; ~ **acoustique** acoustic noise; ~ **aléatoire** random noise; stochastic noise; ~ **atmosphérique** atmospheric noise; atmospherics (QRN); ~ **BF** (basse fréquence) flicker noise; ~ **blanc** white noise; broadband noise; uniform (spectrum) random noise; flat random noise; Gaussian noise; thermal noise; ~ **continu** continuous disturbance; sustained noise; ~ **cosmique** cosmic noise; extra-terrestrial noise; inter-stellar noise; ~ **d'agitation thermique** thermal noise; Brownian motion of electrons; Gaussian noise; Johnson noise; resistance noise; ~ **d'agrément** comfort noise (level); ~ **d'alimentation** battery supply circuit noise; hum; ~ **d'allure erratique** random noise; ~ **d'amplificateur** amplifier noise; ~ **de circuit** line/circuit noise; ~ **de circuit erratique** random circuit noise; ~ **de commutation** switch clicks; ~ **de commutation et de friture** switching noise; contact noise; ~ **de cornemuse** bagpipes; wailing;

howling; ~ **de diaphonie** babble; ~ **de fond** background noise; random noise; hum; ambient noise; receiver/set noise; ~ **de friture** frying noise; contact noise; ~ **de Gauss** Gaussian noise; ~ **de grenaille** shot effect; hiss; Gaussian noise; shot noise; ~ **de la voie au repos** idle-channel noise; ~ **de l'ambiance** ambient noise; ~ **de large bande** broadband noise; wideband noise; ~ **de ligne** line noise; ~ **de microphone** transmitter noise; hiss; burning; frying; microphone noise; ~ **de modulation** modulation noise; ~ **de phase** phase jitter; ~ **de quantification** quantizing distortion; quantizing noise; quantizing error; ~ **de salle** room noise; ~ **de saturation** saturation noise; ~ **de scintillation** flicker noise; flicker effect; ~ **de secteur** mains hum; AC hum; ~ **de sélecteurs** dial effect; dialling effect; ~ **de signal** signal noise; ~ **de télégraphie** telegraph noise; thump; ~ **de terre** earth noise; ~ **de troncature** truncation noise; ~ **d'écoute** listening tone; ~ **des contacts** contact noise; ~ **d'impulsion** pulse noise; ~ **d'intermodulation** intermodulation noise; intermodulation distortion; crosstalk; ~ **d'origine thermique** thermal noise; ~ **électromagnétique** electromagnetic noise; ~ **en créneau** popcorn noise; ~ **équivalent d'entrée** equivalent noise input (ENI); ~ **erratique** random noise; shot noise; hiss; Gaussian noise; ~ **erratique triangulaire** triangular random noise; ~ **extra-terrestre** cosmic noise; extra-terrestrial noise; inter-stellar noise; ~ **gaussien** Gaussian noise; thermal noise; shot noise; ~ **impulsif** impulse noise; click; burst; ~ **induit** induced noise; power induction; ~ **large bande** wideband noise; ~ **mécanique** non-electrical noise; ~ **naturel** natural interference; natural noise; ~ **non pondéré** flat (unweighted) noise; ~ **parasite** extraneous noise; spurious interference; ~ **parasite d'ambiance** sidetone; ~ **périodique** periodic noise; intermittent interference; ~ **permanent** steady noise; ~ **pondéré** psophometric noise; weighted noise; ~ **pondéré d'une voie au repos** idle-channel weighted noise; ~ **propre** inherent noise; set noise; receiver noise; residual noise; ~ **pseudo-aléatoire** pseudo-random noise; ~ **psophométrique** psophometric noise; ~ **quasi-impulsif** pseudo-random noise; ~ **radioélectrique** radio noise; ~ **récurrent** periodic noise; intermittent noise; ~ **résiduel** ripple; ~ **rose** pink noise; random noise; ~ **sonore de commutation** switching noise; ~ **soutenu** steady

B

noise; sustained noise; ~ **subjectif** subjective noise; ~ **sur une seule fréquence** single-frequency noise; ~ **sur une voie au repos** idle-channel noise; ~ **télégraphique** telegraph noise; ~ **thermique** thermal noise; resistance noise; ~ **triangulaire** triangular noise

bruitage *m* key click; positive key presssure

brûlé *adj* scorched; charred; adj.

brûlure *f* **d'écran** screen burn; ~ **d'un redresseur à cristal** burn-out (of crystal rectifier); ~ **ionique** ion burning

brut *adj* raw; unprocessed; gross; original; crude; unrefined; coarse; basic; natural; ~ **de fonderie** rough-cast

brutal *adj* sudden; abrupt; sharp

bruyant *adj* noisy

BT (v. base de temps); ≈ (v. binaire translatable)

BTG (v. base de temps générale)

bufférisation *f* buffering

builder *v* assemble; construct; build

bulle *f* blister; bubble; air-hole

bulletin *m* **de dérangement** fault report; fault docket

bureau *m* desk; office; exchange; ~ **automatique** dial exchange; ~ **avec retour** desk with modesty panel; ~ **central** central office; exchange; ~ **central automatique** automatic exchange; ~ **central de téléimprimeurs** teleprinter (telex) exchange; ~ **central interurbain** trunk exchange; ~ **central manuel** manual exchange; ~ **central non surveillé** unattended exchange; unmanned exchange; ~ **central télégraphique** central telegraph office; ~ **d'arrivée** called exchange; terminating exchange; ~ **de départ** originating exchange; calling exchange; ~ **de destination** office of destination; ~ **d'études** drawing office; design centre; planning office; research department; ~ **d'origine** office of origin; ~ **émetteur** forwarding office; sending office; ~ **interurbain extrême** terminal trunk exchange;

~ **local** local exchange; ~ **manuel** manual exchange; operator-controlled exchange; ~ **ministre** double-pedestal desk; ~ **mixte** auto-manual exchange; ~ **récepteur** receiving office; ~ **satellite** satellite exchange; remote line unit (RLU); ~ **télégraphique** telegraph office; ~ **téléphonique** telephone exchange; ~ **téléphonique automatique rural** rural automatic exchange (RAX); ~ **téléphonique en projet** hypothetical exchange; ~ **téléphonique local** local exchange; ~ **téléphonique manuel** manual exchange; ~ **urbain** local central office

bureauticienne word processor operator

bureautique *f* office automation

bureaux connectés linked exchanges

bus *m* bus; trunk; highway; ~ **A** A-bus; ~ **à rallonge** bus extension; expansion bus; ~ **bidirectionnel** two-way bus; bus transceiver; ~ **coaxial** coaxial trunk; ~ **d'adresses** address bus; ~ **d'autorisation** enable bus; ~ **de confirmation d'exécution** all-seems-well bus; ~ **de contrôle** control bus; ~ **de données** data bus; ~ **de liaison programmée** data link; ~ **de marquage** marking bus; ~ **de transfert d'informations** data bus; ~ **déporté** (peripheral) bus extension; ~ **des mémoires d'appel** call store bus; ~ **rapide** high-speed bus

buse *f* pipe; nozzle; tip; spout (of waveguide); ~ **chauffante** heat gun; hot air blower; ~ **de flux** flux chimney

but *m* object(ive); aim; purpose; goal; target

butée *f* positive stop; abutment; buffer; bracket; spacer; yoke; gate; stand-off; spur; residual screw (of relay); limiting value; crowbar protection device; ~ **d'arrêt** end stop; bracket; back stop; ~ **de cadran** finger stop; ~ **de descente** downward travel stop; ram stroke gap; gap clearance; ~ **progressive** buffered stop; cushioned stop; ~ **réglable** adjustable dead stop

butoir *m* buffer

C

c (v. crête)

ca (v. courant alternatif)

CAA (v. centre à autonomie d'acheminement); ∴ (v. comptabilité automatique des
appels)

CAB (v. code à barres)

cabestan *m* capstan (of tape deck); ~ **d'entraînement** capstan

cabine *f* kiosk; booth; enclosure; blimp;
shelter; ~ **(à) paiement** callbox; coinbox;
prepayment kiosk; payphone; ~ **de nuit**
night kiosk; ~ **de programme** (en sonore)
continuity equipment room; ~ **publique**
public callbox; coinbox; paystation; pay-
phone; prepayment kiosk; ~ **publique à
prépaiement** pay-phone; ~ **technique** (de
prise de son) sound-recording cubicle;
~ **téléphonique** call booth/box; telephone
booth/box

cabinet consultancy

câblage *m* wiring; cable run; cables; bus;
laying-up; ~ **arrière** backplane wiring;
~ **bifilaire** two-core cable; dual-conductor
wiring; ~ **chantier** field wiring; ~ **coaxial**
HF HF coaxial cable; concentric cable;
~ **en fil nu** bare wiring; ~ **en nappe** cable
bundle; ribbon-cable wiring; ~ **imprimé**
printed wiring; ~ **inter-alvéoles** inter-shelf
wiring; ~ **manuel** manual wiring; ~ **marguerite** daisychain (wiring); ~ **orthogonal**
right-angled wiring; ~ **par points de souture**
stitch wiring; ~ **prévu pour** wired(-up) for;
pre-wired; ~ **semi-automatique** semi-automatic wiring; ~ **sub-local A (CSL-A)**
four-wire cluster network; ~ **sub-local B
(CSL-B)** two-wire cluster link; ~ **usine**
factory wiring

câble *m* cable; feeder; wire; lead; conductor;
~ **à charge continue** continuously-loaded
cable; ~ **à courants porteurs sur paire
symétrique** balanced-pair carrier cable; ~ **à
deux conducteurs** twin-core cable; (twisted)
pair cable; dual-conductor cable; ~ **à fibre
gainée** sheathed (direct strand) cable; ~ **à
fibre libre** loose tube fibre cable; ~ **à
grande distance** long-distance cable; ~ **à
isolement enroulé** belted cable; ~ **à jonc
rainuré** slotted-core cable; helical groove
cable; ~ **à paires** paired cable; twin cable;
non-quad cable; ~ **à paires combinables**
multiple-twin quad cable; ~ **à paires en
étoile** quad-pair cable; ~ **à paires symétriques** balanced pair cable; ~ **à paires
torsadées** paired cable; twin cable; ~ **à
plusiers quartes** quad-pair cable; ~ **à
plusieurs conducteurs** multi-core cable; ~ **à
quartes** multiple twin cable; quad cable;
~ **à quartes DM** (Dieselhorst-Martin)
multiple-twin quad cable; ~ **à quartes en
étoile** star-quad cable; ~ **à structure cylindrique rainurée**
slotted (V-grooved) cylindrical former; ~ **à
tresse métallique** screened cable; ~ **aérien**
overhead cable; aerial wire; ~ **armé**
armour-clad cable; shielded cable; ~ **auxiliaire** (feeder) relief cable; ~ **blindé**
shielded cable; armour-clad cable;
~ **chargé** (coil) loaded cable; ~ **coaxial**
coax(ial) cable; concentric cable; ~ **composite** composite cable; ~ **conjoncté** connectorized cable; ~ **creux** hollow conductor;
~ **croisé** inverter cable; null modem cable;
~ **cylindrique de rainure** V-grooved cylinder cable; ~ **d'alimentation** power cable;
feeder; ~ **d'allumage** ignition lead; ~ **d'atterissage** approach cable; ~ **de branchement** branch cable; drop wire; ~ **de
campagne** field cable; ~ **de distribution**
distribution cable (line connection); ~ **de
garde** earth wire; ~ **de jonction** connecting
cable; trunk cable; ~ **de ligne** distribution
cable; ~ **de masse** earthing conductor;
~ **de multiple** bank cable; ~ **de raccord**
cable link; patching cord; ~ **de raccordement** connecting cable; ~ **de radiodiffusion**
transmission cable; ~ **de radioguidage**
leader cable; ~ **de service** office cable;
~ **de télévision** television cable; ~ **de terre**
earth cable; ~ **de traction** snake; ~ **de
transport** feeder; ~ **de transport primaire**
primary cable feeder; ~ **d'énergie** power
cable; ~ **d'immeuble** house cable; residential building cable; ~ **d'interconnexion
batterie** battery interconnection cable
(BIC); ~ **en fils d'acier** steel wire armoured
cable; ~ **en nappe** ribbon cable; ~ **enfichable** connectorized cable; plug-in cable;
~ **enterré** buried cable; ~ **équibrins**
conductor with equal-diameter strands;
~ **équipé** connectorized cable; plug-ended

cable; ~ **expansé** expanded conductor; ~ **haute fréquence** HF feeder; ~ **interurbain** trunk cable; toll cable; ~ **krarupisé** continuously-loaded cable; ~ **lisse** (clos) smooth-bodied conductor; ~ **méplat** bell wire; ribbon cable; flat cable; ~ **mixte** composite cable; ~ **monobrin** solid-conductor cable; ~ **monoconducteur** single-conductor cable; ~ **monofilaire** single-conductor cable; ~ **multiple** multi-core cable; poly-core cable; ~ **nappé** ribbon cable; harness; ~ **non armé** unarmoured cable; unshielded cable; unclad cable; ~ **non blindé** armourless cable; unarmoured cable; ~ **non chargé** unloaded cable; ~ **non pupinisé** non-loaded cable; unloaded cable; ~ **nu** plain cable; lead-covered cable; ~ **optique** optical fibre cable; ~ **plat** flat cable; ribbon cable; band cable; ~ **porteur** track load; messenger wire; bearer cable; catenary; ~ **principal** main cable; ~ **prolongateur** extension lead; extension cable; ~ **pupinisé** coil-loaded cable; loaded cable; ~ **pupinisé en fantôme** composite loaded cable; ~ **ruban** ribbon cable; ~ **sec** dry core cable; ~ **souple** flex(ible) wire; ~ **sous caoutchouc** rubber-insulated cable; ~ **sous écran** screened cable; ~ **sous papier** paper-insulated cable; ~ **sous plomb** lead-sheathed cable; ~ **sous pression** gas-filled cable; ~ **sous-marin** submarine cable; undersea cable; ~ **sous-marin de grand fond** submarine cable; deep-sea cable; ~ **souterrain** buried cable; underground cable; ~ **télégraphique** telegraph cable; ~ **téléphonique** telephone cable; ~ **torsadé** stranded cable; ~ **tracteur** hauling cable; ~ **transatlantique** transatlantic cable; Atlantic cable

câblé hard-wired; jumper-selected; firmware; ~ **en peigne** wired-in; harnessed in cable form; ~ **en usine** factory-wired

câblerie f cable manufacturers

câbles à paires combinables multiple-twin quad cable; ~ **d'adduction** supply cables; ~ **groupés** bunched cables

câblette f bond wire; pulling wire

câbleur m wireman

câbleuse f wire-wrapper (person); wiring machine

câblier m cable-laying vessel

câbliers m pl cable-laying contractors; cable manufacturers

câblodistribution f wired broadcasting; cable distribution

câblogramme m cable; cablegram; wire

cabochon m dimmer cap; (hooded) reflector; (hooded) lens; faceplate (of button); lamp cap

cache f cover; mask; guard; protection; blank; surround (of screen); overlay; ~ **cadran** dial blank; dial cover; ~ **intermédiaire PF** fuse-panel intermediate cover; blanking plate; ~ **sommet** vertex plate (of aerial reflector)

CAD (poste à cadran) (rotary) dial set; dial-up telephone; ⁓ (v. connexion auto-dénudante); ⁓ (v. contact auto-dénudant)

cadenas m padlock

cadence f rate; tempo; speed; frequency; timing signal; throughput; quota; ~ **de balayage** sweep rate; ~ **de base** basic repetition rate; interrupt rate; ~ **de battement** bounce rate (of relay contacts); ~ **de rafales** burst rate; ~ **de taxation** metering rate; ~ **de test** test rate; ~ **de transfert** transfer rate; ~ **d'échange cumulée** cumulative interchange rate; ~ **d'échantillonnage** sampling rate; sampling frequency

cadencé adj interrupted

cadencement m repetition rate; timing; interrupt rate; time base; pulsing

cadencer v interrupt; clock; pulse; ~ **en 0** transmit at rate zero

cadenceur m rate regulator; interrupt cam

cadmié adj cadmium-plated

cadrage m scaling; alignment; synchronization; justification; framing; boundary; phasing; tabulation; adjustment; registration; ~ **du temps de réponse** response time alignment

cadran m rotary dial; dial plate; dial; gauge; meter; indicator panel; ~ **blindé** screened loop aerial; shielded loop aerial; ~ **d'appel** fingerwheel; finger plate; dial; ~ **de numérotation** rotary dial; ~ **double croisé** double crossed-loop aerial; ~ **numéroté** numeral ring; ~ **sans effet de nuit** spaced-frame aerial; spaced-loop aerial

cadre m retaining ring; frame; shelf; aerial; dial; panel; rack; bay; section; gate; loop aerial; balanced frame aerial; context; environment; sash; box

cadre(s) senior staff; management; professional and executive personnel (P&E)

cadre arrière backplane; ~ **arrière câblé** wired backplane; ~ **arrière équipé** backplane assembly; ~ **de manutention** handling frame; ~ **de page** page frame; ~ **de positionnement des alvéoles** shelf positioning frame; ~ **de soudage** welding frame; soldering frame; ~ **de travail** wiring bench; ~ **Epstein** (de 25 cm) Epstein hysteresis tester; Epstein square; ~ **équilibré** balanced-coil; balanced-frame aerial; ~ **haut de serrurerie** rack-top (amplifier shelf);

~ **pivotant** gate; ~ **professionnel** line manager; ~ **radiocompas** (directional) loop aerial; ~ **radiogoniométrique** (v. cadre radiocompas); ~ **rotatif** rotating frame aerial; ~ **roulant** mobile frame; ~ **simple** torque band (of galvanometer); ~ **supérieur** senior; top executive; management official

cadré à gauche left justified; ~ **par** between; enclosed in; surrounded by

cadrer (à droite/à gauche) scale; adjust; (right/left) justify; align

cadres jumelés twin loop

cadreur *m* phaser

CAF (v. commande automatique de fréquence); ~ **à verrouillage** clamped AFC (automatic frequency control)

CAG (v. commande automatique de gain)

cage *f* cabinet (of rheometer, etc.)

cahier *m* log book; ~ **de charges (CdC)** specifications; technical data sheet; generic specifications; ~ **de recette** factory acceptance test report; ~ **de suivi** log; progress report

caisse *f* case; crate; box; receptacle; housing; ~ **de bobines** coil box

caisson *m* cubicle; enclosure; housing; console; ~ **d'isolement (diélectrique)** insulating wall; ~ **émetteur-récepteur** transceiver container; ~ **enterrable** underground vault; ~ **étanche** watertight enclosure

CALA (v. comptabilité automatique locale des appels)

calage *m* timing; setting; calibration; adjustment; clamping; lead(ing); advance; jamming; stalling; keying; fitting; mounting; securing; loop alignment; displacement; incidence; ~ **de la fréquence** frequency setting; ~ **du faisceau** beam positioning; ~ **du niveau du noir** black-level clamping; ~ **par radar** radar calibration

calamine *f* (mill) scale; sludge

calcinateur *m* asher

calcul *m* computing; computation; arithmetic operation; calculation; reckoning; calculus; evaluation; algebra; theory; analysis; assessment; processing; design; logic; logical operation; ~ **approché** smoothing; ~ **d'adresse** address computation; ~ **d'arbre minimal** optimal (merge) tree computation; ~ **de phase** program counter; ~ **de résistance** stress analysis; ~ **d'itinéraire** path analysis; route analysis; ~ **en double précision** double-precision arithmetic; ~ **et stockage de la taxe** bulk billing; ~ **formel** formal logic; ~ **vidéo** double-precision arithmetic

calculateur *m* computer; processor; minicom-

puter; calculator; mainframe; CPU (central processing unit); ~ **à incréments** incremental computer; ~ **à programme câblé** wired program computer; firmware processor; ~ **à programme enregistré** stored program computer; ~ **à réseau analogique** analogue array computer; ~ **analogique** analogue computer; ~ **arithmétique** arithmetic computer; digital computer; ~ **de consultation** enquiry computer; ~ **de mise à jour de la base de données** data base updating computer; ~ **de réserve** standby processor; ~ **d'exécution** target computer; ~ **en temps réel** real-time computer; ~ **hybride** hybrid computer; ~ **incrémentiel** incremental computer; ~ **industriel** process-control computer; ~ **intégrateur de la hauteur d'avions** radar aircraft altitude calculator (RAAC); ~ **microprogrammé** microprogrammed computer; ~ **numérique** digital computer; ~ **par accroissements** incremental computer; ~ **parallèle** parallel computer; ~ **pilote** control computer; ~ **réseau** front-end processor; ~ **séquentiel à enchaînement arbitraire** arbitrary sequence computer; ~ **série** serial computer; ~ **universel** general-purpose computer

calculatrice *f* (desk-top/pocket) calculator; ~ **perforatrice** calculating punch; multiplying punch

calculé *adj* diversity-processed

calculer *v* calculate; compute; evaluate; assess

calculographe calculograph; traffic recorder/logger

cale *f* (c. d'épaisseur) spacer; wedge; chock; shim; packing piece; washer; block; gauge; ~ **biaise** taper washer; ~ **de contrôle** gauge block; ~ **de surélévation** stand-off spur; clearance shim; ~ **étalon** standard shim; stop measure; (feeler) gauge; ~ **position machine** machine positioning shim

calendrier *m* schedule; calendar; timetable; ~ **d'exploitation** operating schedule

calepinage *n* floor slab layout; balanced distribution

caleur *m* clamp

calibrage *m* rating; rating plate; timing; adjustment; calibration; ~ **de la distance** range calibration

calibrateur *m* calibrator; ~ **découpleur** decoupler (isolated data transmitter) calibrator

calibre *m* range; size; bore; template; rated; measuring instrument; gauge; graph; rating; insertion gauge; capacity; ~ **de calage** document gauge; ~ **de fusible** fuse rating; ~ **de pointage** peg insertion gauge; ~ **entre/n'entre pas** GO/NO-GO gauge

calibré à partir du logiciel software-controlled
calibre-mâchoires gap gauge
calibrer v calibrate; gauge; frame; time
caloduc m heat duct
calorifuge adj flame-resistant; heatproof; insulated
calorifugé adj thermally-insulated
calorifugeage m lagging
calotte f cap; cover; crown; dome; canopy; hood; shroud; flash
calque m transparency; print master; original
cambouis m swarf
cambrage m bending
cambrer v bend; shape; form
cambreur m bending tool
came f channel release conditions; cam timer; cam; time signal; ~ **de signe** code cam
caméra f **de télévision** television camera
camouflage m (contre la radiodétection) radar camouflage
campagne f drive; campaign
CAN (convertisseur analogique-numérique) A/D converter (analogue-to-digital converter)
canal m channel; level (of tape); time slot; band; highway; horizontal channel; track; broadband channel; interface; bus line; link; trunk; path; port; ~ **à large bande** broadband channel; wideband channel; ~ **à large bande à trafic simultané dans les deux sens** broadband duplex channel; ~ **adjacent** adjacent channel; ~ **aller** go path; ~ **auxiliaire** backward channel; return path; ~ **banalisé** CB channel; citizen's band channel; ~ **collecteur de données** data bus line; ~ **conducteur** on-state channel; driving channel; ~ **d'accès à la mémoire** data bus; ~ **d'adaptation** peripheral interface channel; ~ **de commande** control channel; ~ **de communication** signalling channel; ~ **de communication système** system communications interface; ~ **de déviation** alternate channel; ~ **de données** data bus line; ~ **de fréquences** frequency channel; channel passband; ~ **de gestion** signalling channel; data link channel; ~ **de liaison directe** direct data channel; ~ **de protection** protection channel; ~ **de protection à large bande** broadband protection channel; ~ **de radio** radio channel; ~ **de réception** receive channel; ~ **de réserve** standby channel; on-call channel; ~ **de retour** backward channel; feedback channel; return path; ~ **de service** service channel; ~ **de signal** signal channel; signal transmission path; ~ **de télévision** television channel; ~ **de test** test interface; ~ **de transmission de données**

data link; ~ **desservant une imprimante** printer port; ~ **direct** television channel using upper sideband; ~ **du signal relais** relay channel; ~ **d'une voie** highway; bus (of multiplex channel); ~ **électronique à trois anodes** triode electron gun; ~ **hertzien** microwave channel; ~ **interdit** unauthorized channel; ~ **inversé** lower sideband television channel; ~ **multiple** multiplex channel; ~ **multiplexeur de blocs** block multiplexer channel; ~ **multiplexeur de multiplets** byte multiplexer channel; ~ **particulier** dedicated time slot; ~ **pour usage commun** common-user channel; ~ **radioélectrique** radio-frequency channel; ~ **rapide** high-speed channel; ~ **réservé** dedicated channel; ~ **retour** return channel; ~ **RF** RF channel; ~ **sac** storage access channel (SAC); ~ **secondaire** sub-channel; ~ **sélecteur** selector channel; ~ **sémaphore** common signalling channel; PCM data channel; ~ **sémaphore (à l'état) actif** active signalling link; ~ **téléphonique** voice-grade channel; ~ **vocal** voice-grade channel; ~ **vocal sol-air** ground-air voice channel; ~ **vocal vaisseau-vaisseau** ship-to-ship channel; ~ **voie par voie** channel-associated signalling channel
canalisation f (de réseau électrique) duct; feeder; conduit
canalisations électriques wiring
canaux à distribution égale de périodes equal-ratio channels; ~ **bouchés** blocked channels; ~ **de communications à courant simple d'un circuit télégraphique** quadruplex single-current message channels of a quadruplex telegraph circuit; ~ **d'E/S** I/O channels; ~ **d'intercommunication** communication channels; ~ **partiellement superposés** overlapping channels
canevas m background; field; raster; outline; sketch; thumbnail description
caniveau m cable trench; cable runway; raceway; floor chase; duct
canne f probe
cannelé adj grooved; fluted; serrated; splined; slotted
canon m spacing washer; bush; guide; (electron-)gun; (lamp socket) securing ring; insulation displacement tool; barrel; ~ **de compression** compression barrel; ~ **de métallisation** plated-through bush; ~ **électronique** electron gun
canton m section (of overhead cable); block
cantonnement m blocking
CAO (v. conception assistée par ordinateur)
CAP (v. commande autonome programmé)

capacimètre *m* capacitance meter
capacité *f* capacity; capacitance; capacitor;
pick-up; transducer; sensor; size (of fuse,
memory, etc.); throughput; calibre; ~ **commutée** switched capacitance; ~ **concentrée**
lumped capacitance; ~ **d'accueil** acceptance capacity; ~ **de canal** channel
capacity; ~ **de charge** load (carrying)
capacity; load factor; wattage; load point;
power rating; ~ **de jonction** junction
capacitance; depletion layer capacitance;
~ **de la zone de transition du collecteur**
collector depletion layer capacitance; ~ **de
la zone de transition de l'émetteur** emitter
depletion layer capacitance; ~ **de l'autocommutateur** exchange capacity; ~ **de
liaison** coupling capacitor; ~ **de raccordement** terminal capacity; ~ **de réaction**
reverse transfer capacitance; ~ **de signalisation** signalling capacity; ~ **de sonde**
mutual capacitance; ~ **de sortie** output
capacitance; ~ **de sortie, en base commune**
output capacitance in common-base configuration; ~ **de sortie, en émetteur commun**
output capacitance in common-emitter
configuration; ~ **de sortie, entrée en
court-circuit** output capacitance (input
short-circuited to AC); ~ **de sortie, entrée
en court-circuit, en source commune** short-
circuit output capacitance in common-
source configuration (drain-source short-
circuited to AC); ~ **de sortie, entrée en
circuit ouvert** output capacitance (input
open-circuited to AC); ~ **de trafic** traffic
capacity; ~ **de transfert inverse en source
commune, entrée en court-circuit** common-
source reverse transfer capacitance (input
short-circuited to AC); ~ **de transfert
inverse, entrée en court-circuit** reverse
transfer capacitance (input short-circuited
to AC); ~ **de transfert inverse, en émetteur
commun** reverse transfer capacitance in
common-emitter configuration; ~ **de transfert inverse, en base commune** reverse
transfer capacitance in common-base configuration; ~ **de transition** depletion layer
capacitance; junction capacitance; ~ **de
voie** channel capacity; ~ **d'écoulement de
trafic** traffic handling capacity; traffic
flow; ~ **d'électrode** total electrode capacitance; ~ **d'entrée** input capacitance;
~ **d'entrée en base commune** input capacitance in common-base configuration;
~ **d'entrée en émetteur commun** input
capacitance in common-emitter configuration; ~ **d'entrée, sortie en circuit ouvert**
input capacitance (output open-circuited to
AC); ~ **d'entrée, sortie en court-circuit**
input capacitance (output short-circuited to
AC); ~ **d'entrée, sortie en court-circuit, en
source commune** short-circuit input capacitance in common source configuration;
gate-source capacitance, drain-source
short-circuited to AC; ~ **d'entretien** maintainability; ~ **différentielle** small-signal
capacitance; ~ **directe** direct capacitance;
~ **du circuit combinant** side-circuit capacitance; ~ **d'un circuit oscillant** tank-circuit
capacitance; ~ **d'une couche d'arrêt** barrier-layer capacitance; ~ **d'une mémoire**
memory capacity; ~ **effective** mutual
capacitance; ~ **effective de l'espace d'interaction** effective gap capacitance; ~ **effective d'entrée** effective input capacitance;
~ **entre deux paires** side-to-side capacitance; ~ **entre enroulements** inter-winding
capacitance; ~ **entre paires** phantom
capacity; ~ **entre spires** inter-winding
capacitance; ~ **grille-plaque** anode-grid
capacitance; ~ **grille-source** gate-source
capacitance (in the equivalent circuit);
~ **interélectrode** direct (inter-)electrode
capacitance; ~ **inutilisé** dead space; void;
~ **linéique** capacitance per unit length;
~ **mémoire** storage capacity; ~ **nominale**
rated capacitance; ~ **par rapport à la masse**
earth capacitance; ~ **parasite** stray capacitance; ~ **plaque-cathode** plate-cathode
capacitance; ~ **propre** self-capacitance;
internal capacitance; ~ **réel-terre** earth
capacitance; ~ **répartie** self-capacitance;
distributed capacitance; ~ **résiduelle** residual capacitance; zero capacity; ~ **statique**
static capacitance; ~ **sur picot** (PCB-mounting) trimmer; ~ **terminale** capacity terminal; ~ **théorique de charge** design load
capacity; ~ **totale d'affichage** display
capacity
capillaire *adj* pin-point; capillary
capital *m* equity shares; assets; capital stocks
capot *m* hood; casing; surround; fascia; cap;
guard; canopy; enclosure; cowling;
shroud; cover; fairing; panel; fillet; ~ **anti-
poussière** dust cover; ~ **de protection**
fender; protection cap; (connector) shroud
capsule *f* capsule; can; insert; cap; cartridge;
stud; ~ **microphonique** transmitter capsule;
microphone capsule; ~ **réceptrice** receiver
insert
captage *m* **de données** capture; intercept;
detection; sensing; acquisition
captation *f* intercept routine; absorption;
~ **des vapeurs** fume cupboard; steam trap
capter *v* intercept; sense; pick-up; detect
capteur *m* pick-up; transducer; sensor;
proximity switch; pick-off; sensing device;

C

detector; gauge; ~ **de compression** strain gauge; ~ **de mesure** measuring sensor; metering unit; ~ **optique** optical receiver; photodetector

CAPU (concentrateur-aiguilleur public) public concentrator/message-switching unit

capuchon *m* cap; cover; hood; shroud; boot; ~ **en caoutchouc** rubber boot

car de reportage outside broadcast van; OB van

caractère *m* character; digit; type font; ~ **additionnel** additional character; special character; ~ **blanc** blank; idle character; space; NULL; ~ **codé** control character; coded character; ~ **codé (en) binaire** binary-coded character; ~ **d'accusé réception** acknowledge character; ~ **d'acheminement** code-directing character; ~ **d'annulation** cancel character; ~ **d'annulation de bloc** block cancel character; ~ **d'appoint** filler character; ~ **d'arrêt** terminator; X-off; ~ **de bourrage** stuffing character; ~ **de chargement de code** escape character (ESC); ~ **de code spécial** shift-out character; coded character; ~ **de commande** control character; instruction character; ~ **de commande d'appel** call control character; ~ **de commande de transmission** transmission control character; ~ **de contrôle** check character; check bit; ~ **de contrôle de justesse** accuracy control character; ~ **de contrôle d'erreur** error control character; check digit; ~ **de contrôle par bloc** block-check character; ~ **de correction** correction character; ~ **de fin de message** message terminal load (MTL); ~ **de fonction** control character; end-to-end character (of EBCIDIC system); ~ **de liaison** break character; separator; ~ **de mise en page** format effector; layout character; ~ **de rejet** ignore character; erase character; error character; ~ **de remplissage** filler character; gap digits; ~ **de répétition** continuation character; ~ **de repris** transmitter on (X-on); ~ **de saut de papier** paper-throw character; ~ **de séparation** separator; separating character; ~ **de service** (transmission) control character; ~ **de signe** sign character; ~ **de substitution** wild-card character; ~ **de synchronisation** synchronous character; ~ **d'effacement** ignore character; rub-out character (DEL); ~ **d'effacement par bloc** block-ignore character; ~ **d'espace arrière** backspace character; ~ **d'oblitération** ignore character; rub-out character (DEL); ~ **d'omission de bloc** block ignore character; ~ **encliquetable** clip-on character;

~ **espace** blank character; space character; ~ **fin de bloc** sentinel; ETB character; block mark; ~ **fin de ligne (CFL)** end-of-line character; ~ **fin de support** end-of-medium character (EM); ~ **graphique** graphic character; ~ **gras** bold character; ~ **imprimable** graphic character; alphanumeric character; printing/printable character; ~ **inactive** passive (idle) character; blank; space; ~ **indicateur** prompt; flag; ~ **interdit** disguised character; illegal character; ~ **inutile** void; redundant character; ~ **mobile** drifting character; ~ **non imprimable** non-printing character; null character; idle character; control character; ~ **non imprimable** control character; ~ **nul** blank character; NULL; idle character; ~ **parasite** (character) ghost; ~ **redondant** redundant character; ~ **romain** roman character; ~ **séparation** separating character; separator

caractére tampon pad

caractère variable mask

caractères par pouce (CCPP) characters per inch (CPI); pitch; ~ **par seconde (car/s)** characters per second (CPS)

caractérisation *f* reference; distinctive features; title; designation; denomination; code; typology

caractériser *v* signify; indicate; represent; symbolize; typify; distinguish; define; code; depict

caractéristique(s) *f* characteristic; characteristic curve; feature; parameter; exponent; rating; typical applications data; performance data; specifications; index; response; attribute; customer benefits; profile

caractéristique *adj* individual; distinctive; distinguishing; critical; usual; typical; customary; appropriate; characteristic; intrinsic; inherent; ~ **à déphasage minimal** minimum-phase frequency characteristic; ~ **affaiblissement-fréquence** attenuation-frequency characteristic; ~ **amplitude-fréquence** frequency characteristic; ~ **bidirectionnelle** bidirectional characteristic; ~ **couple** torque rating; ~ **courant-tension** current-voltage characteristic; ~ **d'amplitude** amplitude/response characteristic; ~ **de commande** control characteristic; ~ **de décharge** flashover characteristic (discharge); ~ **de diode** diode characteristic; ~ **de fréquence** frequency response; ~ **de gain** (en fonction de la fréquence) frequency response; ~ **de grille** grid characteristic; ~ **de lecture** reproduction characteristic; playback characteristic;

~ de l'équivalent overall attenuation curve; ~ de niveau level characteristic; ~ de persistance d'écran decay factor; ~ de plaque anode characteristic; plate characteristic; ~ de propagation propagation characteristic; ~ de qualité performance characteristic; quality factor; figure of merit; ~ de réponse amplitude/fréquence amplitude-frequency characteristic; ~ de réponse aux impulsions pulse response curve; ~ de réponse d'onde carrée square-wave response; ~ de temps de transit de groupe group-delay characteristic; ~ de transfert transfer characteristick; ~ de transfert du récepteur receiver transfer characteristic; ~ de transformation de l'impédance impedance transformation characteristic; ~ d'écran screen characteristic; ~ d'électrode electrode characteristic; ~ d'émission primary emission (characteristic); ~ d'émission (thermo-électronique) primary) emission characteristic; ~ d'émission secondaire secondary emission (characteristic); ~ d'enregistrement recording characteristic; ~ d'extinction decay characteristic; ~ d'insertion insertion loss data; ~ d'oscillation oscillation characteristic; ~ du réseau network parameter; ~ du saut surge characteristic; transient response; unit function response; ~ dynamique dynamic characteristic; AC parameter; ~ efficacité-fréquence sensitivity-frequency characteristic; ~ électrique des points de test scan point electrical characteristic; ~ en charge load factor; fan-out; ~ extérieure external characteristic; ~ gain-fréquence gain-frequency characteristic; ~ grille-plaque grid-plate (grid-anode) characteristic; ~ instantanée instantaneous characteristic; ~ intérieure internal characteristic; ~ mutuelle mutual characteristic; ~ mutuelle (de deux électrodes) transfer characteristic; ~ prépondérante dominant feature; ~ puissance de sortie/fréquence de travail output power; operating frequency characteristic; bandwidth characteristic; ~ puissance de sortie/fréquence à accord fixe output power; frequency characteristic within the RF range; frequency characteristic within the passband; ~ série series characteristic; ~ spectrale spectral response (characteristic); ~ statique static characteristic; DC parameter; ~ uniforme flat characteristic
caractéristiques d'affaiblissement attenuation characteristics; ~ de gabarit recommended conditions of use and associated characteristics; operating characteristics; limiting conditions of use (absolute maximum ratings); ~ du signal appliqué applied signal characteristics; ~ dynamiques dynamic parameters; AC characteristics; ~ électriques electrical properties; ~ fonctionnelles performance rating; ~ naturelles (travailler sur ses c.) (run) normally; ~ statiques static parameters; DC characteristics
carcasse f former (of coil); bobbin; yoke; spool; casing; ~ moulée moulded spool; ~ transformateur transformer casing
carcinotron backward-wave oscillator; carcinotron
cardan m (joint c.) universal joint (UJ)
carénage m grand/petit major/minor refit (of ship)
carence f deficiency
caret m caret (typographical symbol) ($\hat{m}$)
carillon m chime
cariste m forklift truck driver
carlingage m bed; seating
carnet m de commandes order book
carotte f sprue; moulding stalk; core
carre f heel (of angle iron)
carré m (symbole: #) gate (symbol); hash sign; octothorpe; ~ blanc white spot; ~ Gouriaud Alford loop; ~ vide hollow square; box
carrousel m rotary indexing table ("Lazy Susan")
car/s (v. caractères par seconde)
carte f printed circuit board (PCB); module; map (of memory); circuit card; circuit pack; punched card; credit card; chart; diagram; pattern; file; ~ à fenêtre aperture card; ~ à fenêtre à 8 images eight-up aperture card; ~ à graphiter mark-sense card; ~ à lecture graphique mark-sense card; ~ à mémoire smart card; ~ à microfilm aperture card; ~ à pistes magnétiques mark-sense card; ~ à pointes plug-board; ~ à talon stub card; ~ à variante variant card; ~ à version version card; ~ analogique analogue circuit board; ~ binaire binary card; ~ binaire par colonne column binary card; ~ binaire par ligne row binary card; ~ câblée pre-wired circuit board; ~ calcul arithmetic circuit board; arithmetic and logic unit (ALU); ~ clic snap-in card; ~ commande control circuit board; driver; ~ commande moteur motor control circuit board; ~ compte account card; ~ coupleur de périphériques peripheral controller board; ~ d'abonnés subscriber line interface circuit (SLIC); ~ de base de temps clock card; timing signal circuit board; ~ de champ (d'un ensemble

émetteur radioélectrique) field strength pattern; ~ **de circuit imprimé** printed circuit board (PCB); ~ **de commande** control unit; control board; driver; drive board; ~ **de commande auto** automatic control card; ~ **de commutation** switching circuit board; ~ **de contrôle** test card; statement; ~ **de conversion** converter circuit board; ~ **de correction** patch card; ~ **de crédit** credit card; ~ **de débit** charge card; ~ **de fin de groupe** trailer card; ~ **de la zone de service** (d'un émetteur de radiodiffusion) service area diagram; ~ **de Lyon** pressboard; ~ **de passage** piggyback board; ~ **de programmation** mini-switch (programming) card; ~ **de pupitre** console board; ~ **de rapatriement** mapping file; ~ **de recherche** aspect card; ~ **de reconnaissance et de synthèse vocale** voice recognition and voice synthesis board; ~ **de voie** channel unit (circuit pack); ~ **d'échange interprocesseurs** processor interchange card; ~ **d'équipement de ligne** line-circuit pack; ~ **des zones desservies** coverage diagram; ~ **détail** transaction card; detail card; ~ **d'initialisation** bootstrap board; ~ **en code Hollerith à 80** (colonnes) 80-column Hollerith card; ~ **enfichable** plug-in circuit pack; edge card; daughter board; ~ **en-tête** header card; ~ **équipée** PCB assembly; printed circuit assembly; ~ **étalon** known-good board; ~ **filigrane** flip card; ~ **fille** daughter board; slave card; ~ **futée** smart card; chip card; microprocessor card; ~ **horloge** clock card; ~ **hypso** hypsometer card; ~ **imprimée** printed circuit board (PCB); ~ **imprimée double face** double-sided printed circuit board; ~ **imprimée nue** (unpopulated) printed circuit board; ~ **imprimée usinée** printed circuit board; ~ **ionosphérique TU UT** (universal time) chart; ~ **lecture** read circuit board; ~ **magnéto-lecture** mark-sense card; ~ **maîtresse** master card; ~ **mécanographique** (perforée) punched card; tab card; EAM card; ~ **mémoire** memory map; ~ **mère** mother board; backplane; piggyback board; ~ **mise en cause** suspect card; ~ **mixte** hybrid card (magnetic stripe with microprocessor); ~ **moniteur** monitor card; ~ **mouvement** transaction card; ~ **nue** (v. carte imprimée nue); ~ **ordre** control card; ~ **outil** function card; ~ **paramètre** control card; parameter card; job card; ~ **perforée** control card; punched card; ~ **pilote** pilot card; ~ **pour test** test card; ~ **pré-perforée** pre-punched card; ~ **processeur** CPU processor card; ~ **programmable** PROM card; ~ **prolongateur/prolongatrice** extender card; ~ **récapitulative** summary card; ~ **régulation convoyeur** conveyor control card; ~ **régulation moteur** motor control card; ~ **stock** balance card; bin card; ~ **suiveuse** traveller (card); ~ **support** mother board; ~ **synoptique** mimic display card

cartelette f mini-PCB; daughter board

carter m housing; enclosure; crank-case; sump; gearbox; ~ **céramique** nozzle (of wave-soldering machine)

cartes multiples multiple cards

cartographie f **du territoire survolé** ground mapping

carton m pulp; cardboard; ~ **comprimé** presspahn; pressboard; ~ **isolant** presspahn; pressboard; ~ **ondulé** corrugated cardboard

cartons portfolio

cartothèque f card library

cartouche m (c. de plan) title block; draughtsman's panel; ~ f cartridge; cassette; magazine; pack; ~ **chauffante** heater element; ~ **cylindrique** (c/c) cartridge fuse; ~ **de bande magnétique** magnetic tape cartridge; ~ **de filtre** filter element; ~ **de gaz** canister; ~ **de lecteur** pick-up cartridge; ~ **de sauvegarde** streamer (tape) cartridge; ~ **étalon** standard cartridge; ~ **fusible sans percuteur** silent fuse; ~ **magnétique** magnetic tape cartridge

cas m example; case; situation; circumstance; event; occasion; instance; ~ **de figure** profile; ~ **de force majeure** Act of God; natural disaster; unforeseen circumstances; ~ **d'emploi** where used (information, file, etc.); ~ **d'équipement** equipment option; ~ **d'exploitation** working example(s)

cascade f cascade; chaining; tandem connection; ~ (dans une arborescence) level; indention; indent

cascode f cascode

case f box; magazine; pocket; stacker; hopper; rack; bin; partition; cell; compartment; panel; bucket; slot (in PCB frame); ~ **de fusion** card stacker; ~ **de réception** hopper; pocket; ~ **de sélection** sorter pocket; ~ **rebut** reject pocket

casier m bin; box; compartment; magazine; hopper; pigeon-hole; tote bin; ~ **de réception** stacker; ~ **visserie** box of securing components

casque m headset; earphones; headphones; ~ **à oreillettes** earphones; ~ **d'écoute** earphones; earpiece; headset; ~ **radio** headphones; headset; ~ **téléphonique**

headphones; headset

cassant *adj* brittle; frangible; breakable; fragile

casse *f* (-bas/-haut) (lower/upper) case; figures/letters shift

casser *v* shatter; break; sever; dispel (of vacuum); ~ **les angles** (vifs) (sharp) edges rounded off; chamfer; trim; deburr; buff

cassette *f* **de bande magnétique** magnetic tape cassette

cassure *f* crack; cracking; shattering

catalectique *adj* (due to) shortfall; deficient; partial; incomplete

catalogue *m* catalog(ue); ~ **de pièces détachées** component parts catalogue; spares catalogue

catalogues des formats format catalogue

catastrophe *f* runaway

catégorie (**cie**) *f* category; class-of-service; class marking; ~ **d'abonné** subscriber category; class-of-service; ~ **d'appels** call category; ~ **de la ligne** class-of-service; ~ **de service** class-of-service; ~ **d'exigence** application class

catène *m* frame

cathode *f* cathode; filament; ~ **à arc** arc cathode; ~ **à bain de mercure** mercury pool cathode; ~ **à chauffage direct** filament cathode; hot cathode; directly-heated cathode; ~ **à chauffage indirect** indirectly-heated cathode; ~ **à chauffage ionique** hot cathode; ~ **à oxyde** oxide-coated cathode; ~ **chaude** hot cathode; ~ **compensée** dispenser cathode; ~ **équipotentielle** indirectly-heated cathode; ~ **froide** cold cathode; ~ **incandescente** hot cathode; ~ **liquide** pool cathode; ~ **photoélectronique** photo-electric cathode; ~ **poreuse** capillary cathode; porous cathode; ~ **thermoélectronique** thermoelectronic cathode; ~ **virtuelle** virtual cathode (potential minimum surface)

Cathodéon [A.C.] crystal oscillator [T.N.]

cathodoluminescence *f* cathodoluminescence; afterglow

causer *v* cause; provoke; perpetrate

causerie pour la radio radio talk

cautionnement *m* guarantee; surety

CAV (v. commande automatique de volume)

cavalier *m* (shorting) link; jumper lead; jack plug; bridge; coupling; clip; patching cord; insulating staple; dropper; cylindrical socket; cordless plug; tappet; insert; strap; U-link; shunt; stud; ~ **de rebouclage** loopback link; ~ **d'isolement** shorting link

cavité *f* chamber; cavity; recess; resonator; ~ **à longueur variable** variable-length cavity; ~ **accordable** tuned cavity; ~ **hélicoïdale** helical resonator; ~ **résonnante** resonant cavity; cavity resonator; resonant chamber

CB (v. vis cylindrique (à tête) bombée)

CBL (v. vis à tête cylindrique bombée large)

CBLX (v. vis à tête cylindrique bombée large à six lobes internes)

c.c. (v. court-circuit)

c/c (v. cartouche cylindrique)

c-c (v. crête á crête)

cc (v. courant continu)

CCA (v. comptabilité centralisée des appels)

CCD (v. centre de commutation de données)

CCE (v. centre de commutation et d'essais)

CCEI (v. centre de commutation et d'essais internationaux)

CCG (v. circuit commun du groupement d'opérateur)

CCITT (v. Comité Consultatif International Télégraphique et Téléphonique)

CCP (v. compte courant postal)

CCPP (v. caractères par pouce)

CCQ (v. contrôle centralisé de qualité)

CCR (v. centre de commande de rétablissement du service)

CCS (v. centaine de communication-secondes)

CdC (v. cahier de charges); ⁓ (v. chemin de câbles)

CDC (v. centre de calcul); ⁓ (v. centre de communication); ⁓ (v. centre de commutation) ⁓ (v. cœur de chaîne)

cde (v. commande)

CDG (v. centre distant de gestion)

CDM (v. centre de démodulation et modulation)

CE (v. couche épaisse); ⁓ (v. chercheur enregistreur)

cébiste *m* CB enthusiast; "breaker"

CEF (v. chariot élévateur à fourche(tte)s)

ceinture *f* girdle; back panel; ~ **de Van Allen** Van Allen (radiation) belt

Céleron [A.C.] 'Tufnol' (laminated board) [T.N.]

cellulaire *adj* foam; honeycomb; cellular

cellule *f* cell; pad; module; detector (of control system); airframe; section (of filter of delay line); bit location; stage; bin; ~ **à couche d'arrêt** photovoltaic cell; ~ **à sélenium** selenium (rectifier) cell; ~ **à vide** vacuum photocell; ~ **complexe** complex filter cell; ~ **d'affaiblissement** attenuation pad; pad; ~ **d'atténuation** attenuator pad; ~ **de bouclage** terminating impedance; ~ **de couplage** coupling stage (of transmitter); ~ **de filtre** filter section; ~ **de l'espace de phase** phase-space cell; ~ **d'enregistrement** recording room; studio; ~ **électrolytique** electrolytic cell; ~ **émission-réception à**

C

bande étroite high-Q cell; ~ émission-réception à large bande band-pass cell; ~ en pi pi-network; ~ LC LC network (inductance-capacitance); ~ mémoire storage cell; memory location; ~ non protégée unlocked cell; unprotected cell; ~ non vide active cell; ~ passe-bande bandpass filter section; ~ photoconductive/-trice photo-electric (PE) cell; light cell; ~ photoélectrique photo-electric (PE) cell; photosensor; ~ photoémettrice light-emitting cell; ~ photorésistante resistive photocell; photoconductive cell; ~ photovoltaïque photovoltaic cell; ~ RC resistance-capacitance network

CEM (v. central électromécanique); ∴ (v. centre d'exploitation et de maintenance)

cémenté (et trempé) case-hardened (and quenched)

centaine f hundreds-group; hundred(s); ~ de communication-secondes (CCS) centum call second (CCS = 1/36 Erlang); ~ de directions hundred O/G lines

centipoint m centipoint (1/7200 inch)

centrage m alignment; mating; registration; locating (to centre); centring; matching (of impedance)

central m exchange; central processor; central station; central office; switching centre; data switching exchange; host (computer); mainframe; ~ à commande par enregistreurs register-controlled exchange; ~ à lignes d'extension exchange with extension lines; ~ à sélecteurs plans panel office; ~ amont up-line exchange; backward exchange; ~ automatique automatic switching centre; automatic exchange; dial exchange; ~ automatique de téléimprimeurs automatic teleprinter exchange; ~ automatique interurbain automatic trunk exchange; ~ automatique privé avec accès au réseau private automatic branch exchange (PABX); ~ automatique privé sans accès au réseau private automatic exchange (PAX); ~ automatique rural rural automatic exchange; ~ aval down-line exchange; forward exchange; ~ controlé par ordinateur computerized exchange; ~ d'abonnés central office; subscriber office; ~ d'alarme ring-out point; ~ d'alarme d'incendie call-bell point; ~ d'arrivée called exchange; terminating exchange; ~ de radiodiffusion central radio station; ~ de rattachement parent exchange; ~ de réception d'alarme alarm receiver unit; alarm signalling control unit; ~ de secours emergency exchange; ~ de secteur sector exchange; minor exchange; ~ de service

échelonné branch-off telegraph office; ~ de structure simplifiée unit automatic exchange (UAX); ~ de système (tout) à relais all-relay exchange; ~ de transit principal main transit exchange; ~ des téléimprimeurs central telex station; ~ distant distant exchange; remote exchange; far-end exchange; ~ électrique generating plant; ~ électromécanique (CEM) electromechanical (analogue) exchange; ~ électronique electronic exchange; ~ en conteneur containerized exchange; ~ entièrement satellite full-satellite exchange; ~ intermédiaire intermediate exchange; spill office; ~ international international exchange; ~ international de contrôle controlling exchange; ~ interurbain trunk exchange; toll office; ~ local end office; local exchange; central office; ~ manuel manual exchange; ~ manuel privé private manual exchange (PMX); ~ manuel privé avec opérateur ayant accès au réseau private branch exchange (PBX); ~ manuel sans cordons dial(-up) exchange; ~ mobile mobile exchange; ~ national national exchange; ~ nodal tandem exchange; ~ partiellement satellite discriminating satellite exchange; ~ pas-à-pas step-by-step exchange (Strowger); ~ père parent exchange; ~ pour trafic mixte auto-switching exchange; ~ principal main exchange; ~ privé private exchange; private branch exchange (PX/PBX); ~ privé automatique private automatic exchange (PAX); ~ privé relié au réseau public private branch exchange (PBX); ~ public public exchange; ~ régional regional centre; regional exchange; ~ rural rural exchange; ~ satellite satellite exchange; remote line unit (RLU); ~ semi-automatique semi-automatic exchange; ~ suburbain district transmitter; ~ tandem tandem exchange; ~ téléphonique telephone central office; ~ télex teleprinter exchange; telex exchange; ~ terminal terminal exchange; ~ urbain intra-city exchange; local exchange

centrale f power plant; generating station; blower; depot; compressor; generator; ~ d'achat catalogue showroom; ~ de cap gyro compass; ~ de verticale vertical reference unit; ~ d'énergie power plant; ~ thermoélectrique thermoelectric power station

centralisateur m supervisor; concentrator; coordinator; host; ~ d'informations central processing unit (CPU); mainframe

centralisé adj mainstream; common; central;

end-to-end
centraliser v centralize; collate; coordinate;
marshal
centralographe fault recorder; malfunction
indicator
centre m centre; exchange; station; unit; ~ **à
autonomie d'acheminement (CAA)** group
exchange; group centre (GC); ~ **adjacent**
adjacent centre; ~ **amont** up-line exchange; backward exchange; ~ **autonome**
stand-alone centre; ~ **d'abonnés** class five
office; end exchange; subscriber exchange;
~ **d'amplification** repeater station;
~ **d'analyse du réseau** network analysis
point; ~ **d'arrivée** destination (terminating)
exchange; ~ **d'autonomie d'acheminement**
group exchange; primary centre; ~ **de
calcul (CDC)** computer centre; ~ **de calcul
décentralisé** distributed data processing
centre; outlying computer centre; ~ **de
commande de rétablissement du service
(CCR)** restoration control point; ~ **de
communication (CDC)** communications
centre; (switching) exchange; data link;
~ **de commutation (CDC)** switching centre;
exchange (console); ~ **de commutation de
données (CCD)** data switching exchange
(DSE); broadband exchange; ~ **de commutation de messages** message switching
centre; ~ **de commutation de paquets** packet
switching centre; hot-potato link; ~ **de
commutation du réseau de télévision** television network switching centre; ~ **de
commutation en transit** tandem switching
centre; ~ **de commutation et d'essais (CCE)**
switching and test centre (STC); ~ **de
commutation et d'essais internationaux
(CCEI)** international switching and test
centre; ~ **de commutation numérique** digital
switch; ~ **de commutation principal** main
switching centre; ~ **de commutation radiophonique** programme-switching centre;
~ **de commutation régional** district switching centre; ~ **de commutation temporel**
digital switch; ~ **de compartiment** regional
centre; ~ **de démodulation et modulation
(CDM)** transmission centre; ~ **de départ et
d'arrivée** gateway exchange; ~ **de district**
district centre; class 2 sectional centre;
~ **de facturation** billing centre; ~ **de
facturation de taxe (CFT)** billing centre;
billing department; ~ **de gestion** management centre; operation and maintenance
centre (OMC); ~ **de gestion du réseau**
network management point; ~ **de groupement** group switching centre; group exchange; primary centre; ~ **de maintenance**
maintenance centre; ~ **de modulation de**

télévision television programme switching
centre; ~ **de production** production centre;
~ **de raccordement à l'arrivée** incoming
local centre; ~ **de raccordement au réseau
terrestre** terrestrial network interface
switching equipment; data switch; ~ **de
raccordement effectif** effective local centre;
~ **de raccordement numérique** digital
gateway; digital connection unit; ~ **de
rattachement** parent exchange; own exchange; ~ **de rattachement nominal** end
office; home office; parent exchange; ~ **de
réception d'alarme** alarm receiver unit;
alarm signalling control unit; ~ **de
réception des appels** central despatching
unit; ~ **de réglage par radar d'approche**
radar approach control centre; ~ **de
réparation** repair centre; ~ **de retransmission de messages** message forwarding
centre; relay station; ~ **de secteur** minor
exchange; ~ **de tête de ligne international**
international terminating exchange; ~ **de
traitement** processing centre; ~ **de traitement des informations (CTI)** operation and
maintenance centre (OMC); ~ **de transit**
transit exchange; tandem switch; tandem
exchange; (main trunk) exchange; sub-zonal centre; ~ **de transit (CT)** transit centre
(TC); ~ **de transit automatique** automatic
transit exchange; ~ **de transit de détournement** alternative tandem exchange; ~ **de
transit deux/(quatre) fils** two-/(four-)wire
transit centre; ~ **de transit international**
international transit centre; gateway exchange; ~ **de transit interurbain** toll switch;
trunk tandem exchange; ~ **de transit nodal**
tandem exchange; ~ **de transit principal
(CTP)** main transit exchange; main transit
centre (MTC); ~ **de transit régional**
regional transit exchange; tandem exchange; ~ **de transit secondaire (CTS)**
secondary transit centre (STC); ~ **de zone**
area exchange; ~ **d'échange** handing-over
office; ~ **d'émission** (broadcast) transmitting station; ~ **d'enregistrement distant**
remote billing centre; ~ **d'essais** test
centre; ~ **d'études de communications
optiques** optical communications research
centre; ~ **d'exploitation** network supervision centre; ~ **d'exploitation et de maintenance (CEM)** operation and maintenance
centre (OMC); management and control
system (MCS); ~ **diffusant** scattering
centre; ~ **directeur** controlling exchange;
~ **distant de gestion (CDG)** remote
management centre; ~ **distribué** distributed centre; ~ **distributeur de modulation**
central control room; ~ **éloigné** distant/re-

mote/far-end exchange; ~ **émetteur** forwarding centre (telegraphy); forwarding office; sending office; ~ **(en) aval** distant exchange; ~ **intermédiaire** intermediate exchange; spill office; ~ **international** international exchange; international centre; gateway exchange; ~ **international automatique** international exchange; ~ **international d'arrivée** incoming international exchange; ~ **international de départ** outgoing international exchange; ~ **international de maintenance** international maintenance centre; ~ **international de maintenance de la commutation (CIMC)** international switching maintenance centre (ISMC); ~ **international de maintenance de la transmission (CIMT)** international transmission maintenance centre (ITMC); ~ **interurbain** trunk exchange; toll office; class four toll centre (TC); transit exchange; ~ **local (CL)** local exchange; end office; local centre; end exchange; ~ **local primaire** minor exchange; sub-centre; ~ **local satellite** local satellite exchange; remote line unit; ~ **local secondaire** dependent exchange; ~ **luminogène** luminescent centre; ~ **manuel** manual exchange; ~ **mixte d'abonnés et de transit** combined subscriber and transit exchange; ~ **multibrique** multi-level exchange; ~ **national d'arrivée** incoming national exchange; ~ **national de gestion** national management centre; ~ **national vidéotex** national videotex centre; ~ **nodal (CN)** nodal exchange; tandem exchange; main trunk exchange; transit centre (TC); ~ **nodal de transit** tandem exchange; ~ **nodal de triage** nodal sorting centre; ~ **primaire** primary switching centre; primary centre; ~ **principal** main (trunk) exchange; class three primary centre (PC); ~ **principal de commutation** main switching centre; ~ **principal de transit** main transit exchange; tandem exchange; through-trunk exchange; ~ **principal d'exploitation** main operating centre; ~ **principal d'exploitation (CPE)** main operating centre; ~ **privé de type centrex** customer centrex; ~ **quaternaire** quaternary centre; ~ **rattaché** dependent exchange; ~ **régional** regional centre; ~ **régional de gestion** regional management centre; ~ **régional transmission** regional transmission centre; ~ **régional vidéotex** regional videotex centre; ~ **satellite** satellite centre; satellite exchange; remote line unit (RLU); ~ **satellite numérique** digital satellite exchange; ~ **satellite numérique distant** remote digital satellite exchange; ~ **satellite numérique** local local digital satellite exchange; ~ **satellite sans autonomie d'acheminement** local exchange with no multi-routing capability; ~ **secondaire** secondary (switching) centre; ~ **serveur** (host) computer centre; ~ **tarifaire** rate centre; ~ **télégraphique** telegraph centre; ~ **téléphonique de transfert** transfer exchange; ~ **terminal** terminal exchange; ~ **tertiaire** tertiary centre; ~ **tête de ligne** gateway exchange; ~ **tête de ligne internationale d'arrivée** incoming international terminating exchange; ~ **tête de ligne internationale de départ** outgoing international terminating exchange; ~ **translateur** (dans le service international) incoming terminal exchange (in the international service); ~ **urbain** intra-city exchange; local exchange (LE); metropolitan subscriber exchange (MC); ~ **voisin** adjacent exchange

centreur *m* guide pin

centrex centrex

CEP (v. contrôle d'endurance par prélèvement)

CEPT (v. Conférence Européenne des Postes et Télécommunications)

CEQ (v. code d'équipement)

cerclage strapping; ~ **des circuits monophasés** binding of single-phase circuits

cercle *m* **de distance** range circle; ~ **trigonométrique** trigonometrical calculation

cercleuse *f* **de colis** packet binding machine

certificat *m* **de conformité** compliance statement

certificateur smart card PIN code authenticator (personal identification number)

cessation *f* **du contrat** expiry of agreement

cession *f* assignment; relinquishment; disposal; sale; transfer (of capital); ~ **de licence** licence transfer; licensing

cessionnaire *m* **du transfert** assignee; licensee

cf (v. conforme à)

CFAO (v. conception et fabrication assistées par ordinateur)

CFL (v. caractère fin de ligne)

CFT (v. centre de facturation de taxe)

CG (v. convertisseur de gestion)

ch. (v. chiffre)

ch (centième d'heure) hundredth of an hour (0.6 sec); ~ (cheval-vapeur = CV) h.p. (horsepower)

chaînage *m* chaining; linking; stringing; cascading; linkage; serial call; polling; ~ **de données** data chaining

chaînage de ressources resource chaining

chaîne *f* chain; system; network; channel; cascade; subsystem; circuit; sequence; string; measurement system; switch path;

band; assembly line; series; ~ **à quatre fils** four-wire chain; ~ **alphabétique** alphabetic string; ~ **amplificateur** cascade amplifier; DC coupling chain; ~ **amplificatrice** amplifier chain; ~ **binaire** bit string; ~ **cataloguée** stored order
chaîne cinématique operational diagram
chaîne d'appel call string; ~ **d'appels imbriqués** interleaved calling sequence; ~ **de bits** bit string; ~ **de caractères** character string; chain printer; ~ **de commande** central network; control system; ~ **de commande et de gestion** control complex; ~ **de commutation** crossover network; ~ **de connexion** connection; switch path; ~ **de connexion complète** complete connection; ~ **de contrôle** monitoring subsystem; ~ **de conversation téléphonique** speech-path subsystem; ~ **de distribution** timing chain; ~ **de dorure** gold-plating production line; ~ **de listes** list(ing) chain; ~ **de marquage** marking subsystem; ~ **de mesure d'effort** stress measurement system; ~ **de micro-instructions** firmware; ~ **de montage** assembly line; ~ **de mots d'état** status word string (SWS); ~ **de parole** speech path; speech-path subsystem; ~ **de poursuite** tracking system; ~ **de production** flow line; production or manufacturing line; assembly line; ~ **de production de logiciel** linkage editor; ~ **de radar** radar chain; ~ **de radionavigation** navigator chain; ~ **de régulation** closed loop; ~ **de signalisation** signalling subsystem; ~ **de stations de radar** radar chain; ~ **de stations émettrices de télévision** television station link; ~ **de stations radio** radio link; ~ **de symboles** symbol string; ~ **de taxation** charging subsystem; ~ **de texte** text string; ~ **de traitement** job string; ~ **de transmission** transmission path; speech-path subsystem; ~ **d'émetteurs** chain of transmitters; ~ **d'isolateurs** (cable) insulator set; ~ **émission-réception** go-and-return path; ~ **haute fidélité** high-fidelity system; ~ **interurbaine** trunk system; ~ **potentiométrique** voltage divider; ~ **radar défensive d'alerte avancée** early-warning radar chain; ~ **sélective** selection subsystem; ~ **unitaire** unit string; ~ **vide** null string; empty string
chaîné *adj* in daisy-chain configuration; cascaded
chaîner *v* chain; string; catenate; cascade; link
chaîne(s) de positionnement(s) et de faute(s) positioning and fault-handing subsystem; signalling subsystem
chaînette *f* catenary (math.); sag

chaînon *m* link
chaise *f* chassis; bracket
chaleur *f* **humide** damp heat; ~ **sèche** dry heat
chalumeau *m* burner; torch
chambrage *m* counter-bore; bushing
chambre *f* camera; oven; kiln; chamber; enclosure; port; ~ **à vide** toroid; doughnut; donut; ~ **de compression** horn speaker; ~ **d'écho** echo chamber; ~ **d'essai** test enclosure; ~ **sourde** anechoic chamber; ~ **souterraine** manhole; vault (of cables)
champ *m* field; region; area; argument (field); ~ **à courte distance** short-range field; ~ **acoustique** acoustical field; sound field; ~ **acoustique libre** free sound field; free-field air path; ~ **alternatif** alternating field; ~ **coercitif** coercive force; ~ **continu superposé** superimposed DC field; ~ **couplé** linked field; control field; ~ **d'accélération** accelerating field; ~ **d'accessibilité** availability; ~ **d'action** sensitivity; response; ~ **d'adresse** address field; ~ **d'application** field of application; ~ **de bits** (v. champ d'éléments binaires); ~ **de désaimantation** demagnetizing field; ~ **de déviation** deflection field; ~ **de dispersion** leakage field; ~ **de données** data field; ~ **de fuite** leakage field; ~ **de multiplage** (de contrôle de connexion) check multiple; ~ **de rayonnement** radiation field; ~ **de relèvement** bearing field; ~ **de sécurisation** open field; ~ **d'éléments binaires** bit field; ~ **des services inter-réseau** network utility field; ~ **d'induction** induction field; ~ **d'information de vol** flight information region (FIR); ~ **d'interférence** interference field; fringe area; ~ **d'ondes moyennes** medium-frequency field; ~ **du signal** signal field; ~ **électrique** electric field; ~ **électromagnétique** electromagnetic field; ~ **électrostatique** electrostatic field; ~ **en l'absence d'absorption** unabsorbed field strength; ~ **exploré** scanning field; ~ **extérieur** extraneous field; ~ **focalisateur** focussing field; ~ **infini** free field; ~ **magnétique** magnetic field; ~ **magnétique terrestre** earth's magnetic field; ~ **magnétique unidirectionnel** unidirectional magnetic field; ~ **multiple** bank multiple; ~ **multiple à sélecteur final** final selector multiple; ~ **parasite** stray field; disturbing field; ~ **perturbateur** noise field; interference field strength; disturbing field strength; ~ **protégé** protected field; locked field; ~ **répétitif** indexed field; ~ **tournant** rotating field; ~ **variable** variable field
chandelle *f* prop; stay; pillar
chane *m* soldering iron

chanfrein *m* chamfer(ed edge); lead-in (of pin)

chanfreinage *m* bevelling

changement *m* change; alteration; conversion; ~ **d'année** end-of-year flag; ~ **de canal radio** hand-off; chop; ~ **de chaîne** connection changeover; ~ **de code** escape codes; ~ **de fréquence** frequency changing; frequency conversion; ~ **de l'adresse de facturation** change of billing address; ~ **de ligne** line feed; lead feed; ~ **de mode** mode change; ~ **de phase** phase shift; phase change; ~ **de position temporelle** time slot interchange; ~ **d'échappement** change of pitch; ~ **d'état** loop-state transition; state change; status transition; mismatch; ~ **d'état** (signalisation à) continuous (signalling); ~ **graduel du signal** compensation; ~ **saisonnier d'horaire** daylight saving

changer d'état move; change state

changeur *m* changer; converter; inverter; ~ **de code** code converter; ~ **de fréquence** frequency changer; converter; mixer; conversion detector; first detector; ~ **de phases** phase inverter

chantier *m* installation; site; exchange; field; ~ **naval** shipyard

chape *f* yoke; fork; saddle; cleat; cover; shell; cap

chapeau *m* beam (of square)

chapelet *m* string; chain; series; stick; item

char de dépannage recovery vehicle

charge *f* load; charge; logic input; payload; batch; stress; resistive load; ballast; burden; impedance; workload; commitment; format; ~ **à eau** water load; ~ **à la rupture** yield strength; ~ **à vide** overhead; ~ **active** active load; ~ **adaptée** matched load; matched termination; ~ **admissible** safe load; ~ **annuelle** annual charge; ~ **anodique** anode load; ~ **artificielle** dummy load; ~ **au plancher/au sol** floor loading; ~ **capacitive** capacitive load; leading load; ~ **capacitive concentrée** lumped capacitive loading; ~ **cathodique moyenne** mean cathode loading; ~ **chaude** hot load (of satellite); ~ **continue** continuous loading; ~ **d'anode** anode load; ~ **de crête** peak load; ~ **de cristal** level of drive; ~ **de débordement** overflow load; ~ **de fond** boost charge; ~ **de l'électron** electron charge; ~ **de l'espace d'interaction** multipactor gap loading; ~ **de pointe** peak load; ~ **de rupture** ultimate tensile stress; breaking load; ~ **de service** working load; ~ **d'égalisation** equalizing charge; ~ **d'entrée** fan-in; input load; ~ **d'entretien** trickle charge; floating charge; ~ **d'épreuve** proof load; ~ **d'espace** space charge; gap load;

~ **d'essai** test load; dummy load; ~ **d'exploitation** operation function; ~ **du circuit fantôme** composite loading; phantom loading; ~ **d'un câble** cable loading; ~ **d'un tube électronique** electron valve load; ~ **d'une ligne** line load; loading; ~ **électrique** electric charge; ~ **en égalisation** equalization charging; ~ **en floating** floating charge; ~ **en tampon** trickle charge; floating charge; ~ **encombrante** bulky load; wide load; ~ **équilibrée** balanced load; ~ **fictive** dummy load; ~ **inductive** inductive load; lagging load; ~ **instantanée** instantaneous load; ~ **interne de tirage** load pull-down; ~ **liquide** water load; ~ **maximale** maximum rating; top load; ~ **mémoire** core input; ~ **militaire** warhead; ~ **minimale** base load; minimum rating; ~ **mobile** moving charge; ~ **moyenne** off-peak load; ~ **optimale** optimum load impedance; ~ **partielle** light load; ~ **ponctuelle** concentrated load; ~ **postiche** dummy load; ~ **réactive** reactive load; ~ **recouvrée** recovered charge; ~ **répartie** distributed load; ~ **résistante** resistive load; ~ **résistive** non-reactive load; ~ **spatiale** space charge; ~ **spécifique de l'électron** electron-charge mass ratio; ~ **spécifique d'un porteur électrisé** mass ratio; charge ratio; ~ **stockée** stored charge; ~ **superficielle** surface charge; bound charge; free charge; ~ **supplémentaire** extra load; surcharge; ~ **symétrique** balanced load; ~ **utile** payload

chargé *adj* gated (of register); busy; loaded; set; with full complement

chargement *m* loading; load; lading; consignment; cargo; payload; formatting; ~ **bande pilote** verical format unit load (VFL); ~ **et exécution** load-and-go; ~ **initial** bootstrap routine; cold start; ~ **un baladeur** marching-ones load

charger *v* load; store; charge; page-in; poke; ~ **(en)** copy (to); input; load; transfer; down-load; ~ **(en mémoire) à la place de** overlay; down-load

charges *f pl* overheads; ~ **financières** overheads; ~ **industrielles** industrial workload

chargeur *m* loader; loading program; cartridge; disk-pack; handler; charger; bootstrap routine; absolute loader; cassette; magazine; hopper; ~ **absolu** absolute loader; ~ **autonome** data module; ~ **d'accus (à régime lent)** (trickle-charge) battery charger; ~ **de circuit intégré** integrated circuit handler; ~ **de disques** disk-pack; whirly-bird; ~ **de disques autonome** disk-pack; ~ **d'égalisation** battery charger; ~ **d'entretien** battery charger; ~ **éditeur de liens** link-loader; link-editor; ~ **en mémoire** bootstrap loader; ~ **image-mémoire** core image loader

chargeur-translateur relocatable loader

chariot *m* carriage; dolly; trolley; transporter; cart (for forms); truck; caddy; ~ **automatique** automatic carriage; ~ **baladeur** traverse mounting; ~ **de manutention** handling trolley; ~ **élévateur à fourche(tte)s (CEF)** fork-lift truck; ~ **porte-balais** brush carriage; ~ **porte-bâti** rack transporter; ~ **pour fonds de panier** backplane transporter; ~ **pour oscilloscope** oscilloscope carriage; ~ **sans roulette** stillage; ~ **support de bâti** rack transporter

charioté fin fine-machined

charnière *f* hinge; bend (of cable); ~ **montée en feuillure** hidden flange

charnières montées en feuillure concealed hinges

charpente *f* (rack) framework; structure

chasse-goupilles *m* pin drift; drift (pin)

châssis *m* chassis; frame(work); rack; subrack; crate; cage; welded rack; shelf; ~ **d'adaptation** adaptor subrack; ~ **de ventilation** cooling shelf; ~ **d'élements d'abonnés** subscriber line equipment subrack; ~ **des amplificateurs** amplifier shelf; amplifier subrack; ~ **d'extension** add-on subrack; ~ **fonctionnel** subrack; ~ **pivotant** gate; ~ **visu** display subrack

Chatterton [A.C.] *m* adhesive (insulating) tape; masking tape

chauffage *m* **électrique** electric heating

chauffe-eau *m* immersion heater

chaufferette *f* (chaufrette) heater element; heat gun; hot air blower

chef *m* **de file** prime contractor

chemin *m* route; run; track; bed; path; duct; ~ **de câbles (CdC)** cable duct; raceway; trench; floor chase; ~ **de câbles (CdC)** cable run; duct; cable tray; chase; cable rack; trench; cable runway; raceway; floor chase; ~ **de cartes** card path; ~ **de parole** speech path; ~ **de perçage** hole layout (interconnections); ~ **de propagation** audit trail; ~ **de roulement** ball race; ~ **émission** go path; ~ **hamiltonien** Hamiltonian path; ~ **hiérarchique normal** backbone route; ~ **réception** return path; ~ **suivi** main path

cheminée *m* raised platform; doughnut; base; dish

cheminement *m* routing; wiring layout; interconnection; flow; tracking; dressing (of wires); creep; ~ **du travail** job flow

chemise *f* bush; bushing; plating; coating; jacket; liner; sleeve; shroud

chemisé *m* coated; plated; shrouded; slugged

chenille(tte) *f* **à ergots** pin-feed tractor

chercher *v* seek; search; hunt; find; select; fetch

chercheur *m* catswhisker; finder; selector; hunter; searcher; line finder; development engineer; ~ **d'appels** call finder (selector); ~ **d'auxiliaire** service circuit(s); finder stage; ~ **de ligne appelante** finder; ~ **de ligne libre** hunter; ~ **de lignes** line finder; call finder; ~ **d'enregistrement** register finder; sender selector; ~ **distributeur** line finder with allotter; ~ **d'organes** circuit finder; ~ **enregistreur (CE)** register finder; sender selector; ~ **(radiogoniométrique)** radio direction-finder (RDF); ~ **secondaire** second line finder; secondary line switch

chevalet *m* trestle; support

chevauchement *m* overlap; ~ **des spires** overlapping of turns

chevelure *f* subscriber drop (wire); tail (of comet)

cheveux de lumière optical fibre video

cheville *f* plug; dowel pin; peg

chicane *f* baffle; chute

chien *m* **de garde** watchdog (timer)

chiffon non pelucheux lint-free cloth

chiffrage *m* encryption; coding; ciphering

chiffraison *f* digits (numerical layout)

chiffre (ch.) *m* figure; digit; number; numeral; ~ **binaire** binary digit (bit); ~ **caractéristique** code letter; characteristic digit; ~ **clé (sum)** check digit; check number; ~ **d'acheminement** routing digit; ~ **d'affaire** turnover; gross income; total sales; ~ **de contrôle** (sum) check digit; ~ **de discrimination** class-of-service digit; ~ **de langue** language digit; ~ **de poids faible** least significant bit (LSB); ~ **de poids fort** most significant bit (MSB); ~ **de service** gap character; gap digit; service bit; ~ **de taxation** fee digit; charging digit; ~ **de traduction** translation digit; ~ **décimal** decimal digit; ~ **dièse** gate key; gate button; hash symbol; ~ **étoile** star button (digit); asterisk; ~ **n-aire** n-ary digit; ~ **significatif** significant figure

chiffré *adj* quantified; costed; enciphered; coded

chiffrement *m* coding; encryption; ciphering

chiffrer *v* encode; encipher; cost; quantify

chignole *f* (à main) hand drill

chiné *adj* mottled

chlorure *m* **de polyvinyle** polyvinyl chloride (PVC)

choc *m* impact; sudden blow; surge; rough treatment; rough handling; shock; collision; ~ **acoustique** acoustic shock; ~ **de basse fréquence** motorboating; ~ **de courant** current surge; ~ **de première espèce** collision of the first kind; ~ **de tension** voltage surge; ~ **thermique** rapid change of temperature; thermal shock

choisir *v* elect; select; choose; opt

choix *m* selection; choice; identification bit; ~ **de l'imprimante** printer select; ~ **de longueur de la file d'attente de datagramme** datagram queue length selection; ~ **du profil normalisé** standard profile selection; ~ **libre** user-defined

chrominance *f* chrominance; chromaticity; colour

chronogramme *m* timing diagram

chronographe *m* **électrique** (electromagnetic) tape chronograph

chronométrage *m* timing

chronomètre *m* stopwatch; timer; ~ **numérique** digital clock

chronotaximètre *m* chargeable time clock

chrysocal *m*; **chrysocolle** *f* pinchbeck alloy (red brass); copper orthosilicate; chrysocolla

chrysocolle *f* (v. chrysocal)

chute *f* drop-out (of relay); ~ **d'alimentation** power fail; ~ **dans l'arc** arc-drop; ~ **de niveau** drop-out; ~ **de potentiel** potential drop; voltage drop; ~ **de pression** pressure drop; ~ **de tension** voltage drop; ~ **(de tension) anodique** anode drop; anode fall; ~ **(de tension) cathodique** cathode (potential) fall; ~ **(de tension) dans l'arc** arc drop (voltage); ~ **libre** gravity-feed; free fall

CI précaractérisé pre-built block IC

cibiste CB enthusiast; breaker

cible *f* collector electrode; target; test pattern; ~ **composée** compound target; ~ **de radar** radar target; ~ **fantôme** phantom radar target; ~ **fausse de radar** phantom radar target; ~ **simple** isotropic target

ci-dessus foregoing

cie (v. catégorie)

CIE (circuit imprimé équipé) PCB assembly

CIF (v. contact à insertion forcée)

CIHS (circuit imprimé hors service) defective PCB

cimblot *m* (simbleau) locating key; positioning block; spider; centring bridge

CIMC (v. centre international de maintenance de la commutation)

CIMT (v. centre international de maintenance de la transmission)

cinéscope *m* television tube; picture tube; kinescope

cinétique *adj* kinetic

cinquantaine *f* fifties-group

cinquante grammes par cinquante grammes in 50g increments

cintreuse *f* pipe-bending machine

circonscription *f* **de taxe** base rate (charging) area; ~ **téléphonique** exchange-wide; exchange area

circonvolution *f* revolution (of disk)

circuit *m* circuit (cct.); layout; system closed path; channel; element; gate; flow (of data); pattern; tour; line; outline; facility; process; trunk; network; ~ **integrated** circuit (IC); microcircuit; ~ **à anticoïncidence** inclusive-OR gate; non-equivalence; EXCEPT gate; ~ **à bande étroite** narrowband circuit; ~ **à bouchon** tank circuit; ~ **à boucle de phase** phase-locked loop; ~ **à coïncidence** coincidence (equivalence) circuit; ~ **à commande unique** ganged circuit; ~ **à comptage** counter circuit; ~ **à constante de temps** delay line; ~ **à constantes localisées** delay line (lumped circuit); ~ **à constantes réparties** distributed circuit; ~ **à contrôler** circuit under test; ~ **à couplage de charges** charge-coupled device (CCD); ~ **à courant porteur** carrier circuit; ~ **à déclenchement** trigger circuit; ~ **à déclenchement périodique** double limiter; gate; window; ~ **à découpage** switch-mode power supply; chopper circuit; ~ **à détente** trigger circuit; ~ **à deux fils** two-wire circuit; two-wire channel; ~ **à effet de volant** flywheel synchronization circuit; ~ **à exploitation automatique** automatic circuit; ~ **à exploitation manuelle** manual circuit; ~ **à fort trafic** high-usage trunk; ~ **à grande distance** long-haul trunk; long-haul circuit; ~ **à haute fréquence** high-frequency circuit; ~ **à large bande** wideband circuit; ~ **à limitation en tension** crowbar circuit; ~ **à longue distance** long-haul trunk circuit; ~ **à maintien** holding circuit; ~ **à plusieurs stations réceptrices** divided circuit; ~ **à précharge** ratio-less circuit (of MOS logic); ~ **à prise par mise d'une terre sur un fil** earth-start circuit; ~ **à quatre fils** four-wire circuit; four-wire channel; ~ **à résonance en série** series-resonant circuit; ~ **à retard** delay circuit; ~ **à retour par la terre** earth-return circuit; ~ **à signalisation manuelle** ring-down circuit; ~ **à signalisation multifréquence** multifrequency circuit; MF signalling circuit; ~ **à utilisation élevée** high-usage trunk; ~ **absorbant** absorber circuit; sink; ~ **accepteur** acceptor circuit; ~ **accordé** tuned circuit; ~ **accordé décalé** stagger-tuned circuit; ~ **additif** add-on circuit; applique circuit; ~ **additionneur**

binaire binary (full) adder; adder; ~ **aérien** overhead circuit; aerial circuit; open-wire circuit; ~ **amortisseur** damping circuit; ~ **amplificateur** amplifying circuit; booster; repeater; ~ **amplifié** repeatered circuit; ~ **analogique** analogue trunk; linear integrated circuit; ~ **anodique** plate circuit; anode circuit; ~ **anticoïncidence** exclusive OR circuit; anticoincidence circuit; ~ **anti-effet local** anti-sidetone circuit; ~ **anti-étincelles** spark-quench (circuit); ~ **anti-local** anti-sidetone circuit; feedback suppressor circuit; ~ **antiparasité** suppressor circuit; ~ **antirésonnant** wave trap; stopper circuit; suppressor circuit; bandstop circuit; anti-resonant circuit; parallel resonant circuit; ~ **apériodique** aperiodic circuit; damped circuit; non-resonant circuit; ~ **approprié** phantom circuit; bunched circuit; composite circuit; superposed circuit; simplex circuit; earth-return phantom circuit; ~ **approprié de combiné** earth-return double-phantom circuit; ~ **approprié de fantôme** earth-return double-phantom circuit; ~ **arithmétique** arithmetic circuit; ~ **asymétrique à deux fils** asymmetrical two-wire circuit; balanced two-wire circuit; ~ **au repos** idle-circuit condition; ~ **auto-élévateur** bootstrap circuit; ~ **auxiliaire** ancillary circuit; auxiliary circuit; ~ **basse fréquence** voice-frequency circuit; ~ **bidirectionnel** bothway circuit; duplex circuit; ~ **bifilaire** two-wire (loop) circuit; metallic circuit; double-line circuit; ~ **bifilaire double** four-wire circuit; ~ **bistable** bistable circuit; lockover; flip-flop; scale-of-two circuit; toggle circuit; ~ **bloqué** blocked circuit; ~ **bouchon** antiresonant circuit; bandstop filter; interference suppressor; stopper; rejector (circuit); tank circuit; wave trap; band-rejection filter; band elimination filter; absorption circuit; roll-off; ~ **bouclé** loop-around circuit; loop-feeder; ~ **brouilleur** jammer; scrambler; ~ **bruyant** swamped circuit; noisy circuit; ~ **capteur** pick-up circuit; intercept circuit; ~ **codeur** encoder; ~ **combinable** phantom circuit; ~ **combinant** side circuit; (double) phantom circuit; ~ **combiné (double)** (double) phantom circuit; side circuit; ~ **commun** bus; ~ **commun du groupement d'opérateur (CCG)** operator group common circuit (GCC); ~ **commuté** dial-up circuit; switched circuit; ~ **commuté en tandem** tandem switched circuit; ~ **comparateur** comparator; ~ **compensateur** corrector circuit; linearizer; stretcher; equalizer; compensator; ~ **composant** side circuit;

~ **composite** composite circuit; ~ **compteur démultiplicateur 4:1** count-by-four circuit; ~ **concentré** concentrated (lumped constant) circuit; ~ **conditionneur** AND circuit/gate; ~ **configurateur d'impulsions** pulse-shaping circuit; pulse shaper; ~ **conformateur d'onde carrée** squarer; squaring circuit; ~ **convertisseur** converter; ~ **correcteur d'amplitude** amplitude equalizer; ~ **correcteur d'atténuation à bande de base** baseband attenuation equalizer; ~ **correcteur de distorsion** compensating circuit; ~ **couplé** coupled circuit; ~ **d'absorption** absorber circuit; ~ **d'accentuation** emphasizer; ~ **d'accès** access circuit; port; ~ **d'accord** tuned circuit (LC); ~ **d'addition** adder; ~ **d'alarme** call-out installation; alarm circuit; ~ **d'alimentation** feeder line; power-feed circuit; ~ **d'alimentation double** twin feeder; ~ **d'amorçage** firing circuit; trigger circuit; ~ **d'annonce** indicator circuit; warning circuit; ~ **d'annotation** trunk-record circuit; ~ **d'antenne** aerial circuit; ~ **d'appel** ringing current circuit; ~ **d'appel des traducteurs** translator-register interface; ~ **d'arrêt** terminating circuit; ~ **d'arrivée** incoming circuit; ~ **d'aspiration** filter circuit; ~ **d'attaque** driver; drive circuit; ~ **d'attaque de cristaux liquides** LCD driver; ~ **d'augmentation de la pente** peaking circuit; ~ **d'autogénération mutuelle** bootstrap feedback; ~ **de base de temps** time-base circuit; ~ **de blocage temporaire** intercept circuit; ~ **de bouclage à diode** diode clamp; ~ **de calage manipulé** keyed clamping circuit; ~ **de charge** load circuit; loading circuit; output circuit; application; ~ **de charge fictif** dummy load; ~ **de charge réel** normal load; ~ **de chauffage** filament (heater) circuit; ~ **de collage** holding (coil) circuit; ~ **de commande** pilot (wire) circuit; control circuit; driver; ~ **de commande de push-pull** push-pull control circuit; ~ **de compensation** absorber; compensating circuit; roll-off; ~ **de compensation de charge** absorber circuit; ~ **de compensation interne** internal roll-off; ~ **de comptage** counting circuit; metering circuit; ~ **de conférence** conference circuit; bridge; ~ **de conférence par téléimprimeurs** telex conference circuit; teleprinter conference circuit; ~ **de connexion** link circuit; power feed bridge; junctor; connecting circuit; interface (circuit); ~ **de connexion local** own-exchange junctor; ~ **de contre-réaction** feedback circuit; ~ **de contrôle** monitoring circuit; test circuit; check circuit; ~ **de conversation** speech circuit; connection circuit; connecting circuit; link circuit; link; speech path; ~ **de conversation d'un poste téléphonique** network; speech network; speech circuit; speech path; ~ **de couplage** coupling circuit; ~ **de courant d'appel** ringing-current circuit; ring-down circuit; ~ **de déblocage** line-free circuit; ~ **de décision** decision circuit; ~ **de déclenchement** trigger circuit; ~ **de déclenchement à coup unique** single-shot trigger circuit; ~ **de déclenchement à cycle simple** (v. circuit de déclenchement à coup unique); ~ **de démarrage** starter circuit; ~ **de départ** outgoing circuit; ~ de **désaccentuation** de-emphasizer; post-emphasis circuit; ~ **de détection** detector circuit; ~ **de détournement** alternative routing; re-routing; ~ **de deux groupes** two-group combining circuit; ~ **de déviation d'appel** ringing repeater; ~ **de différentiation** differentiating circuit; peaking circuit; peaking network; ~ **de distribution** branch circuit; ~ **de données** data circuit; ~ **de faute d'abonné** (parking) live lock-out circuit; ~ **de fiche** cord circuit; ~ **de filtrage** smoothing circuit; ~ **de fixation d'amplitude** clamping circuit; ~ **de fonctionnement de duplex** full-duplex circuit; ~ **de garde** guard circuit; ~ **de garde pour le parcage** parking circuit; ~ **de génération de courant** (ca/cc) (AC/DC) power supply system; ~ **de génération d'horloge** (self-contained) timing circuitry; ~ **de jonction** trunk; interchange circuit; interface; ~ **de jonction connecté en deux fils** two-wire switched trunk junction; ~ **de liaison** link circuit; interchange circuit; order-wire circuit; ~ **de liaison entre opérateurs** order-wire circuit; locked loop; ~ **de liaison secondaire** virtual circuit; ~ **de ligne** line circuit; locked loop; ~ **de limitation de durée des communications** call-duration limiting circuit; ~ **de maintien** holding circuit; ~ **de manipulation** keying circuit; ~ **de mesure** measuring circuit; metering circuit; ~ **de mesure flottante** damped measuring circuit; ~ **de Miller** Miller circuit; ~ **de mise à la terre** earthing circuit; grounding circuit; ~ **de mise en forme** pulse shaping circuit; ~ **de neutrodynage** (en croix) (cross-coupled) balancing circuit; neutrodyning circuit; neutralizing circuit; push-pull circuit; ~ **de numérotation par interruption de boucle** loop disconnect dialler; ~ **de parole** speech circuit; speech path; ~ **de plaque** plate circuit; anode circuit; ~ **de porte** gate (circuit); port; ~ **de poste à poste** point-to-point circuit; ~ **de**

prolongement extension circuit; trunk circuit; link line extension; ~ **de protection** protective circuit; ~ **de puissance** main (power) supply circuit; ~ **de qualité téléphonique** voice-grade circuit; ~ **de rayonnement** radiating circuit; ~ **de réactance** reactance circuit; ~ **de réaction** feedback circuit; ~ **de reconstitution du rythme** timing recovery circuit; ~ **de référence** reference circuit; ~ **de référence pour la transmission téléphonique** telephone transmission reference circuit; ~ **de relaxation** relaxation circuit; ~ **de renvoi** order-wire circuit; transfer circuit; (inter-position) trunk; ~ **de renvoi sur garde** parking orbit; call park; ~ **de répétition** repeat circuit; ~ **de réserve** fall-back circuit; standby circuit; ~ **de résonance parallèle** tank circuit; resonator; ~ **de secours** (v. circuit de réserve); ~ **de service** engineering circuit; speaker circuit; order-wire circuit; ~ **de seuil à diode** diode clipper; ~ **de Sheffer** NAND gate; ~ **de sortie** signalling circuit; outgoing circuit; output circuit; load circuit; ~ **de sortie à relais** relay output circuit; ~ **de sortie à relais alternatif** AC relay output circuit; ~ **de suivi** locked loop; ~ **de télécommunication** circuit; communication channel; telecommunications circuit; ~ **de télédictée** dial-dictation trunk; ~ **de télésurveillance** remote monitoring circuit; ~ **de transfert** transfer circuit; ~ **de transit** through line; tandem trunk; inter-exchange trunk; ~ **de transmission de données** data circuit; data channel; ~ **de triage de signaux** separation circuit; ~ **de type téléphonique** voice-grade circuit; ~ **de verrouillage** clamp; ~ **de voisinage** short cross-border circuit; ~ **d'eau** cooling circuit; ~ **décade** decade (tens) counting circuit; ~ **décade indicateur numérique** digital indicator encoder; ~ **décalé** staggered circuit; ~ **déclencheur** enabling circuit; trigger circuit; ~ **d'écrêtage** amplitude limiter; amplitude lopper; amplitude separation circuit; clipper; ~ **de/en garde** guard circuit; ring-down circuit; ~ **d'égalisation à réaction négative** feedback equalizer; ~ **d'entrée** incoming circuit; driver; input circuit; ~ **dérivateur** differentiator; peaking circuit; ~ **dérivé** branch circuit; ~ **d'essai des dicordes** cord test circuit; ~ **détecteur** detector; ~ **d'excitation** energizing circuit; exciting circuit; ~ **d'identification** identification circuit; identifier; ~ **d'identification d'opérateur** operator identification circuit; ~ **diffusé** (full-)custom circuit; ~ **dilemme** exclusive-

OR circuit; ~ **d'impulsions inverses** revertive pulse circuit; ~ **d'induit** armature circuit; ~ **d'intercommunication** intercom; talk-back circuit; ~ **d'interconnexion** interconnection circuit; ~ **d'interface** interface circuit; ~ **d'interphone** (v. circuit d'intercommunication); ~ **direct de transit** direct toll (trunk) circuit; ~ **direct spécialement désigné** nominated direct circuit; ~ **directeur** pilot circuit; control circuit; ~ **discriminateur** sampling circuit; sampler; ~ **discriminateur de temps** interval selector; time selector; ~ **disponible** available circuit; idle circuit; ~ **dissymétrique** unbalanced wire circuit; ~ **distributeur de message** message distribution circuit (MDC); ~ **d'occupation** track circuit; busy circuit; ~ **d'occupation totale** no free-path circuit; ~ **d'opératrice** operator circuit; locked loop; ~ **d'ordres** talk-back circuit; order-wire circuit; ~ **dual** reflex circuit; reciprocal circuit; ~ **duplex** duplex circuit; ~ **duplex à branchement** split duplex circuit; ~ **duplex à courant de repos** incremental duplex; ~ **d'utilisation** load (circuit); ~ **échelonné** series circuit; ~ **écrêteur** peaking circuit; amplitude lopper; clipper; limiter; separation circuit; ~ **élargisseur** pulse stretcher; ~ **élémentaire** blocking circuit; ~ **éliminateur** rejector circuit; acknowledgement circuit; stopper circuit; roll-off; ~ **éliminateur de bruit de fond** squelch circuit; ~ **éliminateur d'étincelles** spark-quench circuit; ~ **en dérangement** faulty circuit; ~ **en évolution** driven circuit; ~ **en L** L-network; L-section; ~ **en pi** pi-network; ~ **encadreur** (facsimile) frame; ~ **entrant** incoming junctor; ~ **équilibré** balanced(-wire) circuit; ~ **équivalent** equivalent circuit; quadripole; four-terminal circuit; four-pole equivalent network; ~ **équivalent d'un cristal** crystal equivalent circuit; ~ **ET** AND circuit; AND gate; ~ **exploité en duplex** duplex circuit; ~ **extérieur d'entrée** driving circuit; ~ **fantôme** phantom circuit; side circuit; ~ **fantôme avec retour par la terre** earth-return phantom circuit; ~ **fantôme double** double-phantom circuit; side circuit; ~ **fermé** closed circuit; loop; ~ **feuilleté** laminated (magnetic) circuit; ~ **fictif de référence** hypothetical reference circuit; nominal maximum circuit; ~ **fritureux** noisy circuit; ~ **générateur de cadence en pont** bridge timing circuit; ~ **hacheur** chopper circuit; ~ **hybride** hybrid circuit; two-wire/four-wire circuit; term set; ~ **hypothétique de référence** hypothetical reference circuit; ~ **imprimé** printed circuit;

~ **imprimé découpé à la presse** stamped circuit; ~ **imprimé multicouche** multilayer printed circuit board; ~ **indifférent** don't-care gate; ~ **inductif** inductive circuit; ~ **intégrateur** integrating circuit; ~ **intégré à grande échelle** large-scale integrated circuit (LSI); ~ **intégré à poutre** beam lead; ~ **intégré brasé** side-brazed IC; ~ **intégré hybride** hybrid integrated circuit; ~ **intégré linéaire** analogue integrated circuit; linear IC; ~ **intégré logique** digital integrated circuit; ~ **intégré monolithique** monolithic integrated circuit; ~ **intercontinental** intercontinental circuit; ~ **interrégional** inter-regional trunk; ~ **intersection-négation** NOT-AND gate; ~ **interurbain** intertoll trunk; trunk circuit; trunk tie line; long-distance circuit; toll (switching) circuit; ~ **interurbain à quatre fils** four-wire trunk circuit; ~ **interurbain avec sélection à distance** trunk circuit with dialling facility; ~ **interurbain national** national trunk circuit; ~ **interurbain pris** seized trunk circuit; ~ **inverse** (= circuit NON PAS) NOT gate (inverting gate); ~ **inverseur** inverter; NOT gate; ~ **inverseur** (= circuit NON) NOT gate; ~ **LC** (inductance/capacitance) tuned circuit; ~ **libre** free-condition circuit; ~ **limiteur de courant** current limiter; ~ **linéaire** differentiating network; peaking circuit; ~ **linéariseur** linear compensating circuit; ~ **local** local circuit; toll circuit; closed circuit; trunk junction; ~ **local d'écoute** closed control circuit; ~ **longitudinal** earth-return circuit; ~ **loué** leased circuit; ~ **LSI** large-scale integrated circuit (LSI); ~ **magnétique** magnetic circuit; ~ **manuel** ring-down circuit; manual circuit; ~ **mémoire commandée** monitored memory; ~ **métallique** DC telegraph circuit; loop (circuit); ~ **MF** (v. circuit moyenne fréquence); ~ **MIC** PCM trunk; ~ **microphonique** microphone circuit; speech circuit; ~ **miniaturisé** miniature circuit; microcircuit; ~ **mixte** bothway circuit; two-way trunk; up-and-down circuit; ~ **monolithique** micromodule; monolithic IC; ~ **moyenne fréquence** intermediate-frequency circuit; IF circuit; ~ **multiconférence** multiconference circuit; ~ **multicouche** multilayer circuit; ~ **multiplex à courant porteur** carrier multiplex circuit; ~ **multipoint** multipoint circuit; ~ **national de prolongement** national extension (trunk) circuit; ~ **NI** NOR gate; ~ **NI sans capacité** non-saturated NOR circuit; ~ **NON** NOT gate; ~ **non chargé** unloaded line; ~ **non combinable** non-phantom circuit; ~ **NON-ET** NAND gate; ~ **NON-OU** NOR gate; ~ **numérique fictif de référence** hypothetical reference digital path; ~ **numérique-analogique** digital-to-analogue converter; ~ **oscillant** resonant/ tuned circuit; tank circuit; ~ **oscillant final** tank circuit; ~ **oscillateur** tank (tuned) circuit; oscillator; ~ **OU** OR gate; ~ **ouvert** open circuit; ~ **par satellite** satellite circuit; ~ **par satellite à altitude moyenne** medium-altitude satellite circuit; ~ **par satellite à haute altitude** high-altitude satellite circuit; ~ **par satellite sur orbite stationnaire** stationary orbit satellite circuit; ~ **permanent** leased line(s); ~ **perturbé** hostile circuit; ~ **phantastron** phantastron (delayed-pulse) circuit; ~ **pilote** control circuit; pilot (wire) circuit; ~ **planaire** flip-chip; ~ **plurifilaire** multi-wire circuit; ~ **point-à-point** point-to-point circuit; ~ **porte complémenteur** complementer gate; ~ **porteur** carrier circuit; ~ **pour transmission radiophonique** sound programme circuit; ~ **prédiffusé** semi-custom circuit; ~ **primaire** primary circuit; ~ **privé** private wire; private circuit; ~ **pupinisé** coil-loaded circuit; ~ **radioélectrique** radio circuit; ~ **radiophonique** music circuit; programme circuit; ~ **radiotéléphonique** radiotelephone circuit; ~ **redresseur de crêtes** peak rectifier circuit; ~ **réel** side circuit; ~ **réel bifilaire** two-wire side circuit; ~ **réjecteur** rejector (circuit); stopper circuit; ~ **résistance capacitance** (RC) resistance-capacitance network; ~ **résistant** resistive circuit; ~ **résonnant** resonant circuit; acceptor circuit; tuned circuit; ~ **rural à courants porteurs** rural carrier circuit; ~ **rural métallique** rural metallic (loop) circuit; ~ **sans influence** don't-care gate; ~ **sans perte** zero-loss circuit; ~ **sélectif** selective circuit; ~ **sémaphore** common-channel signalling circuit; ~ **semi-intégré** hybrid integrated circuit; ~ **sensible à l'électricité statique** static-sensitive device (SSD); ~ **séparateur** buffer; ~ **simplex** simplex circuit; ~ **solide** solid-state circuit; ~ **sortant** outgoing junctor; ~ **spatial** satellite circuit; satellite link; ~ **spécialisé** private wire; private circuit; ~ **stabilisateur de courant** current-stabilizing circuit; ~ **standard** standard inter-exchange telephone circuit; ~ **statique** solid-state circuit; steady-state circuit; ~ **superfantôme** double-phantom circuit; side circuit; ~ **superfantôme à retour par la terre** earth-return double-phantom circuit; ~ **superposé** superposed circuit; by-product circuit; virtual

circuit; ~ **support** bearer circuit (telegraphy); ~ **supprimé** eliminated circuit; ~ **symétrique** balanced circuit; ~ **syntonisé** tuned circuit; ~ **tampon** buffer; ~ **télégraphique à retour par la terre** earth return telegraph circuit; ~ **télégraphique de jonction** trunk (telegraph) circuit; ~ **télégraphique direct** direct telegraph circuit; ~ **télégraphique fantôme** phantom telegraph circuit; ~ **télégraphique superfantôme** double-phantom (balanced) telegraph circuit; ~ **téléphonique** speaking circuit; voice-grade circuit; ~ **téléphonique à deux fils** two-wire telephone circuit; loop; ~ **téléphonique bifilaire** telephone loop; ~ **téléphonique de radiodiffusion** programme circuit; ~ **téléphonique de terre** terrestrial telephone circuit; ~ **téléphonique double** phantom telephone connection; ~ **téléphonique étalon de travail** working reference telephone circuit (WRTC); ~ **téléphonique étalonné de référence** standard reference telephone circuit; ~ **téléphonique international** international telephone circuit; ~ **téléphonique interurbain** trunk circuit; toll circuit; ~ **téléphonique loué à temps partiel** part-time leased circuit; part-time private telephone wire; ~ **téléphonique loué en permanence** leased circuit; private wire circuit; ~ **temporisation** time-delay circuit; ~ **terminal** terminal circuit; ~ **unidirectionnel** one-way circuit; simplex circuit; ~ **unifilaire** earth-return circuit; longitudinal circuit; ~ **virtuel (CV)** virtual circuit; by-product circuit; ~ **virtuel commuté (CVC)** switched virtual circuit; ~ **virtuel permanent (CVP)** permanent virtual circuit

circuit(s) à chapelet bucket-brigade device (BBD)

circulateur m circulator (of waveguide); ~ **Y** Y-circulator

circulation f traffic; flow; stepping; ~ **d'air** airflow; ~ **d'information** information flow

circuler un courant pass/generate a current

cire f wax impregnation

cisaillage m cropping; shearing; cutting; snipping

cisaille f **à couper les boulons** bolt croppers; ~ **coupe-câble** cable-cutting shears; ~ **d'établi** workbench shears; bench shears

cisaillement m shear

ciseaux m pl scissors; shears; cutters; snips; ~ **à becs courts pointus** short pointed-tip shears; ~ **à becs longs pointus** long pointed-tip shears; ~ **de câbleur** wiring scissors; ~ **d'électricien coupe-fils** electrician's wire-cutting shears; ~ **papier** scis-

sors
CL (v. centre local)
clair (texte etc.) clear text; plain language; hard copy; uncoded; unshaded; highlighted
clapet *m* pocket; rectifier; valve
claquage *m* arcing; insulation breakdown
claqué *adj* burned-out; blown (of fuse)
claquement *m* (de manipulation) key click; click
clarté *f* clarity; articulation; ~ **de réception** clarifier range
classe *f* grade; category; class; group; series; ~ **de fibre** fibre class; ~ **de service** (user) class-of-service; ~ **de trafic** grade of service; ~ **Didot** (approximate) Pica type (12,8 British points); ~ **mécanique** mechanical class
classement *m* collating; filing; sequencing; sorting; ordering; classification; ranking; grading; rating; ~ **alphabétique** alphabetical sorting
classer *v* classify; sort; file; sequence; collate,v.
classeur *m* (document) file; director instrument; binder
classeuse *f* **totalisatrice** proof machine
classification *f* grading; ranking; ~ **verbale arbitraire d'ondes** arbitrary verbal classification
classique *adj* conventional; standard; orthodox; formal; traditional; ordinary; classic(al); run-of-the-mill; typical; practical
clause *f* **échappatoire** escape clause
clauses techniques type specifications
clavette *f* spline; cotter; locking key
clavier *m* keyboard; keysender; keypad; digit key strip; keyset; DTMF station keypad; fingerboard; ~ **à action directe** sawtooth keyboard; ~ **à dimensions réduites** condensed keyboard; compact keypad; ~ **(à entraînement) mécanique** motorized keyboard; ~ **à nappe élastomère** silicone conductive keypad; membrane keypad; ~ **à rappel magnétique** positive magnetic return (action) keypad; ~ **à transfert** storage keyboard; ~ **alphanumérique** alphanumeric keyboard; ~ **avec garde d'inversion** shift-lock keyboard; ~ **dactylographique** typewriter keyboard; ~ **d'appel** keysender; ~ **de fonctions** function keypad; ~ **de numérotation** pushbutton dial; ~ **décimal** decadic keypad; loop-disconnect pushbutton; ~ **d'impulsions** digit key-strip; ~ **émetteur-récepteur** keyboard sender-receiver (KSR); ~ **mobile** independent keyboard; detachable keyboard; ~ **mobile plat** low-profile independent

keyboard; ~ **multifréquence (MF)** dual-tone multifrequency (DTMF) push-button keypad; tone-dialling keypad; ~ **numérique** numeric keypad; ~ **perforateur** keyboard perforator; ~ **perforateur avec impression** printing keyboard perforator; ~ **séparé** independent keyboard; detachable keyboard; ~ **standard** universal keyboard
clavier-bande keytape
clayette *f* (refrigerator) rack; tray; shelf
cle (contrôle) inspection
clé *f*; **clef** *f* key; cipher; pushbutton; button; switch; code; wrench; spanner; argument; ~ **à cadran** torque wrench; ~ **à crémaillère** monkey wrench; adjustable spanner; ~ **à enclenchement** locking key; ~ **à ergot** spanner wrench; pin spanner; hook spanner; ~ **à fourche** open-ended spanner; ~ **àgroupement** operator position coupling key; ~ **à levier** lever key; ~ **à molette** adjustable spanner; ~ **à pipe** offset socket wrench; ~ **à retour** non-(self-)locking key; ~ **à tube** nut spinner; nut driver; ~ **anglaise** monkey wrench; adjustable spanner; ~ **d'accès** (data) access key; password; personal access code; ~ **d'annulation** cancel key; ~ **d'appel** ringing key; call(ing) key; ~ **d'appel et de conversation** speaking and ringing key; ~ **d'arrêt** hold-over key; ~ **de boucle** loop-disconnect key; ~ **de configuration** call status key; ~ **de contact** switch key; ~ **de contrôle** folded checksum; check key; hash total; ~ **de conversation** talking key; speaking key; ~ **de coupure de sonnerie** mute key; ~ **de désignation** assigment key; ~ **de jour** daily-keying instrument; ~ **de liaison** position grouping key; grouping key; ~ **de prise** busying key; ~ **de rappel** recall key; loopbreak switch; ~ **de rappel du demandeur** reverting switch; ring-back key; ~ **de renvoi** transfer key; ~ **de renvoi de nuit** night service key; ~ **de rupture** cut-off key; interruption key; ~ **de sécurité** interlock switch; ~ **de séparation** split key; ~ **de suppression** (timing) override; ~ **de surveillance** monitoring key; ~ **de tri** sort key; ~ **de validité** protection key; ~ **de voûte** cornerstone; keystone; ~ **d'écoute** listening key; answering key; audio switch; monitoring key; ~ **d'écoute silencieuse** monitoring key; ~ **d'espacement** blank key; ~ **d'occupation** busy key; ~ **dynamométrique** torque wrench; ~ **égale** matching key; ~ **emmanchée** nut spinner; nut driver; ~ **en tube** box wrench; ~ **en tube coudée** offset box wrench; ~ **fractionnable** split keyboard;

C

~ **mâle** (six pans) hexagon key; hex socket wrench; ~ **manivelle** crank; ~ **mixte** combination spanner; ~ **plate** open-ended spanner; ~ **plate à fourche** flat open-ended spanner; ~ **polygonale** ring spanner; ~ **pour couple de tête** head torque wrench; ~ **programme** program access key; ~ **réel court** short real key (four byte real number); ~ **réel long** long real key (eight byte real number)

clef f (v. clé)

clé-pilote keysender

clic n click; transient

cliché m block; negative; layout; format; record; photographic mask; profile; print; ~ **d'anomalie** fault-tracing program; ~ **de carte** card format; ~ **de faute** fault profile; snapshot; fault report

client m client; customer; ~ **pilote** first customer shipment; FCS user

clignotant adj recurrent; cyclic; intermittent; pulsed; bistable; flashing; ~ **lent** slow blinking; ~ **rapide** fast flashing; fast blinking

clignote (voyant) fast flashing

clignotement m flashing speed; blinking; ~ **de caractère** character blink

clignoter v flash; blink

clignoteur m flasher unit; clock

climat m **salin** salt-laden environment

climatisation f air conditioning; controlled temperature conditions

clinquant m foil (for use in cables)

clip m **de connexion** connecting clip; in-line receptacle

clips circlip; snap ring

cliquet m pawl; latch; dog; ratchet; detent; catch; ~ **de recul** backspace pawl; ~ **de retenue (pour) tête** head retaining pawl; detent arm; ~ **rappel** (v. cliquet de recul); ~ **réversible** reversible ratchet

cliquetis m chatter; click

clivage m isolator

cloche f (disk pack) canister

cloison f compartment; partition; screen; wall; bulkhead; ~ **isolant** insulating barrier; screen; partition

cloisonné adj partitioned; divided; modularized

cloisonnement m insulating panel; wall; partition; modularization; boundary

cloquage m blistering

cloque f kink; blister

clore v sign-off; close down; log-off

clos enclosed (of speaker)

clôture f SYSEND; closing (of file); log-off; seal; fastener

clou m peg; stud; nail

CM (v. couche mince)

CN (v. centre nodal)

co-actif adj cluster

coaxial adj coaxial; concentric

cobrette f (cable) support structure

cocher v tick; flag; mark off

codage m coding; encoding; discriminating (key); ~ **à segments** A-law encoding; segmented quantization; ~ **à somme bornée** balanced code; ~ **aléatoire** hash coding; ~ **automatique** automatic coding; ~ **binaire** binary coding; ~ **de base** basic coding; ~ **d'impulsions** pulse coding; ~ **en absolu** absolute coding; ~ **en durée d'impulsions** pulse-width coding; ~ **en ligne** line coding; ~ **en treillis à huit états** eight-state trellis coding; trellis-coded modulation (TCM); ~ **individuel** per-line codecs (system); ~ **multiniveau** multi-level coding; ~ **non uniforme** non-uniform (continuous) quantization; mu-law encoding; ~ **numérique** digital coding; ~ **par découpage** gap coding; ~ **par groupe** shared codecs (system); ~ **par transition** differential encoding; ~ **pseudo-ternaire** high-density bipolar coding (HDB 3); ~ **symbolique** symbolic coding; ~ **uniforme** uniform encoding

code m code; cipher; crypto; data alphabet; ~ **16** hex code; ~ **à accès mimimum** minimum access code; latency code; optimum code; delay code; ~ **à barres (CAB)** universal product code; bar code; ~ **à bâtonnets** bar code; ~ **à cinq couches** five-level code; five-unit (Baudot) code; ~ **à cinq moments** (v. code à cinq couches); ~ **à deux fréquences parmi six** two-out-of-six multifrequency code; ~ **à disparité compensée** paired disparity code; alternative code; ~ **à disparité restreinte** low disparity code; paired disparity code; ~ **à éléments** equal-length (multi-unit) code; unit code; ~ **à enchaînement** chain code; ~ **à excédent trois** excess-three code (XS 3); ~ **à huit moments** eight-level code; ~ **à moments** (v. code à éléments); ~ **à plusieurs niveaux** multi-level code; ~ **à somme bornée** balanced code; ~ **absolu** direct code; one-level code; machine code; specific code; ~ **alphabétique** alphabet code; ~ **alphanumérique** alphanumeric code; ~ **articulé** combination code; ~ **asservi** compelled code; ~ **autocorrecteur** error correction code; Hamming code; forward-acting code; ~ **Baudot** Baudot code; ~ **BHD** (v. code bipolaire à haute densité (d'ordre 3)); ~ **bifréquence** multi-frequency code; ~ **binaire chinois** Chinese binary (code); ~ **binaire MIC PCM** binary code; ~ **binaire naturel** pure binary; ~ **binaire objet translatable** relocatable binary object code; ~ **binaire réfléchi** Gray code; reflected binary code; cyclic code; ~ **binaire symétrique** symmetrical binary code; ~ **bipolaire** bipolar code; ~ **bipolaire à haute densité (d'ordre 3) (code BHD)** (third-order) high density bipolar code (HDB3 code); ~ **biquinaire** biquinary code; ~ **bivalent** two-condition code; ~ **bivalent pour câble** two-condition cable code; double-current cable code (DCCC/ DC3); ~ **caractère** character code; ~ **carte** card code; ~ **clavier** keyboard code; ~ **cliché** profile code; ~ **correcteur d'erreurs** (Hamming) (Hamming) error-correcting code; forward-acting code; ~ **créateur** parent code; ~ **cyclique** cyclic code; Gray code; reflected binary code; signal-distance code (= Hamming distance); ~ **d'accès** access code; ~ **d'adresse** address code; ~ **d'appel** calling code; call-directing code (CDC); ringing code; ~ **d'arrêt** interrupt code; barrier code; stop code; ~ **d'attribut de caractère** character code; ~ **DCB** (v. code décimal codé binaire); ~ **de base** absolute code; ~ **de bouton** button-jammed code; ~ **de bureau** exchange code; office code; ~ **de caractères** character code; ~ **de déclenchement** start code; ~ **de données** data code; telegraph alphabet; ~ **de fin d'étape** step termination code; ~ **de fonction** function code; ~ **de Gray** reflected binary (Gray) code; ~ **de Hamming** (Hamming) error-correcting code; ~ **de masquage** privacy code; ~ **de modulation d'impulsions à plusieurs niveaux** multi-level pulse code; ~ **de nombre de pas égal** equal-length code; ~ **de région** area code; ~ **de remplissage** filler code; stop code; ~ **de renvoi** return code; ~ **de réponse** answer-back code; ~ **de service** function code; ~ **de signalisation** signalling code; ~ **(de signalisation) associé** associated mode (of signalling); ~ **(de signalisation) non-associé** non-associated mode (of signalling); ~ **(de signalisation) quasi-associé** quasi-associated mode (of signalling); ~ **de signaux de ligne** line signal code; ~ **de taxe** charging code; ~ **de téléimprimeur** telex code; teleprinter code; ~ **de tonalité** tone code; ~ **de travail** signal wave; ~ **de verrouillage** interlock code; ~ **de verrouillage de trame** framing code; ~ **de zone** area code; ~ **d'échec** non-completion code; ~ **décimal** decadic (signalling) code; ~ **décimal codé binaire** binary-coded decimal code; BCD code; ~ **d'enchaînement** next-instruction code; ~ **d'en-tête** header code; heading code; ~ **d'équipement (CEQ)** equipment code; ~ **(des) couleur(s)** colour code; colour coding; ~ **d'état** status code; ~ **détecteur d'erreur(s)** error-detecting code; self-checking code; ~ **détecteur d'erreurs vers l'avant** forward error-detecting code; forward-acting code; ~ **deux parmi cinq/sur cinq (2/5)** two-out-of-five code; ~ **d'instructions** instruction code; ~ **d'opération** operation code; OP code; ~ **d'ordre** OP code (operation code); instruction set; ~ **d'ordres unique** common instruction set; ~ **EBCDIC** EBCDIC (Extended Binary Coded Decimal Interchange Code); ~ **émetteur** issuing bank code; ~ **en ligne** line code; ~ **enregistreur** inter-register signalling code; ~ **équilibré** fixed-count code; fixed-ratio code; balanced code; ~ **exécutable** object code; ~ **fonctionnel** function code; ~ **H** Hollerith code; ~ **H** (v. code Hollerith); ~ **hâché** hash code; ~ **hexa (&)** hex(-adecimal) code; ~ **Hollerith** Hollerith code; ~ **indicateur** routing code; ~ **informatique** computer(ized) code; ~ **instruction** instruction code; ~ **interne** keyboard code; ~ **interprétable** machine(-readable) code; ~ **machine** machine code; computer (instruction) code; absolute code; actual code; ~ **majoré de trois** excess-three code (XS3); ~ **MF à impulsions** MF signalling; ~ **mnémonique** mnemonic code; ~ **monnaie** currency code; ~ **morse** Morse alphabet; Morse code; ~ **mouvement** transaction code; ~ **multifréquence** multifrequency code (MF); ~ **multifréquence asservi** compelled multifrequency code; ~ **multifréquence non asservi** non-compelled multifrequency code; ~ **multifréquence semi asservi** semi-compelled multifrequency code; ~ **N dont M** M out of N code; ~ **normal** shift-in code (SI); ~ **numérique** numerical code; ~ **objet translatable** relocatable object code; ~ **octal** octal code; ~ **opération** operation code; OP code; ~ **par tout ou rien** binary code; ~ **paramétrable** skeletal code; ~ **perforation** card code; ~ **plus trois** excess-three code; ~ **pondéré** weighted code; ~ **pseudo-ternaire** pseudo-ternary code; ~ **quibinaire** quibinary code; ~ **quinaire** two-out-of-five code; ~ **redondant** redundant code; ~ **réel** direct code; ~ **réfléchi à excédent trois** Pertheric code; excess-three code; ~ **résultant** object code; ~ **retour** follow-on code; return code; ~ **sans retour à zéro** non-return-to-zero code; NRZ code; ~ **sé-lectionné** select code; ~ **série à huit moments** eight-bit serial code; ~ **spécial** shift-out code (SO); ~ **symbolique** pseudo-code; ~ **télégraphique à cinq moments** five-unit code; ~ **télégraphique internatio-nal** international telegraph code; ~ **télégra-phique Q** Q-code; ~ **télégraphique trivalent** three-condition telegraph code; ~ **télépho-nique** telephone code; ~ **télex** teleprinter code; telex code; ~ **temporel** timing track; ~ **ternaire** ternary code; ternary alphabet; ~ **trivalent pour câble** three-condition cable code; cable morse code; ~ **unique** common code; common language; ~ **utilisateur** user code; ~ **vitesse** data rate

codé *adj* object

codec (codeur-décodeur) *m* codec (coder-de-coder); ~ **monovoie voie par voie** per-chan-nel codec; ~ **par voie** (v. codec monovoie voie par voie)

codeur *n* encoder; coder; ~ **angulaire** angular encoder; ~ **d'arrêt extérieur** external stop code(r); break encoder; ~ **de contrôle** check coder; ~ **de position** (v. codeur angulaire); ~ **de rotation** shaft encoder; angular position encoder; ~ **d'ordres de télécommande** remote control order encod-er; ~ **monovoie** per-channel codec; ~ **nu-mérique** digitizer; quantizer; ~ **quadriphase** QPSK encoder (quadrature phase-shift keying)

codeur-décodeur *m* (v. codec)

codificateur *m* coder; code selector

codification *f* coding; codifying; classifica-tion; ~ **commerciale** ordering code; ~ **de la longueur de trajet** run-length coding; ~ **séquentielle directe** direct sequential encoding

codifier *v* encode; code; codify; classify; document; ~ **en numérique** digitize; quan-tize

coefficient *m* coefficient; factor; constant; figure; modulus; ~ **d'accouplement** cou-pling coefficient; ~ **d'activité moyen** mean activity factor; ~ **d'adaptation** return current coefficient; ~ **d'amélioration** im-provement factor; ~ **d'amortissement** damping coefficient; decay factor; ~ **d'am-plification** gain (constant/coefficient); ~ **d'atténuation** attenuation coefficient; ~ **de cadrage** bit stuffing rate; stuffing rate; ~ **de couplage** (v. coefficient d'accouple-ment); ~ **de courants réfléchis** return-cur-rent coefficient; reflection coefficient; ~ **de déviation** deflection coefficient; deviation factor; ~ **de dilatation** (linear) expansion coefficient; ~ **de dispersion**

leakage factor; leakage coefficient; ~ **de dispersion magnétique** magnetic dispersion coefficient; ~ **de distorsion harmonique** harmonic distortion factor; K-rating; ~ **de foisonnement** growth factor; expansion coefficient; ~ **de frottement** coefficient of friction; ~ **de majoration** weighting (fac-tor); qualifying; ~ **de modulation** modula-tion factor; ~ **de multiplication** error multiplication factor; ~ **de pénétration** penetration factor; ~ **de pertes due aux réflexions** reflection factor; mismatch fac-tor; ~ **de pondération** weighting (coeffi-cient); ~ **de pratique expérimentale** crew factor (of articulation measurements); practice factor; ~ **de protection électrique** screening factor; shield factor; ~ **de qualité** figure of merit; quality factor; Q-factor; ~ **de rayonnement** radiation efficiency; aerial efficiency; ~ **de récipro-cité** reciprocity coefficient; ~ **de réduction** de-rating factor; ~ **de réflexion** reflection factor; return current coefficient; return loss; ~ **de réflexion de la tension** voltage-re-flection coefficient; ~ **de réflexion relatif à l'intensité** return-current coefficient; reflec-tion coefficient; ~ **de sécurité** safety factor; load factor; ~ **de self-induction** self-induc-tion coefficient; ~ **de sensibilité** response; sensitivity coefficient; ~ **de surcharge** load(ing) factor; ~ **de surtension** Q-factor; quality factor; ~ **de température** tempera-ture coefficient; ~ **de température de la tension de fonctionnement** temperature coef-ficient of working voltage; ~ **de transmis-sion** transmittance; ~ **d'efficacité de la luminescence** luminous efficiency; ~ **d'émission secondaire** secondary-emis-sion coefficient; ~ **d'équilibrage** return-current coefficient; ~ **d'induction mutuelle** mutual inductance coefficient; ~ **d'inser-tion** insertion transfer function; ~ **d'inter-action** interaction factor; ~ **d'intermodula-tion** inter-modulation distortion ratio; ~ **d'occupation d'un circuit** circuit usage; percentage occupied time; ~ **d'ondulation** ripple; ~ **d'utilisation** fill; duty factor; demand factor; duty cycle; ~ **électro-acoustique de couplage** electro-acoustic force factor; electro-acoustic coupling impedance; ~ **électromécanique de cou-plage** electromechanical force factor; elec-tromechanical coupling impedance; ~ **hié-rarchique** relative status; ranking; ~ **spéci-fique d'ionisation** specific ionization coeffi-cient

cœur *m* core; kernel; ~ **de chaîne (CDC)** (exchange) central units coexistence *f* overlay

coffret *m* enclosure; cabinet; cubicle; container; stunt box; switch unit; external unit; processor; casing; housing; console; casket; ~ à fusibles fuse box; ~ chaîne de mesure measurement system module; ~ codeur stunt box (of teleprinter); ~ de commande line unit; control unit; dialling unit; control box; signalling unit; stunt box; ~ de contrôle test console; ~ de disques souples pedestal; disk drive unit; ~ de distribution splitter switch; ~ de manœuvre control unit; line unit; control box; ~ de raccordement (CRU) adaptor unit; ~ d'électricien electrician's toolbox; ~ extérieur switch house; ~ filière stock and die set; ~ hyper de réception RF receiver unit; ~ isolant insulated enclosure; ~ logique central processing unit (CPU); control logic pack; ~ mécanicien mechanic's toolbox; ~ métallique sheet metal enclosure; ~ TUT terminal unit tester (TUT)

COFIDEC codec-filter chip

cohérence *f* consistency; coordination; conformity; compatibility; integration; harmony; correspondence; integrity; ~ d'une modulation modulation coherence; ~ temporelle temporal coherence (of fibre optics)

cohérent *adj* homogeneous; consistent; integrated; coordinated; uniform; compatible; integral; synchronized

cohéreur *m* acoustic shock absorber; coherer

coin *m* wedge; termination; corner

coincer *v* trap; jam; seize; squash

coïncidence *f* congruence; register; coincidence; ~ de phase phase coincidence

col *m* neck (of tube)

collaborateur(s) *m* associate(s); staff; colleague(s)

collaboration *f* mutual assistance; joint venture

collage *m* operation; bonding; sticking; welding (of contacts); mounting details; latching; ~ à 0 sticking at zero (of bit)

colle *f* adhesive; bonding substance; glue; cement

collé *adj* bonded; energized (of relay)

collecte d'abonnés subscriber access subsystem; *f* de(s) données data collection; data retrieval; logging; accumulation; acquisition; data sink; collation; polling

collecteur *m* commutator; bus; collector; ~ commun common collector; emitter follower; ~ de courant current collector; commutator; brush; ~ de dissipation heat sink; ~ de données data sink; data logger; ~ HF electron collector (of microwave tube)

collectif *adj* pooled

coller *v* hold; stick; latch(-over); lock; pick up

collerette *f* flange; band; ring; hook; trim; skirt; ~ carrée square flange; ~ de cuivre copper ring; ~ frontale fascia; surround; bezel; trim

colleuse *f* paper tape splicer

collier *m* clip; clamp; tie; collar; ~ à plaquette tab collar; identification sleeve; ~ cranté notched (cable) clip; band; tie; ~ de déviation yoke assembly (of CRT); ~ PC jubilee clip; ~ pour câbles cable clamp; cable clip; tie; ~ TY-RAP [A.C.] cable tie

collision *f* clash; access contention; ~ d'appel à l'interface ETTD/ETCD data collision at the DTE/DCE interface; ~ frontale head-on collision; ~ même jonction double seizure (of trunk from both ends)

colloque *m* (de reconnaissance) handshake

colmatage *m* settling; clogging; sealing

colonne *f* stack; column; frame; field; ~ de carte card column; ~ galopante running column (of bit pattern); ~ journalistique snake column; newspaper column; ~ positive positive column; ~ serpentine snake column; ~ serpentine forcée forced snake column; running newspaper column

colonnette *f* stanchion; pillar

colophane *f* colophony; solder flux; resin

coloration *f* dans la masse de l'enveloppe self-colouring (of insulation); colour-impregnated; ~ superficielle surface colouring

coloris *m* livery; colour scheme; colour code

combat *m* abatement; ~ d'interférences radio-électriques RFI-EMI combat

combinaison(s) strap(ping); configuration; pattern; (code) combination; intercommunication; amalgam

combinaison binaire bit pattern; ~ d'antennes antifading spaced aerials; ~ des contacts contact arrangement; ~ diplexeur-filtre de bande latérale filterplexer

combinateur *m*; combineur *m* adder; combiner; controller; multiple-contact switch; sequence switch; step switch; selector switch; multiplexer; multiplexor; register control device; ~ de bande de base baseband combiner

combinatoire *adj* combinational

combiné *m* handset; receiver; desktop telephone; microtelephone

combineur *m* (v. combinateur)

Comité Consultatif International Télégraphique et Téléphonique (CCITT) International Telegraph and Telephone Consultative

Committee (CCITT); ~ **d'automatisation** feasibility committee; ~ **d'organisation** steering committee; ~ **d'orientation** (v. comité d'organisation)

commande (cde) f control; operating; piloting; drive; actuation; command; instruction; order; activation; signal; lever; control stick; control signal; control character; ~ **à distance** remote control; ~ **à quantification d'amplitude** amplitude-quantized control/synchronization; ~ **à quantification temporelle** time-quantized control; ~ **à repliage** foldback control; ~ **aide** help command; ~ **amont** (commutateur temporel) backward control; ~ **automatique de fréquence (CAF)** automatic frequency control (AFC); ~ **automatique de gain (CAG)** automatic gain control (AGC); ~ **automatique de gain à seuil** biased automatic gain control; delayed automatic gain control; ~ **automatique de gain avec (réglage) silencieux** automatic gain control with squelch; ~ **automatique de gain par impulsions** keyed automatic gain control; pulsed automatic gain control; ~ **automatique de sélectivité** automatic selectivity control (ASC); ~ **automatique de volume (CAV)** automatic volume control; ~ **autonome programmé (CAP)** programmed off-line control; ~ **aval** (commutateur temporel) forward control; front-end control; output control; ~ **bilatérale** bilateral control; ~ **centrale** common control; central control; ~ **centralisée** common control; ~ **commune** (v. commande centralisée); ~ **d'abandon du transfert** transfer abort command; ~ **d'appareil auxiliaire** device control; ~ **d'attente musicale** music-on-hold (signal); ~ **d'avance** stepping control; feed control; drive; ~ **de bout en bout** end-to-end control; ~ **de chaînon (de données) à haut niveau (HDLC)** high-level data link control (HDLC); ~ **de contact** contact operate; ~ **de coup par coup** inching control system; ~ **de flux** (transmit) flow control; ~ **de largeur d'image** width control (of TV); ~ **de liaison (de données) à haut niveau** (v. commande de chaînon (de données) à haut niveau (HDLC)); ~ **de mise en page** formatter; ~ **de processus** process control; ~ **de puissance à l'émission** up-link power control; ~ **de sélectivité** bandwidth control; ~ **de sensibilité** sensitivity control; ~ **décentralisée** distributed control; ~ **d'échelle** range select; ~ **d'équilibrage** balance control; ~ **desmodromique** positive control; ~ **d'implantation** address assignment command; ~ **d'inhibition** inhibition control;

disabling signal; ~ **d'invitation à transmettre** polling command; proceed-to-send signal; ~ **directe** direct control; direct drive; ~ **du relais de signalisation** synchronizing relay control scan point; ~ **du troisième fil** third-wire control; ~ **électronique** electronic control; ~ **géométrique** geometric control; ~ **horizontale de synchronisation** horizontal hold (control); ~ **indirecte** indirect control; indirect drive; ~ **linéarisée** constant; ~ **locale** single-ended control; ~ **locale et distante** double-ended control; ~ **mécanique** actuator; ~ **musicale d'attente** music-on-hold; ~ **numérique** numerical control; ~ **par calculateurs** stored program control; ~ **par courants vocaux** voice-operated switching; ~ **par cristal** crystal control; ~ **par enregistreurs** register control; ~ **par la grille** grid control; ~ **par logiciel** software control; ~ **par logique câblée** hardwired control logic; ~ **par processeurs** processor control; ~ **par programme enregistré (CPE)** stored program control (SPC); ~ **polarisation** polar drive; ~ **programme** ordering schedule; ~ **répartie** distributed control; ~ **verticale de synchronisation** vertical hold; ~ **visualisation** display command; ~ **voie** path command

commandé par l'amont input-controlled; ~ **par l'aval** output-controlled

commander v control; drive; order; start; initiate

commandes en sortie address latch enable (ALE); ~ **enregistrées** order book; ~ **opérateur** dedicated commands

commanditaire backer

commentaire m narrative; commentary; comment; statement; annotation

commenté adj annotated

commerce extérieur foreign trade

commercial adj trade; marketing; business

commercialisé adj marketed

commettant principal

commodité f **d'accès** accessibility

commun adj joint; public; common; collective

communicant adj; **communiquant** adj networked; interactive

communication f call; connection; communication; message; intelligence; signal; transmission; ~ **à grande portée** long-distance connection; trunk call; long-haul communications; ~ **à sens unique** one-way simplex; ~ **alternée dans les deux sens** simplex; ~ **avec indication de taxe** call with cost notification; advise duration and charge (ADC); ~ **avec préavis (PAV)** personal call;

~ **bidirectionnelle** duplex call; duplex connection; ~ **bifurquée** forked working; ~ **bilatérale** duplex; two-way simplex; ~ **collective** conference call; conference connection; ~ **conférence unilatérale** lecture call; ~ **d'arrivée** terminating (incoming) call; ~ **de conférence** conference call; ~ **de départ** originating (outgoing) call; ~ **de détresse** distress call; emergency call; ~ **de données** data communications; ~ **de personne à personne** person-to-person call; ~ **de service** service call; ~ **de transit** transit call; single-switch call; ~ **de transit simple** one-switch call; ~ **d'entrée** incoming call; ~ **d'erreur** alarm message; ~ **d'essai** test call; ~ **différée** deferred call; ~ **directe** direct call; direct connection; ~ **échelonnée** echelon telegraphy; extended telegraph circuit; ~ **effective** effective call; ~ **efficace** completed call; successful call; ~ **en chaîne** transfer call(ing); link signalling; ~ **en cours d'établissement** connection in progress; ~ **en semiduplex** half-duplex operation; ~ **établie** (v. communication effective); ~ **fictive de référence** hypothetical reference connection; ~ **guidée** controlled communication; ~ **internationale** international call; ~ **internationale de transit** international transit call; ~ **internationale de transit simple** two-link international call; one-switch connection; ~ **internationale de transit double** three-link international call; two-switch connection; ~ **internationale directe** direct international call; ~ **locale** local call; intra-city call; ~ **maritime par satellite** maritime satellite communication; ~ **nationale** national call; ~ **nocturne** night call; ~ **non établie** uncompleted call; ~ **non taxée à la durée** untimed call; ~ **numérique** digital connection; ~ **par commutation** switched connection; ~ **par fil** wire communication; line communication; ~ **par satellite** satellite communications (SATCOM); ~ **payable à l'arrivée (PCV)** collect call; transfer charge call; ~ **personnelle** personal call; ~ **personnelle avec messager** messenger call; ~ **phototélégraphique** phototelegraph call; ~ **pour conférence** conference call; conference connection; ~ **privative** call privacy; ~ **refusée** refused call; ~ **régionale** regional call; ~ **routinière** routine message; ~ **sol-air** ground-air communications; ~ **sous-marine** underwater communications; ~ **superposée** crossed line; ~ **taxée à la durée** timed call; ~ **télégraphique circulaire** multi-address message; ~ **téléimprimée** teleprinter message; telex message;

~ **téléphonique** telephone connection; telephone call; message; ~ **transhorizon** over-the-horizon communications; ~ **unidirectionnelle** simplex call; simplex connection; ~ **urbaine entrante** incoming local call; ~ **urgente** urgent call; ~ **virtuelle** virtual call; ~ **vocale** voice communications

communication-minute call-minute
communications optiques light-wave communications
communiquant *adj* (v. communicant)
commutable *adj* variable; changeable; interchangeable
commutateur *m* selector switch; changeover switch; crossbar switch; toggle switch; switch module; switching unit; subswitch; transfer switch; exchange; ~ **à action retardée** delay switch; ~ **à anneau** ring switch; ~ **à barres croisées** crossbar switch; ~ **à bascule** throw-over switch; toggle switch; ~ **à commande amont** time-switch with backward control; ~ **à commande aval** time-switch with forward control; ~ **à couteaux** knife switch; ~ **à deux directions** double-throw switch; ~ **à gaz** gas-filled switch; ~ **à levier** lever switch; ~ **à plots** step switch; ~ **à plots isolées** non-shorting switch; ~ **à prises** tap switch; ~ **à tige** reed switch; ~ **à une direction** single-throw switch; ~ **antenne-terre** aerial-earth switch; ~ **automatique** (private) automatic exchange (PAX); automatic switch; ~ **automatique privé** private automatic exchange; ~ **automatique télégraphique** telegraph switch; telegraph exchange; ~ **auxiliaire d'abonné** hunting selector; hunting switch; ~ **barillet** drum switch; drum controller; ~ **combiné d'écoute et de conversation** combined listening and speaking key; ~ **d'accès** access selector switch; ~ **d'altitude** height change-over switch; ~ **de bande** band switch; tape switch; ~ **de données** data switch(ing unit); ~ **de fonction** function selector; ~ **de gammes** magnifier (of oscilloscope); ~ **de gammes d'ondes** waveband switch; wave range selector; ~ **de groupes locaux** local group switch; ~ **de guide d'ondes** waveguide switch; ~ **de message spécialisé** dedicated message switching centre; ~ **de nuit** night-alarm key; night-alarm switch; ~ **de protection (du contenu du disque)** floppy disk write-protect switch; ~ **de sélection d'adresse** address selector; ~ **de sélection de groupe** group selector switch; ~ **de shuntage** shunt switch; ~ **de sonnerie** ringing changeover switch; ~ **de sortie** output time switch;

~ **de transit privé** private transit exchange; ~ **de verrouillage** keylock switch; interlock switch; ~ **d'entrée** input time switch; ~ **d'équilibrage** balance selector; ~ **d'octets** byte switch; ~ **du sens de relèvement** bearing sense switch; ~ **d'unités** input-output switch; ~ **électromécanique** crossbar switch; analogue exchange; ~ **élémentaire** switch module; (quarter) switching plane; central matrix subswitch; ~ **émission-réception** send-receive switch; ~ **étoile-triangle** star-delta switch; ~ **interurbain** trunk switchboard; ~ **jumelé** ganged switch; ~ **manuel** switchboard; ~ **manuel à supervision par pont de transmission** bridge-control switchboard; ~ **manuel à dicorde** double-cord switchboard; ~ **manuel à supervision par troisième fil** sleeve-control switchboard; ~ **marche-arrêt (MA)** on/off switch; ~ **OC/OL** (ondes courtes/ondes longues) SW/LW selector (short-wave/long-wave); ~ **optique** optical switch; ~ **parole-écoute** intercom switch; ~ **pas-à-pas** stepping relay; step-by-step exchange; ~ **privé** (à postes supplémentaires) private branch exchange (PBX); ~ **sélectif** rotary (selector) switch; uniselector; ~ **spécialisé** dedicated switch; ~ **temporel** time switch; ~ **temporel à commande amont** time switch with backward control; ~ **temporel à commande aval** time switch with forward control; ~ **temporel carré** input time switch; incoming time switch; ~ **unipolaire à deux directions** single-pole double-throw switch (SPDT); ~ **universel** Swiss exchange; ~ **va-et-vient** two-way switch

commutation *f* switching (over); interlock(ing); circuit switching; interchange; interchanging; scheduling; ~ **à commande successive** step-by-step switching; ~ **à deux fils** two-wire switching; ~ **à sélection rotative** rotary switching; ~ **à sélection successive** (v. commutation à commande successive); ~ **à travers les enroulements des transformateurs** tail-eating switching; ~ **analogique** analogue switching; ~ **avec retransmission par bande perforée** reperforator switching; ~ **bit à bit** bit switching; ~ **caractère par caractère** character switching; ~ **de caractères** character switching; ~ **de circuits** circuit switching; line switching; ~ **de circuits virtuels** virtual circuit packet switching; ~ **de la bande** band switching; ~ **de lignes** line switching; circuit switching; ~ **de longueur d'onde** frequency-division switching; ~ **de messages** message switching; store-and-forward switching; ~ **de paquets** packet switching; hot-potato (network); ~ **de puissance** power conversion; ~ **de transit** tandem switching; ~ **de transitions asynchrones** asynchronous-transition switching; ~ **de voies** channel switching; protection switching; ~ **d'éléments** bit switching; ~ **électromécanique** crossbar switching; ~ **électronique de messages** (electronic) message switching; ~ **électronique spatiale** space-division switching; ~ **électronique temporelle** time-division electronic switching; ~ **élément par élément** bit switching; ~ **embarquée** on-board switching; ~ **émission-réception** transmit-receive switching; ~ **en mode courant** current-mode switching; ~ **(en) tandem** tandem switching; ~ **en télécommunication** switching; ~ **et commande** switching and control; ~ **fréquentielle** wavelength switching; frequency-division switching; ~ **manuelle** manual switching; ~ **numérique** digital switching; time-division switching; ~ **par enveloppes** envelope switching; ~ **par paquets** packet switching; hot-potato (network); ~ **par répartition dans l'espace** space-division switching; ~ **par répartition dans le temps** time-division switching; ~ **par volet** wipe; ~ **pas-à-pas** step-by-step switching; SxS switching; ~ **semi-électronique** semi-electronic switching; ~ **spatiale** space-division switching; space switching; analogue switching; ~ **spatiale multiplexée** space-multiplex switching; ~ **Strowger** Strowger switching; ~ **téléphonique** telephone switching; ~ **temporelle** time-division switching; time switching; digital switching; ~ **tout ou rien** saturated logic (transistors)

commutatrice *f* rotary (single-armature) converter; inverter; transverter; commutator-rectifier; dynamotor; commutator ring; ~ **triphasée continue** three-phase to DC converter

commuté *adj* switched; interchanged; dialled-up

commuter *v* switch over; interchange; chop; select

compacité *f* compactness; packing density

compact *adj* sturdy; massive; rigid; dense; high-density

compactage *m* high-density assembly; ~ **des données** data packing; ~ **des tables** table packing

compagnie *f* **exploitante** operating company; ~ **téléphonique** telephone company (telco)

comparaison *f* matching; sampling; ~ **à zéro** floating point compare; ~ **des enregistrements** sampling; ~ **logique** logical comparison; ~ **par paires** paired comparison

comparateur *m* comparator; comparing element; gauge; ~ **à hystérésis** hysteresis comparator; ~ **de phase** phase comparator; ~ **électronique** electronic comparator; ~ **impédance de table** bench-mounted impedance comparator; ~ **modulateur de largeur** pulse-width modulating comparator; PWM comparator; ~ **Zivy** micrometer dial gauge

compartiment *m* partition; bucket (in core memory); cubicle; region; ~ **à monnaie** cash box (of bank teller machine)

compas *m* hinged stays; bracket; ~ **d'ouverture** hinged stay

compatibilité *f* compatibility; interfaceability; direct interfacing

compatible dans le sens croissant upward-compatible

compensateur *m* **d'affaiblissement** line residual equalizer; attenuation equalizer; ~ **de la distorsion d'affaiblissement** attenuation equalizer; ~ **de niveau** level compensator; ~ **de phase** phase equalizer; delay equalizer; modifier; ~ **d'écho** echo canceller; ~ **du temps de propagation** delay equalizer; phase equalizer; ~ **préréglé** preset equalizer

compensation *f* compensation; equalization; balancing; offset; trade-off; roll-off; ~ **avec boucle d'avance de phase** feed-forward compensation; ~ **d'affaiblissement** attenuation equalization; ~ **d'atténuation** (v. compensation d'affaiblissement); ~ **de dérive** drift compensation; ~ **de la charge réactive** reactive load compensation; ~ **de l'erreur quadrantale** quadrantal error correction; ~ **de longueur de câble** cable length compensation; ~ **de température** thermal compensation; ~ **de variations de température** temperature error offset; ~ **d'erreurs** error correction; ~ **des hautes fréquences** high-frequency compensation; HF equalization; ~ **du temps de propagation de phase** phase equalization; ~ **en fréquence** frequency compensation; ~ **interne** roll-off; ~ **linéaire** linear correction; ~ **par dopage** doping compensation

compenser *v* balance; modify; correct; equalize; compensate; redress

compétence discipline; skill

compilateur *m* compiler; translator; ~ **monopasse** one-pass compiler; single-pass compiler

compilation *f* compiling

compiler *v* compile

complément *m* additional element; extra; filler; back-up; buttressing; build-out circuit; mate; rider; adjunct; add-on; boost; supporting details; ~ **à blanc** padded with blanks; ~ **à la base** radix component; ~ **(binaire) à un** diminished radix component; ones complement; ~ **(binaire) restreint** (v. complément (binaire) à un); ~ **de cable** (cable) simulator; ~ **de formation** consolidation; ~ **de ligne** building-out network; pad; attenuator; line simulator; artificial line; simulated line; ~ **de ligne à affaiblissement fixe** transit pad; ~ **de ligne escamotable** switchable pad; ~ **de ligne numérique** digital pad; ~ **de longueur** line build-out network (LBO); ~ **d'une section de pupinisation** building-out section; ~ **vrai** twos complement

complémentaire *adj* additional; back-up; backing; secondary; filler (of characters); trailer; extra; auxiliary; supporting; reciprocal; correlative; mutual; add-on; mating; building-out; follower

complémentation *f* **d'un registre** complement register

complémenté self-compensating; ~ **amplified**

complémenter *v* support; boost; back up; build out

complémenteur *n* complement

complet *adj* full; full-scale; total; exhaustive; integrated; fully-equipped

compléter *v* (par) round-off; add to; complement; fill in; top up; boost; compensate (for); augment; consolidate

complexe *adj* sophisticated; ~ **verre-résine** fibre-glass

compliance *f* interface adaptor

comportement *m* performance; behaviour; action; ~ **à la flamme** flame resistance; ~ **au feu ou à la chaleur** exposure to fire and heat; ~ **du mode** mode behaviour; ~ **en température des caractéristiques dynamiques** AC thermal characteristics

composant *m* component; constituent; compound; device; ~ **discret** discrete component; ~ **électronique de qualité contrôlée** electronic component of assessed quality; ~ **imprimé** printed component; ~ **logiciel** program; ~ **opto-électronique** opto-electronic component; opto-electronic device; ~ **réactif** reactive component; ~ **sensible** sensitive component

composante *f* **à polarisation transversale** cross-polarized component; ~ **active** active component; ~ **active de la tension** real/active component of voltage; ~ **alternative** AC component (of rectified current); ~ **continue** DC component; direct component; ~ **continue inutile** standing DC component; ~ **continue utile** DC component; ~ **de la fréquence zéro** zero-frequency component; ~ **du signal de télévision** waveform component; ~ **d'un signal** signal component; ~ **fondamentale** fundamental component; ~ **harmonique** harmonic component; ~ **magnéto-ionique** ion-magnetic component; ~ **ondulatoire** ripple component; ~ **porteuse** carrier component; ~ **réactive** quadrature component (of voltage/current); ~ **réactive** quadrature component; ~ **résiduelle de courant porteur** residual carrier; ~ **sinusoïdale octantale de l'erreur** octantal component of error; ~ **sinusoïdale quadrantale de l'erreur** quadrantal component of error; ~ **sous-harmonique** sub-harmonic component; ~ **transversale** transverse voltage; ~ **transversale d'une force électromotrice** longitudinal electromotive force; ~ Z Z component; impedance

composants *pl* componentry; ~ **en vrac** loose components; bulk-packaged components; ~ **rapportés** add-on components; ~ **solides** solid-state components; ~ **sous assurance de qualité** components of assessed quality; ~ **sous licence** licensed components

composé *adj* compound; composition; synthetic; lumped

composer *v* compose; consist of; comprise; constitute; format; ~ **au clavier** key-out; dial-up; select; ~ **un chiffre** dial (up); select (number, address); ~ **un numéro** (d'appel) (v. composer un chiffre); ~ **un numéro d'appel** dial-up

composeur *m* **automatique** automatic dialler; ~ **automatique de numéros** automatic dialler; repertory dialler; autodialler; automatic call-maker; ~ **automatique de numéros à cartes perforées** card reader dial; card dialler

composite *adj* overall; compound; combined; ~ **climatique** (essai combiné climatique, essai composite climatique) climatic sequence (tests)

compositeur *m* **automatique de numéros** autodialler

composition *f* composition; formatting; environment; typesetting; setting up (on keyboard); structure; dialling; dial up; keying in; subdivision; component parts; membership; lay-up (of cable); content; ~ **de la multitrame** multi-frame structure; ~ **du conducteur** lay-up; ~ **d'un circuit approprié** compositing; ~ **d'un numéro** dialling; ~ **d'un programme** (computer) programming; ~ **froide** cold typesetting; ~ **stoichiométrique** stoichiometric composition; ~ **vocale** voice-actuated dialling

Composphère [A.C.] composer (typewriter)
composteur *m* stamp; punch
compréhensible *adj* intelligible
compresseur *m* compressor; compander; automatic volume contractor; ~ **de volume** volume compressor
compresseur-extenseur *m* compander (compressor-expander); ~ **syllabique** syllabic compander
compression *f* compression; blocking; packing; squeezing; crowding; reduction; ~ **d'amplitude** amplitude compression; ~ **de bits** bit packing; ~ **de chiffres binaires** bit packing; digit compression; ~ **de données** data reduction; bit packing; ~ **de fréquence** frequency compression; ~ **de la bande de fréquences** frequency band compression; ~ **de largeur de bande** bandwidth compression; bandwidth reduction; ~ **des luminances** luminance compression; ~ **des nuances** grey-scale compression; ~ **d'impulsions** pulse stuffing; bit packing; data compression; ~ **données numériques** digital data packing
compression-extension companding; ~ **de syllabes** syllabic companding; ~ **instantanée** instantaneous companding
comprimer *v* squeeze; compress; pack; block; crowd
compromis *m* trade-off
comptabiliser *v* evaluate; enumerate; compile statistics; levy
comptabilité *f* accounting; statistics; ~ **analytique** cost accounting; ~ **automatique des appels (CAA)** automatic message accounting (AMA); ~ **automatique et centralisée des appels** centralized automatic message accounting (CAMA); ~ **automatique locale des appels (CALA)** LAMA (local automatic message accounting); ~ **centralisée des appels (CCA)** centralized automatic message accounting (CAMA); ~ **en partie double** double-entry book-keeping; ~ **internationale** international accounting
comptage *m* counting; up-counting; metering; tallying; peg count (of calls); ~ **à la distance et à la durée** time-and-distance metering; ~ **d'appels** peg count; peg counting; call registration; ~ **de caractères** character counting; ~ **de prises** peg count; peg counting; ~ **d'impulsions** pulse counting; ~ **du trafic** traffic metering; ~ **progressif** count up; tally up; ~ **régressif** count down; tally down; ~ **simple** single-fee metering; ~ **traceur extérieur** external trace count; ~ **vers l'arrière** backward metering; backward counting
compte *m* **courant postal (CCP)** French

post-office bank account; ~ **d'amortissement** depreciation; ~ **de taxe** charge account; ~ **tenu** allowing for
compte-rendu (CR) status report; proceedings; situation report (sitrep)
comptes d'exploitation générale operating account; operating costs
compte-tours turns counter
compteur *m* counter; meter; recorder; register; timer; checker; scaler; pooler; accumulator; ~ **à cinq étages** five-stage counter; ~ **à tarifs multiples** multi-rate meter; ~ **à voyant** meter with indicator; ~ **annulaire** ring counter; ~ **auxiliaire** subsequent counter; ~ **binaire décimal synchrone** synchronous decade counter; ~ **circulaire** ring counter; ~ **comptable** tally counter; ~ **d'abonné** subscriber meter; message register; ~ **d'accusation** fault-rate counter; ~ **d'adresse** register; program counter; address counter; ~ **d'adresse de la mémoire** memory address register; ~ **d'appels** message register; subscriber register; call register; subscriber meter; ~ **d'assemblage** program counter; instruction (address) register; control register; ~ **de boucles** cycle-index counter; ~ **de charge** load counter; ~ **de débordement** overflow meter; ~ **de défilement de bande** tape footage counter; ~ **de durée de conversation** call timer; call-duration meter; ~ **de durée taxable** chargeable time clock; ~ **de fréquences** frequency counter; frequency meter; ~ **de lignes (de la logique)** logic line counter; ~ **de nombre d'appels** traffic recorder; peg counter; ~ **de périodes** cycle-rate counter; interval timer; ~ **de phase** program counter; step counter; ~ **de positionnement** location counter; ~ **de prise** bid counter; ~ **de séquence** sequence counter; ~ **de spires électronique** electronic turns counter; ~ **de taxation** charge meter; ~ **de taxe à domicile** own-premises meter; private meter; message register facility; ~ **de taxes d'abonné** subscriber meter; ~ **de temps d'emploi** efficiency meter; CPU timer; ~ **de temps d'occupation de groupe** group-occupancy meter; ~ **de tentatives de prise** bid counter; ~ **de trafic** traffic meter; peg(-count) meter; register; traffic usage recorder (TUR); ~ **de trames** frame counter; ~ **décimal** decimal scaler; ripple counter; decade counter; ~ **d'encombrement** congestion meter; ~ **d'impulsions** pulse counter; pulse meter; scaler; ~ **d'instructions** program counter; P-counter; instruction (address) register; control register; ~ **d'intervalles de temps** interval timer;

~ **d'itérations** cycle-index counter; ~ **diviseur par deux** divide-by-two counter; ~ **d'observation** peg counter; ~ **d'occupation totale** all-trunks-busy register (ATB); ~ **électromécanique d'impulsions** pre-determined counter; pulse counter; ~ **en anneau** ring counter; ~ **Geiger-Müller** Geiger counter; ~ **horaire** elapsed hour meter; timer; ~ **intégré** integral counter; ~ **manuel de communications** peg-count meter; ~ **ordinal** ordinal counter; location counter; program counter; ~ **programmable** programmable counter; ~ **réversible** up-down counter; ~ **synchronisable** synchronizing counter; ~ **télétaxe** private meter; ~ **temporisateur** interval timer; ~ **totalisateur** accumulating counter; integrating meter; running total counter; peg counter; batch counter; cumulative register; ~ **triphasé** three-phase counter; ~ **universel** (reciprocal) universal frequency counter; ~ **volumétrique** displacement meter
compteur-décompteur reversible counter (accumulator/scaler); up-down counter
compteur-enregistreur de conversations call demand counter
compteuse *f* counting scales
compulser *v* examine
concaténation *n* concatenation; chaining; stringing
concaténer *v* string; chain; cascade
concentrateur *m* concentrator; line concentrator; remote line unit; pooler; ~ **à interface MIC** electronic line concentrator; ~ **de circuits** circuit concentrator; ~ **de communications** communication concentrator; ~ **de lignes** telephone line concentrator; ~ **de messages** message concentrator; ~ **de terminaux annuaire** communication terminal concentrator; directory terminal concentrator; subscriber terminal concentrator; ~ **électronique d'abonnés distants** remote electronic subscriber connection unit; remote concentrator; ~ **électronique d'abonnés locaux** local electronic subscriber connection unit; local concentrator; ~ **électronique d'abonné** electronic subscriber (line) concentrator; ~ **numérique** digital concentrator; ~ **numérique éloigné** remote digital concentrator; ~ **numérique local** local digital concentrator; ~ **régional** regional concentrator; ~ **satellite électronique distant** remote electronic subscriber line concentrator; ~ **satellite électronique local** local electronic subscriber line concentrator; ~ **satellite électronique rural** rural electronic subscriber connection unit; rural electronic subscriber line concentrator;

C

~ **satellite électronique** electronic subscriber line concentrator; ~ **spatial électronique (CSE)** electronic subscriber connection unit; electronic space-division concentrator; ~ **spatio-temporel** space-time concentrator

concentrateur-aiguilleur public (v. CAPU)

concentrateur-diffuseur *m* concentrator-distributor

concentration *n* concentration tag block/strip; focussing; intensification; commoning; multiplex; ~ **de conversation** speech interpolation (SI); ~ **des atomes excités** excited-atom density (of gas); ~ **des conducteurs** density of conductors; ~ **des conversations** speech interpolation (SI); ~ **électrostatique** electrostatic focussing; ~ **magnétique** magnetic focussing; ~ **numérique de conversation** digital speech concentration; ~ **par gaz** gas focussing; ~ **spatiale** space-division concentration; ~ **temporelle analogique BF-BF** analogue time-division concentration

concentré *adj* bunched; lumped

concentrique *adj* concentric; coaxial

concepteur *n* designer

conception *f* design (philosophy); ~ **assistée par ordinateur (CAO)** computer-aided design (CAD); ~ **automatisée** design automation; ~ **ciselée** full-custom design; ~ **de réseau au moindre coût** least-cost network design; ~ **de système** systems design; ~ **du produit** product design; ~ **et fabrication assistées par ordinateur (CFAO)** computer-aided design and manufacture (CAD/CAM); ~ **logique** logical design; ~ **technique** hardware design

concertation consolidation

concession *f* **de brevet** patent licence; ~ **de service public** privatization; ~ **exclusive** exclusive grant; ~ **non exclusive** non-exclusive grant

concessionnaire exclusif sole agent

conclure un protocole enter into a protocol; sign an agreement

concordance *f* coincidence; compatibility; synchronization; match; correlation; ~ **angulaire** angular alignment (of rotors)

concrétionner sinter (of lamp filament)

concrétiser roundly demonstrate

concurrent *m* rival; competitor

concurrentiel *adj* third-party vendors; other suppliers

condamner à l'ouverture (de) lock

condensateur *m* capacitor; condenser; ~ **à air** air-insulated capacitor; ~ **à armatures** foil capacitor; ~ **à blocs combinés** ganged capacitor; ~ **à mica** mica capacitor;

~ **àsoufflage** quench(ing) capacitor; ~ **au tantale goutte** tantalum-bead capacitor; ~ **bouton** button capacitor; ~ **céramique** ceramic capacitor; ~ **céramique plaquette** ceramic plate capacitor; ~ **chimique** electrolytic capacitor; ~ **d'accord** tuning capacitor; ~ **d'antiparasitage** suppression capacitor; ~ **d'appoint** trimming capacitor; trimmer; ~ **d'arrêt** blocking capacitor; ~ **de blocage** (v. condensateur d'arrêt); ~ **de couplage** coupling capacitor; ~ **de découplage** by-pass capacitor; decoupling capacitor; ~ **de dérivation** (v. condensateur de découplage); ~ **de filtrage** smoothing capacitor; ~ **de filtration** smoothing capacitor; filter capacitor; ~ **de fuite** feedthrough capacitor; by-pass capacitor; ~ **de recalage** smoothing capacitor; ~ **d'équilibrage** neutralizing capacitor; neutrodyning capacitor; balancing capacitor; ~ **d'étalement de bande** band-spread capacitor; ~ **d'intégration** integrating capacitor; ~ **d'isolement** shunt capacitor; decoupling capacitor; by-pass capacitor; ~ **électrolytique** electrolytic capacitor; ~ **enrobé** moulded capacitor; ~ **fixe** fixed capacitor; ~ **fixe au mica** fixed mica dielectric capacitor; ~ **multicouches autocicatrisant** self-healing layer capacitor; ~ **neutrodyne** neutralizing capacitor; ~ **non selfique** non-inductive capacitor; ~ **polarisé** polarized capacitor; ~ **polyester métallisé** metallized polyester film capacitor; ~ **réglable** variable capacitor; ~ **série d'équilibrage** padder; padding capacitor; ~ **shunt d'équilibrage** trimmer; ~ **tantale** tantalum capacitor; ~ **variable (CV)** variable capacitor

condensateurs jumelés twin-ganged capacitor

condensation *f* packing; ~ **de données** bit packing

condensé *adj* short-form (of catalogue)

condenser *v* pack; squeeze; compress; implode

condenseur *m* condenser lens

condition *f* condition; state; term; requirement; ~ **de livraison** condition of supply; ~ **de repos** idle condition; ~ **d'encombrement** congestion; busy condition; ~ **d'oscillation propre** natural mode; ~ **en vigueur** prevailing condition; ~ **limite** boundary condition; ~ **non modulée** zero modulation; ~ **relationnelle** relational condition; ~ **un** (1) mark; ~ **zéro** (0) space

conditionnement *m* conditioning; packaging and storage; original packaging; training; ~ **(de sortie)** (output) gating; ~ **en bande** strip packaging; bandolier packaging

("Ammo-pak") [T.N.]; tape-roll (packaging)

conditions atmosphériques ambient conditions; **~ d'approbation** approval conditions; **~ de guidage** waveguide conditions; **~ de prélèvement et d'acceptation** sampling and acceptance conditions; **~ de réception** acceptance conditions; goods inward inspection requirements; incoming goods inspection requirements; **~ d'injection** launch conditions; **~ nominales de fonctionnement** rated operating conditions

conductance (U) *f* conductance (in siemens); **~ de tube électronique** anode conductance; **~ directe** forward conductance; **~ grille-source** gate-source conductance; **~ inverse** back conductance

conducteur *m* conductor; feeder; cable; lead; wire; core; driver; rail; **~** *adj* forward-biased; ON; driving; **~ aérien** overhead conductor; **~ bimétallique** bimetallic conductor; **~ de câble** cable wire; conductor; **~ de jonction** junction wire; **~ de neutre** neutral lead; neutral wire; **~ de phase** live wire; phase lead; **~ de raccordement** (v. conducteur de jonction); **~ de repérage de la température** temperature reference conductor; **~ d'électricité** current conductor; **~ d'entrée** entrance wire; **~ étamé** tinned wire; **~ extérieur** outer conductor; **~ hyperfréquence** RF conductor; **~ intérieur** inner conductor; centre conductor; core; **~ isolé** insulated wire; **~ monobrin** solid-conductor cable; single-core conductor; **~ multiple** multiple conductor; **~ neutre** neutral wire; zero conductor; **~ nu** bare conductor; **~ optique** optical conductor; **~ poutre** beam lead; **~ ras** flush conductor; **~ relié à l'extrémité d'une fiche bipolaire** tip-side; tip-wire; **~ rigide** solid wire; **~ souple** flexible lead; flex; **~ sous écran** screened wire; **~ toronné** stranded conductor; **~ torsadé** twisted wire; **~ triplaque** strip-line

conductibilité *f* (électrique) conductivity; conductance; conduction

conduction *f* conduction; forward-biasing; ON; **~ ionique** ionic conduction

conductivité *f* specific conductivity; **~ au sol** earth conductivity; **~ thermique** thermal conductivity; **~ type n** (type p) n-type (p-type) conductivity

conduire *v* drive (of amplifier)

conduit *m* conduit; duct; pipe; channel; trough; trench; chase; path; raceway; **~ atmosphérique** atmospheric duct; **~ de ligne numérique** digital line path; **~ de surface** surface duct; ground-based duct;

~ élevé overhead duct; **~ hertzien numérique** digital radio path; **~ numérique** digital path; **~ numérique de référence** hypothetical reference digital path

conduite *f* control; drive; behaviour; procedure; **~ d'essai** test procedure; **~ secondaire** sub-feeder

cône d'acceptance *m* acceptance cone; **~ de diffusion** cone of unreliability; **~ de silence** cone of silence; **~ de soudure** solder shroud

confection *f* preparation; mixing; cable wrapping; lay-up (of cables)

conférence *f* three-party conference; conference call; **~ à trois** three-way conference; **~ additive** add-on conference; three-way calling; **~ Européenne des Postes et Télécommunications (CEPT)** European Conference of Postal and Telecommunications Administrations; **~ programmée** (v. conférence additive); **~ rendez-vous** meet-me conference

conférenceur *m* conferencing circuit; conferencing device

confetti(s) *m* chad; chips; computer punchings

confidentialité *f* confidentiality; privacy

configurable par commutateur switch-selectable

configurateur *m* program generator; bulk tape generator; tape generator; system data generator; data generator; (pulse) shaper; configuration sheet; exchange configuration program; generating routine/program; **~ commercial** marketing configuration; sales pattern

configuration *f* configuration; layout; design; pattern; array; circuit; arrangement; shaping; bit pattern; call status; structure; map; system build; **~ de la trame** frame structure; framing structure; **~ de verrouillage de trame** framing pattern; **~ du test** test configuration; **~ facturière** accounting machine layout (of numeric keypad); **~ repliée** folded configuration; **~ saisie de données** data punch layout (of numeric keypad); **~ téléphonique** telephone layout (of numeric keypad); **~ usine** restore default (options); RAM loader (mode)

confinement *m* **transverse électrique** transverse electrical confinement; **~ transverse optique** transverse optical confinement

confirmation *f* confirmation; **~ d'appel** call confirmation; **~ de libération** clear confirmation; **~ de remise** delivery confirmation

confirmé *adj* practised; sophisticated; confirmed

conflit *m* (d'accès) contention; clash

confondu *adj* overlapping; intermeshed; indistinguishable; inclusive

conformage *m* alignment

conformateur *m* **de signaux** signal shaper; ~ **d'impulsions** pulse-shaping network; shaper; corrector

conformation d'onde carrée squaring

conforme à (cf) rating; compliant with

conformité *f* conformance; conformity; compliance; ~ **de qualité** assessed quality; ~ **des commandes** order checking

congé *m* (de soudure) fillet

congé(s) *m* shutdown; non-working period (holiday); leave; vacation

conjoncteur *m* jack; switch; connector; key; cut-in; circuit-breaker; coupling unit; telephone junction box (jack socket); plug; ~ **femelle** female connector; ~ **gigogne** modular (tee) telephone jack; dual-outlet line jack; doubler socket

conjoncteur-disjoncteur *m* circuit-breaker; make-and-break key; cut-out

conjonction *f* AND function (conjunction); voltage drop

conjoncture *f* financial year; the economy; economic climate; ~ **morose** depressed market

conjugué *adj* composite; two-way simplex; mating

connaissance *f* familiarization; acquaintance; knowledge; skill; insight; cognition; ~ **de** conversant with; familiar with; ~ **pratique** hands-on experience; practical skill

connaître *v* ascertain; establish; determine; learn

connectable *adj* interfaceable; plug-to-plug-compatible

connecté *adj* on-line; on-hook; logged-on; in-circuit; interfaced; on-net

connecter *v* link; couple; connect; attach; interface; sign on; log on; hook up; plug in; ~ **au réseau** come on stream

connecteur *m* connector; plug; coupling unit; pointer; linking statement; selector; cable terminal; final selector; terminal block; ~ **à barres croisées** crossbar-type jack field; ~ **à contacts glissants** side contact connector; ~ **à contacts pincés** crimped contact connector; ~ **à procédé champ** field-wiring connector; ~ **chantourné** ninety-degree double tongue connector; ~ **de bord** edge connector; spring strip; ~ **de bout de carte** edge connector; ~ **de câble** cable connector; ~ **de transition** transition connector; ~ **d'énergie** edge plug; ~ **d'essai** test connector; ~ **d'interface** interface connector; ~ **dix-sept points** seventeen-pin/seventeen-way connector; ~ **droit** straight connector; cable extension link; ~ **d'usure**

wearing connector; floating connector; cable-ended connector; ~ **en face arrière** back (plane) connector; ~ **en face avant** front (panel) connector; ~ **encartable** board-mounted connector; edge connector; PCB-mounted edge plug; ~ **enfichable** cable-mounting connector; plug-in connector; ~ **femelle** female connector; ~ **final** final selector; line selector; ~ **interurbain** trunk selector; trunk connector; ~ **inversé** reversed connector; ~ **local interurbain** trunk offering final selector; ~ **mâle** plug; ~ **monofibre** pigtail connector; ~ **monovoie** single-channel connector; ~ **multibroches** multi-way connector; ~ **multicontact encartable** board-mounting multi-way connector; ~ **multicontact enfichable** cable-mounting multi-way connector; ~ **multicontacts** (v. connecteur multibroches); ~ **multiple** multiple connector; multiple plug; ~ **multivoie** multi-channel connector; multiple-channel connector; ~ **pour transmission de données** data connector; data access arrangement (DAA); ~ **trapézoïdal** D-series connector (ISO 2110)

connecteurs reliés entre eux connectors wired pin-to-pin

connectique *f* connectors; connector applications; connector engineering; connector technology; connector systems; interconnect glue

connectivité *f* connectorization

connectorisé *adj* connectorized

connexe *adj* allied; related; associated; connected

connexion *f* connection; coupling; attachment; link; wiring; jack-plugging; interfacing; logging on; signing on; junction; networking; lead; terminal; hook-up; block; mating; cable connector; ~ **à deux fils** two-wire connection; ~ **à enroulement** wire-wrap connection; ~ **à fiches et prises de 12 voies** twelve-way plug and socket connection; ~ **à grande distance** long-distance connection; trunk connection; ~ **agressive** projecting/rough connection; ~ **arrière** rear connection; ~ **auto-alarme** auto-alarm connection; ~ **auto-dénudante (CAD)** insulation displacement connection (IDC); ~ **automatique en séquence** automatic sequential connection; ~ **aux voies de marquage** marking path interference; ~ **coaxiale** coaxial terminal; ~ **d'arrivée** incoming connection; ~ **de câble** cable connection; cable junction; cable terminal; ~ **de départ** outgoing connection; ~ **de fichiers** file linking; ~ **de fils par enroulement** wire wrapping; ~ **de grille** grid

terminal; grid clip; grid cap; ~ **de l'interrupteur** switch connection; ~ **de mesure** test connection; ~ **de pont** bridge connection; bridge circuit; lattice network; ~ **de relais** relay connection; ~ **de réseau** (électrique) mains supply connection; power supply connection; ~ **de satellite à plusieurs faisceaux** multi-beam satellite link; ~ **de sections** point-to-point communication; ~ **de tableau** switchboard connection; ~ **de terre** earth connection; ~ **de transit** transit connection; ~ **d'essai** test call; trial connection; ~ **différentielle** differential arrangement; ~ **d'induit** armature end connection; ~ **d'interrupteur à huile** oil-switch connection; ~ **directe** hot-line connection; ~ **double** double connection; ~ **électrique** electrical connection; ~ **en cascade** cascade connection; notching; tandem connection; ~ **en étoile** star connection; Y-connection; ~ **en parallèle** parallel connection; parallel circuit; paralleling; shunt connection; ~ **en série** series connection; ~ **en triangle** delta connection; ~ **en U** U-link; jumper; ~ **enroulée** wire-wrap connection; ~ **enroulée miniature** (W) miniature wire-wrap connection; ~ **équivalente** equivalent circuit; equivalent network; ~ **établie** call in progress; ~ **étoile-triangle** star-delta connection; ~ **instantanée** instantaneous connection; ~ **interurbaine** long-distance connection; trunk connection; ~ **locale** local connection; ~ **métallique** physical connection; ~ **multiple** multiple connection; ~ **par commutation de circuits** circuit-switched connection; ~ **par enroulement** wire wrap; wrapping; ~ **par fiches** plug connection; ~ **par pression** pressurized connection; ~ **point à point par clips** termipoint wiring; ~ **privée** private connection; ~ **sans soudure** solderless connection; ~ **semi-permanente** (par groupes de voies temporelles) multi-slot connection; ~ **télégraphique** telegraph connection; ~ **téléphonique** telephone connection; ~ **temporaire** temporary connection; ~ **temporelle** time-division switching; ~ **terrestre** terrestrial connection; ~ **transversale** cross connection; tie trunk; ~ **tressée** pigtail connector; ~ **triangle-triangle** delta-delta connection; ~ **unidirectionnelle** simplex connection; ~ **volante** jumper; jumper wire
connexion/fin line/local
connexions superposées piggyback connections
connexité f connectivity; connectorization; ~ **topologique** map of network dynamic

status
consécutif adj contiguous (of memory cells)
consécutivement adv in strict sequence
conseil(s) m hint; tip; recommendation; advice
conseil d'administration board of directors; ~ **de direction** executive board; governing body
conseillé adj recommended
conséquence f implication; impact; outcome
considérer v judge; deem; be regarded; be treated
consignation f recording; logging
consigne f load; controlled magnitude; setting; instruction; datum; order; reading
consigner v store; record; set; note; instruct; log; post; load; enter
consignes d'exploitation operating instructions
console f console; bracket; pedestal; desk; control desk; ~ **d'accueil** host terminal; ~ **de dialogue** interactive terminal; ~ **de saisie** data input console; entry terminal; ~ **de visu télévidéo** visual display console; ~ **de visualisation (CV)** display device; visual display unit (VDU); screen monitor; video terminal; data display unit
consommables consumables; saleable products; common hardware; expendable items
consommation f consumption; (current) drain; usage; power drawn; inrush current; power requirements; power component (in VA); rated power; ~ **au maintien** sealed consumption; ~ **d'appel** inrush consumption; induced current; ~ **d'énergie** power consumption; ~ **des bobines** coil consumption; ~ **en phonie** power drawn in speech mode; ~ **en veille** standby consumption
constante f constant; ~ **d'adresse** address constant; ~ **d'adresse indexée** indexed address constant; ~ **d'affaiblissement** attenuation constant; ~ **de déphasage** phase constant; wavelength constant; ~ **de diffusion** diffusion constant; ~ **de dissipation** decay factor; ~ **de fréquence** frequency stability; ~ **de Hall** Hall constant; ~ **de ligne de répartition** distributed transmission line constants; ~ **de phase** phase constant; ~ **de porte** port (constant); ~ **de propagation** propagation constant; ~ **de temps** time constant; response time; ~ **de temps d'amplification à résonance** time constant of resonant amplification; ~ **de temps électrique à la charge d'un détecteur** electric charge time constant of detector; ~ **de temps électrique à la décharge d'un détecteur** electric discharge time constant of detector; ~ **de temps thermique** thermal time constant; ~ **de texte** text (constant); ~ **de**

transfert transfer constant; ∼ **diélectrique** permittivity (dielectric constant); ∼ **diélectrique absolue** absolute capacitivity; absolute dielectric constant; permittivity; ∼ **d'intégration lente** slow time constant; ∼ **en virgule flottante** real constant; ∼ **littérale** literal constant; ∼ **réelle** real constant; ∼ **sur bits** bit string constant **constantes localisées** lumped constants; ∼ **réparties** distributed constants

constater v observe

constellation f signal structure diagram; constellation

constitué de configured; sized (of memory)

constitution f composition; structure; configuration; selection; dispersion; design details; component parts; taking (of checkpoint); building (of table, string, queue); mapping; assembly; installation; institution; ∼ **de câble** cable lay; ∼ **de la trame MIC** PCM frame format; ∼ **de monotonie** string-building

constructeur m manufacturer; designer; draughtsman; builder; handler

construction(s) f strapping; set-up; straps; rig; rigging; jumper field

construire v set up; build; take (of map); strap; ∼ **sur mesure** tailor; custom-build

consultation n look-up; interrogation; examination; table look-up; browsing; polling; enquiry; ∼ **(d'un) demandeur en attente** consultation on hold; ∼ **de base de données** data base look-up procedure; ∼ **de mise à jour** read-write access; ∼ **de table** table interrogation; examination; table look-up; ∼ **de vidéotex** videotex enquiry; ∼ **double** dual-track consultation; ∼ **horloge** interrogate clock; clock read; ∼ **séparée** two-way split; ∼ **seule** read-only access; ∼ **sur attente** consult a party on hold

consulter v interrogate; query; enquire; search; look up; reference; consult; read; retrieve; browse

contact m contact; contact-breaker; switch; point; pin; ∼ **à air libre** mechanically-latching contact; ∼ **à balai** brush contact; ∼ **à commande mécanique** (rupture brusque) snap switch; ∼ **à deux directions** double-pole single-throw switch (DPST); ∼ **à double coupure** double break contact; ∼ **à insertion forcée (CIF)** force-fit contact; press-fit contact; ∼ **à lyre** forked-arm limit switch; ∼ **à ouverture** normally-closed contact (NC); ∼ **à permutation** changeover contact; ∼ **à picot** spill; ∼ **à pont** bridge contact; ∼ **à tige** reed contact; ∼ **à vitesse élevée de recombinaison** high-recombination rate contact; ∼ **antirebond** bounceless

contact; ∼ **arrière** back contact; ∼ **auto-dénudant (CAD)** insulation displacement contact (IDC); ∼ **auto-nettoyant** self-wiping contact; ∼ **d'alarme** alarm contact; ∼ **d'auto-alimentation** hold-in contact; ∼ **d'automaintien** locking contact; self-holding contact; ∼ **de balai** brush contact; ∼ **de décade** level contact; decade contact; ∼ **de fermeture** make contact; ∼ **de masse** earthing switch; earth contact; ∼ **de pointe** point contact; ∼ **de repos** break contact; back contact; normally-closed contact (NC); ∼ **de rupture** break contact; ∼ **de tête** off-normal contact; ∼ **de travail** make contact; normally-open contact (NO); front contact; ∼ **débitmètre** flow-meter switch; ∼ **élastique** spring contact; accordion; ∼ **en ampoule** reed switch; ∼ **en ampoule scellée** reed switch; ∼ **(en) tulipe** turned-pin contact; screw-machined contact; ∼ **fixe** fixed contact; ∼ **glissant** sliding contact; ∼ **hermétique** reed switch; ∼ **inverseur** make-break contact; changeover switch; ∼ **mobile** moving contact; ∼ **mouillé** mercury-wetted contact; ∼ **OF (ouvert/fermé) temporisé** timed changeover switch; ∼ **ohmique** ohmic contact; ∼ **prioritaire** early-make contact; ∼ **redresseur** electronic (contact) rectifier; ∼ **repos** break contact; normally-closed contact (NC); back contact; reset contact; ∼ **repos-travail (RT)** break-before-make contact (BBM); ∼ **ressort** bellows contact; ∼ **scellé** sealed contact; ∼ **sec** dry contact; dry-reed relay; reed switch; ∼ **simple** single contact; ∼ **temporisé** time-delay; ∼ **travail** make contact; normally-open contact (NO); set contact; ∼ **travail-repos (TR)** make-before-break contact (MBB)

contacteur m contactor; trip switch; NO contact; heavy-duty relay; multi-way switch; ∼ **à courant inverse** reverse current trip; ∼ **à lame ressort** strap key; tapping key; ∼ **à touches** (pushbutton) multi-pole/multi-way switch; ∼ **auxiliaire** control relay; ∼ **de puissance** block contactor; ∼ **disjoncteur** trip switch; ∼ **multipolaire** multiple switch; multi-way switch; multi-pole switch; multi-switch

contacts des impulsions du cadran d'appel dial pulse contacts; ∼ **doublés** twin-contact elements; bifurcated contact; ∼ **jumelés** twin contacts; ganged contacts; bifurcated contacts

contamination n contamination; corruption

contaminomètre m (PCB) contamination tester

contenance f size; capacity

conteneur m container

contenu *m* content(s); ~ **binaire équivalent** equivalent binary content; ~ **conditionnel moyen de l'information** average conditional information content; ~ **de la transinformation** transinformation content; ~ **de signal** signal content; ~ **de stage** syllabus; programme; ~ **décisif** decision content; ~ **d'une information** intelligence; ~ **en information par symbole** information content per symbol; ~ **moyen de l'information** average information content; entropy [deprecated]; negentropy; ~ **total en information** gross information content; information rate

contestation *f* **de taxe** billing complaint; dispute; challenge; query

contexte *m* mode; environment; context; setting; ~ **canal** channel mode; ~ **de traitement par lots** batch processing; ~ **sauvegarde** (dump storage) mode; ~ **système** system context; ~ **usager** user context

contigu *adj* adjacent; consecutive; contiguous

contiguïté *f* adjacency

continu *adj* sustained; round-the-clock; continuous; continuously variable; stepless

continu-continu DC-DC

continuer *v* proceed; press ahead; resume

continuité *f* continuity; ~ **de blindage** screen link; ~ **des conducteurs** conductor continuity; ~ **électrique** electrical continuity

contour *m* outline

contournement *m* arcover; flashover; ~ **d'isolement** insulation breakdown

contours de découplage (de polarisation) à l'émission transmit cross-polarization isolation contours

contractant *m* contractor

contradiction *f* discrepancy; conflicting; contradiction

contrainte *f* limiting condition; stress; strain; rule; constraint; ~ **de temps** (d'un système) system time restriction

contraintes *f pl* design limits; performance data; ~ **industrielles** design parameters; ~ **mécaniques** mechanical restrictions

CONTRAPOL cross-polarization (XPOL)

contraste *m* contrast; ~ **accentué** heightened contrast; ~ **d'image** image contrast; ~ **inversé** reverse video; ~ **maximale** contrast range

contrat *m* agreement; contract; ~ **de location** leasing agreement; ~ **de plan** agreement of intent

Contrave à 3 chiffres [A.C.] three-digit thumbwheel

contre-calque *m* duplicate master; reproducible copy

contre-courant *m* back current; counterflow

contre-couteau *m* **droit** righthand counter cutter; ~ **gauche** lefthand counter cutter

contre-dépouille *f* undercut; back-taper

contre-écrou *m* lock nut

contrefaçon *f* **de brevets** infringement of patents

contrefort *m* support; leg; buttress; spur

contre-lame *f* spring shaft (of relay)

contremaître *m* foreman

contremesures électroniques actives active electronic countermeasures (ECM)

contrepercer au montage drill back-to-back on assembly

contre-plaque *f* back-plate; reinforcing panel

contre-plaqué *m* plywood

contrepoids *m* **d'antenne** capacity earth; artificial earth; counterpoise aerial; ~ **parasite double** double-parasitic counterpoise

contre-point tailstock

contre-réaction *f* feedback; degenerative feedback; reverse coupling; degeneration

contre-vérification *f* cross-checking

contribuer à help; assist; promote; feed; inject

contrôle *m* detection; monitoring; inspection; checking; regulating; governing; testing; controlling; auditing; debugging; analysis; examination; supervision; check; control; test; scrutiny; surveillance; quality control; survey; gauging; assessment; appraisal; confirmation; ~ **acoustique** acoustic control; acoustic survey; ~ **alphabétique** test alphabetic; ~ **arithmétique** arithmetic check; ~ **automatique** built-in check; monitoring; ~ **câblé** wired-in check; hardware check; ~ **carré** cross-check; ~ **cartes** card testing; ~ **centralisé de qualité (CCQ)** central quality control (CQC); ~ **croisé** (v. contrôle carré); ~ **cyclique d'un émetteur** sequential monitoring; ~ **d'accès** access control; ~ **d'appartenance** validity check; ~ **de cohérence** consistency check; ~ **de conformité** discrepancy check; consistency check; ~ **de continuité** continuity check; ~ **de correspondance** cross-check; ~ **de disponibilité** availability check; ~ **de fabrication** production control; ~ **de flux** transmit flow control; ~ **de fréquence** frequency check; ~ **de la qualité** quality control; ~ **de l'intégrité des données** audit; ~ **de modulation** monitoring of transmission level; ~ **de niveau** level monitoring; ~ **de parité** parity check; odd-even check; ~ **de parité impaire-paire** odd-even check; ~ **de parité longitudinale** longitudinal redundancy check (LRC); ~ **de parité transversale** vertical redundancy check (VRC); ~ **de phase** phase check; ~ **de prise** seizure acknowledgement; ~ **de production** production control; ~ **de programmation** desk check; dry run; ~ **de qualité** quality control; ~ **de qualité à la réception** incoming goods quality inspection; goods inward quality control; ~ **de récurrence** recursion check; ~ **de redondance cyclique** cyclic redundancy check (CRC); ~ **de ronde** nightwatchman service; ~ **de stocks** stocktaking; ~ **de transmission du flux** flow control function (FCF); ~ **de vraisemblance** reasonableness check; validity check; absurdity check; ~ **d'écho** echoplex; echo checking; ~ **d'écoute** audio-monitoring; ~ **d'endurance par prélèvement (CEP)** endurance test on samples; ~ **d'enregistrement** playback; ~ **d'entrée** incoming goods inspection; quality inspection; ~ **d'erreurs** error control; ~ **des pièces mécaniques** inspection of mechanical components; ~ **des signaux d'entrée** input signal check; ~ **des superpositions** overlay check; ~ **des tolérances** marginal testing; ~ **des travées** suite tests; ~ **d'existence** forbidden-combination check; forbidden pulse combination/digit; improper instruction; unused command/code; unallowable digits; false code; non-existent code check; ~ **d'identité** discrepancy check; log-on (password); ~ **d'immatriculation** block serial number check(ing); ~ **d'imparité** odd parity check; ~ **d'inventaire** inventory check; stocktaking; ~ **du flux** flow control; ~ **du niveau** level control; ~ **du temps** time check; ~ **d'uniformité** consistency check; ~ **dynamique** dynamic test; ~ **dynamique des cartes** dynamic card testing; ~ **effacement** erase test; ~ **électrique** electrical test; ~ **entrée** goods-inward inspection; incoming-goods inspection; quality assurance; ~ **final** final inspection; ~ **forcé** spot check; ~ **global** total monitoring; overall check; ~ **insertion** insertion test; ~ **intégral** screening inspection; ~ **local** local check; home record; ~ **longitudinal par blocs** longitudinal redundancy check; ~ **modulo N** modulo N check; ~ **par attributs** inspection by attributes; ~ **par bloc** block check; longitudinal check; ~ **par boucle** loop testing; ~ **par caractère(s)** character check; transverse check; ~ **par comparaison** loop checking; ~ **par duplication** copy check; duplication check; twin check; ~ **par écho** echo check; read-back check; echoplex; ~ **par imparité** (odd) parity check; ~ **par la voix** voice control; ~ **par marges** bias check; marginal testing; ~ **par parité** (even) parity check; ~ **par prélèvements** sampling

inspection; ~ **par redondance** redundancy check; ~ **par retour de l'information** loop checking; message feedback; information feedback; ~ **partiel** partial monitoring; ~ **passif de continuité (CP)** passive continuity check; ~ **qualificatif et dimensionnel** qualification and dimensional inspection; ~ **réduit** reduced test; ~ **reprise** repair inspection; reinspection; ~ **unitaire** individual component test; individual inspection; ~ **visuel** visual examination; ~ **visuel renforcé** in-depth visual examination; walk-through; tightened visual inspection

contrôler v control; monitor; check; inspect; survey; test; analyse; scrutinize; checkpoint; restrict; oversee

contrôleur m tester; meter; monitoring device; controller; monitor; handler; analyser; ~ **automatique d'émission** automatic radio monitor; ~ **coupure de ligne** line split tester; ~ **d'accès direct en mémoire** DMA controller; ~ **de circuit** line fault analyser (of time-domain reflectometry, pulse return pattern); ~ **de communication** communications controller; ~ **de fréquence** frequency monitor; ~ **de gestion** central communications controller; ~ **de grappe** cluster controller; ~ **de modulation** modulation meter; ~ **de périphériques** peripheral unit controller system (PUCS); ~ **de séquence** watch-dog; invigilator; ~ **de signal** signal indicator; ~ **de tâches** job handler; job controller; ~ **de transmission** transmission controller; communications control unit (CCU); controller; ~ **de visualisation** display control; ~ **d'échanges** I/O controller; ~ **d'entrée/sortie** input/output controller; I/O controller; ~ **d'événements de programme** program event recording (PER); ~ **d'interruptions** interrupt controller/handler; ~ **du système** (de base de données) processing manager; control manager; system handler; ~ **E/S** (v. contrôleur d'entrée/sortie); ~ **et régénérateur de tube cathodique** CRT tester/rejuvenator; ~ **frontal** front-end controller; ~ **programmable d'interruptions** programmable interrupt controller (PIC); ~ **universel** multimeter; volt-ohm-milliammeter (VOM)

controversé adj inconclusive
convenance f convention (of syntax)
conversation f conversation; interactive mode; call; speech(-path); speech phase; interchange; talk; dialogue; ~ **à deux** two-party call; ~ **avec avis d'appel (AVP)** messenger call (in the international service); appoint-

ment call; ~ **avec préavis** personal call (international); pre-arranged call; person-to-person call; ~ **avec priorité** precedence call; ~ **collective** conference call; ~ **de bourse** stock-exchange call; ~ **de départ** outgoing call; ~ **de service** service call; official call; ~ **de test** test call; ~ **diurne** day-time call; ~ **éclair** flash call; ~ **en cours** call in progress; ~ **en série** serial call; sequence call; ~ **fortuite à heure fixe** occasional fixed-time call; appointment call; ~ **interurbaine** trunk call; toll call; ~ **normale** ordinary call; ~ **par abonnement** subscription call; ~ **payable à l'arrivée (PCV)** collect call; transfer charge call; ~ **privée** private call; ~ **privée ordinaire** ordinary private call (in the international service); ~ **privée urgente** urgent private call; ~ **radiophonique** radio conversation; ~ **retardée** delayed call; ~ **sans fils** radio conversation; radiotelephone call; ~ **taxable** chargeable call; ~ **téléphonique** telephone call; call; telephone conversation; ~ **urbaine** local call

conversion analogique-numérique (conversion A/N) analogue-to-digital conversion (A-D conversion); ~ **binaire** analogue-to-digital conversion; ~ **binaire-décimal** binary-to-decimal conversion; ~ **bipolaire** analogue-to-digital conversion; ~ **bipolaire-unipolaire** bipolar-to-unipolar conversion; ~ **de code** code conversion; ~ **de fréquence** frequency conversion; ~ **de protocole** protocol conversion; ~ **de support** media conversion; ~ **du signal d'appel** ringing current conversion; decoding; ~ **en numérique** digitization; quantization; ~ **entier flottant** float; ~ **numérique-analogique** (conversion N/A) digital-to-analogue conversion (D-A conversion); ~ **parallèle-série** parallel-to-serial conversion; ~ **série-parallèle** serial-to-parallel conversion; ~ **unipolaire-bipolaire** unipolar-to-bipolar conversion

convertir v convert; translate; transform
convertisseur m inverter (A/C generator); code-converter; digitizer; dynamicizer; transducer; outscriber; frequency changer; DC-DC converter; translator; formatter (S-P/P-S); motor generator; modem; ~ **à cascade** cascade converter; motor converter; ~ **à courant continu** direct-current converter; DC converter; ~ **à vapeur de mercure** mercury arc converter; ~ **abaisseur** bucking converter; step-down converter; ~ **A/N** (CAN: convertisseur analogique-numérique) A-D converter (analogue-to-digital converter); digitizer; ~ **asynchrone**

induction motor-generator; ~ **continu-alternatif** DC to AC converter; inverter; ~ **continu-continu** DC converter; DC voltage transformer; ~ **de canal de télévision** television frequency converter unit; ~ **de canaux** channel converter; channel translating equipment; ~ **de charge** charging converter; ~ **de code** code converter; ~ **de courant** current converter; static power converter; ~ **de courant d'appel à fréquence vocale** VF signal(ling) transformer; ~ **de définition** television system converter; ~ **de données** data converter; ~ **de fréquence** frequency converter; frequency changer; frequency transformer; ~ **de fréquence à faible bruit** low-noise frequency converter; ~ **de gestion (CG)** charge-metering converter; ~ **de groupes** group modulator; group modulating equipment; group translating equipment; ~ **de mesure** measuring transducer; ~ **de normes** standards converter (of TV); ~ **de phase** phase converter; phase changer; ~ **de signal** (signal) converter; frequency changer; ~ **de sortie** outscriber; ~ **de thyratron** thyratron converter; ~ **d'exploitation** traffic converter; ~ **d'images** image converter; ~ **d'impédance négative** negative impedance converter; ~ **d'informations** data transducer; ~ **du courant d'appel pour appel sélectif** dial pulse translator for selective calling; ~ **dynamoteur** dynamotor; ~ **logarithmique** logarithmic converter; ~ **N/A** (CNA: convertisseur numérique-analogique) D-A converter (digital-to-analogue converter); ~ **parallèle-série** dynamicizer; parallel-serial converter; outgoing formatter; ~ **rotatif à induit unique** rotary converter; single-armature converter; synchronous converter; dynamotor; ~ **série-parallèle** staticizer; serial-parallel converter; ~ **statique** static inverter; ~ **vers le bas** down converter

convivialité f (du système) user-friendliness; ~ **(en temps réel)** on-line user assistance
convoi exceptionnel wide load; long load
convoyeur m conveyor; ~ **à doigts** pawl conveyor; finger conveyor; ~ **de CI** PCB conveyor; ~ **élément de liaison** link unit conveyor
coopérant adj networked; pooled
coopération f mutual assistance; joint venture; aid; inter-working; ~ **technologique** technological cooperation
coordinatographe m profile projector
coordonnées f pl address
copeaux m pl swarf; burr
copie f replica; crib; copy; ~ **de déchargement**

C

safeguard copy; back-up copy; ~ **d'écran** hard copy; screen echo; ~ **diazoïque** (dry) photocopy; dyeline reproduction; hard-copy enlargement; ~ **en clair** hard copy; plain language text (P/L); ~ **fugitive** soft copy; ~ **libre** blind copy; ~ **support** media copy (MC); ~ **sur bande** tape copy; dump; ~ **(sur) papier** hard copy; page copy; print-out

copie-antenne broadcast copy

copier v copy

COPOLAR copolarization (COPOL)

copolymère d'éthylène tetrafluoroéthylène (ETFE) fluorinated ethylene polypropylene (FEP); Tefzel [T.N.]

coprocesseur séquentiel inference crunching machine (ICM)

corbeille f buffer; ~ **haute** shift-lock (upper case)

cordeau m **à tracer** tracing line; chalk line

cordon m lead; wire; cord; connecting cable; plug cord; ~ **à deux fiches** double-ended cord; ~ **à tracer + boîte poudreuse** chalk line with chalk box; ~ **à trois fils** (v. cordon trifilaire); ~ **biplex** biplex probe; ~ **blindé** armoured cord; ~ **d'alimentation** power cord; ~ **d'antenne** stranded wire; ~ **d'appel** calling cord; front cord; ~ **de casque téléphonique** head cord; ~ **de combiné** handset cord; ~ **de connexion** cord circuit; ~ **de connexion avec pont** bridge-control cord circuit; ~ **de connexion avec troisième fil** sleeve control cord circuit; ~ **de frettage** thermo-fit sleeve; heat-shrinkable sleeve; ~ **de liaison** cord; connecting wire; lead; ~ **de mesure** test lead; ~ **de raccordement** extension cable; connecting cable; ~ **de renvoi** transfer wire; patch cord; ~ **de réponse** answering cord; back cord; ~ **de soudure** fillet weld; ~ **d'essai** test lead; ~ **enfichable** connectorized lead; plug-ended cable; ~ **inter-alvéoles** inter-shelf connecting cable; ~ **monofibre** pigtail; ~ **plat** flat cord; ribbon cable; bell wire; ~ **pointe de touche** (shrouded) test lead; ~ **trifilaire** three-conductor cable

cordonnet m slitting cord

cornet n mouthpiece (of microphone); flare; horn; cone (of speaker); ~ **à correction de phase** phase-corrected horn; ~ **à source périscopique** beam waveguide feed; ~ **conique équiangulaire** equi-angular conical horn; ~ **ondulé** corrugated horn; ~ **parabolique** hoghorn; ~ **pyramidal** pyramidal horn; ~ **rectangulaire** rectangular horn; ~ **sectoriel E** E-plane (E-bend) sectoral horn; ~ **sectoriel H** H-plane sectoral horn

cornière f angle-iron; bracket; ~ **perforée** perforated angle-iron; 'Dexion' [T.N.]

corps m shank (of bolt); sleeve (of jack); body; casing; substructure; framework; shell; housing; carcase; text; form (of document); ~ **composé** compound; ~ **de boucle** loop body; ~ **de chauffe** heater element; ~ **de composant** component body; ~ **de connecteur** connector casing; connector housing; ~ **de jack** jack sleeve; ~ **de voyant** lamp housing; ~ **du message** message format; text; ~ **étranger** scraps; litter; waste (material); foreign bodies; ~ **isolant** insulating wafer; ~ **pur** pure substance; ~ **simple** element

correcteur m compensator; equalizer; corrector; ~ **d'affaiblissement** attenuation equalizer; ~ **de compromis** compromise equalizer; ~ **de distorsion de phase** frequency equalizer; phase equalizer; ~ **de forme d'onde** pulse stretcher; ~ **de ligne** line equalizer; ~ **de phase** delay equalizer; ~ **de temps de propagation de groupe (CTPG)** group-delay equalizer (GDE); ~ **d'écho** time equalizer; ~ **d'effet de température** temperature compensation equalizer; ~ **d'erreur de base de temps** time-base error correction; ~ **différentiel** derivative equalizer; ~ **d'impulsions** pulse corrector; pulse shaper; pulse stretcher; ~ **du temps de transit** delay equalizer

correction f correction; equalization; compensation; patching; editing; ~ **automatique des erreurs** automatic error-correction; ~ **C-message** C-message weighting; ~ **d'amplitude** amplitude correction; ~ **de défauts d'amplitude** amplitude error correction; ~ **de dentelures** skew (adjustment); ~ **de la distorsion** equalization; correction; ~ **de la distorsion du temps de transit** delay distortion correction; ~ **de la distorsion en coussinet** pincushion distortion equalizing; ~ **de signes à la réception** local (polarity) correction; ~ **de synchronisme** synchronous correction; ~ **d'erreur de phase** phase error correction; ~ **d'erreurs** error correction; ~ **d'erreurs par retransmission** error correction by repetition; ~ **des aiguës** treble correction; ~ **des lignes** line equalizing; lumped loading; phase compensation; ~ **d'ombrage** shading correction; ~ **du temps de montée** rise-time correction; ~ **par pièces** patching; ~ **ponctuelle** error-correcting patch

corrélation f **à caractère réciproque** positive correlation

correspondance f correlation; reciprocity; equivalence; interaction; association;

matching; complementarity; validity; correspondence; relationship; connection; analogy; coincidence; combinational settings; resemblance; register; hit; congruence; ~ **entre filtres passe-haut et filtres à élimination de bande** band-stop/high-pass analogy
correspondant *m* called/calling party; subscriber; party; partner; ~ *adj* respective; relevant; requisite; representing; coinciding; ~ **préenregistré** hotline subscriber (extension)
corrosion *f* etching; corrosion; ~ **électrochimique** electrochemical etching/corrosion; ~ **intercristalline** intergranular corrosion; ~ **intergranulaire** range match
corset *m* waist (of lattice tower)
cos φ (**v. cosinus phi**); ~ **phi avant** phase difference (leading)
cosinus phi (cos φ) power factor
cosse *f* tag; tab; lug; strip; terminal; stud; crimp connector; ~ **à fourches** spade terminal; ~ **à insérer** (picot) insert; ~ **à sertir pré-isolée** crimp connector/terminal; ~ **à visser** (v. cosse à fourches); ~ **de câble** cable eye (shoe); ~ **de raccordement** connecting clip; ~ **drapeau** flag-type terminal/connector; ~ **pour languette** crimp terminal
cotation *f* price quotation; dimensioning
cotations (des adresses) (address) coordinates
cote *f* dimension; benchmark; datum line; quota; share; reference; assessment; classification ~ **nominale** basic dimension
côte *f* rib; side; groove; slope; gradient; hill; coast; shore
côté *m* side; aspect; end; direction; ~ **basse fréquence** primary side/winding; ~ **broches à raccorder** mating face; ~ **demandé/demandeur** forward/backward (end); ~ **du courant bidirectionnel** (v. côté réception); ~ **éléments** (côté composants) component side (V_{cc}); front; ~ **émission** B-side~ **réception** A-side; ~ **recto** component side (of PCB); front; ~ **soudure** solder side (V_{ss}); back; wiring side (of PCB); ~ **verso** solder side (of PCB); back
coté en bourse quoted on the stock market
coter un prix quote a price
coton tige cotton swab; Q-Tips [T.N.]; cotton bud
cou *m* **de cornet** throat
couche *f* film; layer; coat; surface; level (of signalling code); junction (of transistor); case (of case hardening); stratum; ply; ~ **acheminement** network layer (ISO protocol); ~ **antireflet** anti-reflection coating; ~ **brusque E/H** E/H corner; ~ **d'arrêt**

depletion layer; barrier layer; boundary; ~ **d'arrêt p-n** p-n boundary; ~ **de barrage** barrier layer; depletion layer; boundary; ~ **de carbone** carbon film; ~ **de confinement** confinement layer; ~ **de conversion** primer; passivating film; conversion coating; ~ **de liaison** bonding layer; ~ **d'émail** enamel glaze; ~ **déposée** film deposited; ~ **d'oxyde** oxide coating; ~ **E** E-layer; Kennelly-Heaviside layer; Heaviside layer; ionized layer; ~ **E anormale** anomalous E layer; ~ **E aurorale** auroral E layer; ~ **E sporadique** sporadic E layer; ~ **électronique** electron shell (of atom); ~ **en formation** deposited layer; ~ **enterrée** buried layer; ~ **enterrée fortement dopée** heavily-doped buried layer; ~ **épaisse (CE)** thick film; ~ **épitaxiée** epitaxial layer; ~ **externe** outer layer; ~ **F** F-layer; Appleton layer; ~ **interne** inner layer; internal layer; ~ **ionosphérique** ionospheric layer; ~ **mince (CM)** thin film; ~ **photosensible** emulsion; ~ **physique** connection layer (ISO protocol); ~ **progressive E/H** E/H bend; ~ **sensible** (v. couche photosensible)
coude *m* bend; drop (of voltage level); knee; corner; pinch-off (of voltage); ~ **brusque** corner; sharp edge; elbow; ~ **d'amorçage** breakdown knee; ~ **de la caractéristique** characteristic; ~ **de saturation** saturation; bottoming; ~ **progressif** bend
coudé offset; right-angled
couiner *v* send morse (code)
couineur *m* morse key
couleur *f* (lambda p) peak wavelength (of LED)
couleurs *pl* livery; colour scheme
coulisseau *m* slideway; runner; slide(r)
couloir *m* lane; passageway; corridor; track; chute; clearance
coulomb-mètre *n* voltameter; coulometer
couloscope *m* polarograph
coulure *f* break-out; run-out; seepage; trickling; exudation; dip; precipitation
coup *n* cycle; stroke; hit; count; ~ **au but** hit; ~ **de bouton** flashing; ~ **de came** cam time-out; ~ **de crochet commutateur** flash; ~ **de poing** (mushroom-head) emergency-stop button
coupe *f* **à (la) longueur** cutting to length; ~ **AT** AT-cut (of crystal); ~ **biaise** crop; ~ **du cristal** crystal cut; ~ **métallographique** microsection; ~ **micrographique** microsection; ~ **queues** lead cutting
coupé off; de-energized; stopped; ~ **en fer silicium orienté** pre-cut grain-oriented silicon iron
coupe-câble *m* cable cutter; ~ **dénudeur** cable

C

cutter; cable stripper

coupe-circuit *m* circuit-breaker; cut-out; short-circuit; fuse; isolator; switch; ~ **à fusible** safety fuse; fused breaker; ~ **sectionnable** modular fuse-carrier

coupe-fil *m* wire cutter

coupelle *f* core cup; cap; half-core; ~ **métallique** metal bubble key

couper *v* sever; cut out/off; switch off; isolate; de-activate; interrupt; turn off; disrupt; break

coupe-tout *m* master switch

couplage *m* interlocking; coupling; (mesh) connection; interfacing; linking-up; linkage; ganging; mutual induction; ~ **acoustique** acoustic coupling; ~ **auto-inductif** auto-inductive coupling; ~ **automatique** automatic interlocking; ~ **capacitif** capacitive coupling; ~ **cathodique** interstage coupling; ~ **conductif** direct coupling; DC coupling; ~ **critique** critical coupling; ~ **d'antenne** aerial coupling; ~ **de filtre de bande** filter coupling; ~ **de modes** mode coupling (of propagation); ~ **direct** direct coupling; ~ **en carré** four-phase mesh connection; ~ **en dents de scie** sawtooth coupling; ~ **en diaphonie** crosstalk coupling; ~ **en opposition** differential connection; ~ **en triangle** three-phase mesh connection; delta connection; ~ **entre étages** inter-stage coupling; ~ **entre processeurs auxiliaires** auxiliary processor interface (module); ~ **fort** tight coupling; close coupling; ~ **inductif** inductive coupling; electromagnetic coupling; ~ **lâche** loose coupling; weak coupling; ~ **L-C** choke coupling; inductance-capacitance coupling; ~ **mutuel** mutual coupling; transformer coupling; ~ **par bobine d'arrêt** choke coupling; ~ **par impédance commune** common-impedance coupling; ~ **par inductance mutuelle** mutual-inductance coupling; ~ **par rayonnement** radiation coupling; ~ **par résistance** resistance coupling; ~ **par résistance-capacité** resistance-capacitance coupling (R-C); ~ **par transformateur** transformer coupling; mutual coupling; ~ **parasite** interference coupling; stray coupling; cross-coupling; spurious coupling; ~ **polygonal** mesh connection; ~ **serré** close coupling; tight coupling

couple *m* torque; armature current (I_a - of DC motor); thermocouple; cell; junction; moment of force; frame; spar; pair; combination; ~ **de codes** code combination; ~ **de modulation** pair of modulation currents; ~ **de rotation** running torque; ~ **de serrage** torque; ~ **en démarrage direct** direct on-line starting torque; ~ **moteur** driving torque; ~ **photoélectrique** photovoltaic cell; ~ **résistant** (moteur à cage) resisting torque; resistive torque; ~ **résistant constant** constant starting torque; ~ **résistant en marche normal** normal running torque; ~ **thermoélectrique** thermocouple; thermojunction; ~ **utile** running torque

couplé *adj* interconnected

coupler *v* couple; gang

coupleur *m* controller; make-and-break; coupler; combining filter; diplexer; splitter; combining unit; transceiver; ~ **à 3 dB** hybrid coupler; ~ **acoustique** acoustic coupler; line set; ~ **asynchrone** asynchronous communication interface; ~ **canal** channel controller; ~ **continu-continu** squegger; blocking oscillator; ~ **de machines parlantes** recorded announcement unit interface controller; ~ **de périphérique** peripheral controller; ~ **de piles** battery-holder; ~ **de raccordement** interface controller; ~ **de réception** splitter; ~ **de référence** reference coupler; ~ **de sortie** output coupler; ~ **de taxation** metering coupler; ~ **d'émission** combiner (of carrier system); ~ **différentiel** hybrid coupler; ~ **directif** directional coupler; directive feed; ~ **en Y** Y-coupler; ~ **monopulse** monopulse coupler; ~ **optique** optical coupler; optocoupler; ~ **opto-électronique** optocoupler; ~ **parallèle** parallel controller; ~ **pour écouteur** earphone coupler; ~ **sélectif de canaux** channel branching filter; channel-combining unit diplexer; ~ **série** serial controller; ~ **série asynchrone** asynchronous serial controller; ~ **spécifique d'un périphérique** dedicated peripheral controller; ~ **UHF** RF coupler; ~ **V24** serial interface controller

coups de bouton flashing

coupure *f* cut-out; failure; break; rupture; disconnection; interruption; drop-out (of relay); splitting; severance; (power) dump; truncation (of word); cut; discontinuation; separation point; down; outage; outance; release; off; breakdown; demarcation; ~ **calibrée** timed loop-break; ~ **centrifuge** centrifugal clutch; ~ **d'appel** call release; ~ **de colonne statique** static column break; ~ **de faisceau** trunk group down; ~ **de la communication** call disconnection; ~ **de ligne** line break; ~ **de mot** hyphenation; ~ **de page statique** static page break; ~ **de phase** phase failure; ~ **de piste** track cutting; ~ **d'émission** emission cut-out; ~ **des aiguës** treble damping; top cut; ~ **flottante** floating break; ~ **moteur lancé**

normal starting duty; ~ **progressive** roll-off; ~ **sèche** air break; ~ **secteur** mains failure; power down

courant *m* (cf. intensité) current; flow; drive current; stream; ~ *adj* prevalent; widespread; common; current; contemporary; standard; normal; on the market; commercially available; bread-and-butter; routine; fluent; ordinary; ~ **à dents de scie** sawtooth current; ~ **à vide** no-load current; ~ **absorbé** sink current; ~ **actif** marking current; active current; ~ **alternatif (ca)** alternating current (AC); ~ **anodique** anode current; ~ **au blocage** off-state current; ~ **au démarrage** pre-oscillation current; starting current; ~ **basse fréquence** low-frequency current; ~ **biphasé** two-phase current; ~ **cathodique** cathode current; ~ **commuté** switching current; ~ **continu (cc)** direct current (DC); ~ **(continu) à l'état bloqué** continuous (direct) off-state current; ~ **(continu) à l'état passant** continuous (direct) on-state current; ~ **(continu) de base** base (DC) current; ~ **(continu) de collecteur** collector (DC) current; ~ **(continu) de gâchette d'amorçage** gate-trigger continuous (direct) current; ~ **(continu) de grille** gate (DC) current; ~ **(continu) de maintien** continuous (direct) holding current; ~ **(continu) de retournement** continuous (direct) breakover current; ~ **(continu) de source** source (DC) current; ~ **(continu) d'émetteur** emitter (DC) current; ~ **continu pulsé** varying direct current; ~ **continu superposé** superimposed DC field; ~ **court-circuit** short-circuit current; flash current; ~ **cyclique** mesh current; circulating current; ~ **d'accrochage** latching current; ~ **d'action nerveuse** action current; ~ **d'alimentation** supply current; feed current; ~ **d'alimentation du microphone** transmitter feed current; microphone current; ~ **d'amorçage** trigger current; striking current; ~ **d'antenne** aerial current; ~ **d'appel** ringing current; inrush current; induction current (of solenoid); ~ **d'appel cadencé** interrupted ringing current; ~ **d'appel superposé** superposed ringing current; ~ **d'attaque** drive current; control current; ~ **d'attraction (I$_A$)** operate current; pick-up current; ~ **de base** base current; ~ **de blocage** blocking current; stall current; load current; ~ **de boucle** loop current; ~ **de charge** charging current; load current; ~ **de chauffage** heater current; filament current; ~ **de choc** surge current; ~ **de collage** cut-in current; ~ **de commande** working

current; drive current; ~ **de conductibilité** conduction current; ~ **de consommation** drain current; ~ **de convection** convection current; ~ **de court-circuit** short-circuit current; flash current; ~ **de court-circuit à la terre** current to earth; current loss; ~ **de crête** peak current; ~ **de décalage** offset current; ~ **de décharge** discharge current; ~ **de déclenchement (I$_D$)** release current; drop-out current; breaking current; tripping current; operating current; ~ **de déclin** transfer-decay current; ~ **de décollage** cut-out current; ~ **de défaut** fault current; ~ **de démarrage** starting current; ~ **de déplacement** displacement current; ~ **de désamorçage** turn-off current; ~ **de diaphonie** crosstalk current; ~ **de disjonction** break current; ~ **de drain** drain (DC) current; ~ **de filtrage** smoothing current; ~ **de Foucault** eddy current; ~ **de fuite** leakage current; cut-off current; sneak current; dielectric current; ~ **de fuite à la terre** earth leakage current; ~ **de fuite de grille** gate leakage current; ~ **de fuite total au repos** total quiescent leakage current; ~ **de fusion** fusing factor (as function of rated current); ~ **de gâchette** trigger current; ~ **de grille** grid current; ~ **de l'électrode d'amorçage** starter current; ~ **de maintien** fold-back current; holding current; hold-back current; sealed current; ~ **de maintien (au collage)** holding current; ~ **de masse** ground current; earth current; ~ **de mesure** holding-wire current; measuring current; ~ **de modulation** modulation current; ~ **de mouillage** wetting current; ~ **de non amorçage** non-trigger current; ~ **de non fusion** non-fusing factor; ~ **de non retombée** hold current; ~ **de perte à la terre** earth current; ~ **de phase** phase current; ~ **de pic** peak current; ~ **de plaque** anode current; ~ **de pointe** (v. courant de pic); ~ **de pointe accidentelle non répétitif à l'état passant** surge (non-repetitive) on-state current; ~ **de polarisation** bias current; ~ **de polarisation moyen** average bias current; ~ **de prépolarisation** pre-bias current; ~ **de rabattement** fold-back current; hold-back current; sealed current; ~ **de rayon** beam current; ~ **de recouvrement** recovery current; ~ **de ré-équilibrage** bridge input current; ~ **de relâchement** release current; drop-out current; ~ **de rémanence** latching current (of relay); ~ **de repliage** fold-back current; hold-back current; ~ **de repos** quiescent current; spacing current; standing current; ~ **de retour** back current; feedback current; earth current;

return (reflected) current; current reversal; foldback current; ~ **de retournement** breakover current; ~ **de saturation** saturation current; ~ **de seuil** threshold current; ~ **de signal** signal current; ~ **de signalisation** signalling current; marking current; ~ **de sonnerie** ringing current; ~ **de sortie** output current; load; ~ **de substrat** substrate current; ~ **de suite** follow-on current; ~ **de surcharge** (non répétitif) surge current; ~ **de surcharge prévisible à l'état passant** overload (direct) forward current; ~ **de télégraphie** telegraph current; ~ **de terre** earth(-return) current; stray current; ~ **de trafic (CT)** switched loop; traffic relations; traffic flow; ~ **de traînage** transfer-decay current; ~ **de transfert** transfer current; ~ **de travail** marking current; active current; operating current; signalling current; ~ **de vallée** valley (point) current; ~ **de veille** quiescent current; ~ **de vidéo-fréquence** video current; ~ **d'échange** transfer current; ~ **d'écran en absence de signaux** zero signal screen current; ~ **d'écrêtage** clipping current; ~ **d'effluve** glow current; ~ **d'égalisation** equalizing current; ~ **d'électrode** electrode current; ~ **d'émission** emission current; ~ **d'emploi** current rating; rated current; ~ **d'enclenchement** inrush current; ~ **d'entrée** input current; inrush current; ~ **déphasé en arrière** lagging current; ~ **déphasé en avant** leading current; ~ **dérivé** shunt current; leakage current; ~ **d'espace** space current; ~ **déwatté** idle current; ~ **d'excitation** pull-up current; sealing current; ~ **d'extinction** decay current; ~ **d'ionisation** ionization current; ~ **direct** forward current; ~ **direct (continu)** continuous (direct) forward current; ~ **direct (continu) de gâchette** gate continuous (direct) forward current; ~ **direct de crête** peak forward current; ~ **direct (de pointe) de surcharge** surge forward current; ~ **direct de pointe répétitif à l'état passant** repetitive peak on-state current; ~ **direct moyen** average output rectified current; ~ **d'obscurité** dark current; ~ **d'ondulation résiduelle** ripple current; ~ **d'oscillation** oscillating current; ~ **du bruit** noise current; ~ **du faisceau** beam current; ~ **efficace** effective current; r.m.s. current; ~ **électronique** electron current; ~ **en dent de scie** sawtooth current; ~ **en ligne** line current; ~ **faible** weak current; ~ **filtré** smoothed current; ~ **fort** strong current; heavy current; ~ **fourni** (IOL) source current; supply current; ~ **fourni**

(par les alimentations) source current; supply current (IOL); ~ **haute fréquence** high-frequency current; ~ **hypostatique** holding current; ~ **inactif** non-operate current; ~ **induit** induced current; ~ **initial** incident current; initial current flow; ~ **instantané** instantaneous current; ~ **intermittent** intermittent current; ~ **inverse** continuous (direct) reverse current within the working voltage range; reverse current; echo current; back current; singing current; ~ **inverse (continu)** continuous (direct) reverse current; ~ **inverse (continu) de blocage** continuous (direct) reverse blocking current; ~ **inverse de crête** peak reverse current; ~ **inverse de grille** backlash current; ~ **inverse de pointe répétitif** repetitive peak reverse current; ~ **inverse de recouvrement** reverse recovery current; ~ **inverse d'électrode** reverse electrode current; ~ **inverse moyen** (avec IO spécifié) average reverse current (with IO specified); ~ **lacunaire** hole current; ~ **magnétisant** magnetizing current; ~ **maximal** peak current; ~ **maximal de non opération** peak non-operate current; ~ **maximal de résistance/basculement** peak current at onset of increase in resistance; ~ **minimal de commande** minimum operate current; ~ **minimal de fonctionnement** minimum operate current; ~ **modulé** pulsating current; ~ **monophasé** single-phase current; monophase current; ~ **nominal** (thermique) rated (thermal) current; ~ **ondulé** ripple current; ~ **ondulé nominal** rated ripple current; ~ **parasite** eddy current; ~ **périodique** mesh current; ~ **permanent d'anode** quiescent anode current; steady anode current; zero signal current; ~ **perturbateur** disturbing current; interference current; noise current; ~ **perturbateur équivalent** equivalent disturbing current; ~ **photoélectrique** photo(-electric) current; ~ **plaque** anode current; ~ **porteur** carrier (current); current mode; carrier wave; ~ **porteur sur ligne à haute tension** power line carrier; ~ **porteur téléphonique** telephone carrier current; ~ **pulsatoire** pulsating current; ~ **pulsé** pulsating current; ~ **réactif** reactive current; ~ **redressé** rectified current; ~ **redressé de diode** diode current; ~ **réfléchi** back current; echo current; feedback current; return current; ~ **résiduel** earth leakage current; residual current; cut-off current; ripple current; ~ **résiduel de collecteur** collector cut-off current; ~ **résiduel de drain** drain current; ~ **résiduel de la base** base cut-off current;

~ **sinusoïdal** sinusoidal current; ~ **tellurique** earth current; ~ **thermique** thermal rating; ~ **tourbillonnaire** eddy current; ~ **transitoire** transient current; ~ **triphasé** three-phase current; ~ **vagabond** leading current; stray current; ~ **vocal** speech current

courants spéciaux tone-and-pulse distribution

courbe f curve; slope; characteristic; trend; plot; graph; diagram; response pattern; ~ **caractéristique** characteristic curve; ~ **d'affaiblissement** attenuation curve; ~ **d'aimantation** magnetization curve; ~ **de correction** correction curve; ~ **de décalage en baignoire** bath-tub characteristic; ~ **de détérioriation** failure curve; ~ **de dispersion** dispersion curve; ~ **de fusion** fusing factor; ~ **de Gauss** normal distribution curve; ~ **de pondération** roll-off; ~ **de réduction de puissance** de-rating curve; ~ **de réponse** response curve; ~ **de réponse à une action** waveform response; ~ **de réponse uniforme** uniform response curve; ~ **de résonance à deux bosses** double-peak resonance curve; ~ **de tension d'amorçage au choc en fonction du temps d'un parafoudre** impulse sparkover voltage; ~ **d'écoute** (TV) audience profile; ~ **d'énergie potentielle** potential energy curve; ~ **d'erreur** error curve; ~ **d'étalonnage** calibration curve; ~ **d'évolution** trend; evolute; ~ **linéaire** (loi de variation A) linear (of potentiometer track); ~ **logarithmique** (loi de variation B) logarithmic (of potentiometer track); ~ **sectoriel** (v. graphe sectoriel); ~ **spectrale** spectrum; ~ **théorique** theoretical graph; ~ **typique** characteristic

courbure f **à froid** cold bending

couronne f ring-main; rocker; number disk (of dial); ellipse; coil (of wire); ~ **d'antenne** aerial turntable; ~ **de contacts** bank of contacts; ~ **d'enregistrement** recording surface; ~ **porte-balai** brush rocker

courrier m message(s); mail; ~ **électronique** electronic mail; text messaging

courroie f drive belt; ~ **crantée** V-belt; notched belt; toothed belt; ~ **d'alimentation** picker belt; ~ **trapézoïdale** V-belt

course f run; distance; travel; cycle; stroke; ~ **acquittée** length of travel

court adj brief; short-lived

court-circuit (c.c.) m short-circuit; skip; ~ **à la masse** earth leakage; accidental ground; body contact; ground leakage; ~ **entre électrodes** electrode short-circuit; ~ **entre spires** fault between turns; shorted turns; ~ **franc** dead short(-circuit)

court-circuitage m shunting; bridging; by-pass

court-circuité adj short-circuited

court-circuiter v short-circuit; short; bridge; shunt; by-pass

courtier m (= façonnier) broker

coussinet m **de montage** mounting pad (for resistor)

coût m **actualisé** present value cost (pvc); ~ **de non qualité** failure cost (of quality control); ~ **d'exploitation** operating cost; overheads

couteau m blade; knife; cutter; ~ (d'une balance) fulcrum; knife-edge; ~ **d'électricien** electrician's knife; ~ **d'impression** writing bar; writing edge; chopper bar; ~ **d'interrupteur** switch blade; ~ **pince à dénuder** combination knife/wire strippers; ~ **pour tête** insertion cutter for insertion head; ~ **scalpel à lame interchangeable** scalpel with interchangeable blades

coûts de raccordement (per line) connection costs; ~ **de transport** freight charges; shipping costs

couvercle m cover; lid; cap; housing; plug; ~ **anti-bruit** acoustic hood

couverture f coverage; volume/volumetric coverage; footprint; ~ **d'aire** area coverage; ~ **de la surface de la terre** earth coverage; ~ **des stocks** stock endurance; ~ **étendue** extended coverage

couvre-écran control overlay

CP (v. contrôle passif de continuité)

CPE (v. commande par programme enregistré); ≂ (v. centre principal d'exploitation)

CPM (v. méthode du chemin critique)

CR (v. compte-rendu)

crachement m buzz

craint not to be brought into contact with; reacts to; -sensitive

cran m increment; notch; step

crantage m clinch; self-locking barb; offset

cranté adj notched; serrated; perforated; offset

craquelure f fissure

cratère m crater; pit

crayon conducteur conductive pencil; ~ **de graphitage** electrographic pen; ~ **lumineux** light pen

CRC (contrôle de redondance cyclique) CRC (cyclic redundancy check)

créateur m originator

création f line creation

crédit d'impôt tax credit; deduction

créditer v (de) clock (at)

créer v construct; generate; build (up); take (checkpoint); write; set up; devise

créneau m gate; gating pulse; strobe marker; gap; square pulse/wave; mark; slot; niche; marker pulse; strobe pulse; outlet; timing pulse; sync pulse; time slot; frame; timing signal; well strobe; marker; ~ **de tension square(-wave)** voltage; ~ **écriture de comptage** count transfer

crépine f strainer; suction screen

crépitage m crackling

crépitement m clicking (of contacts); acoustic shock

crête (c) f peak (of power); crest (of amplitude); ~ **à crête (c-c)** peak-to-peak (p-p; pk-pk); pit-to-pit; ~ **d'absorption** absorption peak; ~ **d'amplitude** amplitude peak; ~ **de bruit** noise peak; ~ **de résonance** resonance peak; ~ **de tension anodique inverse** peak reverse anode voltage; ~ **de tension inverse** peak reverse voltage; ~ **d'onde** wave peak; ~ **d'oscillation** oscillation peak; ~ **du blanc** peak white

creuset m skillet

creux space (of dial code)

cri crackling (of tin); tin-cry

crique saisonnière season cracking

cristal m **à électrodes en couches métalliques** plated crystal; ~ **à harmoniques** overtone crystal; ~ **à intervalles entre électrodes** gapped crystal; ~ **changeur de fréquence** frequency-changer crystal; ~ **de filtre** filter crystal; ~ **encastré** clamped crystal; ~ **facetté** faceted crystal; ~ **fondamental** fundamental crystal; ~ **idéal** ideal crystal; ~ **monté sur fil métallique** wire-mounted crystal; ~ **non-facetté** unfaceted crystal; ~ **oscillateur** oscillator crystal; ~ **résonateur** resonator crystal

cristallisoir m **en verre** crystallizing dish

cristaux intermétalliques salts (in wave soldering pot)

critère m key; criterion; enabling condition; condition flag; parameter; feature; ~ **composite** composite key; ~ **d'acceptation** acceptance criterion; ~ **de décision** decision element; threshold element; ~ **de défaillance** post-test endpoint (PTE); ~ **de dégénérescence** criterion of degeneracy; ~ **de recherche** search key; ~ **de refus** rejection criterion; ~ **de tri** sort key

critique adj critical

crochet m hook; cradle; rest; latch; brace; ~ **commutateur** cradle switch; gravity switch; hook switch; switch hook; ~ **d'arrêt** ratchet; pawl; retaining clamp; binding cradle; ~ **du récepteur** receiver rest; cradle

croisement m transposition; crossing; traverse; crossover; junction (data transmission); glare; ~ **d'onde** wave transposition

croisière f **d'essais** shake-down (cruise)

croisillon m brace; ~ **inducteur** field spider

croissance f growing (semiconductor); ~ **en ralentissement** slowing-down; slow-down; deceleration

croissant adj ascending; rising (order); incremental; forward; gathering

croix f dagger; plus sign (+)

Cronar component location guide (marked transparent sheet)

croquis m sketch

CRU (v. coffret de raccordement)

cryptographie f cryptography

CSE (v. concentrateur spatial électronique)

CSL-A (v. câblage sub-local A)

CSL-B (v. câblage sub-local B)

Cste (constante) constant

CT (v. centre de transit); $\simeq$ (v. courant de trafic)

cte (constante) constant

CTI (v. centre de traitement des informations)

CTP (v. centre de transit principal); $\simeq$ (v. résistance à coefficient de température positif)

CTPG (v. correcteur de temps de propagation de groupe)

CTS (v. centre de transit secondaire)

cuirassé adj iron-clad; armoured

cuite au four (peinture) oven-fired; stoved

cuivre m copper; ~ **raffiné électrolytique** electrolytic tough pitch (ETP) copper; ~ **recuit étamé** annealed tin-plated copper

cuivreux adj cuprous; copper

culasse f core jig (yoke)

culbuteur m indicator switch

culot m base; cap; socket; ~ **Edison** Edison screw cap

culture f corporate approach; ethic

cumul cumulative; aggregate; inclusive; total

cumulande m augend

cumulateur m addend

cumulé adj accrued; cumulative

cupule f cup (of crystal)

curseur m cursor; slider; sliding contact; selector; ~ **arrêté** cursor off (COF); ~ **de correction** edit cursor; ~ **de stop** margin stop; ~ **(de suivi/de contrôle)** shadow cursor; ~ **en marche** cursor on (CON); ~ **mobile** interactive cursor; moving cursor

curviligne pendular

cuve f cable vault; ~ **rhéographique** electrolytic tank

cuvette f housing; dish; bowl; ~ **de potentiel** potential trough; ~ **labo** laboratory dish

CV (v. circuit virtuel); $\simeq$ (v. condensateur variable); $\simeq$ (v. console de visualisation)

CVC (v. circuit virtuel commuté)

CVP (v. circuit virtuel permanent)

CX/RCX (v. réseau de connexion)

cybernétique f cybernetics (communication

and control theory)

cycle *m* cycle; step; loop; revolution; ~ **blanc** idling cycle; ~ **complet** full cycle; ~ **de base** basic clock rate; ~ **de production** production cycle; ~ **de rétention** retention (grandfather) cycle; ~ **d'échange** transfer cycle; ~ **d'exploitation** operating cycle; ~ **d'hystérésis** hysteresis loop; ~ **d'information** information cycle; ~ **écriture** write cycle

cycles par seconde cps (cycles per second)

cyclique rotary; periodic; cyclic; dynamic

cylindre *m* platen; drum; seek area; cylinder; ~ **à fentes** slotted cylinder; ~ **d'impression** print roll

cylindricité *f* concentricity

cymomètre *m* wave meter

D

D (v. décrochage)
DAA (v. distributeur d'appels automatique)
dactyle (dactylique) tactile
dactylocodage *m* keypunching
dactylographier type; key
dactylographique word-processing; typing
dalle *f* (en aggloméré) (particle-board) slab; chip-board panel
DAN (v. droit à l'annotation)
dangereux *adj* hazardous; risky; dangerous
Darlington de puissance darlington driver
datagramme *m* datagram
date de création release date; creation date; ~ de figeage freeze date; ~ de l'arrêté (comptable) cut-off date; ~ de mise en service cut-over date; launch/commissioning date; ~ de mise en vigueur 'from' date; ~ de mise en vigueur de l'abonnement date of commencement of service; ~ de parution issue date; release date; publication date; ~ de péremption purge date; retention date; scratch date; void date; ~ *f* d'écriture write date; ~ d'enregistrement creation date; release date; ~ d'épreuve test date; ~ du mouvement transaction date; ~ limite deadline; ~ limite de validité purge date
dB (v. décibel)
DC (v. double creuset)
DCA (v. défense contre avions)
DCB (v. numération décimale codée en binaire)
DCC (v. dispositif à couplage de charges)
d.d.p. (v. différence de potentiel)
DDS (v. dents de scie)
DDT (v. distributeur de tâches)
DE (v. demandé); ~ (v. abonné demandé)
débanalisé *adj* dedicated; special-purpose; assigned
débasculer *v* lower
débattement *m* (grande surcourse) (max.) overtravel (of limit switch)
débavurage *m* deburring
débit *m* flow rate; output; throughput; drain; circulation; transfer rate; current rating; (line) speed; drain(age) (of battery); capacity; bit stream; ~ (d'une voie) channel capacity; ~ binaire data signalling rate; binary digit rate; bit rate; ~ binaire cumulé d'un multiplex multiplex aggregate bit rate; ~ binaire équivalent equivalent bit rate;

~ binaire série binary serial signalling rate; ~ de masse mass rate of flow; ~ de repli fallback data rate; ~ de symboles symbol rate; ~ d'information information flow; transfer rate; bit rate; ~ en ligne line bit rate; ~ massique mass rate of flow; ~ moyen de l'information average information rate; ~ numérique digit rate; ~ réel (de transfert) effective data transfer rate; effective transmission rate; ~ voie composite aggregate data rate; ~ volumique volume rate of flow
débiter *v* (sur) draw (of current); feed; cut (of metal); be supplied by; powered by
débitmètre *m* flow meter; ~ totalisateur fuel consumption meter; flow meter
déblocage *m* reset; releasing; unlocking; thawing (interrupt enable); disengagement; reinstatement; read mode (of file records)
débloquer *v* thaw; re-activate; free; re-instate; (cause) to conduct; re-enable
débobiné *adj* run-off
déboîter *v* disconnect; uncouple; unconnect; dislodge
débordement *m* overflow; spill-over; time-out; expiry; spill-forward; spillage; ~ de la temporisation time-out; ~ de mémoire store spillage; ~ de signal signal spill-over; ~ de temporisation time-out; expiry; ~ du dispositif chien de garde watchdog time-out
débottelage *m* unbundling
déboucher *v* terminate (at); discharge
débouchure *f* chad; chips; punched-card scraps
débouclage *m* loop disconnection
déboucler *v* loop-disconnect
débranchement *m* trap
débrancher *v* disconnect; uncouple; unconnect; switch off; plug out; re-route
débridé rimless; without flange
débris *m* de perforation chad; chips; punchings
débrochable detachable; plug-in (type)
débrocher *v* disconnect; detach
débrouillement *m* degarbling; improvisation
débrouilleur *v* descrambler
début *m* start; beginning; commencement; home; leader (of tape); outset; onset; ~ de incipient; ~ de cases start box; ~ de description de feuille begin form description

(BFD); ~ **de feuille** (v. début d'écran); ~ **de la fibre** fibre launch end; ~ **de la mémoire** top of memory; ~ **de message** start of message (SOM); ~ **de numérotation** start of pulsing; ~ **de page** home (position); ~ **de renforcement** start timing; ~ **de sélection** mark; start defining; ~ **de texte** start of text (STX); ~ **de volume** beginning-of-tape (BOT); ~ **d'écran** home (position); ~ **d'en-tête** start of heading (SOH); ~ **du bloc** frame start; ~ **feuille** home (position); ~ **image** memory start address

déc. (v. décuples)

décade *f* ten storage locations; ~ (décomptante/comptante) down-/up-counting decades (tens)

décadrage *m* misalignment; off-registration; off-punching; offset

décalage *m* off-setting; shift(ing); drift; overhang; lag(ging) stepping; staggering; skew; slippage; indention; delay; disparity; deviation; discrepancy; displacement; computer shift; argument; lead(ing); ~ **angulaire** angular displacement; ~ **angulaire électrique** phase shift; ~ **arithmétique** arithmetic shift; ~ **circulaire** cyclic shift; end-around shift; ring shift; circular shift; cycle delay; ~ **cyclique** cyclic shift; end-around shift; ring shift; circular shift; cycle delay; ~ **de cycle** cycle delay; cyclic shift; ring shift; end-around shift; ~ **de fréquence** frequency shift; detuning; ~ **de la courbe en baignoire** bath-tub characteristic (of aging cycle graph); ~ **de la porteuse** carrier offset; ~ **de phase** phase displacement; phase shift; ~ **de temps** time lag/discrepancy; ~ **de trame** web offset (of screen printing); ~ **du déclenchement** trigger delay; ~ **du point d'exploration** displacement of sampling point; ~ **du ronflement** hum displacement; ~ **en arrière** lag; ~ **en avant** lead; ~ **horaire** daylight-saving time change; ~ **temporel** time lag/discrepancy; ~ **vectoriel** vector shift

décalcomanie *f* transfer; sticker; decal

décalé *adj* staggered; offset; realigned; shifted; delayed; slipped

décaler à droite right shift

décalés en phase de 90° in quadrature

décaleur *m* phase converter; phase changer

décalibration out of calibration

décalibré (v. décalibration)

décapage *m* pickling; scouring; dipping; scaling; etching; degreasing; stripping

décapant *m* (solder) flux; degreasing agent

décelable à l'ongle discernible by touch

décentrage *m* **de l'image** off-centring

décentralisation *f* devolution; dispersal; de-

tachment; distribution

décentralisé satellite; peripheral; delegated; distributed; dispersed; outlying; scattered; remote; common

déchaînage *m* deserializing; scattering

décharge *f* discharge; leakage; dump; dumping; deposit; off-load; ~ **autonome** self-maintained discharge; ~ **d'arc** electric arc; arc discharge; ~ **disruptive** disruptive discharge; breakdown (of gas); ~ **électrique** electrical discharge; ~ **en arc** arc discharge; ~ **en retour** back discharge; ~ **luminescente** glow discharge; ~ **luminescente anormale** abnormal glow discharge; ~ **luminescente normale** normal glow discharge; ~ **obscure** dark discharge; ~ **par effet corona** corona discharge; ~ **par étincelles** spark discharge; ~ **semi-autonome** semi-self-maintained discharge; ~ **superficielle** surface discharge

déchargé *adj* vented; run down; discharged

déchargement de bit store bit

décharger *v* off-load; dump; discharge; run down; vent; deposit; quench (of laser printer)

déchargeur *m* arrester; conductor

déchet *m* loss of power (of transponder)

déchets scrap; failure; waste; off-cuts; ~ **infantiles** early failures; incipient faults

déchiffrage *m* (déchiffrement) decryption; decoding; unscrambling; decipherment

déchirure *f* tearing; foldover (of TV)

décibel (dB) *m* decibel; volume-unit of sound (VU)

décibelmètre *m* VU-meter; volume-unit meter

décideur *m* decision-maker

décimal *adj* decimal; decadic; ~ **condensé** packed decimal

décinéper *m* decineper

décisionnel decision-oriented

déclamper *v* unclamp

déclaration *f* declaration; (control) statement; declarative statement

déclaré bon tried and tested; proven; passed

déclassé out of sequence; declassified

déclassement *m* de-rating

déclenché triggered mode

déclenchement *m* releasing; tripping; initiating; dropout; disengagement; firing; triggering; falling-off (of relay); gating; activation; trigger slope; ~ **cyclique** gating; ~ **de la temporisation** gating; ~ **par impulsion** pulse triggering; ~ **par prise de terre** ground start; ~ **périodique** gating; ~ **sur état** edge-triggering; ~ **sur front** level-triggering

déclencher *v* release; activate; trip; trigger;

generate (of interrupt); disengage

déclencheur *m* release mechanism; trigger device; trigger pulse; ~ **à manque de tension** no-voltage trip; ~ **à surintensité** tripping device; over-current trip

déclic *m* positive stop; contact release

déclin *m* decay; drop; fallback; decline

décodage *m* interpretation; decoding; ~ **des mots programme** instruction decoding; ~ **topologique** address decoding

décoder *v* decode; decipher; decrypt

décodeur *m* decoder; ~ **DCB décimal à collecteur ouvert** (BCD) logic driver; ~ **DCB excès gray à sortie passive** excess three-to-Gray decimal decoder (BCD); ~ **décimal** decimal decoder; ~ **pour signaux de chrominance** colour signal processing

décodification séquentielle directe direct sequential decoding

décollage *m* take-off; release; drop-out

décollé *adj* detached

décollement *m* peeling (of PCB track); ~ **du niveau du noir** pedestal

décoller *v* drop-out (of relay); peel; detach

décolletage *m* screw cutting; trimming; turning

décomètre *m* decometer

décomposer *v* dissect (of instruction); unblock; break down; parse (of syntax); partition; segment; subdivide; ~ (se) format

décomposition *f* format; structure; parsing; partitioning; segmentation; subdivision; breakdown; ~ **du travail en éléments** job breakdown

décompression *f* expansion; unpacking; unblocking; unbundling; debunching

décomprimer *v* unpack; unblock; expand; unbundle; debunch; decompress

décomptage *m* down-counting (decades); tally down (of power); decrementation

décompte *m* countdown; decrement

décompteur *m* **programmable** run-out timer

décondenser *v* unpack; unblock; expand

déconnectable *adj* switchable

déconnecté *adj* off-line; off-hook; unplugged; disconnected; released; disabled

déconnecter *v* disconnect; dump; disable

déconnexion *f* disconnection; release; releasing; unconnect; disabling; dumping; logging-off

déconseillé *adj* (fortement ~) not recommended; highly inadvisable; to be discouraged/avoided; deprecated

décor (d'un plan) aspect (even-handed assembly)

décors background features; system simula-

tion utility

découpage *m* breakdown (into sections); chopping (of transponder); structure; subdivision; zoning; splicing; parsing; analysis; segmentation; partitioning; trimming; splitting; organization; dissection; format; formation; switching; layout; ~ **de phase** phase splitting; ~ **du temps** scheduling; ~ **électronique** masking; ~ **en dés** dicing

découpe *f* notch; slot; structure; segment; panel cut-out; aperture; splitting; ~ **en blocs** blocking factor; ~ **en cartes** (circuit) board configuration; ~ **fonctionnelle** layout; simplified; schematic; ~ **logique** exclusive-OR

découper *v* switch off; split; partition; organize; segment; structure; chop; arrange; ~ **en canaux** channelize; ~ **en voies** channelize; ~ **en zones** segment

découpeur *m* (= hacheur électronique) chopper

découplage *m* by-pass; uncoupling; isolation; shunt; decoupling; ~ **de signaux logiques** logic signal (input) isolation

découpler *v* isolate; decouple; by-pass

découpleur *m* decoupler (rectifier); (optal) decoupler; ~ **de prégroupes** pre-group decoupler; ~ **galvanique/galvanométrique** isolated data transmitter (IDT); ~ **optique** optal decoupler

découpure *f* chad

décourt-circuiter *v* unblock; release; restore

découverte *f* detection

découvrir *v* ascertain; establish; detect; expose

décrément *m* decrement; decay factor; damping factor; ~ **logarithmique** logarithmic decrement

décrémètre *m* decremeter

décrochage (D) *m* stalling (of motor); receiver pick-up; lifting handset; unhooking; jitter; off-hook (condition); out-of-sync; mismatching; call-connect signal (set up); unlocking

décroché *adj* off-hook

décrochement *m* drop-out characteristic (of voltage regulator); stand-off; offset

décrocher *v* reply; unhook; go off-hook; ~ **lift handset**; go off-hook

décroissance *f* damping; decay; downward trend

décroissant *adj* backward; descending; top-down; decremental; diminishing; falling

décroissement *m* decrement

décuplé increased tenfold (by a factor of 10)

décuples (déc.) levels

DED (v. détecteur d'état défavorable)

dédouanement *m* customs clearance

dédoublement *m* splitting; shunting; dividing; halving; subdivision; partitioning; ~ **d'image** double-beam display

défaillance *f* bug; outance; outage; failure; unserviceability

défaillant faulty; defective

défaut *m* failure; defect; fault; flaw; lack; bug; malfunction; breakdown; aberration; drop-out; imperfection; disorder; ~ **à la terre** earth fault; ground fault; ~ **admissible** permitted defective; ~ **catalectique** catastrophic failure; ~ **d'accouplement** scoop(ing) (of contacts); ~ **de jeunesse** early failure; incipient defect; infant mortality (of components); ~ **de linéarité de gain** linear gain distortion; ~ **de magnétisation** (v. défaut d'oxyde); ~ **de parallélisme** misalignment; skew; ~ **de qualité** deterioration; ~ **d'isolement** insulation fault; ~ **d'oxyde** drop-out (of magnetic tape); ~ **erratique** machining error; ~ **non accepté (DNa)** "not accepted" fault; ~ **non effacé (DNe)** "not cleared" fault; ~ **permanent** sustained fault

défauts inopérants électriques short-circuit/open-circuit faults

défavorable detrimental

défavoriser *v* militate against

défectueux *adj* corrupt (of file); defective; runaway; faulty; abortive; spurious

défense *f* security; ~ **contre avions (DCA)** AA/ack-ack (anti-aircraft defence)

défiabilité *f* unreliability

défichage *m* unplugging; removal of plug; plugging out

défiché *adj* unplugged; plugged out

défilement *m* throughput; advance; motion; move; drive; movement; traversing; scrolling; feeding; crawl (of TV lines); analysis; transport; ~ **dans une vague d'alliage** drag soldering; ~ **de texte** scrolling; ~ **des pages** paging

défini *adj* evolved; defined; prescribed

définir *v* define; describe; resolve

définitif *adj* final; definitive

définition *f* definition; resolution; ~ **de produit** (product) engineering; ~ **d'image** (image) definition; picture resolution

déflecteur baffle

déflection *f* deflection; swing

défocalisation *f* (deflection) defocussing; ~ **ionosphérique** ionospheric defocussing

défonçage *m* indentation

défoncement *m* **du niveau du noir** black level shift

déformable *adj* ductile; flexible

déformation *f* distortion; deformation; damage; droop (of pulse); garbling; offset

deviation; ~ **à froid** cold forming

défretter *v* unbind; uncoil; unclamp

dégagement *m* clearance; passageway; offset; retraction; displacement; ~ **d'angle** corner slot; milling channel; groove; ~ **de fraise** milling channel; slot; groove

dégager *v* extricate; release; retract

dégarni *adj* exposed

dégâts *m pl* **irréversibles** irreparable damage

dégazage *m* degassing; out-gassing; gettering

dégazeur *m* getter

dégénérescence *f* degeneracy; negative feedback condition

dégradation *f* impairment; degradation; fall-off; ~ **de la qualité de l'émission** transmission impairment; ~ **des teintes** deterioration of shade; ~ **progressive** wear-out

dégrader *v* impair; degrade; fall off; reduce

dégraissage *m* trimmed cable sheath; sleeving

dégraisser *v* trim down (of memory); consistency checking; eliminate superfluous (hardware and software) functions

degré *m* **conventionnel de distorsion** conventional degree of distortion; ~ **d'adaptation** degree of mismatch; ~ **d'amortissement** degree of damping; ~ **d'amplification** degree of gain; ~ **d'assurance** degree of assurance; ~ **de dissymétrie** degree of unbalance; ~ **de distorsion** degree of distortion; ~ **de distorsion arythmique au synchronisme** degree of synchronous start-stop distortion; ~ **de distorsion arythmique global** degree of gross start-stop distortion; ~ **de distorsion d'opération** degree of distortion in service; ~ **de distorsion d'un signal** signal distortion rate; ~ **de distorsion en service** degree of distortion in service; ~ **de distorsion individuelle d'un instant significatif déterminé** (d'une modulation ou d'une restitution) degree of individual distortion of a particular significant instant (of a modulation or a restitution); ~ **de distorsion isochrone** degree of isochronous distortion; ~ **de distorsion pour le synchronisme d'émetteur et de récepteur** degree of synchronous start-stop distortion; ~ **de distorsion pour le texte d'essai normalisé** degree of standardized text distortion; ~ **de distorsion propre** degree of inherent distortion; ~ **de distortion totale dans le système de déclenchement automatique** degree of gross start-stop distortion; ~ **de liberté** degree of freedom; ~ **de perturbation** degree of disturbance/interference; ~ **de saturation** freeze-out fraction; ~ **d'équilibrage** degree of balance

dégressif sliding-scale; decreasing; diminishing

dégroupage m deblocking; ~ (tarifaire) unbundling

dégroupement m debunching; unbundling; unblocking; unpacking

DEL (v. diode électroluminescente)

délai m completion date; contract date; interval; delivery date; lead time; period; ~ **d'appel** polling interval; ~ **d'approvisionnement** purchasing lead time; ~ **d'attente** waiting time; lead time; delay time; ~ **d'attente acceptable** tolerable delay; ~ **d'attente après numérotation** post-dialling delay; ~ **d'attente de tonalité** dial tone delay; dialling speed; ~ **d'attente en présélection** incoming response delay; ~ **d'attente entre caractères** pacing (function) (PAC); ~ **de basculement** turnaround time; ~ **de déclenchement** tripping time; ~ **de garde** guard delay; ~ **de livraison** lead time; ~ **de maintien** holding time; ~ **de mise en œuvre** turnaround time; ~ **de montage** lead time; ~ **de postsélection** post-selection time; ~ **de réparation** mean time to repair (MTTR); ~ **de réponse** (d'opératrice) speed of answer; answering time of an operator; operator's time to answer; turnaround time; ~ **de réponse à un échelon** delay (of receiver or amplifier) to step function excitation; ~ **de réponse en présélection** incoming response delay; ~ **de restitution** turnaround time; restitution delay; ~ **de satisfaction** (de la demande) connection time; waiting time; lead time; ~ **de transmission** transmission time; ~ **d'établissement** (de la communication) call set-up time; ~ **d'exécution** turnaround time; ~ **d'exploitation** turnaround time; ~ **d'intervention** mean time between failures (MTBF); ~ **d'inversion** turnaround time; data set delay; modem turnaround; clear-to-send time; ~ **d'invitation à numéroter** dial tone delay (DTD); ~ **moyen d'attente** average delay; ~ **moyen de raccordement** (DMR) mean connection time; average waiting time; ~ **réduit** pressing deadline

délamination f delamination (of PCB)

délégation régionale branch office

délégué m representative

déléguer v second

délestage m load-shedding; ballast shift; unloading; alternative route; by-pass; relief; unshipping; jettisoning

déliassage m decollation; de-leaving

délicat adj precarious; sensitive; touch-and-go; exacting; meticulous; complex; formidable; vexed

délimitation f demarcation; boundary; flag; frame; ~ **des blocs** block framing

délimiter v delimit; bound; circumscribe; annotate; flag; demarcate

délimiteur m delimiter; separator; fence; flag; tag; bracket; boundary; sentinel

délitage m chipping

délivrer v apply (of potential); output; furnish

délocalisation f centralization; re-location

déloquetage m unlocking; unlatching

DELRIN [A.C.] (acetal resin) plastic

démagnétisation f demagnetization; degaussing

démagnétiseur m bulk eraser (of tapes); degausser

demande f call; request; enquiry; inquiry; query; selection; booking; application; subscription; bid; ~ **d'accès** access request; ~ **d'action** action request; ~ **d'affectation** assignment demand (AD); ~ **d'appel** call request; ~ **d'attributs d'appareil** device attributes (DA); ~ **de basculement** transfer request; ~ **de communication** call booking; call request; ~ **de communication avec indication de taxe** advise-duration-and-charge call; ~ **de libération** clear request; ~ **de location** booking; ~ **de renseignements** request for information; ~ **de réponse** enquiry (ENQ); ~ **de réveil** dial-scheduled alarm call; ~ **de service** service request; ~ **de travail** job request; ~ **d'émission** request to send (RTS); ~ **desservie avec attente** queued-call request; ~ **desservie avec perte** lost-call request; ~ **d'état d'appareil** device status report (DSR); ~ **d'indicatif** WRU (who are you?) signal; identification code request; answerback code request

demandé (DE) (aval) m called party; called subscriber; addressee; B-subscriber; forward end; destination; ~ adj selected; requested; booked; polled; ~ **non taxé** charge-free subscriber

demander l'avis canvass/seek opinion; ~ **une communication téléphonique** book a call

demandeur (DR) (= amont) m; Deur caller; calling party/subscriber; source; A-subscriber; (access) originator; enquirer; inquirer; backward end; claimant; petitioner; patron; customer; applicant; end-user; ~ **en demandé** forward(-end) calling party

démantèlement m divestiture

démarche f introduction; preamble; canvassing; policy; petition(ing); ~ **administrative** formality (red tape); approach; deposition; usual channels

démarrage m starting; start-up; commissioning; ignition; activation; triggering; ~ **à chaud** warm start; re-initialization; reset;

~ **à froid** cold start; initialization; ~ **en asynchrone** asynchronous starting; ~ **progressif** soft start-up

démarreur étoile-triangle star-delta starter; ~ **rotorique** rotor resistance starter; ~ **statorique** primary resistance starter

démasquer *v* unmask; thaw; release; vector (of interrupt); enable

dématérialiser *v* phase out

d'emblée from scratch; readily

démétallisant *m* metal-stripping agent

demi-additionneur *m* half-adder

demi-alternance *f* half-cycle; half-wave

demi-appel half-call (incomplete address digits)

demi-capot half-shell (of connector)

demi-cisaillage pre-scoring

demi-coquille *f* half-bore (of fibre-optic cable)

demi-faute *f* called subscriber off-hook

demi-intervalle de temps half a unit time interval

demi-mot *m* segment; half-word

demi-octet *m* half-byte; nibble; nybble

demi-période *f* half-cycle

demi-pots appairés matching half-cores

demi-primaire *m* primary half-winding

demi-produit *m* semi-finished product

demi-répéteur half transponder

demi-secondaire *m* secondary half-winding

demi-suppresseur *m* **d'écho** half-echo suppressor; ~ **d'écho terminal** terminal half-echo suppressor

demi-système *m* half-system

demi-teinte *f* half-tone

demi-trame *f* half-frame

démodulateur *m* demodulator; detector; speech inverter; ~ (**téléphonie cryptée**) speech inverter; ~ **à extension du seuil** threshold extension demodulator (TED); ~ **à talon** Nyquist demodulator; ~ **amplitude-phase** phase detector; ~ **annulaire** ring demodulator; ~ **apériodique** damped demodulator; ~ **de données** data demodulator; ~ **fac-similé** keyer adaptor; ~ **télégraphique** telegraph demodulator

démodulation *f* demodulation; ~ **dans le temps** time demodulation

démonstrateur *m* commissioning engineer

démontable *adj* detachable; removable; collapsible

démontage *m* disassembly; scrapping; dismantling; takedown; removal; unloading

démonter *v* disassemble; dismantle; unrig; scrap; unload (of tape, disk); remove; detach; de-mount

démouillage *m* de-wetting

démultiplexage *m* demultiplexing; segregation

démultiplexer *v* demultiplex

démultiplexeur *m* demultiplexer (DEMUX)

démultiplicateur *m* counter; divider; reduction gear; scaler (of pulses); vernier; ~ **de vitesse** vernier (arrangement); scaler

dénivellation *f* drop (in level)

dénivellement *m* through-level; expected level

dénombrement *m* counting; inventory check; statistical analysis; population counting; census

densimètre *m* hydrometer

densité *f* density; specific gravity; ~ **de bits** bit density; ~ **de caractères** character density; pitch; ~ **de charge d'espace** space-charge density; ~ **de courant** current density; ~ **de fuite** dielectric density; ~ **de l'énergie radiante** radiant flux density; ~ **de probabilité** probability density; ~ **de puissance** field intensity; power flux density; ~ **d'énergie acoustique** sound-energy density; ~ **d'enregistrement** recording density; packing density; ~ **diffuse** diffuse density; ~ **d'impression** pitch; ~ **du flux énergétique** radiant flux density; ~ **d'un faisceau électronique** density of electron (ion) beam; ~ **électronique** density of electrons; ~ **ionique** ion density; ~ **linéique** (**d'un courant**) current density (flow per unit cross-sectional area of conductor); ~ **relative** specific gravity; relative density

densitomètre *m* densitometer

dent *f* pole (of magnetron segment); tooth; cog; ~ **de scie** (DDS) sawtooth (waveform); serrated; timebase; triangular waveform; jag; ramp (waveform)

dents de scie (DDS) sawtooth (waveform)

denture *f* **d'accouplement** sprocket

dénudage *m* stripping (of wire); clearing; skinning

dénudé *adj* bare; stripped; cleared

dénumérotage *m* number change

dénumérotation *f* directory number change

dénuméroté *adj* renumbered

déontologie *f* code of practice; ethic

DEP (v. déplacement)

dépannage *m* fault-clearing; fault repairing; troubleshooting; debugging; repair; problem-solving

dépanner *v* troubleshoot; repair; debug; check-out

déparasité *adj* interference-free

départ *m* lead-out; outlet (mains distribution supply); outgoing (O/G); outward line; originating; go path; outbound; feeder; start; head; derivation; ~ **usine** ex-works; ~ **vers baie** outgoing feeder; rack feeder

dépassé *adj* superseded

dépassement *m* projection; protrusion; lead-out; excess; overshoot; overflow; overhang; over-consumption; violation; ~ **d'amplitude** whiter than white; ~ **de (capacité de) page** page overflow (PGOF); ~ **de capacité inférieur** undershoot; underflow; ~ **de capacité supérieur** overflow; overshoot; ~ **de l'octet** byte boundary overflow; ~ **de page (DP)** page overflow (PO); PGOF; ~ **de seuil** out-of-limits condition; ~ **du temps d'émission** overrun; ~ **négatif** underflow

dépêche f newsflash; despatch; communique

dépêches commerciales commercial acumen; business skills

dépendance f **de l'amplitude** fundamental component distortion

déperditeur m **de potentiel** static discharger

déperdition f overhead; leak; leakage

déphasage m outphasing; phase shift; phase inverting/displacement; phase error; lag/lead; phase splitting/change; ~ **d'insertion** insertion phase change; ~ **en arrière** phase lag; phase splitting; ~ **en avant** phase lead; ~ **itératif** iterative phase-change coefficient; iterative phase-change constant; ~ **linéique** phase-change coefficient; ~ **sur image(s)** image phase-change coefficient; image phase(change) constant

déphasé adj out-of-phase; ~ **de 180°** push-pull; ~ **en arrière** lagging; ~ **en avant** leading

déphaseur m phase converter; phase shifter; phase changer; phaser; ~ **à deux tubes** long-tailed pair; ~ **directif** directional phase changer; ~ **multiple** phase splitter; ~ **non réciproque** directional phase-changer/phase-shifter; ~ **rotatif** rotary phase changer/phase-shifter

déphaseuse f phase inverter

dépistage m locating; tracking down; tracing; trace (program); recuperation; isolation; identification; ~ **des appels malveillants** malicious call tracing; ~ **d'un défaut/dérangement** trouble-shooting

déplacement m travel; displacement; excursion; offset; shift; swing; move; movement; secondment; transfer; relative address (RA); migration; base address displacement; relocation; reconfiguration; ~ **(DEP)** MOVE key; ~ **angulaire** angular displacement; offset; ~ **avant** step-in; ~ **crête-à-crête** peak-to-peak displacement; ~ **dans le champ** (d. de champ) field displacement; ~ **de fréquence** frequency shift; ~ **de la porteuse** carrier shift; ~ **de phase à quatre états** quadrature phase-shift keying (QPSK); ~ **du curseur** cursor movement; ~ **du flanc postérieur** end distortion; ~ **(en) arrière** step-out; ~ **(en)**

avant step-in; ~ **maximum** full-scale deflection (FSD); carrier shift; ~ **répartiteur** patch-board reconfiguration; strapping panel reconfiguration; ~ **vertical** vertical movement; ~ **zone mémoire** block move

déplacer v move; shift; transfer; clear (of fault)

dépoli adj pearl; frosted (of lamp bulb)

déport m entrance link; extension; mismatch; retransmission; offset; back-haul; relay(ing); remote; ~ **bus** bus extension; ~ **hertzien** optical fibre link; ~ **numérique** digital entrance link (DEL)

déporté offset; off-site

déporter v divert; re-route

déposer v file (of patent)

dépositionné adj cleared; reset

dépôt m deposit; sediment; deposition; residue; submission

dépôt chimique en phase vapeur vapour (phase axial) deposition (VAD)

dépôt conducteur land

dépot d'alliage étain-plomb tin-lead alloy plating

dépôt de garantie initial initial deposit on account; caution money; ~ **électrolytique** electro-deposition; electrolytic/galvanic deposition; ~ **épitaxique** epitaxial deposit; ~ **galvanique** electro-deposition; electrolytic/galvanic deposition

dépouille f (moulding) flash; scrap; stripped (side); delivery (side)

dépouillement m processing; interpretation; breakdown; data reduction; analysis; sifting; scrutiny; ~ **des données** data examination; processing; data reduction

dépoussiérage m dusting; dust removal

déramer v fan out; riffle (of paper)

dérangement m failure; (line) fault; trouble; disorder; bug; malfunction; ~ **du téléphone** telephone breakdown

dérangements telephone engineer; maintenance service (engineer)

dérapage m wander

déréglage m maladjustment; misalignment; slewing; detuning; mismatch; offset; skew

déréglé adj out of step (dial); offset; misaligned; askew; incorrect; deviant; drifted off-centre; slewed

déréglementation f de-regulation

dérivable adj with drop-and-insert capability

dérivateur m differentiator (logic)

dérivation f branch; branching; derivation; fork; leg; bypass; shunt; diversion; junction; tapping; stub; bifurcation; bridging; ~ **à la terre** earth leakage/fault; ~ **de secours** emergency bypass; ~ **des canaux**

channel extraction; ~ **et insertion** drop and insert

dérive *f* loss of accuracy; drift; departure; slip; shift; divergence; discrepancy; leak; deviation; aberration; offset; error; reduction; (temperature) coefficient; ~ **de bits** bit slip; ~ **de fréquence** frequency drift/ shift; ~ **de la tension de décalage** offset null voltage; ~ **de pente** gradient error; offset deviation; ~ **de trajet ionosphérique** ionospheric defocussing; ~ **du zéro** null shift; ~ **en température** temperature deviation; temperature drift; ~ **en température (des valeurs de résistances)** temperature coefficient (of resistance, measured in p.p.m.)

dérivé *f adj* coefficient; slave; shunted; off-shoot

dernier contact par radio last radio contact

dérogation *f* deferment; exemption; waiver; departure (from); deviation; exception; special case; special concession; override

déroulement *m* run; looping (of routine); unwinding; execution; operating sequence; procedure; control sequence

dérouleur *m* unwrapping tool; ~ **de bande** tape deck; tape transport/drive; ~ **de bande magnétique** tape transport; magnetic tape drive (unit)/handler; tape handler

dérouleuse *f* cable drum/payout spool

déroutement *m* trap; unprogrammed branch; re-routing; flow; ~ **par canal** channel trap

dérouter *v* side-track (of traffic)

désaccentuation *f* de-emphasis; post-emphasis

désaccord *m* imbalance; tuning error; mismatch; disparity; discrepancy; divergence; difference; variance

désaccordage *m* de-tuning

désaccorder *v* de-tune; mismatch

désaccouplement *m* uncoupling

désaccoupler *v* uncouple

désactiver *v* terminate; de-activate; kill; deselect

désaffecter *v* de-allocate; re-deploy

désaffleurant *adj* proud; offset; out of level

désagrégation *f* **intercristalline** intercrystalline disintegration

désaimantation *f* demagnetization; degaussing

désalignement *m* skew; misalignment; out-of-true; offset

désamorçage *m* de-energizing; extinction (of thyristor)

désamorcer *v* de-fuse

désarmé *adj* idle; disarmed; reset; cleared

désassemblage *m* **de paquets** packet disassembly

désassembleur *m* **de paquets** packet disassembler

désaxé *adj* askew; offset; misaligned; off-cen-

tre; out-of-true; unbalanced

descendant *adj* down-link (of satellite relay); downward; falling; backward; sliding; top-down; dropping; trailing; decreasing

descente *f* lead down; lead wire; drop; ~ **d'antenne** aerial lead; down lead; ~ **du curseur** cursor down (CUD)

descripteur *m* descriptor; identifier; tag; specifier; term; ~ **d'emplacement** location identifier; ~ **d'octet** byte descriptor; byte specifier

descriptif *m* perspective diagram; ~ **matériel de l'affaire** contract hardware description

description *f* **de la tâche** job description

désembrouilleur *m* descrambler

désenclaver *v* liberate; release from seclusion

désencombrement *m* load shift; decongestion

désenficher *v* dislodge; unplug; plug out

déséquilibrage *m* **des impédances** impedance mismatch; impedance unbalance

déséquilibre *m* centre shift; imbalance; mismatch; slew; maladjustment; unbalance; offset; balance return loss; ~ **de résistance** resistance unbalance; ~ **d'impédance par rapport à la terre** impedance unbalance to earth; ~ **du trafic** traffic load imbalance; ~ **par rapport à la terre** unbalance about earth; unbalance to earth

désérialiseur *m* serial-parallel converter

désexcitation *f* de-excitation; de-energizing

désexciter *v* de-energize

déshabillage *m* stripping; dismantling; uncladding

DESIETER French telex standard

désignation *f* identification; title; name; reference; description; allotting; selection; labelling; writing; nomenclature; type code; ~ **commerciale** trade name; brand; proprietary mark; ~ **en mémoire** (memory) write; ~ **et appel des codes géométriques** naming and invocation of geometric codes

désigner *v* single out; stand for; represent; denote; identify; write; indicate; select; specify; label; allot; nominate; address

désinhiber *v* reactivate; release; free; re-enable

désinstaller *v* discard

désintégration *f* decay

désionisation *f* de-ionization

désoperculer *v* flatten; smooth out

désordonné *adj* unruly

dessaisir *v* release

déssécheur *m* **à air** air desiccator

dessein *m* design

desserrer *v* loosen; unscrew; slacken off; free; release

desserte *f* pay-out stand; trolley

desservi en automatique automated

desservir *v* cater for; host; serve; service; connect; assign; accommodate; attend

dessicateur *m* desiccator; drying agent; desiccant

dessin *m* drawing; plan; scheme; draughting; artwork; pattern; ~ **d'assemblage** assembly drawing; ~ **d'atelier** working drawing; ~ **de construction** constructional drawing; ~ **de coupe** sectional view/representation; ~ **de montage** assembly drawing; construction plan; erection drawing; ~ **d'écran** screen painting; ~ **d'ensemble** assembly drawing; ~ **détaillé** detail drawing; ~ **d'exécution** working drawing; ~ **imaginé** artist's impression; ~ **industriel** mechanical drawing

dessinateur *m* draughtsman

dessouder *v* desolder; unsolder

destinataire *m* f *ou adj* addressee; consignee; recipient; sendee; target; (traffic) sink

destination *f* destination; direction; (traffic) sink

destiné à dedicated to

destructeur *m* shredder (of documents)

destruction *f* irreparable damage; blow-out; deletion

désuet *adj* obsolete

désuétude calculée planned obsolescence

détachable *adj* burstable (continuous stationery)

détail *m* detail; breakdown; itemization; member

détaillé *adj* detailed

détalonnage *m* undercutting; de-rating; stepping down

détasser *v* unpack

détaxe *f* rebate; remission

détectable par machine machine-sensible

détecter *v* detect; sense; discriminate

détecteur *m* detector; sensor; demodulator; finder; ~ **àcristal** crystal detector; crystal receiver; ~ **à deux limites** window detector; pulse-height selector; ~ **à diode** diode detector; ~ **à double seuil** pulse height selector; window detector; ~ **d'anomalies** fault switch; ~ **de champ tournant** rotating field detector; ~ **de crête** peak (overload) detector; ~ **de défaut de tension** voltage failure detector; ~ **de faute** fault finder; ~ **de fréquences** tone detector; ~ **de parole** speech detector; ~ **de polarités** polarity detector; ~ **de quasi-crête** quasi-peak detector; ~ **de rapport** ratio detector; ~ **de signaux** (télégraphiques) recording unit; ~ **de tonalité** tone detector; ~ **de valeur moyenne** average detector; ~ **d'état défavorable (DED)** adverse state detector (ASD);

~ **d'isolement terre** leakage indicator (earth fault detector); ~ **en quadrature de phase** quadrature detector; ~ **linéaire** linear detector; ~ **quadratique** square-law detector

détecteur-amplificateur amplifier detector

détection *f* discrimination; warning; sensing; detection; demodulation; ~ **à réponse linéaire** linear detection; ~ **à réponse quadratique** square-law detection; ~ **automatique d'erreurs** automatic error detection; ~ **d'appel** call detection; ~ **de signaux cohérents** coherent signal detection; ~ **de signaux incohérents** garbled signal detection; ~ **de tonalité** tone presence scan point; ~ **début de feuille** registration sensor; ~ **d'enveloppe** envelope detection; ~ **d'erreurs** error detection; ~ **et correction d'erreurs** error detection and correction; ~ **linéaire** linear detection; ~ **onde porteuse** carrier detect; ~ **parabolique** square-law detection; ~ **plaque** anode detection; ~ **sensible à la phase** phase-sensitive detection; ~ **sortie papier** paper exit sensor; ~ **vidéo** video detection

détendeur *m* payout reel; relief valve; release mechanism; trigger; expansion chamber

détente *f* decompression; expansion; release; triggering; relief; stress relief (of metal); ~ **moyenne** average delay

détérioration *f* mutilation; damage; decay; failure

détermination *f* **automatique des coordonnées** automatic range; bearing or elevation measurement

déterminer *v* perceive; ascertain; establish; localize; define; specify; indicate; evaluate; assess; quantify; select; sort; grade; ~ **la valeur de** evaluate

déterministe *adj* sufficient in isolation; diagnostic; symptomatic

détimbrage *m* de-rating

détonation *f* **balistique** sonic boom

détour *m* **productif** lateral thinking

détourage *m* PCB profile; profiling; final dimensioning and cutting; trim(-line)

détourné *adj* diverted; re-routed; redirected; skewed

détournement *m* deviation; re-routing; alternate routing; diversion; hi-jacking; spill-forward (feature)

détrompage *m* locating; polarizing; discriminating

détrompeur *m* polarizer; discrimination key; coding key; mating device (spigot/cavity); ~ **femelle** polarizing cavity/receptacle; ~ **mâle** mating spigot; locating key

détruire *v* discard; destroy; delete; overwrite

Deur (v. demandeur)
deutéron *m* deuteron
deux alternances full-wave; ~ **circuits décalés** staggered pair; ~ **entrées sur** two-port input to; ~ **fils de conversation** talking pair; ~ **fils en main** two pair-wound wires
deuxième décharge de Townsend second Townsend discharge; ~ **harmonique** second harmonic; ~ **opérande** addend
devant in comparison with; relative to
développé *adj* discussed
développement *m* extension; upgrading; progress; growth; expansion; advancement; ~ **du réseau** network development
développer *v* upgrade; extend; devise; develop
devenir nul expire
déverminage *m* burn-in; screening; soak testing; early failure test
déverminé *adj* burned-in; screened; soak-tested
déverrouillage *m* unlocking; enabling; releasing; misalignment
déversoir *m* earth bed; current leak
déviateur *m* yoke; fender; deflector
déviation *f* deviation; rerouting; alternate routing; displacement; swing; (call) forwarding; deflection; departure; shift; sweep; relay; diversion; intercept; ~ **asymétrique** asymmetrical deflection; ~ **brusque de phase** sudden phase anomaly; ~ **de fréquence** frequency deviation; frequency swing; ~ **de fréquence crête à crête** frequency swing; ~ **de relèvement** bearing deviation; ~ **d'inclinaison** offset deviation; droop; ~ **électrique** electrostatic deflection; electric deflection; ~ **magnétique** magnetic deflection; ~ **maximale** full-scale deflection (FSD); ~ **opto-acoustique** opto-acoustic deflection; ~ **symétrique** symmetrical deflection; ~ **trapézoïdale** trapezoidal deflection
dévidage *m* unwinding
dévidoir *m* reel; payout drum
devis *m* equipment schedule; job estimate
dévolteur *m* negative booster; step-down transformer
dévoyé *adj* errant
déwatté *adj* wattless; reactive; idle
diable *m* **à caisse** crate trolley/dolly
diabolo *m* bobbin; (cable) drum
diadique *adj* dyadic; binary
diagnose *m* fault-finding (chart)
diagnostic *m* diagnostic report; fault analysis; diagnostic message
diagonale *adj* (staggered) diagonal (of bit pattern)
diagramme *m* diagram; flowchart; chart; graphic/pictorial representation; outline;

performance chart; pattern; symbolic representation; low-level timing diagram; signal waveform; configuration; ~ **de Bode** Bode plot/diagram; ~ **de brassage** strap configuration; ~ **de charge** load diagram; ~ **de communication** communications chart; ~ **de couverture** coverage diagram; ~ **de déroulement** flowchart; ~ **de diffraction** diffraction pattern; ~ **de directivité** radiation pattern; radiation diagram; directivity pattern; aerial gain pattern; ~ **de directivité verticale** vertical directivity pattern; ~ **de fonctionnement** performance chart; timing diagram; ~ **de jonctions** trunking diagram; ~ **de liaisons** trunking diagram; ~ **de rayonnement** radiation/beam pattern (of antenna); ~ **de rayonnement primaire** primary radiation pattern; ~ **de rétrodiffusion** back-scatter diagram/pattern; ~ **de Rieke** Rieke diagram; ~ **de transition des états** state transition diagram; ~ **de transition du statut** state transition diagram; ~ **de Veitch** Veitch diagram; ~ **de Venn** Venn diagram; ~ **d'émission** transmission diagram; ~ **des états** state transition diagram; ~ **des itinéraires** channel graph; ~ **des niveaux** level diagram; ~ **des temps** timing diagram; switching time waveforms; ~ **d'impédance de charge** load impedance diagram; ~ **d'interconnexion** interconnection diagram; ~ **du marché** contract outline; ~ **en cardioïde** cardioid (heart-shaped) diagram; ~ **en huit** figure-of-eight diagram; ~ **énergétique** energy-level diagram; ~ **logique** logic diagram; ~ **polaire de rayonnement** polar radiation pattern; ~ **polaire secondaire** secondary radiation pattern; ~ **proportionné de rayonnement** tailored radiation pattern; ~ **secondaire** secondary pattern; ~ **séquentiel théorique** theoretical timing diagram; ~ **solide de rayonnement** solid radiation pattern; ~ **temporel** timing diagram; ~ **vectoriel** signal space diagram
diagraphie *f* log; logging
dialogue *m* conversation; communication; interchange; dialogue; menu; man-machine language; ~ **initial** initial menu; ~ **interactif** question-and-answer dialogue
dialoguer (avec) communicate (with)
diamètre *m* (= module/calibre) shell size; ~ **de la surface cathodique efficace** cathode emitting diameter; ~ **du spot** spot-size aperture
diapason *m* tuning fork
diaphonie *f* crosstalk; cross-feed (of disk tracks); inter-modulation noise; cross-modulation; splash; cross-coupling; ~ **causée**

par la voix speech crosstalk; ~ d'écho inverted crosstalk; ~ entre les bandes latérales sideband splash; ~ entre les deux sens de transmission go-to-return crosstalk; ~ entre voies inter-channel crosstalk; ~ inintelligible inverted crosstalk; non-intelligible crosstalk; ~ intelligible intelligible crosstalk; ~ multiple babble; multiple crosstalk; ~ par la fréquence frequency crosstalk; ~ télégraphique telegraph crosstalk

diaphonomètre *m* crosstalk attenuation meter
diaphragme *m* diaphragm; membrane; aperture; gauge (of wire); iris (of waveguide); ~ de centrage spider; ~ des teintes tone control aperture
dibi (v. distributeur de billets)
dicorde *f* double(-ended) cord circuit; twin pair (tip and sleeve); cord pair; ~ double de croisement double-switching dicord
dictée centralisée central dictation service; dial dictation access
dictionnaire *m* dictionary; directory; ~ diagnostique de défauts fault dictionary
didacthèque *f* educational software library
didacticiel *m* educational software
didactique *adj* educational; instructional; teaching
diélectrimètre *m* insulation tester
diélectrique dielectric; non-conductive; insulating; ~ artificielle artificial dielectric; ~ non uniforme dans le sens longitudinal longitudinally non-uniform dielectric
dièse *m* number sign; hash symbol; pound sign; gate symbol; octothorpe
différation *f* d'une communication call deferring
différé *adj* off-line; deferred; delayed; lagging; postponed; lag; batch (mode); held; spooled; pre-recorded; store-and-forward; time-sharing
différence *f* discrepancy; disparity; difference; ~ de fréquence de mode mode separation; ~ de niveau level difference; ~ de niveau de fréquence de signalisation twist (of tone dialling frequencies); ~ de niveau de puissance power level difference; ~ de niveau de tension voltage level difference; ~ de phase phase difference; path difference; ~ de potentiel (d.d.p.) potential difference (p.d.); voltage between lines; electromotive force; electric potential; ~ de potentiel au contact contact potential difference; ~ juste perceptible just-noticeable difference (j.n.d.)
différencier *v* distinguish (between); differentiate
différent *adj* several; various; distinct; other;

varying; disparate; different; individual; ~ de other than; not; ~ de zéro non-null; non-zero
différentiateur *m* differentiating circuit; peaking network
différentiation *f* des produits product mix
différentiel *adj* differential; derivative; hybrid; small-signal; balanced; discriminating; time-base sync (phase difference)
différer une communication defer a call
diffusant *adj* non-specular; diffusing
diffuser *v* disseminate; circulate; distribute; release; broadcast; disperse; spread; scatter; issue; ~ par la télévision telecast
diffuseur *m* porous stone (of foam fluxer)
diffusiomètre *m* drift meter (of radar system)
diffusion *f* broadcasting; dissemination; distribution; circulation; scatter(ing); paging; multi-line transmission; diffusion; ~ à relais chain broadcasting; ~ arrière back scatter; ~ avant forward scatter; ~ de données data distribution; ~ de Rayleigh Rayleigh scattering; ~ directe de la télévision par satellite direct TV (broadcast) by satellite (DTS); ~ du signal auroral auroral signal scattering; ~ par voie radioélectrique radio broadcasting; ~ restreinte classified; restricted (circulation); ~ troposphérique tropospheric scatter
digigraphie *f* man-machine communication
digramme *m* digraph; directed graph
digraphie *f* double-entry book-keeping
DIL verre céramique CERDIP package
dilatation *f* scaling; expansion; enlargement
diluant *m* thinner
dimension *f* moyenne des messages average message size
dimensionnable *adj* open-ended; variable capacity
dimensionné *adj* traffic-engineered; sized; configured; structured
dimensionnement *m* dimensioning; sizing; scaling; traffic-engineering; design ratings
dimensionner *v* design; traffic-engineer; size; dimension; scale; set (of memory partition); quantify
diminuende *m* minuend
diminuer *v* decrement; reduce; decrease; fall; fade; diminish; dip; drop; dwindle; decline
diminuteur *m* subtrahend
diminution *f* de l'activité activity dip; ~ du gain decrease of gain
diode *f* diode; rectifier; clamp; ~ à avalanche P-PN avalanche photodiode (APD); ~ à capacité variable variable capacitance diode; varactor; ~ à cristal crystal rectifier/diode; ~ à double hétérostructure double heterojunction diode; ~ à pointe cats-

whisker diode; point-contact diode; ~ à **quatre couches** four-layer diode; ~ **à redressement rapide** fast-recovery diode; ~ **antirecul** clamping diode; catching diode; ~ **anti-retour** blocking diode; clamping diode; ~ **asymétrique** asymmetrical starting diode; ~ **avalanche** breakdown diode; avalanche diode; ~ **BARITT** BARITT diode (barrier injection transit time); ~ **d'amortissement** damping diode; damping tube; ~ **de calage** DC restorer diode; DC clamp diode; ~ **de clamping** clamping diode; catching diode; ~ **de commutation** breakdown diode; ~ **de commutation rapide** step-recovery diode; snap-off diode; snap-back diode; charge-storage diode; fast switching diode; breakdown diode; ~ **de contrôle** pilot light; indicator; ~ **de déclenchement** gate trigger diode; ~ **de découplage** cut-out diode; ~ **de limitation** voltage clamp; ~ **de récupération** (fast) recovery diode; ~ **de réglage** AGC detector; ~ **de restitution du niveau de noir** clamping diode; catching diode; clamp; ~ **de roue libre** free-wheel diode; ~ **de verrouillage** clamping diode; catching diode; clamp; ~ **de Zener** avalanche diode; Zener diode; ~ **d'écrêtage** catching diode; clamping diode; ~ **double** binode; duo-diode; double diode (epitaxial rectifier); ~ **économisatrice** booster diode; efficiency diode; ~ **électroluminescente (DEL)** light-emitting diode (LED); ~ **en basse Q** low-Q diode; ~ **en régime d'avalanche** avalanche diode; ~ **équivalente** equivalent diode; ~ **Impatt** IMPATT diode (impact ionization avalanche transit time); ~ **laser** laser diode; ~ **limitatrice** limiter diode; ~ **linéaire** p-i-n photodiode; ~ **multijonctions** multi-layer diode; ~ **rapide** high-speed switching diode; fast recovery diode; ~ **redresseur au silicium** silicon-controlled rectifier (SCR); ~ **Schottky de puissance** Schottky barrier rectifier; hot-carrier diode; ~ **symétrique** symmetrical diode; ~ **tunnel** Esaki (tunnel-effect) diode; ~ **ultrarapide** superswitch

diphasé *adj* diphase; biphase; two-phase

diplexeur *m* diplexer; ~ **à deux ponts** double-bridge diplexer; ~ **à filtre passebande** bandpass filter diplexer; ~ **en pont** bridge diplexer

dipôle *m* dipole; ~ **à impédance négative** repeater (negative impedance dipole); ~ **à large bande** broadband dipole; wideband dipole; ~ **accordé** tuned dipole; ~ **asymétrique** asymmetrical dipole; ~ **demi-onde** half-wave dipole; doublet; ~ **double**

double dipole; ~ **électrique** infinitesimal dipole; radiating doublet; ~ **en rideau** dipole curtain; ~ **en triangle** triangular dipole; ~ **excité** driven dipole; ~ **magnétique** magnetic doublet radiator; ~ **replié** (trombone) folded dipole; bow-tie dipole

direct *adj* direct; on-line; forward; home; primary; incident; private (of telephone line)

directeur *m* manager; controller; driver; conductor; master; executive

direction *f* case line; direction; route; guidance; management; control circuit; trend; outgoing line; approach; ~ **constante** search-lighting (of aerial); ~ **de polarisation** direction of polarization (of waveguide); ~ **de réception** receiving direction; ~ **d'émission** transmitting direction; ~ **d'un projectile radioguidé sur le but** homing target finding

directive *f* command; directive (control statement); pseudo-instruction; declarative macro; policy guideline; construct; ~ **d'assemblage** assembly pseudo-instruction

directivité *f* radiation (pattern); aerial gain; ~ **d'antenne** aerial directivity; aerial gain; ~ **de radiateur élémentaire** elementary radiator directivity; ~ **de réseau** array directivity; ~ **microphone** microphone directivity

diriger *v* steer; guide; direct; channel

dirupteur *m* diruptor (two-way circuit-breaker)

discontacteur *m* switching unit; starter; overcurrent release; overload release; ~ **de puissance** starter; ~ **en coffret** enclosed starter; ~ **inverseur** reversing starter; ~ **sans relais** less-relay starter; ~ **tripolaire** three-pole starter

discontinuité *f* break; non-transparency; ~ **de dépôt** void; ~ **d'indice** stepped index

discordant unmatched; detuned

discret *adj* discrete; low-profile; discreet; runaway; freak

discrétion *f* radio silence

discrétisation *f* quantizing

discriminateur *m* toll discriminator; discriminator; kicksorter analyser; ~ **d'amplitude** pulse-height analyser; ~ **de phase** phase detector; phase discriminator; ~ **numérique** digital discriminator; ~ **passif** passive discriminator

discrimination *f* call restriction; class-of-service entitlement; (COS); distinguishing feature; distinction; discrimination; selection; classification; branch; class marking; skip; jump grading; ~ **adaptative** adaptive discrimination; ~ **arrivée** terminating

D

class-of-service; ~ **automatique** automatic toll-call restriction; ~ **d'abonné** line category; subscriber class-of-service; ~ **de cibles** target discrimination; ~ **départ** originating class-of-service

disjoint discrete; non-contiguous

disjoncteur *m* circuit-breaker; switch; / tripping device; isolator; automatic switch; ~ **à fusible** fuse cut-out; ~ **à huile** oil-break switch; ~ **automatique** automatic (circuit-)breaker; automatic switch; ~ **cyclique** cyclic switch; ~ **de sécurité** limit switch; ~ **différentiel** quick-trip circuit-breaker; ~ **instantané** instantaneous cut-out; quick cut-out; ~ **protecteur** overload switch; maximum cut-out; ~ **rapide** quick-break automatic switch

disjonction *f* exclusive-OR; tripping; break; EITHER-OR

disparition *f* cancellation (of alarm)

dispatcheur *m* despatcher

dispenser *v* administer

dispersé *adj* diffuse; separate(d); widespread; scattered; distributed; colloidal

dispersion *f* spread; scatter; leakage; dispersion; separation; divergence; ~ **de la commande** non-centralized control; ~ **de la qualité de transmission** spread in transmission performance; ~ **de l'affaiblissement** loss dispersion; ~ **des temps de propagation entre voies** channel-to-channel data skew (of logic analyser); ~ **d'intelligence** distributed intelligence; ~ **du gain dynamique** dynamic range; ~ **intermodale** mode dispersion; ~ **interstitielle** gap leakage; ~ **magnétique** magnetic leakage; ~ **matériau/chromatique** material/chromatic dispersion

disponibilité *f* accessibility; free condition; availability; up-time

disponible *adj* available; free; not busy; idle; unassigned; accessible; vacant; ready

dispositif *m* appliance; device; contrivance; system; gadget; mechanism; apparatus; jig; attachment; feature; layout; unit; arrangement; network; ~ **à amplification variable** variable gain device; ~ **à bande étalée** bandspreading device; ~ **à couplage de charges (DCC)** charge-coupled device (CCD); image sensor; ~ **à semiconducteurs** solid-state device; ~ **à transfert de charges** charge-transfer device (CTD); bucket-brigade device; image sensor; ~ **anti-local** anti-sidetone device; ~ **antiparasite** noise eliminator; ~ **anti-surtension** crowbar protection device; ~ **automatique de commutation** automatic protection switch (APS); ~ **auxiliaire de radioralliement** homing aid;

~ **chien de garde** watch-dog timer; ~ **chiffreur** cipher equipment; encoder; ~ **contre les réflexions de mer** anti-clutter facility; ~ **d'acceptation de basculement** transfer-enable unit; ~ **d'accord** tuning set; tuner; ~ **d'accord décalé** tracking device; ~ **d'affaiblissement** attenuator; ~ **d'alignement** clamp; ~ **d'appel** calling device; ringer; ~ **de blocage** blocking device; clamp; ~ **de constitution (du bus)** (bus) generator; ~ **de contact à permutation** changeover contact unit; ~ **de contact de fermeture** make-contact unit; ~ **de contact de rupture** break-contact unit; ~ **de couplage** coupler; ~ **de couplage acoustique** acoustic coupler; ~ **de coupure** splitting arrangement; ~ **de demande de basculement** transfer-request unit; ~ **de déplacement de charge** bucket-brigade device; charge transfer device; image sensor; ~ **de diffusion** recorded announcement unit; multi-line transmission circuit; fan-out facility; ~ **de mesure de distances** distance-measuring equipment (DME); ~ **de plombage** sealing kit; ~ **de prise directe** direct access controller; ~ **de quart de tour** quarter-turn device; ~ **de raccordement** (au réseau) network interface module (NIM); ~ **de RAZ** (remise à zéro) reset facility; ~ **de réglage de la linéarité** linearity control; ~ **de réglage de l'amplification** gain control; ~ **de réglage précis** clarifier; ~ **de secours** standby (charge-)recording unit; ~ **de suralimentation** loop extender; ~ **de taxation** metering unit; ~ **de temporisation chien de garde** watch-dog timer; ~ **de verrouillage de trame** slot aligner; ~ **d'écoute** monitoring equipment; ~ **d'émission de la télétaxe** metering pulse transmitter; ~ **d'émission de tonalités** tone feeder; ~ **d'essai automatique** automatic tester; ~ **d'exclusion** override device; ~ **d'intercommunication** talk-through facility; intercom; ~ **en attente** device wait (DW); ~ **extérieur** external feeder; ~ **magnétothermique** thermal shutdown device; thermomagnetic device; ~ **transistorisé** solid-state device

dispositifs de coupure splitting arrangement

disposition *f* provision; stipulation; layout; array; format; arrangement; organization; availability; structure; principle; ~ **à adresse** address format; ~ **à bloc fixe** fixed-block format; ~ **à bloc variable** variable-block format; ~ **de message** message format; ~ **en rangées** array

disque *m* disk/disc; platter (individual disk in disk pack); plate; ~ **à cartouche amovible**

removable cartridge disk; ~ **analyseur** scanning disk; ~ **archive** disk storage; dump storage disk file; ~ **audionumérique** compact disk; ~ **banalisé** scratch disk; scratch file; ~ **circulaire** (magnetic) disk; ~ **d'appel** dial plate; ~ **de manœuvre** scratch disk; ~ **de Rayleigh** Rayleigh disk; ~ **d'évacuation** swapping disk; ~ **d'exploitation** system disk; ~ **du combinateur** combiner disk; ~ **dur** winchester disk; hard disk; ~ **interrupteur** chopper disk; ~ **magnétique** magnetic disk; ~ **magnétique à tête fixe** fixed-head disk (unit); ~ **magnétique à tête mobile** moving-head disk (unit); ~ **magnétique amovible** removable magnetic disk; ~ **non démontable** undemountable disk; ~ **numéroté** number plate (of rotary dial); dial plate; ~ **optique** optical video disk (OVD); ~ **rigide** hard disk; rigid disk; winchester disk; ~ **sectorisé** stroboscopic (reflector) disk; ~ **souple** floppy disk; diskette; flippy; flexidisk; ~ **souple banalisé** file floppy disk; scratch disk

disquette *m* diskette; floppy disk; flippy; mini-disk

dissecteur *m* **d'image** image dissector

disséminer *v* disperse; broadcast; scatter

dissipateur *m* (thermique) heat sink

dissipatif *adj* lossy

dissipation *f* loss; decay; dissipation; power rating; ~ **de chaleur** heat loss; ~ **totale des électrodes** total electrode dissipation

dissociation *f* unbundling

dissocier *v* preclude

dissymétrie *f* imbalance; misalignment; unbalance; ~ **par rapport à la terre** unbalance about earth; unbalance to earth

dissymétrique *adj* asymmetrical; unbalanced

distance *f* range; span; distance; ~ **critique d'approche** nearest approach; ~ **de conversation** speaking distance; ~ **de la cible** target distance; ~ **de l'horizon** (radioélectrique) radio-horizon distance; ~ **de saut** skip distance; ~ **d'écrasement** upset distance (of welding); ~ **électrique** electrical distance; ~ **entre canaux** inter-channel spacing; ~ **entre émetteurs** spacing between transmitters; ~ **franchissable** range; ~ **optique de l'horizon** optical horizon distance; ~ **terrestre** ground distance

distant *adj* distant; remote; far-end; outlying

distilleuse *f* solvent still; degreasing unit

distinct *adj* discrete; separate; individual

distinguer *v* differentiate

distorsiomètre *m* distortion analyzer; telegraph distortion measuring set (TDMS); ~ **arythmique** start-stop distortion measur-

ing set

distorsion *f* distortion; clutter; skew; mush; flare; clipping; deformation; delay; noise (QRN); flicker; tracking; ~ **à l'émission** transmitter distortion; ~ **accidentelle** fortuitous distortion; jitter; ~ **admissible des signaux** distortion tolerance/margin; ~ **arythmique** start-stop distortion; ~ **asymétrique** bias distortion; skew; asymmetrical distortion; ~ **au voisinage du point d'amorçage** near-singing distortion; ~ **biaise** bias distortion; skew; asymmetrical distortion; ~ **caractéristique** characteristic distortion; ~ **cubique** third-order distortion; ~ **cyclique** cyclic distortion; ~ **d'affaiblissement** amplitude (versus) frequency distortion; frequency distortion; attenuation distortion; ~ **d'amplitude** amplitude distortion; ~ **dans l'émission** send distortion; ~ **de balayage horizontal** line non-linearity; ~ **de balayage vertical** field non-linearity; ~ **de demi-teinte** half-tone distortion; ~ **de déviation** deflection distortion; skew; ~ **de dynamique** volume range distortion; ~ **de forme d'onde** waveform distortion; ~ **de la crête de l'amplitude** peak distortion; ~ **de la réponse en fréquence** frequency response distortion; ~ **de la transmission** transmission distortion; ~ **de l'harmonique impair** odd harmonic distortion; ~ **de ligne** fortuitous distortion; jitter; ~ **de l'ouverture** aperture distortion; ~ **de luminance horizontale** (horizontal) luminance flicker; ~ **de modulation** modulation frequency harmonic distortion; envelope distortion; ~ **de niveau** level distortion; ~ **de non linéarité** non-linear distortion; ~ **de numérotation** dial-pulse distortion; loop-break distortion; ~ **de phase** phase distortion; delay distortion; ~ **de quantification** quantizing distortion; ~ **de raccordement** crossover distortion; ~ **de rebroussement** fold-back distortion; ~ **de retard** lagging distortion; ~ **de signaux télégraphiques** bias distortion; ~ **de suroscillation** overshoot distortion; overthrow distortion; ~ **de temps de propagation** delay distortion; non-linear distortion; ~ **de temps de propagation de groupe** group-delay distortion; envelope-delay distortion; ~ **d'exploration** aperture distortion (of facsimile); ~ **diagonale du signal** diagonal clipping; ~ **d'image** on-screen distortion; skew; smear; picture distortion; ~ **d'impulsion** pulse distortion; ~ **d'intermodulation** intermodulation noise; cross-modulation/combination-tone distortion; ~ **d'intermodulation par la fréquence de modulation** modulation frequency intermodulation distortion; ~ **dissymétrique** bias distortion; skew; ~ **du front de phase** phase-front distortion; ~ **du spectre de la puissance** power-spectrum deformation; ~ **du temps de montée** rise-time distortion; ~ **du temps de propagation de groupe** envelope-delay distortion; ~ **du temps de transit de groupe** delay distortion; envelope delay; frequency distortion; group distortion; ~ **due aux phénomènes transitoires** transient distortion; ~ **en avance** leading distortion; ~ **en barillet** barrel distortion; ~ **en coussinet** pincushion distortion; pillow distortion; ~ **en drapeau** tearing; ~ **en niveau** gain tracking; ~ **en parallélogramme** skew; ~ **en tonneau** barrel distortion; ~ **en trapèze** keystone distortion; trapezium distortion (of CRT); ~ **fortuite** fortuitous distortion; irregular distortion; chance distortion; jitter; ~ **géométrique** geometrical distortion; ~ **harmonique** harmonic distortion; waveform distortion; amplitude distortion; non-linear distortion; ~ **harmonique totale** overall harmonic distortion; ~ **inhérente** inherent distortion; ~ **irrégulière** fortuitous distortion; chance distortion; jitter; irregular distortion; ~ **isochrone** isochronous distortion; ~ **linéaire** linear distortion; frequency distortion; ~ **linéaire de phase** linear phase distortion; ~ **multimode** multi-mode distortion; ~ **non linéaire** delay distortion; harmonic distortion; non-linear distortion; waveform distortion; amplitude distortion; ~ **oblique** skew; ~ **par écrêtage** clipping; ~ **phase/amplitude** phase-amplitude distortion; ~ **quadratique** quadrature (second-order) distortion; ~ **sur une seule fréquence** harmonic distorsion; ~ **télégraphique** (d'une modulation ou d'une restitution) telegraph distortion (of a modulation or a restitution); ~ **trapézoïdale** keystone distortion; trapezium distortion (of CRT); ~ **unilatérale** bias distortion

distribué adj operating (of lamps); lighted; 'on'

distribuer v spread (over); despatch

distributeur m distributor; despatcher; trunk; selective digit emitter; dispenser; highway; bus; fee handler; allotter; stick (of ICs); driver; sender; ~ **agréé** franchised distributor; licensed dealer; ~ **d'appels** call distributor; allotter; traffic distributor; ~ **d'appels automatique (DAA)** automatic call distributor (ACD); ~ **de billets (dibi)** banknote/bill dispenser; cash-point; ~ **de chercheurs** allotter; ~ **de circuits intégrés** IC

stick (dispenser); chip handler; ~ **de cycles** cycle distributor; ~ **de manchons** sleeve dispenser; ~ **de phase** digit emitter; clock-pulse driver; ~ **de tâches (DDT)** task despatcher; ~ **d'enregistreur** register sender; ~ **d'impulsions** pulse distributor; ~ **lent (DL)** slow driver (SDR); ~ **secteur** mains distribution board; ~ **trois socles** triple outlet

distribution f driving; distribution; spread; broadcasting; ~ **aléatoire** random distribution; ~ **de Poisson** Poisson distribution; ~ **de signaux** signal spread; ~ **des appels** call distribution; ~ **lente (DL)** slow driver (SD); ~ **rapide (DR)** fast driver (FD)

divergence f discrepancy

divers adj incidental; sundry; miscellaneous; ancillary; various; assorted

diversifié adj eclectic; diffuse; all-embracing; universal; diversified

divertissements light entertainment

dividende m antecedent (math.); dividend

diviseur m divider; bleeder; scaler; splitter; consequent (math.); multiplier; divisor; ~ **binaire** binary rate multiplier; ~ **de fréquence** binary rate multiplier; ~ **de fréquence** (d'un oscillateur synchronisé) locked-out frequency divider; ~ **de fréquence à intégration** integrating frequency divider; ~ **de tension** voltage divider; bleeder resistor; volt box; potential divider; Kelvin-Varley slide; ~ **par deux** divide-by-two circuit; (phase) splitter

division f scaling; clearing (of optical fibres); ~ **des positions de temps** split-phase; ~ **du canal** channel splitting

divisionnaire splitting

divulgation f disclosure; communication to third party

dizaine f tens-group

DL (v. distributeur lent)

DM (v. quarte Dieselhorst-Martin)

DMR (v. délai moyen de raccordement)

DNa (v. défaut non accepté)

DND (v. numérotation directe)

DNe (v. défaut non effacé)

document m artwork format; hard copy; document form; ~ **aller-retour** turnaround document; round-trip document; re-entry document; ~ **de base** source document; ~ **en clair** hard copy; plain-language (PL) text; ~ **navette** turnaround document; round-trip document; re-entry document; ~ **tournant** turnaround document; round-trip document; re-entry document

documentation f literature; paperwork; documentation; manual

doigt m finger; pawl; dog; post; peg; stud;

pin; spigot; pointer; ~ **d'arrêt** finger stop; pawl; ~ **d'avance** feed pawl; ~ **de blocage** locking pin; ~ **de sélection** selecting finger; selection pawl; ~ **de verrouillage** locking pin

doigts gris service aisle

domaine *m* field; domain; extent (of file); section; region; range; area; category; ~ **anodique** anode region; ~ **cathodique** cathode region; ~ **d'activité** sphere of interest; ~ **d'application** scope; ~ **de contraste** contrast range; ~ **d'information de signalisation** signal information field; ~ **d'utilisation** safe operating area (S.O.A.)

domino *m* connecting strip (sectional); terminal block; barrier strip

donné *adj* single

donnée *f* datum; bit; signal; data element; ~ **de sortie** output bit; ~ **d'entrée** input bit; ~ **primaire** prime data

données *f pl* data; signals; facts; particulars; ~ **analogiques** analogue data; ~ **brutes** raw data; ~ **communes** common data; ~ **commutables** downstream data; ~ **d'acheminement** routing data; ~ **de configuration** (exchange) configuration data; ~ **de sensibilité** threshold data; ~ **de verrouillage de trame** framing data; ~ **d'entrée immédiate** input data; ~ **échantillonnées** sampled data; ~ **fictives** pseudo-data; dummy data; ~ **invalides** garbage; ~ **liées** linked-list data; ~ **numériques** digital data; numeric(al) data; ~ **particulières** selected data; ~ **permanentes** (semi-)permanent data; ~ **pilotes** master file; ~ **variables** transaction data; ~ **virtuelles** virtual data

donner *v* yield; endow; afford; confer; ~ **la main** give priority (to); ~ **l'image** transmit; convey (e.g. temperature via thermocouple); ~ **naissance à un courant** generate a current

donneur *m* donor

dont (X dont Y) including (Y out of X)

dopage *m* doping

dopant *m* dopant

dosage *m* titration

dossier *m* document file; fact file; ~ **carton** cardboard folder; ~ **d'application** documentation book; ~ **de travail** working document; ~ **des programmes** software file; ~ **d'exploitation** run book

dotation *f* inventory; stock(s)

doté de endowed with

doublage *m* dubbing; ~ **de fréquence** frequency doubling

double *adj* twin; copy; duplicate; back-up; two-way; dual; double; duplex; split; replicated; twofold; ~ **action hétérodyne**

double-super effect; ~ **appel** consultation; enquiry call; consultation hold; consultation call; ~ **appel courtier** (va-et-vient) split call; consultation call (with split); broker's call; call hold flip-flop; hold for enquiry; ~ **appel et transfert** consultation call with transfer; ~ **appel extérieur** consultation call on exchange line; consultation call - incoming; ~ **bande latérale** double sideband; ~ **bascule** dual flip-flop; ~ **changement de fréquence** dual conversion; ~ **coloration** dual colouring (e.g. earth lead); ~ **creuset (DC)** double crucible process (DC); ~ **densité** double density; ~ **face** double-sided; ~ **implantation** duplication; back-up installation; ~ **interligne** double line-spacing; ~ **largeur** double (letter) width; ~ **modulation** double modulation; ~ **multiplexeur-démultiplexeur** differential multiplexer-demultiplexer; ~ **multivibrateur** dual (retriggerable) multivibrator; ~ **précision** double precision; ~ **prise** collision; dual seizure; glare; ~ **sens** bothway; ~ **trace** double beam; dual trace; ~ **trigger de Schmitt** dual 4-input NAND gate; Schmitt trigger; ~ **triode** dual triode

doublé *adj* duplicated; shunted; ~ **par** backed-up by

doublement *m* duplexing; redundancy; replication; ~ **en écriture** slip-repeat

doublet *m* set of two parameters (pair); dipole; diad; doublet; two-bit byte; duplicated operation; ~ **électrique** radiating double dipole; infinitesimal dipole; electric dipole/doublet; ~ **(en) demi-onde** half-wave dipole; ~ **(en) onde entière** full-wave dipole; ~ **magnétique** magnetic doublet radiator; ~ **replié** folded dipole; ~ **replié multiple** multiple folded dipole; ~ **symétrisé par coaxial fendu** slot-fed dipole

doubleur de fréquence frequency doubler; ~ **de tension** voltage doubler; voltage doubling circuit; ~ **de tension pour impulsion de retour** flyback generator

douille *f* bush; insert; socket; barrel; jack; duct; holder; turnbuckle; box spanner; shackle; ~ **à baïonette** bayonet coupling; socket; ~ **d'antenne** aerial jack; ~ **de fusible** fuse clip; fuse contact; ~ **de guidage** screwdriver finder; ~ **de jack** jack bush; jack socket; ~ **de lampe** tube socket; lamp-holder; ~ **femelle** tip jack; ~ **filetée intervis** thread insert (wire type)

douvage *m* application of timber slats (on spool drum)

douzaine *f* twelve-group

DP (v. dépassement de page)

DPMM blown-fuse indicator/tripping con-

D

tact
DR (v. demandeur); ⁓ (v. abonné demandeur); ⁓ (v. distribution rapide)
drageoir *m* bezel; trim; fascia; surround
drain *m* grid leak; drain (of FET, etc); ⁓ **ouvert** bare drain; ⁓ **thermique** heat sink
drainage *m* **électrique** electric drainage; ⁓ **électrique avec réglage aux potentiels négatifs minima** controlled electric drainage; ⁓ **électrique direct** direct electric drainage; ⁓ **électrique polarisé** polarized electric drainage; ⁓ **forcé** forced electric drainage
drap *m* buffing pad
drapeau *m* flag; marker; sentinel; separator; delimiter; boundary marker; mark; blanking plate; ⁓ **bloc** block marker; ⁓ **de structure de trame** frame definition flag; ⁓ **de verrouillage** alignment flag; ⁓ **d'intervention** service flag; ⁓ **fin de bloc** end-of-frame flag; ⁓ **indicateur de défaut** fault flag; ⁓ **intervention** service flag
dresser *v* schedule; draft; compile; plot
drisse *f* halyard; guy; cable; cord; rope
droit *m* entitlement; facility; privilege; right-of-way; clearance; authorization; ⁓ **à la répétition automatique du dernier numéro composé** entitlement to automatic exchange line (PSN) last number redial; ⁓ **à l'aboutement réseau** entitlement to through-connect trunk lines; ⁓ **à l'annotation (DAN)** automatic call-back; automatic camp-on busy extension; ⁓ **au renvoi temporaire** dial-controlled call diversion; ⁓ **au réseau** exchange right-of-way; ⁓ **au verrouillage de poste** outgoing call restriction; ⁓ **aux justifications** itemized billing entitlement; detailed billing facility; ⁓ **de charge** load line
droits d'accès access privileges
ds (dans) in
duodécuple *m* twelve-level multiple; twelves-group
duodiode *f* double diode
duoplex diplex
duplex *adj* duplex; full duplex; go-and-return; ⁓ **intégral** full duplex; ⁓ **par addition** incremental duplex; ⁓ **par opposition** opposition duplex
duplexeur *m* duplexer; ⁓ **à quatre accès** four-port duplexer
duplication *f* dubbing
dupliqué *adj* duplicated
dur *adj* hard-grade (of plastics)
durcir *v* cure; harden; set
durcissement *m* curing; setting; gettering
durcisseur *m* thickening agent; emulsifier; stabilizer; setting compound

durée *f* duration; width (of pulse); length; life; time interval; delay; schedule; ⁓ **à mi-amplitude** half-amplitude duration; ⁓ **à mi-hauteur** half-amplitude duration; ⁓ **d'accord** tuning time; ⁓ **d'activation** time-out; ⁓ **d'affaiblissement d'impulsion** trailing edge; ⁓ **d'appel** call-holding time; ⁓ **d'attente** waiting time; ⁓ **d'attente après numérotation** post-dialling delay; ⁓ **d'attente de tonalité** dial-tone delay; ⁓ **d'autonomie** discharge time (batteries); ⁓ **de communication** call holding time; connect time; ⁓ **de commutation** switching time; ⁓ **de conservation** shelf-life; ⁓ **de conversation** connect time; call time; speech time; speech period; call-holding time; ⁓ **de fonctionnement** run time; ⁓ **de la parole** active active-speech time; ⁓ **de l'émission** duration of transmission; ⁓ **de l'interchiffre** inter-digit pause; ⁓ **de l'occupation de ligne** occupancy; ⁓ **de parcours** transmit time; ⁓ **de perte du verrouillage de trame** out-of-frame alignment time; ⁓ **de présélection** incoming response delay; ⁓ **de prise** call duration; holding time; ⁓ **de reconnaissance** recognition time; ⁓ **de réponse** ringing time; ⁓ **de reprise** settling period; recovery time; ⁓ **de réverbération** reverberation time; ⁓ **de sauvegarde** discharge time (of battery); ⁓ **de sélection** (d'un autocommutateur) (exchange) call set-up delay; ⁓ **de signal** signal duration; ⁓ **de sonnerie** answering delay; ⁓ **de suppression** decay time (of pulse); ⁓ **de traitement** execution time; ⁓ **de vie** shelf life; lifetime; durability; life expectancy; life span; service life; ⁓ **d'échauffement** run-up time; warm-up time; readying time; ⁓ **des manœuvres** circuit operating time; ⁓ **d'établissement** (d'un appel) call set-up time; ⁓ **d'établissement** (d'un autocommutateur) through-connection delay; ⁓ **d'identification** recognition time; ⁓ **d'impulsion** pulse duration; pulse length (t_d); pulse period; pulse time; pulse width; ⁓ **d'occupation** holding time; occupancy time; ⁓ **d'occupation de la voie** channel-busy time; ⁓ **d'une unité** time per unit; ⁓ **en ligne** on-line; connect time; ⁓ **entre révisions** overhaul life; mean time to repair (MTTR); ⁓ **limite de stockage** shelf life; ⁓ **minimale d'abonnement** minimum period of service; ⁓ **moyenne d'appel** average call duration; ⁓ **moyenne de communication** mean (call) holding time; ⁓ **moyenne de la tentative d'appel** (v. durée moyennne de communiation); ⁓ **moyenne des messages** average message service time; ⁓ **moyenne d'occupa-**

tion average holding time; ~ **moyennne de communiation** mean (call) holding time; ~ **prévue** target(ed) schedule; ~ **taxable** chargeable duration; chargeable time; chargeable unit; ~ **taxée** charged duration; ~ **théorique d'un intervalle significatif** (de modulation ou de restitution) theoretical duration of a significant interval (of modulation or restitution)

dureté *f* hardness; temper; toughness; ~ **superficielle** skin hardness

duromètre *m* hardness tester

dus *m* back-order

dynamique *f adj* dynamic range; volatile; volume range; swing; dynamic ratio; contrast range; AC (alternating current); ~ **de sortie** output voltage swing; ~ **porteuse d'avenir** open-ended (system)

dynamo *f* **tachymétrique** tachogenerator

dynamomètre *m* dynamometer; torsion tester; spring balance; torque-meter; force tester

dynode *f* dynode; electron mirror

E

EA (v. écoute amplifiée)

EAN (v. enregistrement automatique des numéros)

EAO (v. enseignement assisté à l'ordinateur)

eau *f* **déminéralisée** de-ionized water (distilled water)

eb (élément binaire) bit; binary digit; ~ **superflu** redundant bit

ébauche *f* blank; cut-out; draft; sketch

ébavurage *m* deburring

ébrèchure *f* fissure; crack

écaillement *m* swelling; flaking; scaling

écart *m* deviation; difference; scatter; drift; dispersion; fluctuation; divergence; variation; spacing; hop; lag; lead; bias; misalignment; departure from the norm; offset; discrepancy; interval; separation; differential; ~ **angulaire** angular run-out (angular misalignment loss); ~ **de capacité** difference of capacity; ~ **de fréquence** frequency deviation; frequency shift; ~ **de fréquence instantané** instantaneous frequency deviation; ~ **de régulation** system deviation; ~ **de temps** lag; lead; ~ **diaphonique** signal-to-crosstalk ratio; ~ **d'isolement** clearance; separation; spacing; ~ **d'ordre** ordering bias; ~ **d'usinage** machining allowance; ~ **en échelon** step deviation/swing; offset deviation; ~ **en fréquence à l'onde porteuse** carrier deviation; ~ **énergétique** (entre deux bandes) energy gap; ~ **entre les courants porteurs** carrier interval; ~ **entre porteuse et bruit** carrier-to-noise ratio; ~ **entre signal et bruit** signal-to-noise ratio; ~ **équivalent** equivalent resistance error; ~ **équivalent corrigé** corrected equivalent resistance error; ~ **faible** minor discrepancy; ~ **intervoies** channel spacing; channel separation; ~ **paradiaphonique** signal-to-near-end crosstalk; ~ **télédiaphonique** signal to far-end crosstalk ratio; ~ **type** standard deviation

écarté *adj* put aside; offset

écartement *m* distance; remoteness; separation; lead pitch; spacing; gap; spread; ~ **des faces** separation; ~ **entre canaux** channel spacing; ~ **équivalent** equivalent separation

écarteur *m* separator

écartométrie *f* angle-error measurement

ECF (enroulement champ fixe) stationary field winding

éch. (v. échelle)

échafaudage *m* scaffolding

échancré *adj* notched; scalloped; indented

échancrure *f* notch; opening; rebate; dent

échange *m* swap; transfer; change; interchange; conversation; transaction; assignment; message; communication; session; handshaking; flow; signalling; dialogue; refurbishment; ~ **d'informations** signalling; ~ **document** document swapping; ~ **entre bâtiments** ship-to-ship signalling; ~ **standard** service exchange; ~ **sur liaison** handshaking; ~ **télégraphique d'informations** telegraph conversation

échanger *v* exchange; interchange; swap; trade

échanges *m pl* signalling; ~ **extérieurs** foreign trade

échangeur *m* exchanger; interchange unit; ~ **de chaleur** heat exchanger; ~ **de refroidissement** heat exchanger

échantillon *m* sample; specimen; ~ **de conversation** speech sample; ~ **de parole** speech sample; ~ **de signal** sample intelligence; ~ **de signal de parole** speech sample; ~ **pour acceptation** acceptance sampling; ~ **reconstitué** reconstructed sample; ~ **témoin** control group; ~ **vocal** speech sample; voice-frequency signal

échantillonnage *m* sampling; strobe (output); quantizing; ~ **adresse** address strobe output; ~ **au hasard** random sampling; ~ **d'acceptation** acceptance sampling; ~ **de voies** channel sampling; ~ **écriture** write strobe output; ~ **et mémorisation** sample-and-hold (function); ~ **lecture** read strobe output

échantillonneur-bloqueur *m* sample-and-hold (circuit)

échappement *m* escape; pitch; character spacing; pad-to-track separation/clearance; ~ **proportionnel** proportional spacing; ~ **standard implicite** default pitch; ~ **transmission** data link escape (DLE)

échauffement *m* heating; reheating; warm-up; ~ **des broches** lead temperature

échéance *f* due date; expiry date; time-table; maturity date; time-out

échéancé subject to fixed (contract) date; timed-out

échéancier *m* scheduler; elapsed time indicator; agenda

échec *m* unsuccessful attempt; failure; ~ **de la transmission** transmission failure

échelle (éch.) *f* scale; schedule; range; sweep; comb; ~ **de mesure** measuring scale; ~ **de nuances** shading scale; (grey) step wedge; tone scale; ~ **de sélectivité** (spectral) response range; ~ **des teintes** grey scale; ~ **fixe** fixed spacer comb; ~ **mobile** switching comb

échelon *m* step; level; grade; rank; ramp; ~ **de quantification** quantizing step; ~ **de vitesse** ramp function; ~ **d'indice** step index

échelonné *adj* graded; stepped; staggered; ranked

échelonnement *m* staggering

échiquier *m* grid; chequerboard

écho *m* echo; ghost; multiple image; clutter; copy; read-back check; reflection; ~ **arrière** backward echo; back echo; ~ **artificiel** feather; ~ **avant** forward echo; ~ **corrigé en amplitude** amplitude-corrected echo; ~ **de câble** cable echo; ~ **de mer** sea clutter; ~ **de pluie** rain clutter; ~ **de sol** ground clutter; ground return; ~ **de vagues** sea clutter; ~ **étranger** extraneous echo; ~ **fictif** dummy echo; ~ **fixe** stationary echo; fixed (target) echo; ~ **indirect** mirror reflection echo; ~ **interne** parasitic echo; ~ **latéral** side echo; ~ **mobile** moving echo; ~ **par nuages** cloud return; ~ **parasite** unwanted echo; clutter; ghost; ~ **permanent** permanent echo; ~ **radioélectrique** radio echo; ~ **rapproché** near echo; ~ **retardé** long-delay echo; ~ **tour de terre** round-the-world echo

échomètre *m* **à impulsions** pulse echometer

échomètre-réflectomètre reflectometer

échométrie *f* echo ranging

échoplex (échoplexage) echoplex

échos à conduction conducted echoes; ~ **à conduction conjuguée** conjugate conducted echoes; ~ **parasites** clutter; ghosting

éclaboussure *f* spatter

éclairage *m* lighting; illumination; ~ **de secours** emergency lighting; ~ **par la tranche** edge lighting

éclairement *m* illumination

éclat *m* surface irregularity

éclaté *adj* remote; distributed; decentralized; unpacked; split; scattered; de-bunched

éclatement *m* scatter; unpacking; bursting; dispersal; explosion; exploded view; distribution; scattering; split; cutaway view; fragmentation; breaking-out (of cable);

disbanding; dissolution; ~ **à l'entrefer** gap scatter; ~ **d'un intervalle** gap scatter

éclater *v* subdivide; distribute; scatter; unpack

éclateur *m* spark gap; discharger; arrester; ~ **à air** air-gap (lightning) arrester; ~ **àétincelle pilote** trigatron; ~ **à étincelles** spark gap; ~ **à étincelles amorties** quenched spark gap; ~ **de jonction(s)** distribution bus; ~ **déclenché** triggered spark gap; ~ **tournant** rotary spark gap

écliptique *f* ecliptic

éclisse *f* fish-plate; fish bar; splice piece; shin

éclosion *f* eruption; outbreak; upsurge

économique *adj* cost-effective; inexpensive; money-saving; beneficial

économiser *v* husband; save

économiseur de lampe dimmer control; ~ *m* **d'énergie** power miser

écoulé *adj* elapsed; flowed; carried; ult. (ultimo)

écoulement *m* **de trafic** handling of calls; traffic flow; traffic handling

écouler *v* elapse (of time); carry; flow; handle

écourté *adj* shortened; reduced; abridged

écoute *f* monitoring; listening-in; tapping; intercepting; eavesdropping; ~ **amplifiée (EA)** speaker-phone (facility); ~ **avec séparation** two-way splitting; ~ **clandestine** eavesdropping; bugging; tapping; ~ **discrète** observing; monitoring; tapping; ~ **préalable** pre-fade listening; ~ **téléphonique** wire-tap

écouter *v* listen; monitor; intercept; tap; eavesdrop

écouteur *m* earphone; headset; receiver; audio monitoring device; listener; ~ **audiométrique** audiometric earphone; ~ **interne** insert earphone

écran *m* screen; phase shield; barrier; display; screen page; monitor; display page; isolating screen; video page; menu; soft copy; ~ **à courte persistance** short-persistence screen; ~ **à longue persistance** long-persistence screen; ~ **à tube cathodique** cathode ray tube (CRT); ~ **absorbant** dark-trace screen; ~ **acoustique** (acoustic) baffle; ~ **aluminisé** aluminized screen; ~ **cathodique** cathode ray tube (CRT); ~ **choix de fonctions** menu (display); ~ **de visualisation** visual display unit; ~ **d'étiquette** transparent label cover; ~ **filtrant** anti-dazzle screen; ~ **graphique** graphic display; ~ **haute résolution** high-definition display; ~ **isolant** separator; shield; screen; ~ **latéral** (sur borne) side screen; ~ **luminescent** ultra-violet screen; ~ **magnétique** magnetic shield; ~ **métallisé** metallized screen;

~ **partagé** split screen; ~ **protecteur** protective screen; ~ **séparé** (v. écran partagé); ~ **thermique** heat shield; ~ **utilisable** usable display area; ~ **vidéo** video display; display page

écrasé *adj* overwritten (of data); deleted

écrasement *m* cancellation; scooping; stubbing (of contacts); overwriting; ~ **système** system crash

écraser *v* discard

écrêtage *m* chopping; clipping; peaking; ~ **avant la modulation** pre-modulation clipping; pre-modulation limiting; ~ **d'impulsions** pulse clipping

écrêteur *m* limiter; AF peak limiter; amplitude clipper; peak sensor; ~ **d'impulsions** pulse clipper; ~ **symétrique** symmetrical clipper

écrire write; enter; input; put (aside)

écriture *f* letters; lettering; writing (in); entry; printing; set; setting; receiving (section of tape store); output (write memory); poke; put; transcription; ~ **avant** write forward; ~ **avec rassemblement** gather-write; ~ **avec regroupement** gather-write; ~ **disque** write to disk; ~ **éclair** flash; form flash; form overlay; ~ **électronique** tele-writing

écrou *m* nut; clamp; collar; ~ **à agrafe** rail fixing nut; ~ **à oreilles** wing nut; ~ **à sertir** crimp nut; clinch nut; ~ **borgne** cap nut; ~ **cage** captive nut; cage nut; inset nut; ~ **clips** fixing nut; ~ **coulissant** sliding clamp; ~ **frein** lock nut; ~ **moleté** cap nut; milled nut; acorn nut; box nut; ~ **Nylstop** [A.C.] stiffnut; ~ **O** wing nut; butterfly nut; thumb nut; ~ **Pal** light-duty lock nut; ~ **prisonnier** cage nut; caged nut; ~ **raccord** coupling nut

écroui *adj* cold-drawn; cold-hammered; cold-rolled; cold-worked

écusson *m* badge

éd. (v. édition;)

EDF (v. Electricité de France)

édité *adj* re-issued; printed out

éditer *v* edit; output; print; issue; format; dump; ~ **une libellé** print; display

éditeur *m* editor; report generator; writer; scriber; ~ **conversationnel** display-based editor; ~ **de bande magnétique** magnetic tape editor; ~ **de documents** document print-out facility; ~ **de liens (EL)** link editor; linkage editor; link loader; patch editor; ~ **de sortie** outscriber; output writer; ~ **de textes** text editor; ~ **d'images** picture editor

édition; (éd.) *f* editing; formatting; issue; output; print(-out); version code; index; dump; dumping; report; revision (rev.); release (rel.)

édition de lancement release version; ~ **des courriers** mail shots; ~ **des liens** (EL) link(age) editing; patch editing; link loading; ~ **sur imprimante** printout; hard copy

éducatique *f* educational technology

effaçage et passage à couleur actuelle clear-to-current colour

effacement *m* deletion; reset; cancellation; erasure; discarding; clearance; blanking out; override; destruction; scratching; obliteration; demodulation effect; modulation suppression; shunting; ~ **automatique d'écran** screen clear; ~ **basse** clearing; ~ **cellule** pad shunting; ~ **dans la ligne** erase in line (EL); ~ **dans la partition** erase in display (ED); ~ **dans la zone** erase in area (EA); ~ **de bits** erase bit pattern; ~ **défaut** fault cancel; fault clearing; ~ **du termineur** hybrid disconnection; ~ **ligne** blanking (of TV); ~ **ligne et trame** horizontal and vertical blanking

effacer *v* clear; erase; delete; scrub; obliterate; purge; scratch; blank; letter-out; rub out; kill

effaceur *m* degausser; ~ **ultra-violet** ultraviolet (UV) eraser

effectif *m* staff; manpower; workforce; personnel; liveware; ~ *adj* actual; absolute; effective; real; prevailing; operative; ~ *m* **du lot** lot size; batch size

effectuer *v* execute; perform; implement; accomplish; ~ **la sommation** combine; sum

effet *m* effect; ~ **Barkhausen** Barkhausen effect (magnetization); ~ **Becquerel** Becquerel (photo-electrolytic) effect; ~ **Compton** Compton effect; ~ **d'antenne** aerial effect; radiation effect; radiation efficiency; vertical effect; ~ **de bruit** Schottky Schottky noise; ~ **de champ** field effect; ~ **de charge superficielle** surface-charge effect (S-effect); ~ **de couplage** mutual induction; ~ **de grêle** shot effect; fluctuation noise; Schottky effect; Johnson noise; ~ **de grenaille** shot-effect; fluctuation noise; Schottky effect; Johnson noise; ~ **de masque** masking; blanket effect; ~ **de nuit** night effect; polarization error; ~ **de peau** skin effect; Kelvin effect; ~ **de persiennes** Venetian blind effect; ~ **de pincement** pinch effect; ~ **de proximité** proximity effect; ~ **de réflexion des bords** edge-reflection effect; ~ **de roue** spoking; ~ **de rupture** pinch effect; ~ **de sablier** hourglass effect; ~ **de scintillation** flicker effect; ~ **de seuil** threshold effect; ~ **de sol** ground effect; ~ **de tassement** packing effect; ~ **de traînage** carrying effect; ~ **d'écho** ghost;

double image; echo effect; ~ **Dellinger** radio fade-out; Dellinger effect; ~ **d'entraînement** knock-on effect; ~ **d'évanouissement** fading effect; ~ **d'îlot** island effect; ~ **directif** directional effect; ~ **directionnel** directional effect; ~ **Doppler** Doppler effect; ~ **Edison** Edison effect; Thomson effect; rectifying effect; thermionic emission; ~ **élasto-optique** elasto-optic effect; ~ **électro-optique** Kerr effect; electro-optical effect; ~ **galvanomagnétique** Hall effect; galvanomagnetic effect; ~ **Hall** Hall effect; galvanomagnetic effect; ~ **Larsen** Larsen effect; acoustic feedback; ~ **local** sidetone; ~ **Luxembourg** ionospheric cross-modulation; Luxemburg effect; ~ **magnéto-optique** magneto-optic(al) effect; ~ **microphonique** microphone effect; acoustic feedback (Larsen effect); ~ **papillon** jitter effect; ~ **pelliculaire** skin effect; Kelvin effect; ~ **Peltier** Peltier (thermo-electric) effect; ~ **photoélectrique** photo-electric effect; ~ **photovoltaïque** photovoltaic effect; ~ **Raman** Raman effect; ~ **redresseur** Edison effect; Thomson effect; rectifying effect; thermionic emission; ~ **résiduel** after-effect; ~ **sonore** sound effect; ~ **thermique** thermal effect; thermal agitation (voltage); ~ **thermoélectrique** thermo-electric effect; Peltier effect; Seebeck effect; ~ **tonneau** rain-barrel effect; ~ **transitoire** transient effect; ~ **trapézoïdal** trapezium effect; ~ **tunnel** tunnel effect

efficace *adj* effective; efficient; operative; virtual (r.m.s.) value; successful; completed; true

efficacité *f* effective bandwidth; efficiency (power handling capacity); feasibility; performance; sensitivity; response; (call) completion rate; ~ **à émission** sending sensitivity; ~ **à réception** receiving sensitivity; ~ **de l'oreille artificielle** sensitivity of the artificial ear; ~ **d'émetteur** emitter injection ratio (efficiency); ~ **d'une cathode thermoélectronique** emission efficiency; ~ **paraphonique** close-talking sensitivity; ~ **relative** relative sensitivity; relative response

efflorescence *f* blooming

effluvage *m* glow discharge

effluve *m* brush discharge; glow discharge; corona

efforcer *v* (s') strive

effort *m* **d'arrachement** pull-off strength; ~ **de compression** compressive stress; ~ **de serrage** clamping force (torque)

effraction *f* intrusion; theft; burglary

égalisateur *m* equalizer; ~ **de niveau** level equalizer; ~ **de ronflement** hum balancer

égalisation *f* line-up; equalization; alignment; match; ~ **adaptative** adaptive equalization; ~ **d'amplitude** amplitude equalizing; ~ **de ligne** line equalization; ~ **des échos** echo matching; ~ **différentielle** differential equalization; ~ **du niveau** level equalization; ~ **du temps de transit de groupe** group-delay equalization

égaliseur *m* equalizer; ~ **auto-adaptatif** automatic adaptive equalizer; ~ **automatique** automatic equalizer; line equalizer; ~ **d'affaiblissement** attenuation equalizer; ~ **de retardation de groupe** group-delay equalizer

égalité *f* match; correspondence; coincidence; equality

éjecter *v* bump; eject

éjecteur *m* knock-out pin (of injection moulding)

éjection *f* **du papier** form feedout; paper throw; form ejection

EL (v. éditeur de liens)

E/L (v. essai aux limites)

élaboration *f* R & D (research and development); generation; creation; formulation; preparation; compiling; ~ **des créneaux d'horloge** generation of clock signals; ~ **des messages** transmission; ~ **du "pas prêt"** "not ready" signal generator; ~ **du produit** product development

élaboré *adj* sophisticated; developed; generated; perfected; refined

élaborer *v* formulate; generate; prepare; produce; compose; establish; compile; evaluate; compute; analyse; process

élancement *m* slenderness (ratio)

élargissement *m* spread; ~ **du spot** deflection defocussing

élargisssement des impulsions pulse spreading

élastance *f* elastance (C/1: unit = daraf)

élasticité *f* yield point (of plastic deformation); proof stress; compliance; ~ **acoustique** acoustic compliance

élastique *adj* elastic; resilient; spring; yielding; compliant

élastomère *m* silicone rubber

électricité *f* electricity; ~ **atmosphérique** atmospheric electricity

Electricité de France (EDF) French national electricity grid; domestic electrical utility

électricité libre free electricity; ~ **statique** static electricity

électrique *adj* electric; electrical

électrisation *f* **d'un gaz** electrification of a gas

électro-aimant *m* solenoid; electromagnet; ~ **de rotation** rotating-field magnet; ~ **im-**

primeur printer magnet; ~ **polarisé** polarized electromagnet; ~ **télégraphique** telegraph electromagnet
électro-aimanter v electromagnetize
électro-analyse f electro-analysis
électrocinétique f electrokinetics
électro-comptable adj tabulating
électrode f electrode; ~ **à capsule** dished electrode; ~ **auxiliaire** auxiliary electrode; ~ **d'accélération** accelerating electrode; ~ **de base** base electrode; ~ **de charge** charge corona unit; ~ **de commande** control electrode; modulation electrode; ~ **de concentration** focussing electrode; ~ **de déclenchement** trigger electrode; ~ **de déviation** deflector plate; deflector; ~ **de focalisation** focussing electrode; ~ **de mise à la masse** earth electrode; ~ **de modulation** modulation electrode; ~ **de post-accélération** intensifier electrode; post-deflection accelerating electrode; ~ **de ralentissement** decelerating electrode; ~ **de sortie** output electrode; ~ **de transmission** carry electrode; ~ **de zéro** reference electrode; ~ **d'entrée** input electrode; ~ **d'entretien** keep-alive electrode; ~ **diviseuse** splitting electrode; ~ **émettrice** emitter electrode; ~ **pilote** pilot electrode; keep-alive electrode; ignitor; trigger electrode; starter
électrodynamique adj electromagnetic
électrofrein m electric brake
électrofuge adj anti-static
électroluminescent adj electroluminescent; light-emitting
électrolyte m electrolyte
électromagnétique adj electromagnetic
électromécanique (EM) electromechanical; analogue; electrical engineering
électroménager m ou adj domestic appliances
électron m electron; ~ **célibataire** lone electron; ~ **de conduction** free electron; conduction electron; ~ **de recul** knock-on electron; recoil electron; ~ **de valence** outer-shell electron; valence electron; ~ **incident** primary electron; ~ **interne** inner-shell electron; ~ **libre** free electron; ~ **lié** bound electron; ~ **optique** outer-shell electron; valence electron; ~ **périphérique** outer-shell electron; valence electron; ~ **primaire** primary electron
électronique f adj electronics; electronic; solid state; ~ **professionnel** business electronics
électrophone m record player; turntable; gramophone; phonograph
électropince f clamp meter
électrotechnique f electrical engineering
électro-vanne (EV) f electro-valve; solenoid
électro-ventilateur m electric fan; blower; cooling unit

élément m subassembly; element; component; unit; cell; module; item; material (of program); level; entry; bit; character; detail; subsystem; constituent; part; stage (of circuit); ingredient; ~ **à dix encoches** ten-fibre element; ~ **actif** active aerial; driven aerial; exciter; primary radiator; driven radiator; ~ **anticoïncidence** anti-coincidence element (inclusive-OR gate); non-equivalence circuit; biconditional operation; EXCEPT; equality; ~ **asymétrique d'un circuit** asymmetrical circuit element; ~ **binaire** (eb) bit; binary digit; ~ **binaire de bourrage** stuffing bit; ~ **binaire d'imparité** odd parity bit; ~ **bistable** flip-flop module; ~ **chauffant** heater element; ~ **d'accumulateur** accumulator cell; battery; ~ **dans l'espace radar** radar cell; ~ **d'antenne** aerial element; ~ **de base** basic cell; ~ **de batterie** cell; ~ **de câble** conductor; core; ~ **de chauffage** heating element; ~ **de circuit** circuit element; component; ~ **de code** code element; unit; ~ **de contact** contact element; sense switch; ~ **de cristal** crystal element; ~ **de filerie** (cable) trunking; ~ **de fixation** fastener; ~ **de forme d'onde du signal** (line) signal waveform element; ~ **de goulotte** trunking; ~ **de modulation** restitution element; modulation element; ~ **de parité** parity bit; ~ **de rechange** spare; replacement part; ~ **de réglage** (core) adjuster (of pot core); ~ **de réglage en ferrite** (ferrite) core adjuster; ~ **de restitution** restitution element; ~ **de sélection de groupe (ESG)** group selection unit (GSU); ~ **de sélection de joncteurs (ESJ)** trunk selection unit (TSU); ~ **de sélection de ligne (ESL)** line switching unit (LSU); ~ **de sélection intermédiaire (ESI)** intermediate selection unit (ISU); ~ **de signal** signal element; signal component; digit; ~ **de signal composite** compound signal element; ~ **de signal télégraphique** telegraph signal element; ~ **de signal télégraphique à courant double** double-current mark; ~ **de signal utile** valid signal element; ~ **de surélévation** stand-off; plinth; ~ **de surface** patch; ~ **de temporisation** delay element; ~ **de trame** time slot; ~ **détecteur** sensing element; ~ **d'image** picture element; ~ **droit** straight section (of waveguide); ~ **enfichable** plug-in module; ~ **fusible** fuse link; ~ **logique** functor; ~ **majoritaire** majority element; ~ **numérique** digit; bit; ~ **numérique de justification** justifying digit; stuffing bit; ~ **numérique de service** service digit;

service bit; housekeeping bit; ~ **numérique de service de justification** housekeeping stuffing bit; ~ **passif** parasitic aerial; parasitic radiator; passive aerial; radiation-coupled reflector; secondary radiator; ~ **photochimique** Becquerel cell; photo-electrolytic cell; photochemical cell; ~ **porteur central** central strength member; ~ **primaire** primary radiator; driven element; active aerial; exciter; ~ **rayonnant primaire** primary radiator; driven element; active aerial; exciter; ~ **réfléchissant** reflector; ~ **réflecteur** reflector; ~ **secondaire** secondary radiator; parasitic aerial; passive aerial; ~ **semiconducteur Impatt** impact avalanche transit device; IMPATT device; ~ **transmetteur** sensing element (of strain gauge); ~ **unitaire** unit element; ~ **unitaire de signal télégraphique** single-current mark

élémentaire adj primary; basic; fundamental; elementary; primitive

éléments binaires par seconde bits per second; ~ **de répertoire** directory entries; ~ **de signalisation à la réception** receiver signal element timing; ~ **de signalisation à l'émission** transmitter signal element timing; ~ **en cascade** tandem connection of items; ~ **numériques de service** service digits; ~ **parasites** effective noise source; stray capacitance

élévation f **à une puissance** exponentiation; rise

éliminateur m destaticizer; frictional machine; induction machine; electrostatic generator; influence machine; suppressor

élimination f shorting out; disconnection; rejection; suppression; deletion; removal; dropping; stripping; discarding; disposal; ~ **de bande** band rejection; band elimination; ~ **de fichier** file purge; ~ **de la fréquence image** image frequency rejection; ~ **de l'affaiblissement de filtre** filter attenuation compensation; ~ **de parasites** interference suppression; ~ **des lignes isolées** widow adjust; ~ **d'interférence** disturbance elimination; interference suppression

éliminer v delete; eliminate; stop; reject; discard; ~ **les perturbations** de-noise

éloigné adj remote; far-end; distant

éloignement m receding; recession

EM (v. électromécanique); **≈** (électromagnétique) electromagnetic (relay)

émaillage m enamel glaze

émaillé parallèle sous filin de soie sd (soudé) (EP) enamel-insulated (wire) with silk identification thread

emballage m (secondary/outer) packaging; wrapping; ~ **global** outer packaging; bulk delivery packaging; ~ **particulier** individual packaging; ~ **perdu** non-returnable packaging

emballement m thrashing; ~ **thermique** thermal runaway

embarqué adj on-board (of PCB components); shipborne

embase f (connecteur fixe) mounting base; plinth; flange; connector; receptacle; bottom plate; socket; cable-mounting socket/receptacle; frame-mounting socket/receptacle; ~ **à fixation par écrou** jam nut receptacle; ~ **à piquer** (sur CI) PCB-mounting socket; receptacle; ~ **mâle** shrouded (chassis) plug; I.E.C. mains plug

embauche f engagement; recruitment; hiring

emboîtement m nesting

emboîter v plug in; nest

embouchure f mouthpiece; aperture; mouth

embout m adaptor; end-piece; ferrule; tip; bush; fitting lug; nipple; connector; bung; coaster; coupling; stopper; pad; stub; bumper; cap; insert; ~ **de fusible** fuse cap; ~ **de visseuse** bit holder (of power driver); ~ **pour câble** cable end

embouteillage m swamping; overcrowding; congestion; jam; jamming; blocking; bottleneck

emboutissage m swaging; stamping; pressing; punching; lamination; drawing; dishing; embossing; ~ **(ERICHSEN)** Erichsen dishing test; ~ **à flans bloqués** (drop) stamping (with matching fixed dies)

embouts protégés plated caps (of fuse)

embranchement m branch (connection)

embrayeur m selecting finger

embrochable board-mounting; surface-mounting; plug-in

embrochage m series mounting; wiring

embrouillage m scrambling

embrouiller v scramble

embrouilleur m scrambler

Emc (v. excursion en mode commun)

émetteur m ou adj emitter; transmitter; sender; radiator; signal generator; issuing; originator; source; sending; keyer; repeater; signalling; forwarding; beacon; station; ~ **à arc** (Poulsen) arc converter; ~ **à bande latérale unique** single-sideband transmitter; ~ **à bande perforée** tape transmitter; ~ **à bandes latérales indépendantes** independent sideband transmitter; ~ **à clavier** keyboard transmitter; ~ **à cylindre** drum transmitter; ~ **à fréquence fixe** fixed-frequency transmitter; ~ **à fréquence variable** wide-band sweep transmitter; ~ **à fré-**

quences préréglées multifrequency transmitter; ~ à numéroter automatique automatic numbering transmitter; auto-dialler; ~ à ondes courtes short-wave transmitter; ~ à ondes longues long-wave transmitter; ~ à plat flat-bed transmitter; ~ à plusieurs porteuses multicarrier transmitter; ~ à suppression de porteuse suppressed carrier transmitter; ~ arythmique start-stop transmitter; ~ autocommandé automatic transmitter; ~ automatique automatic transmitter/key; ~ automatique à commande par impulsion automatic transmitter with controlled tape-feed mechanism; ~ automatique d'indicatif answer-back unit; ~ auto-oscillateur self-excited transmitter; ~ auxiliaire de signalisation interchange signalling sender; ~ avec distorsion distortion signal generator; ~ brouilleur interfering transmitter; ~ clandestin illicit transmitter; clandestine transmitter; ~ clavier keysender; ~ commun common emitter; grounded emitter; ~ d'appel automatique automatic calling unit (ACU); automatic calling equipment (ACE); ~ d'appoint auxiliary transmitter; gap filler; ~ d'avion airborne transmitter; ~ DC DEC (number) sender; decadic sender; ~ de cadence (cadence) tapper; ~ de Chireix Chireix transmitter; ~ de clavier keysender; ~ de détresse emergency sender; ~ de détresse maritime ship's emergency transmitter; ~ de données data transmitter; ~ de faible portée short-haul transmitter; ~ de ligne line driver; ~ de l'indicatif answer-back unit; ~ de lumière light emitter (laser source); ~ de radioguidage à signaux équilibrés localizer beacon; ~ de relais translator; repeater station; relay station; ~ de réserve standby transmitter; ~ de réserve actif active standby transmitter; ~ de signalisation signal sender; ~ de télétaxe own-premises meter; pulse transmitter; ~ de télévision portatif pack-carrier television station; mobile television station; ~ décimal decadic sender; ~ différentiel differential voltage transmitter; ~ d'images fixes still-picture transmitter; ~ d'impulsions impulse sender; pulse emitter; key pad; key sender; ~ d'indicatif answer-back unit; ~ directionnel beam transmitter; ~ d'ordres talk-back circuit; speak-back circuit; radio control transmitter; ~ du trajet d'atterrissage glide-path beacon; ~ en service operating transmitter; ~ HF (à hyperfréquence) radio transmitter; ~ linéaire optically aligned emitter; ~ manuel à cinq touches five-key transmitter; ~ mo-

bile mobile transmitter; ~ Morse Morse sender; ~ multiplex multiplex transmitter; ~ multiplex à répartition dans le temps time-division multiplex transmitter; ~ optique optical emitter; light source; ~ pilote master transmitter; parent station; challenger; interrogator; ~ piloté driven transmitter; ~ Poulsen Poulsen arc converter; ~ pour hyperfréquences à modulation d'amplitude amplitude-modulated VHF transmitter; ~ radioélectrique radio transmitter; ~ radioélectrique à plusieurs canaux multichannel radio transmitter; ~ radioélectrique de son de télévision television sound transmitter; ~ radioélectrique multiple multiple transmitter; ~ radiogoniométrique direction-finding transmitter; ~ relais link transmitter; re-broadcast transmitter; repeater; ~ relayeur link transmitter; re-broadcast transmitter; repeater; ~ télégraphique telegraph transmitter; ~ télégraphique à bande perforée tape transmitter; ~ vidéo video transmitter
émetteur-récepteur transceiver; regenerative repeater; pulse repeater; converter; ~ asservi par impulsions transponder; ~ combiné transceiver; ~ de ligne bus transceiver; ~ en bande de base baseband converter; ~ portatif walkie-talkie
émetteurs sur ondes égales simultaneous broadcasting transmitters
émettre v transmit; emit; send; key; generate; radiate; read (of message relay system); issue; ~ des impulsions outpulse
EMG (v. équipement de modulation de groupe primaire)
émidyne f emitter follower
émission f transmission; conveying; issuing; outpulsing; despatching; sending; reading (of message relay system); originating; emitting; logging; output; on (of tones); down link; go path; generating; programme; broadcast; ~ à bande latérale résiduelle vestigial-sideband transmission; ~ à bande latérale unique single-sideband transmission; ~ à bandes latérales indépendantes independent-sideband transmission; ~ à double bande latérale double-sideband transmission; ~ à porteuse réduite reduced-carrier transmission; ~ à porteuse supprimée suppressed-carrier transmission; ~ actuelle topical programme; ~ au clavier key-sending; ~ automatique automatic telegraphy; ~ de l'étranger relay from abroad; overseas relay; ~ de télévision telecast; TV broadcast; ~ de télévision en direct live TV transmission; ~ didactique educational broadcast; schools broadcast;

~ **dirigée** directional transmission; ~ **du signal de télétaxe** metering pulse transmission; ~ **électronique** electron emission; ~ **multiple d'un programme à fréquences multiples** diagonalizing; ~ **radioélectrique** radio transmission; ~ **sous plusieurs angles** multi-path transmission; ~ **spontanée** spontaneous emission; ~ **sur bande interdite** spurious radiation; ~ **télégraphique** telegraph transmission; ~ **télévisée** telecast; television broadcast; ~ **thermionique** thermionic emission; ~ **thermoélectronique** thermionic emission

émission-réception (E/R) send/receive; TX/RX; up/down; ~ **automatique** automatic send-receive (ASR)

emmagasinage *m* storage; reading in (of data); input to memory; recording; (data) logging

emmagasiner *v* store

emmanché dur press fit

emmanchement *m* **dur** press fit; ~ **juste** transition fit

empattement serif

empiètement *m* displacement; spread

empilage *m* stack; sandwich; laminations; tier; accumulation; pile-up (of relay contacts)

empilement *m* sandwiching; stacking; push-up

emplacement *m* (memory) location; (cell) position; space; site; slot; ~ **(de) mémoire** memory location; cell position; ~ **défectueuse** bad spot; bad location; bad cell position; ~ **d'un bit** bit location; ~ **privilégié** protected (location)

emplacements contigus consecutive locations

emploi *m* use; usage; application; job

empreinte *f* imprint; embossment; stamp; mould; (moulding) shell; ~ **(de fonction)** signature

emprunter (un circuit) pass via; trace a path through (of circuit); traverse

émulateur *m* emulator; control unit; clone

émuler *v* emulate

en reset

EN (v. entrée de procédure)

encadré *adj* inset

encadrement *m* bezel; trim; framing; management; supervisory staff; sponsorship;

encaissement *m* (coin) collection

encaisseur *m* **de monnaie** coin box

encastré *adj* flush-mounted; inset; recessed; couched; anchored; clamped; built-in; integral; incorporated; embedded; countersunk; secure; bracket-mounted

enceinte *f* chamber; enclosure; cabinet; enclosed space; ~ (à thermostat) crystal oven; ~ (régulée en T°) (heated) enclosure;

oven; ~ **acoustique** (loud-)speaker cabinet; ~ **acoustique à voies multiples** composite loudspeaker; ~ **essais climatiques** climatic test enclosure; ~ **isotherme** crystal oven

enchaînement *m* interconnection; chaining; sequencing; cascade; (con)catenation; linking; reeling; itemization; next-function stringing; linkage; scheduling; call progress; interworking; path; catena; allocation of run time; binding; continuity; threading; scheduling; ~ (de programmes) suite (of programs); ~ **de segments** call link; ~ **de tâches** task scheduling; ~ **en radiodiffusion** continuity

enchaîner append; concatenate; catenate; chain; string; cascade

enchevêtrement *m* welter; tangle; entanglement

enclenchement *m* interlock; switching-in; lock-in

enclencher *v* trigger; activate; start; set off; pick up; couple; close (of contacts); throw (of switch); operate (of relay); engage; set (of flip-flop)

encliquetage *m* snap-fitting

enclume *f* bar (of printer head)

encoche *f* notch; groove; slot; polarizing recess; ~ **de protection en écriture** write-protect notch/hole

encombré congested; overloaded

encombrement *m* overall dimensions; congestion; floor space (usage/requirements); size; contention; space occupied; geometry (of PCB); bandwidth; ~ **mémoire** memory size; ~ **spectral réduit** reduced bandwidth (of quad PSK)

encrage *m* inking

encrasser *v* clog

encre *f* toner; ~ **conductrice** electromagnetic ink; ~ **siccative** quick-drying ink

endroit *m* cell position; memory location; ~ **défectueux** bad spot

enduit *m* coat; coating; layer; dressing

endurance *f* life; viability; fatigue limit; ~ **au choc de courant maximal** endurance at maximum impulse current

énergie *f* power; energy; force; capacity; ~ (en dBm) transmission level; power level; ~ **au zéro absolu** zero-point energy; ~ **cinétique** kinetic energy; ~ **d'activation des impuretés** impurity activation energy; ~ **de servitude** power supplies; ~ **dénaturante** aliasing energy; ~ **d'entrée** input (power); ~ **des signaux vocaux** speech signal power; ~ **d'excitation** excitation energy; ~ **d'ionisation** ionization energy; ~ **électrique** electrical power; ~ **magnétisante** magnetic field strength; magnetizing

E

force; magnetic field intensity; ~ **mécanique** work (energy, heat); ~ **potentielle** potential energy; ~ **radiante** radiant energy; ~ **rayonnante** radiant energy; ~ **résiduelle** settling time; ~ **tertiaire** tertiary power supplies (of converters); ~ **transitoire** surge voltage; ~ **volumique acoustique totale instantanée** instantaneous sound-energy density

énergies nouvelles alternative energy sources

enfermé *adj* enclosed

enfichable *adj* plug-in; detachable; patching

enfichage *m* patching; plugging in; insertion; field-replaceable; connectorized; plug-ended; ~ **sur ligne occupée** overplugging

enfiché *adj* plugged-in; patched; inserted

enficher *v* plug in; insert; patch

enfilage *m* threading; stringing

enfin et surtout last but not least

enfoncement *m* nip; dimple; pit

enfoncer *v* depress; engage; press

engagé *adj* in contact (with); linked; joined; in service; connected; seized

engagement *m* free/busy condition

engendrer *v* generate; be derived from

engin *m* missile; drone; rocket; projectile; probe; ~ **d'aiguillage** duct rodding equipment; ~ **radioguidé bord-air** ship-air guided missile; ~ **téléguidé d'avion** aircraft guided missile; ~ **téléguidé sol-air** ground-air guided missile

engorgement *m* obstruction; congestion; overrun; contention (of lines); bottleneck

engrenage *m* **de synchronisation** timing gear

engrener *v* mesh; intermesh; engage

enjoliveur *m* trim; bezel; escutcheon; sash

enlever *v* remove; delete

énoncé *m* statement; formulation

enr. (v. enregistreur)

enrayage *m* (card) jam

enregistrement *m* recording; posting; writing; booking; logging; storing; storage; record; setting; recorded programme; order placed; indexing; spooling; ~ **à amplitude constante** constant amplitude recording; ~ **automatique des numéros (EAN)** automatic number identification (ANI); ~ **automatique du numéro d'appel** automatic repeat dialling; ~ **d'annulation** deletion record; ~ **de détail** change record; amendment record; transaction record; ~ **de données** data record; ~ **de mouvement** change record; amendment record; transaction record; ~ **de norme** (date of) issue of standard; ~ **de trafic** call-count record; traffic record; ~ **d'en-tête** header record; ~ **des erreurs** error logging; ~ **des justificatifs de taxe** local automatic message accounting (LAMA); ~ **direct** direct recording; live recording; ~ **du son** sound recording; ~ **du trafic** traffic recording; ~ **d'un message reçu** call answering; ~ en différé spooling; store-and-forward; ~ **et calcul automatique** automatic message recording and accounting; ~ **logique** unit record; logical record; ~ **magnétique longitudinal** longitudinal magnetization; ~ **numérique** stored (physical) record; ~ **numérique de mesure** digital measurement recorder; ~ **par faisceau électronique** electron-beam recording; ~ **physique** stored record; ~ **sur bande** tape recording; ~ **sur disque** disk recording; ~ **taxe** charge recording

enregistrer *v* record; log; write; store; register; post; down-load

enregistreur (enr.) *m* recorder; logging device; register; data logger; chart recorder; graphic instrument; ~ **à décalage** shift register; ~ **à siphon** siphon recorder; ~ **àstylet** ink recorder; ink writer; inker; ~ **automatique** (v. enregistreur chronologique automatique); ~ **chronologique automatique** logger; ~ **d'appels infructueux** overflow meter; ~ **d'arrivée** terminating register; ~ **de départ** originating register; sender; ~ **de dérangements** fault recorder; docket printer; alarm logger; ~ **de données** data logger; ~ **de fautes** fault recorder; docket printer; alarm logger; ~ **de graphiques** (strip) chart recorder; ~ **de niveau** level recorder; ~ **de son** sound recorder; ~ **de trafic** traffic recorder; ~ **de transit** transit register; ~ **magnétique** magnetic recorder; ~ **mécanique** mechanical recorder; ~ **multiple de départ** call handling processor; ~ **R2 arrivée** incoming R2 register; ~ **sonore** sound recorder; ~ **sur disque** disk recorder; ~ **X-Y** X-Y plotter; data plotter

enregistreur-traducteur register-translator

enrichissement *m* upgrading; refinement; enhancement

enrobage *m* encapsulation; conformal coating; cladding; jacket (of fibre cable); potting; ~ **par fluidisation** powder coating

enrobé *adj* covered; coated; clad; packaged; encapsulated; dipped; ~ **fluidisé** (epoxy-resin) dipped

enroulé en hélice wound spirally; coiled

enroulement *m* winding; coil; balancing coil; wire-wrap; ~ **à cage d'écureuil** squirrel-cage winding; ~ **à pas entier** diametral winding; ~ **à plusieurs couches** multilayer winding; ~ **amortisseur** damper/damping (winding) grid; ~ **bifilaire** two-wire wind-

ing; **~ champ fixe** (ECF) stationary field winding; **~ d'amortissement** damping winding; **~ de commande** advance winding; control turn; control winding; signal winding(s); **~ de compensation** compensation winding; **~ de désaimantation** demagnetizing winding; **~ de l'induit** armature winding; armature coil; **~ de maintien** locking winding (of relay); **~ de réaction** feedback winding; **~ d'excitation** exciting winding; **~ différentiel** differential compound winding; **~ en fond de panier** chain winding; **~ en nid d'abeille** honeycamb winding; **~ en série** series winding; **~ inducteur** exciting winding; **~ ondulé** wave winding; **~ parallèle** shunt winding; parallel winding; **~ polyphasé** polyphase winding; **~ primaire** primary winding; line winding; input winding; **~ secondaire** secondary winding; **~ supérieur** (en demi-alternance) forward winding; advance winding; **~ sur gabarit** diamond winding
enrouleur m **de bande** tape winder; take-up spool
enrubannage m tape
enseignement m **assisté à l'ordinateur (EAO)** computer-assisted teaching (CAT); **~ automatisé** CAI (computer-aided instruction)
ensemble m installation; equipment; set; group; kit; unit; assembly; array; package; total; system; cluster; aggregate; one or more; circuitry; subsystem; complex; conglomerate; assortment; collection; convoy; integral; whole; combination; plant; repertoire; (statistical) population; suite (of programs); **~ constitué** (integral) PCB assembly; **~ d'antennes** aerial array; **~ de caractères** character set; font; **~ de données** data set; data array; (data) field; data unit; **~ de filtrage** executive-secretary system; manager-secretary system; director/chief-secretary system; ripple filter; smoothing circuit; **~ de programmes d'une application** applications package; **~ d'éléments directeurs** director; **~ fonctionel** sub-system; **~ hiérarchisé de programmes de traitement** hierarchical set of processing routines; **~ industriel** industrial plant; **~ logiciel** software package; **~ logique** processing subsystem; **~ moto-réducteur** motor gearbox assembly; **~ prise billets** bill pick-off unit; plucker
ensemblier m project management
ensimage m sizing
entâché d'erreurs error-prone
enterré adj buried; underground
en-tête m heading; header
entier adj complete; whole; intact; integral;

~ (nombre **~**) integer; **~ non signé** unsigned integer
entière discrétion sole discretion
entièrement duplex full duplex
entité f item
entourage m framework; surround
entraide(s) m inter-aid; mutual aid; take-over facilities; inter-exchange links; inter-working; remote power feed (RPF)
entraînement m drive; tractor feed; feed; traction; run; training; tracking; transport; **~ à vitesse constante** constant speed drive (CSD); **~ croix de Malte** Geneva drive; **~ de papier** chart drive; **~ du sélecteur** selector drive; **~ par ergots** sprocket feed; pin feed; **~ par roues à picots** sprocket feed
entraîner v entail; incur
entraîneur m **papier** paper-feed sprocket
entrance f fan-in
entrant adj inward; incoming (I/C)
entr'axe m spacing; pitch; centre-to-centre distance; **~ des pattes** lead-to-lead distance
entre centraux adj inter-exchange; inter-office
entre-axe m (entr'axe) pitch; spacing; centre-to-centre distance; **~ de fixation** fixing centre
entre-bloc m inter-block gap (IBG); inter-record gap (IRG)
entrée f inlet; input; entrance; ingress; entry; receipt; storage; shift-in (SI); input port; driver; access; admission; intake; loading; driving point; **~ analogique** analogue input; **~ d'antenne** lead-in; aerial input; **~ d'antenne asymétrique** asymmetrical aerial input; **~ d'antenne symétrique** symmetrical aerial input; **~ de commande** control input; **~ de données** data entry; digital input; **~ de données et réponse vocale** digital input - voice answerback (DIVA); **~ de poste** lead-in; **~ de procédure (EN)** procedure-oriented input; **~ de transfert** gate (G); **~ décalage série droite** data shift right; **~ décalage série gauche** data shift left; **~ d'inhibition** override function; **~ d'onde sinusoïdale** sine-wave input; **~ en ligne** intrusion; **~ en tiers** third-party entry; barge-in; call offering; break-in; intrusion; cut-in; (executive) override facility; **~ en tiers prioritaire** override; executive busy override; executive right-of-way; **~ initialisation** reset input; **~ inversée** inverting input; **~ inverseuse** inverting input; **~ logique** sense input; digital input; **~ non inversée** non-inverting input; **~ non inverseuse** non-inverting input; **~ son** audio input; speech input; **~ tout ou rien** on-off telegraphy; **~ utile** access area; **~ vocale** speech input

entre-enregistrement *m* (inter)block gap; inter-record gap

entrée/sortie (E/S) input/output (I/O); interface

entrefaces *f pl* **d'entrée/sortie** interface functions

entrefer *m* gap; head gap; air gap; flux gate; ~ (d'un relais) residual air gap; ~ **de travail** active air gap; air gap

entrepositaires cash-and-carry (stores)

entrepreneur *m* contractor; businessman

entreprise *f* **de télécommunications** common (communications) carrier

entretenir *v* service; sustain

entretien *m* servicing; maintenance; upkeep; ~ **correctif** remedial maintenance; ~ **courant** routine maintenance; ~ **du réseau de transmission** transmission maintenance work; ~ **en cours d'usage** day-to-day upkeep; routine servicing; ~ **préventif** preventive maintenance; ~ **téléphonique** telephone conversation

entretoise *f* insulating bush; grommet; spacer; strut; brace; wedge; chock; shim; separator; distance piece; reinforcement; ~ **transistor** transistor pad

entre-touches lands (of micrometer)

énumération *f* census

enveloppe *f* jacket; casing; shroud; bulb; envelope; sheathing; enclosure; cladding; lobe; sleeve; window; insulation; ceiling; shell; wrapper; compass; mantle; ~ (paquet de 544 bits) 544-bit packet (envelope); ~ **antidéflagrante** flameproof enclosure; ~ **de la modulation** modulation envelope; ~ **de l'âme** core wrap; ~ **de transmission** transmission envelope; ~ **du signal** signal envelope; ~ **lisse** smooth jacket; ~ **ondulée** corrugated jacket; ~ **verrouillée en permanence** permanently-locked envelope

environnant *adj* prevailing; surrounding

environnement *m* background; (economic) climate

envoi *m* despatch; transmission; conveyance; sending; signalling; out-pulsing; report; message; shipment; consignment; ~ **avec chevauchement** overlap out-pulsing; ~ **de la position curseur** cursor position report (CPR); ~ **de sonnerie** transmission of ringing current; ~ **des signaux au clavier** keysending; key pulsing; ~ **différé ou à l'heure fixe** advance calling; ~ **d'un message différé** advance calling; ~ **en arrière** backward signalling

envoyer *v* send; despatch; convey; transmit; apply; read in; ~ **des impulsions** out-pulse

envoyeur *m* sender; out-sender; coder; ~ **d'appel** ringing current transmitter

envoyez antépénultime send last but two digit; ~ **le chiffre suivant** send next digit; ~ **précédent** send last but one digit; ~ **précédent l'antépénultime** send last but three digit

eólien *adj* wind

EP (v. émaillé parallèle sous filin de soie sd (soudé))

épaisseur *f* **de conduit** duct thickness

épanouissement *m* fanning(-out); dispersal; fulfilment

épargne *f* thrift; economy; land gap (of PCB)

épaulé *adj* ridged; profiled

épaulement *m* stand-off; kneck; rounded tip; spur; ridge; boss; rib

épavé *adj* wrecked; derelict; abandoned

EPD (v. équipement périphérique distant)

éphasage *m* phase shift

épine *f* **dorsal** backbone

épisodique *adj* transient

épisser *v* splice

épissurage *m* splicing; ~ **de masse** mass splicing

épissure *f* splice; splicing; ~ **collective** multi-fibre splicing (mass splicing); ~ **multifibres** (v. épissurage de masse)

épitaxie *f* epitaxy; ~ **liquide** liquid epitaxy

épouser *v* marry; interlock

épreuve *f* test; trial; proving; proof; ~ **de charge** load test; ~ **de sensibilité** sensitivity test

éprouver *v* check-out; diagnose; test

éprouvette *f* specimen; test piece; test tube; test coupon (of PCB)

épuisé *adj* exhausted; depleted; out of stock; out of print

épuisement *m* depletion; ~ (de temporisation) time-out

épurateur *m* suppressor

épuration *f* audit (of files); data purification; decontamination

épure *f* drawing; diagram; definitive design

épuré *adj* cleaned

équarriseur *m* square-wave (generator)

équerre *f* bracket; angle iron; armature (of coil); ~ **à centrer** centring square; ~ **métallique à chapeau** metal square with beam

équidirective *adj* isotropic

équilibrage *m* neutralization; balancing; matching; offset null; equalizing; tuning out/neutralizing (of load reactance); ~ **actif** active balancing; ~ **de canal** channel balancing; ~ **de circuits** balancing of circuits; ~ **de résistance** resistance matching; resistance balancing; ~ **de trafic** traffic balancing; ~ **des termineurs** hybrid balance network; ~ **d'impédance** impedance match-

E

ing; ~ **zéro** null-point detection
équilibrateur m balancing network
équilibre m balance; break-even; trade-off;
~ **différentiel** double-ended
équilibré adj balanced; trimmed; compensated; equalized; neutralized
équilibrer v trim; balance; match
équilibreur m balancing network (circuit); line impedance; line balance; hybrid set; counterweight; balance; building-out circuit; building-out section; ~ **avant-arrière** fader; ~ **de ligne aérienne** open-wire balancing network
équilibromètre m impedance unbalance measuring set; return loss measuring set
équipage m crew; ship's company; ~ **mobile** moving coil
équipe f shift; workshift; team; crew; gang; syndicate
équipé adj populated; installed; equipped; fitted
équipement m equipment; installation; fitting out; plant and equipment; equipping; fixtures; subsystem; gear; appointment(s); system; ~ **à courant porteur pour lignes d'abonnés** subscriber carrier equipment; ~ **à fréquences vocales** voice frequency equipment; ~ **au sol** ground equipment; ~ **bivocal** speech-plus-duplex equipment (S + D); ~ **commun** common equipment; ~ **d'abonné** subscriber-loop equipment; line circuit; ~ **de codage par ligne d'abonné analogique** per-line codec; ~ **de commande** control equipment; ~ **de commutation automatique** automatic switching equipment; ~ **de contrôle** monitoring equipment; ~ **de ligne** subscriber-loop equipment; line circuit; ~ **de ligne à pot compensé** line unit with magnetic biasing; ~ **de ligne à signalisation par changement d'état** three-state line unit; ~ **de ligne longue** loop extender; ~ **de modulation** translating equipment; ~ **de modulation de groupe primaire (EMG)** group modulating equipment (GME); ~ **de modulation de voie** channel translating equipment (CTE); ~ **de multiplexage** multiplexing equipment; ~ **de multiplexage MIC PCM** multiplex equipment; ~ **de multiplexage numérique** digital multiplex equipment; ~ **de parasitage** interference suppression equipment; ~ **de protection contre les erreurs** error control equipment; ~ **de raccordement** concentrator; connecting equipment; ~ **de raccordement d'abonné** network circuit terminating equipment (NCTE); ~ **de réponse multiple** multiple answering equipment; ~ **de secours** standby equipment;

~ **de télécommunication** ground communications equipment (GCE); ~ **de transcodage** code converter; ~ **de transfert de groupe primaire** group modulating equipment (GME); ~ **de transmission par porteuse monovoie** single-channel-per-carrier (SCPC); ~ **de transposition de fréquence** up and down converters; ~ **de transposition de voie** channel modulator; channel translating equipment; ~ **de transposition du groupe primaire** group translating equipment; group modulating equipment (GME); ~ **de voie** channel equipment; ~ **de voie complémentaire** channel-associated equipment; ~ **d'émission mobile** mobile transmission equipment; ~ **d'essai** test equipment; ~ **d'essais systématiques** routiner; ~ **d'extrémité de voie de données** data circuit terminating equipment (DTE); ~ **d'extrémité de voies** channel bank; ~ **d'extrémité MIC** PCM channel bank; ~ **d'infrastructure** capital equipment; producer goods; plant; installed base; ~ **duplex à pont** bridge duplex system; ~ **intermédiaire** intermediate equipment; ~ **modulation de voie** channel translating equipment (CTE); ~ **multiplex numérique** digital carrier equipment; ~ **périphérique** peripheral equipment; hardware; ~ **périphérique distant (EPD)** remote peripheral equipment (RPE); ~ **sous test (EST)** equipment under test; ~ **téléphonique** telephone equipment; ~ **terminal** terminal circuit; outside plant; ~ **terminal de réception** receive-only (RO) terminal; ~ **terminal de traitement de données (ETTD)** data terminal equipment (DTE); ~ **terminal de transmission de données (ETTD)** data terminal equipment (DTE); ~ **terminal du centre** office terminal; ~ **univocal** speech-plus-simplex (S + S) equipment
équipements BF spécialisés dedicated VF equipment; ~ **d'automatisme** control gear; process control equipment; ~ **électriques** electrical gear/installation; ~ **téléphoniques** telephone plant
équirépartition f **de charge** balanced load distribution; least-busy method; ~ **de distribution** least-busy method
équivalence f (logique) IF-and-only-IF; equivalent-to; match; bi-conditional (element); identity
équivalent m net loss; analogue; equivalent; ~ **à la réception** receive reference equivalent (RRE); ~ **à l'émission** send reference equivalent; ~ **de référence** reference equivalent; ~ **de référence à la réception**

receiving reference equivalent; ~ de **référence à l'émission** sending reference equivalent; ~ **de référence de l'effet local** side-tone reference equivalent; ~ **de référence global (ERG)** overall reference equivalent (ORE); ~ **de référence nominal** nominal reference equivalent; ~ **de référence pour l'articulation** articulation reference equivalent; ~ **de transmission** net transmission equivalent; overall attenuation; total attenuation; ~ **de traversée** insertion loss; (speech path) transmission equivalent; ~ **en transit** via net loss; ~ **relatif** relative equivalent

équivoque *adj* ambiguous

E/R (v. émission-réception)

ERG (v. équivalent de référence global)

ergot *m* spigot; pin; detent; dowel; gaff

ERICHSEN *m* (v. emboutissage)

erlang *m* erlang (E)

erlangmètre *m* erlang meter

erreur *f* error; fault; bug; mistake; ~ **absolue** actual error; absolute error; ~ **accumulée** inherited error; ~ **aléatoire** random error; ~ **angulaire** angular error; ~ **câblée** hard error; ~ **centrée** balanced error; ~ **d'accord** tuning error; mismatch; ~ **d'adaptation** matching error; mismatch; ~ **d'alignement** field-alignment error; ~ **d'ambiguïté** ambiguity error; ~ **d'arrondi** rounding-off error; generated error; ~ **d'assortiment** mismatch; ~ **de bit** bit error; ~ **de bloc** block error; ~ **de câblage** wiring fault; wiring error; ~ **de cadence** timing error; ~ **de cadrage** misregistration; framing error; ~ **de calage** loop-alignment error; ~ **de case** mispocket; ~ **de chute** truncation error; ~ **de classement** sequence error; misfile; misfiling; ~ **de coïncidence** coincidence error; ~ **de dérive** drift error; ~ **de déviation latérale** lateral deviation error; ~ **de directivité** squint (angle); ~ **de distance** distance error; ~ **de linéarité** linearity error; mis-keying; ~ **de manipulation** keying error; mis-keying; ~ **de manœuvre** operating error; dialling error; ~ **de nuit** polarization error; night error; ~ **de parité** parity error; ~ **de polarisation** polarization error; ~ **de polarisation maximale** total polarization error; ~ **de programmation** soft error; program bug; ~ **de propagation** propagation error; ~ **de propagation ionosphérique** ionospheric-path error; ~ **de quantification** quantizing error; ~ **de recherche** seek error; ~ **de réflexion locale** re-radiation error; ~ **de relèvement** bearing error; direction-finding error; ~ **de rencontre** contention (error); ~ **de rythme**

over-run (of data channel capacity); ~ **de simultanéité** coincidence error; ~ **de trajets multiples** heiligtag effect; wave-interference error; ~ **de transmission bénigne** soft error; retrievable (transmission) error; ~ **de tri** mis-sort; ~ **de troncature** truncation error; ~ **de zéro** residual deflection; null error; ~ **d'émetteur** source error; transmitter site error; ~ **d'équilibrage** balancing fault; balance error; ~ **d'espacement** spacing error; octantal error; ~ **d'espacement résiduelle** residual spacing (octantal) error; ~ **d'excentrement** (pointer) centring error; ~ **d'inclinaison** rotation axis orientation error; ~ **d'installation** total system error; ~ **d'interpolation de signaux** signal interpolation error; ~ **d'oscillation** oscillation error; ~ **dynamique** dynamic error; ~ **fatale** fatal error; ~ **héritée** inherited error; ~ **instrumentale** instrument error; ~ **intermittente** random error; ~ **irrémédiable** fatal error; ~ **logique** logical error; software error; ~ **machine** hard error; ~ **mortelle** fatal error; ~ **non centrée** bias error; bias; ~ **non récupérable** hard error; ~ **numérique** digital error; ~ **octantale** spacing error; octantal error; ~ **physique** hard error; hardware error; ~ **propagée** inherited error; propagated error; ~ **propre** inherited error; propagated error; ~ **récupérable** recoverable error; non-fatal error; ~ **régionale** distant site error; inter-site error; ~ **(relative) de fréquence** (à long terme) (long-term) frequency departure ($\Delta f/f$); ~ **répercutée** inherited error; propagated error; ~ **résiduelle** residual error; ~ **simple** single error; ~ **statique de phase** phase error; ~ **sur la durée** time interval error (TIE); ~ **symétrique** balanced error; ~ **systématique** biased error; ~ **télémétrique** ranging error; ~ **type de polarisation** standard-wave error

erroné *adj* incorrect; garbled; erroneous; corrupt; freak; mutilated; bad; wrong; false

E/S (v. entrée/sortie); ~ **banalisées** memory mapped I/O ports

escamotable *adj* retractable

esclave *m* controlled by; subordinate to; slave

ESG (v. élément de sélection de groupe)

ESI (v. élément de sélection intermédiaire)

ESJ (v. élément de sélection de joncteurs)

ESL (v. élément de sélection de ligne)

espace *m* blank; space; gap; ~ **à droite** terminal blank; ~ **à gauche** leading blank; ~ **adresse** virtual address space; ~ **aérien** air space; ~ **arrêt-marche** inter-record gap; inter-block gap; ~ **arrière** back-space (BS);

~ **d'adressage** (configuration de l'~) address mapping; ~ **d'adresse** address space; ~ **de captation** catcher space; ~ **de glissement** drift space; ~ **de modulation** buncher space; ~ **de réflexion** reflector space; ~ **d'interaction** input gap; buncher gap; ~ **d'interaction de sortie** output gap; ~ **insécable** hard space; connecting space; protected space; required join; ~ **interbloc** inter-block gap; ~ **invisible** unwritten space; blank space; ~ **libre** gap; ~ **mémoire utilisateur** user memory space; ~ **partageable** common storage space; shared storage; ~ **sombre** dark space; ~ **sombre anodique** anode dark space; ~ **sombre cathodique** cathode dark space; Crookes dark space; Hittorf dark space

espacement *m* (pas) resolution; spacing; pitch; clearance; ~ **arrière** backspace; ~ **d'antenne** aerial spacing; ~ **de radiateurs** element spacing; ~ **de voies** channel spacing; ~ **des caractères** character spacing; ~ **entre impulsions** pulse spacing

espaces vierges de gauche leading blanks

espérance mathématique (statistical) expectation (E)

esperluète *f* ampersand

espionnage *m* **système** system monitoring/checkout; fault/error detection; debugging; ~ **téléphonique** wire tapping; eavesdropping

essai *m* test; ~ **à distance** remote testing; ~ **à l'étude** test at design stage; test under consideration; ~ **à vide** no-load test; off-circuit test; ~ **accéléré** accelerated test; ~ **au brouillard salin** salt-mist test; ~ **au frottement** friction test; ~ **au percement** breakdown test; ~ **automatique** automatic test; ~ **aux limites (E/L)** limit test; destructive test; marginal test; high/low bias test; ~ **combiné climatique** composite climatic sequence; ~ **complet** exhaustive test; ~ **contradictoire** control test; ~ **d'ambiance** environmental test; ~ **d'approbation** approval test; ~ **d'arbitrage** selective (contention) test; ~ **de chute** drop test; ~ **de cisaillement** shear test; ~ **de claquage** insulation breakdown test; ~ **de continuité** continuity test; ~ **de court circuit et faux potentiels** false cross and ground test (FCG); ~ **de dissolution à la goutte** jet test; ~ **de dureté** hardness test; ~ **de fatigue** fatigue test; ~ **de flexion** bending test; flexure test; ~ **de fluage** creep test; ~ **de fonctionnement** functional test; diagnostic test; ~ **de fragilité** brittleness test; '~ **de percussion** impact test; ~ **de pliage** bending test; ~ **de poussée** compression test;

push-in test; ~ **de qualification** (industrielle) qualification-approval test; ~ **de réception** acceptance test; goods-inward testing; ~ **de recette** acceptance test; goods-inward testing; ~ **de régime permanent** continuous-duty test; ~ **de résilience** impact test; elasticity test; ~ **de résistance à la traction** tensile test; pull-off test; ~ **de surcharge** overload test; ~ **de traction** tensile test; pull-off test; ~ **de transmission** transmission test; ~ **de vibration** vibration test; ~ **de vieillissement** aging test; endurance test; early-failure testing; burn-in; soak test; ~ **d'homologation** prototype test; approval test; certification test; ~ **d'isolement** flash test; insulation resistance test; ~ **en fonctionnement** dynamic test; ~ **en laboratoire** laboratory test; ~ **fonctionnel** field test; performance test; dynamic test; ~ **in situ** field test; ~ **inopérant** static test; laboratory test; ~ **lampe** lamp test; ~ **manuel** manual testing; operator-assisted test; ~ **par paliers** step-by-step test (SST); ~ **par tout ou rien** go/no-go test; yes/no test; ~ **périodique** routine test; ~ **pratique** field trial; field test; ~ **probatoire** feasibility test; ~ **prolongé d'occupation** extended busy test; ~ **rapide de circuit** overall circuit routine test; ~ **statique** static test; laboratory test; ~ **statistique** random test; ~ **sur site** field test; field trial; ~ **systématique** routine test

essayer *v* test; endeavour; try; attempt

essence *f* petrol; gasoline; benzine; motor spirit; motor fuel; species (of timber)

essentiel *adj* salient

essor *m* leap forward; future growth and prosperity; boom

essoreuse *f* centrifugal drier; spin drier; wringer; mangle

EST (v. équipement sous test)

estampage *m* drop forging

esthétique *f* design standards; style; industrial design; elegance; aesthetics; ~ *adj* stylish; elegant

estrade *f* dais; rostrum; platform; steps

estrope *f* strap

ET (organe/fonction) AND operator; AND gate; AND circuit; AND element; coincidence element

'et' commercial (perluète: S) ampersand; 'and' sign (&)

établir *v* set up

établissement *m* build-up; turn-on; setting-up; ~ **d'appel hors canal de conversation** off-air call set-up; ~ **de communication** hook-up; call set-up; ~ **de fiches** ticketing;

~ **des objectifs** planning; ~ **des priorités** set priority; ~ **d'un appel** call set-up; ~ **d'une communication** call set-up; hook-up; trunking

étage *m* stage; level; unit; bank; ~ **amplificateur** amplifier stage; ~ **basse fréquence** audio stage; ~ **cathodyne** cathode follower; ~ **changeur de fréquence** frequency changer; ~ **d'abonnés** subscriber stage; ~ **d'amplification** amplifier stage; ~ **de brassage** mixing stage; ~ **de commutation** switching stage; ~ **de commutation numérique** digital switching stage; time(-switching) stage; ~ **de commutation spatiale** multiplex space(-division) stage; ~ **de commutation temporelle** time(-division) stage; time-switching stage; digital-switching stage; ~ **de commutation temporelle d'entrée** input time stage; ~ **de concentration** concentration stage; concentrator stage; ~ **de fréquence intermédiaire** intermediate frequency stage; ~ **de présélection** preselection (line) stage; ~ **de sélecteurs** bank of selectors; bank of switches; ~ **de sélection** selection (group) stage; ~ **démodulateur** demodulation stage; ~ **excitateur du modulateur** modulator driver; ~ **final** output stage; ~ **mélangeur** mixer; ~ **modulé** modulated stage; ~ **pilote** driving stage; ~ **présélecteur HF** RF preselection stage; ~ **séparateur** buffer; ~ **T** highway junction; ~ **temporel de sortie** output time stage

étagé *adj* staggered; stacked
étagère *f* rack; shelf
étai *m* strut
étain *m* tin
étalage *m* interlacing
étalement *m* **de bande** band spreading
étaleur *m* **de bande** up-converter
étalon *m* standard; reference; master; gauge; norm; ~ **de fréquence** frequency standard
étalonnage *m* calibration; logging; graduation; gauging
étalonnement *m* logging; scaling; grading
étalonner *v* calibrate; graduate; log; scale
étalonneur *m* standard calibration oscillator
étamage *m* tinning; tin-lead plating; ~ **à chaud** hot tinning; reflow soldering; ~ **au trempé** dip tinning
étamé *adj* tinned; tin-plated; tin-lead plated
étanche *adj* insulated; sealed; tight; impervious; waterproof; non-porous; waterproof; impermeable; leakproof; ~ **normal** dust and damp-proof
étanchéité *f* seal; sealing (test)
étape *f* step; stage; phase
état *m* state; status; statement; condition;

report; position; situation; status report; schedule; 'status now' report; mode; list; log; ~ **A** space; ~ **actuel** state of the art; ~ **anhydre** moisture content; water content; ~ **attente** wait stage; ~ **autonome** out-of-traffic mode; ~ **auxiliaire d'une modulation** auxiliary condition of a modulation; ~ **bloqué** off-state; ~ **bloqué direct** forward blocking state; ~ **bloqué inverse** reverse blocking state; ~ **d'arrêt** stop state; halt condition; ~ **d'attente** waiting state; ~ **d'avancement** progress report; status report; linkage data; ~ **d'avancement de l'appel** call progress; ~ **de bon fonctionnement** serviceability; ~ **de boucle** loop status; loop state; ~ **de canal** channel status; ~ **de colisage** consignment note; packing list; ~ **de demi-faute** semi-fault condition; ~ **de fonctionnement** running order; working order; ~ **de gestion** inventory; administrative returns; schedule; ~ **de la cassure** end-face condition; ~ **de livraison** as delivered; 'as manufactured' condition (of materials); condition of supply; delivery form; ~ **de mémoire** contents of memory; ~ **de repos** idle condition; quiescent state; ~ **de stock** inventory position/status report; ~ **de surface** mating; surface finish; surface texture; ~ **de veille** search condition; standby state; ~ **décroché** off-hook condition; ~ **défavorable** adverse state (of scrambling); ~ **demandé** final status; ~ **d'exécution** running; ~ **d'impression** report; ~ **d'occupation** busy condition; ~ **du crochet commutateur** on-hook/off-hook condition; ~ **du site** exchange software resources; ~ **d'un traitement** process status; ~ **d'un organe** device status; ~ **et perspectives** present and future (developments/prospects); ~ **H** high state; ~ **hebdomadaire** weekly return; weekly log; ~ **hors service** out-of-service state; ~ **imprimante** continuous stationery; ~ **incident** I/C status bit; ~ **indifférent** state immaterial; don't-care (0 or 1 state); ~ **industriel** engineering design-revision statusl; ~ **initial** entry condition; ~ **instantané** snap(-shot condition); ~ **journalier** daily log; daily return; ~ **L** low state; ~ **libre** free condition; ~ **masqué** masked state; ~ **métastable** metastable state; ~ **mise à jour** updating state; ~ **normal** (énergétique) normal energy level; normal state; ~ **occupé** busy condition; ~ **ouvert** 'off' condition; ~ **passant** on-state; conducting state; ~ **prêt** (paré) ready state; ~ **pupitre** console status; ~ **raccroché** on-hook condition; ~ **récapitulatif** summary; ~ **sauvegardé** last-stored state; ~ **secondaire** sub-status; ~ **significatif** significant condition (mark/space); ~ **significatif d'une modulation** significant condition of a modulation; ~ **significatif d'une restitution** significant condition of a restitution; ~ **technique;** ~ **transfert de grille** form transfer state; ~ Z mark

étau m vice; ~ **instantané** toggle clamp

ETCD (équipement de terminaison du circuit des données) data circuit terminating equipment (DCE)

éteint adj out; off

étendu adj protracted

étendue f span; range; band; extent; scale; spread; ~ **de la zone de silence radio** skip distance; ~ **de mesure** rated range; ~ **des relèvements** range of bearings; spread

ETFE (v. copolymère d'éthylène tetrafluoro-éthylène); ∻ (v. téfzel)

étincelage m flash

étincelle f spark; flashover

étiquetage m labelling; docketing

étiquette f tag; label; sticker; decal; flag; ticket; marker; logo; tab; notice; ~ **auto-collante** self-adhesive label; ~ **d'acheminement** routing label; ~ **de baie** rack identification label; ~ **de bandeau** strip label; ~ **de blocage d'organe** isolating switch label; ~ **de constructeur** manufacturer's logo/name plate; mechanical specifications label; ~ **de début de bande** sticker; beginning-of-tape label (BOT); ~ **de repérage de niveaux** subrack level label

étirage m drawing; pulling; ~ **des préformes** preform drawing process

étiré support mounting frame

étoile f wye (Y) connection; quad; turntable

étoilé adj radial

étouffer v suppress; dampen; quench; stifle; absorb

étouffeur m **d'étincelles** spark quench circuit

étranger adj extraneous; foreign (body); alien; stray; spurious

être susceptible à might; be likely to; prone to; liable (to)

étrier m terminal clamp; cleat; saddle; jumper; connector; bridge; lug; bracket; clip; U-link; stirrup; yoke; clevis; brace; shackle; cradle; lifting tackle; ~ **de court circuit** U-link; jumper; ~ **de masse** earth strap; ~ **de transformateur** yoke

étroit adj narrow; slim; slender; close; slim-line; compact

ETTD (équipement terminal de traitement de données) data terminal equipment (DTE); ∻ (v. équipement terminal de transmission

de données); ∻ **non prêt commandé** DTE controlled not ready

étude f study; survey; observation; analysis; subject; design; examination; research; engineering; planning; ~ **approfondie** survey; in-depth examination; ~ **automatisée** computer-aided design (CAD); ~ **chronométrique** time-and-motion study; work study; ~ **de marché** market survey; market research; ~ **d'interférences radio-électriques** RFI survey (radio-frequency interference); ~ **d'opportunité** feasibility study; ~ **prévisionnelle** forward planning; forecasting; ~ **théorique** feasibility study

études de réseaux network planning

étudié (l' ~) (the) unknown

étudier v consider; examine

étui m stick; pouch; holster; case; sheath; ~ **piqué** padded case; Jiffy bag [T.N.]

étuvage m curing; drying; oven conditioning

étuve f oven; stove; heated enclosure; incubator; temperature-controlled environment; furnace; ~ **à air brassé** fan-assisted oven; ~ **à vide** vacuum drier; ~ **de déverminage** burn-in stove; burn-in oven

EV (v. électro-vanne)

évacuateur m outlet

évacuation f (d'un porteur) dispelling (of stored charge carriers); ~ **d'air** blow-off; ~ **des calories** heat dissipation/discharge system

évacuer v dump

évaluation f benchmarking; assessment; appraisal; ~ **de l'image radar** image interpretation; ~ **d'une transmission téléphonique** telephone transmission rating

évanouissement m fading; decay; ~ **atmosphérique** atmospheric fading; ~ **brusque** radio fade-out; Dellinger effect; ~ **ionosphérique** ionospheric fading; ~ **par interférence** interference fading; ~ **sélectif** selective fading; ~ **sous plusieurs angles** multi-path fading

évasé adj opened-out

évasion f **du radar** radar evasion

événement m event; occurrence; ~ **téléphonique d'interfonctionnement vers l'arrière** backward interworking telephone event (BITE)

éventualité f contingency

éventuel adj optional; future; possible; planned; as required; allowed for; occasional

éventuellement adv where applicable; in certain cases

évidement m window (in tape reel); cavity; recess; slot

évidemment adv clearly; obviously

évitement *m* by-pass

éviter *v* dispense with the need to; avert; avoid; obviate; prevent; side-step

évolué *adj* high-level; open-ended; upgraded; advanced; sophisticated; developed

évoluer *v* progress; advance; develop; upgrade; grow

évolutif open-ended; upgraded; modifier; subject to alteration; liable to change; tentative; expandable; future-proof

évolution *f* upgrading; refinement; elaboration; growth; design level/status; progress; product status; development; trend; advancement; expansion; transformation (process); retrofit; flux; enhancement; migration; ~ de programme program sequence

EXA (v. explorateur d'abonnés)

exactitude *f* accuracy

examineur *m* processor test routine

excédants et manquants overs and shorts

excédent surplus; excess

excentrage *m* offset

excentré *adj* out-of-true; off-centre; skewed; breakout; misaligned; out-of-register; misregistered

excentrement *m* concentricity

excentrique *m* null adjust pin; cam

exceptionnel *adj* outstanding; unusual; abnormal; non-standard

exceptionnellement *adv* seldom; unusually

excitateur *m* energizer; exciter; driver; actuator; magnetizer; ~ électrostatique electrostatic actuator

excitation *f* energization; excitation; pick-up (of relay); driving; stimulus; ~ différentielle differential excitation; ~ d'un guide d'ondes waveguide excitation; ~ dynamique dynamic drive; ~ en dérivation shunted derivation; ~ en série series excitation; ~ par choc impulse excitation; collision excitation; ~ par impulsion impulse excitation; collision excitation; ~ par rayonnement radiation excitation (of gas); ~ rémanente residual excitation; ~ séparée separately excited (shunt field); independent power supply/source; ~ transitoire à modes différents multi-modal transient excitation

excitatrice *f* exciter; ~ pilote pilot exciter

exciter *v* energize

exclu *adj* excluded; omitted

exclusion *f* NOT-IF-THEN; exclusion; EXCEPT; AND-NOT; lock-out (of operator); exclusivity; ~ de recherche en mémoire memory search exclusion; ~ réciproque exclusive-OR (non-equivalence) operation; symmetric difference

exclusivement *adv* solely

exclusivité *f* exclusive priority (bit)

excroissance *f* accretion

excursion *f* d'amplitude amplitude excursion; logic swing; ~ de fréquence frequency swing; deviation; ~ de la tension voltage swing; ~ de la tension de sortie output voltage swing; ~ en continu DC deviation; DC swing; ~ en mode commun (Emc) common-mode output voltage; ~ maximale peak excursion

EXEC GO (key) (carriage return function)

exécutable *adj* ready (queue); load; run; running

exécuter *v* perform; execute; GO; run

exécution *f* de la boucle loop iteration

exemplaire *m* copy; duplicate; unit; specimen

exemple *m* typical; representative

exercer *v* apply; exert

exercice *m* trading year; fiscal year; financial year; accounting period

exfoliation *f* scaling; flaking

exhaustive *adj* comprehensive

exigence *f* imperative

exiger *v* warrant; demand; require

exister *v* obtain; prevail

EXJ (v. explorateur de jonction)

expanseur *m* automatic volume expander; expandor; expander; ~ d'échelle scale expander

expansion *f* expander

expéditeur sending terminal

expédition *f* sur chantiers despatch to site

expérience *f* (academic/professional) discipline; ~ à caractère subjectif uncontrolled experiment; ~ acquise track record

expérimenté *adj* accomplished; skilled

expertise *f* systems analysis

EXPL (v. exploitation)

explicite *adj* self-explanatory

exploitant *m* operating authority; end-user; telco (telephone company); common carrier; system operative

exploitation *f* working; operation; handling; traffic; administration; evaluation; network controller; analysis; ~ (EXPL) run; ~ à l'alternat half-duplex working; up-and-down working; alternate operation; ~ à porte fermée closed-shop operation; hands-off working; ~ à porteuses distinctes spaced-carrier operation; ~ automatique automatic operation; dial-operated; ~ automatique intégrale fully-automatic working; ~ automatique interurbaine subscriber trunk dialling (STD); ~ avec appel sur le circuit ring-down operation; ~ avec attente delay working; ~ avec permutation des fréquences reverse-frequency operation; ~ bidirectionnelle bothway operation;

~ **de classe B** switched-loop operation; ~ **derrière autocommutateur** PABX interworking; ~ **des renseignements** information retrieval; ~ **des résultats** result processing; result analysis; ~ **en alternat** up-and-down working; ~ **en duplex** duplex working; duplex operation; ~ **en mode associé** associated signalling mode; ~ **en mode complètement dissocié** fully-dissociated signalling mode; ~ **en mode dégradé** crippled mode (operation); ~ **en mode non asssocié** non-associated signalling mode; ~ **en mode quasi-associé** quasi-associated signalling mode; ~ **en tandem** tandem operation; tandem working; ~ **et maintenance** operation and maintenance (O & M); ~ **manuelle** manual working; ~ **multiporteuse** multicarrier operation; ~ **par central tandem automatique** automatic tandem-working dial system; tandem operation; ~ **par courant simple** neutral (DC) operation; ~ **par satellite** satellite operation; ~ **par voies conjuguées** two-way simplex system; ~ **privée** private operating agency (POA); ~ **privée reconnue** recognized private operating agency (RPOA); ~ **sans attente** demand service; demand working; ~ **sans personnel** unmanned operation; ~ **semi-automatique** semi-automatic operation; ~ **simplex** simplex operation; ~ **sur deux fréquences** dual-frequency operation; ~ **sur une fréquence** single-frequency operation; ~ **tandem** link-by-link connections; ~ **télésurveillée** unattended operation; ~ **unidirectionnelle** one-way operation

explorateur *m* scanner; ~ **d'abonnés (EXA)** subscriber line scanner (SLS); ~ **de jonction (EXJ)** junction scanner (JSC); ~ **de lignes** line scanner

explorateur-distributeur scheduler and despatcher; scanner and driver; scanner-distributor

exploration *f* scanning; sampling; sweeping; scrolling; ~ **à vitesse constante** constant speed scanning; ~ **arborescente** branch and bound (search); ~ **des voies** pathfinding; ~ **panoramique** circular scanning; ~ **rapide** fast scroll; high-speed scan; rapid sweep;

~ **sectorielle** sector scanning; ~ **table** scan table (mnemonics); ~ **temporelle** (d'une ligne) polling

exploreur *m* scanner

exposant *m* exhibitor; exponent; superscript; index; power; ~ **itératif de transfert** iterative transfer coefficient; ~ **linéique de propagation** propagation coefficient

exposé *m* statement

expression *f* (logiciel) statement; ~ **arithmétique** arithmetical expression; formula; ~ **insécable** protected expression

expulsion *f* kicking out

extenseur *m* expander; expandor; expansor; stretcher

extensibilité *f* modularity; expansion potential; stretch (of memory)

extensible *adj* open-ended; upgradable; modular; expandable

extension *f* upgrading; expansion; add-on memory pack (random access memory RAM); stretching

extérieur *adj* extraneous; outdoor; outside; external; exterior; outer; outward; non-system; foreign; off-site; ancillary

externe *adj* ancillary; priority; outside; external; non-system; built-out

extincteur *m* extinguisher; quencher; ~ (de luminescence) quencher

extinction *f* decay (of oscillations)

extracteur *m* **de cartes** board extractor; ~ **de fumée** fume extractor; ~ **de valeur efficace** rms-to-DC converter

extraction *f* transfer; read-out; dump; fetching; output; printout; retrieval; delivery; masking; swap-out (of overlay); ~ **de l'horloge distante** recovery of distant end signal element; ~ **de l'information** data retrieval; ~ **de partie d'un programme** swapping-out

extraire *v* fetch; access; swap; get

extrémité *f* switching point; ~ **avec rayon** radiused tip; ~ **d'arrivée** incoming end; ~ **de départ** outgoing end; ~ **de réception** receiving end; ~ **d'émission** sending end; ~ **MIC** PCM code converter; ~ **ouverte** open end; ~ **virtuelle** virtual switching point

F

"F" (fermé) (= "T": travail/out) NO (normally open) (= "ON": operate/make - of relay contacts)

fabrication *f* manufacture; product; ~ **à la chaîne** assembly-line production; ~ **en série** mass production; full-scale production

fabriquer *v* derive; contrive; manufacture; produce

façade *f* front panel

face *f* side; surface; face; panel; ~ **avant** front panel; edge strip; ~ **d'appui** bearing surface; mating face; ~ **éléments (FE)** component side (of PCB); ~ **parlante** front panel; ~ **soudure (FS)** solder side (of PCB)

facilement *adv* readily

facilité d'emploi ease-of-use; ~ **d'intervention** forward transfer facility

faciliter *v* facilitate; clarify; expedite; smooth the way for; aid; assist; promote; foster; afford

facilités de manœuvre manoeuvrability; steerability

façonnage *m* routing; machining; modelling

façonnement *m* forming; machining; tooling

façonnier *m* (c.f. courtier) broker

fac-sim *m* hard copy

fac-similé *m* facsimile; fax; ~ **à impression directe** direct recording facsimile; ~ **chiffré** cifax; enciphered facsimile communication; ~ **demiteinte** facsimile type B

facteur *m* factor; coefficient; constant; operand; figure; rate; ratio; ~ **adresse** data address; ~ **ajusté d'utilisation de lignes** adjusted line usage factor; ~ **d'accroissement** growth factor; ~ **d'activité** activity factor; ~ **d'affaiblissement** attenuation factor; ~ **d'amplification** amplification factor; mu-factor; voltage factor; gain; ~ **d'amplification de courant** current amplification factor; current gain; ~ **d'amplification de gaz** gas amplification factor; ~ **d'amplification de tension** voltage gain; voltage factor; mu-factor; ~ **d'amplitude** crest factor; peak factor; ~ **de blocage** blocking factor; block size; ~ **de bruit** noise figure; ~ **de câblage** take-up factor; cable bundle factor; ~ **de charge de sortie (en sortie)** fan-out; output load factor; ~ **de charge d'entrée (en entrée)** fan-in; input load factor; ~ **de choix** choice factor;

~ **de commande** control ratio; ~ **de compensation de charge** absorber circuit factor; ~ **de compensation de l'erreur de relèvement** (bearing) error compensation value; ~ **de concentration** day-to-busy-hour ratio; concentration factor; ~ **de confiance** confidence factor; ~ **de conversion** conversion coefficient; ~ **de coopération** factor of cooperation; ~ **de correction** weighting; ~ **de couplage** coupling coefficient; coupling factor; ~ **de couplage pour signaux faibles** small-signal coupling coefficient; ~ **de crête** peak factor; crest factor; ~ **de cylindre** drum factor; ~ **de débordement** spill-over loss; ~ **de déphasage** (cos phi) phase difference; ~ **de déviation** deviation ratio; ~ **de diffraction** shadow factor; ~ **de directivité** aerial power gain; directional gain; ~ **de dissipation** dissipation factor; dissipation constant; ~ **de distorsion** distortion factor; ~ **de distorsion nonlinéaire** non-linear distortion factor; ~ **de divergence** divergence coefficient; ~ **de forme** form factor; influence factor; ~ **de fréquence** frequency factor; ~ **de fréquence maximale** maximum usable frequency factor (MUF); ~ **de groupage** blocking factor; block size; ~ **de linéarité** figure of linearity; ~ **de marche** duty factor/rating (of motor: in %); ~ **de mérite** figure of merit; quality factor; ~ **de modulation** modulation index; ~ **de multiplication** multiplication factor; ~ **de multiplication du courant de collecteur** collector-current multiplication factor; ~ **de pertes** loss factor; figure of loss; dissipation factor; dissipation constant; ~ **de pointe** peak factor; ~ **de pondération** weighting (factor); ~ **de puissance** power factor (p.f.); ~ **de qualité** quality factor; Q-factor; magnification factor; storage factor; figure of merit; ~ **de qualité** (v. facteur de mérite); ~ **de rebondissement** overshoot (factor); ~ **de réduction** de-rating factor; ~ **de réflexion** reflection factor; reflectance; ~ **de réflexion sur les irrégularités** irregularity reflection coefficient; ~ **de surtension** quality factor; Q-factor; magnification factor; storage factor; figure of merit; ~ **de transfert** transfer coefficient; ~ **de visibilité** visibility factor; ~ **d'échelle**

scaling factor; ~ **d'efficacité dans le temps** efficiency factor in time; ~ **d'élimination** cancellation ratio; ~ **d'émission secondaire** secondary-emission factor; ~ **d'émission télégraphique** telegraph-transmission coefficient; ~ **d'impédance d'onde** normalized impedance; ~ **d'indication stimulant** incentive; ~ **d'intensité de contrainte critique** plane-strain fracture; toughness; ~ **d'interférence** interference factor; ~ **d'irrégularité** peakedness factor; ~ **d'ombre** shadow factor; ~ **d'utilisation** efficiency; plate effect; demand factor; duty factor; duty cycle; load factor; occupancy; spill-over loss; service factor; ~ **d'utilisation de lignes** line usage factor; ~ **maximum d'utilisation de lignes** maximum line usage factor; ~ **pyramidal de sortie** fan-out; ~ **pyramidal d'entrée** fan-in; ~ **Q** Q-factor; figure of merit; ~ **téléphonique de forme** telephone influence factor (TIF); ~ **téléphonique de forme du courant** current telephone influence factor; ~ **TIF** telephone influence factor (TIF)
factice adj dummy; pseudo; false; artificial
faction f shift
facturable adj chargeable; billed
facturation f billing; invoicing; revenues; receipts; ~ **au compteur** bulk billing; ~ **cumulée** (v. facturation au compteur); ~ **détaillée** detailed billing; itemized billing; ~ **globale** bulk billing; ~ **personnalisée** personalized billing (ABC - auto bill calling service); ~ **séparée** unbundling
facture f bill; invoice; structure; ~ **détaillée** itemized bill; detailed bill; ~ **électronique** electronic billing; ~ **téléphonique** telephone bill
facturer v bill
facturière f billing machine; accounting machine
facultatif adj optional
faculté f facility
fading local short-range fading; ~ **rapproché** local fading; short-range fading; ~ **sélectif** selective fading
faible adj low-order; least significant; small; limited; weak; rightmost; trailing; ~ **besoin** limited demand; ~ **courant de repos** low standby current drain; ~ **diaphonie entre amplis** high channel separation; ~ **dissipation** low loss; ~ **encombrement** compactness; ~ **lobe latéral** low side-lobe; ~ **trafic** light traffic; low traffic (level); lull; ~ **vitesse** low speed
faire appel à embody; incorporate; ~ **état de** delineate; ~ **face** (à) cope with; accommodate; cater for; ~ **le point** take stock;

~ **passer** toggle; switch; ~ **un appel** invoke (of subroutine); call up; dial
faisabilité f **industrielle** industrial feasibility
faisceau m (wiring) loom; core; bundle; beam; trunk; trunk group; circuit group; bus; bunch; route; cluster; multi-channel system; link; ~ **à cosécante carrée** cosecant-squared beam; ~ **à signaux équilibrés** equi-signal beam; ~ **à utilisation élevée** high-usage route; ~ **cohérent** coherent beam; ~ **connecteur** information bus; ~ **crayon** pencil beam; ~ **d'acheminement unique** only-route trunk group; ~ **de câbles** cable loom; ~ **de circuits** circuit group; trunk group; ~ **de circuits à utilisation élevée** high-usage circuit group; ~ **de circuits directs** direct circuit group; ~ **de conducteurs** cable core; ~ **de débordement** overflow trunk group; ~ **de dernier choix** last-choice route; last-choice circuit group; ~ **de deuxième choix** second-choice trunk route; ~ **de faisceaux** network cluster; ~ **de fibres** fibre bundle; ~ **de guidage** guide beam; ~ **de jonctions communes** common trunk group; junction group; ~ **de jonctions de premier choix** first-choice trunk group; ~ **de lignes** trunk group; ~ **de lignes à acheminement direct** direct group access trunk; ~ **de lignes d'abonnement** central office line group; ~ **de lignes entrantes** incoming (I/C) trunk group; ~ **de lignes groupées** line hunting group; ~ **de lignes sortantes** outgoing trunk group; ~ **de lignes spécialisées** group of tie-lines; ~ **de premier choix** high-usage circuit group; ~ **de radioguidage** radio beam; ~ **de rattachement** final trunk group; ~ **de rayons de radar** radar beam; ~ **de régénération** holding beam; ~ **de reportage** electronic news-gathering (ENG); ~ **de système de télégraphie harmonique** voice frequency telegraph (VFT) system; ~ **de télégraphie harmonique** voice-frequency multi-channel system; ~ **de transit local d'arrivée** tandem completing trunk group; ~ **de transit local de départ** tandem originating trunk group; ~ **de tubes** nest; bank; cooling coil; ~ **débordant** high-usage circuit group; ~ **départ** outgoing (O/G) trunk group; ~ **direct** (high-usage) direct route; ~ **direct à débordement** primary high-usage trunk group; ~ **direct non débordant** fully-provided trunk group; only-route trunk group; ~ **directionnel** directional beam; ~ **dirigé** radio beam; ~ **échelonné** extended telegraph circuit; ~ **électromagnétique** (radio) beam; ~ **(électromagnétique) plat horizontal** beaver-tail

beam; ~ **(électromagnétique) plat** fan beam; ~ **électronique** electron beam; ~ **elliptique** elliptical beam; ~ **en éventail** fan beam; ~ **en queue de castor** beaver-tail beam; ~ **équivalent** equivalent random circuit group; ~ **est** east spot; ~ **étagé** stacked beam; ~ **explorateur** scanning beam; ~ **filiforme** pencil beam; ~ **final** final circuit group; ~ **hertzien (FH)** radio-relay system; radio link; microwave link/beam; ~ **hertzien à visibilité directe** line-of-sight radio link; ~ **hertzien de déport** back-haul radio link; ~ **hertzien transhorizon** over-the-horizon radio link; ~ **incident** incident beam; ~ **non débordant** final-choice (backbone) route; ~ **ouest** west spot; ~ **parallèle** aligned bundle; ~ **plat** fan beam; ~ **principal** main beam; ~ **saturé** all (trunk group) lines busy; ~ **totalement fourni** fully-provided circuit group; only-route trunk group; ~ **transversal** high-usage trunk group

fait foi definitive

famille *f* product family; ~ **d'ensemble de données** generation data group

fanion *m* flag; flag sequence

fantaisie *f* freak

fantôme *m* phantom; echo; ghost; superposed circuit

FAO (v. file d'attente d'ordre)

FAR (v. file d'attente des réponses)

faradmètre *m* capacitance meter

farde *f* jacket (of film)

fastidieux *adj* irksome; time-consuming

fatidique *adj* pre-ordained; stipulated; inevitable

fatigue visuelle eyestrain

fausse carte dummy circuit board; ~ **connexion** wrong connection; ~ **équerre** bevel square; ~ **manœuvre** false trip; misoperation; user error; misdial(ling); dialling error; false operation; ~ **prise** false (seizure) attempt

faute *f* fault; mistake; defect; error; failure; malfunction; flaw; disorder; bug; ~ **câblée** hardware-generated fault (message); hard error; ~ **d'adressage** addressing incorrect; ~ **de jeunesse** teething trouble; early failure; ~ **de la logique (FLOG)** logic unit fault; ~ **déterministe** primary fault; symptom; ~ **d'imparité** parity error; ~ **échange** interchange fault; ~ **logicielle** bug; soft error; ~ **prématurée** inadvertent error; pre-emptive fault; ~ **programmée** program-generated fault message; soft error; bug; program-detected error; ~ **propre** known error

faux *adj* counterfeit; dummy; false; bad;

wrong; blank; imaginary; phantom; ~ **appel** permanent line condition; line lockout; receiver off-hook (ROH); ~ **contact** bad contact; ~ **fusible** blank fuse; dummy fuse; ~ **numéro** wrong number; ~ **plafond** suspended ceiling; false ceiling; ~ **plancher** false floor; raised floor; concealed trench; free-access floor; raceway floor; ~ **problème** blind alley; ~ **tour** lap (of winding)

favorable *adj* preferred

favoriser *v* foster; promote; encourage

FC (v. fin de course)

f.c.é.m. (force contre-électromotrice) back e.m.f. (electromotive force)

FdP/FdeP/FDP (v. fond de panier)

FE (v. face éléments)

FEC (v. fin d'échange)

fédérateur *adj* unifying; networking

fédération network(-ing)

fêlure *f* crack; split

f.é.m (force électromotrice) e.m.f. (electromotive force)

fendu *adj* slit

fénétrage *m* windowing

fenêtre *f* aperture; window; slot; port; gate; frame; blank; opening; ~ **d'accusé de réception** acknowledgement window; ~ **d'anticipation** channel width; window (of pulse height selector); ~ **de commande** command frame; ~ **de déplacement** movement window; ~ **de mesure** counting gate; ~ **étanche** (de guide d'ondes) pressure-tight window; seal; ~ **fin de récurrence** end-of-repetition gate; ~ **temporelle** time slot

fente *f* (guide d'ondes) slot; ~ **rayonnante** slot radiator

fer à dessouder desoldering iron; ~ **à souder** soldering iron; ~ **blanc** tin(-plate); white (cast) iron; ~ **de garde** guard iron; retaining bar/rod; ~ **doux** ductile iron; ~ **en C** channel (extruded section); ~ **plat** flat bar; ~ **silicium orienté** grain-oriented silicon iron

ferme *f* vertical bar (of distribution frame); main beam; upright; ~ *adj* binding; firm; ~ **radiale** radial truss

fermé *adj* NO (normally operated = "make" relay); on (of switch)

fermer *v* complete (of circuit); de-activate (of file); close

fermeture *f* latch; clasp; closure; seal; enclosure; sign-off; log-off; ~ **à froid** (sous vide) cold-welded (of crystal case); ~ **de faisceau** beam-off position; ~ **de fichier** file closure; ~ **transitive** transitory closure

ferrite *m* ferrite core; ~ **hyperfréquence** RF inductor

ferrorésonance *f* **multiple** multiple ferroresonance
feu *m* lamp; ~ **clignotant** flashing lamp; blinking indicator; ~ **fixe** (allumage) steady glow
feuillard *m* core wrap (of cable); (clamping) band
feuille *f* sheet; leaf; folio; page; form; ~ **d'acheminement** routing form; ~ **de calcul** spreadsheet; ~ **de caractéristiques** data sheet; ~ **de dessin** sketch pad; ~ **de planification** (et de modélisation) **financière** spreadsheet; ~ **de programmation** coding sheet; source document; ~ **de référence** line-up record; ~ **de route** waybill; ~ **mécanographique** source document; coding sheet; ~ **mécanographique imprimante** (computer) print-out; ~ **particulière** detail specification; ~ **récapitulative** summary sheet
feuillet *m* data cell; magnetic leaf; ~ **de procédé de fabrication** manufacturing process sheet
feuilleté *adj* laminated (of magnetic circuit)
feuilleter *v* browse
feutre de nettoyage cleaning fleece
feutrine *f* baize
FF (fusibles) fuses
FH (v. faisceau hertzien)
FI (v. fréquence intermédiaire)
fiabilité *f* reliability; MTBF indicator; fail-safe; ~ **prévisionnelle** reliability forecast
fiable *adj* reliable; trusted
fibrage *m* fibre drawing
fibre à double fenêtre double-window fibre; ~ **à échelon d'indice** step-index fibre; ~ *f* **à gradient d'indice** graded index fibre; ~ **à gradient d'indice parabolique** parabolic-index profile fibre; ~ **à répartition parabolique d'indice** parabolic-index profile fibre; ~ **à saut d'indice** (v. fibre à échelon d'indice); ~ **amorce** pigtail; fibre tail; ~ **conique** conical fibre; optical taper fibre; ~ **de verre** glass-reinforced plastic (GRP); fibre-glass; ~ **émettrice** emitting fibre; ~ **en travers** cross-fibre (coupling); ~ **enrobée** tight fibre; ~ **guide de lumière** optical fibre waveguide; ~ **intermédiaire** (de couplage) optical fibre pigtail; pigtail; ~ **libre** loose fibre; ~ **monomode** single-mode fibre; monomode fibre; ~ **moyenne** mean axial plane; ~ **moyenne de la borne** mean axial plane of terminal; ~ **multimode** multimode fibre; ~ **nue** fibre tail; ~ **optique** fibre-optics; optical fibre; ~ **optique à cœur liquide** liquid core fibre; ~ **réceptrice** receiving fibre; ~ **selfoc** self-focussing fibre; selfoc fibre

ficeler *v* lash; bind; tie
fiche *f* (jack) plug; peg; pin; patch cord; record form; chit; index card; data sheet; slip; profile; ~ **à diode** diode plug; ~ **àpincer** edge connector; ~ **américaine** chassis plug; ~ **banane** banana plug; ~ **bipolaire** twin plug; two-pin plug; double-pole plug; ~ **d'accompagnement** support card; ~ **d'appel** calling plug; call jack; ~ **de casier** bin card; ~ **de configuration** configuration sheet; workstation layout sheet; ~ **de connexion** plug; connector; patching cord; ~ **(de) consigne** instruction sheet; ~ **de définition du matériel** equipment definition sheet; ~ **de formation** training scheme information sheet; ~ **de jack** jack plug; ~ **de manœuvre** scratch file; ~ **de mesure** test sheet; ~ **de mouvement** maintenance sheet; transaction file; tape change; ~ **de poste** workstation instruction sheet; ~ **de produits** product specification; ~ **de qualité** quality control sheet; ~ **de régie** parameter sheet; ~ **de réglage** alignment sheet; ~ **de relevé de défauts** fault record; ~ **de renseignements** information card; ~ **de réponse** answering jack; subscriber jack; ~ **de signalisation de dérangement** fault docket; fault report sheet; ~ **de suivi** progress record card; traveller; route card; move ticket; history file; progress chaser sheet; ~ **de synthèse** aggregate record sheet; ~ **de travail** scratch file; ~ **de travaux** job order; ~ **d'écoute** answering plug; ~ **d'essais** sample file; ~ **d'évolution** product status sheet; ~ **d'instruction** instruction card; ~ **d'instruction de contrôle** sub-assembly inspection instructions; ~ **d'isolement** isolating plug; ~ **double** squid (on control panel); ~ **droite** straight jack (plug); ~ **femelle** socket; plug socket; chassis plug; straight cable socket (IEC mains plug socket); shrouded plug; ~ **fiabilité** quality monitoring report; ~ **fictive** dummy plug; blanking plug; ~ **gigogne** dual outlet plug adaptor; modular (telephone) jack; ~ **inversé** inverted file; dual dictionary; ~ **isolante** dummy plug; blanking plug; ~ **localisation de panne** fault location sheet; ~ **mâle** plug; ~ **mobile** free plug; ~ **monopolaire** single-pole plug; ~ **N** N-type coaxial connector; ~ **opérateur** operator command sheet; operator data sheet; ~ **permanent** master file; permanent file; ~ **principal** master file; permanent file; ~ **produit** product data sheet; ~ **réflexe** (dépannage) remedial maintenance sheet; ~ **relevé de défaut** fault report data sheet; fault report

sheet; ~ **signalétique** document profile; ~ **suiveuse** process inspection label; route card (tag); move ticket; traveller card; history file; ~ **synthétique** aggregate record sheet; ~ **technique** technical sheet; maintenance data sheet; instruction manual

fiché *adj* shown; given

fichier *m* (software) file; edge connector; data base; ~ **à méthode d'accès direct** direct access file; ~ **agenda** routine task file; ~ **ancien** back file; ~ **bibliographique** data file; ~ **commun** permanent data file; ~ **compte-rendu** error log; ~ **consigné sur disquette** floppy disk file; ~ **contigu** contiguous file; ~ **d'activités** activity file; movement file; ~ **d'archivage** archive file; ~ **d'attente** parking file; suspense file; follow-up file; tickler file; ~ **de base** master file; permanent file; ~ **de brassage** device interconnection and hardware configuration file; ~ **de consultation** direct access file; ~ **de manœuvre** scratch file; working file; transaction file; ~ **de mouvement** change file; detail file; transaction file; activity file; maintenance file; ~ **de pièces** patch file; ~ **de réception** input (job) file; ~ **de recherche** directory file; index file; search file; ~ **de relance** parking file; suspense file; tickler file; ~ **de signalement** postings file; ~ **de sortie** output file; exit run file; ~ **de suivi** tickler file; follow-up file; suspense file; parking file; ~ **de taxation** charging file; ~ **de texte** data file; message file; ~ **de travail** scratch file; work file; transaction file; ~ **de vidage** crash (dump) file; ~ **définition des symboles** compool (symbol definition file); ~ **d'émission** output (job) file; ~ **d'entrée** input file; ~ **d'erreurs** log file; error-logging file; ~ **des faisceaux** trunk group file; ~ **destinataire** destination file; file-to; ~ **détail** detail file; change file; modification file; activity file; transaction file; maintenance file; ~ **différentiel** difference file; ~ **d'inscription** log-in file; sign-on file; ~ **direct** linear file; direct access file; ~ **direct séquentiel** random sequential file; ~ **disque** disk file; ~ **électrique** edge plug; ~ **encartable** PCB mounting edge plug; edge connector; ~ **enchaîné** threaded file; chained file; ~ **exécutable** run file; ~ **gazette** journal; notice file; ~ **guide (opérateur)** help file; ~ **image** object file; dump file (disk copy); ~ **implicite** default file; ~ **impression** print file; ~ **indexé** index file; ~ **indirect** indirectly-addressed file; ~ **indirection** at file; ~ **interne** system file; ~ **inverse** inverted file; ~ **logique**

d'édition print-out file; ~ **maître** permanent file; master file; ~ **modèle** template file; ~ **mouchard** snoop file; ~ **mouvement** maintenance file; transaction file; detail file; activity file; change file; amendment file; ~ **non permanent** buffer file; ~ **notice** notice file; ~ **numéro d'annuaire** last-digits file; ~ **or** gold contact edge connector; ~ **origine** source file; ~ **page de garde** banner file; banner page; ~ **partitionné** partitioned file; ~ **permanent** permanent file; master file; ~ **pilote** permanent file; master file; ~ **principal** master file; permanent file; ~ **séquentiel** sequential file; ~ **sur bande magnétique** magnetic tape file; ~ **vidéo** image file

fictif *adj* dummy; pseudo-; simulated; artificial; hypothetical (exchange); waste (of instruction); shadow; phantom; virtual; imaginary

fidélisation *f* brand loyalty

fidélité *f* accuracy; fidelity; response; ~ **de modulation** audio-frequency response; ~ **de répétition** repeat accuracy; reproducibility

FIFO (pile directe) FIFO queue (shift register)

figé *adj* held in abeyance; disabled; stalled; finalized; stuck; unchangeable; formatted; frozen; set; stationary

figeage *m* setting; stalling; disabling

figer *v* disable; set

figure *f* **de bruit** noise figure; ~ **de bruit d'un système** system noise figure (SNF)

figurine *f* illustration; model; diagram; graphic image; pictorial representation

fil *m* wire; lead; conductor; track; thread; line; pick; spike; bar; ~ **à bobiner** coil-winding wire; ~ **à isolement caoutchouc** rubber-insulated wire; ~ **à plomb** plumb line; ~ **à souder** jumper wire; ~ **aérien** overhead wire; ~ **blindé** shielded wire; ~ **compteur** meter wire (M-wire); ~ **d'abonné** drop wire; ~ **d'attache** tie wire; ~ **de batterie** battery lead; ~ **de blocage** test wire; C-wire; sleeve wire; ~ **de bobinage** coil-winding wire; ~ **de câblage** bus wire; ~ **de câblage monobrins** single-stranded wire; ~ **de comptage** meter wire; ~ **de continuité** earth wire; continuity wire; ~ **de conversation** speaking wire; talking wire; speech wire; ~ **de corps** sleeve wire; S-wire; third wire; ~ **de démarrage** start wire; ~ **de douille** S-wire; sleeve wire; third wire; ~ **de fer** (metallic) wire; ~ **de freinage** safety wire; ~ **de gué** lead-through wire; ~ **de lecture** sense wire; ~ **de libération** release wire; ~ **de ligne** line wire; ~ **de maintien** private wire; P-wire; guard wire; third wire; control wire; C-wire; sleeve wire; S-wire; test wire; path-holding wire; ~ **de masse** ground conductor; earthing wire; ~ **(de masse) d'accompagnement** earth conductor; ~ **de métallisation** bonding wire; ~ **de nuque** ring wire; R-wire (connected to subscriber line B-wire); ~ **de pilotage** (d'appel) call pilot wire; ~ **de pointe** tip wire; T-wire (connected to subscriber line A-wire); ~ **de procédure** protocol wire; ~ **de signalisation** signalling wire; ~ **de sonnerie d'appel** ringing lead; ~ **de soudure** solder wire; ~ **de test** test wire; C-wire; S-wire; P-wire; ~ **de test et blocage** C-wire; control wire; third wire; ~ **de tirage** fish(ing) wire; grip wire; ~ **d'épreuve** pilot wire (lead wire); ~ **d'état** sleeve wire (S-wire); ~ **d'information** data wire; ~ **émaillé** enamel-insulated wire; glazed wire; ~ **embouti** swaged lead; ~ **en l'air** open wire; floating lead; flying lead; ~ **fourré** cored wire; ~ **froid** neutral conductor; middle wire; ~ **gainé** insulated wire; ~ **guipé** lapped wire; ~ **jarretière** jumpering wire; jumper wire; cross-connect wire; patching lead; strap; ~ **machine** wire rod; ~ **métallique** wire; ~ **négatif** negative wire; ~ **nu** bare wire; open wire; ~ **nu aérien** open wire; bare wire; ~ **omnibus** bus wire; ~ **paratonnerre** earth wire (lightning); ~ **pilote** pilot wire; ~ **plein** solid wire; ~ **recuit** annealed conductor; ~ **RON** (réception) E-wire; backward signal wire (E = "ear"); inbound lead; ~ **secteur** line wire; mains lead; ~ **sensible** live wire; ~ **simple** single-core wire; ~ **simple isolé** insulated single-core wire; ~ **soudable** solderable wire; ~ **soudé** soldered wire; ~ **sous écran** screened wire; ~ **sous tension** live wire; ~ **torsadé** bridle wire; twisted wire; ~ **TRON** (transmission) M-wire; forward signal wire (M = 'mouth'); ~ **unitaire** single conductor (of wire pair); ~ **verni** enamelled wire; ~ **volant** lead; jumper wire

filament *m* heater (of a valve); filament (directly heated cathode)

file *f* FIFO list; push-up list; row; stream; line; queue; ~ **circulaire** FIFO queue; rubber-band store; ~ **d'accusés d'exécution** acknowledgement queue; ~ **d'attente** queue; waiting time; latency; queuing; ~ **d'attente de canal** channel queue; ~ **d'attente de commutation** incoming queue; ~ **d'attente de lignes** outgoing queue; ~ **d'attente de périphérique** device queue; ~ **d'attente de planification** scheduling group; ~ **d'attente de réception** input job queue; ~ **d'attente de sortie** output job queue; results hopper; ~ **d'attente de voie** channel queue; ~ **d'attente d'émission** output job queue; ~ **d'attente des réponses (FAR)** output job queue; output work queue; results hopper; ~ **d'attente d'exécution** ready queue; work-in-progress queue; run queue; active job queue; ~ **d'attente dirigée** controlled queue; ~ **d'attente d'ordre (FAO)** input job queue; input work queue; order hopper; ~ **d'attente (fichier)** temporary work queue; ~ **d'attente réception** input job stream; ~ **de réception** input job queue; ~ **de tâches en exécution** active job queue; ready queue; work-in-progress queue; run queue; ~ **de tâches logicielles armées** armed software task queue; ~ **de tâches logicielles prêtes** ready software task queue; ~ **de travail** (informatique) work queue; job queue; ~ **des échanges** message queue; ~ **double** deque; double-ended queue

filé *adj* extruded

filerie *f* cabling; wiring; ~ **préfabriquée** prefabricated wiring

filet *m* mesh; thread; net; fillet; line (of graphics image)

filetage *m* **gaz** gas taper

fileté threaded; tapped

filiale *f* chain store; affiliate; subsidiary

filière *f* card throat; (feed) gate; chain of command (hierarchy); die-stock; drawing frame; sequence; specialization; sector; discipline; training scheme; curriculum; ~ **submicronique** ultra-fast high-density IC technology; ~ **technologique** technology

filigrane *m* imprint; measling; monogram (inlaid in PCB)

filin *m* separation thread; identification thread; binder; core belt (of fibre optics); ~ **d'acier** central strength member; ~ **de couleur** colour binder; ~ **de reconnaissance** identification thread; tracer; ~ **de tirage** winch line (of cable laying); ~ **en soie** silk binder

film de conversion primer; passivating layer; conversion coating; ~ **de dissuasion** recorded announcement; ~ **de parole** recorded announcement; ~ **parlant** recorded announcement; ~ **sonore** recorded announcement

fils de conversation speech wires; talking pair; speaking pair; ~ **en main** pair-wound wires; ~ **groupés** bunch; ~ **RON et TRON** E and M wires

filtrage *m* interception; filtering; masking; smoothing; screening; n.; restriction; abridging; diversion; re-routing; secretarial call pick-up service; ~ **des entrées** input filtering

filtre *m* smoothing circuit; filter; mask; extractor; clarifier; ~ **à air** air filter; ~ **à bande étroite** narrow-bandpass filter; ~ **à compression** up-chirp filter; compression filter; ~ **à cristal** crystal filter; ~ **à deux circuits accordés** double-tuned filter; ~ **à diaphragme annulaire** diaphragm-ring filter; ~ **à fils** wire grating; mesh; ~ **à large bande** broadband filter; wideband filter; ~ **à quartz** crystal filter; ~ **absorbant** absorbing filter; ~ **accordable** tuned filter; ~ **actif** active filter; ~ **adapté** matched filter; ~ **anti-parasites** line filter; interference filter; noise filter; ~ **BLU** (de réjection image) (SSB) image reject filter; ~ **céramique** (monolithic) ceramic filter; ~ **complexe** composite wave filter; ~ **correcteur** line equalizer; ~ **coupe-bande** band-elimination filter; band-stop filter; ~ **coupure forte** sharp cut-off filter; sharp-cutting filter; ~ **d'adresses** address mask; ~ **d'aiguillage** directional filter; power separation filter; ~ **d'arrêt** suppression filter; blocking filter; band-elimination filter; ~ **de bande** decoupling network; band filter; ~ **de canal** channel filter; ~ **de cliquetis** click filter; keying filter; ~ **de compatibilité** compatibility filter; ~ **de conversion** conversion filter; ~ **de correction** correction filter; equalizer; ~ **de découplage** decoupling filter; decoupling network; ~ **de désaccentuation** de-emphasizing filter; ~ **de fréquence à absorption** absorption frequency meter; ~ **de groupe** group filter; ~ **de guide d'ondes** waveguide filter; ~ **de haute déviation** high-pass filter; ~ **de manipulation** keying filter; ~ **de mode** mode filter; ~ **de mode à anneaux** ring mode filter; ~ **de mode à réflexion** reflection mode filter; ~ **de mode résonnant** resonant mode filter; ~ **de pondération de bruit** random noise weighting network; ~ **de préaccentuation** pre-emphasis filter; ~ **de réception** receive filter; ~ **de redresseur** smoother; ~ **de réjection** rejection filter; ~ **de réjection à flancs raides** notch filter; band-stop filter; ~ **de résonance** tuned filter; ~ **de sortie** output filter; ~ **de suppression de la diaphonie** crosstalk suppression filter; ~ **de synthèse** synthesizer filter; ~ **de télétaxe** pulse filter; ~ **de transfert** through-connection filter; (FDM) connector; ~ **de transfert de groupe primaire** through-group filter (TGF); ~ **de transmission** transmission filter; ~ **de voie** channel filter; ~ **de Zobel** Zobel (electric-wave) filter; ~ **d'élimination de bande** band-stop filter; band-elimination filter; ~ **d'émission** send filter; ~ **différentiateur** differentiating filter; ~ **différentiel d'aiguillage** differential separating filter; ~ **diplexeur** diplexer (filter); ~ **dispersif** dispersive delay line; ~ **dispersif linéaire** chirp filter; linearly-dispersive delay line; ~ **d'ondes** wave filter; ~ **duplexeur** duplexer (filter); ~ **échelonné** graded filter; ~ **égaliseur** equalization filter; ~ **électrique** electric wave filter; smoothing filter; ~ **électromécanique** electromechanical filter; ~ **éliminateur** (de bande) band elimination filter; band-rejection filter; band-stop filter; suppression wave; suppression trap; ~ **en peigne** digital filter (line); comb filter; (inter-)digital filter; ~ **en pont** bridge filter; ~ **en T** T-section filter (Butterworth/Chebyshev filter); ~ **en treillis** lattice filter; ~ **image** image reject filter; ~ **interchangeable** slip-on filter; ~ **numérique** digital filter; ~ **passe-bande** bandpass filter; ~ **passe-bande à capacités commutées** switched-capacitance bandpass filter; ~ **passe-bas** low-pass filter; ~ **passe-haut** high-pass filter; ~ **piézoélectrique** crystal filter; ~ **présélecteur HF** RF preselection filter; ~ **quadruplex de sélection** four-terminal transmitter; combining unit; ~ **redresseur** ripple filter; ~ **secteur** RFI (radio-frequency interference) assembly; mains filter; ~ **séparateur** separation filter; ~ **séparateur de canal** channel separating filter; ~ **séparateur d'Ericsson** Ericsson separating filter; ~ **suppresseur d'harmoniques** harmonic suppressor; ~ **télégraphique** keying filter; ~ **transversal** transverse filter; ~ **tubulaire** tubular filter; ~ **vidéométrique** random noise weighting network

fin *f* end; trailer; termination; close-down; clear-forward; release; ~ *adj* thorough; ~ **anormale** abend; ~ **bloc canal** end-of-channel block; ~ **de bande** trailing end; end of tape; ~ **de bloc** (de transmission) end-of-transmission block (ETB); ~ **de cases** end box; ~ **de communication** end of transmission; ~ **de contrôle de ligne** link control; ~ **de course** (FC) *m* limit switch; ~ **de course** *f* end of travel; ~ **de description de grille** end form description (EFD); ~ **de dialogue** end of dialogue; ~ **de fichier** filemark; end of file (EOF); ~ **de jalon** trace off; ~ **de la mémoire** bottom of memory; ~ **de message** end-of-transmission block (ETB); ~ **de numérotation** end of dialling; end of selection; end-of-pulsing (signal); ~ **de papier** paper out; ~ **de paquet** end of (scanning) cycle; ~ **de sélection** bound; stop defining; ~ **de sélection (FIN SEL)** bound (key); stop defining; ~ **de sortie** end of output; ~ **de support** end of medium; ~ **de texte** end of text (ETX); ~ **de transmission** end of transmission (EOT); ~ **de volume** end of data; end-of-tape; ~ **d'échange (FEC)** end of exchange; end of message (EOM); ~ **d'émission** end of transmission; close of broadcasting; ~ **du bootstrap disque** disk-based bootstrap end address; ~ **du travail** sign-off

FIN SEL (v. fin de sélection)
finesse *f* **de la trame** scanning density
finition *f* finish; dressing; ~ **soignée** meticulous finish
fixation *f* mounting; ~ **de l'affaiblissement** controlled losses
fixe *adj* stationary; wired-in; pre-defined; preset
fixé *adj* defined; established; stationary; set; stipulated; mounted; specified; stabilized
flanc *m* sidewall; edge; ~ **arrière** trailing edge; ~ **arrière de l'impulsion** pulse trailing edge; ~ **descendant** trailing edge; ~ **d'impulsion** pulse edge
flasque *m* side-panel; end-plate; supporting member; rim; flange; frame; cheek
flèche *f* warp; bow; sag; curvature; bending; indent; pointer; knob; flow-line (of chart); ~ **horizontale droite** right arrow; ~ **horizontale gauche** left arrow; ~ **verticale basse** down arrow; ~ **verticale haute** up arrow
FLOG (v. faute de la logique)
flot (de commande) d'entrée input job stream; ~ **d'information** data stream; bit stream; ~ **d'octets** byte stream
flottant *adj* damped; floating; drifting
flou *m* (en télévision) blurring; blooming
fluage *m* creep
fluctuation *f* **de phase** phase fluctuation
fluide frigorigène cooling fluid; refrigerant
fluidique *f* fluid logic
fluidisé *adj* (resin-)dipped
fluorure d'éthylène ETFE; Tefzel [T.N.]
flux *m* (de trafic) traffic relation; traffic stream; stray current; unwanted current; switched loop; traffic item; parcel of traffic; point-to-point traffic; ~ **calorifique** enthalpy; ~ **de trafic** (v. courant de trafic); ~ **électronique** electron flow; ~ **énergétique** radiant flux; ~ **lumineux** luminous flux; ~ **magnétique** magnetic flux
fluxeur à mousse foam fluxer
focalisation *f* focussing; telescoping; ~ **électromagnétique** (electro-)magnetic focuss-

ing; ~ **électrostatique** electrostatic focussing; ~ **ionosphérique** ionospheric focussing
fonction *f* **attente** standby function; ~ **bis** last number repetition; ~ **booléenne** Boolean function; ~ **caractéristique** (d'un réseau d'antenne) array factor; ~ **de commande** control function; ~ **de commande d'affichage** display control function; ~ **de commande d'extension de code** code extension control function; ~ **de commande pour la présentation** presentation control function; ~ **de corrélation** correlation function; ~ **de dialogue** dialogue function; ~ **de gain** (d'une antenne) gain function; ~ **de parité** parity function; ~ **de phase** phase-change coefficient; ~ **de positionnement** positioning function; ~ **de répartition des durées entre appels** call inter-arrival distribution; ~ **de service** utility function; ~ **de transfert de modulation** modulation transfer function; ~ **du temps** time function; ~ **échelon** step function; ~ **flottante** floating-point function; ~ **haute permanente** shift lock; ~ **moniteur** monitor function; ~ **rampe** ramp function; ~ **répétition** re-do feature; ~ **secret** mute function; call privacy; ~ **télétraitement par lots** remote batch system
fonctionnalités *f pl* standard functions; services
fonctionnel *adj* performance; service
fonctionnement *m* operation; working; running; duty; mode; service; ~ **alterné** alternate mode (of oscilloscope); ~ **asynchrone** asynchronous working; ~ **bidirectionnel optimisé** bidirectional logic-seeking operation (of printer); ~ **dégradé** degraded (mode) operation; ~ **en duplex total** full-duplex operation; ~ **en mode dégradé** crippled mode (operation); ~ **en périodique régulier** periodic duty; ~ **en semi-duplex** half-duplex operation; ~ **en temps réel** real-time operation; ~ **en vol de cycles** cycle-stealing mode; ~ **intermittent** intermittent service; ~ **non surveillé** unattended operation; ~ **synchrone** synchronous working; ~ **vrai-faux** true-false qualifier
fonctionner *v* operate; function; work; ~ **en maître bus** operate in bus master mode
fonctions annexes housekeeping; overheads
fond *m* underside; base; bottom; back; rear; background; content(s); ~ **de filet** bottom of fillet; ~ **de gorge** base of yoke; ~ **de page** overlay; ~ **de panier (FdP/FdeP/FDP)** back panel; backboard; backplane; mother board; chassis; ~ **de panier imprimé** printed wiring backplane; ~ **de plan** base (border layout of PCB/backplane); ~ **sous-**

brillant half-tone; subdued background; ~ **transparent** transparent background

fondamental *adj* radical; basic; fundamental; dominant

fondamentalement *adv* inextricably

fonderie *f* casting

fonds de commerce goodwill; business; ~ **de roulement** working capital; reserve; cash-flow

fondu *adj* (fusible) blown (of fuse); burnt-out; ~ **enchaîné** cross-fade

fongibles *pl* expendable items; perishable items; interchangeable stocks; accessories

fontaine céramique nozzle (of wave-soldering machine)

fonte grise cast iron; ~ *f* **mécanique** grey iron

forçage *m* forcing; setting; next; ~ **avance** next phase; ~ **de bit à 1/0** set/reset bit; ~ **d'une nouvelle page** forcing a new page

force *f* **attractive** attractive force; ~ **coercitive** coercive force; ~ **contre-électromotrice** (f.c.é.m.) back e.m.f.; ~ **cymomotrice** cymomotive force (of aerial); ~ **d'accouplement** coupling force; ~ **d'adhérence** adhesion force; bond strength; ~ **de contact** contact force; ~ **de dénudage** stripping force/effort; ~ **de frappe** hammer intensity; strike force (nuclear deterrent); ~ **de rétention** mating strength; ~ **du son** loudness; ~ **électromagnétique** electromagnetic force; ~ **électromotrice** (f.é.m.) electromotive force (e.m.f.); electric potential; ~ **électromotrice constante** constant e.m.f.; ~ **électromotrice psophométrique** psophometric e.m.f.; ~ **magnétomotrice** magnetomotive force; magnetic potential; ~ **majeure** Act of God; unforeseen circumstances (hostilities/embargo, etc); extenuating circumstances; ~ **motrice** motive (driving) power; ~ **photoélectromotrice** photo-electromotive force; ~ **thermoélectromotrice** thermo-electromotive force

forcé *adj* next; preset; forced

forcer *v* (à) inject; set (of bit); go to next

foret *m* drill; drill bit; ~ **mécanicien** jobber's drill

forfait *m* flat rate; non-returnable deposit; fixed charge; fixed fee

forfaitaire *adj* flat rate; fixed-charge; lump-sum

formage à chaud hot working; ~ **à froid** cold working

format *m* size; format; pattern; ~ **compact** compact format; ~ **court** short format; ~ **de paquet** packet format; ~ **de texte** text format; ~ **d'enregistreur** régister size; ~ **détaillé** detailed format; indented

format; ~ **long** long format

formatage *m* formatting

formateur *m* formatter; instructor; trainer; shaper

formation *f* training; formatting; shaping; building; instruction; assimilation; ~ **automatisée** computer-assisted training; ~ **de base** basic training; ~ **de circuits superposés** superposing; ~ **de groupe de base** basic group formation; ~ **des cadres** executive training; management training; ~ **des signaux par déplacement de fréquence** frequency-shift signalling; frequency-shift keying (FSK); ~ **des signaux par modulation de fréquence** frequency-change signalling; ~ **des signaux par modulation d'amplitude** amplitude-change signalling; ~ **des signaux par mutation de fréquence** frequency-exchange signalling; ~ **directe** (sur l'équipement) hands-on training; ~ **électrique** electrical forming; ~ **professionnelle** vocational training; ~ **sur le tas** on-the-job training; hands-on training; ~ **technique** technical training

forme *f* pattern; format; structure; shape; syntax (of message); ~ **binaire** binary form; ~ **de câbles** cable harness; cable form; ~ **de réalisation** embodiment (of patent); ~ **d'onde** waveform; gating signal; ~ **d'onde carrée** square waveform; ~ **d'onde de télévision** television waveform; ~ **d'onde en dents de scie** sawtooth waveform; ramp; ~ **d'onde périodique** periodic waveform; ~ **d'onde pulsatoire** pulsating waveform; ~ **d'onde rectangulaire** rectangular waveform; square waveform; ~ **d'onde triangulaire** triangular waveform; sawtooth; ~ **d'une impulsion** pulse shape; ~ **intégrale** unsampled form; ~ **interne** high-speed format; fast-core format; ~ **libre** free-format; ~ **numérique** digital form

formule *f* terms; equation; formula; expression; ~ **d'Erlang** erlang formula

fort *adj* marked; singular; ~ **calibre** heavy-duty; ~ **régime** heavy-duty; ~ **trafic** heavy traffic; high usage

fortement déconseillé highly inadvisable; strongly deprecated

fortuite *adj* occasional; chance; incidental; fortuitous; haphazard

fossé *m* well; ditch; trench

FOT (v. fréquence optimale de trafic)

foudre *f* lightning

fouillis d'écho clutter; ~ **du sol** ground clutter; ~ **par la pluie** rain clutter; ~ **par nuage** cloud clutter

four *m* oven; ~ **à passage** oven with

conveyor; ~ **de refusion** reflow oven

fourche f (cosse/plot à) spade terminal/connector; lug; IDC terminal contact (tuning fork); ~ **opto(-électronique)** slotted optoswitch

fourchette f deviation; bracket; span; limits; range; gap; scope; dead zone (of galvanometer); dual trace; set; ~ **d'abonnés** set of consecutive subscriber numbers; ~ **de pourcentage** constituent concentrations

fournir v submit; source; provide; supply; deliver

fournisseur m supplier; manufacturer; producer; vendor; ~ (d'information) service (information) provider

fournisseur-système data base operator/supplier

fourniture f (de courant) power supply; electricity

fourniture(s) f (pl) fixtures and fittings; appointments; accoutrements

fourniture clés en main turnkey delivery

fourreau m stick (IC container); sheath

foyer m focal point; seat (of fire); focus

FP (feuille particulière) detail specification

fractionnement m splitting; modularization; segmentation; dissection; ~ **de blocs** block-splitting; ~ **de la charge** load-splitting

fractionner v dissect (of instruction); split; segment

fragilisant adj stressful; fatigue inducing

fragmentation f disassembly

frais m petty cash (file); ~ m pl **de déplacement** travelling expenses; ~ **de fabrication** manufacturing overheads; ~ **de séjour** subsistence expenses; living expenses; ~ **de voyage** travelling costs; ~ **financiers** financial costs; outlay; ~ **généraux** overheads

fraise f spin

fraisure f countersinking

franc adj **à bord** free on board (FOB)

franchir v clear; release; open; override; span; ~ **le seuil** cross the threshold; step outside the range/limits

franchise f **d'impôt** tax concession

franchissement m **de seuil** out-of-limits condition; overload; ~ **des tonalités intermédiaires** intermediate tone override; ~ **des tonalités PTT** exchange (PSN) tone bridging

franco gare free on rail (FOR); ~ **quai** free on wharf (FOW)

franges f pl ringing

frappe f key(-stroke); stroke; typing; character transfer; ~ **anticipée** rollover; type-ahead feature; ~ **de texte en colonnes**

tabular entry; ~ **non encrée** stencil (of typing)

frapper v key; enter; type

frein m inhibitor; sealant; retardant; absorber; lock; brake; repellent; drag; ~ **à court-circuit** short-circuit brake; ~ **de fluage** deformation inhibitor; resin-flow barrier; ~ **thermique** deformation inhibitor; heat-transfer link

freinage m drag; retardation; deceleration

fréquence f frequency; rate; periodicity; tone; ~ **à battement nul** zero-beat frequency; ~ **acoustique** audiofrequency; ~ **angulaire** angular frequency; pulsatance; radian angular frequency; ~ **assignée** assigned frequency; ~ **au repos** non-modulated frequency; ~ **audible** audio-frequency (AF); ~ **autorisée** authorized frequency; allowed band; ~ **basse** low frequency; ~ **caractéristique** characteristic frequency; ~ **centrale** centre frequency; ~ **conjuguée** image frequency; second-channel frequency; ~ **critique** critical frequency; threshold frequency; cut-off frequency; ~ **critique de saut** zero-skip frequency (ZSF); ~ **d'absorption** absorption frequency; ~ **d'accord** tuned frequency; resonant frequency; ~ **d'alignement** tie-down point; ~ **d'appel** calling frequency; ringing frequency; ~ **de balayage horizontal** line frequency; ~ **de balayage vertical** field frequency; ~ **de base** fundamental (frequency); clock frequency; clock rate; ~ **de battement** beat frequency (of heterodyne); ~ **de boucle** loop frequency; ~ **de chocs** collision frequency; ~ **de code** code frequency; ~ **de combinaison** combination frequency; combination tone; ~ **de contrôle** test frequency; acknowledgement frequency; barrier frequency; ~ **de coupure** cut-off frequency; barrier frequency; theoretical cut-off frequency; critical frequency; ~ **de coupure effective** effective cut-off frequency; ~ **de courant d'appel** ringing frequency; ~ **de découpage** quench frequency; chopping frequency; ~ **de demi-ligne** half-line frequency; ~ **de denture** slot-ripple frequency; ~ **de dépassement** dip frequency; ~ **de déviation** alternate frequency; ~ **de fonctionnement** working frequency; operating frequency; ~ **de garde** guard frequency; ~ **de groupe primaire** group frequency; ~ **de groupe secondaire** supergroup frequency; ~ **de la base de temps** time-base frequency; ~ **de la porteuse** carrier frequency; bearer frequency; ~ **de (la) sousporteuse** sub-carrier frequency; ~ **de ligne** line frequency; scanning line frequency; ~ **de mesure** test frequency; ~ **de**

F

modulation modulation frequency; ~ de neutralisation disabling tone; ~ de phase phase frequency; ~ de points dot frequency; ~ de porteuse radio radio-carrier frequency; ~ de radar radar frequency; ~ de radiodiffusion broadcast-band frequency; ~ de réception receive frequency; receiving frequency; ~ de recouvrement crossover frequency; ~ de récurrence (pulse) repetition frequency (PRF); pulse rate (reciprocal of pulse period); ~ de référence reference frequency; ~ de réjection rejection frequency; ~ de répétition repetition frequency; repetition rate; ~ de répétition (d'impulsion) pulse repetition frequency (PRF); ~ de répétition des impulsions pulse repetition frequency (PRF); ~ de répétition d'impulsions échelonnée staggered pulse repetition frequency; ~ de résonance (self-)resonant frequency; ~ de résonance en parallèle parallel-resonant frequency; ~ de résonance en série series-resonant frequency; ~ (de) secteur line frequency; mains frequency; ~ de signal signal frequency (SF); ~ de signalisation signalling frequency; ~ de train d'ondes group frequency; wave-train frequency; ~ de trame picture frequency; frame frequency; ~ de transition transition frequency; crossover frequency; turnover frequency; ~ de travail nominal frequency; ~ de travail bateau-côte ship-shore working frequency; ~ de veille search frequency; ~ de verrouillage locking frequency; ~ de wobulation sweep frequency; ~ décalée staggered frequency; ~ d'échantillonnage sampling frequency; sampling rate; ~ d'erreurs error rate; ~ des bits bit rate; ~ des interruptions interrupt rate; ~ descendante frequency falling (of right-hand polarized radiation band); ~ d'essai test frequency; ~ d'étalonnage calibration frequency; ~ d'évanouissement fading frequency; fading rate; ~ d'exploration field frequency; ~ d'horloge clock frequency; clock rate; ~ différentielle intermodulation frequency; ~ d'image picture frequency; frame frequency; ~ d'impulsion pulse frequency (PF); ~ d'interférence interfering frequency; ~ d'intermodulation intermodulation frequency; ~ d'interrogation challenge frequency; interrogation frequency; ~ d'ondes carrées square-wave frequency; ~ du courant d'appel ringing frequency; ~ du faisceau directionnel range frequency; ~ du jour day frequency; ~ élevée treble tone; ~ étalon calibrated (standard) frequency; ~ étrangère extrane-

ous frequency; ~ fixe spot frequency; narrow-band; ~ fondamentale fundamental frequency; principal frequency; ~ harmonique harmonic frequency; ~ hétérodyne heterodyne frequency; ~ horloge clock frequency; clock rate; ~ identique à battement nul zero-beat frequency; ~ image image frequency; second-channel frequency; ~ infra-acoustique sub-sonic frequency; infrasonic frequency; ~ infratéléphonique sub-telephone frequency; ~ instantanée instantaneous frequency; ~ intermédiaire (FI) intermediate frequency (IF); ~ internationale d'appel international calling frequency; ~ latérale side frequency; ~ libre free-running frequency; ~ limite limiting frequency; limit frequency; ~ limite équivalente equivalent limit frequency; ~ maximale d'oscillation maximum oscillation frequency; ~ maximale utilisable maximum usable frequency (MUF); junction frequency; ~ minimale utilisable lowest usable (high) frequency (LUF); ~ montante frequency rising (of left-hand polarized radiation band); ~ moyenne medium frequency (MF); intermediate frequency (IF); ~ moyenne de la porteuse mean carrier frequency; ~ musicale audio-frequency (AF); ~ nominale assigned frequency; fundamental frequency; ~ optimale de fonctionnement optimum working frequency; ~ optimale de trafic (FOT) optimum traffic frequency; optimum working frequency; ~ partielle partial frequency; ~ pilote pilot frequency; control frequency; ~ pompe pump frequency (of paramp/maser); ~ porteuse carrier frequency; carrier; ~ porteuse commune common carrier frequency; ~ porteuse (de) son sound carrier frequency; ~ porteuse d'image picture tone; ~ porteuse virtuelle virtual carrier frequency; ~ préréglée preset frequency; ~ principale master frequency; ~ propre natural frequency; ~ pure pure tone; simple tone; ~ radioélectrique radio frequency; ~ résultante sum(mation) frequency; ~ singulaire single frequency; ~ sonore étalon standard tone; concert pitch; ~ sous-harmonique sub-harmonic frequency; ~ supra-acoustique super-audio frequency; ultrasonic frequency; supersonic frequency; ~ supratéléphonique super-telephone frequency; ~ téléphonique voice frequency; telephone frequency; ~ ultra acoustique super-audio frequency; ultrasonic frequency; ~ ultra sonore super-audio frequency; ultrasonic frequency; ~ vocale (FV) telephone frequency; voice frequency (VF); audio-frequency (AF); ~ **zéro** zero frequency

fréquencemètre *m* frequency meter; wave meter; frequency counter; ~ **à cavité** cavity frequency meter; ~ **à résonance** resonant (cavity) frequency meter; ~ **compteur** counting-rate meter; frequency counter; ~ **numérique** digital frequency meter

fréquentiel *adj* frequency-domain

frettage *m* heat shrinking; shrinking; thermofit

fretter *v* attach/mount/apply cable ties; fit heat-shrinkable sleeve

frigorie *f* negative kilo-calorie

frisure *f* curling; ripple (of solder mask)

frittage *m* sintering

fritté *adj* sintered

friture *f* sizzle; sizzling noise; frying; crackling; contact noise; radio interference; acoustic shock; side tone

front *m* (wave-)front; leading edge; ~ **arrière** trailing edge; ~ **avant** leading edge; ~ **de descente** negative-going transition; falling edge; ~ **de l'onde** wave front; ~ **de montée** rise time; positive-going transition; rising edge; ~ **de retombée** fall time; ~ **descendant** falling edge; negative-going transition; ~ **montant** positive-going transition; rise time; rising edge; ~ **positif** positive-going edge; ~ **raide** wave surge; steep edge (of pulse); ~ **tombant** falling edge

frontal *adj* front-end; ~ **d'accès** network gateway; ~ **de transmission en mode caractères** asynchronous line controller; ~ **d'échange et de commande** front-end control logic

frontière *f* boundary; border

fronton *m* facade; front panel; top section

frotteur *m* brush; wiper; sliding contact; ~ **d'essai** test brush

fruste *adj* primitive; rudimentary; unsophisticated

FS (v. face soudure)

ft (fonction) function

FU (unité fonctionnelle) building block; hardware unit; ~ **support** (unité fonctionnelle) data carrier; data medium

fugitif *adj* transient; fleeting; elusive; momentary; spurious

fugitive (clé f.) non-locking (of key); momentary-action (switch)

fugitivement *adv* momentarily

fuite *f* loss; drop; leakage; leak; ~ **de grille** grid leak; ~ **d'onde porteuse** carrier leak; ~ **franche** gross leak

fus. (v. fusible)

fuseau *m* plait; braid (set of wire strands); spindle; bobbin; bunch; ~ **de radioguidage** homing band; homing range; ~ **horaire** time zone

fusée *f* rocket; fuse; ~ **d'avion téléguidée** guided aircraft rocket (GAR); ~ **de proximité** proximity fuse

fusiblage *m* fuses; fuse system

fusible (fus.) *m* fuse (element); circuit-breaker; cut-out; ~ **à cartouche** cartridge fuse; ~ **à couteau** knife(-blade) fuse; switch fuse; ~ **à haut pouvoir de coupure (HPC)** high-rupture capacity fuse (HRC); (heavy duty) protector block; ~ **bon** fuse intact; ~ **classe aM** (accompagnement moteur) motor-protection fuse; A motor-rated fuse; ~ **classe gF** normal distribution fuse; ~ **classe gI** heavy-duty fuse; industrial fuse; ~ **cylindrique** cartridge fuse; ~ **de fort calibre** heavy-duty fuse (high rating); ~ **de protection** security fuse (to protect proprietary logic); ~ **fondu** burnt-out fuse; blown fuse; ~ **instantané** quick-break fuse; fast-blow fuse; ~ **rapide** fast-blow fuse; ~ **retardé** anti-surge (delay) fuse; slow-blow fuse; ~ **sauté** blown fuse; ~ **sectionneur** fuse disconnector; cut-out; fuse isolator; ~ **temporisé** slow-blow fuse; time-lag fuse; delayed action fuse; antisurge fuse

fusion *f* merging; (s)melting; fusion; merger; charge (burden)

fusionner *v* (= unir) coalesce (data files); merge; collate

fût *m* butt (of contact); cask

FV (fréquence vocale) VF (voice frequency)

G

gabarit *m* reference (parameters); standard/ limiting curves(s); absolute maximum values; extreme operating conditions; upper/ lower thresholds; boundaries; tolerance limits; acceptance/rejection criteria; signal waveform; timing diagram; envelope; pattern; clearance gauge; template; jig; range; transmission envelope; mask; model; format; curve; contours; ~ **à trois joncs** three-wire gauge; ~ **d'affaiblissement** attenuation limiting curves; ~ **d'arrêt d'appel** ring trip; ~ **de centrage** centring jig; ~ **de ligne** line envelope; line reference parameter; ~ **de ligne d'abonné** limit values for electrical parameters (of subscriber line); ~ **de l'impulsion** pulse limiting curves; ~ **de perçage** hole layout (diagram); ~ **de tension** voltage range; typical voltages; ~ **d'essai** test parameters; ~ **d'essai de ligne** line test curve; ~ **d'indexage** indexing template

gâche *f* punching-error rate; staple

gâchette *f* tumbler; trigger; pawl; catch; follower; gate; ~ **de triac** triac gate

gain *m* amplification (factor); gain; increase; ~ **absolu d'une antenne** power gain (referred to isotropic radiator); ~ **composite** overall gain; ~ **d'antenne** aerial gain; ~ **de transmission** transmission gain; ~ **d'étage** gain per stage; ~ **différentiel** differential gain; ~ **d'insertion** insertion gain; ~ **d'un amplificateur** amplifier gain; amplification factor; ~ **d'un répéteur** repeater gain; ~ **en fonction du niveau d'entrée** gain tracking; ~ **en module** absolute gain; gain ratio; ~ **en puissance** power gain; increased power; increment; ~ **en tension** transfer function; ~ **hors axe** off-axis gain; ~ **isomorphe** transfer function; ~ **isotrope d'une antenne** power gain referred to an isotropic radiator; ~ **paramétrique** parametric gain; ~ **pour courant continu** direct current (DC) amplification factor; ~ **statique** (hFE) (common emitter) DC current gain; static value of the forward current transfer ratio (in common-emitter configuration); ~ **statique en tension** DC voltage gain; ~ **transductique** transducer gain; ~ **unitaire** unity gain; ~ **variable dans le temps (GVT)** swept gain

gaine *f* boot; duct; shield; sheath; conduit; sleeve; support; braid(ing); case; cladding; jacket; ~ **aluminium** aluminium jacket; ~ **anodique** anode glow; ~ **de poubelle** bin liner; ~ **d'électrons** (ions) electron (or ion) sheath; ~ **en téflon rétractable** heat-shrinkable PTFE sheath; ~ **extérieure** (outer) sheathing; ~ **isolante** insulated tubing; ~ **PE** polyethylene sheath; ~ **plastique** plastic sheath; ~ **téflon** PTFE sheathing; ~ **thermorétractable** heat-shrinkable tube/ sheath(ing)

gainé *adj* sheathed

galbage *m* tenting

galbe *m* curvature; projection

galerie *f* **commerciale** shopping arcade

galet *m* roller; idler; ~ **bourreur** feed roller; ~ **d'alimentation** feed roller; picker; ~ **récepteur** interlocking roller

galette *f* disk-pack; contact disk; spool (of tape); pad; plate; wafer; flat coil; section; slab; billet; stack

galettes jumelées twin wafers (of switch)

galon *m* edging tape; trimming tape

galopin *m* idler wheel

galvanique *adj* electrical; galvanic; sacrificial; anodic

galvanisé *adj* hot-dipped

galvanomètre *m* galvanometer; ammeter; single-needle system; ~ **à câble mobile** moving coil galvanometer; ~ **à cordes** Einthoven (string) galvanometer; ~ **balistique** ballistic galvanometer; ~ **différentiel** differential galvanometer

galvanoplastie *f* electro-plating; electro-deposition

gamme *f* job description schedule; manufacturer's instructions; range; scale; plan; pad; format; layout sheet; product line; product mix; spectrum; specification; ~ **d'accord** tuning range; ~ **d'ajustement de la tension de décalage** offset voltage drift; ~ **de contrôle** inspection plan; general inspection procedure; ~ **de fabrication** job description schedule; production master; ~ **de fréquences** frequency range; frequency band; ~ **de radiodiffusion** broadcasting range; ~ **d'ondes** wave range; ~ **dynamique** dynamic range

garage *m* temporary storage area (of register)

garantie *f* warranty; collateral; ~ **pièces et main d'œuvre** warranty against material defects

garde *f* guard; hold; blank; clearance; ~ **de double-appel** brokerage call; broker's call; ~ **de rétro-appel** brokerage call; broker's call; hold consulted party; ~ **d'inversion** shift-lock (mechanism); ~ **jusqu'à liberation complète** extended engaged condition

garni *adj* (d'espaces/de zéros) zero-filled; padded with blanks

garnir *v* load; pad; fill; line; pack; add to; ~ **de caractères** character fill

garnissage *m* accessories

garniture *f* armature; fittings; lining; packing(-piece); 'O'-ring; seal; gasket

gauche *adj* most significant; high-order; leftmost; leading

gauchissement *m* buckling; warp; bow

gaufrage *m* puckering (of paper); embossment

gaufre *f* embossment; figure

gaufrer *v* crimp

gaussien *adj* Gaussian

gaz *m* **de remplissage inerte** inert filling gas; ~ **électronique** electron gas; ~ **frigoporteur** chilled gas

GE (v. groupe électrogène)

GEC (v. groupe éclaté de concentration)

gélification *f* gelation

gêne *f* inconvenience; annoyance effect; stress; nuisance; impairment; discomfort

général *adj* sundry; general; common; main; broad

généralisé *adj* widespread; in common use; standard; extended; vernacular

généralités *f pl* preamble; introduction; general comments; main aspects; design features; basic outlines; overview; thumbnail sketch

générateur *m* generator; dynamo; generating program; disturbing source; signal source; ~ **air chaud** hot-air blower; ~ **automatique de caractères** automatic character generator; ~ **basse fréquence (BF)** signal generator; ~ **capacitif de dents de scie** capacitive sawtooth generator; ~ **d'air chaud** hot-air blower; ~ **d'appel** ringing-current generator; ~ **de balayage** sweep generator; ~ **de balayage vertical** framing generator (television); ~ **de bande** system tape generator; ~ **de base de temps** time base; time-base generator; ~ **de bruit** noise generator; ~ **de bruits impulsifs** impulse (noise) generator; click generator; surge generator; ~ **de chocs** impulse generator; surge generator; ~ **de compte-rendus** report generator; ~ **de conditionnement** training generator; ~ **de courant d'appel** ringing (current) generator;

~ **de courant simple** neutral-current generator; ~ **de dents de scie** ramp generator; sweep generator; time-base generator; sawtooth generator; ~ **de fonction(s)** function generator; ~ **de fréquences** frequency generator; tone generator; ~ **de grille** forms generator; ~ **de la bande système** system tape generator; ~ **de mélodie** chime generator; ~ **de mot de verrouillage de trame** frame generator; ~ **de parité huit digits** eight-bit parity generator/ checker; ~ **de parole** speech generator; ~ **de programme d'édition** report program generator (RPG); ~ **de rampe** ramp (voltage) generator; threshold generator; time-base generator; sweep generator; sawtooth generator; ~ **de rampe synchronisable** triggerable ramp generator; ~ **de report anticipé de retenue** (high-speed) carry look-ahead generator; ~ **de rythme** timer; clock; timing signal generator; time-base generator; ~ **de séquences** pattern generator; ~ **de seuils** reference-voltage generator; ~ **de signal-standard** reference signal generator; ~ **de signaux** signal generator; ~ **de signaux carrés** square-wave generator; ~ **de signaux de balayage ligne** line-scan generator; ~ **de signaux de balayage trame** field-scan generator; ~ **de signaux de temps** coded time-signal generator; ~ **de tension** voltage generator; ~ **de tonalités (GT)** tone generator; ~ **de tri** sort generator; ~ **d'échos fictifs** dummy echo generator; ~ **d'effacement** blanking-pulse generator; ~ **délivrant des signaux carrés** square-wave (signal) generator; ~ **d'état** report generator; ~ **d'harmoniques** harmonic generator; ~ **d'impulsions** pulse generator; impulse generator; surge generator; ~ **d'impulsions arythmiques** jitterbug; ~ **d'impulsions de radar** keyer; ~ **d'ondes** wave generator; ~ **d'ondes carrées** square-wave generator; ~ **d'ondes sinusoïdales** sine-wave generator; ~ **d'ordres** instruction generator; ~ **d'oscillations** oscillation generator; ~ **électro-optique** opto-electronic generator; ~ **électrostatique** frictional machine; induction machine; static machine; influence machine; electrostatic generator; ~ **haute fréquence (HF)** audio generator; ~ **pseudo-aléatoire** pseudo-random generator; ~ **solaire héliotrope** heliotropic solar generator; ~ **TBF** low-frequency waveform generator; ~ **transfert** generator

génération *f* generating routine; creation; ~ **accidentelle** drop-in; ~ **de système** system building; ~ **d'horloge (GH)** timing control

génératrice   132

génératrice f ou adj generator; dynamo; specimen; driving; generating line; ~ de câble common cable specimen; ~ polyphasée polyphase generator; ~ shunt shunt generator

générique adj type; suite of configuration programs (for exchanges of the same class)

génie m civil earthworks; civil engineering; public building and works; ~ informatique computer engineering; ~ nucléaire nuclear engineering

gentex m gentex (automatic international telegram exchange system); overseas telegram service

gerbage m stacking; ~ statique et dynamique stacking height for storage and transit

gestion f handling; management; maintenance; servicing; control; translator; housekeeping; operation and maintenance; scheduling; CONTROL key; processing; ~ automatisée automated management; process control; ~ d'abonnés subscriber line administration; ~ d'agenda task activation calendar; ~ de base de données data base management system; ~ de boîte aux lettres mailbox management; ~ de la signalisation signalling processor; ~ de l'accès des processeurs au bus de communication par microprogramme firmware processor communications handler for bus control (PCH); ~ de l'écran screen management; ~ de messages message handling; ~ de pile stack control; ~ de positionnements unit-status signalling functions; ~ des abonnés subscriber line connection; ~ des acheminements route administration; ~ des files d'attente des tâches task queue management; ~ des files d'attente d'événements event queue management; ~ des fonds de page forms overlay; ~ des informations data handling; ~ des périphériques device management; ~ des sociétés centralized extension service (CENTREX); ~ des stocks stock control theory; ~ des tâches task scheduling; ~ du fichier file maintenance; trap handling; ~ du réseau network management; ~ du temps time management; ~ impair odd translator; ~ informations mémoire memory processing card; memory management card;

~ mémoire memory management; storage allocation; ~ mot programme program word servicing; instruction handler; ~ occupé signal busy; ~ par canal sémaphore common channel (signalling) management; ~ physique resource management; materials handling; product despatch; ~ prévisionnelle management forecasting; budgeting; ~ pupitre console management

gestionnaire m handler; manager; custodian; keeper; (data) administrator; ~ d'accès périphériques device management; ~ de contexte context manager; ~ de file d'attente queue handler; ~ de terminal tamponné buffered terminal manager

GH (v. génération d'horloge)

GIE (v. groupement d'intérêt économique)

gisement m bearing; direct bearing; relative bearing; ~ vers l'arrière back bearing

glissement m slip; sliding; drift; shift; Doppler drift; ~ commandé controlled slip; ~ de fréquence frequency slip; frequency drift; ~ du zéro zero shift; ~ graduel de la fréquence slow drift; ~ (défilement) horizontal de l'image line slip; ~ par inertie cinching (of tape); ~ (défilement) vertical de l'image picture slip; frame slip

glissière f slide(r); runner; gliding track; slideway; rail; card guide; ~ droite R.H. (righthand) slide/runner; ~ gauche L.H. (lefthand) slide/runner

global adj aggregate; inclusive; gross; overall; comprehensive; total; universal; common; cumulative; whole; integral; unified; bulk; company-wide; batch

GO (v. grandes ondes)

gomme f eraser (graphics); rubout (mode); ~ détersive PCB eraser; PCB cleaner

goupille f spring pin; cotter pin; ~ conique taper pin; ~ cylindrique cotter pin; spring pin; ~ élastique spring pin; ~ fendue split pin; cotter pin; ~ Mécanindus [A.C.] spring pin; ~ rapide quick-release pin

gousset *m* plate; corner-piece; fillet

goutelette *f* globule; droplet

goutte *f* (= dépôt) deposit; blob (of solder)

gouttière *f* channel; trough; gutter; trunk(ing); trench; duct

GPL (gaz à pétrole liquifié) LPG (liquid petroleum gas)

GQ (v. groupe quaternaire)

grâce à owing to; by virtue of; due to

gradateur *m* **de lumière** dimmer

gradient *m* rate of rise; slope; gradient

grading *m* grading pattern

grain *m* track; path; guide head; die; grit; pad; tip; point (of contact); ~ **de contact mobile** path of moving contact

graissage *m* emboldening (of print)

graisseur *m* lubricator

grammage *m* density (of paper); substance (unit: g/m^2)

grand public consumer applications

grande densité de fibres high fibre-packing density; ~ **distance** long-haul; ~ **puissance** heavy duty; ~ **série** full-scale production; mass production; ~ **station** high traffic capacity station; ~ **vitesse** high speed; ~ **vitesse de défilement** fast mode (of tape)

grandes ondes (GO) long-wave (LW)

grandeur *f* magnitude; value; size; length; quantity; variable; parameter; strength; scale; (statistical) population; ~ **de champ** field strength; ~ **d'influence** governing parameter; ~ **nature** to scale; actual size; ~ **naturelle** to scale; actual size; ~ **perturbatrice** disturbance variable; ~ **réelle** actual size; to scale

granule *m* granule (smallest logical unit of storage)

granulé (grandeur du bloc transféré entre disque et mémoire centrale) size of disk storage block (in sectors); (physical) block

granulométrie *f* particle-size (analysis); particle distribution

graphe *m* graph; status; ~ **antisymétrique** antisymmetric graph; ~ **connexe** connected graph; ~ **courbe** line graph; connected graph; ~ **non orienté** non-oriented graph; undirected graph; ~ **orienté** oriented graph; directed graph; ~ **planaire** planar graph; ~ **point-à-groupe** point-to-group graph; ~ **secteurs** pie chart; ~ **sectoriel** pie chart; ~ **sectoriel** ("camembert") pie chart

graphie *f* CW communication (morse)

graphique *n* graph; chart; diagram; illustration; graphics; plot; ~ **enregistré** level recorder chart

graphiques décisionnels decision-making graphics

graphisme *m* artwork; graphics; graphic

symbol(s); ~ **par points** bit-mapped graphics; dot graphics; ~ **spécial** special symbol

graphitage *m* mark-sensing

graphite *m* **sphéroïdal** nodular cast iron

grappe *f* cluster; ~ **de stations** workstation cluster

graticule *m* reference grid; graticule; reticule; ~ **est** grid east; easting

grave *adj* serious; ominous; severe

gravé *adj* etched; engraved; inscribed

graver en mémoire load into memory; permanently store

gravité *f* seriousness; severity

gravure *f* etching; printing (of film); engraving; lithography; ~ **en creux** incised marking; die sinking; inset etching; engraving; embossing; ~ **en profondeur enregistrement vertical** vertical recording; hill-and-dale recording; ~ **sous-jacente et saillie** undercut and overhang

greffé *adj* retro-fitted

grenaillage *m* shot blasting

grenaille *f* shot; damper; granule

grésillement *m* sizzling; crackling; contact noise

griffage *m* crimping

griffe *f* spur; prong; dog; climber; ~ **de monteur** lineman's climber

grignoteuse *f* nibbler

grille *f* guard; grill; grid; deflector; shield; grate; lacing; aperture plate; chart; mesh; damper; slot; lattice; matrix; gate; command form; (screen) page; (screen) format; ~ **à volets réglables** adjustable blade damper; ~ **alignée** shadow grid; ~ **au silicium** silicon gate; ~ **codée** scan matrix; ~ **d'accueil** introduction ("hello") page; sign-on form; log-on form; ~ **d'alimentation** power distribution interface; ~ **d'arrêt** suppressor grid; ~ **de commande** (control) grid; ~ **de défilement** diffuser (mesh/grid); ~ **de désionisation** de-ionizing grid; ~ **de distribution d'énergie** power supply grid; ~ **de l'exécutif** executive form; ~ **de modulation** modulation electrode; modulation grid; ~ **de programmation** programme schedule (of TV); ~ **de saisie** format (page); ~ **d'émargement** sign-on form; sign-on page; ~ **d'énergie** power distribution cabinet; ~ **d'imprimante** printer spacing chart; ~ **filtre** filter mesh; ~ **inactinique** (polyester film) PCB drafting sheet

grillé *adj* burned out

grip-fil *m* probe

grippage *m* seizing; bonding

grip-test *m* probe; test prod; ~ **grand modèle**

long-reach probe (with spring-loaded hook); ~ **petit modèle** (plunger-action) compact hook-grip probe
gris foncé charcoal (grey)
grisé *adj* cross-hatched; shaded
gros industriels blue-chip companies
grossier *adj* coarse (of setting)
grossièrement *adv* broadly speaking
groupage *m* blocking; batching; joint understanding; gathering; bunching; clustering; ~ **par lots** batching
groupe *m* bank; plant; cluster; group; unit; batch; battery; division; party; pack; bunch; installation; complete assembly; set; ~ **à accessibilité partielle** limited availability group; ~ **à accessibilité totale** full availability group; ~ **à douze canaux** twelve-channel group; primary group; ~ **adaptateur de signalisation** signalling adaptor group; ~ **bâton** dummy group; ~ **contrôle qualité sur site** installation quality group; ~ **convertisseur** motor generator (set); converter set/unit; ~ **d'abonnés** subscriber group; ~ **d'abonnés temporel éclaté** remote subscriber terminal group; ~ **d'alimentation** electrical power unit; ~ **de bits consécutifs** byte; ~ **de boîtiers** package group; ~ **de canaux** channel group; ~ **de charge** battery charger; ~ **de cinq bits** quintet; five-bit byte; ~ **de code** code group; ~ **de contacts** contact set; ~ **de deux bits** dibit; ~ **de douze bits** slab; ~ **de gestion physique** product despatching group; ~ **de lignes** (dans un multiplage partiel) grading group; sub-group; ~ **de moments** code group (e.g. tetrad); ~ **de positions binaires** byte; ~ **de quatre bits** (= tétrade) tetrad; four-bit byte; nibble (nybble); quartet; ~ **de relais** relay set; ~ **de six bits** (= hexet) sextet; six-bit byte; ~ **de travail** working party; ~ **de trois bits** (= triade) triplet; triad; three-bit byte; ~ **d'équipement de synchronisation** synchronization equipment group; ~ **d'études réseaux** network planning group; ~ **d'identification** identification group; ~ **d'octets** gulp; ~ **d'ondes périodiques** periodic pulse train; ~ **d'usagers** user group; ~ **éclaté de concentration (GEC)** remote concentration group (RCG); ~ **électrogène (GE)** generator set; ~ **fermé d'abonnés** closed user group (CUG); ~ **fermé d'usagers** closed user group (CUG); ~ **moteur** power plant; ~ **moteur-générateur** motor generator set; ~ **moto-ventilateur** motor-ventilator bank; ~ **opérateur** operator set; ~ **primaire** channel group; primary group; twelve-channel group (of carrier current system);

carrier group; basic group; ~ **primaire de base** basic group; ~ **primaire non démodulé** through group; ~ **produits** product marketing group; ~ **quaternaire (GQ)** supermastergroup; ~ **quinaire** jumbo group; ~ **réfrigérant** cooling plant; ~ **secondaire** (de voies téléphoniques à courants porteurs) supergroup; ~ **secondaire de base** basic supergroup; ~ **secondaire non démodulé** through supergroup; ~ **terminal** terminal group; ~ **tertiaire** mastergroup
groupement *m* line group; multi-line hunting group; accumulator; switch multiple; bunch; bunching; array; cluster; pool; bank; ~ **de diodes** diode array; ~ **de lignes** line group; hunt group; ~ **de lignes réseau** trunk group; ~ **de postes** station group; ~ **de transistors** transistor array; ~ **d'intérêt économique (GIE)** joint (business) venture group; ~ **excessif** overbunching; ~ **inférieur** underbunching; ~ **mixte** both-way group; ~ **optimal** optimum bunching; ~ **préférentiel** priority group; ~ **principal** principal (main) group
groupes éclatés de concentration remote concentration groups/units; ~ **partiels** component parts; sub-assemblies
GT (v. générateur de tonalités)
guerre *f* **électronique** electronic warfare
guichet *m* teller terminal; ~ **automatique bancaire** (de banque) automatic teller machine (ATM)
guide *f* slide bar; guide; rail; comb; prompt character; fairlead; ~ **carte** card guide; ~ **carte double** double card guide; ~ **carte modifié** modified card guide; ~ **carte simple** single card guide; ~ **coudé** waveguide bend; ~ **d'affaire** project guide; site documentation; ~ **de conception** designer's guide; ~ **de recette** acceptance procedure guide; ~ **de recueil de données** telephone data acquisition handbook; ~ **d'onde(s)** waveguide; ~ **d'ondes à deux modes** two-mode waveguide; ~ **d'ondes à diaphragme tubulaire** pipe-diaphragm waveguide; ~ **d'ondes à moulures** ridge waveguide; ~ **d'ondes à ruban** stripline; ~ **d'ondes circulaire** circular waveguide; ~ **d'ondes coaxial** coaxial waveguide; ~ **d'ondes coudé** waveguide bend; ~ **d'ondes diélectrique** dielectric waveguide; ~ **d'ondes elliptique** elliptical waveguide; ~ **d'ondes évanescent** cut-off waveguide; ~ **d'ondes hélicoïdal** helical waveguide; ~ **d'ondes homogène** uniform waveguide; ~ **d'ondes optique** optical waveguide; ~ **d'ondes rayonnant** radiating waveguide; ~ **d'ondes rectangulaire** rectan-

gular waveguide; ~ **d'ondes souple** flexible waveguide; ~ **d'ondes sphérique** spherical waveguide; ~ **d'unisélection** uniselector guide; ~ **en torsade binomial** binomial twist; step twist; ~ **opérateur** prompt; cue; HELP function; ~ **papier** bill feed; ~ **pour jacks** jack guide; ~ **utilisateur** designer's guide
guide(-câble) fairlead
guide-fils grommet; fanning strip
guillemets *m pl* quotation marks; inverted commas

guipage *m* lap winding
guipé *adj* lapped
guiper tape (of splice); lap
guirlandage *m* (coloured) ring(s)
guirlande *f* coiled wire; spiral lead; flex; festoon; daisy-chain
guitare *f* break plate
GVT (v. gain variable dans le temps)
gyrateur *m* gyrator
gyrofréquence *f* (dans l'ionosphère) gyro frequency; ~ **transversale** transverse gyro frequency

H

HA (v. horloge asservie)
habilitation *f* entitlement; authorization
habilité *adj* accredited; concessionary
habillage *m* cladding; covering; shroud; format; label; enclosure; casing; trim; ~ **lateral** side cladding; ~ **transformateur** transformer casing/dressing; shroud
habillé *adj* labelled; clad
habité *adj* manned (of spacecraft)
habituel *adj* commonplace; routine; customary
hacheur *m* **électronique** (= découpeur) chopper
hachuré *adj* cross-hatched; shaded
haie *f* statutory hedge
halte *f* break-point (of program); ~ **à l'adresse** halt on address; ~ **sur adresse** address stop
hampe *f* ascender (of printed character)
handler *m* **de périphérie informatique** computer peripheral handler; input/output peripheral handler; ~ **programme de dialogue** communications controller
harmonie *f* resonance
harmonieux *adj* integrated; well-ordered; rationalized
harmonique *m* harmonic; overtone; voice-frequency; ~ **d'ordre impair** odd harmonic; ~ **d'ordre pair** even-order harmonic; ~ **inférieur** sub-harmonic
harmonisation *f* standardization; assimilation; establishing a common reference point
harnais *m* (cable) harness; loom(s)
harpon *m* securing staple; retaining clip; connector clamp
hauban *m* stay rope; truss wire; anchoring wire; shroud
haubanage (haubannage) *m* staying; bracing; anchoring; anchor tie; guying; ~ **anti-torsion** anti-twist guying; ~ **d'antenne** antenna span
hausse tarifaire rate increase
haut (de baie) *m* (rack) top; ~ **de casse (hdc)** upper case (u.c.); caps; ~ **de gamme** top of the range; up-market; ~ **de page** top of form; header
haute densité polaire d'ordre trois third-order high-density bipolar coding (HDB3); ~ **fréquence** *f* high frequency (HF); ~ **tension** high voltage; ~ **vitesse** high

speed
hauteur *f* amplitude; height; ~ **de son** pitch; tone pitch; ~ **double** double height; ~ **hors tout** overall length; gross height; ~ **libre** vertical clearance; ~ **sous poutre** floor-to-beam height; underbeam height; clearance
haut-parleur *m* loudspeaker; ~ **à bobine mobile** moving-coil loudspeaker; ~ **à induction** induction loudspeaker; moving-iron loudspeaker; ~ **à magnétostriction** magnetostriction loudspeaker; ~ **d'aiguës** tweeter; ~ **de graves** boomer; woofer; bass unit; ~ **médium** squawker; ~ **multicellulaire** multicellular loudspeaker; ~ **piézo-électrique** crystal loudspeaker; ~ **pour basses fréquences** boomer; woofer; ~ **pour fréquences élevées** tweeter; ~ **pour fréquences moyennes** squawker
havane *adj* manilla (colour); buff
HDB3 high-density bipolar/binary (3rd order) code converter
hdc (v. haut de casse)
hélice *f* **d'inscription** helix
hélicoïdal *adj* vaned; spiral; lobed; helical-grooved
hémitropie *f* **combinée** combined twinning; ~ **optique** optical twinning
herméticité *f* gas seal; sealing
hermétique *adj* sealed; air-tight; gas-tight; solid-state (of relay)
hermétisme *m* impenetrability; impermeability
herse *f* signal lamp panel; connecting box; board; external lamp panels; alarm lamps; bank (of lamps); local alarm rack; indicator; distribution panel; batten; cabinet; concealed lighting; ~ **de synthèse d'alarmes** rack alarm indicator panel
hertz (Hz) hertz; cycles per second (cps; c/s)
hertzien *adj* microwave; radio-wave; radio-frequency (RF)
hétérochrone *adj* heterochronous
hétérodynation *f* heterodyning
hétérodyne *f* heterodyne signal generator; beat oscillator
hétérogène *adj* diffuse; diverse (non-uniform); mixed; disparate; dissimilar; open (of system architecture); multi-source
hétérogénéité *f* multi-sourcing
hétéropolaire *adj* heteropolar; polyvalent

heure *f* time of day; ~ **centrale** exchange time; mean time; ~ **chargée** peak load period; busy hour; ~ **chargée moyenne** time-consistent busy hour; ~ **creuse** off-peak period; slack period; ~ **de dépôt** acceptance time; (telegram) handing-in time; ~ **de pointe** peak busy hour; post-selected busy hour; prime time; ~ **de pointe variable** bouncing busy hour; ~ **du réveil** wake-me call time

heures d'arrêt down time; ~ **de faible trafic** off-peak times; ~ **productives** productive hours; ~ **rouges** peak times

heuristique *adj* heuristic; rule-of-thumb; trial-and-error (problem-solving)

hexadécimal *adj* hexadecimal; to the base 16

hexafluorure de soufre sulphur hexafluoride

hexet *m* six-bit byte

HF (v. générateur haute fréquence); ~ (v. hyperfréquence)

hiérarchie *f* ranking; hierarchy; level (of data); graded network; pyramid; ~ **de multiplexage** multiplex hierarchy; ~ **de multiplexage numérique** digital multiplex hierarchy; ~ **des interruptions** interrupt hierarchy; ~ **des traitements** processing hierarchy; ~ **descendante** top-down; ~ **générale** general hierarchy

hiérarchisation *f* hierarchization; ranking

hiérarchisé *adj* multi-level

hirondelle *f* crop mark; fold mark

hisser *v* hoist; pull up

histogramme *m* histogram; bar graph; pillar graph; ~ **des déchets** failure histogram

historique *m* account; record; report; log; background; original; history file

HOF (hauteur de l'outil fermé) height of tool when closed

homochrone *adj* homochronous

homofocal *adj* confocal

homogène *adj* consistent; intermeshed; integrated; uniform; clustered; (universally) compatible; standardized

homogénéité *f* consistency; uniformity

homologation *f* approval; certification; authorization; licence; listing; endorsement

homologue *adj ou m* similar; matching; identical; associated; corresponding; counterpart; duplicate; replica; stand-by

homologué UL UL-listed (Underwriters' Laboratories); UL-recognized

homologuer *v* confirm; endorse; acknowledge; approve; authorize; certify; license

homopolaire *adj* homopolar; covalent

homothétie *f* scaling

honoraire *m* fee

horaire *adj/m* timetable; schedule; hourly; periodic

horaires de taxation metering time schedule; ~ **variables** flexi-time

horamètre *m* elapsed hour meter

horizon 2000 next generation; twenty-first century; ~ **radioélectrique** radio horizon

horloge *f* clock; timer; clock pulse; timing signal; ~ **à discontinuités** blanked clock; ~ **asservie (HA)** slave clock; ~ **centrale** central clock; exchange clock; ~ **chien de garde** watchdog timer; ~ **de comptage** up(-counting) clock; ~ **de contact** automatic timer; ~ **de référence** reference clock; ~ **de taxation** metering clock; ~ **distante** remote clock; distant clock; ~ **du central** exchange clock; ~ **émission** transmitter signal element timing; ~ **en temps réel** real time clock (RTC); ~ **enregistreur** register clock; ~ **incidente** remote clock; ~ **intégrée** on-chip clock; ~ **interne** on-chip oscillator/clock; time-of-day clock; ~ **locale** local clock; ~ **logicielle** software clock; ~ **maîtresse** master clock; ~ **mère** master clock; ~ **parlante** speaking clock; ~ **pilote** master clock; ~ **principale** master clock; ~ **régénérée** recovered clock (signal); ~ **retour (HR)** flyback; ~ **temps réel** real-time clock; time-of-day clock; ~ **temps réel secteur ou à entrée externe** mains sync or external input real-time clock

horodatage *m* time-and-date coding

horodateur *m* time-and-date stamp; chronopher

hors set (memory signal); ~ **bande** out-band; out-of-band; ~ **circonscription** foreign; ~ **circuit** off-circuit; down; ~ **code** shift out (SO); ~ **configuration** configured-off; ~ **conversation** off-air; ~ **d'ouvrage** incidental; ~ **d'usage** unserviceable; not in use; off; ~ **exploitation** out of operation; ~ **fonctionnement** unserviceable (U/S); inoperative; down; off-line; ~ **gabarit** out-of-range; out-of-limits; unformatted; non-standard; ~ **lieux** off-premises; ~ **ligne** off-line; ~ **meuble** not installed; ~ **norme** out-of-limits; ~ **numérotation** supernumerary; ~ **œuvre** external dimensions; ~ **parc** third-party vendor equipment; outside suppliers; (penetration of) new markets; ~ **service (h.s.)** unserviceable; out of action; not in use; inoperative; not working; out-of-service; busied out; at rest; off; failed; down; de-selected; ~ **signal** reset; ~ **taxe (HT)** gross; pre-tax; before tax; ~ **tension** off load; powered down; ~ **texte** (bit de) zone (bit); ~ **tolérance(s)** out-of-limits; non-standard; ~ **tout** inclusive; overall; gross; width; ~ **trafic** out of operation; off-line

H

hostile *adj* enemy
hotte *f* canopy; hood; cowl; booth; ~ **aspirante** suction hood; ~ **d'extraction** extractor hood
housse *f* dust cover; case
HPC (v. fusible à haut pouvoir de coupure)
HR (v. horloge retour); ~ (v. humidité relative)
h.s. (v. hors service)
HT (v. hors taxe)
hublot *m* window; porthole; wall light
huilée *adj* with airline lubrication
huitaine abonné eight-subscriber group
humecté *adj* impregnated; damped; soaked; lightly dipped
humidité *f* moisture; ~ **relative (HR)** relative humidity
hurleur *m* howler
hydraulique *adj* hydraulic; cooling; ~ **mécanique** hydraulic engineering; hydraulics

hydrofuge *adj* water-repellent; watertight
hygrométrie *f* relative humidity (in %)
hyper de réception RF receiver
hyperfréquence (HF) RF (radio frequency); microwave
hyperluminosité *f* **de l'écho** blooming
hypothèse *f* assumption; theory; design objective; ~ **de calcul** design assumption
hypsogramme *f* level diagram; hypsogram
hypsographe *m* level recorder
hypsomètre (= népermètre/décibelmètre) level measuring set; hypsometer; automatic trunk test device; transmission (level-)measuring set; ~ **arrivée** incoming hypsometer; ~ **départ** outgoing hypsometer; ~ **urbain** local automatic trunk testing device
hystérésis *f* (= hystérèse) hysteresis; eddy current; backlash
HZ high impedance (NOT Hz)
Hz (v. hertz)

I

I_A (v. courant d'attraction)
IA (v. indicateur d'acheminement); ≃ (v. indicatif d'acheminement); ≃ (v. interurbain automatique)
IB (v. inversion de batterie)
I_{cc} (intensité courant continu) DC current
ICE (v. information et communication d'entreprise)
ICO (v. indicateur de connexion opérateur)
icône *f* icon; ikon (of graphics); system configuration display
iconoscope *m* iconoscope
iconoscope-image à dimensions réduites photicon
ID (v. courant de déclenchement)
ID (indication et durée, appel avec) advise duration and charge (ADC)
idéal *adj* nominal
idem *adj* ditto; as above; ibid.; ibidem
identificateur *m* identifier; descriptor; handle (= callsign); ~ **d'abonnés** subscriber selector; ~ **de communication** call identifier; ~ **de début de bande** beginning-of-tape label (BOT); ~ **de début de données** beginning-of-data block label/identifier (BLID); ~ **de début de fichier** beginning-of-file label/identifier (BOFI); ~ **de fin de bande** end-of-tape label/identifier (EOT); ~ **de fin de fichier** end-of-file label (EOF); ~ **de jonction** line finder; routing selector; ~ **de procédure** protocol identifier
identification *f* recognition; identity; trace; tracing; ~ **automatique d'objets volants** automatic flying object identification; ~ **cyclique** repeated identification; ~ **de la cible** target identification; ~ **de la ligne appelante** calling line identification; originating number display; station number display; station call identification; ~ **de la ligne appelée** called line identification; ~ **de la ligne d'appel** calling line identification; ~ **de zone** area identification (AID); ~ **des appels malveillants** malicious call tracing; ~ **des correspondants** remote line identification; ~ **du terminal distant** remote terminal identification; ~ **unique** one-shot identification
identité *f* uniformity; identification; identifier; consistency; descriptor
IDF (Ile de France) Ile de France (French

telephone network charging area)
IDT (v. indice de durée et de taxation)
IF (v. indicatif)
ignifuge *adj* non-flammable; flame-resistant; flame-proof; fire-retardant
ignitron *m* ignitron
ignoré *adj* no-op; not serviced; unknown
ignorer *v* disregard; be unaware of
IGQS (v. indice global de qualité de service)
illégal *adj* illegal
illicite *adj* unauthorized
illumination *f* (d'un objet) illumination (of a target); feed (aerial)
illustré *adj* exalted; distinguished
îlot *m* pocket; cluster; land (of PCB)
ILS (v. interrupteur à lame souple)
image *f* memory core; frame; image; picture; display; dump; storage data; screen page; soft copy; facsimile; mirror; reflection; recorded audio signal; identical (to); video signal; status indication; video frame; ~ (sur disque) data (copied on disk); ~ (visible) picture; reflection; ~ **bande pilote** loop parameters; ~ **brillante** high-key trace; ~ **complexe** complex display; ~ **de carte** card image; ~ **de courant** foldback current; ~ **de télévision** television image; television picture; ~ **électronique** electronic image; ~ **électro-optique** picture; ~ **excentrique** offset PPI (plan position indicator); ~ **fantôme** ghost; multiple image; ~ **fixe** still picture; ~ **fugitive** soft copy; ~ **latente** latent image; ~ **mémoire** core dump; core image; program binary; binary memory image; executable memory image; ~ **mémoire rééditable** operational program binary; ~ **non rémanente** volatile display; ~ **optique** (sur un tube analyseur) optical image (in a television camera); ~ **panoramique** plan position indicator (display) (PPI); ~ **par image** step and repeat; ~ **stéréoscopique** vectograph; ~ **sur disque** data (copied on disk); dump file; ~ **synthétique** composite image; ~ **système** system core storage; ~ **tâche** task image; ~ **télévisée** video image; video picture; ~ **utile** test pattern
image-mémoire core image
imagerie *f* image processing; imagery (remote

terrain sensing)

images f pl graphics; ~ **animées en temps réel** live pictures; ~ **des organes** stored states of hardware devices; ~ **par seconde** scan frequency (in Hz)

imbrication f; imbriquage m (loop) nesting; interleaving; interlacing

imbriquage m (v. imbrication)

imbriqué adj interlaced; nested; interleaved; embedded

imbriquer v interleave; nest; interlace
¡me ¡th

imitation f **des signaux** signal imitation

immédiat adj direct; prompt; on-line; urgent; immediate; real-time

immersion f dipping

immobilisation f hang-up

immobilisations f pl fixed assets; capital stocks; cumulative outlay

immobilisé adj out of action; down; stopped; shut-down

immunité f **dynamique au bruit** dynamic noise immunity

impact m repercussion

impair adj odd

imparité f odd parity

impasse f dead end (of program); deadlock; deadly embrace

impédance f impedance; (apparent) resistance; ~ **à ailettes** ribbed insulator; ~ **àcourt-circuit** short-circuit impedance; ~ **à la résonance** resonant impedancee; ~ **à l'accès** driving-point impedance; ~ **à l'antirésonance** dynamic impedance; ~ **acoustique** acoustic impedance; ~ **acoustique intrinsèque** specific acoustic impedance; ~ **caractéristique** characteristic impedance; surge impedance; ~ **caractéristique d'ondes** characteristic wave impedance; ~ **cinétique** motional impedance; ~ **conjuguée** conjugate impedance; ~ **d'antenne** aerial impedance; ~ **de base** base impedance; ~ **de charge** load impedance; load circuit; ~ **de couplage** coupling impedance; interaction impedance; ~ **de ligne** line impedance; ~ **de sortie** output impedance; ~ **de terminaison** terminating impedance; terminal impedance; ~ **de transfert** transfer impedance; mutual impedance; ~ **de transfert en circuit ouvert** open-circuit transfer impedance; ~ **d'électrode** electrode impedance; ~ **d'entrée** driving-point impedance; feedpoint impedance; input impedance; source impedance; ~ **d'entrée** (sortie en court circuit) small-signal value of the short-circuit input impedance; ~ **d'équilibrage** balancing impedance; ~ **d'étouffement** parasitic stop-

per; ~ **d'étouffement anode** anode stopper; ~ **d'étouffement de grille** grid stopper; ~ **directe** direct impedance; ~ **d'onde** wave(-guide) impedance; ~ **d'onde caractéristique** characteristic wave impedance; waveguide characteristic; surge impedance; ~ **effective d'entrée** effective input impedance; ~ **électronique de l'espace d'interaction** electronic gap impedance; ~ **en charge normale** loaded impedance; ~ **en circuit ouvert** open-circuit impedance; blocked impedance; ~ **en court circuit** short-circuit impedance; ~ **image** image impedance; ~ **itérative** iterative impedance; ~ **libre** free impedance; ~ **mécanique** mechanical impedance; ~ **mécanique de transfert** transfer mechanical impedance; ~ **négative** expedance; ~ **réciproque** inverse impedance; ~ **réfléchie** reflected impedance; coupled impedance

impédances conjuguées d'un quadripôle conjugate impedances of a quadripole

impératif m constraint; obligation; ~ adj compelling; mandatory

implantation f mounting; matrix; grid; installation; layout; location; site; residence; residency; base; structure; insertion grid; map; topology; pattern; configuration; ~ **biposes** double-up layout; ~ **mémoire** memory map; ~ **multiposes** multiple-mount assembly; multi-up layout

implanté adj based; located; installed; resident

implanter v enter; locate; install

implication f IF-THEN operation; inclusion; (material) implication; conditional implication instruction

implicite adj default; unprogrammed; unqualified; unspecified

impliqué adj involved; concerned

importance f scale; magnitude; immensity

important adj immense; major; considerable; substantial; tremendous; huge; wide-ranging; vast; key; significant

imposé adj forced; enforced

impossible adj impracticable; forbidden; not permitted; barred; denied; inoperable

imprégnation cire wax impregnated; wax coated

impression à l'italienne landscape printing; ~ f **conductrice** track; conductive strip; conductive pattern; land; ~ **de points** chopper-bar recording; ~ **de travers** slewed printing; ~ **décentralisée** decentralized printing; ~ **déportée** off-line printing; spooling; ~ **différée** spooling; time-sharing I/O system; ~ **directe** direct printing; on-line printing; ~ **en creux** imprint; ~ **en**

différé spooling; pseudo-offlining; ~ **en écho** echo printing; screen echo; ~ **en transparence d'écran** hard copy; ~ **immédiate** on-line printing; real-time I/O system; ~ **locale** off-line printing; ~ **pâle** low-density print; ~ **par report** offset printing; ~ **sélective** snapshot printout; ~ **spoulée** spooling; off-line printing; ~ **trait** solid printing
imprévisible *adj* unpredictable; unforeseeable
imprimante *f* printer; line printer; ~ **à aiguilles** dot-matrix printer; stylus printer; wire printer; spin printer; ~ **à bande** band printer; ~ **à barre** bar printer; ~ **à boule** golfball printer; ~ **à chaîne** chain printer; ~ **à cylindre** barrel printer; ~ **à cylindre hélicoïdal** spiral cylinder printer; ~ **à dépôt ionique** ion deposition printer; ~ **à électro-érosion** electrographic printer; ~ **à espacement proportionnel** proportional spacing printer; ~ **à jet d'encre** ink-jet printer; ~ **à la volée** fly printer; ~ **à laser** laser printer; ~ **à marguerite** daisywheel printer; ~ **à papier** tractor-feed printer; ~ **à peigne** comb printer; ~ **à tambour** drum printer; ~ **balistique** ballistic matrix printer; ~ **caractère par caractère** at-a-time printer; ~ **de guichet** document and journal printer; ~ **de recopie d'écran** screen dump printer; ~ **de sortie** terminal printer; ~ **électrostatique** electrostatic printer; ~ **matricielle** dot-matrix printer; wire printer; ~ **mosaïque** dot matrix printer; ~ **par ligne** line printer; ~ **par page** page printer; ~ **par points** stylus printer; matrix printer; wire printer; dot matrix printer; ~ **parallèle** parallel printer; line printer; ~ **rapide (IR)** high-speed printer; ~ **série** serial printer; ~ **thermique** thermal printer
imprimé *m* hard copy; page copy; form; print; ~ **en continu** continuous form; ~ **suite** continuation form
imprimer *v* print; output; record; datalog
imprimeur *m* **de fac-similé** facsimile recorder; ~ **direct** deciphering printer; ~ **en relief** embosser
impulsation *f* pulse; impulse
impulser *v* promote
impulsion *f* pulse; trigger pulse; (magnetic) charge; bit; impulse; signal; marker; pip; impetus; echo; spike; strobe; ~ **à crête fractionnée** serrated pulse; ~ **à front raide** steep pulse; ~ **à longue durée** broad pulse; ~ **chaotique** chaotic pulse; ~ **d'alignement** clamping pulse; ~ **d'asservissement** lock(ing) pulse; ~ **d'attaque** driving pulse; trigger pulse; ~ **de blocage** inhibit pulse; disabling pulse; re-phasing pulse; ~ **de**

charge charging pulse; ~ **de code** code pulse; ~ **de commande** drive pulse; ~ **de commutation** signalling pulse; switching pulse; commutator pulse; position pulse; p-pulse; ~ **de comptage** metering pulse; ~ **de contrôle** check bit; ~ **de courant** current pulse; ~ **de courte durée** short-duration pulse; spike; ~ **de décalage rapide** fast-shift pulse; ~ **de déclenchement** trigger pulse; ~ **de demi-ligne** broad pulse; half-line pulse; ~ **de discrimination** identifying pulse; ~ **de durée T** T-pulse; ~ **de fermeture** make pulse; ~ **de garde** holding pulse; ~ **de marquage** timing pulse; ~ **de mise au repos** release pulse; ~ **de numérotation** dial pulse; dialling pulse; ~ **de porte** gating pulse; ~ **de positionnement** p-pulse; position pulse; commutator pulse; ~ **de prise** (de la ligne) line seizure pulse; ~ **de retour de ligne** flyback pulse; ~ **de rythme** timing pulse; strobe pulse; clock pulse; ~ **de sélection** drive pulse; ~ **de strobage** strobe pulse; ~ **de strobage progressive** walking strobe pulse; ~ **de suppression** blanking pulse; ~ **de synchronisation** synchronizing pulse; marker; ~ **de taxe** meter pulse; metering pulse; ~ **de test** interrogating pulse; ~ **de verrouillage** clamp pulse; clamping pulse; ~ **de verrouillage de trame** framing pulse; ~ **d'échantillonnage** sampling pulse; burstgate pulse; strobe; ~ **décimale** dial pulse; ~ **d'égalisation** equalizing pulse; ~ **d'étalonnage** calibration pulse; marker; ~ **d'horloge** clock pulse; ~ **d'ouverture** break pulse; clear pulse; ~ **en dent de scie** sawtooth pulse; ~ **en sinus carré** sine-squared pulse; ~ **en triangle** triangular pulse; sawtooth pulse; ~ **fine** narrow pulse; ~ **idéale** nominal pulse; ~ **lumineuse** light pulse; ~ **négative** negative-going pulse; ~ **parasite** pulse spike; spike; ~ **permanente** permanent-line signal; ~ **rectangulaire** rectangular pulse; square-wave pulse; ~ **réfléchie** echo; ~ **triangulaire** triangular pulse; sawtooth pulse; ~ **unidirectionnelle** unidirectional pulse; ~ **unitaire** Dirac function; ~ **vidéo** video pulse
impulsionnel *adj* pulsed; dynamic; AC (alternating current)
impulsions de télétaxation pulses to subscriber's private meter; ~ **modulées en amplitude** pulse amplitude modulation (PAM); ~ **périodiques** time-and-distance metering; ~ **sonores** tone burst
impulsographe *m* pulse(-width) recorder; impulse machine

imputation *f* apportionment; levy; attribution; itemization; ~ **sur le compte de l'abonné** incrementing message register (subscriber's private meter)

imputer *v* levy; charge

Iₙ (intensité nominale) rated current

inabordable *adj* intractable

inaccessible *adj* unobtainable; access barred; down; denied

inachevé *adj* outstanding

inactif *adj* idle

inadmissible *adj* forbidden; unacceptable; unavailable

inaltérable *adj* weather-resistant

inamovible *adj* fixed

incassable *adj* unbreakable; shatter-proof

incidence *f* repercussion

incident *m ou adj* malfunction; (system) failure; disorder; hitch; trouble; alert; bug; crash; contingency; eventuality; problem; incoming; fall-back; ~ **sur démarrage à froid** cold fault; ~ **système** system crash

incitation *f* cueing message; cue

inciter *v* prompt

inclinaison *f* skew (of character); tilt; slope; pitch; dip; rake; bank; taper

inclinasion de l'onde de sol wave tilt

inclus *adj* installed

inclusion *f* IF-THEN

incohérence *f* inconsistency; incongruity; incompatibility; bug; garbling; impairment

incohérent *adj* inconsistent; garbled; mutilated

incolore *adj* clear; plain; colourless; unpigmented

incombe à is vested in

incombustible *adj* fireproof; non-combustible

incompatibilité *f* NOT-AND (NAND) operation; non-conjunction

incomplet *adj* less than full complement; mutilated; garbled

inconnu *adj* not recognized; unknown

inconscient *adj* automatic

inconvénient *m* disadvantage; drawback; risk

incorporé *adj* built-in; integral; embodied; on-chip

incrémenter *v* increment

incrémentiel *adj* incremental

incriminé *adj* offending; source of fault; suspect

incriminer *v* test; check; implicate; indicate (of fault); write (to address); diagnose

incrustation *f* boxing (of graphic display)

indépendance *f* **de la séquence des bits** bit transparency

indépendant *adj* unrelated; individual; discrete; free; ~ **du temps** time-invariant

indépendemment *adv* irrespective; immaterial

indesserrabilité *f* self-locking function; immobilization

indeterminé *adj* not known; undefined

index *m* set point/value; controlled magnitude; trip temperature; marker; pointer; indicator; index; list; directory

indexage *m* registration

indexation *f* indexing; posting; ~ **générique** generic posting; up-posting

indexé sur geared to

indiçage *m* index marking

indicateur *m* marker; flag; indicator (lamp); meter; status bit; sentinel; tag; display; pointer; ~ **à double spot** two-spot display; ~ **à modulation d'intensité** intensity modulated display; ~ **cathodique** CRT display; ~ **d'accord** tuning indicator (meter); ~ **d'accusé de réception** acknowledgement flag (ACK); ~ **d'acheminement (IA)** routing indicator; ~ **d'acheminement détourné** alternative routing indicator; ~ **d'aiguillage** flag (switch indicator); sentinel; ~ **d'amplitude et de distance** range-amplitude display; ~ **d'appel de maintenance** test call indicator; ~ **d'appel de transit** transit call indicator; ~ **d'appel en instance** call-waiting tone; ~ **d'azimut automatique** omnibearing indicator (OBI); ~ **de catégorie du demandeur** calling line category indicator; ~ **de connexion d'opératrice** operator connection indicator; ~ **de connexion opérateur (ICO)** operator connection indicator; ~ **de distance et de gisement** (d'azimut) range-bearing display; type B display; ~ **de distance et de site** elevation-position indicator (EPI); ~ **de fin à volet** ring-off indicator; ~ **de fin d'appel** ring-off indicator; ~ **de hauteur et de distance** height-position indicator (HPI); range-height indicator; ~ **de la portée** communications zone indicator (COZI); ~ **de lever de doute** sense finder; ~ **de niveau sonore** volume indicator; ~ **de position et de cours d'approche** position and homing indicator; ~ **de sortie** output meter; ~ **de taxe** charge indicator; ~ **de transit** transit indicator; ~ **de volume** volume-unit meter; VU-meter; ~ **de volume du SFERT** SFERT speech level meter; ~ **d'écart** drift meter; ~ **d'enveloppe** envelope indicator; ~ **d'état** flag; status indicator; ~ **d'ordres de phase** instruction op-code indicator; ~ **du numéro demandé** call indicator; home indicator; ~ **fin d'appel** ring-off indicator; ~ **lumineux** signal lamp; ~ **lumineux d'appel** call lamp; ~ **numérique** digital (display) indicator; ~ **optique en étoile** white-star indicator;

~ **panoramique** plan position indicator (PPI); ~ **panoramique à centre dilaté** expanded centre plan display; ~ **panoramique à excentration** off-centre plan display; ~ **panoramique stabilisé** azimuth-stabilized PPI; ~ **sectoriel** sector display; ~ **type E** elevation-position indicator (EPI)

indicatif (IF) *m* routing code; station identification; answer-back code; office code; prefix; call number; dialling code; access code; key; "handle" (of CB operator); callsign; ~ **d'acheminement (IA)** routing code; ~ **d'appel** (= préfixe) access code; call sign; ~ **d'appel abrégé** short callsign; abbreviated dialling prefix; ~ **d'appel d'une opératrice d'assistance** assistance code; ~ **de central** exchange code; office code; ~ **de pays** country code; ~ **de service restreint** barred code; barred numerical code; ~ **de tri** sort key; ~ **international** international code; access prefix to the international network; ~ **interurbain** trunk code; ~ **littéral** alphabetical code; code letter; ~ **(local)** exchange code; ~ **numérique** numerical code; ~ **régional (IR)** area code; numbering plan area (NPA) code; regional code

indication *f* identifier; prompt; signal; instruction; direction; cue; clue; hint; ~ **audible donnée par une machine parlante** recorded announcement tone; ~ **d'appel en instance** call-waiting notification; ~ **de position par impulsion d'émetteur** identification of position; ~ **du coût d'appel** call charge notification

indications *f pl* directions; instructions

indice *m* index; code; rating; radix base; suffix; subscript; (address) modifier; ratio; figure; digit; factor; ~ **de durée et de taxation (IDT)** advise duration and charge (ADC); ~ **de fabrication** software status code; ~ **de force des sons** loudness rating; ~ **de glissement aval** frequency pulling figure; pulling figure; ~ **de modulation** deviation ratio; modulation index; ~ **de performance** evaluation index; figure of merit; rating; ~ **de préservation** protection code; ~ **de puissance d'un émetteur** power rating of a transmitter; ~ **de qualité de raccordement** connection quality index; ~ **de qualité de réception (IQR)** reception quality; grade-of-service index; figure of merit; ~ **de qualité de transmission** transmission performance; rating; ~ **de qualité objective** attitude index; ~ **de recette** grade-of-service index; GOS indicator; ~ **de réfraction** refractive index; ~ **de réfraction modifié** modified refractive in-

dex; ~ **de réfraction modifié à excès** excess modified refractive index; ~ **de version** hardware/(software) release code; ~ **d'exploitation** interchangeability index; series index; (design) revision status; ~ **d'interchangeabilité** (design) revision status; ~ **d'oxygène** (limiting) oxygen index (of combustion); ~ **du cœur** refractive index of core; ~ **du milieu** refractive index; ~ **global de qualité de service (IGQS)** cumulative grade-of-service indicator; ~ **inférieur** subscript; ~ **préservation** protection code; privacy code; ~ **supérieur** (= exposant) superscript

indifféremment *adv* immaterial; neutral; indiscriminately

indifférencié *adj* ordinary; undistinguished; identical

indiqué par pointed to by

indiquer *v* depict; point; direct; prompt; denote; show; signify; indicate; point (to)

indirection *f* indirect addressing

indiscernable *adj* identical

indisponibilité *f* unavailability; outage; shutdown; down-time

indisponible *adj* out of commission; engaged; inaccessible; unavailable; ~ **libre** unavailable idle; ~ **occupé** unavailable busy; quiescent

individuel exclusive; separate; distinct; discrete

indivisible *adj* per whole or part (thereof); integral; inseparable; (unified) whole

inductance *f* inductance; coil; choke; reactor; inductor; ~ **concentrée** concentrated inductance; ~ **d'apex** apex inductor; ~ **de découplage** decoupling inductor; ~ **de dispersion** leakage inductance; ~ **de filtrage** smoothing choke; ~ **de fuite** stray inductance; leakage inductance; ~ **de relèvement** peaking coil; ~ **distribuée** distributed inductance; ~ **électrique** (coefficient of) mutual inductance; ~ **magnétique** (uniforme) magnetic flux density; ~ **mutuelle** mutual inductance; ~ **propre** (coefficient of) self inductance; ~ **saturable** saturable reactor (= transductor); ~ **spécifique** inductance factor (A_L); ~ **spécifique nominale** rated inductance factor

inducteur *adj ou m* inductor; inductance coil; field magnet (with induction coils); magnet wheel; magnet rotor; stator; exciting; field winding

induction *f* induction; magnetic flux density; electrical flux density; effective flux density (unit: mT = millitesla); ~ **de bruit** noise induction; ~ **électrostatique** electrostatic

induction; ~ **magnétique** magnetic induction; ~ **mutuelle** mutual induction; ~ **parasite de fréquence intermédiaire** intermediate frequency breakthrough; ~ **télégraphique** cross-fire
induire v induce
induit m armature; rotor (DC motor); induced coil
industrialisation f industrial application(s); marketing
industriel adj industry-standard
inéluctablement adv invariably; always
inertance f **acoustique** acoustic inertia
inertie f **calorifique** thermal inertia; ~ **magnétique** inductance; ~ **thermique** thermal inertia; temperature lag
inexécution f non-execution
inexistant adj non-existent; no-such
inexploitable adj inoperable
infantile adj premature; early; incipient; emergent
inférieur adj lower-ranking; lesser; subordinate
infidèle adj defective; incorrect
infini adj indefinite; unlimited
infiniment variable random setting
infirme adj false
infirmer v refute; rebut
inflammable adj flammable
infléchi adj bent; warped; buckled
infléchissement continu sinusoidal oscillation
influence f **capacitive** electrostatic induction
influences parasites spurious effects; stray signals
infoduc m maintenance register; pipeline register
infographie f data graphics (stored graph display)
informateur m message transfer control circuit
informathèque f data base; data bank
informaticien m EDP specialist; systems analyst; computer scientist; programmer
information(s) f communication(s) (feedback); signal; data; parameter; information; details; message; news (bulletin); datum
information analogique analogue information (data); ~ **d'acheminement** routing information; ~ **d'aménagement** housekeeping information; ~ **de commande** control signal; ~ **de retour disponible (IRD)** return information available; ~ **de sécurisation** automatic protection switching data; APS data; ~ **d'état de boucle** loop-status information; ~ **et communication d'entreprise (ICE)** management information systems (MIS); ~ **massive** bulk data; ~ **numériques décimales** dialling signal(s); ~ **pa-**

quetée multiplexed information; ~ **par attributs** specification data; ~ **par mesures** test data; ~ **parasite** drop-in; garbage; ~ **tout ou rien** bit; binary digit
information(s) de sortie receive-data (signal); ~ **d'entrée** transmitted-data (signal)
informations d'ordre control information; ~ **fournies par l'abonné** address digits; ~ **internes** inside information; ~ **invalides** garbage; drop-in; ~ **ponctuelles** up-to-the-minute details
informatique f data processing; computer science; computing; ~ **distribuée** distributed (data) processing; ~ **répartie** distributed processing
informatisation f computerization
informatisé adj computerized
informer v cue
infra-acoustique sub-audio
infranoir adj blacker-than-black
infraréfraction f sub-refraction
infrastructure f substructure; base; plant; (military) infrastructure; ~ **matérielle** plant
infratéléphonique adj sub-voice; narrowband
ingénierie f contract engineering; project management; marketing; ~ **informatique** computer systems engineering; software design
ingénieur m engineer; ~ **d'affaires** project engineer; contract manager; ~ **de mise en circuit** commissioning engineer; field engineer; ~ **de projet** designer; planner; ~ **technico-commercial (ITC)** systems engineer; marketing engineer; field engineer; technical sales representative
ingénieur-conseil consultant engineer
inhiber v inhibit; disable; cancel (of lamp); blind
inhibiteur m inhibit gate; ~ **de corrosion** corrosion inhibitor
inhibition f inhibition; disabling; muting; masking; ~ **du microphone** transmitter mute; ~ **partie transmission** speech circuit muting; ~ **sonnerie** anti-tinkle (circuit); ring-trip
ininflammable adj non-flammable
initialisation f bootstrapping; initialization; cold start; enquiry; ~ **à froid** cold start
initialiser v reset; clear; bootstrap; initialize; re-arm; ~ **à 1** preset
initiateur m originator
initiative f discretion; incentive; instigation; behest
injecter v inject; apply (of voltage); launch (of light wave); feed; insert
injecteur m **d'électrons** electron injector
injection f launch (of light signal); ~ **de transfert** drop-and-insert

injurieux *adj* deleterious; harmful; slanderous
inopérant *adj* not executed; impossible; inoperative; unserviceable (U/S); static; laboratory (of tests)
inopiné *adj* ad hoc
inox *m* (acier inoxydable) stainless steel
inscripteur *m* recorder; logger
inscription *f* write-in; entry; recording; logging; booking; registration; listing; legend; caption (of switch); posting (of file); ~ **d'appel** call booking; ~ **des matrices** data written to core (array); ~ **fugitive** echoplex; soft copy; ~ **machine** idiomatic feature; machine entry
inscrire *v* (sur) enter; write; log; record; copy (to); enshrine
insensibilité *f* **aux brouillages** immunity to interference
insensible (aux chocs) robust; resilient; impervious; shock-proof; immune; ~ **aux chocs** robust; shock-resistant; shockproof
inséparable *adj* hard; connected; protected
insertion *f* break-in; insertion; ~ **de bit de verrouillage de trame** frame bit insertion; ~ **de la composante continue** direct current (DC) insertion; ~ **de ligne** insert line (IL); ~ **en activité** hot slide-in; ~ **sans soudure** (ISS) solderless insertion; force-fit; press-fit; quick-connect
insigne *m* badge; insignia; mark
insolation *f* radiation; exposure (to heat/light)
insonorisation *f* sound-proofing
instabilité *f* instability; jitter; ~ **de l'impulsion** pulse jitter; ~ **d'image** jitter; ~ **du niveau** level instability; ~ **du niveau de la composante continue** direct current (DC) level instability
instable *adj* fickle
installation *f* plant; assembly; installation; ~ **automatique d'abonné avec postes supplémentaires** private automatic branch exchange (PABX); ~ **d'abonné** user facility; ~ **d'abonné avec postes supplémentaires à exploitation manuelle** private manual branch exchange (PMBX); ~ **d'abonné avec postes PBX** (private branch exchange); ~ **de commutation** relay facility; ~ **de commutation automatique** automatic switching equipment; ~ **de direction de tir** fire control equipment; ~ **de filtrage** manager-secretary telephone system; ~ **de l'alerte avancée transportable** mobile base early warning equipment; ~ **manuelle d'abonné avec postes supplémentaires** private manual branch exchange (PMBX); ~ **motrice** power plant; ~ **multiplex** channeling equipment; ~ **privée (IP)** private (branch)

exchange (PBX); ~ **technique** plant; ~ **télégraphique à courant continu** DC telegraph system; ~ **terminale d'abonné (ITA)** customer premises equipment (CPE)
installations d'éclairage et de force motrice lighting and power plant; ~ **extérieures** outside plant
installé au sol free-standing
instant *m* **de décision d'un signal numérique** epoch of a digital signal; ~ **de départ de la dent de scie** line scan start; ~ **de transfert** transfer time-slot; transfer link; ~ **d'écriture** write time slot; write instant; ~ **significatif** significant instant; epoch
instantané *adj* instant; instantaneous; immediate; direct; casual; on-the-spot; snapshot; momentary
instantanément *adv* at any (one) time
instants idéaux d'une modulation (ou d'une restitution) ideal instants of a modulation (or of a restitution)
instauration *f* setting (of mode); selection; ~ **de mode** set mode (SM)
instruction *f* instruction; statement; operation; ~ **à 1, 2, ... n adresses** one, two, ...n-address instruction; ~ **à adresse n-plus-une** n-plus-one instruction; ~ **à plusieurs adresses** multiple-address instruction; ~ **à une adresse** single-address code/instruction; ~ **arithmétique** arithmetic instruction; ~ **assembleur** assembly-language instruction; ~ **composée** compound statement; ~ **d'affectation** assignment statement; ~ **d'aiguillage** branch instruction; ~ **d'arrêt** halt instruction; ~ **d'arrêt conditionnel** conditional halt instruction; ~ **d'arrêt facultatif** optional halt instruction; ~ **d'assemblage** assembler instruction; ~ **de branchement** jump instruction; branch instruction; control transfer instruction; discrimination instruction; trap; ~ **de branchement conditionnel** conditional branch instruction; conditional transfer/ jump; arithmetic IF; computed GOTO; conditional transfer of control; ~ **de lecture** read instruction (RD); ~ **de programme** program instruction; code line; ~ **de retour** return instruction; ~ **de saut conditionnel** conditional jump instruction; ~ **de service** service instruction; housekeeping instruction; ~ **d'écriture** write instruction (WD); ~ **effective** actual instruction; ~ **élémentaire** primary instruction; basic instruction; ~ **en language assembleur** assembler instruction; ~ **fictive** dummy instruction; no-op instruction (NOP); do-nothing instruction; null instruction; waste instruction; ~ **ineffective**

(v. instruction fictive); ~ **insignifiante** (v. instruction fictive); ~ **machine** machine (language) instruction; ~ **macroprogramme** macroinstruction; ~ **primitive** basic instruction; presumptive instruction; unmodified instruction; ~ **priviligiée** master mode instruction; ~ **réelle** actual instruction; effective instruction; ~ **sans adresse** zero-address instruction; no-address instruction **instrument** *m* **à cadre mobile** moving coil instument; ~ **de mesure de précision** precision sweep; ~ **de mesure du taux d'ondes stationnaire** standing-wave meter; ~ **écouteur** listener

instrumenté *adj* recorded (of program)

instrument(s) de mesure meter; measuring instruments; panel-ware

insufflation *f* **d'air** air blast; ~ **pulmonaire** mouth-to-mouth resuscitation; kiss-of-life

intégral *adj* complete; full; comprehensive; unaltered; incorporated; unabridged

intégrateur *m* integrating circuit; ~ **de Miller** Miller integrator; ~ **de phase** phase integrator

intégration *f* merging; ~ **à densité moyenne** medium-scale integration (MSI); ~ **à forte densité** large-scale integration (LSI); ~ **à grande échelle** large-scale integration (LSI)

intégré *adj* pre-defined; ~ **dans le bâti** built-in; integral; rack-mounted

intégrer *v* (à) incorporate (into); integrate (with); merge; embody; blend in (with)

intégrité *f* sanity

intelligence artificielle artificial intelligence; ~ **de communication** communications intelligence; ~ **répartie** distributed intelligence; dispersed intelligence

intelligibilité *f* intelligibility

intempéries *f pl* weathering

intempestif *adj* sneak; inopportune; inadvertent; early; untimely; unwanted; irregular; false; unauthorized; pre-emptive; for no apparent reason; incidental; sporadic; premature; precipitate; random; indiscriminate

intensification *f* **de signaux parasites** enhancement of spurious signals

intensité *f* current (r.m.s. value); intensity; rate; strength (of magnetic field) load; amperage; volume; peak value; depth; capacity; rating; brightness; loudness; tone; incident energy (of UV tube); ~ **absorbée** current drain; sink current; ~ **absorbée par moteur** motor current; ~ **acoustique** sound intensity; acoustic intensity; loudness; volume; ~ **au démarrage** starting current; ~ **courant continu** (I_{CC}) direct current (DC); current r.m.s.

value; ~ **d'aimantation** magnetic field strength; magnetic field intensity; magnetizing force; ~ **de champ** field strength; ~ **de courant** current r.m.s. value; ~ **de faisceau** beam current; ~ **de puissance** peak value (of power); ~ **de rabattement** hold-back current; fold-back current; sealed current; ~ **de trafic acheminé** traffic flow; ~ **d'écho** echo intensity; ~ **des raies** line intensity; ~ **du bruit** noise intensity; ~ **du champ de réception** incoming signal level; ~ **du champ électrique** electric current; ~ **du trafic instantanée** instantaneous traffic load; ~ **lumineuse** luminous intensity; ~ **micro** microphone current; ~ **moyenne de trafic** mean traffic intensity; ~ **radiante** radiant intensity; ~ **réduite** subdued brightness; half-tone; lowlight; dimness; ~ **résiduelle** ripple current; ~ **sonore** loudness; volume; amplification

inter (v. interurbain)

interactif *adj* conversational; interactive

interaction *f* interference; ~ **mutuelle** mutual interaction

interactivité *f* audience participation (of TV); armchair interactive TV

interarmées *adj* joint services (of military specifications)

inter-auto (IA) tie-line; trunk

inter-bâtiment *m* ship-to-ship; ship/ship

intercalaire *m* insert; separator; liner; envelope

intercaler *v* interpolate; integrate; insert; embed

intercepter *v* intercept

intercepteur *m* intercepting trap; interceptor fighter

interception *f* interception; intercept; ~ **d'appel** call intercept; override; group pick-up

interchangeable *adj* interchangeable

interclassement *m* merging; collating

interclasser *v* collate; coalesce; merge

interclasseuse *f* collator

intercommunication *f* cross-feed; intercom(munication)

interconnecter *v* interconnect; interlink; cross-connect; interface

interconnexion *f* patching; topology; interconnection; hook-up; cross-connect; interface; networking; ~ **des réseaux hétérogènes** open systems interconnection (OSI); ~ **des systèmes ouverts** open-systems interconnection (OSI) (ISO); ~ **en boucles** loop topology; ~ **en étoile** star topology; ~ **en matrice** mesh topology; ~ **manuelle** manual patching; ~ **totale** fully-meshed interconnection

interdiction *f* inhibiting; barred access;

lock-out; denial; ~ **alternative** alternative denial; NAND function; ~ **d'appels longue distance** toll denial; ~ **de débordement** do-not-overflow; ~ **d'écoute** exclusion; ~ **d'écriture** read-only
interdire v bar; forbid; prohibit; deny; proscribe; preclude
interdit adj prohibited; barred; illegal; denied/barred (access); disguised; proscribed; inaccessible
interentreprise adj intercorporate; business-to-business
intéressant adj cost-effective; viable proposition; advantageous
intérêt m advantage; benefit; advisability
interface f interface; coupling; junction; liaison; boundary; ~ **cœur gaine** core/cladding boundary; ~ **d'abonné** subscriber line interface card (SLIC); ~ **de ligne** line interface; ~ **de terminal** terminal interface; ~ **émission** communications interface; ~ **HDB3** HDB3 code converter; ~ **par coordonnées** coordinate addressing; ~ **parallèle** parallel interface; ~ **série programmable** serial programmable interface
interférence f disturbance; interference; thump (of telephony); ~ **d'avion** aeroplane flutter; ~ **de mire** pattern interference; ~ **due aux courants du secteur électrique** interference from power lines; ~ **en télévision** television interference (TVI); ~ **hétérodyne** heterodyne interference; ~ **intermode** inter-mode interference; ~ **non stationnaire** non-stationary interference; ~ **par canal commun** co-channel interference; ~ **par impulsions chaotiques** chaotic pulse interference; ~ **par symboles** inter-symbol interference
interférences variées (signal channel) miscellaneous interference
interfonctionnement m interworking
intérieur adj local; interior; internal; inside; in-house; inner; built-in; integral; home; domestic
intérimaire adj medium-term
interlignage m underlap
interligne m line feed (LF); row pitch; line spacing; ~ **moyen** half-line feed
interlocuteur m counterpart; audience
intermanuel m manual trunk
intermariable adj compatible
intermédiaire adj intermediate; booster; buffer
intermittent adj sporadic; casual; transient; irregular; infrequent
intermodulation f crosstalk; intermodulation; cross-modulation; ~ **du troisième ordre** third-order intermodulation

intermodulomètre m inter-modulation meter
inter-MOM inter-digit pause
interne adj local; interior; internal; inside; inner; built-in; on-chip; on-board; in-plant; in-house; inward; resident; innate; intrinsic; inherent; integral; indigenous; domestic
interpellation f interrogation; scanning
interphone m interphone control system (ICS); intercommunication equipment; talk-back circuit; intercom
interpolation f interpolation; ~ **d'un signal** signal interpolation
interporteuse f intercarrier
interprétable adj machine-readable
interprétation f legend; key; meaning; notation; version
interpréteur m interpreter program; interpretive trace routine; ~ **de commandes** shell (of Unix operating system)
interrogateur m interrogator; challenger
interrogation f enquiry; test; question-answer routine; polling; challenge; interrogation; query; ~ **de groupe** group polling; ~ **par impulsions** pulse interrogation; ~ **sélective** polling; round robin; ~ **séquentielle** selective calling; round robin; ~ **systématique** polling
interrompre v interrupt; disrupt; halt; discontinue; ~ **en cascade** cycle off; ~ **pas à pas** cycle off; ~ **une émission** break in on a transmission
interrupteur m on-off switch; selector switch; contact breaker; ~ **à action brusque** snap switch; ~ **à bascule** toggle switch; tumbler switch; tappet switch; reversible switch; ~ **à commande photoélectrique** photo-electric controlled switch; ~ **à cornes** horn-break switch; horn-gap switch; ~ **à couteau** knife switch; ~ **à culbuteur** tumbler switch; ~ **à double rupture** double-break switch; ~ **à force centrifuge** dynamic relay; ~ **àgalets** roller switch; ~ **à genouillère** toggle switch; ~ **à gradin** step switch; ~ **à lame souple (ILS)** reed switch; reed relay; ~ **à levier** toggle switch; ~ **à mercure** mercury switch; ~ **à poussoir** pushbutton switch; ~ **à temps** time switch; ~ **bipolaire** double-pole switch; ~ **blindé** explosion-proof switch; ~ **de blocage** lock-out switch; ~ **de fin de course** limit switch; ~ **de ligne** line switch; ~ **de mise à la terre** earthing switch; earth switch; ground switch; Home Office switch; ~ **de protection** protection switch; ~ **de service** ON/OFF switch; mains control switch; ~ **déportable** remote switch; ~ **électronique** electronic switch; ~ **fugitif** keyboard switch; momentary-ac-

I

tion switch; ~ **général** main power switch; ~ **haute tension** high-voltage switch; ~ **horaire** automatic timer; time switch; ~ **RG déporté** (renvoi général) assigned night answer (ANA) switch; ~ **thermique** thermal switch; ~ **va-et-vient** three-way switch

interruptible *adj* enabled; interruptible

interruption *f* interrupt; trap; interlock; stoppage; halt; shutdown; disruption; pause; break; disconnection; ~ **automatique** automatic interrupt; ~ **claquée** interrupt timed-out; ~ **courte** short break; ~ **logique** software interrupt; ~ **longue** long break; ~ **physique** hardware interrupt; priority interrupt; ~ **vectorisée** vectored interrupt

intersecteur *m* AND-gate intersector

intersection *f* AND function; AND operation

intersélection *f* interdialling

intertrain *m* inter-digit pause/period/interval/gap

intertravée *f* inter-suite; cross-aisle

interurbain (inter) trunk; toll; long-distance; ~ **automatique (IA)** direct distance dialling (DDD); standard trunk dialling (STD); tie trunk; automatic trunk exchange

intervalle *m* gap; slot; interval; period; pause; increment; pitch; spacing; clearance; ~ **d'amorçage d'allumage** starter gap; ~ **de contrôle** control interval; ~ **de déclenchement** trigger gap; ~ **de manipulation** keying pulse; time between pulses; ~ **de mots** word interval; ~ **de pointage** plotting interval; ~ **de quantification** quantizing interval; ~ **de silence** silent period; ~ **de suppression** blanking interval; ~ **de suppression de ligne** line-blanking interval; ~ **de suppression de trame après synchronisation** post-sync field-blanking interval; ~ **de temps (IT)** (internal) time slot (TS); ~ **de temps de signalisation** signalling time slot; ~ **de temps de verrouillage de trame** frame-alignment time slot; ~ **de temps de voie** channel time slot; ~ **de temps pour élément numérique justifiable** justifiable digit time slot; ~ **d'échantillonnage** sampling interval; ~ **d'espacement des fréquences porteuses** carrier spacing; ~ **d'exploration** scanning interval; ~ **entre blocs** block gap; ~ **entre les chiffres** inter-digit pause; ~ **minimum** minimum interval; ~ **non protégé** unguarded interval; ~ **significatif** significant interval; ~ **unitaire** unit interval

intervallomètre *m* interval timer; frequency counter/timer; pulse period meter

intervenant *m* party

intervention *f* rectification; attention; repair; call-out; servicing; maintenance; remedial action; overriding; taking control; barge-in; cut-in; break-in; forward transfer; intrusion; challenge; assistance; ~ **de cames** channel-release conditions; time-out; ~ **en tiers** executive (busy) override; barge-in; break-in; ruthless pre-emption; executive right-of-way; ~ **manuelle** operator assistance; operator control; ~ **opératrice** operator override; break-in; cut-in; intrusion; ~ **prioritaire** executive busy override; ruthless preemption; barge-in; break-in; exclusive right-of-way

interversion *f* **de conducteurs** poling; ~ **des numéros d'appel** transposition of subscribers' numbers

interzone *f* **entrant** incoming (I/C) trunk

intime *adj* intimate; sensitive; confidential; classified

intitulé *m* title; header; prompt

intolérance *f* non-compliance; breach

intra-central intra-exchange; operator-to-operator

intrants *m pl* overheads

intrinsèque *adj* built-in

introducteur *m* **frontal** automatic front feed (AFF)

introduction de document forms handling; ~ *f* **en temps réel** real-time input

introduire *v* input; insert; feed; write(-in); enter

intrusion *f* crossed lines

inutile *adj* of no benefit; superfluous; redundant; irrelevant; not applicable; unnecessary; garbage; extraneous

inutilisable *adj* unserviceable (U/S)

inutilisé *adj* unused; not used; spare; vacant; redundant; not assigned; left blank

invalidation d'entrée manuelle disable manual input (DMI)

invalide *adj* void; garbage; bad; false; wrong

invariant *adj* re-enterable; re-entrant

inverse *adj* reciprocal; opposite; reverse; backward; complement

inversé *adj* complemented (of sign bit)

inversement *adv* conversely; by contrast; vice versa

inverseur *m* changeover switch; toggle switch; sense switch; driving unit; alteration switch; inverting gate; NOT gate; ~ **à charge** load inverter; ~ **de baie** rack inverter; ~ **de courant** changeover switch; ~ **de parasites** noise inverter; noise limiter; noise suppressor; white spot inverter; ~ **de polarité** paraphase amplifier; see-saw amplifier; ~ **émission-réception** transmit-receive (T-R) switch; ~ **fugitif unipolaire CI**

PCB-mounting keyboard rocker switch; ~ **sextuple** hex inverter

inversion *f* shift; reversal; inversion; case shift; turn-around; ~ **automatique** automatic case shift; ~ **chiffres** figure shift; ~ **codée des 1** coded mark inversion (CMI); ~ **de batterie (IB)** battery reversal; ~ **de phase** phase reversal; ~ **de polarités** polarity reversal; ~ **de signal** signal inversion; ~ **de température** temperature inversion; ~ **des nuances** tone reversal; ~ **lettres** letter shift; ~ **partielle des nuances** partial tone reversal

inverteur (circuit i.) *m* inverter (logic switching circuit)

inviolable *adj* tamper-proof; foolproof

invisibilité *f* secrecy; transparency

invisible *adj* code-insensitive; transparent; concealed

invitation *f* **à émettre** polling; interrogation; ~ **à numéroter** dial tone; proceed-to-select; ~ **à recevoir** selection; selective calling; ~ **à transmettre (IT)** invitation-to-transmit signal ('K' in morse code); 'over' cue

inviter à frapper cue

involontaire *adj* spontaneous

invoquer *v* call (up)

ion *m* **excité** excited ion

ionisation *f* ionization; ~ **sporadique** sporadic ionization

ionogramme *m* ionogram

ionosphère *f* ionosphere

ions OH hydrogen ion concentration (pH value)

IP (v. installation privée)

IQR (v. indice de qualité de réception)

IR (v. imprimante rapide); ⩭ (v. indicatif régional)

IRD (v. information de retour disponible)

irradiation (d'un objet) *f* illumination (of a target)

irradié *adj* irradiated (electron bombardment)

irrécupérable *adj* irretrievable; unrecoverable

irrégularité *f* **du diagramme de rayonnement** circularity ratio

irrégulier *adj* sporadic; fortuitous

isochrone *adj* isochronous; in phase

isolant *m* insulator; insulation; insulating (material); dielectric base; ~ **électrique** insulating pad (for IC)

isolateur *m* insulator; isolator; transistor-mounting pad; ~ **à cloche** bell-shaped insulator; ~ **à cloche double** double-shed insulator; ~ **à ferrite** ferrite isolator; ~ **à nervures** ribbed insulator; ~ **à tige** rod insulator; stick insulator; ~ **de traversée** partition insulator; ~ **de vibration** resilient mounting; ~ **en forme de noix** egg-shaped insulator; ~ **en porcelaine** porcelain insulator

isolation *f* insulation; ~ **entre spires** inter-turns insulation; inter-winding insulation; ~ **galvanique** isolation voltage; ~ **phonique** sound-proofing

isolé *adj* stand-alone; high-and-dry; unconnected; glass-encapsulated (of thermistor); free-standing; self-contained; integral; out-of-service

isolement *m* insulation (resistance); disconnection; shorting; breakdown; leakage; busying out; isolation; segregation; secrecy; separation; spacing; clearance; gap; outage; crossed-path; ~ **au papier** paper insulation; ~ **d'air** air insulating gap; ~ **électrique** electrical insulation; ~ **entre barres** busbar isolation; ~ **galvanique** electrical separation; ~ **terre** earth breakdown; earth leakage

isoler *v* isolate; insulate; busy-out; segregate

isomorphie *f* one-to-one correspondence

isotope *m* (d'un élément) isotope

ISS (v. insertion sans soudure)

issu de originating from; derived from; emanating from; stemming from

IT (v. intervalle de temps); ⩭ (v. invitation à transmettre)

ITA (v. installation terminale d'abonné)

ITC (v. ingénieur technico-commercial)

item *m* parameter value

itératif *adj* iterative; ladder; tandem; recurrent

itération *f* loop; iteration

itinéraire *m* route; path; switch path

J

JA (joncteur d'arrivée) incoming trunk junctor (ITJ)

jack *m* jack; hub; ~ **à rupture** break jack; cut-off jack; ~ **auxiliaire** auxiliary jack; ~ **court** earthing connection; ~ **d'appel** calling jack; ~ **de conférence** conference jack; ~ **de coupure** break jack; ~ **de dérivation** branch jack; drop jack; ~ **de renvoi** transfer jack; ~ **de réponse** answering jack; ~ **de sortie** out-jack; ~ **d'écoute** listening jack; monitor; ~ **d'entr'aide** auxiliary jack; ~ **d'entrée** in-jack; ~ **d'essai** test jack; bridging jack; ~ **double de rupture** double-break jack; ~ **libre** idle jack; ~ **local** local jack; answering jack; ~ **micro-monitrice** monitor micro-jack; ~ **multiple** multiple jack; ~ **triple** triple jack

jaillir *v* (hors de) be ejected (from)

jalon *m* sample; specimen; step; trace on

jalonner *v* (de points de reprise) checkpoint

jambage *m* descender

JAN (v. joncteur d'abonné)

jappement *m* whine

jaquette *f* sleeve

jarretiérage *m* strapping

jarretière *f* bonding strip; jumper; coupling; cross connection; link strap; bridle; pigtail

jauge *f* gauge; size; calibre; ~ **de contrainte** strain gauge; ~ **de profondeur** depth gauge

jaugeur *m* gauge; size; calibre

jetable *adj* non-returnable; disposable

jeter *v* pitch; discard; dispose (of)

jeton *m* coin-box token

jeu *m* clearance; play; backlash; set; kit; assembly; repertory; package; (character) font; repertoire; ~ **de caractères** character set; font; ~ **de caractères alphabétique** alphabetic character set; ~ **de caractères codés** code; coded character set; ~ **de caractères étendu** extended character set; ~ **de transcodage** code conversion set; ~ **d'essais** test deck; ~ **d'instructions** instruction set; instruction repertoire; ~ **partiel** (de caractères) subset; ~ **partiel de caractères alphabétiques** alphabetic character subset

j^me j^th

JME (v. jonction multiplex d'entrée)

JMS (v. jonction multiplex de sortie)

joint *m* **abouté** butt joint; ~ **d'étanchéité** waveguide gasket; ~ **plein** waveguide shim; ~ **torique** (= segment) O-ring; gasket; sealing ring; ~ **tournant** rotary joint

jointage *m* fibre soldering

jointer *v* joint; splice

jointif *adj* contiguous

jonc *m* retaining band; tie; binding wire; saddle; junction; optical fibre cable; cable former; rod; ~ **cylindrique** V-grooved cylinder (cable); fibre support element; rod; ~ **d'arrêt** circlip; ~ **nominal** standard interface; ~ **rainuré** slotted (corrugated) waveguide

joncteur *f* line circuit; transmission bridge; trunk; bus; intra-office trunk circuit; interface; (trunk) relay set; supervisory unit; matching equipment; analogue trunk; terminal circuit; junctor; ~ **alimentateur** power-feed junctor; ~ **bicéphale** double junctor; ~ **d'abonné (JAN)** subscriber line interface circuit (SLIC); ~ **de conférence** conference junctor; three-way conference call circuit; ~ **de films** recorded announcement junctor; ~ **discriminé** special subscriber line equipment; ~ **disponible** free trunk; ~ **entrante** incoming junctor; ~ **local** local junctor; trunk junctor; ~ **ordinaire** ordinary subscriber line equipment; ~ **réseau/usager** extension/exchange line SLIC; ~ **sortante** outgoing junctor

jonction *f* connection; interface; terminal; bond; junction; bus; trunk; tie line; interchange circuit; interchange trunk; PCM link; point of convergence; station line circuit (of telex system); ~ **adapté** matched junction; ~ **affluente** associated interface; tributary; ~ **arrivée** incoming trunk; ~ **BF** analogue trunk; VF trunk; ~ **commune** common trunk; ~ **contradirectionnelle** contradirectional interface; ~ **d'abonné** subscriber line interface; ~ **de collecteur** collector junction; ~ **départ** outgoing trunk; ~ **différentielle** hybrid junction; ~ **disponible** idle trunk; ~ **EH en T** EHT-junction; ~ **électronique numérique** multiplex interface; ~ **en té** T-junction; tee junction; ~ **entrante** incoming trunk; ~ **externe** interface; ~ **interautomatique** tie trunk; ~ **MIC** PCM trunk; ~ **multiplex** time-space (T-S) junction; space-time (S-T) junction; ~ **multiplex de sortie (JMS)** space-time junction (S-T); ~ **multiplex d'entrée (JME)** time-space junction (T-S); ~ **numérique** digital trunk; digital junction; digital interface (DIF); ~ **p-n** p-n junction; ~ **sortante** outgoing trunk; ~ **temporelle** PCM-TDM multiplex

jonctionnement *m* connection; coupling; interfacing; splicing; jointing

jonctions intercentraux inter-exchange trunks

joue *f* side plate; flange; rim

jouer sur match (of resistors)

jour *m* aperture; light; day; daylight; ~ **(au) poussoir** armature clearance (of relay); ~ **chargé** busy day; ~ **d'échéance** due date; ~ **férié** public holiday; non-working day; non-weekday; ~ **non ouvrable** non-weekday; non-working day; ~ **ouvrable** week-day; working day

journal *m* log; journal; day-file; ~ **de bord** status report; ~ **de transmission** transmission log; ~ **parlé** radio news; newscast

journalisation *f* log-roll printing

journée *f* **d'information** seminar

journées *f pl* proceedings (of conference)

judicieux *adj* prudent; shrewd

juger *v* deem; consider

jumelé *adj* ganged; twin; bifurcated; articulated

jupe *f* shroud; skirt

justesse *f* accuracy; precision; consistency

justification *f* bit stuffing; ~ **de taxe** ticketing; ~ **des choix possibles** criteria; ~ **négative** negative justification; ~ **positive** positive justification

justifier *v* vindicate

juxtaposabilité *f* butt-mounting

juxtaposition *f* contiguity

J

K

K7 cassette
kénétron *m* kenetron; valve tube; vacuum rectifier
kerdomètre *m* gain-measuring set
kHz (v. kilohertz)
kilohertz (kHz) kilohertz (kHz)
kilomètre-circuit circuit-kilometre
kilovolt *m* kilovolt
kilovoltampère *m* kilovolt-ampere
kilowatt *m* kilowatt
kilowattheure *m* kilowatt-hour
kinéscope *m* picture tube

kiosque *m* **point-argent** cashpoint kiosk
KL (kiloligne) thousand lines; kiloline
klystron *m* klystron; klystron tube; electron-beam generator; ~ **à glissement** drift-tube klystron; ~ **fonctionnant en sustension** overbunching klystron; ~ **réflexe** reflex klystron; backward-wave tube
KO (non conforme) NOK (non-compliant); unsatisfactory; incorrect; defective
krarupisation *f* continuous loading
kyrielle *f* panoply

L

l (longueur) length
L (largeur) width
LA (v. ligne acoustique)
label de bande interior label; tape marker;
 ~ **début d'information sur bande** beginning
 of information marker
label-fin *m* trailer label
laboratoire *m* orbital habité manned orbiting
 laboratory
laborieux *adj* arduous
lâche *adj* loose; slack
laconisme *m* limited extent
lacune *f* gap; drop-out; split; hole
lacune-trou electron hole
laine *f* **de verre** glass wool
laiton *m* étamé tin-plated brass
lamage *m* spot-facing; counter-bore
lame *f* knife-blade; reed; flake; slice; vane;
 spring; segment (of commutator); bar; n.;
 ~ **à retard pour microondes** path-length
 microwave lens; ~ **cristalline** crystal blank;
 ~ **de redressement** trimming tool; ~ **d'inscription** chopper bar; ~ **fixe** back contact
 (of relay); ~ **mobile** moving contact (of
 relay); ~ **porte-contact** contact member;
 contact spring; ~ **radiale** segment (of
 commutator); ~ **(radiale) de collecteur**
 commutator segment; commutator bar;
 ~ **ressort** leaf spring; ~ **vibrante** vibrating
 reed
lamé *adj* spot-faced
lamelle *f* pad (airgap); contact strip (of PCB);
 terminal pad/land; finger (of edge connector); ~ **d'entrefer** air-gap pad
lampe *m* lamp; valve; bulb; vacuum tube; ~ **à
 arc** arc lamp; ~ **à décharge au gaz**
 gas-discharge lamp; ~ **à effluve** glow lamp;
 ~ **à filament bispiralé** coiled-coil lamp;
 ~ **à incandescence** incandescent lamp;
 filament lamp; ~ **à mercure** mercury
 vapour lamp; ~ **à néon** neon lamp;
 ~ **àpente variable** mu-tube (variable);
 ~ **articulée** swivel-arm lamp; ~ **chauffante**
 fusing heater; ~ **d'alarme** alarm lamp;
 ~ **d'appel** calling lamp; line lamp; alerting
 lamp; ~ **d'avertissement** warning lamp;
 ~ **de clôture** all-clear signal lamp; all-ready
 signal lamp; supervisory lamp; clearing
 lamp; ~ **de disponibilité** idle indicator
 lamp; free-line signal indicator; ~ **de fin**

end-of-call lamp; clearing lamp; all-clear
 lamp; ~ **de fin de conversation** all-clear
 signal lamp; all-ready signal lamp; supervisory lamp; clearing lamp; ~ **de message**
 message waiting lamp; message lamp; ~ **de
 quartz** quartz lamp; ~ **de réponse** answer
 lamp; ~ **de réponse et de fin** answer lamp;
 ~ **de signalisation** signalling lamp; indicator lamp; ~ **de signalisation de retard** delay
 lamp; ~ **de supervision** (SUPER) (answering) supervisory lamp; clearing lamp; ~ **de
 surveillance** pilot lamp; ~ **de tableau**
 switchboard indicator; ~ **de visualisation**
 lamp; indicator; ~ **d'infrarouge** infra-red
 lamp; ~ **d'inoccupation** free-line signal
 (FLS); ~ **d'occupation (LO)** busy lamp;
 visual busy signal; ~ **électrique** electric
 lamp; ~ **filament** filament bulb; ~ **indicatrice** indicator lamp; ~ **Liliput** wedge
 lamp; midget lamp; ~ **lumière du jour**
 daylight lamp; ~ **navette** festoon lamp;
 ~ **par fluorescence** fluorescent lamp;
 ~ **radiotechnique** radio valve; ~ **témoin**
 signal lamp; pilot lamp; ~ **témoin de canal**
 channel calling lamp
lancé *adj* in progress; running
lancement *m* introduction; release; launch;
 float; start-up; ~ **en atelier** workshop
 procurement; replenishment; re-stocking
lancer *v* initiate; trigger; activate; start; run;
 issue; launch; instigate
langage *m* language; code; ~ **adapté aux
 procédures** procedure-oriented language;
 procedural language; ~ **algorithmique**
 algorithmic language; ~ **artificiel** synthetic
 language; ~ **assembleur** assembler language; assembly language; ~ **clair** clear
 test; plain language; ~ **d'application**
 problem-oriented language; ~ **d'assemblage** assembly language; assembler (language); ~ **de commande** control language;
 command set; ~ **de programmation** programming language; ~ **de service** service
 language; ~ **d'exécution** object language;
 catalanguage; ~ **d'origine** source language;
 ~ **évolué** high-level language; ~ **homme-
 machine** man-machine language; ~ **machine** machine language; object language;
 direct code; absolute code; catalanguage;
 ~ **mémoire rééditable** relocatable binary

object (code); ~ **naturel** plain language; ~ **objet** target language; object language; catalanguage; ~ **procédurier** procedure-oriented language; ~ **résultant** target language; object language; catalanguage; ~ **symbolique** symbolic language; pseudo-code; ~ **universel** universal language; multipurpose language

langue naturelle living language

languette f connector blade (clip mounting); tab; pin; reed/tongue (of relay); strip; lug; terminal; edge-board contact; ~ **à souder** solder spill; ~ **de connexion** connecting pin; push-on terminal blade; ~ **de masse** earthing strip; grounding lug

LAPS (v. logique d'accès partagé au satellite)

laqué adj enamelled

LAR (v. ligne à retard)

large bande broad-band; wide-band

largement adv predominantly; ~ **dimensionné** conservatively-rated

largeur f width; breadth; depth; ~ **(angulaire) d'un faisceau électromagnétique** beam width; ~ **de bande** bandwidth; ~ **de bande de base** baseband bandwidth; ~ **de bande de canal** channel bandwidth; channel width; ~ **de bande de phase** phase bandwidth; ~ **de bande d'impulsion** pulse bandwidth; ~ **de bande du bruit propre** inherent-noise bandwidth; ~ **de bande effective** effective bandwidth; ~ **de bande effective du bruit** effective noise bandwidth; ~ **de bande instantanée** instantaneous bandwidth; ~ **de bande occupée** occupied bandwidth; ~ **de bande pour transmission satellite-terre** bandwidth down; ~ **de bande relativement constante** constant-percentage bandwidth; ~ **de bande spectrale** spectral-response range; spectral sensitivity; ~ **de bit** bit width; ~ **de conduction** conduction band; ~ **de faisceau** beam width; ~ **de faisceau effective** effective beam width; ~ **de fenêtre** channel width (of pulse height selector); ~ **de puissance moyenne** half-power beam width; ~ **d'impulsion** pulse width (t_w); pulse average time (t_pav); pulse spacing; ~ **du canal** channel width; ~ **équivalente d'entrefer** equivalent air-gap width; ~ **réelle d'entrefer** effective air-gap width .

laryngophone m throat microphone

laser m **à modes verrouillés** mode-locked laser; ~ **à semiconducteur** diode laser; ~ **de découpe** scribing laser; ~ **de réglage** trimming laser

LAS.HP (ligne asynchrone - haute performance) high-performance asynchronous line controller

latté f blockboard

LB (local banalisé) bothway (B/W) local

LC (v. lecteur de cartes)

lecteur m reader; scanner; viewer; ~ **acoustique** acoustic pick-up; sound box; ~ **de badges** badge reader; ~ **de bande** tape reader; transmitter distributor (TD); ~ **de bandes perforées** paper-tape reader; punched-tape reader; ~ **de cartes (LC)** card reader (CR); ~ **de cartes perforées** punched-card reader; ~ **de ruban** tape reader; ~ **de son** sound-head; pick-up; ~ **enregistreur de disque souple** floppy disk drive unit; ~ **magnétique** magnetic character reader; ~ **optique** optical character reader; bar-code scanner; light reader; microfilm reader; ~ **optique de marques** optical mark reader; ~ **optique de son** optical sound reproducer

lecteur-perforateur de bande tape reader-punch

lecture f read; read-out; sensing; retrieval; peek; fetching; reset(ting); input; pick-up; play(-back); transmitting (of section of tape store); down-loading; copying; GET function; ~ **adresse curseur** read cursor address (RCA); ~ **arrière** read backward; ~ **auto-rythmeuse** self-clocked read; ~ **avant** read forward; ~ **avec éclatement** scatter read; ~ **avec effacement** destructive read; ~ **date** fetch date; ~ **destructive** destructive read; ~ **directe** direct read; ~ **d'une broche** pin readout; ~ **graphique** mark sense; ~ **incorrecte** reading error; ~ **non destructive** non-destructive read; ~ **optique** optical character recognition (OCR); ~ **par clé** get key; ~ **par rang** get index (GETI); ~ **rapide** flying-head read; fly mode; ~ **sans effacement** non-destructive read; ~ **sans tolérance** direct reading

légal adj statutory; lawful

légende f caption; legend; key; decal

léger adj lightweight; compact

légibilité f legibility

lentille f lens; ~ **à échelons** zoned lens; ~ **à lames parallèles** parallel-plate lens; ~ **à lames parallèles dans le plan H** H-plane lens; ~ **à lames parallèles dans le plan E** E-plane lens; ~ **à retard de phase** phase delay lens; ~ **à retard pour microondes** path-length microwave lens; ~ **diélectrique** dielectric lens; ~ **électronique** electron lens; ~ **électrostatique** electrostatic lens; ~ **magnétique** electromagnetic lens; ~ **multicellulaire** egg-box lens; ~ **radioélectrique** lens

lessive f detergent

lettergramme m data-link message; lettergram

lettre de relance reminder (letter); ~ de transport aérien (LTA) air waybill (AWB); ~ recommandée avec accusé de réception recorded-delivery registered letter; ~ type standard letter; circular letter
lever de doute sensing; resolving dilemma/ambiguity; sense-finding; ~ un dérangement clear a fault
levier *m* lever; latch; catch; detent arm; ~ à galet lever roller (of microswitch); ~ d'arrêt detent arm; ~ de calage detent arm; ~ de commande operating lever; joystick; ~ de commutation control lever
lexicologique *adj* grammatical
LF (v. ligne de filtrage)
liaison *f* link; linkage; coupling; connection; communication (data-link)n.; trunk; bus; tie; bond; strap; highway; interface; path; ~ à fort porteur carrier link; ~ à fort trafic high-usage trunk; ~ à fréquences vocales voice-frequency link; ~ à grande distance long-haul link; ~ à manque de tension break-type connection; ~ à microondes microwave link; ~ à mise de tension make-type connection; ~ à paires coaxiales coaxial link; ~ automatique automatic tie-line; ~ compte-rendu de marquage marking report link; ~ d'alarme alarm bus; ~ de compte-rendu de contrôle monitoring report link; ~ de données data link; ~ de masse earth connection; ~ de parole speech link; ~ de réaction feedback line; ~ de secours protection line; ~ de sécurité safety connection; ~ de signalisation signalling link; ~ de signalisation commune common-signalling link; ~ de signalisation de réserve alternative signalling link; ~ de signalisation quasi-associé quasi-associated signalling link; ~ de test test bus; ~ de transmission de données data link; ~ d'échange control link; ~ décimale ten-wire connector; ~ d'énergie power connections; ~ dérivable drop-and-insert line; ~ d'information message link; signal transmission medium; ~ directe direct call; direct connection; direct interface; ~ duplex duplex communication link; ~ duplex euphonie one duplex voice channel; ~ duplex intégral full-duplex link; ~ en groupe primaire group link; ~ en groupe secondaire supergroup link; ~ en ligne à paires symétriques carrier line link; ~ entre-voies channel-to-channel connection; ~ équipotentielle earth plane; equalizing bar; equalizing ring; ground plane; ~ fixe de télécommunication aéronautique aeronautical fixed circuit; ~ harmonique (deux fils et retour commun) radio link; VF link;

~ hertzienne microwave link; radio link; ~ hertzienne à visibilité directe line-of-sight radio link; ~ hertzienne par satellite satellite relay microwave link; ~ hertzienne transhorizon over-the-horizon radio link; tropospheric scatter radio link; ~ information machine data bus; ~ intercalculateur interprocessor link; ~ interurbain inter-toll trunk; ~ logique signal connection; ~ maritime ship-shore communications; ~ métallique physical line; wire connection; metallic loop; ~ MIC PCM link; ~ MIC/LTX PCM/LTX (local terminal exchange) link; ~ microondes microwave link; ~ multiplex à haute vitesse high speed multiplex link; ~ multipoint multipoint circuit/link; multidrop (line); ~ normale working line; ~ numérique digital span line; T-span; ~ numérique entrante (LNE) input digital highway (IDH); ~ numérique sortante (LNS) output digital highway (ODH); ~ optique optical fibre link; ~ par câble cable link; ~ par lignes de télévision television link; ~ par reprise directe de la télévision television direct pick-up link; ~ par satellite satellite link; ~ point à point point-to-point link; ~ radio radio communication link; ~ radioélectrique radio link; ~ radioélectrique sur ondes décamétriques high frequency (HF) radio link; ~ radiophonique radio link; ~ radiotéléphonique radiotelephone link; ~ satellite-côte satellite-shore link; ~ série doublée (serial) inter-processor data link; ~ simplex simplex communication (link); ~ spatiale satellite circuit; satellite link; ~ spécialisée leased line; dedicated line; private line; ~ station-relais radio-relay link; ~ symétrique balanced line; ~ téléinformatique communication link; ~ téléphonique speech communication; ~ terre-satellite earth-to-satellite link; ~ terrestre terrestrial link; land line; ~ V24 V24 interface
liant *m* binder; binding agent; agglutinant; ~ agglomérant binding agent
liasse *f* form set; ~ dupli-autocopiant NCR paper (non-carbon ribbon)
libellé *m* literal; motto; label; wording; preamble; message label; text; description; terms; field (of prompt); identifier; text; title; ~ d'une commande ordering details
libération *f* clearing; release; clear-down; ring-off; clearing-back; clearing-forward; blow-off; disconnection; exit; ~ anticipée premature release; ~ arrière forcée forced clear-back; ~ au raccrochage des deux correspondants called and calling subscriber released; ~ de garde release guard; ~ de

l'état grille release forms (RLF); ~ d'une ligne releasing a line; ~ forcée forced release; ~ par l'abonné demandé called party release; called subscriber release; ~ par le dernier abonné (à raccrocher) last party release; last subscriber release; either-party release; ~ par le premier abonné (à raccrocher) first party release; either-party release; first subscriber release
libérer v cleardown; clear; release; de-assign; free; disconnect; ~ sur temporisation time-out
liberté f play (of contact)
libre adj idle; available; free; vacant; unrestricted; spare; clear; cleared down; unoccupied; uncommitted (of gate array cell); unassigned; ~ appel free-phone; toll-free (call); ~ de devoid of; ~ jouissance usufruct
libres adj assorted
licencié m licensee; franchisee
lié adj (à) oriented; associated (with); tied (to)
lien m relationship; link; tie; lashing; patch; nexus; ~ de flexion articulated joint
lier v attach
lieu m locus
lieux m pl premises
LIFO (pile refoulée) LIFO stack (pushdown stack)
ligature f diphthong; tied letters; lashing; tie; tie wire; binding wire
ligne f line; cable; feeder; lead; channel; loop; row; stroke; highway; path; trunk; bus; circuit; junction; wire; PCM multiplex; tuple (= row); ~ à accès direct hot line; ~ à charge très légère very lightly-loaded coil; ~ à constantes non stationnaires distributed-parameter line; ~ à courant porteur carrier line; ~ à deux fils two-wire line; ~ à paires coaxiales coaxial line; ~ à prise directe (du réseau) dial-up line; dial-out line; ~ à quatre fils leased line; ~ à répéteurs repeatered line; ~ à retard (LAR) artificial line; acoustic delay line; sonic delay line; ~ à retard à magnétostriction magnetostrictive delay line; ~ à retard à mercure mercury delay line; tank; ~ à retard (acoustique) acoustic delay line; sonic delay line; ~ à signalisation par changement d'état three-state line unit; ~ acoustique (LA) acoustic delay line; sonic delay line; artificial line; ~ acoustique multiple bucket-brigade delay line; ~ active current line (of screen display); ~ aérienne open-wire line; overhead line; open wire; ~ aérienne pour la téléphonie open-wire telephone line; ~ appelante calling line; ringing line; ~ appelée called

line; ~ artificielle pad; artificial line; attenuator; line simulator; ~ artificielle de complément artificial building-out line; ~ auto exchange line; ~ automatique dial-up line; ~ auxiliaire junction; trunk; ~ avec répéteurs repeatered line; ~ banalisée party line; two-way line; ~ bidirectionnelle duplex line; ~ bifilaire two-wire (line) circuit; ~ blindée screened line; ~ bus optique optical bus; ~ coaxiale coaxial line; ~ coaxiale à remplissage de ferrite ferrite-filled coaxial line; ~ coaxiale à résidence ondulaire à chargement continu coaxial tapered line; tapered coaxial line; ~ coaxiale d'alimentation d'antenne coaxial aerial feeder; ~ coaxiale non homogène dans le sens transversal transversely unhomogeneous coaxial line; ~ collective omnibus circuit; multi-party line; ~ collective pour quatre connexions four-party line; ~ commune (dans un multiplage partiel) common trunk (in a grading); party line; ~ commutée switched line; dial-up line; ~ commutée par numérotation dial-up line; PSN line; ~ d'abonné subscriber line; local loop; subscriber loop; residential line; ~ d'abonné libre tone-on condition; ~ d'abonné pour l'interurbain long-distance loop; ~ d'abonné spécialisée pour l'interurbain PABX subscriber trunk line; ~ d'abonnement always-open line; ~ d'accès access line; trunk; bus line; ~ d'accès à une machine parlante announcement trunk; ~ d'acheminement principale basic routing line; ~ d'adresse address line; address bus; ~ d'adresse de lecture read address bus; ~ d'adresse de voie channel address bus; ~ d'adresse d'écriture write address bus; ~ d'affaiblissement attenuator; pad; ~ d'alimentation feeder; ~ d'alimentation coaxiale coaxial feeder; ~ d'analyse scanning line; ~ d'annotatrice record circuit; recording trunk; record position; ~ d'appel calling line; ~ d'appel de l'opératrice d'inscription et de départ recording completing trunk; ~ d'appel entre positions interurbaines interposition circuit; ~ de base base line; ~ de branchement branch circuit; tie line; drop; ~ de câble cable line; ~ de cadrage phasing line; reference line; ~ de central terminal final exchange line; terminal exchange line; ~ de code source line; ~ de commande (command) line; control bus; ~ de communication de pannes fault-testing junction; ~ de concentration concentration line; ~ de départ outgoing line; O/G line;

~ de filtrage (LF) executive-and-secretary line; ~ de jonction tie line; tie trunk; ~ de jonction de départ outgoing junction; ~ de jonction de transit tandem tie trunk; ~ de jonction libre idle junction; idle trunk; ~ de jonction locale local trunk circuit; ~ de jonction utilisée dans les deux sens bothway junction; two-way trunk; ~ de liaison flow line; ~ de modulation programme line; music line; ~ de partage demarcation line; boundary; ~ de poste supplémentaire extension line; extension loop; station line; ~ de programmation code line; ~ de rattachement analogue line; ~ de référence reference circuit; reference line; ~ de renvoi transfer line; transfer circuit; line loop; order wire; intercepting trunk; ~ de réseau (LR) exchange line (X-line); PCM highway; dial-up line; PSN line; central office trunk; PCM multiplex; switched line; ~ de réserve fall-back circuit; ~ de retard delay line; delay network; ~ de retour return line; ~ de service order wire; service wire; service circuit; control line; speaker circuit; ~ de signaux équilibrés equi-signal line; ~ de sonnerie bell line; ~ de surveillance alarm circuit; ~ de synthèse scanning line; ~ de télécommande remote-control circuit; ~ de télécommunication (tele-)communications line; ~ de télécommunication à station radio-relay communications; ~ de télécommunication multiplex multi-channel communications line; ~ de télégraphie telegraph line; ~ de télégraphie simultanée superposed telegraph circuit; ~ de télévision television line; ~ de télévision à grande distance long-haul television circuit; television line; ~ de test test line; test bus; ~ de tête master line; ~ de transfert through line; ~ de transmission transmission line; ~ de transmission à isolateurs d'écartement beaded transmission line; ~ de transmission à quart d'onde quarter-wave transmission line; ~ de transmission avec transpositions transposed transmission line; ~ de transmission de données data line; ~ de transmission équilibrée balanced transmission line; ~ de transmission HF en cascade cascaded HF transmission line; ~ de transmission unidirectionnelle unidirectional line; unidirectional transmission line; simplex circuit; ~ de transport power line; feeder; ~ de transport d'énergie électrique electrical power line; feeder; ~ de va et vient go-and-return line; ~ débanalisée dedicated line; ~ dégagée free line; ~ d'énergie electric line; power

line; ~ d'équilibrage balancing line; ~ dérivée spur; drop wire; ~ désignable line with directory number assigned; addressable line; callable line; ~ d'état d'un document document status line; ~ d'exploration scanning line; scan line; ~ d'extension artificielle artificial extension line; ~ d'extension locale local extension circuit; ~ d'information data line; data bus; ~ directe private line; direct line; fire telephone; hot line; ~ directe entre fonctionnaires du premier plan command hot loop; ~ d'ordre order wire; attendant trunk; ~ d'une carte card row; ~ duplexée duplex line; ~ d'usager station line; ~ en attente line on hold; ~ en boucle ouverte open-loop line; ~ en cascade cascaded line; ~ en dérangement faulty line; ~ en faux appel permanent line; ~ en fils nus aériens open-wire line; overhead line; ~ en garde line on hold; camped-on line; ~ en quart d'onde quarter-wavelength line; ~ en trait plein solid line; ~ entre centraux privés tie-line; ~ équilibrée balanced line; balanced (signal) pair; ~ essentielle essential line; priority line; always-open line; ~ extérieure exchange line; external line; trunk; ~ fendue de mesure slotted line; slotted measuring section; ~ formatrice d'impulsions pulse shaping line; ~ haute tension high-voltage line; ~ inactive dead line; ~ individuelle (d'abonné) exclusive exchange line; individual trunk (direct exchange line); ~ individuelle (dans un multiplage partiel) individual trunk (in a grading); ~ industrielle power line; ~ interautomatique tie line; tie trunk; automatic tie line; automatic tie trunk; ~ intérieure extension line; station line; ~ interinstallations tie line; tie trunk; ~ intermédiaire trunk junction; toll switching trunk; ~ interstandard (LIS) manual tie line; manual tie trunk; inter-switchboard line; switchboard incoming trunk junctor (SWIJ); ~ interurbaine trunk line; toll line; inter-toll trunk; ~ isochrone isochronous line; ~ isochrone en phase in-phase position line; ~ isolée widow; club line; break line; ~ jonction entrante (LJE) incoming trunk; ~ jonction sortante (LJS) outgoing trunk; ~ libre free line; idle line; available line; useful line; ~ local d'enregistrement local record line; ~ locale de bureau rural local terminal exchange line; LTX line; ~ locale de renvoi local transfer line; ~ locale pour service immédiat local demand-traffic circuit; ~ locale pour télévision local television line; ~ longue

L

off-premises line; long line; ~ **longue** (avec suralimentation) loop extender; ~ **louée** leased line; leased common carrier; ~ **médiane d'un guide d'ondes** centre-line (of waveguide); ~ **mémoire** long-format shift register; ~ **métallique** metallic line; wire; ~ **mixte** dot-dashed line; chain-dotted line; ~ **multipartie** multi-party line; ~ **multiplex** carrier line; ~ **neutre** neutral line; ~ **non affectée** spare line; ~ **non chargée** unloaded line; ~ **non groupée** non-equivalent line; exclusive line; ~ **non partagée** exclusive exchange line; direct exchange line; non-party line; ~ **non pupinisée** unloaded line; ~ **numérique** digital line; ~ **occupée** engaged line; busy line; ~ **omnibus** bus line; bus; ~ **orpheline** orphan; ~ **partagée** party line; shared line; rural party line; ~ **partagée à deux directions** shared service line; ~ **partagée à magnéto** magneto party line (hand ringer); ~ **pilote** pilot wire; ~ **pleine** full line; ~ **pointillée** dotted line; ~ **pour le trafic entrant** incoming one-way circuit; ~ **précédente** scroll down; ~ **principale** main line; bus; exclusive exchange line; ~ **principale d'abonné** main subscriber line; ~ **privée** inter-switchboard line; tie-line; private line; private common carrier; direct line; tie trunk; ~ **PTT** exchange line; central office trunk; public switched network (PSN) line; dial-up line; PCM highway/ multiplex; ~ **pupinisée** loaded line; ~ **réseau (LR)** exchange line; central office trunk; PCM highway; switching network link; PCM multiplex; dial-up line; PSN line; ~ **réseau entrante (LRE)** switching network input line; (PCM) go multiplex; ~ **réseau privée** PABX network line; ~ **réseau sortante (LRS)** switching network output line; (PCM) return multiplex; ~ **résiliée** suspended line; ~ **sans comptage (LSC)** free originating line; ~ **sans numérotation** hot line; ~ **sans répéteurs** non-repeated circuit; repeaterless line; ~ **sans taxation (LST)** free terminating line; charge-free line; ~ **sans taxation (LST)** free terminating line; charge-free line; ~ **secondaire** secondary line; ~ **simple** ordinary line; ~ **souterraine** underground circuit; ~ **SPA** (spécialisée en départ) outgoing-only line; denied termination line; ~ **SPB** (spécialisée en arrivée) incoming-only line; denied origination line; ~ **spéciale** leased line; ~ **spécialisée** private line (local loop); leased line; tie line; direct line; ~ **spécialisée en arrivée (SPB)** denied origination; ~ **spécialisée en départ (SPA)** denied

termination (subscriber line); ~ **suite** continuation line; ~ **suivante** line feed (LF); scroll up; ~ **supplémentaire** extension line; ~ **suspendue** ceased line; line temporarily out of service; ~ **télégraphique privée** private telegraph wire; ~ **téléphonique** telephone line; voice-grade line; dial-up line; ~ **téléphonique croisée** transposed telephone line; ~ **téléphonique internationale** international telephone line; ~ **terminale** subscriber line; ~ **terrestre** land line; terrestrial line; ~ **tête de groupement** pilot line; ~ **tiretée** dashed line; ~ **translatée** line with isolating transformer; repeatered line; ~ **triphasée** three-phase line; ~ **unidirectionnelle** unidirectional line; simplex line; ~ **urbaine de jonction** inter-office trunk; ~ **urbaine entrante** incoming junction; incoming trunk; ~ **vers un central public autre que le central de rattachement** foreign exchange line; ~ **veuve** widow; club line; break line; ~ **zéro** zero line

lignes banalisées et maillées common carrier grid (lines); ~ **d'impulsions** stepping lines; ~ **groupées** line group; PBX group; line-hunting group; collecting line; ~ **par pouce (LPP)** lines per inch (LPI)

Liliput courte small wedge lamp; midget lamp

limande f ribbon cable

limitateur m limiter; ~ **d'amplitude** amplitude limiter; peak limiter; clipper

limitatif adj finite; restricted; confined; exhaustive

limitation f **absolue** bottoming; ~ **d'amplitude** amplitude limiting; ~ **de courant** current limiting; ~ **de crête** peak limiting; ~ **de la bande de fréquences** frequency band limiting; ~ **de la dynamique** peak limiting; ~ **des parasites** noise suppression; ~ **d'interférence** interference limiting; ~ **thermique** thermal shutdown

limitations de la largeur de bande de télévision television bandwidth restrictions

limitative adj exhaustive; finite; restricted; confined

limite f ou adj compass; bounds; boundaries; critical; (current) limiting; cut-off; bound (of bucket); ~ **de bande** band limit; ~ **de confiance** confidence limit; ~ **de signalisation** signalling limit; ~ **de transmission** transmission limit; ~ **de validité** purge date; ~ **d'élasticité** yield point; proof stress; ~ **d'octet** byte boundary; ~ **élastique** yield point; proof stress; ~ **inférieure de la spécification (LIS)** lower specification boundary; specified lower limit; ~ **puissance** maximum power; ~ **supérieure de la**

spécification (LSS) upper specification boundary; specified upper limit

limité à confined (to); restricted (to)

limites absolues d'emploi absolute maximum ratings; ~ d'utilisation performance details; application; ~ incluses inclusive; ~ maximum d'utilisation absolute maximum ratings

limiteur m limiter; limiting device; clipper; peak limiter (AF); ~ à diode blocage du canal audio diode rate-of-rise noise limiter; ~ automatique des parasites automatic noise limiter (ANL); ~ de bruit noise limiter; ~ de courant current limiter; ~ de parasites noise limiter; noise inverter; noise suppressor; ~ de surmodulation overmodulation limiter

linéairement adv in linear progression

linéariseur m linearizer

linéarité f linearity; hold; ~ d'amplitude amplitude linearity; ~ verticale vertical hold

liquidation f aborting

liquide adaptateur d'indice index-matching liquid (material); ~ m frein securing fluid; "Loctite" [T.N.]

lire v read; fetch; sense; scan; transmit; access; get

LIS (v. ligne interstandard); ≃ (v. limite inférieure de la spécification); ≃ (v. logiciel individuel de site)

liseret m (liseré) stripe (of ribbon cable); reference edge

lisibilité f legibility

lissage m smoothing; trimming; adjustment

listage m listing; dump (output)

liste f list; roster; rota; directory; index; ~ à permutation circulaire circular (logical shift) list; cyclic list; ~ à rotation circular (logical shift) list; cyclic list; ~ d'assemblage assembly list; ~ de blocs block list; ~ de bornage from-to list; terminal assignment list; ~ de messages log listing; ~ des besoins where-used list; ~ d'indicateurs dialling code; office code; prefix code; ~ directe push-up list; FIFO; ~ d'options menu; ~ en anneau wraparound list; ~ inverse push-down list; LIFO; cellar; ~ linéaire dense list; linear list; ~ mécanographique computer printout; ~ noire void list; ~ non vide non-null list; ~ normalisée authority file; ~ refoulée push-down list; LIFO; ~ rouge ex-directory numbers; ~ vide null list

lister v list; print; dump; view (of file index)

listing m listing

littéral adj literal; alphabetical

livraison f shipping; consignment; package;

~ à lettre lue off-the-shelf shipment; ~ clés en main turnkey delivery; ~ contrôlée first-customer shipment (FCS)

livre m technique workshop manual

livrer v despatch; send; forward; supply; deliver

livret m record

LJE (v. ligne jonction entrante)

LJS (v. ligne jonction sortante)

LNE (v. liaison numérique entrante)

LNS (v. liaison numérique sortante)

LO (v. lampe d'occupation)

lobe m lobe; ~ arrière back lobe; ~ de rayonnement (radiation) lobe; ~ latéral minor lobe; side lobe; ~ principal main lobe; ~ réfléchissant reflection lobe; ~ secondaire minor lobe; side lobe

local m premises; room; building; quarters; ~ adj local; in-plant (system); short-range; own-exchange; off-line; single-ended; home; short-haul; ~ à archive file vault; storage vault; archive(s); ~ technique plant room

localisateur m location counter

localisation f tracing (of faults); radio direction-finding (RDF); ~ d'avaries fault tracing; fault-finding diagnostic; ~ des défauts fault tracing; ~ des dérangements fault tracing; ~ des équipements défectueux fault tracing; ~ d'un émetteur locating a transmitter; ~ radio-électrique radio direction-finding (RDF); ~ sommaire des dérangements broad fault tracing

location f leasing; hire; rental; booking

locaux m pl premises; ~ de servitude ancillary equipment rooms

logarithme en base 10 natural logarithm; ~ népérien natural logarithm

logarithmo-normal log-normal

logatome m logatom; discrete word

logement m seating; housing; location; recess

logiciel m ou adj software; ~ adapté à l'utilisateur middleware; ~ adapté aux sites exchange software; office software; ~ banalisé common software; ~ câblé hardwired programming; ROM; wired-in software; ~ combinatoire combinational logic; ~ d'application applications software; ~ de base system software; firmware; ~ de défense et localisation d'avaries security and fault-handling software; ~ de support support software; ~ d'exploitation system software; firmware; ~ figé ROM software; firmware; ~ individuel de site (LIS) dedicated exchange software; ~ informationnel information management software; ~ opérationnel operational software; ~ pilote control logic unit software; ~ proche

du matériel firmware; ~ **réserve** stand-by logic unit software

logigramme *m* **de test** test chart

logique *f* logic (unit); processing subsystem; processor; wired logic circuit; digital; sensing; switching; arithmetic unit; ~ **auxiliaire** standby processor; ~ **bipolaire (à) haute vitesse** emitter-coupled logic; current-mode logic (CML); ~ **câblée** hard-wired logic; firmware; ~ **cellulaire** cellular logic; ~ **combinatoire** combination(al) logic; ~ **d'accès partagé au satellite (LAPS)** (satellite) TDMA terminal; ~ **d'acquisition** signal processing subsystem; signal processing unit; ~ **d'arrêt** stop logic; interrupt logic; halt logic; ~ **de basculement** timing logic; ~ **de décision** decision logic; ~ **de déroulement** sequencing logic; ~ **de marquage** marking logic; ~ **de traitement** processing logic; ~ **d'effacement** erase logic; ~ **d'enchaînement** chain code; ~ **d'extrémité** MIC (PCM) code converter; ~ **d'horloge** timing logic; ~ **d'inversion** negation logic; ~ **DTL** diode-transistor logic (DTL); ~ **intégrée à injection** integrated injection logic (I^2L); ~ **majoritaire** majority (voting) logic; timing-signal distribution; ~ **non proportionnel** ratio-less circuit; ~ **pilote** control logic unit; ~ **réserve** stand-by logic unit; ~ **séquentielle** sequential logic; ~ **simple** non-duplicated logic circuit; ~ **statique** wired logic; firmware; ROM; ~ **TTL** transistor-to-transistor logic (TTL)

loi *f* law; rule; equation; principle; method; ~ **d'arrivée** call arrival (probability) distribution; ~ **de Child-Langmuir** Child-Langmuir equation; ~ **de codage** encoding law; ~ **de codage A** A-law coding; ~ **de codage à segments** segmented encoding law; ~ **de compression** compression law; (en-)coding law; ~ **de distribution des vitesses de Maxwell-Boltzmann** Maxwell-Boltzmann velocity distribution law; ~ **de Lambert** Lambert's law (surface illumination); ~ **de Lenz** Lenz's law (direction of current); ~ **de Paschen** Paschen's law (breakdown voltage); ~ **de Poisson** Poisson distribution; ~ **de quantification hyperbolique** hyperbolic quantizing law; ~ **de quantification logarithmique** logarithmic quantizing law; ~ **de recherche** hunt method; ~ **de Richardson-Dushmann** Richardson-Dushmann equation (emission of electrons); ~ **de service** call-holding time (probability distribution); ~ **de Stokes** Stokes law (particles in a fluid); ~ **de transformation logarithmique** logarithmic compression;

~ **de variation A/B** linear/logarithmic (tracking of potentiometer); ~ **d'Einstein** Einstein's law; ~ **d'Ohm** Ohm's law; ~ **statistique** statistical distribution

longeron *m* spar; side member

longévité *f* durability

longitudinal *adj* lengthwise

longrine *f* traverse; length-wise member

longue distance (à) long-distance; long-haul; ~ **durée** long-term; ~ **expérience** proven track record

longueur *f* length (of data block); capacity (of register); ~ **contrôlée** check length; ~ **d'absorption** absorption length; ~ **d'article** item size; ~ **de bloc** block length; ~ **de bloc fixe** fixed record length; ~ **de cohérence** coherence length; ~ **de cohérence d'un train d'ondes** coherence length of wavetrain; ~ **de dégainage** stripping length; ~ **de diffusion** diffusion length; ~ **de feuille** form length; ~ **de mot** word length; ~ **de parallélisme** length of parallelism; ~ **de pas** step length; ~ **de rayonnement** effective length; ~ **de trait** dash length; ~ **d'enregistrement** record length; ~ **d'équilibre** equilibrium (coupling) length; ~ **d'onde** wavelength; ~ **d'onde au pic d'émission** peak emission wavelength; ~ **d'onde critique** critical wavelength; cut-off wavelength; ~ **d'onde dans le guide** guide wavelength; ~ **d'onde de coupure** critical wavelength; cut-off wavelength (of waveguide); ~ **d'onde de détresse maritime** distress (signal) wavelength; ~ **d'onde de seuil** threshold wavelength; ~ **d'onde propre** natural wavelength; ~ **d'une section de rapprochement oblique** length of oblique exposure; ~ **effective** effective path length; electrical length; ~ **fixe** fixed (word) length; ~ **non compensée** non-compensated length; ~ **utile hors chanfrein** effective length excluding chamfer; ~ **variable** variable (word) length

loquet *m* latch; catch; clasp; clip

losange *m* rhombus (decision box); diamond-shaped

lot *m* batch; kit; set; package; lot; outfit; shipment; consignment; aids; ~ **de livraison** shipment; delivery lot; ~ **de maintenance** spare parts; maintenance kit; ~ **de production** production batch; production lot

louche *f* ladle; scoop

loué *adj* leased; private

loupe *f* zoom (of CRT display); magnifier; ~ **de contrôle** magnifier; ~ **micrométrique** eye-piece graticule

LPP (v. lignes par pouce)
LR (v. ligne de réseau)
LRE (v. ligne réseau entrante)
LRS (v. ligne réseau sortante)
LSC (v. ligne sans comptage)
LSS (v. limite supérieure de la spécification)
LST (v. ligne sans taxation)
LTA (v. lettre de transport aérien)
lueur f **anodique** anode glow; ~ **cathodique** cathode glow
lumière f light; glow; slot; aperture; orifice; opening; hatch; hole; brightness; louvre; ~ **anodique** anode glow; ~ **cohérente**

coherent wave; ~ **négative** negative glow; ~ **tombante** overhead lighting
lumières visibles ou invisibles visible and invisible spectrum
luminaire m light fixtures; light fittings
luminance f **de fond** background lighting
luminescence f luminescence; ~ **cathodique** cathodoluminescence; afterglow
luminosité f intensity; brightness; ~ **d'image** brightness (picture)
lyre f tuning fork contact; tine (of IDC connector); cable clip; prong

M

M (main) **gauche/droite** lefthand/righthand
m̂ (même) same (shorthand symbol)
m! (factorielle «m») factorial n
MA (v. commutateur marche-arrêt); ∼ (v. marche); ∼ (v. marque d'arrêt); ∼ (v. multivibrateur astable); ∼ (v. multiplexeur-aiguilleur)
machine f machine; mechanism; motor; computer; CPU (central processing unit); tester; device; tool; processor; generator; ∼ **à bobiner** (coil-)winding machine; ∼ **àcalculer** desk calculator; calculating machine; ∼ **à calculer de bureau** desk-top calculator; ∼ **à couper et cambrer** cropping and lead-bending machine; ∼ **à couper les composants** component lead-cropping machine; ∼ **à dénuder** stripping machine; ∼ **à dessouder** de-soldering machine; ∼ **à écrire (MAE)** teletypewriter (TTY); service TTY; typewriter; word processor; ∼ **à insoler** UV exposure unit (of PCB etching); ∼ **à pointes** pin-tester; bed-of-nails; ∼ **à sécher centrifuge** centrifugal drier; spin drier; ∼ **à sertir** crimping machine; ∼ **à souder à la vague** wave-soldering machine; ∼ **à traitement de texte** word processor; ∼ **cible** target machine; ∼ **d'appel** ringing machine; ringer; magneto; tone generator; ∼ **de contrôle polyvalent** multi-purpose tester; ∼ **de microgravure** micro-etching machine; ∼ **de Pétri** Petri network; ∼ **de projection** optical comparator; verification projector; ∼ **de travail** prime mover; driver; motor; ∼ **d'entraînement** drive mechanism; driver; ∼ **électrique à induction** induction generator; ∼ **grosses consommatrices** heavy-duty machine; ∼ **logique** virtual machine; logical machine; ∼ **(logique de traitement) d'appel** call-handling processor; ∼ **motrice** prime mover; motor; driver; ∼ **parlante** recorded announcement equipment; ∼ **tampographique** marking machine
machine-assimilable machine-readable
mâchoire f **de cadran** dial socket; ∼ **pistolet** rivet gun jaw; ∼ **quadruple** four-pin socket
macroassembleur m macro-assembler; macro-assembly language
macroélément m data element chain; macro-element
macrofonction f macro-logic function

macroinstruction f macro-instruction
macromachine f macroprogram subsystem
macroprogramme macroprogram
macrosynchronisme m duplex file updating
maculage m offset (blur); smudging
MAD (v. mise à disposition)
MAE (v. machine à écrire)
magasin m hopper; stacker; store(s); warehouse; magazine; repository; ∼ **à fils** wiring magazine; ∼ **d'alimentation** hopper; ∼ **d'alimentation en cartes** card hopper
magasinier m storekeeper
magnéto f hand-cranked ringer (ringing machine); manual ringer; megohmmeter; megger
magnétographie f video recording
magnétolecture f magnetic reading; mark-sensing
magnétomètre m magnetometer
magnétophone m tape recorder; reproducer
magnétorésistance f magnetic resistance
magnétoscope m video (cassette) recorder
magnétron à anode fendue split-anode magnetron; ∼ **à cavités** cavity magnetron; ∼ **à ondes progressives** travelling-wave magnetron; ∼ **accordable tout-métal** all-metal tuned magnetron
maillage m grid configuration; linking
maille f transfer link (= time slot); trunk; path; switching matrix; circuit; mesh link; grid; channel; junctor; cross-point matrix; lattice; ∼ **d'accès** switch path; ∼ **disponible** free link; ∼ **du réseau** lattice parameter
maillé adj meshed; mesh (of network topology)
maillechort m nickel silver; German silver
mailler v link; mesh
maillet m mallet
maillon m link
main f quire (25 sheets of paper); hand; ∼ **d'œuvre** manpower; labour; workforce
mains libres (à) hands-free; speaker-phone facility
maintenabilité f maintainability; mean time to repair (MTTR) indicator
maintenance f maintenance; upkeep; ∼ **à distance** remote maintenance; ∼ **corrective** corrective maintenance; modification; ∼ **courante** routine maintenance; ∼ **curative** remedial maintenance; troubleshoot-

ing; ~ **de circuits** circuit maintenance; ~ **de la commutation** switching maintenance; ~ **de la transmission** transmission maintenance; ~ **dirigée** directed maintenance; ~ **périodique** routine maintenance; ~ **préventive (MP)** preventive maintenance; ~ **qualitative** qualitative maintenance

maintenir v (se) hold; lock; ~ **l'historique** log out

maintenu au repos (in) mark hold

maintien m hold; lock; latching; hold-over; dwell; ~ **au collage** latching (of relay contact); ~ **au repos** mark-hold; ~ **électrique** electrical latching; ~ **magnétique** magnetic latching; ~ **manuel** manual hold; ~ **mécanique** magnetic latching; mechanical latching; ~ **par l'arrière** backward hold; ~ **par l'avant** forward hold

maître m master (of servo-system); owner; keeper; in absolute authority; key; ~ **d'oeuvre** lead contractor; prime contractor; project coordinator; supervisor; ~ **d'ouvrage** foreman/superintendent of public works

maître-esclave master-slave (system)

maître-oscillateur master oscillator

maîtresse f ou adj master; parent; mother

maîtrise f solving; supervision; assimilation; expertise; skill; middle management; proficiency; commanding lead; ~ **d'œuvre** project management; prime contractor status

maîtriser v be fully conversant with; master

MAJ (v. majoration); ~ (v. mise à jour)

majeur m major control

majorant adj upper bound; upper boundary

majoration (MAJ) upward adjustment; index-linking; weighting (factor); qualifying

majoré adj (avec garde) over-estimated (with error margin); ~ **de** qualified by

majorité f majority

majuscule(s) f pl shift (function); upper case; capitals

mal sectionné unevenly trimmed

malentendant m hard-of-hearing; aurally handicapped

manche m lever; handwheel; handle; column; stick; ~ f ferrule; sleeve

manchon m sleeve; slug; bush; jacket; ~ **de câble** cable stub; ~ **d'épissure** compression sleeve

manchonnage m bushing; sleeving

manchon(-repère) (identification-)sleeve

mandrin m drift; (coil) former; chuck; mandrel; ~ **à pince** collet chuck; ~ **métallique** metal former

maneton m crank pin

manette f lever; handle

maniabilité f user-friendliness; controllability

manipulateur (télégraphique) telegraph key; ~ m **de commutation** shift key; ~ **de fichiers** file handler

manipulation f kneading; folding; keying; handling; ~ **dans la grille** grid keying; ~ **dans le circuit d'antenne** back-shunt keying; ~ **dans le circuit primaire d'alimentation** primary keying; ~ **entre intervalles** break-in keying; ~ **par tout ou rien** on-off keying; ~ **par variation de fréquence** frequency-shift keying; ~ **parfaite** perfect modulation; ~ **sans destruction** blowout-free handling; ~ **télégraphique** keying

manivelle f **de magnéto** magneto crank

manocontact m pressure switch

manœuvrable en rotation rotatable

manœuvre m unskilled worker; casual labourer; ~ f manoeuvre; operation; call selection; dialling; driving; steering; ~ **à vide** dummy run; trial (run); ~ **intempestive** mistake

manœuvrer v actuate; throw (of key); drive; steer

manomètre m pressure gauge

manquant m deficit; shortage; short(fall); back-order

manque m failure; loss; inadequacy; ~ **de produit d'enrobage** void; ~ **de revêtement** void; ~ **fugitif du réseau** transient undervoltage; brown-out

manquement m discrepancy

mantisse f mantissa; coefficient; fixed-point part; fractional part (of logarithm)

manuel m ou adj manual; ringdown (circuit); operator-assisted; operator position; ~ **d'utilisation** user manual

manutention f handling; porterage

MAP (v. mise au point)

maquettage m breadboarding; prototyping; cut-and-paste presentation

maquette f mock-up; module; unit; kit; set; scale model; artwork; breadboard; dummy; original drawing; specimen; pattern; prototype; ~ **de déverminage** burn-in unit; ~ **de maintenance** portable routine tester; routiner; ~ **de traction** tensile tester; ~ **d'essais** signal analyser; data logger; tester; logic analyser; break-out box

marbre m surface plate

marbré adj veined

marbrier m surface plate

marche f step; ~ **(MA)** on; operating; start; running; ~ **à blanc** dummy run; ~ **à vide** no-load operation; idling; ~ **arrière** reverse; ~ **arrière du dérouleur** reverse tape transport mode; ~ **courante (MC)** current (production); ~ **rapide** fly

marché *m* contract; market; ~ **d'étude** development contract; ~ **intérieur** home market; domestic market; ~ **mondial** open market; ~ **porteur** buoyant market

marchepied *m* step-stool

marge *f* margin; threshold; tolerance; boundary; gutter; ~ **au synchronisme des appareils arythmiques** synchronous margin of start-stop apparatus; ~ **basse** page-skip margin; bottom margin; ~ **brute d'autofinancement** cash-flow; liquid assets; ~ **d'amorçage** singing margin; ~ **de gain** gain margin; ~ **de protection contre les perturbations** noise margin; ~ **de sécurité** safety margin; ~ **de service** dead sector; margin of service; ~ **d'un appareil télégraphique** margin of a telegraphic apparatus; ~ **effective** effective margin; ~ **gauche** offset (left margin); ~ **haute** top margin; ~ **nette** net margin; ~ **nette des appareils arythmiques** normal/net margin of start-stop apparatus; ~ **nominale** nominal margin; ~ **théorique** design tolerance

marginal *adj* supply tolerance control; fringe; borderline; marginal; threshold; edge

marguerite *f* daisywheel; pinwheel; daisy-chain

mariabilité *f* plug-to-plug compatibility; interchangeability; matability

mariage *m* convergence

maritime *adj* off-shore; seaborne; marine

marquage *m* marking; indication; recording; response; ~ **centralisé** end-to-end path-finding; ~ **des connexions** speech-path marking

marque *f* sticker; mark; label; flag; brand; trade mark; proprietary name; ~ **d'arrêt (MA)** stop mark; ~ **de bande** tape mark; file mark; control mark; ~ **de bloc** block mark; ~ **de fin** end mark; ~ **de repère** benchmark; reference mark; flag; ~ **de synchronisation** timing mark; ~ **DE/DR** called party/caller code; ~ **déposée** registered trade mark; proprietary name; trade name; logo

marqueur *m* marker; marking/(keying) wave; plotter; inscriber; logger; tracer; message distributor; ~ **de distance** range marker; ~ **stroboscopique** strobe marker

martelé *adj* hammer finish; crackle finish; stoved

masquable *adj* maskable

masquage *m* freeze; (solder-)mask; masking; privacy

masque *m* mask extractor; filter

masquer *v* mask; blind; shield; render transparent

masse *f* mass; volume; weight; bulk; bond; frame; earth; ground; reference potential; neutral; ~ **acoustique** acoustic mass; ~ **analogique** analogue earth; analog ground; ~ **armoire** frame earth; ~ **d'air** air mass; ~ **de l'électron** electron mass; ~ **du bâti** positive polarity connected to chassis; frame earth; ~ **électrique** earth; ground; ~ **logique** logic earth; digital ground (GRDD); ~ **mécanique** frame earth; ~ **métallique (Mm)** frame earth; metal weight; ~ **moléculaire** molecular weight; ~ **salariale** wagebill; wages fund; ~ **volumique** relative density

massette *f* **plastique** plastic-faced mallet

massif *m* bed; block; body; base; mounting; bulk; field; bank; ~ *adj* (massive) solid; bulky; massive; block; ~ **de jacks** jack field; ~ **de lampes d'occupation** busy lamp field; ~ **des clés** key field

mastic *m* putty; cement; sealant; filler

mat *adj* matt; dull; drab

mât *m* **télescopique** telescopic mast

matelas thermique thermal padding

matelassé *adj* padded

mâter *v* beat in (of cables)

matérialiser *v* implement; execute; realise; effect; evince; incorporate

matériau *m* material; ~ **composé** synthetic material; ~ **isolant** dielectric material; insulating base

matériel *m ou adj* equipment; hardware; appliances; plant; implements; stock; property; aids; ~ **d'abonné** private attachment; ~ **de commutation** switching equipment; ~ **de péritéléphonie** telephone accessories; ~ **de servitude** utility hardware; ~ **d'énergie** power plant; ~ **d'extrémité** terminal equipment; ~ **roulant** rolling stock; ~ **téléphonique** telephone equipment

matériels en fabrication de série batch-produced equipment

matière *f* **de l'isolant** insulating material; ~ **de remplissage** filling elements; filler material; ~ **plastique** plastic(s); ~ **première** raw material(s); ~ **tendre** resilient material

matriçage *m* swaging

matrice *f* switching plane; matrix; grid; array; table; chart; ~ **de brassage** link matrix; ~ **de commutation** switching array; switching matrix; ~ **de connexion** crosspoint array; ~ **de diodes** diode array; ~ **de points de croisement** crosspoint matrix; ~ **de tores** core array; core matrix; ~ **de trafic** traffic matrix; ~ **d'éléments d'image** picture element matrix; pixel grid; ~ **des phases** function table; truth table; ~ **et poinçon** die and stock; ~ **repliée** folded matrix;

~ **scellée multicontacts** (à maintien magnétique) (magnetic-latching) sealed multicontact matrix; ~ **temporelle symétrique** symmetrical time-division matrix

mauvais acheminement misrouting; ~ **aspect** untidy; ~ **cadrage** mistabulation; unjustified; ~ **contact** unsound contact; bad contact; ~ **isolement** faulty insulation; dielectric breakdown

mauvaise manipulation mis-keying; incorrect keying; ~ **soudure** bad joint

maximum m d'intensité peak current

MC (v. marche courante); ≃ (v. mémoire de commande)

MDF (v. modulation par déplacement de fréquence)

MDP2 (v. modulation à deux états de phase)

mécanique f ou adj (mechanical) engineering

mécanisme m mechanism; technique; function; device; procedure; expedient; contrivance; ~ **d'assemblage** unifying architecture (network); ~ **de cadran** dial mechanism; ~ **de progression** stepping mechanism; ~ **d'entraînement** drive mechanism

mécanographique adj punched-card (system)

mèche f drill; filament(s) (of aramid, in optical fibre cable)

méconnaissance f confusion

médiatisé adj media-oriented

méganomètre m (vern.) megger (megohmmeter)

mégohmmètre m megohmmeter; megger (vern.)

meilleur adj optimum

mélange m crossed-wire fault (shorting); conversion (e.g. of two HF signals); mix; blend

mélangeur m mixer; blender; conversion detector; frequency changer; first detector; combiner; ~ **à cristal** crystal mixer; ~ **d'entrée** input mixer; ~ **équilibré** balanced mixer; ~ **OU** OR-gate; inclusive-OR circuit

mélodie f jingle; chime; tone; warble; ~ **de sonnerie** ringing tone

mélographe m melograph (intonation emulator)

membrane f diaphragm

membre m member (of indexed data set); limb

mémento m notes; memorandum

mémoire f storage; (main) memory; store; map; core; latch; dump storage; buffer; ~ **à accès aléatoire** random-access memory (RAM); ~ **à accès rapide** high-speed memory; zero-access store; ~ **à accès sélectif** direct-access storage/memory; ~ **à boucle inductive** plated-wire memory; ~ **à boucle magnétique** magnetic-loop memory;

~ **à bulles** magnetic bubble memory; ~ **à circulation** circulating memory; delay-line store; dynamic store; dynamic RAM (DRAM); ~ **à connexion** crosspoint (memory); ~ **à disques** disk storage; ~ **à faisceau** beam store; ~ **à ferrites** core storage; core memory; ~ **à feuillets** data cell; ~ **à fil** twistor (memory); permanent magnet twistor; plated-wire memory; ~ **à films minces** thin-film memory; ~ **à films minces (magnétiques)** (magnetic) thin film storage; ~ **à lecture majoritaire** read-mostly memory; ~ **à lecture seule** read-only memory (ROM); ~ **à ligne de retard** delay-line store; circulating memory; ~ **à liste directe** push-up store; rubber-band store; first-in/first-out (FIFO); ~ **à liste inversée** push-down store; cellar; last-in/first-out (LIFO); ~ **à liste refoulée** push-down store; cellar; last-in/first-out (LIFO); ~ **à magnétostriction** magnetostrictive memory; ~ **à propagation** delay-line store; dynamic store; dynamic RAM (DRAM); circulating storage; ~ **à régénération** regenerative memory; Cheshire-cat store; destructive storage; ~ **à tambour** drum memory; drum storage; ~ **à tores** core memory; core storage; ~ **acoustique** acoustic memory; acoustic store; ~ **active** RAM (random access memory); ~ **adressable** (content-)addressed memory (CAM); content-addressed storage; ~ **annexe** bump; ~ **associative** content-addressed storage; associative storage; searching storage; ~ **auxiliaire** backing store; auxiliary store; dump; ~ **banale** working storage; scratch-pad memory; cut-and-paste buffer; ~ **basse** low core; low memory (LOWMEM); ~ **bloc-notes** scratch-pad memory; jotter; cut-and-paste buffer; ~ **boucle intermédiaire** scratch-pad memory; ~ **cache** cache memory; ~ **centrale** central memory; main memory; core storage; ~ **circulante** delay-line store; dynamic store; dynamic RAM (DRAM); circulating memory; ~ **commune** common memory; shared memory; ~ **courte durée** short-life memory (SL); ~ **cyclique** circulating memory; delay-line store; dynamic store; dynamic RAM (DRAM); ~ **d'adresse temporelle** channel-associated signalling memory; ~ **d'appels** call-data store; ~ **d'appoint** backing store; ~ **de boucle intermédiaire** scratch-pad memory; ~ **de commande (MC)** control memory; ~ **de commande des tonalités** tone-feeder control memory; ~ **de commande des voies sources** tone-feeder control memory; ~ **de commande spatiale** space-switch control memory; ~ **de commande temporelle d'entrée/de sortie** input/output time-switch control memory; ~ **de correspondance** matching memory; correspondence memory; ~ **de diffusion** one-to-n (connection) memory; ~ **de discrimination d'abonnés** line equipment status (memory); ~ **de la zone des variables** call-data memory; call-data store; ~ **de maille** link status memory; ~ **de masse** bulk memory; backing store; dump storage; ~ **de masse rapide** high-speed backing store; ~ **de masse tournante** disk unit; ~ **(de) programme** program memory; ~ **de rafraîchissement** regenerative store; Cheshire-cat store; ~ **de réception** receive memory; ~ **de resynchronisation** resynchronisation memory; ~ **de sélection de tonalités** tone select memory; ~ **de temporisation** time-delay memory; timing memory; ~ **de trame** frame store; frame memory; ~ **de transit** buffer store; ~ **de travail** working storage; operating memory; cut-and-paste buffer; scratch-pad; ~ **débanalisée** dedicated storage; ~ **d'échanges entre processeurs** processor data interchange memory; ~ **d'entrée** input buffer; ~ **d'état d'équipement** line equipment status memory; ~ **d'image** display memory; ~ **d'itinéraire** switch-path map; ~ **d'occupation** operating/output status memory; ~ **dynamique** delay-line store; dynamic store; dynamic RAM (DRAM); circulating storage; ~ **économiseuse** data save store; ~ **électrostatique** CRT storage; ~ **état des voies (MEV)** channel status memory; ~ **fictive** fictitious memory; virtual memory; ~ **fixe** read-only memory (ROM); permanent memory; nonvolatile memory; ~ **géante** bulk memory; backing store; dump storage; ~ **grande/de grande capacité** bulk memory; backing store; dump storage; ~ **holographique** holographic storage; ~ **inaltérable** nonerasable storage; read-only memory (ROM); non-volatile memory; ~ **intermédiaire** buffer memory; ~ **longue durée** long-life memory (LL); ~ **magnétique** magnetic storage; ~ **matricielle** matrix store; coordinate store; ~ **micro-coup** interrupt memory; ~ **morte** read-only memory (ROM); programmable read-only memory (PROM); static (non-volatile) memory; ~ **morte à fusible** fusible/fusable read-only memory (FROM); ~ **morte programmable (MMP)** programmable read-only memory (PROM); ~ **non effaçable** non-erasable storage; ~ **non inscriptible par le logiciel** electrically-programmable

read-only memory (EPROM); ~ **non volatile** EPROM (electrically programmable read-only memory); non-volatile memory; ~ **nue** unprogrammed memory; blank storage; ~ **permanente** non-volatile memory; ROM; ~ **principale** main memory; ~ **privée** cache (memory); ~ **rapide** zero-access store; high-speed memory; fast-access memory; ~ **rapprochée** associative memory; parallel search storage; content-addressed memory; ~ **rémanente** non-volatile memory; ~ **sauvegardable** non-volatile memory; ~ **semi-permanente** programmable ROM (EPROM); ~ **statique** static dump; non-volatile memory; ~ **statique programmable et reprogrammable** electricallly programmable and UV-erasable (static) read-only memory (EPROM); ~ **supplémentaire** backing store; ~ **tampon** buffer memory/store; ~ **tampon de chaînage** chaining buffer store; ~ **tampon de sortie** output buffer; ~ **tampon de tonalités** tone buffer memory; ~ **tampon d'entrée** input buffer; ~ **tampon du clavier (SUR IMP)** type-ahead feature; rollover function; ~ **tampon émission (MTE)** send buffer memory (SBM); ~ **tampon réception (MTR)** receive buffer memory (RBM); ~ **temporaire** buffer; put-aside store; ~ **temporelle d'entrée/de sortie** input/output time-switch buffer memory; ~ **topographique** real/virtual address mapping table; ~ **unitaire** direct input-output (I/O) indicator; latch; bistable memory; ~ **utilisable** programmable memory; non-dedicated storage; ~ **virtuelle** virtual storage/memory; ~ **vive** random-access memory (RAM); dynamic RAM; ~ **vive huit digits** dualquad bistable latch

mémorisation *f* store; storage; reading-in; copying; writing; dumping; keeping; buffering; put-aside function; latching; ~ **de phrase** text put-aside; vocabulary; glossary; library; boiler-plating; ~ **du dernier numéro** last stored number redial; last number repetition; ~ **et retransmission** store-and-forward; ~ **temporaire** keeping; put-aside storage; buffering

mémoriser *v* copy; store; record; write; dump; keep

mener *v* spearhead

mention *f* message; indication; injunction

méplat *m ou adj* flat

mère *adj* master; parent; mother

mériter *v* warrant; deserve

mésochrone *adj* mesochronous

méson *m* meson

message *m* message; call; prompt; ~ «**arrêt de**

l'émission de la tonalité» stop-sending-tone message; ~ attendu en réception expected return message; ~ collectif multi-address message; ~ d'adresse initial initial address message (IAM); ~ d'adresse subséquent subsequent address message (SAM); ~ d'anomalie fault message; ~ d'appel paging; ~ de connexion connection message; ~ de contrôle status message; ~ de durée d'appel call duration message; ~ de faute fault message; ~ de faute câblée hardware-generated fault message; ~ de guidage prompt; system information message; ~ de nouvel appel (NA) new-call message; ~ de patience please-hold-on message; hold-the-line message; trying-to-connect-you message; ~ de raccrochage (RAC) on-hook message; ~ de repos idle message; ~ de service memorandum; ~ de signalisation signal message; signalling message; ~ de surveillance supervisory message; ~ déconnexion release message; ~ d'état status message; prompt; status report; ~ détourné re-directed message; straggler message; ~ d'exploitation et de maintenance operation and maintenance message; ~ d'identification prompt; cue; ~ d'information information message; ~ distinct discrete message; ~ «émission de tonalités» send-tone message; ~ en attente message waiting (MW); ~ enregistré recorded announcement; ~ guide prompt; ~ irrationnel unreasonable message; ~ isolé one-unit message; ~ multiple multi-unit message (MUM); ~ non spontané compelled message; ~ publicitaire advertising jingle; commercial break; ~ réponse answer message; ~ sémaphore common-channel (signalling) message; ~ simple one-unit message; ~ spontané non-compelled message; ~ synthétisé dummy message; synthesized message; ~ vide null message; ~ vidéo image message; ~ virtuel virtual call; ~ voie par voie channel-associated message

messagerie f messaging; electronic mail; ~ de l'écrit messaging; telewriting; electronic mail; ~ vocale voice messaging; message calls

mesure(s) f measurement; parameter; action; step; metering; test(ing); benchmarking

mesure de distance range-finding; ~ de l'erreur error measurement; ~ de trafic traffic measurement; ~ défensive countermeasure; ~ d'équivalent net loss measurement; ~ du bruit noise measurement; ~ en boucle go-and-return measurement; loop measurement; ~ en cours d'épreuve in-test measurement; ~ en impulsions pulse characteristics; ~ par rétrodiffusion backscatter measurement; ~ potentiométrique potentiometer measurement

mesuré adv parsimoniously; cautiously

mesures de charge load and traffic data; ~ de défense security procedure; ~ de performances benchmarking; ~ de trafic traffic observation; ~ en impulsions pulse characteristics; ~ finales post-test end-point measurements

mesureur m measurement coordinator; measuring set; meter; tester; ~ de champ field meter; ~ de la grandeur du champ field-strength meter; ~ de la tension de bruit psophometer; noise meter; ~ de marge receive margin measuring set; ~ de vitesse (teleprinter speed)/modulation rate measuring set

métacaractère m wild card character; meta-character

métacompilateur m metacompiler; compiler writing system

métal m de base basis metal (NOT base metal); ~ embouti swaged metal; ~ précieux precious metal; noble metal; ~ vil base metal

métallique adj hard-wired; metallic; wire

métallisation f metallization; metal plating; bonding; through-hole plating; sputtering; passivation; ~ aluminium aluminium plating

métallisé adj metallized; through-hole plated

méthode f technique; procedure; method; strategy; ~ canonique canonical form; ~ d'accès avec file d'attente queued access method; ~ de deux points directeurs two-control-point method; ~ de simple appel A-position working; ~ de simple appel à service rapide A-position demand working; ~ d'écoute intercept method; ~ d'écriture avec retour à zéro dipole recording method; ~ du chemin critique critical path method (CPM); ~ par coupure cut-back method; ~ quatre points four-terminal resistor measurement system; ~ voltampèremétrique voltameter test

mètre ruban metre tape

métropolitain adj domestic; non-tropical

metteur m à jour de textes symboliques symbolic text updating facility; ~ au point debugging routine

mettre à jour update; debug; maintain; ~ à la disposition de refer to; ~ à la terre earth; ~ à un set; ~ à zéro clear; reset; zeroize; ~ au repos place on stand-by; set to idle; ~ en cause implicate; identify primary source of fault; spoil; impair; challenge;

jeopardize; ~ **en circuit** cut-in; commission; ~ **en court circuit** short(-circuit); ~ **en dérivation** shunt; bypass; tap; ~ **en écoute** listen-in; monitor; eavesdrop; intercept; ~ **en état** repair; recondition; overhaul; ~ **en évidence** reveal; ~ **en faute** inhibit; disable; implicate; incriminate; ~ **en forme** shape; format; edit; ~ **en garde** park; hold; ~ **en jeu** deploy; ~ **en marche** turn-on; start; activate; ~ **en occupation** busy-out; ~ **en oeuvre** activate; institute; instigate; operate; invoke; ~ **en service** bring into service; commission; enable; cut-over; bring on stream; activate; inaugurate; ~ **hors circuit** disconnect; ~ **hors tension** de-energize; switch off; ~ **le contact** switch on; ~ **une ligne en dérivation** tap a line; shunt

meuble m panel; rack; shelving; cabinet; stand; console; housing; operator position; desk; turret; ~ **interurbain** trunk desk; toll desk; toll board

meuleuse d'angle angular grinder

MEV (v. mémoire état des voies)

MF (v. modulation de fréquence); ≃ (v. moyenne fréquence); ≃ (v. multifréquence); ≃ (v. clavier multifréquence)

MIA (v. modulation d'impulsions en amplitude)

MIC (v. modulation par impulsions et codage); ≃ **actif** PCM link with CCS and CAS signalling; ≃ **passif** PCM link with channel-associated signalling only

micable adj configured for PCM transmission

MIC-DA (v. modulation par impulsions et codage différentiel adaptatif)

mi-course adv mid-travel; mid position; centre

micro m microphone; microinstruction; microprocessor; microswitch; microprogram; microcomputer

microampèremètre m microammeter

microboîtier m **plat** flat-pack

microbulle f tiny air bubble; blow-hole

microcalculateur m microcomputer

microcarte f microcard

microcasque m light-weight headphones

microcentral m micro-exchange

microcircuit m microcircuit

microcommande f micro-instruction

microcontact m microswitch

microcoup m interrupt; interruption

microcoupure f brown-out (of electricity); transient; drop-out; ~ **secteur** brown-out (of electricity)

microcourbure f micro-bending (of fibre optics)

microdossier m jacket

microélectronique f micro-electronics

microenrobage m micro-potting

microfiche m microfiche

microfilm m microfilm

microforme f micromedium; microtext

micro-image m (vidéo/magnétique) (video) chip

micro-informatique f microcomputer; microcomputing

micro-instruction f micro-instruction

micro-interrupteur m miniature switch; microswitch

micrologiciel m firmware

micrologie f firmware

micromachine (MR) f microprogram subsystem

micromodule m micromodule; bead

micro-onde f microwave

micro-ordinateur m microcomputer

micropavé m flip-chip

microphone m microphone; transmitter; ~ **à bobine mobile** moving-coil microphone; (electro-)dynamic microphone; ~ **à charbon** carbon microphone/transmitter; ~ **à condensateur** capacitor microphone; electrostatic microphone; electret microphone; ~ **à conducteur mobile** moving-conductor microphone; ribbon microphone; ~ **à cristal** piezo-electric crystal microphone; ~ **à électret** electret microphone; ~ **à fer mobile** moving-iron microphone; ~ **à gradient de pression** pressure-gradient (velocity) microphone; ~ **à grenaille de charbon** carbon-granule microphone; ~ **à magnétostriction** magnetostriction microphone; ~ **à pression** pressure(-gradient) microphone; ~ **à quartz piézoélectrique** piezoelectric quartz-crystal microphone; ~ **à réluctance variable** variable reluctance microphone; ~ **à ruban** ribbon microphone; moving-conductor microphone; band microphone; ~ **à sonde** probe-tube microphone; ~ **clandestin** bug; ~ **de bouche** close-talking microphone; ~ **de boutonnière** lapel microphone; button-hole microphone; ~ **de masque** mask microphone; ~ **de proximité** close-talking microphone; ~ **électrodynamique** electrodynamic (moving-coil) microphone; ~ **électromagnétique** electromagnetic microphone; ~ **en réflecteur** parabolic (reflector) microphone; ~ **étalon** standard microphone; ~ **labial** close-talking microphone; ~ **omnidirectionnel** non-directional microphone; ~ **piézoélectrique** quartz-crystal microphone; ~ **plastron** breast-plate microphone/transmitter; ~ **thermique** thermal microphone

microphonicité *f* howl; microphone effect
microphoto *f* chip
microplaquette *f* wafer; chip
microplastron *m* breast-plate microphone
micropoutre *f* beam lead
microprocesseur *m* microprocessor; ~ **à tranches** (en technologie bipolaire) bit-slice bipolar microprocessor; ~ **intégré** on-chip microprocessor
microprogrammation *f* firmware
microprogrammé *adj* firmware-based
microréseau *m* **de génération** static inverter
microrupteur *m* microswitch; snap switch
microscope *m* **de mesure** measuring microscope; ~ **électrostatique** electron (electrostatic) microscope; ~ **protonique** proton microscope
microscopie *f* microfilming
microsélecteur *m* miniature crossbar switch
microsillon *m* microgroove; fine groove
microstructure *f* microcircuit; chip; integrated circuit; micro-assembly; ~ **logique** digital integrated circuit
microtore *m* miniature core
microvue *f* micro-exposure; microcopy; microprint; micro-transparency
MIC/SPA PCM serial/parallel conversion
migration *f* shift; wander; straying; precipitation; upgrading; transitional aid; porting
mi-hauteur *m* half-amplitude
milieu *m* environment; medium; mid-way; centre; ~ **acoustique** acoustic environment; ~ **agressif** hostile environment; ~ **chaud** hot well; ~ **d'indice** refractive index; ~ **froid** cold well; ~ **industriel** industrial environment; ~ **virtuel** virtual machine environment (VME)
millésime *m* year (of manufacture)
millième *m* **de pouce** mil (10⁻³ in./0.0254 mm)
millier *m* thousands-group
millionième(s) *m(pl)* part(s) per million (p.p.m. = 1.10⁻⁶)
millivoltampèremètre *m* millivoltammeter
mineur *m* minor control (sorting); primary
miniaturisation *f* miniaturisation; solid-state circuitry
miniaturisé *adj* solid-state
minibandeau *m* miniature overlay; mini-strip
minicalculateur *m* minicomputer
minidisque *m* diskette; floppy disk; flippy; ~ **souple** floppy disk; diskette; flippy
mini-interrupteur *m* DIP switch
minimum basic; standard; short-form
mini-ordinateur *m* minicomputer
miniprocesseur *m* miniprocessor
minirépartiteur *m* miniature crossbar switch
miniréseau de connexion flexibility point; patch panel

minirupteur *m* snap switch; microswitch
minisélecteur *m* mini-selector; mini-crossbar switch; mini-switch; ~ **à maintien électromécanique** mechanically-latched mini-crossbar switch; ~ **électromécanique** mini-switch; mini-crossbar switch
minuscule *f ou adj* lower case (letter)
minuterie *f* timer; timing device; cyclic time switch; minute switch; ~ **(impulsions pour régime) périodique** periodic-pulse time switch
minutes *f pl* **taxées** paid minutes
mirage *m* reflection
mire *f* television test pattern; resolution grid; pattern generator; prompt; raster; ~ **de définition** resolution grid; ~ **de demi-teinte** half-tone grid/pattern; ~ **de géométrie** tooling feature; locating pattern; ~ **de télévision** television test card; ~ **électronique** pattern generator
miroir *m* mirror; light-reflecting surface; ~ **de sortie** output beam mirror; ~ **électronique** electron mirror; ~ **grille** rod reflector; rod mirror
mis en bloc(s) blocking
mise *f* **à disposition (MAD)** submission; hand-over; conveyance; retrieval; ~ **à jour (MAJ)** up-dating; revision; modification; amendment; retrofit; ~ **à jour date et heure** set time; ~ **à jour de fichier** file maintenance; file updating; ~ **à la masse** earthing; bonding to earth; in leak; single-ended; referred to earth; ~ **à la terre** earthed; grounded; earthing; ~ **à l'échappement** venting (of air valves); ~ **à l'état** set status; ~ **à l'heure** setting; resetting; ~ **à niveau** upgrading; elevating; retrofit; streamlining; reconfiguration; ~ **à palier** upgrading; retrofit; ~ **à terre de protection** protective earth(ing); ~ **à un** (d'un bit) set bit; ~ **au calendrier** schedule; ~ **au courant** inform; keep up-to-date; ~ **au point (MAP)** debugging; rectification; adjustment; definition; development; focussing; final adjustment; troubleshooting; refinement; integration tests; ~ **au rebut** scrap; ~ **au travail** activating; ~ **de l'installation en renvoi** night service; ~ **de tension** (schéma à ~) make-type circuit layout; ~ **en accusation** identified as symptomatic (of fault condition); implication; ~ **en attente** hold in abeyance; camp-on; camp-on busy; ring-when-free; queuing; ~ **en attente de messages** message queuing; ~ **en attente devant la ligne occupée** camp-on busy; ~ **en attente par l'opératrice** attendant camp-on; ~ **en attente sur abonné libre/occupé** camped-on free/busy subscriber; ~ **en**

autonomie (off-line) arbitration (of inter-lock/contention situation); ~ **en bâtis** rack assembly; racking; ~ **en blocage** isolation; disabling; turn-off; biasing to cut-off; ~ **en boîte** packaging; modularizing; ~ **en boîtier** circuit partitioning; ~ **en cause** challenge; implicate; singled out; diagnosed; ~ **en circuit** switching-on; commissioning; ~ **en conduction** turn-on (time); ~ **en consultation** data collation; ~ **en conteneur** containerization; ~ **en disponibilité** handover; deployment; release; ~ **en équation** finding the equation; ~ **en équilibre** balancing; ~ **en état** set status; ~ **en état d'occupation** busying; ~ **en évidence** highlighted; ~ **en exergue** demonstration; ~ **en faute** incrimination piloting; ~ **en faux-appel** line lockout; permanent line; isolation; call park; ~ **en file d'attente** queueing; camping-on; ~ **en fonction** selection; select mode; ~ **en forme** editing; formatting; shaping (of pulses, signals); ~ **en forme du spectre** spectrum shaping; ~ **en garde** three-party conference; call parking; warning notice; precaution(s); ~ **en garde** (circuit de) clamp-on (circuit); camp-on; ~ **en garde par indicatif** call parking; ~ **en garde par l'opératrice** attendant hold; ~ **en garde pour appel antérieur** enquiry call; ~ **en garde pour information** consultation hold; ~ **en indisponible** isolation (of PCM highways); ~ **en marche (MM)** start(-up); activation; operation; ~ **en mémoire** storage; ~ **en occupation** busy out; ~ **en œuvre** implementation; initiation; application; procedure; initialization; fulfilment; institution; installation; deployment; inauguration; instigation; preliminary adjustments; mobilization; production; ~ **en page** paging; format(ting); layout; ~ **en phase** phase synchronization; phasing; ~ **en phase du train incident** synchronization of received signals; ~ **en phase sur blanc** phase white; ~ **en phase sur noir** phase black; ~ **en pile** pushing into the stack; ~ **en place** installing; mustering; setting-up; fetching (of data); introduction; fitting; deployment; threading; laying; erection; evolving; institution; inauguration; ~ **en points communs** commoning; ~ **en présence (MP)** switching control unit (SCU); party connector unit (PCU); "through" signal; handshaking (protocol); ~ **en régie** succession in the hands of the public trustee; ~ **en relation** (avec) establish contact (with); connection; handshaking; correlation; ~ **en route** run up; warm up; activation;

switching-on; ~ **en séquence** sequencing; ~ **en service** cut in service; lead time; creation; cutover; come on stream; enabling; inauguration; commissioning; operating; procedure; ~ **en service du ronfleur** audio on; ~ **en service massive** block cut-over; ~ **en sonnerie** ringing; rung; ~ **en surveillance** (message de) (start) supervision (message); ~ **en tampon** buffering; ~ **en tiers** executive busy override facility (intrusion); cut-in; ~ **en travail** pick-up; ~ **en travers** skew (of tape); ~ **en valeur** show one's mettle; ~ **en veilleuse** do-not-disturb facility; station forced busy; ~ **hors fonction** de-select mode; ~ **hors service** (HS) disabling; override; busying out; out-servicing; isolation; ~ **hors service brutale** (system) crash; ~ **hors service douce** graceful degradation; crippled mode; ~ **hors service manuelle de jonctions** busying-out of trunks; ~ **hors tension** powering down; ~ **hors trafic** shedding of traffic; ~ **sous cocon** mothballing; ~ **sous écran** screening; shielding; ~ **sous tension** (MST) powering-up; switching-on; energizing; ~ **sous vide** inducing vacuum

misé sur opt for

mission *f* role; function; tour of duty; errand; brief; business; activities; mandate; responsibility; task; commitment; vocation; (operating) assignment; sphere of influence; ~ **d'identification** fact-finding visit/tour

mixage *m* combination

mixer *v* merge; blend; combine

mixte *adj* bothway (B/W); trunk and local; joint; compound; combined/shared (switch-board); hybrid (circuit); improper (fraction); partitioned; (in) common; reversible; composite; up-and-down

mle (v. modèle)

Mm (v. masse métallique)

MM (v. mise en marche)

MMP (v. mémoire morte programmable)

MMT (v. moniteur multifonctions multitâches)

mobile *adj* rotary; moving (part); detachable; plug-in; removable; volatile (of file); flying (of magnetic drum head); free; roaming; roving; mobile (cellular R/T); floating; vehicular; back-pack; independent; ~ **demandé** terminating mobile; ~ **demandeur** originating mobile

mobilité *f* **du porteur** Hall mobility; carrier mobility

modalités *f pl* **de reprise** corrective action

mode *f* mode; procedure; method; ~ **à quantification d'amplitude** amplitude-quantized control; ~ **additionné** add mode; ~ **alterné** alternate mode; ~ **arythmique** start-stop mode; asynchronous (byte) mode; ~ **asservi** slave mode; ~ **associatif** content-addressed mode (search); ~ **associé** associated-signalling mode; ~ **autonome** local mode; ~ **caractère** character mode; byte mode; asynchronous (= arythmic) transmission mode; ~ **cascadable** pipeline (architecture); ~ **circuit virtuel** virtual circuit mode; ~ **commun** common mode; ~ **complètement dissocié** fully-dissociated signalling mode; ~ **continu** burst mode; time-compression multiplex; ping-pong; ~ **conversationnel** speech mode; interactive mode; on-line; conversational mode; dialogue mode; ~ **courant** current mode; emitter-coupled; ~ **datagramme** datagram mode; ~ **de communication** communication mode; ~ **de livraison** delivery method; ~ **de propagation** propagation mode; ~ **de propagation guidé** trapped mode; ~ **de refroidissement** heat sink; ~ **de secours** stand-by mode; ~ **de vibration fondamental** fundamental thickness-shear mode; ~ **découpé** chopped (display) mode; ~ **dégénéré** degenerate mode; run-down state; ~ **d'emploi** instructions for use; operating procedure; ~ **d'exécution** processing mode; ~ **d'exploitation associé** associated mode of operation; ~ **dialogué** speech mode; conversational mode; interactive mode; on-line; ~ **différé** store-and-forward; ~ **discontinu** byte mode; character mode; asynchronous transmission mode; ~ **dominant** dominant mode (of waveguide); ~ **émulation** emulation mode; ~ **entrée de données** data entry mode; ~ **étendu** extended mode; ~ **évanescent** evanescent mode; ~ **fondamental** dominant mode (of waveguide); ~ **grille** mode format; ~ **image** image mode; ~ **interactif** interactive mode; speech mode; ~ **inverse** invert mode; ~ **ligne** line-driven; ~ **local** local mode; ~ **magnétique transversal** transverse magnetic (TM) mode; E mode; ~ **menu** menu-driven; ~ **non adressé** stand-by mode; ~ **non associé** non-associated signalling mode; ~ **non connecté** off-line; ~ **opératoire** (operating) procedure; instructions; ~ **phonique** speech mode; ~ **pi** pi mode; ~ **pilote** master mode; ~ **plume baissée** pen-down mode; ~ **quasi-associé** quasi-associated signalling mode; ~ **réduction de consommation** stand-by mode; power-down mode (PDN); ~ **repli** fallback-rate mode; ~ **restreint**

restricted mode; ~ **rouleau** roll mode; rack-up; ~ **secours** standby mode; ~ **transparent** code-insensitive data communication; code-independent/code transparent data communication; ~ **transversal** shear mode; ~ **V$_{dd}$ pulsé** clocked V$_{dd}$ operation

modèle (mle) m specimen; pattern; trial model; type; pro forma; example; sample; version; ~ **associable** structurally-similar device; related model; ~ **de circuit imprimé** land pattern (PCB track layout); ~ **mathématique** mathematical model; ~ **réduit** small-scale model

modem m (modulateur-démodulateur) modem; data set; ~ **à sous-canaux** channelized data set; ~ **retournable** reversible modem; ~ **supra-vocal** DOV (data-over-voice) modem

modems sur groupe primaire group modems

moderne adj state-of-the-art

moderniser v streamline

modifiable par cavalier jumper-selectable; strap-selected

modificateur m modifier

modification f patch; change; alteration; upgrading; retrofit; amendment; revision; refinement; ~ **d'adresse** address modification; ~ **de protection** reprotect; ~ **de texte** editing; ~ **d'état** status transition; state change; ~ **sur segment de recouvrement transféré** patching of swapped-in overlay

modulaire adj modular

modularité de panne failure modularity; ~ **d'extension** f modular expansion

modulat m modulated wave

modulateur m modulator; ~ **à bande latérale unique** single-sideband modulator; ~ **à basse distorsion** low-distortion modulator; ~ **à phase rectangulaire** quadriphase modulator; ~ **annulaire** ring modulator; ~ **d'amplitude** amplitude modulator; ~ **de brouillage** jammer modulator; ~ **de densité d'impulsion** pulse density modulator (PDM); ~ **de données** data modulator; ~ **de fréquence** frequency modulator; ~ **de largeur** pulse-width modulator; ~ **de lumière** light modulator; ~ **de phase** phase modulator; ~ **en anneau** ring modulator; ~ **en pont** modulation bridge; ~ **équilibré** balanced modulator; ~ **multiple** speech scrambler; ~ **optique** optical modulator; ~ **push-pull** balanced modulator; ~ **statique** static modulator

modulation f modulation; keying; translation; pulsing; ~ **à bande laterale unique** single-sideband modulation; ~ **à bas niveau** low-power modulation; ~ **à deux états de phase (MDP2)** binary PSK (phase-shift keying); ~ **à double courant** polar keying; ~ **à impulsions codées** (MIC) pulse-code modulation (PCM); ~ **à interruption de porteuse** quiescent-carrier modulation; ~ **à simple courant** neutral keying; ~ **à trait permanent** modulated continuous wave (MCW) keying; ~ **arythmique** start-stop modulation; restitution; ~ **combiné d'amplitude et de phase** combined amplitude and phase modulation; ~ **d'amplitude** on-off signalling; amplitude modulation (AM); amplitude (shift) keying (ASK); ~ **d'amplitude en classe A** class-A modulation; ~ **d'amplitude en quadrature de phase** quadrature amplitude modulation (QAM); ~ **d'amplitude par absorption** absorption modulation; ~ **(d'amplitude) par variation de charge** pulse amplitude modulation (PAM); ~ **de densité** beam-current modulation; density modulation; ~ **de fréquence (MF)** frequency modulation (FM); ~ **de fréquence à bande étroite** narrow-band frequency modulation; ~ **de fréquence en fonction du temps** frequency-time modulation; ~ **de fréquence et d'amplitude simultanée** simultaneous frequency and amplitude modulation (FAM); ~ **de la sousporteuse** subcarrier modulation; ~ **de phase** phase modulation; ~ **de phase avec phase de référence** phase modulation with reference phase; ~ **de phase différentielle** differential phase modulation; ~ **de phase différentielle et d'amplitude** combined amplitude and phase modulation; ~ **de phase et d'amplitude combinée** combined phase and amplitude modulation; ~ **de phase nulle** zero-phase modulation; ~ **de phase par inductance à noyau magnétique** phase modulation by inductance variation; ~ **de voie** channeling; ~ **delta** delta modulation; ~ **d'espacement des impulsions** pulse-position modulation (PPM); ~ **différentielle** differential modulation; ~ **d'impulsion** pulse modulation; ~ **d'impulsions à variation de temps** pulse-position modulation (PPM); ~ **d'impulsions dans le temps** pulse-time modulation (PTM); ~ **d'impulsions en amplitude (MIA)** pulse-amplitude modulation (PAM); ~ **d'impulsions en durée** pulse-duration modulation; (PDM); pulse-width modulation (PWM); pulse-length modulation (PLM); ~ **d'impulsions en espacement** pulse-interval modulation (PIM); ~ **d'impulsions en fréquence** pulse-frequency modulation (PFM); ~ **d'impulsions en position** pulse-position modulation (PPM);; pulse-phase modulation (P-PH-M); ~ **en amplitude** amplitude modulation;

~ **en fréquence** frequency modulation; ~ **en fréquence d'une sousporteuse** subcarrier frequency modulation; ~ **en phase avec phase de référence** phase modulation with reference phase; ~ **extérieure de l'harmonique** external harmonic modulation; ~ **fragmentée** curbed modulation; ~ **incorrecte** (m. infidèle) defective modulation; ~ **multiple** multiple modulation; ~ **negative** negative modulation; ~ **par absorption** absorption modulation; ~ **par déplacement de phase** phase-shift keying (PSK); ~ **par déplacement de fréquence (MDF)** frequency-shift keying (FSK); ~ **par impulsions** pulse modulation; ~ **par impulsions codées (MIC)** pulse-code modulation (PCM); ~ **par impulsions et codage (MIC)** pulse code modulation (PCM); ~ **par impulsions et codage différentiel adaptatif (MIC-DA)** adaptive differential pulse code modulation (ADPCM); ~ **par inversion de phase** phase-inversion modulation; phase-shift keying; ~ **par saut de phase** phase-shift keying; ~ **par tout ou rien** on-off keying; ~ **positive** positive (amplitude) modulation; ~ **seize QAM (16 QAM)** sixteen-state quadrature-amplitude modulation; ~ **sur deux fréquences audibles** two-tone modulation (TTM); ~ **sur l'anode** anode modulation; ~ **télégraphique** telegraph modulation; ~ **(télégraphique) par tout ou rien** on-off keying; ~ **tout ou rien** on-off keying; binary modulation; ~ **type spectre étalé** spread-spectrum modulation; ~ **vocale** speech modulation

module *m* module; program; calibre; size; quotient; factor; shell; (circuit) board; index; absolute value; routine; patch (group of instructions); device; daughter board; modulus (absolute value norm); ~ **16 sorties optocoupleur** sixteen-pin opto-isolator; ~ **à agrafes** jumper-connected daughter board; ~ **à effet Peltier** thermo-electric module; Peltier element; ~ **chargeable** load module; ~ **d'adressage** addressing module; ~ **d'amplification en émission** send amplifier card; ~ **d'amplification en réception** receive amplifier card; ~ **de choix** selection module; ~ **de circuit** circuit module; ~ **de communication locale de sécurité** local security-call module; ~ **de coopération** index of cooperation; ~ **de couplage** interface module; ~ **de reconnaissance de parole** speech recognition module; ~ **de réfraction** refractive modulus; ~ **de regroupement** marshalling unit; ~ **de résistance** resistor network module; ~ **de sécurité** (défense) security module; ~ **de**

synchronisation synchronization module; timing module; ~ de synthèse vocale speech synthesis module; ~ d'échange interchange module; ~ d'échange(s) sémaphore CCS tester; ~ d'élasticité modulus of elasticity; ~ d'enchaînement linking module; ~ d'essais (= robot d'essais) tester; routiner; ~ d'impression engine driver (of laser printer); ~ exécutable load module; mainline program; ~ interne resident module; ~ mémoire storage device; ~ objet object module; ~ physique crate (controller); ~ résultant object module; ~ sans agrafes direct-wired daughter board; ~ seize sorties isolées photocoupleur sixteen-pin opto-isolator (optically-coupled-isolator); ~ source source module; ~ terminal de distribution driving terminal module

moduler v modulate; pulse; key; translate

modulomètre m modulation meter

moins encombrant more compact; smaller; less bulky

moins-value f cost reduction

moirage m (en télévision) moiré (effect); interference pattern

moisissure f mould growth (test); mildew

moletage croisé m diamond knurling

MOM (v. moment)

moment (MOM) m moment; unit/code element; level; time instant; ~ (angulaire) cinétique angular momentum; ~ d'absence de courant no-current pulse; ~ de torsion twisting moment; ~ d'inertie moment of inertia; ~ (linéaire) cinétique momentum

monétique f electronic funds transfer (EFT); electronic money

moniteur m supervisor; scheduler; monitor; ~ de l'émetteur transmitter monitor; ~ de ligne line monitor; ~ de ligne de transmission transmission line monitor; ~ de référence reference monitor; ~ d'image picture monitor; ~ multifonctions multitâches (MMT) multi-function multi-tasking monitor

monitrice f charge hand

mono-alternance f half-wave (rectifier)

monobloc m ou adj (keypad) array; single housing; one-piece case; single-part unit

monochromatique adj single-frequency; monochromatic; homogeneous

monochrome adj black-and-white; monochrome

monocoaxial adj monocoaxial; single-tube

monoconnecteur m single-fibre connector

monocorde m single-ended cord circuit; ~ de mise en attente des circuits interurbains trunk camp-on cord circuit

monocouche adj single-layer

monocoup m ou adj monostable; single-shot; ~ réglable single-pulse circuit

monocourbe f single trace (of oscilloscope)

monocristal m single crystal

monofilaire adj single-wire; one-wire

monofilament m strand (of wire)

monoïde m libre free monoid (math.)

monolithique adj monolithic; passivated

monolocuteur m single-speaker system

monophase adj single-phase

monopolaire adj single-pole; unipolar

monoposte adj stand-alone; single-terminal

monoprogrammation f single programming; uniprogramming

mono-séparateur m unit separator (data delimiter)

monostable f one-shot; monostable circuit

monotension f single power supply

monotiés adj in ascending order

monotonie f string

monovariant adj one degree of freedom (of phase rule)

monovoie adj single-channel; per channel

montage m mounting; installation; erection; stack; assembly; circuit; configuration; circuitry; housing; (test) jig; ~ à anode à la masse cathode follower; ~ à blanc trial installation; ~ à cathode asservie cathode follower; ~ à diodes diode stack; diode array; ~ à OU câblé wired-OR circuit; ~ à résilience resilient mounting; ~ auto-élévateur bootstrap feedback; ~ autoélévateur cathodique bootstrap amplifier; ~ cloison partition hardware; ~ collecteur commun emitter follower; ~ de mesure hypso-kerdo level/gain measurement circuit; ~ différentiateur differentiator; differentiating circuit/network; ~ différentiel long-tailed pair; ~ en étoile three-phase/full-wave rectifier; ~ en parallèle parallel connection; ~ en pont lattice network; ~ en push-pull push-pull circuit; ~ en série series connection; ~ en triangle delta connection; ~ expérimental (d'un circuit) breadboard circuit; ~ Hartley three-point connection; ~ intégrateur integrator; integrating circuit/network; ~ inverseur de phase phase inverter (circuit); ~ symétrique push-pull circuit; ~ symétrique en étoile symmetrical star connection; ~ thermosonique de fil wire bonding; ~ vertical stand-off

montage/amplificateur cathodyne cathode follower

montant m ou adj upright; pillar; column; up-link (of satellite relay); ~ autorisé credit limit; ~ perforé pre-drilled upright/col-

umn
monté en configured as
montée f (de signal) slewing
montées en opposition in head-to-tail configuration (of diodes); ~ **tête-bêche** in head-to-tail configuration (of diodes)
monter v pick up (of relay); load (of disk, tape); mount; assemble; go high (of signal); increment; rig
montés en symétrie in push-pull configuration;
monteur-câbleur m installer/wireman
montrer v illustrate; depict; show; demonstrate
monture f socket; frame; mount; ~ **pour bolomètre** bolometer mount; ~ **tripode** tripod mount; ~ **type carrousel** wheel-and-track mount (of aerial)
moquette aiguillé tufted fabric
morceau m subset
mort adj neutral; dummy; idle; dead; blind
mortalité f failure
mot m sample; signal; flag; word; cell; instruction; prompt
MOT (v. moteur)
mot binaire channel word; ~ **clé** keyword; ~ **(d')adresse de canal** channel address word (CAW); ~ **de commande** control word; ~ **de commande de canal** channel command word (CCW); ~ **de contrôle** password; ~ **de déclenchement** trigger word (of logic state analyser); ~ **de double appel** consult call word; ~ **de masques** masking word; ~ **de passe** password; ~ **de service** service word; housekeeping word; ~ **de totalisation** summation word (checksum); ~ **de verrouillage de trame** frame alignment word (FAW); ~ **de verrouillage multitrame** multiframe alignment word; ~ **d'enchaînement** call progress word; ~ **d'en-tête** header word; heading; preamble; ~ **d'état** status word; flag; ~ **d'état de canal** channel status word (CSW); ~ **d'état de programme** program status word (PSW); ~ **d'état d'organe** unit status word; indicator; flag; device flag; device status word; ~ **d'état machine** CPU flag register; ~ **d'index** modifier; index word; ~ **directeur** descriptor; ~ **double** doubleword; ~ **enregistreur** register word (page of 1 Kbit); flag; ~ **entier** fullword; ~ **fin d'article** end-of-record word; ~ **machine** byte; computer word; ~ **macroprogramme** macro-instruction; ~ **mémoire** storage location; register; latch; ~ **programme** instruction; program word; ~ **qualificatif** status word; ~ **sigle** acronym; logo(-type); mnemonic; ~ **somme** signal; ~ **télégraphique** telegraph word; ~ **vedette** headword

moteur (MOT) m motor; engine; driver; ~ **à bague** slip-ring motor; ~ **à cage** squirrel-cage motor; ~ **à service intensif** heavy duty motor; ~ **à un sens de marche** non-reversing motor; ~ **compound à flux additionnel** cumulative compound motor; ~ **de synchronisation** synchronous motor; ~ **fractionnaire** stepper motor; fractional HP motor; ~ **hydraulique** rolling-vane motor; ~ **polyphasé** polyphase motor; ~ **shunt** shunt motor
motif m frame sync word; pattern; theme; subject; meaning; text; ~ **(de cellule)** (cell) cluster (of R/T system)
motopompe f motor-driven pump
moto-réducteur m gear-train (motor); geared motor; ball drive motor; friction drive motor; reduction gear motor; stepping motor
motorisation f drive unit
mots en vedette catch-phrase; headline; ~ **par minute** words per minute (w.p.m.); ~ **taxés** paid words
mou m slack (of cable)
mouchard m watch-dog; invigilator; tell-tale; tapper; snooper
mouche excentrée offset hole (of PCB pad)
mouché adj trimmed; rounded-off; radiused
mouillabilité f wetting capacity; solderability
mouillage m wetting
mouillé à la mercure mercury-wetted (of relay)
moulé adj encapsulated; ~ **sous pression** pressure-cast; die-cast
moulinette f software routine
mouvance f **harmonique** harmonic mobility
mouvement m motion; movement; transaction; change; detail; activity; ~ **alternatif** reciprocating motion; ~ **de va-et-vient** reciprocating motion; ~ **dirigé** linear motion; ~ **ondulatoire** wave motion
moyen m ou adj aggregate; moderate; mean; average; ~ **arithmétique** arithmetic mean; ~ **de transmission** transmission facility
moyennage m integration count; averaging
moyennant prep provided (that); subject to; on condition that
moyenne cumulative rolling average; ~ **des temps de bon fonctionnement (MTBF)** mean time between failures (MTBF); ~ **fréquence (MF)** intermediate frequency (IF); ~ **mobile** sample mean; harmonic mean; ~ **quadratique** root mean square (r.m.s.); ~ **technique des temps de réparation (MTTR)** mean time to repair (MTTR)
moyens m pl wherewithal; means; resources; facilities; ~ **de production** capital equipment; producer goods; ~ **d'exploitation rigoureuse** sound management (structures);

~ **d'information** news media; ~ **optiques de l'imagerie** optical imaging resources
MP (v. maintenance préventive); ≈ (v. mise en présence)
MPF (v. multiplexage par partage des fréquences)
MR (v. micromachine)
MST (v. mise sous tension)
MTBF (v. moyenne des temps de bon fonctionnement)
MTE (v. mémoire tampon émission)
MTR (v. mémoire tampon réception)
MTTR (v. moyenne technique des temps de réparation)
muet *adj* dead (of telephone line)
multi-adresse *adj* multiple-address
multibrins *adj* stranded; multi-core
multibroche *adj* multi-point; multi-pin
multicontact *adj* multi-way
multiconversion *adj* background; spool; multiple conversion
multicopie *adj* multi-ply (of paper roll)
multi-émission *adj* multileaving
multi-enregistreur *m* multiregister; call-handling processor
multifilaire *adj* many-wire
multiforme *adj* diverse
multifréquence (MF) multi-frequency
multigarde *f* multi-stage call holding
multigraphe *m* polygraph (P-graph); multigraph
multimètre à aiguille analogue multimeter; ~ **numérique** digital multimeter
multiniveau *adj* multi-level
multipériodique *adj* parallel-running (of pilot program)
multiplage *m* (sur) commoning (with); multipling over/to; ~ **décalé** slipped band; multiple; ~ **partiel** grading; ~ **partiel asymétrique** unsymmetrical grading; ~ **partiel symétrique** symmetrical grading
multiple *adj* mixed; common; multiple; ganged
multiplé (sur) commoned/multipled (with/over)
multipler *v* multiple; common; bunch
multiplés point à point commoned (contact-to-contact)
multiplet *m* byte; ~ **de synchronisation** synchronization byte
multiplex *m ou adj* multiplex (carrier); ~ **de données** data line concentrator; ~ **de signalisation** signalling multiplex; ~ **hétérogène** heterogeneous multiplex; ~ **homogène** homogeneous multiplex; ~ **MIC** PCM link/multiplex; PCM highway; ~ **numérique** digital carrier; digital multiplex; ~ **numérique à modulation MIC**

PCM-TDM multiplexer (MUX); ~ **par partage des fréquences** frequency-division multiplex (FDM); ~ **terrestre** terrestrial MUX
multiplexage *m* multiple access; multiplexing (mixing); subscriber carrier technique; channeling; channelizing; ~ **à transfert capacitif** multiplexing with flying capacitor; ~ **analogique** frequency division multiplexing (FDM); ~ **cyclique** round-robin; ~ **dans le temps** time-division multiplexing (TDM); ~ **en fréquence** frequency-division multiplexing (FDM); ~ **par partage des fréquences (MPF)** frequency-division multiplexing (FDM); ~ **par partage du temps** time-division multiplexing (TDM); ~ **par répartition en fréquence** frequency-division multiplexing (FDM); ~ **temporel** time-division multiplex; time-division multiple access (TDMA)
multiplexage-démultiplexage muldem
multiplexer *v* channelize; multiplex
multiplexeur *m* multiplexer; multiplexor (MUX); ~ **de huit vers une voie** eight-to-one-line multiplexer; ~ **télégraphique point-multipoint** point-to-multipoint telegraph multiplexer
multiplexeur-aiguilleur (MA) cross-connect unit (CCU); ~ **de transit** hub cross-connect unit
multiplexeur-démultiplexeur muldex (digital multiplexer plus demultiplexer)
multiplicateur *m* multiplexer; multiplier; intensifier; ier; ~ **analogique/numérique** analogue-digital multiplier; ~ **de fréquence non linéaire** non-linear frequency multiplier; ~ **d'électrons** (secondaires) electron multiplier; ~ **Q** Q-multiplier
multiplication *f* proliferation; multiplication; ~ **de fréquence** frequency multiplication; ~ **logique** AND operation; logical product
multiplicité *f* plurality
multiplieur *m* multiplier; ier
multiplis *m* plywood
multipoint *m ou adj* multidrop; multipoint (line); multi-way; ~ **local** drop; ~ **urbain** drop
multipolaire (borne ~) multi-way terminal
multipose *f* bulk insertion; multiple-mount assembly
multiposte *adj* clustered-terminal working; shared logic
multiprogrammation *f* multiprogramming; concurrent processing
multiroutage *m* path diversity routing; multirouting
multisignaleur *m* multi-signaller

multitâche *adj* multi-tasking
multitraitement *m* multiprocessing
multitrame *adj* multiframe
multivalent *adj* multiple-bit; polyvalent
multivibrateur *m* multivibrator; latch; relaxation oscillator; ~ **astable (MA)** free-running multivibrator; ~ **bistable** bistable (multivibrator); latch; half-shift register
multivoies *adj* multipath; multitone
mumétal "Mumetal" [T.N.] (high permeability magnetic zinc alloy)
mur *m* **du son** sound barrier; supersonic threshold
murmure *m* **confus** babble
musique d'attente music-on-hold; ~ **de fond** background music
mutateur *m* rectifier; frequency converter; ~ **de puissance** chopper amplifier; synchronous vibrator; power vibrator; vibrating-reed amplifier; contact-modulated amplifier
mutation *f* changeover; patching; line transfer; equipment number change; ~ **automatique** automatic changeover; ~ **manuelle** manual changeover; ~ **massive** block changeover
mutations jumpering; strapping
muter *v* change over; transfer; switch (over)
mutilation *f* clipping; garbling; ~ **de la parole** clipping (voice); ~ **de mots** clipping of words; ~ **de signaux** signal clipping; ~ **de syllabe finale** final clipping; ~ **de syllabes** clipping of syllables; ~ **du code** code garbling; ~ **initiale** initial clip; ~ **supplémentaire** extended clip
mutilé *adj* erroneous; mutilated (of message packet); scrambled; garbled; clipped

N

NA (v. message de nouvel appel)
nacelle *f* cup; beat
NAK (v. accusé de réception négatif)
nanoseconde *f* nanosecond
nappe *f* wire group; cable loom; cable harness; cable form; ribbon cable; bundle; array; ~ **de câbles** cable loom; bundle; ribbon cable; ~ **de dipôles verticaux** dipole array; group aerial; ~ **de fils** wire bundle; cable form; ribbon cable; ~ **de haubannage** guying system
nat. *adj* (v. nature)
national *adj* national; domestic; home
nature (nat.) *adj* to scale; (in) full; category; type
naturel *adj* plain; pure; untreated; raw; straight; unmachined; intrinsic; clear (uncoloured); colourless
navette *f ou adj* shuttle; turnaround; re-entry; ~ **spatiale** space shuttle
nb. *m*, **nbre** (v. nombre)
NC (v. non cumulatif)
ND (v. numéro de désignation)
n^e (n-ième) nth
ne pas déranger do not disturb
néant not applicable (NA); none
nécessaire *adj* requisite
nécessité conjoncturelle market forces
NEF (Normes d'Exploitation Françaises) French PTT administration operating standards
négaton *m* electron
néper *m* neper
net *adj* clear; net; nett
netteté *f* articulation; clarity; intelligibility; definition; ~ **des mots** word intelligibility; ~ **idéale** ideal articulation; ~ **pour les bandes** band articulation; ~ **pour les logatomes** logatom articulation; syllable articulation; ~ **pour les mots** word articulation; discrete word intelligibility; ~ **pour les phrases** sentence articulation; ~ **pour les sons** sound articulation
nettoyage *m* consistency check; debugging; state forcing; purging; audit; refining; screening; vetting; filtering; garbage collection; purification (of data); ~ **au solvant** degreasing; solvent cleaning; ~ **du logiciel** audit; auditing; data purification; unpatching; upgrading; file tidying; ~ **rapide** flash

strip
neuf *adj* fresh; new
neutralisateur de tonalité tone disabler
neutralisation *f* balancing out; lock-out (of line); ~ **de suppresseur d'echo** echo suppressor disabling; ~ **en pont** neutralizing bridge
neutraliser *v* disable; neutralize; cancel (of contact); override; isolate; conceal; blank
neutraliseur *m* **de tonalité** tone disabler
neutre *m ou adj* neutral; inert; ~ **sorti** voltage to neutral; line-to-neutral
neutrodynage *m* neutrodyning; ~ **en croix** cross-neutralization; neutrodyning
nez *m* nozzle; nose; ~ **de marche** step trim; nosing
NI (= NON-OU) NOR (= NOT OR)
niche *f* **insonorisée** soundproof booth; ~ **téléphonique** wall-telephone booth
nid *m* nest; ~ **d'abeilles** honeycomb
niveau *m* level; stage; shelf; step; rate; grade; line; category; state; voltage; logic; potential; gain; standard; electromotive force (e.m.f.); ~ **0** (zéro) base line; zero level (of oscilloscope); earth plane; reference earth potential; ~ **absolu** absolute (power) level; ~ **absolu de puissance** absolute power level; ~ **absolu de puissance moyenne** mean absolute power level; ~ **absolu de puissance réelle** absolute power level; ~ **absolu de tension** through level (600 ohms); (absolute) voltage level (referred to 0.775 V); ~ **absolu d'intensité de courant** current level (referred to 1.29 mA); ~ **composite adapté** terminated level; ~ **d'anomalie** fault category; ~ **d'appel** ringing level; ~ **de base** basic qualifications; basic operating system; ~ **de bruit** noise figure; static level; ~ **de bruit admissible** permissible noise level; acceptable noise level; ~ **de bruit d'un circuit** circuit noise level; ~ **de champ** field strength; ~ **de commande** driving (voltage) level; ~ **de confiance** confidence level; ~ **de crête du blanc** peak white (level); ~ **de crête du signal** peak (signal) level; ~ **de diaphonie** crosstalk volume; crosstalk level; ~ **de diffusion** confidentiality; ~ **de fonctionnement** operate level; ~ **de fréquence** tone level; ~ **de gravité** degree of severity; ~ **de la composante continue** DC

level; ~ **de mesure** test level; ~ **de pression** pressure level; ~ **de pression acoustique** sound-pressure level; ~ **de priorité** priority level; ~ **de puissance** power level; ~ **de puissance relatif** relative power level; ~ **de qualité admissible (NQA)** acceptable quality level (AQL); ~ **de quantification** quantizing step; quantum; ~ **de référence** reference level; ~ **de repos** non-active; ~ **de résonance** resonance state/level; ~ **de saturation** overload level; ~ **de sévérité** (job) error count; ~ **de signal** signal level; ~ **de signal transmis** transmitted signal level; ~ **de sortie** output level; ~ **de suppression** blanking level; ~ **de suppression ligne** line blanking level; ~ **de tonalité** tone level; ~ **de transmission** transmission level; ~ **d'écoute BF** volume (audio level); ~ **d'écrêtage** clipping level; ~ **d'efficacité** completed call rate; ~ **d'énergie d'excitation** excitation state (level); ~ **d'entrée** input level; send level; ~ **des fréquences vocales** audio level; ~ **d'essai** test level; ~ **d'essai non adapté** through level; transit level; ~ **d'habilitation** assigned access level; grade of entitlement; ~ **d'interférence** interference level; ~ **d'interruption** interrupt level; ~ **donneur** donor level; ~ **du blanc** picture white; white level; ~ **du noir** picture black; ~ **du rayonnement non ionisant** non-ionizing radiation level; ~ **du signal de télévision** television signal level; ~ **du son** sound level; ~ **énergétique** energy level (of particle); ~ **(énergétique) normal** normal (energy) level/state; ~ **haut** high level; ~ **inaccessible** blocked level; dead level; ~ **inchangé** unaffected level; ~ **logique 0/(1)** low-/(high-)level output; ~ **maximal de bruit admissible** maximum permissible noise level; ~ **maximal de porteuse** maximum carrier level; ~ **maximal de sortie** maximum output level; ~ **mémoire** store level; ~ **minimal de porteuse** minimum carrier level; ~ **prioritaire** priority level; ~ **relatif** relative level; ~ **relatif de puissance** relative level; transmission level; ~ **relatif de puissance réelle** relative power level; ~ **relatif de tension** relative voltage level; ~ **relatif d'intensité de courant** relative current level; ~ **relatif zéro** zero relative level; ~ **sonore** electrical speech level; volume level; ~ **spectral élémentaire** spectrum pressure level; ~ **vocal** voice level; ~ **zéro** zero level; reference voltage; earth plane; earth potential; base line
niveaux de gris grey scale; shades of grey
nivelage *m* levelling
nivellement *m* resource allocation; ~ **en zones** zone levelling/splitting
noble *adj* master; upper-echelon; noble (of metal)
nœud *m* node; knot; ~ **coulant** slip knot; ~ **de commutation** switching node; ~ **double** granny knot; reef knot; ~ **du maillage** node of grid store; ~ **principal** host node
noir artificiel artificial black; nominal black; ~ **d'une image** picture black; ~ **et blanc** monochrome; black-and-white; ~ **perturbé** noisy blacks
noirci blacked over; charred; passivated
noircissement *m* **chimique** passivation; blackodizing
nom *m* identification (ID); name; label; handle; ~ **courant** common designation; vernacular; ~ **de fichier** file name; ~ **de fonction** function code; ~ **de l'information** signal (name); signal ID; ~ **de volume implicite** default volume ID; ~ **des disques** disk label; ~ **symbolique** identifier; symbolic name; mnemonic; ~ **utilisateur** user ID (identifier)
nombre (nb., nbre) *m* number; quantity (qty); integer; count; ~ **aléatoire** random number; ~ **atomique** atomic number; ~ **binaire** binary number; ~ **complexe** phasor; ~ **de base** base number; ~ **de défauts tolérés** permitted defectives; ~ **de mérite** figure of merit; ~ **de paires** pair count; ~ **décimal condensé** packed decimal; ~ **d'impulsions** pulse repetition frequency (PRF); ~ **d'octets** length (in bytes); ~ **en double précision** double-length number; double-precision number; ~ **entier** integer; whole number; ~ **ordinal** serial number; ordinal number; ~ **quantique** quantum number; ~ **quantique interne** total angular momentum quantum number; ~ **quantique principal** main (first) quantum number; ~ **quantique secondaire** orbital (second) quantum number
nomen(clature) (Nre.) *f* parts list; nomenclature; inventory
Nomex [A.C.] anti-wicking wafer (for IC sockets)
nominal *adj* rated; standard; nominal; optimum; ideal; ostensible; basic; design; typical
NON (organe) NOT (element)
non adapté lay; ~ **armé** unclad; unshielded; not set; ~ **asservi** without handshaking; free-running; ~ **bien reçu** negative acknowledgement (NAK); ~ **branché** offline; ~ **câblé** not connected (NC); ~ **conforme** not to standard; non-compliant; ~ **connecté** off-line; ~ **cumulatif (NC)** non-cumulative (tolerance); ~ **désignation**

f random selection; ~ **désigné** uncommitted; unassigned; ~ **dessiné** not shown; ~ **dissipatif** non-lossy; lossless; ~ **doublé** non-duplicated; ~ **entretenu** without boosting; ~ **équipé** not installed; not connected; unpopulated; ~ **équivalence** exclusive-NOR; biconditional operation; except; equality
NON ET (= ON/ET-NON) NAND (= NOT AND); non-conjunction; Sheffer stroke (function); NOT-BOTH; alternative denial; dispersion
non exécutable not implemented; ~ **filtré** unsmoothed; ~ **fonctionnement** *m* non-operation; ~ **gravé** unmarked; without caption (keys); ~ **hiérarchisé** meshed; ~ **influencé par** immune (to); ~ **informaticien** lay user; ~ **inscription dans l'annuaire (liste rouge)** non-entry (ex-directory subscriber); ~ **juxtaposition** underlap; ~ **linéaire** looped; ~ **linéarité** non-linearity; distortion; ~ **linéarité d'amplitude** amplitude (non-linearity) distortion; ~ **modulé** unmodulated; ~ **mouillage** non-wetting; ~ **nul(le, d'une valeur)** non-zero; ~ **observation** disregarding; failure to comply
NON OU (= NI) NOR (= NOT OR); dagger operation; non-disjunction; NEITHER-NOR; joint denial; Pierce function
non plaqué upstanding (of component on PCB); upright; ~ **polarisé** neutral; non-polarized; ~ **pondéré** unweighted; unadjusted; uncorrected; ~ **prêt** not ready; ~ **programmé** unscheduled; ~ **qualifié** lay; ~ **redéclenchable** non-retriggerable; ~ **relative** unbiased (address); ~ **rémanent** volatile; ~ **répétitive** one-time; ~ **réponse** don't answer; ~ **résident** swappable; ~ **retour à zéro** non-return to zero (NRZ); ~ **satisfaction** *f* non-fulfilment; ~ **seulement...mais** as (much)...as; ~ **spécialisé** lay; ~ **spécifique** generic; ~ **surveillé** unattended; ~ **uniformité d'aspect** dissimilarity; ~ **utilisé** illegal; spare; not used; ~ **vide** non-vacant; assigned; ~ **vierge** impure; used (of tape); ~ **vitrifié** unfired; non-fired; ~ **volatile** non-volatile
nord extrême far north
normal *adj* typical; on-line; generic; ordinary
normalement *adv* typically
normalisé *adj* standard; standardized; compliant; ~ **CCITT** CCITT compliant; to CCITT standards
normaliser *v* standardize
norme *f* standard; ~ **de modulation** modulation standard; ~ **tarifaire** tariff standard
normes *f pl* rules; standards; practice; ethics; ~ **de construction** equipment practice;

~ **de télévision** television standards; ~ **de transmission** transmission standards
notamment *adv* inter alia; primarily; including; of which; chiefly; for instance
notation *f* **à base multiple** mixed radix notation; ~ **polonaise** (reverse) Polish notation
note *f* (de bas de page) footnote; ~ **d'accord** tuning note; ~ **de service** memorandum
noter *v* log
notice *f* brochure; leaflet; manual; handbook; ~ **de réglage** maintenance handbook; workshop manual; ~ **d'emploi** user's handbook; user manual; instructions for use; ~ **d'exploitation** user manual
notificateur (nr.) *m* routing distributor; ~ **d'information** translator-distributor (TD); paper-tape transmitter
notoriété *f* renown
nourrice *f* (fused) distribution board; multiple outlet strip; mains extension lead; trailer socket; trailing socket
nourriture *f* **et hébergement** board and lodging; bed and breakfast
nouveau *adj* (nouvel/nouvelle) fresh; further; subsequent; new
nouvel abonnement/changement de titulaire changeover (of subscriber account); re-allocation; ~ **appel** (NA) new call event signalling; off-hook condition; ~ **article** addition record
nouvelle ligne line feed (LF)
novateur *adj* innovative; pioneering; original
novénaire *adj* novenary (to the base nine)
noyau *m* core; nucleus; slug; kernel; main monitor; ~ **à air** air core; ~ **aggloméré** dust core; ~ **de commutation** switch core; ~ **de ferrite** ferrite core; ~ **feuilleté** laminated core; ~ **plongeur** slug; ~ **résident** resident kernel
noyaux appairés matching cores
noyé *adj* embedded; inset; caged; captive
NQA (v. niveau de qualité admissible)
nr. (v. notificateur)
Nre. (v. nomen(clature))
NRJ (énergie) power
nu *adj* bare; stripped; unequipped; unmachined; sleeveless; basic; unpopulated
nuage *m* cloud; ~ **de bandelettes** "chaff"; "window" (of ECM foil strips); ~ **d'électrons** electron cloud
nucléon *m* nucleon; nuclear particle
nuire *v* impair; adversely affect; compromise
nuisant au bon fonctionnement liable to impair operation
nul *adj* null; nil; zero
numérateur *m* numerator; numbering machine

N

numération f **à base fixe** fixed-radix notation; ~ **à base multiple** mixed radix notation; ~ **binaire** binary notation; ~ **de base** base notation; radix notation; ~ **décimale codée en binaire (DCB)** binary-coded decimal notation (BCD); ~ **hexadécimale** hexadecimal notation; ~ **pondérée** fixed-count code

numérique adj numerical; digital; discretely variable; ~ **étendu** extended character set

numérisation f digitization (A/D conversion); quantization; ~ **des réseaux** network digitization

numérisé adj digitized; quantized

numériser v digitize; quantize

numériseur m digitizer; quantizer; ~ **d'images** image digitizer

numéro (N₀.) m (cardinal) number; serial number; ~ **abrégé (NA)** short-code number; abbreviated dialling number; ~ **appelant** calling subscriber number; ~ **appelé** called subscriber number; ~ **changé** changed number; ~ **court** short (code) number; ~ **d'abonné** subscriber directory number; ~ **d'annuaire** directory number; ~ **d'appel** call number; directory number; subscriber number; ~ **d'appel de nuit** night-call number; ~ **de bande de site** installation tape number; ~ **de code d'indicatif** routing code number; ~ **de compte** logical code number; ~ **de désignation (ND)** (pseudo-)directory number; ~ **de dotation** stock number; ~ **de ligne** circuit number; ~ **de page forcé** forced page number; ~ **de route** traffic code; ~ **de séquence vers l'arrière** backward sequence number; ~ **de séquence vers l'avant** forward sequence number; ~ **de série de l'autocommutateur** exchange code; ~ **de téléphone** telephone number; ~ **de trame** frame number; ~ **demandé** wanted number; called subscriber number; ~ **demandeur** calling number; ~ **d'équipement** equipment number; ~ **d'individualisation** serial number; ~ **d'instruction** statement number; ~ **d'ordre** serial number; ~ **erroné** wrong number; ~ **inaccessible** unobtainable number; ~ **incomplet** incomplete number; ~ **indicatif** dial prefix; code; ~ **inutilisé** vacant number; ~ **libre** unallotted number; unassigned number; unused number; ~ **logique d'édition** logical output number; ~ **national** national number; ~ **national significatif** significant national number; ~ **non attribué** vacant number; ~ **non utilisé** unallocated number; unassigned number; unused number; ~ **ordinal d'une harmonique** harmonic number; ~ **principal** listed directory number; ~ **privé** private

number; ~ **significatif** significant number; ~ **simplifié** short code number; short number; ~ **vert** toll-free number; freephone number

numérotage m dialling; numbering; ~ **en boucle** loop-disconnect pulsing; loop-break dialling

numérotation f dialling; pulsing; (number) notational representation; digital (of dialling); number selection; address signals; touch calling; numbering; keying; ~ **à circuit de retour par la terre** battery dialling; loop pulsing; ~ **à clavier** pushbutton dialling; touch-tone dialling; ~ **à fréquences vocales** tone dialling; ~ **abrégée** abbreviated dialling; speed dialling; speed calling; repertory dialling; ~ **abrégée collective** short-code dialling (central repertory); pool abbreviated dialling; ~ **abrégée individuelle** short-code dialling (individual repertory); unique abbreviated dialling; ~ **abrégée ouverte** open-numbering plan short-code dialling; ~ **au cadran** dial selection; decadic pulse dialling; ~ **au clavier** pushbutton dialling; pushbutton calling; signalling; permutation code; ~ **au clavier (télégraphique)** teleprinter keyboard selection; ~ **au clavier multifréquence** tone dialling; DTMF dialling; ~ **au clavier multifréquences** teltouch dialling; key tone selection; touch calling; DTMF dialling; ~ **clavier** pushbutton dialling; ~ **combiné raccroché** on-hook dialling; ~ **de message** message numbering; ~ **décimale** ((decadic) pulse dialling; ~ **directe (DND)** direct distance dialling (DDD); standard trunk dialling (STD); ~ **directe d'un poste supplémentaire** direct in-dialling (DID); direct inward dialling; ~ **directe entrante** direct in-dialling; direct inward dialling (DID); ~ **d'une traite** direct through-dialling; ~ **en bloc** block address; ~ **en boucle** loop dialling; loop-disconnect pulsing; loop-break dialling; ~ **en courant alternatif** AC pulsing; ~ **extérieure** trunk dialling; ~ **fermée** closed/fixed-length numbering; closed numbering (plan); ~ **incohérente** vacant number; unassigned number; ~ **intégrée** intermediate tone override; ~ **interurbaine** toll dialling; ~ **interurbaine automatique** direct distance dialling (DDD); ~ **mixte** combined tone-and-pulse dialling; ~ **ouverte** open/variable length numbering; open numbering plan; ~ **par ouverture de boucle** loop dialling; loop disconnect pulsing; loop-break dialling; ~ **par rupture de boucle** loop dialling; loop-break dialling; disconnect pulsing; ~ **pondérée**

positional notation; ∼ **sans décrocher** on-hook dialling; hands-free dialling

numéroter *v* dial; key (of keysender); select; number; ∼ **au clavier** key-out; touch-dial; ∼ **vers le réseau public** out-dial

numéroteur *m* auto-dialler; ∼ **à fréquence** vocale tone dialler; ∼ **à molettes** number-stamping device; numerator; ∼ **automatique** automatic numbering transmitter; dialler

nuque *f* (de jack) (jack) ring

O

O (ouvert) (= «R»: repos/rien⁾ NC (normally closed = OFF = "break"; de-energized: of relays)

OB (barre zéro) reference potential; earth plane

OBA (v. abonné observé à l'arrivée)

objectif *m* target; objective lens; ~ complexe complex target; ~ composé compound target; ~ simple single target

objet *m* physical item; functional entity; aim; subject; purpose; parameter; (data) sink; target; ~ de localisation distant object; ~ dérivé object

obligation *f* duty; forcing; ~ en coupure split-and-insert

obligatoire *adj* mandatory; compulsory; essential; not optional; definite

obligatoirement *adv* without exception

oblique *adj f* solidus; oblique stroke; slash; slant; angular; sloped

obliquité *f* skew

oblitérable *adj* amendment

oblitération *f* deletion: cancellation; erasure

OBs stabilized reference potential; signal ground

OBS (v. abonné observé par sondage)

obscurcisseur *m* dimmer

obscurcission *f* (= «dimage») dimming

observation *f* monitoring; observation; traffic measurement; processed data; ~ de service service observation; ~ de trafic traffic observation; traffic measurement

observations *f pl* comments; remarks

obstacle *m* clutter

obtenir *v* procure; retrieve; access; acquire; derive

obtention *f* retrieval; acquisition; ~ des bits bit retrieval

obturateur *m* mask; blanking panel; occluder; ~ électrique shutter; electric shunting

obturation *f* masking; blanking

OC (v. ondes courtes); ~ (v. octet de contrôle)

occupation *f* busy; busy tone; seizing (signal); occupancy; content; blocking; loading; holding; engaged (tone); ~ (au) deuxième degré busy (extension) with call camped-on; ~ (au) premier degré busy (extension) with no calls camped-on; ~ automatique automatic holding; ~ de bus busy bus;

~ de leviers des types character assignment of type lever; ~ de ligne line occupancy; ~ des canaux channel loading; ~ des lignes lines busy; line occupancy; ~ fictive dummy connection; ~ marginale marginal occupancy; ~ privée busy local; ~ totale all-trunks-busy; ~ toutes jonctions (OTJ) all-trunks-busy (signal)

occupé *adj* busy (BY); engaged; occupied

occuper *v* seize (of line); engage; busy; occupy

occurrence *f* indexed item; event; iteration; ~ courante current item

Océanie *f* Australasia

octal *adj* octal; byte (mode)

octet *m* eight-bit byte; string; bite; ~ cible target byte; ~ de bourrage stuffing byte; ~ de contrôle (OC) check byte; ~ de données (OD) data byte; ~ de signalisation signalling byte; ~ par octet in byte mode; sequentially

octode octode

octomot *m* eight-word segment

octuple *m* eight-level multiple; eight group; eight-coil relay; ~ bascule type D avec RAZ octal D-type flip-flop with clear

octuplicateur *m* de fréquence octupler

OD (v. octet de données)

œil *m* magique ·magic-eye tube; tuning indicator

œillet *m* eyelet; stud

œuvre *f* enterprise

office *m* practice; function; routine

officieux *adj* informal; casual

offre *f* break-in; override; trunk offering; barge-in; product line; integrated package (of solutions); ~ d'appel call offering; busy verification; override; trunk offering; ~ d'appels interurbaine trunk offering; override; ~ discrète discrete trunk offering; ~ d'un appel call offering; ~ en tiers trunk offering; (busy) override; barge-in; ~ principale flagship product; ~ sur poste intérieur occupé busy (station) override

offrir une communication announce a call

ogive *f* nose cone; (loudspeaker) cone

ohmique *adj* resistive; linear; DC; non-inductive; non-reactive; in-phase; wattful

ohmmètre *m* ohmmeter; ~ à magnéto megger; megohmmeter

OI (v. ordinateur individuel)

OL (v. onde longue); ~ (v. oscillateur local)
oléopneumatique oil-and-air; pneumo-oil (of circuit-breaker)
OM (v. onde moyenne)
ombre f shadow region; ~ **du col** neck shadow
oméga m PCB track detour/offset; ~ [A.C.] rail; mounting track
omnidirective adj omnidirectional; isotropic
omniprésent adj ubiquitous
O/N (oui/non) yes/no; go/no-go; pass/fail
ON (= NON-ET) NAND (= NOT AND); ~ (v. ouverture numérique)
on a donc providing; hence; thus; consequently
onde f wave; ripple; undulation; cycle; ~ **à front raide** steeply-rising wave; ~ **à modulation vocale** speech-modulated wave; ~ **à moyenne fréquence** medium-frequency wave; ~ **à polarisation horizontale** horizontally-polarized wave; ~ **à polarisation verticale** vertically-polarized wave; ~ **absente** tone off; ~ **acoustique** acoustic wave; sound wave; speech wave; ~ **amortie** damped wave; ~ **atmosphérique** downcoming radio wave; ~ **carrée** square wave; ~ **centimétrique** centimetric wave (SHF band); ~ **cohérente interrompue** coherent wave; ~ **commune** common wave; shared channel; ~ **continue** continuous (undamped)/sustained wave; ~ **continue manipulée** keyed continuous wave; ~ **continue non modulée** pure continuous wave; undamped wave; ~ **cylindrique** cylindrical wave; ~ **d'appel** calling wave; ~ **de charge d'espace** space-charge wave; ~ **de choc** shock wave; ~ **de réponse** answering wave; ~ **de repos** stationary wave; standing wave; spacing wave; compensating wave; back wave; ~ **de service** traffic wave; ~ **de signalisation** tone-on signal; ~ **de sol** ground wave; ~ **de surface** surface wave; ground-reflected wave; ground wave; ~ **de surface acoustique** surface acoustic wave (SAW); ~ **décamétrique** decametric (short) wave (HF band); ~ **décimétrique** decimetric wave (UHF band); ~ **décimillimétrique** decimillimetric wave (ultramicrowaves); ~ **d'espace** space wave; sky wave; indirect wave; ~ **d'interférence** interference wave; ~ **directe** ground wave; direct wave; fundamental wave; surface wave; forward wave; ~ **dominante** fundamental wave; dominant wave; principal wave; ~ **électrique circulaire** circular electric wave; ~ **électromagnetique** electromagnetic wave; ~ **en dents de scie** saw-tooth oscillation; saw-tooth wave; ~ **en retour** return tone (of level measuring set); ~ **entrante à valeur**

variable fading radio wave; ~ **entretenue** continouus wave (CW); ~ **entretenue modulée** modulated continuous wave (MCW); ~ **enveloppe** wave front; ~ **extraordinaire** extraordinary wave; ~ **fondamentale** fundamental wave; dominant wave; ~ **gaussienne** Gaussian wave; ~ **guidée** guided wave; ~ **H** transverse electric wave; TE wave; H wave; ~ **hectométrique** hectometric wave; ~ **hertzienne** electromagnetic (radio) wave (VLF to SHF); ~ **incidente** incident wave; ~ **indirecte** indirect wave; reflected wave; back wave; ~ **inverse** backward wave; ~ **ionosphérique** sky wave; ~ **kilométrique** kilometric wave (LF band); ~ **limite** maximum usable frequency (MUF); ~ **longue (OL)** long wave (LW); ~ **lumineuse** wavelength of light (lightwave); ~ **magnétique circulaire** circular magnetic wave; ~ **métrique** metric wave (VHF band); ~ **millimétrique** millimetric (dwarf) wave (EHF band); ~ **modulante** modulating wave; ~ **modulée** modulated wave; ~ **moyenne (OM)** medium wave (MW); ~ **myriamétrique** myriametric wave (VLF band); ~ **non amortie** continuous (sustained) wave; undamped wave; ~ **périodique** periodic wave; ~ **pilote** pilot carrier; pilot wave; reference pilot; ~ **pilote de commutation** switching control pilot; switching pilot; ~ **pilote de groupe** group pilot; ~ **pilote de groupe primaire** group reference pilot; ~ **pilote de groupe secondaire** supergroup reference pilot; ~ **pilote de régulation** regulating pilot; ~ **pilote de synchronisation** synchronizing pilot; ~ **polarisée circulairement** circularly-polarized wave; ~ **polarisée elliptiquement/(circulairement dextrorsum)** clockwise polarized wave; right-hand polarized wave; ~ **polarisée elliptiquement/(circulairement sinistrorsum)** anti-clockwise polarized wave; counter-clockwise polarized wave; left-hand polarized wave; ~ **polarisée rectilignement** plane-polarized wave; ~ **porteuse** carrier wave; (frequency) carrier; carrier current; ~ **porteuse intermédiaire** sub-carrier; ~ **porteuse sur ligne de transport** power line carrier (PLC); ~ **présente** tone on; ~ **progressive** travelling wave; ~ **propre** natural wave; ~ **radio** radio wave; ~ **radioélectrique** radio wave; ~ **rectangulaire** rectangular wave; ~ **récurrente** reflected wave; recurrent wave; back wave; ~ **réfléchie** reflected wave; indirect wave; back wave; ~ **réfléchie par le sol** ground-reflected wave; ~ **résiduelle (de fréquence)** (carrier) leak; ~ **spatiale** indirect (space) wave; sky wave; ~ **stationnaire** standing wave; spacing wave; back wave; ~ **transitoire** spurious wave; ~ **transversale** transverse wave; ~ **très longue** very long wave (VLF band); ~ **ultra-courte (OUC)** ultrashort wave (VHF band); ~ **vagabonde** spurious wave

ondemètre m wave-meter; ~ **à cavité** cavity wave-meter; frequency meter; ~ **à résonance** resonance wave-meter; ~ **hétérodyne** heterodyne wave-meter

ondes courtes (OC) short wave (SW); ~ **décamétriques** decametric (short) wave (HF band)

ondomètre m wave-meeter

ondulateur m tone keyer

ondulation f kink; crimp; ripple; corrugation; waviness; constant-k (residual response); ~ **relative** ripple factor; ~ **résiduelle** ripple

onduleur m DC-AC inverter; ~ **d'appel** ringing inverter; ~ **monophasé** DC-AC single-phase inverter

onglet m **de protection** write-protect sticker; tab

OP (v. ouvrier professionnel)

opacimètre m densitometer

opale adj clear; white; colourless

opérande m **immédiat** immediate operand

opérateur m element; operator; gate; (logical) connective; device; craftsperson; ~ **booléen** (Boolean) logical operator/connective; ~ **de commande** handler; ~ **de concaténation** AND operator (&); ~ **de mémoire temporelle** time-switch buffer memory board; ~ **de prélèvement des échantillons pour contrôle partiel** partial monitoring sampling board; ~ **de prélèvement et d'injection de code** code sampling and injection board; ~ **de puissance** buffer; ~ **de réception des positonnements** positioning board; ~ **de recherche et d'identification par le contenu** content search board; ~ **de relation** relational operator; ~ **de son** sound operator; ~ **de transformation** conversion circuit; ~ **de transformation orthogonale** multiplex-demultiplex circuit; ~ **de visualisation et d'émission des fautes** fault-handling card; ~ **décalage arrière** backward difference operator; ~ **dérivation** differentiation operator; ~ **des signaux de temps** timing-signal card; ~ **d'étendue** range operator; ~ **d'exploitation** routine operation; ~ **double aiguillage spatiale** space-switching card; ~ **logique** arithmetic and logic unit (ALU); gate; logical connective; ~ **nabla** del (math.); ~ **relationnel** relational operator; logical connective

opération f transaction; operation; ~ **à largeurs de bande égales** equi-band operation; ~ **à modulation complète d'un émetteur** operating a transmitter of high modulation percentage; ~ **annexe** housekeeping; ~ **arithmétique** arithmetic operation; ~ **arithmétique binaire** binary arithmetic operation; ~ **booléenne diadique** dyadic/binary Boolean operation; ~ **d'aménagement** housekeeping/overhead operation; ~ **de central automatique** automatic exchange operation; ~ **de répondeur à porteuses multiples** multi-carrier transponder operation; ~ **de service** housekeeping operation; ~ **de servitude** overhead operation; housekeeping; ~ **en circuit série** series working; ~ **en simultané** simultaneous operation; ~ **ET** AND operation; conjunction; meet; logical product; intersect; intersection; ~ **ineffective** no-operation (NOP); ~ **inverse** inverse function; ~ **OU** alteration; inclusive OR; disjunction; EITHER-OR; non-identity operation; logical-add; logical sum; ~ **quadruplex** quadruplex service/operation; ~ **unaire** monadic operation

opérations de blocage sur fichier buffering and debuffering operations on file; ~ **d'exploitation** routine operations

opératrice f operator; attendant; agent; ~ **aveugle** blind operator; ~ **d'arrivée** incoming operator; B-board; B-position; ~ **d'assistance** assistance operator; ~ **de départ** outgoing operator; A-board; A-position; local operator; ~ **de renseignements** enquiry desk; information operator; ~ **de réponse** answering operator; ~ **de trafic** traffic operator; ~ **d'interception** intercept operator; ~ **directrice** controlling operator; ~ **locale** local operator; A-board; A-position; ~ **translatrice** incoming operator; B-board; B-position

opérer v perform; execute; transact; operate; proceed

opposable adj interfaceable; compatible; may be connected to

opposition de phase opposite phase; phase opposition; anti-phase; in phase opposition (180° out of phase); phase inversion; balanced

optimal adj ideal; preferred; optimum

optimalisation f optimization; ~ **du retard** delay optimization; ~ **du temps de montée** rise-time optimization; ~ **du temps de transit** delay optimization

optimisation de logiciel debugging (of software)

optimiser v optimize; rationalize; enhance;

fully exploit

optimiseur *m* optimizer

option(s) *f* optional extras; accessories; alternatives; menu

option implicite default option

optique *f ou adj* optic(s); optical; ~ **de radar** radar optics; ~ **électronique** electron optics; opto-electronics

optoélectronique *f* opto-electronics

opto-seuil *m* opto-isolator

optronique *f* light-wave communications; optronics

or *m* **faux** Dutch gold (copper-leaf finish); ~ **flash** gold flashing

orage *m* **ionosphérique** ionospheric storm; ~ **magnétique** magnetic storm

orbite *f* orbit; ~ **circulaire** circular orbit; ~ **de satellite** satellite orbit; ~ **d'expansion** expansion orbit; ~ **dilatée** expansion orbit

ordinaire *adj* straightforward; commonplace; routine; run-of-the-mill; standard; everyday

ordinateur *m* computer; mainframe; ~ **central** host computer; mainframe; ~ **frontal** communication computer; front-end computer; ~ **hôte** mainframe; host computer; ~ **individuel (OI)** personal computer (PC); ~ **lourd** mainframe computer; ~ **principal** host processor; host computer; mainframe; ~ **réseau** front-end processor; ~ **universel** general-purpose computer; all-purpose computer; analytical engine

ordinogramme *m* flow chart; flow diagram; process chart; logic diagram

ordinothèque *f* system library

ordonnancement *m* job flow; sequencing; scheduling; planning; collating; production engineering; merging

ordonnanceur *m* scheduler; ordinator; collator; sequencer

ordonné *adj* computed; processed; classified; scheduled; collated

ordonner *v* collate; schedule; sequence; configure

ordre *m* instruction; statement; sequence; rank; OP code (part of instruction); order; mnemonic; request; command; discipline; ~ **assembleur** assembly language; ~ **croissant** ascending order; ~ **de classement** collating sequence; ~ **de correction** change order; ~ **de grandeur** order of magnitude; ~ **de grandeur des temps** estimated time; ~ **de passage** sequence (of execution); queue discipline; ~ **décroissant** descending order; ~ **d'instrumentation** trace utility command; ~ **du jour** agenda; ~ **homologue** duplicate unit; ~ **inférieur** lower order; ~ **machine** machine language op code;

~ **macroprogramme** macro-instruction (op code); ~ **supérieur** higher order

ordres de gestion (job) control language

oreille *f* **artificielle** artificial ear

organe *m* component; constituent part; element; unit; terminal; device; instrument; circuit; control unit; peripheral; chip; apparatus; ~ **annexe** ancillary device/unit; ~ **d'accès au réseau** network access device; ~ **d'appel** calling equipment; ringer; ~ **d'appui** support chip; ~ **de calcul** computer; processor; ~ **de commande** control finder; control unit; driver; ~ **de contrôle** monitoring unit; ~ **de liaison** data link interface; ~ **de maintenance** test unit; maintenance device; ~ **de puissance** power point; ~ **de raccordement** connecting device; interface; ~ **de service** input/output terminal; I/O port; ~ **de sortie/d'entrée** input/output terminal; I/O port; ~ **de visualisation** display field; ~ **d'exploitation** operation and maintenance terminal; ~ **périphérique** interactive operator terminal

organes apparatus; equipment; ~ **centraux** switching equipment; exchange core subsystem; ~ **communs** exchange core subsystem; ~ **d'adaptation et d'accord** matching and tuning devices; ~ **de commutation** switchgear; ~ **de commutation et coupure** switchgear; ~ **d'extrémité** connection and signalling units; ~ **d'utilisation** user terminal; interface equipment

organigramme *m* flow chart; organizational diagram; ~ **d'analyse** system (flow-)chart; flow-process diagram; ~ **détaillé** low-level flowchart; ~ **du bâti** rack configuration

organique *adj* intrinsic; inherent

organisation *f* planning; engineering; ~ **dispersée** distributed switching; ~ **en trame** framing

organisme *m* body; organization

orientable *adj* directional; rotatable; steerable

orientation *f* attitude; trend; direction; steering; guidance; lay; disposition; tilt; inclination; slope; ~ (sur un poste) switching; routing; (call) forwarding; ~ **professionnelle** vocational guidance

orienté (vers) routed to; directed towards; ~ **opérateur** user-friendly

orienté-problème (langage) problem-oriented language

orienter *v* channel; transfer; direct; forward; aim; route; switch; steer; guide; train; align; point; sweep; tilt

orienteur *m* selection-finder; guider

origine *f* datum; origin; source; home (position); ~ **de l'interruption** interrupt source; ~ **de portée zéro** zero-range origin; ~ **décalée** offset; ~ **technique** technical source

orthogonal *adj* reversible (serial-parallel); right-angled; bidirectional

OS (v. ouvrier spécialisé)

oscillateur *m* oscillator; multivibrator; generator; ~ **à autoexcitation** standard oscillator; ~ **à barres parallèles** parallel rod oscillator; ~ **à battement** beating oscillator; local oscillator (LO); ~ **à blocage** blocking oscillator; blocking generator; ~ **à blocage déclenché** triggered blocking oscillator; ~ **à circuit anodique accordé** tuned-anode oscillator; ~ **à circuit d'anode accordé** tuned-anode oscillator; ~ **à circuit de grille accordé** tuned-grid oscillator; ~ **à commande par tension** voltage-controlled oscillator (VCO); ~ **à compensation de température** temperature-compensated oscillator; ~ **à couplage électronique** electron-coupled oscillator (ECO); ~ **à cristal** (quartz-)crystal oscillator; ~ **à déphasage** quadrature oscillator; ~ **à extinctions** (self-)quenching oscillator; quencher; squegging oscillator; squegger; ~ **à haute fréquence** radio-frequency oscillator; ~ **à plaques parallèles** parallel-plate oscillator; ~ **à pont de Wien** Wien bridge oscillator; ~ **à quartz** quartz-crystal controlled oscillator; ~ **à quartz thermostaté** temperature-compensated crystal oscillator (TCXO); (field-replaceable) thermostatically-controlled crystal oscillator (TCXO); ~ **à relaxation** relaxation oscillator; sweep generator; ~ **à relaxation commandé par le courant** current-controlled relaxation (sweep) oscillator; ~ **à télécommande** labile oscillator; remotely-controlled oscillator; ~ **à transitron** transitron oscillator; ~ **à tube à vide** vacuum-tube/thermionic-valve oscillator; ~ **à tube de réactance** reactance tube oscillator; ~ **agile** agile oscillator; ~ **asservi en phase** phase-locked oscillator (VCXO); ~ **autodyne** autodyne oscillator; ~ **bloqué** locked oscillator; ~ **cohérent** coherent oscillator; ~ **commandé en tension** voltage-controlled (crystal) oscillator (VCXO); ~ **commandé par oscillations de relaxation** squegging oscillator; self-quenching oscillator; ~ **de base de temps** time-base generator; ~ **de battement** beating oscillator; local oscillator (LO); ~ **de blocage** blocking oscillator; ~ **de calibrage** standard calibration oscillator; ~ **de Colpitts** Colpitts oscillator; ~ **de découpage** quench oscillator; squegger; ~ **de dents de scie** saw-tooth oscillator;

sweep generator; ~ **de freinage** retarding-field oscillator; ~ **de Hartley** Hartley oscillator; ~ **de puissance** power oscillator; ~ **de relaxation** sweep (relaxation) oscillator; ~ **de synchronisation** timing oscillator; ~ **de transposition** translation oscillator; ~ **en bande X** X-band oscillator; ~ **en dents de scie** sweep oscillator; ~ **Hartley à couplage électronique** ECO-Hartley circuit; ~ **hétérodyne** heterodyne (beat-frequency) oscillator (BFO); ~ **incorporé** timing hardware; ~ **local (OL)** beating oscillator; local oscillator (LO); ~ **local à réglage numérique** digitally-controlled local oscillator; ~ **local final** beating oscillator; local oscillator (LO); ~ **local stabilisé** stabilized local oscillator; ~ **paramétrique** parametric oscillator; ~ **pilote** master oscillator; crystal driver; ~ **pilote thermostaté** temperature-compensated crystal oscillator (TCXO); ~ **R-C** R-C oscillator; resistance-capacitance oscillator; relaxation oscillator; ~ **stabilisé** stabilized oscillator; ~ **symétrique** push-pull oscillator; ~ **taux d'erreur(s)** phase-shift oscillator; line oscillator; ~ **toutes ondes** all-wave oscillator; ~ **variable** variable(-frequency) oscillator (VFO); ~ **verrouillé en phase** phase-locked oscillator

oscillation *f* oscillation; singing; swinging; shift; switch-over; motorboating; ~ **amortie** damped oscillation; ~ **apériodique** transient oscillation; overdamped oscillation; ~ **BF parasite** motorboating; relaxation oscillation; ~ **de relèvement** bearing oscillation; ~ **dynatron** dynatron oscillation; ~ **électromagnétique** electromagnetic oscillation; ~ **en dents de scie** saw-tooth oscillation; saw-tooth wave; ~ **fondamentale** fundamental oscillation; first harmonic; ~ **forcée** forced oscillation; ~ **harmonique** overtone; ~ **hétérodyne** local oscillation; ~ **interne spontanée** self-oscillation; spurious oscillation; singing; ~ **libre** force-free oscillation; free oscillation; ~ **modulée en fréquence** amplitude-modulated oscillation; ~ **parasite** singing (uncontrolled oscillations); stray/spurious oscillations; ~ **pendulaire** hunting; phase oscillation; ~ **sans pointe** spikeless oscillation; ~ **stationnaire** steady-state oscillation; ~ **transitoire** ringing

oscillo bicourbes dual-trace oscilloscope

oscillogramme *m* oscillogram; pattern (scope); waveform; ~ **du mode** mode pattern

oscillographe *m* oscillograph

oscilloscope *m* oscilloscope; ~ **à mémoire**

storage oscilloscope; ~ **bicourbe** dual-trace oscilloscope; ~ **de contrôle de télévision** waveform monitor; ~ **de mesure d'intervalle de temps** interval-timer oscilloscope; ~ **deux traces** dual-trace oscilloscope; double-beam oscilloscope

oscilloscope-intervallomètre interval-timer oscilloscope

OSI ISO (International Standards Organisation)

ossature *f* framework; chassis; ironwork

ossivibrateur *m* bone-conduction headphone/receiver

ostéophone *m* bone-conduction headphone/receiver

OT (ordre de travail) job order; job sheet

OTJ (v. occupation toutes jonctions)

OU (cf. union, réunion) OR gate; OR element; one gate; one element; OR circuit; ~ **2 x 3 entrées** dual three-input OR gate; ~ **câblé** (hard-)wired OR; dot AND circuit

où en est the state of play

OU exclusif exclusive-OR; non-equivalence; OR only; diversity; except gate; exjunction; symmetric difference; distance; modulo two sum; addition without carry

OUC (v. onde ultra-courte)

ouie *f* **d'aération** air vent; louvre

outil *m* facility; device; aid; appliance; tool; standard; reference; utility; ~ **à déwrapper** unwrapping tool; wire-wrap remover; ~ **de clipsage** lead-forming tool; pin-setting tool; ~ **de développement** development system; ~ **de mise au point** debugging aid; ~ **de montage** gap gauge; ~ **de rangement** trimming tool; ~ **de sertissage** crimping tool; lever press; riveter; ~ **de trace** tracer

outillage *m* tools; tooling; tools and equipment

outils informatiques computerized management system

ouvert *adj* off (of switch); in-line; NC (break) contact

ouverture *f* opening; aperture; orifice; foothold; gate (of thyristor); interruption; opening; divergence (of beam); gateway; ~ **angulaire** angular aperture; ~ **de boucle** loop-disconnect; ~ **de document** document opening; ~ **du faisceau** beam aperture; ~ **numérique** numerical aperture (of fibre optics); ~ **numérique (ON)** numerical aperture (NA)

ouvrier *m* **non spécialisé** unskilled worker; labourer; ~ **professionnel (OP)** skilled worker; skilled operative; ~ **spécialisé (OS)** semi-skilled worker/operative

OVNI (objet volant non identifié) unidentified flying object (UFO)

oxydant *m* oxidizing agent

oxydation *f* **anodique** anodizing; ~ **extérieure à l'état vapeur** outside vapour phase oxidation (OVPO); ~ **intérieure à l'état vapeur** inside vapour phase oxidation (IVPO)

oxygénation *f* passivation

oxymétal *m* metal oxide (of rectifier)

P

PA (préamplificateur) pre-amplifier; ≂ (v. prise optique d'appartement)

padding *m* padding capacitor; padder

page *f* page; leaf; sheet; folio; frame; screen; ~ **d'articulation** (document) administration page; ~ **de garde** banner; fly-leaf; title page; ~ **de mise en service** initial page; ~ **enregistreur** register; ~ **mémoire de travail** worksheet; ~ **précédente** previous page; ~ **suivante** next page

page-écran screen page; video page; display page

page-guide index

pages face à face facing pages

pagination *f* paging; ~ **à la demande** demand paging

paie *f* payroll

paiement *m* **électronique** electronic funds transfer (EFT); ~ **pour solde** final instalment

paille *f* (metal) shaving

paillette *f* flake

pair *adj* even(-numbered)

pairage *m* pairing; twinning; matching

paire *f* pair; ~ **blindée** screened pair; ~ **coaxiale** coaxial pair; ~ **combinable** interchangeable pair; ~ **conversation** speech junction; talking pair; ~ **de fils** wire pair; ~ **de service** order-wire pair; ~ **différentielle** differential pair; ~ **électron-trou** hole-electron pair; ~ **équilibrée** balanced (signal) pair; balanced line; ~ **métallique** wire pair; loop; ~ **sous écran** screened pair; shielded pair; ~ **symétrique** balanced pair; symmetric cable pair; balanced line; ~ **torsadée** twisted pair

palette *f* tongue; spill (of edge connector); plunger (of head load); platform; vane (of galvanometer); flapper (of armature); blade; armature (of relay); pallet; ~ **équilibrée** balanced armature

palier *m* plateau (of graph); level; pulse top; increment; platform; phase; sector; porch; pedestal; standard; bearing; bearing plane (of balance beam); release (version); ~ **arrière** back porch; ~ **avant** front porch; ~ **de taxe** metering rate; charge level; call charge rate/scale; charge band; tariff rate; time-and-distance metering rate; ~ **d'effacement** blanking level; ~ **incliné** pulse tilt; ~ **technique** engineering development level; release

pallier *v* mitigate; alleviate; relieve; offset

palmer *m* micrometer; ~ **à friction** friction micrometer

palonnier *m* compensating arm

palpeur *m* pecker (of computer); sensor; notch-tracer/-follower; data pick-off element; feeler gauge

pan *m* flat (of nut); turn; revolution (of handwheel)

panachage *m* mixing; mingling; combining; merging; multiplexing

panier *m* compartment; subrack; circuitry; wiring panel; card cage; crate; case; basket; magazine; box (of batteries); ~ **arrière** backplane; ~ **d'adaptation** adaptor subrack; ~ **d'alimentation** mother board; backplane; ~ **de brassage** strapping connector module; ~ **de commutation** switching subrack; ~ **de lavage** cleaning basket; cleaning cage; ~ **de manutention** handling basket; ~ **percé** leaky bucket

panne *f* breakdown; failure; malfunction; trouble; shutdown; fault; crash; outage; disorder; defect; mishap; dump; ~ **d'alimentation** power failure; AC dump; ~ **de fer** tip of soldering iron; ~ **de l'émetteur** transmitter outage; ~ **du secteur** AC dump; mains failure; ~ **franche** unconditional fault; ~ **frontal** front-end crash; ~ **mortelle** non-recoverable failure; irretrievable loss; deadly embrace; deadlock

panneau *m* panel; instrument display; console; menu; ~ **à fentes** panel of slot radiators; ~ **arrière** backplane; backboard; rear panel; ~ **avant** front panel; ~ **d'affichage** display panel; ~ **d'affichage graphique** graphic display panel; ~ **d'appareils de mesure** metering panel; ~ **d'assemblage** mounting panel; ~ **de câblage (PC)** wiring panel; ~ **de commande** control panel; ~ **de coupure** test panel; ~ **de distribution** distribution panel; switchboard; ~ **de doublets** panel of full-wave dipoles; ~ **de fusibles** fuse panel; ~ **de jacks** jack field; jack panel; ~ **de lampes** lamp field; indicator panel; ~ **de lampes d'occupation** busy lamp field; busy lamp panel; ~ **de mutation (PM)** switchboard; plugboard;

patch panel; ~ **de papillons** array of bat-wing aerials; ~ **de raccordement** patch panel; plugboard; switchboard; ~ **de renvoi** transfer panel; ~ **d'éléments rayonnants** aerial array; ~ **d'essai** test board; ~ **d'essai des lignes** line test board; ~ **Isorel** [A.C.] hardboard; ~ **particule** chipboard

panoplie *f* reference display panel (of PCB components); choice; spectrum

PAP *adv ou adj* (v. pas à pas)

papeterie *f* stationery

papier *m* hard copy; ~ **autocopiant** NCR paper (National Cash Registers: T.N.); ~ **autorévélateur** self-inking paper (for dot matrix printer); ~ **buvard** absorbent paper; blotting paper; ~ **cadrié** (quadrillé) squared paper; ~ **calque** tracing paper; ~ **de nettoyage** cleaning tissue; ~ **de soie** tissue paper; ~ **de tournesol** litmus paper; ~ **dépliant** continuous form paper; ~ **diagramme** graph paper; ~ **kraft** kraft (paper); strong brown paper; ~ **pliage paravent** fanfold paper; ~ **réactif** litmus paper; ~ **replié en accordéon** fanfold paper; ~ **sensible** sensitized paper; ~ **sulfurisé** grease-proof paper

papillon *m* (repair) chit; voucher; butterfly (of bit pattern); fast Fourier transform

papillotement *m* wow; flicker

paquet *m* deck; pack; package; message packet; burst; multiplexed data; ~ **bref** short burst; ~ **de cartes** deck of (punched) cards; ~ **de données** data packet; ~ **d'erreurs** error burst

parabole *f* **de coupure** critical voltage; cut-off parabola

parabolique *adj* square-law

paradiaphonie *f* near-end crosstalk (NEXT); side-to-side crosstalk; go-to-return crosstalk; reverse crosstalk

parafoudre *m* lightning arrester; surge arrester; diverter; lightning conductor; atmospheric discharge; lightning rod; ~ **à gaz** gas arrester; ~ **de charbon** carbon black protector

paragraphe *m* paragraph (16-kbyte division of segment)

parallèlement *adv* concurrently

parallélépipède *m* six-sided case; box; solid

parallélisme *m* parallel processing; parallel exposure; parallelism; alignment

paramétrable *adj* dynamic; preset; skeletal; (field-)programmable; adjustable; operator-selected; variable; adjusted; controlled (value)

paramétrage *m* parameterization; storage; parameter assignment

paramètre *m* parameter; control message;

operand; ~ **bureau** exchange parameter; ~ **chaîné** string parameter; ~ **classique** formal parameter; ~ **d'aiguillage** program switching data; ~ **de dimensionnement** sizing parameter; ~ **de groupement** bunching parameter; ~ **de résistance** Z-parameter; ~ **défectueux** spurious parameter; runaway; ~ **electrique** electrical parameter; ~ **impulsionnel** dynamic parameter; ~ **serré** close(-tolerance) parameter

paramètres caractéristiques du bruit characteristic noise parameters; ~ **d'aiguillage** (program) switching information; ~ **de bureau** exchange parameters; ~ **de commutation** switching parameters

paramétrisation *f* parameterization; storage

parasite(s) *m ou adj* interference; stray; spurious; noise; extraneous; unwanted; disturbing; clutter; disturbance; drop-in; noise spike; garbage; false drop; false retrieval; glitch

parasite erratique discontinu discontinuous random noise; ~ **industriel** man-made noise; ~ **naturel** natural interference; natural noise

parasites à peine perceptibles just-perceptible noise; minimum perceptible noise; ~ **atmosphériques** interference; atmospherics; static; ~ **d'agitation thermique** thermal noise; ~ **de récurrence** recurrent noise; ~ **industriels** man-made noise; ~ **intolérables** intolerable noise; ~ **radio** radio disturbance; interference; noise

parasoleil *m* viewing hood (of oscilloscope)

parasurtenseur *m* surge arrester; surge diverter; ~ **amortisseur d'ondes** surge absorber; surge arrester

paratonnerre *m* lightning conductor; lightning arrester

paravent *m* fan-fold

parc *m* total number; inventory; lines installed; installed base; ~ **de voies** number of channels

parcage *m* parking orbit; ~ **d'appel** call park; call parking; ~ **et distribution d'appels** call parking and distribution; ~ **renvoi sur garde** call parking

parcourir *v* scan; search

parcours *m* path; round; route; ~ **de la diaphonie** crosstalk path; ~ **de ronde** round (of exchange nightwatchman service); ~ **d'écho** singing path; ~ **des ondes** propagation path; ~ **moyen libre** (PML) (d'un porteur électrisé) mean free path (of charged particle)

paré *adj* ready

pare-étincelles *m* spark quench; spark arrester

pare-poussières *m* dust-trap

P

parfait *adj* ideal; peak; optimum
PARIS - BORDEAUX - LE MANS - SAINT-LEU - LEON - LOUDUN Joe took father's shoe bench out
Paris et région parisienne metropolitan
parité *f* (even) parity; redundancy; ~ **des monnaies** foreign exchange rates; ~ **impair transversale** vertical redundancy check (VRC); ~ **longitudinale** horizontal parity; ~ **transversale** vertical parity
parler *v* speak
parleur *m* sounder
parmi *prep* out of
paroi *f* **de bloc** domain wall
parole *f* speech; word(s); wording; voice; ~ **codée** coded speech
paroles brouillées slurred speech; scrambling
part *f* segment (of pie chart); share
partage *m* sharing; splitting; ~ **de charge** load-sharing; traffic-sharing; ~ **de fenêtre** split frame; ~ **de fichiers** file-sharing; ~ **de fréquence** frequency-sharing; ~ **de maille** link-sharing; ~ **de temps** time-sharing; ~ **de trafic** load-sharing; traffic-sharing; ~ **des imprimantes** spooling; ~ **d'orbite** orbit-sharing
partagé *adj* collective; common; shared
partageable *adj* shared (resource); common
participation *f* involvement; holding; share; contribution; equity; ~ **des salariés** profit-sharing
particularité *f* departure from the norm; characteristic
particule *f* particle; ~ **alpha** alpha particle; ~ **bêta** beta particle; ~ **nucléaire** nucleon; nuclear particle
particulier *m ou adj* singular; individual; special; private; incidental; private user; dedicated; user-defined; salient; feature
partie *f* part; attachment; element; segment; end; portion; component; section; field; compartment; bucket; ~ **additive** attachment; add-on element; ~ **adresse** address field; address part; ~ **conductrice** core (of cable); ~ **d'adresse** address part; ~ **de bloc** blockette; ~ **de décodage** decode (section); ~ **états** status portion; ~ **fractionnaire** fixed-point part; ~ **linéaire** linear section; ~ **locale** exchange end; ~ **machine** (du bloc enregistreur) core (of register unit); ~ **noble** master; salient; spur; prominent; heart; core; ~ **opérande** operand field (of instruction); ~ **programme** program segment; ~ **réelle** active component; ~ **utile** mating area (of contact); wipe area
partiel *adj* slight; limited; discriminating
partition *f* partition; work area; segment; chapter

partitionnement *m* **mémoire** (dynamic) allocation
paru au J.O. (Journal Officiel) published in the official gazette
parution *f* release; publication; issue
pas *m* step; pitch; position; interval; spacing; increment; centre-to-centre distance; gap; decrement; progression; lay(-up); ~ **à pas** (PAP) *adv ou adj* by process of elimination; step-by-step; incrementally; single-shot; alternate; gradual; progression; ~ **axial** pitch (of thread); ~ **d'amplification** repeater spacing; ~ **de câblage** length of lay; ~ **de débordement** overflow area; ~ **(de filetage)** lead; pitch; ~ **de filin** lay of binder; ~ **de fixation** fixing centre(s); ~ **de grille** grid pitch; ~ **de progression** increment; ~ **de quantification** quantizing step; ~ **de rebouclage** exit from test loop; ~ **de régénération** repeater spacing; ~ **de régression** decrement; ~ **de rotation** rotary step; ~ **de toronnage** lay-up; lay; lay ratio; ~ **de torsade** lay-up; ~ **(de vis)** lead; ~ **d'enregistrement** inter-record gap; ~ **d'entraînement** feed pitch; ~ **d'espacement** centre-to-centre spacing; ~ **d'exploration** scanning pitch; ~ **(d'hélice)** lead; ~ **d'implantation** (PCB) mounting pitch (in subrack); insertion pitch; spacing; ~ **d'installation en travée** rack spacing; ~ **du gaz** (conique) gas taper
passable *adj* fair
passage *m* transfer; run; branch; switch; cycle; through-connection; transition; shift; conversion; changeover; walk-through; chop; pin; lead; duct; gap; toggling; posting; threading (of flux); propagation; ~ **(en)** switching to; through-connection; shift-in (SI); porting (of programs to another device); ~ **à la ligne suivante** line feed (LF); ~ **au code B** change to B signals; ~ **automatique** automatic changeover; ~ **came** cam time-out; ~ **de câble** gland; ~ **de fil** wire guide; grommet; channel; duct; ~ **de trains d'ondes** burst firing (fast cycle); ~ **délicat** smooth transition; ~ **deux fils-quatre fils** two-wire/four-wire term set; hybrid; ~ **en conversation** through-switching; ~ **en faux appel** permanent line status; ~ **en local** unload; ~ **en machine** machine run; ~ **en métallique** metallic (through-)connection; through-switching; ~ **en séquence** no-operation (NO-OP); next instruction; ~ **en supervision** forward transfer; ~ **grossier** general test (cycle); ~ **sur liaison de réserve** changeover; chop (to standby link)
passager *adj* short-lived; transitory; ephemeral; temporary; fleeting; incidental

passant *adj* conducting; energized; driving; active; open; on-state; forward-biased; "on"

passation *f* placement; concluding

passe *f* job; run; transaction; event; pass; ~ **bas** *adj* low-pass; ~ **de facturation** billing transaction; ~ **haut** high-pass

passé *m* history sheet

passe-bande bandpass; bandwidth

passe-fil(s) grommet; conduit; wire bush; strain relief bushing

passe-perches probe hatch

passer (une commande) lodge/place (of order); ~ **à l'état 1/(0)** change to the 1 (or 0) state; go high/(low); ~ **en code** shift-in (SI); ~ **en revue** scan; monitor; survey; scrutinize; ~ **hors code** shift-out (SO)

passerelle *f* gangway; aisle; catwalk; gateway; transitional link; interface; bridge

passe-vue *f* microtext reader

passif *adj* passive; stand-by

passivé *adj* passivated; dormant; masked (of metal electropotential)

pastille *f* lozenge; pellet (of transistor); label; chip; pad; caption; decal; land; ~ **lumineuse** caption light; ~ **prédéfoncée** knock-out (of plastic/metal housing)

pâte *f* compound; paste; ~ **de scellement** sealing compound; ~ **diamantée** diamond paste

patin *m* base plate; coaster; pad; bumper

patrimoine *m* legacy; heritage

patte *f* tab; lug; mounting plate; bracket; foot; pin; pedestal; termination; tag; ~ **à souder** soldering tag; solder tail; ~ **à wrapper** wire-wrap lug; tag; pin; foot; ~ **orientable** adjustable lug; swivel base; ~ **support** mounting bracket

PAV (v. communication avec préavis); ~̇ (v. appel avec préavis)

pavé *m* bank (of keys); mounting stud; wiring duct; block (of data); pad; scraps; chad; chips; tab; key cap; ~ (bloc d'informations chaîné) storage block (chained record); ~ **clignotant** blinking reverse (video) block; ~ **de centrage** centring block; ~ **de fixation** mounting tab; ~ **sérigraphié** silkscreened pad

pavillon *m* earpiece; earcap; mouthpiece; horn; ~ **acoustique** horn; ~ **de haut-parleur** loudspeaker horn; ~ **microphone** mouthpiece

pays *m* country; ~ **d'arrivée** terminating country; ~ **de départ** originating country; ~ **de destination** country of destination; ~ **de transit** transit country; ~ **de transit direct** direct transit country; ~ **de transit en commutation** switched transit country;

~ **d'origine** country of origin; ~ **terminal** terminating country

PC (prise de courant) electrical point; mains outlet; socket; ~̇ (v. panneau de câblage); ~̇ (v. porte-cartouche)

pc (v. poste de contrôle)

PC (v. pied à coulisse); ~̇ (v. point de concentration); ~̇ (v. point de consigne)

Pce (v. puissance); ~ (v. pièce)

PCU (v. poste à correspondant unique)

PCUD (v. poste à correspondant unique différé)

PCUI (v. poste à correspondant unique immédiat)

PCV (v. communication payable à l'arrivée); ~̇ (v. conversation payable à l'arrivée); ~̇ (payable à l'arrivée = percevoir) (code 10 en France) reverse-charge call; transfer-charge call; collect service; ~̇ (v. polychlorure de vinyle)

PCX (v. point de connexion)

PD et MO (v. pièces détachées et main d'œuvre)

pdt (pendant) during; in the course of

PE (v. pleine échelle); ~̇ (v. porte-étiquette)

péage *m* toll collection

peau d'orange *f* elephant skin; dimpling

pédagogique *adj* instructional

pédale *f* hook-switch; ~ **d'alternat** (foot) pressel switch; ~ **de secret** privacy switch

peignage *m* combing

peigne *m* clamp; harness; loom (of cables); cable form; comb; fanning strip; cleat; reed; fan (of cable loom); ~ **de câblage** wiring harness; ~ **de câble** cable harness; cable form; fanned cable; pre-formed cable; ~ **de masse** earth form; ~ **de quadrillage** notched plate for wiring board; wiring tool; ~ **du combinateur** combiner comb; ~ **séparé** cable form

peinture *f* **d'impression** undercoat; primer; ~ **finition** top coat (of paint); ~ **glycérophtalique** alkyd resin coating; glyptal resin coat; ~ **par poudrage** powder coating; "plastic" coating; ~ **primaire** primer; undercoat

pelliculé *adj* laminated; coated with film

pelure *f* flimsy (print)

penché *adj* tilted; not upright; italic (of print); sloping; slanted; skewed

pénétration *f* break-through; ingress; ~ **de la moyenne fréquence** IF rejection; ~ **du tapis de nuages** burn-through

pente *f* mutual conductance; transconductance; slope conductance; gradient; roll-off; rake; slope; incline; offset; goodness (of valve); slew; curve; pitch; tilt; ~ **d'accord** curve; slope; pitch; ~ **de conversion**

conversion transconductance; ~ **de dimi-nution** roll-off; ~ **d'une courbe** roll-off; ~ **maximale du signal de sortie** slew rate; ~ **moyenne du signal de sortie** average rate of change of output signal; slew rate (SVOAV)

pentode f pentode; ~ **de sortie** output pentode

perçage m **cloison** panel cut-out (diagram)

percée f break-through; spearhead(ing)

percer v bore; punch; drill; pierce; perforate; puncture

perceuse f power drill; ~ **tamponette percussion** percussion power drill; hammer drill; impact drill

perche f **de masse** earth rod; ~ **d'étalonnage** calibration probe

perchlorure m **de fer** ferric chloride (PCB etchant)

percuteur m plunger (of fuse); striker; ~ **électrique** firing pin

perditance f leakance; leakage

perdre le contact lose contact; sever contact

père adj parent; master

perfectionnement m refinement

perforateur m punch; perforator; ~ **à clavier** keyboard perforator; keypunch; ~ **de bande** paper tape punch; ~ **imprimeur à clavier** printing keyboard perforator; ~ **pour téléimprimeur** teleprinter/telex perforator; ~ **pour télex** teleprinter/telex perforator

perforation f punch; (code) hole; puncture; (insulation) breakdown; ~ **à la touche** touch-typing (of tape punch); ~ **d'entraînement** centre hole; feed hole; ~ **diélectrique** dielectric puncture; ~ **électrique** breakdown; punch-through; ~ **hors texte** zone-punching; over-punching; ~ **partielle** chadless perforation (of tape); ~ **significative** code hole; ~ **totale** chadded (tape)

perfo.(-ratrice) f tape punch

perforatrice f **de bande** tape punch

perfo.(-ratrice) réproductrice duplicating punch; gang-punch

performance f **de seuil** threshold performance

performant adj high-performance; powerful; sophisticated

périmé adj obsolete; superseded

période f cycle; period; interval; ~ **creuse** slack period; off-peak period; ~ **d'abonnement** rental period; ~ **d'accusation** suspect period; down time; ~ **d'atténuation d'écho** hangover time; ~ **de faible trafic** light traffic period; ~ **de jeunesse** early-failure period; ~ **de mise au point** preliminary stages; early stages; ~ **de pointe** peak period; ~ **de réglage** line-up period; ~ **de silence** silent period; ~ **de taxation** charge period; metering rate period; ~ **d'échantillonnage** sampling period; ~ **d'évanouissement** fading period; ~ **hors service** down-time; overhead; ~ **préparatoire** preparatory period; run-up; warm-up; ~ **propre** natural period; ~ **transitoire du fac-similé** facsimile transient; ~ **transitoire finale** decay time

périodemètre m **numérique** digital period counter

périodicité f frequency; (servicing) interval; repeat interval; recurrence; ~ **d'appel** ringing interval

périodique adj cyclic; intermittent; recurrent; routine

périodiquement adv intermittently

péripétie f vicissitude; vagary

périphérie f fringe; edge; rim; brim

périphérique m ou adj peripheral device; ancillary; terminal; fringe; ~ **d'entrée/de sortie** input/output device; I/O terminal; ~ **horloge générale** interrupt clock; ~ **léger** teletypewriter (TTY); ~ **nul** null device; ~ **programmé** control module

péritéléphonie f telephone support facilities; accessories

péritélévision f television accessories

perle f bead; ~ **en agathe** agate bead (stylus of disk recorder)

perluète f (&'et' commercial) ampersand (&'and' sign: &)

permanence f **de secours** 24-hour assistance (centre)

permanent adj sustained; uninterrupted; permanent; non-volatile; master; continuous-duty; steady; round-the-clock; non-stop; ongoing; constant; indefinite

perméabilité f permeability; ~ **du vide** permeability of vacuum; ~ **initiale** initial permeability; ~ **magnétique (absolue)** magnetic permeability; ~ **relative** relative permeability

perméamètre m permeameter

perméance f permeance

permettre v cater for; allow; enable

permis m licence; permit; authorization; ~ adj authorized; legal (of command)

permittivité f permittivity; ~ **du vide** permittivity of vacuum

permulettre f key letter in context (KLIC)

permutable adj swappable

permutation f changeover; interchange; switching; indexing; rotation; switchover; shift; ~ **automatique** automatic changeover; ~ **circulaire** turned/rotated through 180°; cyclic shift; round robin; end-around shift; ~ **cyclique** turned/rotated through 180°; cyclic shift; round robin; end-around

shift
permuter *v* change over; switch over/around; rotate; interchange; convert; index; shift
persienne(s) *f* *(pl)* louvre(s); blind(s); shutter(s)
persistance *f* (d'écran) persistence; afterglow; decay; retentivity
personnalisable *adj* customized; made-to-order; user-defined; field-programmed
personnalisation *f* customizing
personnalisé *adj* application; user-friendly; user-defined; dedicated; custom-designed; customized; bespoke
personnel *m* staff; personnel complement; liveware; ~ **compétent** qualified service engineer; skilled technician; ~ **direct** internal (resident) staff; ~ **indirect** outside staff (non-resident)
personnes physiques ou morales individual or legal entities
perspective *f* trend; prospect; persuasion; ~ **cavalière** isometric projection; oblique projection
perte *f* loss; leakage; drop; failure; breakdown; waste; discharge; drop-out; attrition; dissipation; ~ **à la terre** earth leakage; ground leak; ~ **à l'accord** tuning losses; ~ **à l'injection** launch loss; ~ **accidentelle** drop-out; ~ **atmosphérique** atmospheric loss; ~ **au couplage** coupling loss; ~ **d'absorption** absorption loss; ~ **d'amplification** gain loss; attenuation; ~ **d'antenne** aerial loss; ~ **de conversion** conversion loss; ~ **de cuivre** copper loss; ~ **de déviation angulaire** angular deviation loss; ~ **de lumière** light loss; ~ **de multitrame** multiframe loss; ~ **de niveau** level breakdown; ~ **de pilote** pilot loss; ~ **de porteur** carrier loss; carrier drop-out; ~ **de propagation** propagation loss; ~ **de puissance** power loss; ~ **de synchronisation** synchronization failure; lock-out; ~ **de trame** frame loss; ~ **de transmission** transmission loss; ~ **de verrouillage** loss of frame alignment; ~ **de verrouillage de (multi-)trame** loss of (multi-)frame alignment; out-of-frame sync; ~ **d'enregistrement** recording loss; ~ **diélectrique** dielectric loss; ~ **d'information** drop-out; walkdown; ~ **d'insertion** insertion loss; ~ **dissipative** power loss; ~ **du lecture** playback loss; ~ **du signal de rythme** loss of bit timing; ~ **due aux réflexions** mismatch loss; return loss; reflection loss; ~ **en charge** impedance loss; ~ **en ligne** line loss; ~ **en puissance apparente due à une dérivation** bridging loss; tapping loss; ~ **irrémédiable** irretrievable loss; walk-

down; irreversible magnetic process; ~ **lors d'une mise en dérivation** tapping loss; ~ **magnétique résiduelle** loss of residual magnetism; ~ **ohmique** ohmic loss; resistance loss; wattful loss; in-phase loss; ~ **par courant de Foucault** eddy-current loss; ~ **par couronne** corona loss; ~ **par diaphonie** crosstalk loss; ~ **par effet Joule** copper loss; ~ **par excitation** excitation loss; ~ **par hystérésis** hysteresis loss; ~ **par rayonnement** radiation loss; ~ **par réflexion** return loss; ~ **rotorique** rotor loss; ~ **thermique** thermal loss; heat loss
pertes dans l'arc arc-drop loss; arc loss; ~ **de charge** voltage drop; ~ **de taxation** loss of revenue; ~ **en charge** impedance drop; ~ **par hystérésis** eddy current loss
pertinence *f* dependability
perturbateur *m* interference source; noise source; noise generator; jammer
perturbation *f* disturbance; disruption; interference; noise jamming; hit-on-the-line; garbling; clutter; corruption; turbulence; ~ **atmosphérique** atmospheric interference; static; ~ **de données** corruption of data; ~ **électromagnétique** electromagnetic disturbance; ~ **industrielle** man-made noise; ~ **ionosphérique** ionospheric disturbance; ~ **ionosphérique à début brusque** sudden ionospheric disturbance; ~ **par appareils électriques** electrical interference; ~ **par la fréquence image** image frequency interference; ~ **par onde continue manipulée** keyed CW jamming; ~ **quasi-impulsive** quasi-impulsive noise/disturbance; ~ **radioélectrique** radio disturbance; ~ **réciproque** mutual interference
perturber *v* disrupt; disturb; impair; degrade; adversely affect
peste pourpre *f* purple plague
pétale *m* lobe; petal (of print-wheel); spoke (of print-wheel); ~ **de rayonnement** radiation lobe
petite mécanique small-scale mechanical engineering; ~ **série** limited production (run); pilot scheme
petites ondes (PO) medium wave
pétrole *m* (lampant) paraffin; kerosene; lamp oil
peu apparent just noticeable; ~ **encombrant** compact; ~ **ou pas** rarely if ever; seldom; ~ **profond** shallow;adj.; ~ **répandu** little used; scarce; ~ **sensible** virtually immune
peut ne pas is not necessarily
PF (v. porte-fusible); ~ (v. poids fort)
pf (v. poids faible)
PF *m* str (v. phénoplaste stratifié)
pg (v. programme)

phanotron *m* phanotron
phantastron *m* phantastron
phare *m* beacon
phase *f* instruction; step; stage; run; pass; leg; instruction address; instruction time; lane; cycle; state; trip; clock pulse; ~ **d'appel** ringing interval; ~ **de départ** start address; start instruction; ~ **de renvoi** transfer address; return address; ~ **de retour** return address; return instruction; ~ **de signal** signal phase; ~ **de supervision** answer supervision; ~ **de travail** pass; run; current instruction; stage; step; ~ **dépendant du niveau** level-dependent phase; ~ **d'exécution** execute phase; ~ **en cours** current instruction (address); ~ **et gain appariés** gain and phase match; ~ **préparée** instruction (addressed); next instruction address; ~ **suivante** next instruction (address); ~ **systématique** housekeeping task
phasemètre *m* phase meter
phases opératoires main steps; procedure
phénomène *m* effect; ~ **transitoire** transient
phénoplaste *m* **stratifié (PF str)** cotton-fibre laminated (board)
phénylène *m* **polyoxide (NORYL)** polyphenylene oxide
philosophie *f* theory; approach
phimètre *m* phase meter; PF meter
phonème *m* phoneme
phonie *f* speech; audio; ~ (radio-) R/T voice transmission
phosphorescence *f* phosphorescence
phosphorogène *m* activator
phosphoroscope *m* phosphoroscope
photocathode *f* photocathode
photocomposeuse *f* phototypesetter; film-setter
photoconduction *f* photoconductive effect
photocoupleur *m* optocoupler; optical ammeter
photodétecteur *m* photodetector; light detector
photodiode *f* photodiode
photoélectron *m* photo-electron
photoémission *f* photo-electric emission/effect
photographier *v* (l'écran) store (screen display)
photogravé *adj* photo-engraved; etched
photoluminescence *f* photo-luminescence
photon *m* photon
photonique *f* lightwave communications (photonics); optical communications
photopile *f* photovoltaic cell; photocell
photorécepteur *m* photodetector; light detector
photosensible *adj* optical; photo-electric; light-sensitive
photostyle *m* light pen; light sensor

phototélégramme *m* phototelegram
phototélégraphie *f* phototelegraphy; picture transmission; photofacsimile telegraphy
photothyristor *m* light-activated silicon-controlled rectifier (LASCR)
phrase préenregistrée *f* put-aside vocabulary
phrase-type *f* standard sentence
pianoter *v* key; type
pic *m* peak (of curve); spike; ~ **de commutation** switching spike; ~ **d'entrée** launch peak
pichet *m* beaker; pitcher; jug
picofarad *m* picofarad (pF); micromicrofarad (uuF)
picot *m* tapping; soldering pot; peg; stud; pin; spike; termination; (solder) spill; ~ **à souder** solder spill (of connector); ~ **de masse** earth spike (of pot core)
pictogramme *m* special (pictorial) symbol; ideogram; pictogram
PID PID (proportional integral and derivative action); three-term control; anticipatory control
pièce (pce) part; component; spare; unit; article; specimen; item; (program) patch; document; ~ **cassante** fragile part; brittle component; ~ **de contact** contact (element); ~ **de détail** minor part; detail; ~ **de fixation** fastener; securing component; ~ **de rechange** spare part; ~ **détachée** accessory; spare part; ~ **d'indexation** polarizing key; ~ **d'usure** wearing part; ~ **jointe (PJ)** enclosure(s); ~ **lisse** plain work-piece; ~ **montée (PM)** original equipment (OE); as fitted; ~ **ouvrée** finished article; wrought article; ~ **polaire** pole-piece; ~ **polaire supérieure** upper pole-piece; ~ **sous tension** live part; ~ **symétrique** reversible assembly
pièces détachées et main d'œuvre (PD et MO) parts and labour
pied *m* foot; stand; base; butt; stud; pod; stem; stalk; step; heel; toe; stub; tab; ~ **à coulisse (PC)** (vernier) caliper; ~ **de fixation** mounting stud; ~ **de lavage** stand-off rim; ~ **de levage** crowbar; ~ **de mesure** measurement adaptor; ~ **de microphone** microphone stand; ~ **support** pedestal; plinth
pied-de-biche pinch bar; crowbar; spike bar
piège *m* choke (of waveguide); trap(ping) centre; ~ **à absorption** absorption trap; ~ **de radar** radar decoy; radar trap; ~ **d'ions** ion trap; ~ **électrique** absorption circuit; trap circuit; ~ **son du canal adjacent** adjacent channel rejector
piéger *v* seize; trap
pierre *f* **de diffusion** porous stone (of foam

fluxer)

piètement *m* plinth; stand

pieuvre *f* interface kit

pige *f* limit gauge (GO/NO-GO); measuring rod; standard line (of printed text); ~ **publicitaire** advertising copy; press-cutting agency

pigeonneau *m* ram spigot (of press)

piget *m* **de montage** mounting

pignons hélicoïdaux bevel gear (assembly)

pile *f* cell; battery element; stack; primary cell; pile-up (of relay contacts); ~ **alcaline** alkaline cell; ~ **au lithium** lithium cell; ~ **directe** (file) push-up stack (FIFO); queue; ~ **électrique** cell; battery; ~ **galvanique** electric cell; battery; ~ **liquide** wet cell; ~ **photovoltaïque** photocell; ~ **refoulée** push-down stack (LIFO); cellar; ~ **sèche** dry cell

pilier *m* **d'adaptation** matching pillar

pilotage *m* pilot(ing); driving; control; ~ **son** audio on/off (control)

pilote *m ou adj* pilot; master; oscillator; drive(r); control circuit; ~ **à circuit oscillant** resonant-circuit drive; ~ **à cristal** crystal-oscillator drive; ~ **à diapason** tuning-fork oscillator drive; ~ **à ligne résonnante** line-stabilized oscillator drive; ~ **d'appels** call director; ~ **d'émetteur** master oscillator; ~ **électromécanique** electromechanical drive; ~ **logique** worker logic unit; ~ **régulateur** regulating pilot

piloter *v* control; drive; pilot; operate; steer; channel

pince *f* collet; clip; prong; pliers; grip; clamp; tongs; nippers; clippers; forceps; extraction tool; chuck; insertion tool; pincers; tweezers; snips; gripper; claw; ~ **à becs demi-ronds** half round-nose pliers; snipe-nose pliers; ~ **à décaper** scraping pliers; ~ **à décoffrer** crowbar; ~ **à dénuder** stripping pliers; skinning pliers; ~ **à dessin** bulldog clip; ~ **à ébarber** trimming pliers; ~ **à gratter à mors** stripping and scraping pliers; ~ **à main sertissage** crimping pliers; ~ **à manchonner** sleeving pliers; ~ **à morille** clamping pliers; ~ **à mors** collet clamp; jaw clamp; ~ **à sertir** crimping pliers; ~ **à souder** welding tongs; ~ **absorbante** absorbing clamp; ~ **américaine** stripping pliers; strippers (of wire insulation); collet; ~ **ampèremétrique** clamp meter; clamp-on ammeter; ~ **bec de canard** duck-bill piers; ~ **bec rond** round-nose pliers; ~ **brucelle(s)** (= précelles) tweezers; ~ **coupante** side cutters; ~ **coupante articulée** slip-joint wire cutters; ~ **coupante devant** edge cutters; ~ **coupante diagonale** side cutters; ~ **coupe câble** cable-cutting pliers; ~ **crabe** crocodile clip; alligator clip; ~ **crocodile** crocodile clip; alligator clip; ~ **de blocage** mole grips; "Vise-grip" [T.N.]; locking wrench; locking pliers; self-grip wrench; ~ **de préhension** insertion/extraction tool; gripper; ~ **de test** test clip (of IC); ~ **d'essai** test clip (of IC); ~ **étau** self-grip wrench; locking pliers; mole grips; Vise-Grip [T.N.]; ~ **extraction** extraction tool; ~ **flanc** nippers; clippers; side cutters; grip; ~ **insertion** insertion tool; finger (of insertion machine); ~ **plate** flat pliers; duck-bill pliers; ~ **radio réglable** adjustable 'radio' pliers; ~ **réglable** adjustable pliers; ~ **téléphone** 'telephone' pliers; ~ **télévision** long-nose pliers; ~ **universelle** combination pliers

pinceau *m* beam; brush

pincement *m* pinch; nip; crimp(ing)

pinoche *f* pin

pion *m* **de centrage** locating pin; spline; polarizing key; spigot; guide pin; registration stud; ~ **détrompeur** locating pin; spline; spigot

piquage *m* (sur CI) pitting; tapping

piqué *adj* padded

pique-fil *m* wire clinch

piqûre *f* (surface) pitting; blowhole; pinhole

PIRE (v. puissance isotropique rayonnée équivalente)

pis *m* **aller** makeshift procedure

pissette *f* washing bottle

pistage *m* artwork; layout; ~ **d'appel** call tracing

piste *f* track; area; strip; stripe; band; rail; ~ **de rythme** clock (master) track; ~ **de synchronisation** clock track; ~ **horloge** clock track; ~ **magnétique** stripe; band; ~ **voleur** (= voleur de courant) thief track; robber bar

pistes concentriques décalées staggered concentric tracks

pistolet *m* **à dessin** french curve (stencil); ~ **à wrapper** wire-wrap tool

piston *m* plunger key; piston; ~ **à contact** contact plunger

pistonphone *m* pistonphone

pivotant *adj* swing-out; swivelling; hinged

PJ (v. pièce jointe)

placage *m* flush-mounting; seating

placard *m* closet; cubicle

place *f* space; room (in memory); area; ~ **libre** free space; ~ **mémoire** storage space

placer *v* fetch

plafonnier *m* overhead light; ceiling light

plage *f* band; range; span; sweep; scale;

region; swing; ~ **d'accord** tuning range; ~ **d'admission** modulation range; control range; ~ **d'asservissement** output frequency (of crystal oscillator); ~ **de blocage** cut-off region; ~ **de blocage de la diode** diode cut-off region; ~ **de capture** pull-in range (of PLL); ~ **de fonctionnement** working range; ~ **de lecture** reading range/band; ~ **de maintien** hold-in range (of PLL); ~ **de masse** earth plane; ~ **de régulation** fade margin; ~ **de relèvement** swing; ~ **d'entraînement** pulling range; ~ **d'erreurs** error range; ~ **d'insensibilité** dead band; ~ **d'inversion de courant** commutation zone; ~ **d'orientation** orientation range; swing; ~ **droite/inclinée** straight/inclined terminal tag; plate

plaider en faveur (de) promote; foster

plan *m* approach; drawing; scheme; plane; plan; field; level; layout; diagram; ~ *adj* linear; flat; plane; level; flush; ~ **à séquence immuable** fixed-sequence automation device; ~ **d'acheminement** routing plan; ~ **d'affectation** allocation scheme; ~ **d'alimentation** power supply plane; ~ **d'aménagement** floor layout; ~ **d'appui** bearing surface; support plane; ~ **de blocage** blocking plan; ~ **de câblage** wiring plane; from-to list; ~ **de calcul** flow diagram; flow chart; ~ **de déviation** deflection plane; ~ **de groupe** trunking diagram; ~ **de masse** earth plane; ~ **de numérotage** numbering plan; numbering scheme; ~ **de numérotage coordonné** linked numbering scheme/plan; ~ **de numérotage fermé** fixed-length (closed) numbering plan; ~ **de numérotage intégré** integrated numbering plan; ~ **de numérotage national** national numbering plan; ~ **de numérotation** numbering plan; numbering scheme; ~ **de numérotation fermé** fixed-length (closed) numbering plan; ~ **de numérotation international** international numbering plan; ~ **de numérotation national** national numbering plan; ~ **de numérotation ouverte** open numbering plan; variable-length numbering plan; ~ **de perçage** hole layout (drawing); ~ **de polarisation** plane of polarization; ~ **de pose** seating plane; ~ **de présentation** detail drawing; ~ **de sol** ground plane; ~ **de taxation** charging plan; ~ **de tension** voltage plane; ~ **de tores** core plane/matrix; ~ **de transmission** transmission plan; ~ **d'échantillonnage** sampling plan; ~ **d'équipement** equipment layout drawing; ~ **d'équivalence composant** interchangeability list; ~ **des planches à peigne** cable harness layout drawing;

~ **directeur** master plan; master drawing; strategic development plan; ~ **du fond** underside; ~ **du réseau** exchange area layout; ~ **graphique** (graphics) bit plane; ~ **mémoire** memory plane; ~ **qualité** quality control plan; ~ **unifilaire** single-line diagram; ~ **zéro** zero plan (null attenuation)

planage *m* dwell time

planche *f* sheet; folio; diagram (figure); board; ~ **à câbler** wiring board; ~ **à clous** peg board; bed-of-nails; ~ **à dessin** drawing board; ~ **de bord** instrument panel; head-up display

planchette *f* **de bornes** terminal block; terminal strip; ~ **lumineuse** light box

planéité *f* flatness; seating

planificateur *m* scheduler; (network) planner

planification *f* scheduling; planning; ~ **des réseaux** network planning

planifieur *m* scheduler

planning *m* schedule; time-table

plantage *m* stall(ing); crash dump

planter *v* crash; blow (of system); stall

plaquage *m* conductive foil; plating

plaque *f* plate; strip; panel; board; label; anode; ~ **à oxyde rapporté** pasted plate (of battery); ~ **anti-bourrage** joggle plate; ~ **antimaculage** mackle plate; ~ **collectrice** signal electrode; signal plate; ~ **cuivrée** copper-clad board; ~ **d'adaptation** adaptor plate; matching plate; adaptor dial; ~ **d'agrément** PTT approval plate; licence plate; ~ **d'assise** base plate; plinth; pattress; sole plate; ~ **de balayage** deflecting plate; ~ **de base** base plate; plinth; sole plate; pattress; ~ **de chauffe** heating plate; ~ **de circuit imprimé** printed circuit board; ~ **de constitution de baie** rack equipment label; ~ **de constructeur** manufacturer's name-plate; ~ **de déviation** baffle plate; deflector; ~ **de fermeture** end plate; ~ **de fond** back plate; plinth; pattress; ~ **de percussion** striker plate; ~ **de raccordement des terres** earthing plate; ~ **de relais** relay strip; ~ **de terre** earth plate; ~ **d'étude** strip-board ("Veroboard": T.N.); ~ **d'identification** badge; name plate; ~ **d'obturation** blanking plate; blanking panel; ~ **Faure** pasted plate; Faure plate; ~ **Planté** formed plate; Planté plate; ~ **postiche** blanking panel; ~ **présensibilisée** photo-resist copper-clad (epoxy glass) board; ~ **signalétique** rating plate; ~ **stratifiée** base (material); laminated base board; ~ **support** (= platine) mounting plate; panel; board; card; strip; pattress; back plate; ~ **tournante** turntable; swivel stand

plaqué *adj* in contact with; flat against; flush-mounted; seated; ~ (= métallisé) through-hole plated

plaquette *f* PCB (printed circuit board); card; slice; strip; wafer; brochure; pamphlet; stirrup (of fuse-carrier); plate; ~ **à cosses** tag strip; lug connection strip; ~ **compensatrice** adaptor plate; ~ **d'alumine** alumina blade; ~ **de connexion** fanning strip; connecting block; terminal board; ~ **gaufrée** wafer; ~ **imprimée** printed circuit board; ~ **micro-élément** wafer

plastique *adj* plastic effect

plastron *m* enclosure; protective casing; shell (of switch); front panel

plasturgie *f* plastic enclosure

plat *adj* low-profile; flat-bed; shallow

plateau *m* pedestal; platter (of disk pack); ~ **de potentiel** potential plateau; ~ **partagé** split platen; ~ **récepteur papier** forms stacker; ~ **rotatif** indexing table; "Lazy Susan" (component mounting stand); ~ **roulant** platform truck; ~ **tournant** turntable (of aerial)

plate-forme *f* stillage; pallet; ~ **d'antenne stabilisée** stabilized aerial platform; ~ **d'intégration** test bed; in-plant testing; ~ **technologique** technological infrastructure (mainframe, microcomputers, etc.)

platine *f* unit; stage; mounting plate; board; card; chassis; mother board (PCB); (outer) pole-piece; strip; base-plate; panel; deck; disk drive; control panel; bed; platinum; ~ **d'assemblage** (fibre) organizer; ~ **de bouchement** blanking plate; blanking panel; ~ **de fixation** mounting plate; ~ **d'insertion** insert (of PCB); ~ **disquette** disk drive; ~ **porte-objet** stage plate (of microscope)

plein *m* mark (of dial plate); ~ *adj* full; maximum; complete; unperforated; solid

pleine échelle (PE) full-scale deflection (FSD)

plénum *m* canopy; platform

plésiochrone *adj* plesiochronous

pleurage *m* wow (of radio); flutter (of tape)

Plexiglas *m* acrylic sheet; thermoplastic acrylic resin; polymethyl methacrylate; Plexiglas; Altuglas; Lucite; Perspex [T.N.]; ~ **fumé** tinted acrylic

pliage *m* (du spectre de fréquences) aliasing error; fold-over distortion

plié en accordéon fan-fold; ammunition-pack (storage)

plinthe *f* base board; plinth; skirting board

pliure *f* bend(ing)

plot *m* contact; stud; terminal; tapping; hub; collector; pad; ~ **à fourches** spade lug; spade terminal; ~ **de contact** bonding pad;

~ **élastique** (resilient) isolating block

PLSD (v. prise de ligne sans déchrochage)

pluie *f* **saline** salt spray

pluri-annuel long-term; multi-annual

plus et moins-values dividends; ~ **ou moins** to a certain degree; relatively

plus-value(s) cost increase; capital gains; yield; profit margin

PM (v. panneau de mutation); ~ (v. pièce montée); ~ (v. présence message); ~ (v. point milieu); ~ (v. position manuelle); ~ (v. pour mémoire); ~ (v. prise médiane)

PML (v. parcours moyen libre)

PMMA (Altuglas) [A.C.] polymethyl methacrylate; acrylic resin

PO (v. petites ondes); ~ (v. poste opérateur)

po (pouce) inch (in.)

pochette *f* pack; packet; sleeve (of disk)

poids *m* weight(ing); significance; clout; ~ **atomique** atomic weight; ~ **d'adresse** address bit; address bus; ~ **faible (pf)** underflow; low-order; trailing; least significant bit (LSB); rightmost; ~ **fort (pF)** most significant bit (MSB); high-order; leading; leftmost; ~ **linéaire d'un câble** weight per unit length (of conductor); ~ **moléculaire** molecular weight; ~ **psophométrique** psophometric weight

poignard *m* **de test** test probe; prod

poignée *f* haft; handle; knob; grip; stem

poinçonnage *m* punching

poinçonneuse *f* punching pin; punch knife

point *m* point; pin; tapping; tag; fix (radio); count (logic); tip; spot; setting; dot; position; contact; way (of multiple conductor cable); terminal; full stop; period; subsection (of clause); ~ **à point** point-to-point; pin-to-pin; ~ **acnodal** conjugate point; ~ **brusque de trafic** traffic surge; ~ **chaud** live part; ~ **d'accès** port; gateway; inlet; outlet; entry point; access point; log-in point; ~ **d'accès à un circuit** circuit access point; inlet; port; ~ **d'accès à une ligne** line access point; ~ **d'accumulation** bottleneck; ~ **d'alarme** hot spot; ~ **d'alimentation décalé** displaced feed point; ~ **d'amorçage** singing point; ~ **d'amorçage actif** active singing point; ~ **d'amorçage des oscillations** singing point; ~ **d'amorçage passif** passive singing point; ~ **d'appui** fulcrum; pivot; bearing position; ~ **d'arrêt** break-point; cut-off; ~ **d'arrêt conditionnel** conditional breakpoint; ~ **de basculement** triggering level; ~ **de branchement** branchpoint; fork; ~ **de cassure** breakpoint (of rectifier diode); ~ **de commutation** switching point; ~ **de commutation à quatre fils** four-wire switching point; ~ **de commuta-**

tion de Jonction interface switching point; ~ **de concentration (PC)** distribution point; ~ **de conduite** written space; leader dot; linking space; ~ **de connexion (PCX)** crosspoint; pin; ~ **de consigne (PC)** set point; set value; ~ **de contrôle** control point; control value; trip setting; test point; check point; test pin; ~ **de croisement** crosspoint; ~ **de croisement scellé** reed crosspoint; ~ **de détection** operating point; quiescent bias point; ~ **de division** split point; ~ **de fonctionnement** quiescent bias point; operating point; ~ **de goutte** drop point; ~ **de mesure** measuring point; measurement position; ~ **de niveau relatif zéro** zero transmission level point; zero (relative level) point; ~ **de passage** walk-through; ~ **de passage par zéro** zero (relative level) point; ~ **de réference pour la transmission** transmission reference point; ~ **de repère** benchmark; ~ **de répétition** repeater point; ~ **de réponse spécifiée** explicit return point; ~ **de reportage extérieur** outside broadcast (OB) point; ~ **de repos** quiescent point; ~ **de reprise** checkpoint; restart point; return point; re-entry point; rescue point; ~ **de retour** re-entry point; rescue point; ~ **de rosée** dew point; ~ **de rupture** break-point; ~ **de sortie** output point; ~ **de soudure** blob; welding bulge; ~ **de test** scan point; test pin; ~ **de transfert de signaux** signal transfer point (STP); ~ **de transfert sémaphore (PTS)** signalling transfer point (STP); ~ **de transformation** transformer point; ~ **de transit** transit point; ~ **de vente** point of sale (POS); ~ **d'éclair** flashpoint; ~ **d'entrée** input; inlet; entry point; port; ~ **d'équilibrage** balance point; null point; ~ **d'équilibre** null point; ~ **d'examination** sample; ~ **d'image** picture element; pixel; pel; ~ **d'impact** discontinuity; ~ **d'inflexion** turn-over point; ~ **d'injection** sprue (of moulding); ~ **d'intensité** inrush current; current peak; ~ **d'interconnexion** interconnect point; ~ **éclair** flash-point; ~ **fictif** hypothetical (reference) point; ~ **figuratif** state point; ~ **graphique** pixel (pel); picture element; ~ **interruptible** interrupt point; authorized break-point; ~ **milieu (PM)** centre tap (CT); ~ **morse** Morse dot; ~ **mort** dead centre; idling position; neutral; aural null; ~ **neutre** neutral; ~ **nodal** node; ~ **sémaphore (PS)** signalling point (SP); ~ **terminal** terminal

pointage *m* training; tracking; plotting; aiming; itemization; poking; loading (to known address); steering; pointing; select-

ing; ~ **automatique** angle tracking; automatic aiming; ~ **d'une case du segment menu** selecting menu option; addressing menu pocket; ~ **fin** fine steering accuracy; ~ **vrai** true plot

pointant sur addressed to; selecting

pointe *f* peak value; spike (of pulse); surge; tip; power/supply point; stylus; probe; scriber; transient; glitch; pin; stud; ~ **à câbler** stud; forming peg; ~ **à tracer** scriber; ~ **brusque de trafic** traffic surge; ~ **carrée** bradawl; ~ **conique** taper pin; ~ **de charge** peak load; ~ **de commutation** switching spike; glitch; ~ **de démarrage** starting peak; ~ **de dépassement inférieur** peak undershoot; ~ **de fiche** tip (of jack); ~ **de lecture** pick-up stylus; ~ **de puissance vocale** peak speech power; ~ **de temporisation de garde** hold time-out; ~ **de touche** test prod; ~ **d'intensité** inrush current; current peak; ~ **du jack** tip of jack; ~ **longue** long-reach test prod; ~ **transitoire** spike

pointé *adj* current; selected; addressed

pointeau *m* centre-punch

pointeur *m* pointer; link address; return address; ~ **à coordonnées** X-Y plotter; ~ **de cellules** cell pointer; ~ **de chaînage** link pointer; return address; ~ **de pages** page pointer; ~ **de piles** stack pointer; ~ **de remplissage** queue-loading pointer; ~ **de vidage** queue-unloading pointer; ~ **d'instructions** instruction pointer (IP)

pointillé *m* dotted (line)

point-mémoire bit; latch (one-bit storage device)

points de suspension ellipsis; ~ **et traits** dots and dashes; ~ **forts et points faibles** pros and cons; ~ **sémaphores adjacents** adjacent signalling points

poire *f* switch (floating cable pushbutton type)

polarisation *f* bias; polarization; soak (of dielectric); reference supply; ~ **automatique (de grille)** automatic grid bias; ~ **circulaire droite** right-hand circular polarization; ~ **circulaire gauche** left-hand circular polarization; ~ **croisée** cross-polarization (XPOLAR); ~ **de coupure** grid bias; cut-off bias; ~ **de grille** grid bias; ~ **d'entrée** input bias; ~ **diélectrique** dielectric soak; soakage; ~ **directe** forward bias; ~ **en courant continu** direct current (DC) biasing; ~ **inverse** reverse bias; back bias; ~ **négative** negative bias; back bias; ~ **principale** nominal polarization; ~ **rectiligne** linear polarization

polarisé *adj* biased; polarized; directional; ~ **en inverse** back-biased

polarité f polarity; ~ **A** A polarity; ~ **d'arrêt** stop polarity; ~ **de départ** start polarity; ~ **Z** Z polarity

pôle m pole; gateway; way (of multicore cable); pin (of connector); node; ~ **de commutation** commutating pole; ~ **magnétique** magnetic pole; ~ **négatif** negative pole; ~ **positif** positive pole; ~ **saillant** salient pole

police f (type) font; character set/repertoire

police-secours (code 17 en France) police and ambulance services

polisseuse f buffing machine

politique d'acheminement traffic routing strategy

pollution f corrupt(ion); contamination; mutilation; ~ **d'orbite** orbit pollution

polychloroprène m Neoprene [T.N.]

polychlorure de vinyle (PCV) polyvinyl chloride (PVC)

polychrome adj colour

polyéthylène m polythene; polyethylene

polyfluorure de vinylidène (PVF2) polyvinylidene fluoride; Kynar [T.N.]

polynôme m **câblé** fixed polynomial; ~ **de base** primitive polynomial

polyode f multi-electrode valve

polyplexeur m multiplexer

polysème m plurivalent term

polystyrène m **expansé** expanded polystyrene

polytechnique adj multidisciplinary

polytéréphtalate d'éthylène polyethylene terephthalate (PETP)

polyuréthane alvéolé cellular polyurethane

polyvalence f non-specialization; broad-based skills

polyvalent adj versatile; multi-purpose; many-valued; general-purpose; universal; common; interdisciplinary

POM (polyoxyméthylène) polyformaldehyde; polyacetal

pompage m hunting (of control system); squegging

pompe f **à dessouder** de-soldering pump

pompiers (code 18 en France) fire service

ponctuel adj concentrated; individual; localized; pinpoint; local; peak-hour; one-time

pondérateur adj weight (coefficient)

pondération f weighting

pondéré adj weighted; positional; adjusted; corrected

pondeuse f call-testing device; load box

pont m bridge; traverse; jumper; strap; array; crossover; network; lattice; span; inverse; stack; reciprocal; link; rear axle; long weekend; ~ **aérien** airlift; ~ **alternatif** AC bridge; ~ **bascule** weighing machine; ~ **conducteur** conducting bridge; ~ **d'ali-**mentation supply bridge; transmission bridge; feed bridge; battery supply; power pack; ~ **de conversation** link circuit; connection circuit; ~ **de diodes** diode bridge; diode array; ~ **de mesure** measuring bridge; test circuit; ~ **de modulation** modulation bridge; ~ **de puissance** thyristor stack; power pack; ~ **de rapport de transformation** inverse (reciprocal) of turns ratio; ~ **de redresseurs** bridge rectifier; ~ **de résistance** resistance bridge; ~ **de transmission** transmission bridge; ~ **de Wheatstone** Wheatstone bridge; ~ **différentiel** differential bridge; ~ **d'impédance** impedance bridge; ~ **diviseur** bridge/lattice network; section; voltage divider bridge; crossover network; ~ **Kelvin** Kelvin bridge; ~ **local** link/bridge circuit; power feed bridge; ~ **magnétique** magnetic bridge; ~ **mixte** (series) bridge network; ~ **redresseur** rectifier bridge; ~ **roulant** travelling (overhead) crane

pontage m strapping; shunt; by-pass

ponter v by-pass; insert jumper; strap

pontet m bridge; (cable-fixing) saddle; (wiring) cleat; strap; sweep lock-out; mounting bracket; rail

pool m (de machines) cluster; bank; ~ **commun** compool; common pool (of symbolic values); ~ **des libellés** literal pool

portabilité f (d'un programme) portability

portage m porting

portatif adj portable; back-pack

porte f gate (element); port; door; hatch; ~ **analogique** analogue gate; ~ **d'accès** gateway; ~ **de visite** inspection hatch; ~ **de voie** channel gate; ~ **d'échantillonnage** sampling gate; ~ **ET** AND gate; ~ **fermée** closed-shop; limited access; hands-off; ~ **interdiction** inhibit gate; ~ **logique** logic gate; switching gate; ~ **logique rapide** high-speed logic gate; ~ **NI** NOR gate; ~ **NON** NOT gate; ~ **NON-ET** NAND gate; ~ **OU** OR gate; ~ **ouverte** open-shop; unlimited access; ~ **passante** active scan point; ~ **silencieux** squelch; ~ **tri-état** tri-state port; three-state port

porté à la connaissance disclosed; declared

porte-balais m brush holder

porte-cartouche (PC) m fuse-carrier; electrical point; mains outlet; socket

porte-copies m copy-holder; lectern

portée f scope; range; reach; seating; haul; span; ~ **de charbon** (carbon) brush bearing/seating; ~ **diurne** day range; daylight service range; ~ **du poste fixe** talk-out range; ~ **du poste mobile** talk-back range; ~ **du relèvement** direction-finding

P

range; ~ **mininale** minimum range; ~ **no-minale** nominal range; ~ **zéro** zero range

porte-embout *m* **magnétique** bit holder

porte-étiquette (PE) *m* label-holder

porte-fusible (PF) *m* fuse-carrier; fuse-holder

porte-molette *m* knurling tool

porte-objet *m* stage (of microscope)

porter *v* enter; set; carry; ~ **au niveau bas** set low

porte-stylo *m* pen stall (of graph recorder)

porteur *m* (charge) carrier (of semiconductor); bearer; card-holder; ~ *adj* enterprising; promising; auspicious; propitious; profitable; lucrative; ~ **dérivé** derived carrier; ~ **électrisé** charged particle carrier; ~ **majoritaire** majority carrier; ~ **métallique** metal strength member; ~ **minoritaire** minority carrier

porteuse (fréquence p.) carrier (frequency); ~ (onde p.) carrier (wave); ~ *f* **àmodulation par la parole** voice-controlled carrier (VCC); ~ **à niveau réduit** reduced-level carrier; ~ **à suppression partielle** partially-suppressed carrier; ~ **commutée** controlled carrier; ~ **complète** full carrier; ~ **constante** steady carrier; ~ **de canal** channel carrier; ~ **de données** data carrier; ~ **de groupe** group carrier; ~ **de groupe secondaire** supergroup carrier; ~ **de modulation** modulation carrier; ~ **décalée** offset carrier; ~ **interrompue dans les silences** quiescent carrier; ~ **modulée** modulated carrier; ~ **modulée par le pseudo-bruit** pseudo-noise carrier; ~ **modulée par une fréquence vocale** voice-modulated carrier; ~ **monovoie** (à) single-channel-per-carrier; ~ **non modulée** unmodulated carrier; ~ **optique** optical carrier wave; ~ **permanente** continuous carrier; ~ **pilote** pilot carrier; ~ **principale** main carrier; ~ **réduite** reduced carrier; ~ **renforcée** exalted carrier; ~ **secondaire** secondary carrier; ~ **supprimée** suppressed carrier; ~ **zéro** zero carrier

porte-voix *m* loudspeaker; ~ **à amplification électrique** public address; PA system

portier *m* port; ~ **CAG** AGC killer; ~ **électronique** electronic door-answering system; janitor

portillon *m* gate; gate circuit

portillonnage *m* gating

portique *m* gantry; frame

pose *f* installation; attachment; application; mounting; fixture; lay; fitting; setting; ~ **de tabulation** horizontal tabulation set (HTS); ~ **d'épargne** masking

posé au soudage welded on; soldered on

poser *v* affix; lay; apply; position; set; table

(of motion); ~ **une question** raise a question; ask/put a question; query

positif *adj* positive; substantive

position *f* (telegraph) set; position; station; desk; setting; location; situation; status; (lamp) field; order turret; console; ~ **alternatif** (AC) mains setting; ~ **automatisée de téléphoniste** traffic operator position system (TOPS); ~ **auxiliaire** stand-by position; ~ **aveugle** blind operator position; ~ **binaire** bit location; binary position; ~ **d'annotation** booking position; ~ **d'annotatrice** trunk-record position; ~ **d'appel** calling position; ~ **d'arrivée** incoming position; B-position; ~ **de communication inter-réseaux** joint trunk position; inter-exchange trunk position; ~ **de concentration** calling concentrator; ~ **de contrôle du trafic téléphonique international** international control station; ~ **de conversation** speech position; ~ **de départ** outgoing position; A-position; ~ **de file** queue place; ~ **de la radioborne extérieure** outer marker site; ~ **de nuit** night position; ~ **de réclamations** complaints desk; customer enquiries; ~ **de repos** off position; idle position; ~ **de repos anormale** off-normal rest position; ~ **de rotation jusqu'au bout de course** overflow position; ~ **de surveillante** supervisor position; ~ **de trafic** traffic position; ~ **de transit** transit position; ~ **de transmission de groupes secondaires** supergroup allocation; ~ **de travail** on-position; ~ **d'écoute** listening position; ~ **des télégrammes téléphonés** phonogram position; ~ **d'essais** test desk; ~ **d'inscription** trunk-record position; ~ **d'intensité maximale** position of maximum signal; ~ **directrice** controlling position; ~ **dirigeuse** operator position; console; turret; ~ **d'opératrice** operator position; ~ **d'un élement de signal** digit position; ~ **d'un élement numérique** digit position; ~ **fantôme** limbo position (column 81 of data line); ~ **initiale** home position; ~ **interurbaine** toll board; trunk board; ~ **interurbaine de départ** outward toll board; ~ **manuelle (PM)** manual position; operator position; ~ **mixte d'inscription et de départ** (position A) A-position; A-board; ~ **occupée** occupied position; ~ **pour exploitation sans attente** demand position; ~ **repos** home (of cursor); ~ **sans fiches ni cordons** cordless position; ~ **télégraphique** telegraph position

positionnement *m* positioning; setting; status; configuration; state; programming; ~ **absolu du curseur** horizontal and vertical absolute position (HVP); ~ **du préfixe fichier** set file prefix; ~ **en 1/0** setting (of bit) to (state) 1 or 0; ~ **sur eb** bit state; bit pattern

positionner *v* position; set; configure; program; ~ (un événement) set (of event); ~ **dans le temps** synchronize

positionneur *m* locator; directional control valve

positon *m* positron; positive electron

possession *f* **de l'écran** device ownership

possibilité(s) *f* possibility; capability; facility; menu; feature; option; contingency; alternate; configuration

possibilité d'entrer en tiers preference facility; override feature

possibilités de discrimination grading facilities

possible *adj* incidental; contingent; ready

post-accélération *f* post-deflection acceleration

postage *m* mailing

postambule *m* postamble

poste *m* extension; station; telephone set; console; position; desk; subset; entry; item; (order) turret (of PABX); situation (of employment); ~ **à appel direct de l'opératrice** direct operator signalling station; ~ **à appel individuel** direct operator signalling station; VIP executive station; ~ **à authentification** coded-access extension; ~ **à cadran** dial telephone (set); ~ **à clavier** keypad telephone set; pushbutton set; ~ **à clavier bidirectionnelle** pushbutton telephone; ~ **à clavier multifréquence** touchtone telephone; DTMF set; ~ **à correspondant unique (PCU)** hot-line station; ~ **à correspondant unique différé (PCUD)** deferred hotline station; ~ **à correspondant unique immédiat (PCUI)** immediate hotline station; ~ **à poste** point-to-point; station-to-station; ~ **à pourvoir** situation vacant; ~ **à prépaiement** public callbox; coin box; coin station; public pay station; ~ **à prise directe** unrestricted station/extension; direct-dialling extension; ~ **à prise directe intégrale** unrestricted direct-dialling extension; ~ **à prise directe libre** unrestricted extension; ~ **à prise directe restreinte** toll restricted station; locally-unrestricted extension; ~ **à réception amplifiée** loudspeaking telephone; ~ **à sélection directe** hot-line telephone; ~ **à socle** table model telephone set; ~ **abaisseur** step-down station; ~ **asservi** substation; ~ **central** operator station; attendant console; ~ **central de commande** central control position; ~ **central de contrôle** central monitoring position (CMP); ~ **coactif** cluster (work-)station;

~ **collecteur** collecting office; ~ **contrôlé** semi-restricted extension/station; fully-restricted extension; ~ **d'abonné** outstation; subscriber station/set; ~ **d'abonné filtré** manager extension; ~ **d'affaires** business telephone; ~ **d'agent** operator station; operator position; ~ **d'appel** callbox; ~ **de cerclage** binding station; ~ **de contrôle (pc)** observation post; test position; station; ~ **de débordement** least-cost routing station; ~ **de données** data set; ~ **de filtrage** manager-secretary station; ~ **de ligne partagée** party line extension; ~ **de pilotage** cockpit; flight deck; ~ **de pointage** reporting station (of nightwatchman service); ~ **de renvoi ANA** (assigned night answer) station; ~ **de saisie** input terminal; ~ **de service** service extension; attendant console; operator station; ~ **de servitude** duty extension; ~ **de soudure** welding set; ~ **de test** test station; ~ **de travail** operator terminal; work station; ~ **de travail protégé** safe workstation; ~ **décimal** rotary dial telephone; ~ **d'écoute** intercept station; monitoring post; ~ **d'indexation** postal coding desk; ~ **d'intercommunication** key telephone system (KTS); ~ **d'intérieur** decorator set (of telephone); ~ **directeur-secrétaire** manager-and-secretary station; ~ **dirigeur** operator station; attendant console; ~ **discriminé** restricted-access station; ~ **d'opératrice** operator console; operator's telephone set; ~ **d'usager** station user; ~ **élévateur** step-up station; ~ **émetteur** transmitting station; broadcasting station; ~ **émetteur d'amateur** amateur transmitter; ~ **émetteur-récepteur** transceiver; ~ **en attente** station camped-on; camp-on extension; ~ **en sonnerie** ringing extension; ~ **étanche** weatherproof telephone; watertight installation; ~ **extérieur** outstation; ~ **filtrant** secretary station; ~ **filtré** manager station; ~ **filtreur** secretary station; ~ **individuel** stand-alone workstation; ~ **intérieur** extension; station; ~ **interne** extension; station; ~ **mains libres** hands-free set; ~ **mobile** desk-top telephone set; ~ **mobile de contrôle de radar** mobile radar control post; ~ **multiligne** multi-line extension; ~ **mural** wall telephone set; ~ **opérateur (PO)** operator position (OP); attendant's desk; operator console; order turret; ~ **phototélégraphique** phototelegraph station; ~ **prédéterminé** transfer extension; ~ **prêt pour données** ready for data; ~ **principal** master set; main station; ~ **principal d'abonné** main subscriber station; ~ **prioritaire** executive override station; right-of-way station; priority extension/station; ~ **privé** fully-restricted extension; ~ **privilégié** direct operator signalling station; ~ **relais** repeater station; ~ **renvoyé** call-forwarding extension; ~ **répétiteur** repeater station (remote monitoring); ~ **serveur** server workstation; ~ **superprivilégié** executive station with direct operator signalling; VIP executive station; ~ **supplémentaire (PS)** extension telephone; extension station; PABX station; out-station; ~ **supplémentaire avec prise directe du réseau** (public) direct-dialling extension; ~ **supplémentaire avec prise contrôlée du réseau** (public) partially-restricted extension; ~ **supplémentaire contrôlé** semi-restricted extension/station; ~ **surveillé** semi-restricted extension/station; ~ **télégraphique** telegraph station; telegraph position; ~ **téléphone public** public telephone; ~ **téléphonique** telephone station; extension; subscriber station; telephone set; console; ~ **téléphonique à appel magnétique** magneto telephone set; hand-ringing set; ~ **téléphonique à cadran** dial telephone set; ~ **téléphonique à clavier** key (pushbutton) telephone set; ~ **téléphonique à haut-parleur** loudspeaker telephone set; ~ **téléphonique d'abonné** subscriber station; telephone station; subset; ~ **téléphonique de table** desk telephone set; ~ **téléphonique principal** subscriber main station; main station; ~ **téléphonique public** pay station; public telephone station; public call office; ~ **téléphonique supplémentaire** subscriber extension station; ~ **terminal** remote terminal; terminal equipment; ~ **unique** stand-alone workstation; ~ **usager** extension; station user

postfixer v retro-fit
postiche adj blank; dummy
postindexation f post-indexing
postluminescence f afterglow
post-synchronisé adj (sound-)dubbed
post-transformation retro-fit
pot (de ferrite) m (ferrite) pot core; ~ **carré** square pot-core assembly; ~ m **compensé** magnetic biasing; ~ **d'abonné** subscriber (line) transformer; ~ **(de ferrite) taillé** pot core with trimmed air-gap; ~ **de répéteur** repeater housing; chamber; ~ **de répétiteur** repeater housing; chamber; ~ **de soudure** solder pot; ~ **pour inductance** pot core
poteau m pole; stanchion; post; ~ **centrifuge** spun concrete pole (cable mast); ~ **électrique** telegraph pole; ~ **métallique** stanchion; ~ **téléphonique** telegraph pole

potelet m stanchion
potence f boom
potentiel m potential (difference); e.m.f.; voltage; ~ **de comparaison** reference potential; reference voltage; ~ **d'excitation** excitation potential; ~ **d'ionisation** ionization potential; electron-binding energy; radiation potential; ~ **électrique** electric potential; voltage; ~ **flottant** floating potential; ~ **magnétique** magnetomotive force (m.m.f.); magnetic potential
potentiomètre m potentiometer; ~ **à piste moulée** moulded-track potentiometer; ~ **ajustable à couche de carbone** carbon-track trimmer; preset trim potentiometer; ~ **bobiné** wire-wound potentiometer; ~ **bobine multitours** multiturn wire-wound potentiometer; ~ **d'affichage** setting potentiometer; ~ **d'ajustage** trim potentiometer; trim-pot; preset potentiometer; ~ **de compensation** balancing potentiometer
potentiomètre de concentration focussing pot
potentiomètre de lumière brightness (control) potentiometer; ~ **de réglage** trimmer; ~ **de réglage du gain** gain control potentiometer; ~ **(double) à curseur** dual-track slide potentiometer; ~ **graphite** carbon-track potentiometer; ~ **hélicoïdal** helipot; ~ **multitour** ganged potentiometer; ~ **rectiligne** linear potentiometer; slider pot; ~ **rotatif** (avec interrupteur) rotary potentiometer (with switch)
poubelle f garbage (collector)
poudrage m powder coating
poudre d'alliage molybdène-permalloy powdered molybdenum-permalloy
poulie f **folle** idler pulley; guide pulley
poupée f **mobile** moving tailstock
pour faciliter l'explication in the interests of clarity; ~ **mémoire (PM)** or similar; variable; memorandum (NB); typical; as required; non-contractual; ~ **ordre** under consideration; ~ **suite à donner** for further action; response; ~ **voir** tentative; prototype; for trial purposes
pourcent(age) m percent(age)
pourcentage m **de débordement** percentage overflow; ~ **de distorsion** harmonic content; ~ **de modulation** percentage modulation; ~ **de signe** marking percentage; ~ **des demandes satisfaites** percentage of effective-to-booked calls; per-cent completion; ~ **du temps de mise à la terre** earthing percentage; ~ **d'utilisation** cable loading; line load; cable fill
poursuite f tracking; ~ **automatique** automatic tracking; ~ **monopulse** monopulse tracking; ~ **pas à pas** step track

poursuivre *v* accomplish
pourtant *adv* admittedly; yet; all the same
pourtour *m* periphery
poussé *adj* sophisticated
poussée *f* thrust
pousseur *m* thrust arm; plunger; (component) pusher
poussoir *m* insertion tool; push-rod; pressure plate; ~ **à enclenchement** latching pushbutton; ~ **rivet** rivet clincher
poutre *f* rack
pouvant recevoir accommodating; catering for; hosting
pouvoir *m* power; rating; potential; capacity; strength; ~ **absorbant** absorbing power; ~ **agglomérant** bond strength; ~ **de coupure** (d'un contact) contact rating; ~ **de coupure** (d'un fusible) rated breaking capacity (of fuse); ~ **d'écoulement** current(-carrying) capacity; ~ **diélectrique** electric flux density; dielectric strain; electric displacement; ~ **électrique** electric flux density; displacement; dielectric strain; ~ **émissif d'une surface** emissivity; ~ **émissif spécifique d'une surface** specific emissivity; ~ **inducteur spécifique** (relative) permittivity; dielectric constant; specific inductive capacity; inductivity; ~ **réfléchissant** (absolute) reflectance; ~ **séparateur** resolution; discrimination; ~ **séparateur angulaire** angular resolution; ~ **séparateur de relèvement** (range) resolution; ~ **séparateur radial** range discrimination/ resolution
PPO polyphenylene oxide; Noryl [T.N.]
PQ (MCDU) (milliers-centaines-dizaines-unités) access code
pratiquement *adv* virtually; to all intents and purposes
préaccentuation *f* pre-emphasis
préaffichage *m* pre-setting; loading
préalable *adj* previous; prior; look-ahead; early; antecedent
préambule *m* (en p.) prelude; run-up (to); preamble
préamplificateur *m* pre-amplifier; head amplifier; ~ **d'antenne** aerial pre-amplifier
préamplification *f* pre-amplification; ~ **variable** variable gain
préanalyse *f* pre-analysis
préassignation *f* **fixe** fixed pre-assignment; ~ **variable dans le temps** time pre-assignment
précâblé *adj* pre-wired; ready-wired; factory-wired
précalculé *adj* (message) pre-stored
précambrage *m* clinching (of terminations)
précaractérisé *adj* semi-custom

précelles *f pl* tweezers
précession *f* **des électrons** electron spin
préchargeur *m* bootstrap routine
préchauffage *m* warm-up period
précis *adj* sharp; accurate; specific; precise
préciser *v* give a detailed account; specify; detail; stipulate; outline; define; prescribe
précision *f* accuracy; definition; resolution; ~ **de l'objet** terms of reference; ~ **de pointage** steering accuracy; ~ **relative** linearity error (of A-D converter); ~ **télémétrique** ranging accuracy
précoce *adj* early
précompensation d'écriture shift forward (SF)
précomptage *m* public telephone coin counting
préconcentrateur *m* pre-concentrator
préconditionnement *m* pre-selection; conditioning
préconisé *adj* recommended; specified
précontrainte *f* pre-stress
précorrection *f* pre-correction; pre-emphasis; ~ **de phase** phase pre-compensation
précoupleur *m* I/O controller
précurseur *m* herald; trend-setter; forerunner; pioneer
prédécoupage *m* perforations
prédécoupe *f* scribing; scoring
prédécoupé *adj* scored
prédéfini *adj* predetermined; preset
prédétermination *f* **du facteur d'échelle** fixed pre-scaling
prédéterminé *adj* preset; pre-arranged
prédéveloppement *m* advanced prototype production
prédicteur *m* **de retenue** carry look-ahead (generator)
prédiction *f* look-ahead
prédiffusé *adj* semi-custom
prédiffusion *f* circulated for preview
prédistortion *f* pre-distortion
prédivision *f* pre-scaling
prédomination *f* **vers le côté négatif** marking bias
pré-écriture avant sélection early write
pré-égalisation *f* pre-equalization
préemptible *adj* can be overridden
pré-enrobé *adj* resin-bonded; pre-preg
préétabli *adj* stored
préférentiel *adj* priority
préfigurer *v* foreshadow; pave the way for
préfixe *m* access code; prefix; ~ **d'accès** access code; ~ **de message** message prefix; prosign (precedence indicator); ~ **de prise** dialling code; trunk access code; ~ **de service** facility code; ~ **de surveillance de l'acheminement** route monitoring access code; ~ **d'inscription** (du renvoi tempo-

P

raire) (follow-me call forwarding) facility code; call-diversion code; ~ **international** international access code; ~ **interurbain** trunk access code

préforme *f* preform; boule

prégroupe *m* pre-group

préhenseur *m* automatic-tripping fuse-carrier

préhension *f* grip

préimpulsion *f* pre-knock pulse; pre-trigger pulse

préindustrialisation *f* production engineering

prélecture *f* (de vérification) read-back check

prélevé *adj* tapped; sampled; read; recorded; levied; debited; charged; fetched; picked up

prélèvement *m* sampling; separating; stealing; tapping; ~ (sur) fetching (data from memory); pick-up; pick-off; ~ **automatique** direct debiting; ~ **numérique** digital readout

prélever *v* fetch; sample; read; record; levy; steal; tap; measure

préliminaire *adj* draft (of manual); short-form

prémagnétisation *f* bias

prémarqué *adj* labelled

prématuré *adj* early; pre-emptive; inadvertent; forced

premier article de chaîne home record; first (production) article; ~ **assemblage du gainage** first cladding phase; ~ **entré, premier sorti** FIFO (first in, first out); ~ **nombre** prime number

première décharge de Townsend first Townsend discharge; ~ **frappe** initial draft; ~ **harmonique** fundamental harmonic; first harmonic

prendre *v* acquire; take; accept; select; ~ **en charge** service (of interrupt); write; accept; ~ **en compte** service; recognize; enable; validate; incorporate; ~ **un déroutement** take a trap; ~ **une commande** accept a call

preneur *m* **de son** technical operator

prenons par exemple consider

prépaiement *m* pre-payment; pay tone(s)

préparateur *m* initiator

préparer un circuit set up a circuit; rig; lay

préposé *m* operator; agent

prépositionner *v* set; preset

préprocesseur *m* **de signalisation** signalling pre-processor; front-end processor

préprogrammé *adj* preliminary schedule

préréglé *adj* preset; factory-adjusted

prérequis *m* prior qualifications; admission requirements

présager *v* herald

prescription *f* convention

présélecteur *m* access selector; pre-selector; subscriber uniselector; multi-switch

(thumbwheel switch)

présélection *f* presetting; pre-emption; pre-selection; dial-tone connection; line preference; ~ **automatique** prime-line preference; automatic selection

présélectionné *adj* preset; currently selected (of task)

présence *f* connection; attendance; access; installed; ~ **de fils** wire-connected lamp; ~ **de tonalité** tone present; ~ **message (PM)** message present (bit); ~ **porteuse** receiver ready (RR); carrier detect (CD)

présensibilisé *adj* sensitized

présent *adj* installed; resident; set (of bit); in-circuit; connected

présentation *f* aspects; design features; handshaking; basic features; display; overview; introduction; feed; format; layout; configuration; construction; finish; offering; conveyance (of goods); view; ~ **aéroportée de la situation du trafic** airborne traffic situation display; ~ **d'appel** call announcement (by operator); call offering; ~ **de formule** form feed; ~ **de l'instruction** training manual; ~ **générale** overview; outline specifications; ~ **numérique** digital display; numerical display; ~ **par instruments de mesure** meter display

présenté au rythme de clocked by

présenter *v* apply (of current); offer; feed; harbour; pose; constitute; exhibit; reveal; submit; hand over

présérie *adj* pre-production (advance prototype)

présignal *m* prefix; access code

presse à platine flat-bed press; ~ **flan** blanking press

presse-étoupe *f* cable gland; stuffing box; pressure seal; compression gland; coaxial plug

pressentir *v* anticipate; pre-empt

presseur *m* clamping plate; bail arm

pression *f* **acoustique** acoustic pressure; sound pressure; ~ **acoustique de la voix** electrical speech pressure/power; speech voltage; ~ **acoustique instantanée** instantaneous sound pressure; ~ **de refoulement** upset pressure (of welding); ~ **de touche** keystroke; ~ **du son** acoustic pressure; ~ **uniforme** (= contrainte) stress; pressure

pressostat *m* pressure controller

pressurisation *f* pressurization

pressurisé *adj* pressurized

prestataire *m* service and equipment supplier; service provider

prestation *f* workmanship

prestation(s) *f(pl)* services rendered; commitments; (package of) products and services

prêt *adj* ready; ~ (signal p.) request-to-send (signal) (RTS); ~ **à émettre** clear-to-send; ~ **á l'émploi** off-the-peg; ~ **bail** lend-lease
prétraitement *m* pre-processing; conditioning
prétraiter *v* pre-process
prévaloir *v* override
prévenir *v* anticipate; foresee; alert; plan
prévention *f* **de bruit** noise prevention
prévisible *adj* likely; expected; predicted; forecast
prévision *f* forecast; projection; plan; prediction; ~ **de la demande** demand forecasting; ~ **du réseau** network planning; ~ **ionosphérique** ionospheric prediction
prévisionnel *adj* projected; planned; forecast; predicted; expected
prévoir *v* install; plan; forecast; predict; make allowance for; provide; design; anticipate; envisage; set aside; intend; specify; arrange; write (in); earmark
prévu *adj* provided (for); designed; prospective; future; catered for; envisaged; due; built-on; expected; forecast; planned; predicted; anticipated; installed; projected; intended; scheduled; earmarked; ~ **pour l'èxtension à n étages** cascadable to n micro-words
primaire *adj* primary (winding); ~ **de transformateur** transformer primary
primitif *adj* virgin; original; source
primitive *f* processor interface macro-instruction; primitive routine; ~ **d'activation** call subroutine; primary source (origin) of fault; ~ **géométrique** geometric primitive; ~ **graphique** graphics primitive
primordial *adj* fundamental; elementary; of paramount importance; vital
principal *adj* host; master; main; dominant; chief; mainline
principe *m* philosophy; ~ **de réciprocité** reciprocity principle; ~ **d'exclusion de Pauli Fermi** Pauli Fermi principle
prioritaire *adj* foreground
priorité *f* override; right-of-way; foreground; ~ **d'arrivée** order of arrival (of messages); ~ **lente** low priority; ~ **tournante** cyclically
pris *adj* busied; ~ **dans** selected from; constructed from; ~ **en charge** contracted
prise *f* (female) socket; plug; connector; tap; tapping; busy; seizing; seizure (of line); power outlet; receptacle; supply point; busying; acquisition; ~ **d'air** air intake; ~ **d'appel** answer a call; pick-up; call selection; ~ **de commandes** order booking; ~ **de contact** handshaking; sign-on; ~ **de courant** connector; power socket; current outlet; receptacle; mains power point; ~ **de courant murale** wall socket; outlet;

~ **de données** data link connector; ~ **de liaison** link seizure; ~ **de ligne sans déchrochage (PLSD)** on-hook dialling; ~ **de masse** earth connection; earth plate; ~ **de pression** pressure connector; ~ **de réglage** adjustment tapping; ~ **de relais** shoulder tap (to standby processor); ~ **(de) secteur** convenience outlet; ~ **de son** studio operation; ~ **de terre** earthing system; earth connection/plate; ~ **de terre élémentaire** earthing conductor; ~ **de test** (plug-in) test bush; test receptacle; test point; test terminal; ~ **de vue** shooting; snapshot; photography; imagery; exposure; remote terrain sensing; ~ **de vue multispectrale** multi-spectral imagery; multi-spectral photography; ~ **de vue panchromatique** panchromatic photography; ~ **d'enregistreur** register assignment (to a call); ~ **d'essai** test point; ~ **directe** direct (trunk) access; direct outward dialling (DOD); part-restricted; ~ **directe contrôlée** through-dialling; ~ **directe libre** unrestricted; ~ **directe urbaine** local direct trunk access; direct outward dialling (DOD); ~ **en charge** accepting; servicing; writing; handling; ~ **en compte** servicing; obeying; enabling; handling; detection; monitoring; observation; response; ~ **fixe** receptacle; socket; chassis socket/plug; ~ **inefficace** unsuccessful seizure; ~ **initiale** pre-emption; ~ **intermédiaire** tap (of delay line); ~ **largable** lanyard-release plug; ~ **mâle** socket; ~ **médiane (PM)** centre tap (CT); ~ **mobile** plug; flying connector; plug-ended cable; ~ **mobile roulante** trailing socket; ~ **optique d'appartement (PA)** optical entrance unit; ~ **par établissement d'un boucle** loop start; ~ **par mise d'une terre sur un fil** ground start; earthing connection; earth calling; ~ **péritélévision SCART** SCART (single-channel asynchronous receiver/transmitter) TV peripheral connector; ~ **pour antenne** aerial connection socket; ~ **rapide** spring-loaded connector block; ~ **sabot** collector; sliding contact; ~ **secteur** mains outlet; mains supply socket; ~ **simultanée** double seizure; ~ **sur une bobine** coil tap; ~ **vampire** insulation displacement connector (IDC)
privative *adj* exclusive
privé *adj* exclusive; leased; private
privilégié *adj* privileged; protected; reserved; exclusive; high-ranking; priority; VIP
prix *m* **brut** wholesale price; ~ **de revient** prime cost
probabilité *f* probability; likelihood; ~ **conditionnelle** conditional probability; ~ **d'at-**

tente waiting probability; ~ **de blocage** blocking probability; ~ **de choc** probability of collision; ~ **de perte** grade of service; lost-call probability; ~ **de signal** signal probability; ~ **de transition** transition probability; ~ **d'échec** lost-call probability; ~ **d'erreur** error probability; ~ **d'être occupé** busy probability; ~ **d'ionisation** ionization probability

problématique *adj* problem area

problème *m* **d'exclusion** exclusion problem

procédé *m* **de transparence électronique** overlay; ~ **itératif** iterative procedure; ~ **photomultiplication** step-and-repeat process; ~ **physique** material process; ~ **stochastique** stochastic process

procédure *f* action; procedure; protocol; sub-routine; formality; ~ **asservie** compelled-signalling protocol; ~ **d'abandon** abort procedure; ~ **d'appel-réponse** handshaking protocol; sign-on procedure; ~ **de chargement initial** bootstrap routine; ~ **de commande à haut niveau** high-level data link control procedure (HDLC); ~ **de commande d'appel** call control procedure; ~ **de commande de chaînon** (de données) high-level data link control procedure (HDLC); ~ **de liaison** link protocol; link control procedure; ~ **de ligne** line (control) procedure; link protocol; ~ **de réapprentissage** training pattern; ~ **de reprise** back-up procedure; restart procedure; ~ **de transmission** link control procedure; ~ **d'échange** handshaking protocol; sign-on; ~ **d'initialisation de chargement** bootstrap loader; ~ **objet** object procedure; ~ **réseau** network protocol

processeur *m* processor; ~ **central** main processor; ~ **de dépouillement** interpretive processor; ~ **de gestion** administrative processor; ~ **file** single-stream processor; ~ **frontal** front-end processor; ~ **principal** main processor; ~ **répartie** distributed processor (assembly-disassembly) (PAD)

processus *m* process

procès-verbal (PV) *m* minutes; report; ~ **de réception** final acceptance certificate

proche *adj* prevailing; approximate; near; ~ **infrarouge** near-infrared

procurer *v* acquire; obtain; buy-in; requisition

producteur *m* data-base producer; ~ **de base de données** data base producer; ~ **de données** information provider; data-base producer; ~ **d'harmoniques** harmonic generator

production de porteurs carrier supply; ~ **des cames** timing-signal generation; ~ *f* **d'oscillations propres non désirées** squitter

productique *f* production engineering; computer(-integrated) production

produit(s) *m* *(pl)* substance; product; merchandise

produit amplification/largeur de bande gain-bandwidth product; ~ **croisé** cross-product; ~ **de convolution** convolution (integral); ~ **de distorsion** distortion product; ~ **de modulation** modulation product; ~ **d'intermodulation** intermodulation product; ~ **gain bande réel** gain bandwidth product; ~ **haut de gamme** top-of-the-range product; ~ **mètre x ampères** metre-amperes

produits (recettes) revenue; ~ **consommés** utilities; ~ **de départ** OEM products (original equipment manufacturer); ~ **d'intermodulation** inter-modulation products

profane *m* ou *f* lay user

professionnel *adj* trade; professional-grade; business; industrial

profil *m* standard enquiry; set question-and-answer routine; access privileges; ~ **binaire** bit pattern; ~ **d'indice** index profile

profilé *m* extruded section; ~ **en U** U-section; rail (Omega); ~ **extrudé** extruded section; ~ **traverse** cross-section; mounting rail/track

profondeur *f* depth; volume; capacity/size (of store); ~ **de modulation** depth of modulation; modulation factor; ~ **de modulation de vitesse** depth of velocity modulation

progiciel *m* (software) package; applications software; ~ **d'application** applications package

programmateur *m* sequence timer; interval timer; ~ **de travaux** job scheduler

programmathèque *f* program library

programmation *f* programming; coding; scheduling; planning; pre-setting; selection; ~ **automatique** machine-aided programming; ~ **câblée** firmware; ~ **et ordonnancement** critical path scheduling; ~ **fixe** firmware; ~ **linéaire** linear programming; ~ **optimum** maximum access programming; ~ **sans boucle** straight-line coding; ~ **symbolique** symbolic coding; ~ **technique** hardware configuration; jumper and switch settings

programme (pg) *m* program; programme (other than DP context); scheme; schedule; syllabus; routine; software; ~ **amovible** non-resident program; overlay program; ~ **appelant** calling program; ~ **autonome de test** self-contained test program; ~ **auto-organisateur** self-organizing program; ~ **câblé** firmware; ~ **chargeur** (bootstrap) loader; loading routine; ~ **d'adaptation** postprocessor; interface routine; ~ **d'aide**

à la mise au point debugging (aid) routine; check-out routine; ~ **d'analyse** interpretive trace program; ~ **d'analyse sélective** snapshot (trace) program; ~ **d'application** application program; ~ **d'avant-plan** foreground program; priority routine; ~ **de bibliothèque** library program; ~ **de chargement de carte** board loader; ~ **de cohérence** audit program; ~ **de contrôle** checking routine; test program; ~ **de diagnostique** diagnostic program; ~ **de gestion** handler; management routine; ~ **de gestion des interruptions** interrupt-handling program; ~ **de localisation de pannes** diagnostic routine; fault-tracing program; ~ **de mise au point** debugging (aid) routine; check-out routine; ~ **de reprise** roll-back routine; ~ **de service** message-sending routine; utility program; ~ **de support** operational software development program; support software; ~ **de test de bon fonctionnement** self-test program; ~ **de traduction** assembly routine; ~ **de traitement** handler; processor; ~ **de traitement des tampons** buffer handler; ~ **de trésorerie** cash-management program; ~ **d'édition** report generator; output program; ~ **d'enchaînement** sequencing program; ~ **d'essai** test program; ~ **d'études** study program; ~ **d'exploitation** operating program; ~ **diagnostic** diagnostic routine; ~ **d'introduction** input program; ~ **directeur** executive (routine); monitor; supervisory program; director; scheduler; ~ **enregistré** stored program; ~ **exécutif** supervisor; monitor; ~ **explorateur** (= moniteur) system scheduler; ~ **figé** stalled program; ~ **interpréteur** interpreter; ~ **invariable** re-entrant program; re-enterable program; ~ **moniteur** scheduler; monitor; supervisory routine; executive; ~ **opérationnel** operational program; ~ **pilote** driver; ~ **prêt-à-porter** pack programme (of cable TV); ~ **principal** enregistreur macroprogram; ~ **prioritaire** foreground program; ~ **relogeable** relocatable program; ~ **résident** resident program; ~ **secondaire** background program; ~ **spécifique de test** self-test program; ~ **subordonné** dependent program; ~ **superviseur** supervisory program; executive control program (ECP); executive routine; director; ~ **translatable** relocatable program; ~ **utilisateur** application program; field-programmable routine; ~ **vedette** blue-ribbon program; star program
programmé adj program-controlled; field-programmable; scheduled; software; software-controlled

programme-produit m package
programmer v program; select; preset; pre-select
programmerie f software
programmes d'adaptation bridgeware
progresser (faire ~) increment; inch; step; advance; jog
progressif adj sequential; gradual; step-by-step; soft; by increments; walking; eventual
progression f sequence; advancement; progress; driving; stepping; increment(ation/-ing); inching; feed; ~ **circulaire** cyclic shift; end-around-carry; ~ **des prix** inflation level
projecteur m spotlight; lamp; optical comparator; profile projector; searchlight; ~ **de profil** profile projector; shadowgraph; optical comparator
projection f spatter; spraying; splashing
projet m scheme; ~ **de** draft; provisional
prolongateur m expander; filler; extension; extender; outrigger; ~ **à reprise arrière** (in-line) stackable test lead; ~ **de carte** board extender; outrigger; ~ **d'informations** expander (= elongation circuit); filler element; ~ **mâle/mâle à reprise** stackable plug/socket shrouded test lead
prolongement de ligne de base base-line extension; ~ **national** national extension
prolonger v extend; elongate
promoteur cheer-leader
promouvoir militate in favour of; promote; foster
prononciation f enunciation
propagation anormale anomalous propagation; ~ **d'ondes radioélectriques** radio wave propagation; ~ **guidée** guided propagation; ~ **normale** standard propagation; ~ **par trajets multiples** multipath propagation; ~ **rectiligne** linear propagation; ~ **transhorizon** over-the-horizon propagation; tropospheric scatter; ~ **transhorizon troposphérique** over-the-horizon scatter propagation; ~ **troposphérique** scatter propagation
propagé adj inherited (of error)
proportion f **d'appels perdus** proportion of lost calls
proportionellement adv commensurately; pro-rata
proportionner v scale
proposition f (menu) option
propre adj inherent; intrinsic; natural; innate; individual; on-chip; resident; real; exclusive; unique; clean
propreté f cleanness; cleaning; finished quality

propriétaire *m* file keeper; occupant; host; owner

protection *f* protection; fuse system; shutdown; mask; ~ **à l'écriture** write-protect; ~ **cathodique avec anode enterrée** cathode protection with sacrificial anode; ~ **civile** environmental conservation; ~ **contre la foudre** lightning protection; ~ **contre les erreurs** error control; ~ **contre les interventions** station override security; ~ **contre les surtensions** over-voltage protection; surge protection; crowbar protection; ~ **de réserve** back-up protection; ~ **différentielle** differential protective system; ~ **électrique** electric protection; ~ **en courant** over-current protection; ~ **galvanique** galvanic protection; sacrificial protection; ~ **mémoire** storage protection; ~ **sélective** selective protection; ~ **sur la voie utile** co-channel rejection; ~ **thermique** thermal shutdown (of regulator)

protégé **contre les intrusions** override security facility; ~ **contre l'offre** override security facility; ~ **normal** general-purpose

protéger *v* mask; plate; lock; protect; save; inhibit

protocole *m* protocol; logical and procedural interface; ~ **à jeton** token(-passing) protocol; ~ **d'appareil** device protocol; ~ **de mise en présence** access protocol; handshaking protocol; ~ **de présentation** handshaking protocol; ~ **standard d'accès** standard network access protocol (SNAP); ~ **standard d'appareil** standard device protocol

proton *m* proton

provient **de** stems from; emanates from; originates in

provision *f* allowance; stipulation

provisoire *adj* draft; tentative; heuristic; temporary; makeshift; expedient

provoqué **par** prompted by; instigated by

provoquer *v* induce; activate; trigger; start; set; initiate; prompt; precipitate; generate (of interrupt); instigate; force

PS (v. poste supplémentaire); ~ (v. point sémaphore)

pseudo-aleatoire *adj* pseudo-random

pseudo-code *m* pseudo-code

pseudo-défaut *m* program-sensitive fault

pseudo-enregistreur *m* pseudo-register

pseudo-incidence **brewstérienne** (pseudo-)-Brewster angle

pseudo-instruction *f* pseudo-instruction; quasi-instruction; pseudo-code

pseudonyme *m* alias

pseudo-radiostation *f* deceive station

pseudo-tarage *m* simulated fault measurement

pseudo-ternaire *adj* pseudo-ternary

pseudo-total *m* hash total

psophomètre *m* psophometer; noise meter

PTS (v. point de transfert sémaphore)

publicité *f* **radiophonique** radio advertising; commercial break; advertising jingle

publimatique *f* advertising communications

publiphone *m* pay-phone

publipostage *m* mailing; mailshots; promotional circulars

puce *f* chip; wafer; die; ~ **à protubérance** flip-chip; ~ **seule** single chip

puces *f pl* dice

puiser *v* fetch (of data)

puissance (Pce) power rating; force; capacity; potency; energy; output; duty; strength; intensity; ~ **absorbée** power drawn; ~ **acoustique** sound power; ~ **active** active power; real power; ~ **anodique absorbée** anode power input; ~ **anodique d'entrée** direct current (DC) anode power input; ~ **apparente** apparent power; ~ **apparente rayonnée** effective radiated power (ERP); ~ **apparente rayonnée équivalente dans l'axe** effective isotropic radiated power (EIRP); ~ **appliquée** applied power; ~ **calorifique unitaire** thermal unit rating; ~ **consommée** power consumption; power drawn; ~ **coupée** breaking capacity; ~ **d'alimentation (anodique)** DC anode power input; ~ **d'antenne** aerial capacity; ~ **d'appel** attractive force (pull of coil); ~ **d'attaque de grille** grid driving power; ~ **de bruit** noise power; ~ **de bruit disponible** available noise power; ~ **de bruit disponible à l'entrée** available input noise power; ~ **de calcul** number-crunching power; ~ **de crête** peak envelope power (PEP); ~ **de crête de bande latérale** peak side-band power (PSP); ~ **de distorsion de quantification** quantizing distortion power; ~ **de la porteuse** carrier power; ~ **de l'émetteur** transmitted power; ~ **de l'onde porteuse** carrier power; ~ **de pompage** pump power; ~ **de signal disponible à l'entrée** available input signal power; ~ **de signal offerte par la sortie** available output signal power; ~ **de sortie (W sous ohms)** output power; power output; delivered power (W into ohms); service capacity (of motor); ~ **de sortie de crête** peak-power output; ~ **de sortie d'un microphone** microphone output; ~ **de sortie d'un récepteur** receiver output; ~ **de sortie harmonique non modulée** harmonic unmodulated output power; ~ **de sortie instantanée** instantaneous power output; ~ **de sortie nominale** rated output power; ~ **de sortie non essentielle** unwanted output power; ~ **de sortie utile** effective output power; ~ **de traitement** call-handling capacity; ~ **débitée** delivered power; ~ **délivrée** incident energy (of UV lamp, in mW/cm2); rating; apparent power (in VA); ~ **d'émission** transmitting power; ~ **d'emploi** power rating; ~ **d'entrée** input power; grid-driving power; ~ **d'excitation de grille** grid-driving power; ~ **directe** incident (transmitted) power; ~ **disponible** available power; ~ **dissipée d'une impulsion** pulse dissipation; ~ **dissipée par la plaque** anode dissipated power; ~ **du bruit** noise output; noise power; ~ **du circuit d'antenne** aerial circuit power; ~ **efficace** effective power; ~ **émise** radiated power; ~ **émise isotropiquement** isotropic radiated power; ~ **en crête de modulation** peak envelope power (PEP); ~ **équivalente du bruit de la bande latérale** equivalent side-band input; ~ **frigorifique** cooling power; ~ **instantanée** instantaneous power; ~ **isotropique rayonnée équivalente (PIRE)** effective isotropic radiated power (e.i.r.p.); ~ **limite** maximum power; ~ **limite admissible** operating limit; overload level; ~ **magnétique** magnetizing force; ~ **magnétisante** magnetic (field) strength; magnetic intensity; magnetizing force; ~ **maximale d'une impulsion** peak pulse power; ~ **maximale moyenne de sortie** maximum average power output; ~ **maximum admissible** operating limit; ~ **maximum disponible** maximum available power; ~ **mécanique** power; energy; ~ **moyenne** mean power; ~ **nominale** rated power; ~ **nominale de crête** peak envelope power (PEP); ~ **optique incidente** incident optical power; ~ **perturbatrice** interference power; disturbance power; ~ **phonétique de parole** speech power; ~ **psophométrique** psophometric power; ~ **rayonnée** radiated power; ~ **rayonnée dans une direction** radiated power per unit in a given direction; ~ **réactive** reactive power; ~ **réfléchie** reflected power; indirect power; return power; ~ **surfacique acoustique instantanée** instantaneous acoustical power (sound energy flux) per unit area; ~ **théorique** rated power; ~ **totale anodique d'entrée** total anode power input; ~ **utile de sortie** useful output power; ~ **vocale** acoustical speech power; vocal level; ~ **vocale de référence** reference speech

power; ~ **vocale instantanée** instantaneous acoustical speech power; sound energy flux; ~ **vocale phonétique syllabique** phonetic/syllabic speech power; ~ **volumique** power density

puissant adj effective; powerful; high-performance; formidable; immense

puits m well; recess; trough; pit; bin; ~ **de chaleur** heat sink; ~ **de données** data sink; ~ **de potentiel** potential trough; ~ **de terre** (général) earth-electrode system; earth pit; earth plate; ~ **de test** test recess

pulsation f **du secteur** mains pulsatance; angular frequency; radian frequency

pulsé adj clocked; pulsed; AC

pulvérisation f spraying; sputtering; ~ **cathodique** cathode sputtering

pulvérulent adj friable

punaise f lunar bug

pupinisation f coil loading; ~ **lourde** heavy loading

pupinise adj loaded; pupinized

pupitrage m console operation(s)

pupitre m rack-top test panel; console; desk; panel; instrument panel; benchboard; order turret (PBX); system log; ~ **activateur** operator console; ~ **de commande** control desk; instrument panel; control panel; ~ **de dispatcheur** despatcher's console; ~ **de maintenance** maintenance console; ~ **de mélange** mixing console; ~ **de nuit** night console; ~ **de service** operator console; attendant console; ~ **d'essai** test console; ~ **d'exploitation** rack console; ~ **d'interrogation** enquiry desk; ~ **dirigeur** call director; ~ **d'opératrice** operator console; order turret; attendant desk; ~ **exploitant** rack console; ~ **organe** rack console

pupitreur m console operator; supervisor

pureté f content-graded

purger v flush; dump; evacuate; bleed; drain; discharge; vent; delete; blast; zap

PV (v. procès-verbal); ~ (cosse) tag; lug

PVF2 (v. polyfluorure de vinylidène)

pvt (par voie télégraphique) by telegraph

pylône m tower; mast; ~ **autostable** self-supporting tower; ~ **d'antenne** aerial tower; mast; ~ **en treillis haubanné** guyed lattice tower

pyramide de décodage decoding pyramid

Q

QS (v. qualificateur-scripteur)

qté (v. quantité)

quadratique *adj* square-law

quadribit *m* quad bit

quadrillage *m* surface pattern; partitioning; cross-hatching; coordinate layout; grid

quadripôle *m* quadripole; four-terminal network; black box; bridge network; ~ **à accès symétriques** balanced two terminal-pair network; ~ **électrique** electric quadripole; ~ **symétrique** balanced quadripole

quadrivalent *adj* four-condition

quadruple coupleur de bus bidirectionnel à trois états quad tri-state bus transceiver

quadruplet *m* double line pair

quadruplex *m* quadruplex

quai *m* (loading) dock; bay; platform

qualificateur-scripteur (QS) quality-of-service supervisory (QOS)

qualification *f* grading; ~ **de zone** define area qualification (DAQ); ~ **industrielle** qualification approval

qualifié *adj* skilled

qualité absolue imperative; ~ *f* **correspondance** letter quality (LQ); ~ **courante** draft quality; ~ **courrier** letter quality (LQ); ~ **courrier approché** near-letter quality (NLQ); memo quality; ~ **de fonctionnement** performance; ~ **de service** quality of service; ~ **de transmission** transmission quality; ~ **de transmission de la parole** speech transmission quality; ~ **de transmission téléphonique** telephone transmission quality; ~ **d'écoulement** grade of traffic; grade of service; ~ **d'écoulement du trafic**

grade of service (GOS); grade of traffic; ~ **du son** sound quality; ~ **grossière** coarse pitch (of screw thread); ~ **listing** draft quality; ~ **moyenne** medium pitch (of screw thread)

quantième *m* date; day of month

quantificateur *m* quantizer; digitizer; A-D converter

quantification *f* quantization; analogue-digital conversion; digitizing

quantifier *v* quantize; digitize

quantité (qté) *f* quantity; volume (of data); amperage; ~ **de matière** amount of substance; ~ **d'électricité** quantity of electricity; electric charge; electric flux; ~ **non conforme** overs and shorts

quantum *m* connection charge; quantum

quarte *f* quad (cable); quadruple; ~ **de plan** quarter-plane (of switching matrix); ~ **Dieselhorst-Martin (DM)** multiple-twin (quad) cable; ~ **étoile** star quad

quartet *m* four-bit byte; nibble; half-byte; quartet

quartz *m* quartz crystal unit; ~ **de base** quartz-controlled generator

quasi-logarithmique nearly-logarithmic

question *f* query; enquiry; inquiry

questionnaire *m* customer enquiry form

queue *f* termination; lead (of component); ~ **d'aronde** dovetail; ~ **de signal** signal tail

queusot *m* stem

qui est là? who-are-you? (WRU)

quinte *f* five-wire cable; quintuple

quitter *v* exit; sign-off; log-off

quota *m* threshold

R

rabat *m* flap

rabattable hinged; articulated

rabattement *m* clinching; clinch (of terminations)

rabattre *v* lower; fold back

RAC (v. message de raccrochage)

raccord *m* splice; connection; end-bell; adaptor; joint; patch; kludge; back-shell; ~ **à bride lisse** butt joint; ~ **à piège** choke coupling; ~ **directif** directional coupler; ~ **mécanique** adaptor; coupling; ~ **progressif** taper (of waveguide)

raccordement (racct.) *m* connection; coupling; joint; patching; local line; subscriber line; station line; jumper; interface; splice; hook-up; wiring; junction; linkage; ~ **de masse** mass splicing; ~ **des phases** phase interlinking; ~ **distant** remote trunk arrangement (RTA); ~ **inter-alvéoles** inter-shelf wiring; ~ **inter-cartes** board-to-board wiring; ~ **intra-alvéoles** shelf-wiring

raccorder *v* attach; host; interface; patch; wire; join; connect; couple; link; hook up; splice

raccourcissement *m* **de la longueur d'onde** wavelength shortening

raccrochage *m* hanging-up; securing; attaching; ringing-off; replacing receiver; going on-hook; on-hook (condition); on-hook signal; call-release signal; clear-back signal; ~ **du demandé** clear-back (signal); ~ **du demandeur** clear-forward (signal)

raccroché *adj* on-hook

raccrocher *v* hang up; clear; release; go on-hook; replace receiver/handset

racct. (v. raccordement)

racine *f* root; root segment; radix; base; ~ **carrée de cosinus** square-root cosine

radar *m* radar; ~ **à courte distance** short-range radar; ~ **à deux lobes directifs** double-beam radar; ~ **à exploration latérale** side-looking airborne radar; ~ **à impulsions** pulse radar; ~ **à impulsions synchronisées** coherent pulse radar; ~ **à ouverture synthétique** synthetic-aperture radar; ~ **à portée moyenne** medium-range radar; ~ **à rayons infrarouges** infra-red range and direction-finding equipment; ~ **aéroporté** airborne radar; ~ **auxiliaire à faisceau mince** zone position indicator (ZPI); ~ **cô-**

tier coastal radar; shore-based radar; ~ **d'acquisition** acquisition radar; ~ **d'acquisition et de poursuite** acquisition (lock-on) and tracking radar; ~ **d'alerte** early-warning radar; ~ **d'alerte avancée** distant early-warning radar; ~ **d'altimétrie** height-finding radar; ~ **d'approche à multiplexage** multiplexed homing radar; approach radar; ~ **d'avion** airborne radar; ~ **de bord** ship's radar; shipborne radar; ~ **de piste d'atterrissage** airport surface detection equipment (ASDE); ~ **de port** port radar; ~ **de poursuite** tracking radar; ~ **de poursuite d'engins** missile-tracking radar; ~ **de route vraie** true-motion radar; true-plot radar; ~ **de service de bac** ferry service radar; ~ **de surveillance** all-round search radar; ~ **de surveillance d'aéroport** airport surveillance radar; ~ **d'identification** IFF (identification friend or foe); ~ **directeur de tir** accurate position finder (APF); ~ **dirigé en avant** forward-looking radar; ~ **localisateur de mortiers** mortar-locating radar; ~ **maritime** marine radar; ~ **mesureur d'altitude** height finder; ~ **panoramique d'avion** airborne all-round radar search apparatus; ~ **portatif** hand radar; portable radar; ~ **pour bombardement à faible altitude** low-altitude bombing radar (LAR); ~ **pour faible portée** very short-range radar; ~ **récepteur d'avion de guet** zero catcher; ~ **rétroviseur** backward-looking radar; ~ **secondaire de surveillance** secondary surveillance radar (SSR); ~ **terrestre** ground radar; ~ **tridimensionnel** three-dimensional radar

radiateur *m* heat sink; cooling fins; ~ **de chaleur** heat sink; ~ **de puissance** power heat sink; ~ **d'électrode** electrode radiator

radiation *f* radiation; ~ **directive** directional radiation; ~ **électromagnétique** electromagnetic radiation

radier *m* reinforced concrete mesh

radio(graphie) *f* X-ray; gamma ray; photography; radiogram; radiograph

radio aéronautique aircraft radio; airborne radio; ~ **amateur** amateur radio; ~ **du service de pilotage** pilot radio service; ~ **fac-similé** radio facsimile; ~ **maritime** ship-borne radio

radioalignement *m* track guidance system; ~ à **comparaison** signal comparison tracking; ~ à **enchevêtrement** interlocking equi-signal system; ~ de **piste** localizer beacon

radioaltimètre *m* radio altimeter

radioamateur *m* radio amateur ("ham")

radioborne *m* marker beacon; ~ **en éventail** fan marker beacon; ~ **en route** en-route marker beacon; ~ **intermédiaire** middle marker beacon

radiocommandé *adj* radio-controlled

radiocommunication *f* radio communication; ~ **bateau-bateau** ship-ship communication

radiodéction à basculement de diagramme beam switching; split aerial switching; lobe switching/swinging; lobing

radiodétecteur à diagramme en V V-beam system; ~ **aéroporté d'interception** air-intercept radar (AI); ~ **d'approche** approach control radar; ~ **d'approche aux instruments** beam-approach beacon system; ~ **d'approche de précision** precision approach radar (PAR); ~ **d'avertissement** airborne weather radar; cloud and collision warning system; ~ **de mouvement au sol** aerodrome surface movement indicator (ASMI); ~ **de navigation** navigational radar; ~ **de surveillance** surveillance radar; ~ **de surveillance d'approche** surveillance radar element (SRE); ~ **panoramique** panorama radar (PANAR); wide-sweep radar

radiodétection à effet Doppler-Fizeau moving-target indication radar; MTI radar; ~ à **élimination des échos fixes** moving-target indication radar (MTI); ~ à **goniométrie instantanée d'amplitude** static split; ~ à **modulation de fréquence** frequency-modulated radar; ~ **primaire** primary radar; ~ **secondaire** secondary radar

radiodiffusion *f* radio broadcasting service; broadcast; ~ à **ondes communes** mutual broadcasting system; ~ **différée** recorded broadcast; ~ **directe** live broadcast; ~ **météorologique** meteorological broadcast; weather report; ~ **par réseau d'émetteurs** simultaneous broadcast (SB); ~ **spécialisée** narrow-casting; ~ **visuelle** television broadcasting

radiodistribution *f* wire broadcast

radioémetteur *m* radio transmitter

radioémission *f* broadcast transmission

radiofréquence *f* radio frequency (RF)

radiogoniomètre *m* radio direction finder; ~ à **antenne fixe** fixed direction finder; fixed-aerial finder; ~ à **antennes espacées** spaced-aerial direction finder; ~ à **bascule-ment du diagramme** switched-beam direction finder; ~ à **cadre** rotating-loop direction finder; ~ à **cadres croisés** Bellini-Tosi (crossed-loop) direction finder; ~ à **cadres espacés** spaced-loop direction finder; ~ à **chercheur** rotating direction finder; ~ à **grande ouverture** wide-aperture direction finder; ~ à **lecture directe** direct-reading direction finder; ~ à **réajustage automatique à zéro** direction finder with automatic reset; ~ **Adcock** Adcock direction finder; ~ **(Adcock) à équilibreurs** balanced Adcock direction finder; ~ **Adcock en H** elevated (H-type) Adcock direction finder; ~ **auditif** aural direction finder; ~ **automatique double** dual automatic direction finder; ~ **de bord automatique** automatic radio compass; ~ **secondaire** direction-finding slave (sub-)-station; ~ **Watson-Watt** double-channel cathode-ray direction finder (CRDF)

radiogoniométrie *f* radio direction-finding (RDF)

radiogramme *m* message; radiogram

radioguidage *m* radio guidance; direct command guidance

radiolocalisation *f* radio determination; radiolocation

radiomesure *f* radiotelemetry; radiotelemetering

radiomètre *m* radiometer; ~ **acoustique** acoustic radiometer

radionavigation *f* radionavigation; ~ **hyperbolique** hyperbolic navigation system

radiophare *m* radio beacon; ~ à **basse puissance** low-power radio beacon; ~ à **deux modulations différentes** radio beacon with double modulation; ~ à **diagramme circulaire** non-directional radio beacon (NDB); ~ à **diagramme oscillant** sector-scanning beacon; ~ à **faisceau en éventail** radio fan marker; ~ à **impulsions** pulsed beacon; ~ à **indication d'azimut** directional radio beacon; ~ à **quatre voies et antenne en boucle** loop range; ~ à **quatre voies et indication optique et acoustique** visual/aural range (VAR); ~ **d'alignement** track beacon; ~ **d'alignement** quadrantal four-course radio beacon; radio range; ~ **d'approche** homing beacon; ~ **d'attente** holding beacon; ~ **d'atterrissage** landing beacon; ~ **d'identification** identification beacon; ~ **omnidirectionnel** directional radio beacon; ~ **protégé des erreurs de nuit** night-effect-free radio beacon; ~ **répéteur d'impulsions** directional radar beacon; ~ **tournant** revolving radio beacon

radiophonique *adj* (sound) broadcasting

radioralliement *m* homing
radiorécepteur *m* radio receiver
radiorecherche de personnes radiopaging
radiorepérage *m* radiolocation; (passive) radar; radio direction finding (RDF); radio navigation
radioscopie *f* X-ray photography
radiosonde *f* radiosonde (meteorological sounding balloon)
radiostation *f* radio station; ~ **côtière** coastal/shore-based radio station; ~ **maritime** shipborne radio station; off-shore radio; ~ **stationnaire** fixed radio station; ~ **transportable** mobile radio station
radiotechnique *f* radio engineering
radiotélégramme *m* radiogram; message
radiotélégraphie *f* radio telegraphy; wireless telegraphy; ~ **dirigée** directional radio telegraphy
radiotélégraphiste *m f* radio operator
radiotéléimprimeur *m* radio teleprinter
radiotélémètre *m* base range-finder
radiotélémétrie *f* radio range-finding
radiotéléphone *m* radiotelephone; radiophone; ~ **mobile** mobile radiotelephone
radiotéléphonie *f* radiotelephony; ~ **cellulaire** cellular radiotelephony
radôme *m* (= radome) radome; ~ **conique** tapered radome
rafale *f* glitch; burst; ~ **d'erreurs** error burst
rafales *f pl* gusting
rafraîchissement *m* (d'écran) (screen) regeneration; refresh; update
raideur *f* **acoustique** acoustic stiffness
raidisseur *m* stiffener; brace
raie *f* (spectral) line (of radiation: in KeV); dual-frequency component; spot frequency; ~ **latérale** sideband
raies parasites stray radiation
rainure *f* keyway; groove; slot; channel; ditch (of waveguide trap); ~ **en vé** V-groove; vee groove; ~ **hélicoïdale** helical groove
raisons *f pl* **d'exploitation** operational reasons
ralliement *m* **actif** active homing
rallonge *f* extender; extension
rame *f* (= 20 mains) ream (500 sheets = 20 quires)
ramener *v* restore; reduce; reset
rampe *f* ramp; bank; rail; stacker; ~ **de tension** ramp voltage; ~ **lumineuse** illuminated indicator bank; lamp field
rang *m* rank; variable indicator (i,j); order; row; sequence; position; location; digit position; place; number; index; address; ~ **donnée** data location; data position
rangée *f* row; bank; suite; frame; array
rangement *m* store; storing; storage; stowage; filing; sequencing; buffering; ~ **par inter-**

classement balanced (merge) sort
ranger *v* put aside; store; shelve
rapatriement *m* loading; copying; fetching; retrieval; relocation; transferring back; mapping; re-storing; getting; boiler-plating; porting
rapatrier *v* load; copy; fetch; retrieve; relocate; transfer back; redirect; re-store; map; GET (from backing store); port
rapide *adj* high performance; fast; high-speed; volatile; flying-head operation
rapidité *m* **de modulation** modulation rate; telegraph speed; ~ **de service** speed of service; ~ **de transfert de données** data transfer rate
rapiécer *v* patch
rappel *m* recall; call-back; loop-back; ring-back; recapitulation; résumé; summary; outline; (procedural) survey; prompt; get; pull-down; explanation; revision notes; review; ~ **automatique** automatic call-back; executive ring-back; ~ **automatique après occupation** automatic call-back - ring again; ~ **automatique du poste opérateur** automatic operator recall; ~ **automatique sur poste occupé** camp-on busy extension; automatic call-back; ~ **de l'opératrice** operator recall; ~ **d'enregistreur** register recall; hook-switch flash; ~ **du demandeur** camp-on; ~ **du distant** recall distant-end subscriber; recall far-end subscriber; ~ **d'une phrase** get (put-aside) vocabulary/glossary; boiler-plating; ~ **rendez-vous** appointments reminder; programmed call placement; ~ **sur supervision** flashing; ~ **temporisé** automatic recall; automatic time-out; timed reminder
rappeler *v* recall; prompt; call-back
rapport *m* ratio; relationship; proportion; record; comparison; report; characteristic; ~ **B** (bruit) signal-to-noise ratio; ~ **certifié d'essais** certified test record (CTR); ~ **cyclique** make-break ratio; duty cycle; mark-space ratio; on-off ratio; ~ **d'affaiblissement dans le mode commun** common-mode rejection ratio; ~ **d'amplification** amplification ratio; gain; ~ **d'amplitude** amplitude ratio; ~ **d'amplitude de synchronisation** picture ratio; synchronizing ratio; ~ **d'amplitude de tension** voltage standing-wave ratio (VSWR); ~ **de commande** control ratio; ~ **de concentration** concentration ratio; ~ **de découplage** (d'antennes) coupling coefficient; coupling factor; ~ **de densité du courant** electron gun convergence ratio; electron gun density multiplication; ~ **de déviation** deviation ratio; deflection ratio; ~ **de dimensions** aspect ratio; ~ **de**

R

division division ratio (DR); ~ **de format** aspect ratio; ~ **de mélange** specific humidity; ~ **de pondération** weighting factor; ~ **de pondération d'un courant** current weighting factor; ~ **de protection** protection ratio; ~ **de puissance** power ratio; ~ **de réjection en mode commun** common mode rejection ratio; ~ **de reproduction** reproduction ratio; ~ **de suroscillation** overshoot ratio; overswing ratio; ~ **de transfert de courant continu pour une tension collecteur-émetteur** DC current transfer ratio (CTR: $I_c/I_f = T$ [tau]); ~ **de transformation** turns ratio; voltage ratio; ~ **d'équilibrage** balance ratio; ~ **d'équilibre des signaux** signal balance ratio; ~ **des hauteurs d'entrée** pick-up ratio; ~ **des rayonnements avant et arrière** front-to-back ratio; ~ **d'état** status report; ~ **d'impulsions** make-break ratio; pulse ratio; mark-space ratio; on-off ratio; duty cycle; ~ **d'onde stationnaire (ROS)** standing-wave ratio (SWR); ~ **d'ouverture sur fermeture** break-to-make ratio; ~ **du shunt** shunt ratio; ~ **du trafic journalier au trafic à l'heure chargée** day-to-busy-hour ratio; ~ **largeur/hauteur** aspect ratio; ~ **phase/fréquence vidéo** phase(-frequency) response characteristic; ~ **prix/performance** price/performance trade-off; ~ **signal à bruit de quantification** signal-to-quantizing noise ratio; ~ **signal à distorsion totale** signal-to-quantization noise ratio; ~ **signal sur bruit** (v. rapport signal-bruit); ~ **signal sur ronflement** signal-to-hum ratio; ~ **signal-bruit** signal-to-noise ratio (S/N)

rapporté *adj* add-on; detachable
rapporteur *m* **d'angle** protractor
rapprochement *m* exposure; comparison; ~ **oblique** oblique exposure
rarement *adv* seldom
rassemblement électronique electron bunching
rassembler *v* combine; rally; marshal; muster; bunch; gather; accumulate; collate
raté *m* **d'allumage** misfire; ~ **de blocage** arc-through; loss of control
rattachement *m* deployment; assignment; subscriber line; station line; ~ **en MIC** PCM link
rattrapage *m* retro-fit; ~ **de gain** gain compensation
RAV (v. robot d'arrivée)
raviver *v* refresh; regenerate
rayon *m* ray; trajectory; radius; daisywheel; ~ **alpha** alpha ray; ~ **axial** axial ray; ~ **bêta** beta ray; ~ **cosmique** cosmic ray; ~ **de courbure** radius of curvature; bending radius; ~ **de raccordement** transition

radius; ~ **direct** direct ray; incident ray; ~ **électrique (ionique)** electron (ion) trajectory; ~ **entrant** guided ray; ~ **gamma** gamma ray; ~ **incident** incident ray; ~ **incliné** angled ray; ~ **indirect** indirect ray; ~ **ionosphérique** ionospheric ray; ~ **non axial** non-axial ray; ~ **optique** light ray; light beam; ~ **tangent** tangential wave path; tangent ray; ~ **terrestre** radius of the earth; ~ **terrestre fictif** effective radius of the earth

rayonnement *m* radiation; spin-off; incident energy (of UV source); ~ **acoustique** acoustic radiation; ~ **diffusé** scattered radiation; ~ **direct** free-space propagation; ~ **en avant** forward radiation; ~ **hors de bande** out-of-band radiation; ~ **indirect** indirect radiation; reflected radiation; ~ **non essentiel** spurious emission; ~ **paramétrique** parametric radiation; ~ **parasite** stray radiation; ~ **primaire** primary radiation; ~ **secondaire** secondary radiation

rayure *f* scratch; score mark
raz-de-marée *m* tidal wave; major upsurge; landslide; upturn; breakthrough
RBF (v. répartiteur basse fréquence)
RC (v. répartiteur de croisement); ⁓ (v. retour de chariot); ⁓ (resistance-capacitance) circuit RC network
R$_{cc}$ (v. résistance courant continu)
RCE (v. réseau de communication d'entreprise)
RCP (v. réseau à commutation par paquets)
RDC (v. réseau de protection); ⁓ (v. réseau d'aide à la commutation)
RE (v. répartiteur d'entrée)
réacheminement *m* re-routing; redirecting; diversion; ~ **automatique** call forwarding - don't answer
réactance *f* reactance; coil; choke; ~ **acoustique** acoustic reactance; ~ **acoustique intrinsèque** specific acoustic reactance; unit area acoustic reactance; ~ **capacitive** capacitive reactance; capacitance; ~ **capacitive de câble** cable capacitance; ~ **d'électrode** electrode reactance; ~ **effective** effective reactance; ~ **inductive** inductive reactance; inductance; ~ **mécanique** mechanical reactance
réacteur à surrégénération breeder reactor; ~ **limiteur de courant** current-limiting reactor
réaction capacitive capacitive feedback; ~ **de tension** voltage feedback; ~ **électrostatique** capacitive feedback; ~ **équilibrée** bridge feedback; ~ **parasite** stray feedback; ~ **positive** regenerative feedback; positive feedback; ~ **tout ou rien** quantal response

réactiver v restore

réactivité f à froid cold hardening/setting (reaction)

réaffichage m reload; reloading

réaiguillage m re-routing

réaiguiller v re-route; divert; redirect

réajustement m du rythme re-timing

réajuster v re-adjust

réalisable adj feasible

réalisateur m programmer; designer; manufacturer

réalisation f installation; manufacture; production; implementation; operating; execution; design; generation; assembly; practice; ~ des programmes software; programming; ~ logicielle modify software; programming; ~ matérielle erection; construction; manufacture

réaliser v accomplish; build; construct; make; effect; implement; install; execute; manufacture; produce; realise; create; design; fulfil; crystallize; ~ un chiffre d'affaire gross

réaménagement m re-organization

réapprovisionnement m re-ordering; replenishment; buying-in; re-stocking

réarmement m reset; resetting; reinstatement

réarmer v re-enable; reset; reinstate

réavaler v retrieve; confiscate

rebaptisation f renaming (of files)

rebobinage m rewind(ing); ~ rapide review (function)

rebondissement m (contact) bounce; chatter(ing) (of relays); recoil; backlash; reflex action; toggling; backswing; overswing; overshoot

rebord m (de manchon) rail

rebouclage m loop-back; wraparound; dynamic stop; loop iteration; strapping; always running; feedback (of programmed array logic); ~ de MIC PCM link loop-back

rebut m garbage; reject; ~ à l'entrée et à la sortie garbage-in/garbage-out (GIGO)

recadrage m re-phasing; realignment

recalage m shift; re-adjustment; coordination; retiming; synchronization; reset

recalcul de feuille recalculation

récapitulatif m check list; survey; summary; résumé; memorandum

récepteur m ou adj receiver; handset; earphone; stacker; sink; load (circuit); destination; downstream; input; ~ à amplification directe direct detection receiver; straight circuit; ~ à amplification directe avec plusieurs canaux multi-channel straight receiver; ~ à bande étalée bandspread receiver; ~ à bande latérale single-sideband receiver; ~ à batteries battery receiver; ~ à bobine mobile moving-coil receiver; ~ à conduction osseuse bone-conduction receiver; ~ à cristal crystal receiver; ~ à ondes courtes short-wave receiver; ~ à projection projection TV receiver; ~ à superhétérodyne superheterodyne receiver; ~ à superréaction super-regenerative receiver; ~ autodyne autodyne receiver; ~ auxiliaire de signalisation signalling receiver; ~ clavier DTMF digit receiver; ~ d'alarme alarm receiver; ~ d'approche homing receiver; ~ de cartes card stacker; ~ de documents stacker; ~ de données data sink; ~ de faible portée short-range receiver; short-haul receiver; ~ de fréquence (RF) frequency receiver; ~ de Hell Hell printer; Hell receiver (mosaic telegraphy); Hellschreiber; ~ de la fréquence pilote pilot receiver; ~ de ligne line receiver; ~ de lumière light detector; ~ de poche pocket receiver; ~ de poursuite tracking receiver; ~ de radio radio set; ~ de radiodiffusion broadcasting receiver; ~ de réémission relay receiver; re-broadcast receiver; ~ de retransmission direct pick-up receiver; ~ de signaux signal receiver; ~ de télévision television receiver; ~ de veille watch receiver; ~ d'images picture receiver; ~ électro-optique opto-electronic receiver; ~ fac-similé facsimile receiver; ~ FIFO push-up list; ~ hétérodyne heterodyne receiver; ~ imprimeur printer; ~ morse rapide high-speed Morse receiver/recorder; ~ ondes courtes short-wave receiver; ~ optique light detector; ~ parfait ideal receiver; ~ piézoélectrique crystal receiver; ~ portable pocket receiver; back-pack; ~ radar radar receiver; ~ radar d'alarme radar detector; ~ radio radio set; radio receiver; ~ radioélectrique radio receiver; radio set; ~ radiotéléphonique à fréquence fixe spot-frequency RT receiver; ~ secteur mains receiver; ~ séparé remote receiver; ~ serre-tête headphone(s); ~ sur page page receiver; ~ synchrodyne passif passive synchrodyne receiver; ~ téléphonique telephone receiver; earphone; ~ tous courants AC/DC receiver; ~ toutes ondes all-wave receiver; ~ traducteur imprimeur (cable-code) direct printer; ~ universel all-mains receiver

récepteur-perforateur receiving perforator; reperforator; ~ imprimeur printing reperforator; printer perforator; ~ imprimeur (= reperforateur-imprimeur) receive-only typing reperforator; ~ non imprimeur

R

receive-only non-typing reperforator; ~ **transmetteur** reperforator-transmitter

réception *f* reception (RX); receipt; stacking; input; return; acceptance; goods inward; incoming goods; R-wire (ring of jack); up-link; writing (section of tape store); sinking; ~ **à amplification directe** tuned RF (straight) reception; ~ **à bande latérale unique** single-sideband reception; ~ **à correlation croisée** cross-correlation reception; ~ **à diagramme en huit** figure-of-eight reception; ~ **à impression** printing reception; ~ **à l'écoute** aural reception; sound reception; ~ **à polarisation multiple** polarity diversity reception; ~ **à réaction** regenerative reception; ~ **à superréaction** super-regenerative reception; ~ **au casque** earphone reception; ~ **autodyne** autodyne reception; ~ **automatique d'une image transmise par satellite** satellite automatic picture reception; ~ **avec porteuse locale** local carrier reception; ~ **avec régénération de la porteuse** reconditioned carrier reception; ~ **avec renforcement de la porteuse** exalted carrier reception; ~ **avec restitution de la porteuse** local carrier demodulation; local carrier reception; ~ **de télévision** television reception; ~ **dirigée** directional reception; ~ **d'un télégramme** telegram reception; ~ **en diversité** diversity reception; ~ **en diversité à gain égal** equal-gain diversity reception; ~ **enregistrée** visual reception; ~ **hétérodyne** heterodyne reception; beat reception; ~ **homodyne** demodulation of an exalted carrier; homodyne reception; ~ **logarithmique** logarithmic reception; ~ **multiple** diversity reception; ~ **noir et blanc** black and white reception; ~ **superhétérodyne** superheterodyne reception; ~ **synchrone** homodyne reception; monodyne reception; zero-beat reception

recette *f* acceptance (testing); goods inward inspection; incoming goods inspection

receveur *m* recipient; addressee; call-forwarding

recevoir *v* receive

recharge *f* refill; top-up; spare

rechargement export (of data base files); hard-facing (of metals)

recharger *v* overlay; reload; replenish

rechargeur *m* replenisher

réchaud *m* **électrique** hot plate

recherche *f* research; search; seek; hunt; find; study; fetch; research and development (R & D); retrieval; polling; tracking; scan; locating; ~ **binaire (dichotomique)** binary chop; dichomotizing search; ~ **conjuguée** end-to-end pathfinding; ~ **cyclique** circu-

lar hunting; round-robin hunting; ~ **d'appel** call-finding; ~ **de chemin** path search; pathfinding; ~ **de dénombrement et de sélection** request-driven system; ~ **de dérangements** fault-finding; trouble-shooting; ~ **de fautes** fault-tracing; ~ **de ligne appelante** line-finding; ~ **de l'information** information retrieval; ~ **de message** message retrieval; ~ **de personnes** call paging; ~ **de personnes au moyen de signaux d'appel codés** code calling; ~ **de voies** path-finding; ~ **des limites** destructive tests; ~ **dichotomique** binary chop; dichotomizing search; binary look-up; ~ **d'informations** information retrieval; ~ **d'itinéraire** pathfinding; ~ **d'organes** hunting; ~ **d'un dérangement** fault finding; ~ **d'une ligne** (libre) hunting; ~ **d'une ligne appelante** (line-)finding; ~ **en distance** range search; ~ **en mémoire** fetch; ~ **et substitution** search and replace (S & R); find and exchange; ~ **multicritères** multi-aspect search; multi-criterion search; ~ **par contremesures électroniques** ECM search; ~ **par décalage** round-robin hunting; ~ **par le contenu** content-addressed search; ~ **progressive** distributed hunting; ~ **rapide en bobinage** cue; ~ **rapide en rebobinage** review; ~ **sélective** peek; ~ **sur critères** conditional search

rechercher *v* establish; ascertain; seek; identify; hunt; find; search; investigate; examine; canvass opinion; ~ **les pannes** fault-finding; trouble-shooting

récipient *m* vessel; container

réciproquement *adv* vice versa

réclamations (code 10 en France) complaints; customer enquiries; customer assistance

reclassement *m* re-grading; re-categorization

recombinaison *f* recombination

recommandé *adj* typical; advisable; recommended

recommencer *v* restart

recomposition *f* re-formatting

reconfigurable *adj* software-defined

reconfiguration *f* reconfiguration; error recovery; ~ **automatique** automatic reconfiguration

reconnaissance *f* recognition; reconnaissance (recce); acknowledgement; identification; ~ **de caractères** character recognition; ~ **de forme** pattern recognition; ~ **de la parole** speech recognition; ~ **magnétique de caractères** magnetic ink character recognition (MICR); ~ **optique de caractères** optical character recognition (OCR); ~ **par radar** radar reconnaissance; ~ **par télévision** television reconnaissance; ~ **radioélectrique** radio reconnaissance

R

reconnaître v single out; recognize; identify; trace; acknowledge

reconstitution f **du rythme incident** bit timing recovery; ~ **du signal de rythme** timing signal recovery

reconstruit adj reconditioned

reconsulter v reconnect to (another party)

reconversion f re-training

reconvertir v convert back

recopie f **d'écran** guard copy; screen echo; print page

recopier v transcribe; duplicate; copy; roll-out; reproduce; put aside; ~ **en bloc** block copy; ~ **sur disque** dump (to disk); duplicate

recouvrement m overlay; overlap(ping); lands; intersection; coincidence; swapping; stimulation (carrier-photon); ~ **de faits** fact retrieval; ~ **du temps** time overlap

recouvrir v embrace; encompass; intersect; overlay; swap

rectangulaire adj rectangular; oblong; flat; square(-wave)

rectification f repair; correction; grinding; milling; machining; amendment

recto m component side (of PCB)

recto-verso A-side/B-side; right-hand/left-hand page; front/back; face/back; back-to-back; obverse/reverse; odd-even; right-left; component/solder side (of PCB)

recueil m batch; collection; compilation; compendium; ~ **de l'état de boucle** loop status management; ~ **des données** data acquisition

recuit adj annealed; ~ **de détente** stress-relief annealing

recul m backspace (BS); back-off (BO); ~ **codé** coded backspace; ~ **de sortie** output back-off; ~ **du curseur** cursor backward (CUB)

récupération f retrieval; recovery; restoration; recall; recouping; detection; identification; fetching; retrieval; recycling; ~ **de messages** message retrieval; ~ **d'énergie sans distorsion** phase-less boost; ~ **d'horloge** clock recovery; timing signal extraction; ~ **du rythme** timing signal extraction; timing (signal) recovery; ~ **état neuf** reconditioned as new

récupérer v retrieve; call up; fetch; harness; get; recover; extract; restore; salvage

récurrence f recursivity; recursion; period; ~ **de balayage** hold-off

récurrent adj recursive

récursif adj recursive; re-entrant

récursivité f recursion; recursivity

recyclage m reprocessing; re-run; restart; roll-in

rédaction f writing; compiling; editing; ~ **de ticket** (fault) docket printing

redécrochage m re-answer

redémarrage à chaud quick start; warm restart; ~ **lent** slow restart; cold start; reset

redevance f bill; charge; rental; royalty; fee; ~ **annuelle** annual rate; subscription; licence; ~ **d'abonnement** rental (charge); ~ **de télévision** television licence

redhibitoire adj invalidated; eliminated; nullified

rediffusion f radio relay; re-broadcasting

redondance f redundancy; replication

redondant adj redundant; don't care; replicated facility

redoublement m redundancy

redressement m conversion; rectification; recovery; correction; re-formatting; ~ **à enroulement fractionné** split-winding rectification

redresseur m rectifier; ~ **à argon** argon rectifier; ~ **à cathode liquide** pool rectifier; ~ **à contact par pointe** point-contact rectifier; ~ **à contact par pointe soudé** welded-contact rectifier; ~ **à contact par surface** surface-contact rectifier; ~ **à crête de tension inverse** high inverse-voltage rectifier; ~ **à cristal** crystal rectifier; crystal diode; ~ **à cristal vidéo** crystal video rectifier; ~ **à deux alternances** full-wave rectifier; ~ **à gâchette** silicon-controlled rectifier (SCR); ~ **à germanium** germanium rectifier; ~ **à mercure** mercury-vapour rectifier; ~ **à oxyde de cuivre** copper-oxide rectifier; ~ **à sélénium** selenium rectifier; ~ **à silice** silicon(-controlled) rectifier (SCR); reverse-blocking triode thyristor; ~ **à simple alternance** half-wave rectifier; ~ **à tube** electron-tube rectifier; ~ **à une alternance** half-wave rectifier; ~ **à vapeur de mercure** mercury-vapour rectifier; ~ **à vide poussé** diode rectifier; ~ **en pont** bridge rectifier; ~ **excitateur** booster; ~ **ignitron** ignitron rectifier; ~ **mono-alternance** half-wave rectifier; ~ **sec** dry-plate rectifier; metal rectifier; ~ **vibratoire** vibrator rectifier

réducteur m getter

réduction f cutback; de-rating; back-off; step-down; ~ **au minimum de distorsion** distortion minimization; ~ **d'accessibilité** limited availability; ~ **d'amplitude** amplitude reduction; ~ **d'articulation** clipping; ~ **de charge** de-rating; ~ **de consommation** standby mode; ~ **de données** data reduction; ~ **de la bande latérale** sideband reduction; ~ **de la pointe** peak reduction; ~ **de la qualité de transmission** transmission

R

impairment; distortion; ~ **de la vitesse de groupe** group retardation; ~ **de netteté** articulation reduction; ~ **de qualité** impairment; ~ **du bruit** noise reduction; ~ **du lobe latéral** side-lobe reduction; ~ **du pourcentage de distorsion** harmonic content reduction

réduire v dwindle; scale (down); de-rate; attenuate; minimize; restrict

réduit adj partial; low-capacity; small-scale; compact; abridged; condensed; short; shortened; miniature; compressed; selective; off-peak; skeleton; de-rated; dim; primitive; unsophisticated; rudimentary

réel adj real; true; actual; absolute; effective; genuine; specific; ~ **court** short real key (4-byte real number); ~ **long** long real key (8-byte real number)

réémetteur m relay transmitter; translator (station)

réémettre v retransmit; relay; repeat; send back

réémission f relay; retransmission; repeating; backward transmission; out-pulsing; redial; redialling; ~ **d'appel sur ligne occupée** automatic repeat dialling; ~ **passive** passive retransmission

réemploi m repetition; re-cycling; recovery; reset

réenclenchement m resetting; re-activation; re-connection; cancelling (of alarm); ~ **automatique rapide** automatic reset

réenregistrement m store back; re-recording

réenrouleur m spooler

réexpédition f retransmission; intermediate handling; (message) forwarding; relay

refaire v renovate

référence f reference; yardstick; benchmark; credential; testimonial; track record; ~ **de distance** range; ~ **de temps zéro** zero-time reference; ~ **nominative** label; name (as reference)

référencé à referred to

réfléchi (sur écran) screen echo

réflecteur f reflector; repeller; sticker; tape mark; ~ **à surface continue** continuous-surface reflector; ~ **à tiges** rod reflector; rod mirror; ~ **actif** active reflector; ~ **cylindrique** cylinder reflector; ~ **d'antenne** aerial reflector; ~ **de bande** sticker; ~ **de confusion** (de radar) (radar) confusion reflector; ~ **de klystron** klystron reflector; klystron repeller; ~ **déviateur** passive reflector; ~ **en dé** cheese; ~ **en segment** cheese; ~ **en trièdre** corner reflector; ~ **parabolique** parabolic reflector; ~ **parabolique excité par un dipôle** dipole-excited parabolic reflector; ~ **paraboloïde** dish

(reflector); parabolic reflector; ~ **sphérique** dish

réflectomètre m reflectometer

refléter v mimic; echo; reflect; bounce back

réflexion f reflection; echo; hop; return (current); mirror image; reflected impedance; ~ **à phénomènes auroraux** auroral reflection; ~ **diffuse** diffuse reflectance; ~ **du signal** signal return; ~ **par plusieurs voies** multi-path reflection; ~ **plane** specular reflectance; ~ **totale** total reflection; ~ **troposphérique** tropospheric reflection

réflexions multiples zig-zag reflection; ~ **successives** multi-hop

refonte f rewritten; revised; altered (structurally)

reformer v re-format

refoulement m overflow; rejection; delivery; discharge; output

réfraction f **côtière** coastal refraction; ~ **normale** standard refraction

refroidi à air brassé fan-assisted cooling; forced-draught cooling

refroidisseur m heat sink; cooling vane; cooling fin

refus m denial; lock-out; no-go; fail (of test); ~ **de prise** no-free-trunk condition

refuser v disable; reject; deny; refuse; decline; not accept; not permit

refusion étain-plomb reflow soldering; fusing; sweating; ~ **par flux d'air chaud** reflow soldering

regarnir v reload

régénérateur m signal amplifier; repeater; rejuvenator; ~ **de la composante** direct current (DC) restorer; ~ **de synchronisation** sync regenerator; synchronizing pulse repeater; ~ **d'impulsions** pulse repeater; pulse corrector; ~ **tube cathodique** CRT rejuvenator

régénération f regeneration; reload(ing); refresh; restoration; restart; ~ **d'impulsions** pulse regeneration; ~ **du train numérique** bit-stream regeneration

régénérer v equalize; recover; refresh; reload; rejuvenate; re-cycle; repeat; boost; ~ **l'écran** re-draw screen (display)

régie f control desk (of cable TV network); ~ **d'abonnés** controller; subscriber multiservice control unit; interface; ~ **d'installation d'abonnés** network termination (NT); ~ **intelligente** smart terminal supervisor; intelligent subscriber interface

régime m power; rate; rating; state; operating conditions; system; load; procedure; governing factor(s); mode; duty; norm; standard; range; speed; (tax) category; ~ **accidentel** undervoltage condition(s); ~ **conti-**

R

nu CW (morse) operation; continuous wave; ~ **de courant résiduel** residual-current state; ~ **de décharge** discharge current; ~ **de saturation** saturation state; ~ **du neutre** neutral point; neutral conductor; ~ **dynamique** dynamic operation; ~ **frontalière** frontier relations; ~ **isolé** isolated phase; ~ **moteur (RM)** rating (of motor); ~ **permanent** steady state; ~ **statique** steady-state operation; ~ **transitoire** transient state; waveform response

région *f* region; area; bucket (of memory); ~ **contiguë** bucket; ~ **de diffraction** diffraction region; ~ **de Fresnel** Fresnel region; ~ **d'induction** (reactive) near-field region

régional *adj* regional

régisseur *m* **d'abonné** intelligent subscriber interface

registre *m* register; latch; counter; flag; ~ **à approximations successives** successive-approximation register; ~ **à circulation** delay-line register; circulating register; ~ **à décalage** shift register; offset register; ~ **à décalage long** long-shift register; ~ **à empilement** stack register; ~ **à glissement** shift register; ~ **à quatre éléments binaire** quad bistable latch; ~ **accumulateur** accumulator (register); tally register; ~ **adressable** addressable latch; ~ **arithmétique** accumulator; arithmetic register; ~ **arrivée** destination register; ~ **banalisé** general register; ~ **d'addition** A-register (augend register); ~ **d'adresse d'instruction** instruction address register; location counter; instruction counter; ~ **d'adresses** base register; index register; B-box; ~ **d'affichage** console display register; ~ **d'aiguillage de données** memory switch; ~ **d'aiguillage d'octets** memory switch; ~ **de base** base register; B-register (addend register); index register; B-box; B-line; ~ **de contrôle** check register; status register; ~ **de cumul** accumulator (register); B-register; index register; addend register; B-box; ~ **de décalage** (cyclique) shift register; circulating register; ~ **de fautes (RF)** fault register; ~ **de masquage** mask register; ~ **de microinstruction** pipeline register (control register = program counter); ~ **de phase** program counter; instruction address register (IAR); ~ **de processus** process register; ~ **de retenue** latch; put-aside register; ~ **de segment** segment register; overlay register; ~ **de sortie** output register; ~ **de travail** scratchpad register; cut-and-paste register; ~ **d'émission** send register; ~ **d'état de périphérique** device flag; ~ **d'état pro-**

gramme program status register; ~ **d'index** B-register; addend register; index register; ~ **d'information** order register; ~ **d'instruction** instruction counter; location counter; ~ **d'opérations échelonnées** instruction address register (IAR); ~ **espion** transfer register; console display register; ~ **index** B-box; index register; modifier register; accumulator register; B-line; B-store; B-register (addend register); ~ **mémoire** storage register; memory register (distributor); exchange register; high-speed bus; arithmetic register; auxiliary register; ~ **opérateur** arithmetic register; ~ **parallèle** parallel register; ~ **pointeur** pointer (link-address) register; ~ **programme** control register; program counter; ~ **réduit** short(-format) register

réglable *adj* controlled; ~ **à l'infini** random setting; infinitely variable

réglage *m* setting; adjustment; line-up; control; tuning; ~ **à l'infini** random setting; ~ **approximatif** coarse adjustment; ~ **automatique** automatic control; ~ **automatique d'accord** automatic frequency control (AFC); ~ **automatique d'amplitude** automatic amplitude control; ~ **automatique de fréquence** automatic frequency control (AFC); ~ **automatique de sélectivité** automatic selectivity control; ~ **automatique de sensibilité** automatic gain control (AGC); ~ **automatique de surcharge** automatic overload control (AOC); ~ **automatique du gain** automatic gain control (AGC); ~ **d'accord** trimming; tuning; ~ **de fréquence** locking; tuning; ~ **de gain compensé** compensated volume control; ~ **de la dynamique** volume range control; ~ **de la linearité** linearity control; ~ **de l'amplitude** amplitude control; ~ **de l'équivalent** transmission loss adjustment; ~ **de précision** fine adjustment; vernier control; ~ **de puissance** gain control; volume control; ~ **de sélectivité** selectivity control; ~ **de tonalité** tone control; ~ **des aiguës** treble control; ~ **des fréquences élevées** treble control; ~ **des graves** bass control; ~ **du seuil** set value; threshold setting; ~ **du zéro** null adjustment; offset(ting); zero setting (of amplifier); ~ **fin** fine setting; precision adjustment; fine tuning; jogging; inching; ~ **fin de vitesse** pitch setting (of tape or disk speed); ~ **grossier** coarse setting; ~ **haut de page** vertical registration; ~ **intensité normale** set highlight; ~ **intensité réduite** set lowlight; ~ **précis** fine adjustment/setting; fine tuning; ~ **silencieux** squelch; muting

R

control; ~ **silencieux compensé** compensated squelch; ~ **systématique** routine adjustment; ~ **usine (RU)** factory-set
règle f **de bipolarité** plus-minus rule; ~ **de formage** shaping rule
réglé en butée set to limiting value
règlement m regulations; ruling; payment; settlement
réglementation f regulations
régler v set; adjust; tune; line up
règles d'acheminement traffic routing rules; ~ **de l'art** prevailing standards; rules of the art; code of practice; ~ **de syntaxe** syntax rules; ~ **de tarification** charging rules; ~ **et tables d'échantillonnage** (text-)naming rules
réglet m rule; reglet
réglette (rg.) f strip; graduated scale; tag strip/block; terminal block (TB); bank; mounting; format line; control line (of screen); ruler line; ~ **à bornes** barrier strip; screw-type terminal; ~ **à broches** terminal strip (tag type); ~ **à coupure** splitting terminal block; ~ **à couteau** knife-switch tag board; ~ **à profil U** IC stick; ~ **de connexion(s)** terminal block (TB); terminal strip; ~ **de décharge** quenching lamp; ~ **de dérivation** bridging connector; ~ **de jacks** jack strip; ~ **de raccordement** terminal block (TB); ~ **de répartition** fanning strip
régleur (professionnel) (skilled) fitter
régression v loss of compatibility
regroupé (dans) subsumed (under)
regroupement m collection; marshalling; assembly; pooling; mustering; consolidation; combination; assimilation; gathering; relating; collating; ~ **des données** data collection
regrouper v gather(-write); marshal; assemble; muster; combine; harness; collect; pool; consolidate; assimilate; correlate (with); collate; batch; ~ (sous un numéro) subsume (under); assimilate
régularisation f up-dating; up-grading
régulateur m governor; controller; regulator; ~ **à découpage** switching regulator; ~ **à trois actions** three-term controller (PID); ~ **automatique d'accord** automatic frequency control (AFC); ~ **automatique d'amplification** automatic volume control (AVC); ~ **automatique de fréquence** automatic frequency control (AFC); ~ **automatique de gain** automatic gain control (AGC); ~ **automatique de niveau** automatic volume control (AVC); ~ **automatique de sensibilité** automatic gain/volume control (AGC/AVC); ~ **automatique de tension** automatic voltage regulator; ~ **de brillance** brightness control; ~ **de phase** phase regulator; ~ **de**

rapport cyclique duty cycle regulation device; ~ **de sensibilité temporisé** anti-clutter gain control; swept gain; sensitivity time control; gain time control; ~ **de tension** voltage regulator; line regulator; ~ **d'excitation** excitation regulator; ~ **d'induction** induction regulator; ~ **d'intensité** volume control; ~ **série** series regulating device; ~ **suiveur** zero detector
régulation f control; regulation; direction; ~ **amont** line regulation; ~ **aval** load regulation; ~ **de charge** load shedding; ~ **des flux d'information** flow control; ~ **en cascade** cascade control; ~ **en charge** load regulation; ~ **en entrée/d'entrée** line regulation; ~ **linéaire** series regulation; linear regulation; ~ **numérique directe** direct digital control; ~ **PID** three-term control (proportional-integral-derivative PID)
régulier adj symmetrical; geometrically-aligned; steady; uniform; consistent
rehausse f canopy; extender; elevating rail; form; stand-off; clearance ledge
réimplantation f relocation
réimplanter v relocate; re-site
réinitialisation f warm start; restart; re-boot; ~ **à froid** cold start; initial program load
réinitialiser v reset; re-initialize; reload; restart; re-boot
réinjection f feedback; reflection; ~ **de tension alternative** AC ripple; ~ **sur la source** output ripple (noise) (in mV p-p)
réinscriptible re-enterable
réintroduction de la porteuse re-insertion of carrier
réintroduire v retro-fit; re-enter
réjecteur m **de canal** channel rejector
réjection f **de la bande Q** Q-band rejection; ~ **de la fréquence image** image frequency rejection; ~ **de signaux parasites** clutter rejection; ~ **en mode commun (RMC)** common-mode rejection ratio (CMRR)
relâchement m drop-out (of relay); release; ~ (d'un appel) (call) release; ~ **arrière différé** delayed backward release; ~ **différé** slow release; ~ **général** general release; ~ **retardé** slow release
relâcher v drop out (of relay); release
relais m relay; protection; switch; repeater; way station; base station; ~ **à accrochage** latching relay; locking relay; ~ **à action différée** time-delay relay; slow-acting relay; ~ **à action échelonnée** stepping relay; two-step relay; ~ **à action lente** slow-acting relay; time-delay relay; ~ **à action répétée** repeating relay; ~ **à adhérence** latching relay; locking relay; ~ **à ampoule** reed

R

relay; ~ à **ampoule scellée** reed relay; ~ à **armature double** twin-armature relay; ~ à **attraction retardée** slow-acting relay; time-delay relay; ~ à **blocage** latching relay; ~ à **bobine plongeante** plunger relay; ~ à **cascade** stepping relay; ~ à **champ de shunt** shunt-field relay; ~ à **contact en ampoule hermétique** sealed-contact relay; ~ à **contact mouillé au mercure** mercury-wetted relay; ~ à **contacts scellés** sealed-contact relay; reed relay; ~ à **dérivation magnétique** shunt-field relay; ~ à **deux positions stables** side-stable relay; ~ à **deux seuils** two-step relay; ~ à **deux temps** two-step relay; ~ à**diaphragme** diaphragm relay; ~ à **enclenchement** latching relay; ~ à **fiches** plug-in relay; ~ à **fort pouvoir de coupure** heavy-duty relay; ~ à **haute impédance** high-impedance relay; ~ à **induction** induction relay; ~ à **lames souples** reed relay; ~ à l'**indifférence** neutral relay; ~ à **maximum** surge relay; ~ à **mémoire** locking relay; latching relay; ~ à **mercure** mercury-wetted relay; ~ à **minimum** undercurrent/undervoltage relay; ~ à **palette** armature relay; ~ à **point nul** residual relay; locking relay; ~ à **portée optique** line-of-sight repeater; ~ à **redresseurs secs** rectifier relay; ~ à **rémanence** remreed; ~ à**résonance** tuned relay; ~ à **tige** reed relay; ~ à **tiges à maintien magnétique** remreed; ~ à **tout ou rien** all-or-nothing relay; (electromagnetic) changeover (on/off) relay; ~ **amplificateur** amplifier-operated relay; ~ **auxiliaire** relief relay; ~ **bagué** slugged relay; coupled relay; ~ **bistable** side-stable relay; two-step relay; ~ **chemisé** slugged relay; coupled relay; ~ **compteur** counting relay; ~ **convertisseur** converter relay; ~ **d'accès** access relay; ~ **d'accouplement** interlocking relay; latching relay; ~ **d'adressage** access relay; ~ **d'aiguillage** changeover relay; ~ **d'alimentation** feeder relay; ~ **d'annonciateur** line relay; ~ **d'appel** line relay; call relay; ringing relay; ~ **d'avance** stepping relay; ~ **de blocage** latching relay; ~ **de commande** control relay; ~ **de commande de sonnerie** ringing-current connect relay; ~ **de connexion** connecting relay; cut-through relay; ~ **de coupure** cut-off relay; supervisory relay; stepping relay; ~ **de courant** current relay; ~ **de déclenchement** tripping relay; release relay; ~ **de décodage** decoding relay; ~ **de défaut en série** failed cascade relay stages; ~ **de dérivation** shunt-field relay; ~ **de faute** fault relay; lock-out relay; ~ **de fonction** function relay; ~ **de fréquence** frequency relay; ~ **de liaison** coupling relay; connecting relay; cut-through relay; ~ **de libération** release relay; tripping relay; ~ **de ligne** line relay; calling relay; ~ **de mise en faute** lock-out relay; ~ **de mise en faux appel** lock-out relay; permanent-line relay; ~ **de mise en marche** starting relay; ~ **de passage** visited base station; ~ **de protection** protection relay; ~ **de puissance** power relay; ~ **de radiodétection** radar relay; ~ **de renvoi en faux-appel** lock-out relay; permanent-line relay; ~ **de retour de courant** reverse-current relay; directional relay; ~ **de sectionnement** isolating relay; ~ **de signal** signal relay; ~ **de signalisation** signal relay; ~ **de sonnerie** ringing current (relay); ~ **de supervision** supervisory relay; ~ **de surcharge** overload relay; ~ **de test** test relay; ~ **de tirage** pulling station; ~ **de verrouillage** locking relay; latching relay; ~ **d'écoute** listening-in relay; intercept relay; ~ **d'enclenchement** interlocking relay; ~ **d'entraide** inter-aid relay; ~ **détecteur** sensing relay; ~ **différentiel** differential relay; balancing relay; ~ **d'impédance** impedance relay; distance relay; ~ **d'inversion de batterie** battery-reversal relay; ~ **directionnel** reverse-current relay; directional relay; ~ **d'isolement** isolating relay; ~ **d'itinéraire** routing relay; ~ **double** double-coil relay; twin-armature relay; ~ **du signal de fin** clearing relay; ~ **électro-magnétique** electromagnetic relay; ~ **électro-thermique** thermal relay; ~ **enfichable** plug-in relay; ~ **étanche** sealed relay; ~ **européen** continental relay; ~ **hermétique à gaz inerte** dry-reed relay; ~ **hertzien** microwave link; radio relay; ~ **homopolaire** homopolar relay; ~ **huilé** oil-filled relay; oil-break relay; oil-insulated relay; ~ **instantané** instantaneous relay; tripping relay; cut-through relay; ~ **intégrateur d'impulsions** notching relay; ~ **interchangeable** relay set; ~ **intermédiaire** transfer relay; ~ **itinéraire** routing relay; ~ **limiteur d'intensité** current-limiting relay; ~ **magnéto-thermique (Rmt)** thermal relay; ~ **miniature** miniature relay; ~ **miniature (polarisé)** cradle relay; telegraph relay; ~ **modulateur** chopper; ~ **multiple (RM)** multiple coil relay; multiple relay; access relay set; ~ **nominal** home base station; ~ **non polarisé** neutral relay; non-polarized relay; ~ **pas à pas** single-step relay; one-step relay; ~ **photosensible** photo-electric relay; ~ **polarisé** polarized relay; directional relay; ~ **polyphasé** phase-balance relay;

~ **primaire** initiating relay; ~ **progresseur** selector relay; single-step relay; ~ **quadruple** four-coil relay; ~ **quintuple** five-coil relay; ~ **rapide** high-speed relay; ~ **retardé** time-delay relay; time-lag relay; ~ **scellé sous ampoule** reed relay; ~ **sélecteur** discriminating relay; ~ **simple** single-coil relay; ~ **statique** static relay/modulator; solid-state relay; ~ **téléphonique** telephone relay; ~ **temporisé** time-delay relay; slow-acting relay; ~ **thermionique** thermionic relay; ~ **thermique (Rt)** electro-thermal relay; thermal relay; ~ **totalisateur** integrating relay; ~ **tout ou rien** changeover relay; on-off-relay; all-or-nothing relay; ~ **translateur** repeating coil; ~ **vibrateur** vibrating relay

relance automatique des demandes de rappel automatic reactivation of call-back requests; ~ **de sonnerie** ringing tone reactivated

relancer v restart; re-activate; re-instate; resume; re-order (of supplies); re-issue

relation f affinity; relation; handshaking; connection; signalling; relationship; link; interaction; ~ **bilatérale à grande distance** two-way long-haul link/connection; ~ **de phase** phase relationship; ~ **d'impulsions** mark-space ratio; ~ **directe** direct relation; ~ **directe de trafic** direct relation; ~ **source-collecteur** source-sink relationship; ~ **télégraphique** telegraph relation; telegraph traffic; ~ **téléphonique** telephone relation; telephone traffic

relations frontalières frontier traffic; cross-border traffic; ~ **homme-machine (RHM)** man-machine language (MML); operator commands; interactive working

relaxateur m **horizontal** horizontal oscillator

relaxation de câblage strand setting

relayer v relay

relecture f write-then-read; read-back; echo check; echoplex

relève f **des défauts** troubleshooting

relevé m plot(ting); reading; record; map; acquisition; ticket; docket; ~ **de bits** bit map; ~ **de communication** toll ticket; ~ **de données** data acquisition; ~ **de facturation** bill; statement; ~ **de la mémoire** memory map; ~ **de taxes** toll readout

relèvement m (taking a) bearing; ~ **approximatif** course bearing; ~ **croisé** cross-bearing; ~ **de la cible** target bearing; ~ **graduel du niveau** fade up; ~ **par impulsions** pulse direction-finding; ~ **précis** fine bearing; ~ **radiogoniométrique** radio direction-finding (RDF); ~ **tridimensionnel** three-dimensional direction-finding; ~ **visuel** visual direction-finding; ~ **vrai station-station** true bearing ground-to-ground

relever v raise; record; read (off); map; chart; fetch; clear (of fault); measure

relié à mated with

relier v connect (up); link; join; couple; span; route; wire; interconnect; bind; plug

reliés entre eux connected pairwise; bunched; commoned

reliquat m residue; back-order; back-log; balance

réluctance f reluctance

rémanence f afterglow; residual magnetism; non-volatility; ~ **par la compression** compression set

rémanent adj non-volatile; retentive; residual; persistent; lingering

remblai m back-fill(ing)

rembobinage m rewinding

remettre à blanc clear; ~ **à zéro** reset; clear; zeroize; store zero (STZ)

remis en sonnerie re-rung

remise f (au client) handover; transfer; ~ **à zéro (RZ/RAZ)** reset; clear; zeroizing; store zero (STZ); cancelling (of lamp/alarm); ~ **au contrôle** control hand-over; relinquishing control; ~ **au repos** release; ~ **des télégrammes** delivery of telegrams; ~ **en cause** (major) overhaul; reassessment; ~ **en état** re-instatement; overhaul; reconditioning; ~ **en marche** re-start; ~ **en service** re-instatement; re-enabling

remodulation f remodulation

remontée f wicking; migration; (call) tracing; pick-up (of relay); capillary action; precipitation; posting (of data); up-loading; ~ **à vide** latch-up; ~ **de soudure** wicking; precipitation; capillary action; ~ **du curseur** cursor up (CUU); ~ **par le chemin de propagation** (propagation) path-tracing process; backward recovery; audit trail

remorqué adj articulated

remplacement m substitution; swapping; exchange; refurbishment

remplacer v supplant; swap

remplage m filler

remplir v fill; pad; complete; blank (off)

remplissage m filler; blanking (plate); padding; replenishment; charge; ~ **au fur et à mesure** most-busy method; ~ **numérique** digital filling

remue-méninges brainstorming

rendement m performance; yield; output; efficiency; main characteristic; occupancy; throughput; ~ **anodique** (RF stage) anode efficiency; conversion efficiency; plate efficiency; ~ **d'antenne** aerial efficiency; ~ **de conversion** conversion efficiency;

plate efficiency; anode efficiency; ~ d'écran screen efficiency; ~ du trafic diurne all-day efficiency; ~ énergétique energy efficiency; ~ global overall efficiency; ~ horaire hourly percentage paid time; paid time ratio; ~ quantique quantum yield; quantum efficiency; ~ supérieur heavy duty

rendre disponible enable access; ~ étanche waterproof; ~ la main relinquish control; control transfer; ~ opérationnel come on stream; ~ robuste ruggedize

rendu de l'écran background image (normal/reverse video); ~ visuel screen attribute; video attribute; graphics attribute

renforcé adj in-depth; intensified; heavy-duty

reniflard m sniffer

renifleur m sniffer (nitrous explosive detector)

renommé adj prestigious

renoncer v waive; discard

renouement m wrap-around

renouvellement d'appel extérieur trunk re-dial

renseignement(s) m(,pl) intelligence; information; detail(s)

renseignements (code 12 en France) directory enquiries; directory

renseigner (rubrique) complete (field)

rentabiliser v recoup investment(s)

rentabilité f return on investment; profitability; cost-effectiveness; economic viability

rentable adj commercially viable

rentré adj retracted; withdrawn; up-locking

rentrées f pl en devises foreign earnings

renversement m reversal; ~ de la polarité polarity reversal; ~ des phases phase reversal; phase inversion

renvoi m transfer; cross-reference; referral; return; extension; re-routing; branch; relay; patching; re-direction; GET; ~ (d'organigramme) connector (flow chart); flow-line; ~ automatique sur opératrice call forwarding - follow me; ~ aux essais switching to test circuits; test circuit transfer; ~ commandé on-demand call forwarding; variable call forwarding; call forwarding - don't answer (busy line); call diversion - all calls; ~ conditionnel call forwarding - don't answer; ~ d'abonné follow-me call forwarding; ~ d'appel call forwarding; call transfer; follow-me facility; call diversion; ~ d'appel forcé abbreviated ringing-station busy; delayed ringing; forced call forwarding; ~ d'appel temporaire poste-à-poste follow-me facility; call diversion; ~ d'appels en cas d'absence de demandé automatic call forwarding (where the subscriber is absent); ~ de jour day-time transfer; ~ de lignes line transfer;

~ de nuit common night service; night (trunk) answer; pre-assigned station night answering service; ~ début go to home position; ~ des appels vers les numéros changés changed-number intercept; ~ des lignes pour le service de nuit night-service connection; ~ différé call forwarding - don't answer; call diversion - no reply; ~ en arrière backward signalling; ~ en cas d'absence call forwarding - when absent/don't answer; ~ en cas de non réponse call forwarding - don't-answer; ~ en cas d'occupation call forwarding - busy line; ~ en cascade cascaded forwarding; serial call forwarding; chain call; tandem call forwarding; ~ en faute lock-out; ~ en faux appel line lock-out; ~ fixe call forwarding - preset; call diversion - preset; ~ général (RG) assigned night answer (ANA); fixed night service; predetermined night answer; ~ si poste occupé call diversion on engaged; call diversion when busy; ~ sur garde parking orbit; ~ sur non réponse timed-out call forwarding; call forwarding - don't answer; ~ sur occupation call forwarding - when busy; busy transfer; call forwarding - busy line; ~ sur position de renseignements service intercept; ~ temporaire temporary call forwarding - follow me; call diversion; ~ temporaire (commandé) variable on-demand call forwarding; meet-me call forwarding; follow-me call forwarding; automatic transfer; call forwarding - variable; call forwarding - all calls; call diversion; ~ temporaire poste à poste follow-me facility; ~ temporaire variable (v. renvoi temporaire); ~ temporisé timed-out call forwarding; call forwarding when absent; call forwarding - don't answer; ~ variable call forwarding - follow me; meet-me call forwarding; on-demand call forwarding

renvoyer v forward; redirect; relay; re-route; transfer; postpone; defer; lock-out

répandre v (se) proliferate

répandu adj prevalent; widespread

réparabilité f repairability

réparateur m repairman; faultsman

réparation f fault-clearing routine; repair; reconditioning (of data record); making good; overhaul

réparer v revoke

répartis adj deployed; assigned; divided

répartiteur m distribution frame; scheduler; handler; patch board; flexibility point; splitter; dispatcher; distributor; cross-connect panel; patch panel/board; fanning strip; ~ à haute fréquence HF repeater

distribution frame; ~ **à sorties horizontales** horizontal distribution frame (HDF); ~ **à vis** barrier strip; ~ **basse fréquence (RBF)** repeater distribution frame (RDF); ~ **de croisement (RC)** intermediate distribution frame (IDF); ~ **de distribution** serving area interface; ~ **de groupes primaires (RGP)** group distribution frame (GDF); ~ **de groupes secondaires (RGS)** supergroup distribution frame (SDF); ~ **de jonctions MIC** PCM trunk distribution frame; switching interface; ~ **de masse (RM)** earth (bus-)bar; earth rail; ~ **de puissance** power divider; ~ **de signaux** signal splitter; ~ **d'entrée (RE)** main distribution frame (MDF); ~ **en cuivre** distribution frame; busbar; ~ **général (RG)** main distribution frame (MDF); ~ **intermédiaire (RI)** intermediate distribution frame (IDF); ~ **interurbain** trunk distribution frame; ~ **mixte** combined distribution frame (CDF); ~ **numérique** digital distribution frame; ~ **principal** main distribution frame (MDF)
répartition f distribution; sharing; splitting; budgeting; scheduling; fanning (strip); patching; cross-connection; multiplexing; apportionment; dividing; ~ **de l'équivalent de référence** budgeting of the reference equivalent; ~ **des groupes primaires/secondaires** group (or supergroup) allocation; ~ **des tâches** job scheduling; job handling; ~ **du champ sur l'ouverture** aperture illumination; ~ **en cloche** gabled distribution; tapered distribution; ~ **temporelle** time-division multiplexing
repasser le contrôle au pupitre return control to console
repérage m labelling; identification; component parts; reference
répercussion f knock-on effect
répercuter v reflect; carry forward; impinge (upon); influence; reproduce; transfer
repère m identification mark; item (number); reference; benchmark; label; feature; key; tag; guide; index mark; terminal identification; locator; flag; imprint; stamp; sign; inscription; seal; datum; embossment; ~ **de distance** range rings; ~ **d'étalonnage** calibration mark
reperforation f reperforation
répertoire m directory; (file) index; catalogue; repertory; inventory; instruction set; dictionary; record; auto-dial list; pre-recorded list; ~ **d'accès** log-in directory; ~ **de caractères** character set; character repertory; font; ~ **de fichiers** file directory; file index; ~ **de volume** volume index; ~ **des pages actives** translation look-aside buffer

répertorié adj indexed; listed; catalogued; enumerated; documented; itemized
répéter v roll-back; repeat; re-run; iterate; amplify; boost; regenerate; reflect; relay
répéteur m repeater; telephone amplifier; radio relay; transponder; ~ **à deux voies** go-and-return repeater; ~ **à deux voies et deux ponts** double-bridge two-way repeater; ~ **à impédance négative** negative-impedance repeater; ~ **correcteur de la distorsion** equalizing repeater; regenerative repeater; ~ **dans un seul sens** one-way repeater; ~ **de conférence** conference repeater; ~ **de cordon** cord repeater; ~ **de ligne** line repeater; ~ **de satellite** satellite repeater; transponder; ~ **de satellite passif** passive satellite transponder; ~ **d'impulsions** pulse repeater; ~ **embroché** through-line repeater; transit-line repeater; ~ **faisceau global** global beam transponder; ~ **fixe** fixed repeater; ~ **immergé** submerged repeater; ~ **intermédiaire pour circuit à deux fils** two-wire intermediate repeater; ~ **loué** leased transponder; ~ **négatif téléphonique pour circuit à deux fils** negative two-wire repeater; ~ **pour circuit à deux fils** two-wire repeater; ~ **pour circuit à quatre fils** four-wire repeater; ~ **régénérateur** regenerative repeater; ~ **régénérateur d'impulsions** regenerative pulse repeater; ~ **sur cordon** cord-circuit repeater; ~ **télégraphique** telegraph repeater; ~ **téléphonique** telephone repeater; ~ **terminal** terminal repeater; ~ **unidirectionnel** simplex repeater; one-way repeater; ~ **universel** universal repeater
répétiteur m repeater; tie-line; tie-trunk
répétiteur de signal signal repeater; ~ **numérique** digital repeater; digit-sending repeater
répétitif adj recurrent; iterative
répétition f repetition; iteration; retransmission; re-dialling; echo; ~ **automatique** automatic trunk redial; automatic last number repetition; ~ **automatique de tentative** automatic repeat attempt; ~ **de boucle** loop iteration; ~ **de caractères** repeat (REP)
rephasage m referencing
repliage m fold-back; folding; aliasing; fold-over; clinching (of terminations); ~ **de mise en boîte** modular folding
replié adj folded; crinkled; crumpled
repliement m **de lignes** line-shortening facility
replier v replicate
répondeur m transponder; (radar) beacon; answering machine; ~ **à deux fréquences** cross-band transponder; ~ **automatique fournissant une annonce pré-enregistrée**

custom announcement service; ~ **statique** announcement-only answering chip; ~ **téléphonique** answering machine; ~ **téléphonique automatique** automatic telephone answering machine

répondeur-enregistreur answering machine

réponse *f* reply; response; answer; reaction; blip; answer-back signal/code; return message; reflex; ~ **à l'échelon** step-function response; ~ **à une action impulsive de Dirac** Dirac pulse response; unit pulse response; ~ **au courant** response to current; ~ **automatique** automatic answering; call forcing; ~ **aux phénomènes transitoires** transient response; ~ **de la cible** target blip; ~ **d'identification de position** positional response; ~ **en fréquence** frequency response; ~ **en tension** voltage response; ~ **impulsionnelle à un échelon de courant de sortie** load transient response; ~ **impulsionnelle à un échelon de tension d'entrée** line transient response; ~ **non pertinente** false drop; alien; ~ **parasite** response to interference; ~ **percussionnelle** pulse response; ~ **pertinente** hit; ~ **transitoire** step response; ~ **vocale** audio response; voice answer-back

report *m* carry (over); transfer; postpone; ~ **à nouveau** amount carried forward; ~ **accéléré** high-speed carry; ripple-through-carry; ~ **bloqué à neuf** standing-on-nines (carry); ~ **circulaire** end-around-carry; wrap-around; ~ **d'impulsions en crédit** carry; ~ **d'impulsions en débit** borrow; ~ **en boucle** end-around-carry; ~ **en cascade** cascaded carry; ~ **en surface** surface-mounting; ~ **négatif circulaire** end-around-borrow; ~ **simultané** standing-on-nines; high-speed carry; ripple-through-carry; ~ **temporaire d'appels** follow-me call forwarding

reportage *m* outside broadcast; documentary programme; ~ **extérieur** outside broadcast (OB)

reporter *v* write back

reporteuse *f* (= machine de report) automatic account card feed; facsimile posting machine

repos *m* break (of NC contact); back (contact); home position (of contact); vigil; passive; space; quiescent; idle state; dwell; late; neutral; rest; pause; off (of tones); disconnected; ~ **téléphonique** do-not-disturb facility

repositionner *v* re-calibrate

repoussage *m* spinning (of metal)

repousser *v* repel; reject; spin; coil

reprendre *v* restore; reset; revert; restart;

retry; repair; re-establish; resume; pick up; retrieve; reproduce; replace; realign; incorporate; overhaul; collate; re-connect; refurbish; synchronize; recover; GO TO (instruction); adjust; re-enter; rescue; recycle; adapt; GET (of data); re-dial; ~ **le réglage** re-align; reset; re-adjust

représentant *m* salesman; representative; agent

représentation *f* **analogique** analogue representation; ~ **codée** coded representation; ~ **décimale codée binaire** binary-coded decimal representation; ~ **en transparence** phantom view; ~ **en virgule fixe** fixed-point representation; ~ **en virgule flottante** floating-point representation; ~ **exclusive** sole agency; ~ **graphique** schematic diagram; illustration; ~ **par accroissements** incremental representation

représenté en médaillon inset

représenter *v* account for; display; show

reprise *f* (action) replay; adaptation; adjustment; alteration; amendment; collation; de-update; GET (of data); GO TO (address); incorporation; iteration; loop-back; making good; modification; overhaul; pick-up; rallying; realignment; rebuilding; recall; reconnection; reconstitution; recovery; recuperation; recycling; redesign; re-dialling; re-entry; refurbishment; reinstatement; renovation; repair; repeat; reproduction; re-run; rescue; reset; restart; restoration; resumption; retest; retrieval; re-try; retrofit; review; revision; roll-back; upsurge; settling period; ~ **automatique** roll-back; automatic relocation/realignment; ~ **automatique d'appel** automatic callback; automatic recall (when free); ~ **connecteur** header (of connector); edge plug; ~ **d'abonnement** reconnection; ~ **d'appel** return to call on hold; call-back; call pick-up; recall; ~ **de présélection** repeat call attempt; automatic recall; re-dial; ~ **de tonalité** dial tone repetition; ~ **de transmission** put-back; X-on (transmitter on); ~ **de verrouillage de trame** reframing; ~ **du système** warm start; ~ **du trafic** resumption of load-sharing; ~ **d'un appel parqué** call pick-up; ~ **d'une ligne en garde** return to line on hold; answer hold; call pick-up and hold; ~ **en horloge locale** synchronization with local clock; ~ **partielle** warm start; ~ **sur erreur** roll-back; restart; ~ **sur incident** roll-back; restart; ~ **totale** cold start

reproductibilité *f* repeat accuracy; reproducibility; ~ **dans les gradients** uniform grading

reproduction *f* reproduction; restitution; ~ **de**

son sound reproduction; ~ **parfaite** perfect restitution

reproduire *v* reproduce; copy; duplicate

répulsion *f* repulsion

réputé *adj* (de) acknowledged (to)

requête *f* inquiry; request

réseau *m* circuit; mains (supply); network; system; lattice; exchange; pattern; array; raster; plant; installation; cluster; grid; spring; layout; line (voltage); ~ *adj* front-end; network(ed); ~ **à accords décalés** stagger-tuned circuit; ~ **à blocage** blocking network; ~ **à commutation de circuits** circuit-switching network; ~ **à commutation par paquets (RCP)** packet-switching network; hot-potato network; ~ **à compensation de température** temperature compensation network; ~ **à déphasage minimal** minimum-phase network; ~ **à entraide** mutual-aid network; inter-working network; ~ **à étages** multi-stage network; ~ **à mémoires tampons** buffered network; ~ **à neutre isolé** network with isolated neutral; ~ **à paires de bornes** N-port network; N-terminal network; ~ **à points multiples** multi-point network; ~ **à pôles** N-terminal network; N-port network; ~ **à programme enregistré** stored program (control) network; ~ **à résistance constante** constant resistance network; ~ **à synchronisation despotique** despotic (synchronized) network; ~ **à synchronisation mutuelle** mutually-synchronized network; ~ **actif linéaire** linear active network; ~ **actif passe-tout** all-pass active network; ~ **additionnel** add-on circuit; ~ **aérien** open-wire system; ~ **alternatif** AC mains supply; ~ **analogique** analogue network; ~ **automatique** dial-up network; ~ **banalisé** shared network; open systems network; ~ **bidirectionnel** two-way network; ~ **câblé** cable network; ~ **câblé de vidéocommunications** broadband cable network; ~ **centralisé** centralized (topology) network; star network; ~ **commuté** switched network; dial-up network; (public) switched network (PSN); ~ **commuté automatique** dial-up network; ~ **commuté avec numérotation** dial-up network; ~ **conformateur d'impulsions** pulse-shaping network; pulse-forming network (PFN); ~ **correcteur** equalizer; ~ **d'adaptation** matching network; ~ **d'aide à la commutation (RDC)** snubber circuit; snubber network; ~ **d'alimentation** power supply network/grid; ~ **d'alimentation sans pertes** loss-less feed network; ~ **d'antennes** aerial array; ~ **d'antennes à fentes** slot array; ~ **d'antennes diélectriques**

dielectric array; ~ **d'antennes phasé pour bande L** L-band phase array; ~ **de brassage** mixing network; grading network; ~ **de brassage commun** common mixing network; ~ **de Clos** Clos network; ~ **de commande** control network; ~ **de communication** communication network; ~ **de communication d'entreprise (RCE)** local area network (LAN); ~ **de commutation** switching network; ~ **de commutation de messages** message-switching network; store-and-forward network; ~ **de commutation de paquets** hot-potato network; packet-switching network; ~ **de concentration** concentration network; ~ **de connexion (CX/RCX)** switching network; (hybrid) term set; line terminating network; ~ **de connexion à blocage nul** non-blocking switching network; ~ **de connexion numérique** digital switching network; ~ **de connexion temporel** time-division switching network; ~ **de connexion temporel replié** folded time-division switching network; ~ **de connexion terrestre** terrestrial connecting network; ~ **de contre-distorsion** equalizer; ~ **de conversation** switching network; speech-path subsystem; ~ **de décalage** (data) shift network; ~ **de découplage** decoupling network; ~ **de désaccentuation** post-emphasis/de-emphasis network; ~ **de dipôles** dipole array; ~ **de dipôles pour réception** all-channel aerial; ~ **de distribution** distribution network; loop plant; ~ **de distribution public** mains (supply); ~ **de distribution tiers** third-party vendors; dealer network; ~ **de données** data network; ~ **de donnees spécialisees** dedicated data network; ~ **de fentes rayonnantes** slot array; ~ **de force motrice** power network; ~ **de grande ville** metropolitan network; ~ **de n prises** (TV) network reaching out to n households; ~ **de parole** switching network; speech-path subsystem; ~ **de protection (RDC)** snubber circuit; snubber network; ~ **de radiodiffusion** radio network; broadcast(ing) network; ~ **de sonnerie** common alerting system; ~ **de surveillance par radar** radar warning net; ~ **de télécommunication** telecommunications network; ~ **de télécopie** facsimile network; ~ **de télédistribution** cable TV network; ~ **de téléinformatique** data (communications) network; ~ **de télévision** television network; ~ **de traction électrique** electric traction network; ~ **de transfert** transmission network; ~ **de transit** transit network; ~ **de transmission** transmission network; ~ **de transmission de données** data network; ~ **de transmission de l'image** radar link; ~ **de transport** transmission network; ~ **de transport de données** data communications network; ~ **de transport d'énergie électrique** power transmission/ distribution network; ~ **d'éclairage** lighting circuit; lighting system; ~ **démocratique** democratic (mutually synchronized) network; ~ **d'équilibrage** balancing network; ~ **d'équilibrage duplex** duplex artificial circuit; duplex balance; ~ **despotique** despotic (synchronized) network; ~ **d'images** video network; ~ **d'information** information network; ~ **d'information temporelle** serial) inter-processor data link; ~ **dissimulé** out-of-sight plant; ~ **diviseur** dividing network; ~ **d'opérateurs ET/OU NON** AND/OR INVERT gate array; ~ **droit** non-folded network; rectangular network; ~ **droit replié par ses sorties** rectangular network with folded outlets; ~ **droit replié par un étage supplémentaire** rectangular network folded using an additional stage; ~ **droit replié sorties vers entrées** rectangular network with outlets folded back to inlets; ~ **en delta** delta network; ~ **en double T** twin-T network; ~ **en échelle** ladder network; ~ **en étoile** star network; centralized topology; ~ **en I** H-network; ~ **en mailles** meshed network; closed-loop network; ~ **en pi** pi-network; ~ **en spirale** spiral array; ~ **en T ponté** bridged-T network; ~ **en treillis** lattice network; ~ **équipé au moyen de bobines d'extinction** network equipped with arc-suppression coils; ~ **équivalent** equivalent network; ~ **étoile** umbrella; star network; centralized network (topology); ~ **filtrant** filter network; weighting network; ~ **hiérarchisé** hierarchical (mutually-synchronized) network; ~ **infini d'antennes accordées** infinite periodic array; ~ **intégrateur** integrating network; ~ **intégré** integrated network; ~ **interconnexion (RI)** interconnecting network (IN); ~ **international** international network; ~ **interrégional** inter-regional network; ~ **interurbain (RI)** trunk network; long-distance network (LDN); toll network; ~ **interurbain pour exploitation sans attente** demand trunk network; ~ **ligne à retard** bucket-brigade delay line; ~ **linéaire d'antennes** linear (aerial) array; end-to-end array; ~ **linéaire flexible** flexible linear array; ~ **local** local network; ~ **local d'entreprise (RLE)** local area network (LAN); ~ **local d'établissement (RLE)** local area network (LAN); ~ **logique fixe** hard-array logic (HAL);

~ **logique préprogrammé** hard-array logic (HAL); ~ **logique programmable** programmable array logic (PAL); ~ **maillé** fully-meshed (grid) network; closed-loop network; lattice network; ~ **mis en garde** trunk call held; ~ **multipoint** multi-drop network; multi-point network; ~ **multiservices** integrated services digital network (ISDN); ~ **neutre relié à la terre** network with earth-connected neutral; ~ **non linéaire** non-linear network; ~ **numérique à intégration de services (RNIS)** integrated services digital network (ISDN); ~ **numérique avec intégration des services** integrated services digital network (ISDN); ~ **numérique intégré (RNI)** integrated digital network (IDN); ~ **oligarchique** oligarchic (synchronized) network; ~ **optique multiservices** ISDN optical fibre network; ~ **P et T** public switched network; dial-up network; ~ **partiel** network cluster; ~ **passif** passive network; ~ **plan** planar network; ~ **plésiochrone** plesiochronous network; ~ **pondérateur** weighting network; ~ **prédiffusé** semi-custom circuit; gate array; ~ **primaire** primary network; ~ **privé à téléimprimeurs** private telegraph network; ~ **public** public telephone network; ~ **public de transmission de données** public data network; ~ **radioélectrique pour communications à grande distance** long-haul radio network; ~ **radiogoniométrique** direction-finding network; ~ **rapide** quick-chip; ~ **réfléchissant** reflective network; ~ **répartiteur** dividing network; ~ **replié** folded network; ~ **résistif** resistor network; ~ **retardateur** delay network; ~ **rural** rural network; ~ **sans blocage** non-blocking network; ~ **secondaire** secondary network; ~ **serveur** (videotex) server network; ~ **symétrique** balanced network; ~ **synchrone** synchronous network; ~ **synchrone de données** synchronous data network; ~ **synchrone de transmission de données** synchronous data network; ~ **tandem de lignes de jonction** tandem tie trunk network (TTTN); ~ **télégraphique** telegraph network; ~ **télégraphique privé** private telegraph network; ~ **télégraphique public** public telegraph network; ~ **téléphonique asynchrone** asynchronous telephone network; ~ **téléphonique commuté (RTC)** (public) switched telephone network (PSTN); ~ **téléphonique local** local exchange network; ~ **téléphonique privé** private telephone network; ~ **téléphonique public** public telephone network; ~ **télex** telex network; ~ **temporel-temporel** time-time network (TT); ~ **terrestre**

terrestrial network; ~ **TV en circuit fermé** closed-circuit TV system; ~ **unidirectionnel** one-way network; ~ **urbain** local network

réseaux trunk groups; ~ **hiérarchisés en anneau** ring priority networks; ~ **parallèles** multi-bus system; ~ **réciproques** structurally dual networks

réserve f **d'atténuation** provision for future splices (of optic cable); ~ **de bande** reserve tape (at end of roll); ~ **de linéarité** overload factor

réservé adj dedicated; ~ (à l'extension) spare; for future expansion/development; standby

réserver v reserve; book

réservoir m bin; tank; well; ~ **à pensée** "think tank"

résidant adj resident

résidu du courant porteur carrier leak

résiduel adj residual; vestigial; leak(age)

résidus de flux flux residue

résiliation f termination; cancellation

résilié adj cancelled; revoked; annulled; rescinded; withdrawn; terminated

résilier v cancel; revoke; rescind; withdraw; annul

résine f potting compound; resin; gum; rosin; ~ **époxyde** epoxy resin; ~ **glycérophtalique** alkyd resin; glyptal resin; glycerol-phthalic anhydride; ~ **phénolique** phenolic resin; ~ **photosensible** (photogravure à r.) photoresist

résistance f resistor; resistance; strength; impedance; drag; ~ **à coefficient de température positif (CTP)** positive temperature coefficient (PTC) thermistor; ~ **à couche de carbone** carbon-film resistor; ~ **à couche métallique** metal-glaze (thick film) resistor; metal film resistor; ~ **à la lumière** light-fastness; ~ **à la pression** compression strength; ~ **à la rupture** breaking strength; ultimate tensile strength; ~ **à la soudure (choc thermique)** resistance to solder heat (thermal shock); ~ **à la traction** tensile strength; ~ **à l'abrasion** scratch resistance; ~ **à l'arc** arc resistance; ~ **à l'arrachement** pull-off strength; ~ **à l'éclatement** burst strength; ~ **à l'isolement** leakage resistance; insulation resistance; ~ **à plots** stepping resistor (rheostat); ~ **acoustique** acoustic resistance; ~ **additionnelle** dropping resistor; ~ **agglomérée** carbon composition resistor; ~ **ajustable** trimmer; trimpot; ~ **apparente** impedance; ~ **apparente à l'état passant** on-state slope resistance; ~ **au feu** flammability; ~ **ballast** load impedance; ballast resistor; ~ **bobinée (vitrifiée)** (vitreous) wire-wound resistor;

~ **chauffante** heater; heating element; ~ **chutrice** dimming resistor; load-limiting resistor; ~ **courant continu (R$_{cc}$)** DC (ohmic/true) resistance; ~ **d'adaptation** load-matching resistor; ~ **d'amortissement** damping resistance; ~ **dans l'état passant** on-state resistance (R$_{on}$); ~ **d'antenne** aerial resistance; ~ **de blocage** blocking resistance; ~ **de boucle** loop resistance; ~ **de bruit** noise resistance; ~ **de capacité** capacitance; ~ **de carbone aggloméreé** carbon composition resistor; ~ **de champ** diverter; ~ **de charge** load impedance; ballast resistor; resistor bulb; barretter; charging resistor; ~ **de chauffe** heater element; ~ **de contact** contact resistance; ~ **de couplage** coupling resistor; ~ **de décharge** discharge resistance; buffer resistance; ~ **de découplage** decoupling resistor; ~ **de démarrage** starting resistor; ~ **de filtrage** filter resistance; ~ **de fuite** leakage resistance; bleeder resistance; ~ **de fuite de grille** grid-leak (resistor); ~ **de grille** grid-leak resistor; ~ **de la masse** earth resistance; ~ **de limitation** current-limiting resistor; ~ **de polarisation** bias resistor; ~ **de puissance** power resistor; ~ **de rappel** pull-down resistor; pull-up resistor; ~ **de rayonnement** radiation resistance; ~ **de terminaison** load resistor; matched load; termination; ~ **de tirage** pull-down resistor; ~ **de tirage extérieur** external pull-down resistor; ~ **d'économie** economy resistance; ~ **d'électrode** electrode resistance; ~ **d'électrode en courant alternatif** electrode slope resistance; ~ **d'équilibrage** ballast resistor; barretter; ~ **des enroulements** winding resistance; ~ **différentielle** differential resistor; ~ **d'isolement** insulance; insulation resistance; input-output isolation; ~ **d'obscurité** dark resistance; ~ **drain-source** drain-source off-state resistance; ~ **économiseuse** (v. résistance d'économie); ~ **effective** AC resistance; effective resistance; ~ **électrique** heater element; ~ **en boucle** loop resistance; ~ **en continu** ohmic resistance; DC resistance; true resistance; electric resistance; linear resistor; ~ **en courant alternatif** slope resistance; incremental resistance; differential anode resistance; ~ **en court-circuit** short-circuit resistance; ~ **équivalente** equivalent resistance; ~ **équivalente du faisceau** electron-beam DC resistance; ~ **fixe à forte dissipation** fixed high-power resistor; ~ **intérieure** internal resistance; ~ **interne** anode/plate resistance; internal resistance; source resistance; ~ **interne de** la base base spreading resistance; ~ **interne différentielle** differential anode resistance; slope resistance; AC resistance; incremental resistance; ~ **limite à la rupture** break-down point; ~ **linéaire** ohmic resistor; linear resistor; ~ **linéique** resistance per unit length; ~ **mécanique** tensile strength; mechanical strength; ~ **non inductive** non-inductive resistance; ~ **non réactive** non-reactive resistance; ~ **normale à dissipation nulle** zero power resistance (R$_T$); ~ **ohmique** ohmic resistance; DC resistance; true resistance; electric resistance; linear resistor; ~ **parallèle** parallel resistance; ~ **parallèle équivalente** equivalent parallel resistance; ~ **protégée** candohm resistor; ~ **pure** pure resistance; intrinsic resistance; ~ **répartie d'antiparasitage** distributed resistance; ~ **rotorique** rotor resistance; ~ **série** dropping resistor; series resistor; ~ **série équivalente** equivalent series resistance; ~ **spécifique** specific resistance; ~ **statorique** primary resistance; ~ **thermique** thermal resistance (R$_{th}$); ~ **thermique jonction-boîtier** junction-case thermal resistance (R$_{th(j-c)}$); ~ **thermométrique** thermistor (thermo-resistor); ~ **variable** variable resistor (rheostat); ~ **VDR** voltage-dependent resistor (VDR); transient suppressor; varistor; ~ **vitrifiée** vitreous (wire-wound) resistor

résistant *adj* hardy; strong; resilient; sturdy; robust; ~ **à la propagation de la flamme** flame-retardant

résistivité *f* (volume) resistivity; specific resistance; specific insulation; ~ **(en volume ohmique) transversale** volume resistivity; ~ **superficielle** surface resistivity; ~ **transversale** mass resistivity; ~ **volume ohmique transversale** volume resistivity

résite *f* C-staged resin

résitol B-staged resin

résol A-staged resin

résolution *f* definition

résonance *f* resonance; ~ **aiguë** sharp resonance; ~ **de tension** voltage resonance; syntony; tuning; ~ **optique** optical resonance; ~ **série** series resonance; ~ **shuntée** parallel resonance; anti-resonance; shunt resonance

résonateur *m* resonator; tank circuit; ~ **à quartz** quartz-controlled resonator; ~ **de sortie** catcher; output resonator; output gap; ~ **d'entrée** buncher; input resonator; input gap

résonner *v* ring back

résorber (un dérangement) clear (of fault)

respecter *v* be compatible with; comply with;

observe; conform to; achieve; attain; uphold

responsable *f ou adj* supervisor; manager

resserrement des tolérances tighter tolerance limits

resserrer *v* contract; increase the severity of (test); tighten (-up)

ressort *m* spring; ~ **à épingle** torsion spring; ~ **à spires jointives** closed pattern (extension) spring; ~ **cylindrique** (à action angulaire) torsion spring; ~ **d'appel/de rappel** return spring; ~ **de commande** main spring; ~ **de compression** compression spring; ~ **de traction** extension spring

ressource *f* resource; facility

ressources humaines manpower; work force; liveware

ressuage *m* bleeding; sweating; weeping

restauration *f* regeneration; refresh; reload; restore; ~ **collective** cafeteria service; catering; canteen services; dining room facilities; ~ **de la composante continue** DC restoration; DC re-insertion; ~ **des modes** mode reset; ~ **normale de la composante continue** normal DC restoration

restaurer de la pile pop (from stack)

rester à l'appareil hold a circuit; hold the line

restituer *v* recover; restore; retrieve

restitution *f* reassembly; restitution; re-shaping; display attributes (of terminal); salvaging (of files); output; ~ **(de l'impulsion)** pulse (re-)shaping; ~ **de la composante continue** DC restoration; DC re-insertion; ~ **erronée** incorrect restitution; ~ **isochrone** isochronrous restitution

restockage en mémoire store-back

résultats *m pl* **obtenus en exploitation** field experience

résumé *m* abstract; summary; collation; subject matter; ~ **succinct** compendium; abstract

résumer *v* collate

rétablir *v* restore; reset

retaper *v* re-type

retard *m* delay; lag; error; stand-off; skew; ~ **à la croissance** turn-on time (t$_{on}$); ~ **à la décroissance** turn-off time (t$_{off}$); ~ **à la mise en conduction** turn-on time (t$_{on}$); ~ **absolu** absolute delay; ~ **aller-retour en extrémité** round-trip end delay; ~ **aux extrémités** end delay; ~ **de codification** coding delay; ~ **de phase** phase lag; ~ **de tonalité** dial(ling) tone delay (DTD); ~ **statistique** statistical delay

retardateur *m* delay unit; (digit) delay element

retardé *adj* delayed

retassement *m* condensing; squeezing; packing (of data)

R

retassure *f* shrinkage hole; void; recession; pipe

retenir *v* hold (in abeyance)

rétention *f* compression set

retentir *v* (sonnerie) ring (of bell)

retenue *f* deduction; borrow; carry digit; ~ **anticipée** carry look-ahead; ~ **complète** complete carry; ~ **de sortie** output carry; ~ **d'entrée** input carry; ~ **d'impulsions en débit** borrow (negative carry); ~ **mécanique** strain relief; ~ **négative** borrow (negative carry); ~ **propagée** carry look-ahead; ripple-through carry; high-speed carry

réticule *m* graticule; cross-hair; lattice

réticulé *adj* cross-linked

retirer separate out; withdraw

retombée *f* fall-out; spin-off; drop-out; decay; by-product; ~ **technologique** technological spin-off

retomber *v* drop out (of relay); release

retouche *f* patch; re-touch

retour *m* reverse/reversal; backwash (= overswing diode); re-entry; reset; return; backward; flash-back; back-track; change-back; ~ **à la ligne** new line (NL); ~ **à zéro** return to zero; reset; ~ **arrière** backspace (BS); ~ **au repos** homing; homelanding; ~ **chariot** (RC) carriage return CR); ~ **commun** common return; earth return; ~ **courant** reverse (blocking) current; ~ **d'appel** ringing signal; ring-back tone; ~ **d'appel cadencé** interrupted ring-back tone; ~ **d'appel immédiat** immediate ring-back tone; ~ **d'appel permanent** continuous ring-back tone; ~ **d'arc** back-fire; arc-back; ~ **de chariot (RC)** carriage return (CR); ~ **de l'information** feedback; ~ **d'écoute** feedback circuit; ~ **du faisceau** flyback (of CRT spot); ~ **du spot** flyback; retrace; ~ **libre** without resistance; ~ **par trajets multiples** multi-path return; ~ **sur la liaison normale** change-back

retour-image video relay link

retournement *m* turnover; turnaround (of modem)

retourneur de baie rack inverter

retrait *m* withdrawal; operator release; recession; shrinkage; contraction; ~ **avec chaînage** withdraw - serial call; ~ **de la pile** pop (from stack); ~ **de lignes** line withdrawal

retrancher *v* subtract

retranscription *f* re-copy

retransmetteur *m* repeater (e.g. telegraph relay); ~ **à bande perforée** reperforator; ~ **à bande perforée** (à lecture automatique totale) coupled reperforator and tape reader; fully automatic reperforator trans-mitter-distributor (FRXD)

retransmettre *v* retransmit; relay; forward; repeat

retransmission *f* retransmission; forwarding; relaying; intermediate handling; repeat transmission; ~ **automatique** automatic retransmission; ~ **des alarmes** alarm forwarding; alarm reporting; ~ **des numéros** automatic number identification; ~ **du numéro demandeur** automatic number identification

rétrécissant à la chaleur (heat-)shrinkable

rétrécissement *m* taper; shrinkage; necking

rétroaction *f* feedback

rétro-appel *m* consultation; consult/enquiry call; consultation hold; call pick-up; ~ **courtier** brokerage call; broker's call

rétrocouplage *m* positive feedback; regeneration

rétrodiffusion *f* backscattering; ~ **directe** short-distance backscatter; ~ **indirecte** long-distance backscatter; ~ **par la terre** ground backscatter

rétroprojecteur *m* overhead projector

rétroviseur *m* rear mirror

réunion *f* combination; OR operation; one gate; conference; ~ (circuit-) inclusive-OR (circuit); OR function; union; ~ **à distance** teleconferencing; ~ **d'information** press conference; briefing; ~ **téléphone** teleconferencing

réunir *v* convene; pool

réunis entre eux bunched; commoned

réutilisation de fréquence par double polarisation dual-polarization frequency re-use

revalider *v* re-enable

revalorisé *adj* reset to initial value

réveil *m* activation; wake-me/wake-up call; ~ **automatique** wake-me call service; automatic alarm call; wake-up call

révélation *f* foreground

revendeur *m* dealer; agent; retailer

réverbération *f* reverberation; echo; reflection

réversible *adj* double-ended; up-down

revêtement *m* surface coating; lining; coat; ~ **anticorrosif** anti-rust coating; corrosion-resistant coating; ~ **primaire (RP)** primary coating (extramural cladding)

revêtir *v* (de) face (with); coat; plate; clad

revêtu *adj* clad; coated

révision *f* overhaul; amendment; revision; editing; review

RF (v. récepteur de fréquence); ∼ (v. registre de fautes)

rg. (v. réglette)

RG (v. renvoi général); ∼ (v. répartiteur général)

RGP (v. répartiteur de groupes primaires)

RGS (v. répartiteur de groupes secondaires)
rhéostat *m* rheostat; dimmer; variable resistance; **~ bobiné** wire-wound rheostat; **~ de champ** field rheostat; **~ de démarrage** starting rheostat; **~ de glissement** (rotorique) slip regulator; **~ d'excitation** exciting rheostat
RHM (v. relations homme-machine)
rhodoïd *m* celluloid; transparency (cellulose acetate)
rhodoviol *m* polyvinyl alcohol
RI (v. répartiteur intermédiaire); ⩰ (v. réseau interconnexion); ⩰ (v. réseau interurbain)
riche *adj* versatile; detailed; abundant
richesse *f* **sémantique** signal repertoire
rideau *m* **à plat directionnel** billboard array; **~ Chireix-Mesny** Chireix array; broadside array; **~ d'antennes** tiered array; stacked array; aerial array; **~ de dipôles horizontaux à réflecteurs** pinetree (radar) array; **~ de Dolph-Tchebychev** Chebyshev array; **~ de doublets** pinetree (aerial) array; **~ de huit dipôles** eight-element dipole array; **~ de radar** radar array; **~ en dents de scie** Chireix array; broadside array; **~ gazeux** backflow; **~ multiple de doublets** Kooman's array; pinetree array; end-fire array; **~ rayonnant** radiating curtain; **~ réfléchissant** reflecting curtain
rigide *adj* torsion-resistant; rigid; solid
rigidité *f* tension (of spring); **~ diélectrique** dielectric strength; voltage proof; flash test; dielectric withstanding voltage; disruptive gradient
rigoureux *adj* exacting; stringent
risque commercial customer overdraft
river *v* clinch; rivet
rivet *m* **goutte de suif** mushroom-head rivet; button-head rivet; brazier-head rivet; snap(-head) rivet; **~ tubulaire** blank rivet; Chobert rivet; explosive rivet; blind rivet
RLE (v. réseau local d'entreprise); ⩰ (v. réseau local d'établissement)
RM (v. régime moteur); ⩰ (v. relais multiple); ⩰ (v. répartiteur de masse)
RMC (v. réjection en mode commun)
Rmt (v. relais magnéto-thermique)
RNI (v. réseau numérique intégré)
RNIS (v. réseau numérique à intégration de services)
robot *m* (d'appels) automatic system; robot transponder (exchange automatic answering service); (call) routiner; remote tester; end-to-end routiner; **~ d'arrivée (RAV)** incoming test call responder; (inward) call routiner; **~ d'essais** (end-to-end) call routiner
robotique *f* robotics; automatic control

robustesse *f* life; endurance; strength; robustness; ruggedness; sturdiness; **~ des sorties** robustness of terminations
rôdage *m* refining; burn-in; shakedown; soak test
rôder *v* hone; lap; burn-in; shakedown
rôle *m* function; **~ d'interface** liaison
rompre *v* break off (of call); disconnect; sever
RON et TRON E and M (wires) (= Ear/Mouth: backward and forward signal wires); inbound/outbound wires
rondelle *f* washer; spacer; distance piece; pad (of PCB); slice; **~ Belleville** conical (spring) washer; Belleville washer; **~ brute** black washer; **~ cuvette** dished washer; finishing washer; **~ de sécurité à crans** (notched) stop washer; lock washer; **~ d'éloignement** spacer; distance piece; **~ éventail** fan washer; star washer; **~ Grower** [A.C.] split (locking) washer; spring washer; **~ Onduflex** [A.C.] wave washer; flexible washer; spring washer; crinkle washer; **~ précise** machined washer; **~ Supergrower** [A.C.] (helical) split washer; spring washer; **~ Z** notched washer
ronflement *m* hum; **~ d'anode** anode hum; **~ de la modulation** modulation hum; **~ de secteur** mains hum; **~ résiduel** residual hum; ripple (noise)
ronflette *f* dither
ronfleur *m* buzzer
roquette *f* reel; spool
ROS (v. rapport d'onde stationnaire)
rosace *f* junction box; **~ de connexion** connection box; connection rose; **~ de plafond** ceiling rose
rosette *f* **de branchement** connection box
rotacteur *m* rotary switch; uniselector
rotation de bits cyclic shift; circular shift; **~ jusqu'au bout de course** level overflow motion
rotor *m* impeller; rotor; **~ à cage** squirrel-cage rotor; **~ à enroulement** phase-wound rotor; **~ en court-circuit** short-circuited rotor; **~ inductif** search coil
roue *f* **à ailettes** impeller; **~ codeuse** thumbwheel; code selector; **~ dentée** gear wheel; toothed wheel; cog wheel; **~ d'impression** printwheel; **~ phonique** phonic wheel; **~ polaire** rotor; armature
rouleau *m* rolling (mode); wrap-around; rack-up (of VDU display)
roulement *m* RY test loop and repeated R-Y (5-unit) code transmission
roulette(s) *f (pl)* castor(s)
routage *m* (chemin physique) circuit routing (physical path)

R

route *f* route; path; ~ **d'approche** homing

routeur *m* PCB auto-router

routine *f* routine

RP (v. revêtement primaire)

RQ automatique error-detection and feedback system; decision feedback system; request repeat system; (ARQ) system

RT (v. contact repos-travail)

Rt (v. relais thermique)

RTC (v. réseau téléphonique commuté)

RTT signalling code with metering pulse train

RU (v. réglage usine)

ruban *m* tape; band (of colour code); ribbon; ~ **à perforation partielle** chadless tape; ~ **cache** masking tape; ~ **de niveau** level bar; ~ **de protection** protective tape; ~ **de sélection** select bar; ~ **du papier** paper tape; ~ **encreur** fabric ribbon (cartridge); printer ribbon; ~ **isolant** insulating tape; masking tape; ~ **magnétique** magnetic tape; ~ **plat** microstrip; stripline; ~ **serré** tight fibre (of cable)

rubanage *m* taping; ribbon (of optical fibre cable)

rubrique *f* data element; record; reference; field; section; detail; parameter; heading; item; label

rudimentaire *adj* primitive

rugosité *f* surface finish; roughness; surface tension (SI unit)

ruissellement *m* trickling

rupteur *m* NC (normally-closed) contact; breaker; ~ **à tige** wobblestick; ~ **de charge** contact-breaker (load cut-out)

rupture *f* break; breakdown; disconnection; release; severance; opening (of verticals); fracture; breakage; interrupt; cleardown; discontinuity; branch; jump; clearing (of connection); break-off; separation; depletion; ~ **brusque** snap (action of contacts); ~ **d'appel** call release; ~ **DE** B-subscriber release; ~ **de boucle** loop-opening; loop-break; ~ **de communication** call release; ~ **de contact** sign-off; ~ **de liaison** outage; ~ **de ligne** line break; outage; ~ **de monotonie** string break; ~ **de réception** break; receive interruption; ~ **de séquence** sequence break; ~ **de stocks** stock depletion; ~ **DR** A-subscriber release; ~ **retardée** slow release

rural *adj* rural; countryside

rustine *f* kludge; patch

rythme *m* clock pulse; timing; strobe (marker pulse); ~ **de bits** bit timing

rythmeur *m* master clock; timing circuit; interval timer; digit emitter; clock-pulse driver

RZG (remise à zéro générale) general reset; initialization

RZP (remise à zéro partielle) partial reset

RZ/RAZ (v. remise à zéro)

S

sablage *m* (air) abrading; sand blasting
sablier *m* down-counter; timer
sabordage *m* aborting; abandonment
sabot *m* contact; shoe; collector; skid; ~ **de rangement** storage ramp
sabre *m* spindle; shaft (of rotary switch); warp; warping; curvature
sachet *m* **déshydratant** desiccant; siccative
SAD (v. sélecteur d'adresse)
saillie *f* overhang
sain *adj* hygienic; unimpaired; uncorrupted
saisie *f* interception; (data) entry; acquisition; capture; input; seizure; retrieval; recording; ~ **de données** data capture; input; entry; retrieval; ~ **de l'information** transaction; retrieval; ~ **de masse** bulk storage; mass storage; secondary storage
salissure *f* stain; smudge; blemish; grime; contamination; sludge; contaminant
salle (anéchoïde) **anéchoïque** free field room; anechoic chamber; ~ **blanche** laboratory; clean room; ~ **de l'autocommutateur** switching equipment room; switchroom; ~ **de l'automatique** switchroom; ~ **de visioconférence** videoconference studio; ~ **d'énergie** power room
salve *f* **d'erreurs** error burst
SAMU (service d'aide médicale d'urgence) (code 15 en France) emergency medical service; SOS team
sanction *f* acceptance criterion; tolerance limit(s); test conditions; post-test end-point
sang-froid *m* composure
satellite *m* remote line unit (RLU); sub-centre; orbital (earth) satellite; experimental space vehicle (ESV); ~ **à accès limité** limited-access satellite; ~ **à haute altitude** high-altitude satellite; ~ **à plusieurs accès** multiple-access satellite; ~ **à simple accès** single-access satellite; ~ **actif** active satellite; ~ **artificiel** artificial (earth) satellite; ~ **de communications** communications satellite; bird; ~ **de radiodiffusion** broadcasting satellite; ~ **de télécommunication** communications satellite; ~ **de télévision** television satellite; ~ **géostationnaire** geo-stationary satellite; ~ **géosynchrone** geo-stationary satellite; ~ **météorologique** weather satellite; ~ **passif** passive satellite; ~ **relais** relay satellite; ~ **spécifique** dedicated satellite; ~ **synchrone** geo-stationary satellite; ~ **tactique de communication** tactical communication satellite; ~ **télécommandé** station-keeping satellite

satiné *(adj)* brushed; spun (of aluminium)
satinisation *f* abrading (chemical etch)
satisfaisant *adj* conclusive (of test results)
saturation *f* bottoming; overflow; swamping; soak(-ing); congestion; ~ **en départ** all-trunks-busy (ATB); ~ **magnétique** magnetic saturation; soak
sauf *prep* NOT-IF-THEN; AND-NOT; exclusion; EXCEPT; ~ **dérogation** unless otherwise specified; unless (explicitly) waived; ~ **indication au contraire** unless otherwise specified/indicated
saut *m* skip (of page); shift; jump; ejection; slew; throw; leap; hop; slip; branch; GO TO (instruction); control transfer; ~ **après impression** post-slew; ~ **arrière de bloc** data block backward jump; ~ **avant de bloc** data block forward jump; ~ **avant impression** pre-slew; ~ **avant/arrière** position (jump) forward/backward; ~ **bas de page** bottom of form skip; ~ **de colonne** indent; tabulate; ~ **de colonne forcé** jump to next column; ~ **de feuillet** form feed; ~ **de fréquence** frequency jump/skip; frequency hopping; ~ **de fréquences** frequency hopping; ~ **de ligne** line feed; ~ **de ligne arrière** negative line feed; ~ **de page** form feed; next page (instruction); ~ **de papier** skip(ping) device; paper throw; paper slew; page eject; ~ **de phase** instruction step; (GOTO) next instruction; ~ **de tension** (voltage) surge; ~ **dernière position curseur** jump to last cursor position; ~ **d'espaces à haute vitesse** white-space tabulation; ~ **en écriture** slip-delete; ~ **inter-secteurs** sector interleaving; ~ **systématique** unconditional jump
sauter *v* skip; jump; branch
sauterelle *f* catch; latching mechanism
sautillement (d'image) jitter
sauvegarde *f* rescue dump; protection; (data) saving; back-up recording; (disk) copy; ~ (contexte s.) (data) integrity; dump; mode protection; context sensitivity; ~ **de contexte** context save; context switch; ~ **des comptes de taxe** charge account

dumping; ~ **des données** data integrity; ~ **des pavés** on-roll program block recording; ~ **et régénération** dump and restart (procedure); ~ **incrémentielle** programmed selective dump; periodic dump; dump and restart; ~ **par batteries** non-volatility; battery back-up; ~ **sélective** daily back-up; selective dump; snapshot dump

sauvegarder v copy; dump; save; protect; rescue; secure; ~ **dans la pile** push in the stack

SAV (v. service après-vente)

savoir-faire m skill(s); expertise; know-how; mastery; proficiency; versatility; talent

S + B/B (signal + bruit/bruit) signal-to-noise ratio (SNR)

scalaire m scalar

SCAO (v. système de commande d'assiette et d'orbite)

scaphandre m space suit

scellement m bedding-in; foundation; sealing; ~ **à disque** disk seal

scénario m **de cadrage** analytical model; ~ **vidéo** voice-over; script

schéma m diagram; layout; doctrine; outline; configuration; pattern; arrangement; flowchart; blueprint; structure; scheme; ~ **à manque de tension** break-type circuit layout; ~ **à mise de tension** make-type circuit layout; ~ **cinématique** operational diagram; ~ **conceptuel** research design; ~ **de câblage** wiring diagram; ~ **de circuit unifilaire** block diagram; ~ **de fonction** block diagram; ~ **de fonctionnement** block diagram; ~ **de montage** wiring diagram; ~ **de multiplage partiel** grading diagram; ~ **de principe** basic (theoretical) diagram; ~ **de synchronisation** synchronization pattern; ~ **de verrouillage** frame alignment pattern; framing pattern; ~ **d'ensemble** block diagram; ~ **d'ensemble et de niveaux** block and level diagram (BL); ~ **des connexions** wiring diagram; ~ **développé** circuit diagram; ~ **fonctionnel** block diagram; ~ **synoptique** block diagram

schémathèque f drawings; drawing library

scie f **à métaux** hacksaw; ~ **sauteuse** jig saw

scinder v segment; subdivide

scintillation f scintillation; flicker; flutter; ~ **de fréquence** frequency scintillation

scintillement m flutter; flicker; jitter; ringing; fading

scintiller v flash; flicker; sparkle; glitter; glisten

scission f hiving off

scorie f dross

scrutateur m scanner

scrutation f scanning; polling

SCTT (Service de Contrôle Technique des Télécommunications) French Telecom inspectorate

SDA (v. sélection directe à l'arrivée)

Sdt (v. station de transfert)

seau m pail; bucket

sécable adj soft; unprotected; segmented

sécant adj intersecting

sécheuse f **centrifuge** centrifugal drier; spin drier

second enroulement secondary winding

seconde gravement erronée severely errored second; ~ **qualité** sub-standard; second-rate

secours m **automatique** hot standby; ~ **croisé** mutual back-up; ~ **semi-automatique** warm standby

secouru par le secteur with back-up AC source

secousse(s) f (pl) bump (test)

secteur m mains; half-byte (4 bits: = nibble); arm; sector; segment (of commutator); bin; (data) block; slice (of pie chart); line; field; ~ **à grande diffusion** consumer sector; chain stores; market; ~ **alternatif** AC mains (supply); ~ **d'alimentation** mains supply; ~ **de 256 octets** 256-byte sector; ~ **de routage (SR)** routing area (RA); ~ **de trame** sub-frame; ~ **d'exploration** scan area; ~ **électrique** (power) line; mains; ~ **inutilisable** bad block; ~ **mort** clip position; dead segment (of commutator); blind sector; ~ **primaire** agriculture; ~ **public** the state; ~ **secondaire** industry; ~ **spatial** (en télégraphie) space segment (for telegraph transmission); ~ **tertiaire** tertiary sector (offices, shops, services and research organisations)

section f sub-routine; segment (of program); hop; section; cross-section; (wire) gauge; ~ **base** base segment; ~ **d'acheminement** routing section; routing office; ~ **d'adaptation** matching section; transforming section; ~ **de groupe primaire** group section; ~ **de groupe secondaire** supergroup section; ~ **de ligne** line section; link; section of circuit; ~ **de pupinisation** loading-coil section; ~ **de régénération** repeater section; ~ **de régulation de ligne** line regulating section; ~ **de répéteurs** repeater section; ~ **d'équilibrage à câble à deux conducteurs** twin-line matching section; ~ **d'essais** test section; ~ **droite** transverse cross-section; ~ **effective** effective cross-section; ~ **efficace de choc** effective collision cross-section; ~ **homogène** homogeneous section; ~ **locale** (physical) extension circuit; tail

sectionnable adj modular (of fuse-carrier)

sectionnement m isolation; power supply/feed

(group); mains supply spur; ~ **général** outgoing trunk multiple; full multiple; ~ **particulier** partial multiple

sectionneur *m* (fused) isolator

sectionneur-commutateur double-throw isolating switch

sectorisation *f* zooming (of satellite photography)

sectorisé *adj* graduated; segmented; sectored (of disk)

sécurisation *f* introducing safeguards; system security; fail-safe protection; fall-back system; standby system; replication; system back-up

sécuriser *v* provide back-up (fail-safe) facilities; replicate; back-up

sécurité *f* safety; security; protection; adhesion; reliability; dependability; control; continuity; protective relay; ~ **de contact à l'extraction** contact grip on extraction; ~ **de fonctionnement** operational security; ~ **intrinsèque** intrinsically safe; ~ **protecteur** interlock; ~ **thermique** thermal shutdown

sécurités *f pl* safety features; protective measures

SED (v. système d'exploitation sur disque)

séduire *v* entice; attract

segment *m* sealing ring; gasket; stroke; circlip; section; overlay; routine; segment; allocation; component; chapter; partition; slice (of pie chart); ~ **actif** overlay; ~ **de recouvrement** overlay (segment)

segmentation *f* overlay; segmentation; splitting

séjour *m* secondment; period of duty

sélecteur *m* selector; discriminator/(-ing); dialling unit tuner; ~ **à balais** brush selector; ~ **à cinq cent points** five-hundred point selector; ~ **à deux mouvements** bank-and-wiper switch; two-motion selector; Strowger selector; ~ **à dix sorties** ten-point selector; ~ **à double mouvement** Strowger selector; two-motion selector; bank-and-wiper switch; ~ **à mouvement unique** uniselector; ~ **à plusieurs étages** multi-point selector; ~ **à relais** all-relay selector; ~ **absorbeur** digit absorber; digit-absorbing selector; discriminating selector (repeater); ~ **auxiliaire** special code selector; ~ **crossbar miniaturisé** miniswitch; ~ **d'adresse (SAD)** peripheral address selector switch; ~ **d'amplitude** amplitude disciminator; ~ **d'arrivée** incoming selector; ~ **de central** exchange selector; service selector; ~ **de départ** outgoing selector; out-trunk switch; ~ **de désignation** allotting switch; assignment

selector; ~ **de données** data selector; ~ **de gamme** range switch; band selector; ~ **de groupe** group selector; ~ **de groupe du centre terminal** terminal exchange group selector; ~ **de position** position selector; ~ **de préfixe** code selector; ~ **de route** director selector; ~ **de tension** voltage adaptor; ~ **de voie d'acheminement** code selector; ~ **de zone** zone selector; ~ **directeur** director selector; director switch; ~ **discriminateur** discriminating selector; routing selector; ~ **discriminateur répéteur de signaux** discriminating selector repeater (DSR); ~ **double** dual-purpose selector; ~ **du chiffre A** A-digit selector; ~ **du débit binaire** data signalling rate selector (DTE/DCE); ~ **Ericsson** Ericsson line selector; ~ **final** final selector; tandem selector; ~ **marqueur** marker switch; ~ **pas à pas** pulse-controlled selector; ~ **plan** panel selector; ~ **rapide** high-speed selector/switch; ~ **répéteur** repeater selector; ~ **rotatif** rotary switch; selector; uniselector; ~ **rotatif à moteur** motorized uniselector; ~ **rotatif de groupe** rotary group selector; ~ **tandem** tandem selector; ~ **XY** XY selector

sélectif *adj* snapshot (= selective trace program); flexible; polling

sélection *f* routing; dialling; (address) selection; call set-up; discrimination; separation; hunting; defining (of text); pathfinding; ~ **à distance de l'abonné demandé** subscriber trunk dialling (STD); ~ **à distance de l'abonné demandé** (en exploitation semi-automatique) trunk operator dialling; ~ **à quatre fréquences** four-frequency dialling; ~ **abrégée** speed dialling; short-code dialling; ~ **automatique** automatic selection (Strowger); hunting; ~ **automatique à distance** through-dialling; transit dialling; ~ **conjuguée** conjugate pathfinding and selection; end-to-end selection; ~ **conjuguée avec entraide** partial secondary working; ~ **de boîtier** chip select; ~ **de fréquence** frequency discrimination; ~ **de la configuration de multiplexage** data signal rate selection; ~ **de portée** range selection; ~ **de signes** sign selection; ~ **de texte** defining text; ~ **décimale** decade selection; ~ **des données** data select; ~ **directe à l'arrivée (SDA)** direct in-dialling; direct inward dialling; through-dialling; ~ **du boîtier** chip select (CS); ~ **du périphérique** device select; ~ **en avant** forward selection; ~ **implicite** direct connection call; ~ **interurbaine automatique** subscriber trunk diall-

S

ing (STD); toll dialling; ~ **libre à plusieurs niveaux** level hunting; ~ **numérique** numerical selection; ~ **par cadran** dial selection; ~ **par impulsions** pulse action; ~ **par signaux de code** (à moments) equal-length code switching; ~ **pas à pas** (étage par étage) link-by-link selection/pathfinding; step-by-step selection; ~ **rendu de zone** select zone rendition (SZR); ~ **rendu graphique** select graphics rendition (SGR); ~ **sur plusieurs niveaux** multi-level discrimination; ~ **technique** mode switch; reconfiguration; user-selectable option; ~ **vers l'aval** forward selection; ~ **X** (entrée) chip select (CS)

sélectionner v select; dial; key; filter out; ~ **une tâche** set a currently-selected task

sélectivité f selectivity; spectral response; ~ **spectrale** spectral response

self f inductance; choke; coil; filter; suppressor; inductor; ~ **à air** air-spaced coil; ~ **à grande surtension** high-Q coil; ~ **d'antenne** aerial tuning coil; ~ **d'arrêt et de découplage (VHF)** VHF choke; ~ **de blocage** choke coil; reactance coil; ~ **de bouclage** coupling coil; ~ **de filtrage** smoothing choke; ~ **de ligne** line inductance; feeder choke; ~ **d'équilibrage des débits** current (compensating/balancing) coil; ~ **doubleuse** charging choke; ~ **inductance HF** RF choke; ~ **interphase** interphase reactor; phase equalizer; absorption inductor; ~ **transversale** shunt inductance

selfique adj self-inductive

selon les cotes (s.l.c.) not to scale

selsyn m synchro; autosyn; magslip; selsyn

sémaphore m common-channel (signalling); flag; separator; message queue; read-modify-write (function)

sématème m basic signal; signal train

sémateur m (bivalent) generator; driver

semblable adj identical; similar; comparable

semelle f base-plate; base; plinth

semi-asservi semi-compelled

semi-autonome off-host

semi-brillance half-tone

semiconducteur m semiconductor; ~ **extrinsèque** extrinsic semiconductor; ~ **intrinsèque** intrinsic semiconductor; ~ **ionique** ion semiconductor; ~ **par défaut d'électrons** p-type semiconductor; ~ **par excès d'électrons** n-type semiconductor

semi-duplex half duplex; either-way

semi-permanent non-temporary (of data set)

semi-produit semi-finished product

semi-rigide reinforced

sénaire adj senary (six-base)

sens m direction; trend; (electrical) polarity;

orientation; lay; path; ~ **aller** go path; ~ **d'attaque** direction of actuating force; ~ **de câblage** direction of lay; ~ **de lecture** reading direction; ~ **de montage** orientation; mounting direction; ~ **de transmission** transmission direction; ~ **d'écoulement du trafic** direction of traffic flow; ~ **des aiguilles d'une montre** clockwise; ~ **direct** (passant) forward; ~ **du relèvement** bearing sense; ~ **d'utilisation** load direction; ~ **en arrière** backward direction; ~ **en avant** forward direction; ~ **inverse** (bloqué) reverse; ~ **inverse des aiguilles d'une montre** anti-clockwise; counter-clockwise; ~ **retour** return direction; ~ **trigonométrique** counter-clockwise; anti-clockwise; ~ **trigonométrique inverse** clockwise; ~ **unique** one-way

senseur m sensor

sensibilisateur m sensitiser

sensibilité f sensitivity; response; accuracy; range; tolerance; resolution; definition; ~ **au tungstène** tungsten sensitivity; ~ **d'accord électronique** electronic tuning sensitivity; ~ **de déviation** deflection sensitivity; ~ **dynamique** dynamic range; ~ **lumineuse** luminous sensitivity; ~ **lumineuse dynamique** dynamic luminous sensitivity; ~ **lumineuse statique** static luminous sensitivity; ~ **rapportée au niveau zéro** zero-level sensitivity

sensible adj acute; notable; singular; responsive; prone

sensiblement adv substantially; appreciably; more or less; to a greater or lesser degree

sentinelle f separator; sentinel; flag; delimiter; boundary marker

séparateur m separator; resolver; decoupler; isolating circuit; delimiter; diverter; filter; deflector; splitter; trap; clipper; buffer; ~ **d'article** record separator; item delimiter; buffer; ~ **de blocs** block separator; ~ **de colonne** column split; ~ **de fichier** file separator; ~ **de groupe** group separator; ~ **de phases** phase splitter; ~ **de signaux** signal separator; ~ **de sous article** unit separator; ~ **de synchronisation** sync separator; ~ **de zone** area separator (AS); ~ **d'informations** data separator; delimiter

séparatif m long break

séparation f splitting; ~ **fractionnaire** radix point; ~ **galvanique** electrical separation; electrical isolation

séparé adj separate; remote; stripped; isolated; split; diverted; filtered; adrift

séparer v segregate; isolate

septénaire adj septenary (seven-base)

séquence f sequence; step; cycle; rota; series;

~ **d'alarme** alarm sequence; ~ **d'appel** calling sequence; ~ **de classement** collating sequence; ~ **de contrôle de trame** frame-check sequence (FCS); ~ **de contrôle par bloc** block-check sequence (BCS); ~ **de Markov** Markov chain; Markov series; ~ **d'entrelacement** interlaced scanning; ~ **des émissions** communications priority; ~ **d'initialisation** bootstrap routine; ~ **d'invitation à émettre** interrogation frame; polling; ~ **uniquement composée de l** all ls sequence

séquencement *m* sequencing; chaining

séquenceur *m* sequence controller

séquentiel *m* sequence switch; sequence controller; interval timer; sequencer; timing diagram; ~ *adj* in-line; batch; serial; sequential; ~ **indexé** indexed sequential; ~ **taxation** charge sequence timer

sérialisateur *m* (sérialiseur) serial interface adaptor; serial I/O controller; parallel-serial converter; ~ **de données** serial data communications controller

série *f ou adj* (en ~) series; serial; tandem; family; string; train; progression; mass production; array; bank; batch; successive; burst; consecutive; pattern; cascaded; ~ **arithmétique** arithmetic progression; ~ **chiffres** figures-case; ~ **de dipôles** broadside dipole array; ~ **d'impulsions** pulse train; (tone) burst; ~ **légère** light-duty; ~ **lettres** letters-case; ~ **lourde** heavy-duty; ~ **synchrone** synchronous serial

sérigraphie *f* screen process printing; silk-screening; screen printing

serpentin *m* ring main; cooling coil; heat exchanger

serre *f* clip; ferrule

serré *adj* close (of tolerance); dense; compact; narrow; tight

serre-bornes terminal clamp

serre-câble cable grip; cable clamp; cable tie

serre-fils clamp; saddle; binding post

serre-gaine conduit

serrer en croix tighten (screws) alternately at opposite corners

serrurerie *f* **de salle** room ironwork; fixtures

sertir *v* crimp; clinch; seam

sertissage *m* wire crimping

servante *f* (mobile) subrack; housing (for PCBs, disks and PSU)

server *v* cater for

serveur *m* videotex centre; host computer centre; cluster controller; service provider; information provider; ~ **central** central server; ~ **concentrateur** cluster controller; ~ **d'images** image processor; ~ **d'informa-**tions data host; ~ **documentaire** document processing centre

serveuse *f* cluster controller; master workstation

service *m* duty; department; section; facility; ~ **à plein temps** wide-area telephone service (WATS); ~ **à tarif fixe** flat-rate service; ~ **à tarif forfaitaire** flat-rate service; ~ **après-vente (SAV)** field support; after-sales service; customer service; sales back-up; ~ **bout-en-bout** end-to-end servicing; ~ **centralisateur** program booking centre; ~ **centrex** centrex service (business telephone direct dialling facility); ~ **centrex fourni par un central public** central office centrex; ~ **chantier** site management department; ~ **complémentaire d'attente autorisée** waiting-allowed facility; ~ **continu** continuous duty; heavy duty; ~ **de communication conférence unilatérale** lecture call; ~ **de communication en espace** space communications service; ~ **de communication par satellite** satellite communications service; ~ **de communications téléphoniques** message-taking service; ~ **de contrôle et d'alerte aérien** aircraft control and warning service (ACW); ~ **de double appel** consultation-hold facility; ~ **de lancement** launch service; ~ **de l'heure** speaking clock; ~ **de lignes groupées** equivalent service; overline service; ~ **de location de circuits** leased circuits service; ~ **de nuit** assigned night answering service; common night service; ~ **de radio côtier** ship-shore radio service; ~ **de radiocommunication entre satellites** inter-satellite service; ~ **de radiodiffusion** broadcasting service; ~ **de radiodiffusion aéronautique** aeronautical broadcasting service; ~ **de radiophares** radio beacon service; ~ **de radiotéléphonie** radiotelephone service; ~ **de satellite fixe** fixed-orbit satellite service; ~ **de sélection automatique** automatic dial service; ~ **de télécommunication** telecommunications service; ~ **de téléphonogrammes** telemessage (phonogram) service; ~ **de transmission de données à commutation de circuits** circuit-switched data transmission service; ~ **de transmission de données à commutation par paquets** packet-switched data transmission service; ~ **de transmission des télégrammes par téléimprimeur** printergram service; ~ **de voies de transmission louées et partagées par plusieurs entreprises** shared private line service; ~ **d'écoute** intercept service; ~ **des abonnés absents** absent subscriber service; answering service; ~ **des télégrammes**

S

téléphonés phonogram (service); ~ **d'exploitation** programme service; ~ **d'indication d'appel en instance** call waiting notification facility (tone); ~ **du journal parlé** newscasting; news service; ~ **du transfert automatique** follow-me facility; ~ **intercontinental** intercontinental service; ~ **international** international service; ~ **international avec préparation** (international) advance-preparation service; ~ **international rapide** international demand service; rapid service; ~ **interurbain automatique** automatic long-distance service; subscriber trunk dialling (STD); direct distance dialling (DDD); ~ **interurbain planifié** wide-area telephone service (WATS); ~ **mixte** combined service; ~ **mobile de radiodiffusion** aeronautical mobile radio service; ~ **par satellite météorologique** weather satellite service; ~ **permanent** continuous (24-hour) service; round-the-clock service; ~ **privé** private service; ~ **public de données** public data service; ~ **public de radiocommunications** public radio service; ~ **public de télécommunications** common carrier; ~ **radio de port** port operations service; ~ **réduit** standby service; console back-up; universal/unassigned night answer service (UNA); ~ **restreint** off-peak; barred access; restricted service; ~ **réveil** alarm-clock service; wake-me facility; ~ **semi-automatique** semi-automatic service; ~ **semi-duplex** half-duplex operation (teletype); ~ **sévère** heavy-duty; ~ **simplifié** night-answer service; ~ **spécial** special service; ~ **supplémentaire** new subscriber service; supplementary service; additional service; special feature; ~ **technico-commercial** sales engineering department; ~ **télégraphique** telegraph service; ~ **téléphonique** telephone service; ~ **télex** telex service; ~ **vert** (code 14 en France) free-phone service
services m pl utilities; functions; facilities; ~ **d'assistance** delegation; ~ **paratéléphoniques** non-telephone services; ~ **simplifiés** night-answer service
serviette f **en papier** paper tissue
servitude(s) f service; overhead; utility; housekeeping; auxiliary plant; ancillary; red-tape
servodyne f actuator; servo-control
session f sequence
SET (v. signal étalon de télévision)
seuil m threshold; boundary; limit; critical value; trip point; trigger level; ~ **d'alarme** out-of-limits alarm condition; ~ **d'audibilité** audibility threshold; ~ **de basculement** switching threshold; ~ **de conduction** (diode) forward voltage; ~ **de disparition d'alarme** alarm-off threshold; ~ **de longueur d'onde photo-électronique** threshold wavelength; ~ **de luminescence** threshold of luminescence; ~ **de rentabilité** break-even point; ~ **de réponse** operating threshold; ~ **de sensibilité** sensitivity threshold; ~ **d'erreur** cliff effect; error threshold; ~ **précis** error-free trigger level; ~ **statique** static threshold (servo-system); ~ **toléré** permissible threshold
seul adj in isolation; just; only
sévère adj exacting; stringent; severe; grave
sévérisé adj made more stringent; tightened up
sévérité f rigour; gravity
sextuple inverseur hex inverter
shunt m shunt; by-pass; parallel resistor; override; PCB selector plug; ~ **de mesure d'intensité calibré** current-rated measuring shunt; ~ **logé dans l'appareil** built-in shunt; ~ **sonnerie** anti-tinkle (circuit)
shuntage m shunting
shunter v shunt; place in parallel; by-pass
SI (v. taux de signalisation)
SIA (v. signal d'indication d'alarmes)
siège m seat(ing) (of semiconductor)
siemens m reciprocal ohm (mho)
sifflement m **hétérodyne** heterodyne whistles
sifflet m **de fût** splayed side of soldering pot
sigle m acronym; logo(-type); symbol; mnemonic; motif; code; trade mark; ~ **de constructeur** manufacturer's name-plate; logo(-type)
signal m signal; pulse; charge; flag; marker; indicator; sign; code; tone; output; input; carrier; strobe; message; bit; ~ **à large bande** broadband signal; wideband signal; ~ **à un élément** single-component signal; ~ **acoustique d'occupation** engaged click; ~ **aléatoire** random signal; ~ **alphabétique** alphabetic signal; ~ **analogique** analogue signal; ~ **arrière** backward signal; ~ **audible d'appel** audible ringing signal; ~ **bipolaire** bipolar signal; alternate mark inversion signal; ~ **bipolaire modifié** modified alternate mark inversion; ~ **brouillé** mushy signal; ~ **brouilleur** unwanted signal; ~ **calibré** calibrated signal; ~ **carré** square-wave signal; ~ **codé** coded signal; ~ **commutateur** keying signal; ~ **complémentaire** reciprocal; complement; ~ **comportant une barre** bar waveform; ~ **comportant une impulsion et une barre** pulse and bar test signal; ~ **composé** compound signal; multi-component signal; composite signal; ~ **composite** compound signal;

S

~ **d'abonné libre** subscriber line free; ~ **d'abonné occupé** subscriber-busy signal; ~ **d'accès interdit** access-barred signal; ~ **d'accompagnement de masse** earth signal; ~ **d'accusé de réception** (digit) acknowledgement signal (ACK); answer signal; ~ **d'acquittement** acknowledgement signal; ~ **d'adresse** address signal; register signal; ~ **d'alarme** alarm signal; warning signal; ~ **d'allumage** bright-up signal; ~ **d'antenne** aerial signal; ~ **d'appel** ringing signal; calling signal; polling signal; offering signal; seizure signal; alerting signal; prompt; ~ **d'appel audible** audible ringing signal; alerting signal; ~ **d'appel de fin** ring-off signal; ~ **d'appel d'enregistreur** register recall signal; ~ **d'appel en avant** ring-forward signal; ~ **d'appel interurbain** trunk-call signal; ~ **d'arrêt** stop bit; ~ **d'arrêt d'émission** stop-send signal; ~ **d'attente** waiting signal; ~ **d'autorisation** enabling signal; ~ **de basculement** transfer signal; gating pulse; ~ **de base** basic signal; ~ **de blanc artificiel** artificial white signal; ~ **de blocage** blocking signal; test-busy signal; ~ **de blocage vers l'amont** backward-busying signal; ~ **de bourdonnement** buzzer signal; ~ **de bruit** noise signal; ~ **de cadrage** phasing signal; framing signal; ~ **de cadran** forward transfer signal; ~ **de caractère** character signal; PCM word; ~ **de classe de trafic** class-of-traffic signal; ~ **de commande** control signal; pilot signal; pilot carrier; ~ **de commutation sur liaison de réserve** changeover signal (to standby link); ~ **de confirmation d'appel** call-confirmation signal; ~ **de confirmation de libération** clear-confirmation signal; ~ **de confusion** confusion signal; ~ **de connexion** connection signal; call-connected signal; ~ **de continuité** continuity signal; ~ **de contrôle** check signal; ~ **de correction** correction signal; ~ **de correction parabolique de ligne** line bend (correction); ~ **de coupure** cut-off signal; ~ **de début** start bit; ~ **de début de bloc** start-of-block signal; ~ **de déclenchement** trip signal; seising signal; ~ **de décrochage du demandé** answer signal; answer supervision; ~ **de demande d'appel** call-request signal; ~ **de demande de chiffres** proceed-to-send signal (PTS); ~ **de détresse** distress signal; ~ **de données** data signal; carrier; ~ **de fin** clear-forward signal; release signal; disconnect signal; on-hook signal; stop bit; ~ **de fin automatique** automatic clearing signal; ~ **de fin de bloc** end-of-block signal; ~ **de fin de communication** clear-forward signal;

disconnect signal; on-hook signal; stop bit; clearing signal; ~ **de fin de conversation** clearing signal; on-hook signal; disconnect signal; ~ **de fin de numérotation** end-of-pulsing signal; forward end-of-selection signal; end-of-address signal; ~ **de fin de sélection** number-received signal; end-of-selection signal; ~ **de fonction aléatoire** random-function signal; ~ **de garde** guard signal; ~ **de gestion** management signal; ~ **de gestion du réseau** network management signal; ~ **de (la bande de) base** baseband signal; ~ **de libération** clear signal; release signal; breakdown signal; clear-forward signal; ~ **de libération de circuit** backward release signal; ~ **de libération de garde** release-guard signal; ~ **de libération en amont** clear-back signal; ~ **de libération en arrière** clear-back signal; ~ **de libération en aval** clear-forward signal; ~ **de ligne** line signal (supervisory signal); ~ **de ligne hors service** line out-of-service signal; ~ **de maintenance** maintenance signal; ~ **de manœuvre** pulsing signal; dialling tone; ~ **de manœuvre immédiat** dial tone first (DTF); ~ **de marquage** marker signal; ~ **de mesure** measuring signal; test signal; ~ **de mise en attente** waiting-in-progress signal; ~ **de mise en marche** start signal (of start-stop system); ~ **de mise en phase sur blanc** phase white; ~ **de mise en phase sur noir** phase black; ~ **de modulation** program signal; modulation signal; ~ **de multitrame** multiframe signal; ~ **de noir artificiel** artificial black signal; ~ **de noir nominal** nominal black signal; ~ **de numéro complet** address-complete signal; ~ **de numéro non utilisé** number not-in-use; vacant number signal; ~ **de numéro reçu** number-received signal; end-of-selection signal; ~ **de numérotation** dialling signal; address signal; ~ **de numérotation incomplet** address incomplete signal; ~ **de perturbation** clutter signal; ~ **de portillonnage** gating signal; ~ **de positionnement** setting-up signal; ~ **de poste à prépaiement** coin-box signal; ~ **de prise** seize signal; connect signal; busying signal; seizing signal; trunk seizure signal; ~ **de prise pour transit** transit seizure signal; ~ **de prise terminal** terminal seizing signal; ~ **de raccrochage** clear signal; on-hook signal; clear-forward signal; ~ **de raccrochage (du demandé)** clear signal; clear-back signal; ~ **de rappel** flashing signal; register recall signal; ring forward (signal); ~ **de rappel du demandeur** ring-back signal; ~ **de rappel sur supervi-**

sion flashing signal; ~ **de rappel vers l'arrière** backward-recall signal; ~ **de rappel vers l'avant** forward-recall signal; ~ **de relèvement** direction-finding signal; ~ **de remise à zéro** reset signal; ~ **de renvoi** transfer signal; ~ **de réponse** answer signal; off-hook signal; return light (of radio broadcasting); ~ **de repos** interval signal; spacing wave; ~ **de retard** delay signal; ~ **de retour d'appel** ringing-tone signal; ringing tone; ~ **de retour sur liaison normale** change-back signal (to primary link); ~ **de rythme** timing signal; ~ **de salutation** handshake (signal); ~ **de service** service signal; ~ **de service sans impression** non-printing service signal; ~ **de sonnerie** bell signal; ~ **de sortie** output signal; outgoing signal; ~ **de sortie décimale** decimal read-out signal; ~ **de supervision** supervisory signal; ~ **de suppression** blanking signal; ~ **de surveillance** supervisory signal; pilot tone/signal; ~ **de synchronisation** synchronizing signal; sync pulse; trigger signal; ~ **de synchronisation d'octet** byte timing signal; ~ **de synchronisation ligne** line synchronizing signal; ~ **de synchronisation trame** field synchronizing signal; ~ **de téléimprimeur** teleprinter signal; telex signal; ~ **de télévision** television signal; ~ **de télévision étalon** standard television signal; ~ **de télex** telex signal; ~ **de travail** marking wave; ~ **de validation** authentication signal; enabling pulse; ~ **de validation d'adresse** address strobe; ~ **de verrouillage de trame** frame alignment signal; ~ **de verrouillage de trame concentré** bunched frame alignment signal; ~ **de verrouillage de trame distribué** distributed frame alignment signal; ~ **de verrouillage de trame réparti** distributed frame alignment signal; ~ **de vision** video signal; ~ **décalé** offset signal; ~ **d'échantillonnage** strobe output; ~ **d'échec de l'appel** call-failure signal; ~ **déclencheur** keying signal; ~ **d'effacement** erase signal; erasure signal; ~ **d'encombrement** congestion signal; ~ **d'enregistrement** call sign; call signal; ~ **d'enregistreur** address signal; register signal; inter-register signal; ~ **d'entrée** input signal; incoming signal; ~ **d'entrée de référence** reference input signal; ~ **d'erreur** error signal; ~ **désiré** wanted signal; intelligence signal; ~ **d'espace** space signal; ~ **d'espacement** spacing signal; ~ **d'essai** test signal; test tone; ~ **d'exploitation** operation and maintenance signal; ~ **d'identification** identification signal; ~ **d'identification de la position**

positional signal; ~ **d'image** picture signal; ~ **d'image à radiofréquence** vision signal; video signal; ~ **d'image complet** video signal; ~ **d'indication d'alarmes (SIA)** alarm indication signal (AIS); ~ **d'information** dead-level signal; no-such-number tone; ~ **d'interdiction** inhibiting signal; ~ **d'interruption** breakdown signal; ~ **d'intervalle** interval signal; ~ **d'intervention d'une opératrice** (côté demandé) forward-transfer signal; ~ **d'inversion chiffres** figures-shift signal; ~ **d'inversion lettres** letters-shift signal; ~ **d'invitation à numéroter** proceed-to-select signal; start-dialling signal; start-pulsing signal; ~ **d'invitation à transmettre** proceed-to-select signal; start-pulsing signal; start-dialling signal; ~ **discret modulé en fréquence** discrete frequency modulation signal; ~ **d'occupation** busy tone; busy signal; busy flash; engaged signal; ~ **d'occupation complète** all-trunks-busy signal; ~ **d'occupation de ligne** number-unobtainable tone; ~ **d'offre** offering signal; ~ **d'ordre** order signal (of radio broadcasting); ~ **double** split response; ~ **d'urgence** urgency signal; ~ **en amont** backward signal; ~ **en arrière** backward signal; ~ **en avant** forward signal; ~ **en bande de base** baseband signal; ~ **en trait permanent** continuous-wave signal (CW); ~ **étalon** standard signal; reference signal; ~ **étalon de télévision (SET)** standard television signal; ~ **faible** weak signal; ~ **fin de bloc** end-of-block signal; ~ **horaire** time signal; ~ **horodateur** date-time group; ~ **imprimé** (par aimantation) (magnetically) induced charge; ~ **incident** input signal; ~ **international** international signal; ~ **invitant à différer la numérotation** delay-dialling signal; ~ **isochrone** isochronous signal; ~ **lumineux** luminous signal; ~ **magnétique** magnetic charge (impulse/signal); ~ **modulant** modulating wave; program signal; modulation signal; ~ **noir** black signal; ~ **numérique** digital signal; ~ **numérique affluent** tributary digital signal; ~ **numérique binaire** binary digital signal; ~ **numérique unique** single digital signal; ~ **par impulsion** pulse signal; ~ **parasitaire** drop-in signal; ~ **parasite** spurious signal; ~ **perceptible minimal** just-discernible signal; ~ **pilote** pilot signal; cueing signal; ~ **primaire** primary signal; ~ **qui est là?** who-are-you signal (WRU); ~ **rectangulaire** rectangular waveform; square wave; ~ **réfléchi** echo; ~ **répété** repeated signal; ~ **répété jusqu'à accusé de réception** repeated-until-acknowledged signal; ~ **sonore** audible signal; beep; bell (BEL); hoot stop; ~ **télégraphique** telegraph signal; ~ **temporel discret** discretely-tuned signal; ~ **triangulaire symétrique** symmetrical triangular waveform; ~ **unitaire vide** empty signal unit; ~ **utile** positive pulse; effective signal; wanted signal; incident signal; active signal; ~ **vers l'arrière** backward signal; ~ **vers l'avant** forward signal; ~ **vidéo** video signal; ~ **vidéo transitoire** bounce; ~ **vocal** speech signal; voice signal; ~ **zéro** null signal; zero signal

signalé adj with signal applied; flagged; posted

signalement m posting

signaler v post (an event); report; signal; alert; flash; warn; notify; advise; display; flag; annotate; mark; blink; ring; buzz

signaleur m signalling unit; signalling relay set; ringer; signalling module; digital switching equipment (DSGE); signaller; signalling converter; ~ **50 Hz AC** receiver; ~ **à fréquence basse** ringing repeater; signalling equipment; ~ **à fréquence vocale** (FV) VF signalling relay set; VF receiver; ~ **mixte** composite signalling module

signalisation f signalling; warning (system); indication; display; reporting; marking; flag; handshaking signals; lamp field; ~ **à canal commun** common-channel signalling; ~ **à changement d'état** continuous signalling; ~ **à courant alternatif** AC signalling; ~ **à courant double** (v. signalisation à double courant); ~ **à deux fréquences** dual-tone multifrequency signalling; ~ **à double courant** bipolar signalling; double-current signalling; ~ **à fréquence vocale** voice-frequency signalling; ~ **à fréquence zéro** zero-frequency signalling; ~ **à impulsion** semi-compelled signalling (pulse); ~ **à une fréquence** single-frequency signalling; ~ **acoustique** audible alarm; tone indicators; ~ **asservie** compelled signalling; ~ **asservie par l'avant et par l'arrière** forward and backward fully-compelled signalling; ~ **associée dans la bande** channel-associated in-slot signalling; ~ **asynchrone** asynchronous signalling; ~ **audible** audible signalling; ~ **automatique** automatic signalling; ~ **avec chevauchement** overlap signalling; ~ **bifréquence** DTMF signalling; ~ **bout-à-bout** end-to-end signalling; ~ **continue** continuous signalling; ~ **dans la bande** in-band signalling; ~ **de bout en bout** end-to-end signalling; ~ **de commande** control signalling; ~ **de commande centralisée** centralized

control signalling; ~ **de gestion** management signalling; ~ **de ligne libre** idle-line indication; free-line signalling (FLS); ~ **de ligne par impulsions** earth-pulse signalling; ~ **de positionnement zéro** null-point detector; ~ **de prépaiement** pay tones; ~ **de télétaxe** remote metering pulses; ~ **décimale** decadic (pulse) signalling; ~ **d'enregistreur** inter-register signalling; ~ **dissociée** common-channel signalling; ~ **du type clavier à multifréquences** MF pushbutton dialling; ~ **émission parée** 'transmission ready' indication; ~ **en bande de base** baseband signalling; ~ **en intervalle de temps** in-slot signalling; ~ **enrichie** enhanced signalling; ~ **entre autocommutateurs** inter-exchange signalling; ~ **hachée** flashing warning signals; ~ **hors bande** out-band (out-of-band) signalling; out-slot signalling; ~ **hors bande** (voie par voie) channel-associated out-slot signalling; ~ **hors bande par changement d'état à bas niveau** tone-on-idle signalling out of band; ~ **hors intervalle de temps** out-slot signalling; ~ **impulsionnelle** pulse(d) signalling; ~ **intempestive par imitation de signaux** signal imitation; ~ **inter-centraux** inter-exchange signalling; ~ **manuelle** ring-down; ~ **monofréquence** single-frequency signalling; ~ **multifréquence** MF signalling; ~ **multi-fréquence asservie** compelled MF signalling; ~ **multiple** superimposed ringing; ~ **non associée** non-associated signalling; ~ **par canal sémaphore** common-channel signalling (CCS); common-channel inter-office signalling; ~ **par changement d'état** continuous (two-state) signalling; ~ **par courant alternatif** AC signalling; ~ **par courant continu** direct-current signalling; DC signalling; ~ **par courants porteurs** carrier signalling; ~ **par impulsions** pulsed signalling; ~ **par ondes musicales** tonic-train signalling; VF signalling; ~ **par voie commune** common-channel signalling; ~ **section par section** link-by-link signalling; ~ **sémaphore** common-channel signalling; ~ **semi-continue** semi-continuous signalling; ~ **sur la ligne d'abonné** signalling over subscriber loop; ~ **sur voie associée** channel-associated signalling; ~ **sur voie commune** common-channel signalling (CCS); common-channel inter-office signalling; ~ **synchrone** synchronous signalling; ~ **télégraphique par courants à amplitudes différentes** amplitude-change signalling; ~ **TRON-RON** E and M signalling; ~ **vers l'arrière** backward signalling; ~ **vers l'avant** forward

S

signalling; ~ **voie par voie** (v/v) channel-associated signalling (CAS)

signalogramme *m* **magnétique** magnetic signalogram

signaux *m pl* **à bande commune** band-sharing signals; ~ **à plusieurs voies** multi-path signals; ~ **arrières** backward signals; ~ **dans la bande** in-band signals; ~ **de gestion** handshaking (bus-access) signals; control signals; ~ **de numérotation** digital signals; (im)pulsing signals; address digits; ~ **de parole** speech signals; ~ **de supervision** supervisory signals; ~ **de type à impulsions** pulse signals; ~ **de type changements d'état** continuous signals; ~ **d'égalisation** equalizing pulses; ~ **horodateurs** time-and-date signals; ~ **instables** keying chirps; ~ **normaux** straight signals; ~ **parasites** clutter; spurious signals; ~ **parasites hors bande à la sortie** spurious out-band signals at output; ~ **vers l'arrière** backward signals

signe *m* sign bit; polarity; signal; character; tone; unit; ~ **alinéa** pilcrow; paragraph sign; blind P; ~ **allemand** sharp S (German ß); ~ **d'appel** ringing tone; ~ **de change** shift signal; ~ **de la phase** phase difference; ~ **d'écho** echo sign; ~ **dièse** number sign (#); gate symbol; hash symbol; ~ **d'occupation** holding-code signal; ~ **final** message-ending character; ~ **indiquant les taxes** metering digit; ~ **initial** start-of-message character; ~ **monétaire** general currency symbol; ~ **morse** Morse character; ~ **multiple** multiple signal; ~ **nouveau paragraphe** (alinéa) pilcrow; paragraph sign; blind P; ~ **paragraphe** section sign

signes contraires alternate polarity; ~ **en chiffres** numerical digits

signifiant *adj* valid

significatif *adj* relevant; pertinent

signification *f* legend; caption; key; meaning

silane *m* silicon compound

silencieux *m* squelch

silentbloc *m* resilient mounting

silice *f* silica; ~ **fondue** fused silica

silicium *m* silicon

sillon *m* channel (of timer disk); track; groove; ~ **fin** microgroove

simbleau *m* (= cimblot) centring bridge; locating key; spider; positioning block

simple single; common; basic; standard; one-off; straightforward; ordinary; isotropic; subsidiary; local; primitive; ~ **densité** single-density (of disk); ~ **face** single-sided; ~ **interligne** single-line spacing

simplex *adj* simplex; single-processor mode

simplification *f* expediency

simulateur *m* simulator; ~ **d'appel téléphonique** test call generator; ~ **d'appels** artificial call generator; routiner; ~ **d'équilibre de mode** stable mode simulator; ~ **émetteur d'indicatif** answer-back unit simulator

simulation *f* simulation; ~ **discrète** Monte Carlo simulation

simultané *adj* concurrent; in-line; coincident; parallel

simultanéité *f* simultaneity; overlap

simultanément *adv* concurrently

sinon faire ELSE DO (instruction)

sintonisateur *m* (= syntonisateur) tuner

sinus *m* sine

sinusoïdal *adj* sine; sinusoidal; pulsed; AC; swept-frequency

sinusoïde *f* sine wave; sinusoid

sirène modulée pulsating siren

site *m* elevation; site; locus; exchange; installation; ~ **radiogoniométrique** direction-finding (DF) site

situation *f* **nette** net worth; ~ **radiogéographique de l'émetteur** transmitter site

situés sur des frontières de mots situated on full-word boundaries

sixte *f* six-level (wire) multiple

skiatron *m* dark-trace tube; skiatron

s.l.c. (v. selon les cotes)

S-mètre *m* signal-strength meter; S-meter

SMK (v. somme modulo K)

société *m* **aéronautique** aerospace company; ~ **des télécommunications** common carrier; ~ **filiale** subsidiary

sociétés de service et d'ingénierie informatique (SSII) computer systems and (software) services market

socle *m* base; pedestal; stand; support; plinth; sole plate; PCB-mounting plug; ~ **de fusible** fuse-carrier; fuse-holder; ~ **de lampe** (= culot) valve base

soie *f* **de verre** spun glass

soigneusement *adv* thoroughly; scrupulously; meticulously

soit take; let; assuming (that); in other words; that is to say; given (that)

solde *m* balance; closure; remnant

solenoïde *m* solenoid

solidaire *adj* integral; embodied; interdependent; joint; incorporated; interlocked; built-in

solidarisé *adj* interlocked

solide *adj* dependable; sturdy; robust; rugged

solidité à la lumière light fastness

sollicitation *f* invocation; summons; summoning; calling (up); driving; addressing; tripping; triggering; operating; activating; polling; prompt (message); ~ **des entrées**

en progression binaire hub polling; ~ **extérieure** interruption

sollicité adj driven; called; addressed; polled

solliciter address (of memory); drive; trigger; trip; activate; operate; busy; call/invoke (of file); poll; prompt

solution f integrated product; package of products and services; ~ **informatique** application

solvabilité f credit rating

sommaire m menu; (file) index; ~ adj partial; incomplete; brief; perfunctory

sommairement adv perfunctorily

sommateur m adder (logic)

sommation f **pondérée** weighted sum

somme f **de contrôle** check-sum; hash total; gibberish total; ~ **globale** checksum; ~ **modulo K (SMK)** modulo K sum; ~ **numérique** digital sum; ~ **numérique courante** running numeric sum •

sommet m apex; cusp; peak; crest; vertex; point; summit; branch point; node; tip; beginning; top (of memory); ~ **de la pile** top of stack; current stack frame

son m sound; tone; audio signal; ~ **complexe** complex sound; ~ **grave** low tone; bass; ~ **pur** pure sound; ~ **ululé** warble tone

sonar m **ultrasonore** active sonar (sound navigation and ranging)

sondage m sampling; polling; ~ **atmosphérique** air sounding; ~ **ionosphérique** ionospheric sounding; ~ **ionosphérique à incidence oblique** oblique-incidence ionospheric sounding; ~ **ionosphérique par rétrodiffusion** backscatter ionospheric sounding; ~ **ionosphérique vertical** vertical-incidence ionospheric sounding

sonde f sensor; probe; prod; thermistor; detector; ~ **capacitive** straight-wire probe; ~ **de qualification** qualifier probe; ~ **inductive** coupling loop; ~ **Pt100** resistance thermometer

sondeur m **ionosphérique** ionospheric recorder; ~ **ionosphérique oblique** oblique-incidence ionospheric recorder; ~ **ionosphérique vertical** vertical-incidence ionospheric recorder

sonie f (sone) sone (unit of loudness)

sonnage m continuity testing; buzzing-out test

sonnant adj ring(ing)

sonner (un circuit) check (a circuit); test continuity

sonnerie f bell; buzzer; ringer; chime(s); ringing current (connect signal); ringing current (transmission); ringing tone; ringing; bell set; ~ **à coups espacés** single-stroke bell; ~ **à courant alternatif** alternating-current ringer; ~ **à courant continu**

direct-current bell; ~ **accordée** harmonic telephone ringer; ~ **bip** bleeper; ~ **cadencée** interrupted ringing; ~ **continue** machine ringing; ~ **d'alarme** alarm bell; ~ **d'appel** ringing; bell; ~ **d'appel à courant continu** DC bell; ~ **de nuit** night alarm; night bell; ~ **de poste téléphonique** bell set; telephone ringer; ~ **d'oubli** alarm bell; ~ **extérieure** common alerting system; ~ **forte** loud ringing bell; ~ **générale** common alerting system; ~ **lente** slow interrupted ringing; ~ **monocoup** machine ringing; ~ **permanente** continuous ringing; ~ **trembleuse** trembler; buzzer

sonnette f bell; continuity tester; bell character (BEL)

sonomètre m (objective) noise meter; acoustimeter; sound level device; sound-level meter (SLM); monochord

sonore adj audible; acoustic; tonal

sonorisation f public address system

sonothèque f tape library

sonotrode f ultrasonic electrode

sortance f fan-out

sortant adj outgoing (O/G); outgoing selector

sortie f exit; outlet; output; discharge; issue; clearing; downstream end; outgoing; lead-out; delivery; outflow; port; gate; receiver (as opposed to driver); escape; lead; termination; pin; read-out; emergence; print(-out); closing (of file); ~ **anormale** abnormal exit; ~ **axiale** axial lead; axial termination; ~ **complémentée** complementing output; ~ **d'alarme** alarm output; ~ **d'antenne** aerial output; ~ **de code pour une commande** data-link escape (DLE); ~ **directe** direct output; ~ **hors dialogue** non-interactive output; ~ **IEEE/RS 232** serial output interface; ~ **non validée** data out invalid; ~ **page** print margins; ~ **trois états** tri-state port; ~ **V** dip-solder termination

sorties en l'air outputs floating; ~ **non connectées** outputs floating; not connected (NC); ~ **unilatérales** single-in-line (flatpack) terminations; SIL terminations

sortir v display; print out; exit; output

soubresaut m judder

souche f stocks

soudabilité f solderability

soudage m soldering; welding; ~ **à flux d'air chaud** reflow soldering; ~ **à la flamme** gas welding; flame welding; oxy-acetylene welding; ~ **au fer** bit soldering; hand soldering; ~ **autodécapante** self-fluxing solder; cored solder; ~ **en pattes d'araignée** spider bonding; ~ **froide** cold junction (compensation)

S

soude *f* sodium hydroxide; caustic soda

soudé *adj* welded; soldered; brazed

souder *v* weld; solder

soudeuse *f* welding set

soudure *f* fusion; welding; bonding; solder (joint); ~ **à âme de résine** resin-core solder; ~ **à bain mort** dip soldering; draw soldering; ~ **à la vague** wave soldering; flow soldering; ~ **à l'autogène** gas welding; oxy-acetylene welding; ~ **à résistance élevée** high-resistance joint (HR); ~ **au trempé** dip soldering; ~ **autodécapante** self-fluxing solder; ~ **bouton** mushroom-head joint; ~ **continue** seam welding; ~ **défectueuse** dry joint; ~ **électrique** resistance welding; arc welding; ~ **étain-plomb 60/40** tinsmith's solder; tinman's solder; tin-lead solder; soft solder; ~ **étanche** leak-proof welded joint; ~ **froide** cold solder joint; ~ **par points** spot welding; ~ **par recouvrement** lap joint; ~ **résistante** brazing (arc welding); ~ **sèche** dry joint

soufflage *m* air-jet cleaning (dust removal); ~ **magnétique** magnetic blow-out (circuit)

souffle *m* hiss; total continuous spectrum noise; ~ **cosmique** cosmic noise

soufflette *f* **air comprimé** compressed air blower

soufflure *f* blow-hole

soulager *v* ease the load on; relieve

soulignement *m* underscoring; underlining

soumission *f* **des travaux à distance** remote job entry (RJE)

soupape *f* rectifier; valve; relay; trap; regulator; ~ **à cathode liquide** pool rectifier; ~ **ionique** gas-filled rectifier; gas-discharge relay; ~ **sèche** (electronic) contact rectifier

souple *adj* versatile; compliant; flexible; user-friendly

souplesse *f* versatility; resilience; pliability; compliance; flexibility; ~ **d'adaptation** interfaceability; compatibility; ~ **de mise en œuvre** operational versatility; ~ **d'emploi** flexibility; versatility; compliance; ~ **extrême** great versatility; user-friendliness

souplisseau *m* insulated sleeving; tubing; sheathing

source *f* origin; source; fountainhead; feed; ~ **annulaire** ring source; ~ **chaude** hot well; ~ **d'alimentation** power (supply) source; ~ **d'antenne** aerial feed; ~ **de bruit** noise source; ~ **de courant +ve et -ve** bilateral current source; ~ **de données** data source; ~ **de messages** message source; ~ **d'énergie** power supply; ~ **d'énergie de**

secours emergency power supply; ~ **d'énergie en bande K** K-band power source; ~ **d'illumination** (aerial) feed; ~ **d'interférence** interference source; (radio) noise source; ~ **divergente** divergent light source; ~ **froide** heat sink; cold well; ~ **monochromatique stable** stable monochromatic source; ~ **périscopique** beam-waveguide feed; ~ **primaire** aerial feed; ~ **primaire décalée** offset feed; ~ **semi-conductrice** semiconductor source (s/c laser; diode laser; injection laser); ~ **sonore** acoustic source; ~ **stationnaire** ergodic source; stationary source

sous in (of mode); using; sub-; infra-; under; at (of potential); into (of power delivered into load)

sous-bloc *m* routine

sous-brillant *adj* dim

sous-canal *m* sub-channel

sous-carte *f* daughter board

sous-centre *m* sub-centre

sous-commandiers *m pl* foremen; charge-hands; middle management

sous-dépassement *m* underflow

sous-dimensionné *adj* (lines) congested

sous-division *f* **de la fréquence de répétition d'impulsions** skip keying

sous-domaine *m* sub-field

sous-dossier *m* discussion document

sous-ensemble *m* subset; subassembly (s/assy)

sous-excitation *f* under-excitation

sous-fichier *m* file section

sous-fonction *f* sub-function

sous-groupe *f* pre-group; sub-group

sous-indicatif *m* sub-code

sous-jacence *f* undercut (of PCB layers)

sous-jacent *adj* underlying; sub-surface

sous-modulation *f* insufficient modulation; under-modulation

sous-multiple *m* sub-multiple; aliquot part

sous-paquet *m* sub-burst

sous-paramètre *m* sub-parameter

sous-porteuse *f* sub-carrier; ~ **modulée en fréquence** frequency-modulated sub-carrier

sous-position(nement) *f* sub-position

sous-poutre *f* joist

sous-programme *m* subroutine; procedure; patch; ~ **bouclé** recursive subroutine; ~ **de bibliothèque** library (sub-)routine; ~ **de traitement d'anomalies** malfunction routine; ~ **fermé** closed subroutine; linked subroutine; ~ **ouvert** direct (insert) subroutine; open routine; ~ **paramétrable** dynamic subroutine

sous-programmes imbriqués nested (sub-routines)

sous-répartiteur *m* line concentrator; cable terminal; ~ **automatique (SRA)** line concentrator
sous-répartition (SR) *f* cross-connect point
sous-réseau *m* switching plane; cross-connect point
sous-schéma *m* outline; sub-table
sous-station *f* substation
sous-système *m* subsystem; part; ~ **de télémesure trajectographie et télécommande** telemetry tracking and command (TTC); ~ **de transport de messages (SSTM)** message transfer part (MTP); ~ **utilisateur téléphonique (SSUT)** telephone user part (TUP)
sous-tension *f* undervoltage
soustracteur *m* (full) subtractor
sous-traitant *m* subcontractor
soustraire *v* delegate
sous-trame *f* sub-frame
sous-tranche sub-assembly
sous-voie *f* time-derived channel
souterrain *adj* buried; underground
soutirage *m* **électrique** forced electric drainage
soyage *m* joggling; slide-on (of terminal)
SPA (v. ligne spécialisée en départ); ≃ (v. station principale asservie)
spatial *adj* space-domain
spatule *f* burnisher
SPB (v. ligne spécialisée en arrivée)
SPC = **vis CHc** (v. vis à six pans creux)
speaker *m* (speakerine) (TV/radio) announcer; broadcaster
spécialisation *f* **de trafic** call queuing; switched-loop operation
spécialisé *adj* leased; bespoke; dedicated
spécialisée arrivée (SPB) denied origination; ~ **départ (SPA)** denied termination
spécification *f* type; specification; ~ **de définition** detail specification; ~ **générale** generic specification; ~ **particulière** detail specification
spécificités *f pl* dedicated features
spécifique *adj* individual; dedicated; user-defined; non-standard; job-oriented; categorical; exclusive; unique; bespoke; selected; select; home-grown; made-to-measure; inherent; purpose-built; native
spectre *m* spectrum; ~ **acoustique** sound spectrum; ~ **continu** continuous spectrum; ~ **de bruit** noise spectrum; ~ **de fréquences** frequency spectrum; ~ **de longueurs d'ondes électromagnétiques** electromagnetic spectrum; ~ **de puissance** power spectrum; ~ **d'émission** output spectrum; ~ **d'énergie (émis en ligne)** energy spectrum; line (signal power density) spectrum; ~ **d'énergie en cosinus élevé** raised cosine energy spectrum;

~ **d'une impulsion** pulse spectrum; ~ **étalé** spread spectrum
spectres de résonance pour micro-ondes microwave resonance spectrum
spire *f* winding drum (for film); turn; lap; fuse; ~ **de désaimantation** demagnetizing turn; ~ **jointive** contiguous turn (of coil winding); lap; ~ **morte** idle/dead turn; lap; winding (of coil)
spires jointives closed-pattern (of spring)
spitage *m* bolting down
SPM (v. station principale maîtresse)
spontané *adj* non-compelled
spontanément *adv* non-compelled; automatically; impromptu; ad hoc
spot *m* spot; fly-back; trace; ~ **analyseur** scanning spot; ~ **commercial** advertising slot
SR (v. sous-répartition); ≃ (v. secteur de routage)
SRA (v. sous-répartiteur automatique)
ssens (sous-ensemble) subassembly (s/assy)
SSII (v. sociétés de service et d'ingénierie informatique)
SSTM (v. sous-système de transport de messages)
SSUT (v. sous-système utilisateur téléphonique)
stabilisateur *m* **de courant** current stabilizer; ~ **de tension** voltage stabilizer
stabilisation *f* settling; ~ **automatique de bruit** automatic gain stabilization; ~ **d'amplitude** amplitude stabilization; ~ **dans les trois axes** spin-stabilized; triaxially stabilized; de-spun; ~ **de couleur** colour lock (control)
stabiliser *v* settle
stabilité *f* stability; consistency; settling; station-keeping (of satellite); ~ **de fréquence** frequency stability; ~ **de la transposition** converter frequency stability; ~ **de phase** phase stability; ~ **de point zéro** zero stability; ~ **en orbite** station-keeping (of satellite)
stable *adj* neutral; centre-biased (of switch); blinking (of lamp); clear
stade *m* **d'amplification** amplifier stage; ~ **d'attaque** driver stage; ~ **de déclenchement périodique** blanking stage; ~ **de puissance** power stage; ~ **final** output stage; ~ **oscillateur** oscillator stage
stage *m* instruction; training course
stagiaire *m ou f* trainee
standard *m* multi-position switchboard; ~ *adj* default; ~ **d'abonné** private branch exchange (PBX); ~ **manuel** manual switchboard; ~ **téléphonique** telephone exchange; switchboard
standardiste *m ou f* telephone operator;

S

stati-contact 246

switchboard operator; attendant
stati-contact *m* proximity switch
statif *m* stand (of microscope)
station *f* station; (logic) path; ~ **amplificatrice** repeater station; relay station; ~ **asservie** slave station; remote station; ~ **autocommandée** automatic station; ~ **coactive** cluster workstation; ~ **connectée au réseau** on-net station; ~ **côtière** shore station; coastal station; ~ **de base** base station; ~ **de connexion** networking station; ~ **de contrôle** control station; ~ **de contrôle** (d'un faisceau) system control station; ~ **de contrôle du réseau** net control station; radio control station; ~ **de conversion** converter station; ~ **de diffusion de renseignements météorologiques** weather-reporting station; ~ **de distribution** distribution (despatching) station; ~ **de données** data station; ~ **de fac-similé** facsimile broadcast station; ~ **de localisation radiogoniométrique** direction-finding control station; ~ **de poursuite radar** radar tracking station; ~ **de radiodiffusion** broadcasting station; radio; ~ **de radiotélégraphie** radiotelegraphy station; ~ **de réception** receiving station; ~ **de rediffusion** fill-in transmitter; ~ **de relais électronique** radio-relay station; ~ **de relais radioélectrique** radio-relay station; ~ **de relèvement tridimensionnel** three-dimensional DF station; ~ **de répéteurs** repeater station; ~ **de télévision** television centre; ~ **de transfert (Sdt)** transfer station; ~ **de transformation** transformer station; ~ **d'émission** transmitting station; broadcast station; ~ **d'énergie** power source; power plant; ~ **d'évaluation** repetition station; ~ **directrice** controlling test station; ~ **directrice coaxiale** coaxial control station; ~ **directrice de groupe** group control station; ~ **émettrice** transmitting station; ~ **expérimentale** experimental station; ~ **hertzienne** radio-relay station; ~ **maîtresse** master station; ~ **mobile** mobile station; roamer; ~ **non surveillée** unattended station; ~ **normalement exploitée** attended station; ~ **orbitale** space station; ~ **principale asservie (SPA)** remote terminal station; ~ **principale de répéteurs** main repeater station; ~ **principale maîtresse (SPM)** main terminal station; ~ **radar** radar station; ~ **radioélectrique** radio station; ~ **radioélectrique appelée** answering station; ~ **radiogoniométrique** direction-finding station; ~ **réceptrice** receiving station; ~ **relais** relay station; ~ **sans connexion au réseau** off-net station; ~ **semi-surveillée** semi-attended station; ~ **serveur** cluster controller; ~ **sous-directrice** sub-control station; auxiliary telephone; ~ **spatiale tournante** spinning space station; ~ **surveillée** attended station; ~ **téléalimentée** dependent station; ~ **télésurveillée** unattended station; ~ **terminale** terminal station; ~ **terrestre** earth station; ground station; ~ **terrestre asservie** slave ground station; ~ **terrienne** (earth) satellite relay station; tracking station; terrestrial station; ~ **terrienne côtière** shore station; ~ **tributaire** subordinate station; dependent station
stationnaire *adj* steady; standing; stationary; fixed
stations émettrice/réceptrice up and down stations (of satellite)
statique *adj* steady-state; static; non-operational; still; DC (direct-current); solid-state; wired; stable; stationary
statisme *m* droop (of control system)
stator *m* stator; field winding; ~ **inductif** field coils
statoréacteur *m* ramjet
stéréoscopie *f* stereography; 3-D photography; stereoscopic photography
stimulateur *m* (électrique de cœur) pacemaker
stimulis *m* test and diagnostic data; test signals
stock *m* storage; inventory; repertory
stockage *m* shelf life; warehousing; storage; ~ **et retransmission** store-and-forward
stocker *v* store; read-in; preserve; log; down-load
strap *v* shunt; shorting link; strap; jumper
strappage *m* strap(ping)
strapper *v* strap
stratifié *m ou adj* laminated; laminate; substrate
stratifil *adj* roving
stricto sensu in the strict sense; strictly speaking
strié *adj* fluted; serrated
structure *f* syntax; form; structure; configuration; pattern; ~ **à deux niveaux** split control; ~ **à ruban** ribbon structure; ~ **cylindrique rainurée** V-grooved cylinder structure; ~ **d'accueil** host computer; ~ **de données liées** linked-list data structure; ~ **de l'adresse** address format; ~ **de l'information** data format; ~ **de message** message format; message structure; syntax; ~ **d'octet** byte pattern; ~ **du logiciel** software partitioning; ~ **hiérarchique** multi-level; ~ **logique** operating system; resource allocation; reconfiguration; ~ **passive** repeaterless system; ~ **physique** mono-processor; multi-processor; comput-

er network environment; ~ **plane épitaxiée** planar epitaxial structure; ~ **répartie** distributed structure

studio *m* studio; ~ **de radiodiffusion** broadcast studio; ~ **sourd** soundproofed studio; anechoic studio

stylique *adj* design

stylo-marqueur *m* (etch-resist) ink pen

SU (unité symbolique) logical unit; symbolic unit

subfascination *f* subliminal technique (psychological induction in advertising)

subir *v* sustain; undergo; be subjected (to)

subordination *f* **à la capacité de mémoire** memory-bound

subordonné à limited; bound; oriented

substance *f* agent; matter; ~ **luminescente** phosphor

substitution *f* swapping

substrat *m* substrate; bulk

subvention *f* funding; grant; subsidy

succession de signaux sequence of signals; ~ **d'ordre des phases** phase sequence; instruction steps

successivement *adv* in turn; consecutively

succinct *adj* concise; crash; impromptu; swift; compact; condensed; abridged; summary

sucette *f* snap-on connector

sucre *m* insulating screw joint

suffixe *m* in-call facility code; suffix; subscript; ~ **d'intrusion** intrusion suffix (dialling code)

suicide *m* hardware reset (function)

suintement *m* sweating; weeping; percolation; bleeding

suite *f* continuation; sequence; series; run; train; succession; stream

SUITE NEXT (key)

suite à prompted by; in pursuance of; ~ **de câbles** cable run; ~ **de zéros** string of spaces; ~ **d'éléments binaires** bit string

suivant *adj* next; neighbouring; subsequent; following

suiveur *m ou adj* (= non-inverseur) non-inverting (buffer/driver); tracking; ~ *adj* tracking; ~ **de tension** voltage follower

suivi *m* product design consistency; uniformity; conformity; monitoring; progress chasing; modification sequence; liaison; review; progress check; audit; tracking; ~ **de** backed by

superfantôme *m* double-phantom

superficiel *adj* cosmetic

supergroupe *m* supergroup

supericonoscope *m* image iconoscope

supérieur *adj* higher-ranking; uppermost; top; upper; upward(s); ~ **à** better than; greater than; in excess

supermodulation *f* overmodulation

supermultiplex *m* superhighway

superposé *adj* overlaid; superposed; virtual; stacked; one above the other; superimposed; bias; phantom

superposer *v* superpose; superimpose; overlay

superréaction *f* super-regeneration

superréfraction *f* super-refraction

superviser *v* monitor

superviseur *m* executive (supervisory) program; (task) scheduler; ~ **d'entrée-sortie** I/O (data) handler; ~ **temps réel** real-time monitor

supervision *f* supervision; ~ **des accès** I/O supervision; ~ **des appels** call supervision

supplémentaire *adj* add-on; party-line; back-up

support *m* bed; former; medium; receptacle; plinth; mount; base; holder/carrier; frame; rack; plate; path (of PCM trunk); socket; peripheral (device); terminal; processing; jacket; back-up; backing medium; stationery; host; carrier; (training) aids; backing (of adhesive label); memory board; ~ **amovible reprogrammable** EPROM device; ~ **banalisé** scratch file; ~ **blanc** empty medium; ~ **commutateur** gravity switch; ~ **de données** data medium; ~ **de lampe** valve-holder; ~ **de microphone** microphone stand; ~ **de transmission** transmission medium; ~ **de transmission de données** data transmission medium; ~ **de travail** I/O device; input-output terminal; ~ **de tube** valve-holder; ~ **d'électrode** electrode support; ~ **d'enregistrement** data recording medium; ~ **d'indicateur** display console; ~ **d'information** data recording medium; ~ **émission** go path; ~ **fer à souder** soldering iron rest; ~ **informatique** data-processing support facilities; ~ **isolant** insulated base (of PCB); ~ **paiement** credit card; payment card; plastic money; ~ **pédale** hook-switch mounting; ~ **perforé** pre-drilled plate; ~ **plastique** plastic support element; ~ **pour coupe-circuit** fuse-holder; ~ **profilé** mounting rail/track; pre-formed (standard) fixing rail; ~ **réception** return path; ~ **relais** relay socket; ~ **serre-câble** base (for cable ties); ~ **stratifié plaqué cuivre** foil-clad laminate; ~ **transparent** transparency

supporté *adj* compatible

supports publicitaires advertising media

supposé *adj* ostensible

supposer *v* presuppose; be predicated on; assume

suppresseur de gigue jitter suppressor; ~ **de réaction** singing suppressor; ~ *m* **d'écho**

S

echo suppressor; (echo) killer; ~ **d'écho à action discontinue** relay type echo suppressor; ~ **d'écho différentiel** differential echo suppressor; ~ **d'écho intermédiaire** intermediate echo suppressor; ~ **d'écho terminal** terminal echo suppressor; ~ **d'harmoniques** harmonic filter; ~ **différentiel d'écho** differential echo suppressor; ~ **d'impulsions** impulse suppressor

suppression *f* elimination; removal; stop(-page); cut-out; deletion; cancellation; override; discontinuation; blanking; inhibiting; withdrawal; isolation; suppression; clearing; purge; scratching; ~ **de bande latérale unique** single-sideband suppression; ~ **de caractères** delete character (DCH); ~ **de la bande latérale** sideband suppression; ~ **de la porteuse** carrier suppression; ~ **de ligne** delete line (DL); ~ **de l'onde directe** ground-wave suppression; ~ **de l'onde porteuse** carrier suppression; ~ **de rebondissement** debounce; ~ **de rebondissements** de-bounce; bounce elimination; ~ **de tabulation** tabulation clear (TBC); ~ **d'écho** echo suppression; ~ **d'écho fixe** permanent echo cancellation; ~ **d'éléments** (binaires) truncation; ~ **des blancs** (leading) zero suppression; ~ **des erreurs** debugging; ~ **des parasites** noise blanking; ~ **d'harmoniques** harmonic discrimination; ~ **du faisceau** blanking; ~ **d'un secteur** zone blanking

supprimer *v* delete; cancel; withdraw; scratch; purge; discard

supraconducteur *adj* (à supraconductivité) cryogenic

supraphonique *adj* superaudio (AC telegraphy, above 3.4 kHz)

SUR IMP (v. mémoire tampon du clavier)

surabondant *adj* generously applied

suralimentation *f* battery boosting; voltage boosting; supercharging; bucking

suralimenteur *m* booster; supercharger

suramplificateur *m* booster

surblanc *m* whiter-than-white

surbrillance *f* high-lighting

surcharge *f* overload; overflow; overdrive; surge; overwrite; burn-out; ~ **admissible** overload capacity; ~ **des répéteurs** repeater overloading; ~ **passagère** transient overload; surge

surcharger *v* overload; ~ **en écriture** overwrite

surcourse *f* overtravel

surdéviation *f* overswing

surdimensionnement *m* (du réseau) (network) overdimensioning; overkill

surécrire *v* over-write; over-print

surélévation *f* clearance; stand-off

surépaisseur *m* wall thickness; coating thickness; cover lay; cover layer; ~ **d'usinage** machining allowance

sûreté *f* integrity; safety; ~ **intégrale** fail-safe

surexcitation *f* over-excitation

surface *f* **caractéristique de directivité** beam width; ~ **de captation** absorption cross-section; effective area; ~ **de diffusion** echoing area; scattering cross-section; radar cross-section; ~ **de séparation** interface; ~ **effective** absorption cross-section; effective area; ~ **effective de diffusion** echoing area; ~ **en regard** aligned portion; ~ **granitée** crackle finish

surfrappe *f* strikeover

surfusion *f* fusing

surimpression *f* flash; overprint; overtype; emboldening; double strike

surindicatif *m* supercode

surinscrire *v* overwrite

surintensité *f* current surge; overload; over-current; ~ **de courant** overcurrent

surlignement *m* overscoring; vinculum

surluminance *f* edge flare

surmodulation *f* (= dépassement) overshoot (logic); over-modulation; swing; backwash

surmoulé (enrobé de plastique) encapsulated; shrouded

surnumérotation *f* over-pulsing; dialling excess digits

suroscillation *f* ringing (of pulse); squegging; overshoot; damped oscillation

surpresseur *m* booster

surpuissance *f* overkill capacity

surtaxe *f* surcharge; ~ **d'avis d'appel** messenger call fee

surtension *f* overvoltage; (voltage) surge; high-Q; ~ **de commutation** switching spike; ~ **de retour** flyback voltage; ~ **inverse** reverse voltage surge

survaleur *f* goodwill

surveillance *f* supervision; monitoring; watch; ~ **de contacts** contact monitoring; ~ **de l'acheminement** route monitoring; ~ **du taux d'erreurs d'alignement** alignment error rate monitoring; ~ **qualité** quality monitoring; quality assurance

surveillant(e) *m* (*f*) supervisor; watchdog

surveillé *adj* guarded against; attended; monitored; manned

survolteur *m* booster; ~ **continu-continu** DC-DC voltage booster

susceptance *f* susceptance (imaginary part of admittance); ~ **d'électrode** electrode susceptance

susceptibilité en conduction immunity to conducted interference; ~ **non linéaire**

non-linear susceptibility
susceptible *adj* prone; liable; likely
susciter *v* evince
suspendu *adj* temporarily out of service; overhead; top-mounted; aborted
suspension *f* **d'appel** delay working; ~ **élastique** resilient mounting
SVC (appel du superviseur) supervisor(y) call
Sylvanier (circline) [A.C.] circular(-form) fluorescent tube
symbole *m* symbol; digit; (special) character; multiline extension; ~ **abstrait** abstract symbol; ~ **binaire** binary digit; bit; ~ **commun** public symbol; ~ **de décision** decision box (of flowchart); ~ **N-aire** N-ary symbol
symbolique *adj* symbolic
symbolisé *adj* denoted
symétrie *f* equalizing; balance; push-pull; ~ **de la tension** voltage balance; ~ **par rapport à la terre** balance to earth; balance about earth
symétrique *adj* reverse; balanced; opposite-handed; construction; reversible; push-pull; matching; mirror image; matched; ~ **par rapport au 0V** balanced to earth potential
symétriseur *m* quarter-(wave) bar; sleeve; quarter-wave line; stub; ~ **à écran coaxial** quarter-wave sleeve; ~ **à ligne symétrique** Pawsey stub; quarter-wave(length) coaxial line; ~ **à manchon** quarter-wave sleeve
synchro *m* magslip; autosyn; selsyn
synchrone *adj* synchronous
synchronisateur *m* phaser; synchroscope; synchronizer; phase-shifting transformer; phasing transformer
synchronisation *f* gating; synchronization; alignment; coinciding; timing; triggering; ~ **de trame** frame alignment
synchronisé *adj* in phase; ~ **Dₜ RS** positive-edge triggered
synchroniser *v* de-skew (of data)
synchroniseur *m* phaser
synchronisme *m* synchronism; simultaneity
synchronoscope *m* synchronous machine
synergie *f* synergistic relationship; concerted action; harmony; inter-working
synoptique *f* skeleton diagram; circuit diagram; brief survey; overview; structural breakdown; configuration
syntaxe *f* syntax; message structure
synthèse *f* composite picture; consolidation; résumé; aggregate; collection; conclusion; summary; cumulation; scanning; summation; artifice; artefact; conspectus; amalgamation; synthesis; evaluation; correlation; trial and error; ~ **de la forme d'onde**

waveform synthesis; ~ **de la gamme supérieure** time-domain synthesis; ~ **ligne par ligne non entrelacée** sequential scanning
synthétique *adj* integrated; composite; consolidated; man-made; cumulative; false; dummy
synthétiser *v* re-integrate
synthétiseur *m* frequency synthesizer; ~ **de voix** voice synthesizer; ~ **évolutif** subscriber carrier system
syntonisateur *m* tuner
syntonisation *f* tuning
systématique *adj* regular; routine; systematic; methodical; housekeeping; persistent; invariable
systématiquement *adv* methodically; invariably; on a routine basis; as a matter of course; standard
système *m* system; ~ **à barres croisées** crossbar system; ~ **à batterie centrale** common-battery system (CB); ~ **à boucle** loop ringing; ~ **à canaux multiples adaptatif** adaptive multi-channel system; ~ **à canaux multiples décentralisé** multichannel decentralized system; ~ **à commande commune** common control system; ~ **à commande par enregistreurs** register-controlled system; ~ **à courant porteur** carrier system; ~ **à courant porteur sur câble coaxial** coaxial carrier system; ~ **à courants porteurs à haute fréquence** high-frequency (HF) carrier system; ~ **à décades** decade system; ~ **à double appel** direct trunking; ~ **à enregistreurs** register-controlled system; director system; ~ **à entraînement mécanique** power-driven system; ~ **à impulsions en arrière** revertive pulse system; ~ **à large bande** broadband system; wideband system; ~ **à magnéto** magneto system; ~ **à microondes** microwave system; ~ **à mosaïque** mosaic telegraphy; ~ **à ondes porteuses décalées** offset carrier system; ~ **à plusieurs porteuses sur voies multiples** multi-channel multi-carrier system; ~ **à plusieurs voies de radio-téléimpression** multi-channel radio teletype; ~ **à postes embrochés** omnibus (telegraph) system; way circuit; ~ **à signal décalé** offset signal method; ~ **acoustique stéréophonique** stereophonic sound system; ~ **actif-réserve** worker-standby system; ~ **aéroporté de prévention** airborne collision avoidance system; ~ **antirebond** bounce eliminator; ~ **antivibratoire** anti-hunting system; ~ **arythmique** start-stop system; ~ **arythmique cadencé** stepped start-stop system; ~ **asservi** positive-feedback system; ~ **au synchronisme** synchronous

duplex operation; ~ **auditif** auditory system; ~ **automatique** automatic system; ~ **automatique à commutateurs rotatifs** rotary system; ~ **automatique à entraînement mécanique** power-driven system; ~ **automatique pas à pas** step-by-step automatic system; ~ **automatique tout à relais** all-relay (dial) system; relay automatic system; ~ **auto-oscillant** self-oscillating system; ~ **avec attente** delay system; ~ **avec marqueur** marker system; ~ **avec mise en file des appels** call-queuing system; ~ **avec perte** loss system; ~ **binaire** binary system; ~ **combinateur de diversité** diversity combining system; ~ **correcteur d'erreurs (RQ automatique)** error correcting telegraph system (ARQ); ~ **correcteur d'erreurs par retour de l'information** information feedback system; ~ **D** (débrouillez-vous) do-it-yourself (DIY); makeshift; home-made; ~ **d'alarme** alarm system; ~ **d'alarme d'incendie** call bell system; ~ **d'asservissement** master/slave system; ~ **d'assignation à la demande** demand-assignment multiple access (DAMA); ~ **d'atterrissage sans visibilité** blind-landing system; ~ **de bande latérale unique comprimée dans le temps** time-compressed single-sideband system (TICOSS); ~ **de base** basic system; ~ **de batterie locale** local battery system (LB); ~ **de commande** control system; ~ **de commande d'assiette et d'orbite (SCAO)** attitude and orbital control system (AOCS); ~ **de communication binaire** binary ccmmunications system; ~ **de communication numérique** digital communications system; ~ **de commutation** switching system; ~ **de commutation automatique** automatic switching system; ~ **de commutation manuelle** manual switching system; ~ **de commutation privé** private switching system; ~ **de commutation semi-automatique** semi-automatic switching system; ~ **de compteur** tally system; ~ **de dérivation** drop-and-insert connection; ~ **de détection et de mesure de distance par énergie visible** visible energy detection and ranging (VEDAR); ~ **de liaison intercalculateur** interprocessor link system; ~ **de mémoire vocale** voice storage system (VSS); ~ **de navigation par satellites** satellite navigation system; ~ **de numération** numbering system; ~ **de radar LANAC** laminar navigation and anti-collision system (LANAC); ~ **de radar pour planeurs** radar glider positioning system; ~ **de radiolocation à réseau à éléments en phase** phased array radar system; ~ **de radionavigation SHO-**RAN short-range navigation system (SHORAN); ~ **de radionavigation TACAN** tactical air navigation system (TACAN); ~ **de reconnaissance vocale** voice information processing (VIP); ~ **de référence** master telephone transmission reference system; ~ **de référence pour la transmission** transmission reference system; ~ **de signalisation** signalling system; ~ **de signalisation asynchrone** start-stop signalling system; ~ **de signalisation sur voie commune** common-channel signalling system; ~ **de signalisation synchrone** synchronous signalling system; ~ **de téléimpression duplex** opposition duplex; ~ **de téléphonie duplex** full-duplex operation; ~ **de télévision** television system; ~ **de télévision à modulation de vitesse du faisceau** velocity modulation television system; ~ **de transmission** transmission system; ~ **de transmission par fibre optique** optical-fibre transmission system; ~ **Decca** Decca navigation system; ~ **décimal** decimal system; ~ **dégivreur** de-icing system; ~ **demiteinte** half-tone system; ~ **des limites absolues** (d'emploi) absolute maximum ratings; ~ **détecteur d'erreurs avec demande de répétition** error-detecting and feedback system; ARQ system; decision-feedback system; request-repeat system; ~ **détecteur d'erreurs sans répétition** error-detecting system; ~ **d'exploitation** operating system; ~ **d'exploitation échangé** swapping operating system; ~ **d'exploitation sur disque (SED)** disk operating system (DOS); ~ **d'interruption** interrupt system; ~ **diplex** diplex; ~ **d'ordonnance** sequence system; scheduling; ~ **dorsal** back-end system; ~ **duplex** duplex system; ~ **dupliqué** dual-processor system; ~ **embarqué de communication avec un satellite** shipborne satellite communications system; ~ **étalon de travail** working standard; ~ **harmonique** VF telegraph system; carrier telegraphy; wired wireless; ~ **hautbois** oboe (radar distance measuring system); ~ **Hell** Hellschreiber system; Hell (mosaic telegraphy) printer system; ~ **hertzien** radio-relay system; microwave system; ~ **hyperbolique à modulation par impulsions** pulse-modulated hyperbolic system; ~ **intégré de communications** integrated communications system; ~ **interne** in-plant system; in-house system; ~ **LIDAR** light-detection and ranging (LIDAR); ~ **LORAC** long-range accuracy radar system (LORAC); ~ **LORAN** long-range navigational system (LORAN); ~ **microondes hybride** hybrid microwave system; ~ **monoprocesseur** single-processor system; ~ **multiplex carrier** system; ~ **multiplex numérique d'abonnés** digital subscriber carrier system; ~ **non quantifié** classical system (pre-Newtonian); ~ **océanique de satellites** oceanic satellite system; ~ **pas à pas** step-by-step system; directly-controlled progressive system; ~ **quadruplex** quadruplex system; ~ **quantifié** quantized system; ~ **radar à monoimpulsion** monopulse radar system; ~ **radar continu hyperbolique** hyperbolic continuous radar system; ~ **radiotéléphonique** radiotelephone system; ~ **semi-automatique** semi-automatic system; ~ **spatial** register processing sub-system; ~ **standard d'approche à radiophare** let-down approach; standard beam approach (SBA); ~ **synchrone** synchronous system; ~ **télé-** graphique duplex équilibré en pont bridge duplex connection; ~ **téléphonique** telephone system; ~ **téléphonique à appel magnétique** magneto telephone set; ~ **téléphonique à batterie centrale** common battery system (CB); ~ **téléphonique à batterie locale** local battery system (LB); ~ **téléphonique à douze voies** twelve-channel telephone system; ~ **téléphonique à poussoirs** key telephone set (KTS); ~ **téléphonique automatique** automatic switching system; ~ **téléphonique manuel** manual telephone system; ~ **temporel** register transfer system; ~ **tout à relais** all-relay system; ~ **Van Rysselbergh** composited circuit; ~ **Verdan** Verdan system; ~ **Wheatstone** Wheatstone automatic transmission system

S

T

'T' (v. travail)

T hybride hybrid-T junction; magic-T junction

T magique hybrid-T junction; magic-T junction

T plan E series T; shunt-T

table *f* table; desk; panel; bed; map; board; box; ~ **à accès direct** single-stage index table; ~ **à digitaliser** digitizing pad; digitizing tablet; ~ **à double entrée** two-dimensional array; ~ **à lumière** light box; ~ **à organisation directe** direct-access table; ~ **à tiroir** multi-stage index table; ~ **chaînée** search table; ~ **compacte** continuous table; ~ **d'accusation** fault-finding chart; look-up table; ~ **d'acheminement** routing table; ~ **d'affectation binaire** bit map; ~ **d'affectation des sections** program relocation table; ~ **d'aiguillage** correspondence table; ~ **de branchement** cross-connect panel; ~ **de codes de bureau** exchange code table; ~ **de correspondance** (bit) map; conversion table; cross-reference table; correlation table; map; truth table; function table; status map; ~ **de coupure** test rack; ~ **de décision** decision table; ~ **de définition** truth table; Boolean operation table; ~ **de données** light box; ~ **de fonction booléenne** Boolean operation table; ~ **de fonctions** truth table; function table; ~ **de Karnaugh** Karnaugh map; ~ **de mémoires communes** common memory map; ~ **de référence** cross-reference table; ~ **de taux de taxe** charge rate table; ~ **de traduction** translation table; ~ **de vérité** truth table; ~ **d'équivalence** look-up table; ~ **des écarts** table of differentials; ~ **des matières** contents; ~ **des reprises en secours** rescue dump; check-point/dump-point table; ~ **d'essais** test desk; test board; ~ **d'essais et de mesure** test desk; trunk test rack; test board; ~ **desserte** payout stand; ~ **d'état des canaux** channel status table; ~ **d'opérateur** toll board; ~ **d'opératrice** operator desk; operator position; ~ **éclairante** light box; ~ **éclatée** split table; ~ **interurbaine** toll board; trunk position; ~ **logiciel** software table; ~ **mobile en X-Y** X-Y axis cross-slide; X-Y traversing table; ~ **optique** photoplotter; ~ **rase** wind of change; spring-clean; ~ **répartie** distributed table; ~ **sémaphore** data link table; common-channel signalling table; ~ **traçante** plotter; chart recorder; ~ **X-Y** traversing bed; traversing table; X-Y plotting table

tableau *m* chart; diagram; panel; array; report; escutcheon; schedule; index; roster; board; illustration; table; mimetic diagram; multi-position switchboard; lamp field; (order) turret; bulletin; bezel; ~ **à fusibles** fuse board; cut-out panel; ~ **basse tension LT** distribution board; ~ **commutateur** telephone switchboard; ~ **commutateur à batterie centrale** common-battery switchboard; ~ **commutateur à batterie locale** local-battery switchboard; ~ **commutateur à clés** key switchboard; ~ **commutateur interurbain** toll switchboard; ~ **commutateur manuel** manual switchboard; ~ **commutateur manuel à clés** cordless switchboard; ~ **commutateur multiple** multiple switchboard; ~ **commutateur téléphonique** telephone switchboard; ~ **comprimé** packed array; ~ **d'affectation des séries** callsign block allocation table; ~ **d'affichage** bulletin board; ~ **de bord** mimic diagram; management information system; instrument panel; dashboard; situation report; status panel; status report; lamp field; mimetic diagram; management; information system; ~ **de brassage** jumper field; mixer panel; ~ **de commande** instrument panel; control panel; ~ **de commutation** switchboard; ~ **de connexions** plugboard; ~ **de contrôle de vraisemblance** reasonableness check table; ~ **de conversion** conversion table; ~ **de distribution** switchboard; switch panel; distribution board; ~ **de jacks** jack field; jack panel; ~ **de voies** track diagram; ~ **d'essai** test panel; ~ **électrique** electrical control panel; switchboard; ~ **indicateur optique** diagram panel; mimetic diagram; mimic diagram; lamp field; ~ **manuel** manual switchboard; ~ **multiple** multiple switchboard; ~ **synoptique** mimic diagram; mimetic diagram

tablette *f* (rack) plate; ~ **de travail** working surface; ~ **digitalisante** digitizer pad; ~ **graphique** graphics tablet; keypad

tableur *m* spread sheet

tablier *m* apron

tabulateur *m* tabulation key; tab key

tabulation *f* key-stroke; ~ **avant** horizontal tabulation (HT); ~ **horizontale** horizontal tabulation; skip; ~ **horizontale arrière** cursor backward tabulation (CBT); ~ **verticale** vertical tabulation; skip

tabulatrice *f* **alphanumérique** alphanumeric accounting machine

tache *f* blemish; stain; spot; mark; ~ **cathodique** cathode spot; ~ **de diffraction** diffraction fringe; ~ **d'exploration** scanning spot; ~ **d'imprégnation** measling; ~ **ionique** ion burn; ~ **noire** toner fleck

tâche *f* routine; task; project; job; ~ **d'aide à la mise au point** debugging aid; ~ **de chargement des programmes** program loader task; ~ **de défense** security task; ~ **de fond** background task; ~ **de gestion** housekeeping routine; ~ **déconcentrée** common task; decentralized task; ~ **demanderesse** calling task; ~ **élémentaire** basic task; ~ **émettrice** sending task; ~ **en cours** running task; current task; task in progress; ~ **en exécution** running task; ~ **exécutable** ready task; ~ **périodique** recurrent task; routine task

tachy *m* (dynamo tachymétrique) tachogenerator; ~ *f* (tachymètre) tachometer

taille *f* (de zone/secteur) capacity; length (of storage area/element); boundary; ~ **d'un segment** segment size; ~ **mémoire** memory occupancy; ~ **par défaut d'une région** default bucket size

talkie walkie *m* walkie-talkie

talon *m* Nyquist interval bandwidth; stub; lug; reference period; maximum (pulse) transmission rate; tab

tambour d'enroulement filament drum; ~ **magnétique** magnetic lug

tampon *m* buffer; bushing; plug; pad; stamp; plug gauge (GO/NO-GO); ~ **amplificateur** buffer; ~ **d'alvéole** shelf buffer; ~ **de baie** rack buffer; ~ **de feutre** felt pad; ~ **de sortie** output buffer; ~ **de travail** cut-and-paste buffer; ~ **d'entrée** input buffer; ~ **encreur** inked pad

tamponnage *m* buffering

tandem *m ou adj* tandem; en bloc MF signalling; cascaded series

tangente *adj* border-line; ~ *f* **de l'angle de pertes** tangent of loss angle

tant soit peu rather; somewhat

tantale goutte tantalum bead (of capacitor)

TAO (v. test assisté par ordinateur); ~ (v. traduction assisté par ordinateur)

tapis *m* **de présence** touch-sensitive mat; ~ **de sol** earth mat; ~ **isolant** insulating mat; ~ **mousse** foam pad

tapoter *v* hammer/tap (lightly)

taquet *m* cleat; ~ **de marge** margin stop; ~ **de tabulation** tab stop; tabulating stop

TAR (v. tout au réseau)

tarage *m* calibration; setting-(up); ~ **automatique** automatic calibration

taraud *m* tap

taré *(adj)* pre-set; calibrated

tarif *m* tariff; rate; scale of charges; price list; ~ **de nuit** night rate; ~ **de taxation** charge rate table; ~ **forfaitaire** flat rate; fixed charge; ~ **hors pointe** off-peak tariff; off-peak rate; ~ **réduit** reduced rate; ~ **unitaire** message rate; ~ **vert** flexible tariff

tarification *f* charging (scale); rate fixing; billing; ~ **séparée** unbundling; ~ **sur réservation** reservation charging

tarifs dissociés unbundling

tasseau *m* bracket; stay; support; lath; batten; hoop; girdle; brace; ~ **de surélévation** stand-off; ledge; rim

tassement *m* compaction; packing; crowding; ~ **de caractères** character crowding; ~ **du microphone à charbon** carbon microphone packing

taux *m* rate; ratio; scale; coefficient; factor; degree; percentage; probability; ~ **d'accusation** fault rate; ~ **d'activité** activity ratio; ~ **d'appels** calling rate; ~ **d'appels efficaces** completion rate; ~ **de balayage** slew rate; ~ **de blocage** blocking probability; all-trunks-busy rate; access-denial probability; ~ **de blocage interne** internal blocking probability; ~ **de bridage** earthing percentage; ~ **de compréhension immédiate** immediate appreciation percentage; ~ **de compression de la transadmittance** transadmittance compression ratio; ~ **de coupure progressive** roll-off; ~ **de couverture** coverage; ~ **de décalage** stagger (ratio); ~ **de défaillance** (component) failure rate; ~ **de défaillance moyen** average failure rate; ~ **de distorsion** degree of distortion; distortion factor; ~ **de distorsion harmonique** k-rating; harmonic distortion; ~ **de facturation** billing rate; ~ **de faute** (bit) error rate; ~ **de filtrage** ripple rejection; ~ **de justification** justification ratio; stuffing ratio; ~ **de modulation** degree of modulation; modulation factor; modulation depth/percentage; smoothing factor; ripple (ratio); ~ **de modulation de vitesse pour signal faible** small-signal depth of velocity modulation; ~ **de mouvement** (file) activity ratio; ~ **de perte(s)** loss probability; attrition rate; depletion rate; dissipation factor; ~ **de PIP**

plug-in-and-play; ~ **de prélèvement** sampling rate; sampling level (SL); ~ **de rapiéçage** patching rate; ~ **de rappel** hit rate; ~ **de réaction** feedback ratio; ~ **de réflexions** voltage standing wave ratio (VSWR); ~ **de refus** percent denial; ~ **de refus d'échos fixes** sub-clutter visibility; ~ **de réjection en mode commun** common mode rejection ratio; ~ **de rejet** call-rejection rate; failure rate; ~ **de rejet d'infrastructure des lignes (TRIL)** rejection rate due to inadequate provision of plant; ~ **de relâchement** premature-release rate; ~ **de remplissage** duty cycle; mark-space ratio; pattern density; usage/allocation demand factor; ~ **de répétition** repetition rate; ~ **de répétition de trames** (Hz) frames per second (fps); ~ **de répétition d'impulsions** pulse repetition rate (PRR); ~ **de signalisation (SI)** number of reported faults; engineer call-out rate; ~ **de silence** idle ratio; inactivity ratio; ~ **de suppression de la modulation** modulation suppression rate; ~ **de surmodulation** overshoot factor; ~ **de taxe** charge rate; ~ **de transit** base transmission factor; diminution factor; transport factor/ratio; ~ **de travail** marking percentage; ~ **d'ébasage** base clipping; ~ **d'échantillonnage** sampling rate; ~ **d'échec** non-completion rate (of calls); call-completion rate; abort rate; access-denial probability; failure rate; ~ **d'écrêtage d'impulsions** pulse limiting rate; ~ **d'efficacité** completion rate; completion ratio; ~ **d'efficacité** (d'un faisceau) circuit group efficiency; ~ **d'ellipticité** axial ratio; ~ **d'ellipticité** axial ratio; ~ **d'émission secondaire** secondary-emission rate (of a surface); ~ **d'encombrement** grade of service; ~ **d'erreur d'une manipulation** keying error rate; ~ **d'erreurs** error rate; ~ **d'erreurs résiduelles** residual (undetected) error rate; ~ **d'erreurs sur les bits (TEB)** bit error rate (BER); ~ **d'erreurs sur les blocs** block-error probability; ~ **d'erreurs sur les caractères** bit error rate; block-error probability; ~ **d'erreurs sur les éléments** element error rate; bit error rate; ~ **d'erreurs sur une modulation** transmission error rate; ~ **d'expansion** expansion ratio; ~ **d'exploitation** duty cycle; duty factor; ~ **d'extension** expansion ratio; ~ **d'harmoniques** harmonic content; ~ **d'impulsions** pulse duty cycle; ~ **d'indisponibilité** down-time ratio; access-denial probability; ~ **d'interruption** down-time ratio; ~ **d'occupation** occupancy (rate); content ratio; ~ **d'occupation moyen** mean occupancy;

~ **d'ondes stationnaires** (voltage) standing wave ratio (VSWR/SWR); ~ **d'ondulation** ripple (ratio); ~ **d'usure** attrition rate; ~ **d'utilisation** (de câbles) cable fill; ~ **hygrométrique** relative humidity; ~ **interne de récupération (TIR)** internal rate of return (IRR); ~ **moyen d'occupation** mean occupancy

taxant *(adj)* levying charges

taxateur *m* charge meter; charging system; charging unit

taxation *f* ticketing; charging; billing; metering; charge metering; call metering; ~ **à domicile** own-premises metering; residential metering; ~ **à la distance** charging by distance; ~ **à l'arrière** reverse charging (collect); ~ **à l'arrivée** reverse charging; ~ **à mémoire centrale (TMC)** central storage charging system; ~ **à tarif réduit** cheap rate charging; ~ **au compteur** bulk billing; ~ **automatique** automatic message accounting (AMA); ~ **automatique avec justification** automatic message accounting; automatic toll ticketing; ~ **automatique avec justificatifs** automatic message accounting (AMA); automatic toll ticketing; ~ **automatique centralisée avec justification** centralized automatic message accounting (CAMA); ~ **avec renvoi des impulsions de taxe** revertive metering; backward metering; ~ **de base facturée (TBF)** (annual) billings; metered unit; ~ **différée** delayed charge metering; ~ **du demandé** transfer charge (collect) calls; reverse charging; ~ **en arrière** metering over junction; backward charge metering; ~ **fixe** flat-rate charging; ~ **forfaitaire** flat fee; flat-rate charging; ~ **indépendante de la durée** flat-rate charge metering; ~ **par impulsions périodiques** charge metering by periodic pulses; multimetering; ~ **par unités de conversation** speech-unit charge metering; ~ **par zone et la durée** time-and-zone metering; ~ **périodique** time-and-distance metering

taxe *f* (call) charge; duty; fee; ~ **d'annulation** (call) cancellation charge; ~ **de base** basic metered unit; ~ **de mise en présence** initial charge; ~ **de mise en relation** initial charge; ~ **de perception** collection charge; ~ **de préparation** report charge; ~ **de répartition** accounting rate; ~ **de transit** transit charge; ~ **d'envoi de messager** messenger charge; ~ **fixe** flat-rate metering; ~ **frontalière** cross-border charge; ~ **incriminée** disputed charge account; ~ **réduite** reduced charge; cheap rate; ~ **supplémentaire** additional charge; ~ **téléphonique** call charge; call fee; ~ **terminale** terminal charge; ~ **terrestre** land-station charge(s); ~ **unitaire** basic metered unit

taxeur *m* charge meter; charging system/unit

TBF (v. taxation de base facturée); ≂ (v. très basse fréquence)

TBT (v. très basse tension)

té *m* **hybride** hybrid-T junction; magic-T junction; ~ **magique** hybrid-T junction; magic-T junction; ~ **parallèle** shunt-T; ~ **série** series-T

TEB (v. taux d'erreurs sur les bits)

TEC (v. transistor à effet de champ)

technicien *m* engineer (semi-skilled)

technique *f ou adj* engineering; workshop; technical; plant; technological; industrial; ~ **de bouclage** re-entrant technique; ~ **des communications** communications equipment engineering; ~ **du transfert résonnant** resonant-transfer technique

technologie *f* state of the art; ~ **à haute intégration** large-scale integration (LSI); ~ **à hélice brasée** brazed-helix technology

Téflon [A.C.] polytetrafluoroethylene (PTFE)

téfzel (ETFE) fluorinated ethylene polypropylene (FEP)

teinte *f* shading; tone; hue; colour

téléachat *m* videotex buying facility

téléactions *f* remote functions; teleservices

téléaffichage *m* remote display; remote indication

téléalarme *f* remote alarm; distributed alarm

téléalimentation *f* remote power feed; exchange-powered

téléautographe *m* tele-autograph; telewriter

téléautographie *f* telewriting

téléavertisseur *m* paging device; Bellboy [T.N.]

télébouclage *m* remote loop-back

téléboutique *f* telephone sales office; telephone sales outlet; telephone showroom

télébureautique *f* interactive electronic office automation

téléchargement *m* down-loading; remote job entry (RJE)

télécinématique telecine (equipment)

télécollecte *f* telepayment; telecontrol; telearchics; electronic funds transfer (EFT); point-of-sale polling

télécommande *f* remote control; telecontrol; telearchics; ~ **d'avion** aircraft wireless control; ~ **de radio** radio remote control

télécommunication(s) telecommunications

télécommunication aéronautique aeronautical communications

télécommunications spatiales satellite communications

téléconduite *f* telecontrol

téléconférence *f* teleconferencing

télécontrôle *m* remote monitoring; telewatch

télécopie *f* facsimile; ~ **contrastée** document facsimile telegraphy; two-level facsimile; two-tone fax; ~ **nuancée** picture facsimile telegraphy; half-tone facsimile; multi-level fax

télécopieur *m* facsimile system; fax transceiver

télédétection *f* remote sensing

télédiagnostic *m* remote diagnostics

télédiaphonie *f* far-end crosstalk (FEXT); forward crosstalk; ~ **entre circuits combinants** side-to-side far-end crosstalk; ~ **entre réel et fantôme** side-by-phantom far-end crosstalk

télédictée *f* dial dictation

télédiffusion *f* line/wire broadcasting; public address; ~ **par fil** line/wire broadcasting

télédistribution *f* cable distribution; cable TV

télé-écriture *f* telewriting; messaging

téléenregistrement *m* telerecording

téléexploitation *f* **et télémaintenance** remote operation and maintenance

télégestion *f* remote management; remote processing; distributed management system

télégramme *m* telegram; wire; message; ~ **alphabétique** alphabetic telegram; ~ **annulatif** cancelling telegram; ~ **de service** service telegram; ~ **de transit** transit telegram; ~ **d'état** government telegram; ~ **différé** deferred telegram; ~ **en transit** transit telegram; ~ **en transit direct** direct transit telegram; ~ **fac-simile** facsimile telegram; ~ **privé** private telegram; ~ **téléphoné** telephone telegram; phonogram; ~ **urgent** urgent message; urgent telegram

télégraphe *m* telegraph; ~ **à signes de longueur inégale** unequal-letter telegraph

télégraphe alphabétique alphabetic telegraph

télégraphe Baudot Baudot printing telegraph; ~ **imprimeur** printing telegraph; ~ **imprimeur de page** page-printing telegraph; ~ **morse** Morse telegraph; ~ **multiplex en circuit échelonné** series multiplex telegraph; ~ **pas** step-by-step telegraph

télégraphie *f* telegraphy; ~ **à bande perforée** automatic telegraph transmission; ~ **à bande vocale** carrier telegraphy; voice-frequency telegraphy; wired wireless; ~ **à courant continu** direct-current (DC) telegraphy; ~ **à courant simple** neutral-current telegraphy; single-current telegraphy; ~ **à fréquence acoustique** voice-frequency telegraphy; ~ **à fréquence moyenne** medium-frequency telegraphy; ~ **à fréquences vocales** VF (multi-channel) telegraphy (VFT3); ~ **à mosaïque** mosaic telegraphy; ~ **à ondes**

T

courtes short-wave telegraphy; ~ à plusieurs canaux multichannel telegraphy; ~ arythmique start-stop telegraphy; ~ autographique facsimile telegraphy; ~ compensée à circuit fantôme double double-phantom balanced telegraphy; ~ dans la bande vocale dans un sens (= univocal) speech-plus-simplex; ~ diplex diplex telegraphy; ~ diplex à quatre fréquences four-frequency diplex telegraphy; twinplex; ~ duplex duplex telegraphy; twinplex; ~ en fantôme phantom telegraphy; ~ en quadruplex quadruplex telegraphy; ~ entretenue pure on-off telegraphy; ~ et téléphonie simultanées intra-band telegraphy; ~ fac-simile facsimile telegraphy; ~ harmonique VF telegraphy; carrier telegraphy; wired wireless; voice frequency (multichannel) telegraphy; audio frequency telegraphy; ~ harmonique à double modulation AC telegraphy with double VF modulation; ~ harmonique à plusieurs voies multichannel VF telegraphy; ~ HF HF telegraphy; ~ infra-acoustique sub-audio telegraphy; ~ inter-bandes interband telegraphy; ~ intrabande intra-band telegraphy; ~ multiple TD multiplex (transmission); ~ multiplex multiplex telegraphy; ~ multiplex à branchement split multiplex; ~ multiplex en circuit de branchement forked multiplex telegraph; ~ non modulée continuous wave telegraphy; ~ numérique multipoint multipoint TDM telegraphy; ~ par appareils imprimeurs printing telegraphy; type printing; ~ par courant continu direct current (DC) telegraphy; ~ par courants porteurs HF carrier (current) telegraphy; ~ par décomposition des signes mosaic telegraphy; ~ par enregistrement des signaux signal-recording telegraphy; ~ par manipulation par tout ou rien telegraphy by on-off keying; ~ par multivoie à deux fréquences porteuses two-tone keying; two-tone telegraph system; ~ par porteuse HF HF carrier telegraphy; ~ par répartition dans le temps time-division multiplex telegraphy; ~ par superfantôme octuplex telegraphy; ~ pendulaire pendulum start-stop telegraphy; ~ sans fil (TSF) radio telegraphy; wireless; ~ supra-acoustique super-audio telegraphy; superimposed telegraphy; ~ sur ligne aérienne open-wire telegraphy

télégraphiste m ou f telegraphist; wireless operator; radio operator

téléguidé (porteur d'informations) guided (of missile); drone courier

téléimprimeur m teleprinting apparatus; teleprinter; teletype(writer) TTY; printing telegraph; ~ à distance remote teleprinter; ~ arythmique teleprinter; teletypewriter (TTY); ~ de maintenance maintenance teleprinter; ~ électronique electronic teleprinter; ~ rapide high-speed teleprinter; ~ spécialisé pour la réception receive-only teleprinter

téléindicateur m remote indicating instrument

téléinformatique f data communications; compunications; ~ domestique data base interrogation

télélocalisation f des fautes remote fault tracing

télémaintenance f remote maintenance

télémate m remote controller

télématique f information technology; telematics; videotex; ~ bancaire videobanking

télématisation f data communications

télémessagerie f messaging; electronic mail

télémesure f telemetering; telemetry; remote sensing; ~ à modulation de fréquence frequency modulation telemetry; ~ de ligne d'abonné loop reporting

télémètre m range finder

télémétrie f range-finding

télépaiement m electronic funds transfer (EFT)

téléphone m telephone; ~ à cadran incorporé au combiné dial-in-handset telephone; compact telephone; ~ à clavier touch-tone (pushbutton) telephone; ~ à dispositif antilocal anti-sidetone telephone; antinoise telephone; ~ à haut-parleur loudspeaking telephone; ~ à magnéto magneto telephone; ~ à poussoirs pushbutton telephone; ~ à prépaiement pay-phone; ~ à tige candlestick telephone; ~ autogénérateur sound-powered telephone; ~ avec bloque-cadran locking dial telephone; ~ compact compact telephone; ~ d'affaires business telephone; ~ de bord interphone; intercom; ~ de confort convenience telephone; ~ domestique home telephone; ~ électronique electronic telephone; digital telephone; ~ en coffret chestphone; ~ haute fidélité hi-fi telephone; ~ mural wall telephone; ~ rouge hot line (USA-USSR); ~ rouge d'administration command hot line/loop; ~ sans cordon de raccordement cordless phone; ~ vert hot line (France-USSR)

téléphoner v call; telephone; ring; buzz

téléphonie f telephony; ~ à batterie centrale common battery telephone system; ~ à fréquence vocale VF telephony; ~ à inversion de fréquence garbled telephony; scrambled telephony; ~ à rayons infra-

rouges infra-red telephony; ~ **à trafic dispersé** thin-route telephony; ~ **automatique** automatic telephony; ~ **automatique à génération directe d'impulsions** direct-pulse automatic telephone system; ~ **chiffrée** ciphony; enciphered telephony; ~ **codée** enciphered telephony; ciphony; ~ **duplex** duplex telephony; ~ **multiplex** multiplex telephony; ~ **par courants porteurs** carrier telephony; multiplex system; ~ **sans fils** wireless telephony

téléphonique *adj* voice-grade (VG); telephone
téléphoniste *m ou f* telephone operator; telephonist; ~ **des positions A** A operator; ~ **des positions B** B operator
téléphonométrie *f* reference equivalent (quality); telephonometry
téléphotographie *f* phototelegraphy; picture transmission
téléphotomètre *m* telephotometer
téléprogrammation *f* down-loading; down-line loading
télépupitre *m* operation and maintenance centre console; remote console; OMC console
téléréglage *m* remote regulation; remote control; ~ **du gain** remote gain control
téléréunion *f* teleconference
téléscope *m* **électronique** electron telescope
téléscripteur *m* teletype(writer) (TTY); teleprinter; telewriter (= teleautograph machine)
télésécurité *f* remote surveillance
télésélection de nombres téléphoniques avec un clavier key pulsing; pushbutton dialling; key selection; keysending; ~ **par fréquences vocales** VF dialling
téléservice *m* networked services
télésignalisation *f* remote indication
télésoumission *f* **de travaux** remote job entry (RJE)
télésous-titrage *m* sub-titling
téléspectateur *m* (TV) viewer
télésurveillance *f* remote supervision; unattended operation
télétaxation *f* remote metering pulse
télétaxe (TLT) *f* message register pulse; private charge metering; metering pulses to subscriber's premises; remote charging; residential charge metering
télétex *m* (télétraitement de texte) word-processor networking
télétraitement *m* teleprocessing; remote processing; remote job entry (RJE); ~ **de texte** (télétex) word-processor networking; ~ **par lots** remote batch processing
télétransmission *f* remote transmission
télétravail *m* out-working (with IT resources);

telecommuting; teleworking; home distributed data processing
télétype de dialogue *m* teleprinter; conversational terminal
télévidéothèque *f* on-line TV programme library
téléviseur *m* television receiver; television set; ~ **et émetteur-récepteur radar de bord** airborne television receiver and radar transponder; ~ **portatif** portable television receiver (walkie-lookie)
télévision *f* television (TV); ~ **à accès conditionnel** pay-television; coin-operated television; ~ **à antenne centrale** community antenna television (CATV); ~ **à antenne collective** community antenna television (CATV); ~ **à haute définition** high-resolution TV (over 100 scanning lines/frame); ~ **à péage** pay-television; coin-operated television; ~ **à plusieurs canaux** multichannel television; ~ **bilatérale** two-way television; ~ **dans les deux sens** two-way television; ~ **direct** cable television; direct-broadcast; ~ **en circuit fermé** closed-circuit television; ~ **en couleur** colour television; ~ **en relief** stereoscopic television; ~ **par câble** cable television; ~ **payante** pay-television; coin-operated television; ~ **scolaire** TV broadcasting to schools
télévision-réception seule television receive-only (TVRO)
téléwattmètre *m* telewattmeter
télex *m* telex; printergram; ~ **sans fil** radio teletype
téléxérographie *f* long-distance xerography
témoin *m ou adj* reference; guide; control
température *f* **ambiante** ambient temperature; room temperature; in free air conditions; ~ **dans la masse** bulk temperature; ~ **de basculement** operating temperature; ~ **de bruit** noise temperature; ~ **de fonctionnement** operating temperature; working temperature; ~ **de fusion** melting temperature; ~ **de jonction** junction temperature; ~ **de mercure condensé** condensed mercury temperature; ~ **de régime** working temperature; operating temperature; ~ **de service** working temperature; operating temperature; ~ **de stockage** storage temperature; ~ **de transition vitreuse** glass-transition temperature; ~ **extérieure** outside temperature; ~ **humide** wet-bulb temperature; ~ **interne** indoor temperature; ~ **intrinsèque** intrinsic temperature; ~ **thermodynamique** thermodynamic temperature; ~ **virtuelle de jonction** virtual junction temperature

tempête *f* **ionosphérique** ionospheric storm

temporel *adj* time-domain; time-division

temporellement transparent time-transparent

temporisateur *m* timer; timing unit; time-delay unit; delay counter; interval timer; ~ **programmable** programmable interval timer

temporisation *f* time lag/delay; (call) timing; time-out; ~ **aléatoire** random back-off; ~ **avant transmission** post-dialling delay; ~ **d'arrêt** time-out; ~ **d'attente** wait delay; ~ **de garde** guard time-out; guard delay; ~ **de raccrochage du demandé** called party release guard; abort timing; ~ **écoulée** time-out; ~ **interchiffre** inter-digit pause; ~ **repos** delay on de-energization; ~ **travail** delay on energization

temporisé *adj* slow-acting; timed-out; delayed

temps *m* phase(s); stroke; cycle; time; timing; clock signal; overhead; interval; ~ **à trafic nul** overhead (machine time with zero traffic); out-of-traffic time; ~ **à vide** processor overhead; ~ **actif** (CPU) execution time; ~ **clair** clear sky; ~ **couvert** cloudy weather; ~ **d'accélération** start time; acceleration time; ~ **d'accès** access time; ~ **d'acquisition** acquisition time; ~ **d'addition** add time; ~ **d'aiguillage** timing signals; ~ **d'amorçage commandée par la gâchette** gate-controlled turn-on time; ~ **d'appel** call time; dialling time; ~ **d'arrêt** stop time; deceleration time; ~ **d'attente** waiting time; queueing time; delay; latency (time); ~ **de basculement** setting time; switch-over time; gating time; ~ **de blancs** black-out time; ~ **de blocage** turn-off time (t_{off}); blocking period; access-denial time; ~ **de blocage du courant** off period; ~ **de chauffage** pre-heating time; warm-up time; ~ **de collage** operate time; bridging time (of relay); ~ **de commutation** switching time; ~ **de conduction** turn-on time ($t_{on} = t_d + t_r$); ~ **de coupure** cut-off; turn-off; splitting time; ~ **de croissance** rise time (t_r); build-up time; ~ **de croissance commandée par la gâchette** gate-controlled rise time; ~ **de cycle** cycle time; ~ **de décroissance** decay time; fall time (t_f); ~ **de désamorçage par commutation du circuit** circuit commutated turn-off time; circuit commutated recovery time; ~ **de désaturation** turn-off time ($t_{off} = t_s + t_f$); ~ **de descente** fall time (t_f); decay time; ~ **de désionisation** recovery time; de-ionization time; ~ **de déstockage** fall time; turn-off time; ~ **de fermeture** (loop-)make time (of dial pulses); cut-off; turn-off; recovery time; off time; ~ **de**

fermeture partielle partial restoring time; ~ **de fonctionnement** operate time; run time; ~ **de fonctionnement d'un suppresseur d'écho à action continue** operate time of a rectifier type echo suppressor; ~ **de gélification** gel time; pot life; ~ **de libération** release time; clear-down time; ~ **de maintien** hangover time; ~ **de maintien d'un suppresseur d'écho à action discontinue** hangover time of a relay type echo suppressor; ~ **de maintien pour intervention** break-in hangover time; ~ **de maintien pour la suppression** suppression hangover time; ~ **de mise en blocage** turn-off time (t_{off}); ~ **de mise en conduction** turn-on time (t_{on}); ~ **de mise en marche** start time; acceleration time; ~ **de mise en route** warm-up time; warming-up period; ~ **de montée** build-up time; rise time (t_r); slew rate; ~ **de parcours** transit time; ~ **de passage** changeover time; transfer time; run time; transit time; ~ **de période** periodic time; ~ **de pointage** levelling time; ~ **de portillonnage** gate width; gating time; ~ **de pose** exposure time; ~ **de précharge** pre-load time; ~ **de préparation** set-up time; ~ **de prépositionnement** set-up time; ~ **de présélection** incoming response delay; ~ **de présence** attendance time; ~ **de prise** access time; seizure time; acquisition time; ~ **de propagation** propagation time; propagation delay; ~ **de propagation absolu** absolute delay; ~ **de propagation de groupe** envelope delay; group delay; ~ **de propagation de phase** phase delay; ~ **de propagation du X à la sortie** deselection of data output in OR-tie operation; ~ **de propagation en boucle** loop propagation time; ~ **de réaction** response time; ~ **de rebondissement** bounce time; ~ **de recherche** search time; seek time; ~ **de recherche et d'exécution** fetch and execute time; ~ **de recouvrement à l'état bloqué** off-state recovery time; ~ **de recouvrement direct** forward recovery time; ~ **de recouvrement inverse** reverse recovery time; ~ **de relâchement** (call) release time; drop-out time; clear-down time; ~ **de renversement** turnaround time; data set delay; clear-to-send-delay; ~ **de réponse** operating time; pick-up time; response time; turnaround time; ~ **de réponse à U_n** nominal operating time (of relays); rated voltage pick-up time; ~ **de repos** idle period; quiescent period; dwell; ~ **de reprise** repeat interval; recovery time; settling time; machine-spoilt work time; ~ **de reprise de verrouillage de trame**

re-framing time; frame alignment recovery time; ~ **de rétablissement** recovery time; settling time; ~ **de retard** delay time (t_d); ~ **de retard à la croissance** delay time; ~ **de retard à la descente** carrier storage time (t_s); ~ **de retard à la montée** delay time (t_d); ~ **de retenue** carry time; ~ **de retombée** fall time; decay time; release time; ~ **de retour** reset time; ~ **de retour au repos** recovery time (of expander); ~ **de retour image** flyback time; spot retrace time; ~ **de rotation** turnaround time; ~ **de sélection** selection time; ~ **de silence** silent period; ~ **de stockage** carrier storage time (t_s); ~ **de transfert** transfer time; swap time; ~ **de transfert dans un central** cross-office transfer time; ~ **de transfert de messages** message transfer delay; ~ **de transfert des signaux** signal transfer time; ~ **de transfert des signaux dans un centre** cross-office signal transfer time; ~ **de transit** transit time; delay; ~ **de transit d'un écho** echo delay time; ~ **de transition** attack time; rise time (of pulse); ~ **de transition d'un amplificateur** amplifier attack time; ~ **de transition d'un limiteur** attack time; limiter attack time; ~ **d'écrêtage** clipping time; ~ **d'émission** air time; ~ **d'entretien** idle time; ~ **des blancs** black-out time; ~ **des fronts** rise time; ~ **d'établissement** turn-on time; settling time; ramping time; ramp response time; attack time (of expander); ~ **d'établissement en conduction** turn-on time; ~ **d'établissement en inhibition** turn-off time; ~ **d'exploitation** working time; run time; ~ **d'exploration** search time; scan time; ~ **d'indisponibilité** down time; coasting time; ~ **d'intégration** electrode current averaging time; ~ **d'ionisation** ionization time; ~ **d'occupation** holding time; ~ **d'ondulation** ripple time; ~ **d'ouverture** (loop-)-break/interrupt time (of dial pulses); on period; turn-on; ~ **écoulé** elapsed time; run-out time; ~ **en service** up time; ~ **exploitable** up time; ~ **gamme** measured operation times (of work study); ~ **hors service** down time; ~ **imparti** allotted time; ~ **machine** machine time; CPU time; accountable time; ~ **mort** down time; idle time; insensitive time; dead time; guard time; ~ **mort entre chiffres** inter-digit pause; ~ **moyen d'attente** average delay; ~ **moyen de bon fonctionnement** mean time between failures (MTBF); ~ **moyen de réparation** mean time to repair (MTTR); ~ **moyen d'intervention** mean time to repair (MTTR); ~ **moyen entre défaillances** mean

time between failures (MTBF); ~ **non imputable** debatable time; ~ **partagé** time sharing; ~ **réel** real time; on-line (application); ~ **total de coupure** turn-off time (t_{off} = t_s + t_f); ~ **total de croissance** turn-on time (t_{on} = t_d + t_r); ~ **total de décroissance** turn-off time (t_{off} = t_s + t_f); ~ **total d'établissement** turn-on time (t_{on} = t_d + t_r); ramp response time; ramping time

tenant adj from; current

tendage des câbles cable tensioning

tendance f **à l'amorçage** near-singing condition

tendeur m turnbuckle; screw shackle; tensioner

teneur m content; concentration; ~ **en cendres** ash content

tenseur m tension pulley

tensiomètre m spring balance; tension/compression scale (tester); tensimeter

tension f tension; voltage; potential; bias; ~ **à l'état bloqué** off-state voltage; ~ **à l'état passant** on-state voltage; ~ **à rampe symétrique** triangular waveform; ~ **à vide** no-load voltage; open-circuit voltage; off-load voltage; ~ **admissible** rated voltage; ~ **alternative** alternating voltage; AC voltage; ~ **alternative superposée** superposed AC voltage; virtual value; r.m.s. value; ~ **alternative/continue d'amorçage d'un parafoudre** AC/DC spark-over voltage of a protector; ~ **anodique** anode voltage; ~ **anodique d'amorçage** anode breakdown voltage; ~ **asymétrique** asymmetrical voltage; ~ **(au) secondaire** secondary voltage; ~ **avalanche** avalanche voltage; ~ **composée** line voltage (of polyphase system); ~ **constante** constant voltage; ~ **continue** DC voltage; ~ **(continue) à l'état bloqué** continuous (direct) off-state voltage; ~ **(continue) à l'état passant** continuous (direct) on-state voltage; ~ **(continue) d'amorçage par la gâchette** gate trigger continuous (direct) voltage; ~ **(continue) de non amorçage par la gâchette** gate non-trigger continuous (direct) voltage; ~ **(continue) de retournement** breakover continuous (direct) voltage; ~ **(continue) grille-drain** gate-drain (DC) voltage; ~ **(continue) grille-source** gate-source (DC) voltage; ~ **crénelée** square-wave voltage; ~ **critique de grille** critical grid voltage; ~ **d'accélération** acceleration/accelerating voltage; ~ **d'alimentation** supply voltage; ~ **d'alimentation stabilisée** stabilized supply voltage; ~ **d'allumage** anode breakdown voltage; ~ **d'amorçage** turn-on voltage; striking voltage; trigger voltage; starting voltage; **~ d'amorçage au choc d'un parafoudre** impulse spark-over voltage of a protector; **~ d'appel** ringing voltage; **~ d'arc** flashover voltage; **~ d'asservissement** control voltage (of VCO); **~ d'assistance** assisted voltage; **~ d'avalanche** breakdown voltage (BDV); **~ de balayage** sweep voltage; **~ de basculement** switchover voltage; gating voltage; switching voltage; transfer voltage; **~ de blocage** sticking potential; grid cut-off voltage; blocking bias; **~ de bruit** noise voltage; **~ de charge** charging voltage; **~ de chauffage** heater voltage; **~ de choc** surge voltage; **~ de claquage** breakdown voltage (BDV); **~ de conjonction** voltage drop; **~ de contournement** (wet) flashover voltage; **~ de coude** pinch-off voltage; **~ de coupure** cut-off voltage; target voltage; **~ de court-circuit** short-circuit voltage; **~ de crête** peak voltage; crest voltage; **~ de crête à l'état bloqué** peak off-state voltage; **~ de crête de fonctionnement à l'état bloqué** peak off-state working voltage; **~ de crête de l'espace d'interaction** peak alternating gap voltage; **~ de crête en sens conducteur** peak forward voltage; **~ de décalage** offset voltage; **~ de décalage en entrée** input offset voltage; **~ de décharge** discharging voltage; sweep voltage; **~ de déchet** breakdown voltage; **~ de démarrage** starting voltage; **~ de déport** offset voltage; **~ de désamorçage** turn-off voltage; **~ de déséquilibre** unbalancing voltage; **~ de désexcitation** drop-out voltage; **~ de déviation** deflecting voltage; sweep voltage; ramp voltage; **~ de diode équivalente** equivalent diode voltage; **~ de drain** sink voltage; drain voltage (V_{DD}); **~ de fonctionnement** operating voltage; working voltage; **~ de gâchette** gate voltage; **~ de grille** grid voltage; gate voltage; **~ de lever de doute** stick-off voltage; sense voltage; **~ de ligne** voltage between lines; voltage between phases; line voltage; **~ de maintien** holding voltage; sustaining voltage; **~ de masse** earth potential; **~ de modulateur** modulator voltage; **~ de modulation** modulation voltage; modulator voltage; sample voltage; **~ de non amorçage** non-trigger voltage; **~ de pénétration** punch-through voltage (V_{pt}); reach-through voltage; **~ de perçage** punch-through voltage; reach-through voltage; **~ de percement** puncture (impulse) voltage; **~ de phase** phase voltage; **~ de pic** peak voltage; **~ de pincement** pinch-off voltage; **~ de pointe** peak (point) voltage; **~ de**

pointe à l'état bloqué continuous (direct) off-state voltage; **~ de polarisation** bias (voltage); operating voltage; working voltage; **~ de polarisation de grille** grid bias; **~ de rallumage** re-striking voltage; **~ de rampe** sweep voltage; ramp voltage; **~ de recouvrement** recovery voltage; **~ de référence** reference voltage; comparison voltage; **~ de régime** operating voltage; **~ de réinjection** ripple; **~ de repos** (d'une électrode) electrode bias; **~ de retard** delay bias; **~ de retour** backward potential; **~ de retournement** breakover voltage ($V_{(BO)}$); **~ de ronflement** hum voltage; ripple voltage; **~ de rupture** breakdown voltage (BDV) ($V_{(BR)}$); **~ de saturation** collector-emitter saturation voltage (of phototransistor); saturation voltage; **~ de secteur** mains voltage; line; **~ de service** service voltage; working voltage; **~ de seuil** threshold voltage; **~ de seuil à l'état passant** on-state threshold voltage; **~ de seuil grille-source** gate-source threshold voltage; **~ de signal** signal voltage; **~ de sortie** output voltage; **~ de source** source voltage (V_{SS}); **~ de suppression de faisceau** blanking voltage; **~ de surcharge** (accidentelle/non-répétitive) surge (non-repetitive) voltage; **~ de synchronisation** reference voltage; **~ de tenue** isolation voltage; peak withstand(ing) voltage; voltage proof; flash test; dielectric withstanding voltage; **~ de terre** earth potential; **~ de verrouillage** blanking voltage; **~ d'éclairage** driving potential (of phototransistor); **~ d'éclairement** driving potential (of phototransistor); **~ d'écrêtage** peak limiting voltage; clipping voltage; **~ d'électrode** electrode voltage; **~ d'emploi** working voltage; **~ d'enclenchement** pull-in voltage; **~ d'entrée** input voltage; line; **~ d'entrée d'un signal** applied signal voltage; **~ d'entretien** sustaining voltage; **~ d'équilibrage** phase(-balance) voltage; **~ d'essai** test voltage; **~ d'excentrement** off-centre voltage; **~ d'excitation** sealing voltage; **~ d'extinction** extinction voltage; **~ différentielle** differential voltage; **~ différentielle d'entrée** differential input signal; **~ d'image** image potential; **~ d'information** signal voltage; signal potential; **~ d'ionisation** ionization voltage; **~ directe** forward voltage; turn-on voltage; forward(-acting) bias; **~ directe (continue)** forward continuous (direct) voltage; **~ directe (continue) de gâchette** forward gate continuous (direct) voltage; **~ directe (continue) grille-source** forward gate-source (DC) voltage; **~ directe de pointe de** gâchette peak forward gate voltage; ~ directe de pointe répétitive peak value of forward recovery voltage; ~ directe moyenne average forward voltage; ~ directe transitoire de crête crest forward voltage; ~ directe transitoire de pointe peak forward voltage; ~ d'isolement rated voltage; isolation voltage; ~ disruptive flashover voltage; ~ d'onde carrée square-wave voltage; ~ du secteur line voltage; mains voltage; ~ du seuil threshold voltage; trigger level; ~ du signal de commande drive voltage; ~ d'utilisation working voltage; ~ efficace r.m.s. voltage; effective voltage; ~ en dents de scie saw-tooth voltage; ramp voltage; sweep voltage; ~ en opposition bucking voltage (opposed to reference voltage); ~ en triangle delta voltage; mesh voltage; hexagon voltage; ~ entre phase et neutre phase(-balance) voltage; star voltage; voltage to neutral; ~ entre phases interlinked phase voltage; ~ fugitive (d'impulsion) impulse (flashover) voltage; ~ grille-source de blocage gate-source cut-off voltage; ~ image image potential; ~ initiale initial voltage; ~ instantanée instantaneous voltage; ~ inverse reverse bias; reverse voltage; ~ inverse (continue) reverse continuous (direct) voltage; ~ inverse (continue) de gâchette reverse gate continuous (direct) voltage; ~ inverse (continue) grille-source reverse gate-source (DC) voltage; ~ inverse de crête peak reverse voltage; ~ inverse de crête à l'état bloqué peak reverse off-state voltage; ~ inverse de pointe de gâchette peak reverse gate voltage; ~ inverse de pointe d'ionisation flash-back voltage; ~ inverse de pointe non répétitive non-repetitive peak reverse voltage; peak transient reverse voltage; ~ inverse de pointe répétitive repetitive peak reverse voltage; maximum recurrent reverse voltage; ~ limite sticking voltage; ~ maximale de blocage hold-off voltage; ~ modulatrice modulating voltage; ~ nominale (U_n) rated voltage; ~ nominale d'isolement rated (isolation) voltage; ~ perturbatrice disturbing voltage; noise voltage; ~ perturbatrice équivalente equivalent disturbing voltage; ~ polygonale mesh voltage; ~ préferentielle preferred voltage; ~ primaire primary voltage; ~ psphométrique psophometric voltage; ~ pulsatoire pulsating voltage; ~ réactive reactive voltage; ~ réfléchie return voltage; ~ résiduelle ripple; ~ résiduelle (d'une ligne industrielle) residual voltage (of power line); ~ retardatrice

restraining voltage; ~ simple d'onde carrée neutral square-wave voltage; single square-wave voltage; ~ stabilisée controlled voltage; ~ superficielle (= rugosité) surface tension; ~ symétrique balanced terminal voltage; ~ synchrone synchronous voltage; ~ transversale transverse voltage; ~ variable variable voltage; ~ vidéo video voltage

tentative *f* attempt; bid; ~ d'appel call attempt; bid; ~ d'appel à l'heure chargée busy hour call attempt (BHCA); ~ de prise seizure attempt; ~ infructueuse abortive call attempt; unsuccessful call

tentatives de prise par circuit et par heure bids per circuit per hour (BCH)

tenue *f* performance; strength; resistance; ~ à jour maintenance; updating; ~ au cheminement creep strength; ~ aux fuites de ligne line insulation; ~ aux solvants resistance to solvents; ~ axiale axial strength; ~ de fichier file maintenance (up-dating); ~ de la lame contact grip; ~ en température en régime permanent steady-state temperature resistance; ~ transversale transverse strength; right-angled pull-off strength

terme *m* à éviter deprecated (term); ~ à proscrire deprecated (term); ~ de métier technical term; jargon; vernacular; ~ documentaire docuterm

terminaison *f* port; termination; ~ à deux fils two-wire termination; ~ à quatre fils four-wire termination; ~ adaptée matched termination; matched load; ~ du programme en moins de temps prévu under-burn

terminal *m* terminal; out-station; device; ~ à consultation seule dumb terminal; ~ à quatre fils hybrid (terminal); ~ actif exchange-end terminal; ~ activateur operator terminal; ~ au repos non-dedicated terminal; ~ cathodique visual display unit (VDU); ~ conversationnel interactive terminal; ~ d'affichage (visual) display terminal; ~ d'affichage de paramètres control message display; ~ d'archivage dump terminal; backing store device; ~ de circuit à quatre fils hybrid (terminal); ~ de consultation data retrieval terminal; look-up terminal; enquiry terminal; ~ de dénumérotation change-of-directory-number recorded announcement device; ~ de dialogue conversational terminal; interactive terminal; man-machine dialogue terminal; ~ de guichet teller terminal; ~ de jonction interface module; ~ de ligne line terminal; ~ de multiplexage numérique digital multiplex terminal; ~ de prise de liaison link connection terminal; ~ de réception receiving terminal; ~ **de recouvrement** collection terminal; ~ **de saisie** input terminal; entry terminal; ~ **de service** service terminal; ~ **de télégestion** data (communications) terminal; ~ **de transaction** queued task terminal; ~ **d'échange** interactive terminal; ~ **d'émulation** emulation terminal; ~ **d'exploitation** administration terminal; ~ **d'impression** printer terminal; ~ **en mode paquet** packet mode terminal; ~ **grande diffusion** interactive (public) broadcast terminal; ~ **habilité** job-oriented terminal; ~ **implicite** default configuration terminal; ~ **(inter)actif** smart terminal; ~ **léger** low-speed terminal; ~ **lourd** remote (batch) terminal; ~ **MIC** PCM line terminal; PCM multiplex; ~ **mobile** mobile terminal; ~ **multicanaux sémaphore** CCS transceiver; ~ **numérique de ligne** digital line terminal; ~ **numérique de multiplexage** digital multiplex terminal; ~ **numérique d'extrémité** PCM multiplex; digital group; ~ **passif** dumb terminal; ~ **point de vente (TPV)** point-of-sale terminal (POST); ~ **spécifique** job-oriented terminal; ~ **synchrone** block-mode terminal; ~ **téléautographique** facsimile terminal; picture telegraphy terminal

terminateur *m* interrupted task consistency checking program

terminé *adj* out (end of communication); done; completed

terminer *v* conclude

termineur *m* terminating unit; hybrid set; four-wire term set; ~ **à douze voies** twelve-channel term set; ~ **à quatre fils** four-wire term set; ~ **équilibreur** hybrid coil

terre *f* earth; ground (system); shore; ~ **commutable** variable earth; interchangeable earth; ~ **de maintien** holding earth potential; ~ **de protection** protective ground; protective earth; ~ **de retour** earth return; ~ **de signalisation** signal ground; signalling earth; ~ **électronique** electronic earth; ~ **franche** solid earth; direct earth; dead earth; full earth; open ground; clear ground; ~ **générale** common earth; earth electrode system; earth plate; ~ **parafoudre** lightning conductor; ~ **résistante** earth impedance; ~ **téléphonique** telephone earth

test *m* check; test; interrogation; trial; ~ **assisté par ordinateur (TAO)** computer-assisted testing; ~ **baladeur** sequential memory test; ~ **complet** exhaustive test; ~ **croisé** cross test; ~ **DAMIER** checkerboard test; ~ **de cohérence** consistency check; ~ **de l'abonné demandé** called subscriber free/busy check; ~ **de lever de doute** ambiguity test; ~ **de rétention** mating strength test; ~ **de sonnerie** ring-back facility; ~ **de totalisation** summation check; totalizing check; check-sum procedure; ~ **défilant** rolling test; ~ **dichotomique** dichotomizing test; ~ **d'isolement** crossed-path test; insulation (resistance) test; ~ **d'occupation** engaged test; busy test; ~ **du demandé** called line free/busy check; called party free/busy check; ~ **en rebouclage** loopback test; ~ **fonctionnel** field test; dynamic test; ~ **interne** self-test; ~ **khi deux** chi-squared test; ~ **oui-non** go/no-go test; ~ **par la batterie** battery testing; ~ **par la terre** earth testing; ground testing; ~ **saute-mouton** leapfrog test; ~ **saute-mouton restreint** crippled leapfrog test; ~ **sélectif** leapfrog test; ~ **statique** laboratory test; static test; ~ **unitaire** partial test

testable *adj* pollable; testable

testeur *m* test set; tester; data logger; logic analyser; signal analyser; break-out box

tête *f* head; point; tuner; termination; ~ **à radiofréquence** RF head; ~ **de câble** cable terminal; cable termination; ~ **de coupe** cutting head; ~ **de coupure** splitting terminal block; ~ **de file** head of queue; ~ **de grappe** cluster controller; ~ **de groupement** group master line; ~ **de lecture** read head; playback head; reproduction head; scanner (of facsimile); sensor; ~ **de lecture de bande** tape reader; tape-reading head; play-back head; ~ **de liste** group master extension; ~ **de message** message preamble; ~ **de mesure** measurement panel; test matrix; ~ **de mort** skull-and-crossbones (danger symbol); ~ **de radiodétecteur** radar head; ~ **de réception** terminal; ~ **de réseau** head end (of CTV network); ~ **de série** first article; ~ **de vidage** message unloading start point; ~ **d'écriture** write head; recording head; ~ **d'effacement** erase head; ~ **d'enregistrement** recording head; record head; ~ **d'impression** print head; element; ~ **d'inscription** record head; write head; ~ **d'insertion** insertion head; ~ **flottante** floating head; ~ **magnétique** magnetic head; ~ **optique** optical termination unit; ~ **P et T** exchange line termination; ~ **verticale** vertical (side) terminal block

tête-bêche head to tail; ~ **(carte)** tumble card

tête-pied (impression) tumble-mode (printing)

téton *m* **de positionnement** locating stud

tétrapôle *m* four-terminal network/resistor

tetrode *f* tetrode

texte *m* text; message; copy; ~ **centré** centred text; ~ **justifié** justified text; ~ **ombré** shadow printing; ~ **rayé** (over-)scored text; overstrike text

textuelle *adj* documentary

théorème *m* **de Norton** Norton's theorem (equivalent to Thévenin's theorem = Helmholtz' theorem); ~ **de Thévenin** Thévenin's theorem; Helmholtz' theorem

théorie *f* **de l'information** information theory; ~ **des files d'attente** queueing theory

théorique *adj* design; ideal; planned; desired; assumed; nominal; conceptual

thermi-point wire soldering; termipoint soldering

thermistance *f* thermistor; temperature-compensating diode; thermal resistor; ~ **à coefficient de température positif (CTP)** positive temperature coefficient (PTC) thermistor; ~ **CTP** (à coefficient de température positif) (direct-heating) positive-temperature coefficient (PTC) thermistor

thermocontact *m* thermal switch

thermocouple *m* thermocouple

thermodurcissable *adj* thermo-setting

thermoformage *m* thermo-forming

thermographie *f* thermal infra-red mapping; thermography; thermal imaging

thermophone *m* thermophone

thermoplongeur *m* immersion heater (portable)

thermo-régulé *adj* temperature-controlled

thermorésistance *f* (= thermistance) thermistor

thermo-rétrécissant *adj* heat-shrinkable

thermostat *m* thermostat

thyratron *m* thyratron; hot-cathode gas-filled triode

thyristor bidirectionnel triac

thyristor-interrupteur gate turn-off thyristor

ticket *m* (fault) docket; ticket(-ting); ~ **d'appel** metering docket/ticket; call ticket; ~ **d'appel différable** deferred call ticket; ~ **de dérangement** fault docket; ~ **de facturation** soft ticket; bill; ~ **taxable** chargeable docket

tient lieu et place de supersedes

tierce majeure major third

tiers *m* third party; ~ **en garde** third party on hold

tige *f* peg; rod; bar; pin; reed; post; stud; ~ **d'adaptation** matching post; ~ **en +** cruciform rod ('T' rod); ~ **filetée** threaded rod; ~ **polaire** terminal post; ~ **rémanente** remreed; ~ **souple** catswhisker (of limit switch)

timbre *m* chime; gong

timistor *m* timistor

tintement *m* tinkle; tinkling

TIR (v. taux interne de récupération)

tirage *m* hard copy; ~ **héliographique** blueprint; ~ **naturel** natural draught

tirant fixation fixing rod

tirer une ligne install a (power) line

tiret *m* underline symbol; hyphen; dash; ~ **clignotant** cursor; ~ **de coupure de mot** soft hyphen; temporary hyphen; ~ **insécable** hard hyphen; ~ **inséparable** hard hyphen; connected hyphen

tirette *f* pull-out knob; retractable button; ~ **de largage** lanyard

tiroir *m* plug-in module; crosspoint panel; tray; slide valve; ~ **d'éclatement** interface unit; ~ **d'effacement** UV eraser (drawer); ~ **MIC** PCM module

tissu *m* **de verre** fibre glass; glass cloth; ~ **métallique** gauze; mesh

titre *m* chapter; section; part; caption; header; destination; title; content

titulaire du marché contractor

TL (v. trou lisse)

TLT (v. télétaxe)

TM (v. tolérance maximum)

TMC (v. taxation à mémoire centrale)

TNC (v. tolérance non cumulable)

toc *m* dog; stub; pawl

toile *f* canvas; fabric; tissue; emery cloth; web; fin; moulding flash

tôle *f* **forte** heavy-gauge sheet steel

tolérance *f* margin; acceptable deviation; ~ **aux échos** echo tolerance; ~ **de fréquence** frequency tolerance; ~ **FM** FM tolerance; ~ **maximum (TM)** maximum tolerance; ~ **non cumulable (TNC)** non-cumulative tolerance; ~ **totale de la variation de gain** overall tolerance in gain variation

tomber *v* drop-out (of relays); release; ~ **en panne** lay up; break down; fail

ton *m* **discriminateur** discriminating tone

tonalité *f* tone; ~ **cadencée** interrupted tone; howler; ~ **continue** continuous tone; ~ **d'abonné inaccessible** number unobtainable tone; ~ **d'acceptation de manœuvre** facility acceptance tone; ~ **d'acheminement** routing tone; ~ **d'annotation** camp-on tone; ~ **d'appel** ringing tone; ~ **d'appel en attente** call waiting tone; ~ **d'attente** comfort tone; ~ **d'avertissement** warning tone; ~ **d'avertissement d'entrée** break-in alert tone; intrusion tone; ~ **de contrôle** test tone; ~ **de faux appel** permanent-line tone; perm signal; howler; ~ **de garde** waiting tone; hold tone; ~ **de manœuvre** dial tone; ~ **de neutralisation** disabling tone; ~ **de**

niveau **interdit** barred level tone; ~ **de numéro inaccessible** number unobtainable tone; NU tone; ~ **de patience** comfort tone; ~ **de précomptage** (prepayment) advance warning tone; ~ **de présence** listening-in tone; ~ **de refus de service** facility not-accepted tone; ~ **de réponse** answering tone; ~ **de retour d'appel** ringing tone; buzz-back tone; audible ringing signal; ring-back tone; ~ **de vérification de numéro** check number tone; ~ **d'empilage** call-waiting tone; ~ **d'encombrement** congestion tone; re-order tone; ~ **d'envoi** dial tone; ~ **d'essai** check tone; test tone; ~ **d'intervention** intrusion tone; override warning tone; ~ **d'intervention interdictive** number-unobtainable tone; ~ **d'invitation à numéroter** dial tone; proceed-to-dial tone; ~ **d'invitation à transmettre** proceed-to-dial tone; dialling tone; ~ **d'occupation** busy tone (= engaged signal); audible busy signal; ~ **d'occupation interdictive** level-2 busy tone; ~ **modulée** warble (tone); ~ **musicale d'attente** music-on-hold; ~ **superposée** uninterrupted tone; ~ **trois plus trois** (3 + 3) three-minute (warning) tone/pip

tonalités cadencées interrupted tones; ~ **et annonces parlées** tones and spoken messages; recorded announcements

tonnelage m barrel distortion; barrelling

top m time signal; stroke; pip; (clock) pulse marker; spike; sync pulse

TOP (v. tube à onde progressives)

top d'annotation (de rappel automatique) automatic callback; reservation callback; ~ **de ligne** line synchronization pulse; ~ **de radiodétection** radar pulse; ~ **de synchronisation** sync signal; sync pulse; ~ **d'écho** blip; ~ **d'image** picture synchronizing pulse; frame (sync) pulse; ~ **fractionné** serrated pulse; ~ **sonore** (brief) tone burst; audio signal; ~ **trame** field pulse; framing pulse; picture

topage m synchronizing

topogramme m memory map

topographie f mapping (mode); ~ **d'interligne** new-line mapping mode

topologie f (memory) map; device internal storage structure

TOR (v. acquisition tout ou rien); ~ (v. tout ou rien)

tordon m single ply (of cable wires)

tordu adj twisted; bent; crumpled; kinked

tore m core; toroidal core; ring core; ~ (de ferrite) ferrite rod/core; torus (doughnut/donut); toroid; ferrite toroidal core; ring core

torique (aimant ~) toroid (annular magnet); doughnut

toron m strand; lead; (wire) bundle; harness; cable form; ply

toronnage m stranding; twisting (of wires); lay(-up); ~ **des brins** twisting of strands

torsadé adj twisted

torsadeur m wire-twisting tool

tortiller v kink

tortue f turtle

tosseau m distance piece

total m sum; total; global; overall; gross; ~ **de contrôle** check sum; proof total; control total; ~ **de vérification** hash total; check sum; gibberish total; ~ **mêlé** hash total; check sum; gibberish total

totalisateur m integrator; counter; totalizer; ~ **soustracteur** balance counter

totaliser v accumulate; integrate

touche f key; button; probe; test prod; pushbutton; ~ **à courant double** double-current key; ~ **à la terre** earth detector; ~ **d'appel** calling key; ~ **de contrôle** check key; CTRL key; CODE key; function key; ~ **de coupure** cut-off key; ~ **de mise en mémoire temporaire d'un numéro** save dialled number key; ~ **de passage** mode-change key; ~ **de relance du dernier numéro composé** last number repetition button; ~ **de retour-arrière** backspace key; ~ **d'effacement** erase key; ~ **d'expansion** expansion key; ~ **dièse** hash key; gate key; gate button; ~ **d'interruption** break key; ~ **fugitive** shift-lock key; momentary-action button; ~ **maintien majuscule** caps-lock key; ~ **programmée** programmable key; ~ **secret** privacy key; mute button; ~ **semi-automatique** bug key; semi-automatic key

tour f de télécommunication telecommunications tower; ~ **d'horizon** keynote (speech); ~ **hertzienne** micro-wave tower; radio mast

tourelle f turret

touret m drum; reel; spool; ~ **à abrasion** rotary drum sander; ~ **moteur** wire twister (motor-driven)

tourie f carboy

tourne-à-gauche m tap wrench

tourne-disque m record player

tourner en coïncidence rotate in step

tournevis m coudé offset screwdriver; ~ **cruciforme** cross-head screwdriver; ~ **dynamométrique** torque(-limiting) screwdriver; ~ **fixe-vis** screw-retaining screwdriver

tournoi m (tournoiement) tournament (sorting algorithm)

tous azimuts omnidirectional

tout au réseau (TAR) all-exchange; exchange-wide; ~ **ou rien (TOR)** all-or-nothing;

on/off; start/stop; mark-space; 1/0; saturated logic; digital or binary; make-break; go/no-go; changeover; alternating; open/shut; ~ **va bien** OK (prompt)

tout-à-relais all-relay

toutes clauses cumulées worst-case (conditions); ~ **lignes occupées** all paths busy; ~ **pages confondues** all pages included

toutes-ondes multifrequency; all-channel; band-wide

TPV (v. terminal point de vente)

TR (v. contact travail-repos); ~ (v. transformateur redresseur)

traçage *m* marking out; artwork; outline; ~ **d'appels malveillants** malicious call-tracing

trace *f* speck; permanent record; snapshot; copy; ~ **à amplitude variable/(fixe)** (fixed)/variable area track; ~ **à densité variable** variable density track; ~ **acoustique** sound track; ~ **acoustique symétrique** push-pull sound track; ~ **du chemin suivi** program trace; propagation path-tracing method; audit trail; ~ **fugitive** blip; ~ **pilote** control track; ~ **repère** strobe

tracé *f* plot; trace (recording); curve; line; track layout; pattern; ~ **(de carte)** wire routing; layout; artwork; ~ **graphique** graphics element; graphics symbol; ~ **optique** photoplotting technique; ~ **squelettique** outline

tracer *v* position; align; plot

traceur *m* pen-plotter; trace mode; ~ **de courbes** data plotter; plotting table; X-Y; ~ **numérique** digital incremental plotter

tracteur *m* sprocket drive; tractor feed

traction *f* (d'un bouton) release; disengagement; withdrawal; unlocking

traducteur *m* converter; conversion unit; translator; interpreter; transducer; ~ **analogique-numérique** analogue-digital converter; ~ **d'appel** call converter/translator; ~ **de prégroupes** pre-group translator; ~ **de réception** receiver VF modulator/translator; ~ **de tension** voltage transducer; ~ **imprimeur** Morse (or 5-unit) printer; ~ **imprimeur en page** page printer; page printing receiver; page teleprinter

traduction *f* translation; conversion; assembly; ~ **assisté par ordinateur (TAO)** computer-assisted translation; ~ **d'arrivée** final translation; ~ **de code** code translation; ~ **de départ** initial translation; ~ **décimal/5 MOM moments** decimal to five-unit code conversion; ~ **jurée** translation authenticated under oath; sworn translation

traductrice *f* interpreter; ~ **reporteuse** transfer interpreter

trafic *m* traffic; ~ **à grande distance** long-distance traffic; ~ **à l'heure chargée** busy-hour traffic; ~ **aléatoire** random traffic; ~ **artificiel** artificial traffic; ~ **automatique** automatic traffic; ~ **automatisé** automated traffic; ~ **bilatéral** two-way working; ~ **canalisé** channelized traffic; ~ **d'amateur** radio-amateur traffic; ~ **d'arrivée** incoming traffic; terminating traffic; ~ **de débordement** overflow traffic; spillover traffic; ~ **de départ** originating traffic; outgoing traffic; ~ **de transit** tandem traffic; through traffic; transit traffic; ~ **d'essai** test traffic; ~ **direct** real-time communication; ~ **écoulable** traffic handling; ~ **écoulé** traffic carried; traffic handled; volume of traffic; ~ **efficace** effective traffic; ~ **en instance** traffic on hand; traffic waiting; ~ **entrant** incoming traffic; ~ **faible** light traffic; ~ **fictif** dummy traffic; ~ **intense de téléphonie** heavy telephone traffic; ~ **international** international traffic; ~ **interurbain** trunk traffic; long-distance communication; ~ **interzone** trunk traffic; ~ **local** local communication; local traffic; ~ **moyen d'un jour ouvrable** average traffic per working day; average traffic per business day; ~ **national** national traffic; ~ **offert** traffic offered; ~ **ponctuel** peak-hour traffic; ~ **radioélectrique** radio traffic; ~ **réel** effective traffic; ~ **régional** regional traffic; ~ **régularisé** smooth traffic; ~ **semi-automatique** semi-automatic traffic; ~ **suburbain** junction traffic; ~ **terminal** terminal traffic

train *m* series; train; succession; stream; burst; string; ~ **binaire** bit stream; ~ **de bits** bit stream; ~ **de bits composite multiplexé** multiplex aggregate bit stream; ~ **de sonnerie** tone burst; ~ **d'éléments binaires** bit stream; ~ **d'impulsions** pulse train; pulse group; (tone) burst; ~ **d'ondes** wave-train; burst-firing; ~ **MIA PAM** bit stream; ~ **MIC PCM** bit stream; ~ **numérique** digital train; bit stream; ~ **porteur** pulse carrier

traînage *m* streaking; transient decay current; after-glow; viscosity; trailing; after-image; tailing

traînard *m* cable harness; distribution board; trailing socket

traîne *f* **de l'impulsion** pulse tail

traînée *f* lag; streaking

trains de travaux job batches; job streams;

T

~ d'ondes fast cycle wavetrains; burst firing

trait *m* **de découpe au ciseau** pre-scored lines; **~ double** double dash; **~ morse** Morse dash; **~ permanent** continuous wave; **~ plein** solid line

traite *f* bill; draft

traitement *m* processing; handling; routine; process; finish; surface coating; servicing; **~ antirebond** bounce elimination; **~ automatique de données** datamation; automatic data processing; **~ automatique de textes** word processing; **~ d'anomalies** fault handler; **~ d'appel** taking a call; returning a call; **~ d'arrière-plan** background processing; **~ d'avant-plan** foreground processing; **~ de données** data processing; **~ de fiches** forms processing; **~ de fond** backgrounding; **~ de l'information** data processing; **~ de masse** batch processing; **~ de surface** surface coating (process); **~ de texte** word processing; **~ des anomalies** fault handler; **~ des appels** call processing; **~ des erreurs** error checking and recovery; debugging; **~ des images** image processing; **~ des informations** data processing; **~ des interruptions** interrupt servicing; interrupt handling; **~ des ordres** command processing; **~ des phases** instruction processing; **~ des signaux** signal processing; **~ d'informations généralisées** generalized data management system; **~ du renvoi par réacheminement** forwarding by re-routing; **~ du renvoi par transit** forwarding with transit; **~ du signal de conversation** speech processing; **~ du signal de parole** speech (signal) processing; **~ électronique des données** EDP (electronic data processing); **~ immédiat** demand processing; in-line processing; real-time processing; **~ intégré de données** integrated data processing; **~ inverse** back-tracking; **~ momentané** real-time processing; **~ non prioritaire** backgrounding; **~ par lots** batch processing; **~ par priorité** rippling; foregrounding; **~ parallèle** simultaneous operation; **~ prioritaire** foregrounding

trajectographie *f* tracking

trajectoire *m* trajectory; path; trend; strategy; **~ visuelle** path (microwave line-of-sight)

trajet *m* (communications) path; microwave line-of-sight; link (of satellite); hop; **~ ascendant** up-link; **~ auroral** auroral path; **~ d'air** air path; **~ de décharge auxiliaire** auxiliary gap; **~ de signalisation** signalling path; **~ de transmission** transmission path; **~ descendant** down-link; **~ d'une onde réfléchie** hop

trame *f* raster; screen; frame; graticule; field; slot; loop transmission; dot pattern; **~ de signalisation en distribution** driving signalling frame; **~ de signalisation en exploration** scanning signalling frame; **~ d'exploration** scanning raster; **~ impaire** odd(-number) frame; **~ incidente** received frame; **~ paire** even(-number) frame; **~ primaire** colour frame/field; **~ sémaphore** signal unit; **~ sémaphore de message** message signal unit; **~ sémaphore de remplissage** fill-in signal unit; **~ sémaphore d'état canal** link status signal unit; **~ vide** Pierce ring

tramé *adj* half-tone

tranche *f* allocation; segment; slice; section; field; partition; wafer; phase; **~ de bits** bit slice; **~ de mot** word slice; bit field; **~ horaire** time band; time slot; **~ programme** program section

tranquille *adj* quiescent; inactive; idle

transadmittance *f* transadmittance

transbordable *adj* trans-shipped

transcepteur *m* transceiver

transcodage *m* code conversion; transcoding

transcodeur *m* (transcodeuse) code converter; conversion mixer/transducer; frequency changer; **~ imprimeur** printing code converter; five-unit code teleprinter

transcodification *f* **de caractères** character translation

transconductance *f* transconductance; mutual conductance

transcription *f* transcription; dump; copy

transcrire *v* transcribe; copy; dump; duplicate

transducteur *m* (pair of) saturable reactors (= transductor = magnetic amplifier); register; **~ actif** active transducer; **~ électroacoustique** electro-acoustic transducer; **~ électromécanique** electromechanical transducer; **~ idéal** ideal transducer; **~ linéaire** linear transducer; **~ passif** passive transducer; **~ réversible** reversible transducer

transférer *v* transfer; dump; copy; load; port; **~ en mémoire auxiliaire** roll-out; dump

transfert *m* transfer; branch; load; roll-out (of data); throw; migration; page-out; swap-in (of cverlay); call forwarding; basic diversion; up-loading; down-loading; porting; **~ d'appel** call transfer; call forwarding; **~ de connaissances** inculcation of skills; **~ de fichiers** down-line loading; up-loading; file transfer; **~ différé** call forwarding - don't answer; **~ d'information** information transfer; **~ en Z** Z transfer function; **~ par blocs** block transfer; **~ radial** trans-put process; **~ réseau** divert outside call; **~ sur non réponse** call forwarding -

don't answer; ~ **sur poste occupé** call diversion when busy; call diversion on engaged; ~ **sur sonnerie** call diversion on ringing

transfluxeur *m* multi-aperture core; Transfluxor [T.N.]

transformable *adj* convertible

transformateur *m* transformer; converter; rectifier; translator; repeating coil; balun; ~ **à induction** mutual inductance coupling transformer; ~ **à large bande** broadband transformer; ~ **à primaire étoile** star-connection transformer; ~ **à prises** tapped transformer; ~ **à secondaire triangle** delta-connection transformer; ~ **abaisseur** step-down transformer; ~ **asymétrique-symétrique** push-pull transformer; balun; ~ **basse fréquence** low-frequency transformer; ~ **d'adaptation** matching transformer; ~ **d'alimentation** mains transformer; ~ **d'appel** bell transformer; ringing-current transformer; ~ **de code** code converter (e.g. Gray to binary); ~ **de couplage** coupling transformer; ~ **de courant** current transformer; ~ **de liaison** coupling transformer; ~ **de ligne** line repeating coil; ~ **de mesure** measuring transformer; ~ **de mode** mode changer; mode transformer; mode transducer; ~ **(de mode) en bouton de porte** door-knob transformer; ~ **(de mode) par barre transversale** crossbar transformer; bar-and-post transformer; ~ **de modulation** modulation (stage) transformer; ~ **de préamplificateur** pre-amplification transformer; ~ **de puissance** power transformer; ~ **de sonnerie** bell(-ringing) transformer; ~ **de sortie** output transformer; ·send transformer; ~ **de symétrie** balanced transformer; ~ **de tension** voltage transformer; ~ **d'entrée** input transformer; ~ **d'équilibrage** balancing transformer; balanced transformer; ~ **d'essai** test transformer; ~ **différentiel** hybrid transformer; two-to-four wire term set (terminating set); hybrid coil; induction coil; ~ **différentiel à équilibreur** hybrid termination; ~ **différentiel adaptatif** adaptive hybrid transformer; ~ **différentiel équilibré** hybrid coil; hybrid transformer; ~ **d'impulsion** pulse transformer; ~ **d'isolement** barrier transformer; isolation transformer; ~ **double** matched transformer; ~ **élévateur** step-up transformer; booster transformer; ~ **en bouton de porte** door-knob transformer; ~ **en quart d'onde** quarter-wave line; quarter-wave aerial; ~ **équilibreur** phase equalizer; interphase reactor; absorption inductor; ~ **guide** (d'ondes) grating con-

verter; ~ **haute fréquence** high-frequency transformer; ~ **parfait** ideal transformer; ~ **redresseur (TR)** transformer-rectifier; ~ **réducteur** step-down transformer; ~ **rotatif** magslip; ~ **survolteur** booster transformer; ~ **symétriseur** balun; bazooka; ~ **torique** toroidal transformer; toroid

transformateursonde probe transformer

transformateursuceur booster transformer

transformation *f* conversion; mapping (into); ~ **à froid** cold-working (of metal); ~ **aléatoire** hash coding; randomization; ~ **de Laplace** Laplace transform; ~ **HDB3 binaire** HDB3-binary code conversion; ~ **non linéaire** non-linear transformation; ~ **orthogonale** serial-parallel/parallel-serial conversion; multiplex/demultiplex; ~ **série/parallèle** serial-parallel conversion

transformée *f* **de Fourier** Fourier transform; ~ **en Z** Z transform

transhorizon *adj* tropospheric scatter

transimpédance *f* mutual impedance

transinformation *f* **moyenne** average transinformation

transistor *m* transistor; ~ **à barrière superficielle** surface-barrier transistor; ~ **à champ interne** drift transistor; graded-base transistor; ~ **à contacts de pointe et à jonction** point-junction transistor; ~ **à couches d'arrêt** hetero-junction transistor; ~ **à effet de champ (TEC)** FET (field-effect transistor); ~ **à gradient de champ** drift transistor; ~ **à jonction** junction transistor; ~ **ballast** series (regulating) transistor; pass transistor; ~ **de commutation** switching transistor; ~ **MOS canal n à enrichissement** enhancement type N-channel MOS transistor; ~ **n-p-i-n** n-p-i-n transistor

transistorisé *adj* solid-state

transit *m* transit; through(-connection); relay; retransmission; end-to-end MF signalling; ~ **de lignes** tandem trunking (of PABX); ~ **direct** direct through-connection; direct transit; ~ **manuel** retransmission; intermediate handling; ~ **manuel par bande perforée** torn tape relay; manual tape relay; ~ **normal** normal transit; ~ **par bande perforée** tape relay; ~ **simple** two-link/one-switch international call

transitaire *m* forwarding agent; shipping company

transiter *v* (sur) be routed (over)/via; interchange

transition *f* branch; transition; change; ~ **active** positive-going transition; ~ **brutale de courant** current swing; ~ **de signal** signal transition; ~ **électronique** electron transition; ~ **négative** negative-going tran-

sition; ~ **positive** positive-going transition
transitoire *adj* transient; interim; ephemeral;
fleeting; surge
transitron *m* **intégrateur** phantastron
translatable (adresse ~) relocatable (address)
translateur *m* repeating coil; line transformer;
level converter; I/C terminal exchange;
~ **de ligne à méandre** meander-line
transformer; ~ **de niveau** level converter;
~ **de niveau continu** voltage offset transistor; ~ **rectificateur** regenerative repeater;
~ **télégraphique** telegraph repeater
translation *f* retransmission; relaying; boosting; ~ **convertisseuse** converter; ~ **de débit**
rate change; ~ **de vitesse** rate change;
~ **d'exploration** scanning traverse; ~ **régé-
nératrice** regenerative repeater; ~ **télégraphique** telegraph repeater; ~ **télégraphique
pour diffusion** broadcast telegraph repeater;
~ **télégraphique pour conférence** conference
telegraph repeater
transmetteur *m* transmitter; sender; forwarding; driver; relay(ing); ~ **d'alarme** tele-
alarm; (remote) alarm sender; ~ **de ligne**
line driver; repeater; ~ **fac-similé** facsimile
transmitter
transmettre *v* forward; convey; relay; down-
load
transmis par télémesure telemetered; transmitted by telemetry
transmission *f* transmission; ~ **à bandes
latérales asymétriques** asymmetric sideband
transmission; ~ **à basses fréquences** audio-
frequency transmission; ~ **à courant
porteur** carrier transmission; ~ **à modulation négative** negative transmission; ~ **à
monocanal** single-channel transmission;
~ **analogique** frequency division multiplex
transmission; FDM transmission; analogue
transmission; ~ **anisochrone** anisochronous transmission; ~ **arrière** backward
sending; backward signalling; ~ **arythmique** start-stop transmission; ~ **asynchrone**
asychronous transmission; ~ **au coup par
coup** message sequence control; ~ **avec
bande latérale résiduelle** vestigial sideband
transmission; ~ **avec chevauchement** overlap transmission; ~ **avec composante
continue utile** DC transmission; ~ **avec
signal de référence additionnel** additional
reference transmission; ART method;
~ **basse fréquence** (BF) voice-frequency
(VF) transmission; ~ **binaire synchrone**
binary synchronous communication (BSC,
BISYNC); ~ **bivalente** double-current
transmission (mark-space DC line current);
~ **de bande perforée** punched tape transmission; ~ **de documents** document trans-

mission; ~ **de données** data transmission;
data communications; ~ **de données en
bande téléphonique** data in voice (DIV);
~ **de données infratéléphoniques** data under
voice (DUV); ~ **de données infravocales**
data under voice (DUV); ~ **de données par
paquets** packet data transmission; ~ **de
données supratéléphoniques** data above
voice (DAV); ~ **de données supravocales**
data over voice; data above voice (DOV,
DAV); ~ **de données vocales** data in voice
(DIV); ~ **de journaux** newspaper transmission; ~ **de la parole** speech transmission; ~ **de signaux** signal transmission;
~ **de signaux par courant continu** DC
transmission; ~ **des télégrammes par
téléphone** telegram tranmsission by telephone; telemessage; ~ **d'images** picture
transmission; ~ **du message au lecteur de
badge** set transmit state (STS); ~ **en boucle**
loop transmission; ~ **en parallèle** parallel
transmission; ~ **en série** serial transmission; ~ **en vue directe** line-of-sight
transmission; ~ **fac-similé** facsimile transmission; ~ **guidée** guided-wave transmission; ~ **interurbaine** inter-exchange
transmission; ~ **ligne ou page** media copy
(MC); ~ **multiple d'images** simultaneous
facsimile transmission; ~ **multiplex à
répartition temporelle** time-division multiplexing; ~ **normalisée** effective transmission; ~ **numérique** digital transmission;
~ **optique** optical transmission; ~ **par
batterie centrale** closed-circuit wiring;
~ **par câble** cable transmission; ~ **par
courant double** double-current transmission; polar direct current system; ~ **par
courant simple** single-current transmission;
~ **par courants porteurs** carrier transmission; ~ **par double courant** double-current transmission; ~ **par envoi de courant**
open-circuit working; ~ **par fermeture de
circuit** closed-circuit working; ~ **par
interruption de courant** closed-circuit working; ~ **par laser** laser communications;
~ **par microondes dépassant l'horizon**
over-the-horizon microwave transmission;
~ **par modulation en amplitude** amplitude-
modulated transmission; ~ **par ouverture
de circuit** closed-circuit working; ~ **par
paquets** packet transmission; ~ **par rafales**
burst transmission; ~ **par réflexions successives** multi-hop transmission; ~ **par rupture**
closed-circuit working; ~ **par satellite**
satellite transmission; ~ **par secteurs**
time-division multiplex; ~ **par signal noir**
black-signal transmission; ~ **par simple
courant** single-current transmission; (in-

verse) neutral direct-current system; ~ **par trajets multiples** multi-path propagation; ~ **parallèle** parallel transmission; ~ **point à point** directional radio transmission; ~ **radiophonique** sound programme transmission; broadcast; ~ **sans composante continue utile** AC transmission; ~ **série** serial transmission; ~ **sonore** sound transmission; ~ **sous incidence oblique** oblique-incidence transmission; ~ **sur ondes porteurs** carrier transmission; ~ **télévisuelle** television transmission; ~ **transparente au code** code-transparent transmission

transmission-réception automatique automatic send-receive (ASR)

transmittance *f* transmittance; ~ **isomorphe** transfer function

transmodulation *f* cross-modulation; gibberish; chatter; ~ **ionosphérique** ionospheric cross-modulation; Luxembourg effect

transmultiplexeur *m* transmultiplexer

transnational *adj* multi-national; supra-national

transpalette *f* pallet handler

transparence *f* **de code** code transparency; ~ **de grille** inverse/reciprocal amplification factor

transpondeur *m* transponder; slave/satellite transmitter

transport *m* feeder cable; main cable; transmission

transportabilité *f* interchangeability; compactness

transporteur *m* carrier

transpositeur *m* frequency converter; ~ **de/en fréquence** frequency translator; frequency converter

transposition *f* serial-parallel/(parallel-serial) conversion; ~ **à double changement de fréquence** dual-conversion frequency converters; ~ **coordonnée** coordinated transposition; ~ **de canal** channel modulation; channel translation; ~ **de fréquence** frequency translation; up and down converters; ~ **de groupe de base** basic group translation; ~ **des codes** code conversion; ~ **émission** up-converter (U/C); ~ **en fréquence** frequency translation; ~ **par croisement** transposition (by crossing); ~ **par rotation** twist transposition system; ~ **réception** down-converter (D/C)

trappe *f* absorption circuit; trap circuit; hatch; trap-door

travail ('T') *m* make (contact); job; task; normally-open (NO) contact; ~ **à distance** off-location working (of telematics); ~ **de sortie** electron affinity; work function; ~ **gratifiant** job satisfaction; ~ **interne** inner work function; ~ **pénible** difficult chore; fastidious task

travail-repos make-before-break

travaux de masse batch processing

travée *f* suite (of racks); bay; aisle

traverse *f* cross-arm (of telegraph pole); cross-member

traversée *f* transition; cross-over; feed-through; bushing (of transformer); propagation; ~ **de commutateur** switch path; ~ **étanche** pressure seal

traverser thread (of flux)

tréfilage *m* **à froid** cold drawing

tréfileuse *f* wire-pulling device

trèfle *m* occultable dimmer

treillis *m* (filter) lattice; ~ **détecteur** detection grating

treiz. *f* (treizaine) thirteen-group

tréma *m* diaeresis; umlaut (¨)

tremblement *m* **de l'image** picture bounce

trembleur *m* vibrator unit

trémie *f* hopper

trempe *f* immersion; dip; ~ **et revenu (TRR)** quenched and hardened

trempé dans un bain statique dipped in a still bath

très basse fréquence (TBF) very low frequency (VLF); ~ **basse tension (TBT)** very low voltage; ~ **bonne tenue aux impulsions** low loss (of capacitor); ~ **grande portée** very long range (VLR); ~ **haute fréquence** very high frequency (VHF); ~ **peu** seldom; rarely

tresse *f* braid; plait; tress; strand; ~ **de blindage** screening braid; ~ **de métallisation** braided bonding strip

treuil *m* winch

tri *m* sort; separation; GO/NO-GO test; ~ **à plusieurs niveaux** multi-level sort; ~ **alphanumérique** alphanumeric sort; ~ **ascendant** forward sort; ~ **descendant** backward sort; ~ **lexicographique** alphabetical sort; ~ **par blocs** block sort; ~ **par dichotomie** key sort; binary chop sort; ~ **par fusion (équilibrée)** (balanced) merge sort; ~ **par grands groupes** block sort; ~ **par interclassement** merge sort; ~ **stable** stable sort

triage *m* sorting; separation

triangle *m* **de modulation** modulation triangle; ~ **des couleurs** chromaticity diagram

tributaire *m* remote; subordinate; source; derivative

tridondance *f* triple redundancy

trieuse *f* sorter; sorting machine

trieuse-liseuse sorter-reader

TRIL (v. taux de rejet d'infrastructure des lignes)

triode *f* **à cristal** transistor; ~ **au germanium**

transistor
triode-pentode triode pentode
triple entrée statique triple input
triplicateur *m* **de fréquence** tripler
tripôle *m* (d'aiguillage) three-terminal circuit
(hybrid); Deplistor
triturer *v* merge
trochotron *m* hot-cathode stepping tube
troisième fil sleeve conductor; sleeve wire;
S-wire; third wire (control)
trolley *m* bus; trunk; highway; rail; track
tromperie *f* **par radio** radio deception
TRON M-wire (forward signal wire: M =
mouth)
tronc *m* **commun** common core; ~ **synchro**
metronome; time-keeper; pacemaker
troncature *f* **à gauche** left-truncated
tronçon *m* stub; section; segment; link;
(trunk) subgroup/section; ~ **de câble** cable
stub; cable segment
tronçonique *adj* tapered
tronçonner *v* sectionalize; segment; divide up
tronqué *adj* truncated
trop important too copious; ~ **plein** overflow;
escape
tropicalisé *adj* able to withstand tropical
environments; suitable for use in tropical
conditions; tropicalized
tropopause *f* tropopause
troposphère *f* troposphere
trottoir *m* stand-off; ledge
trou *m* gap; hole; aperture; orifice; ~ **borgne**
recessed hole; blind hole; closed hole;
~ **d'ancrage** mating hole; ~ **de dégagement**
clearance hole; back-off hole; ~ **de passage**
entry/exit hole; via hole; ~ **de pilotage**
access hole; via hole; ~ **de régristration**
locating hole; alignment hole; ~ **de
traversée** feed-through; ~ **(débouchant)
taraudé** (TT) tapped (through) hole; ~ **lisse**
(TL) untapped hole; ~ **mécanique** non-
electrical hole; unsupported hole; ~ **métallique** plated-through hole; supported hole;
~ **métallisé** plated-through hole; supported hole; ~ **non métallisé** unsupported hole
troubles *m pl* interference; problems
trouver *v* locate; identify
TRR (v. trempe et revenu)
trusquin *m* scribing block; surface gauge
TSF (v. télégraphie sans fil)
TTC (toutes taxes compris) net; nett (after
tax; tax paid)
TTL de puissance buffer
tube *m* valve; tube; link; pipe; ~ **à cathode
chaude** hot-cathode tube; ~ **à cathode
froide** cold-cathode tube; ~ **à cathode
froide à plusieurs électrodes** multi-electrode
voltage stabilizer; ~ **à chauffage indirect**

indirectly-heated tube; ~ **à décharge en arc**
arc-discharge tube; arc-discharge valve;
~ **à décharge luminescent** glow discharge
tube; ~ **à disques scellés** disk seal tube; disk
seal valve; ~ **à éclat** xenon flash tube; ~ **à
faisceau électronique** electron beam valve;
~ **à gaz** gas-filled valve; ~ **à grille-écran**
screen-grid valve; ~ **à mémoire** storage
tube; ~ **à modulation de vitesse** velocity-
modulated tube (VM); ~ **à onde progressives (TOP)** travelling wave tube (TWT);
~ **à pente réglable** variable mutual-conductance valve; remote cut-off valve;
variable-mu valve; ~ **à polarisation nulle**
zero-bias tube; ~ **à rayon double** beam
tube; ~ **à rayons cathodiques** cathode-ray
tube (CRT); ~ **à rayons cathodiques à deux
faisceaux** double-beam CRT; split-beam
CRT; ~ **à rayons cathodiques à deux canons**
double-gun cathode-ray tube; ~ **à trace
sombre** dark-trace tube; skiatron; ~ **à vide**
vacuum valve; ~ **actinique** ultra-violet
tube; UV fluorescent tube; ~ **alternat TR**
tube; TR cell; ~ **amplificateur** amplifier
tube; ~ **analyseur** scanner tube; ~ **analyseur à accumulation** storage camera tube;
~ **analyseur à électrons rapides** high
electron-velocity camera tube; anode-voltage stabilized camera tube; ~ **analyseur de
télévision** camera tube; ~ **bouton** acorn
valve; shoebutton tube; ~ **cathodique** CRT
(cathode-ray tube); ~ **cathodique à écran
absorbant** dark trace tube; skiatron; ~ **cathodique à écran luminescente** luminescent-
screen tube; ~ **cathodique à image** television tube; picture tube; kinescope; ~ **cathodique à persistance** long-persistence
CRT; ~ **cathodique à plusieurs canons**
multiple-gun CRT; ~ **cathodique asservi**
slave tube; ~ **cathodique de projection**
projection CRT; ~ **cavalier** isometric
(projection/perspective) tube; ~ **changeur
de fréquence** frequency converter tube;
~ **cinéscope** television picture tube; kinescope; ~ **compteur** beam-switching tube;
~ **compteur à aiguille** needle counter tube;
~ **compteur autocoupeur** self-quenched
counter tube; ~ **d'attaque** driver tube;
~ **de commutation** switching tube; ~ **de
contact** guide tube (of MIG welder); ~ **de
puissance** power tube; ~ **de puissance à
faisceau électronique** beam-power valve;
~ **de sectionnement** isolating link; ~ **de
télévision** television tube; ~ **détecteur**
detector tube; ~ **du neutre** neutral link;
~ **électromètre** electrometer valve; ~ **électronique** electronic valve; electron tube;
~ **électronique en verre** glass valve; ~ **en**

métal metal valve; ~ **étalon de tension** voltage reference tube; ~ **gland** acorn tube/valve; ~ **image** image converter; ~ **indicateur** Nixie tube [T.N.]; digitron; ~ **indicateur à néon** neon indicator tube; ~ **indicateur cathodique** electron-ray indicator tube; ~ **isolant** isolating tube; ~ **mâle** external screw-thread screw; ~ **miniature** miniature valve; midget valve; ~ **modulateur** modulator tube; ~ **Nixie** digitron; Nixie tube [T.N.]; ~ **oscillateur** oscillator tube; ~ **parafoudre** lightning arrester; ~ **phare** lighthouse tube; ~ **photoélectronique** photovalve; ~ **plongeur** release valve (of gas cylinder); ~ **radio** radio tube; ~ **redresseur** (à gaz) (gas-filled) rectifier tube; ~ **régulateur de tension** voltage-stabilized tube; voltage-regulator valve; ~ **scellé** sealed-off tube/valve; ~ **stabilisateur à plusieurs électrodes** multi-electrode voltage stabilizer; ~ **stabilisateur de tension** voltage-stabilizing tube; ~ **stroboscopique** stroboscopic tube;

~ **tout-verre** all-glass valve; ~ **transformateur d'image** image converter tube; ~ **trichrome à pénétration** shadow mask tricolour kinescope; colourtron; dot-matrix tube

tulipe f printer thimble (print drum)

tunnel m **de glissement** drift tunnel

turbine f impeller

tuteur m (component) support; prop; pillar

tuyère f pipe; nozzle; spout

type m **à enrichissement** enhancement type; ~ **à mémoire** latched type (of relay); ~ **administratif** executive style (model, type); ~ **de caractère** character font; ~ **de coupure** break type; ~ **de table** desk-top model; ~ **mobile** upright; organ-console model; desk-top; ~ **mural** wall(-mounted); ~ **piano** organ console (model); floor pattern

typon m artwork; offset plate/film; half-tone positive transparency; master; stencil; first-generation master film

typotélégraphie f printing telegraphy; type printing

T

U

U (v. conductance)

U (différence de potentiel) potential difference (p.d.)

Ua (tension d'alimentation) supply voltage

UC (unité centrale) central processing unit (CPU); main frame

UCT (v. unité centrale de traitement)

UE (v. unité d'échange)

UHF (v. ultrahaute fréquence)

UIT (v. Union Internationale des Télécommunications)

ultérieur *adj* further; subsequent; later; forthcoming

ultérieurement *adv* shortly; subsequently

ultra-blanc whiter-than-white

ultradyne *f* ultradyne

ultra-fiable *adj* highly reliable

ultrahaute fréquence (UHF) ultra-high frequency (UHF)

ultrason *m* ultrasound; ultrasonic frequency

ululation *f* sweep modulation; warble (tone)

un *m* mark; ~ **galopeur/baladeur/migrant** marching one; walking one

unicité *f* uniqueness; consistency; convergence

unidirectionnel *adj* one-way; unilateral; simplex; unidirectional; up-and-down (working)

unigraphie *f* single-entry book-keeping

unilatéral *adj* one-way; single-sided; single-in-line

union *f* OR operation; ~ **Internationale des Télécommunications (UIT)** International Telecommunications Union (ITU)

unique *adj* second-to-none; exclusive; incomparable; stand-alone

unisélection *f* uniselection

unitaire *adj* individual; single (of wire); unit

unité *f* units group/digit; ~ **à bande magnétique** magnetic tape unit; ~ **à disque à tête fixe** fixed head disk unit; ~ **américaine de volume** volume-unit (VU); ~ **arithmétique et logique** arithmetic and logic unit; ~ **centrale de traitement (UCT)** main frame; central unit; central processing unit (CPU); ~ **d'adaptation** (de données) data adaptor unit (DAU); ~ **d'adaptation des lignes** line processing unit; ~ **d'adaptation et de contrôle** (de données) data adaptor unit (DAU); ~ **d'affichage** (visual) display

unit (VDU); ~ **d'appel** calling equipment; ringer; ~ **d'appel automatique** automatic calling unit (ACU); ~ **de bande magnétique** magnetic tape unit; tape drive; ~ **de base** (de taxation) basic metered unit; ~ **de calcul** arithmetic and logic unit (ALU); ~ **de charge** unit load; tariff unit; ~ **de commande** director equipment; (network control) signalling unit; control section; ~ **de commande centrale** central control unit; ~ **de commande de réseau** network control signalling unit; ~ **de communication** call unit; ~ **de commutation temporelle à autonomie d'acheminement** multi-routing time switch; ~ **de connexion numérique** digital switching subsystem; ~ **de conversation** speech unit; ~ **de défense de signalisation** signalling security unit; ~ **de distribution de signaux** signal mixer unit; ~ **de gestion** handler; control unit; ~ **de gestion des distributeurs** signalling sender monitor; ~ **de gestion du réseau de connexion** switching network control unit; ~ **de gestion mémoire** memory management unit (MMU); ~ **de gestion programmée** programmable logic (unit); ~ **de gestion sémaphore** common channel signalling monitor; ~ **de liaison** controller; ~ **de liaison de mémoire de masse** fixed-head disk controller; ~ **de liaison solitaire** lone signal unit (LSU); ~ **de marche** logging unit; ~ **de raccordement** connection unit; ~ **de raccordement** (au réseau) network interface machine (NIM); ~ **de raccordement d'abonnés (URA)** subscriber (line) connection unit (= concentrator); ~ **de raccordement des circuits ou jonctions BF** (analogue) trunk connection unit; ~ **de raccordement distant** remote subscriber connection unit; ~ **de raccordement distante** remote switching system; ~ **de raccordement local** local subscriber connection unit; ~ **de raccordement multiplex** multiplex connection unit; ~ **de réponse vocale (URV)** audio response unit (ARU); ~ **de réverbération** echo chamber; ~ **de sélection** routing unit; ~ **de signalisation** pilot light; ~ **de signalisation d'accusé de réception** acknowledgement signal unit (ASU); ~ **de signalisation de synchronisation** synchronization signal

unit; ~ **de signalisation erronée** error signal unit; ~ **de signalisation initiale** initial signal unit (ISU); ~ **de signalisation pour la commande du système de signalisation** system control signal unit; ~ **de signalisation solitaire** lone signal unit (LSU); ~ **de signalisation subséquente** subsequent signal unit (SSU); ~ **de taxation** charging processor; ~ **de taxe** unit charge (of international service); basic metered unit; ~ **de traduction objet** object module; ~ **de trafic** traffic unit; ~ **de traitement (UT)** activity; job step; processing unit; processing action; processor; ~ **(de traitement) centrale** central processing unit; ~ **de traitement de texte** word processor; ~ **de transmission** transmission unit; ~ **de volume** volume unit (VU); ~ **d'échange (UE)** input-output (I/O) units; peripheral; interchange unit; ~ **d'extraction de la signalisation de ligne** line signalling controller; ~ **d'information** information unit; bit; element; ~ **d'information binaire** bit; ~ **d'inspection** specimen; ~ **disque** disk unit; ~ **disque amovible** removable disk unit; ~ **électrostatique** electrostatic unit; ~ **fonctionnnelle** hardware subsystem; ~ **mixte abonnés/transit** local/tandem switch; ~ **périphérique** peripheral; terminal; ~ **physique** device; ~ **témoin** logging unit; ~ **vendable** catalogue item
unités défectueuses tolérées permitted defectives
universel *adj* general-purpose; generic
univocal *adj* speech + simplex
univoque *adj* single-valued; non-ambiguous
URA (v. unité de raccordement d'abonnés); ∻ **distante** remote subscriber connection unit

urgence *f* warning; emergency; urgency; alert; alarm; flash (of service)
URV (v. unité de réponse vocale)
usage *m* **multiple de voies de transmission** channeling of transmission paths
usager *m* customer; extension; subscriber; user; field; ~ **de la société** centralized exchange group extension; CENTREX extension; ~ **en communication** busy extension; ~ **interne** local subscriber
usé *adj* spent; contaminated; dead (of battery)
usinage *m* machining; finishing; shaping; styling; working; cutting (of PCB); ~ **d'entrefer** air-gap trimming
usiné avec surepaisseur fine-machined with extra surface allowance
usuel *adj* prescriptive
usure *f* degradation; wear; smear(ing); attrition
UT (v. unité de traitement)
utile *adj* usable; significant; effective
utilisable *adj* serviceable; ~ **en entraide** standby facility
utilisateur *m* end-user; user; customer; field
utilisation *f* load; application; ~ **collective** time-sharing; ~ **commune de bande de fréquence** band sharing; ~ **des circuits fantômes** use of phantom circuits; ~ **du matériel** (equipment) functions; ~ **éventuelle** for use as required; for future use
utilisations *pl* file
utilisé dans les deux sens bothway; duplex
utilitaire *f* utility program; service routine; ~ **de moniteur** scheduler utility; ~ **des traitements** process utility
UVPROM electrically-erasable PROM

V

V inversé caret
VACA (valeur actuelle des charges annuelles) p.v. of a.c. (present value of annual charges)
vacation *f* system; run; session; proceedings; attendance; time slice; period; shift
vacillement *m* jitter (of time base)
vacuomètre *m* vacuum gauge
va-et-vient *m* two-way switch; single-pole double-throw switch; change-over switch; split (of broker's call); see-saw; (exclusive) OR gate; reciprocating action
V$_{AK}$ anode-cathode voltage
valable *adj* applicable; valid; relevant; pertinent
valence *f* number of signification conditions (of a modulation or a restitution)
valeur *f* value; magnitude; efficiency; quantity; rating; parameter; **~ à mesurer** measurand; measured variable; **~ absolue** magnitude; absolute value; modulus; **~ absolue du courant de sortie du signal** signal output current; **~ accidentelle** anomalous value; **~ actualisée nette (VAN)** net present value (NPV); **~ ajoutée** added value; bonus; extra yield; goodwill; invisible earnings/assets; **~ crête à crête** peak-to-peak value; **~ de consigne** desired value; reference value; **~ de crête** peak value; crest value; **~ de crête de choc du courant** impulse current peak value; **~ de l'information** information value; **~ de repos** quiescent value; **~ décimale tronquée à ... entier** decimal rounded to the nearest whole number; **~ désirée** set point; desired value; **~ efficace** r.m.s. value; root-mean-square; effective value; virtual value; **~ entière** integer value; **~ implicite** default value; standard value; assumed value; **~ limite absolue** absolute maximum rating; **~ limite d'une perturbation** limit of interference; **~ lissée** adjusted value; **~ lue** measured value; **~ mixte** mixed number; **~ moyenne** mean value; average; **~ moyenne quadratique** r.m.s. value; root mean square value; virtual value; effective value; **~ nominale** face value; **~ nominale maximale** continuous maximum rating; **~ normalisée la plus proche** nearest preferred value; **~ pondérée d'un courant** weighted value of a current; **~ pondérée d'une tension** weighted value of

a voltage; **~ prise** default value; **~ propre** eigenvalue; **~ quelconque** non-null value; **~ réelle** absolute (real) value; modulus; positive value; **~ sémantique** semantic content; **~ statique du rapport de transfert direct du courant en émetteur** static value of the forward current transfer ratio in common-emitter configuration; **~ théorique** design value; assumed value; **~ type de centrage** centre value
valeurs brutes unadjusted values; uncorrected/unweighted values; **~ de conditionnement** ambient conditions; **~ limites** limiting conditions of use
validation *f* confirmation; endorsement; vetting; enabling; authentication; ratification; entry (prompt); **~ de l'écriture** write enable; **~ d'entrée manuelle** enable manual input (EMI); **~ des données** data purification; **~ des erreurs arithmétiques** enable arithmetic errors; **~ d'un transfert** handshake
validation/masque des erreurs arithmétiques enable/disable arithmetic errors
valider *v* enable; validate; ready; authorize; prove; authenticate; ratify; enter; confirm; endorse
valise *f* console; tester; tool kit; **~ de maintenance** portable maintenance console; **~ de réglage** maintenance console
valorisation *f* index-linking
valorisé *adj* priced; costed
valoriser *v* assign values; enhance; refine; upgrade; quantify
VAN (v. valeur actualisée nette)
vanne *f* **HF** (hyperfréquence) RF gate
vantail *m* flap; shutter
vapeur *f* fume(s); **~ d'eau** steam
variable *f* variable; argument; **~ aléatoire** random variable; **~ binaire** binary variable; two-valued variable; **~ entière** discrete variable (integer value only); **~ fictive** shadow variable; **~ indépendante** argument; independent variable; **~ logique** (tout ou rien) bit; binary signal; **~ logique binaire** logic state (0 or 1); **~ pointée** based variable
variateur de vitesse variable speed (transmission) controller; regulator
variation *f* swing; fluctuation; shift; change;

~ (brusque) (sharp, sudden) fluctuation; hit; ~ **accidentelle** transient surge; ~ **brusque** hit; ~ **brusque de phase** phase hit; ~ **d'affaiblissement en fonction de l'amplitude** variation of attenuation with amplitude; ~ **d'amplitude** amplitude variation; amplitude hit; ~ **de charge** load variation; step load change; ~ **de flux lumineux** luminous flux variation; ~ **de fréquence due à l'effet Doppler** Doppler shift; ~ **de la luminosité** brightness variation; ~ **de la somme numérique** digital sum variation; ~ **de niveau** level shift; level variation; ~ **de phase** phase shift; ~ **discrète** step change; ~ **d'offset** offset variation; ~ **d'orientation d'un faisceau** beam lobe switching; ~ **du champ de fréquences d'un magnétron** magnetron moding; ~ **fugitive** transient charge; brown-out (of power); ~ **linéaire** linear tracking; ~ **linéaire de fréquence** straight-line frequency

variocoupleur *m* variocoupler

varioplex *m* varioplex

variplotter *m* X-Y recorder

varistance *f* varistor (non-linear resistor)

vasque *f* diffuser; bowl (of lamp fitting)

vaste *adj* ambitious; extensive

VE (v. vernis épargne)

vecteur *m* medium; dimension; characteristic; vector; ~ **de phase** phasor; ~ **indépendant** free vector; ~ **représentatif** phasor

véhiculer *v* convey; carry; deliver

veille *f* search; standby; watch; quiescent state; ~ **permanente** round-the-clock watch-keeping; ~ **réponse** standby for answer

veilleuse *f* pilot light; subdued lighting; night light

vélotraitement batch transmission

vendable *adj* marketable; saleable; catalogue(d)

venir (faire) proceed to; ~ **déjà de...** to have only just...

vent *m* **de sable** sand storm; ~ **de survie** survival wind

vente *f* **par correspondance** mail order supplies

ventilateur *m* cooling unit; fan; distributor; helicopter

ventilation *f* distribution; circulation; cooling; apportionment; ~ **forcée** fan-assisted cooling; forced draught

ventiler *v* classify; circulate; disperse

ventouse *f* ventilation panel; duct; air vent; (soldering iron) fume absorber

ventre *m* anti-node; loop; ~ **de tension** voltage loop

vérificateur *m* gauge; measuring instrument; vernier caliper

vérification *f* checking; verifying; inspection; proving; ascertaining; confirmation; audit; ~ **à rebours** audit trail; ~ **de fichier** file maintenance; ~ **de la cohérence** consistency check; ~ **de la fonction logique** truth table; function table; ~ **de l'étalonnage** recalibration

vérin *m* actuator; jack; adjustable locking guide; ~ **motorisé** motor-driven actuator

véritable *adj* genuine; actual

vernier *m* vernier (scale)

vernis *m* varnish; (solder) mask; protective overlay; lacquer; ~ **antifongique** fungicidal varnish; ~ **épargne (VE)** solder resist; mask; lacquer; varnish; ~ **isolant** insulating varnish; mask; ~ **soudable** solderable lacquer

vérolé *adj* corrupt

véroler *v* corrupt (of disk files)

verre *m* **céramique** ceramic glaze; ~ **de cœur** glass core; ~ **de gaine** glass cladding; ~ **de scellement** vitreous coating; sealing glaze; ~ **dévitrifiable** crystallizable glass; ~ **époxy** (époxyde) impregnated fibreglass; epoxy (epoxide resin

verrine *f* (lamp) shell; glass

verrou *m* interlock; ~ **de page** memory page lock; ~ **de récepteur** T-R cell; ~ **d'émetteur** transmitter-blocker (T-B) cell; ~ **virtuel** virtual address lock

verrouillage *m* (inter)locking; mating; lock-out; DC restoration; clamping (of circuit); latching; 'freeze' function; synchronization; alignment; lock-in; protection (of files); call barring; ~ **corbeille haute** shift-lock (key); ~ **de fréquence** frequency locking; ~ **de poste** outgoing call restriction; ~ **de trame** frame alignment (multiplex synchronization); ~ **des articles** record blocking; ~ **du niveau du noir** black-level clamping; ~ **haut** latch-up (phenomenon) (of op. amp.); ~ **multi-trames** superframe alignment pattern; multiframe alignment pattern; ~ **par zone** zonal blocking; ~ **quart de tour** quarter-turn catch

verrouillé *adj* latched; biased beyond cut-off (transistor); protected (of data)

verrouiller *v* clamp

verrouilleur *m* (signal) lock

verrue de taxation charge-limiting subroutine; ~ **d'opératrice** *f* interlock

vers *prep* in the vicinity of; jump to (instruction); connected to; communicating with

version *f* module

verso *m* solder side (of PCB)

verticale d'entraide inter-aid vertical (path)

vestiaire *m* locker
veuillez patienter hold-the-line; trying-to-connect-you; please wait
VHF (v. self d'arrêt et de découplage)
vibrations *f pl* vibration (fatigue test); ~ **à fréquence balayée** swept-frequency vibration (test); ~ **à fréquence variable** swept-frequency vibrations; ~ **sinusoïdales** swept-frequency vibration
vibreur *m* chopper; buzzer (trembler); vibrator; ~ **électronique miniature** miniature solid-state buzzer; ~ **synchrone** synchronous vibrator
vibromètre *m* vibration meter
vibrotest *m* buzzer (continuity tester)
vice *m* fault; defect; flaw
vicésimal *adj* vicenary (twenty-base)
victime *f* casualty
vidage *m* disaster dump; erasure; crash dump; ~ **à l'arrêt** static dump; ~ **de mémoire** dump; ~ **par instant** snap/snapshot dumping; ~ **sur catastrophe** disaster dump; crash dump
vidage-reprise dump and restart
vide *adj* empty; dump; purge; flush; blank; null
vidé *adj* dumped
vidéo *f ou adj* image; video; ~ **inversée** reverse video; highlighting; ~ **mélangée** composite video; ~ **mire** test pattern
vidéocommunication picture communication
vidéoconférence *f* videoconference; videophone conference
vidéodiffusion *f* one-way teletext; Oracle; Ceefax [T.N.]
vidéodisque *m* video disk
vidéo-enregistreur magnétique video recorder; ~ **sur film** video recorder
vidéofréquence *f* video-frequency; picture transmission frequency
vidéographie *f* videotex; Viewdata; Prestel [T.N.] (two-way interactive videography)
vidéophone *m* videophone
vidéophonie *f* visual telephony
vidéotex *m* videotex; Viewdata; Prestel [T.N.]
vidéotexte *m* Videotext (interactive videography system) [T.N.]
vidéothèque *f* video library
vidigraphe *m* video recorder
vidiophone *m* videophone
vie *f* **moyenne du porteur minoritaire** bulk lifetime; volume lifetime
vieillissement *m* aging; burn-in; endurance testing; life test; ~ **à la chaleur** high-temperature aging; ~ **accéléré** accelerated aging; accelerated life test; soak testing; early-failure testing; ~ **aux radiations UV** ultra-violet aging; ~ **d'un composant**

burn-in; soak testing; early-failure testing; ~ **en blocage** off-state aging; ~ **en fonctionnement** on-state aging
vient de attempts to
vierge *adj* clear; virgin (blank); unperforated; unprogrammed; un-exposed (of film)
vigitherme *m* heat sensor
vignette *f* specimen
ville *f* **câblée** wired city
viol *m* violation; ~ **de bipolarité** alternate mark-inversion violation; bipolar violation
violation *f* breach; violation; ~ **de (la règle de) bipolarité** (v. violation de l'alternance des polarités); ~ **de l'alternance des polarités** alternate mark-inversion violation
virement des frais reversing charges
virginité *f* virgin memory check; unprogrammed status
virgule *f* decimal point (math.); decimal comma; radix point; ~ **binaire** binary point; ~ **flottante** floating point (arithmetic)
vis *f* screw; bolt; ~ **à baïonette** snap fastener; ~ **à billes** recirculating ball screw; ~ **à bout pointu** conical/tapered point (set) screw; dog-point (set) screw; ~ **à déformation** set screw; ~ **à métaux** machine screw; ~ **à six pans creux (SPC = vis CHc)** hexagon socket screw; cap screw; ~ **à tête cylindrique (C)** cheesehead screw (flat fillister head); pan head screw; ~ **à tête cylindrique bombée large (CBL)** binding-head screw; pan head screw; ~ **à tête cylindrique bombée large à six lobes internes (CBLX)** hexagon-recess pan head screw; ~ **à tête fendue** slotted-head screw; ~ **à tête fraisée (F/90˚)** flat-head screw; ~ **à tête fraisée bombée (FB/90˚)** oval-head screw; ~ **à tête moletée** knurled screw; ~ **à téton** dog-point (set) screw; ~ **à tôle** (sheet-)metal screw; drive screw; self-tapping screw; ~ **à vis** facing; on opposite sides; ~ **Allen** (ST HC cuvette) cup-point set screw; ~ **américaine** crosshead screw; ~ **autotaraudeuse** self-tapping screw; drive screw; thread-cutting screw; ~ **BTR** round-headed wood screw; ~ **CHc** (cylindrique à six pans creux) socket-head cap screw; cap screw; ~ **CLT** cheesehead self-tapping screw; ~ **C/P fendue** slotted cheesehead drive screw; ~ **cruciforme** cross-head screw; Phillips screw [T.N.]; ~ **cylindrique (à tête) bombée (CB)** fillister (head) screw; ~ **d'accord** tuning screw; ~ **d'adaptation** matching screw; ~ **d'assemblage** machine screw; ~ **de purge** bleed screw; ~ **de réglage** adjusting screw; trimming screw; ~ **de vidange** drain screw; ~ **FHc/90˚** CSK

(countersunk) hex socket screw; ~ **imperdable** captive screw; ~ **Parker** self-tapping screw; drive screw; sheet metal screw; ~ **Poêlier** mushroom-head screw; ~ **pointeau** (cone tip) set screw; ~ **pour métaux** machine screw; ~ **sans fin** lead screw; grub screw; worm (gear); ~ **sans tête** grub screw; set screw; ~ **sans tête à cuvette** cup point set screw; ~ **SPC** (six pans creux) hex socket screw; cap screw

visa *m* confirmation; authorization; stamp; signature; ~ **d'homologation** endorsement; ~ **pour application** official endorsement; clearance

viscosité *f* **cinématique** kinematic viscosity; ~ **diélectrique** dielectric viscosity; ~ **dynamique** dynamic viscosity

visé *adj* target

visée *f* aim; target; objective; pointing; sight; n.; orientation; view-finding; ~ **directe** (photoélectrique) direct projection (PEC emission)

visibilité de la trame line visibility; ~ **des lignes** line visibility; ~ **directe** line-of-sight; ~ **d'objets malgré les échos de sol** sub-clutter visibility

visière *f* viewing hood; ~ **anti-chaleur** heat-protective visor; shield

visioconférence *f* videoconference

vision globale (comprehensive) overview

visionneuse *f* viewer; video display; monitor; screen

visiophonie *f* (still-picture) videophony

visite *f* conducted tour; guided tour

vissage *m* **inter-pistes** skew (of disk tracks)

vissement *m* **inter-pistes** (v. vissage inter-pistes)

visser à fond screw home; screw tightly; ~ **légèrement** hand-tighten; ~ **sans serrer** hand-tighten

visserie *f* fixing hardware; securing components; nuts and bolts; fasteners

visseuse *f* power driver

visu *m* (console de visualisation) visual display unit (VDU); (screen) monitor; video terminal; display device

visualisateur *m* visual display unit (VDU); (screen) monitor; video terminal; display device

visualisation *f* visual display; ~ **du curseur** cursor on/off (CON/COF); ~ **locale** local copy

visualiser *v* display; view; indicate

visuel *m* visual display unit (VDU)

vitesse *f* speed; velocity; rate; tempo; ~ **acoustique** sound particle velocity; ~ **angulaire** angular velocity; ~ **d'accord thermique** thermal tuning rate; ~ **d'attaque**

drive speed; ~ **d'avance papier** paper slew rate (in inches per second); ~ **d'aveuglement** blind speed; ~ **de balayage** sweep velocity; scanning speed; ~ **de déroulement** drive speed; ~ **de formation d'une paire** generation rate; ~ **de groupe** group velocity; envelope velocity; ~ **de lumière dans le vide** velocity of light; ~ **de manipulation** keying speed; ~ **de phase** phase velocity; ~ **de propagation** propagation velocity; ~ **de recombinaison superficielle** surface-recombination velocity; ~ **de recombinaison volumique** volume recombination rate; ~ **de régénération** (RAM) loading rate; refresh rate; ~ **de repli** fallback data rate; ~ **de révolution** speed of revolution; r.p.m.; ~ **de tambour** drum speed; ~ **de transfert** transfer rate; ~ **de transmission** data rate; ~ **de transmission d'eb** bit rate; ~ **de variation de la tension de sortie** slew rate; ~ **d'émission télégraphique** signalling speed/rate; speed of telegraph transmission; ~ **d'exploration** scanning speed; ~ **d'exploration à la réception** writing speed; ~ **d'impression** printing speed; ~ **d'une particule** sound particle velocity; ~ **en bauds** baud rate; ~ **en ligne** line speed; ~ **linéaire** velocity; ~ **maximale d'exploration à la réception** maximum writing speed; ~ **moyenne** medium speed; average speed; ~ **spécifique de désionisation** de-ionization rate; ~ **spécifique d'ionisation** ionization rate; ~ **télégraphique** telegraph speed; modulation rate

vitre *f* glaze; glazing; ~ **pare-balles** bulletproof glass

vobulateur *m*; wobulateur sweep generator

vobulation *f*; wobulation sweep modulation

vocalisé *adj* with vowels; vowelized

Vodas voice-operated device (anti-singing)

Vodat voice-operated device for automatic transmission

Vogad voice-operated gain-adjusting device

voie *f* channel; input/output signal; track; n.; band; sweep; trace; path; highway; bus; port; ~ **à courants porteurs** carrier channel; ~ **à deux fréquences vocales** two-frequency channel; ~ **à duplex intégral** full-duplex channel; ~ **à fréquences vocales** voice-grade channel; VG channel; ~ **à large bande** broadband channel; wideband channel; ~ **adjacente** adjacent channel; ~ **aller** go path; forward path; primary channel; ~ **analogique** analogue channel; ~ **balise** marker channel; beacon channel (of R/T); ~ **bidirectionnelle** duplex channel; ~ **bidirectionnelle à l'alternat** either-way operation; half-duplex channel; two-way simplex channel; ~ **binaire** bit track; ~ **commune** bus; trunk; common channel; ~ **composite** multiplex channel; ~ **d'accès** access channel; ~ **d'acheminement** routing path; card track; route; ~ **d'acheminement auxiliaire** auxiliary route; ~ **d'acheminement de secours** emergency route; ~ **d'acheminement normale** normal route; ~ **d'aller** forward channel; go path; primary channel; ~ **de basse fréquence** audio-frequency channel; ~ **de communication** telecommunications circuit; ~ **de communication bilatérale** telegraph circuit/channel; ~ **de communication par porteuse de haute fréquence** HF carrier current telephone channel; ~ **de communication télégraphique** telegraph circuit/line; ~ **de conversation** speech path; ~ **de débordement** alternate route/overflow route; ~ **de départ** go path; ~ **de dernier choix** last-choice route; final-route chain; ~ **de détournement** alternative route; ~ **de deuxième choix** second-choice route; ~ **de diffusion** broadcast channel; ~ **de données** data channel; data path; ~ **de fréquence porteuse** carrier channel; ~ **de gestion** common channel signalling path; CCS channel; signalling channel; ~ **de haute fréquence** HF channel; ~ **de marquage** marking path; ~ **de parole** (speech) channel; speech path; ~ **de premier choix** first-choice route; ~ **de qualité téléphonique** voice-grade channel; ~ **de radiocommunication** radio link; radio channel; ~ **de remplacement** alternate route/overflow route; ~ **de retour** reverse channel; return path; backward channel; secondary channel; ~ **de secours** emergency route; ~ **de service** service channel; order wire; service line; ~ **de service de réserve** spare order-wire channel; ~ **de signal** signal transmission path; signal channel; ~ **de télécommunication** telecommunications channel/circuit; ~ **de transfert des informations** information channel; ~ **de transit** transit route; ~ **de transmission** transmission path; transmission channel; ~ **d'émission télégraphique** telegraph route; ~ **dérivée en fréquence** frequency-derived channel; ~ **dérivée en temps** time-derived channel; ~ **des courants de réaction** singing path; ~ **d'état** status channel; ~ **détournée** emergency route; alternative route; alternate route; overflow route; deviation; ~ **directe** direct route; ~ **dispersive** dispersive channel; ~ **disponible** not busy channel; idle channel; free channel; bus grant; ~ **d'oscilloscope** oscilloscope channel; ~ **du trafic** traffic channel;

~ **duplex** full-duplex channel; ~ **émission** (v. voie de départ); ~ **entrante** inlet; ~ **hertzienne** microwave channel; ~ **infratéléphonique** sub-voice channel; narrowband channel; ~ **libre** free channel; ~ **matérielle** signalling channel; ~ **micro-ondes** microwave link; ~ **normale** primary route; normal route; forward channel; ~ **numérique** time slot; digital channel; ~ **par voie (v/v)** channel-associated (signalling); ~ **porteuse** carrier channel; bearer channel; ~ **primaire** primary route; forward channel; ~ **radioélectrique** radio channel; ~ **rapide** high-speed highway; ~ **retour** return path; backward path; ~ **sans signalisation** non-associated signalling channel; ~ **secondaire** secondary route; backward channel; ~ **semi-duplex** half-duplex channel; ~ **sortante** outlet; ~ **source** digital tones and announcements channel; ~ **support** bearer channel; ~ **support d'information** information bearer channel; ~ **télégraphique** telegraph channel; ~ **téléphonique** speech path; voice-grade channel; telephone channel; ~ **temporelle (VT)** (external) time slot (telephone channel); time slot (TS); time channel; digital channel; ~ **transversale** transverse route; ~ **unidirectionnelle** simplex channel; up-and-down circuit; ~ **utile** information channel; ~ **verticale** vertical channel (of oscilloscope)

voie/voie channel-associated signalling (CAS)
voilage *m* buckling; warp; bow
voile *f* rib; warp; twist; bow
voilé *adj* out-of-true
voix *f* language; voice; speech; ~ **artificielle** artificial voice
vol de cycles cycle stealing; ~ **sans portance** ballistic flight
volant *m* handwheel; flywheel
volatiliser *v* evaporate
volée *f* burst; train
volet *m* voucher; certificate; credentials; flap; n.; docket; panel; door (of disk drive); ~ **d'annonciateur** annunciator disk; drop
voleur *m* **de courant** robber bar; thief track; thief (bar)
volontaire *adj* deliberate
volontairement *adv* intentionally; by design; deliberately
voltampère réactif volt-ampere reactive (VAR)
voltampèremètre *m* voltameter; VA meter
voltmètre *m* voltmeter; ~ **à diode** diode-type voltmeter; ~ **à induction** induction-type voltmeter; ~ **à lampe** DC) valve voltmeter; slide-back voltmeter; vacuum-tube voltmeter; ~ **continu** DC voltmeter; ~ **de crête**

peak programme meter; peak voltmeter; crest voltmeter; ~ **de parole** speech voltmeter; ~ **de quasi-crête** quasi-peak voltmeter; ~ **efficace** r.m.s. voltmeter; ~ **électronique** electronic voltmeter; valve voltmeter; vacuum-tube voltmeter (VTVM); ~ **électrostatique** electrostatic voltmeter; ~ **programmable** programmable voltmeter; ~ **quadratique** square-law detector; ~ **rapide** direct-reading voltmeter; ~ **sélectif** selective level meter synthesizer; level-measuring set; level generator; ~ **thermique** hot-wire voltmeter

voltohmampèremètre m Avometer (VOM) (amp-volt-ohmmeter: T.N)

voltohmmètre m voltohmmeter

volume m volume (bulk direct access store); disk-pack (removable disk cartridge); data recording medium; tape file; disk; ~ **acoustique** volume; loudness; sound level; ~ **bande** tape reel; ~ **de conduit** ducting space; ~ **de couverture** volumetric coverage; (volume) coverage; ~ **de référence** reference volume; ~ **d'encombrement** packing density; occupancy (of PCB); ~ **d'impulsion** echoing volume; ~ **d'information** information volume; ~ **du trafic** acheminé amount of traffic carried; ~ **multi-fichier** multi-file volume

volumètre m electrical speech level meter; volume indicator; volume level meter (VU-meter)

volumineux adj copious

volumique adj bulk; mass

voûte f cable duct

voyant m tell-tale lamp; indicator (lamp); pilot light; status light; ~ **de synthèse** rack alarm indicator; ~ **du clavier** control indicator light (CIL)

Voyez la brique géante que je jette auprès du wharf The quick brown fox jumps over the lazy dog

vrai adj explicit; true; real; actual

VT (v. voie temporelle)

vue m frame; ~ (face avant/arrière) (front/rear) elevation; ~ **de dessus** top view; ~ **de profil** side view; ~ **d'en bas** bottom view; ~ **d'ensemble** general view; overall view; ~ **éclatée** exploded view; ~ **en coupe** sectional view; cut-away view; ~ **en plan** plan view; ~ **partielle** cut-away view

vumètre m VU (volume-unit) meter

v/v (v. voie par voie)

W

watt efficace true watt
wattmètre optique optical wattmeter

wobulateur (v. vobulateur)
wobulation (v. vobulation)

Z

Z entrée différentielle differential input impedance

ZAA (v. zone à autonomie d'acheminement)

Zamak Mazak [T.N.] (U.K.); Zamak [T.N.] (U.S.) special high-grade low melting-point zinc alloy

zéro *m* zero; null; neutral; reset; blank; space; ~ **analogique** frame ground; ~ **barré** slashed zero (0); ~ **de transmission** transmission zero; ~ **logique** signal ground; digital earth; ~ **migrant** marching zero

zingué *adj* galvanized

ZL (v. zone locale)

zone *f* area; zone; field; belt; lane; band; section; range; space; region (of semiconductor); segment; portion; sector; block (of data); extent; keyfield; ~ **à autonomie d'acheminement (ZAA)** group centre area (GCA); ~ **à habitat dispersé** under-populated area; ~ **à numérotation fermée** closed numbering area; ~ **à signaux équilibrés** equi-signal zone; ~ **adresse de seize bits** address syllable; ~ **algébrique** signed field; ~ **amovible** overlay area; ~ **argument** argument field; ~ **auditeur** listening zone; ~ **aurorale** auroral belt; ~ **banalisée** non-dedicated area; ~ **blanche** blank field; ~ **commune** common area; ~ **couverte primaire** primary service area; ~ **d'appel de mobile** (mobile) paging area; ~ **d'attraction** catchment area; ~ **d'audibilité** audible range; ~ **de chaînage** sequencing zone; ~ **de charge d'espace** space-charge region; barrier layer; ~ **de charge spatiale** space-charge region; ~ **de comptage de blocs** block count; ~ **de confusion** confusion region; ~ **de contact** (utile) (contact) wipe area; ~ **de couplage** link-pack area (LPA); interface zone; ~ **de couverture** coverage area; ~ **de couverture verticale** vertical coverage; ~ **de diffusion** diffusion length; ~ **de disque** disk (file) extent; ~ **de distorsion** distortion area; ~ **de la fenêtre atmosphérique** atmospheric window region; ~ **de longueur fixe** fixed-length field; ~ **de longueur variable** variable-length field; ~ **de manœuvre** working area; ~ **de mémoire** storage area/block; ~ **de nuit** night reception zone; ~ **de numérotage**

numbering area; numbering plan area; local area; ~ **de numérotage mondial** world numbering zone; ~ **de perforation** card field; zone punch; overpunch; ~ **de pièces** patch field; ~ **de raréfaction** depletion layer; ~ **de rattachement** local area; exchange area; home area; ~ **de réception** received digits zone; ~ **de réception du numéro demandé** received digits zone; ~ **de recherche de mobile** (mobile) paging area; ~ **de recouvrement** overlay area; ~ **de responsabilité** catchment area; ~ **de retouche** patch area; ~ **de réversibilité** reversible (deformation); ~ **de service** service area; ~ **de service primaire** primary service area; ~ **de service secondaire** secondary service area; ~ **de silence** blind area; skip area; silent zone; skip zone; ~ **de taxation** charging area; meter fee zone; metering zone; ~ **de taxation locale** local service area; ~ **de taxation urbaine** local service area; ~ **de temporisation** time delay zone; ~ **de traduction** translation zone; ~ **de travail** scratchpad area; buffer; working area; ~ **d'écoute** listening zone; ~ **défectueuse** bad block (of data); ~ **d'émetteur** emitter (region); ~ **d'empiètement** displacement area; spread; ~ **d'enchaînement** call progress zone; ~ **d'enclenchement** hold-in range; ~ **d'envoi** signal transmission area; ~ **déplétée** depletion region; ~ **des constantes** constant area; ~ **des données** data area (DA); ~ **des variables** call data; ~ **desservie** service area; ~ **d'incertitude** indeterminate band; dead band; ~ **d'induction** induction zone; near zone; proximity zone; ~ **d'information** information field; ~ **d'insensibilité** dead band; ~ **d'interférence** interference region/area; ~ **d'inversion** commutating zone; ~ **discriminante** convention; discriminating field; ~ **d'ombre** shadow region; ~ **du col** neck region; ~ **d'un centre nodal** tandem area; ~ **dynamique** dynamic area; ~ **équiphase** equiphase zone; Decca lane; ~ **fixe** fixed(-length) field; ~ **frontalière** frontier zone; ~ **gardée** guarded area; ~ **indicatif** index area; key field; ~ **industrielle** industrial estate; ~ **insécable** protected field; ~ **interdite** prohibited area;

Z

~ **interurbaine** trunk zone; ~ **isolante** isolated region; ~ **locale (ZL)** local area (LA); ~ **mémoire** memory field; ~ **morte** dead space; dead spot; radar gap; hole; ~ **neutre** dead/neutral zone; ~ **non gardée** unguarded area; ~ **non protégée** unprotected area; ~ **primaire de silence** primary skip zone; ~ **prise** seize area; ~ **protégée** protected area; ~ **rapiécée** patch area; ~ **réceptrice** receiving area; ~ **réservée à la** fréquence de détresse guard band; ~ **sautée** skip area; ~ **sécable** unprotected area; ~ **sécante** intersecting area; ~ **secondaire** secondary service area; ~ **surbrillante** highlighted area; ~ **tampon** buffer area; ~ **téléphonique** telephone area; ~ **urbaine (ZU)** metropolitan (urban) area (MA); local area; ~ **utile** objective; target area; ~ **variable** variable(-length) field

ZU (v. zone urbaine)

Z

ENGLISH/FRENCH

A

AA/ack-ack (anti-aircraft defence) DCA (défense contre avions)

abacus *n* abaque; boulier

abandon *v* abandonner

abatement *n* abaissement; baisse; combat

abbreviate *v* abréger

abbreviated dialling numérotation abrégée; ~ **dialling number** numéro abrégé (NA); ~ **dialling prefix** indicatif d'appel abrégé; ~ **ringing-station busy** renvoi d'appel forcé

ABC - auto bill calling service (s. personalized billing)

abend arrêt anormal; fin anormale

aberration *n* aberration; dérive; défaut

abnormal exit sortie anormale; ~ **glow discharge** décharge luminescente anormale

abnormality *n* anomalie (de fonctionnement)

abnormal termination arrêt anormal

A-board *n* opératrice de départ; opératrice locale; position mixte d'inscription et de départ (position A)

abort *v* abandonner; arrêter

aborted *adj* suspendu; à l'arrêt; ~ **call** appel abandonné

aborting *n* sabordage; liquidation

abortive call appel inefficace; appel infructueux; appel sans aboutissement; appel instable; ~ **call attempt** tentative infructueuse

abort procedure procédure d'abandon; ~ **rate** taux d'échec; ~ **timing** temporisation de raccrochage du demandé

abrading *n* (chemical etch) satinisation; (air) ~ sablage

abridged *adj* écourté; réduit; succinct

abrupt *adj* brutal

absence of ground absence de terre

absent subscriber service abonné absent (service d'a.)

absolute (power) **level** niveau absolu; ~ (real) **value** valeur réelle; ~ **address** adresse absolue; adresse directe; adresse domiciliaire; adresse effective; adresse électrique; adresse fonctionnelle (AF); adresse-machine; adresse modifiée; adresse primitive; adresse réelle; adresse spécifique; ~ **addressing** adressage absolu; ~ **binary** binaire absolu; ~ **capacitivity** constante diélectrique absolue; ~ **code** code de base; code machine; langage machine; ~ **coding** codage en absolu; ~ **conditional branch** branchement conditionnel à une adresse réelle; ~ **delay** temps de propagation absolu; ~ **dielectric constant** constante diélectrique absolue; ~ **error** erreur absolue; ~ **gain** gain en module; ~ **loader** chargeur absolu; ~ **maximum ratings** limites absolues d'emploi; limites maximum d'utilisation; système des limites absolues (d'emploi); ~ **maximum values** gabarit; ~ **power level** niveau absolu de puissance réelle; ~ **value** module; valeur absolue

absorb *v* étouffer

absorbent paper papier buvard

absorber *n* circuit de compensation; ~ **circuit** circuit d'absorption; circuit de compensation de charge; ~ **circuit factor** facteur de compensation de charge

absorbing clamp pince absorbante; ~ **filter** filtre absorbant; ~ **power** pouvoir absorbant

absorption *n* absorption; captation; **non-deviation** ~ absorption ionosphérique sans déviation de vitesse de groupe; ~ **band** bande d'absorption; ~ **circuit** circuit bouchon; piège électrique; trappe; ~ **cross-section** surface de captation; surface effective; ~ **fading** affaiblissement dû à l'absorption; ~ **frequency meter** filtre de fréquence à absorption; ~ **inductor** self interphase; transformateur équilibreur; ~ **length** longueur d'absorption; ~ **loss** affaiblissement d'absorption; perte d'absorption; ~ **modulation** modulation d'amplitude par absorption; ~ **of charged particles** absorption de porteurs électrisés; ~ **peak** crête d'absorption; ~ **trap** piège à absorption

absorptive attenuator affaiblisseur à absorption; affaiblisseur résistif

abstract *n* résumé succinct

abstractor *n* analyste

abstract symbol symbole abstrait

absurdity check contrôle de vraisemblance

A-bus *n* bus A

abusive call appel malveillant; appel importun

abutment *n* butée

AC *adj* pulsé; impulsionnel; en impulsions;

sinusoïdal; dynamique; $\sim$ (s. alternating current); $\sim$ **bridge** pont alternatif
accelerated aging vieillissement accéléré; $\sim$ **life test** vieillissement accéléré; $\sim$ **test** essai accéléré
accelerating electrode électrode d'accélération; $\sim$ **field** champ d'accélération
acceleration n accélération linéaire; $\sim$ **time** temps d'accélération; temps de mise en marche; $\sim$ **voltage** tension d'accélération
accelerator n accélérateur; $\sim$ (catalyst) activateur
accelerometer n accéléromètre
acceptable deviation tolérance; $\sim$ **noise level** niveau de bruit admissible
acceptance n réception; $\sim$ (testing) recette; $\sim$ **angle** angle d'illumination; $\sim$ **capacity** capacité d'accueil; $\sim$ **conditions** conditions de réception; $\sim$ **cone** cône d'acceptance; $\sim$ **criterion** critère d'acceptation; sanction; $\sim$ **procedure guide** guide de recette
acceptance/rejection criteria gabarit
acceptance sampling échantillonnage d'acceptation; $\sim$ **test** essai de réception; essai de recette; $\sim$ **time** heure de dépôt
acceptor n accepteur; bouchon d'absorption; $\sim$ **circuit** circuit accepteur; circuit résonnant
access v accéder (à); extraire; lire; obtenir; $\sim$ n accès; entrée; $\sim$ **area** entrée utile; $\sim$ **arm** bras d'accès; bras d'écriture; bras de lecture; $\sim$ **barred** inaccessible
access-barred signal signal d'accès interdit
access channel voie d'accès; $\sim$ **circuit** circuit d'accès; $\sim$ **code** code d'accès; indicatif (IF); indicatif d'appel; préfixe d'accès; présignal; $\sim$ **contention** collision; $\sim$ **control** contrôle d'accès; $\sim$ **denial** blocage système
access-denial probability taux de blocage; taux d'échec; taux d'indisponibilité; $\sim$ **time** temps de blocage
access hole trou de pilotage
accessibility n commodité d'accès; disponibilité
accessible adj abordable; accessible; disponible
access line ligne d'accès
accessories n pl garnissage; péritéléphonie
accessory n accessoire; pièce détachée
access point point d'accès; $\sim$ **prefix to the international network** indicatif international; $\sim$ **privileges** droits d'accès; profil; $\sim$ **protocol** protocole de mise en présence; $\sim$ **relay** relais d'accès; relais d'adressage; $\sim$ **relay set** relais multiple (RM); $\sim$ **request** demande d'accès; $\sim$ **selector** présélecteur; $\sim$ **selector switch** commutateur d'accès;

$\sim$ **time** temps d'accès. temps de prise
AC characteristics caractéristiques dynamiques
accidental ground court-circuit à la masse
accomplish v réaliser; effectuer; assurer; poursuivre
accomplished adj expérimenté
AC component (of rectified current) composante alternative
accordion n contact élastique
accountable time temps machine
account card carte compte
accounting n comptabilité; $\sim$ **machine** facturière; $\sim$ **machine layout** (of numeric keypad) configuration facturière; $\sim$ **period** exercice; $\sim$ **rate** taux de répartition
accoutrements n pl fourniture(s)
accretion n excroissance
accrued adj cumulé
accumulating counter compteur totalisateur
accumulator n batterie; $\sim$ (register) registre arithmétique; registre accumulateur; registre de cumul; registre index; $\sim$ **cell** élément d'accumulateur
accuracy n sensibilité; exactitude; fidélité; justesse; précision; $\sim$ **control character** caractère de contrôle de justesse
accurate adj précis; $\sim$ **position finder (APF)** radar directeur de tir
ACD (s. automatic call distributor)
AC/DC receiver récepteur tous courants; $\sim$ **ringing** appel bi-courants; appel par courant superposé; $\sim$ **spark-over voltage of a protector** tension alternative/continue d'amorçage d'un parafoudre
AC dump panne d'alimentation; panne du secteur
ACE (s. automatic calling equipment)
AC generator alternateur
achromatic aerial antenne achromatique
AC hum bruit de secteur
ACK (s. acknowledgement flag)
acknowledge v accuser réception; $\sim$ **bit** bit de bonne réception; $\sim$ **character** caractère d'accusé réception
acknowledgement n acquittement; $\sim$ **(ACK)** accusé de réception (AR)
acknowledge(ment) bit bit bien reçu (BR); bonne réception (BR)
acknowledgement flag (ACK) indicateur d'accusé de réception; $\sim$ **frequency** fréquence de contrôle; $\sim$ **queue** file d'accusés d'exécution; $\sim$ **signal (ACK)** signal d'accusé de réception; signal d'acquittement; $\sim$ **signal unit (ASU)** unité de signalisation d'accusé de réception; $\sim$ **window** fenêtre d'accusé de réception
AC mains (supply) secteur alternatif; réseau

alternatif

acorn nut écrou moleté; ~ **tube/valve** tube gland; tube bouton

acoustic *adj* acoustique; sonore; ~ **absorption** absorption acoustique; ~ **admittance** admittance acoustique

acoustical field champ acoustique; ~ **speech power** puissance vocale

acoustic chamber abat-son; ~ **compliance** élasticité acoustique; ~ **control** contrôle acoustique; ~ **coupler** coupleur acoustique; dispositif de couplage acoustique; ~ **coupling** couplage acoustique; ~ **damping** amortissement acoustique; ~ **delay line** ligne à retard (LAR); ligne acoustique (LA); ~ **environment** milieu acoustique; ~ **feedback (Larsen effect)** effet microphonique; ~ **feedback (Larsen effect)** effet Larsen; effet microphonique; ~ **hood** couvercle anti-bruit; ~ **impedance** impédance acoustique; ~ **inertia** inertance acoustique; ~ **intensity** intensité acoustique; ~ **mass** masse acoustique; ~ **memory** mémoire acoustique; ~ **noise** bruit acoustique; ~ **pick-up** lecteur acoustique; ~ **pressure** pression acoustique; pression du son; ~ **radiation** rayonnement acoustique; ~ **radiometer** radiomètre acoustique; ~ **reactance** réactance acoustique; ~ **resistance** résistance acoustique; ~ **shock** choc acoustique; crépitement; friture; ~ **shock absorber** amortisseur de chocs acoustiques; cohéreur; ~ **source** source sonore; ~ **stiffness** raideur acoustique; ~ **store** mémoire acoustique; ~ **survey** contrôle acoustique; ~ **wave** onde acoustique

acoustimeter *n* sonomètre (objective)

AC parameter caractéristique dynamique; ⋩ **pulsing** numérotation en courant alternatif

acquire *v* procurer; acquérir; être à portée; obtenir; prendre

acquisition *n* captage de données; collecte de(s) données; prise; saisie; relevé; ~ **and tracking radar** radar d'acquisition et de poursuite; ~ **time** temps d'acquisition; temps de prise

AC relay output circuit circuit de sortie à relais alternative; ⋩ **resistance** résistance effective; résistance interne différentielle; ⋩ **ripple** réinjection de tension alternative

acronym *n* mot sigle

acrylic sheet Plexiglas [A.C.]

AC signalling signalisation par courant alternatif; ⋩ **telegraphy with double VF modulation** télégraphie harmonique à double modulation; ⋩ **thermal characteristics** comportement en température des caractéristiques dynamiques

action current courant d'action nerveuse; ~ **request** demande d'action

activate *v* actionner; déclencher; lancer; mettre en marche; mettre en oeuvre; mettre en service; provoquer; solliciter

activation *n* actionnement; attaque; commande (cde); déclenchement; démarrage; mise en marche (MM); mise en route; ~ (of alarm) bagottement

activator *n* accélérateur

active *adj* passant; ~ **aerial** élément actif; élément rayonnant primaire; ~ **air gap** entrefer de travail; ~ **balance return loss** affaiblissement actif d'équilibrage; ~ **balancing** équilibrage actif; ~ **cell** cellule non vide; ~ **component** composante active; partie réelle; ~ **current** courant actif; courant de travail; ~ **electronic countermeasures (ECM)** contremesures électroniques actives; ~ **filter** filtre actif; ~ **homing** ralliement actif; ~ **jamming** brouillage intentionnel; ~ **job queue** file d'attente d'exécution; file de tâches en exécution; ~ **load** charge active; ~ **power** puissance active; ~ **reflector** réflecteur actif; ~ **(balance) return loss** affaiblissement des courants d'écho; ~ **satellite** satellite actif; ~ **scan point** porte passante; ~ **signal** signal utile; ~ **signalling link** canal sémaphore (à l'état) actif; ~ **singing point** point d'amorçage actif; ~ **sonar** (sound navigation and ranging) sonar ultrasonore; ~ **speech time** durée de la parole active; ~ **standby transmitter** émetteur de réserve actif; ~ **transducer** transducteur actif; ~ **when low** (negative logic) actif (en) état bas

activity *n* activité; (file) ~ **ratio** taux de mouvement; ~ **dip** diminution de l'activité; ~ **factor** facteur d'activité; ~ **file** fichier de mouvement; fichier détail; fichier d'activités; ~ **ratio** taux d'activité

Act of God force majeure

AC transmission transmission sans composante continue utile

actual address adresse absolue; ~ **code** code machine; ~ **error** erreur absolue; ~ **instruction** instruction réelle; instruction effective; ~ **measured loss (AML)** affaiblissement réel; ~ **size** grandeur réelle; grandeur nature; grandeur naturelle; en vraie grandeur

actuate *v* actionner; manœuvrer

actuation *n* actionnement; attaque

actuator *n* actionneur; commande mécanique; excitateur; vérin; servodyne

ACU (s. automatic calling unit)

acute angle angle aigu; angle vif

AC voltage tension alternative
ACW (s. aircraft control and warning service)
acyclic *adj* acyclique
AD (s. assignment demand)
adapter *n* adaptateur
adaptive channel allocation affectation dynamique adaptable des voies; ~ **differential pulse code modulation (ADPCM)** modulation par impulsions et codage différentiel adaptatif (MIC-DA); ~ **discrimination** discrimination adaptative; ~ **equalization** égalisation adaptative; ~ **hybrid transformer** transformateur différentiel adaptatif; ~ **multi-channel system** système à canaux multiples adaptatif
adaptor *n* adaptateur; bloc d'adaptation; embout; raccord; raccord mécanique; ~ **dial** plaque d'adaptation; ~ **plate** plaque d'adaptation; plaquette compensatrice; ~ **subrack** châssis d'adaptation; panier d'adaptation; ~ **unit** coffret de raccordement (CRU)
ADC (s. advise-duration-and-charge)
Adcock aerial antenne à polarisation verticale; antenne polarisée verticalement; ~ **direction finder** radiogoniomètre Adcock
A-D conversion (analogue-to-digital conversion) conversion A/D (conversion analogique-numérique); ~ **converter** quantificateur
added bit bit supplémentaire; ~ **block** bloc supplémentaire; ~ **value** valeur ajoutée
addend *n* cumulateur; deuxième opérande; ~ **register** registre de cumul; registre d'index
adder *n* circuit additionneur binaire; combinateur; circuit d'addition; sommateur
adder-subtractor additionneur-soustracteur
addition *n* addition; adjonction
additional *adj* complémentaire; ~ **character** caractère additionnel; ~ **charge** taxe supplémentaire; ~ **element** complément; ~ **reference transmission** transmission avec signal de référence additionnel; ~ **service** service supplémentaire
addition of lines adjonction de lignes; ~ **record** article supplémentaire; nouvel article; ~ **without carry** OU exclusif
add mode mode additionné
add-on *n* complément; additif; ~ *adj* additif; complémentaire; rapporté; supplémentaire; ~ **circuit** circuit additif; réseau additionnel; ~ **components** composants rapportés; ~ **conference** conférence additive; conférence programmée; ~ **element** partie additive; ~ **memory pack** (random access memory RAM) extension; ~ **subrack** châssis d'extension

address *v* adresser; appeler; désigner; ~ *n* adresse; coordonnées; rang
addressable latch bascule adressable; registre adressable; ~ **line** ligne désignable
address assignment command commande d'implantation; ~ **bit** poids d'adresse; ~ **bus** bus d'adresses; ligne d'adresse; ~ **code** code d'adresse
address-complete signal signal de numéro complet
address computation calcul d'adresse; ~ **constant** constante d'adresse; ~ **coordinates** cotations (des adresses); ~ **counter** compteur d'adresse; ~ **decoding** décodage topologique; ~ **digit analysis** analyse de la numérotation; ~ **digits** signaux de numérotation; informations fournies par l'abonné
addressed *adj* pointé; appelé; sollicité
addressee *n* demandé (DE) (aval); destinataire; receveur
address field champ d'adresse; partie adresse; ~ **format** structure de l'adresse; disposition à adresse; ~ **incomplete signal** signal de numérotation incomplet
addressing *n* adressage; sollicitation; ~ **incorrect** faute d'adressage; ~ **menu pocket** pointage d'une case du segment menu; ~ **module** module d'adressage
address latch enable (ALE) commandes en sortie; ~ **line** ligne d'adresse; ~ **mapping** configuration de l'espace d'adressage; ~ **mask** filtre d'adresses; ~ **modification** modification d'adresse; ~ **part** partie adresse; partie d'adresse; ~ **selector** commutateur de sélection d'adresse; ~ **signal** signal d'adresse; signal de numérotation; signal d'enregistreur; ~ **space** espace d'adresse; ~ **stop** halte sur adresse; ~ **strobe** signal de validation d'adresse; ~ **strobe output** échantillonnage adresse; ~ **syllable** zone adresse de seize bits
add time temps d'addition; ~ **to** garnir; compléter (par)
adhesion force force d'adhérence
adhesive *n* colle; ~ **tape** bande adhésive; Chatterton [A.C.]
adiabatic *adj* adiabatique
A-digit selector sélecteur du chiffre A
adjacency *n* contiguïté
adjacent *adj* adjacent; contigu; ~ **centre** centre adjacent; ~ **channel** canal adjacent; voie adjacente; ~ **channel attenuation** affaiblissement de canaux adjacents; ~ **channel rejector** piège son du canal adjacent; ~ **exchange** centre voisin; ~ **lines** lignes adjacentes; ~ **signalling points** points sémaphores adjacents
adjunct *n* complément

adjust régler; reprendre
adjustable blade damper grille à volets réglables; ~ **dead stop** butée réglable; ~ **lug** patte orientable; ~ **pliers** pince réglable; ~ **'radio' pliers** pince radio réglable; ~ **spanner** clé à molette; clé anglaise; clé à crémaillère
adjusted line usage factor facteur ajusté d'utilisation de lignes; ~ **value** valeur lissée
adjuster (of pot core) élément de réglage
adjusting screw vis de réglage
adjustment n réglage; mise au point (MAP); ajustement; cadrage; calage; calibrage; lissage; reprise; ~ **tapping** prise de réglage
administer v dispenser
administration n exploitation; ~ **terminal** terminal d'exploitation
administrative processor processeur de gestion; ~ **returns** état de gestion
admission n entrée; ~ **requirements** prérequis
admittance n admittance
adopt v adopter
ADPCM (s. adaptive differential pulse code modulation)
adrift adj séparé
advance v évoluer; progresser (faire -); ~ n approche; défilement; avance; ~ **calling** envoi d'un message différé
advanced adj évolué; ~ **prototype production** prédéveloppement
advancement n évolution; progression; développement; avance
advance-preparation service service international avec préparation
advance warning tonalité de précomptage; ~ **winding** enroulement supérieur (en demi-alternance); enroulement de commande
advantage n intérêt; atout
advantageous adj intéressant
adversely affect nuire; altérer; perturber
adverse state detector (ASD) détecteur d'état défavorable (DED)
advertising communications publimatique; ~ **copy** pige publicitaire; ~ **jingle** message publicitaire; publicité radiophonique; ~ **media** supports publicitaires; ~ **slot** spot commercial
advice n conseil(s); ~ **note** accusé de réception (AR); avis
advisability n intérêt
advisable adj recommandé
advise v signaler; ~ **duration and charge (ADC)** indication de durée et de taxation (IDT)
aerial n antenne; cadre; aérien; ~ adj aérien; ~ **amplifier** amplificateur d'antenne; ~ **array** antenne réseau; antenne rideau; ensem-

ble d'antennes; panneau d'éléments rayonnants; ~ **attenuator** affaiblisseur d'antenne; ~ **bay** boîte d'antenne; ~ **capacity** puissance d'antenne; ~ **circuit** circuit d'antenne; circuit aérien; ~ **circuit power** puissance du circuit d'antenne; ~ **coil** bobine d'antenne; ~ **connection** borne d'antenne; ~ **connection socket** prise pour antenne; ~ **coupling** couplage d'antenne; ~ **current** courant d'antenne; ~ **directivity** directivité d'antenne
aerial-earth switch commutateur antenne-terre
aerial effect effet d'antenne; ~ **efficiency** coefficient de rayonnement; rendement d'antenne; ~ **element** élément d'antenne; ~ **feed** source d'antenne; source primaire; ~ **gain** gain d'antenne; directivité d'antenne; ~ **gain pattern** diagramme de directivité; ~ **impedance** impédance d'antenne; ~ **input** entrée d'antenne; ~ **jack** douille d'antenne; ~ **lead** descente d'antenne; ~ **loss** perte d'antenne; ~ **matching device** adaptation d'antenne; ~ **output** sortie d'antenne; ~ **power gain** facteur de directivité; ~ **pre-amplifier** préamplificateur d'antenne; ~ **reflector** réflecteur d'antenne; ~ **resistance** résistance d'antenne; ~ **signal** signal d'antenne; ~ **spacing** espacement d'antenne; ~ **terminal** borne d'antenne; ~ **tower** pylône d'antenne; ~ **tuning** accord d'antenne; ~ **tuning coil** self d'antenne; ~ **turntable** couronne d'antenne; ~ **wire** câble aérien
aerodrome surface movement indicator (ASMI) radiodétecteur de mouvement au sol
aerodynamic adj aérolique
aeronautical broadcasting service service de radiodiffusion aéronautique; ~ **communications** télécommunication aéronautique; ~ **fixed circuit** liaison fixe de télécommunication aéronautique; ~ **mobile radio service** service mobile de radiodiffusion
aeroplane flutter interférence d'avion
aerospace company société aéronautique
aesthetics n esthétique
AFC (s. automatic frequency control)
AFF (s. automatic front feed)
affidavit n attestation
affiliate n filiale
affinity n relation
affixed adj apposé (sur)
afford v faciliter
AF peak limiter écrêteur
A/F socket set boîte composée (de) douilles américaines
after-effect n effet résiduel
afterglow n cathodoluminescence; luminescence cathodique; persistance (d'écran);

postluminescence; rémanence

after-image *n* traînage

after-sales service service après-vente (SAV)

agate bead (stylus of disk recorder) perle en agathe

AGC (s. automatic gain control)

AGC/AVC (s. automatic gain/volume control)

AGC detector diode de réglage; ∼ **killer** portier CAG

agenda *n* agenda; échéancier; ordre du jour

agent *n* agent; préposé; représentant

agglutinant *n* liant

aggregate *n* cumul; ensemble; synthèse; ∼ *adj* global; synthétique; ∼ **data rate** débit voie composite; ∼ **record sheet** fiche de synthèse; fiche synthétique

aggrieved, the ∼ **party** la plus diligente des parties

agile oscillator oscillateur agile

aging *n* vieillissement; ∼ **test** essai de vieillissement

agreement *n* accord; contrat; ∼ **of intent** contrat de plan

Ah (s. ampere-hour)

AI (s. air-intercept radar)

aid *v* faciliter; ∼ *n* aide; assistance; coopération; outil

AID (s. area identification)

aim *v* orienter; ∼ *n* but; objet; visée

aiming *n* pointage; ∼ **angle** angle de visée

air blast insufflation d'air

airborne all-round radar search apparatus radar panoramique d'avion; ∼ **collision avoidance system** système aéroporté de prévention; ∼ **radar** radar aéroporté; radar d'avion; ∼ **radio** radio aéronautique; ∼ **television receiver and radar transponder** téléviseur et émetteur-récepteur radar de bord; ∼ **traffic situation display** présentation aéroportée de la situation du trafic; ∼ **transmitter** émetteur d'avion; ∼ **weather radar** radiodétecteur d'avertissement

air break coupure sèche; ∼ **conditioning** climatisation; ∼ **core** noyau à air

air-core coil bobine à air

aircraft control and warning service (ACW) service de contrôle et d'alerte aérien; ∼ **guided missile** engin téléguidé d'avion; ∼ **radio** radio aéronautique; ∼ **wireless control** télécommande d'avion

air desiccator déssécheur à air; ∼ **filter** filtre à air

air flow *n* circulation d'air

air frame *n* cellule

air-gap (lightning) **arrester** éclateur à air

air-gap entrefer

air-gap pad lamelle d'entrefer; ∼ **trimming**

usinage d'entrefer

air-hole bulle

air inlet arrivée d'air

air-insulated capacitor condensateur à air

air insulating gap isolement d'air; ∼ **intake** prise d'air

air-intercept radar (AI) radiodétecteur aéroporté d'interception

air-jet cleaning (dust removal) soufflage

airlift *n* pont aérien

air-lifted aérotransportable

air mass masse d'air; ∼ **path** trajet d'air

airport surface detection equipment (ASDE) radar de piste d'atterrissage; ∼ **surveillance radar** radar de surveillance d'aéroport

air sounding sondage atmosphérique; ∼ **space** espace aérien

air-spaced coil self à air

air-tight hermétique

air time temps d'émission

air-traffic controller aiguilleur du ciel

air vent ouie d'aération; ventouse; ∼ **waybill (AWB)** lettre de transport aérien (LTA)

AIS (s. alarm indication signal)

aisle *n* passerelle; travée

AJ (s. anti-jamming)

AL (s. inductance factor)

alarm *n* alarme; **(remote)** ∼ **sender** transmetteur d'alarme; ∼ **annunciator** avertisseur; ∼ **bell** sonnerie d'alarme; ∼ **bus** liaison d'alarme; ∼ **circuit** circuit d'alarme; ligne de surveillance

alarm-clock service service réveil

alarm contact contact d'alarme; ∼ **forwarding** retransmission des alarmes; ∼ **indication signal (AIS)** signal d'indication d'alarmes (SIA); ∼ **lamp** lampe d'alarme; ∼ **lamps** herse; ∼ **logger** enregistreur de dérangements; enregistreur de fautes; ∼ **loop** boucle d'alarme; ∼ **message** communication d'erreur

alarm-off threshold seuil de disparition d'alarme

alarm output sortie d'alarme; ∼ **receiver** récepteur d'alarme; ∼ **receiver unit** central de réception d'alarme; ∼ **reporting** retransmission des alarmes; ∼ **sequence** séquence d'alarme; ∼ **signal** signal d'alarme; ∼ **signalling control unit** central de réception d'alarme; ∼ **system** système d'alarme

A-law coding loi de codage A; ∼ **encoding** codage à segments

albedo *n* albédo

ALE (s. address latch enable)

alert *v* prévenir; signaler; ∼ *n* incident

alerting lamp lampe d'appel; ∼ **signal** signal d'appel audible

Alford loop carré Gouriaud

algebra *n* calcul, algèbre
algebraic *adj* algébrique
algorithm *n* algorithme
algorithmic language langage algorithmique
alias pseudonyme
aliasing *n* repliage; ~ **energy** énergie dénaturante; ~ **error** pliage (du spectre de fréquences)
alien *n* réponse non pertinente; ~ *adj* étranger
align *v* cadrer (à droite/à gauche)
aligned aligné; ~ **bundle** faisceau parallèle; ~ **portion** surface en regard
aligner *n* (digroup terminal) aligneur
alignment *n* accord; alignement; cadrage; centrage; conformage; égalisation; parallélisme; synchronisation; verrouillage; ~ **bit** bit de verrouillage de trame; ~ **chart** abaque; ~ **error rate monitoring** surveillance du taux d'erreurs d'alignement; ~ **flag** drapeau de verrouillage; ~ **hole** trou de régistration; ~ **input** accord d'antenne; ~ **sheet** fiche de réglage
aliquot part sous-multiple
alkaline accumulator accumulateur alcalin; ~ **cell** pile alcaline
alkyd resin résine glycérophtalique; ~ **resin coating** peinture glycérophtalique
all lines busy faisceau saturé
all-channel toutes-ondes; ~ **aerial** réseau de dipôles pour réception
all-clear signal lamp lampe de fin (de conversation); lampe de clôture
all-day efficiency rendement du trafic diurne
alleviate *v* pallier
all-exchange tout au réseau (TAR)
all-glass valve tube tout-verre
allied *adj* connexe
alligator clip pince crocodile; pince crabe
all ls sequence séquence uniquement composée de l
all-mains receiver récepteur universel
all-metal tuned magnetron magnétron accordable tout-métal
allocate *v* affecter; attribuer; assigner
allocation *n* segment; tranche; **(dynamic)** ~ partitionnement mémoire; ~ **of run time** enchaînement; ~ **scheme** plan d'affectation
all-or-nothing tout ou rien (TOR)
allot *v* affecter; désigner
allotted time temps imparti
allotter *n* distributeur d'appels; distributeur de chercheurs
allotting switch sélecteur de désignation
allowable *adj* admissible
allowance *n* provision
allowed band bande permise; fréquence autorisée

all pages included toutes pages confondues
all-pass active network réseau actif passe-tout
all paths busy toutes lignes occupées
all-purpose computer ordinateur universel
all-ready signal lamp lampe de clôture; lampe de fin (de conversation)
all-relay (dial) system système automatique tout à relais; ~ **exchange** central de système (tout) à relais; ~ **selector** sélecteur à relais; ~ **system** système tout à relais
all-round aerial antenne omnidirectionnelle; antenne omnidirective; ~ **search radar** radar de surveillance
all-seems-well bus bus de confirmation d'exécution
all-trunks-busy (ATB) occupation totale; occupation toutes jonctions (OTJ); saturation en départ; ~ **rate** taux de blocage; ~ **register (ATB)** compteur d'occupation totale
all-wave oscillator oscillateur toutes ondes; ~ **receiver** récepteur toutes ondes
alphabet *n* alphabet; ~ **code** code alphabétique
alphabetic(al) *adj* alphabétique; littéral
alphabetical code indicatif littéral; ~ **sort** tri lexicographique; ~ **sorting** classement alphabétique
alphabetic character set jeu de caractères alphabétique; ~ **character subset** jeu partiel de caractères alphabétiques; ~ **signal** signal alphabétique; ~ **string** chaîne alphabétique; ~ **telegram** télégramme alphabétique; ~ **telegraphy** télégraphie alphabétique
alphameric *adj* alphanumérique
alphanumeric *adj* alphanumérique; ~ **accounting machine** tabulatrice alphanumérique; ~ **character** caractère imprimable; ~ **code** code alphanumérique; ~ **keyboard** clavier alphanumérique; ~ **sort** tri alphanumérique
alpha particle particule alpha; ~ **ray** rayon alpha
alteration *n* changement; modification; opération OU; reprise; ~ **switch** aiguilleur; inverseur
alternate-action pushbutton bouton poussoir (à tête) pas à pas; ~ **switch** bouton à double effet
alternate channel canal de déviation; ~ **frequency** fréquence de déviation; ~ **mark inversion** bipolarité; ~ **mark inversion signal** signal bipolaire; ~ **mark-inversion violation** violation de l'alternance des polarités; violation de (la règle de) bipolarité; viol de bipolarité; ~ **mode** (of oscilloscope) fonctionnement alterné;

~ **operation** exploitation à l'alternat

alternate/overflow (least-cost) routing acheminement de débordement; acheminement par voie détournée; acheminement alternatif

alternate polarity signes contraires; ~ **route/ overflow route** voie détournée; voie de débordement; voie de remplacement; ~ **routing** acheminement détourné; détournement; déviation

alternating adj alternatif; tout ou rien (TOR); ~ **current (AC)** courant alternatif (ca)

alternating-current ringer sonnerie à courant alternatif

alternating field champ alternatif; ~ **sweep** balayage alterné; ~ **voltage** tension alternative

alternative code code à disparité compensée; code à disparité restreinte; ~ **denial** interdiction alternative; NON ET (= ON/ET-NON); ~ **energy sources** énergies nouvelles; ~ **route** délestage; voie de détournement; voie détournée; ~ **routing** acheminement avec débordement; acheminement sur voie de débordement; acheminement sur voie secondaire; acheminement de secours; circuit de détournement; ~ **routing indicator** indicateur d'acheminement détourné; ~ **signalling link** liaison de signalisation de réserve; ~ **tandem exchange** centre de transit de détournement

alternator n alternateur

altimeter n altimètre

ALU (s. arithmetic and logic unit)

alumina (aluminium oxide) alumine; ~ **blade** plaquette d'alumine

aluminium bar barre d'aluminium; ~ **jacket** gaine aluminium; ~ **plating** métallisation aluminium; ~ **strip** bande d'alu(minium)

aluminized screen écran aluminisé

always-open line ligne essentielle; ligne d'abonnement; ~ **(subcriber) line** abonné essentiel

always running rebouclage

AM (s. amplitude modulation)

AMA (s. automatic message accounting)

amalgamation n synthèse

amateur inventor bricoleur; ~ **radio** radio amateur; ~ **(radio) frequency band** bande de fréquences d'amateur; ~ **transmitter** poste émetteur d'amateur

ambient adj atmosphérique; ~ **conditions** conditions atmosphériques; valeurs de conditionnement; ~ **noise** bruit de fond; bruit de l'ambiance; ~ **temperature** température ambiante

ambiguity error erreur d'ambiguïté; ~ **test** test de lever de doute

ambiguous adj équivoque

amendment n mise à jour (MAJ); modification; rectification; révision; reprise; ~ **file** fichier mouvement; ~ **record** enregistrement de détail; enregistrement de mouvement

AML (s. actual measured loss)

ammeter n ampèremètre; galvanomètre

ammunition depot arsenal; ~ **dump** arsenal

A motor-rated fuse fusible classe aM (accompagnement moteur)

amount of substance quantité de matière; ~ **of traffic carried** volume du trafic acheminé

amperage n intensité

ampere-hour (Ah) ampère-heure; ~ **meter** ampèreheuremètre

ampere-turn (a.t.) n ampère-tour

ampersand n ('and' sign: &) perluète ('et' commercial); esperluète

amplification n amplification; intensité sonore; ~ **addition** addition d'amplification; ~ **factor** facteur d'amplification; gain; ~ **ratio** rapport d'amplification

amplified adj complémenté

amplifier n amplificateur; ~ **attack time** temps de transition d'un amplificateur; ~ **chain** chaîne amplificatrice; ~ **detector** détecteur-amplificateur; ~ **gain** gain d'un amplificateur; ~ **noise** bruit d'amplificateur

amplifier-operated relay relais amplificateur

amplifier rack bâti d'amplificateurs; ~ **shelf** châssis des amplificateurs; ~ **stage** étage amplificateur; ~ **subrack** châssis des amplificateurs; ~ **tube** tube amplificateur

amplify v amplifier; ~ **current component** amplifier en courant

amplifying telephone handset amplificateur à l'émission

amplitude n amplitude; hauteur; ~ **(versus) frequency distortion** distorsion d'affaiblissement; ~ **(non-linearity) distortion** non linéarité d'amplitude; ~ **(shift) keying (ASK)** modulation d'amplitude; ~ **adjustment** ajustage d'amplitude; ~ **analysis** analyse d'amplitude

amplitude-change signalling signalisation télégraphique par courants à amplitudes différentes; formation des signaux par modulation d'amplitude

amplitude clipper écrêteur; ~ **clipping (of sync pulse separation)** alignement sur les fonds; ~ **compression** compression d'amplitude; ~ **control** réglage de l'amplitude

amplitude-corrected echo écho corrigé en amplitude

amplitude correction correction d'amplitude; ~ **discriminator** sélecteur d'amplitude;

~ **distortion** distorsion d'amplitude; distorsion harmonique; distorsion non linéaire; ~ **equalizer** circuit correcteur d'amplitude; ~ **equalizing** égalisation d'amplitude; ~ **error correction** correction de défauts d'amplitude; ~ **excursion** excursion d'amplitude

amplitude-frequency characteristic caractéristique de réponse amplitude/fréquence

amplitude hit variation d'amplitude; ~ **limiter** circuit d'écrêtage; limitateur d'amplitude; ~ **limiting** limitation d'amplitude; ~ **linearity** linéarité d'amplitude; ~ **lopper** circuit d'écrêtage; circuit écrêteur

amplitude-modulated oscillation oscillation modulée en fréquence

amplitude modulation (AM) modulation d'amplitude; ~ **modulator** modulateur d'amplitude; ~ **peak** crête d'amplitude

amplitude-quantized control/synchronization commande à quantification d'amplitude

amplitude ratio rapport d'amplitude; ~ **reduction** réduction d'amplitude

amplitude/response characteristic caractéristique d'amplitude

amplitude separation circuit circuit d'écrêtage; ~ **stabilization** stabilisation d'amplitude; ~ **variation** variation d'amplitude

ANA (assigned night answer) **station** poste de renvoi; ∻ (s. assigned night answer)

analog *adj* analogique; ~ **ground** masse analogique

analogue *n* équivalent; ~ *adj* analogique; électromécanique (EM); ~ **array computer** calculateur à réseau analogique; ~ **channel** voie analogique; ~ **circuit board** carte analogique; ~ **computer** calculateur analogique; ~ **data** données analogiques

analogue-digital conversion quantification; ~ **converter** traducteur analogique-numérique; ~ **multiplier** multiplicateur analogique/numérique

analogue earth masse analogique; ~ **exchange** commutateur électromécanique; ~ **gate** porte analogique; ~ **information** (data) information analogique; ~ **input** entrée analogique; ~ **integrated circuit** circuit intégré linéaire; ~ **line** ligne de rattachement; ~ **loop(-back)** boucle analogique; ~ **multimeter** multimètre à aiguille; ~ **network** réseau analogique; ~ **representation** représentation analogique; ~ **signal** signal analogique; ~ **switching** commutation analogique; commutation spatiale; ~ **time-division concentration** concentration temporelle analogique BF-BF

analogue-to-digital conversion (A-D conversion) conversion binaire; conversion bipo-

laire; conversion analogique-numérique (conversion A/N)

analogue transmission transmission analogique; ~ **trunk** jonction BF; circuit analogique; joncteur

analyser *n* contrôleur; analyseur

analysis *n* analyse; dépouillement; étude; contrôle; calcul; découpage; exploitation

analyst *n* analyste

analytical engine ordinateur universel; ~ **model** scénario de cadrage

anchored *adj* encastré

anchoring *n* haubanage (haubannage); ~ **wire** hauban

anchor tie haubanage (haubannage)

ancillary *adj* divers; annexe; auxiliaire; de servitude; périphérique; ~ **circuit** circuit auxiliaire; ~ **device/unit** organe annexe; ~ **equipment rooms** locaux de servitude; ~ **services** appartements de fonction; ~ **system** asservissement

AND circuit circuit conditionneur; circuit ET; ∻ **element** ET (organe/fonction); ∻ **function** (conjunction) intersection; conjonction; ∻ **gate** circuit ET; porte ET

AND-gate intersector intersecteur

AND-NOT exclusion; sauf

AND operation opération ET; intersection; multiplication logique; ∻ **operator** (&) opérateur de concaténation

AND/OR INVERT gate array réseau d'opérateurs ET/OU NON

'and' sign (&) 'et' commercial (perluète: &)

anechoic chamber chambre sourde; salle (anéchoïde) anéchoïque; ~ **studio** studio sourd

angle *n* angle

angled ray rayon incliné

angle-error measurement écartométrie

angle-iron *n* cornière; équerre

angle of approach angle d'arrivée; ~ **of arrival** angle d'arrivée; ~ **of departure** angle de tir; ~ **of diffraction** angle de diffraction; ~ **of dip** angle d'incidence; ~ **of discrimination** angle de discrimination; ~ **of flow** angle de passage; angle d'ouverture; ~ **of incidence** angle d'incidence; angle de calage; ~ **of site** angle de site; ~ **of weave** angle de tressage; ~ **tracking** pointage automatique

angular alignment (of rotors) concordance angulaire; ~ **aperture** ouverture angulaire; ~ **deviation loss** perte de déviation angulaire; ~ **displacement** déplacement angulaire; décalage angulaire; ~ **encoder** codeur angulaire; codeur de position; ~ **error** erreur angulaire; ~ **frequency** fréquence angulaire; ~ **grinder** meuleuse d'angle; ~ **momentum** moment (angulaire) cinétique; ~ **position encoder** codeur de rotation; ~ **resolution** pouvoir séparateur angulaire; ~ **run-out** écart d'usinage; ~ **spacing** angle d'espacement; ~ **velocity** vitesse angulaire

ANI (s. automatic number identification)

anisochronous *adj* anisochrone; ~ **transmission** transmission anisochrone

anisotropy *n* anisotropie

ANL (s. automatic noise limiter)

annealed *adj* recuit; ~ **conductor** fil recuit; ~ **tin-plated copper** cuivre recuit étamé

annotated *adj* commenté

annotation *n* commentaire

announce a call offrir une communication

announcement-only answering chip répondeur statique

announcement trunk ligne d'accès à une machine parlante

announcer (TV/radio) ~ speaker (speakerine)

annoyance effect gêne

annual charge charge annuelle; ~ **rate** redevance annuelle

annul *v* résilier

annular magnet aimant torique

annulus *n* anneau

annunciator *n* annonciateur; ~ **disk** volet d'annonciateur

anode *n* anode; plaque; anticathode; ~ **battery** batterie d'anode; batterie de plaque; ~ **breakdown voltage** tension anodique d'amorçage; tension d'allumage; ~ **characteristic** caractéristique de plaque; ~ **circuit** circuit anodique; circuit de plaque; ~ **conductance** conductance de tube électronique; ~ **current** courant anodique; courant de plaque; ~ **dark space** espace sombre anodique; ~ **detection** détection plaque; ~ **dissipated power** puissance dissipée par la plaque; ~ **drop** chute (de tension) anodique; ~ **efficiency** rendement de conversion; ~ **fall** chute (de tension) anodique; ~ **feed** alimentation plaque; ~ **glow** lueur anodique; lumière anodique

anode-grid capacitance capacité grille-plaque

anode hum ronflement d'anode; ~ **load** charge anodique; ~ **modulation** modulation sur l'anode; ~ **power input** puissance anodique absorbée; ~ **region** domaine anodique; ~ **resistance** résistance interne; ~ **stopper** impédance d'étouffement anode; ~ **supply** alimentation anodique; ~ **voltage** tension anodique

anode-voltage stabilized camera tube tube analyseur à électrons rapides

anodic *adj* galvanique

anodizing *n* oxydation anodique

anomalous propagation propagation anor-

male; ~ **value** valeur accidentelle

answer *n* réponse

answer-back code code de réponse; indicatif (IF); ~ **code request** demande d'indicatif; ~ **unit** émetteur d'indicatif

answer bit bit de réponse; ~ **hold** reprise d'une ligne en garde

answering cord cordon de réponse; ~ **delay** durée de sonnerie; ~ **jack** fiche de réponse; jack local; ~ **key** clé d'écoute; ~ **machine** repondeur; ~ **operator** opératrice de réponse; ~ **plug** fiche d'écoute; ~ **service** service des abonnés absents; ~ **station** station radioélectrique appelée; ~ **time of an operator** délai de réponse (d'opératrice); ~ **tone** tonalité de réponse; ~ **wave** onde de réponse

answer lamp lampe de réponse et de fin; ~ **message** message réponse

answer-only machine appareil pour annoncer; ~ **set** appareil automatique de réponse

answer signal signal de réponse; signal de décrochage du demandé; signal d'accusé de réception; ~ **supervision** phase de supervision

antecedent *n* (math.) dividende; ~ *adj* préalable

antenna *n* antenne; ~ **span** haubanage d'antenne

anti-blocking *n* antibourrage

anticipated *adj* prévu

anti-clockwise sens inverse des aiguilles d'une montre; sens trigonométrique; ~ **polarized wave** onde polarisée elliptiquement/(circulairement sinistrorsum)

anti-clutter facility dispositif contre les réflexions de mer; ~ **gain control** régulateur de sensibilité temporisé

anti-coincidence element (inclusive-OR gate) élément anticoïncidence

anti-dazzle *adj* anti-éblouissant; antireflet; ~ **screen** écran filtrant

anti-fading *n* anti-évanouissement; ~ **aerial** antenne à rayonnement zénithal réduit

anti-flare anti-éblouissant

anti-hunting antipompage; antivibratoire

anti-jamming (AJ) *n* antibrouillage

anti-node *n* boucle; ventre

anti-noise telephone téléphone à dispositif antilocal

anti-phase *adj* en opposition de phase

anti-reflection coating couche antireflet

anti-resonance résonance shuntée

anti-resonant circuit circuit bouchon; circuit antirésonnant

anti-rust coating revêtement anticorrosif

anti-sidetone circuit circuit anti-local

anti-static *adj* électrofuge

anti-surge (delay) **fuse** fusible retardé; ~ **fuse** fusible temporisé

anti-symmetric graph graphe antisymétrique

anti-tinkle (circuit) inhibition sonnerie; ~ **circuit** (of ringer) anti-tintement; shunt sonnerie

anti-twist guying haubanage anti-torsion

AOC (s. automatic overload control)

AOCS (s. attitude and orbital control system)

A-operator téléphoniste des positions A

APD (s. avalanche photodiode)

aperiodic adj apériodique; acyclique; ~ **aerial** antenne apériodique; ~ **circuit** circuit apériodique; ~ **damping** affaiblissement apériodique

aperture n trou; ouverture; fenêtre; découpe; ajour; lumière; jour; embouchure; ~ **aberration** aberration d'ouverture; ~ **admittance** admittance d'ouverture; ~ **aerial** antenne à ouverture; ~ **area** aire d'ouverture; ~ **card** carte à fenêtre; ~ **distortion** distorsion de l'ouverture; ~ **distortion** (of facsimile) distorsion d'exploration; ~ **illumination** répartition du champ sur l'ouverture; ~ **plate** grille

apex n sommet; ~ **inductor** inductance d'apex

apogee n apogée

A-polarity polarité A

A-position n opératrice de départ; position mixte d'inscription et de départ (position A); opératrice locale; ~ **demand working** méthode de simple appel à service rapide; ~ **working** méthode de simple appel

apparatus n appareil; dispositif; organe

apparent angle of approach angle apparent d'arrivée; ~ **attenuation** affaiblissement apparent; ~ **power (in VA)** puissance délivrée; puissance apparente

append v enchaîner

appendix n annexe

Appleton layer couche F

appliance n appareil; dispositif; outil

appliances n matériel

applicable adj valable

applicant n demandeur

application n application; ~ **class** catégorie d'exigence; ~ **program** programme d'application; programme utilisateur

applications package progiciel d'application; ~ **software** logiciel d'application; progiciel

applied data bit bit de données appliqué; ~ **power** puissance appliquée; ~ **signal characteristics** caractéristiques du signal appliqué; ~ **signal voltage** tension d'entrée d'un signal

applique circuit circuit additif

apply v poser; délivrer; présenter; injecter

appointment call conversation avec avis

d'appel (AVP); conversation fortuite à heure fixe

appointments reminder rappel rendez-vous

apportionment n imputation; répartition; ventilation

appraisal n avis; évaluation; contrôle

appreciably adv sensiblement

approach cable câble d'atterissage; ~ **control radar** radiodétecteur d'approche; ~ **radar** radar d'approche à multiplexage

approval n homologation; agrément; ~ **conditions** conditions d'approbation; ~ **test** essai d'homologation; essai d'approbation

approved adj agréé

approximate(d) adj approché

apron n aire plane; tablier

APS (s. automatic protection switch)

A.R. (s. as required)

arbiter n bascule de prise

arbitrary adj aléatoire; ~ **sequence computer** calculateur séquentiel à enchainement arbitraire

arbitration, (off-line) ~ **(of interlock/contention situation)** mise en autonomie

arbor n arbre; broche; axe

arc v amorcer

arc-back n retour d'arc; allumage en retour

arc cathode cathode à arc; ~ **discharge** décharge en arc

arc-discharge tube tube à décharge en arc; ~ **valve** tube à décharge en arc

arc drop (voltage) chute (de tension) dans l'arc

arc-drop loss pertes dans l'arc

architecture n architecture

archive file fichier d'archivage

arcing n claquage

arc lamp lampe à arc; ~ **loss** pertes dans l'arc

arc-over n contournement; amorçage

arc resistance résistance à l'arc

arc-suppressor coil bobine d'équilibrage; bobine d'extinction

arc-through raté de blocage

arc welding soudure électrique

arduous adj laborieux

area n zone; région; domaine; champ; place; ~ **code** indicatif régional (IR); code de zone; code de région; ~ **coverage** couverture d'aire; ~ **exchange** centre de zone; ~ **identification (AID)** identification de zone; ~ **separator (AS)** séparateur de zone

A-register (augend register) registre d'addition

argon rectifier redresseur à argon

argument n argument; clé; variable; ~ **(field)** champ; zone argument

arithmetical expression expression arithmétique

arithmetic and logic unit (ALU) unité arithmé-

tique et logique; bloc opérateur; opérateur
logique; unité de calcul; carte calcul;
~ **check** contrôle arithmétique; ~ **circuit**
circuit arithmétique; ~ **circuit board** carte
calcul; ~ **computer** calculateur arithmétique; ~ **IF** branchement conditionnel;
~ **instruction** instruction arithmétique;
~ **mean** moyen arithmétique; ~ **module**
(ALU) bloc de calcul; ~ **operation** opération arithmétique; calcul; ~ **progression**
série arithmétique; ~ **register** registre
arithmétique; registre opérateur; registre
mémoire; ~ **shift** décalage arithmétique;
~ **unit** logique
arm v armer; ~ n bras; branche; secteur
armature n armature; induit; roue polaire;
palette; garniture; équerre; ~ **circuit**
circuit d'induit; ~ **clearance** (of relay) jour
(au) poussoir; ~ **coil** bobine d'induit;
enroulement de l'induit; ~ **current** (I$_a$ - of
DC motor) couple; ~ **end connection**
connexion d'induit; ~ **relay** relais à
palette; ~ **winding** enroulement de l'induit
armchair interactive TV interactivité
armed adj activable; ~ **software task queue**
file de tâches logicielles armées
armour n blindage; armature; armure
armour-clad cable câble armé; câble blindé
armoured adj cuirassé; ~ **cord** cordon blindé
armourless cable câble non blindé
armour-plated adj blindé
ARQ (s. error correcting telegraph system)
arrangement n disposition; configuration;
schéma
array n rangée; série; configuration; disposition; ensemble; groupement; réseau; tableau; matrice; antenne; ~ **directivity**
directivité de réseau; ~ **factor** fonction
caractéristique (d'un réseau d'antenne);
~ **of bat-wing aerials** panneau de papillons
arrester n éclateur; déchargeur
arrive v (at) aboutir (à)
artery n artère
article n article; pièce (pce)
articulated adj jumelé; rabattable; remorqué;
~ **joint** lien de flexion
articulation n clarté; netteté; ~ **reduction**
réduction de netteté; ~ **reference equivalent**
affaiblissement équivalent pour la netteté
(AEN); équivalent de référence pour
l'articulation
artificial adj fictif; factice; ~ **aerial** antenne
fictive; antenne sans charge; ~ **black signal**
signal de noir artificiel; ~ **building-out line**
ligne artificielle de complément; ~ **call**
generator simulateur d'appels; ~ **dielectric**
diélectrique artificielle; ~ **ear** oreille
artificielle; ~ **earth** contrepoids d'antenne;

~ **extension line** ligne d'extension artificielle; ~ **intelligence** intelligence artificielle; ~ **line** ligne artificielle; ligne
acoustique (LA); ligne à retard (LAR);
complément de ligne; ~ **mouth** bouche
artificielle; ~ **satellite** satellite artificiel;
~ **traffic** trafic artificiel; ~ **voice** voix
artificielle; ~ **white signal** signal de blanc
artificiel
artist's impression dessin imaginé
ART method transmission avec signal de
référence additionnel
artwork n dessin; graphisme; traçage; tracé
(de carte); pistage; maquette; ~ **format**
document
ARU (s. audio response unit)
AS (s. area separator)
asbestos n amiante
ASC (s. automatic selectivity control)
ascender n (of printed character) hampe
ascending order ordre croissant
ascertain v déterminer; connaître; rechercher;
découvrir; apprendre
ascertained attenuation affaiblissement évalué
ascribe v attribuer; affecter
ASD (s. adverse state detector)
ASDE (s. airport surface detection equipment)
as delivered état de livraison
ASF (s. automatic sheet feed)
as fitted pièce montée (PM)
ash content teneur en cendres
asher n calcinateur
ashore adv à terre
A-side côté réception
A-side/B-side recto-verso
ASK (s. amplitude (shift) keying)
askew adj de côté; déréglé; désaxé; en biais
'as manufactured' condition (of materials) état
de livraison
ASMI (s. aerodrome surface movement
indicator)
aspect (even-handed assembly) décor (d'un
plan); ~ **card** carte de recherche; ~ **ratio**
rapport de dimensions; rapport de format;
rapport largeur/hauteur
ASR (s. automatic send-receive)
as required (A.R.) pour mémoire (PM);
éventuel; au choix; à titre d'information
assemble v monter
assembler n assembleur; autocode; ~ **instruction** instruction d'assemblage; ~ **language**
langage assembleur
assembly n assemblage; montage; jeu; réalisation; constitution; ensemble; installation;
bâti; regroupement; appareil; ~ **drawing**
dessin d'ensemble; dessin de montage;

~ **language** langage assembleur; langage d'assemblage; ordre assembleur; autocode

assembly-language instruction instruction assembleur

assembly line chaîne de production; chaîne; chaîne de montage; banc de montage

assembly-line production fabrication à la chaîne

assembly list liste d'assemblage; ~ **program** assembleur; ~ **pseudo-instruction** directive d'assemblage; ~ **routine** programme de traduction

assessed quality assurance (de la) qualité; conformité de qualité

assessment n évaluation; contrôle; calcul; bilan

asset n atout

assigment key clé de désignation

assign v affecter; attribuer; allouer; assigner

assigned access level niveau d'habilitation; ~ **frequency** fréquence nominale; fréquence assignée; ~ **night answer (ANA)** renvoi général (RG); ~ **night answer switch** interrupteur RG déporté (renvoi général); ~ **night answering service** service de nuit

assignee n cessionnaire du transfert

assignment algorithm algorithme d'assignation; ~ **demand (AD)** demande d'affectation; ~ **selector** sélecteur de désignation; ~ **statement** instruction d'affectation

assign values valoriser

assimilation n regroupement

assistance n assistance; intervention; ~ **code** indicatif d'appel d'une opératrice d'assistance; ~ **operator** opératrice d'assistance

assisted adj, (power-)~ assisté; ~ **voltage** tension d'assistance

associate(s) collaborateur(s)

associated homologue; apparentés; connexe; lié (à); ~ **interface** jonction affluente; ~ **mode** (of signalling) code (de signalisation) associé; ~ **mode of operation** mode d'exploitation associé; ~ **signalling mode** exploitation en mode associé

association n correspondance

associative storage mémoire rapprochée; mémoire associative

assorted adj divers

assumed value valeur théorique; valeur implicite

assuming that il est convenu

assumption n hypothèse

A-staged resin résol

astatic needle aiguille astatique

ASU (s. acknowledgement signal unit)

A-subscriber abonné demandeur (DR); abonné appelant

A-subscriber release rupture DR

asychronous transmission transmission asynchrone

asymmetric adj asymétrique; dissymétrique

asymmetrical aerial input entrée d'antenne asymétrique; ~ **circuit element** élément asymétrique d'un circuit; ~ **deflection** déviation asymétrique; ~ **dipole** dipôle asymétrique; ~ **distortion** distorsion asymétrique; distorsion biaise; ~ **starting diode** diode asymétrique; ~ **two-wire circuit** circuit asymétrique à deux fils; ~ **voltage** tension asymétrique

asymmetric sideband transmission transmission à bandes latérales asymétriques

asymmetry n asymétrie

asynchronous adj arythmique; asynchrone; anisochrone; ~ **communication interface** coupleur asynchrone; ~ **line controller** frontal de transmission en mode caractères; ~ **(byte) mode** mode arythmique; ~ **serial controller** coupleur série asynchrone; ~ **signalling** signalisation asynchrone; ~ **starting** démarrage en asynchrone; ~ **telephone network** réseau téléphonique asynchrone; ~ **transition switching** commutation de transitions asynchrones; ~ **transmission mode** mode discontinu; mode caractère; ~ **working** fonctionnement asynchrone

asyndetic adj (devoid of connectives) asyndétique

a.t. (s. ampere-turn)

at-a-time printer imprimante caractère par caractère

ATB (s. all-trunks-busy)

AT-cut (of crystal) coupe AT

at design stage à l'étude; ~ **equal and opposite potentials** en équilibre différentiel; ~ **eye-level** en regard; ~ **file** fichier indirection; ~ **full voltage** sous pleine tension

Atlantic cable câble transatlantique

at low level au niveau bas

ATM (s. automatic teller machine)

atmosphere n atmosphère

atmospheric adj atmosphérique; ~ **absorption** absorption atmosphérique; ~ **discharge** parafoudre; ~ **duct** conduit atmosphérique; ~ **electricity** électricité atmosphérique; ~ **fading** évanouissement atmosphérique; ~ **interference** perturbation atmosphérique; ~ **loss** affaiblissement atmosphérique; perte atmosphérique; ~ **noise** bruit atmosphérique

atmospherics (QRN) parasites atmosphériques; brouillage; bruit atmosphérique

atmospheric window region zone de la fenêtre atmosphérique

atomic number nombre atomique; ~ **weight**

poids atomique

at random au hasard; dans le désordre; ~ **rest** hors service (h.s.); ~ **sea** au large; ~ **short notice** dans un délai court

'at' sign (@) arobas ('a' commercial); arabesque

at stop à l'arrêt

attached *adj* (to) apposé (sur)

attaching *n* raccrochage

attachment *n* accessoire; adjonction; partie additive; connexion; dispositif

attack time temps de transition; ~ **time** (of expander) temps d'établissement

attempt *n* tentative

attendance *n* vacation; ~ **time** temps de présence

attendant *n* opératrice; standardiste; ~ **camp-on** mise en attente par l'opératrice; ~ **console** pupitre de service; poste central; poste dirigeur; poste de service; ~ **desk** pupitre d'opératrice; ~ **hold** mise en garde par l'opératrice; ~ **trunk** ligne d'ordre

attended *adj* surveillé; ~ **station** station surveillée; station normalement exploitée

attention *n* intervention

attenuate *v* affaiblir (s'); réduire; abaisser

attenuated band bande atténuée

attenuation *n* affaiblissement; atténuation; perte d'amplification; abaissement; ~ **characteristics** caractéristiques d'affaiblissement; ~ **coefficient** affaiblissement linéique; ~ **constant** constante d'affaiblissement; ~ **curve** courbe d'affaiblissement; ~ **distortion** distorsion d'affaiblissement; ~ **equalization** compensation d'affaiblissement; compensation d'atténuation; ~ **equalizer** correcteur d'affaiblissement; compensateur de la distorsion d'affaiblissement; égaliseur d'affaiblissement; ~ **factor** facteur d'affaiblissement

attenuation-frequency characteristic caractéristique affaiblissement-fréquence

attenuation increase augmentation de l'affaiblissement; ~ **limiting curves** gabarit d'affaiblissement; ~ **over a section of radio link** affaiblissement à travers d'un relais hertzien; ~ **pad** affaiblisseur; cellule d'affaiblissement; ~ **peak** affaiblissement maximal; ~ **per unit length** affaiblissement linéique

attenuator *n* affaiblisseur; complément de ligne; ligne d'affaiblissement; ligne artificielle; atténuateur; dispositif d'affaiblissement; ~ **pad** cellule d'atténuation

at the planning stage à l'étude

attitude *n* orientation; ~ **and orbital control system (AOCS)** système de commande d'assiette et d'orbite (SCAO); ~ **index**

indice de qualité objective

attraction *n* appel

attractive force (pull of coil) force attractive; puissance d'appel

attribute *n* attribut; caractéristique

attribution *n* imputation

attrition *n* perte; usure; ~ **rate** taux de perte(s)

audibility *n* audibilité; audition; ~ **threshold** seuil d'audibilité

audible *adj* audible; sonore; ~ **alarm** alarme sonore; avertisseur sonore; signalisation acoustique; ~ **busy signal** tonalité d'occupation; ~ **range** zone d'audibilité; ~ **ringing signal** tonalité de retour d'appel; signal audible d'appel; ~ **signal** signal sonore; ~ **signalling** signalisation audible

audience participation (of TV) interactivité; ~ **profile** courbe d'écoute

audio *n* phonie; ~ *adj* acoustique; audiofréquence; ~ **(VF/AF)** BF (basse fréquence)

audio(-frequency) amplifier amplificateur à basse fréquence; amplificateur basse fréquence; amplificateur BF

audioconference *n* audioconférence

audio control panel boite d'écoute

audio-frequency (AF) *n* audiofréquence; fréquence acoustique; fréquence vocale (FV); basse fréquence (BF); fréquence audible; fréquence musicale; ~ **response** fidélité de modulation; ~ **telegraphy** télégraphie harmonique; ~ **transmission** transmission à basses fréquences

audio generator générateur haute fréquence (HF)

audiogram *n* audiogramme

audiography *n* audiographie

audio input entrée son; ~ **level** niveau des fréquences vocales

audiomatics *n* audiomatique

audiometer *n* audiomètre

audiometric earphone écouteur audiométrique

audio-monitoring *n* contrôle d'écoute; ~ **device** voie d'écoute

audio on mise en service du ronfleur; ~ **on/off** (control) pilotage son; ~ **response** réponse vocale; ~ **response unit (ARU)** unité de réponse vocale (URV); ~ **signal** top sonore; ~ **stage** étage basse fréquence; ~ **switch** clé d'écoute; ~ **sync pulse tape** bande sonore topée

audit *n* contrôle de l'intégrité des données; nettoyage du logiciel; suivi; vérification; épuration

auditory system système auditif

audit program programme de cohérence; ~ **trail** analyse rétrospective; remontée par le chemin de propagation; trace du chemin suivi; vérification à rebours

augend *n* cumulande

aural *adj* acoustique; ~ **acuity** acuïté auditive; audition; ~ **direction finder** radiogoniomètre auditif

aurally handicapped malentendant

aural null accord silencieux; point mort; ~ **reception** réception à l'écoute

auroral absorption absorption aurorale; ~ **belt** zone aurorale; ~ **E layer** couche E aurorale; ~ **path** trajet auroral; ~ **reflection** réflexion à phénomènes auroraux; ~ **signal scattering** diffusion du signal auroral

authentication signal signal de validation

authority file liste normalisée

authorization *n* habilitation; homologation; visa; permis; droit; agrément; autorisation

authorized band bande permise; ~ **breakpoint** point interruptible; ~ **frequency** fréquence autorisée

auto-alarm connection connexion auto-alarme

autoclave (test chamber) autoclave

autocorrelation *n* autocorrélation

autodialler *n* composeur automatique de numéros; émetteur à numéroter automatique; numéroteur

autodialling *n* appel automatique

auto-dial list répertoire

autodyne *n* autodyne; ~ **oscillator** oscillateur autodyne; ~ **receiver** récepteur autodyne; ~ **reception** réception autodyne

auto-inductive coupling couplage auto-inductif

auto-manual exchange bureau mixte

automated *adj* automatisé; desservi en automatique; ~ **management** gestion automatisée; ~ **traffic** trafic automatisé

automatic account card feed reporteuse (= machine de report); ~ **acknowledgement** accusé de réception automatique; ~ **adaptive equalizer** égaliseur auto-adaptatif; ~ **aiming** pointage automatique; ~ **alarm call** réveil automatique; ~ **amplitude control** réglage automatique d'amplitude; ~ **answering** réponse automatique; ~ **calibration** tarage automatique; ~ **call** appel automatique; ~ **call-back** rappel automatique; reprise automatique d'appel); top d'annotation (de rappel automatique); droit à l'annotation (DAN); ~ **call-back - ring again** rappel automatique après occupation; ~ **call distribution system** autocommutateur de position(s) de réponse; ~ **call distributor (ACD)** distributeur d'appels automatique (DAA); ~ **call forwarding** (where the subscriber is absent) renvoi

d'appels en cas d'absence de demandé; ~ **calling equipment (ACE)** émetteur d'appel automatique; ~ **calling unit (ACU)** émetteur d'appel automatique; ~ **callmaker** composeur automatique de numéros; ~ **camp-on busy extension** droit à l'annotation (DAN); ~ **carriage** chariot automatique; ~ **case shift** inversion automatique; ~ **changeover** mutation automatique; passage automatique; permutation automatique; ~ **character generator** générateur automatique de caractères; ~ **circuit** circuit à exploitation automatique; ~ **(circuit-)breaker** disjoncteur automatique; ~ **clearing signal** signal de fin automatique; ~ **coding** codage automatique; ~ **control card** carte de commande auto; ~ **control engineering** l'automatique; ~ **controller** automate; ~ **control systems** les automatismes; ~ **data processing** traitement automatique des données; ~ **design engineering** automatisation des dossiers d'étude; ~ **dialler** composeur automatique de numéros; ~ **dialling** appel automatique; ~ **dial service** service de sélection automatique; ~ **equalizer** égaliseur automatique; ~ **error-correction** correction automatique des erreurs; ~ **error-detection** détection automatique d'erreurs; ~ **exchange** autocommutateur; bureau central automatique; l'automatique; ~ **exchange operation** opération de central automatique; ~ **flying object identification** identification automatique d'objets volants; ~ **free-phone service** appel automatique-service libre; ~ **frequency control (AFC)** commande automatique de fréquence (CAF); réglage automatique d'accord; régulateur automatique de fréquence; ~ **front feed (AFF)** introducteur frontal; ~ **gain control (AGC)** commande automatique de gain (CAG); réglage automatique du gain; réglage automatique de sensibilité; anti-évanouissement; antifading; régulateur automatique de gain; ~ **gain control with squelch** commande automatique de gain avec (réglage) silencieux; ~ **gain stabilization** stabilisation automatique de bruit; ~ **gain/volume control (AGC/AVC)** régulateur automatique de sensibilité; ~ **grid bias** polarisation automatique (de grille); ~ **holding** occupation automatique; ~ **interlocking** couplage automatique; ~ **interrupt** interruption automatique; ~ **last number repetition** répétition automatique; ~ **long-distance service** service interurbain automatique; ~ **message accounting (AMA)** comptabilité automatique des appels (CAA); taxation automatique avec justification; taxation automatique avec justificatifs; ~ **message recording and accounting** enregistrement et calcul automatique; ~ **messaging** boulisterie automatique; ~ **noise limiter (ANL)** limiteur automatique des parasites; ~ **number identification (ANI)** retransmission des numéros; enregistrement automatique des numéros (EAN); ~ **numbering transmitter** numéroteur automatique; émetteur à numéroter automatique; ~ **operation** exploitation automatique; ~ **operator recall** rappel automatique du poste opérateur; ~ **overload control (AOC)** réglage automatique de surcharge; ~ **protection switch (APS)** dispositif automatique de commutation; ~ **protection switching data** information de sécurisation; ~ **radio compass** radiogoniomètre de bord automatique; ~ **radio monitor** contrôleur automatique d'émission; ~ **range** détermination automatique des coordonnées; ~ **reactivation of call-back requests** relance automatique des demandes de rappel; ~ **recall** reprise de présélection; rappel temporisé; ~ **recall (when free)** reprise automatique d'appel; ~ **reconfiguration** reconfiguration automatique; ~ **relocation** reprise automatique; ~ **repeat attempt** répétition automatique de tentative; ~ **repeat dialling** enregistrement automatique du numéro d'appel; réémission d'appel sur ligne occupée; ~ **repeat dialling device** appareil envoyeur automatique; ~ **reset** réenclenchement automatique rapide; ~ **retransmission** retransmission automatique; ~ **ringing** appel dirigé; ~ **ringing (current) trip** arrêt automatique d'appel; ~ **search jammer** brouilleur automatique d'exploration; ~ **selection (Strowger)** sélection automatique; ~ **selectivity control (ASC)** commande automatique de sélectivité; ~ **send-receive (ASR)** émission-réception automatique; ~ **sequential connection** connexion automatique en séquence; ~ **sheet feed (ASF)** alimentation feuille à feuille; ~ **signalling** signalisation automatique; ~ **speed control** accélération automatique; ~ **station** station autocommandée; ~ **station identification device** appareil automatique d'identification de stations; ~ **stop** arrêt automatique; ~ **switch** commutateur automatique; disjoncteur automatique; ~ **switching centre** autocommutateur; central automatique; ~ **switching equipment** équipement de commutation automatique; ~ **switching system** système de commutation automatique; ~ **system** système automatique;

~ **tandem-working dial system** exploitation par central tandem automatique; ~ **telegraph transmission** télégraphie à bande perforée; ~ **telephone answering machine** répondeur téléphonique automatique; ~ **telephony** téléphonie automatique; ~ **teleprinter exchange** central automatique de téléimprimeurs; ~ **teller machine (ATM)** guichet automatique bancaire (GAB); ~ **test** essai automatique; ~ **tester** dispositif d'essai automatique; ~ **tie-line (50 Hz) pulse signalling** à signalisation impulsionnelle automatique; ~ **tie line** ligne interautomatique; ~ **tie trunk** ligne interautomatique; ~ **time-out** rappel temporisé; ~ **timer** interrupteur horaire; ~ **toll-call restriction** discrimination automatique; ~ **toll ticketing** taxation automatique avec justificatifs; ~ **tracking** poursuite automatique; ~ **traffic** trafic automatique; ~ **transfer** renvoi temporaire (commandé); renvoi temporaire variable; ~ **transit exchange** centre de transit automatique; ~ **transmission measuring set** appareil automatique de mesure de la transmission; ~ **transmitter** émetteur autocommandé; ~ **transmitter with controlled tape-feed mechanism** émetteur automatique à commande par impulsion

automatic-tripping fuse-carrier préhenseur
automatic trunk exchange central automatique interurbain; interurbain automatique (IA); ~ **trunk redial** répétition automatique; ~ **trunk test device** hypsomètre; ~ **tuning** accord automatique; ~ **voltage regulator** régulateur automatique de tension; ~ **volume contractor** compresseur; ~ **volume control (AVC)** commande automatique de volume (CAV); régulateur automatique de niveau; ~ **volume expander** expanseur
automation n automatisation
automaton n automate
autonomy n autonomie
auto-switching exchange central pour trafic mixte
autosyn n arbre électrique; selsyn; synchro
autotransformer n autotransformateur
auxiliary circuit circuit auxiliaire; ~ **condition of a modulation** état auxiliaire d'une modulation; ~ **electrode** électrode auxiliaire; ~ **gap** trajet de décharge auxiliaire; ~ **jack** jack auxiliaire; jack d'entr'aide; ~ **plant** servitude(s); ~ **processor interface** (module) couplage entre processeurs auxiliaires; ~ **register** registre mémoire; ~ **route** voie d'acheminement auxiliaire; ~ **store** mémoire auxiliaire; ~ **telephone** station sous-directrice; ~ **transmitter** émet-

teur d'appoint

availability check contrôle de disponibilité

available *adj* disponible; libre; ~ **circuit** circuit disponible; ~ **input noise power** puissance de bruit disponible à l'entrée; ~ **input signal power** puissance de signal disponible à l'entrée; ~ **line** ligne libre; ~ **noise power** puissance de bruit disponible; ~ **output signal power** puissance de signal offerte par la sortie; ~ **power** puissance disponible

avalanche diode diode de Zener; diode en régime d'avalanche; diode avalanche; ~ **photodiode (APD)** diode à avalanche P-PN; ~ **voltage** tension avalanche

AVC (s. automatic volume control)

average *n* valeur moyenne; moyen; ~ **bias current** courant de polarisation moyen; ~ **call duration** durée moyenne d'appel; ~ **conditional information content** contenu conditionnel moyen de l'information; ~ **delay** délai moyen d'attente; temps moyen d'attente; détente moyenne; ~ **detector** détecteur de valeur moyenne; ~ **failure rate** taux de défaillance moyen; ~ **forward voltage** tension directe moyenne; ~ **holding time** durée moyenne d'occupation; ~ **information content** contenu moyen de l'information; ~ **information**

rate débit moyen de l'information; ~ **message service time** durée moyenne des messages; ~ **message size** dimension moyenne des messages; ~ **output rectified current** courant direct moyen; ~ **rate of change of output signal** pente moyenne du signal de sortie; ~ **reverse current** (with I$_O$ specified) courant inverse moyen (avec I$_O$ spécifié); ~ **speed** vitesse moyenne; ~ **traffic per working day** trafic moyen d'un jour ouvrable; ~ **transinformation** transinformation moyenne; ~ **waiting time** délai moyen de raccordement (DMR)

averaging *n* moyennage

Avometer (VOM) (amp-volt-ohmmeter: T.N) voltohmampèremètre

awaiting attention en instance

award *n* (of contract) adjudication

AWB (s. air waybill)

axial lead sortie axiale; ~ **ratio** taux d'ellipticité; ~ **ray** rayon axial; ~ **slot aerial** antenne à fentes axiales; ~ **strength** tenue axiale; ~ **termination** sortie axiale

axis *n* axe; ~ **of symmetry** axe de symetrie

axle *n* arbre; axe

azimuth *n* azimut; ~ **angle** angle d'azimut

azimuth-stabilized PPI indicateur panoramique stabilisé

B

babble n bruit de diaphonie; murmure confus
back n fond; ~ (of circuit board) côté soudure; ~ (of page) côté verso; ~ adj ancien; inverse; ~ (contact) repos; ~ **bearing** gisement vers l'arrière; ~ **bias** polarisation inverse; polarisation négative
back-biased adj bloqué; polarisé en inverse
backboard n fond de panier (FdP/FdeP/FDP); panneau arrière
backbone route artère principale; chemin hiérarchique normal
back conductance conductance inverse; ~ **contact** contact de repos; contact arrière; ~ **contact** (of relay) lame fixe; ~ **cord** cordon de réponse
back-coupling n (à) réaction
back current courant de retour; courant inverse; contre-courant; ~ **discharge** décharge en retour; ~ **echo** écho arrière
backed by suivi de
backed-up by doublé par
back e.m.f. (electromotive force) f.c.é.m. (force contre-électromotrice)
back-end system système dorsal
back file fichier ancien
backfire n retour d'arc; allumage en retour; arc en retour
backflow n rideau gazeux
background n arrière-plan; fond; canevas; acquis; historique; ~ **features** décors; ~ **image** (normal/reverse video) rendu de l'écran
backgrounding n traitement non prioritaire; traitement de fond
background lighting luminance de fond; ~ **music** musique de fond; ~ **noise** bruit de fond; ~ **processing** traitement d'arrière-plan; ~ **program** programme secondaire; ~ **task** tâche de fond
back-haul radio link faisceau hertzien de déport
backing n (of adhesive label) support; ~ **medium** support; ~ **store** mémoire auxiliaire; mémoire d'appoint; mémoire de grande capacité; mémoire de masse; mémoire géant; mémoire supplémentaire; ~ **store device** terminal d'archivage
backlash n jeu; rebondissement; hystérésis (= hystérèse); ~ **current** courant inverse de grille

back lobe lobe arrière
backlog n arriéré; ancienneté; reliquat
backmatter n annexe
back-mounted adj à raccordement arrière
back-off (BO) n recul; **random** ~ temporisation aléatoire; ~ **hole** trou de dégagement
back-order n dus; reliquat; manquant
back-pack n récepteur portable; ~ adj mobile; portatif
back panel fond de panier (FdP/FdeP/FDP); ceinture
backplane n fond de panier (FdP/FdeP/FDP); panier arrière; panier d'alimentation; cadre arrière; bac à fils; carte mère; ~ **assembly** cadre arrière équipé
back (plane) connector connecteur en face arrière
backplane transporter chariot pour fonds de panier; ~ **wiring** câblage arrière
back plate plaque de fond; plaque support (= platine); contre-plaque; ~ **porch** palier arrière
backscatter n diffusion arrière; ~ **diagram/pattern** diagramme de rétrodiffusion
backscattering n rétrodiffusion
backscatter ionospheric sounding sondage ionosphérique par rétrodiffusion; ~ **measurement** mesure par rétrodiffusion
back-shell n raccord
back-shunt keying manipulation dans le circuit d'antenne
backslash barre inversée
backspace (BS) n recul; retour arrière; espace arrière; ~ **character** caractère d'espace arrière; ~ **key** touche de retour-arrière; ~ **pawl** cliquet de recul; cliquet rappel
back stop n butée d'arrêt
backswing n rebondissement
back-taper n contre-dépouille
back-to-back recto-verso
back-tracking n traitement inverse
back-up v sécuriser; ~ n complément; support; aide; auxiliaire; ~ adj complémentaire; supplémentaire; annexe; double; de reprise; de secours; ~ **copy** copie de déchargement; ~ **installation** double implantation; ~ **procedure** procédure de reprise; ~ **protection** protection de réserve; ~ **recording** sauvegarde; ~ **route** acheminement de secours

backward *adj* inverse; de retour; amont (en -); en arrière; décroissant; descendant

backward-acting à réaction

backward busying blocage vers l'arrière

backward-busying signal signal de blocage vers l'amont

backward channel voie de retour; canal de retour; voie secondaire; canal auxiliaire; ~ charge-metering taxation en arrière; ~ control commande amont (commutateur temporel); ~ counting comptage vers l'arrière; ~ difference operator opérateur décalage arrière; ~ direction sens en arrière; ~ echo écho arrière; ~ end demandeur (DR); ~ exchange central amont; ~ hold maintien par l'arrière; ~ indicator bit bit indicateur vers l'arrière; ~ interworking telephone event (BITE) événement téléphonique d'interfonctionnement vers l'arrière

backward-looking radar radar rétroviseur

backward metering comptage vers l'arrière; taxation avec renvoi des impulsions de taxe; ~ path voie retour; ~ potential tension de retour

backward-recall signal signal de rappel vers l'arrière

backward recovery remontée par le chemin de propagation

backward-release signal signal de libération de circuit

backward sending transmission arrière; ~ sequence number numéro de séquence vers l'arrière; ~ signal signal vers l'arrière; signal en arrière; signal en amont; ~ signalling signalisation vers l'arrière; renvoi en arrière; transmission arrière; ~ signal wire (E = "ear") fil RON (réception); ~ sort tri descendant; ~ transmission réémission; ~ wave onde inverse

backward-wave oscillator carcinotron; ~ tube klystron réflexe

back-wash *n* surmodulation; dépassement; ~ (= overswing diode) (diode de) retour

back wave onde réfléchie; onde récurrente; onde indirecte; onde de repos; onde stationnaire

bad *adj* faux; erroné; invalide; ~ block secteur inutilisable; ~ block (of data) zone défectueuse; ~ cell position emplacement défectueuse; ~ contact faux contact; mauvais contact

badge *n* badge; écusson; insigne; ~ reader lecteur de badges

bad joint mauvaise soudure; ~ location emplacement défectueuse; ~ payer abonné défaillant; ~ spot emplacement défectueuse; endroit défectueux

baffle *n* chicane; déflecteur; amortisseur; ~ plate plaque de déviation

bagpipes *n* bruit de cornemuse

bail arm presseur

baize *n* feutrine

balance *v* accorder; compenser; équilibrer; ~ *n* équilibre; symétrie; reliquat; solde; ~ about earth symétrie par rapport à la terre; ~ attenuator atténuateur d'équilibrage; ~ card carte stock; ~ control commande d'équilibrage; ~ counter totalisateur soustracteur

balanced *adj* équilibré; en équilibre différentiel; symétrique; ~ (signal) pair paire équilibrée; ~ (merge) sort rangement par interclassement; ~ Adcock direction finder radiogoniomètre (Adcock) à équilibreurs; ~ amplifier amplificateur symétriseur; ~ armature palette équilibrée

balanced(-wire) circuit circuit équilibré

balanced circuit circuit symétrique; ~ code code à somme bornée; ~ coil cadre équilibré; ~ distribution calepinage; ~ error erreur centrée; erreur symétrique; ~ feed alimentation symétrique d'antenne

balanced-frame aerial cadre équilibré

balanced line ligne équilibrée; liaison symétrique; paire équilibrée; ~ load charge symétrique; charge équilibrée; ~ load distribution équirépartition de charge; ~ mixer mélangeur équilibré; ~ modulator modulateur équilibré; ~ network réseau symétrique; ~ pair paire symétrique

balanced-pair cable câble à paires symétriques; ~ carrier cable câble à courants porteurs sur paire symétrique

balanced quadripole quadripôle symétrique; ~ terminal voltage tension symétrique; ~ to earth potential symétrique par rapport au 0V; ~ transformer transformateur de symétrie; transformateur d'équilibrage; ~ transmission line ligne de transmission équilibrée; ~ two terminal-pair network quadripôle à accès symétriques; ~ two-wire circuit circuit asymétrique à deux fils

balance error erreur d'équilibrage; ~ point point d'équilibrage; ~ ratio rapport d'équilibrage; ~ return loss affaiblissement d'adaptation; affaiblissement d'équilibrage; affaiblissement de symétrie; déséquilibre; ~ selector commutateur d'équilibrage; ~ to earth symétrie par rapport à la terre

balancing *n* équilibrage; compensation; mise en équilibre; ~ capacitor condensateur d'équilibrage; ~ coil enroulement; ~ fault erreur d'équilibrage; ~ impedance impédance d'équilibrage; ~ line ligne d'équili-

B

brage; ~ **loop** boucle d'équilibrage; ~ **net-work** réseau d'équilibrage; équilibrateur; équilibreur; ~ **of circuits** équilibrage de circuits; ~ **out** neutralisation; ~ **poten-tiometer** potentiomètre de compensation; ~ **relay** relais différentiel; ~ **transformer** transformateur d'équilibrage

ball n bille

ballast n charge; ~ **resistor** résistance de charge; résistance d'équilibrage; résistance ballast; ~ **shift** délestage

ball drive motor moto-réducteur

ballistic flight vol sans portance; ~ **galva-nometer** galvanomètre balistique; ~ **matrix printer** imprimante balistique

ballooning n balourd

ball race chemin de roulement

balun n transformateur asymétrique-symétri-que; transformateur symétriseur; boucle d'adaptation

banana plug fiche banane

band n bande; plage; voie; collier cranté; étendue; zone; canal; chaîne; collerette; ~ (of colour code) ruban; ~ **amplifier** amplificateur de bande; ~ **articulation** netteté pour les bandes; ~ **cable** câble plat; ~ **elimination** élimination de bande

band-elimination filter filtre d'élimination de bande; filtre d'arrêt; circuit bouchon; filtre coupe-bande; filtre éliminateur

band filter filtre de bande; ~ **gap** bande interdite

banding strip bande de cerclage

band limit limite de bande; ~ **microphone** microphone à ruban

bandolier packaging ("Ammo-pak") [T.N.] conditionnement en bande

bandpass n bande passante

band-pass amplifier amplificateur passe-bande; ~ **attenuation** affaiblissement de la bande passante; ~ **cell** cellule émission-ré-ception à large bande; ~ **filter** filtre passe-bande; ~ **filter diplexer** diplexeur à filtre passe-bande; ~ **filter section** cellule passe-bande; ~ **loss** affaiblissement de la bande passante

band printer imprimante à bande; ~ **rejection** élimination de bande

band-rejection filter filtre éliminateur (de bande); circuit bouchon

band selector sélecteur de gamme; ~ **sharing** utilisation commune de bande de fréquence

band-sharing signals signaux à bande com-mune

band-spread capacitor condensateur d'étale-ment de bande

band spreading étalement de bande

band-spreading device dispositif à bande étalée

band-spread receiver récepteur à bande étalée

band-stop circuit circuit anterésonant; ~ **filter** filtre d'élimination de bande; filtre coupe-bande; circuit bouchon; filtre de réjection à flancs raides; filtre éliminateur

band-stop/high-pass analogy correspondance entre filtres passe-haut et filtres à élimina-tion de bande

band switch commutateur de bande; ~ **switch-ing** commutation de la bande

band-wide toutes-ondes

bandwidth n bande passante; largeur de bande; passe bande; bande utile; ~ **char-acteristic** caractéristique puissance de sor-tie/fréquence de travail; ~ **compression** compression de largeur de bande; ~ **condi-tioning** adaptation sur la longueur de bande; ~ **control** commande de sélectivité; ~ **down** largeur de bande pour transmission satellite-terre; ~ **reduction** compression de largeur de bande

bank n banque; bâti; batterie; bras; étage; faisceau; groupe; groupement; massif; pool (de machines); rampe; rangée; série (en -); ~ (of resistors) banc; ~ (of lamps) herse; ~ (of keys) pavé; ~ (of contacts) série

bank-and-wiper switch sélecteur à deux mou-vements; sélecteur à double mouvement

bank angle angle d'inclinaison latérale; ~ **cable** câble de multiple

banked (of keyboard layout) en corbeille

bank multiple champ multiple; arc

banknote/bill dispenser distributeur de billets (dibi)

bank of contacts banc de broches; couronne de contacts; ~ **of resistors** batterie de résistances; ~ **of selectors** banc de sélec-teurs; étage de sélecteurs; ~ **of switches** étage de sélecteurs

banner n page de garde; ~ (page) bannière; ~ **file** fichier page de garde

bar v interdire; ~ n barre; barrette; bâtonnet; lame; tige; ~ (of printer head) enclume

bar-and-post transformer transformateur (de mode) par barre transversale

bar code code à barres; code à bâtonnets

bar-code scanner lecteur optique

bare adj nu; dénudé; ~ **conductor** conducteur nu; ~ **drain** drain ouvert; ~ **wire** fil nu aérien; ~ **wiring** câblage en fil nu

barge-in intervention en tiers; offre en tiers; intervention prioritaire; entrée en tiers

bar graph histogramme

BARITT diode (barrier injection transit time) diode BARITT

Barkhausen effect (magnetization) effet Bar-khausen

bar printer imprimante à barre

barrage jammer brouilleur à large bande; ~ **jamming** brouillage volontaire à large bande

barred adj interdit; bloqué; impossible; ~ **access** interdiction; service restreint; accès unilatéral; ~ **code** indicatif de service restreint; ~ **level tone** tonalité de niveau interdit; ~ **numerical code** indicatif de service restreint

barrel n barillet; canon; douille; ~ **distortion** distorsion en tonneau; distorsion en barillet; tonnelage

barrelling tonnelage

barrel printer imprimante à cylindre

barretter n résistance de charge; résistance d'équilibrage

barrier code code d'arrêt; ~ **frequency** fréquence de coupure; ~ **layer** couche d'arrêt; couche de barrage; zone de charge d'espace

barrier-layer capacitance capacité d'une couche d'arrêt

barrier strip réglette à bornes; répartiteur à vis; barrette à visser; domino; ~ **transformer** transformateur d'isolement

barring n interdiction

bar waveform signal comportant une barre

base n base; pied; culot; semelle; socle; support; fond; infrastructure; massif; racine; ~ (border layout of PCB/backplane) fond de plan; ~ (material) plaque stratifiée; ~ (for cable ties) support serre-câble; ~ **address** adresse de base; adresse (de) début; adresse d'implantation; adresse d'origine; adresse logique; adresse primitive; ~ **address displacement** déplacement; ~ **aerial** antenne fixe

baseband n bande de base; ~ **amplifier** amplificateur de bande de base; ~ **attenuation equalizer** circuit correcteur d'atténuation à bande de base; ~ **bandwidth** largeur de bande de base; ~ **combiner** combinateur de bande de base; ~ **converter** émetteur-récepteur en bande de base; ~ **signalling** signalisation en bande de base

base board plinthe; ~ **clipping** taux d'ébasage; ~ **(DC) current** courant (continu) de base; ~ **cut-off current** courant résiduel de la base

based adj implanté; ~ **variable** variable pointée

base electrode électrode de base; ~ **impedance** impédance de base; ~ **line** ligne de base; niveau 0 (zéro)

base-line extension prolongement de ligne de base

base load charge minimale; ~ **metal** métal vil;

~ **notation** base de numération; ~ **number** nombre de base; ~ **of yoke** fond de gorge; ~ **pin** broche de culot; ~ **plate** plaque d'assise; plaque de base; platine; semelle; patin; ancrage; ~ **range-finder** radiotélémètre; ~ **rate (charging) area** circonscription de taxe; ~ **register** registre de base; registre d'adresses; ~ **segment** section base; ~ **spreading resistance** résistance interne de la base; ~ **station** station de base; ~ **terminal** borne de base; ~ **transmission factor** taux de transit

basic cell élément de base; ~ **clock rate** cycle de base; ~ **coding** codage de base; ~ **diagram** schéma de principe; ~ **dimension** cote nominale; ~ **diversion** transfert; ~ **features** présentation; ~ **group** groupe primaire de base; ~ **group formation** formation de groupe de base; ~ **group translation** transposition de groupe de base; ~ **instruction** instruction élémentaire; instruction primitive; ~ **metered unit** unité de taxe; taxe de base; unité de base (de taxation); taxe unitaire; ~ **operating system** niveau de base; ~ **outlines** généralités; ~ **path attenuation** affaiblissement idéal de propagation; ~ **qualifications** niveau de base; ~ **reference atmosphere** atmosphère fondamentale de référence; ~ **repetition rate** cadence de base; ~ **routing line** ligne d'acheminement principale; ~ **signal** signal de base; sématème; ~ **supergroup** groupe secondaire de base; ~ **15 supergroup assembly** assemblage de base de 15 groupes secondaires; ~ **system** système de base; ~ **task** tâche élémentaire; ~ **training** formation de base

basis metal (NOT base metal) métal de base

basket n panier

bass n son grave; ~ **boosting** amplification des graves; ~ **control** réglage des graves; ~ **unit** haut-parleur de graves

batch v regrouper; ~ n lot; série; recueil; groupe; ~ adj global; en série; ~ **counter** compteur totalisateur

batching n groupage par lots

batch mode mode différé; ~ **processing** traitement par lots; traitement de masse; travaux de masse; accès séquentiel; ~ **size** effectif du lot; ~ **transmission** vélotraitement

bath-tub characteristic courbe de décalage en baignoire

batten n herse; tasseau

battery n batterie; groupe; pile électrique; pile galvanique; élément d'accumulateur; ~ **amplifier** amplificateur batterie; ~ **back-up** sauvegarde par batteries;

B

~ **boosting** suralimentation; ~ **capacity indicator** accumètre; ~ **charger** chargeur d'entretien; chargeur d'égalisation; groupe de charge; ~ **dialling** numérotation à circuit de retour par la terre; ~ **discharge time** autonomie de batterie; ~ **element** pile
battery-holder *n* coupleur de piles
battery interconnection cable (BIC) câble d'interconnexion batterie; ~ **lead** fil de batterie
battery-powered *adj* alimentation par pile
battery receiver récepteur à batteries; ~ **reversal** inversion de batterie (IB)
battery-reversal relay relais d'inversion de batterie
battery supply pont d'alimentation; ~ **supply circuit noise** bruit d'alimentation; ~ **testing** test par la batterie
bat-wing aerial antenne en papillon
Baudot apparatus appareil Baudot; ∻ **code** code Baudot; ∻ **printing telegraph** télégraphe Baudot
baud rate vitesse en bauds
bay *n* baie; travée; cadre; quai
bayonet coupling douille à baïonette
bazooka *n* transformateur symétriseur; boucle d'adaptation
BBD (s. bucket-brigade device)
BBM (s. break-before-make contact)
B-board *n* opératrice d'arrivée; opératrice translatrice
B-box registre de base; registre d'adresses; registre index; registre de cumul
BCD (s. binary-coded decimal)
BCH (s. bids per circuit per hour)
BCS (s. block-check sequence)
BDV (s. breakdown voltage)
beacon *n* balise; émetteur; phare; repondeur; ~ **channel** (of R/T) voie balise
bead *n* bille; perle; micromodule
beaded transmission line ligne de transmission à isolateurs d'écartement
beading *n* baguette
beaker *n* pichet
beam *n* faisceau; pinceau; ~ (of square) chapeau; ~ **aerial** antenne à faisceau; antenne apériodique; antenne directionnelle; antenne projecteur; ~ **alignment** alignement du faisceau; ~ **angle** angle de faisceau; ~ **aperture** ouverture du faisceau
beam-approach beacon system radiodétecteur d'approche aux instruments
beam axis axe du faisceau; ~ **current** courant du faisceau; intensité de faisceau; courant de rayon
beam-current modulation modulation de densité
beam direction angle de rayonnement; ~ **lead**

circuit intégré à poutre; conducteur poutre; micropoutre; ~ **lobe switching** variation d'orientation d'un faisceau
beam-off position fermeture de faisceau
beam positioning calage du faisceau
beam-power valve tube de puissance à faisceau électronique
beam splitter à lames semi-réfléchissantes; ~ **store** mémoire à faisceau; ~ **switching** radiodéction à basculement de diagramme
beam-switching tube tube compteur
beam transmitter émetteur directionnel; ~ **tube** tube à rayon double; ~ **waveguide feed** cornet à source périscopique; ~ **width** largeur (angulaire) d'un faisceau électromagnétique; surface caractéristique de directivité
bearer *n* porteur; ~ **cable** câble porteur; ~ **channel** voie porteuse; voie support; ~ **circuit** (telegraphy) circuit support; ~ **frequency** fréquence de la porteuse
bearing *n* gisement; palier; relèvement; ~ **deviation** déviation de relèvement; ~ **error** erreur de relèvement; ~ **field** champ de relèvement; ~ **or elevation measurement** détermination automatique des coordonnées; ~ **oscillation** balancement du relèvement; ~ **pin** axe de roulement; ~ **plane** (of balance beam) palier; ~ **position** point d'appui; ~ **sense** sens du relèvement; ~ **sense switch** commutateur du sens de relèvement; ~ **surface** face d'appui; plan d'appui
beat *n* battement; ~ **amplitude** amplitude de battement; ~ **frequency** (of heterodyne) fréquence de battement; ~ **in** (of cables) mâter
beating *n* battement; ~ **oscillator** oscillateur local final; hétérodyne
beat reception réception hétérodyne
beaver-tail aerial antenne à faisceau étalé; ~ **beam** faisceau (électromagnétique) plat horizontal; faisceau en queue de castor
Becquerel (photo-electrolytic) **effect** effet Becquerel; ∻ **cell** élément photochimique
bed *n* table; berceau; support; massif; carlingage; platine
bedding-in scellement
bed-of-nails *n* planche à clous; machine à pointes
beep *n* bip; signal sonore
be fully conversant with maîtriser
begin form description (BFD) début de description de feuille
beginning *n* début
beginning-of-data block label/identifier (BLID) identificateur de début de données
beginning-of-file label/identifier (BOFI) iden-

tificateur de début de fichier
beginning of information marker label début d'information sur bande
beginning-of-tape (BOT) début de volume; ~ **label (BOT)** étiquette de début de bande; identificateur de début de bande
begit *n* binon
behaviour *n* comportement; conduite
BEL (s. bell character)
bell *n* sonnerie; sonnette
bell(-ringing) transformer transformateur de sonnerie
Bellboy [T.N.] téléavertisseur
bell button bouton poussoir (BP); ~ **character (BEL)** caractère d'appel; sonnette; ~ **crank** genouillère
Belleville washer rondelle Belleville
Bellini-Tosi (crossed-loop) aerial antenne à champ tournant; antenne à cadres croisés; antenne en tourniquet; ~ **(crossed-loop) direction finder** radiogoniomètre à cadres croisés
bell line ligne de sonnerie
bellows contact contact ressort
bell set sonnerie de poste téléphonique
bell-shaped insulator isolateur à cloche
bell signal signal de sonnerie; ~ **transformer** transformateur d'appel; ~ **wire** cordon plat; câble méplat
belt *n* zone
belted cable câble à isolement enroulé
bench *n* banc
benchboard *n* pupitre
benchmark *n* repère; cote; référence
benchmarking *n* évaluation; mesures de performances
bench-mounted impedance comparator comparateur impédance de table
bench shears cisaille d'établi
bend *v* cambrer; ~ *n* angle; coude progressif; ~ (of cable) charnière
bending *n* cambrage; flèche; pliure; ~ **angle** angle de courbure; ~ **radius** rayon de courbure; ~ **test** essai de flexion; essai de pliage; ~ **tool** cambreur
bent *adj* tordu; infléchi
benzine *n* essence
BER (s. bit error rate)
bespoke *adj* sur mesure; spécifique; à la demande; spécialisé; adapté (à)
beta particle particule bêta; ~ **ray** rayon bêta
better than au moins égale; supérieur à
bevel *n* biseau; angle oblique; ~ **gear** (assembly) pignons hélicoïdaux
bevelling *n* chanfreinage
bevel square fausse équerre
Beverage aerial antenne apériodique; antenne à effet directif

bezel *n* enjoliveur; drageoir; encadrement; collerette frontale
BFD (s. begin form description)
BFO (s. heterodyne (beat-frequency) oscillator)
BHCA (s. busy hour call attempt)
bias *v* biaiser; ~ *n* erreur non centrée; écart; polarisation; prémagnétisation; ~ (base address) base; ~ (voltage) tension de polarisation; ~ **check** contrôle par marges; ~ **current** courant de polarisation; ~ **distortion** distorsion asymétrique; distorsion biaise; distorsion dissymétrique; distorsion unilatérale
biased *adj* polarisé; ~ **automatic gain control** commande automatique de gain à seuil; ~ **beyond cut-off** (of transistor) bloqué; verrouillé; ~ **error** erreur systématique
bias error erreur non centrée
biasing *n* biaisage; ~ **battery** batterie de polarisation de grille; ~ **to cut-off** mise en blocage
bias resistor résistance de polarisation
BIC (s. battery interconnection cable)
biconditional operation élément anticoïncidence; non équivalence
biconical aerial antenne biconique
bid *n* tentative; ~ **counter** compteur de tentatives de prise
bidirectional *adj* bidirectionnel; orthogonal; ~ **characteristic** caractéristique bidirectionnelle; ~ **logic-seeking operation** (of printer) fonctionnement bidirectionnel optimisé
bids per circuit per hour (BCH) tentatives de prise par circuit et par heure
bifurcated contact(s) contacts jumelés; contacts doublés
bifurcation *n* dérivation
bilateral aerial antenne bidirectionnelle; ~ **control** commande bilatérale; ~ **current source** source de courant +ve et -ve
bill *v* facturer; ~ *n* facture; relevé de facturation
billable call appel taxé
billboard array rideau à plat directionnel
billet *n* galette
bill feed guide papier
billing *n* facturation; taxation; tarification; ~ **centre** centre de facturation de taxe (CFT); ~ **complaint** contestation de taxe; ~ **department** centre de facturation de taxe (CFT); ~ **machine** facturière; ~ **rate** taux de facturation; ~ **transaction** passe de facturation
bill pick-off unit ensemble prise billets
bimetallic *adj* bimétallique; ~ **conductor** conducteur bimétallique; ~ **strip** bilame
bin *n* case; casier; secteur; réservoir; puits;

cellule; bac à fils; ~ (of data on tape) bloc de données

binary *adj* binaire; bivalent; diadique; ~ **arithmetic operation** opération arithmétique binaire; ~ **card** carte binaire; ~ **chop** recherche binaire (dichotomique); ~ **chop sort** tri par dichotomie; ~ **code** code par tout ou rien

binary-coded character caractère codé (en) binaire; ~ **decimal (BCD)** binaire codé décimal; ~ **decimal notation (BCD)** numération décimale codée en binaire (DCB)

binary coding codage binaire; ~ **communications system** système de communication binaire; ~ **data capture** acquisition tout ou rien (TOR); ~ **digit (bit)** élément binaire (eb); information tout ou rien; chiffre binaire; symbole binaire; bit; ~ **digital signal** signal numérique binaire; ~ **digit rate** débit binaire; ~ **divider** bascule dédoubleuse; ~ **form** forme binaire; ~ **(full) adder** circuit additionneur binaire; ~ **look-up** recherche dichotomique; ~ **memory image** image mémoire; ~ **modulation** modulation tout ou rien; ~ **notation** numération binaire; ~ **number** nombre binaire; ~ **pair** (flip-flop) bascule binaire; ~ **point** virgule binaire; ~ **position** position binaire; ~ **PSK** (phase-shift keying) modulation à deux états de phase (MDP2); ~ **rate multiplier** diviseur binaire; diviseur de fréquence; ~ **serial signalling rate** débit binaire série; ~ **shift** décalage binaire; ~ **signal** variable logique (tout ou rien); ~ **synchronous communication (BSC, BI-SYNC)** transmission binaire synchrone; ~ **system** système binaire

binary-to-decimal conversion conversion binaire-décimal

binary tree arbre binaire; ~ **variable** variable binaire

bin card fiche de casier; carte stock

bind *v* attacher; ficeler; relier

binder *n* liant; filin; bande de cerclage; classeur

binding agent liant agglomérant; ~ **cradle** crochet d'arrêt

binding-head screw vis à tête cylindrique bombée large (CBL)

binding of single-phase circuits cerclage des circuits monophases; ~ **post** borne à vis; serre-fils; borne de connexion; ~ **station** poste de cerclage; ~ **wire** ligature; jonc

bin liner gaine de poubelle

binocular eyepiece binoculaire

binode (epitaxial rectifier) *n* binode; diode double

binomial *n* binôme; ~ **twist** guide en torsade

binomial

biometry (biological statistics) biométrie

biotechnology *n* biotechnique

biphase *adj* diphasé

biplex probe cordon biplex

bipolar *adj* bipolaire; ~ **code** code bipolaire; ~ **op-amp** ampli-op bipolaire; ~ **signal** signal bipolaire; ~ **signalling** signalisation à double courant; signalisation à courant double

bipolar-to-unipolar conversion conversion bipolaire-unipolaire

bipolar-transistor amplifier amplificateur à transistor bipolaire

bipolar violation viol de bipolarité

biquadratic *adj* bicarré

biquinary code code biquinaire

bird *n* satellite de communications

bistable (multivibrator) multivibrateur bistable; ~ **circuit** bascule; circuit bistable; ~ **memory** mémoire unitaire; ~ **trigger** circuit bascule bistable

bit *n* eb (élément binaire); symbole binaire; donnée; bit; élément numérique; impulsion; information tout ou rien; unité d'information binaire; variable logique (tout ou rien); signal; point-mémoire; binon; unité d'information; **(graphics)** ~ **plane** plan graphique; ~ **by bit** à la donnée; ~ **density** densité de bits

bite *n* octet

BITE (s. backward interworking telephone event)

bit error erreur de bit; ~ **error rate (BER)** taux d'erreurs sur les bits (TEB); ~ **field** champ d'éléments binaires; tranche de mot; champ de bits; ~ **holder (of power driver)** embout de visseuse; porte-embout magnétique; ~ **location** cellule; emplacement d'un bit; position binaire; ~ **map** table d'affectation binaire; relevé de bits

bit-mapped graphics graphisme par points

bit packing compression de chiffres binaires; bourrage d'impulsions; compression de données; ~ **pattern** combinaison binaire; positionnement sur eb; profil binaire; ~ **plane** plan graphique; ~ **rate** débit binaire; ~ **retrieval** obtention des bits; ~ **slice** tranche de bits

bit-slice bipolar microprocessor microprocesseur à tranches (en technologie bipolaire)

bit slip dérive de bits; ~ **soldering** soudage au fer

bits per second (bps) éléments binaires par seconde; bits par seconde

bit state positionnement sur eb; ~ **stream** train d'éléments binaires; flot d'information; débit; train numérique

B

bit-stream regeneration régénération du train numérique

bit string chaîne binaire; suite d'éléments binaires; chaîne de bits; ~ **string constant** constante sur bits; ~ **stuck at 1** un permanent; ~ **stuffing** justification; ~ **stuffing rate** coefficient de cadrage; ~ **switching** commutation d'éléments; commutation élément par élément; ~ **timing** rythme de bits; ~ **timing recovery** reconstitution du rythme incident; ~ **track** voie binaire; ~ **transparency** indépendance de la séquence des bits; ~ **width** largeur de bit

bivalent *adj* bivalent

BL (s. block and level diagram)

black-and-white monochrome; noir et blanc

black and white reception réception noir et blanc; ~ **box** automate; quadripôle

black-box approach analyse compartimentale

blacked over noirci

blacker-than-black infranoir

black-level clamping alignement du niveau du noir; calage du niveau du noir; verrouillage du niveau du noir; ~ **shift** défoncement du niveau du noir

blackodizing *n* noircissement chimique

black-out *n* absorption complète; ~ **time** temps des blancs

black signal signal noir

black-signal transmission transmission par signal noir

black washer rondelle brute

blade *n* palette; couteau; becquet (béquet); ~ **aerial** antenne lame; ~ **angle** angle de calage

blank *v* effacer; ~ *n* espace; caractère blanc; caractère inactive; zéro; cache; garde; ébauche; ~ *adj* blanc; postiche; vide; ~ (off) remplir; ~ **character** caractère nul; caractère espace

blanked clock horloge à discontinuités

blanket effect effet de masque

blank field zone blanche; ~ **fuse** faux fusible

blanking *n* obturation; suppression; blocage; ~ (of TV) effacement ligne; ~ (plate) remplissage; ~ **interval** intervalle de suppression; ~ **level** palier d'effacement; niveau de suppression; ~ **out** effacement; ~ **panel plate** obturateur; plaque d'obturation; plaque postiche; platine de bouchement; cache intermédiaire; drapeau; ~ **plug** bouchon obturateur; fiche fictive; fiche isolante; ~ **press** presse flan; ~ **pulse** impulsion de suppression

blanking-pulse generator générateur d'effacement

blanking signal signal de suppression; ~ **stage** stade de déclenchement périodi-

que; ~ **voltage** tension de suppression de faisceau; tension de verrouillage

blank key clé d'espacement; ~ **rivet** rivet tubulaire; ~ **space** espace invisible; ~ **storage** mémoire nue

blast *v* purger

bleed *v* purger

bleeder *n* diviseur; ~ **resistance** résistance de fuite; ~ **resistor** diviseur de tension

bleeding *n* ressuage; suintement

bleed screw vis de purge

bleep *n* bip

bleeper *n* sonnerie bip

blemish *n* tache; salissure

BLID (s. beginning-of-data block label/identifier)

blimp *n* cabine

blind *v* inhiber; masquer

blind(s) *n* persienne(s)

blind alley faux problème; ~ **angle** angle mort; ~ **area** zone de silence; ~ **copy** copie libre; ~ **hole** trou borgne

blind-landing system système d'atterrissage sans visibilité

blind operator opératrice aveugle; ~ **operator position** position aveugle; ~ **P** signe nouveau paragraphe (alinéa); ~ **rivet** rivet tubulaire; ~ **sector** secteur mort; ~ **speed** vitesse d'aveuglement

B-line registre de base; registre index

blink *v* clignoter

blinking *n* clignotement; ~ **indicator** feu clignotant; ~ **reverse (video) block** pavé clignotant

blip *n* top d'écho; trace fugitive

blister *n* ampoule; boursoufflure; bulle; cloque

blistering *n* cloquage

blob *n* bourrelet; point de soudure; ~ (of solder) goutte (= dépôt)

block *v* boucher; bloquer; comprimer; ~ *n* bloc; cale; canton; ~ (of data) pavé; zone; secteur; ~ **address** numérotation en bloc; ~ **and level diagram (BL)** schéma d'ensemble et de niveaux

blockboard *n* latté

block cancel character caractère d'annulation de bloc; ~ **changeover** mutation massive

block-check character caractère de contrôle par bloc; ~ **sequence (BCS)** séquence de contrôle par bloc

block contactor contacteur de puissance; ~ **copy** recopier en bloc; ~ **count** zone de comptage de blocs; ~ **cut-over** mise en service massive; ~ **diagram** schéma synoptique; schéma de fonctionnement; schéma de circuit unifilaire; schéma d'ensemble; schéma fonctionnel

B

blocked channels canaux bouchés; ~ **circuit** circuit bloqué; ~ **impedance** impédance en circuit ouvert; ~ **level** niveau inaccessible
block error erreur de bloc
block-error probability taux d'erreurs sur les blocs; taux d'erreurs sur les caractères
blockette *n* partie de bloc
block framing délimitation des blocs; ~ **gap** espace arrêt-marche; interva'le entre blocs; ~ **header** bloc début d'en-tête
block-ignore character caractère d'effacement par bloc
blocking *n* blocage; cantonnement; groupage; mis en bloc(s); embouteillage; compression; occupation; ~ **acknowlegement** accusé de réception de blocage; ~ **attenuation** affaiblissement de blocage; ~ **bias** tension de blocage; ~ **capacitor** condensateur d'arrêt; condensateur de blocage; ~ **circuit** circuit élémentaire; ~ **current** courant de blocage; ~ **device** dispositif de blocage; ~ **diode** diode anti-retour; ~ **factor** facteur de groupage; facteur de blocage; découpe en blocs; ~ **filter** filtre d'arrêt; ~ **generator** oscillateur à blocage; ~ **network** réseau à blocage; ~ **oscillator** oscillateur de blocage; ~ **period** temps de blocage; ~ **plan** plan de blocage; ~ **probability** taux de blocage; probabilité de blocage; ~ **resistance** résistance de blocage; ~ **signal** signal de blocage
block length longueur de bloc; ~ **list** liste de blocs; ~ **mark** caractère fin de bloc; marque de bloc; ~ **marker** drapeau bloc
block-mode terminal terminal synchrone
block move déplacement zone mémoire; ~ **multiplexer channel** canal multiplexeur de blocs; ~ **of data** bloc de données; ~ **separator** séparateur de blocs; ~ **serial number check(ing)** contrôle d'immatriculation; ~ **size** facteur de groupage; ~ **sort** tri par blocs; ~ **splitting** fractionnement de blocs; ~ **transfer** transfert par blocs
blooming *n* efflorescence; flou (en télévision); hyperluminosité de l'écho
blow *v* (of system) planter
blowback *n* agrandissement cathodique
blower unit bloc de ventilation
blowhole *n* piqûre; soufflure; microbulle
blown *adj* (of fuse) claqué; fondu
blown-in air air insufflé
blow-off *n* évacuation d'air
blowout-free handling manipulation sans destruction
blue-chip companies gros industriels
blueprint *n* schéma; tirage héliographique
blue-ribbon program programme vedette
blurring *n* flou (en télévision)

BO (s. back-off)
board *n* planche; plaque; platine; table; tableau; bloc; herse; ~ **extender** prolongateur de carte; ~ **extractor** extracteur de cartes; ~ **loader** programme de chargement de carte
board-mounted connector connecteur encartable
board-mounting embrochable
board of directors conseil d'administration
board-to-board wiring raccordement intercartes
bobbin *n* bobine; bobineau; carcasse; diabolo; fuseau
Bode plot/diagram diagramme de Bode
body *n* corps; ~ **contact** court-circuit à la masse
BOFI (s. beginning-of-file label/identifier)
boiler-plating *n* mémorisation de phrase; rappel d'une phrase; rapatriement
bold (print) bissé; ~ **character** caractère gras
bolometer *n* bolomètre; ~ **mount** monture pour bolomètre
bolt croppers cisaille à couper les boulons
bolting down spitage
bond *n* liaison; jonction
bonded *adj* collé
bonding *n* collage; grippage; métallisation; soudure; ~ **layer** couche de liaison; ~ **pad** plot de contact; ~ **strip** jarretière; ~ **substance** colle; ~ **to earth** mise à la masse; ~ **wire** fil de métallisation
bond strength force d'adhérence; pouvoir agglomérant; ~ **wire** câblette
bone-conduction headphone/receiver ossivibrateur; ostéophone; ~ **receiver** récepteur à conduction osseuse
book *v* réserver; ~ **a call** demander une communication téléphonique
booking *n* demande de location; enregistrement; inscription; ~ **position** position d'annotation
Boolean algebra algèbre booléenne; algèbre de Boole; ~ **calculus/logic** algèbre booléenne; algèbre de Boole; ~ **function** fonction booléenne; ~ **operation table** table de fonction booléenne; table de définition
boom *n* potence; girafe
boomer *n* haut-parleur de graves
boost *n* capuchon; gaine; ~ **charge** charge de fond
booster *n* survolteur; suralimenteur; suramplificateur; surpresseur; redresseur excitateur; circuit amplificateur; ~ **amplifier** amplificateur de puissance; ~ **battery** batterie tampon; ~ **diode** diode économisatrice; ~ **transformer** transformateur survol-

teur; transformateur élévateur; transformateur-suceur
boosting *n* amplification
booth *n* cabine; hotte
bootlace-lens aerial antenne lentille à lacets de chaussure
bootstrap *v* initialiser; ~ *n* amorce; ~ **amplifier** montage autoélévateur cathodique; amplificateur à contre-réaction; ~ **board** carte d'initialisation; ~ **circuit** circuit auto-élévateur; ~ **feedback** autoréaction mutuelle; circuit d'autogénération mutuelle; ~ **loader** chargeur en mémoire; procédure d'initialisation de chargement
bootstrapping *n* initialisation
bootstrap routine procédure de chargement initial; séquence d'initialisation; chargeur; préchargeur
B-operator téléphoniste des positions B
border *n* frontière
border-line *adj* marginal; tangente
bore *v* percer; ~ *n* calibre
boresight (direction) axe de visée
borne by à la charge de
borrow (negative carry) retenue d'impulsions en débit; retenue négative
boss *n* bossage; épaulement
BOT (s. beginning-of-tape label)
bothway (B/W) *adj* bidirectionnel; banalisé; à double sens; mixte; ~ **circuit** circuit bidirectionnel; circuit mixte; ~ **group** groupement mixte; ~ **junction** ligne de jonction utilisée dans les deux sens; ~ **local call** appel local banalisé (LB); ~ **operation** exploitation bidirectionnelle
bottleneck *n* embouteillage; engorgement; point d'accumulation; goulot d'étranglement
bottom *n* fond; bas
bottoming *n* coude de saturation; limitation absolue
bottom margin marge basse; ~ **of fillet** fond de filet; ~ **of form skip** saut bas de page; ~ **of memory** fin de la mémoire; ~ **of range** bas de gamme; ~ **plate** embase (connecteur fixe)
bottom-up method approche ascendante
bottom view vue d'en bas
boule *n* préforme
bounce *n* battement; signal vidéo transitoire; ~ **back** refléter; ~ **elimination** suppression de rebondissements; ~ **eliminator** système antirebond
bounce-eliminator flip-flop bascule antirebond
bounce-free antirebondissement
bounceless contact contact antirebond
bounce rate (of relay contacts) cadence de

battement; ~ **time** temps de rebondissement
bouncing busy hour heure de pointe variable
bound *v* délimiter; ~ *n* borne; ~ (key) fin de sélection (FIN SEL); ~ (of bucket) limite
boundaries *n,pl* gabarit; limite
boundary *n* borne; délimitation; frontière; marge; bord; cadrage; cloisonnement; seuil; délimiteur; taille (de zone/secteur); couche d'arrêt; couche de barrage; ligne de partage; interface; ~ **condition** condition limite; ~ **definition** alignement; ~ **marker** drapeau; sentinelle
bound charge charge superficielle
bounded *adj* aligné; borné
bound electron électron lié
bow *n* flèche; gauchissement; voilage; voile
bowl *n* (of lamp fitting) vasque
bow-tie aerial antenne papillon; antenne repliée; antenne trombone; ~ **dipole** dipôle replié
box *n* boîte; boîtier; cadre; caisse; carré vide; case; casier; parallélépipède; table; ~ (of batteries) panier
boxing (of graphic display) incrustation
box nut écrou moleté; ~ **of measuring rods** boîte de piges; ~ **of securing components** casier visserie; ~ **spanner** douille; ~ **wrench** clé en tube
B-position *n* opératrice d'arrivée; opératrice translatrice; position d'arrivée
bps (s. bits per second)
brace *n* bielle; croisillon; entretoise; étrier; raidisseur; tasseau; ~ (brackets) accolade crochet
bracing *n* haubanage (haubannage)
bracket *n* équerre; butée d'arrêt; chaise; compas; console; cornière; étrier; fourchette; patte; tasseau
bracket-mounted encastré
bradawl *n* pointe carrée
braid *n* (set of wire strands) fuseau
braid(ing) *n* gaine
braided bonding strip tresse de métallisation
braiding angle angle de tressage
brainstorming remue méninges
brake *n* frein
branch *n* dérivation; aiguillage; arête; bifurcation; branche; passage; renvoi; saut; transfert; transition; ~ (connection) embranchement
branch(ing) box boîte de dérivation
branch address adresse de branchement; adresse d'aiguillage; ~ **and bound** (search) exploration arborescente; ~ **cable** câble de branchement; ~ **circuit** circuit de distribution; circuit dérivé; ligne de branchement
branching *n* branchement; dérivation; ~ **box**

boîte de distribution

branch instruction instruction de branchement; instruction d'aiguillage; ~ **jack** jack
de dérivation

branch-off attenuation affaiblissement de
branchement

branch office délégation régionale

branch-off telegraph office central de service
échelonné

branchpoint *n* adresse de branchement;
bifurcation

brand *n* marque; désignation commerciale;
~ **loyalty** fidélisation

brazed *adj* soudé

brazed-helix technology technologie à hélice
brasée

brazier-head rivet rivet goutte de suif

brazing *n* brasage; brasure; soudure résistante

breach *n* violation

breadboard *n* maquette; avant-projet; ~ **circuit** montage expérimental (d'un circuit)

breadboarding *n* maquettage

break *n* rupture; coupure; interruption;
discontinuité; disjonction; ~ (of NC
contact) repos

breakable *adj* cassant

breakage *n* rupture

break-before-make contact (BBM) contact
repos-travail (RT)

break character caractère de liaison; ~ **contact** contact de repos; contact de rupture

break-contact unit dispositif de contact de
rupture

break current courant de disjonction; ~ **down**
v décomposer

breakdown *n* panne; isolement; perte; rupture; coupure; défaut; ~ (into sections)
découpage; décomposition; dépouillement; ~ (of gas) décharge disruptive;
~ (of insulation) perforation électrique;
~ **diode** diode de commutation rapide;
diode avalanche; ~ **knee** coude d'amorçage; ~ **point** résistance limite à la
rupture; ~ **signal** signal d'interruption;
~ **test** essai au percement; ~ **voltage**
(BDV) (V(BR)) tension de déchet; tension
de claquage; tension de rupture; tension
d'avalanche

break encoder codeur d'arrêt extérieur

breaker *n* rupteur

"breaker" (CB enthusiast) cébiste; cibiste

break-even *n* équilibre; ~ **analysis** analyse de
point mort

break-in *n* intervention opératrice; insertion;
intervention en tiers; offre; entrée en tiers;
intervention prioritaire; ~ **alert tone**
tonalité d'avertissement d'entrée

breaking capacity puissance coupée; ~ **current** courant de déclenchement (ID);
~ **load** charge de rupture

breaking-out *n* (of cable) éclatement

breaking strength résistance à la rupture

break-in hangover time temps de maintien
pour intervention; ~ **keying** manipulation
entre intervalles

break in on a transmission interrompre une
émission; ~ **jack** jack de coupure; jack à
rupture; ~ **key** touche d'interruption;
~ **line** ligne isolée; ligne veuve; ~ **off** (of
call) rompre

break-out *n* coulure; excentrage

break-out box maquette d'essais; testeur;
boîte de contrôle de jonction

breakover continuous (direct) voltage tension
(continue) de retournement; ~ **current**
courant de retournement; ~ **voltage**
(V(BO)) tension de retournement

break plate guitare

break-point *n* point d'arrêt; point de rupture;
halte; point de cassure; ~ **halt** arrêt
dynamique; ~ **instruction** arrêt dynamique

break pulse impulsion d'ouverture

breakthrough *n* raz-de-marée; percée; pénétration

break time (of dial pulses) temps d'ouverture

break-to-make ratio rapport d'ouverture sur
fermeture

break type type de coupure

break-type circuit layout schéma à manque de
tension; ~ **connection** liaison à manque de
tension

breast-plate microphone microplastron;
microphone plastron

breeder reactor réacteur à surrégénération

B-register (addend register) registre de base;
registre de cumul; registre d'index

Brewster, (pseudo-)∼ angle pseudo-incidence
brewstérienne; ∼ **angle** angle de polarisation; angle de Brewster

bridge *n* pont; étrier; cavalier; pontet; circuit
de conférence; passerelle; ~ **circuit**
connexion de pont; ~ **connection**
connexion de pont; ~ **contact** contact à
pont

bridge-control cord circuit cordon de
connexion avec pont; ~ **switchboard**
commutateur manuel à supervision par
pont de transmission

bridge diplexer diplexeur en pont

bridged tap branchement en dérivation

bridged-T network réseau en T ponté

bridge duplex connection système télégraphique duplex équilibré en pont; ~ **duplex
system** équipement duplex à pont; ~ **feedback** réaction équilibrée; ~ **filter** filtre en

pont; ~ **input current** courant de ré-équili-brage

bridge/lattice network pont diviseur

bridge network quadripôle; ~ **rectifier** pont de redresseurs; ~ **terminal** borne à étriers; ~ **timing circuit** circuit générateur de cadence en pont

bridgeware programmes d'adaptation

bridging *n* appontage; dérivation; court-circuitage; ~ **connector** réglette de dérivation; ~ **jack** jack d'essai; ~ **loss** affaiblissement dû à une dérivation; perte en puissance apparente due à une dérivation; ~ **time** (of relay) temps de collage

bridle *n* jarretière; ~ **wire** fil torsadé

brief *n* mission

briefing *n* réunion d'information

brief survey synoptique; ~ **tone burst** bip

brightness *n* brillance; intensité; lumière; luminosité; ~ (control) **potentiometer** potentiomètre de lumière; ~ **control** régulateur de brillance; ~ **variation** variation de la luminosité

bright-up signal signal d'allumage

bring on stream mettre en service

brittle component pièce cassante

brittleness test essai de fragilité

broadband *adj* (à) large bande; ~ **aerial** antenne à large bande; ~ **amplifier** amplificateur à large bande; ~ **cable network** réseau câblé de vidéocommunications; ~ **channel** canal à large bande; voie à large bande; ~ **dipole** dipôle à large bande; ~ **duplex channel** canal à large bande à trafic simultané dans les deux sens; ~ **exchange** centre de commutation de données (CCD); ~ **filter** filtre à large bande; ~ **noise** bruit de large bande; bruit blanc; ~ **protection channel** canal de protection à large bande; ~ **signal** signal à large bande; ~ **system** système à large bande; ~ **transformer** transformateur à large bande

broadcast *v* diffuser; disséminer; ~ *n* émission; radiodiffusion; transmission radiophonique

broadcast(ing) network réseau de radiodiffusion

broadcast band bande de radiodiffusion

broadcast-band frequency fréquence de radiodiffusion

broadcast call appel en diffusion; ~ **channel** voie de diffusion; ~ **copy** copie-antenne

broadcaster *n* speaker (speakerine)

broadcasting *n* diffusion; ~ **range** gamme de radiodiffusion; ~ **receiver** récepteur de radiodiffusion; ~ **satellite** satellite de radiodiffusion; ~ **service** service de radio-diffusion; ~ **station** poste émetteur; station de radiodiffusion

broadcast station station d'émission; ~ **studio** studio de radiodiffusion; ~ **telegraph repeater** translation télégraphique pour diffusion; ~ **transmission** radioémission

broad fault tracing localisation sommaire des dérangements; ~ **pulse** impulsion à longue durée; impulsion de demi-ligne

broadside array rideau en dents de scie; antenne à grande ouverture; antenne à rayonnement transversal; rideau Chireix-Mesny; ~ **dipole array** série de dipôles

broad tuning accord aplati

brochure *n* plaquette

broker *n* courtier; façonnier

brokerage call rétro-appel courtier; garde de double-appel; garde de rétro-appel

broker's call (with split) double appel courtier (va-et-vient)

bromomethane *n* bromure de méthyle

Brownian motion of electrons bruit d'agitation thermique

brown-out *n* (of electricity) microcoupure secteur; baisse accidentelle de la tension; manque fugitif du réseau; variation fugitive

browse *v* consulter; feuilleter

browsing *n* broutage; consultation; balayage

brush *n* balai; brosse de lecture; collecteur de courant; frotteur; ~ (card reader) balai de lecture; ~ **carriage** chariot porte-balais; ~ **contact** contact à balai; ~ **discharge** effluve; aigrette

brushed *adj* satiné; ~ **aluminium** aluminium brossé

brush holder porte-balais; ~ **rocker** couronne porte-balai; ~ **selector** sélecteur à balais

BS (s. backspace)

BSC, BISYNC (s. binary synchronous communication)

B-side côté émission

B-staged resin résitol

B-store registre index

B-subscriber abonné demandé (DE); abonné appelé

B-subscriber release rupture DE

B-tree arbre binaire

bubble *n* bulle

bucket *n* case; région contigue; adresse; compartiment

bucket-brigade delay line ligne acoustique multiple; réseau ligne à retard; ~ **device (BBD)** dispositif à transfert de charges; dispositif de déplacement de charge; circuit(s) à chapelet

bucking *n* suralimentation; ~ **converter** convertisseur abaisseur; ~ **voltage** (opposed to reference voltage) tension en

B

opposition
buckled *adj* infléchi
buckling *n* gauchissement; voilage
budgeting of the reference equivalent répartition de l'équivalent de référence
buff *v* casser les angles (vifs); ~ (colour) havane
buffer *n* tampon; zone de travail; mémoire temporaire; séparateur d'article; tampon amplificateur; TTL de puissance; butée; amplificateur d'isolement; butoir; circuit séparateur; opérateur de puissance; ~ *adj* intermédiaire
buffer/address multiplexer amplificateur aiguillage d'adresses
buffer amplifier amplificateur intermédiaire; amplificateur tampon stabilisé; amplificateur séparateur; ~ **area** zone tampon; ~ **battery** batterie équilibrée
buffered network réseau à mémoires tampons; ~ **stop** butée progressive; ~ **terminal manager** gestionnaire de terminal tamponné
buffer file fichier non permanent; ~ **handler** programme de traitement des tampons
buffering *n* mise en tampon; mémorisation temporaire; tamponnage; rangement; bufférisation; adaptation de la vitesse; ~ **and debuffering operations on file** opérations de blocage sur fichier
buffer memory/store mémoire intermédiaire; mémoire tampon; ~ **put-aside store** corbeille; ~ **register** accumulateur tampon; ~ **resistance** résistance de décharge; ~ **store** mémoire de transit
buffing *n* adoucissage; ~ **machine** polisseuse; ~ **pad** drap
bug *n* défaillance; défaut; dérangement; erreur; faute; incident; incohérence; microphone clandestin; faute logicielle
bugging *n* écoute clandestine
bug key touche semi-automatique
building *n* (of table, string, queue) constitution; ~ **block** unité fonctionnelle
building-out *adj* complémentaire; ~ **network** complément de ligne; ~ **section** équilibreur; complément d'une section de pupinisation
build-out circuit complément
build up (of charge) amorcer
build-up time temps de montée
built-in *adj* solidaire; encastré; incorporé; intégré dans le bâti; intérieur; interne; intrinsèque; ~ **aerial** antenne incorporée; ~ **check** contrôle automatique; ~ **shunt** shunt logé dans l'appareil
bulb *n* lampe; ampoule; enveloppe
bulge *n* bourrelet; bombement

bulk *n* massif; base volumique; substrat; masse; ~ *adj* global; volumique; ~ **billing** calcul et stockage de la taxe; facturation au compteur; facturation globale; taxation au compteur; ~ **data** information massive; ~ **delivery packaging** emballage global; ~ **eraser** (of tapes) démagnétiseur
bulkhead *n* cloison
bulk insertion multipose; ~ **lifetime** vie moyenne du porteur minoritaire; ~ **memory** mémoire de grande capacité; mémoire de masse; mémoire géante
bulk-packaged components composants en vrac
bulk storage archivage; saisie de masse; ~ **tape generator** configurateur; ~ **temperature** température dans la masse
bulky load charge encombrante
bulldog clip pince à dessin
bulletin board tableau d'affichage
bullet-proof glass vitre pare-balles
bump *n* mémoire annexe; ~ (test) secousse(s)
bumper *n* patin; embout
bunch *v* rassembler; ~ *n* faisceau; groupe; groupement; fuseau
bunched *adj* réunis entre eux; concentré; reliés entre eux; ~ **cables** câbles groupés; ~ **circuit** circuit approprié; ~ **frame alignment signal** signal de verrouillage de trame concentré
buncher *n* résonateur d'entrée; ~ **gap** espace d'interaction; ~ **space** espace de modulation
bunching *n* groupage; ~ **angle** angle de groupement; ~ **parameter** paramètre de groupement
bundle *n* faisceau; nappe de câbles; toron
bung *n* embout; bouchée; bouchon
buoy *n* bouée
buoyant market marché porteur
burden *n* charge
burglar alarm alarme effraction
buried aerial antenne enterrée; ~ **cable** câble enterré; câble souterrain; ~ **layer** couche enterrée
burned-in *adj* déverminé
burned out *adj* grillé; claqué
burner chalumeau
burn-in *n* déverminage; essai de vieillissement; rôdage
burning *n* bruit de microphone
burn-in oven étuve de déverminage; ~ **unit** maquette de déverminage
burnisher *n* spatule
burn-out *n* surcharge; ~ (of crystal rectifier) brûlure d'un redresseur à cristal
burn-through pénétration du tapis de nuages
burnt-out fuse fusible fondu

B

burr *n* bavure; copeaux

burst *n* paquet; rafale; série; train; volée; bruit impulsif

burstable (continuous stationery) détachable

burst firing (fast cycle) passage de trains d'ondes

burst-gate pulse impulsion d'échantillonnage

bursting *n* éclatement

burst mode mode continu; à l'alternat; ~ rate cadence de rafales; ~ strength résistance à l'éclatement; ~ transmission transmission par rafales

bus *n* voie; artère; barre; bus; collecteur; distributeur; faisceau; joncteur; jonction; liaison; ligne omnibus; trolley; voie commune; ~ (of multiplex channel) canal d'une voie; (peripheral) ~ extension bus déporté

busback *n* bouclage

busbar *n* barre omnibus; barre bus; barre collective; barre d'alimentation (BA); ~ isolation isolement entre barres

bus controller allocateur; automate de gestion; ~ driver amplificateur de ligne; ~ extension bus à rallonge; déport bus; ~ grant affectation des voies; voie disponible

bush *n* canon; douille; alvéole; chemise; embout; manchon

bushing *n* chambrage; manchonnage; ~ (of transformer) traversée

busied *adj* pris

busied-out *adj* bloqué; hors service (h.s.)

business *n* affaire; activité; ~ *adj* commercial; ~ electronics électronique professionnel

businessman *n* entrepreneur

business-oriented de type professionnel

business skills dépêches commerciales; ~ (rate) subscriber abonné d'affaires; ~ telephone téléphone d'affaires

business-to-business interentreprise

bus line canal; ligne d'accès; ligne omnibus; ~ master mode en maître bus; ~ transceiver bus bidirectionnel; émetteur-récepteur de ligne; ~ wire fil omnibus

busy *v* occuper; solliciter; ~ (BY) *adj* occupé; actif; chargé; ~ (station) override offre sur poste intérieur occupé; ~ bus occupation de bus; ~ circuit circuit d'occupation; ~ condition état occupé; condition d'encombrement; ~ day jour chargé; ~ drop indicator annonciateur d'occupation; ~ extension usager en communication; ~ (extension) with call camped-on occupation (au) deuxième degré; ~ (extension) with no calls camped-on occupation (au) premier degré; ~ flash signal d'occupation; ~ hour heure chargée; ~ hour call attempt (BHCA) tentative d'appel à l'heure chargée; appel à l'heure chargée (AHC)

busy-hour traffic trafic à l'heure chargée

busying *n* prise; blocage; mise en état d'occupation; ~ key clé de prise

busying-out isolement; mise hors service (HS); ~ of trunks mise hors service manuelle de jonctions

busying signal signal de prise

busy key clé d'occupation; ~ lamp lampe d'occupation (LO); ~ lamp field massif de lampes d'occupation; panneau de lampes d'occupation; ~ line ligne occupée; ~ local occupation privée; ~ loop boucle d'attente; ~ probability probabilité d'être occupé; ~ response avis d'occupation; ~ signal signal d'occupation; ~ station override acheminement avec offre sur poste occupé; ~ subscriber abonné occupé; ~ test test d'occupation; ~ tone (= engaged signal) tonalité d'occupation; ~ transfer renvoi sur occupation; ~ verification offre d'appel

butt *n* pied; ~ (of contact) fût

butterfly *n* (of bit pattern) papillon; ~ nut écrou O

Butterworth/Chebyshev filter (s. T-section filter)

butt joint raccord à bride lisse; joint abouté

butt-mounting juxtaposabilité

button *n* bouton; clé; touche; ~ capacitor condensateur bouton

button-head rivet rivet goutte de suif

button-hole microphone microphone de boutonnière

button-jammed code code de bouton

buttress *n* contrefort

buyer *n* acheteur

buy-in *v* procurer

buying-in *n* approvisionnement

buzz *n* crachement

buzz-back tone tonalité de retour d'appel

buzzer *n* ronfleur; sonnerie; sonnerie trembleuse; vibreur; ~ (continuity tester) vibrotest; ~ call appel phonique; ~ signal signal de bourdonnement

buzzing-out test sonnage

B/W (s. bothway)

BY (s. busy)

by-pass *v* ponter; shunter; découpler; court-circuiter; ~ *n* découplage; court-circuitage; délestage; dérivation; shunt; évitement; pontage; ~ capacitor condensateur de découplage; condensateur de fuite; condensateur de dérivation; condensateur d'isolement

by-passed addition addition accélérée

by-product retombée; ~ **circuit** circuit virtuel (CV); circuit superposé

byte *n* multiplet; mot machine; groupe de bits consécutifs; octet; ~ (mode) octal; ~ **alignment** alignement sur l'octet; ~ **boundary** limite d'octet; ~ **boundary overflow** dépassement de l'octet; ~ **descriptor** descripteur d'octet; ~ **mode** mode caractère; mode discontinu; ~ **multiplexer channel** canal multiplexeur de multiplets; ~ **pattern** structure d'octet; ~ **specifier** descripteur d'octet; ~ **stream** flot d'octets; ~ **switch** commutateur d'octets; ~ **timing signal** signal de synchronisation d'octet

C

cabinet *n* armoire; coffret; enceinte; herse; meuble; ~ (of rheometer, etc.) cage

cable *n* câble; ~ (telegram) câblogramme; ~ **armour** armature de câble; ~ **attenuation** affaiblissement du câble; ~ **bundle** câblage en nappe; ~ **bundle factor** facteur de câblage; ~ **capacitance** réactance capacitive de câble; ~ **clamp** serre-câble; collier pour câbles; ~ **clip** lyre; ~ **connection** connexion de câble; ~ **connector** connecteur de câble; ~ **core** faisceau de conducteurs; ~ **cutter** coupe-câble dénudeur

cable-cutting pliers pince coupe câble; ~ **shears** cisaille coupe-câble

cable distribution câblodistribution; télédistribution; ~ **drum/payout spool** dérouleuse; ~ **duct** chemin de câbles (CdC); voûte; ~ **echo** écho de câble; ~ **end** embout pour câble

cable-ended connector connecteur d'usure

cable extension link connecteur droit; ~ **eye** (shoe) cosse de câble; ~ **fill** taux d'utilisation (de câbles); ~ **form** nappe; peigne; toron; ~ **former** jonc

cablegram *n* câblogramme

cable grip serre-câble; ~ **harness** peigne de câble; nappe; traînard; ~ **harness layout drawing** plan des planches à peigne; ~ **junction** connexion de câble; ~ **lay** constitution de câble

cable-laying contractors câbliers; ~ **vessel** câblier

cable-length compensation compensation de longueur de câble

cable line ligne de câble; ~ **link** câble de raccord; liaison par câble; ~ **loading** charge d'un câble; ~ **loom** faisceau de câbles; nappe de câbles; ~ **manufacturers** les cabliers; ~ **morse code** code trivalent pour câble

cable-mounting connector connecteur enfichable; ~ **multi-way connector** connecteur multicontact enfichable; ~ **socket/receptacle** embase (connecteur fixe)

cable network réseau câblé; ~ **rack** chemin de câbles (CdC); ~ **run** chemin de câbles (CdC); ~ **runway** caniveau; chemin de câbles (CdC); ~ **segment** tronçon de câble; ~ **slack compartment** boîte de lovage;

~ **stripper** coupe-câble dénudeur; ~ **stub** tronçon de câble; manchon de câble; ~ **support** balancier d'accompagnement; ~ **television** télévision par câble; ~ **tensioning** tendage des câbles; ~ **terminal** sous-répartiteur; boîte de raccordement; ~ **termination** collier; ~ **tie** collier TY-RAP [A.C.]; serre-câble; ~ **transmission** transmission par câble; ~ **tray** chemin de câbles (CdC); ~ **trench** caniveau; ~ **TV network** réseau de télédistribution; ~ **vault** cuve; ~ **wire** conducteur de câble; ~ **wrapping** confection

cabling *n* filerie

cache *n* antémémoire; ~ **memory** mémoire cache; mémoire privée

CAD (s. computer-aided design)

CAD/CAM (s. computer-aided design and manufacture)

cadmium-plated cadmié

cage *n* alvéole; châssis; bac à cartes; ~ **aerial** antenne en cage

caged *adj* noyé

cage nut écrou cage; écrou prisonnier

caging *n* blocage

calculating machine machine à calculer; ~ **punch** calculatrice perforatrice

calculation *n* calcul

calculator *n* calculateur; (desk-top/pocket) ~ calculatrice

calculograph *n* calculographe

calculus *n* calcul

calendar *n* calendrier

calibrate *v* étalonner

calibrated (standard) **frequency** fréquence étalon; ~ **signal** signal calibré

calibration *n* étalonnage; calage; tarage; calibrage; ajustage; ~ **bench** banc d'étalonnage; ~ **block** bloc étalon; ~ **curve** courbe d'étalonnage; ~ **frequency** fréquence d'étalonnage; ~ **mark** repère d'étalonnage; ~ **probe** perche d'étalonnage; ~ **pulse** impulsion d'étalonnage; ~ **tape** bande étalon

calibrator *n* calibrateur

calibre *n* jauge; capacité; module; jaugeur

caliper *n*, (**vernier**) ~ pied à coulisse (PC)

call *v* appeler; solliciter; ~ *n* appel; communication; conversation; demande; ~ (up) invoquer; (**exchange**) ~ **set-up delay**

durée de sélection (d'un autocommutateur)

callable line ligne désignable

call accepted acceptation d'appel; ~ **address** adresse d'appel; ~ **amplifier** amplificateur du signal d'appel; ~ **announcement** (by operator) présentation d'appel; ~ **answering** enregistrement d'un message reçu; ~ **arrival (probability) distribution** loi d'arrivée; ~ **attempt** tentative d'appel; ~ **awaiting completion** appel en cours de traitement

call-back *n* rappel; appel double; reprise d'appel

call barred appel interdit; ~ **barring** verrouillage

call-bell point central d'alarme d'incendie

call bit bit d'appel; ~ **booking** inscription d'appel; demande de communication; ~ **booth/box** cabine téléphonique

callbox *n* poste d'appel; cabine (à) paiement

call button bouton d'appel; ~ **camped-on** appel en instance; ~ **category** catégorie d'appels; ~ **charge** taxe téléphonique; ~ **charge notification** indication du coût d'appel; ~ **charge rate/scale** palier de taxe

call-completion rate taux d'échec

call-confirmation signal signal de confirmation d'appel

call-connected signal signal de connexion

call-connect signal (set up) décrochage (D)

call-control character caractère de commande d'appel

call converter/translator traducteur d'appel

call-count record enregistrement de trafic

call data zone des variables

call-data store mémoire de la zone des variables

call deferring différation d'une communication

call-demand counter compteur-enregistreur de conversations

call detection détection d'appel

call-directing code (CDC) code d'appel

call director pilote d'appels; pupitre dirigeur; ~ **disconnection** coupure de la communication; ~ **distribution** distribution des appels; ~ **distributor** distributeur d'appels; ~ **diversion** renvoi d'appel; renvoi temporaire; ~ **diversion - all calls** renvoi commandé

call-diversion code préfixe d'inscription (du renvoi temporaire)

call diversion - no reply renvoi différé; ~ **diversion on engaged** renvoi si poste occupé; ~ **diversion on ringing** transfert sur sonnerie; ~ **diversion - preset** renvoi fixe; ~ **diversion when busy** renvoi si poste occupé; ~ **duration** durée de prise

call-duration limiting circuit circuit de limitation de durée des communications; ~ **message** message de durée d'appel; ~ **meter** compteur de durée de conversation

called *adj* appelé; sollicité; ~ **and calling subscriber released** libération au raccrochage des deux correspondants

called/calling party correspondant

called end amont (en -); ~ **exchange** central d'arrivée; ~ **line** ligne appelée; ~ **line free/busy check** test du demandé; ~ **line identification** identification de la ligne appelée; ~ **party** abonné appelé; abonné demandé (DE); ~ **party/caller code** marque DE/DR; ~ **party free/busy check** test du demandé; ~ **party release** libération par l'abonné demandé; ~ **party release guard** temporisation de raccrochage du demandé; ~ **subscriber** demandé (DE); ~ **subscriber free/busy check** test de l'abonné demandé; ~ **subscriber number** numéro demandé; ~ **subscriber off-hook** demi-faute; ~ **subscriber release** libération par l'abonné demandé

called/wanted subscriber abonné demandé (DE)

caller *n* abonné demandeur (DR); abonné appelant; appeleur

call-failure signal signal d'échec de l'appel

call fee taxe téléphonique; ~ **finder** (selector) chercheur d'appels

call-finding recherche d'appel

call-for-bids appel d'offres

call forcing réponse automatique; ~ **forwarding** renvoi d'appel; transfert d'appel; aiguillage des appels; ~ **forwarding - all calls** renvoi temporaire (commandé); renvoi temporaire variable; ~ **forwarding - busy line** renvoi en cas d'occupation; renvoi sur occupation; ~ **forwarding - don't answer** renvoi sur non réponse; renvoi conditionnel; renvoi différé; renvoi temporisé; réacheminement automatique; ~ **forwarding - don't answer** (busy line) renvoi commandé

call-forwarding extension poste renvoyé

call forwarding - follow me renvoi variable; renvoi automatique sur opératrice; ~ **forwarding - preset** renvoi fixe; ~ **forwarding to busy subscriber** acheminement sur abonné occupé; ~ **forwarding to free subscriber** acheminement sur abonné libre; ~ **forwarding - variable** renvoi temporaire (commandé); renvoi temporaire variable; ~ **forwarding when absent** renvoi temporisé; ~ **forwarding - when absent/don't answer** renvoi en cas d'absence; ~ **forwarding - when busy** renvoi sur occupation

call-handling capacity puissance de traitement; ~ **processor** multi-enregistreur; machine (logique de traitement) d'appel; enregistreur multiple de départ

call hold flip-flop double appel courtier (va-et-vient)

call-holding time durée d'appel; ~ **time** (probability distribution) loi de service

call identifier identificateur de communication; ~ **indicator** indicateur du numéro demandé

calling adj appelant; appeleur; ~ (up) sollicitation; ~ **code** code d'appel; ~ **concentrator** position de concentration; ~ **condition** en appel; ~ **cord** cordon d'appel; ~ **device** dispositif d'appel; ~ **end/side** aval (en); ~ **equipment** organe d'appel; ~ **exchange** bureau de départ; ~ **frequency** fréquence d'appel; ~ **jack** jack d'appel; ~ **key** touche d'appel; ~ **lamp** lampe d'appel; ~ **line** ligne appelante; ligne d'appel; ~ **line category indicator** indicateur de catégorie du demandeur; ~ **line identification** identification de la ligne d'appel; ~ **loop** boucle d'appel; ~ **number** numéro demandeur; ~ **party** abonné appelant; ~ **party/subscriber** demandeur (DR) (= amont); Deur; ~ **plug** fiche d'appel; ~ **position** position d'appel; ~ **program** programme appelant; ~ **rate** taux d'appels; ~ **relay** relais de ligne; ~ **sequence** séquence d'appel; ~ **signal** signal d'appel; ~ **subscriber** abonné appelant; ~ **subscriber number** numéro appelant; ~ **task** tâche demanderesse; ~ **tone** tonalité d'appel; ~ **wave** onde d'appel

call in progress conversation en cours; connexion établie; en conversation; ~ **inter-arrival distribution** fonction de répartition des durées entre appels; ~ **intercept** interception d'appel; ~ **jack** fiche d'appel

call(ing) key clé d'appel

call lamp indicateur lumineux d'appel; ~ **link** enchaînement de segments; ~ **metering** taxation

call-minute communication-minute

call number numéro d'appel; ~ **offered** appel présenté; ~ **offering** offre d'appel; entrée en tiers; présentation d'appel

call-out n intervention; ~ **installation** circuit d'alarme

call paging recherche de personnes; ~ **park** circuit de renvoi sur garde; parcage d'appel; mise en faux-appel; ~ **parking** mise en garde; mise en garde par indicatif; parcage d'appel; parcage renvoi sur garde; ~ **parking and distribution** parcage et distribution d'appels; ~ **pick-up** rétro-appel; reprise d'un appel parqué; ~ **pick-up**

and hold reprise d'une ligne en garde; ~ **pilot wire** fil de pilotage (d'appel); ~ **presented to circuit group** appel offert; ~ **privacy** communication privative; fonction secret; ~ **processing** traitement des appels; ~ **progress** état d'avancement de l'appel; ~ **progress word** mot d'enchaînement; ~ **progress zone** zone d'enchaînement; ~ **queuing** spécialisation de trafic

call-queuing system système avec mise en file des appels

call register compteur d'appels; ~ **registration** comptage d'appels

call-rejection rate taux de rejet

call relay relais d'appel; ~ **release** rupture d'appel; coupure d'appel

call-release signal raccrochage

call request demande d'appel

call-request signal signal de demande d'appel

call restriction discrimination; ~ **routiner** robot d'essais; ~ **selection** prise d'appel; ~ **set-up** établissement d'un appel; ~ **set-up time** délai d'établissement (de la communication); ~ **signal** signal d'enregistrement

callsign block allocation table tableau d'affectation des séries

call status configuration; ~ **status key** clé de configuration; ~ **store bus** bus des mémoires d'appel; ~ **string** chaîne d'appel; ~ **subroutine** primitive d'activation; ~ **supervision** supervision des appels

call-testing device pondeuse

call-through test set appeleur (de robots)

call ticket ticket d'appel; ~ **time** durée de conversation; ~ **timer** compteur de durée de conversation; ~ **to distant end** appel du distant; ~ **to marker** appel marqueur; ~ **to subscriber** appel de l'abonné; ~ **tracing** pistage d'appel; ~ **transfer** transfert d'appel; renvoi d'appel

call-transfer button bouton de terre

call unit unité de communication; ~ **up** appeler; faire un appel; se porter en appel/appelant; ~ **waiting** appel en instance

call-waiting notification indication d'appel en instance; ~ **tone** tonalité d'appel en attente; tonalité d'empilage

call with cost notification communication avec indication de taxe

cam n came; excentrique

CAMA (s. centralized automatic message accounting)

camera n chambre; ~ **tube** tube analyseur de télévision

camped-on en attente; ~ **free/busy subscriber** mise en attente sur abonné libre/occupé;

~ **line** ligne en garde

camping-on mise en file d'attente

camp-on n attente sur poste occupé; mise en attente; mise en garde; rappel du demandeur; ~ **busy** mise en attente devant la ligne occupée; ~ **busy extension** rappel automatique sur poste occupé; ~ **busy station** attente sur poste occupé; ~ **busy subscriber** attente signalé sur abonné occupé; ~ **extension** poste en attente; ~ **tone** tonalité d'annotation; ~ **warning tone** attente signalée

cam time-out passage came; coup de came; ~ **timer** came

can n boîtier métallique; capsule

CAN (s. cancel)

cancel v annuler; supprimer; résilier; ~ **(CAN)** annulation; ~ (of lamp) inhiber; ~ (of contact) neutraliser; ~ **character** caractère d'annulation; ~ **key** clé d'annulation

cancellation n suppression; effacement; oblitération; résiliation; écrasement; acquittement; disparition; **(call)** ~ **charge** taxe d'annulation; ~ **ratio** facteur d'élimination

cancelled subscriber abonné résilié

cancelling (of alarm) réenclenchement; remise à zéro (RZ/RAZ); ~ **telegram** télégramme annulatif

candlestick telephone téléphone à tige

candohm resistor résistance protégée

can earthed boîtier à la masse

canister n bidon; boîte; bouteille; **(disk pack)** ~ cloche

canonical form méthode canonique

canopy n hotte; calotte; capot; plénum; rehausse

canteen services restauration collective

canting angle angle d'obliquité

canvas n toile

canvassing n démarche

canvass/seek opinion demander l'avis

cap n capot; calotte; capsule; capuchon; chape; coupelle; couvercle; culot; embout; bouchon

capacitance n capacité; résistance de capacité; ~ **meter** capacimètre; faradmètre; ~ **per unit length** capacité linéique

capacitive coupling couplage capacitif; ~ **feedback** réaction capacitive; réaction électrostatique; ~ **load** charge capacitive; ~ **reactance** réactance capacitive; ~ **sawtooth generator** générateur capacitif de dents de scie

capacitor n condensateur; capacité; ~ **microphone** microphone à condensateur

capacity n capacité; calibre; contenance; débit; énergie; intensité; pouvoir; puissance (Pce); taille (de zone/secteur); ~ (of register) longueur; ~ (of store) profondeur; ~ **earth** contrepoids d'antenne; ~ **terminal** capacité terminale

capillary action remontée de soudure; ~ **cathode** cathode poreuse

capital equipment moyens de production; équipement d'infrastructure; ~ **gains** plus-value(s)

capitals n pl majuscule(s)

cap nut écrou borgne; écrou moleté

caps (capital letters) haut de casse (hdc)

cap screw vis CHc (cylindrique à six pans creux); vis SPC (six pans creux)

caps-lock key touche maintien majuscule

capstan n cabestan d'entraînement

capsule n capsule; boîtier

caption n légende; pastille; signification; inscription; ~ **light** pastille lumineuse

captive adj noyé; ~ **nut** écrou cage; ~ **screw** vis imperdable

capture n acquisition; saisie; captage de données

carbon black protector parafoudre de charbon; ~ **brush** balai de charbon; ~ **composition resistor** résistance de carbone aggloméré; ~ **dioxide (CO2)** anhydride carbonique; ~ **film** couche de carbone

carbon-film resistor résistance à couche de carbone

carbon-granule microphone microphone à grenaille de charbon

carbon microphone packing tassement du microphone à charbon; ~ **microphone/transmitter** microphone à charbon

carbon-track potentiometer potentiomètre graphite; ~ **trimmer** potentiomètre ajustable à couche de carbone

carboy n tourie

carcase n corps

carcinotron n carcinotron

card n plaquette; plaque support; platine

cardboard folder dossier carton; ~ **packing case** boîte américaine

card cage panier; ~ **code** code carte; ~ **column** colonne de carte; ~ **dialler** composeur automatique de numéros à cartes perforées; ~ **feed** alimentation en cartes perforées; ~ **field** zone de perforation; ~ **format** cliché de carte; ~ **frame** bac à cartes; ~ **guide** glissière; guide carte

card-holder n porteur

card hopper magasin d'alimentation en cartes; ~ **image** image de carte

cardioid (heart-shaped) diagram diagramme en cardioïde

card jam bourrage de cartes; ~ **library** cartothèque; ~ **path** chemin de cartes;

~ **reader (CR)** lecteur de cartes (LC);
~ **reader dial** composeur automatique de
numéros à cartes perforées; ~ **row** ligne
d'une carte; ~ **stacker** case de fusion;
récepteur de cartes; ~ **testing** contrôle
cartes; ~ **throat** filière; ~ **track** voie
d'acheminement

caret n (typographical symbol) (^) V inversé;
caret

cargo n chargement

carriage n berceau; chariot; ~ **return (CR)**
retour de chariot (RC); ~ **tape** bande
pilote; boucle d'asservissement

carried adj écoulé

carrier n fréquence porteuse; support; transporteur; onde porteuse; ~ **channel** voie
porteuse; voie à courants porteurs; voie de
fréquence porteuse; ~ **circuit** circuit à
courant porteur; ~ **component** composante
porteuse; ~ **current** onde porteuse; ~ **(current)** courant porteur; ~ **detect (CD)**
détection onde porteuse; présence porteuse; ~ **deviation** écart en fréquence à
l'onde porteuse; ~ **drop-out** perte de
porteur; ~ **frequency** fréquence porteuse;
~ **group** groupe primaire; ~ **interval** écart
entre les courants porteurs; ~ **leak** fuite
d'onde porteuse; résidu du courant porteur; ~ **line** ligne à courant porteur; ligne
multiplex; ~ **line link** liaison en ligne à
paires symétriques; ~ **link** liaison à
courant porteur; ~ **loss** perte de porteur;
~ **mobility** mobilité du porteur; ~ **multiplex circuit** circuit multiplex à courant
porteur; ~ **offset** décalage de la porteuse;
~ **phase angle** angle de phase de la
porteuse; ~ **power** puissance de la porteuse; ~ **route** artère multiplex; ~ **shift**
déplacement de la porteuse; ~ **signalling**
signalisation par courants porteurs;
~ **spacing** intervalle d'espacement des
fréquences porteuses; ~ **storage time** (t_S)
temps de retard à la descente; temps de
stockage; ~ **supply** production de porteurs;
~ **suppression** suppression de la porteuse;
~ **system** système à courant porteur;
système multiplex; ~ **telegraphy** télégraphie harmonique; télégraphie à bande
vocale; ~ **telephony** téléphonie par courants porteurs

carrier-to-noise ratio écart entre porteuse et
bruit

carrier transmission transmission par courants
porteurs; transmission sur ondes porteurs;
~ **wave** courant porteur; onde porteuse

carry v porter; écouler; véhiculer; ~ n report
d'impulsions en crédit; ~ **digit** retenue;
~ **electrode** électrode de transmission;

~ **forward** répercuter

carrying effect effet de traînage

carry look-ahead retenue anticipée; retenue
propagée; ~ **look-ahead** (generator) prédicteur de retenue; ~ **time** temps de
retenue

cart n (for forms) chariot

cartridge n cartouche; capsule; chargeur;
~ **fuse** fusible à cartouche; cartouche
cylindrique (c/c); fusible cylindrique

CAS (s. channel-associated signalling)

cascadable to n micro-words prévu pour
l'extension à n étages

cascade n cascade; chaîne; enchaînement;
~ **amplifier** amplificateur à chaîne; amplificateur en cascade; ~ **connection**
connexion en cascade; ~ **control** régulation en cascade; ~ **converter** convertisseur
à cascade

cascaded carry report en cascade; ~ **forwarding** renvoi en cascade; ~ **HF transmission
line** ligne de transmission HF en cascade;
~ **line** ligne en cascade; ~ **series** tandem

cascading n chaînage

cascode n cascode

case n caisse; boîte; boîtier; étui; gaine;
housse; panier; ~ (of case hardening)
couche

case-hardened (and quenched) cémenté (et
trempé)

case line direction; ~ **shift** inversion

cash box (of bank teller machine) compartiment à monnaie

cash-management programme programme de
trésorerie

cash-point n distributeur de billets (dibi);
~ **kiosk** kiosque point-argent

casing n boîte; boîtier; capot; carcasse;
coffret; corps; enveloppe; habillage

cask n fût

casket n boîtier; coffret

Cassegrain aerial antenne à alimentation
Cassegrain; antenne parabolique

cassette n cassette (K7); cartouche; chargeur

casting n fonderie

cast iron fonte grise

castor(s) roulette(s)

casual labourer manœuvre

CAT (s. computer-assisted teaching)

catalanguage n langage objet; langage d'exécution; langage machine; langage résultant

catalog(ue) n catalogue; répertoire

catalogued adj répertorié

catalogue item unité vendable; ~ **showroom**
centrale d'achat

catastrophic failure défaut catalectique

catch n loquet; arrêtoir; cliquet; gâchette;
levier; sauterelle

catcher *n* résonateur de sortie; ~ **space** espace de captation

catching diode diode antirecul; diode de clamping; diode d'écrêtage; diode de restitution du niveau de noir; diode de verrouillage

catchment area zone d'attraction

catch-phrase *n* mots en vedette

category *n* catégorie (cie); classe; domaine; niveau; nature (nat.)

catena *n* enchaînement

catenary *n* (math.) chaînette; ~ (of cable) câble porteur

catenate *v* chaîner

cathode *n* cathode; ~ **amplifier** amplificateur à charge cathodique; ~ **current** courant cathodique; ~ **dark space** espace sombre cathodique; ~ **emitting diameter** diamètre de la surface cathodique efficace; ~ **follower** amplificateur cathodique; étage cathodyne; montage à anode à la masse; montage à cathode asservie; ~ **glow** lueur cathodique; ~ **(potential) fall** chute (de tension) cathodique; ~ **protection with sacrificial anode** protection cathodique avec anode enterrée; ~ **ray tube (CRT)** écran à tube cathodique; tube à rayons cathodiques; ~ **region** domaine cathodique; ~ **spot** tache cathodique; ~ **sputtering** pulvérisation cathodique

cathodoluminescence *n* luminescence cathodique; cathodoluminescence

catswhisker *n* chercheur; ~ (of limit switch) tige souple; ~ **diode** diode à pointe

CATV (s. community antenna television)

catwalk *n* passerelle

caustic soda soude

caution money dépôt de garantie initial

cavity *n* alvéole; cavité; évidement; ~ **frequency meter** fréquencemètre à cavité; ~ **magnetron** magnétron à cavités; ~ **package** boîtier à cavité; ~ **resonator** cavité résonnante; ~ **wave-meter** ondemètre à cavité

CAW (s. channel address word)

CB (s. citizen's band); ∻ (s. common battery); ∻ **channel** canal banalisé; ∻ **enthusiast** cibiste

CBT (s. cursor backward tabulation)

cc (s. condition code)

CCD (s. charge-coupled device)

CCITT (s. International Telegraph and Telephone Consultative Committee); ∻ **compliant** normalisé CCITT

CCS (s. common-channel signalling); ∻ (s. centum call second); ∻ **channel** voie de gestion; ∻ **tester** module d'échange(s) sémaphore; ∻ **transceiver** terminal multicanaux sémaphore

cct. (s. circuit)

CCU (s. communications control unit); ∻ (s. cross-connect unit)

CCW (s. channel command word)

CD (s. carrier detect)

CDC (s. call-directing code)

CDF (s. combined distribution frame)

CDMA (s. code-division multiple access)

ceased line abonnement résilié; ligne suspendue

ceiling light plafonnier; ~ **rose** rosace de plafond

cell *n* cellule; case; couple; élément; élément de batterie; pile; pile électrique; mot

cellar *n* mémoire à liste refoulée; mémoire à liste inversée; liste inverse; pile refoulée

cell pointer pointeur de cellules; ~ **position** emplacement (de) mémoire; endroit

cellular *adj* cellulaire; alvéolaire; ~ **logic** logique cellulaire; ~ **polyurethane** polyuréthane alvéolé; ~ **radiotelephony** radiotéléphonie cellulaire

celluloid *n* rhodoïd

cement *n* mastic; colle

census énumération; dénombrement

centimetric wave (SHF band) onde centimétrique

centipoint (1/7200 inch) centipoint

central clock horloge centrale; ~ **communications controller** contrôleur de gestion; ~ **control** commande centrale; ~ **control position** poste central de commande; ~ **control room** centre distributeur de modulation; ~ **control unit** unité de commande centrale; ~ **despatching unit** centre de réception des appels; ~ **dial office** autocommutateur d'abonnés; ~ **dictation service** dictée centralisée

centralization *n* délocalisation

centralized automatic message accounting (CAMA) comptabilité centralisée des appels (CCA); taxation automatique centralisée avec justification; ~ **control signalling** signalisation de commande centralisée; ~ **exchange group extension** usager de la société; ~ **extension service (CENTREX)** gestion des sociétés; ~ **topology** réseau en étoile; ~ **(topology) network** réseau centralisé

central matrix subswitch commutateur élémentaire; ~ **memory** mémoire centrale; ~ **monitoring position (CMP)** poste central de contrôle; ~ **network** chaîne de commande; ~ **office** bureau central; central d'abonnés; central local; ~ **office centrex** service centrex fourni par un central public; ~ **office line group** faisceau de lignes d'abonnement; ~ **office trunk** ligne de réseau (LR); ligne PTT; ~ **processing unit** unité (de traitement) centrale; ~ **processing unit (CPU)** unité centrale de traitement (UCT, UC); centralisateur d'informations; coffret logique; ~ **quality control (CQC)** contrôle centralisé de qualité (CCQ); ~ **radio station** central de radiodiffusion; ~ **server** serveur central; ~ **station** central; ~ **storage charging system** taxation à mémoire centrale (TMC); ~ **strength member** âme centrale; élément porteur central; filin d'acier; ~ **telegraph office** bureau central télégraphique; ~ **telex station** central des téléimprimeurs; ~ **unit** unité centrale de traitement (UCT, UC); ~ **units** cœur de chaîne

centre-biased (of switch) stable

centre conductor conducteur intérieur; ~ **decision value** amplitude de décision centrale

centred text texte centré

centre-fed alimentation médiane

centre frequency fréquence centrale; ~ **hole** perforation d'entraînement

centre-line axe; ~ (of waveguide) ligne médiane d'un guide d'ondes

centre-pin axe

centre-punch n pointeau

centre shift déséquilibre; ~ **tap (CT)** point milieu (PM); prise médiane (PM)

centre-tapped à prise centrale

centre-to-centre distance entr'axe; pas; ~ **spacing** pas d'espacement

centre value valeur type de centrage

CENTREX (s. centralized extension service); ~ **extension** usager de la société

CENTREX service (business telephone direct dialling facility) service centrex

centrifugal clutch coupure centrifuge; ~ **drier** essoreuse; machine à sécher centrifuge; sécheuse centrifuge

centring block pavé de centrage; ~ **bridge** cimblot (simbleau); ~ **jig** gabarit de centrage; ~ **square** équerre à centrer

centum call second (CCS = 1/36 Erlang) centaine de communication-secondes (CCS); appel réduit

ceramic capacitor condensateur céramique; ~ **encapsulation** boîtier céramique; ~ **filter** filtre céramique; ~ **glaze** verre céramique; ~ **plate capacitor** condensateur céramique plaquette

CERDIP package DIL verre céramique

certification test essai d'homologation

certified test record (CTR) rapport certifié d'essais

cessation n arrêt

CFA (s. crossed-field amplifier)

chad n débris de perforation; confetti(s); débouchure; découpure; pavé

chadded tape bande perforée; bande à perforation complète

chadless tape bande à perforation partielle; bande semi-perforée; ruban à perforation partielle

"chaff" nuage de bandelettes

chain v chaîner; concaténer; enchaîner; ~ n chaîne; chapelet; ~ **broadcasting** diffusion à relais; ~ **call** appel en série; renvoi en cascade; ~ **code** code à enchaînement

chain-dotted line ligne mixte

chained file fichier enchaîné

chaining n chaînage; concaténation; enchaînement; séquencement; ~ **buffer store** mémoire tampon de chaînage

chain of command (hierarchy) filière; ~ **of transmitters** chaîne d'émetteurs; ~ **printer** imprimante à chaîne; ~ **radar system** chaîne de stations de radar; ~ **stores** secteur à grande diffusion; ~ **winding** enroulement en fond de panier

chairman's address allocution du président

chalk line cordeau à tracer

challenge frequency fréquence d'interrogation

challenger n émetteur pilote; interrogateur

chamber n chambre; enceinte; ~ (of repeater) pot de répétiteur

chamfer v casser les angles (vifs); ~ n angle cassé

chamfered edge n chanfrein

chance adj accidentel; fortuite; ~ **distortion** distorsion fortuite; distorsion irrégulière

changeable adj commutable

change-back signal (to primary link) signal de retour sur liaison normale

changed number numéro changé

changed-number intercept renvoi des appels vers les numéros changés; abonné transféré

changed subscriber abonnement transféré

change file fichier mouvement; fichier détail; ~ **of billing address** changement de l'adresse de facturation

change-of-directory-number recorded announcement device terminal de dénumérotation

change of pitch changement d'échappement; ~ **order** ordre de correction

changeover n permutation; passage; ~ (of subscriber account) nouvel abonnement/ changement de titulaire; ~ **contact** contact à permutation; ~ **relay** relais tout ou rien; relais d'aiguillage; ~ **signal** (to standby link) signal de commutation sur liaison de réserve; ~ **switch** inverseur; inverseur de courant; va-et-vient; ~ **time** temps de passage

changer *n* changeur

change record enregistrement de mouvement;
enregistrement de détail; ~ **state** basculer;
changer d'état; ~ **tape** bande mouvement(s); ~ **to B signals** passage au code B;
~ **to the 1** (or 0) **state** passer à l'état 1/(0)

changing *n* (of polarity) basculement

channel *v* aiguiller; diriger; orienter; piloter;
~ *n* voie; canal; bande; chaîne; circuit;
conduit; gorge; gouttière; ligne; maille;
passage de fils; rainure; ~ (of timer disk)
sillon; ~ (extruded section) fer en C;
(speech) ~ voie de parole; ~ **address bus**
ligne d'adresse de voie; ~ **address word**
(CAW) mot (d')adresse de canal; ~ **allocation** affectation des voies; attribution des
voies de transmission; ~ **amplifier** amplificateur de canal

channel-associated equipment équipement de
voie complémentaire; ~ **in-slot signalling**
signalisation associée dans la bande;
~ **message** message voie par voie; ~ **out-slot signalling** signalisation hors bande
(voie par voie); ~ **signalling (CAS)**
signalisation sur voie associée; signalisation voie par voie (v/v); ~ **signalling**
channel canal voie par voie; ~ **signalling**
memory mémoire d'adresse temporelle

channel balancing équilibrage de canal;
~ **bandwidth** largeur de bande de canal;
~ **bank** baie d'équipements de voie;
équipement d'extrémité de voies;
~ **branching filter** coupleur sélectif de
canaux

channel-busy time durée d'occupation de la
voie

channel calling lamp lampe témoin de canal;
~ **capacity** capacité de voie; débit (d'une
voie); ~ **carrier** porteuse de canal

channel-combining unit diplexer coupleur
sélectif de canaux

channel command word (CCW) mot de
commande de canal; ~ **converter** coupleur
canal; ~ **converter** convertisseur de canaux; ~ **equipment** équipement de voie;
~ **extraction** dérivation des canaux; ~ **filter** filtre de voie; ~ **gate** porte de voie;
~ **graph** diagramme des itinéraires;
~ **group** groupe primaire

channeling *n* multiplexage; modulation de
voie; ~ **equipment** installation multiplex;
~ **of transmission paths** usage multiple de
voies de transmission

channelize *v* découper en voies; multiplexer

channelized data set modem à sous-canaux

channelizing *n* multiplexage

channelled *adj* aiguillé; ~ **traffic** trafic

canalisé

channel loading occupation des canaux;
~ **mode** contexte canal; ~ **mode access**
(CMA) accès mode canal (AMC); ~ **modulation** transposition de canal; ~ **modulator**
équipement de transposition de voie;
~ **passband** canal de fréquences; ~ **queue**
file d'attente de voie; ~ **rejector** réjecteur
de canal

channel-release conditions intervention de
cames

channel sampling échantillonnage de voies

channel-separating filter filtre séparateur de
canal

channel separation écart intervoies; ~ **spacing**
espacement de voies; écart intervoies;
écartement entre canaux; ~ **splitting**
division du canal; ~ **status** état de canal;
~ **status memory** mémoire état des voies
(MEV); ~ **status table** table d'état des
canaux; ~ **status word (CSW)** mot d'état de
canal; ~ **switching** commutation de voies;
~ **time slot** intervalle de temps de voie

channel-to-channel connection liaison entre-voies; ~ **data skew** (of logic analyser)
dispersion des temps de propagation entre
voies

channel translating equipment (CTE) équipement de transposition de voie; convertisseur de canaux; équipement de modulation
de voie; ~ **translation** transposition de
canal; ~ **trap** déroutement par canal;
~ **unit** (circuit pack) carte de voie; ~ **width**
largeur de bande de canal; fenêtre d'anticipation; largeur de fenêtre; ~ **word** mot
binaire

chaotic pulse impulsion chaotique; ~ **pulse**
interference interférence par impulsions
chaotiques

chapter *n* chapitre; segment; titre; partition

character *n* caractère; élément; signe; symbole; ~ **alignment** alignement de caractères; ~ **assignment of type lever** occupation de leviers des types; ~ **blink**
clignotement de caractère; ~ **check**
contrôle par caractère(s); ~ **code** code
caractère; code d'attribut de caractère;
~ **counting** comptage de caractères;
~ **crowding** tassement de caractères;
~ **density** densité de caractères; ~ **fill**
garnir de caractères; ~ **font** type de
caractère

characteristic *n* caractéristique; courbe typique; particularité; ~ **admittance** admittance caractéristique; ~ **band** bande
caractéristique; ~ **curve** courbe caractéristique; ~ **digit** chiffre caractéristique;
~ **distortion** distorsion caractéristique;

~ **frequency** fréquence caractéristique; ~ **impedance** impédance caractéristique; ~ **noise parameters** paramètres caractéristiques du bruit; ~ **wave impedance** impédance d'onde caractéristique

character mode mode caractère; mode discontinu; ~ **recognition** reconnaissance de caractères; ~ **repertory** répertoire de caractères; ~ **set** jeu de caractères; ensemble de caractères; police; répertoire; ~ **signal** signal de caractère; ~ **spacing** espacement des caractères; échappement

characters per inch (CPI) caractère par pouce (CCPP)

character string chaîne de caractères; ~ **switching** commutation de caractères; ~ **transfer** frappe; ~ **translation** transcodification de caractères

charcoal (grey) gris foncé

charge *n* (burden) fusion; **(call)** ~ taxe

chargeable *adj* facturable; avec taxation; ~ **call** appel taxé; conversation taxable; ~ **docket** ticket taxable; ~ **duration** durée taxable; ~ **time clock** compteur de durée taxable; chronotaximètre; ~ **unit** durée taxable

charge account compte de taxe; ~ **account dumping** sauvegarde des comptes de taxe; ~ **band** palier de taxe; ~ **card** carte de débit; ~ **corona unit** électrode de charge

charge-coupled device (CCD) dispositif à couplage de charges (DCC)

charged *adj* prélevé; imputé; ~ **duration** durée taxée

charged-particle carrier porteur électrisé

charge-free line ligne sans taxation (LST); ~ **subscriber** abonné sans taxe; demandé non taxé

charge hand monitrice; sous-commandier; ~ **indicator** indicateur de taxe; ~ **level** palier de taxe

charge-limiting subroutine verrue de taxation

charge meter compteur de taxation; taxateur; taxeur

charge-metering by periodic pulses taxation par impulsions périodiques; ~ **converter** convertisseur de gestion (CG)

charge period période de taxation

charger *n* chargeur

charge rate taux de taxe; ~ **rate table** table de taux de taxe; tarif de taxation; ~ **ratio** charge spécifique d'un porteur électrisé; ~ **recording** enregistrement taxe; ~ **region** barrière de potentiel; ~ **sequence timer** séquentiel taxation

charge-storage diode diode de commutation rapide

charge-transfer device (CTD) dispositif de déplacement de charge; dispositif à transfert de charges

charging *n* taxation; ~ **(scale)** tarification; ~ **area** zone de taxation; ~ **by distance** taxation à la distance; ~ **choke** self doubleuse; ~ **code** code de taxe; ~ **converter** convertisseur de charge; ~ **current** courant de charge; ~ **digit** chiffre de taxation; ~ **file** fichier de taxation; ~ **plan** plan de taxation; ~ **processor** unité de taxation; ~ **pulse** impulsion de charge; ~ **resistor** résistance de charge; ~ **rules** règles de tarification; ~ **subsystem** chaîne de taxation; ~ **system** taxateur; taxeur; ~ **unit** taxateur; ~ **voltage** tension de charge

charred *adj* brûlé; noirci

chart *n* carte; abaque; barème; diagramme; graphique; grille; matrice; tableau; ~ **drive** entraînement de papier; ~ **recorder** table traçante

chase *n* chemin de câbles (CdC); conduit

chassis *n* châssis; ossature; bâti; chaise; fond de panier (FdP/FdeP/FDP); platine; ~ **plug** fiche femelle; fiche américaine; ~ **socket** prise fixe

chatter *n* cliquetis; broutage; transmodulation; ~ **(of relay contacts)** battement; rebondissement

cheap rate charging taxation à tarif réduit

Chebyshev approximation approximation de Tchebychev; ~ **array** rideau de Dolph-Tchebychev

check *n* contrôle; ~ **(a circuit)** sonner (un circuit); ~ **bit** caractère de contrôle; bit clé; bit de contrôle; bit de redondance; ~ **byte** octet de contrôle (OC); ~ **character** caractère de contrôle; ~ **circuit** circuit de contrôle; ~ **coder** codeur de contrôle; ~ **digit** caractère de contrôle d'erreur; bit clé; bit de contrôle; chiffre clé; chiffre de contrôle

checker *n* compteur

checkerboard algorithm algorithme DA-MIER-DAMIER; ~ **test** test DAMIER

checking routine programme de contrôle

check key touche de contrôle; ~ **length** longueur contrôlée

checklist *n* bilan

check list récapitulatif; ~ **loop** boucle pour essais de continuité; ~ **multiple** champ de multiplage pour contrôler une connexion; ~ **number** chiffre clé; ~ **number tone** tonalité de vérification de numéro

check-out *v* dépanner; éprouver; ~ **routine** programme d'aide à la mise au point

checkpoint *v* jalonner (de points de reprise); ~ *n* point de reprise; ~ **table** table des reprises en secours

check register registre de contrôle; ~ **signal** signal de contrôle

check-sum total de contrôle; total mêlé; somme de contrôle; somme globale; ~ **procedure** test de totalisation

check tone tonalité d'essai

cheek *n* flasque

cheese *n* antenne cornet; réflecteur en segment; réflecteur en dé; ~ **aerial** antenne en D; antenne fromage

cheesehead screw (flat fillister head) vis à tête cylindrique (C); ~ **self-tapping screw** vis CLT

Cheshire-cat store mémoire de rafraîchissement; mémoire à régénération

chessboard configuration algorithme DA-MIER-DAMIER

chestphone téléphone en coffret

Child-Langmuir equation loi de Child-Langmuir

chilled gas gaz frigoporteur

chime *n* carillon; mélodie; timbre

chime(s) *n* sonnerie

chime generator générateur de mélodie

Chinese binary binaire (par) colonne; ∻ **binary** (code) code binaire chinois

chip *n* pastille; microphoto; microplaquette; microstructure; boîtier; organe; **(video)** ~ micro-image (vidéo/magnétique)

chipboard *n* panneau particule; aggloméré

chip-board panel dalle (en aggloméré)

chip card carte futée; ~ **handler** distributeur de circuits intégrés

chipping *n* délitage

chips *n pl* débris de perforation; confetti(s); débouchure; pavé

chip select (CS) sélection du boîtier; sélection X (entrée)

Chireix array rideau Chireix-Mesny; rideau en dents de scie

Chireix-Mesny aerial antenne à rayonnement transversal

Chireix transmitter émetteur de Chireix

chirp filter filtre dispersif linéaire

chi-squared test test khi deux

chit *n* bon; fiche; papillon

Chobert rivet rivet tubulaire

chock *n* cale (d'épaisseur); entretoise

choice factor facteur de choix

choke *n* self; bobine; bobine d'amortissement; bobine d'arrêt; bobine de blocage; bobine de choc; bobine self-induction; bobine selfique; inductance; réactance; ~ (of waveguide) piège; ~ **coil** self de blocage; ~ **connector** bride à piège

choke-coupled amplifier amplificateur à impédance

choke coupling raccord à piège; bride à piège; couplage par bobine d'arrêt; couplage L-C

choked *adj* amorti

chop *v* découper; ~ *n* changement de canal radio; ~ (to standby link) passage sur liaison de réserve

chopped (display) mode mode découpé

chopper *n* découpeur; hacheur électronique; relais modulateur; vibreur; ~ **amplifier** mutateur de puissance; amplificateur à interrupteur; ~ **bar** couteau d'impression; lame d'inscription

chopper-bar recording impression de points

chopper circuit circuit à découpage; circuit hacheur; ~ **disk** disque interrupteur

chopper-stabilized amplifier amplificateur écrêteur; amplificateur à découpage

chopping *n* écrêtage; ~ (of transponder) découpage; ~ **frequency** fréquence de découpage

chromatic aberration aberration chromatique

chromaticity *n* chrominance; ~ **diagram** triangle des couleurs

chrominance *n* chrominance

chronopher horodateur

chrysocolla *n* chrysocal; chrysocolle

chubby screwdriver boule courte

chuck *n* mandrin

chute *n* couloir; goulotte; chicane

cifax *n* fac-similé chiffré

CIL (s. control indicator light)

cinching (of tape) glissement par inertie

cipher equipment dispositif chiffreur

ciphering *n* chiffrage; chiffrement

ciphony téléphonie chiffrée; téléphonie codée

circlip *n* anneau; clips; jonc d'arrêt; segment; anneau Truarc

circuit (cct.) *n* circuit; réseau; montage; maille; chaîne; ~ **access point** point d'accès à un circuit

circuit-breaker *n* coupe-circuit; conjoncteur-disjoncteur; fusible (fus.); disjoncteur

circuit card carte; ~ **commutated turn-off time** temps de désamorçage par commutation du circuit; ~ **concentrator** concentrateur de circuits; ~ **diagram** synoptique; schéma développé; ~ **element** élément de circuit; ~ **finder** chercheur d'organes

circuit-gap admittance admittance de l'espace d'interaction

circuit group faisceau de circuits

circuit-group efficiency taux d'efficacité (d'un faisceau)

circuit-kilometre kilomètre-circuit

circuit maintenance maintenance de circuits; ~ **module** module de circuit; ~ **noise level** niveau de bruit d'un circuit; ~ **number** numéro de ligne; ~ **operating time** durée

des manœuvres; ~ **pack** carte; ~ **partition-ing** mise en boîtier; ~ **routing** (physical path) routage (chemin physique)
circuitry *n* montage
circuit-switched connection connexion par commutation de circuits; ~ **data transmission service** service de transmission de données à commutation de circuits
circuit switching commutation de circuits; commutation de lignes
circuit-switching network réseau à commutation de circuits
circuit under test circuit à contrôler; ~ **usage** coefficient d'occupation d'un circuit
circular (logical shift) **list** liste à permutation circulaire; liste à rotation; ~ **electric wave** onde électrique circulaire
circular(-form) fluorescent tube Sylvanier (circline) [A.C.]
circular hunting recherche cyclique
circularity ratio irrégularité du diagramme de rayonnement
circular letter lettre type
circularly-polarized aerial antenne à polarisation circulaire; ~ **feed** alimentation en polarisation circulaire; ~ **wave** onde polarisée circulairement
circular magnetic wave onde magnétique circulaire; ~ **orbit** orbite circulaire; ~ **polarization aerial** antenne à polarisation circulaire; ~ **scanning** balayage circulaire; exploration panoramique; ~ **shift** décalage circulaire; décalage cyclique; rotation de bits; ~ **waveguide** guide d'ondes circulaire
circulate *v* diffuser; ventiler
circulated for preview prédiffusion
circulating current courant cyclique; ~ **memory** mémoire à circulation; mémoire circulante; mémoire cyclique; mémoire à ligne de retard; ~ **register** registre à circulation; registre de décalage (cyclique); ~ **storage** mémoire dynamique; mémoire à propagation
circulation *n* diffusion; ventilation; débit
circulator *n* (of waveguide) circulateur
circumscribe *v* délimiter
citizen's band (CB) bande banalisée; bande (de fréquences) publique; ~ **band channel** canal banalisé
civil engineering génie civil
clad *adj* revêtu; habillé; enrobé; blindé
cladding *n* enveloppe; gaine; habillage; enrobage; blindage
clamp *n* pince; peigne; collier; caleur; bride à capote; bride de serrage; diode de restitution du niveau de noir; diode de verrouillage; dispositif d'alignement; dispositif de blocage; serre-fils

clamped AFC (automatic frequency control) CAF à verrouillage; ~ **crystal** cristal encastré
clamping *n* blocage; arrêt; calage; ~ (of circuit) alignement; ~ **circuit** circuit de fixation d'amplitude; ~ **diode** diode antirecul; diode anti-retour; diode de clamping; diode d'écrêtage; diode de restitution du niveau de noir; diode de verrouillage; ~ **force** (torque) effort de serrage; ~ **plate** presseur; ~ **pliers** pince à morille; ~ **pulse** impulsion d'alignement; impulsion de verrouillage
clamp meter pince ampèremétrique; électro-pince
clamp-on attente; ~ (circuit) (circuit de) mise en garde; ~ **ammeter** pince ampèremétrique
clamp pulse impulsion de verrouillage
clandestine transmitter émetteur clandestin
clarifier *n* filtre; dispositif de réglage précis; ~ **range** clarté de réception
clarity *n* netteté; clarté
clash *n* conflit (d'accès); collision
clasp *n* attache rapide; agrafe; boucle; fermeture; loquet
class-A modulation modulation d'amplitude en classe A
class five office centre d'abonnés; ~ **four toll centre** (TC) centre interurbain
classical system (pre-Newtonian) système non quantifié
classification *n* classement; codification
classified (restricted circulation) diffusion restreinte
class marking discrimination; catégorie (cie)
class-of-service *n* catégorie de la ligne; catégorie d'abonné; ~ **digit** chiffre de discrimination; ~ **entitlement** discrimination
class-of-traffic signal signal de classe de trafic
class three primary centre (PC) centre principal; ~ **two sectional centre** centre de district
claw *n* pince
cleaning basket panier de lavage; ~ **fleece** feutre de nettoyage
clean room salle blanche
clear *v* abandonner; effacer; franchir; initialiser; libérer; mettre à zéro; raccrocher; remettre à blanc; remettre à zéro; acquitter; ~ (of fault) relever; résorber (un dérangement); déplacer; ~ *n* remise à zéro (RZ/RAZ); ~ *adj* blanc; libre; stable; ~ (uncoloured) naturel; incolore
clearance *n* dégagement; angle de garde; autorisation; couloir; écart d'isolement; espacement (pas); garde; hauteur sous

poutre; intervalle; isolement; jeu; suréléva-tion; ~ (of fault/alarm condition) acquitte-ment; effacement; ~ (endorsement) droit; visa pour application; autorisation; ~ **fit** ajustement mobile; ~ **gauge** gabarit; ~ **hole** trou de dégagement; ~ **ledge** rehausse; ~ **shim** cale de surélévation

clear area bande de sécurité

clear-back signal signal de libération en amont; signal de raccrochage (du de-mandé); signal de libération en arrière

clear band bande de sécurité; ~ **button** bouton de libération

clear-confirmation signal signal de confirma-tion de libération

clear-down *n* libération; rupture; relâche-ment; ~ **time** temps de libération; temps de relâchement

cleared *adj* désarmé; dépositionné; ~ **down** libre

clear-forward signal signal de fin de communi-cation; signal de libération en aval; signal de raccrochage

clear ground terre franche

clearing *n* (of connection) rupture; ~ (of optical fibres) division; ~ **bank** banque de compensation; ~ **drop indicator** annoncia-teur de fin de conversation; ~ **lamp** lampe de fin de conversation; lampe de supervi-sion (SUPER); lampe de clôture; ~ **loop** boucle de compensation; ~ **relay** relais du signal de fin; ~ **signal** signal de fin de communication

clear pulse impulsion d'ouverture; ~ **request** demande de libération; ~ **signal** signal de libération; signal de raccrochage (du demandé); ~ **sky** temps clair; ~ **test** langage clair; ~ **text** clair (texte etc.)

clear-to-current colour effaçage et passage à couleur actuelle

clear-to-send (CTS) prêt à émettre; autorisa-tion d'émission; ~ **(signal)** autorisation de lecture

clear-to-send-delay temps de renversement

clear-to-send time délai d'inversion

cleat *n* étrier; chape; peigne; taquet

clevis *n* étrier; ~ **pin** axe goupillé

click *n* bruit impulsif; claquement (de manipulation); cliquetis; clic; ~ **filter** filtre de cliquetis; ~ **generator** générateur de bruits impulsifs

clicking *n* (of contacts) crépitement

clickless sans cliquetis

cliff effect seuil d'erreur

climatic sequence (tests) essai composite climatique (essai combiné climatique); ~ **test enclosure** enceinte essais climatiques

climber *n* griffe

climbing *adj* ascendant

clinch *v* river; sertir; ~ *n* crantage; ~ (of component leads) bouclage; ~ (of termina-tions) rabattement; ~ **angle** angle de rabattement

clinching *n* rabattement; ~ (of terminations) précambrage; repliage

clinch nut écrou à sertir

clip *n* agrafe; attache rapide; cavalier; collier; étrier; loquet; pince; serre

clip-on character caractère encliquetable

clipped *adj* mutilé

clipper *n* circuit d'écrêtage; limiteur; sépara-teur; limitateur d'amplitude; ~ **amplifier** amplificateur limiteur

clippers *n pl* pince flanc

clipping *n* distorsion par écrêtage; écrêtage; mutilation; réduction d'articulation; ~ (voice) mutilation de la parole; ~ **cur-rent** courant d'écrêtage; ~ **level** niveau d'écrêtage; ~ **of syllables** mutilation de syllabes; ~ **of words** mutilation de mots; ~ **time** temps d'écrêtage; ~ **voltage** tension d'écrêtage

clip position secteur mort

clock *v* cadencer; ~ *n* horloge; générateur de rythme; base de temps (BT); clignoteur; ~ **card** carte de base de temps; carte horloge

clocked *adj* actionnée; pulsé; ~ **by** présenté au rythme de; ~ V_{dd} **operation** mode V_{dd} pulsé

clock frequency fréquence horloge; fréquence de base; fréquence d'horloge; ~ **(master) track** piste de rythme; ~ **pulse** impulsion d'horloge; impulsion de rythme; rythme

clock-pulse driver rythmeur; distributeur de phase

clock rate fréquence d'horloge; fréquence de base; fréquence horloge; ~ **read** consulta-tion horloge; ~ **recovery** récupération d'horloge; ~ **signal** temps; ~ **track** piste de synchronisation; piste horloge; ~ **wait** attente d'horloge

clockwise sens trigonométrique inverse; sens des aiguilles d'une montre

clockwise-polarised wave onde polarisée ellip-tiquement/(circulairement dextrorsum)

clog *v* encrasser

clogging *n* colmatage

clone *v* émulateur

close *v* (of contacts) enclencher; ~ (of tolerance) serré; ~ **coupling** couplage serré; couplage fort

closed circuit circuit fermé; circuit local

closed-circuit television télévision en circuit fermé; ~ **TV system** réseau TV en circuit fermé; ~ **wiring** transmission par batterie centrale; ~ **working** transmission par interruption de courant; transmission par rupture; transmission par ouverture de circuit

closed control circuit circuit local d'écoute; ~ **hole** trou borgne

closed-length numbering numérotation fermée

closed loop boucle fermée; chaîne de régulation

closed-loop control à asservissement de phase; ~ **network** réseau en mailles; réseau maillé

closed numbering (plan) numérotation fermée; ~ **numbering area** zone à numérotation fermée

close down v clore

closedown n arrêt; fin

closed pattern (extension) **spring** ressort à spires jointives

closed-shop operation exploitation à porte fermée

closed subroutine sous-programme fermé; ~ **user group** groupe fermé d'abonnés; ~ **user group (CUG)** groupe fermé d'usagers

close fit ajustement serré; ~ **of broadcasting** fin d'émission

closet n placard; armoire

close-talking microphone microphone de bouche; microphone de proximité; microphone labial; ~ **sensitivity** efficacité paraphonique

closing (of file) clôture; sortie

Clos network réseau de Clos

closure n fermeture

cloud and collision warning system radiodétecteur d'avertissement; ~ **clutter** fouillis par nuage; ~ **return** écho par nuages

cloudy weather temps couvert

clover-leaf aerial antenne en trèfle

club line ligne isolée; ligne veuve

cluster n grappe; banc; batterie; bloc; ensemble; faisceau; groupe; groupement; îlot; pool (de machines); réseau; ~ adj co-actif; **(cell)** ~ (of R/T system) motif (de cellule); ~ **controller** tête de grappe; serveur concentrateur; station serveur; serveuse; contrôleur de grappe

clustered-terminal working multiposte

clustering n groupage

cluster workstation station coactive

clutter n échos parasites; fouillis d'écho; obstacle; parasite(s); distorsion; perturbation; ~ **attenuation** affaiblissement au niveau des échos fixes; ~ **rejection** réjection de signaux parasites

CMA (s. channel mode access)

C-message weighting correction C-message

CMI (s. coded mark inversion)

CML (s. current-mode logic)

CMP (s. central monitoring position)

CMRR (s. common-mode rejection ratio)

CO_2 (s. carbon dioxide)

coalesce v interclasser; ~ (data files) fusionner; unir

coarse adj brut; grossier; ~ **adjustment** réglage approximatif; ~ **pitch** (of screw thread) qualité grossière; ~ **scanning** balayage approximatif; ~ **setting** réglage grossier

coastal radar radar côtier; ~ **radio station** radiostation côtière; ~ **refraction** réfraction côtière

coaster n patin; embout

coasting time temps d'indisponibilité

coat n revêtement; enduit; couche

coated adj revêtu; enrobé; chemisé; ~ **with film** pelliculé

coating n enduit; chemise; ~ **thickness** surépaisseur

coaxial adj coaxial; concentrique; ~ **aerial** antenne à jupe; ~ **aerial feeder** ligne coaxiale d'alimentation d'antenne; ~ **cable** câble coaxial; ~ **carrier system** système à courant porteur sur câble coaxial; ~ **control station** station directrice coaxiale; ~ **feeder** ligne d'alimentation coaxiale; ~ **line** ligne à paires coaxiales; ~ **link** liaison à paires coaxiales; ~ **pair** paire coaxiale; ~ **plug** presse-étoupe; ~ **tapered line** ligne coaxiale à résidence ondulaire à chargement continu; ~ **terminal** connexion coaxiale; ~ **trunk** bus coaxial; ~ **waveguide** guide d'ondes coaxial

co-channel interference interférence par canal commun; ~ **rejection** protection sur la voie utile

cockpit poste de pilotage

code n code; alphabet; argument; clé; indice; langage; numéro indicatif; sigle; ~ **bar** barre sélectrice

codec (coder-decoder) codec (codeur-décodeur)

code calling recherche de personnes au moyen de signaux d'appel codés; ~ **cam** came de signe

codec-filter chip COFIDEC

code combination couple de codes; ~ **conversion** conversion de code; transcodage; transposition des codes; ~ **conversion set** jeu de transcodage; ~ **converter** transcodeur (transcodeuse); convertisseur de code; équipement de transcodage; changeur de code; ~ **converter** (e.g. Gray to binary) transformateur de code

coded adj chiffré

coded-access extension poste à authentifica-

tion
coded backspace recul codé; ~ **character set** jeu de caractères codés
code-directing character caractère d'acheminement
code-division multiple access (CDMA) accès multiple par différence de code
coded mark inversion (CMI) inversion codée des 1; ~ **representation** représentation codée; ~ **ringing** appel sélectif; ~ **signal** signal codé; ~ **speech** parole codée; ~ **stop** arrêt sur code; arrêt programmé; ~ **time-signal generator** générateur de signaux de temps
code element élément de code; ~ **extension control function** fonction de commande d'extension de code; ~ **frequency** fréquence de code; ~ **garbling** mutilation du code; ~ **group** (e.g. tetrad) groupe de moments; groupe de code; ~ **hole** perforation significative
code-insensitive invisible; ~ **data communication** mode transparent
CODE key touche de contrôle
code letter chiffre caractéristique; indicatif littéral; ~ **line** ligne de programmation; instruction de programme; ~ **of practice** règles de l'art; déontologie; ~ **pulse** impulsion de code
coder n codeur; codificateur
coder-decoder (s. codec)
code sampling and injection board opérateur de prélèvement et d'injection de code; ~ **selector** roue codeuse; codificateur; sélecteur de préfixe; sélecteur de voie d'acheminement; ~ **translation** traduction de code; ~ **transparency** transparence de code
code-transparent transmission transmission transparente au code
codify v codifier
coding n codification; codage; chiffrage; chiffrement; programmation; ~ **delay** retard de codification; ~ **key** détrompeur; ~ **sheet** bordereau de perforation; feuille de programmation; feuille mécanographique
coefficient n coefficient; facteur; mantisse; taux; dérivé; ~ **of friction** coefficient de frottement
coercive force force coercitive; champ coercitif
COF (s. cursor off)
cog n dent
cogging n à coup (accoup); par saccades
cognate adj apparentés
cognition n connaissance
cog wheel roue dentée
coherence length of wavetrain longueur de

cohérence d'un train d'ondes
coherent beam faisceau cohérent; ~ **oscillator** oscillateur cohérent; ~ **pulse radar** radar à impulsions synchronisées; ~ **signal detection** détection de signaux cohérents; ~ **wave** onde cohérente interrompue; lumière cohérente
coherer n cohéreur
coil n bobine; bobinage; boudinette; enroulement; inductance; réactance; self; ~ (of cable) botte; ~ (of wire) couronne; ~ **aerial** antenne à cadres croisés; ~ **box** caisse de bobines; ~ **consumption** consommation des bobines
coiled adj enroulé en hélice
coiled-coil lamp lampe à filament bispiralé
coiled wire guirlande
coil-loaded cable câble pupinisé; ~ **circuit** circuit pupinisé
coil loading pupinisation; ~ **tap** prise sur une bobine
coil-winding wire fil de bobinage; fil à bobiner
coin-box n cabine (à) paiement; cabine publique; appareil à prépaiement; ~ **signal** signal de poste à prépaiement; ~ **telephone** appareil téléphonique à prépaiement; ~ **token** jeton
coincidence circuit circuit à coïncidence; ~ **element** ET (organe/fonction); ~ **error** erreur de coïncidence; erreur de simultanéité
coinciding adj correspondant
coin-operated television télévision à péage; télévision payante; télévision à accès conditionnel
coin station poste à prépaiement
cold bending courbure à froid
cold-cathode tube tube à cathode froide
cold drawing tréfilage à froid
cold-drawn adj écroui
cold fault incident sur démarrage à froid; ~ **forming** déformation à froid
cold-hammered adj écroui
cold hardening réactivité à froid; ~ **junction** (compensation) soudage froide
cold-rolled adj écroui
cold solder joint soudure froide; ~ **start** chargement initial; démarrage à froid; initialisation à froid; redémarrage lent; réinitialisation à froid; reprise totale; ~ **typesetting** composition froide
cold-welded (of crystal case) fermeture à froid (sous vide)
cold well source froide; milieu froid
cold-worked adj écroui
cold-working (of metal) formage à froid; transformation à froid
collapsible adj démontable

C

collar n collier; bague

collate v rassembler; agréger; centraliser; classer; fusionner; unir; interclasser; ordonner; regrouper; reprendre; résumer

collating n interclassement; ordonnancement; regroupement; ~ **sequence** ordre de classement

collation n collecte de(s) données

collator n ordonnanceur; interclasseuse; assembleuse

colleague(s) collaborateur(s)

collect call appel PCV; communication payable à l'arrivée (PCV)

collecting line lignes groupées; ~ **office** poste collecteur

collection, (coin) ~ encaissement; ~ **charge** taxe de perception; ~ **terminal** terminal de recouvrement

collector n plot; prise sabot; collecteur; ~ **(DC) current** courant (continu) de collecteur

collector-current multiplication factor facteur de multiplication du courant de collecteur

collector cut-off current courant résiduel de collecteur; ~ **depletion layer capacitance** capacité de la zone de transition du collecteur; ~ **electrode** cible

collector-emitter saturation voltage (of phototransistor) tension de saturation

collector junction jonction de collecteur; ~ **terminal** borne de collecteur

collect service PCV (payable à l'arrivée = percevoir) (code 10 en France)

collet n pince américaine; ~ **chuck** mandrin à pince; ~ **clamp** pince à mors

collimation n alignement

collision n double prise; choc; ~ **excitation** excitation par choc; excitation par impulsion; ~ **frequency** fréquence de chocs; ~ **of the first kind** choc de première espèce; ~ **warning** avertissement de collision

colloidal dispersé

colophony n colophane

colour adj polychrome; ~ **aberration** aberration chromatique; ~ **analyser** analyseur de couleur; ~ **binder** filin de couleur; ~ **code** code (des) couleur(s); coloris; ~ **coding** code (des) couleur(s)

colour-coding band (of resistor) anneau de marquage

colour frame/field trame primaire

colour-impregnated coloration dans la masse de l'enveloppe

colourless adj incolore; naturel; opale

colour lock (control) stabilisation de couleur; ~ **scheme** couleurs; ~ **signal processing** décodeur pour signaux de chrominance; ~ **television** télévision en couleur

colourtron tube trichrome à pénétration

Colpitts oscillator oscillateur de Colpitts

column n colonne; montant; manche; ~ **binary card** carte binaire par colonne; ~ **split** séparateur de colonne

coma aberration aberration en coma

comb filter filtre en peigne

(code) combination n combinaison(s)

combination n association; ensemble; mixage; regroupement; réunion; couple

combination(al) logic logique combinatoire

combinational settings correspondance

combination bar barre de sélecteurs; ~ **code** code articulé; ~ **frequency** fréquence de combinaison; ~ **knife/wire strippers** couteau pince à dénuder; ~ **pliers** pince universelle; ~ **spanner** clé mixte; ~ **tone** fréquence de combinaison

combine effectuer la sommation; regrouper

combined adj composite; banalisé; mixte; ~ **amplitude and phase modulation** modulation de phase différentielle et d'amplitude; ~ **distribution frame (CDF)** répartiteur mixte; ~ **listening and speaking key** commutateur combiné d'écoute et de conversation; ~ **service** service mixte; ~ **subscriber and transit exchange** centre mixte d'abonnés et de transit; ~ **tone-and-pulse dialling** numérotation mixte; ~ **twinning** hémitropie combinée

combiner n mélangeur; combinateur; ~ (of carrier system) coupleur d'émission; ~ **comb** peigne du combinateur; ~ **disk** disque du combinateur

combing n peignage

combining n panachage; ~ **filter** coupleur; ~ **unit** filtre quadruplex de sélection

comb printer imprimante à peigne

come on stream mettre en service; rendre opérationnel; connecter au réseau

comfort noise (level) bruit d'agrément; ~ **tone** tonalité d'attente; tonalité de patience

command n commande (cde); directive; ordre; ~ **form** grille; ~ **frame** fenêtre de commande; ~ **hot line/loop** téléphone rouge d'administration; ligne directe entre fonctionnaires du premier plan

commanding lead maîtrise

command processing traitement des ordres; ~ **set** langage de commande

commensurately proportionellement

comment n commentaire

commentary n commentaire

comments observations

commercial break message publicitaire; publicité radiophonique

commercially available du commerce; courant; ~ **viable** rentable

commission *v* mettre en service

commissioning *n* mise en service; démarrage; ~ **engineer** démonstrateur; ingénieur de mise en circuit

commodity *n* bien

common *v* banaliser; multipler; ~ *adj* commun; banalisé; centralisé; courant; décentralisé; général; global; multiple; partagé; partageable; polyvalent; simple; ~ **aerial** antenne commune; ~ **alerting system** appel général; réseau de sonnerie; sonnerie extérieure; ~ **area** zone commune; ~ **base** (of semiconductor) base commune; ~ **battery (CB)** batterie centrale (BC); batterie commune (BC)

common-battery signalling appel à batterie centrale; ~ **switchboard** tableau commutateur à batterie centrale

common battery system (CB) système téléphonique à batterie centrale

common-battery telephone set appareil téléphonique à batterie centrale

common battery telephone system téléphonie à batterie centrale; ~ **cable specimen** génératrice de câble; ~ **carrier** service public de télécommunications; exploitant; ~ **carrier frequency** fréquence porteuse commune; ~ **carrier grid** (lines) lignes banalisées et maillées; ~ **channel** voie commune

common-channel inter-office signalling signalisation par canal sémaphore; signalisation sur voie commune

common-channel management gestion par canal sémaphore

common-channel message message sémaphore; ~ **signalling (CCS)** signalisation sur voie commune; signalisation par canal sémaphore; signalisation dissociée; signalisation par voie commune; ~ **signalling circuit** circuit sémaphore

common-channel signalling monitor unité de gestion sémaphore; ~ **channel signalling path** voie de gestion

common-channel signalling table table sémaphore

common code code unique; ~ **collector** collecteur commun; ~ **control** commande centralisée; commande commune; ~ **control system** système à commande commune; ~ **core** tronc commun; ~ **data** données communes; ~ **designation** nom courant; ~ **earth** terre générale

commoned *adj* réunis entre eux; reliés entre eux; multiplés point à point; ~ **with** en commun avec

common emitter émetteur commun; ~ **equipment** équipement commun; ~ **hardware** consommables

common-impedance coupling couplage par impédance commune

commoning *n* mise en points communs; multiplage (sur); ~ **block** boîtier de compoundage

common instruction set code d'ordres unique; ~ **language** code unique; ~ **memory** mémoire commune; ~ **memory map** table de mémoires communes; ~ **mixing network** réseau de brassage commun; ~ **mode** mode commun

common-mode output voltage excursion en mode commun (Emc); ~ **rejection ratio (CMRR)** rapport d'affaiblissement dans le mode commun; taux de réjection en mode commun; réjection en mode commun (RMC)

common night service renvoi de nuit; service de nuit; ~ **pool** (of symbolic values) pool commun; ~ **return** retour commun; ~ **signal battery** batterie centrale pour la signalisation; ~ **signalling channel** canal sémaphore; ~ **signalling link** liaison de signalisation commune; ~ **software** logiciel banalisé

common-source reverse transfer capacitance (input short-circuited to AC) capacité de transfert inverse en source commune, entrée en court-circuit

common storage space espace partageable; ~ **suppressed frequency band** bande de fréquence commune supprimée; ~ **task** tâche déconcentrée; ~ **trunk** (in a grading) ligne commune (dans un multiplage partiel); ~ **trunk** jonction commune; ~ **trunk group** faisceau de jonctions communes

common-user channel canal pour usage commun

common wave onde commune

communication *n* communication; dialogue; échange; ~ **(data-link)** liaison

communications centre centre de communication (CDC); ~ **channel** circuit de télécommunication; ~ **chart** diagramme de communication; ~ **computer** ordinateur frontal; ~ **concentrator** concentrateur de communications; ~ **controller** contrôleur de communication; handler programme de dialogue; ~ **control unit (CCU)** contrôleur de transmission; ~ **equipment engineering** technique des communications; ~ **intelligence** intelligence de communication; ~ **interface** interface émission; ~ **link** liaison téléinformatique; ~ **mode** mode de communication; ~ **network** réseau de communication; ~ **priority** séquence des émissions; ~ **satellite** satellite de télécommunication; ~ **terminal concentrator** concentra-

teur de terminaux annuaire; ~ **zone indicator (COZI)** indicateur de la portée
communication to third party divulgation
communique n dépêche
community aerial antenne commune; ~ **antenna television (CATV)** télévision à antenne collective; télévision à antenne centrale
commutating bar barre de commutation; ~ **pole** pôle de commutation; ~ **zone** zone d'inversion
commutation zone plage d'inversion de courant
commutator n collecteur de courant; ~ **bar** lame (radiale) de collecteur; ~ **pulse** impulsion de positionnement; impulsion de commutation
commutator-rectifier n commutatrice
commutator ring anneau collecteur; commutatrice; ~ **segment** lame (radiale) de collecteur
compact à encombrement réduit; aggloméré; de faible encombrement; étroit; léger; peu encombrant; réduit; serré; succinct; ~ **disk** disque audionumérique; ~ **format** format compact
compaction n tassement
compact keypad clavier à dimensions réduites
compactness n faible encombrement; compacité; transportabilité
compact telephone téléphone compact; téléphone à cadran incorporé au combiné
companded adj avec compresseurs-extenseurs
compander n compresseur; ~ (compressor-expander) compresseur-extenseur
companding n compression-extension
company-wide global
comparable adj au choix; ~ **to** assimilable à
comparator n comparateur
comparing element comparateur
comparison (of check sums) biais (mettre en); ~ **voltage** tension de référence
compartment n alvéole; case; casier; cloison; panier
compass n boussole
compatibility n compatibilité; concordance; souplesse d'adaptation; cohérence; ~ **filter** filtre de compatibilité
compatible adj adaptable (à); opposable; cohérent; intermariable; supporté
compelled code code asservi; ~ **message** message non spontané; ~ **MF signalling** signalisation multi-fréquence asservie; ~ **multifrequency code** code multifréquence asservi; ~ **signalling** signalisation asservie; asserrissement
compelled-signalling protocol procédure asservie

compendium n résumé succinct; recueil
compensated squelch réglage silencieux compensé; ~ **volume control** réglage de gain compensé
compensating arm palonnier; ~ **circuit** circuit correcteur de distorsion; circuit de compensation; ~ **coil** bobine égalisatrice; ~ **wave** onde de repos
compensation n compensation; ~ **winding** enroulement de compensation
compensator n autotransformateur; correcteur; alternostat; circuit compensateur
competitor concurrent
compiler n autoprogrammeur; compilateur; ~ **writing system** métacompilateur
compile statistics comptabiliser
compiling n rédaction
complaints desk position de réclamations
complement n complémenteur
complementarity n correspondance
complemented (of sign bit) inversé
complementer gate circuit porte complémenteur
complementing output sortie complémentée
complement register complémentation d'un registre
complete v (of circuit) fermer; ~ (of data field) renseigner (rubrique); ~ adj intégral; ~ **carry** retenue complète; ~ **connection** chaîne de connexion complète
completed call communication efficace; appel établi; ~ **call rate** niveau d'efficacité
complete terminal attributes (CTA) attributs complets d'appareil
completion date délai; ~ **rate** taux d'efficacité; taux d'appels efficaces; ~ **to wrong number** appel aboutissant à un faux numéro
complex algorithm algorithme complexe; ~ **display** image complexe; ~ **filter cell** cellule complexe; ~ **sound** son complexe; ~ **target** objectif complexe
compliance n conformité; ~ **statement** certificat de conformité; ~ **with standard** alignement sur norme
compliant adj normalisé; ~ **with** conformé à (cf)
comply with v respecter
component n composant; élément; organe; partie; pièce (pce); ~ **body** corps de composant; ~ **lead-cropping machine** machine à couper les composants; ~ **parts** composition; constitution; ~ **parts catalogue** catalogue de pièces détachées
componentry n composants
component side (of PCB) (V$_{cc}$) côté éléments (côté composants); côté recto; face éléments (FE)
components of assessed quality composants

sous assurance de qualité

compool (symbol definition file) pool commun; fichier définition des symboles

composite *adj* mixte; conjugué; synthétique; ~ **attenuation** affaiblissement résultant; ~ **cable** câble mixte; câble composite; ~ **circuit** circuit approprié; circuit composite; ~ **climatic sequence** essai combiné climatique

composited circuit système Van Rysselbergh

composite image image synthétique; ~ **key** critère composite; ~ **loaded cable** câble pupinisé en fantôme; ~ **loading** charge du circuit fantôme; ~ **loss** affaiblissement composite; ~ **loudspeaker** enceinte acoustique à voies multiples; ~ **picture** synthèse; ~ **signal** signal composé; ~ **signalling module** signaleur mixte; ~ **video** vidéo mélangée; ~ **wave filter** filtre complexe

compositing *n* composition d'un circuit approprié

compound *n* corps composé; ~ *adj* composé; mixte; composite; ~ **parameter argument** argument de paramètre composé; ~ **signal** signal composite; signal composé; ~ **signal element** élément de signal composite; ~ **statement** instruction composée; ~ **target** objectif composé; cible composée

compress *v* comprimer; condenser

compressed air blower soufflette air comprimé

compression *n* compression; ~ **barrel** canon de compression; ~ **filter** filtre à compression; ~ **gland** presse-étoupe; ~ **law** loi de compression; ~ **set** rétention; rémanence par la compression; ~ **sleeve** manchon d'épissure; ~ **spring** ressort de compression; ~ **strength** résistance à la pression; ~ **test** essai de poussée

compressive stress effort de compression

compressor *n* bloque-cartes

compromise equalizer correcteur de compromis

Compton effect effet Compton

compunications téléinformatique

computation *n* calcul

computed *adj* ordonné; calculé; ~ **GOTO** instruction de branchement conditionnel

compute-limited *adj* asservi à la vitesse de calcul

computer *n* ordinateur; calculateur; organe de calcul; machine

computer-aided design (CAD) conception assistée par ordinateur (CAO); étude automatisée; ~ **design and manufacture (CAD/CAM)** conception et fabrication assisté par ordinateur (CFAO); ~ **instruction (CAI)** enseignement automatisé

computer-assisted *adj* automatisé; ~ **learning** apprentissage automatique; ~ **teaching (CAT)** enseignement assisté à l'ordinateur (EAO); ~ **testing** test assisté par ordinateur (TAO); ~ **training** formation automatisée; ~ **translation** traduction assisté par ordinateur (TAO)

computer-based *adj* automatisé

computer centre centre de calcul (CDC); ~ **code** code machine; code informatique

computer-compatible amovible

computer engineering génie informatique

computer(-integrated) production productique

computerization *n* informatisation

computerized *adj* informatisé; automatisé; ~ **exchange** central controlé par ordinateur; ~ **management system** outils informatiques

computer network environment structure physique

computer-oriented *adj* automatisé

computer peripheral handler handler de périphérie informatique; ~ **print-out** liste mécanographique; ~ **punchings** confetti(s); ~ **science** informatique; ~ **scientist** informaticien; ~ **shift** décalage; ~ **systems and (software) services market** sociétés de service et d'ingénierie informatique (SSII); ~ **systems engineering** ingénierie informatique; ~ **word** mot machine

computing *n* informatique; calcul

CON (s. cursor on)

concatenate enchaîner

concatenation *n* concaténation

concave angle angle rentrant

conceal display affichage en attente

concealed hinges charnières montées en feuillure; ~ **lighting** herse; ~ **trench** faux plancher

concentrated *adj* ponctuel; ~ **(lumped constant) circuit** circuit concentré; ~ **inductance** inductance concentrée; ~ **load** charge ponctuelle

concentration factor facteur de concentration; ~ **line** ligne de concentration; ~ **network** réseau de concentration; ~ **ratio** rapport de concentration; ~ **stage** étage de concentration; ~ **terminal circuit connections** brassage

concentrator *n* concentrateur; centralisateur; équipement de raccordement

concentrator-distributor concentrateur-diffuseur

concentrator stage étage de concentration

concentric *adj* coaxial; concentrique; ~ **cable** câblage coaxial HF; câble coaxial

concert pitch fréquence sonore étalon

conclusive (of test results) satisfaisant

CON/COF (s. cursor on/off)

concurrent *adj* simultané; en parallèle
concurrently-tuned jammer brouilleur accordable
concurrent processing multiprogrammation
condensed keyboard clavier à dimensions réduites; ~ **mercury temperature** température de mercure condensé
condenser *n* condensateur; ~ **lens** condenseur
condensing *n* retassement
condition *n* état
conditional assembly assemblage conditionnel; ~ **branch instruction** instruction de branchement conditionnel; ~ **breakpoint** point d'arrêt conditionnel; ~ **breakpoint instruction** arrêt dynamique conditionnel; ~ **halt instruction** instruction d'arrêt conditionnel; ~ **implication instruction** implication; ~ **jump** branchement conditionnel; ~ **jump instruction** instruction de saut conditionnel; ~ **probability** probabilité conditionnelle; ~ **search** recherche sur critères; ~ **transfer of control** instruction de branchement conditionnel
condition code (cc) bascule; ~ **flag** critère
conditioning *n* préconditionnement; prétraitement
condition of supply état de livraison
conductance (in siemens) *n* conductance (U); conductibilité (électrique)
conducted echoes échos à conduction
conducting *adj* passant; ~ **bridge** pont conducteur; ~ **state** état passant
conduction *n* conduction; ~ **angle** (of rectifier) angle de conduction; ~ **band** bande de conduction; largeur de conduction; ~ **current** courant de conductibilité; ~ **electron** électron de conduction
conductive foil plaquage; ~ **pattern** impression conductrice; ~ **pencil** crayon conducteur; ~ **strip** impression conductrice
conductivity *n* conductibilité (électrique)
conductor *n* conducteur; âme; fil; élément de câble; ~ **continuity** continuité des conducteurs; ~ **with equal-diameter strands** câble équibrins
conduit *n* conduit; gaine; passe-fil(s); serre-gaine
cone *n* cornet; ogive; balise; ~ **aerial** antenne en cône; ~ **of silence** cône de silence; ~ **of unreliability** cône de diffusion
conference *n* réunion; ~ **call** appel conférence; communication collective; ~ **circuit** circuit de conférence; ~ **connection** communication collective; ~ **jack** jack de conférence; ~ **junctor** joncteur de conférence; ~ **repeater** répéteur de conférence; ~ **telegraph repeater** translation télégraphique pour conférence

conferencing circuit conférenceur
confidence factor facteur de confiance; ~ **level** niveau de confiance; ~ **limit** limite de confiance
confidentiality *n* confidentialité; le secret; niveau de diffusion
configuration *n* configuration; agencement; arrangement; combinaison(s); constitution; diagramme; montage; positionnement; possibilité(s); présentation; schéma; structure; synoptique; implantation; ~ **sheet** fiche de configuration; configurateur
configured for PCM transmission micable
configured-in *adj* en configuration
configured-off *adj* hors configuration
configured-out *adj* en configuration restreinte; en configuration priviligiée
confinement layer couche de confinement
confirmation *n* confirmation; validation; vérification; visa; contrôle
confirmed loop condition boucle confirmée
confiscate *v* réavaler
confocal *adj* homofocal
conformal coating enrobage
conformance *n* conformité
conformity *n* conformité
conform to respecter
confusion area aire de confusion; ~ **reflector** réflecteur de confusion (de radar); ~ **region** zone de confusion; ~ **signal** signal de confusion
congested *adj* encombré; ~ **arc** arc encombré
congestion *n* encombrement; blocage; embouteillage; engorgement; saturation; ~ **meter** compteur d'encombrement; ~ **signal** signal d'encombrement; ~ **tone** tonalité d'encombrement
congruence *n* correspondance; coïncidence
conical fibre fibre conique; ~ **point (set) screw** vis à bout pointu; ~ **spiral aerial** antenne en spirale conique; ~ **(spring) washer** rondelle Belleville
conjugate attenuation coefficient affaiblissement sur impédances conjuguées; ~ **conducted echoes** échos à conduction conjuguée; ~ **impedances of a quadripole** impédances conjuguées d'un quadripôle; ~ **pathfinding and selection** sélection conjuguée; ~ **point** point acnodal
conjunction *n* opération ET
connect *v* raccorder; brancher (sur); aiguiller; connecter; desservir; relier
connected *adj* en liaison; ~ **call** appel établi; ~ **graph** graphe connexe; graphe courbe; ~ **hyphen** tiret inséparable; ~ **pairwise** reliés entre eux
connecting bar barre de raccordement;

C

~ **block** plaquette de connexion; ~ **box** herse; ~ **cable** câble de jonction; cordon de raccordement; ~ **circuit** circuit de conversation; circuit de connexion; ~ **clip** cosse de raccordement; clip de connexion; ~ **device** organe de raccordement; ~ **equipment** équipement de raccordement; ~ **pin** languette de connexion; ~ **relay** relais de liaison; ~ **space** espace insécable; ~ **strip** barrette de raccordement; ~ **terminal** borne de connexion; ~ **wire** cordon de liaison

connection *n* connexion; raccordement (racct.); branchement; articulation; communication; correspondance; jonction; liaison; mise en relation (avec); ~ **and signalling units** organes d'extrémité; ~ **box** boîte de raccordement; rosace de connexion; rosette de branchement; ~ **changeover** changement de chaîne; ~ **charge** quantum; ~ **circuit** pont de conversation; ~ **fee** abonnement; ~ **in progress** communication en cours d'établissement; ~ **layer** (ISO protocol) couche physique; ~ **message** message de connexion; ~ **quality index** indice de qualité de raccordement; ~ **rose** rosace de connexion; ~ **signal** signal de connexion; ~ **time** délai de satisfaction (de la demande); ~ **unit** unité de raccordement

connectivity *n* connexité

connector *n* connecteur; conjoncteur; embase (connecteur fixe); fiche de connexion; prise de courant; ~ (flow chart) renvoi (d'organigramme); ~ **applications** connectique; ~ **blade** (clip mounting) languette; ~ **casing** corps de connecteur; ~ **clamp** harpon; ~ **engineering** connectique; ~ **housing** corps de connecteur

connectorization *n* connexité; connectivité

connectorized *adj* connectorisé; ~ **cable** câble équipé; câble enfichable; câble conjoncté; ~ **lead** cordon enfichable

connectors *n pl* connectique; ~ **wired pin-to-pin** connecteurs reliés entre eux

connector systems connectique; ~ **technology** connectique

connect signal signal de prise

connect-through aboutissement

connect time durée en ligne; durée de communication

consecutive locations emplacements contigus

consequent *n* (math.) diviseur

conservatively-rated largement dimensionné

consignee *n* destinataire

consignment *n* lot; livraison; envoi; ~ **note** bordereau d'envoi; état de colisage; bordereau d'expédition

consistency *n* cohérence; homogénéité; identité; justesse; stabilité; unicité; ~ **check** contrôle de cohérence; nettoyage; contrôle de conformité; contrôle d'uniformité; vérification de la cohérence; ~ **checking** dégraissage

console *n* pupitre; banc; banquette; caisson; coffret; console; meuble; panneau; poste; valise; position dirigeuse; ~ **back-up** service réduit; ~ **board** carte de pupitre; ~ **display register** registre d'affichage; registre espion; ~ **management** gestion pupitre; ~ **operation(s)** pupitrage; ~ **operator** pupitreur; ~ **status** état pupitre

consolidation *n* synthèse; regroupement; complément de formation; concertation

conspectus *n* synthèse

constant *n* constante; coefficient; commande linéarisée; facteur; ~ **amplitude recording** enregistrement à amplitude constante; ~ **area** zone des constantes; ~ **e.m.f.** force électromotrice constante

constant-k (residual response) ondulation

constant-percentage bandwidth largeur de bande relativement constante

constant resistance network réseau à résistance constante; ~ **speed drive (CSD)** entraînement à vitesse constante; ~ **speed scanning** exploration à vitesse constante; ~ **starting torque** couple résistant constant; ~ **voltage** tension constante

constituent concentrations fourchette de pourcentage; ~ **part** organe

constructional drawing dessin de construction

construction plan dessin de montage

consultancy cabinet

consultant engineer ingénieur-conseil

consult a party on hold consultation sur attente

consultation call double appel; ~ **call** (with split) double appel courtier (va-et-vient); ~ **call - incoming** double appel extérieur; ~ **call on exchange line** double appel extérieur; ~ **call with transfer** double appel et transfert; ~ **hold** mise en garde pour information

consultation-hold facility service de double appel

consultation on hold consultation (d'un) demandeur en attente

consult call word mot de double appel

consult/enquiry call rétro-appel

consumables *pl* consommables

consumer *n* (of electricity) abonné; ~ **applications** grand public; ~ **sector** secteur à grande diffusion

consumption *n* consommation

contact *n* contact; plot; point; sabot; ~ **arrangement** combinaison des contacts;

~ **bank** banc de broches

contact-breaker (load cut-out) rupteur de charge

contact detector détecteur à contact; ~ **disk** galette; ~ **element** élément de contact; ~ **follow** accompagnement; ~ **force** force de contact; ~ **grip** tenue de la lame; ~ **grip on extraction** sécurité de contact à l'extraction; ~ **member** lame porte-contact

contact-modulated amplifier mutateur de puissance; amplificateur à condensateur vibrant; amplificateur à interrupteur

contact monitoring surveillance de contacts; ~ **noise** bruit de commutation et de friture; bruit des contacts; grésillement; ~ **operate** commande de contact

contactor *n* contacteur; ~ **unit** bloc de puissance

contact plunger piston à contact; ~ **potential difference** différence de potentiel au contact; ~ **rating** pouvoir de coupure (d'un contact); ~ **release** déclic; ~ **resistance** résistance de contact; ~ **set** groupe de contacts; ~ **spring** lame porte-contact; ~ **strip** (of PCB) lamelle

container *n* récipient; conteneur; abri; boîte; boîtier; coffret

containerization *n* mise en conteneur

containerized exchange central en conteneur

contaminant *n* salissure

contamination *n* pollution; ~ **tester** contaminomètre

content(s) *n* contenu; composition; occupation; teneur; titre

content-addressed memory mémoire rapprochée; ~ **mode** (search) mode associatif; ~ **search** recherche par le contenu; ~ **storage** mémoire associative; mémoire adressable

content-graded pureté

contention *n* (of lines) conflit (d'accès); encombrement; engorgement; erreur de rencontre

contentious *adj* antagoniste

content ratio taux d'occupation

contents *n* table des matières; ~ (of file) articulation

content search board opérateur de recherche et d'identification par le contenu

contents of memory état de mémoire

context manager gestionnaire de contexte; ~ **save** sauvegarde de contexte

contiguous *adj* contigu; jointif; adjacent; ~ (of memory cells) consécutif; ~ **file** fichier contigu; ~ **turn** (of coil winding) spire jointive

continental relay relais européen

continuation character caractère de répétition;

~ **form** imprimé suite; ~ **line** ligne suite

continuity *n* continuité; ~ **check** contrôle de continuité; ~ **equipment room** cabine de programme (en sonore); ~ **signal** signal de continuité; ~ **test** essai de continuité; ~ **tester** sonnette; ~ **testing** sonnage; ~ **wire** fil de continuité

continuous (sustained) **wave** onde continue; onde non amortie; ~ (signalling) changement d'état (signalisation); ~ (direct) **breakover current** courant (continu) de retournement; ~ **carrier** porteuse permanente; ~ **disturbance** bruit continu

continuous-duty *adj* permanent

continuous duty service continu

continuous-duty test essai de régime permanent

continuous form imprimé en continu; ~ **form paper** papier dépliant; ~ (direct) **forward current** courant direct (continu); ~ (direct) **holding current** courant (continu) de maintien; ~ **loading** krarupisation; charge continue

continuously-loaded cable câble à charge continue; câble krarupisé

continuously variable continu

continuous maximum rating valeur nominale maximale; ~ (direct) **off-state current** courant (continu) à l'état bloqué; ~ (direct) **off-state voltage** tension (continue) à l'état bloqué; tension de pointe à l'état bloqué; ~ (direct) **on-state current** courant (continu) à l'état passant; ~ (direct) **on-state voltage** tension (continue) à l'état passant; ~ (direct) **reverse blocking current** courant inverse (continu) de blocage; ~ (direct) **reverse current** courant inverse (continu); ~ **ring-back tone** retour d'appel permanent; ~ **ringing** sonnerie permanente; ~ (24-hour) **service** service permanent; ~ (two-state) **signalling** signalisation par changement d'état; ~ **signalling** signalisation continue; ~ **signals** signaux de type changements d'état; ~ **spectrum** spectre continu; ~ **stationery** état imprimante

continuous-surface reflector réflecteur à surface continue

continuous table table compacte; ~ **tone** tonalité continue; ~ **wave (CW)** régime continu; onde entretenue

continuous-wave signal (CW) signal en trait permanent

contract *n* contrat; affaire; marché; ~ **engineering** ingénierie; ~ **hardware description** descriptif matériel de l'affaire

contraction *n* retrait

contract manager ingénieur d'affaires

contractor *n* contractant; titulaire du marché;

entrepreneur
contract outline diagramme du marché
contradirectional interface jonction contradirectionnelle
contrast range domaine de contraste; contraste maximale; dynamique
control v commander; piloter; aiguiller; contrôler; ~ n commande (cde); gestion; pilotage; régulation; contrôle; conduite; attaque; asservissement; ~ **and switchgear** appareillage; ~ **axis** axe de commande; ~ **bit** bit de commande; ~ **board** carte de commande; ~ **box** coffret de commande; coffret de manœuvre; ~ **bus** bus de contrôle; ligne de commande; ~ **card** carte paramètre; carte ordre; carte perforée; ~ **channel** canal de commande; ~ **character** caractère de fonction; caractère de commande; caractère de service; caractère codé; caractère non imprimable; commande (cde); ~ **characteristic** caractéristique de commande; ~ **circuit** circuit de commande; circuit pilote; circuit directeur; ~ **circuit board** carte commande; ~ **complex** chaîne de commande et de gestion; ~ **computer** calculateur pilote; ~ **current** courant d'attaque; ~ **desk** pupitre de commande; console; ~ **desk** (of cable TV network) régie; ~ **electrode** électrode de commande; ~ **engineer** automaticien; ~ **equipment** équipement de commande; ~ **field** argument; champ couplé; ~ **finder** organe de commande; ~ **frequency** fréquence pilote; ~ **function** fonction de commande; ~ **gear** équipements d'automatisme; ~ **group** échantillon témoin; ~ **hand-over** remise au contrôle; ~ **indicator light (CIL)** voyant du clavier; ~ **information** informations d'ordre; ~ **input** entrée de commande; ~ **interval** intervalle de contrôle
CONTROL key gestion
control keypad bloc de commande; ~ **knob** bouton de commande
controllability n maniabilité
control language langage de commande; ordres de gestion
controlled adj asservi; réglable; ~ (value) paramétrable; ~ **carrier** porteuse commutée; ~ **communication** communication guidée; ~ **electric drainage** drainage électrique avec réglage aux potentiels négatifs minima; ~ **losses** fixation de l'affaiblissement; ~ **magnitude** consigne; index; ~ **outward dialling** accès au réseau contrôlé par l'opérateur; ~ **queue** file d'attente dirigée; ~ **slip** glissement commandé; ~ **temperature conditions** climatisa-

tion; ~ **trunk group access** accès au réseau controlé (par l'opérateur); ~ **voltage** tension stabilisée
controller n contrôleur; coupleur; asservisseur; directeur; régie; régulateur
control lever levier de commutation; ~ **line** ligne de service; ~ **line** (of screen) réglette (rg.)
controlling exchange centre directeur; ~ **operator** opératrice directrice; ~ **position** position directrice; ~ **test station** station directrice
control link liaison d'échange; ~ **logic pack** coffret logique; ~ **logic unit** logique pilote; ~ **logic unit software** logiciel pilote; ~ **loop** bande pilote; boucle d'asservissement; boucle de commande; boucle de régulation; ~ **manager** contrôleur du système (de base de données); ~ **mark** marque de bande; ~ **memory** mémoire de commande (MC); ~ **message** paramètre; ~ **message display** affichage de paramètres; terminal d'affichage de paramètres; ~ **module** périphérique programmé; ~ **network** réseau de commande; ~ **overlay** couvre-écran; ~ **panel** tableau de commande; pupitre de commande; panneau de commande; platine; ~ **point** point de contrôle; ~ **range** plage d'admission; ~ **ratio** facteur de commande; rapport de commande; ~ **register** compteur d'instructions; registre programme; compteur d'assemblage; ~ **relay** relais de commande; ~ **section** unité de commande; ~ **sequence** articulation; déroulement; ~ **signal** signal de commande; ~ **signalling** signalisation de commande; ~ **signals** signaux de gestion; ~ **station** station de contrôle; ~ **stick** commande (cde); ~ **system** chaîne de commande; système de commande; ~ **tape** bande pilote; boucle d'asservissement; ~ **test** essai contradictoire; ~ **total** total de contrôle; ~ **track** trace pilote; ~ **transfer** branchement; saut; ~ **transfer instruction** instruction de branchement; ~ **turn** enroulement de commande; ~ **unit** bloc de commande; carte de commande; coffret de commande; coffret de manœuvre; émulateur; organe; unité de gestion; organe de commande; régie d'abonnés; ~ **unit coupling** architecture d'association; ~ **value** point de contrôle; ~ **voltage** (of VCO) tension d'asservissement; ~ **winding** enroulement de commande; ~ **wire** fil de test et blocage; fil de maintien; ~ **word** mot de commande
convection-cooled à air brassé
convection current courant de convection

convenience outlet prise (de) secteur; ~ **telephone** téléphone de confort

convention n zone discriminante; ~ (of syntax) convenance

conventional adj classique; ~ **degree of distortion** degré conventionnel de distorsion

convergence n unicité; mariage; ~ **angle** angle de convergence

conversation n dialogue; conversation; échange

conversational adj de dialogue; interactif; ~ **mode** mode dialogué; mode conversationnel; ~ **terminal** terminal de dialogue

conversion n transformation; traduction; changement; conversion; passage; permutation; redressement; ~ (e.g. of two HF signals) mélange; ~ **circuit** opérateur de transformation; ~ **coating** couche de conversion; ~ **coefficient** facteur de conversion; ~ **detector** mélangeur; changeur de fréquence; ~ **efficiency** rendement de conversion; rendement anodique; ~ **film** base d'accrochage; ~ **filter** filtre de conversion; ~ **layer** base d'accrochage; ~ **loss** perte de conversion; ~ **mixer/transducer** transcodeur (transcodeuse); ~ **table** table de correspondance; ~ **transconductance** pente de conversion; ~ **unit** traducteur

converter n changeur; convertisseur; transformateur; traducteur; translation convertisseuse; ~ **circuit board** carte de conversion; ~ **frequency stability** stabilité de la transposition; ~ **relay** relais convertisseur; ~ **set/unit** groupe convertisseur; ~ **station** station de conversion

convertible transformable

convex angle angle saillant

convey transmettre; véhiculer; ~ (e.g. temperature via thermocouple) donner l'image

conveyor n convoyeur; ~ **control card** carte régulation convoyeur

convolution (integral) produit de convolution

cool v aérer

coolant n agent réfrigérant

cooling n ventilation; ~ **circuit** circuit d'eau; ~ **coil** serpentin; faisceau de tubes; ~ **fin** refroidisseur; radiateur; ~ **fluid** fluide frigorigène; ~ **plant** groupe réfrigérant; ~ **power** puissance frigorifique; ~ **shelf** châssis de ventilation; ~ **unit** électro-ventilateur; ~ **vane** refroidisseur; ailette de refroidissement

coordinate addressing adressage par coordonnées

coordinated transposition transposition coordonnée

coordinate layout quadrillage

coordinates pl abscisses et ordonnées; (**address**) ~ cotations (des adresses)

coordinate store mémoire matricielle

coordination loss affaiblissement de coordination

coordinator n centralisateur

copolarization (COPOL) COPOLAR

co-polar loss affaiblissement copolaire

copper n cuivre; ~ adj cuivreux

copper-clad board plaque cuivrée

copper loss perte de cuivre; perte par effet Joule; ~ **orthosilicate** chrysocal; chrysocolle

copper-oxide rectifier redresseur à oxyde de cuivre

copper ring collerette de cuivre; ~ **strap** bande de cuivre

copy v copier; mémoriser; rapatrier; recopier; transcrire; transférer; ~ (to) charger (en); inscrire (sur); ~ n copie; écho; exemplaire; trace; transcription; sauvegarde; ~ adj double; ~ **check** contrôle par duplication

copy-holder n porte-copies

copying n mémorisation; rapatriement; lecture

cord n cordon; ~ **circuit** circuit de fiche; cordon de connexion

cord-circuit repeater répéteur sur cordon

cordless adj sans cordon; ~ **phone** téléphone sans cordon de raccordement; ~ **plug** cavalier; ~ **position** position sans fiches ni cordons; ~ **switchboard** tableau commutateur manuel à clés

cord pair dicorde; ~ **repeater** répéteur de cordon; ~ **test circuit** circuit d'essai des dicordes

core n âme; cœur; conducteur; faisceau; mémoire; noyau; partie machine; tore; anneau (de ferrite); élément de câble; ~ **array** matrice de tores; ~ **belt** (of fibre optics) filin

core/cladding boundary interface cœur gaine

core cup coupelle

cored solder soudage autodécapante

core dump image mémoire

cored wire fil fourré

core image image mémoire; ~ **image library** bibliothèque exécutable; bibliothèque image-mémoire; ~ **image loader** chargeur image-mémoire; ~ **input** charge mémoire; ~ **jig** (yoke) culasse; ~ **material rod** barreau de cœur; ~ **matrix** matrice de tores; ~ **memory** mémoire à tores; mémoire à ferrites; ~ **plane/matrix** plan de tores; ~ **storage** mémoire à tores; ~ **wrap** enveloppe de l'âme; ~ **wrap** (of cable) feuillard

corkscrew aerial antenne en hélice; antenne hélicoïdale

corner-piece n gousset

corner reflector antenne en dièdre; réflecteur en trièdre; ~ **slot** dégagement d'angle

corona n effluve; aigrette; ~ **discharge** décharge par effet corona; ~ **loss** perte par couronne

corporate image bon renom

corrected adj pondéré; ~ **bearing** angle de relèvement corrigé; ~ **equivalent resistance error** écart équivalent corrigé

correcting amplifier amplificateur correcteur; ~ **loop** boucle de compensation

correction character caractère de correction; ~ **curve** courbe de correction; ~ **filter** filtre de correction; ~ **signal** signal de correction

corrective action modalités de reprise; ~ **maintenance** maintenance corrective

corrector n conformateur d'impulsions; correcteur; ~ **circuit** circuit compensateur

correlation n correspondance; synthèse; concordance; mise en relation (avec); ~ **function** fonction de corrélation; ~ **table** table de correspondance

correspondence memory mémoire de correspondance; ~ **table** table d'aiguillage

corridor n couloir

corrosion n agressivité; ~ **inhibitor** inhibiteur de corrosion

corrosion-resistant coating revêtement anticorrosif

corrugated cardboard carton ondulé; ~ **horn** cornet ondulé; ~ **jacket** enveloppe ondulée

corrugation n ondulation

corrupt v altérer; véroler; polluer; ~ adj erroné; vérolé; défectueux; ~ **bit** bit erroné; ~ **(data) block** bloc erroné

corruption n contamination; perturbation

COS (s. class-of-service)

cosecant-squared aerial antenne compensée; ~ **beam** faisceau à cosécante carrée

cosmic noise bruit cosmique; bruit extra-terrestre; souffle cosmique; ~ **ray** rayon cosmique

cost accounting comptabilité analytique

costed adj chiffré; valorisé

cost-effective adj économique; intéressant; à faible coût

cost-effectiveness rentabilité

cotter n clavette; ~ **pin** goupille cylindrique; goupille fendue

Cotton balance balance électrodynamique; ~ **bud** coton tige

cotton-fibre laminated (board) phénoplaste stratifié (PF str)

cotton swab coton tige

coulometer n coulomb-mètre

count-by-four circuit circuit compteur démultiplicateur 4:1

countdown n comptage régressif; décompte

counter n compteur; totalisateur; démultiplicateur; registre

counter-bore n lamage; chambrage

counter circuit circuit à comptage

counter-clockwise sens inverse des aiguilles d'une montre; sens trigonométrique; ~ **polarized wave** onde polarisée elliptiquement/ (circulairement sinistrorsum)

counterfeit adj faux

counterflow n contre-courant

countermeasure n mesure défensive

counterpart n homologue; interlocuteur

counterpoise aerial contrepoids d'antenne

countersinking n fraisure

countersunk adj encastré

counterweight n équilibreur

counting n comptage; dénombrement; ~ **circuit** circuit de comptage; ~ **gate** fenêtre de mesure

counting-rate meter fréquencemètre compteur

counting relay relais compteur; ~ **scales** balance compteuse

country code indicatif de pays; ~ **of destination** pays de destination; ~ **of origin** pays d'origine

count transfer créneau écriture de comptage; ~ **up** comptage progressif

couple v raccorder; relier; connecter; coupler; enclencher

coupled adj accouplé; ~ **circuit** circuit couplé; ~ **impedance** impédance réfléchie; ~ **relay** relais bagué; relais chemisé; ~ **reperforator and tape reader** retransmetteur à bande perforée (à lecture automatique totale)

coupler n coupleur; dispositif de couplage

coupling n accouplement; adaptateur; adaptation; articulation; bague; bride de fixation; cavalier; connexion; couplage; embout; interface; jarretière; jonctionnement; liaison; raccordement (racct.); raccord mécanique; ~ **box** boîte de raccordement; ~ **capacitor** condensateur de couplage; capacité de liaison; ~ **circuit** circuit de couplage; ~ **coefficient** coefficient d'accouplement; facteur de couplage; rapport de découplage (d'antennes); coefficient de couplage; ~ **coil** bobine de couplage; self de bouclage; ~ **factor** facteur de couplage; rapport de découplage (d'antennes); ~ **force** force d'accouplement; ~ **impedance** impédance de couplage; ~ **loop** boucle de couplage; sonde inductive; ~ **loss** perte au couplage; ~ **nut** écrou raccord; ~ **relay** relais de liaison; ~ **resis-**

tor résistance de couplage; ~ **stage** (of transmitter) cellule de couplage; ~ **transformer** transformateur de couplage; ~ **unit** conjoncteur; connecteur
course bearing relèvement approximatif
covalent adj homopolaire
cover n couvercle; cache; calotte; capot; capuchon; chape
coverage n couverture; taux de couverture; **(scanned)** ~ aire de lecture; ~ **area** zone de couverture; ~ **diagram** carte des zones desservies; diagramme de couverture
covered adj enrobé
covering n habillage
cover lay surépaisseur; ~ **layer** surépaisseur
cowl n hotte
cowling n capot
COZI (s. communications zone indicator)
CPE (s. customer premises equipment)
CPI (s. characters per inch)
CPM (s. critical path method)
CPR (s. cursor position report)
cps (s. cycles per second)
CPU (s. central processing unit); ~ **flag register** mot d'état machine; ~ **processor card** carte processeur; ~ **time** temps machine; ~ **timer** compteur de temps d'emploi
CQC (s. central quality control)
CR (s. carriage return); ~ (s. card reader)
crack n fêlure; cassure; ébréchure
cracking n cassure
crackle finish martelé; surface granitée
crackling n friture; grésillement; crépitage; ~ (of tin) cri
cradle n berceau; crochet; étrier; ~ **relay** relais miniature (polarisé); ~ **switch** crochet commutateur
craft n bâtiment
craftsperson agent; opérateur
crank n clé manivelle
crank-case n carter
crank pin maneton
crash v planter; ~ n arrêt imprévu; arrêt inopiné; arrêt intempestif; avalanche; bourrage de cartes; incident; panne; ~ **dump** vidage sur incident; plantage; ~ **(dump) file** fichier de vidage
crashed adj à l'arrêt
crate n alvéole; bac à cartes; boîte d'emballage; caisse; châssis; panier; ~ (controller) module physique
crater n cratère
crate trolley/dolly diable à caisse
crawl n (of TV lines) défilement
CRC (s. cyclic redundancy check)
CRDF (s. double-channel cathode-ray direction finder)

create v générer; réaliser
creation n élaboration; génération; mise en service; ~ **date** date de création; date d'enregistrement
credential référence
credentials n volet
credit n acompte; ~ **card** carte de crédit; support paiement
credited, to be ~ **against the next order** à valoir sur commande suivante
credit limit montant autorisé; ~ **note** avoir; ~ **rating** solvabilité
creep n fluage; cheminement; ~ **strength** tenue au cheminement; ~ **test** essai de fluage
crest n crête (c); sommet; ~ **factor** facteur de crête; facteur d'amplitude; ~ **forward voltage** tension directe transitoire de crête; ~ **value** valeur de crête; ~ **voltage** tension de crête; ~ **voltmeter** voltmètre de crête
crew n équipage; équipe; ~ **factor** (of articulation measurements) coefficient de pratique expérimentale
crib n copie
crimp v sertir; gaufrer; ~ n ondulation; pincement
crimp connector cosse; ~ **connector/terminal** cosse à sertir pré-isolée
crimped contact connector connecteur à contacts pincés
crimping n sertissage; griffage; ~ **machine** machine à sertir; ~ **pliers** pince à sertir; pince à main sertissage; ~ **tool** outil de sertissage
crimp nut écrou à sertir; ~ **press** balancier; ~ **terminal** cosse pour languette
crinkled adj ondulé; replié
crinkle washer rondelle Onduflex [A.C.]
cripple v arrêter
crippled adj arrêt; ~ **leapfrog test** test saute-mouton restreint; ~ **mode** (operation) exploitation en mode dégradé; mise hors service douce
criterion n critère; ~ **of degeneracy** critère de dégénérescence
critical adj critique; caractéristique; limite; ~ **angle** angle critique; ~ **coupling** couplage critique; ~ **damping** amortissement critique; ~ **frequency** fréquence critique; fréquence de coupure; ~ **grid voltage** tension critique de grille; ~ **path method (CPM)** méthode du chemin critique; ~ **path scheduling** programmation et ordonnancement; ~ **value** seuil; ~ **voltage** parabole de coupure; ~ **wavelength** longueur d'onde critique; longueur d'onde de coupure
crocodile clip pince crocodile; pince crabe

Crookes dark space espace sombre cathodique

crop v (of component leads) araser; ~ n coupe biaise; ~ **mark** hirondelle

cropping n cisaillage; ~ **and lead-bending machine** machine à couper et cambrer

cross-aisle intertravée

cross-arm (of telegraph pole) traverse

cross-band transponder répondeur à deux fréquences

crossbar. switch commutateur à barres croisées; commutateur électromécanique; ~ **switch horizontal** barre horizontale de commutateur; ~ **switching** commutation électromécanique; ~ **system** système à barres croisées; ~ **transformer** transformateur (de mode) par barre transversale

crossbar-type jack field connecteur à barres croisées

cross-bearing relèvement croisé

cross-check n contrôle de correspondance; bouclage; contrôle carré

cross-checking n contre-vérification

cross-connect n interconnexion

cross-connection n brassage; répartition; connexion transversale; jarretière

cross-connect panel brasseur; répartiteur; table de branchement; ~ **point** sous-répartition (SR); sous-réseau; ~ **terminal block** bloc de sous-répartition; ~ **unit (CCU)** multiplexeur-aiguilleur (MA); ~ **wire** fil jarretière

cross-correlation reception récepton à correlation croisée

cross-coupling n couplage parasite; diaphonie

crossed-field amplifier (CFA) amplificateur à champs croisés (ACC)

crossed line communication superposée; ~ **lines** intrusion

crossed-loop aerial antenne à cadres croisés; antenne Bellini-Tosi; antenne en tourniquet

crossed-path test test d'isolement

crossed-slot aerial antenne à fentes croisées

crossed-wire fault (shorting) mélange

cross-fade fondu enchaîné

cross-feed n intercommunication; ~ (of disk tracks) diaphonie

cross-fibre (coupling) fibre en travers

cross-fire induction télégraphique

crossfooting n addition horizontale

cross-hair n réticule

cross-hatched adj hachuré; grisé

cross-hatching n quadrillage

cross-head screw vis cruciforme; vis américaine; ~ **screwdriver** tournevis cruciforme

crossing n croisement

cross-linked adj réticulé

cross-member traverse

cross-modulation n intermodulation; diaphonie; distorsion d'intermodulation; transmodulation

cross-neutralization neutrodynage en croix

cross-office transfer time temps de transfert dans un central

crossover n croisement; traversée; pont; ~ **distortion** distorsion de raccordement; ~ **frequency** fréquence de recouvrement; fréquence de transition; ~ **network** pont diviseur; chaîne de commutation

crosspoint n point de connexion (PCX); point de croisement; ~ (memory) mémoire à connexion; ~ **array** matrice de connexion; ~ **matrix** maille; matrice de points de croisement; ~ **panel** tiroir

cross-polarisation jammer brouilleur à polarisation croisée

cross-polarization (XPOLAR) polarisation croisée; ~ **(XPOL)** CONTRAPOL

cross-polarized component composante à polarisation transversale

cross-product produit croisé

cross-reference n renvoi; ~ **table** table de correspondance; table de référence

cross-section n coupe; profilé traverse; section

crosstalk n diaphonie; intermodulation; bruit d'intermodulation; ~ **attenuation** affaiblissement diaphonique; ~ **attenuation meter** diaphonomètre; ~ **coupling** couplage en diaphonie; ~ **current** courant de diaphonie; ~ **level** niveau de diaphonie; ~ **loss** perte par diaphonie; ~ **path** parcours de la diaphonie; ~ **suppression filter** filtre de suppression de la diaphonie; ~ **volume** niveau de diaphonie

cross test test croisé

crowbar n pied-de-biche; pied de levage; pince à décoffrer; ~ **circuit** circuit à limitation en tension; ~ **protection** protection contre les surtensions; ~ **protection device** dispositif anti-surtension; butée

crowding n compression; tassement

crown n calotte

CRT (s. cathode-ray tube); ∻ **display** indicateur cathodique; ∻ **rejuvenator** régénérateur tube cathodique; ∻ **storage** mémoire électrostatique; ∻ **tester/rejuvenator** contrôleur et régénérateur de tube cathodique

cruciform rod ('T' rod) tige en +

crude adj brut

cruising range autonomie

crumpled adj replié; tordu

crusher n broyeur

cryogenic adj supraconducteur (à supraconductivité)

cryptography n cryptographie

crystal activity activité du cristal; ~ **blank** lame cristalline; ~ **control** commande par cristal; ~ **cut** coupe du cristal; ~ **detector** détecteur à cristal; ~ **diode** redresseur à cristal; ~ **driver** oscillateur pilote; ~ **element** élément de cristal; ~ **equivalent circuit** circuit équivalent d'un cristal; ~ **filter** filtre à cristal; filtre à quartz; filtre piézoélectrique

crystallizable glass verre dévitrifiable

crystallizing dish cristallisoir en verre

crystal loudspeaker haut-parleur piézo-électrique; ~ **mixer** mélangeur à cristal

crystal-oscillator drive pilote à cristal

crystal oven enceinte isotherme; ~ **receiver** récepteur à cristal; détecteur à cristal; récepteur piézoélectrique; ~ **rectifier** redresseur à cristal; ~ **video rectifier** redresseur à cristal vidéo

CS (s. chip select)

CSD (s. constant speed drive)

C-staged resin résite

CSW (s. channel status word)

CT (s. centre tap)

CTA (s. complete terminal attributes)

CTD (s. charge-transfer device)

CTE (s. channel translating equipment)

CTR (s. certified test record)

CTRL key touche de contrôle

CTS (s. clear-to-send)

CUB (s. cursor backward)

cubicle *n* coffret; armoire; caisson; compartiment; placard; baie

CUD (s. cursor down)

cue *v* inviter à frapper; appeler; informer; ~ *n* incitation; message d'identification; guide opérateur; indication; recherche rapide en bobinage; appel; ~ (recorder control) bobinage rapide

cueing message incitation; ~ **signal** signal pilote

CUF (s. cursor forward)

CUG (s. closed user group)

cumulative *adj* global; synthétique; cumulé; ~ **compound motor** moteur compound à flux additionnel; ~ **grade-of-service indicator** indice global de qualité de service (IGQS); ~ **interchange rate** cadence d'échange cumulée; ~ **outlay** immobilisations; ~ **register** compteur totalisateur

cup *n* (of crystal) cupule

cup-point set screw vis sans tête à cuvette; vis Allen (ST HC cuvette)

cuprous *adj* cuivreux

curbed *adj* bridé; ~ **modulation** modulation fragmentée

curing *n* durcissement; étuvage

curling *n* frisure

currency code code monnaie

current *n* courant; intensité; ~ (production) marche courante (MC); ~ *adj* actuel; courant; en cours; pointé; tenant

current(-carrying) capacity pouvoir d'écoulement

current (r.m.s. value) intensité; ~ **affairs** actualités; ~ **amplification factor** facteur d'amplification de courant; ~ **balance** balance électrodynamique; ~ **coil** bobine de courant; ~ **collector** collecteur de courant; ~ **commitment(s)** en cours de réalisation; ~ **compensating** self d'équilibrage des débits; ~ **conductor** conducteur d'électricité

current-controlled relaxation (sweep) oscillator oscillateur à relaxation commandé par le courant

current converter convertisseur de courant; ~ **density** (flow per unit cross-sectional area of conductor) densité linéique (d'un courant); densité de courant; ~ **drain** intensité absorbée; ~ **gain** facteur d'amplification de courant; ~ **instruction** phase de travail; ~ **item** occurrence courante; ~ **leak** déversoir; ~ **level** niveau absolu d'intensité de courant; ~ **limiter** limiteur de courant; ~ **limiting** limitation de courant

current-limiting reactor réacteur limiteur de courant; ~ **relay** relais limiteur d'intensité; ~ **resistor** résistance de limitation

current line (of data display) ligne active; ~ **loss** courant de court-circuit à la terre

currently assigned en cours d'affectation; ~ **selected** (of task) présélectionné

current mode mode courant

current-mode logic (CML) logique bipolaire (à) haute vitesse; ~ **switching** commutation en mode courant

current outlet prise de courant; ~ **peak** point d'intensité; ~ **pulse** impulsion de courant

current-rated measuring shunt shunt de mesure d'intensité calibré

current rating courant d'emploi; débit; ~ **relay** relais de courant; ~ **reversal** courant de retour; ~ **r.m.s. value** intensité courant continu (I_{CC}); ~ **source** alimentation en courant; ~ **stabilizer** stabilisateur de courant

current-stabilizing circuit circuit stabilisateur de courant

current stack frame sommet de la pile; ~ **surge** surintensité; choc de courant; ~ **swing** transition brutale de courant; ~ **task** tâche en cours; ~ **telephone influence factor** facteur téléphonique de forme du courant; ~ **to earth** courant de court-circuit à la terre; ~ **transformer** transformateur de courant

current-voltage characteristic caractéristique courant-tension

current weigher balance électrodynamique; ~ **weighting factor** rapport de pondération d'un courant

cursor *n* curseur; tiret clignotant; aiguille; ~ **backward (CUB)** recul du curseur; ~ **backward tabulation (CBT)** tabulation horizontale arrière; ~ **control keys** bloc du curseur; ~ **down (CUD)** descente du curseur; ~ **forward (CUF)** avance du curseur; ~ **movement** déplacement du curseur; ~ **off (COF)** curseur arrêté; ~ **on (CON)** curseur en marche; ~ **on/off (CON/COF)** visualisation du curseur; ~ **position report (CPR)** envoi de la position curseur; ~ **up (CUU)** remontée du curseur

curvature *n* galbe; courbure; sabre

curve *n* courbe; gabarit; pente; tracé

cushioned *adj* amorti; ~ **stop** butée progressive

cusp *n* sommet

custodian *n* gestionnaire

custom announcement service répondeur automatique fournissant une annonce pré-enregistrée

customary *adj* habituel; caractéristique

custom-build *v* construire sur mesure

custom-built *adj* à la carte

custom-designed *adj* spécifique; à la demande; personnalisé

customer *n* client; usager; utilisateur; abonné; acquéreur; ~ **assistance** réclamations (code 10 en France); ~ **benefits** caractéristique(s); ~ **centrex** centre privé de type centrex; ~ **enquiries** position de réclamations; ~ **enquiry form** questionnaire; ~ **overdraft** risque commercial; ~ **premises equipment (CPE)** installation terminale d'abonné (ITA); ~ **service** service après-vente (SAV)

customized *adj* personnalisé; personnalisable

customizing *n* adaptation; personnalisation

customs clearance dédouanement; apurement du dossier douanier

cut *v* (of metal) débiter; ~ *n* coupure

cut-and-paste buffer tampon de travail; mémoire banale; mémoire bloc-notes; mémoire de travail; ~ **presentation** maquettage; ~ **register** registre de travail

cut-away view vue en coupe; éclatement; vue partielle

cutback *n* réduction

cut-back method méthode par coupure

cut-in *v* mettre en circuit; ~ *n* entrée en tiers;

mise en tiers; intervention opératrice; conjoncteur; ~ **current** courant de collage

cut in service mise en service

Cutler feed alimentation par fentes

cut-off *n* blocage; point d'arrêt; temps de fermeture; temps de coupure; limite; ~ **attenuator** affaiblisseur à coupure; ~ **bias** polarisation de coupure; ~ **current** courant résiduel; courant de fuite; ~ **date** date de l'arrêté (comptable); ~ **frequency** fréquence de coupure; fréquence critique; ~ **jack** jack à rupture; ~ **key** clé de rupture; touche de coupure; ~ **parabola** parabole de coupure; ~ **region** plage de blocage; ~ **relay** relais de coupure; ~ **signal** signal de coupure; ~ **voltage** tension de coupure; ~ **waveguide** guide d'ondes évanescent; ~ **wavelength (of waveguide)** longueur d'onde de coupure; longueur d'onde critique

cut-out *n* coupure; suppression; ajourement; ébauche; coupe-circuit; fusible (fus.); conjoncteur-disjoncteur; ~ **current** courant de décollage; ~ **diode** diode de découplage; ~ **fuse** fusible sectionneur; ~ **panel** tableau à fusibles

cutover *n* mise en service; basculement

cut-over date date de mise en service

cutter for insertion head couteau pour tête insertion

cutters *n pl* ciseaux

cut-through relay relais de liaison; relais instantané; relais de connexion

cutting (of PCB) usinage; ~ **head** tête de coupe; ~ *n* **to length** coupe à (la) longueur

CUU (s. cursor)

CW (s. continuous wave); ~ **communication** (morse) graphie

C-wire *n* fil de blocage; fil de maintien; fil de test; fil de test et blocage

CW operation (morse) en régime continu

cybernetics (communication and control theory) cybernétique

cycle *v* boucler un cycle; ~ *n* course; boucle; coup; cycle; onde; passage; période; phase; séquence; temps; **(half)**~ alternance; ~ **delay** décalage cyclique; décalage circulaire; décalage de cycle; ~ **distributor** distributeur de cycles

cycle-index counter compteur de boucles; compteur d'itérations

cycle off *v* interrompre en cascade; interrompre pas à pas

cycle-rate counter compteur de périodes

cycles per second (cps) hertz (Hz)

cycle stealing accès direct en mémoire; vol de cycles

cycle-stealing mode fonctionnement en vol de

cycles

cycle time temps de cycle

cyclic *adj* cyclique; clignotant; périodique

cyclically *adv* en priorité tournante

cyclic code code cyclique; code binaire réfléchi; ~ **distortion** distorsion cyclique; ~ **list** liste à permutation circulaire; liste à rotation; ~ **redundancy check (CRC)** contrôle de redondance cyclique; ~ **shift** décalage cyclique; décalage circulaire;

permutation cyclique; progression circulaire; rotation de bits; ~ **switch** disjoncteur cyclique; ~ **time switch** minuterie

cylinder *n* barillet; bouteille; cylindre; ~ **reflector** réflecteur cylindrique

cylindrical socket cavalier; ~ **spool** bobine cylindrique; ~ **wave** onde cylindrique

cymomotive force (of aerial) force cymomotrice

D

DA (s. device attributes); ≈ (s. data area)
DAA (s. data access arrangement)
dabbler *n* bricoleur
dagger *n* croix; ~ **operation** NON OU (= NI)
daily back-up sauvegarde sélective
daily-keying instrument clé de jour
daily log état journalier; ~ **return** état journalier
daïs *n* allège; estrade
daisy-chain *n* guirlande
daisychain wiring câblage marguerite
daisywheel *n* marguerite; rayon; ~ **printer** imprimante à marguerite
DAMA (s. demand-assignment multiple access)
damage *n* déformation; détérioration
damped *adj* humecté; amorti; flottant; ~ **circuit** circuit apériodique; ~ **demodulator** démodulateur apériodique; ~ **measuring circuit** circuit de mesure flottante; ~ **oscillation** oscillation amortie; suroscillation; ~ **wave** onde amortie
damper *n* amortisseur; grille; grenaille
damper (winding) **grid** enroulement amortisseur
damp heat chaleur humide
damping *n* amortissement; décroissance; atténuation; ~ **circuit** circuit amortisseur; ~ **coefficient** coefficient d'amortissement; ~ **coil** bobine d'amortissement; ~ **diode** diode d'amortissement; ~ **factor** décrément; ~ **resistance** résistance d'amortissement; ~ **tube** diode d'amortissement; ~ **winding** enroulement d'amortissement
DAQ (s. define area qualification)
dark current courant d'obscurité; ~ **discharge** décharge obscure; ~ **resistance** résistance d'obscurité; ~ **space** espace sombre
dark-trace screen écran absorbant; ~ **tube** skiatron; tube à trace sombre; tube cathodique à écran absorbant
darlington driver Darlington de puissance
dash *n* tiret
dashed line ligne tiretée
dash length longueur de trait
DAT (s. digital audio tape)
data données; information(s); ~ (copied on disk) image (sur disque); ~ **above voice (DAV)** transmission de données supratéléphoniques; transmission de données supra-

vocales; ~ **access arrangement (DAA)** connecteur pour transmission de données; ~ **acquisition** acquisition de données; relevé de données; recueil des données; ~ **adaptor unit (DAU)** unité d'adaptation (de données); unité d'adaptation et de contrôle (de données); adaptateur d'interface; ~ **address** facteur adresse; ~ **alphabet** code; ~ **area (DA)** zone des données; ~ **array** ensemble de données; ~ **attribute** attribut; ~ **bank** banque de données; informathèque; ~ **base** base de données; informathèque; ~ **base interrogation** téléinformatique domestique; ~ **base look-up procedure** consultation de base de données; ~ **base management system** gestion de base de données; ~ **base manager** administrateur de base de données; ~ **base operator/supplier** fournisseur-système; ~ **base producer** producteur de base de données
data-base updating computer calculateur de mise à jour de la base de données
data bit bit utile; bit significatif; ~ **block** bloc de données; bloc d'informations; ~ **block backward jump** saut arrière de bloc; ~ **block forward jump** saut avant de bloc; ~ **break** accès direct en mémoire; ~ **bus** bus de données; bus de transfert d'informations; canal d'accès à la mémoire; liaison information machine; ligne d'information; ~ **bus line** canal collecteur de données; ~ **byte** octet de données (OD); ~ **call** appel de données; ~ **capture** saisie de données
data-carrier/medium support; porteuse de données
data cell mémoire à feuillets; ~ **chaining** chaînage de données; ~ **channel** circuit de transmission de données; voie de données; ~ **circuit** circuit de transmission de données; ~ **circuit terminating equipment (DTE)** équipement d'extrémité de voie de données; ~ **code** code de données; ~ **collation** mise en consultation; ~ **collection** collecte de(s) données; regroupement des données; ~ **collision at the DTE/DCE interface** collision d'appel à l'interface ETTD/ETCD; ~ **communications** communication de données; téléinformatique;

télématisation; ~ **communications network** réseau de transport de données; réseau de téléinformatique; ~ **compression** compression d'impulsions; ~ **connector** connecteur pour transmission de données; ~ **converter** convertisseur de données; ~ **(copied on disk)** image sur disque; ~ **demodulator** démodulateur de données; ~ **display unit** console de visualisation (CV); ~ **distribution** diffusion de données; ~ **element** donnée; rubrique; ~ **element chain** macroélément; ~ **entry** entrée de données; ~ **entry mode** mode entrée de données; ~ **examination** dépouillement des données; ~ **field** champ de données; ~ **file** fichier de texte; fichier bibliographique; ~ **format** structure de l'information; ~ **generator** configurateur

datagram *n* datagramme; ~ **mode** mode datagramme; ~ **queue length selection** choix de longueur de la file d'attente de datagramme

data graphics (stored graph display) infographie; ~ **handling** gestion des informations; ~ **host** serveur d'informations; ~ **input console** console de saisie; ~ **integrity** sauvegarde des données; ~ **in voice (DIV)** transmission de données vocales; ~ **library** bibliothèque de données; ~ **line** ligne d'information; ligne de transmission de données; ~ **line concentrator** multiplex de données; ~ **link** liaison de données; bus de liaison programmée; canal de transmission de données; bus de liaison programmée; ~ **link channel** canal de gestion; ~ **link connector** prise de données

data-link escape (DLE) sortie de code pour une commande; échappement transmission

data link interface organe de liaison; ~ **link message** lettregramme; ~ **link table** table sémaphore; ~ **location** rang donnée

datalog *v* imprimer

data logger enregistreur de données; collecteur de données; maquette d'essais; testeur

datamation *n* traitement automatique de données

data medium support de données; ~ **modulator** modulateur de données; ~ **module** chargeur autonome; ~ **network** réseau de transmission de données; ~ **out invalid** sortie non validée; ~ **over voice (DOV)** transmission de données supravocales; ~ **packet** paquet de données; ~ **packing** compactage des données; ~ **path** voie de données; ~ **pick-off element** palpeur; ~ **plotter** enregistreur X-Y; traceur de courbes; ~ **position** rang donnée; ~ **processing** informatique; traitement de don-

nées; ~ **processing centre (DPC)** centre de traitement des informations (CTI)

data-processing support facilities support informatique

data punch layout (of numeric keypad) configuration saisie de données; ~ **purification** nettoyage du logiciel; épuration; validation des données; ~ **record** enregistrement de données; article; ~ **recording medium** support d'enregistrement; volume; ~ **reduction** dépouillement des données; réduction de données; compression de données; ~ **retrieval** collecte de(s) données; extraction de l'information; ~ **retrieval terminal** terminal de consultation; ~ **routing** acheminement de messages; ~ **save store** mémoire économiseuse; ~ **select** sélection des données; ~ **selector** selecteur de données; ~ **separator** séparateur d'informations; ~ **set** ensemble de données; poste de données; modem (modulateur-démodulateur); ~ **set delay** délai d'inversion; temps de renversement; ~ **sheet** feuille de caractéristiques; fiche; ~ **shift left** entrée décalage série gauche; ~ **shift right** entrée décalage série droite; ~ **signal** signal de données; ~ **signalling rate selector (DTE/DCE)** sélecteur du débit binaire; ~ **signal rate selection** sélection de la configuration de multiplexage; ~ **sink** collecteur de données; récepteur de données; puits de données; ~ **source** source de données; ~ **station** station de données; ~ **stream** flot d'information; ~ **switch(ing unit)** commutateur de données; ~ **switch** centre de raccordement au réseau terrestre; ~ **switching exchange (DSE)** centre de commutation de données (CCD); central; ~ **(communications) terminal** terminal de télégestion; ~ **terminal equipment (DTE)** équipement terminal de transmission de données (ETTD); équipement terminal de traitement de données (ETTD); ~ **transducer** convertisseur d'informations; ~ **transfer rate** rapidité de transfert de données; ~ **transfer unit** bloc d'échange; ~ **transmission** transmission de données; ~ **transmission medium** support de transmission de données; ~ **transmitter** émetteur de données; ~ **under voice (DUV)** transmission de données infratéléphoniques; ~ **unit** ensemble de données; ~ **wire** fil d'information; ~ **written to core** (array) inscription des matrices

date *n* date; quantième; ~ **of commencement of service** date de mise en vigueur de l'abonnement

date-time group signal horodateur

datum *n* donnée; consigne; information(s); repère; origine; ~ **by datum** à la donnée; ~ **line** cote

DAU (s. data adaptor unit)

daughter board carte fille; carte enfichable; cartelette; module; sous-carte

DAV (s. data above voice)

day-file *n* journal

day frequency fréquence du jour

daylight lamp lampe lumière du jour; ~ **saving** changement saisonnier d'horaire

daylight-saving time change décalage horaire

daylight service range portée diurne

day of year quantième; ~ **range** portée diurne

day-time call conversation diurne; ~ **transfer** renvoi de jour

day-to-busy-hour ratio rapport du trafic journalier au trafic à l'heure chargée; facteur de concentration

day-to-day upkeep entretien en cours d'usage

DC (ohmic/true) **resistance** résistance courant continu (R_{CC}); ~ (s. double crucible process)

D/C (s. down-converter)

DC (s. direct current)

DC-AC inverter onduleur; ~ **single-phase inverter** onduleur monophasé

DC amplifier amplificateur de courant continu; ~ **anode power input** puissance d'alimentation (anodique); ~ **bell** sonnerie d'appel à courant continu

DCCC/DC3 (s. double-current cable code)

DC characteristics caractéristiques statiques; ~ **clamp diode** diode de calage; ~ **component** composante continue utile; ~ **converter** convertisseur continu-continu; convertisseur à courant continu; ~ **coupling** couplage conductif; ~ **coupling chain** chaîne amplificateur; ~ **current** intensité courant continu (I_{CC}); ~ **current gain** gain statique (h_{FE}); ~ **current transfer ratio** (CTR: $I_C/I_f = T$ [tau]) rapport de transfert de courant continu pour une tension collecteur-émetteur

DC-DC converter convertisseur continu-continu; ~ **voltage booster** survolteur continu-continu

DC deviation excursion en continu

DCH (s. delete character)

DC level niveau de la composante continue; ~ **parameter** caractéristique statique; ~ **re-insertion** restitution de la composante continue; restauration de la composante continue; ~ **resistance** résistance en continu; résistance ohmique; ~ **restoration** verrouillage; ~ **restorer diode** diode de calage; ~ **signalling** signalisation par courant continu; ~ **swing** excursion en continu; ~ **telegraph circuit** circuit métallique; ~ **telegraph system** installation télégraphique à courant continu; ~ **to AC converter** convertisseur continu-alternatif; ~ **transmission** transmission de signaux par courant continu; transmission avec composante continue utile; ~ **voltage** tension continue; ~ **voltage gain** gain statique en tension; ~ **voltage transformer** convertisseur continu-continu; ~ **voltmeter** voltmètre continu

DDD (s. direct distance dialling)

de-activate *v* désactiver; arrêter; couper; fermer

dead *adj* (of telephone line) muet; dans le vide; ~ (of battery) usé; ~ **band** bande vide; plage d'insensibilité; zone d'incertitude; ~ **centre** point mort; ~ **earth** terre franche; ~ **end** (of program) impasse; ~ **halt** arrêt immédiat; ~ **level** niveau inaccessible

dead-level signal signal d'information

deadline date limite

dead line ligne inactive

deadlock *n* impasse; panne mortelle; arrêt forcé

deadly embrace impasse; panne mortelle; arrêt forcé

dead reckoning (DR) à l'estime; ~ **sector** marge de service; ~ **segment** (of commutator) secteur mort; ~ **short(-circuit)** court-circuit franc; ~ **space** accord silencieux; zone morte; capacité inutilisé; ~ **spot** zone morte; ~ **time** temps mort; ~ **zone** zone neutre; ~ **zone** (of galvanometer) fourchette

dealer *n* revendeur; ~ **network** réseau de distribution tiers

de-allocate *v* désaffecter

de-assign *v* libérer

debatable time temps non imputable

debited *adj* prélevé

deblocking *n* dégroupage

de-bounce suppression de rebondissements

debug *v* dépanner; mettre à jour

debugging *n* mise au point (MAP); contrôle; dépannage; espionnage système; nettoyage; suppression des erreurs; ~ (of software) optimisation de logiciel; ~ **aid** outil de mise au point; ~ **(aid) routine** programme d'aide à la mise au point; ~ **routine** metteur au point

de-bunched *adj* éclaté

debunching *n* décompression; dégroupement

deburr *v* casser les angles (vifs)

deburring *n* adoucissage; ébavurage

DEC (number) sender émetteur DC

decade contact contact de décade; ~ counter compteur décimal; ~ (tens) counting circuit circuit décade; ~ resistance box boîte à décades; ~ selection sélection décimale; ~ system système à décades

decadic (signalling) code code décimal; ~ keypad clavier décimal; ~ pulse dialling numérotation au cadran; ~ sender émetteur décimal; ~ signalling signalisation décimale

decal n décalcomanie; étiquette; légende; pastille

decametric (short) wave (HF band) ondes décamétriques

decay v affaiblir (s'); ~ n décroissance; affaiblissement; amortissement; déclin; désintégration; détérioration; dissipation; évanouissement; persistance (d'écran); retombée; extinction; ~ characteristic caractéristique d'extinction; ~ current courant d'extinction

decayed adj amorti

decay factor coefficient d'amortissement; caractéristique de persistance d'écran; constante de dissipation; décrément; ~ time période transitoire finale; temps de décroissance; temps de descente; temps de retombée; ~ time (of pulse) durée de suppression

Decca lane zone équiphase

deceive station pseudo-radiostation

decelerating electrode électrode de ralentissement

deceleration n abaissement; freinage; croissance en ralentissement; ~ time temps d'arrêt

decentralized adj éclaté; ~ printing impression décentralisée; ~ task tâche déconcentrée

decibel n décibel (dB)

decimal comma virgule; ~ decoder décodeur décimal; ~ digit chiffre décimal; ~ point (math.) virgule; ~ read-out signal signal de sortie décimale; ~ rounded to the nearest whole number valeur décimale tronquée à un entier; ~ scaler compteur décimal; ~ system système décimal; ~ to five-unit code conversion traduction décimal/5 MOM moments

decimetric wave (UHF band) onde décimétrique

decimillimetric wave (ultramicrowaves) onde décimillimétrique

decineper n décinéper

decipher v décoder

deciphering printer imprimeur direct

decipherment n déchiffrage (déchiffrement)

decision box (of flowchart) symbole de décision; ~ circuit circuit de décision; ~ content contenu décisif; ~ element critère de décision

decision-feedback system système détecteur d'erreurs avec demande de répétition; RQ automatique

decision logic logique de décision

decision-maker n décideur

decision-making graphics graphiques décisionnels

decision-oriented décisionnel

decision table table de décision; ~ value amplitude de décision

deck n platine; ~ of (punched) cards paquet de cartes

declaration n déclaration

declarative macro directive; ~ statement déclaration

declassified déclassé

decline n baisse; déclin

decode n (section) partie de décodage

decoded chip bit de message

decoder n décodeur

decoding n décodage; déchiffrage (déchiffrement); conversion du signal d'appel; application des critères de reconnaissance; ~ pyramid pyramide de décodage; ~ relay relais de décodage

decollation n déliassage

decometer n décomètre

decompress v décomprimer

decompression n détente

deconcentrated core architecture déconcentrée

decongestion n désencombrement

decontamination épuration

decorator set (of telephone) poste d'intérieur

decoupler n séparateur; ~ (rectifier) découpleur; ~ (isolated data transmitter) calibrator calibrateur découpleur

decoupling capacitor condensateur de découplage; condensateur de dérivation; condensateur d'isolement; ~ filter filtre de découplage; ~ inductor inductance de découplage; ~ network réseau de découplage; filtre de bande; ~ resistor résistance de découplage

decrease v abaisser; diminuer; ~ n abaissement; ~ of gain diminution du gain

decreasing adj descendant

decrement v diminuer; ~ n décrément; pas de régression; décompte; décroissement

decremental adj décroissant

decrementation n décomptage

decremeter n décrémètre

decrypt v décoder

decryption n déchiffrage (déchiffrement)

dedicated adj spécifique; débanalisé; personnalisé; spécialisé; réservé; particulier;

~ **channel** canal réservé; ~ **commands** commandes opérateur; ~ **data network** réseau de donnees spécialisees; ~ **distributed core** architecture à cœur réparti spécialisé; ~ **exchange** software logiciel individuel de site (LIS); ~ **features** spécificités; ~ **line** ligne débanalisée; liaison spécialisée; ~ **message switching centre** commutateur de message spécialisé; ~ **peripheral controller** coupleur spécifique d'un périphérique; ~ **satellite** satellite spécifique; ~ **storage** mémoire débanalisée; ~ **switch** commutateur spécialisé; ~ **tasks** application; ~ **time slot** canal particulier; ~ **to** destiné à; ~ **VF equipment** équipements BF spécialisés

deem v juger; considérer

de-emphasis n désaccentuation; affaiblissement

de-emphasizer n atténuateur; affaiblisseur; circuit de désaccentuation

de-emphasizing filter filtre de désaccentuation

de-energize v désexciter; mettre hors tension

de-energized adj à l'arrêt; coupé; au repos

de-energizing n désamorçage; désexcitation

deep-sea adj de grand fond; ~ **cable** câble sous-marin de grand fond

de-excitation n désexcitation

default address adresse implicite; ~ **attribute** attribut par défaut; ~ **bucket size** taille par défaut d'une région; ~ **configuration terminal** terminal implicite

defaulter n (subscriber account) abonné défaillant

default file fichier implicite; ~ **full-row attributes** attributs par défaut pour ligne complète; ~ **full-screen attributes** attributs par défaut d'écran complet; ~ **option** option implicite; ~ **pitch** échappement standard implicite; ~ **value** valeur implicite; valeur prise; ~ **volume ID** nom de volume implicite

defect n défaut; anomalie; faute; panne; vice; avarie; aléa

defective défaillant; défectueux; en défaut; infidèle; non conforme; ~ **modulation** modulation incorrecte (m. infidèle); ~ **PCB** circuit imprimé hors service (CIHS); ~ **ringing** appel défectueux

defer v ajourner; renvoyer; ~ **a call** différer une communication

deferment n dérogation

deferred adj différé; ~ **action** action différée; ~ **address** adresse différée; ~ **addressing** adressage indirect; adressage différé; ~ **call** communication différée; ~ **call ticket** ticket d'appel différable; ~ **hotline station** poste à correspondant unique

différé (PCUD); ~ **stop** arrêt différé; ~ **telegram** télégramme différé

deficiency n carence

deficit n manquant

define v définir; caractériser; déterminer; préciser; ~ **area qualification (DAQ)** attribut de définition de zone

defining text sélection de texte

definition n résolution; définition; mise au point (MAP); netteté; précision; sensibilité; ~ **parameter** borne

definitive design épure

deflecting coil bobine de balayage; ~ **plate** plaque de balayage; ~ **voltage** tension de déviation

deflection n déviation; déflection; ~ **amplifier** amplificateur de déviation; ~ **angle** angle de déviation; ~ **coefficient** coefficient de déviation; ~ **coils** bloc de déviation; bloc de déflexion; ~ **defocussing** élargissement du spot; ~ **distortion** distorsion de déviation; ~ **field** champ de déviation; ~ **plane** plan de déviation; ~ **ratio** rapport de déviation; ~ **sensitivity** sensibilité de déviation

deflector n déviateur; électrode de déviation; grille; séparateur; plaque de déviation; ~ **coil** bobine de déviation; ~ **plate** électrode de déviation

deform v altérer

deformation n distorsion; déformation; ~ **inhibitor** frein de fluage; frein thermique

de-fuse v désamorçer

degarbling n débrouillement

degassing n dégazage

degausser n démagnétiseur; effaceur

degaussing n démagnétisation; désaimantation

degeneracy n dégénérescence

degenerate mode mode dégénéré

degeneration n contre-réaction

degenerative (negative-feedback) amplifier amplificateur à contre-réaction; ~ **feedback** contre-réaction

degradation n dégradation; usure

degrade v dégrader; perturber

degraded (mode) operation fonctionnement dégradé

degreasing n nettoyage au solvant; décapage; ~ **agent** décapant; ~ **unit** distilleuse

degree of assurance degré d'assurance; ~ **of attack** (of cables) agressivité; ~ **of balance** degré d'équilibrage; ~ **of damping** degré d'amortissement; ~ **of distortion** taux de distorsion; ~ **of distortion in service** degré de distorsion en service; ~ **of disturbance** degré de perturbation; ~ **of freedom** degré de liberté; ~ **of gain** degré d'amplification;

~ **of gross start-stop distortion** degré de distorsion arythmique global; degré de distortion totale dans le système de déclenchement automatique; ~ **of individual distortion of a particular significant instant** (of a modulation or a restitution) degré de distorsion individuelle d'un instant significatif déterminé (d'une modulation ou d'une restitution); ~ **of inherent distortion** degré de distorsion propre; ~ **of isochronous distortion** degré de distorsion isochrone; ~ **of mismatch** degré d'adaptation; ~ **of modulation** taux de modulation; ~ **of severity** niveau de gravité; ~ **of standardized text distortion** degré de distorsion pour le texte d'essai normalisé; ~ **of synchronous start-stop distortion** degré de distorsion arythmique au synchronisme; degré de distorsion pour le synchronisme d'émetteur et de récepteur; ~ **of unbalance** degré de dissymétrie

de-icing system système dégivreur

de-ionization rate vitesse spécifique de désionisation; ~ **time** temps de désionisation

de-ionized water (distilled water) eau déminéralisée

de-ionizing grid grille de désionisation

del (math.) opérateur nabla

DEL (s. digital entrance link); ~ (s. rub-out character)

delamination *n* (of PCB) délamination

delay *n* retard; attente; décalage; distorsion; durée; temps d'attente; temps de transit; ~ (of receiver or amplifier) **to step function excitation** délai de réponse à un échelon; ~ **bias** tension de retard; ~ **call** appel avec attente; ~ **circuit** circuit à retard; ~ **code** code à accès mimimum; ~ **counter** temporisateur

delay-dialling signal signal invitant à différer la numérotation

delay distortion distorsion non linéaire; distorsion de temps de propagation; distorsion du temps de transit de groupe; distorsion de phase; ~ **distortion correction** correction de la distorsion du temps de transit

delayed *adj* différé; retardé; temporisé; décalé; ~ **action** action différée; ~ **action alarm** alarme intervention différée; alarme temporisée; ~ **action fuse** fusible temporisé; ~ **alarm** alarme différée; ~ **automatic gain control** commande automatique de gain à seuil; ~ **backward release** relâchement arrière différé; ~ **blocking** blocage doux; ~ **call** appel différé; conversation retardée; ~ **charge metering** taxation différée; ~ **ringing** renvoi d'appel forcé;

~ **stop** arrêt différé

delay element élément de temporisation; retardateur; ~ **equalizer** compensateur du temps de propagation; compensateur de phase; correcteur de phase; correcteur du temps de transit; ~ **lamp** lampe de signalisation de retard; ~ **lens** lentille à retard de phase; ~ **line** ligne de retard; circuit à constante de temps; ~ **line** (lumped circuit) circuit à constantes localisées

delay-line register registre à circulation; ~ **store** mémoire à propagation; mémoire à circulation; mémoire à ligne de retard; mémoire circulante; mémoire cyclique; mémoire dynamique

delay network réseau retardateur; ligne de retard; ~ **on de-energization** temporisation repos; ~ **on energization** temporisation travail; ~ **optimization** optimalisation du retard; optimalisation du temps de transit; ~ **signal** signal de retard; ~ **switch** commutateur à action retardée; ~ **system** système avec attente; ~ **time** (t_d) délai d'attente; temps de retard à la croissance; temps de retard à la montée; ~ **unit** retardateur; ~ **working** exploitation avec attente; appel avec attente; appel différé; suspension d'appel

de-leaving *n* déliassage

delete *v* effacer; supprimer; annuler; détruire; éliminer; enlever; purger; ~ **character** (DCH) suppression de caractères

deleted *adj* écrasé

delete line (DL) suppression de ligne

deleterious *adj* adverse; injurieux

deletion *n* effacement; suppression; destruction; élimination; oblitération; ~ **record** article éliminé; enregistrement d'annulation

deliberately *adv* à dessein; volontairement

delimit *v* délimiter

delimiter *n* borne; délimiteur; drapeau; sentinelle; séparateur

deliver *v* livrer; fournir; véhiculer

delivered power (W into ohms) puissance de sortie (W sous ohms); puissance débitée

delivery *n* extraction; refoulement; sortie; ~ (side) dépouille; ~ **confirmation** confirmation de remise; ~ **date** délai; ~ **docket** bordereau de livraison (BL); ~ **form** état de livraison; ~ **lot** lot de livraison; ~ **method** mode de livraison; ~ **of telegrams** remise des télégrammes; ~ **schedule** bordereau de livraison (BL)

Dellinger effect effet Dellinger; évanouissement brusque

delta aerial antenne adaptée en delta;

~ **connection** montage en triangle; connexion en triangle; couplage en triangle

delta-connection secondary (winding) à secondaire triangle; ~ **transformer** transformateur à secondaire triangle

delta-delta connection connexion triangle-triangle

delta matching adaptation en delta; ~ **modulation** modulation delta; ~ **network** réseau en delta; ~ **voltage** tension en triangle

demagnetization n désaimantation; démagnétisation

demagnetizing field champ de désaimantation; ~ **turn** spire de désaimantation; ~ **winding** enroulement de désaimantation

demand-assignment multiple access (DAMA) accès multiple avec assignation en fonction de la demande (AMAD)

demand factor facteur d'utilisation; coefficient d'utilisation; ~ **forecasting** prévision de la demande; ~ **paging** pagination à la demande; ~ **position** position pour exploitation sans attente; ~ **processing** traitement immédiat; ~ **service** exploitation sans attente; ~ **tasking** en tâche à la demande; ~ **trunk network** réseau interurbain pour exploitation sans attente; ~ **working** exploitation sans attente

demarcation n délimitation; ~ **line** ligne de partage

democratic (mutually synchronized) **network** réseau démocratique

demodulation n démodulation; ~ **effect** effacement; ~ **of an exalted carrier** réception homodyne; ~ **stage** étage démodulateur

demodulator n démodulateur; détecteur

de-mount v démonter

demultiplex v démultiplexer

demultiplexer (DEMUX) n démultiplexeur

demultiplexing n démultiplexage

DEMUX (s. demultiplexer)

denatured alcohol alcool dénaturé

denial n interdiction; refus; blocage

denied adj impossible; inaccessible; interdit; ~ **origination** ligne spécialisée en arrivée (SPB); ~ **origination subscriber** abonné spécialisé en arrivé (SPB); ~ **termination** ligne spécialisée en départ (SPA)

denied-termination subscriber abonné spécialisé en départ (SPA)

de-noise v éliminer les perturbations

denomination n caractérisation

denote v désigner; indiquer

denoted adj symbolisé

dense adj compact; serré; ~ **list** liste linéaire

densitometer n opacimètre; densitomètre

density n densité; base volumique; ~ (of paper) grammage; ~ **modulation** modulation de densité; ~ **of conductors** concentration des conducteurs; ~ **of electron** (ion) **beam** densité d'un faisceau électronique; ~ **of electrons** densité électronique

dent n bosselure; échancrure

deny v interdire; refuser

departure n dérive; déviation; dérogation; écart; particularité

dependent adj asservi; ~ **exchange** centre rattaché; centre local secondaire; ~ **program** programme subordonné; ~ **station** station tributaire; station téléalimentée

depict v caractériser; indiquer; montrer

depleted adj épuisé

depletion n rupture; épuisement; ~ **layer** couche d'arrêt; couche de barrage; zone de raréfaction; ~ **layer capacitance** capacité de jonction; capacité de transition; ~ **mode** à appauvrissement; ~ **rate** taux de perte(s); ~ **region** barrière de potentiel; zone déplétée

Deplistor tripôle (d'aiguillage)

deploy v mettre en jeu; affecter

deployment n mise en œuvre; mise en disponibilité; mise en place; rattachement; articulation

deposit n dépôt; décharge; goutte

deposited layer couche en formation

deposition n dépôt

depot n centrale; ~ **ship** bâtiment atelier

deprecated adj à proscrire; déconseillé; ~ (term) terme à éviter

depreciation n amortissement

depress v actionner; appuyer; enfoncer; abaisser

depressed market conjoncture morose

depression n abaissement; appui

depth n profondeur; intensité; largeur; ~ **gauge** jauge de profondeur; ~ **of velocity modulation** profondeur de modulation de vitesse

deque n (double-ended queue) file double

de-rated adj réduit; à puissance réduite

de-rating n réduction de charge; déclassement; détalonnage; détimbrage; ~ **curve** courbe de réduction de puissance; ~ **factor** coefficient de réduction

de-regulation n déréglementation

derelict adj épavé

derivation n départ; dérivation

derivative n tributaire; base; ~ adj différentiel; ~ **action** action dérivée; ~ **equalizer** correcteur différentiel

derived carrier porteur dérivé

descender n jambage

descending order ordre décroissant

descrambler n désembrouilleur; débrouilleur

description *n* libellé
descriptor *n* descripteur; identificateur; mot directeur; identité
de-select *v* désactiver
de-selected *adj* hors service (h.s.)
de-selection of data output in OR-tie operation temps de propagation du X à la sortie
de-select mode mise hors fonction
deserializing *n* déchaînage
desiccant *n* dessicateur; sachet déshydratant
desiccator *n* dessicateur
design (philosophy) *n* conception; ~ dessein; étude; configuration; calcul; avant-projet; réalisation; ~ *adj* théorique; nominal; stylique; de calcul; ~ **assumption** hypothèse de calcul
designator *n* bit indicateur
design automation conception automatisée; ~ **centre** bureau d'études; ~ **details** constitution
designer *n* concepteur; constructeur; réalisateur; analyste; ingénieur de projet
designer's guide guide utilisateur; guide de conception
design features présentation; généralités; ~ **level** évolution; ~ **limits** contraintes; ~ **load capacity** capacité théorique de charge; ~ **objective** hypothèse; ~ **parameters** contraintes industrielles; ~ **ratings** dimensionnement; ~ **revision status** état technique; ~ **standards** esthétique; ~ **tolerance** marge théorique; ~ **value** valeur théorique
desired *adj* théorique; ~ **value** valeur de consigne; valeur désirée
desk *n* bureau; console; meuble; position; poste; pupitre; table; ~ **calculator** machine à calculer; ~ **check** contrôle de programmation
de-skew (of data) synchroniser
desk telephone set poste téléphonique de table
desk-top *adj* type mobile; ~ **calculator** machine à calculer de bureau; ~ **model** type de table; ~ **telephone set** poste mobile
desk with modesty panel bureau avec retour
de-solder *v* dessouder
de-soldering iron fer à dessouder; ~ **pump** pompe à dessouder
despatch *v* envoyer; livrer; distribuer; aiguiller; ~ *n* envoi; dépêche
despatcher *n* dispatcheur
despatcher's console pupitre de dispatcheur
despatch note bordereau d'envoi; bordereau d'expédition; ~ **to site** expédition sur chantier
despotic (synchronized) **network** réseau à synchronisation despotique
de-spun *adj* stabilisation dans les trois axes;

~ **aerial** antenne contre-rotative; antenne stable dans l'espace
destaticizer *n* éliminateur
destination address adresse de destination; ~ **file** fichier destinataire; ~ **register** registre arrivée; ~ **side** aval (en); ~ **(terminating) exchange** centre d'arrivée
destroy *v* détruire; altérer
destructive addition addition destructive; ~ **read** lecture avec effacement; lecture destructive; ~ **storage** mémoire à régénération; ~ **test** essai aux limites (E/L); recherche des limites
detachable *adj* amovible; débrochable; démontable; enfichable; mobile; rapporté; ~ **keyboard** clavier séparé; clavier mobile
detachment *n* décentralisation
detail *n* pièce de détail; élément; rubrique; mouvement; ~ **card** carte détail; ~ **drawing** dessin détaillé; plan de présentation
detailed analysis analyse organique; ~ **billing** facturation détaillée; ~ **billing facility** droit aux justifications; ~ **format** format détaillé
detail file fichier mouvement; fichier détail; ~ **specification** feuille particulière (FP); spécification de définition; spécification particulière
detection *n* détection; prise en compte; ~ **grating** treillis détecteur
detector *n* détecteur; sonde; démodulateur; capteur; ~ (of control system) cellule; ~ (of alarm system) avertisseur; ~ **circuit** circuit de détection; ~ **tube** tube détecteur
detent *n* cliquet; ergot; ~ **arm** cliquet de retenue (pour) tête; levier d'arrêt; levier de calage
deterioration of shade dégradation des teintes
de-tune *v* désaccorder
de-tuned *adj* discordant
de-tuning *n* décalage de fréquence; déréglage; désaccordage
de-update *n* reprise
deuteron *n* deutéron
developed *adj* évolué; élaboré
development *n* mise au point (MAP); évolution; ~ **contract** marché d'étude; ~ **engineer** chercheur; ~ **system** outil de développement
deviant *adj* aberrant; déréglé
deviation *n* dérive; décalage; écart; dérogation; détournement; déviation; excursion de fréquence; fourchette; voie détournée; ~ **absorption** absorption ionosphérique à déviation de vitesse de groupe; ~ **factor** coefficient de déviation; ~ **ratio** facteur de déviation; indice de modulation; rapport de déviation

D

device *n* dispositif; appareil; boîtier; composant; machine; mécanisme; module; opérateur; organe; outil; unité physique; terminal; ~ **attributes (DA)** demande d'attributs d'appareil; ~ **configuration** aiguillage; ~ **control** commande d'appareil auxiliaire; ~ **flag** mot d'état d'organe; registre d'état de périphérique; ~ **interconnection and hardware configuration file** fichier de brassage; ~ **internal storage structure** topologie; ~ **management** gestionnaire d'accès périphériques; ~ **ownership** possession de l'écran; ~ **protocol** protocole d'appareil; ~ **queue** file d'attente de périphérique; ~ **select** sélection du périphérique; ~ **status** état d'un organe; ~ **status report (DSR)** demande d'état d'appareil; ~ **status word** mot d'état d'organe; ~ **wait (DW)** dispositif en attente
devolution *n* décentralisation
de-wetting *n* démouillage
dew point point de rosée
'Dexion' [T.N.] cornière perforée
DF (s. direction-finding)
diad *n* doublet
diaeresis *n* tréma
diagnosed *adj* mise en cause
diagnosis *n* accusation
diagnostic *adj* déterministe; ~ **message** diagnostic; ~ **program** programme diagnostique; ~ **report** diagnostic; ~ **routine** programme de localisation de pannes; analyse; programme diagnostic; ~ **test** essai de fonctionnement
diagonal clipping distorsion diagonale du signal
diagonalizing *n* émission multiple d'un programme à fréquences multiples
diagram *n* schéma; diagramme; carte; courbe; épure; figurine; graphique; plan; tableau; planche; ~ **panel** tableau indicateur optique
dial *v* sélectionner; afficher; appeler; faire un appel; numéroter; ~ *n* cadran d'appel; ~ **(up)** composer un chiffre; composer un numéro (d'appel); ~ **blank** cache cadran
dial-controlled call diversion droit au renvoi temporaire
dial cover cache cadran; ~ **dictation** télédictée
dial-dictation access accès à un service de dictée centralisé; ~ **trunk** circuit de télédictée
dial effect bruit de sélecteurs; ~ **exchange** bureau automatique; autocommutateur; central automatique
dial-in-handset telephone téléphone à cadran incorporé au combiné
dialled *adj* appelé

dialled-up *adj* commuté
dialler *n* numéroteur automatique
dialling *n* numérotation; numérotage; sélection; composition d'un numéro; manœuvre; appel; accès; ~ **analysis** analyse de la numérotation; ~ **code** indicatif (IF); préfixe de prise; liste d'indicateurs; ~ **effect** bruit de sélecteurs; ~ **error** fausse manœuvre; erreur de manœuvre; ~ **excess digits** surnumérotation
dialling-out appel au cadran d'un centre manuel distant
dialling pulse impulsion de numérotation; ~ **signal** signal de numérotation; ~ **speed** délai d'attente de tonalité; ~ **time** temps d'appel; ~ **tone** tonalité d'invitation à transmettre; signal de manœuvre; ~ **unit** tuner sélecteur
dial mechanism mécanisme de cadran; ~ **office** autocommutateur
dialogue *n* conversation; dialogue; échange; ~ **function** fonction de dialogue; ~ **mode** mode conversationnel
dial-operated exploitation automatique
dial-out line ligne à prise directe (du réseau)
dial plate cadran; disque d'appel; disque numéroté; ~ **prefix** numéro indicatif; ~ **pulse** impulsion décimale; impulsion de numérotation
dial-pulse contacts contacts des impulsions du cadran d'appel; ~ **distortion** distorsion de numérotation; ~ **translator for selective calling** convertisseur du courant d'appel pour appel sélectif
dial-scheduled alarm call demande de réveil
dial selection numérotation au cadran; sélection par cadran; ~ **socket** mâchoire de cadran; ~ **telephone set** poste téléphonique à cadran; ~ **tone** tonalité d'invitation à numéroter; tonalité de manœuvre; tonalité d'envoi
dial-tone connection présélection; ~ **delay (DTD)** durée d'attente de tonalité; délai d'invitation à numéroter; retard de tonalité
dial tone first (DTF) signal de manœuvre immédiat; ~ **tone repetition** reprise de tonalité
dial-up *v* numéroter (au cadran d'appel); composer au clavier
dial up *n* composition
dial-up *adj* automatique; ~ **access** accès commuté; ~ **circuit** circuit commuté; ~ **conference call** appel en conférence automatique; ~ **exchange** central manuel sans cordons; ~ **line** ligne PTT; ligne à prise directe (du réseau); ligne automatique; ligne commutée par numérotation; ligne réseau (LR); ligne téléphonique;

~ **network** poste à cadran (CAD); réseau automatique; réseau commuté automatique; réseau commuté avec numérotation; ~ **telephone** poste à cadran (CAD)

diametral winding enroulement à pas entier

diamond knurling moletage croisé; ~ **paste** pâte diamantée

diamond-shaped losange; ~ **aerial** antenne en losange

diamond winding enroulement sur gabarit

diaphragm *n* diaphragme; membrane; ~ **relay** relais à diaphragme

diaphragm-ring filter filtre à diaphragme annulaire

diary *n* agenda

dibit *n* groupe de deux bits

dice *n pl* puces

dichomotizing search recherche binaire (dichotomique)

dichotomizing test test dichotomique

dicing *n* découpage en dés

dictionary *n* dictionnaire; répertoire

DID (s. direct inward dialling)

die *n* grain; puce; ~ **and stock** matrice et poinçon

die-cast *adj* moulé sous pression

dielectric amplifier amplificateur à élément ferro-électrique; ~ **array** réseau d'antennes diélectriques; ~ **base** isolant; ~ **breakdown** mauvais isolement; ~ **constant** pouvoir inducteur spécifique; ~ **current** courant de fuite; ~ **density** densité de fuite; ~ **lens** lentille diélectrique; ~ **loss** perte diélectrique; ~ **material** matériau isolant; ~ **puncture** perforation diélectrique; ~ **radiator** antenne diélectrique; ~ **rod radiator** antenne pylône diélectrique; antenne en cierge; ~ **soak** polarisation diélectrique; ~ **strain** pouvoir diélectrique; ~ **strength** rigidité diélectrique; ~ **viscosity** viscosité diélectrique; ~ **waveguide** guide d'ondes diélectrique; ~ **withstanding voltage** tension de tenue; rigidité diélectrique

die sinking gravure en creux

die-stock *n* filière

DIF (s. digital interface)

di-fan aerial antenne en éventail double

difference *n* différence; désaccord; écart; ~ **file** fichier différentiel; ~ **of capacity** écart de capacité

differential *n* écart; ~ **amplifier** amplificateur différentiel; ~ **anode resistance** résistance interne différentielle; résistance en courant alternatif; ~ **arrangement** connexion différentielle; ~ **attenuation** affaiblissement différentiel; ~ **attenuator** atténuateur différentiel; ~ **bridge** pont différentiel; ~ **compound winding** enroulement différentiel;

~ **connection** couplage en opposition; ~ **current amplifier** amplificateur du courant différentiel; ~ **earth ringing** appel direct en connexion simultanée avec retour par la terre; ~ **echo suppressor** suppresseur d'écho différentiel; ~ **encoding** codage par transition; ~ **equalization** égalisation différentielle; ~ **excitation** excitation différentielle; ~ **gain** gain différentiel; ~ **gain control** affaiblissement sélectif; ~ **galvanometer** galvanomètre différentiel; ~ **input impedance** Z entrée différentielle; ~ **input signal** tension différentielle d'entrée; ~ **loss** atténuation différentielle; ~ **modulation** modulation différentielle; ~ **multiplexer-demultiplexer** double multiplexeur-démultiplexeur; ~ **pair** paire différentielle; ~ **phase modulation** modulation de phase différentielle; ~ **protective system** protection différentielle; ~ **relay** relais différentiel; ~ **resistor** résistance différentielle; ~ **separating filter** filtre différentiel d'aiguillage; ~ **voltage** tension différentielle; ~ **voltage transmitter** émetteur différentiel

differentiating circuit circuit de différentiation; différentiateur; ~ **filtre** filtre différentiateur; ~ **network** circuit linéaire

differentiation operator opérateur dérivation

differentiator *n* circuit dérivateur; montage différentiateur; ~ (logic) dérivateur

diffracting edge arête de diffraction

diffraction attenuation affaiblissement de diffraction; ~ **edge** arête de diffraction; ~ **fringe** tache de diffraction; ~ **loss** affaiblissement par diffraction; ~ **pattern** diagramme de diffraction; ~ **region** région de diffraction

diffuse *adj* hétérogène; diversifié; dispersé; ~ **density** densité diffuse

diffused lens package boîtier plastique diffusant

diffuser *n* vasque; ~ (mesh/grid) grille de défilement

diffuse reflectance réflexion diffuse

diffusing *adj* diffusant

diffusion constant constante de diffusion; ~ **length** longueur de diffusion; zone de diffusion

digest *v* assimiler

digit *n* chiffre (ch.); élément numérique; indice; symbole; caractère; élément de signal

digit-absorbing selector sélecteur absorbeur

digital *adj* numérique; logique; ~ **adder** additionneur à trois entrées; additionneur complet; ~ **audio tape (DAT)** bande audionumérique

digital/binary tout ou rien (TOR)

digital block bloc numérique; ~ **carrier** multiplex numérique; ~ **carrier equipment** équipement multiplex numérique; ~ **channel** voie numérique; voie temporelle (VT); ~ **clock** chronomètre numérique; ~ **coding** codage numérique; ~ **communications system** système de communication numérique; ~ **computer** calculateur numérique; ~ **concentrator** concentrateur numérique; ~ **connection** communication numérique; ~ **connection unit** centre de raccordement numérique; ~ **data** données numériques; ~ **data** (bits) information numériques décimales; ~ **data capture** acquisition tout ou rien (TOR); ~ **data packing** compression données numériques; ~ **discriminator** discriminateur numérique; ~ **display** affichage numérique; ~ **distribution frame** répartiteur numérique; ~ **distributor** brasseur (de voies numériques); ~ **earth** zéro logique; ~ **entrance link (DEL)** déport numérique; ~ **error** erreur numérique; ~ **feedback** asservissement numérique; ~ **filling** remplissage numérique; ~ **filter** filtre numérique; filtre en peigne; ~ **form** forme numérique; ~ **frequency meter** fréquencemètre numérique; ~ **gateway** centre de raccordement numérique; ~ **ground (GRD**ᴅ**)** masse logique; ~ **group** terminal numérique d'extrémité; ~ **incremental plotter** traceur numérique; ~ **(display) indicator** indicateur numérique; ~ **indicator encoder** circuit décade indicateur numérique; ~ **indicators** afficheurs numériques; ~ **input** entrée logique; entrée de données; ~ **input - voice answerback (DIVA)** entrée de données et réponse vocale; ~ **integrated circuit** circuit intégré logique; microstructure logique; ~ **interface (DIF)** jonction numérique; ~ **junction** jonction numérique; abonné numérique; ~ **line** ligne numérique; ~ **line path** conduit de ligne numérique; ~ **line terminal** terminal numérique de ligne

digitally-controlled local oscillator oscillateur local à réglage numérique

digital measurement recorder enregistrement numérique de mesure; ~ **multimeter** multimètre numérique; ~ **multiplex** multiplex numérique; ~ **multiplex equipment** équipement de multiplexage numérique; ~ **multiplex hierarchy** hiérarchie de multiplexage numérique; ~ **multiplex terminal** terminal de multiplexage numérique; ~ **or binary** tout ou rien (TOR); ~ **path** conduit numérique; ~ **period counter** périodemètre numérique; ~ **radio path** conduit hertzien

numérique; ~ **read-out** prélèvement numérique; ~ **repeater** répétiteur numérique; ~ **satellite exchange** centre satellite numérique; ~ **signal** signal numérique; ~ **span line** liaison numérique; ~ **speech concentration** concentration numérique de conversation; ~ **stream** train numérique; ~ **subscriber carrier system** système multiplex numérique d'abonnés; ~ **sum variation** variation de la somme numérique; ~ **switch** centre de commutation numérique; centre de commutation temporel; ~ **switching** commutation numérique; commutation temporelle; ~ **switching equipment (DSGE)** signaleur; ~ **switching network** réseau de connexion numérique

digital-switching stage étage de commutation numérique; étage de commutation temporelle

digital switching subsystem unité de connexion numérique; ~ **telephone** téléphone électronique

digital-to-analogue conversion (s. D-A conversion); ~ **converter** circuit numérique-analogique

digital tones and announcements channel voie source; ~ **train** train numérique; ~ **transmission** transmission numérique; ~ **trunk** jonction numérique

digit compression compression de chiffres binaires; ~ **driver** amplificateur d'écriture; ~ **emitter** distributeur de phase; rythmeur

digitization n numérisation; conversion en numérique

digitize v numériser; quantifier; codifier en numérique

digitizer n numériseur; codeur numérique; quantificateur; convertisseur; ~ **pad** tablette digitalisante

digitizing pad table à digitaliser; ~ **tablet** table à digitaliser

digit key-strip clavier d'impulsions; ~ **position** rang; ~ **rate** débit numérique; ~ **receiver** auxiliaire de numérotation

digitron n tube indicateur; tube Nixie

digits (numerical layout) chiffraison

digit-sending repeater répétiteur numérique

digraph n digramme

digroup n bloc primaire

DIL (s. dual-in-line package); ∹ **package** boîtier enfichable (à sorties bilatérales)

dim adj réduit; sous-brillant

dimension n cote

dimensioning n dimensionnement; cotation

diminish v diminuer

diminished radix component complément (binaire) à un; complément (binaire) restreint

diminution factor taux de transit

dimmer *n* gradateur de lumière; trèfle occultable; obscurcisseur; rhéostat; ~ **cap** cabochon; bonnet à trèfle; ~ **control** économiseur de lampe

dimming *n* obscurcission; «dimage»; ~ **resistor** résistance chutrice

dimness intensité réduite

dimple *n* enfoncement

dimpling *n* peau d'orange

din *n* bruit

diode *n* diode; ~ **array** matrice de diodes; pont de diodes; montage à diodes; ~ **bridge** pont de diodes; ~ **characteristic** caractéristique de diode; ~ **clamp** circuit de bouclage à diode; ~ **clipper** circuit de seuil à diode; ~ **current** courant redressé de diode; ~ **cut-off region** plage de blocage de la diode; ~ **detector** détecteur à diode; ~ **laser** laser à semiconducteur; ~ **plug** fiche à diode; ~ **rate-of-rise noise limiter** limiteur à diode blocage du canal audio; ~ **rectifier** redresseur à vide poussé; ~ **stack** montage à diodes

diode-transistor logic (DTL) logique DTL

diode-type voltmeter voltmètre à diode

DIP (s. dual-in-line package)

dip frequency fréquence de dépassement

diphase *adj* diphasé

diphthong *n* ligature

diplex système diplex; duoplex

diplexer *n* diplexeur; coupleur; ~ **filter** filtre diplexeur

diplex telegraphy télégraphie diplex

dipole *n* doublet; antenne dipôle; ~ **aerial** antenne doublet; antenne à doublet; antenne dipôle; ~ **array** antenne en réseau de doublets; nappe de dipôles verticaux; réseau de dipôles; ~ **curtain** dipôle en rideau

dipole-excited parabolic reflector réflecteur parabolique excité par un dipôle

dipole layer barrière de potentiel; ~ **recording method** méthode d'écriture avec retour à zéro

dipped *adj* enrobé; fluidisé; ~ **in a still bath** trempé dans un bain statique

dipping *n* immersion; décapage

dip solder bath bain de soudure; ~ **soldering** soudure à bain mort; soudure au trempé

dip-solder termination sortie V

DIP switch mini-interrupteur

dip tinning étamage au trempé

Dirac function impulsion unitaire; ~ **pulse response** réponse à une action impulsive de Dirac

direct *v* diriger; aiguiller; orienter; ~ **access** accès direct; accès instantané; ~ **access controller** dispositif de prise directe;

~ **access file** fichier à méthode d'accès direct; fichier de consultation; fichier direct; ~ **access storage** mémoire à accès sélectif; ~ **access table** table à organisation directe; ~ **address** adresse directe; adresse absolue; ~ **addressing** adressage direct; ~ **allocation** affectation directe; attribution fixe; ~ **bearing** gisement; ~ **broadcast** télévision direct; ~ **call** appel sans numérotation; communication directe; ~ **capacitance** capacité directe; ~ **circuit group** faisceau de circuits directs; ~ **code** code absolu; langage machine; code réel; ~ **command guidance** radioguidage; ~ **component** composante continue; ~ **connection** liaison directe; ~ **connection call** sélection implicite; ~ **control** commande directe

direct-coupled amplifier amplificateur à couplage direct; ~ **flip-flop** bascule à couplage

direct coupling couplage direct; couplage conductif; ~ **current (DC)** courant continu (cc); ~ **current amplification factor** gain pour courant continu; ~ **current amplifier** amplificateur de courant continu; ~ **current anode power input** puissance anodique d'entrée; ~ **current bell** sonnerie à courant continu; ~ **current biasing** polarisation en courant continu; ~ **current blocking** blocage de la composante continue; ~ **current converter** convertisseur à courant continu; ~ **current (DC) insertion** insertion de la composante continue; ~ **current (DC) level instability** instabilité du niveau de la composante continue; ~ **current restorer** régénérateur de la composante; ~ **current signalling** signalisation par courant continu; ~ **current telegraphy** télégraphie par courant continu; ~ **data channel** canal de liaison directe; ~ **debiting** prélèvement automatique; ~ **detection receiver** récepteur à amplification directe

direct-dialling extension poste à prise directe; poste supplémentaire avec prise directe du réseau (public)

direct digital control régulation numérique directe; ~ **distance dialling (DDD)** interurbain automatique (IA); numérotation directe (DND); ~ **drive** commande directe; attaque directe; ~ **earth** terre franche

directed call appel dirigé; ~ **graph** digramme; graphe orienté; bigramme; ~ **link** (of graph) arc; ~ **maintenance** maintenance dirigée; ~ **tree** arborescence

direct electric drainage drainage électrique direct; ~ **exchange line** ligne non partagée; ~ **group access trunk** faisceau de lignes à acheminement direct; ~ **impedance** impédance directe; ~ **in-dialling** sélection directe à l'arrivée (SDA); numérotation directe entrante; ~ **input-output** (I/O) **indicator** mémoire unitaire; ~ **(inter-)electrode capacitance** capacité interélectrode; ~ **interface** liaison directe; ~ **international call** communication internationale directe; ~ **inward dialling** sélection directe à l'arrivée (SDA); numérotation directe entrante

directional aerial antenne directionnelle; antenne à effet directif; antenne apériodique; antenne de Beverage; antenne orientable; antenne accordée; antenne directive; antenne directrice; antenne dirigée; ~ **beam** faisceau directionnel; ~ **control valve** positionneur; ~ **coupler** coupleur directif; ~ **effect** effet directif; effet directionnel; ~ **filter** filtre d'aiguillage; ~ **gain** facteur de directivité; ~ **loop aerial** cadre radiocompas; cadre radiogoniométrique; ~ **phase changer** déphaseur directif; ~ **phase-shifter** déphaseur non réciproque; ~ **radar beacon** radiophare répéteur d'impulsions; ~ **radiation** radiation directive; ~ **radio beacon** radiophare à indication d'azimut; radiophare omnidirectionnel; ~ **radio telegraphy** radiotélégraphie dirigée; ~ **radio transmission** transmission point à point; ~ **reception** réception dirigée; ~ **reflectance** albédo; ~ **relay** relais directionnel; relais polarisé; relais de retour de courant; ~ **transmission** émission dirigée

direction angle angle de directivité

direction-finder repeater compass boussole répétrice de radiogoniomètre

direction finder with automatic reset radiogoniomètre à réajustage automatique à zéro

direction-finding (DF) n goniométrie; ~ **aerial** antenne radiogoniométrique; ~ **control station** station de localisation radiogoniométrique; ~ **error** erreur de relèvement; ~ **network** réseau radiogoniométrique; ~ **range** portée du relèvement; ~ **signal** signal de relèvement; ~ **site** site radiogoniométrique; ~ **slave (sub-)station** radiogoniomètre secondaire; ~ **station** station radiogoniométrique; ~ **transmitter** émetteur radiogoniométrique

direction of actuating force sens d'attaque; ~ **of lay** sens de câblage; ~ **of polarization** (of waveguide) direction de polarisation; ~ **of traffic flow** sens d'écoulement du trafic

directive n (control statement) directive; ~ **feed** coupleur directif

directivity pattern diagramme de directivité

direct line ligne directe; ligne privée; ligne spécialisée

directly-controlled progressive system système pas à pas

directly-heated cathode cathode à chauffage direct

direct memory access (DMA) accès direct en mémoire; ~ **on-line starting torque** couple en démarrage direct; ~ **(operator) call** appel d'ordres; ~ **operator call** appel individuel; appel privilégié du pupitre opérateur; ~ **operator signalling station** poste à appel direct de l'opératrice; poste à appel individuel; poste privilégié

director n programme superviseur; annotateur ordonnanceur; ensemble d'éléments directeurs

director/chief-secretary system ensemble de filtrage

director equipment unité de commande; ~ **instrument** classeur; ~ **selector** sélecteur de route; sélecteur directeur; ~ **switch** sélecteur directeur; ~ **system** système à enregistreurs

directory n annuaire; répertoire; dictionnaire; index; liste; ~ **enquiries** renseignements (code 12 en France); ~ **entries** éléments de répertoire; ~ **file** fichier de recherche; ~ **number** numéro d'annuaire; numéro d'appel; ~ **number change** dénumérotation; ~ **terminal concentrator** concentrateur de terminaux annuaire

direct output sortie directe; ~ **outward dialling (DOD)** prise directe urbaine; ~ **outward dialling (DOD) on international calls** accès à l'international automatique; ~ **pick-up receiver** récepteur de retransmission; ~ **printer** récepteur traducteur imprimeur (cable-code); ~ **printing** impression directe; ~ **projection** (PEC emission) visée directe (photoélectrique)

direct-pulse automatic telephone system téléphonie automatique à génération directe d'impulsions

direct ray rayon direct; ~ **read** lecture directe; ~ **reading** lecture sans tolérance

direct-reading direction finder radiogoniomètre à lecture directe; ~ **voltmeter** voltmètre rapide

direct recording enregistrement direct; ~ **recording facsimile** fac-similé à impression directe; ~ **relation** relation directe de trafic; ~ **route** voie directe; faisceau direct; ~ **routing** acheminement direct; ~ **sequential decoding** décodification séquentielle directe; ~ **sequential encoding** codification séquentielle directe; ~ **signalling (hot line)**

appel direct (de l'opératrice); ~ **(insert) subroutine** sous-programme ouvert; ~ **telegraph circuit** circuit télégraphique direct; ~ **through-connection** transit direct; ~ **through-dialling** numérotation d'une traite; ~ **toll (trunk) circuit** circuit direct de transit; ~ **transit** transit direct; ~ **transit country** pays de transit direct; ~ **transit telegram** télégramme en transit direct; ~ **(trunk) access** prise directe; ~ **trunking** système à double appel; ~ **TV (broadcast) by satellite (DTS)** diffusion directe de la télévision par satellite; ~ **wave** onde directe

direct-wired daughter board module sans agrafes

diruptor *n* (two-way circuit-breaker) dirupteur

disable *v* inhiber; arrêter; déconnecter; figer; mettre en faute; neutraliser; refuser; ~ **cluster** arrêt grappe

disabled *adj* bloqué; à l'arrêt; déconnecté; figé

disable manual input (DMI) invalidation d'entrée manuelle

disabling *n* inhibition; mise en blocage; mise hors service (HS); ~ **pulse** impulsion de blocage; ~ **signal** commande d'inhibition; ~ **tone** tonalité de neutralisation

disarmed *adj* désarmé

disassembly *n* démontage; fragmentation

disaster dump vidage sur catastrophe

disbanding *n* éclatement

discard *v* abandonner; désinstaller; détruire; écraser; éliminer; jeter; renoncer; supprimer

discernible by touch *v* décelable à l'ongle

discharge current courant de décharge

discharger *n* éclateur

discharge resistance résistance de décharge; ~ **time** (of battery) autonomie; durée de sauvegarde

discharging voltage tension de décharge

disclosure *n* divulgation

discomfort *n* gêne

discone (aerial) antenne discône; antenne disque-cône

disconnect *v* déconnecter; libérer; débrancher; débrocher; rompre; déboîter; mettre hors circuit

disconnected subscriber abonné isolé

disconnect key bouton d'isolement; ~ **pulsing** numérotation par rupture de boucle; ~ **signal** signal de fin de communication

discontinuation *n* coupure

discontinuous random noise parasite erratique discontinu

discrepancy *n* aléa; anomalie; bruit; contradiction; décalage; dérive; désaccord; différence; divergence; écart; manquement;

~ **check** contrôle de conformité; contrôle d'identité

discrete *adj* discret; autonome; disjoint; distinct; indépendant; individuel; ~ **component** composant discret; ~ **frequency modulation signal** signal discret modulé en fréquence

discretely-tuned signal signal temporel discret

discretely variable numérique

discrete message message distinct; ~ **trunk offering** offre discrète; ~ **variable** (integer value only) variable entière; ~ **word** logatome; ~ **word intelligibility** netteté pour les mots

discretionary powers autonomie

discriminating field zone discriminante; ~ **key** codage; ~ **relay** relais sélecteur; ~ **satellite exchange** central partiellement satellite; ~ **selector** (repeater) sélecteur absorbeur; ~ **selector repeater (DSR)** sélecteur discriminateur répéteur de signaux; ~ **tone** ton discriminateur

discrimination (filter) *n* (filtre d')atténuation; ~ **instruction** instruction de branchement; ~ **key** détrompeur

discriminator *n* discriminateur; sélecteur

discussed *adj* développé

discussion document sous-dossier

disengaged *adj* au repos

disengagement *n* déclenchement; déblocage; traction (d'un bouton)

disguised character caractère interdit

dish *n* cuvette; cheminée; réflecteur sphérique; ~ (reflector) réflecteur paraboloïde; ~ **aerial** antenne parabolique; antenne Cassegrain

dished electrode électrode à capsule; ~ **washer** rondelle cuvette

dishing *n* emboutissage

dish-reflector aerial antenne à réflecteur parabolique

disjunction *n* opération OU; addition

disk *n* (disc) disque; ~ **aerial** antenne à disque; ~ **attenuator** affaiblisseur à disque

disk-based bootstrap end address fin du bootstrap disque

disk drive platine disquette; ~ **drive unit** coffret de disques souples

diskette *n* disque souple; disquette; minidisque

disk (file) extent zone de disque; ~ **file** fichier disque; ~ **label** nom des disques; ~ **operating system (DOS)** système d'exploitation sur disque (SED)

disk-pack *n* chargeur de disques autonome; galette; ~ (removable disk cartridge) volume

disk recorder enregistreur sur disque

disk-resident *adj* amovible

disk seal scellement à disque; ~ **seal tube** tube à disques scellés; ~ **storage** mémoire à disques; disque archive; ~ **unit** unité disque

dislodge *v* désenficher; déboîter

dismantling *n* démontage; déshabillage

disorder *n* incident; anomalie; défaut; dérangement; faute; panne

dispel (of vacuum) casser

dispelling *n* (of stored charge carriers) évacuation (d'un porteur)

dispenser *n* distributeur; ~ **cathode** cathode compensée

dispersal *n* éclatement; épanouissement; décentralisation

dispersed *adj* décentralisé; ~ **intelligence** intelligence répartie

dispersion *n* NON ET (= ON/ET-NON); ~ **curve** courbe de dispersion

dispersive channel voie dispersive; ~ **delay line** filtre dispersif

displaced feed point point d'alimentation décalé

displacement *n* déplacement; décalage; dégagement; déviation; empiètement; pouvoir électrique; ~ **address** adresse d'espacement; ~ **area** zone d'empiètement; ~ **current** courant de déplacement; ~ **meter** compteur volumétrique; ~ **of sampling point** décalage du point d'exploration

display *v* afficher; visualiser; ~ *n* affichage; écran; image; ~ *adj* affichable; ~ **attributes** (of terminal) restitution

display-based editor éditeur conversationnel

display capacity capacité totale d'affichage; ~ **command** commande visualisation; ~ **console** support d'indicateur; ~ **control** contrôleur de visualisation; ~ **control function** fonction de commande d'affichage; ~ **device** console de visualisation (CV); visualisateur; ~ **field** organe de visualisation; ~ **memory** mémoire d'image; ~ **page** page-écran; écran vidéo; ~ **panel** afficheur; panneau d'affichage; ~ **subrack** châssis visu

disposable *adj* jetable

dispute *n* contestation de taxe

disputed charge account taxe incriminée

disrupt *v* perturber; couper; interrompre

disruption *n* interruption; perturbation; arrêt

disruptive discharge décharge disruptive; ~ **gradient** rigidité diélectrique; ~ **jammer** brouilleur à grande puissance

dissect *v* (of instruction) décomposer; fractionner

dissection *n* découpage

dissemination *n* diffusion

dissimilarity *n* non uniformité d'aspect

dissipation *n* perte; dissipation; ~ **constant** facteur de pertes; ~ **factor** facteur de pertes; taux de perte(s)

dissipative attenuation affaiblissement par dissipation

distance *n* OU exclusif; ~ **error** erreur de distance

distance-measuring equipment (DME) dispositif de mesure de distances

distance piece rondelle d'éloignement; entretoise; tosseau; ~ **relay** relais d'impédance

distant clock horloge distante; ~ **early-warning radar** radar d'alerte avancée

distant-end subscriber abonné lointain

distant exchange central distant; centre (en) aval; ~ **object** objet de localisation; ~ **site error** erreur régionale; ~ **subscriber** abonné lointain

distinctive *adj* caractéristique

distortion *n* distorsion; bruit; déformation; non linearité; réduction de la qualité de transmission; ~ **analyser** analyseur de distorsion non linéaire; distorsiomètre; ~ **area** zone de distorsion; ~ **factor** facteur de distorsion; taux de distorsion

distortion-free sans distorsion

distortionless sans distorsion

distortion minimization réduction au minimum de distorsion; ~ **product** produit de distorsion; ~ **signal generator** émetteur avec distorsion; ~ **tolerance/margin** distorsion admissible des signaux

distress call communication de détresse; ~ **signal** signal de détresse; ~ **(signal) wavelength** longueur d'onde de détresse maritime

distributed *adj* décentralisé; dispersé; éclaté; ~ **alarm** téléalarme; ~ **amplifier** amplificateur à répartition; ~ **capacitance** capacité répartie; ~ **centre** centre distribué; ~ **circuit** circuit à constantes réparties; ~ **constants** constantes réparties; ~ **control** commande répartie; commande de puissance à l'émission; ~ **(data) processing** informatique distribuée; ~ **data processing centre** centre de calcul décentralisé; ~ **frame alignment signal** signal de verrouillage de trame réparti; ~ **hunting** recherche progressive; ~ **inductance** inductance distribuée; ~ **intelligence** intelligence répartie; dispersion d'intelligence; ~ **load** charge répartie; ~ **management system** télégestion

distributed-parameter line ligne à constantes non stationnaires

distributed processing informatique répartie; ~ **processor** (assembly-disassembly) (PAD) processeur répartie; ~ **resistance** résistance répartie d'antiparasitage; ~ **structure** structure répartie; ~ **switching** organisation dispersée; ~ **table** table répartie; ~ **transmission line constants** constante de ligne de répartition

distribution *n* répartition; distribution; décentralisation; diffusion; éclatement; ventilation; ~ (despatching) **station** station de distribution; ~ **amplifier** amplificateur de distribution; ~ **board** tableau de distribution; traînard; nourrice; ~ **bus** éclateur de jonction(s); ~ **cabinet** armoire de distribution; ~ **cable (line connection)** câble de distribution; câble de ligne; ~ **frame** répartiteur; ~ **network** réseau de distribution; ~ **panel** herse; panneau de distribution; ~ **point** point de concentration (PC)

distributor *n* distributeur; répartiteur; ventilateur

district centre centre de district; ~ **switching centre** centre de commutation régional; ~ **transmitter** central suburbain

disturbance *n* perturbation; parasite(s); interférence; ~ **elimination** élimination d'interférence; ~ **power** puissance perturbatrice; ~ **variable** grandeur perturbatrice

disturbed one/zero (core memory pulse) un/zéro perturbé

disturbing current courant perturbateur; ~ **field** champ parasite; ~ **field strength** champ perturbateur; ~ **source** source perturbatrice; générateur; ~ **voltage** tension perturbatrice

ditch (of waveguide trap) rainure

dither *n* ronflette

ditto idem

DIV (s. data in voice)

DIVA (s. digital input - voice answerback)

divalent *adj* bivalent

divergence *n* écart; dérive; désaccord; dispersion; ~ (of beam) ouverture; ~ **coefficient** facteur de divergence

divergent light source source divergente

diverse *adj* (non-uniform) hétérogène; multiforme

diversion *n* déviation; réacheminement; dérivation; détournement; renvoi

diversity *n* OU exclusif; ~ **combining system** système combinateur de diversité

diversity-processed *adj* calculé

diversity reception réception multiple; réception en diversité

divert *v* déporter; réaiguller

diverted *adj* détourné; séparé; ~ **call** appel détourné

diverter *n* résistance de champ; séparateur; parafoudre

divert outside call transfert réseau

divestiture *n* démantèlement

divide-by-two counter compteur diviseur par deux

divided *adj* cloisonné; ~ **circuit** circuit à plusieurs stations réceptrices

divided-float battery batterie en tampon; batterie équilibrée

dividend *n* dividende

dividends plus et moins-values

divider *n* diviseur; démultiplicateur

divide up tronçonner

dividing *n* dédoublement; répartition; ~ **network** réseau diviseur; réseau répartiteur

division ratio (DR) rapport de division

divisor *n* diviseur

DIY (s. do-it-yourself)

D-I-Y enthusiast bricoleur

DL (s. delete line)

DLE (s. data-link escape)

DMA (s. direct memory access); ~ **controller** contrôleur d'accès direct en mémoire

DME (s. distance-measuring equipment)

DMI (s. disable manual input)

DO (instruction) boucler

docket *n* bon; relevé; volet; ticket

docketing *n* étiquetage

docket printer enregistreur de dérangements; enregistreur de fautes; ~ **printing** rédaction de ticket

dockyard *n* arsenal

document and journal printer imprimante de guichet

documentary data base base de données textuelle; ~ **programme** reportage

documentation documentation; ~ **book** dossier d'application

documented *adj* répertorié

document facsimile telegraphy télécopie contrastée; ~ **file** dossier; ~ **form** document; ~ **gauge** calibre de calage; ~ **opening** ouverture de document; ~ **print-out facility** éditeur de documents; ~ **processing centre** serveur documentaire; ~ **profile** fiche signalétique; ~ **release bulletin** (updates) bordereau de mise à jour; ~ **status line** ligne d'état d'un document; ~ **swapping** échange document; ~ **transmission** transmission de documents

docuterm *n* terme documentaire

DOD (s. direct outward dialling)

dog *n* griffe; cliquet; doigt; toc

dog-point (set) screw vis à bout pointu; vis à téton

do-it-yourself (DIY) système D (débrouillez-vous)

dolly *n* bras d'interrupteur; chariot; bouterolle

domain *n* domaine; ~ **wall** paroi de bloc
dome *n* bombement; calotte
domestic *adj* national; intérieur; interne; métropolitain; ~ **appliances** électroménager; ~ **market** marché intérieur
dominant *n* principal; ~ *adj* fondamental; ~ **feature** caractéristique prépondérante; ~ **mode** (of waveguide) mode fondamental; mode dominant; ~ **wave** onde fondamentale
done *adj* bien effectué; terminé
donor level niveau donneur
do-not-disturb facility mise en veilleuse; repos téléphonique; ne pas déranger
do-nothing instruction instruction fictive; instruction ineffective; instruction insignifiante
do-not-overflow interdiction de débordement
don't answer non réponse; ~ **care (0 or 1 state)** état indifférent; sans influence; redondant; sans importance
don't-care (bit) sans signification; ~ **gate** circuit indifférent; circuit sans influence
donut *n* chambre à vide
doodle (of graphics package) broutille
door *n* (of disk drive) volet
door-knob transformer transformateur (de mode) en bouton de porte
dopant *n* dopant
doping compensation compensation par dopage
Doppler drift glissement; ~ **effect** effet Doppler; ~ **shift** variation de fréquence due à l'effet Doppler
dormant *adj* passivé
DOS (s. disk operating system)
dot *n* point; ~ **AND circuit** OU câblé
dot-dashed line ligne mixte
dot frequency fréquence de points; ~ **graphics** graphisme par points; ~ **(interlace) scanning** analyse par points (successifs); analyse (point par point) entrelacée
dot-matrix printer imprimante par points; imprimante á aiguilles; imprimante matricielle; imprimante mosaïque; ~ **tube** tube trichrome à pénétration
dot pattern trame
dots and dashes points et traits
dotted line ligne pointillée
double beam double trace
double-beam CRT tube à rayons cathodiques à deux faisceaux; ~ **display** dédoublement d'image; ~ **oscilloscope** oscilloscope deux traces; ~ **radar** radar à deux lobes directifs
double-break contact contact à double coupure; ~ **jack** jack double de rupture; ~ **switch** interrupteur à double rupture
double-bridge diplexer diplexeur à deux

ponts; ~ **two-way repeater** répéteur à deux voies et deux ponts
double card-guide guide carte double
double-channel cathode-ray direction finder (CRDF) radiogoniomètre Watson-Watt
double-check *n* bouclage
double-coil relay relais double
double-cone aerial antenne à double cône
double connection connexion double
double-cord switchboard commutateur manuel à dicorde
double crossed-loop aerial cadran double croisé; ~ **crucible process (DC)** double creuset (DC)
double-current cable code (DCCC/DC3) code bivalent pour câble; ~ **key** touche à courant double; ~ **mark** élément de signal télégraphique à courant double; ~ **signalling** signalisation à double courant; signalisation à courant double; ~ **transmission** transmission bivalente; transmission par double courant
double dash trait double; ~ **density** double densité; ~ **diode (epitaxial rectifier)** diode double; ~ **diode** binode; duodiode; ~ **dipole** dipôle double
double-ended équilibre différentiel; réversible; à commande locale et distante; ~ **control** commande locale et distante; ~ **cord** cordon à deux fiches
double(-ended) cord circuit dicorde
double-ended queue (deque) file double
double-entry book-keeping comptabilité en partie double; digraphie
double frequency-changing double changement de fréquence
double-gun cathode-ray tube tube à rayons cathodiques à deux canons
double height hauteur double; ~ **heterojunction diode** diode à double hétérostructure; ~ **image** effet d'écho
double-indexed address adresse doublement indexée
double junctor joncteur bicéphale
double-length add addition en double précision; addition en double longueur; ~ **number** nombre en double précision
double (letter) width double largeur; ~ **limiter** circuit à déclenchement périodique
double-line circuit circuit bifilaire; ~ **pair** quadruplet
double line-spacing double interligne; ~ **modulation** double modulation
double-parasitic counterpoise contrepoids parasite double
double-peak resonance curve courbe de résonance à deux bosses
double-pedestal desk bureau ministre

double-phantom n superfantôme; ~ **balanced telegraphy** télégraphie compensée à circuit fantôme double; ~ **(balanced) telegraph circuit** circuit télégraphique superfantôme

double-pole double-throw (DPDT) bipolaire double course; bipolaire à deux directions; ~ **plug** fiche bipolaire; ~ **single-throw switch (DPST)** contact à deux directions; ~ **switch** interrupteur bipolaire

double precision double précision

double-precision arithmetic calcul en double précision; calcul vidéo; ~ **number** nombre en double précision

doubler socket conjoncteur gigogne

double seizure (of trunk from both ends) collision même jonction; prise simultanée

double-shed insulator isolateur à cloche double

double sideband double bande latérale

double-sideband transmission émission à double bande latérale

double-sided adj double face; ~ **printed circuit board** carte imprimée double face

double squirrel-cage motor Boucherot

double-stream amplifier (of TWT) amplificateur à deux faisceaux

double strike bissé; surimpression

double-super effect double action hétérodyne

double-switching dicord dicorde double de croisement

doublet n dipôle demi-onde; doublet

double-throw isolating switch sectionneur-commutateur; ~ **switch** commutateur à deux directions

double-tuned amplifier amplificateur à deux accords; ~ **filter** filtre à deux circuits accordés

double-up layout implantation biposes

double-window fibre fibre à double fenêtre

doubleword n mot double

doughnut n chambre à vide; cheminée; aimant torique

DOV (data-over-voice) modem modem supravocal

dovetail n queue d'aronde

dowel n ergot; ~ **pin** cheville

down adj baissé; bas; hors circuit; hors fonctionnement; hors service (h.s.); immobilisé; inaccessible; ~ **arrow** flèche verticale basse

down-coming radio wave onde atmosphérique

down converter convertisseur vers le bas

down-converter (D/C) transposition réception

down-counter n sablier

down-counting n (decades) décomptage; ~ **decades** (tens) décade décomptante

down-draught n aspiration

down lead descente d'antenne

down-line exchange central aval; ~ **loading** téléprogrammation; transfert de fichiers

down-link n trajet descendant; émission

down-loading n téléchargement; téléprogrammation; transfert

down-locking n accrochage bas

down-posting n autopostage spécifique

downside adj en aval

downstream adj en aval; récepteur; ~ **data** données commutables; ~ **end** sortie

down time temps d'indisponibilité; temps mort; temps hors service; période d'accusation; heures d'arrêt

down-time ratio taux d'indisponibilité; taux d'interruption

downward adj descendant; ~ **travel stop** butée de descente; ~ **trend** décroissance

DPC (s. data processing centre)

DPDT (s. double-pole double-throw)

3-D photography stéréoscopie

DPST (s. double-pole single-throw switch)

DR (s. division ratio); ≃ (s. dead reckoning)

drab adj mat

draft n avant-projet; ~ adj provisoire; préliminaire; projet de; ~ **quality** qualité courante; qualité listing

drag aerial antenne traînante; ~ **soldering** défilement dans une vague d'alliage

drain v purger; **(current)** ~ consommation; débit; ~ **current** courant de consommation; ~ **(DC) current** courant de drain; ~ **current** courant résiduel de drain; ~ **screw** vis de vidange

drain-source off-state resistance résistance drain-source

drain voltage (V_{DD}) tension de drain

DRAM (s. dynamic RAM)

draughting n dessin

draughtsman n constructeur; dessinateur

draughtsman's panel cartouche

draw v (of current) débiter

drawer n alvéole

drawing n plan; dessin; épure; étirage; ~ (of metal sheet) emboutissage; ~ (of wire) tréfilage; ~ **board** planche à dessin; ~ **frame** filière; ~ **library** schémathèque; ~ **office** bureau d'études

drawings n pl schémathèque

drawn-in air air insufflé

draw soldering soudure à bain mort

dressing n enduit; finition; ~ (of wires) cheminement

drift n dérive; glissement; décalage; écart; mandrin; aberration; ~ (pin) chasse-goupilles; ~ **compensation** compensation de dérive

drift-corrected amplifier amplificateur à compensation de dérive; amplificateur à correction de dérive

drifted off-centre déréglé

drift error erreur de dérive

drifting *adj* flottant; ~ **character** caractère mobile

drift meter indicateur d'écart; diffusiomètre; ~ **space** espace de glissement; ~ **transistor** transistor à gradient de champ; transistor à champ interne

drift-tube klystron klystron à glissement

drift tunnel tunnel de glissement

drill *v* percer; ~ *n* foret; mèche; ~ **back-to-back on assembly** contrepercer au montage; ~ **bit** foret

drilled *adj* ajouré

drilling rig barge de forage

drip *n* coulure

drive *v* commander; piloter; solliciter; alimenter; manœuvrer; conduire; ~ *n* commande (cde); attaque; bloc de puissance; conduite; défilement; entraînement; ~ **belt** courroie; ~ **board** carte de commande; ~ **circuit** circuit d'attaque; ~ **current** courant de commande; courant (cf. intensité); courant d'attaque; ~ **mechanism** machine d'entraînement

driven *adj* sollicité; récepteur; aval (en); ~ **aerial** élément actif; ~ **circuit** circuit en évolution; ~ **dipole** dipôle excité; ~ **element** élément rayonnant primaire; ~ **radiator** élément actif; ~ **transmitter** émetteur piloté

drive operation controller asservisseur commandes; ~ **pulse** impulsion de commande; impulsion de sélection

driver *n* bloc de commande; amplificateur; bloc de puissance; boîtier de puissance; carte de commande; circuit d'attaque; circuit d'entrée; conducteur; directeur; distributeur; entrée; excitateur; machine d'entraînement; machine de travail; machine motrice; moteur (MOT); organe de commande; transmetteur; programme pilote; sémateur (bivalent); ~ **stage** stade d'attaque; ~ **tube** tube d'attaque

drive screw vis à tôle; vis autotaradeuse; vis Parker; ~ **shaft** arbre de couche; arbre d'entraînement; ~ **speed** vitesse de déroulement; vitesse d'attaque; ~ **unit** motorisation; ~ **voltage** tension du signal de commande

driving *n* distribution; pilotage; ~ *adj* passant; conducteur; ~ **channel** canal conducteur; ~ **circuit** circuit extérieur d'entrée; ~ **point** entrée

driving-point admittance admittance d'entrée; ~ **impedance** impédance d'entrée; impédance à l'accès

driving potential (of phototransistor) tension d'éclairage; tension d'éclairement; ~ **pulse** impulsion d'attaque; ~ **signalling frame** trame de signalisation en distribution; ~ **stage** étage pilote; ~ **terminal module** module terminal de distribution; ~ **torque** couple moteur; ~ **unit** inverseur; ~ **(voltage) level** niveau de commande

drone *n* engin; ~ **courier** porteur d'informations téléguide

droop *n* statisme; déformation; déviation d'inclinaison

drop *n* abaissement; baisse; branchement; déclin; descente; fuite; perte; ~ (in level) dénivellation; ~ (of voltage level) coude; ~ (indicator) volet d'annonciateur; ~ **and insert** dérivation et insertion; injection de transfert

drop-and-insert connection système de dérivation; ~ **line** liaison dérivable

drop-dead halt arrêt immédiat

drop forging estampage

drop-in *n* génération accidentelle; information parasite; informations invalides; parasite(s)

drop (indicator) annonciateur d'appel

drop-in signal signal parasitaire

drop jack jack de dérivation

droplet *n* goutelette

drop-out *v* (of relay) décoller; relâcher; retomber; ~ *n* retombée; blocage; chute de niveau; déclenchement; relâchement; décollage; défaut; lacune; perte; coupure; microcoupure; ~ (of magnetic tape) défaut d'oxyde; défaut de magnétisation; ~ **characteristic** (of voltage regulator) décrochement; ~ **current** courant de déclenchement (I_D); courant de relâchement; ~ **time** temps de relâchement; ~ **voltage** tension de désexcitation

dropper *n* cavalier

dropping resistor résistance additionnelle; résistance série

drop point point de goutte; ~ **stamping** (with matching fixed dies) emboutissage à flans bloqués; ~ **terminal** boîte d'éclatement; boîtier de piquage; ~ **test** essai de chute; ~ **wire** fil d'abonné; branchement d'abonné; câble de branchement; ligne dérivée

dross *n* scorie

drum *n* barillet; bobine; cylindre; touret; ~ **controller** commutateur barillet; ~ **factor** facteur de cylindre; ~ **memory** mémoire à tambour; ~ **printer** imprimante à tambour; ~ **speed** vitesse de tambour; ~ **storage** mémoire à tambour; ~ **switch** commutateur barillet; ~ **transmitter** émetteur à cylindre

dry cell pile, sèche; ~ **contact** contact sec; ~ **core cable** câble sec; ~ **heat** chaleur sèche

drying agent dessicateur

dry joint soudure sèche; soudure défectueuse; ~ **loop** boucle sèche

dry-plate rectifier redresseur sec

dry-reed relay contact sec; relais hermétique à gaz inerte

dry run contrôle de programmation

DSE (s. data switching exchange)

D-series connector (ISO 2110) connecteur trapézoïdal

DSGE (s. digital switching equipment)

DSR (s. device status report); ≁ (s. discriminating selector repeater)

DTD (s. dial tone delay)

DTE (s. data terminal equipment); ≁ **controlled not ready** ETTD non prêt commandé

DTE/DCE (s. data signalling rate selector)

DTF (s. dial tone first)

DTL (s. diode-transistor logic)

DTMF (s. dual-tone multi-frequency); ≁ **dialling** numération au clavier multifréquence; ≁ **digit receiver** récepteur clavier; ≁ **push-button keypad** clavier multifréquence (MF); ≁ **set** poste à clavier multifréquence; ≁ **signalling** signalisation bifréquence; ≁ **station keypad** clavier

DTS (s. direct TV (broadcast) by satellite)

dual adj double; ~ **automatic direction finder** radiogoniomètre automatique double; ~ **colouring** (e.g. earth lead) double coloration

dual-conductor adj bifilaire; ~ **cable** câble à deux conducteurs; ~ **wiring** câblage bifilaire

dual-control bistable trigger circuit basculeur bistable à deux entrées

dual conversion double changement de fréquence

dual-conversion frequency converters transposition à double changement de fréquence

dual dictionary fiche inversé; ~ **flip-flop** double bascule; ~ **frequency** bifréquence

dual-frequency component raie; ~ **operation** exploitation sur deux fréquences

dual highway adj bi-canal

dual-in-line (DIL) à sorties bilatérales; ~ **package (DIP)** boîtier enfichable (à sorties bilatérales)

dual-input bus bijoncteur

dual 4-input NAND gate double trigger de Schmitt; ~ **mode** bivalent; ~ **op amp** amplificateur d'écart

dual-outlet line jack conjoncteur gigogne;

~ **plug adaptor** fiche gigogne

dual-polarization frequency re-use réutilisation de fréquence par double polarisation

dual-polarized aerial antenne bipolarisée

dual processor biprocesseur

dual-processor system système dupliqué

dual programming (mode) biprogrammation

dual-purpose selector sélecteur double

dual-quad bistable latch mémoire vive huit digits

dual-reflector aerial antenne à deux réflecteurs

dual (retriggerable) multivibrator double multivibrateur; ~ **seizure** double prise

dual-source repeater jammer brouilleur répéteur à rayonnement double en contrephase

dual three-input OR gate OU 2 x 3 entrées

dual-tone multifrequency (DTMF) **push-button keypad** clavier multifréquence (MF); ~ **multi-frequency (DTMF)** clavier multifréquence; ~ **multifrequency signalling** signalisation à deux fréquences

dual trace double trace

dual-trace oscilloscope oscilloscope bicourbe; oscilloscope deux traces

dual-track consultation consultation double; ~ **slide potentiometer** potentiomètre (double) à curseur

dual triode double triode; ~ **voltage** bi-tension

dubbed post-synchronisé

dubbing n duplication; doublage; post-synchronisation

duck-bill piers pince bec de canard; pince plat

duct n conduit; amenée; canalisation; caniveau; chemin de câbles (CdC); douille; gaine; goulotte; gouttière; passage; passage de fils; ventouse

ductile adj déformable; ~ **iron** fer doux

ductility n allongement à la rupture

ducting space volume de conduit

duct rodding equipment engin d'aiguillage; ~ **thickness** épaisseur de conduit

due date jour d'échéance

dull adj mat

dumb aerial antenne sans charge; antenne artificielle; ~ **terminal** terminal passif; terminal à consultation seule

dumb-waiter n ascenseur

dummy n maquette; ~ adj fictif; artificiel; bidon; factice; faux; mort; postiche; synthétique; ~ **address** adresse fictive; ~ **aerial** antenne fictive; ~ **circuit board** fausse carte; ~ **connection** occupation fictive; ~ **data** données fictives; ~ **echo** écho fictif; ~ **echo generator** générateur d'échos fictifs; ~ **fuse** faux fusible; ~ **group** groupe bâton; ~ **instruction**

instruction fictive; instruction insignifiante; instruction ineffective; ~ **load**
antenne fictive; antenne artificielle; antenne sans charge; charge artificielle;
charge d'essai; charge fictive; charge
postiche; circuit de charge fictif; ~ **message** message synthétisé; ~ **plug** fiche
fictive; fiche isolante; ~ **run** marche à
blanc; manœuvre à vide; ~ **traffic** trafic
fictif

dump v décharger; déconnecter; éditer;
évacuer; lister; mémoriser; purger; transcrire; transférer; vider; ~ (to disk) recopier
sur disque; ~ n analyse-mémoire; autopsie; copie sur bande; décharge; édition;
(éd.); extraction; image; mémoire auxiliaire; panne; sauvegarde; transcription;
vidage de mémoire; ~ (output) listage;
(power) ~ coupure; ~ **and restart** (procedure) sauvegarde et régénération; sauvegarde incrémentielle; vidage-reprise

dumped adj vidé

dump file image sur disque; ~ **file** (disk-copy)
fichier image; ~ **storage** archivage; mémoire de grande capacité; mémoire de
masse; mémoire géante; ~ **storage disk file**
disque archive; ~ **terminal** terminal
d'archivage

duo-diode diode double

duplex adj bidirectionnel; bilatérale; biplex;
double; duplex; utilisé dans les deux sens;
~ **artificial circuit** réseau d'équilibrage
duplex; ~ **balance** réseau d'équilibrage
duplex; ~ **call** communication bidirectionnelle; ~ **channel** voie bidirectionnelle;
~ **circuit** circuit bidirectionnel; circuit
duplex; circuit exploité en duplex; ~ **communications link** liaison duplex; ~ **computer** biprocesseur; ~ **connection** communication bidirectionnelle

duplexer n (filter) filtre duplexeur

duplex file updating macrosynchronisme

duplexing n doublement

duplex line ligne bidirectionnelle; ligne
duplexée; ~ **operation** exploitation en
duplex; ~ **system** système duplex; ~ **telegraphy** télégraphie duplex; ~ **telephony**
téléphonie duplex; ~ **working** exploitation
en duplex

duplicate v recopier sur disque; transcrire;
reproduire; ~ n exemplaire; homologue;
~ adj double; doublé; dupliqué

duplicated operation doublet

duplicate master contre-calque; ~ **unit** ordre
homologue

duplicating punch perfo.(-ratrice) réproductrice

duplication n double implantation; ~ **check**

contrôle par duplication

durability n durée de vie; longévité

duration of transmission durée de l'émission

during normal operation en exploitation

dust-and-damp-proof enclosure boîtier étanche

dust core noyau aggloméré; ~ **cover** capot
anti-poussière; housse

dusting n dépoussiérage

dust-proof enclosure boîtier étanche aux
poussières

dust removal dépoussiérage

dust-trap n pare-poussières

Dutch gold (copper-leaf finish) or faux

duty adj de service; ~ **cycle** rapport cyclique;
taux de remplissage; coefficient d'utilisation; facteur d'utilisation; rapport d'impulsions; taux d'exploitation; ~ **cycle regulation device** régulateur de rapport cyclique;
~ **engineer** agent de service; ~ **extension**
poste de servitude; ~ **factor** (of motor: in
%) facteur de marche

DUV (s. data under voice)

DW (s. device wait)

dwell n temps de repos; repos; ~ **time**
planage

dwindle v diminuer; réduire

dyadic adj diadique

dyadic/binary Boolean operation opération
booléenne diadique

dyeline reproduction copie diazoïque

dynamic adj cyclique; paramétrable; impulsionnel; dynamique; actif; ~ **allocation**
allocation dynamique; ~ **area** zone dynamique; ~ **card testing** contrôle dynamique
des cartes; ~ **characteristic** caractéristique
dynamique; ~ **drive** excitation dynamique;
~ **error** erreur dynamique; ~ **firing**
amorçage dynamique; ~ **impedance** impédance à l'antirésonance

dynamicizer n convertisseur parallèle-série

dynamic luminous sensitivity sensibilité lumineuse dynamique; ~ **noise immunity**
immunité dynamique au bruit; ~ **operation**
régime dynamique; ~ **parameter** paramètre
impulsionnel; caractéristique dynamique;
~ **RAM (DRAM)** mémoire dynamique;
mémoire à circulation; mémoire à propagation; mémoire circulante; mémoire cyclique; ~ **range** dynamique; dispersion du
gain dynamique; gamme dynamique; sensibilité dynamique; ~ **ratio** dynamique;
~ **relay** interrupteur à force centrifuge;
~ **stop** arrêt de rebouclage; arrêt sur
bouc¹e; rebouclage; ~ **storage allocation**
affectation dynamique de mémoire;
~ **store** mémoire dynamique; mémoire à
circulation; mémoire à propagation; mémoire circulante; mémoire cyclique;

~ **subroutine** sous-programme paramétrable; ~ **test** essai en fonctionnement; contrôle dynamique; essai fonctionnel; ~ **viscosity** viscosité dynamique

dynamo *n* générateur

dynamometer *n* dynamomètre

dynamotor *n* convertisseur rotatif; commutatrice; convertisseur dynamoteur

dynatron oscillation oscillation dynatron

dynode *n* dynode

E

E (s. erlang)

EA (s. erase in area)

each-way à la retourne

EAM card carte mécanographique (perforée)

E and M signalling signalisation RON-TRON

E and M wires fils RON et TRON

earcap n pavillon

early adj anticipé; prématuré; préalable; infantile; intempestif; précoce; ~ failure déchet infantile; défaut de jeunesse; faute de jeunesse

early-failure period période de jeunesse

early failure test déverminage

early-failure testing vieillissement accéléré; essai de vieillissement

early-make contact contact prioritaire

early stages période de mise au point

early-warning radar radar d'alerte; ~ radar chain chaîne radar défensive d'alerte avancée

early write pré-écriture avant sélection

earphone n écouteur; récepteur; récepteur téléphonique; ~ coupler coupleur pour écouteur; ~ reception réception au casque

earphones n casque à oreillettes; casque d'écoute

earpiece n pavillon; casque d'écoute

earth v mettre à la terre; ~ n masse; masse électrique; terre; ~ aerial antenne enterrée; ~ bed déversoir; ~ breakdown isolement terre; ~ bus-bar répartiteur de masse (RM); ~ button bouton de manœuvre; bouton de reprise; ~ cable câble de terre; ~ calling prise par mise d'une terre sur un fil; ~ capacitance capacité par rapport à la masse; capacité réel-terre; ~ conductivity conductivité au sol; ~ conductor fil (de masse) d'accompagnement; ~ connection prise de masse; connexion de terre; liaison de masse; ~ contact contact de masse; ~ coverage couverture de la surface de la terre; ~ current courant de masse; courant de perte à la terre; courant de retour; courant tellurique; ~ detector touche à la terre

earthed adj mis à la terre

earth electrode électrode de mise à la masse

earth-electrode system puits de terre (général); terre générale

earth fault défaut à la terre; ~ form peigne de masse; ~ impedance terre résistante

earthing adj mise à la terre; mise à la masse; ~ circuit circuit de mise à la terre; ~ conductor câble de masse; prise de terre élémentaire; ~ connection prise par mise d'une terre sur un fil; ~ percentage pourcentage du temps de mise à la terre; taux de bridage; ~ plate plaque de raccordement des terres; ~ strap bracelet; ~ strip barrette de masse; barrette de terre; languette de masse; ~ switch interrupteur de mise à la terre; contact de masse; ~ system prise de terre; ~ wire fil de masse

earth leakage court-circuit à la masse; isolement terre; perte à la terre; ~ leakage current courant de fuite à la terre; courant résiduel; ~ leakage/fault dérivation à la terre; ~ mat tapis de sol; ~ noise bruit de terre; ~ pit puits de terre (général); ~ plane plan de masse; barre zéro (0B); liaison équipotentielle; niveau 0 (zéro); niveau zéro; plage de masse; ~ plate plaque de terre; prise de masse; puits de terre (général); terre générale; ~ potential tension de terre; niveau zéro

earth-pulse signalling signalisation de ligne par impulsions

earth rail barre de masse; répartiteur de masse (RM); ~ resistance résistance de la masse; ~ return terre de retour; retour commun

earth-return circuit circuit à retour par la terre; circuit longitudinal; circuit unifilaire

earth-return current courant de terre

earth-return double-phantom circuit circuit approprié de combiné; circuit approprié de fantôme; circuit superfantôme à retour par la terre; ~ phantom circuit circuit fantôme avec retour par la terre; circuit approprié; ~ telegraph circuit circuit télégraphique à retour par la terre

earth rod perche de masse

earth's albedo albédo de la terre

earth signal signal d'accompagnement de masse

earth's magnetic field champ magnétique terrestre

earth spike (of pot core) picot de masse

earth-start circuit circuit à prise par mise d'une terre sur un fil

earth station station terrestre; ~ strap étrier

de masse; ~ **switch** interrupteur de mise à la terre; ~ **testing** test par la terre
earth-to-satellite link liaison terre-satellite
earth wire fil de continuité; câble de garde; ~ **wire** (lightning) fil paratonnerre
earthworks *n* génie civil
ease-of-use facilité d'emploi
ease the load on soulager
easting *n* graticule Est
east spot faisceau est
eavesdrop *v* mettre en écoute
eavesdropping *n* écoute clandestine; espionnage téléphonique
EBCDIC (Extended Binary Coded Decimal Interchange Code) code EBCDIC
Eccles-Jordan circuit bascule bistable
echelon telegraphy communication échelonnée
echo *v* refléter; ~ *n* écho; impulsion réfléchie; réverbération; fantôme; réflexion; répétition; ~ **attenuation** affaiblissement de l'écho; ~ **box** boîte d'écho; ~ **canceller** annuleur d'écho; compensateur d'écho; ~ **cancelling** annulation de la réflexion; ~ **chamber** chambre d'écho; unité de réverbération; ~ **check** contrôle par écho; relecture; ~ **checking** contrôle d'écho; ~ **current** courant réfléchi; courant inverse; ~ **delay time** temps de transit d'un écho; ~ **effect** effet d'écho
echoing area surface effective de diffusion; ~ **volume** volume d'impulsion
echo intensity intensité d'écho; ~ **matching** égalisation des échos
echoplex *n* contrôle par écho; inscription fugitive; échoplex (échoplexage); relecture
echo printing impression en écho; ~ **ranging** échométrie; ~ **return loss (ERL)** affaiblissement d'adaptation pour l'écho; ~ **sign** signe d'écho; ~ **suppression** suppression d'écho; ~ **suppressor disabling** neutralisation de suppresseur d'écho; ~ **tolerance** tolérance aux échos
ecliptic *n* écliptique
ECM (s. active electronic countermeasures); ⊷ **search** recherche par contremesures électroniques
ECO (s. electron-coupled oscillator)
ECO-Hartley circuit oscillateur Hartley à couplage électronique
economy resistance résistance d'économie; résistance économiseuse
ECP (s. executive control program)
ED (s. erase in display)
eddy current courant de Foucault; courant parasite; courant tourbillonnaire; hystérésis (= hystérèse)
eddy-current loss perte par courant de Foucault; pertes par hystérésis
edge *n* bord; arête; flanc; angle
edge-board contact languette
edge card carte enfichable; ~ **connector** connecteur de bout de carte; fichier encartable; connecteur de bord; fiche à pincer; ~ **cutters** pince coupante devant; ~ **flare** surluminance; ~ **lighting** éclairage par la tranche; ~ **plug** connecteur d'énergie; fichier électrique; reprise connecteur
edge-reflection effect effet de réflexion des bords
edge strip (of PCB) bandeau; bandeau avant; face avant
edge-triggering *n* déclenchement sur état
edgewise *adj* sur chant
edging *n* bordure; ~ **tape** galon
Edison effect effet redresseur; effet Edison; ⊷ **screw cap** culot Edison
edit *v* éditer; ~ **cursor** curseur de correction
editing *n* rédaction; mise en forme; édition; (éd.); modification de texte; révision; correction
editor *n* éditeur
EDP (electronic data processing) traitement électronique des données; ⊷ **specialist** informaticien
educational broadcast émission didactique; ~ **software** didacticiel; ~ **software library** didacthèque; ~ **technology** éducatique
E = "**ear**" (s. backward signal wire)
EFD (s. end form description)
effect *n* effet; phénomène
effective efficace; effectif; réel; utile; puissant; ~ **address** adresse effective; adresse modifiée; adresse réelle; ~ **air-gap width** largeur réelle d'entrefer; ~ **area** surface de captation; surface effective; ~ **attenuation** affaiblissement composite; atténuation effective; ~ **bandwidth** largeur de bande effective; efficacité; ~ **beam width** largeur de faisceau effective; ~ **bunching angle** angle effectif de transit; ~ **call** communication effective; communication établie; ~ **collision cross-section** section efficace de choc; ~ **cross-section** section effective; ~ **current** courant efficace; ~ **cut-off frequency** fréquence de coupure effective; ~ **data transfer rate** débit réel (de transfert); ~ **flux density** (unit: mT = millitesla) induction; ~ **gap capacitance** capacité effective de l'espace d'interaction; ~ **input admittance** admittance effective d'entrée; ~ **input capacitance** capacité effective d'entrée; ~ **input impedance** impédance effective d'entrée; ~ **instruction** instruction réelle; ~ **isotropic radiated power (EIRP)** puissance apparente rayon-

née équivalente dans l'axe (PIRE); ~ **length** longueur de rayonnement; ~ **length excluding chamfer** longueur utile hors chanfrein; ~ **local centre** centre de raccordement effectif; ~ **loss** affaiblissement effectif; ~ **margin** marge effective; ~ **noise bandwidth** largeur de bande effective du bruit; ~ **noise source** éléments parasites; ~ **output admittance** admittance effective de sortie; ~ **output power** puissance de sortie utile; ~ **path length** longueur effective; ~ **power** puissance efficace; ~ **radiated power (ERP)** puissance apparente rayonnée; ~ **radius of the earth** rayon terrestre fictif; ~ **reactance** réactance effective; ~ **resistance** résistance effective; ~ **signal** signal utile; ~ **traffic** trafic efficace; trafic réel; ~ **transmission** transmission normalisée; ~ **transmission rate** débit réel (de transfert); ~ **value** valeur efficace; valeur moyenne quadratique; ~ **voltage** tension efficace

efficiency *n* rendement; facteur d'utilisation; ~ (power handling capacity) **feasibility** efficacité; ~ **diode** diode économisatrice; ~ **factor in time** facteur d'efficacité dans le temps; ~ **meter** compteur de temps d'emploi

efficient *adj* efficace

EFT (s. electronic funds transfer)

egg-box lens lentille multicellulaire

egg-shaped insulator isolateur en forme de noix

E/H bend coude progressive E/H; ≁ **corner** coude brusque E/H

EHT-junction jonction EH en T

eigenvalue *n* valeur propre

eight-bit byte octet; ~ **parity generator/checker** générateur de parité huit digits; ~ **serial code** code série à huit moments

eight-coil relay octuple

eight-element dipole array rideau de huit dipôles

eight group octuple

eight-level code code à huit moments; ~ **multiple** octuple

eight-state trellis coding codage en treillis à huit états

eight-subscriber group huitaine abonné

eight-to-one-line multiplexer multiplexeur de huit vers une voie

eight-up aperture card carte à fenêtre à 8 images

eight-word segment octomot

Einstein's law loi d'Einstein

Einthoven (string) galvanometer galvanomètre à cordes

EIRP (s. effective isotropic radiated power)

EITHER-OR *n* disjonction; opération OU

either-party release libération par le dernier abonné (à raccrocher)

either-way semi-duplex; ~ **operation** voie bidirectionnelle à l'alternat

ejection *n* saut

EL (s. erase in line)

elapsed *adj* écoulé; ~ **hour meter** compteur horaire; horamètre; ~ **time** temps écoulé; ~ **time indicator** échéancier

elastance (C/1: unit = daraf) élastance

elasticity test essai de résilience

elasto-optic effect effet élasto-optique

E-layer couche E

elbow *n* coude brusque

electret microphone microphone à condensateur; microphone à électret

electrical *adj* électrique; galvanique; ~ **accounting machine department** atelier mécanographique; ~ **connection** connexion électrique; ~ **continuity** continuité électrique; ~ **control panel** tableau électrique; ~ **degree** angle de calage; ~ **discharge** décharge électrique; ~ **distance** distance électrique; ~ **engineering** électrotechnique; ~ **flux density** induction; ~ **forming** formation électrique; ~ **gear** équipements électriques; ~ **insulation** isolement électrique; ~ **interference** perturbation par appareils électriques; ~ **isolation** séparation galvanique; ~ **latching** maintien électrique; ~ **length** longueur effective

electrically-erasable PROM UVPROM

electrically programmable and UV-erasable (static) read-only memory (EPROM) mémoire statique programmable et reprogrammable

electrical parameter paramètre électrique; ~ **point** prise de courant (PC); ~ **power** énergie électrique; ~ **power line** ligne de transport d'énergie électrique; ~ **power unit** groupe d'alimentation; ~ **properties** caractéristiques électriques; ~ **rotation** (of potentiometer) angle de rotation électrique; ~ **separation** isolement galvanique; séparation galvanique; ~ **speech level** niveau sonore; ~ **speech level meter** volumètre; ~ **speech pressure/power** pression acoustique de la voix; ~ **test** contrôle électrique

electric arc décharge d'arc; ~ **brake** électrofrein; ~ **cell** pile galvanique; ~ **charge** charge électrique; quantité d'électricité; ~ **charge time constant of detector** constante de temps électrique à la charge d'un détecteur; ~ **current** intensité du champ électrique; ~ **deflection** déviation électrique; ~ **dipole** doublet électrique; ~ **discharge time constant of detector**

constante de temps électrique à la décharge d'un détecteur; ~ **displacement** pouvoir diélectrique; ~ **drainage** drainage électrique; ~ **fan** électro-ventilateur; ~ **field** champ électrique; ~ **flux** quantité d'électricité; ~ **flux density** pouvoir diélectrique; ~ **heating** chauffage électrique

electrician's knife couteau d'électricien; ~ **toolbox** coffret d'électricien; ~ **wire-cutting shears** ciseaux d'électricien coupe-fils

electricity n électricité

electric lamp lampe électrique; ~ **line** ligne d'énergie; lignes électriques; ~ **potential** potentiel électrique; force électromotrice (f.é.m.); différence de potentiel (d.d.p.); ~ **protection** protection électrique; ~ **quadripole** quadripôle électrique; ~ **resistance** résistance ohmique; résistance en continu; ~ **shunting** obturateur électrique; ~ **traction network** réseau de traction électrique; ~ **wave filter** filtre électrique

electrification of a gas électrisation d'un gaz

electro-acoustic coupling impedance coefficient électro-acoustique de couplage; ~ **force factor** coefficient électro-acoustique de couplage; ~ **transducer** transducteur électroacoustique

electro-analysis n électro-analyse

electrochemical etching corrosion électrochimique

electrode n électrode; ~ **admittance** admittance d'électrode; ~ **bias** tension de repos (d'une électrode); ~ **characteristic** caractéristique d'électrode; ~ **current** courant d'électrode; ~ **current averaging time** temps d'intégration; ~ **impedance** impédance d'électrode

electro-deposition n dépôt électrolytique; dépôt galvanique; galvanoplastie

electrode radiator radiateur d'électrode; ~ **reactance** réactance d'électrode; ~ **resistance** résistance d'électrode; ~ **short-circuit** court-circuit entre électrodes; ~ **slope resistance** résistance d'électrode en courant alternatif; ~ **support** support d'électrode; ~ **susceptance** susceptance d'électrode; ~ **voltage** tension d'électrode

electrodynamic (moving-coil) microphone microphone électrodynamique

electrographic pen crayon de graphitage; ~ **printer** imprimante à électro-érosion

electrokinetics n électrocinétique

electroluminescent adj électroluminescent

electrolyte n électrolyte

electrolytic capacitor condensateur chimique; condensateur électrolytique; ~ **cell** cellule électrolytique; ~ **corrosion** attaque électrolytique; ~ **deposition** dépôt électrolytique;

dépôt galvanique; ~ **tank** cuve rhéographique; ~ **tough pitch (ETP) copper** cuivre raffiné électrolytique

electromagnet n électro-aimant

electromagnetic adj électromagnétique; électrodynamique; ~ **(radio) wave (VLF to SHF)** onde hertzienne; ~ **balancer** balance électrodynamique; ~ **coupling** couplage inductif; ~ **disturbance** perturbation électromagnétique; ~ **field** champ électromagnétique; ~ **force** force électromagnétique; ~ **ink** encre conductrice; ~ **interference (EMI)** brouillage électromagnétique; ~ **lens** lentille magnétique; ~ **microphone** microphone électromagnétique; ~ **noise** bruit électromagnétique; ~ **oscillation** oscillation électromagnétique; ~ **radiation** radiation électromagnétique; ~ **relay** relais électromagnétique; ~ **spectrum** spectre de longueurs d'ondes électromagnétiques; ~ **wave** onde électromagnetique; ~ **wave absorption** absorption d'ondes électromagnétiques

electromagnetize v électro-aimanter

electromechanical adj électromécanique (EM); ~ **(analogue) exchange** central électromécanique (CEM); ~ **coupling impedance** coefficient électromécanique de couplage; ~ **drive** pilote électromécanique; ~ **filter** filtre électromécanique; ~ **force factor** coefficient électromécanique de couplage; ~ **transducer** transducteur électromécanique

electrometer amplifier amplificateur de l'électromètre; ~ **valve** tube électromètre

electromotive force (e.m.f.) force électromotrice (f.é.m.); différence de potentiel (d.d.p.); niveau

electron n électron; négaton; ~ **(or ion) sheath** gaine d'électrons (ions); ~ **affinity** travail de sortie; ~ **beam** faisceau électronique

electron-beam DC resistance résistance équivalente du faisceau; ~ **generator** klystron; ~ **recording** enregistrement par faisceau électronique

electron beam valve tube à faisceau électronique

electron-binding energy potentiel d'ionisation

electron bunching rassemblement électronique; ~ **charge** charge de l'électron

electron-charge mass ratio charge spécifique de l'électron

electron cloud nuage d'électrons; ~ **collector (of microwave tube)** collecteur HF

electron-coupled oscillator (ECO) oscillateur à couplage électronique

electron current courant électronique; ~ **emis-**

sion émission électronique; ~ **flow** flux électronique; ~ **gas** gaz électronique; ~ **gun** canon électronique; ~ **gun convergence ratio** rapport de densité du courant; ~ **gun density multiplication** rapport de densité du courant; ~ **hole** lacune-trou
electronic *adj* électronique; ~ **billing** facturation électronique; ~ **comparator** comparateur électronique; ~ **component of assessed quality** composant électronique de qualité contrôlée; ~ **control** commande électronique; ~ **differential analyser** analyseur différentiel électronique; ~ **directory** annuaire électronique; ~ **door-answering system** portier électronique; ~ **earth** terre électronique; ~ **exchange** autocommutateur électronique; central électronique; ~ **funds transfer (EFT)** télécollecte; télépaiement; paiement électronique; monétique; ~ **gap admittance** admittance électronique de l'espace d'interaction; ~ **gap impedance** impédance électronique de l'espace d'interaction; ~ **image** image électronique; ~ **line concentrator** concentrateur à interface MIC; ~ **mail** courrier électronique; messagerie de l'écrit; télémessagerie; ~ **money** monétique; ~ **news-gathering (ENG)** faisceau de reportage; ~ **(contact) rectifier** contact redresseur
electronics *n* électronique
electronic space-division concentrator concentrateur spatial électronique (CSE); ~ **subscriber (line) concentrator** concentrateur électronique d'abonné; concentrateur satellite électronique; ~ **switch** interrupteur électronique; ~ **telephone** téléphone électronique; ~ **teleprinter** téléimprimeur électronique; ~ **tuning** accord électronique; ~ **tuning sensitivity** sensibilité d'accord électronique; ~ **turns counter** compteur de spires électronique; ~ **two-state device** basculeur électronique; ~ **valve** tube électronique; ~ **voltmeter** voltmètre électronique; ~ **warfare** guerre électronique
electron injector injecteur d'électrons; ~ **(ion) avalanche** avalanche électronique; ~ **lens** lentille électronique; ~ **mass** masse de l'électron; ~ **microscope** microscope électrostatique; ~ **mirror** dynode; miroir électronique; ~ **multiplier** multiplicateur d'électrons (secondaires); ~ **optics** optique électronique
electron-ray indicator tube tube indicateur cathodique
electron shell (of atom) couche électronique; ~ **spin** précession des électrons; ~ **telescope** télescope électronique; ~ **(ion) trajectory** rayon électrique (ionique);

~ **transition** transition électronique; ~ **tube** tube électronique
electron-tube rectifier redresseur à tube
electron valve load charge d'un tube électronique
electro-optical effect effet électro-optique
electro-plated steel acier galvanisé
electro-plating *n* galvanoplastie
electrostatic actuator excitateur électrostatique; ~ **deflection** déviation électrique; ~ **field** champ électrostatique; ~ **focussing** focalisation électrostatique; concentration électrostatique; ~ **generator** générateur électrostatique; éliminateur; ~ **induction** induction électrostatique; influence capacitive; ~ **lens** lentille électrostatique; ~ **microphone** microphone à condensateur; ~ **printer** imprimante électrostatique; ~ **unit** unité électrostatique; ~ **voltmeter** voltmètre électrostatique
electro-thermal relay relais thermique (Rt)
electro-valve *n* électro-vanne (EV)
element *n* élément; article; bit; organe; partie; corps simple; tête d'impression; unité d'information; opérateur
elementary radiator directivity directivité de radiateur élémentaire
element error rate taux d'erreurs sur les éléments; ~ **spacing** espacement de radiateurs
elephant skin peau d'orange
elevated (H-type) Adcock direction finder radiogoniomètre Adcock en H; ~ **aerial** antenne extérieure
elevating rail rehausse
elevation angle angle de site; angle d'élévation
elevation-position indicator (EPI) indicateur de distance et de site; indicateur type E
elevator *n* ascenseur
eliminated circuit circuit supprimé
eliminate superfluous (hardware and software) **functions** dégraisser
elimination *n* suppression
ellipse *n* couronne
ellipsis *n* points de suspension
elliptical beam faisceau elliptique; ~ **waveguide** guide d'ondes elliptique
elongation at rupture allongement à la rupture
ELSE DO (instruction) sinon faire
elusive *adj* fugitif; ~ **one** une fuite
EM (s. end-of-medium character)
emanates from provient de; issu de
embed *v* intercaler
embedded *adj* encastré; imbriqué; noyé
embodied *adj* solidaire; incorporé
embodiment (of patent) forme de réalisation
emboldened *adj* bissé
emboldening (of print) *n* graissage; surimpres-

sion
embosser *n* imprimeur en relief
embossing *n* gravure en creux; emboutissage
embossment *n* empreinte; gaufrage; gaufre; repère
emergency *n* urgence; ~ *adj* d'urgence; de secours; d'intervention; ~ **aerial** antenne de secours; ~ **bypass** dérivation de secours; ~ **call** appel d'urgence; communication de détresse; ~ **exchange** central de secours; ~ **lighting** éclairage de secours; ~ **medical service** SAMU (service d'aide médicale d'urgence) (code 15 en France); ~ **power supply** source d'énergie de secours; ~ **route** voie d'acheminement de secours; voie détournée; voie de secours; ~ **sender** émetteur de détresse; ~ **stop** arrêt d'urgence
emergency-stop button coup de poing
emergent *adj* infantile
emery cloth toile d'émeri
e.m.f. (s. electromotive force)
EMI (s. electromagnetic interference); ≃ (s. enable manual input)
emission current courant d'émission; ~ **cut-out** coupure d'émission; ~ **efficiency** efficacité d'une cathode thermoélectronique
emissivity *n* pouvoir émissif d'une surface
emit *v* émettre
emitter *n* émetteur
emitter-coupled mode courant; ~ **logic** logique bipolaire (à) haute vitesse
emitter (DC) current courant (continu) d'émetteur; ~ **depletion layer capacitance** capacité de la zone de transition de l'émetteur; ~ **electrode** électrode émettrice; ~ **follower** montage collecteur commun; émidyne; ~ **injection ratio** (efficiency) efficacité d'émetteur; ~ **region** zone d'émetteur; ~ **terminal** borne de l'émetteur
emitting *n* émission; ~ **fibre** fibre émettrice
E mode mode magnétique transversal
emphasizer *n* amplificateur sélectif; circuit d'accentuation
emphasizing *n* accentuation
empty band bande vide; ~ **medium** support blanc; ~ **signal unit** signal unitaire vide; ~ **string** chaîne vide
emulation mode mode émulation; ~ **terminal** terminal d'émulation
emulator *n* émulateur
emulsifier *n* durcisseur
emulsion *n* couche photosensible; couche sensible
enable *v* valider; activer; autoriser; mettre en service; mettre en service; permettre; prendre en compte; ~ **access** rendre

disponible; ~ **arithmetic errors** validation des erreurs arithmétiques; ~ **bus** bus d'autorisation; ~ **(code)** autorisation
enabled *adj* actif; active; interruptible
enable manual input (EMI) validation d'entrée manuelle
enabling *n* validation; autorisation; activation; armement; déverrouillage; mise en service; prise en compte; démasquage; ~ **circuit** circuit déclencheur; ~ **condition** critère; ~ **pulse** signal de validation; ~ **signal** signal d'autorisation
enamel glaze couche d'émail; émaillage
enamel-insulated wire fil émaillé; fil verni; ~ **with silk identification thread** émaillé parallèle sous filin de soie
enamelled *adj* laqué
en bloc MF signalling tandem
encapsulated *adj* enrobé; surmoulé; moulé
encapsulation *n* enrobage
encased *adj* blindé
encipher *v* chiffrer
enciphered facsimile communication fac-similé chiffré; ~ **telephony** téléphonie chiffrée; téléphonie codée
enclosed *adj* en coffret; enfermé; cadré par; ~ **(of speaker)** clos; **totally** ~ abrité àventilation forcée; ~ **space** enceinte; ~ **starter** discontacteur en coffret
enclosure *n* enceinte; annexe; armoire; boîte; boîtier; cabine; caisson; capot; carter; chambre; coffret; enveloppe; habillage; plastron
enclosure(s) *n* pièce jointe (PJ)
encode *v* chiffrer; codifier
encoder *n* circuit codeur; dispositif chiffreur; ~ **shaft** axe de codeur
encoding *n* codage; ~ **law** loi de codage
encryption *n* chiffrage; chiffrement
end *n* fin; bout; arrêt; côté; partie
end-around-borrow report négatif circulaire
end-around-carry progression circulaire; report circulaire; report en boucle
end-around shift décalage circulaire; permutation circulaire; décalage cyclique; permutation cyclique
end-bell *n* raccord
end box fin de cases; ~ **delay** retard aux extrémités; ~ **distortion** déplacement du flanc postérieur; ~ **exchange** centre d'abonnés; centre local (CL)
end-face condition état de la cassure
end-fed aerial antenne en J
end-feed alimentation en extrémité; alimentation à la base de l'antenne
end-fire array antenne à rayonnement longitudinal; antenne colinéaire; antenne en arête de poisson; antenne en sapin; antenne

Yagi; rideau multiple de doublets

end form description (EFD) fin de description de grille; ~ **item** article fini

endless loop bande sans fin

end mark marque de fin

endodyne *n* autodyne

end of (scanning) **cycle** fin de paquet

end-of-address signal signal de fin de numérotation

end-of-battery-reversal signal arrêt inversion de batterie

end-of-block signal signal fin de bloc

end-of-call lamp lampe de fin

end-of-channel block fin bloc canal

end of data fin de volume; ~ **of dialling** fin de numérotation; ~ **of dialogue** fin de dialogue; ~ **of exchange** fin d'échange (FEC); ~ **office** centre local (CL); centre de rattachement nominal

end-of-file (EOF) adresse de fin (de fichier); ~ **label (EOF)** identificateur de fin de fichier; ~ **record** article fin de fichier

end-of-frame flag drapeau fin de bloc

end-of-line character caractère fin de ligne (CFL)

end-of-medium character (EM) caractère fin de support

end of message (EOM) fin d'échange (FEC); ~ **of output** fin de sortie

end-of-pulsing signal signal de fin de numérotation

end-of-record word mot fin d'article

end-of-repetition gate fenêtre fin de récurrence

end of selection fin de numérotation

end-of-selection signal signal de fin de sélection; signal de numéro reçu

end of tape fin de bande; fin de volume

end-of-tape label/identifier (EOT) identificateur de fin de bande

end of text (ETX) fin de texte; ~ **of transmission (EOT)** fin d'émission; fin de communication; fin de transmission

end-of-transmission block (ETB) fin de bloc (de transmission); fin de message

end of travel fin de course

end-of-year flag changement d'année

endorsement *n* visa d'homologation; aval; validation

endowed with doté de

end-piece *n* embout

end-plate *n* flasque; plaque de fermeture

end-point *n* aboutissement

end stop butée d'arrêt

end-to-end de bout en bout; centralisé; ~ **array** réseau linéaire d'antennes; ~ **character** (of EBCDIC system) caractère de fonction; ~ **control** commande de bout en bout; ~ **MF signalling** transit; ~ **path-**

finding marquage centralisé; recherche conjuguée; ~ **routiner** robot (d'appels); ~ **selection** sélection conjuguée; ~ **servicing** service bout en bout; ~ **signalling** signalisation de bout en bout; ~ **signalling call** appel transit

endurance *n* robustesse; ~ **at maximum impulse current** endurance au choc de courant maximal; ~ **test** essai de vieillissement; ~ **test on samples** contrôle d'endurance par prélèvement (CEP)

end-user *n* utilisateur; acquéreur; exploitant; usager

end-wise feed alimentation colonne par colonne

enemy *adj* hostile

energize *v* exciter; alimenter; amorcer; appeler

energized *adj* sous tension; appelé; passant; collé

energizing *n* mise sous tension (MST); ~ **circuit** circuit d'excitation

energy *n* énergie; puissance (Pce); ~ **efficiency** rendement énergétique; ~ **gap** écart énergétique (entre deux bandes); ~ **level** (of particle) niveau énergétique

energy-level diagram diagramme énergétique

energy spectrum spectre d'énergie (émis en ligne)

ENG (s. electronic news-gathering)

engage *v* amorcer; enclencher; enfoncer; engrener; occuper

engaged *adj* indisponible; occupé; ~ (tone) occupation; ~ **click** signal acoustique d'occupation; ~ **line** ligne occupée; ~ **signal** signal d'occupation; ~ **test** test d'occupation

engine *n* moteur (MOT); ~ **driver** (of laser printer) module d'impression

engineer *n* agent; ingénieur; ~ (semi-skilled) technicien; ~ **call-out rate** taux de signalisation (SI)

engineering *n* étude; organisation; technique; mécanique; **(mechanical)** ~ mécanique; ~ **circuit** circuit de service; ~ **design-revision status** état industriel; ~ **development level** palier technique; ~ **time** temps d'indisponibilité

engraved *adj* gravé

engraving *n* gravure

enhance *v* améliorer; optimiser; valoriser; amplifier

enhanced *adj* affiné; ~ **signalling** signalisation enrichie

enhancement *n* enrichissement; évolution; ~ **of spurious signals** intensification de signaux parasites; ~ **type N-channel MOS transistor** transistor MOS canal n à

enrichissement
ENI (s. equivalent noise input)
ENQ (s. enquiry)
enquire v consulter
enquirer n demandeur (DR) (= amont); Deur
enquiry (ENQ) consultation; demande de
réponse; ~ **call** mise en garde pour appel
antérieur; double appel; ~ **computer**
calculateur de consultation; ~ **desk** opératrice de renseignements; pupitre d'interrogation; ~ **terminal** terminal de consultation
en-route marker beacon radioborne en route
enshrine v inscrire (sur)
entail v entraîner
entanglement n enchevêtrement
enter v inscrire; afficher; consigner; écrire;
frapper; implanter; introduire; porter;
valider; saisir
enthalpy flux calorifique
entitlement n droit; habilitation; ~ **to**
**automatic exchange line (PSN) last number
redial** droit à la répétition automatique du
dernier numéro composé; ~ **to through-
connect trunk lines** droit à l'aboutement
réseau
entrance link déport; ~ **terminal** borne
d'entrée; ~ **wire** conducteur d'entrée
entry n entrée; accès; acquisition; écriture;
élément; inscription; poste; saisie;
~ **(point)** adresse d'entrée; ~ **(prompt)**
validation; ~ **block** bloc d'entrée; ~ **code**
appel; ~ **condition** état initial; ~ **hole** trou
de passage; ~ **point** point d'entrée; accès
d'entrée; adresse de lancement; ~ **terminal**
console de saisie
envelope n enveloppe; gabarit; ampoule;
intercalaire; ~ **(of lamp bulb)** ballon;
~ **delay** temps de propagation de groupe;
distorsion du temps de transit de groupe
envelope-delay distortion distorsion de temps
de propagation de groupe
envelope detection détection d'enveloppe;
~ **distortion** distorsion de modulation;
~ **indicator** indicateur d'enveloppe;
~ **switching** commutation par enveloppes;
~ **velocity** vitesse de groupe
environment n milieu; contexte; cadre; composition
environmental conservation protection civile;
~ **test** essai d'ambiance
envisage v prévoir
envisaged adj prévu
EOF (s. end of file)
EOM (s. end of message)
EOT (s. end of transmission); ∻ (s.
end-of-tape label/identifier)
EPI (s. elevation-position indicator)
epitaxial deposit dépôt épitaxique; ~ **layer**

couche épitaxiée
epitaxy n épitaxie
E-plane lens lentille à lames parallèles dans le
plan E; ∻ **(E-bend) sectoral horn** cornet
sectoriel
epoch n instant significatif; ~ **of a digital
signal** instant de décision d'un signal
numérique
epoxy (epoxide resin) résine époxyde; verre
époxy (époxyde)
EPROM (electrically programmable read-only memory) mémoire non volatile; ∻ **device**
support amovible reprogrammable
Epstein hysteresis tester cadre Epstein (de 25
cm); ∻ **square** cadre Epstein (de 25 cm)
equal and opposite en différentielle
equal-gain diversity reception réception en
diversité à gain égal
equality n élément anticoïncidence; non
équivalence
equalization charging charge en égalisation;
~ **filter** filtre égaliseur
equalizer n égalisateur; réseau correcteur;
circuit compensateur; correcteur; filtre de
correction; réseau de contre-distorsion
equalizing amplifier amplificateur correcteur;
~ **bar** liaison équipotentielle; ~ **battery**
batterie en tampon; batterie équilibrée;
~ **charge** charge d'égalisation; ~ **current**
courant d'égalisation; ~ **pulse** impulsion
d'égalisation; ~ **repeater** répéteur correcteur de la distorsion; ~ **ring** liaison
équipotentielle
equal-length (multi-unit) code code à éléments; code à moments; ~ **code switching**
sélection par signaux de code (à moments)
equal-ratio channels canaux à distribution
égale de périodes
equation n formule; loi
equi-angular conical horn cornet conique
équiangulaire
equi-band operation opération à largeurs de
bande égales
equilibrium (coupling) length longueur d'équilibre
equi-phase zone zone équiphase
equipment n matériel; équipement; organes;
appareillage; ~ **code** code d'équipement
(CEQ); ~ **definition sheet** fiche de définition du matériel; ~ **for blind operator**
additif aveugle; ~ **layout drawing** plan
d'équipement; ~ **number** numéro d'équipement; ~ **number change** mutation;
~ **option** cas d'équipement; ~ **practice**
normes de construction; ~ **schedule** devis;
~ **under test** équipement sous test (EST)
equipped adj équipé
equiradial aerial antenne omnidirectionnelle;

antenne omnidirective

equi-signal beam faisceau à signaux équilibrés; ~ **zone** zone à signaux équilibrés

equivalence *n* correspondance

equivalent air-gap width largeur équivalente d'entrefer; ~ **articulation loss** affaiblissement équivalent pour la netteté (AEN); ~ **attenuation** affaiblissement équivalent; ~ **binary content** contenu binaire équivalent; ~ **bit rate** débit binaire équivalent; ~ **circuit** circuit équivalent; ~ **diode** diode équivalente; ~ **diode voltage** tension de diode équivalente; ~ **disturbing current** courant perturbateur équivalent; ~ **disturbing voltage** tension perturbatrice équivalente; ~ **limit frequency** fréquence limite équivalente; ~ **network** réseau équivalent; ~ **noise input (ENI)** bruit équivalent d'entrée; ~ **parallel resistance** résistance parallèle équivalente; ~ **random circuit group** faisceau équivalent; ~ **resistance error** écart équivalent; ~ **separation** écartement équivalent; ~ **series resistance** résistance série équivalente; ~ **service** service de lignes groupées; ~ **side-band input** puissance équivalente du bruit de la bande latérale

equivalent-to équivalence (logique)

erasable *adj* amovible

erase *v* effacer; ~ **bit pattern** effacement de bits; ~ **character** caractère de rejet; ~ **head** tête d'effacement; ~ **in area (EA)** effacement dans la zone; ~ **in display (ED)** effacement dans la partition; ~ **in line (EL)** effacement dans la ligne; ~ **key** touche d'effacement; ~ **logic** logique d'effacement

eraser *n* (graphics) gomme

erase signal signal d'effacement; ~ **test** contrôle effacement

erasure signal signal d'effacement

erection drawing dessin de montage

erect sideband bande latérale directe

ergodic source source stationnaire

ergonomics *n* biotechnique

Erichsen dishing test emboutissage (ERICHSEN)

Ericsson line selector sélecteur Ericsson; ~ **separating filter** filtre séparateur d'Ericsson

ERL (s. echo return loss)

erlang (E) erlang; ~ **formula** formule d'Erlang; ~ **meter** erlangmètre

ERP (s. effective radiated power)

errand *n* mission

errant *adj* dévoyé

erroneous *adj* erroné; ~ **bit** bit erroné; ~ **block** bloc erroné

error *n* erreur; anomalie; dérive; faute; ~ **amplifier** amplificateur d'erreur; ~ **burst** paquet d'erreurs; rafale d'erreurs; salve d'erreurs; ~ **character** caractère de rejet; ~ **checking and recovery** traitement des erreurs; ~ **control bit** bit de contrôle d'erreur; ~ **control character** caractère de contrôle d'erreur; ~ **control equipment** équipement de protection contre les erreurs; ~ **control loop** boucle de protection contre les erreurs

error-correcting *adj* autocorrecteur; ~ **code** code correcteur d'erreurs (Hamming); ~ **patch** correction ponctuelle; ~ **telegraph system (ARQ)** système correcteur d'erreurs (RQ automatique)

error-correction by repetition correction d'erreurs par retransmission; ~ **code** code autocorrecteur

error count niveau de sévérité; ~ **curve** courbe d'erreur

error-detecting and feedback system système détecteur d'erreurs avec demande de répétition; ~ **code** code détecteur d'erreur(s); ~ **system** système détecteur d'erreurs sans répétition

error-detection and correction détection et correction d'erreurs; ~ **and feedback system** RQ automatique

error-free trigger level seuil précis

error log fichier compte-rendu; ~ **logging** enregistrement des erreurs

error-logging file fichier d'erreurs

error measurement mesure de l'erreur; ~ **multiplication factor** coefficient de multiplication; ~ **probability** probabilité d'erreur

error-prone entaché d'erreurs

error range plage d'erreurs; ~ **rate** taux d'erreurs; taux de faute; ~ **rate monitor** appareil de surveillance du taux d'erreur; ~ **recovery** reconfiguration; ~ **signal** signal d'erreur; ~ **signal unit** unité de signalisation erronée; ~ **tape** bande de stockage des erreurs; ~ **threshold** seuil d'erreur

Esaki (tunnel-effect) diode diode tunnel

ESC (s. escape character)

escape *n* échappement; ~ **character (ESC)** caractère de chargement de code; ~ **clause** clause échappatoire; ~ **codes** changement de code

escutcheon *n* enjoliveur; tableau

essential line ligne essentielle

establish *v* rechercher; ~ **contact** (with) mise en relation (avec)

established *adj* fixé

establishing a common reference point harmonisation

estimated time ordre de grandeur des temps

ESV (s. experimental space vehicle)

ETB (s. end-of-transmission block); ~

character caractère fin de bloc

etch *n* attaque chimique

etchant *n* agent de gravure

etched *adj* gravé; photogravé

etching *n* gravure; décapage; avivage; corrosion

ETFE fluorure d'éthylène

et seq. et suivant

ETX (s. end of text)

European Conference of Postal and Telecommunications Administrations Conférence Européenne des Postes et Télécommunications (CEPT)

evacuate *v* purger

evaluation *n* synthèse; bilan; calcul; ~ **index** indice de performance

evanescent mode mode évanescent

even(-numbered) *adj* pair

even(-number) frame trame paire

even-order harmonic harmonique d'ordre pair

event *n* événement; occurrence; passe; ~ **flip-flop** bascule d'événement (BEV); ~ **queue management** gestion des files d'attente d'événements

evolute *n* courbe d'évolution

E-wire *n* fil RON (réception)

exacting *adj* sévère; rigoureux; délicat

exalted carrier porteuse renforcée; ~ **carrier reception** réception avec renforcement de la porteuse

example *n* modèle (mle)

EXCEPT élément anticoïncidence; exclusion; sauf; non équivalence; ~ **gate** circuit à anticoïncidence; OU exclusif

excess modified refractive index indice de réfraction modifié à excès

excess-three code (XS3) code majoré de trois; code réfléchi à excédent trois; code plus trois

excess three-to-Gray decimal decoder (BCD) décodeur DCB excès gray à sortie passive

exchange *v* échanger; ~ *n* bureau central; central téléphonique; centre; chantier; commutateur; site; ~ **(PSN) tone bridging** franchissement des tonalités PTT; ~ **area** circonscription téléphonique; zone de rattachement; ~ **area layout** plan du réseau; ~ **call** appel du central; ~ **capacity** capacité de l'autocommutateur; ~ **central units** cœur de chaîne (CDC); ~ **clock** horloge centrale; ~ **code** indicatif de central; code de bureau; indicatif (local); numéro de série de l'autocommutateur; ~ **configuration program** configurateur; ~ **core subsystem** organes centraux; organes communs; ~ **end** partie locale

exchange-end terminal terminal actif

exchange line (X-line) ligne de réseau (LR);

ligne PTT; ligne extérieure; ligne auto; ~ **line termination** tête P et T; ~ **parameter** paramètre bureau; ~ **plant** l'automatique

exchange-powered *adj* (à) téléalimentation

exchanger *n* échangeur

exchange register registre mémoire; ~ **right-of-way** droit au réseau; ~ **selector** sélecteur de central; ~ **software** logiciel adapté aux sites; ~ **software resources** état du site; ~ **termination** accès; ~ **time** heure centrale; ~ **time base** base de temps générale (BTG)

exchange-wide tout au réseau (TAR); circonscription téléphonique

exchange with extension lines central à lignes d'extension

excitation *n* excitation; attaque de grille; ~ **anode** anode d'entretien; anode d'excitation; ~ **band** bande d'excitation; ~ **energy** énergie d'excitation; ~ **loss** perte par excitation; ~ **potential** potentiel d'excitation; ~ **regulator** régulateur d'excitation; ~ **state** (level) niveau d'énergie d'excitation

excited-atom density (of gas) concentration des atomes excités

excited ion ion excité

exciter *n* excitateur; élément actif; élément rayonnant primaire; ~ **coil** bobine d'excitation

exciting circuit circuit d'excitation; ~ **rheostat** rhéostat d'excitation; ~ **winding** enroulement inducteur; enroulement d'excitation

exclusion *n* exclusion; sauf; interdiction d'écoute; ~ **bit** bit d'exclusivité; ~ **problem** problème d'exclusion

exclusive exchange line ligne individuelle (d'abonné); ligne principale; ligne non partagée; ~ **grant** concession exclusive; ~ **line** ligne individuelle; ligne non groupée

exclusive-NOR non équivalence

exclusive-OR *n* disjonction; OU exclusif; découpe logique; ~ (non-equivalence) **operation** addition sans retenue; exclusion réciproque

exclusive OR circuit circuit anticoïncidence; circuit dilemme; ~ **priority** (bit) exclusivité; ~ **right-of-way** intervention prioritaire

exclusivity *n* exclusion

excursion *n* déplacement

ex-directory numbers liste rouge

executable machine language binaire exécutable; ~ **memory image** image mémoire

execute phase phase d'exécution

execution *n* déroulement; réalisation; ~ **time** durée de traitement

executive *n* programme moniteur; directeur; ~ (supervisory) **program** superviseur;

~ (routine) programme directeur

executive-and-secretary line ligne de filtrage (LF)

executive board conseil de direction; ~ **busy override** intervention en tiers; entrée en tiers prioritaire; intervention prioritaire; ~ **busy override facility** (intrusion) mise en tiers; ~ **control program (ECP)** programme superviseur; ~ **form** grille de l'exécutif; ~ **override station** poste prioritaire; ~ **right-of-way** intervention en tiers; entrée en tiers prioritaire; ~ **ring-back** rappel automatique

executive-secretary system ensemble de filtrage

executive station abonné privilégié; ~ **station with direct operator signalling** poste super-privilégié; ~ **style** type administratif; ~ **training** formation des cadres

exemption n dérogation

exhausted adj (of stocks) épuisé

exhaustive adj limitatif; complet; ~ **test** essai complet

exhibitor n exposant

existing adj actuel

exit v quitter; abandonner; sortir; ~ n sortie; libération; ~ **from** se débrancher (dans); ~ **from test loop** pas de rebouclage; ~ **run file** fichier de sortie

exjunction n OU exclusif

expand v décomprimer

expandable adj évolutif; extensible

expanded centre plan display indicateur panoramique à centre dilaté; ~ **conductor** câble expansé; ~ **polystyrene** polystyrène expansé

expander n extenseur; expanseur; prolongateur

expansion bus bus à rallonge; ~ **cascading** banalisation progressive; ~ **chamber** détendeur; ~ **coefficient** coefficient de foisonnement; coefficient de dilatation; ~ **key** touche d'expansion; ~ **orbit** orbite d'expansion; orbite dilatée; ~ **potential** extensibilité; ~ **ratio** taux d'extension

expansor n extenseur

expectation, (statistical) ~ **(E)** espérance mathématique

expected level dénivellement; ~ **return message** message attendu en réception

expedance n impédance négative

expendable items consommables; fongibles

experimental space vehicle (ESV) satellite; ~ **station** station expérimentale

expertise n acquis; maîtrise; savoir-faire

expiry n débordement de temporisation; ~ **date** échéance; ~ **of agreement** cessation du contrat

explicit return point point de réponse spécifiée

exploded view vue éclatée

explosion-proof adj antidéflagrant; ~ **switch** interrupteur blindé

explosive rivet rivet tubulaire

exponent n exposant; caractéristique(s)

exponential atmosphere atmosphère exponentiel

exponentiation n élévation à une puissance

export (of data base files) rechargement

exposed adj apparent; dégarni

exposure n prise de vue; ~ (to heat/light) insolation; ~ **time** temps de pose; ~ **to fire and heat** comportement au feu ou à la chaleur

extended busy test essai prolongé d'occupation; ~ **character set** jeu de caractères étendu; numérique étendu; ~ **clip** mutilation supplémentaire; ~ **coverage** couverture étendue; ~ **engaged condition** garde jusqu'à libération complète; ~ **mode** mode étendu; ~ **telegraph circuit** faisceau échelonné

extender n prolongateur; rallonge; rehausse; ~ **card** carte prolongateur/prolongatrice

extension n adaptateur; augmentation; déport; développement; poste; poste intérieur; poste interne; poste supplémentaire (PS); poste téléphonique; poste usager; prolongateur; rallonge; renvoi; ~ (of file) allongement; ~ (of PABX system) poste supplémentaire; poste d'usager; ~ **cable** cordon de raccordement; câble prolongateur; ~ **call** arrivée intérieure; ~ **circuit** circuit de prolongement; section locale

extension/exchange line SLIC joncteur réseau/usager

extension lead câble prolongateur; ~ **line** ligne intérieure; ligne de poste supplémentaire; ~ **loop** ligne de poste supplémentaire; ~ **spring** ressort de traction; ~ **station** poste supplémentaire (PS); ~ **telephone** poste supplémentaire (PS)

extent n étendue; domaine

extenuating circumstances force majeure

exterior adj extérieur

external adj externe; extérieur; ~ **blocking** blocage externe; ~ **characteristic** caractéristique extérieure; ~ **dimensions** hors œuvre; ~ **feeder** dispositif extérieur; ~ **foil** armature extérieure; ~ **harmonic modulation** modulation extérieure de l'harmonique; ~ **lamp panels** herse; ~ **line** ligne extérieure

externally-heated arc arc à chauffage externe

external pull-down resistor résistance de tirage extérieur; ~ **retaining ring** (circlip) anneau extérieur; ~ **screw-thread screw** tube mâle;

~ **slaving** asservissement extérieur; ~ **stop code(r)** codeur d'arrêt extérieur; ~ **trace count** comptage traceur extérieur; ~ **unit** coffret

extinction *n* (of thyristor) désamorçage; ~ **voltage** tension d'extinction

extinguisher *n* extincteur

extra bit bit supplémentaire; ~ **block** bloc supplémentaire

extraction tool pince; pince extraction

extractor *n* filtre; ~ **hood** hotte d'extraction

extra load charge supplémentaire

extraneous *adj* parasite(s); étranger; extérieur; inutile; ~ **echo** écho étranger; ~ **field** champ extérieur; ~ **frequency** fréquence étrangère; ~ **noise** bruit parasite

extraordinary wave onde extraordinaire

extra-terrestrial noise bruit extra-terrestre; bruit cosmique

extra yield valeur ajoutée

extreme operating conditions gabarit

extrinsic absorption absorption extrinsèque; ~ **semiconductor** semiconducteur extrinsèque

extruded *adj* filé; ~ **section** profilé extrudé

exudation *n* coulure

ex-works *adj* en sortie usine; départ usine

eye amplitude amplitude de l'œil

eyelet *n* œillet

eye-piece graticule loupe micrométrique

eyestrain *n* agression visuelle; fatigue visuelle

F

fabric *n* toile; ~ **ribbon** (cartridge) ruban encreur

facade *n* fronton

face/back recto-verso

face-down feed alimentation colonne par colonne

face-plate (of button) cabochon

faceted crystal cristal facetté

face value valeur nominale

facilities moyen

facility *n* outil; aide; droit; faculté; possibilité; ressource; service; ~ **acceptance tone** tonalité d'acceptation de manœuvre; ~ **code** préfixe de service; ~ **not-accepted tone** tonalité de refus de service

facing pages pages face à face

facsimile *n* télécopie; fac-similé; image; ~ *adj* autographique; ~ **apparatus** appareil de télégraphie fac-similé; ~ **broadcast station** station de fac-similé; ~ **equipment** appareil de fac-similé; ~ **network** réseau de télécopie; ~ **posting machine** reporteuse (= machine de report); ~ **receiver** récepteur fac-similé; ~ **recorder** imprimeur de fac-similé; ~ **system** télécopieur; ~ **telegram** télégramme fac-simile; ~ **telegraphy** bélinogramme; télégraphie autographique; télégraphie fac-similé; ~ **terminal** terminal téléautographique; ~ **transient** période transitoire du fac-similé; ~ **transmission** transmission fac-similé; ~ **transmitter** transmetteur fac-similé; ~ **type B** fac-similé demiteinte

fact file dossier

fact-finding visit/tour mission d'identification

factor *n* facteur; coefficient; indice; module; taux

factorial n m! (factorielle «m»)

factor of cooperation facteur de coopération

factory acceptance test report cahier de recette

factory-adjusted *adj* préréglé

factory-set *adj* réglage usine (RU)

factory-wired *adj* précâblé; câblé en usine

fact retrieval recouvrement de faits

fade margin plage de régulation

fader *n* équilibreur avant-arrière

fade up relèvement graduel du niveau

fading *n* évanouissement; affaiblissement; scintillement; ~ **effect** effet d'évanouissement

fading-free sans évanouissement

fading frequency fréquence d'évanouissement; ~ **period** période d'évanouissement; ~ **radio wave** onde entrante à valeur variable; ~ **rate** fréquence d'évanouissement

fail (of test) refus

failed cascade relay stages relais de défaut en série

fail-safe *adj* autosurveillé; sécurisé; ~ **mode** en sécurité positive; ~ **protection** sécurisation

fail-soft operation fonctionnement en mode dégradé

failure *n* échec; panne; aléa; avarie; coupure; défaillance; défaut; dérangement; détérioration; faute; manque; mortalité; perte; incident; ~ **cost** (of quality control) coût de non qualité; ~ **curve** courbe de détérioriation; ~ **histogram** histogramme des déchets; ~ **modularity** moudularité de panne; ~ **rate** taux de défaillance; taux d'échec; taux de rejet

faint speech amplifier amplificateur à l'émission

fairing *n* capot

fairlead *n* guide(-câble)

fall-back *n* incident; déclin; repli ~ **circuit** circuit de réserve; ligne de réserve; circuit de recours; ~ **data rate** débit de repli; vitesse de repli

fall-back-rate mode mode repli

fall-back system sécurisation

falling *adj* descendant; décroissant; ~ **edge** front de descente; front descendant; front tombant

falling-off *n* (of relay) déclenchement

fall off *v* dégrader

fall-off *n* dégradation

fall-out *n* retombée

fall time (t_f) temps de décroissance; temps de descente; front de retombée; temps de déstockage; temps de retombée; ~ **time** front de retombée; temps de déstockage; temps de retombée

false *adj* artificiel; faux; factice; erroné; infirme; intempestif; invalide; synthétique; ~ **add** addition sans report; ~ **ceiling** faux plafond; ~ **code** contrôle d'existence; ~ **cross and ground test (FCG)** essai de court circuit et faux potentiels; ~ **drop** réponse non pertinente; bruit; ~ **floor** faux plancher; ~ **operation** fausse manœuvre; ~ **retrieval** parasite(s); bruit; ~ **(seizure) attempt** fausse prise

false-start call appel permanent

false trip fausse manœuvre

FAM (s. simultaneous frequency and amplitude modulation)

fan v aérer; ~ n (of cable loom) peigne; ~ **aerial** antenne en éventail

fan-assisted cooling ventilation forcée; refroidi à air brassé; ~ **oven** étuve à air brassé

fan beam faisceau en éventail; faisceau (électromagnétique) plat

fan-beam aerial antenne à faisceau étalé

fan-fold paper papier replié en accordéon; papier pliage paravent

fan-in n charge d'entrée; entrance; facteur de charge d'entrée (en entrée); facteur pyramidal d'entrée

fan marker beacon radioborne en éventail

fanned cable peigne de câble

fanning(-out) n épanouissement

fanning strip réglette de répartition; plaquette de connexion; peigne; guide-fils; répartiteur

fan out v déramer

fan-out n facteur de charge de sortie (en sortie); caractéristique en charge; facteur pyramidal de sortie; sortance; ~ **facility** dispositif de diffusion

fan washer rondelle éventail

far-end adj distant; éloigné; ~ **crosstalk (FEXT)** télédiaphonie; ~ **crosstalk attenuation** affaiblissement télédiaphonique; ~ **exchange** central distant

fascia n collerette frontale; capot; drageoir

fast adj rapide; ~ **access** accès rapide

fast-access memory mémoire rapide

fast blinking clignotant rapide

fast-blow fuse fusible rapide; fusible instantané

fast-core format forme interne

fast cycle wavetrains trains d'ondes; ~ **driver (FD)** distribution rapide (DR)

fast-driving flip-flop bascule de distribution rapide

fastener n élément de fixation; agrafe; clôture

fasteners npl visserie; boulonnerie

fast flashing clignotant rapide; ~ **forward** (recorder control) bobinage avant; ~ **Fourier transform** papillon; ~ **mode** (of tape) grande vitesse de défilement

fast-recovery diode diode à redressement rapide; diode de récupération

fast scroll exploration rapide

fast-select acceptance acceptation de la sélec-tion rapide

fast-shift pulse impulsion de décalage rapide

fast switching diode diode de commutation rapide; ~ **turn-around** à temps de réemploi écourté

fatal error erreur fatale; erreur irrémédiable; erreur mortelle

fatigue inducing adj fragilisant; ~ **limit** endurance; ~ **test** essai de fatigue

fault n défaut; faute; aléa; anomalie; avarie; erreur; panne; vice; ~ **analysis** diagnostic; ~ **between turns** court-circuit entre spires; ~ **cancel** effacement défaut; ~ **category** niveau d'anomalie

fault-clearing n dépannage; effacement défaut; ~ **routine** réparation

fault condition anomalie (de fonctionnement); ~ **current** courant de défaut; ~ **detection** espionnage système; ~ **dictionary** dictionnaire diagnostique de défauts; ~ **docket** ticket de dérangement; fiche de signalisation de dérangement; bulletin de dérangement; ~ **finder** détecteur de faute

fault-finding recherche de dérangements; ~ **chart** table d'accusation; diagnose; ~ **diagnostic** localisation d'avaries

fault flag drapeau indicateur de défaut; ~ **handler** traitement d'anomalies

fault-handling card opérateur de visualisation et d'émission des fautes

faultless adj sans défaut

fault location sheet fiche localisation de panne; ~ **message** message de faute; message d'anomalie; ~ **profile** cliché de faute; ~ **rate** taux d'accusation

fault-rate counter compteur d'accusation

fault record fiche de relevé de défauts; ~ **recorder** enregistreur de fautes; enregistreur de dérangements; centralographe; ~ **register** registre de fautes (RF); ~ **relay** relais de faute; ~ **repairing** dépannage; ~ **report** cliché de faute; bulletin de dérangement; ~ **report sheet** fiche relevé de défaut; fiche de signalisation de dérangement

faultsman n réparateur

fault switch détecteur d'anomalies

fault-testing junction ligne de communication de pannes

fault-tracing n localisation des dérangements; localisation des défauts; localisation d'avaries; recherche de pannes; localisation des équipements défectueux; ~ **program** programme de localisation de pannes; cliché d'anomalie

faulty adj baissé; défaillant; défectueux; ~ **circuit** circuit en dérangement; ~ **insulation** mauvais isolement; ~ **line** ligne en

F

dérangement
Faure plate plaque Faure
FAW (s. frame alignment word)
fax *n* téléscopie; fac-similé; ~ **transceiver** télécopieur
FCF (s. flow control function)
FCG (s. false cross and ground test)
FCS (s. frame-check sequence); ~ (s. first-customer shipment); ~ **user** client pilote
FD (s. fast driver)
FDM (s. frequency-division multiplexing)
FDMA (s. frequency-division multiple access)
FDM transmission transmission analogique
feasibility committee comité d'automatisation; ~ **study** analyse préalable; analyse globale; étude d'opportunité; étude théorique; ~ **test** essai probatoire
feasible réalisable
feather *n* écho artificiel
feature *n* possibilité(s); caractéristique(s); critère
fee *n* redevance; honoraire; taxe
feed (aerial) illumination (d'un objet)
feedback *n* contre-réaction; réinjection; retour de l'information; rétroaction; asservissement; ~ (of programmed array logic) rebouclage; ~ **admittance** admittance de réaction; ~ **channel** canal de retour; ~ **circuit** circuit de contre-réaction; circuit de réaction; retour d'écoute; ~ **coil** bobine de réaction; ~ **current** courant de retour; courant réfléchi; ~ **equalizer** circuit d'égalisation à réaction négative; ~ **line** liaison de réaction; ~ **loop** boucle de réaction; ~ **ratio** taux de réaction
feedback-stabilized amplifier amplificateur contre-réactionné
feedback suppressor circuit circuit anti-local; ~ **winding** enroulement de réaction
feed bridge pont d'alimentation; ~ **control** commande d'avance; ~ **current** courant d'alimentation
feeder *n* artère; câble d'alimentation; câble de transport; canalisation (de réseau électrique); conducteur; départ; ligne d'alimentation; ligne de transport d'énergie électrique; affluent; ~ **cable** transport; ~ **choke** self de ligne; ~ **line** circuit d'alimentation; ~ **relay** relais d'alimentation
feed-forward compensation compensation avec boucle d'avance de phase
feed hole perforation d'entraînement
fee digit chiffre de taxation
feeding *n* défilement
feed junctor alimenteur; ~ **magnet** aimant d'entraînement; ~ **pawl** doigt d'avance; ~ **pitch** pas d'entraînement

feedpoint impedance impédance d'entrée
feed roller galet bourreur; galet d'alimentation; ~ **spool** bobine débitrice; ~ **suppression magnet** aimant interrupteur d'entraînement
feed-through *n* trou de traversée; ~ **capacitor** condensateur de fuite
fee handler distributeur
feeler gauge palpeur
felt pad tampon de feutre
female connector connecteur femelle
fence *n* borne; délimiteur
fender *n* capot de protection; déviateur
FEP (s. front-end processor); ~ (s. fluorinated ethylene polypropylene)
ferric chloride (PCB etchant) perchlorure de fer
ferrite coil bobine à noyau mobile; ~ **core** noyau de ferrite
ferrite-filled coaxial line ligne coaxiale à remplissage de ferrite
ferrite isolator isolateur à ferrite; ~ **rod** bâton de ferrite; bâtonnet
ferrite-rod aerial antenne à tige de ferrite; antenne à noyau magnétique; antenne à ferrites
ferrite toroidal core tore (de ferrite)
ferrule *n* embout; manche; serre
ferry service radar radar de service de bac
festoon *n* guirlande; ~ **lamp** lampe navette
FET (s. field-effect transistor)
fetch *v* prélever; appeler; chercher; extraire; lire; placer; rapatrier; récuperer; relever; puiser; ~ *n* recherche en mémoire; ~ **and execute time** temps de recherche et d'exécution; ~ **date** lecture date
fetched *adj* prélevé
fetching *n* lecture
FEXT (s. far-end crosstalk)
ff. (folios) et suivant
FF (s. form feed)
FHB (s. file header block)
fibre bundle faisceau de fibres; ~ **class** classe de fibre; ~ **cloth** tissu de verre; ~ **drawing** fibrage
fibre-glass *n* fibre de verre; complexe verre-résine
fibre launch end début de la fibre; ~ **optical-transmission system** système de transmission par fibre optique
fibre-optics *n* fibre optique
fibre soldering jointage; ~ **support element** jonc cylindrique; ~ **tail** fibre amorce; fibre nue
fictitious memory mémoire fictive
fidelity *n* fidélité
field *n* champ; zone; libellé; rubrique; canevas; chantier; colonne; domaine; en-

semble de données; massif; partie; plan; secteur; trame tranche; ~ *adj* utilisateur; usager; en exploitation

field-alignment error erreur d'alignement

field cable câble de campagne; ~ **coil** bobinage d'excitation; stator inductif; ~ **displacement** déplacement dans le champ (d. de champ); ~ **effect** effet de champ

field-effect transistor (FET) transistor à effet de champ (TEC)

field engineer ingénieur de mise en circuit; ingénieur technico-commercial (ITC); ~ **experience** résultats obtenus en exploitation; ~ **frequency** fréquence de balayage vertical; fréquence d'exploration; ~ **intensity** densité de puissance; ~ **magnet** (with induction coils) inducteur; ~ **meter** mesureur de champ; ~ **non-linearity** distorsion de balayage vertical; ~ **of application** champ d'application

field-programmable personnalisable; programmé; ~ **routine** programme utilisateur

field pulse top trame

field-replaceable enfichable

field rheostat rhéostat de champ

field-scan generator générateur de signaux de balayage trame

field spider croisillon inducteur; ~ **strength** intensité de champ; grandeur de champ; niveau de champ

field-strength meter mesureur de la grandeur du champ; ~ **pattern** carte de champ (d'un ensemble émetteur radioélectrique)

field support service après-vente (SAV); ~ **sweep** balayage vertical; balayage de trame; ~ **synchronizing signal** signal de synchronisation trame; ~ **test** essai pratique; test fonctionnel; essai fonctionnel; essai in situ; essai sur site; ~ **trial** essai sur site; essai pratique; ~ **winding** bobinage de champ; inducteur; stator; ~ **wiring** câblage chantier

field-wiring connector connecteur à procédé champ

FIFO (s. push-up stack); ∿ (s. first-in/first-out); ∿ **queue** file circulaire; pile directe

fifteen-supergroup assembly assemblage de 15 groupes secondaires

fifties-group *n* cinquantaine

figure *n* chiffre (ch.); coefficient; facteur; indice

figure-of-eight reception réception à diagramme en huit

figure of linearity facteur de linéarité; ~ **of loss** facteur de pertes; ~ **of merit** facteur de qualité; coefficient de qualité; facteur de mérite; nombre de mérite; facteur de surtension; facteur Q; indice de perfor-

mance; caractéristique de qualité; indice de qualité de réception (IQR)

figures blank blanc de chiffres

figures-case série chiffres

figures/letters shift casse (-bas/-haut)

figures-shift signal signal d'inversion chiffres

filament *n* filament; boudinette; cathode

filament(s) (of aramid, in optical fibre cable) mèche

filament battery (A) batterie de chauffage; batterie de filament; ~ **bulb** lampe filament; ~ **cathode** cathode à chauffage direct; ~ **(heater) circuit** circuit de chauffage; ~ **current** courant de chauffage; ~ **drum** tambour d'enroulement; ~ **lamp** lampe à incandescence

file *v* (of patent) déposer; ~ **closure** fermeture de fichier; ~ **directory** répertoire de fichiers; ~ **floppy disk** disque souple banalisé; ~ **handler** manipulateur de fichiers; ~ **header block (FHB)** bloc en tête de fichier; ~ **index** répertoire de fichiers; ~ **keeper** propriétaire; ~ **linking** connexion de fichiers; ~ **maintenance** tenue de fichier; mise à jour de fichier; gestion du fichier; vérification de fichier

file-mark *n* marque de bande; fin de fichier

file name nom de fichier; ~ **name and record** adresse logique

file-protect(ion) ring anneau d'autorisation d'écriture; bague d'autorisation d'écriture; anneau de protection

file purge élimination de fichier; ~ **section** sous-fichier; ~ **separator** séparateur de fichier

file-sharing partage de fichiers

file tidying nettoyage du logiciel

file-to fichier destinataire

file transfer transfert de fichiers; ~ **updating** mise à jour de fichier; ~ **vault** local à archive

filing *n* classement; rangement

fill *n* coefficient d'utilisation

filler *n* remplissage; complément; prolongateur; remplage; bourrage; apport d'alliage; mastic; ~ *adj* (of characters) complémentaire; ~ **character** caractère de remplissage; caractère d'appoint; ~ **code** code de remplissage; ~ **element** prolongateur d'informations; ~ **material** matière de remplissage

fillet *n* filet; bourrelet; capot; congé (de soudure); gousset; arrondi; ~ **weld** cordon de soudure

filling elements matière de remplissage

fill-in signal unit trame sémaphore de remplissage; ~ **transmitter** station de rediffusion

fillister (head) screw vis cylindrique (à tête) bombée (CB)
film *n* couche; ~ **deposited** couche déposée
film-setter *n* photocomposeuse
film strip bande optique
filter *n* filtre; masque; self; séparateur; ~ **attenuation band** bande d'atténuation de filtre; ~ **attenuation compensation** élimination de l'affaiblissement de filtre; ~ **capacitor** condensateur de filtration; ~ **circuit** circuit d'aspiration; ~ **coupling** couplage de filtre de bande; ~ **crystal** cristal de filtre; ~ **element** cartouche de filtre
filtering *n* filtrage; nettoyage
filter mesh grille filtre; ~ **network** réseau filtrant
filter-out *v* sélectionner
filterplexer *n* combinaison diplexeur-filtre de bande latérale
filter resistance résistance de filtrage; ~ **section** cellule de filtre; ~ **stop band** bande d'atténuation de filtre
fin *n* ailette; ~ **aerial** antenne à ailettes
final acceptance certificate procès-verbal de réception; ~ **adjustment** mise au point (MAP); ~ **amplifier** amplificateur de sortie
final-choice (backbone) route faisceau non débordant
final circuit group faisceau final; ~ **clipping** mutilation de syllabe finale; ~ **dimensioning and cutting** détourage; ~ **exchange line** ligne de central terminal; ~ **inspection** contrôle final; ~ **inspection bench** banc final; ~ **instalment** paiement pour solde
final-route chain voie de dernier choix
final selector sélecteur final; connecteur; connecteur final; ~ **selector multiple** champ multiple à sélecteur final; ~ **status** état demandé; ~ **translation** traduction d'arrivée; ~ **trunk group** faisceau de rattachement
financial costs frais financiers; ~ **year** exercice; conjoncture
find and exchange recherche et substitution
finder *n* chercheur; chercheur de ligne appelante; détecteur; ~ **stage** chercheur d'auxiliaire
finding the equation mise en équation
fine adjustment/setting réglage précis; ~ **bearing** relèvement précis; ~ **groove** microsillon
fine-machined *adj* chariôté fin; ~ **with extra surface allowance** usiné avec surépaisseur
fine setting réglage fin; ~ **steering accuracy** pointage fin; ~ **tuning** accord précis; réglage précis; réglage fin; accord fin
finger (of edge connector) lamelle; ~ **(of insertion machine)** pince insertion

fingerboard *n* clavier
finger conveyor convoyeur à doigts; ~ **plate** cadran d'appel; ~ **stop** doigt d'arrêt; butée de cadran
fingerwheel *n* cadran d'appel
finish *n* finition; présentation; traitement
finished article pièce ouvrée; ~ **product** article fini; ~ **quality** propreté
finishing *n* usinage; ~ **washer** rondelle cuvette
FIR (s. flight information region)
fire control equipment installation de direction de tir; ~ **flash call** avertissement téléphonique d'incendie
fire-proof *adj* incombustible
fire-retardant *adj* ignifuge
fire service pompiers (code 18 en France); ~ **telephone** ligne directe
firing *n* amorçage; allumage; déclenchement; attaque; ~ **angle** angle d'ouverture; ~ **circuit** circuit d'amorçage; ~ **pin** percuteur éléctrique
firm *adj* ferme
firmware *n* chaîne de micro-instructions; logiciel d'exploitation; logiciel de base; automate câblé; logiciel figé; logique câblée; logique statique; micrologiciel; micrologie; microprogrammation; programmation câblée; programmation fixe
firmware-based *adj* microprogrammé
firmware processor calculateur à programme câblé; ~ **processor communications handler for bus control (PCH)** gestion de l'accès des processeurs au bus de communication par microprogramme
first article tête de série
first-choice route voie de premier choix; ~ **routing** acheminement premier choix; ~ **trunk group** faisceau de jonctions de premier choix
first cladding phase premier assemblage du gainage
first-customer shipment (FCS) livraison contrôlée; client pilote
first detector mélangeur; changeur de fréquence
first-generation master film typon
first harmonic première harmonique; oscillation fondamentale
first-in/first-out (FIFO) mémoire à liste directe
first-level address adresse absolue; adresse directe
first party release libération par le premier abonné (à raccrocher); ~ **(production) article** premier article de chaîne; ~ **Townsend discharge** première décharge de Townsend
fiscal year exercice

fish(ing) wire fil de tirage
fish bar éclisse
fish-bone aerial antenne en arête de poisson;
antenne en sapin
fish-plate n éclisse
fissure n ébréchure; craquelure
fit n ajustage; ajustement; ~ heat-shrinkable
sleeve fretter
fitted cabinet armoire équipée
fitter, (skilled) ~ régleur (professionnel)
fitting n pose; mise en place; ajustement;
calage; ~ lug embout
five-bit byte groupe de cinq bits
five clear working days cinq jours non chomés
five-coil relay relais quintuple
five-hundred point selector sélecteur à cinq
cent points
five-key transmitter émetteur manuel à cinq
touches
five-level code code à cinq couches; code à
cinq moments
five-stage counter compteur à cinq étages
five-unit alphabet alphabet à cinq éléments;
alphabet à cinq unités; ~ code code
télégraphique à cinq moments; code à cinq
couches; alphabet à cinq unités
five-wire cable quinte
fix n (radio) point
fixed adj stationnaire; inamovible; ~ (target)
echo écho fixe
fixed-aerial finder radiogoniomètre à antenne
fixe
fixed attenuator affaiblisseur fixe
fixed-block format disposition à bloc fixe
fixed capacitor condensateur fixe; ~ charge
forfait; tarif forfaitaire
fixed-charge adj forfaitaire
fixed contact contact fixe; banc
fixed-count code code équilibré; numération
pondérée
fixed direction-finder radiogoniomètre à antenne fixe; ~ fee forfait
fixed(-length) field zone fixe
fixed-frequency transmitter émetteur à fréquence fixe
fixed-head disk disque magnétique à tête fixe;
~ disk controller unité de liaison de
mémoire de masse
fixed head disk unit unité à disque à tête fixe;
~ high-power resistor résistance fixe à forte
dissipation
fixed-length (closed) numbering plan plan de
numérotation fermé
fixed (word) length longueur fixe
fixed-length field zone de longueur fixe;
~ record article de longueur fixe
fixed mica dielectric capacitor condensateur
fixe au mica; ~ night service renvoi général

(RG)
fixed-orbit satellite service service de satellite
fixe
fixed-point arithmetic arithmétique en virgule
fixe; ~ part mantisse; partie fractionnaire;
~ representation représentation en virgule
fixe
fixed polynomial polynôme câblé; ~ pre-assignment préassignation fixe; ~ pre-scaling
prédetermination du facteur d'échelle;
~ radio station radiostation stationnaire
fixed-radix notation numération à base fixe
fixed-ratio code code équilibré
fixed record length longueur de bloc fixe;
~ repeater répéteur fixe; ~ spacer comb
échelle fixe
fixed-time call communication à heure fixe
fixing centre entre-axe de fixation; pas de
fixation; ~ hardware visserie; ~ nut écrou
clips; ~ rod tirant fixation
fixtures serrurerie de salle; ~ and fittings
fourniture(s)
flag v signaler; annoter; baliser; cocher;
délimiter; ~ n drapeau; fanion; indicateur; sentinelle; bannière; bit de présence;
caractère indicateur; délimiteur; étiquette;
marque; mot d'état; mot enregistreur;
registre; repère; sémaphore; signalisation;
~ (switch indicator) indicateur d'aiguillage; ~ bit bit drapeau
flagged adj signalé
flag sequence fanion
flagship product offre principale
flag-type terminal/connector cosse drapeau
flair n aptitude
flake n lame; paillette
flaking n écaillement; exfoliation
flame-proof adj ignifuge; ~ enclosure enveloppe antidéflagrante
flame resistance comportement à la flamme
flame-resistant adj calorifuge; ignifuge
flame-retardant adj résistant à la propagation
de la flamme
flame welding soudage à la flamme
flammability n résistance au feu
flammable adj inflammable
flange n flasque; joue; collerette; embase
(connecteur fixe)
flanged adj à oreilles
flanking adj adjacent
flap n volet; vantail; rabat; ~ attenuator
affaiblisseur à guillotine; affaiblisseur à
lame tournante
flapper n (of armature) palette
flare n cornet; distorsion
flash v clignoter; s'allumer à cadence;
scintiller; ~ n coup de crochet commutateur; écriture éclair; surimpression; étince-

F

lage; bavure; bocage; calotte; ~ (of service) urgence; **(moulding)** ~ dépouille
flash-back *n* arc en retour; ~ **voltage** tension inverse de pointe d'ionisation
flash button bouton à impulsion calibrée; ~ **call** conversation éclair; ~ **current** courant de court-circuit
flasher unit clignoteur
flashing *n* coups de bouton; rappel sur supervision; ~ *adj* clignotant; ~ **button** bouton de rappel; ~ **lamp** feu clignotant; ~ **signal** signal de rappel sur supervision; ~ **speed** clignotement; ~ **warning signals** signalisation hachée
flashover *n* contournement; étincelle; ~ **characteristic** (discharge) caractéristique de décharge; ~ **voltage** tension disruptive; tension d'arc
flash-point *n* point éclair
flash strip nettoyage rapide; ~ **test** essai d'isolement; rigidité diélectrique; tension de tenue
flask *n* ballon
flat *n* (of nut) pan; méplat; ~ **against** plaqué; ~ **bar** fer plat
flat-bed *adj* à plat; ~ **press** presse à platine; ~ **transmitter** émetteur à plat
flat cable câble plat; câble méplat; ~ **characteristic** caractéristique uniforme; ~ **coil** galette; ~ **cord** cordon plat; ~ **fee** taxation forfaitaire
flat-head screw vis à tête fraisée (F/90°)
flat loss affaiblissement uniforme
flatness *n* planéité
flat (unweighted) noise bruit non pondéré; ~ **open-ended spanner** clé plate à fourche
flat-pack *n* microboîtier plat; boîtier plat (à sorties unilatérales)
flat pliers pince plate; ~ **random noise** bruit blanc; ~ **rate** tarif forfaitaire
flat-rate charge metering taxation indépendante de la durée; ~ **charging** taxation fixe; taxation forfaitaire; ~ **metering** taxe fixe; ~ **service** service à tarif fixe; service à tarif forfaitaire
flat-top aerial antenne en nappe
flat tuning accord approximatif
flaw *n* vice; anomalie; défaut
F-layer couche F
fleeting *adj* fugitif; passager; transitoire
flex *n* conducteur souple; guirlande
flexibility *n* souplesse; ~ **point** miniréseau de connexion; répartiteur
flexible *adj* souple; sélectif; déformable; ~ **lead** conducteur souple; ~ **linear array** réseau linéaire flexible; ~ **tariff** tarif vert; ~ **washer** rondelle Onduflex [A.C.]; ~ **waveguide** guide d'ondes souple

flex(ible) wire câble souple
flexiblility *n* souplesse d'emploi
flexidisk *n* disque souple
flexi-time horaires variables
flexure test essai de flexion
flicker *v* scintiller; s'allumer à cadence; ~ *n* scintillement; papillotement; distorsion; ~ **effect** bruit de scintillation; effet de scintillation
flicker-free sans scintillement
flicker noise bruit de scintillation; bruit BF (basse fréquence)
flight deck poste de pilotage; ~ **information region (FIR)** champ d'information de vol
flimsy *adj* (print) pelure
flip *n* (of switch or core) basculement; ~ **card** carte filigrane
flip-chip *n* micropavé; circuit planaire; puce à protubérance
flip-flop *n* alternance; bascule; circuit bistable; ~ **module** élément bistable
flippy *n* disque souple; disquette; minidisque
float *v* (of channel) banaliser; ~ *n* conversion entier flottant; battement; ~ **factor** adresse primitive
floating *adj* flottant; mobile; ~ **accumulator** batterie tampon; ~ **address** adresse relative; adresse symbolique; adresse flottante; ~ **battery** batterie en tampon; batterie équilibrée; batterie flottante; ~ **break** coupure flottante; ~ **charge** charge d'entretien; charge en tampon; ~ **connector** connecteur d'usure; ~ **head** tête flottante; ~ **lead** fil en l'air
floating-point arithmetic arithmétique en virgule flottante; ~ **compare** comparaison à zéro; ~ **function** fonction flottante; ~ **radix** base de la caractéristique; ~ **representation** représentation en virgule flottante
floating potential potentiel flottant
floor chase chemin de câbles (CdC); caniveau; ~ **layout** plan d'aménagement; ~ **loading** charge au plancher/au sol; ~ **pattern** type piano; ~ **slab layout** calepinage; ~ **space** (usage/requirements) encombrement
floor-to-beam height hauteur sous poutre
floppy disk disque souple; disquette; minidisque; ~ **disk drive unit** lecteur enregistreur de disque souple; ~ **disk file** fichier consigné sur disquette; ~ **disk write-protect switch** commutateur de protection (du contenu du disque)
flow *v* écouler
flowchart organigramme; plan de calcul; diagramme; diagramme de déroulement; ordinogramme; schéma
flow control régulation des flux d'informa-

tion; ~ **control function (FCF)** contrôle de transmission du flux; ~ **diagram** ordinogramme; plan de calcul
flow-line *n* renvoi (d'organigramme); chaîne de production; ligne de liaison; flèche
flow meter débitmètre totalisateur
flow-meter switch contact débitmètre
flow-process diagram organigramme d'analyse
flow rate débit; ~ **soldering** soudure à la vague
FLS (s. free-line signal)
fluctuation *n* écart; battement; ballottement; variation (brusque); ~ **noise** effet de grenaille; effet de grêle
fluidizing bath bain fluidisé
fluid logic fluidique
fluorescent lamp lampe par fluorescence
fluorinated ethylene polypropylene (FEP) copolymère d'éthylène tetrafluoroéthylène (ETFE); téfzel
flush *v* purger; ~ **conductor** conducteur ras
flush-mounted *adj* encastré; affleurant; plaqué
flush-mounting *n* placage
fluted *adj* cannelé
flutter *n* pleurage; battement; scintillation; scintillement
flux, (solder) ~ décapant; ~ **chimney** buse de flux; ~ **gate** entrefer; ~ **residue** résidus de flux
fly *n* marche rapide
flyback *n* horloge retour (HR); retour du spot; ~ (of CRT spot) retour du faisceau; ~ **generator** doubleur de tension pour impulsion de retour; ~ **pulse** impulsion de retour de ligne; ~ **time** temps de retour image; ~ **voltage** surtension de retour
flying (of magnetic drum head) mobile; ~ **connector** prise mobile
flying-head read lecture rapide
flying lead fil en l'air; ~ **spot scanning** analyse à spot lumineux
fly-leaf *n* page de garde
fly mode lecture rapide; ~ **press** balancier; ~ **printer** imprimante à la volée
flywheel *n* volant; ~ **synchronization circuit** circuit à effet de volant
FM (s. frequency modulation)
foam fluxer fluxeur à mousse; ~ **pad** tapis mousse
FOB (s. free on board)
focal axis axe focal
focal-fed aerial antenne illuminée du foyer; antenne à alimentation focale
focal point foyer
focussing *n* focalisation; concentration; mise au point (MAP); ~ **coil** bobine de focalisation; bobine de concentration;

~ **electrode** électrode de focalisation; électrode de concentration; ~ **field** champ focalisateur; ~ **magnet** aimant de concentration; ~ **pot** potentiomètre de concentration
foil *n* armature (d'un condensateur); ~ (for use in cables) clinquant; ~ **capacitor** condensateur à armatures
foil-clad laminate support stratifié plaqué cuivre
fold-back *n* repliage; ~ **control** commande à repliage; ~ **current** courant de rabattement; courant de repliage; courant de retour; image de courant; intensité de rabattement; courant de maintien; ~ **distortion** distorsion de rebroussement
folded checksum clé de contrôle; ~ **configuration** configuration repliée; ~ **dipole** antenne trombone; doublet replié; dipôle replié; ~ **matrix** matrice repliée; ~ **network** réseau replié; ~ **time-division switching network** réseau de connexion temporel replié
fold mark hirondelle
fold-over *n* repliage; ~ (of TV) déchirure; ~ **distortion** pliage (du spectre de fréquences)
folio *n* planche
follower *n* gâchette; suiveur
follow-me call forwarding renvoi d'abonné; renvoi temporaire (commandé); ~ **facility** renvoi temporaire poste à poste; service du transfert automatique
follow-on code code retour; ~ **current** courant de suite
follow-up file fichier de suivi; fichier d'attente
font *n* police; répertoire de caractère; jeu
foolproof inviolable
foot *n* patte
footer bas de page
foothold *n* ouverture
footnote *n* note (de bas de page)
footprint *n* couverture
FOR (s. free on rail)
forbidden band bande interdite
forbidden-combination check contrôle d'existence
forbidden-pulse combination contrôle d'existence
force *n* puissance; énergie; pouvoir; force
forced *adj* forcé; prématuré
forced-air (cooling) à air brassé
forced call-forwarding renvoi d'appel forcé; ~ **clear-back** libération arrière forcée; ~ **draught** ventilation forcée
forced-draught cooling refroidi à air brassé
forced electric drainage drainage forcé; soutirage électrique; ~ **oscillation** oscilla-

F

tion forcée; ~ **page number** numéro de page forcé; ~ **release** libération forcée; ~ **snake column** colonne serpentine forcée

force-fit *adj* insertion sans soudure (ISS); ~ **contact** contact à insertion forcée (CIF); ~ **pin** broche à insertion sans soudure

force-free oscillation oscillation libre

forceps *n* pince

force tester dynamomètre

forcing a new page forçage d'une nouvelle page

forecast *v* prévoir

forecasting *n* étude prévisionnelle

foreground *n* avant-plan; ~ *adj* prioritaire; de premier plan

foregrounding *n* traitement prioritaire

foreground processing traitement d'avant-plan; ~ **program** programme d'avant-plan; programme prioritaire

foreign *adj* extérieur; hors circonscription; ~ (body) étranger; ~ **earnings** rentrées en devises; ~ **exchange line** ligne vers un central public autre que le central de rattachement; ~ **trade** commerce extérieur

foreman *n* agent de maîtrise; contremaître

foreman/superintendent of public works maître d'ouvrage

forensic *adj* analytique

forerunner *n* précurseur; avant-coureur

for example par exemple (p.ex.); ~ **further action** pour suite à donner; ~ **future expansion/development** réservé (à l'extension); ~ **future use** utilisation éventuelle; ~ **guidance** à titre indicatif; ~ **information** à titre d'information; à titre indicatif

fork *n* bifurcation; chape; dérivation; point de branchement

forked-arm limit switch contact à lyre

forked multiplex telegraph télégraphie multiplex en circuit de branchement; ~ **working** communication bifurquée

fork-lift truck chariot élévateur à fourche(tte)s (CEF); ~ **truck driver** cariste

form *n* imprimé; ~ (of document) corps

formality *n* (red tape) démarche administrative

formal logic calcul formel; ~ **parameter** paramètre classique

format *v* mettre en forme; composer; ~ *n* forme; aménagement; cliché; décomposition; découpage; disposition; format; gabarit; gamme; présentation; ~ (page) grille de saisie

format(ting) *n* mise en page

format catalogue catalogues des formats; ~ **effector** caractère de mise en page; ~ **line** réglette (rg.); ~ **tape** bande pilote

formatter *n* commande de mise en page;

formateur; ~ (S-P/P-S) convertisseur

formatting *n* mise en forme

formed plate plaque Planté

form ejection éjection du papier

former *n* support; ~ (of coil) carcasse

form factor facteur de forme; ~ **feed (FF)** feuillet; alimentation en papier; ~ **feedout** éjection du papier; ~ **flash** écriture éclair

forming *n* façonnement; ~ **peg** pointe à câbler

form length longueur de feuille; ~ **overlay** écriture éclair; ~ **set** liasse

forms generator générateur de grille; ~ **handling** introduction de document; ~ **overlay** gestion des fonds de page; ~ **processing** traitement de fiches; ~ **stacker** plateau récepteur papier

form stop arrêt de papier; ~ **transfer state** état transfert de grille

formula *n* formule; expression arithmétique

fortuitous *adj* accidentel; ~ **distortion** distorsion accidentelle; distorsion de ligne; distorsion fortuite; distorsion irrégulière

forward *v* acheminer; aiguiller; livrer; orienter; renvoyer; ~ *adj* direct; ascendant; aval (en); croissant

forward(-acting) bias tension directe

forward-acting code code détecteur d'erreurs vers l'avant; code correcteur d'erreurs (Hamming); code autocorrecteur

forward and backward fully-compelled signalling signalisation asservie par l'avant et par l'arrière

forward/backward (end) côté demandé/demandeur

forward bias polarisation directe

forward-biased *adj* passant; conducteur

forward-biasing *n* conduction; ~ **pulse** (cycle) alternance de conduction

forward blocking state état bloqué direct; ~ **channel** voie d'aller; voie normale; voie primaire; ~ **conductance** conductance directe; ~ **continuous (direct) voltage** tension directe (continue); ~ **control** commande aval (commutateur temporel); ~ **crosstalk** télédiaphonie; ~ **current** courant direct; ~ **direction** sens en avant; ~ **echo** écho avant; ~ **end** demandé (DE) (aval)

forward(-end) calling party demandeur en demandé

forward end-of-selection signal signal de fin de numérotation; ~ **error-detecting code** code détecteur d'erreurs vers l'avant; ~ **exchange** central aval; ~ **gate continuous (direct) voltage** tension directe (continue) de gâchette; ~ **gate-source (DC) voltage** tension directe (continue) grille-source; ~ **hold** maintien par l'avant

forwarding *n* acheminement; aiguillage; réexpédition; ~ *adj* émetteur; ~ **agent** transitaire; ~ **by re-routing** traitement du renvoi par réacheminement; ~ **centre** (telegraphy) centre émetteur; ~ **office** bureau émetteur; ~ **with transit** traitement du renvoi par transit

forward-looking radar radar dirigé en avant

forward path voie aller; ~ **planning** étude prévisionnelle; ~ **radiation** rayonnement en avant

forward-recall signal signal de rappel vers l'avant

forward recovery time temps de recouvrement direct; ~ **scatter** diffusion avant; ~ **selection** sélection vers l'aval; sélection en avant; ~ **sequence number** numéro de séquence vers l'avant; ~ **signalling** signalisation vers l'avant; ~ **signal wire (M = 'mouth')** fil TRON (transmission); ~ **sort** tri ascendant; ~ **transfer** passage en supervision; intervention; avance; ~ **transfer facility** facilité d'intervention

forward-transfer signal signal d'intervention d'une opératrice (côté demandé); signal de cadran

forward voltage tension directe; seuil de conduction; ~ **wave** onde directe; ~ **winding** enroulement supérieur (en demi-alternance)

foster *v* faciliter; favoriser; plaider en faveur (de); promouvoir

foundation *n* scellement

four-bit byte groupe de quatre bits (= tétrade); quartet

four-coil relay relais quadruple

four-condition quadrivalent

four-course radio beacon radiophare d'alignement quadrantal

four-digit multiplexed display bloc afficheur de quatre chiffres

four-frequency dialling sélection à quatre fréquences; ~ **diplex telegraphy** télégraphie diplex à quatre fréquences

Fourier transform transformée de Fourier

four-layer diode diode à quatre couches

four-party line ligne collective pour quatre connexions

four-phase mesh connection couplage en carré

four-pin socket mâchoire quadruple

four-pole equivalent network circuit équivalent

four-port duplexer duplexeur à quatre accès

four-quadrant quatre quadrants

four-terminal circuit circuit équivalent; quadripôle; ~ **network/resistor** tétrapôle; ~ **resistor measurement system** méthode quatre points; ~ **transmitter** filtre quadruplex de sélection

four-way *adj* à quatre voies

four-wire *adj* à quatre fils; ~ **chain** chaîne à quatre fils; ~ **channel** circuit à quatre fils; ~ **circuit** circuit à quatre fils; circuit bifilaire double; ~ **cluster network** câblage sub-local A (CSL-A); ~ **repeater** répéteur pour circuit à quatre fils; ~ **switching point** point de commutation à quatre fils; ~ **termination** terminaison à quatre fils; branchement à quatre fils; ~ **term set** termineur à quatre fils; ~ **trunk circuit** circuit interurbain à quatre fils

FOW (s. free on wharf)

fps (s. frames per second)

fractional HP motor moteur fractionnaire; ~ **part** (of logarithm) mantisse

fraction sign barre

fragile part pièce cassante

fragmentation *n* éclatement

frame *v* calibrer; ~ *n* bâti (mécanique); baie; cadre; catène; châssis; colonne; couple; créneau; délimitation; flasque; image; masse; monture; page; portique; rangée; support; trame; vue

frame (sync) **pulse** top d'image; **(facsimile)** ~ circuit encadreur; **command** ~ fenêtre de commande; ~ **aerial** antenne à cadre; ~ **alignment** alignement de trame; synchronisation de trame; ~ **alignment** (multiplex synchronization) verrouillage de trame; ~ **alignment pattern** schéma de verrouillage; ~ **alignment recovery time** temps de reprise de verrouillage de trame; ~ **alignment signal** signal de verrouillage de trame; ~ **alignment time slot** intervalle de temps de verrouillage de trame; ~ **alignment word (FAW)** mot de verrouillage de trame; ~ **bit insertion** insertion de bit de verrouillage de trame; ~ **blank** fenêtre

frame-by-frame au niveau de la trame

frame-check sequence (FCS) séquence de contrôle de trame

frame counter compteur de trames; ~ **definition flag** drapeau de structure de trame; ~ **earth** masse mécanique; masse armoire; masse du bâti; masse métallique (Mm); ~ **frequency** fréquence de trame; fréquence d'image; ~ **generator** générateur de mot de verrouillage de trame; ~ **ground** zéro analogique; ~ **loss** perte de trame; ~ **memory** mémoire de trame

frame-mounting socket/receptacle embase (connecteur fixe)

frame number numéro de trame; ~ **slip** glissement (défilement) vertical de l'image

frames per second (fps) taux de répétition de trames (Hz)

frame start début du bloc; ~ **store** mémoire de trame; ~ **structure** configuration de la

trame; ~ **synchronizing bit** bit de synchronisation de trame; ~ **sync word** motif
framework *n* ossature; bâti mécanique; corps;
entourage
framing *n* encadrement; organisation en
trame; ~ **bit** bit de verrouillage de trame;
~ **code** code de verrouillage de trame;
~ **data** données de verrouillage de trame;
~ **error** erreur de cadrage; ~ **generator**
(television) générateur de balayage vertical;
~ **pattern** configuration de verrouillage de
trame; schéma de verrouillage; ~ **pulse**
impulsion de verrouillage de trame; top
trame; ~ **signal** signal de cadrage;
~ **structure** configuration de la trame
franchised distributor distributeur agréé
franchisee *n* licencié
frangible *adj* cassant
freak *n* fantaisie; ~ *adj* anormal; discret;
erroné
free *v* libérer; débloquer; désinhiber; desserrer; ~ *adj* libre; disponible; indépendant;
mobile
free-access floor faux plancher
free-acting *adj* autonome
free-air *adj* atmosphérique; en ambiance
free/busy condition engagement
free call appel non taxé; ~ **channel** voie
disponible; voie libre; ~ **charge** charge
superficielle; ~ **condition** disponibilité;
état libre
free-condition circuit circuit libre
free-cutting steel acier de décolletage
freedom of action autonomie
free electricity électricité libre; ~ **electron**
électron de conduction; électron libre;
~ **fall** chute libre; ~ **field** champ infini
free-field air path champ acoustique libre;
~ **room** salle (anéchoïde) anéchoïque
free-format forme libre
freehand *adj* à main levée
free impedance impédance libre; ~ **line** ligne
dégagée; ligne libre
free-line signal (FLS) lampe d'inoccupation;
~ **signal indicator** lampe de disponibilité;
~ **signalling (FLS)** signalisation de ligne
libre
free link maille disponible; ~ **monoid** (math.)
monoïde libre; ~ **on board (FOB)** franc à
bord; ~ **on rail (FOR)** franco gare; ~ **on
wharf (FOW)** franco quai; ~ **originating
line** ligne sans comptage (LSC); ~ **oscillation** oscillation libre
free-phone *adj* appel libre; ~ **call** appel en
franchise; ~ **number** numéro vert; ~ **service** service vert (code 14 en France)
free-running *adj* astable; non asservi; auto-oscillateur; ~ **circuit** bascule astable; ~ **fre-**

quency fréquence libre; ~ **multivibrator**
multivibrateur astable (MA)
free sound field champ acoustique libre;
~ **space** place libre
free-space admittance admittance en espace
libre; ~ **aerial** antenne en espace libre;
~ **attentuation** affaiblissement en espace
libre; ~ **loss** affaiblissement en espace
libre; ~ **propagation** rayonnement direct
free-standing *adj* autonome; isolé; autoporteur; installé au sol
free subsriber abonné libre; ~ **terminating
line** ligne sans taxation (LST); ~ **trunk**
joncteur disponible; ~ **vector** vecteur
indépendant
free-wheel diode diode de roue libre
freeze *n* masquage; ~ **date** date de figeage;
~ **frame** arrêt sur image; ~ **function**
verrouillage
freeze-out fraction degré de saturation
freezing *n* blocage
freight charges coûts de transport
french curve (stencil) pistolet à dessin
frequency *n* fréquence; périodicité; cadence;
~ **allocation** attribution de fréquence;
~ **allotment** allotissement de fréquences;
~ **analysis** analyse harmonique; ~ **assignment** assignation de fréquence; ~ **band**
bande de fréquences; gamme de fréquences; ~ **band compression** compression
de la bande de fréquences; ~ **band limiting**
limitation de la bande de fréquences;
~ **changer** changeur de fréquence; convertisseur de fréquence; mélangeur; transcodeur
frequency-changer crystal cristal changeur de
fréquence
frequency-change signalling formation des
signaux par modulation de fréquence
frequency changing changement de fréquence;
~ **channel** canal de fréquences; ~ **characteristic** caractéristique amplitude-fréquence; ~ **characteristic within the pass-
band** (RF range) caractéristique puissance
de sortie/fréquence à accord fixe; ~ **check**
contrôle de fréquence; ~ **compensation**
compensation en fréquence; ~ **compression**
compression de fréquence; ~ **conversion**
changement de fréquence; conversion de
fréquence; ~ **converter** convertisseur de
fréquence; mutateur; transpositeur; ~ **converter tube** tube changeur de fréquence;
~ **counter** compteur de fréquences; fréquencemètre compteur; ~ **counter/timer**
intervallomètre; ~ **crosstalk** diaphonie par
la fréquence; ~ **departure** ($\delta f/f$) erreur
(relative) de fréquence
frequency-derived channel voie dérivée en

fréquence

frequency deviation écart de fréquence; déviation de fréquence; ~ **discrimination** sélection de fréquence; ~ **distortion** distorsion linéaire; distorsion du temps de transit de groupe; distorsion d'affaiblissement

frequency-division multiple access (FDMA) accès multiple par répartition en fréquence (AMRF); ~ **multiplex (FDM)** multiplex par partage des fréquences; ~ **multiplexing (FDM)** multiplexage par partage des fréquences (MPF); multiplexage par répartition en fréquence; multiplexage en fréquence; multiplexage analogique; ~ **multiplex transmission** transmission analogique; ~ **switching** commutation de longueur d'onde; commutation fréquentielle

frequency-domain adj fréquentiel; ~ **analysis** analyse dans le domaine fréquentiel

frequency doubler doubleur de fréquence; ~ **doubling** doublage de fréquence; ~ **drift** glissement de fréquence; dérive de fréquence; ~ **equalizer** correcteur de distorsion de phase

frequency-exchange signalling formation des signaux par mutation de fréquence

frequency excursion balayage de fréquence; ~ **factor** facteur de fréquence; ~ **falling** (of right-hand polarized radiation band) fréquence descendante; ~ **generator** générateur de fréquences; ~ **hopping** saut de fréquence; ~ **jump** saut de fréquence; ~ **locking** verrouillage de fréquence; ~ **meter** compteur de fréquences; fréquencemètre; ondemètre à cavité

frequency-modulated radar radiodétection à modulation de fréquence; ~ **sub-carrier** sous-porteuse modulée en fréquence

frequency modulation (FM) modulation de fréquence (MF); ~ **modulation telemetry** télémesure à modulation de fréquence; ~ **modulator** modulateur de fréquence; ~ **monitor** contrôleur de fréquence; ~ **multiplication** multiplication de fréquence; ~ **pulling figure** indice de glissement aval; ~ **range** gamme de fréquences; ~ **receiver** récepteur de fréquence (RF); ~ **relay** relais de fréquence; ~ **response** caractéristique de fréquence; caractéristique de gain (en fonction de la fréquence); réponse en fréquence; ~ **response distortion** distorsion de la réponse en fréquence; ~ **rising** (of left-hand polarized radiation band) fréquence montante; ~ **scintillation** scintillation de fréquence; ~ **selective attenuation** affaiblissement sélectif en fréquence; ~ **setting** calage de la fréquence

frequency-sharing n partage de fréquence

frequency shift décalage de fréquence; déplacement de fréquence; écart de fréquence; dérive de fréquence

frequency-shift keying (FSK) modulation par déplacement de fréquence (MDF); formation des signaux par déplacement de fréquence; manipulation par variation de fréquence

frequency slip glissement de fréquence; ~ **spectrum** spectre de fréquences; ~ **stability** stabilité de fréquence; constante de fréquence; ~ **standard** étalon de fréquence; ~ **swing** excursion de fréquence; déviation de fréquence; déviation de fréquence crête à crête; ~ **switch** bouton coup par coup; ~ **synthesizer** synthétiseur

frequency-time modulation modulation de fréquence en fonction du temps

frequency tolerance tolérance de fréquence; ~ **transformer** convertisseur de fréquence; ~ **translation** transposition de fréquence; ~ **translator** transpositeur de/en fréquence

Fresnel region région de Fresnel

friable adj pulvérulent

frictional machine générateur électrostatique; éliminateur

friction drive motor moto-réducteur; ~ **micrometer** palmer à friction; ~ **test** essai au frottement

fringe area champ d'interférence

FROM (s. fusible/fusable read-only memory)

'from' date date de mise en vigueur

from-to list liste de bornage; plan de câblage

front n côté recto; ~ (of PCB) côté éléments (côté composants); ~ adj avant (AV); **(wave-)**~ front; ~ **contact** contact de travail; ~ **cord** cordon d'appel

front-end adj frontal; d'arrivée; d'entrée; réseau; ~ **computer** ordinateur frontal; ~ **control** commande aval (commutateur temporel); ~ **controller** contrôleur frontal; automate; ~ **control logic** frontal d'échange et de commande; ~ **crash** panne frontal; ~ **processor (FEP)** calculateur réseau; processeur frontal; préprocesseur de signalisation; antéserveur

front-fed adj alimentation frontale

frontier charge taxe frontalière; ~ **relations** régime frontalière; ~ **traffic** relations frontalières; ~ **zone** zone frontalière

front panel face avant; bandeau avant; façade; face parlante; fronton; panneau avant; plastron; ~ **panel connector** connecteur en face avant; ~ **porch** palier avant

front-to-back ratio rapport des rayonnements avant et arrière

frosted adj (of lamp bulb) dépoli

frozen adj figé; bloqué

FRXD (s. fully automatic reperforator transmitter-distributor)
frying n bruit de microphone; friture
FSD (s. full-scale deflection)
FSK (s. frequency-shift keying)
fuel consumption meter débitmètre totalisateur
fulcrum n point d'appui; couteau (d'une balance)
full adder additionneur à trois entrées; ~ **(three-input) adder** additionneur complet; ~ **availability** accessibilité totale; accès parfait; ~ **availability group** groupe à accessibilité totale; ~ **carrier** porteuse complète
full-custom design conception ciselée
full cycle cycle complet
full-duplex adj bidirectionnel simultané; à duplex intégral; entièrement duplex; ~ **channel** voie à duplex intégral; ~ **circuit** circuit de fonctionnement en duplex; ~ **link** liaison duplex intégral; ~ **operation** fonctionnement en duplex total; système de téléphonie duplex
full earth terre franche; ~ **line** ligne pleine; ~ **load** en pleine charge; ~ **multiple** sectionnement général
full-satellite exchange central entièrement satellite
full-scale adj complet; ~ **deflection (FSD)** pleine échelle (PE); déviation maximale; déplacement maximum; ~ **production** fabrication en série; grande série
full-screen reveal apparition affichage écran complet
full stop point
full-wave adj biphase; à deux alternances; ~ **dipole** doublet (en) onde entière; ~ **rectifier** redresseur à deux alternances
fullword n mot entier
fully automatic reperforator transmitter-distributor (FRXD) retransmetteur à bande perforée (à lecture automatique totale)
fully-automatic working exploitation automatique intégrale
fully-dissociated signalling mode exploitation en mode complètement dissocié
fully-distributed core architecture éclatée
fully-enclosed container boîtier étanche
fully-equipped adj complet
fully-meshed (grid) **network** réseau maillé; ~ **interconnection** interconnexion totale
fully-provided trunk group faisceau totalement fourni; faisceau direct non débordant
fully-restricted extension poste contrôlé; poste privé
fully-steerable adj à débattement complet; ~ **aerial** antenne totalement orientable

fume absorber ventouse; ~ **cupboard** captation des vapeurs; ~ **extractor** extracteur de fumée
functional block bloc fonctionnel; ~ **entity** objet; ~ **test** essai de fonctionnement; ~ **unit** bloc fonctionnel
function card carte outil; ~ **code** code de fonction; code de service; ~ **generator** générateur de fonction(s); ~ **key** touche de contrôle; ~ **keypad** clavier de fonctions; ~ **relay** relais de fonction; ~ **selector** commutateur de fonction; ~ **table** table de correspondance; table de fonctions; matrice des phases; vérification de la fonction logique
functor n élément logique
fundamental component composante fondamentale; ~ **component distortion** dépendance de l'amplitude; ~ **crystal** cristal fondamental; ~ **frequency** fréquence fondamentale; fréquence nominale; ~ **harmonic** première harmonique; ~ **oscillation** oscillation fondamentale; ~ **thickness-shear mode** mode de vibration fondamental; ~ **wave** onde fondamentale; onde dominante; onde directe
funding n subvention
fungicidal varnish vernis antifongique
furnace n étuve
furrow n gorge
further elaboration (of data) ajustement
fuse n fusible (fus.); amorce; coupe-circuit; spire; ~ **board** tableau à fusibles; ~ **box** coffret à fusibles; ~ **cap** embout de fusible
fuse-carrier n porte-fusible (PF); porte-cartouche (PC); socle de fusible
fuse clip douille de fusible; ~ **contact** douille de fusible; ~ **cut-out** disjoncteur à fusible
fused breaker coupe-circuit à fusible
fuse disconnector fusible sectionneur
fused silica silice fondue
fuse-holder n porte-fusible (PF)
fuse intact fusible bon; ~ **isolator** fusible sectionneur; ~ **link** élément fusible; ~ **panel** panneau de fusibles
fuse-panel intermediate cover cache intermédiaire PF
fuse plug bouchon fusible; ~ **rating** calibre de fusible; ~ **system** fusiblage; protection
fusible/fusable read-only memory (FROM) mémoire morte à fusible
fusing n refusion étain-plomb; surfusion; ~ **factor** courbe de fusion; ~ **heater** lampe chauffante
future expansion aménagements futurs
future-proof adj évolutif

G

G (s. gate)
GaAs (s. gallium arsenide)
gabled distribution répartition en cloche
gadget *n* dispositif
gaff *n* ergot
gain (constant/coefficient) coefficient d'amplification; ~ **and phase match** phase et gain appariés
gain-bandwidth product produit gain bande réelle; produit amplification/largeur de bande
gain compensation rattrapage de gain; ~ **control** dispositif de réglage de l'amplification
gain-control potentiometer potentiomètre de réglage du gain
gain-frequency characteristic caractéristique gain-fréquence
gain function fonction de gain (d'une antenne); ~ **loss** perte d'amplification; ~ **margin** marge de gain
gain-measuring set kerdomètre
gain per stage gain d'étage; ~ **ratio** gain en module; ~ **time control** régulateur de sensibilité temporisé; ~ **tracking** gain en fonction du niveau d'entrée; distorsion en niveau
gallium arsenide (GaAs) arséniure de gallium (AsGa)
galvanic protection protection galvanique
galvanized *adj* zingué
galvanomagnetic effect effet galvanomagnétique; effet Hall
galvanometer *n* galvanomètre; boussole
gamma ray rayon gamma
ganged *adj* jumelé; accouplé; à couplage mécanique; multiple; ~ **capacitor** condensateur à blocs combinés; ~ **circuit** circuit à commande unique; ~ **contacts** contacts jumelés; ~ **potentiometer** potentiomètre multitour; ~ **switch** commutateur jumelé
gang-punch *n* perfo.(-ratrice) reproductrice
gangway *n* passerelle
gantry *n* portique
gap *n* espace; créneau; écartement; entrefer; fourchette; intervalle; isolement; lacune; pas; passage; trou; espace libre; ~ **character** chiffre de service; ~ **clearance** butée de descente; ~ **coding** codage par découpage; ~ **digit** chiffre de service; caractère de remplissage; ~ **filler** émetteur d'appoint;

~ **gauge** calibre-mâchoires; outil de montage; ~ **leakage** dispersion interstitielle; ~ **load** charge d'espace
gapped crystal cristal à intervalles entre électrodes
gap scatter éclatement à l'entrefer; éclatement d'un intervalle
GAR (s. guided aircraft rocket)
garbage *n* données invalides; information parasite; ~ **collection** nettoyage
garbage-in/garbage-out (GIGO) rebut à l'entrée et à la sortie
garble *v* altérer
garbled *adj* incohérent; incomplet; mutilé; erroné; ~ **signal detection** détection de signaux incohérents; ~ **telephony** téléphonie à inversion de fréquence
garbling *n* altération; déformation; incohérence; mutilation; perturbation
gas amplification factor facteur d'amplification de gaz; ~ **arrester** parafoudre à gaz
gas-discharge lamp lampe à décharge au gaz; ~ **relay** soupape ionique
gas-filled cable câble sous pression; ~ **rectifier** soupape ionique; ~ **switch** commutateur à gaz; ~ **valve** tube à gaz
gas focussing concentration par gaz
gasket *n* garniture; segment; joint torique
gasoline *n* essence
gas seal herméticité; ~ **taper** filetage gaz; pas du gaz (conique)
gas-tight *adj* hermétique
gas welding soudage à la flamme; soudure à l'autogène
gate *v* (onto read bus) aiguiller (sur le bus de lecture); ~ *n* porte; bascule; butée; cadre; cadre pivotant; châssis pivotant; circuit à déclenchement périodique; créneau; fenêtre; gâchette; grille; opérateur logique; portillon; sortie; ~ (of thyristor) ouverture; ~ **(circuit)** circuit de porte; ~ **(symbol)** carré (symbole: #); ~ **(G)** entrée de transfert; **RF** ~ vanne HF (hyperfréquence); ~ **angle** (of thyristor) angle d'ouverture; ~ **array** réseau prédiffusé; ~ **button** touche dièse; chiffre dièse; ~ **circuit** portillon; ~ **continuous (direct) forward current** courant direct (continu) de gâchette
gate-controlled rise time temps de croissance

commandée par la gâchette; ~ **turn-on time**
temps d'amorçage commandée par la
gâchette

gate (DC) current courant (continu) de grille

gated *adj* aiguillé; ~ (of register) chargé;
~ **multivibrator** bascule monostable

gate-drain (DC) voltage tension (continue)
grille-drain

gate key touche dièse; chiffre dièse; ~ **leakage current** courant de fuite de grille;
~ **non-trigger continuous (direct) voltage**
tension (continue) de non amorçage par la
gâchette

gate-source capacitance (in the equivalent
circuit) capacité grille-source; ~ **capacitance, drain-source short-circuited to AC**
capacité d'entrée, sortie en court-circuit, en
source commune; ~ **conductance** conductance grille-source; ~ **cut-off voltage**
tension grille-source de blocage; ~ **threshold voltage** tension de seuil grille-source;
~ **(DC) voltage** tension (continue) grille-
source

gate symbol dièse

gate-trigger continuous (direct) current courant (continu) de gâchette d'amorçage;
~ **continuous (direct) voltage** tension
(continue) d'amorçage par la gâchette

gate trigger diode diode de déclenchement;
~ **turn-off thyristor** thyristor-interrupteur;
~ **valve** boisseau; ~ **voltage** tension de
gâchette; tension de grille

gateway *n* porte d'accès; accès; passerelle;
pôle; ouverture; ~ **exchange** centre tête de
ligne; centre de départ et d'arrivée; centre
de transit international

gate width temps de portillonnage

gathering *adj* croissant

gather-write *v* écriture avec rassemblement;
écriture avec regroupement

gating *n* basculement; aiguillage; attaque
d'un récepteur; blocage; déclenchement;
déclenchement de la temporisation; déclenchement périodique; portillonnage; synchronisation; **(output)** ~ conditionnement
(de sortie); ~ **pulse** impulsion de porte;
créneau; signal de basculement; ~ **signal**
forme d'onde; ~ **time** temps de basculement; temps de portillonnage; ~ **voltage**
tension de basculement

gauge *n* calibre; cadran; cale (d'épaisseur);
capteur; comparateur; étalon; jauge; jaugeur; vérificateur; ~ (of wire) diaphragme;
~ **block** cale de contrôle

Gaussian noise bruit de Gauss; bruit gaussien;
bruit blanc; bruit d'agitation thermique;
bruit de grenaille; bruit erratique; ~ **wave**
onde gaussienne

gaz à pétrole liquifié GPL (gaz à pétrole
liquifié)

GC (s. group centre)

GCA (s. group centre area)

GCC (s. operator group common circuit)

GCE (s. ground communications equipment)

G-cramp *n* bride de serrage; bride à capote

GDE (s. group-delay equalizer)

GDF (s. group distribution frame)

gearbox *n* carter

geared motor moto-réducteur

gear-train (motor) moto-réducteur

gear wheel roue dentée

Geiger counter compteur Geiger-Müller

gelation *n* gélification

gel time temps de gélification

gender changer adaptateur mâle-femelle

general call appel en diffusion; ~ **comments**
généralités; ~ **currency symbol** signe
monétaire; ~ **hierarchy** hiérarchie générale; ~ **inspection procedure** gamme de
contrôle

generalized data management system traitement d'informations généralisées

general-purpose *adj* universel; à applications
multiples; banal; polyvalent; ~ **computer**
ordinateur universel; ~ **exchange** autocommutateur universel

general register registre banalisé; ~ **release**
relâchement général; ~ **reset** remise à zéro
générale (RZG); ~ **test** (cycle) passage
grossier; ~ **view** vue d'ensemble

generate a current donner naissance à un
courant

generated address adresse synthétique;
adresse calculée; ~ **error** erreur d'arrondi

generating line génératrice; ~ **plant** central
électrique; ~ **program** générateur; ~ **routine** configurateur; ~ **station** centrale

generation data group famille d'ensemble de
données; ~ **of clock signals** élaboration des
créneaux d'horloge; ~ **rate** vitesse de
formation d'une paire

generator *n* centrale; générateur; oscillateur;
sémateur (bivalent); ~ **box** boîtier d'inducteur; ~ **busbar** barre génératrice; ~ **ringing**
appel magnétique; ~ **set** groupe électrogène (GE)

generic posting autopostage générique; indexation générique; ~ **specifications** cahier
de charges (CdC); spécification générale

Geneva drive entraînement croix de Malte

gentex *n* (automatic international telegram
exchange system) gentex

geometrical distortion distorsion géométrique

geometrically-aligned régulier

geometric control commande géométrique;
~ **primitive** primitive géométrique

geometry (of PCB) encombrement
geo-stationary satellite satellite géostationnaire; satellite géosynchrone; satellite synchrone
germanium rectifier redresseur à germanium
German silver maillechort
get *v* acquérir; extraire; lire; récuperer
GET *v* (op code) accéder (à); **get** (put-aside) **vocabulary/glossary** rappel d'une phrase
GET function lecture; renvoi; reprise; acquisition
GETI (s. get index)
get index (GETI) lecture par rang; ~ **key** lecture par clé
getter *n* dégazeur; réducteur
gettering *n* dégazage; durcissement
ghost *n* écho parasite; fantôme; caractère parasite
ghosting *n* échos parasites
gibberish *m* transmodulation; ~ **total** total mêlé; somme de contrôle; total de vérification
GIGO (s. garbage-in/garbage-out)
gimbal angle angle de pivotement; ~ **axis** axe articulé par cardan
gimmick *n* astuce
girdle *n* ceinture; tasseau
gland *n* passage de câble
glare *n* double prise; croisement
glare-free antireflet; anti-éblouissant
glass cladding verre de gaine; ~ **cloth** tissu de verre; ~ **core** verre de cœur
glass-encapsulated (of thermistor) isolé
glass-reinforced plastic (GRP) fibre de verre
glass-transition temperature température de transition vitreuse
glass valve tube électronique en verre; ~ **wool** laine de verre
glaze *n* vitre
glazed wire fil émaillé
glazing *n* vitre
glide-path beacon émetteur du trajet d'atterrissage
gliding track glissière
glitch *n* parasite(s); bruit; pointe de commutation; rafale
global beam transponder répéteur faisceau global
globule *n* goutelette
gloss *n* brillance
glossy *adj* brillant
glow current courant d'effluve; ~ **discharge** effluve; décharge luminescente; effluvage; ~ **discharge tube** tube à décharge luminescente; ~ **lamp** lampe à effluve
glue *n* colle
glycerol-phthalic anhydride résine glycérophtalique

glyptal resin coat peinture glycérophtalique
GME (s. group modulating equipment)
GO (key) (carriage return function) EXEC
go-and-return circuit boucle; ~ **line** ligne de va et vient; ~ **measurement** mesure en boucle; ~ **path** chaîne émission-réception; ~ **repeater** répéteur à deux voies
go band bande aller; ~ **high** (of signal) monter; ~ **high/(low)** passer à l'état 1/o
gold contact edge connector fichier or; ~ **flashing** or flash
gold-plating production line chaîne de dorure
golfball printer imprimante à boule
gong *n* timbre
GO/NO-GO gauge calibre entre/n'entre pas; ~ **test** test oui-non; essai par tout ou rien; tri
goodness *n* (of valve) pente
goods inward réception
goods-inward inspection contrôle entrée; recette; ~ **inspection requirements** conditions de réception; ~ **inspection voucher** avis de réception (AR); ~ **quality control** contrôle de qualité à la réception; ~ **testing** essai de réception; essai de recette
goodwill *n* valeur ajoutée; survaleur
go off-hook décrocher; ~ **on-hook** raccrocher; ~ **path** voie aller; canal aller; chemin émission; départ; sens aller; support émission
GOS (s. grade of service)
GO side amont (en -)
GOS indicator indice de recette
GO TO (address) reprise; saut
GOTO function branchement inconditionnel
go to home position renvoi début; ~ **to next** forcer (à)
go-to-return crosstalk paradiaphonie; diaphonie entre les deux sens de transmission
governing body conseil de direction; ~ **factor(s)** régime; ~ **parameter** grandeur d'influence
government telegram télégramme d'état
governor *n* régulateur
graceful degradation blocage doux; mise hors service douce
grade *n* niveau; échelon; classe
graded *adj* échelonné
graded-base transistor transistor à champ interne
graded filter filtre échelonné; ~ **index fibre** fibre à gradient d'indice; ~ **network** hiérarchie; ~ **rack** baie à multiplage partiel
grade of entitlement niveau d'habilitation; ~ **of service (GOS)** qualité d'écoulement du trafic; taux d'encombrement; probabilité de perte; classe de trafic
grade-of-service index indice de qualité de

réception (IQR); indice de recette
grade of traffic qualité d'écoulement du trafic
gradient *n* pente; gradient; côte; ~ **error** dérive de pente
grading *n* multiplage partiel; brassage; classement; étalonnement; ~ **diagram** schéma de multiplage partiel; ~ **facilities** possibilités de discrimination; ~ **group** groupe de lignes (dans un multiplage partiel); ~ **network** réseau de brassage
gradual *adj* progressif
graduated scale réglette (rg.)
grain-oriented silicon iron fer silicium orienté
gram-atom *n* atome-gramme
gramophone *n* électrophone
grandfather tape bande première génération
granny knot nœud double
grant *v* affecter; ~ *n* subvention
granule *n* grenaille; ~ (smallest logical unit of storage) granule
graph *n* courbe; graphe; graphique; calibre
graphic character caractère graphique; caractère imprimable; ~ **display** écran graphique; ~ **display panel** panneau d'affichage graphique; ~ **image** figurine; ~ **instrument** enregistreur (enr.)
graphics *n pl* graphique; graphisme; images; ~ **attribute** rendu visuel; ~ **element** tracé graphique; ~ **primitive** primitive graphique; ~ **symbol** tracé graphique; ~ **tablet** tablette graphique
graphic symbol(s) graphisme
graphite-metal brush (phosphor bronze) balai métallographique
graph paper papier diagramme
grate *n* grille
graticule *n* réticule; graticule; trame
grating converter transformateur guide (d'ondes)
gravity-feed chute libre
gravity switch crochet commutateur; support commutateur
Gray code code binaire réfléchi; code cyclique
grazing angle angle rasant
GRDD (s. digital ground)
grease-proof paper papier sulfurisé
grey iron fonte mécanique; ~ **scale** niveaux de gris; échelle des teintes
grey-scale compression compression des nuances
grid *n* grille; échiquier; implantation; maille; matrice; quadrillage; réseau; ~ **battery** batterie de grille; ~ **bias** tension de polarisation de grille; polarisation de coupure; ~ **cap** connexion de grille; ~ **characteristic** caractéristique de grille; ~ **clip** connexion de grille; ~ **configuration** maillage; ~ **control** commande par la

grille; ~ **current** courant de grille; ~ **cut-off voltage** tension de blocage
grid-driving power puissance d'attaque de grille; puissance d'entrée; puissance d'excitation de grille
grid east graticule Est; ~ **keying** manipulation dans la grille; ~ **leak** fuite de grille; drain
grid-leak resistor résistance de grille
grid pitch pas de grille
grid-plate (grid-anode) **characteristic** caractéristique grille-plaque
grid stopper impédance d'étouffement de grille; ~ **terminal** connexion de grille; ~ **voltage** tension de grille
grip *n* ancrage; pince; poignée; préhension
gripper *n* pince de préhension
grip wire fil de tirage
grit *n* grain
grommet *n* passe-fil(s); guide-fils; passage de fil
groove *n* rainure; sillon; dégagement de fraise; encoche; gorge; dégagement d'angle; ~ **angle** angle d'ouverture d'un sillon
grooved *adj* cannelé
gross *adj* global; total; brut; hors taxe (HT); hors tout; ~ **height** hauteur hors tout; ~ **income** chiffre d'affaire; ~ **information content** contenu total en information; ~ **leak** fuite franche; ~ **power budget** (in dB) bilan typique
ground *n* masse électrique; ~ **(system)** terre; ~ **absorption** absorption par le sol
ground-air communications communication sol-air; ~ **guided missile** engin téléguidé sol-air; ~ **voice channel** canal vocal sol-air
ground backscatter rétrodiffusion par la terre
ground-based duct conduit de surface; ~ **jammer** brouilleur terrestre
ground bus barre zéro (0B); ~ **button** bouton de terre; ~ **clutter** écho de sol; fouillis du sol; ~ **communications equipment** (GCE) équipement de télécommunication; ~ **conductor** fil de masse; ~ **current** courant de masse; ~ **distance** distance terrestre
grounded *adj* mis à la terre
grounded-anode amplifier amplificateur à anode à la masse
grounded-cathode amplifier amplificateur avec cathode à la masse
grounded emitter émetteur commun
grounded-grid amplifier amplificateur à grille à la masse
ground effect effet de sol; ~ **elevation angle** angle de site au sol; ~ **equipment** équipement au sol; ~ **fault** défaut à la terre
grounding brush brosse de masse; ~ **circuit** circuit de mise à la terre; ~ **lug** languette de masse

ground leak perte à la terre; ~ **leakage** court-circuit à la masse; ~ **mapping** cartographie du territoire survolé; ~ **plane** plan de sol; liaison équipotentielle
ground-plane aerial antenne à polarisation horizontale; antenne à plan de sol; antenne orientée vers la terre
ground radar radar terrestre
ground-reflected wave onde réfléchie par le sol
ground return écho de sol; ~ **start** déclenchement par prise de terre; prise par mise d'une terre sur un fil; ~ **station** station terrestre; ~ **supply** (alternator) alternateur de parc; ~ **switch** interrupteur de mise à la terre; ~ **testing** test par la terre; ~ **wave** onde de sol; onde de surface; onde directe
ground-wave suppression suppression de l'onde directe
group aerial nappe de dipôles verticaux; ~ **alarm** alarme de groupe; ~ **allocation** répartition des groupes primaires; ~ **amplifier** amplificateur de groupe; ~ **backward busying** blocage en arrière d'un groupe; ~ **carrier** porteuse de groupe; ~ **centre (GC)** centre à autonomie d'acheminement (CAA); ~ **centre area (GCA)** zone à autonomie d'acheminement (ZAA); ~ **control** blocage en arrière d'un groupe; ~ **control station** station directrice de groupe; ~ **delay** temps de propagation de groupe
group-delay characteristic caractéristique de temps de transit de groupe; ~ **distortion** distorsion de temps de propagation de groupe; ~ **equalization** égalisation du temps de transit de groupe; ~ **equalizer (GDE)** égaliseur de retardation de groupe; correcteur de temps de propagation de groupe (CTPG)
group distortion distorsion du temps de transit de groupe; ~ **distribution frame (GDF)** répartiteur de groupes primaires (RGP); ~ **exchange** centre à autonomie d'acheminement (CAA); centre de groupement; ~ **filter** filtre de groupe; ~ **frequency** fréquence de groupe primaire; fréquence de train d'ondes
grouping key clé de liaison
group link liaison en groupe primaire; ~ **master extension** tête de liste; ~ **master line** tête de groupement; ~ **modems** modems sur groupe primaire; ~ **modulating equipment (GME)** convertisseur de groupes; équipement de modulation de groupe primaire (EMG); équipement de transfert de groupe primaire; équipement de transposition du groupe primaire; ~ **modulator** convertisseur de groupes

group-occupancy meter compteur de temps d'occupation de groupe
group of tie-lines faisceau de lignes spécialisées; ~ **pick-up** interception d'appel; ~ **pilot** onde pilote de groupe; ~ **polling** interrogation de groupe; ~ **reference pilot** onde pilote de groupe primaire; ~ **retardation** réduction de la vitesse de groupe; ~ **section** section de groupe primaire; ~ **selection unit (GSU)** élément de sélection de groupe (ESG); ~ **selector** sélecteur de groupe; ~ **selector switch** commutateur de sélection de groupe; ~ **separator** séparateur de groupe; ~ **switching centre** centre de groupement; ~ **translating equipment** convertisseur de groupes; équipement de transposition du groupe primaire; ~ **velocity** vitesse de groupe
growing n (semiconductor) croissance
growth factor coefficient de foisonnement; facteur d'accroissement
GRP (s. glass-reinforced plastic)
grub screw vis sans fin; vis sans tête
GSU (s. group selection unit)
guarantee n cautionnement
guard n garde; capot; cache; ~ **band** bande de garde; zone réservée à la fréquence de détresse; ~ **circuit** circuit de garde; ~ **copy** recopie d'écran; ~ **delay** délai de garde; temporisation de garde
guarded area zone gardée
guard frequency fréquence de garde; ~ **iron** fer de garde; ~ **ring** anneau de garde; ~ **signal** signal de garde; ~ **time** temps mort; ~ **time-out** temporisation de garde; ~ **wire** fil de maintien
guide n repère; témoin; ~ **beam** faisceau de guidage
guided (of missile) téléguidé; ~ **aircraft rocket (GAR)** fusée d'avion téléguidée; ~ **propagation** propagation guidée; ~ **ray** rayon entrant; ~ **wave** onde guidée
guided-wave transmission transmission guidée
guide edge bord de référence; ~ **head** grain; ~ **pin** pion de centrage; centreur; ~ **pulley** poulie folle
guider n orienteur
guide tube (of MIG welder) tube de contact; ~ **wavelength** longueur d'onde dans le guide
gulp n groupe d'octets
gum n résine
gun metal bronze
gusting rafales
gutter n marge; gouttière
guy n drisse
guyed lattice tower pylône en treillis haubanné**

G

guying haubanage (haubannage); ~ **system** nappe de haubannage

gyrator *n* gyrateur

gyro compass centrale de cap; ~ **frequency** gyrofréquence (dans l'ionosphère)

G

H

hacksaw *n* scie à métaux
H-aerial antenne en H
haft *n* poignée
HAL (s. hard-array logic)
half-adder *n* demi-additionneur; additionneur élémentaire à deux entrées; additionneur sans retenue
half-adjust *v* arrondir
half-amplitude *n* mi-hauteur; ~ duration durée à mi-amplitude; durée à mi-hauteur
half a unit time interval demi-intervalle de temps
half-bore *n* (of fibre-optic cable) demi-coquille
half-byte (4 bits: = nibble) quartet; demi-octet; secteur
half-call (incomplete address digits) demi-appel
half-cheese aerial antenne à demi-cornet
half-cycle *n* demi-alternance; demi-période
half-duplex *adj* à l'alternat; bidirectionnel non simultané; semi-duplex; ~ channel voie semi-duplex; ~ operation communication en semi-duplex; fonctionnement en semi-duplex; ~ working service semi-duplex; exploitation à l'alternat
half-echo suppressor demi-suppresseur d'écho
half-frame *n* demi-trame
half-line feed interligne moyen; ~ frequency fréquence de demi-ligne; ~ pulse impulsions de demi-ligne
half-power beam width largeur de puissance moyenne; ~ firing angle angle total d'ouverture à mi-intensité
half round-nose pliers pince à becs demi-ronds
half-shell (of connector) demi-capot
half-shift register bascule; bascule bistable; multivibrateur bistable
half-system *n* demi-système
half-tone *n* demi-teinte; fond sous-brillant; intensité réduite; semi-brillance; ~ *adj* tramé; ~ distortion distorsion de demi-teinte; ~ facsimile télécopie nuancée; ~ grid/pattern mire de demi-teinte; ~ positive transparency typon; ~ system système demiteinte
half-transponder demi-répéteur
half-wave *n* alternance; demi-alternance; mono-alternance; ~ aerial antenne demi-onde; ~ dipole doublet (en) demi-onde;

dipôle demi-onde; ~ rectifier redresseur mono-alternance; redresseur à une alternance; redresseur à simple alternance
half-word *n* demi-mot; ~ address adresse secteur
Hall constant constante de Hall; ~ effect effet galvanomagnétique; effet Hall; ~ mobility mobilité du porteur
halt *n* arrêt; interruption; blocage; ~ adress adresse blocage; ~ condition état d'arrêt; ~ instruction instruction d'arrêt; ~ logic logique d'arrêt; ~ on address arrêt sur adresse; halte à l'adresse; ~ on error arrêt sur faute; ~ on instruction blocage sur phase
halving *n* dédoublement
halyard *n* drisse
Hamiltonian path chemin hamiltonien
hammer (lightly) tapoter; ~ drill perceuse tamponette percussion; ~ finish martelé; ~ intensity force de frappe
Hamming error-correcting code code autocorrecteur; code de Hamming
handbook *n* notice
hand-cranked ringer (ringing machine) magnéto
hand drill chignole (à main)
handing-in time heure de dépôt
handing-over office centre d'échange
handle *n* manche; manette; poignée; nom; ~ (= callsign) indicatif (IF); identificateur
handler *n* programme de gestion; gestionnaire; automate; chargeur; constructeur; contrôleur; gérant; opérateur de commande; programme de traitement; répartiteur; unité de gestion
handling *n* gestion; acheminement; exploitation; manipulation; manutention; prise en charge; prise en compte; traitement; ~ basket panier de manutention; ~ frame cadre de manutention; ~ of calls écoulement de trafic; ~ trolley chariot de manutention
hand-over *v* présenter; ~ *n* mise à disposition (MAD); mise en disponibilité; remise (au client)
hand radar radar portatif
hand-ringing set poste téléphonique à appel magnétique
handset *n* combiné; récepteur; ~ cord cordon

de combiné

hands-free *adj* à mains libres; autonome; automatique; ~ **set** poste mains libres

handshake *n* colloque (de reconnaissance); validation d'un transfert; adresser (s'); ~ (signal) signal de salutation

handshaking *n* mise en présence (MP); mise en relation (avec); adressage; échange sur liaison; présentation; prise de contact; ~ (bus-access) **signals** signaux de gestion; ~ **protocol** procédure d'appel-réponse; procédure d'échange; protocole de mise en présence; protocole de présentation

hands-off working exploitation à porte fermée

hand soldering soudage au fer

hands-on experience connaissance pratique; aptitude; ~ **training** formation sur le tas; formation directe (sur l'équipement)

hand-tighten *v* visser légèrement; visser sans serrer

handwheel *n* volant; manche

hanging-up *n* raccrochage

hangover time temps de maintien; période d'atténuation d'écho; ~ **time of a relay type echo suppressor** temps de maintien d'un suppresseur d'écho à action discontinue

hang-up *n* arrêt sur boucle; blocage; arrêt de rebouclage; arrêt involontaire; immobilisation; arrêt imprévu

haphazard *adj* aléatoire; anarchique; fortuite

hard-array logic (HAL) réseau logique préprogrammé

hardboard *n* panneau Isorel [A.C.]

hard copy copie d'écran; copie en clair; copie (sur) papier; document en clair; édition sur imprimante; fac-sim; impression en transparence d'écran; tirage

hard-copy enlargement copie diazoïque

hard disk disque rigide; disque dur; ~ **error** erreur câblée; erreur machine; erreur non récupérable; erreur physique; faute câblée

hard-facing (of metals) rechargement

hard-grade (of plastics) dur

hard hyphen tiret inséparable; tiret insécable

hardness test essai de dureté; ~ **tester** duromètre

hard-of-hearing malentendant

hard over (hard left/hard right) en butée (à gauche/à droite)

hard-soldered joint brasure; brasage

hard space espace insécable; ~ **standing** aire plane

hardware *n* matériel; équipement périphérique; ~ **address** adresse fonctionnelle (AF); adresse-machine; ~ **check** contrôle câblé; ~ **configuration** programmation technique; ~ **design** conception technique; ~ **error** erreur physique

hardware-generated fault message message de faute câblée

hardware interrupt interruption physique; ~ **release code** indice de version; ~ **reset** (function) suicide; ~ **subsystem** unité fonctionnnelle; ~ **unit** unité fonctionnelle

hard-wired *adj* câblé; métallique; ~ **logic** logique câblée; ~ **programming** *n* logiciel câblé

harmonic analyser analyseur d'harmoniques; ~ **analysis** analyse harmonique; ~ **component** composante harmonique; ~ **content** taux d'harmoniques; pourcentage de distorsion; ~ **content reduction** réduction du pourcentage de distorsion; ~ **discrimination** suppression d'harmoniques; ~ **distortion** taux de distorsion harmonique; distorsion non linéaire; ~ **distortion factor** coefficient de distorsion harmonique; ~ **filter** suppresseur d'harmoniques; ~ **frequency** fréquence harmonique; ~ **generator** générateur d'harmoniques; producteur d'harmoniques; ~ **mean** moyenne mobile; ~ **mobility** mouvance harmonique; ~ **multiple telegraph** appareil télégraphique multiple à courants alternatifs accordés; ~ **number** numéro ordinal d'une harmonique; ~ **suppressor** filtre suppresseur d'harmoniques; ~ **telephone ringer** sonnerie accordée; ~ **unmodulated output power** puissance de sortie harmonique non modulée

harmony *n* synergie

harness *n* assemblage (de câbles); peigne; toron; harnais; câble nappé

harnessed in cable form câblé en peigne

Hartley oscillator oscillateur de Hartley

hash addressing algorithme de conversion; ~ **code** code hâché; ~ **coding** codage aléatoire; transformation aléatoire

hashing *n* algorithme de conversion; ~ **alarm** alarme visuelle

hash key touche dièse; ~ **sign** carré (symbole: #); ~ **symbol** dièse; ~ **total** total mêlé; somme de contrôle; clé de contrôle; pseudo-total; total de vérification

hatch *n* trappe; lumière; porte

haul *n* portée

hauling cable câble tracteur

HDB3 (s. third-order high-density bipolar coding)

HDB3-binary code conversion transformation HDB3 binaire

HDF (s. horizontal distribution frame)

HDLC (s. high-level data link control procedure)

head amplifier préamplificateur; ~ **cord** cordon de casque téléphonique; ~ **crash**

accrochage de la tête; ~ **end** (of CTV network) tête de réseau

header *n* en-tête; haut de page; intitulé; titre; ~ (of connector) reprise connecteur; ~ **card** carte en-tête; ~ **code** code d'en-tête; ~ **record** enregistrement d'entête; ~ **word** mot d'en-tête

head gap entrefer

heading *n* mot d'en-tête; rubrique; ~ **code** code d'en-tête

headline *n* mots en vedette

head of queue tête de file

head-on collision collision frontale

headphones *n* casque téléphonique; casque radio; récepteur serre-tête

head retaining pawl cliquet de retenue (pour) tête

headset *n* casque; écouteur

head torque wrench clé pour couple de tête

head-to-tail configuration montés en tête-bêche

head-up display affichage superposé; planche de bord

headword mot vedette

hearing *n* audition

hearing-loss plot audiogramme

heat-carrying agent agent refroidissant

heat coil bobine thermique; ~ **dissipation system** évacuation des calories; ~ **duct** caloduc

heated enclosure étuve

heater (of a valve) *n* filament; ~ banc de mise en chauffe; résistance chauffante; ~ **battery** batterie de chauffage; batterie de filament; ~ **current** courant de chauffage; ~ **element** résistance électrique; cartouche chauffante; chaufferette (chauffrette); corps de chauffe; élément chauffant; résistance de chauffe; ~ **voltage** tension de chauffage

heat exchanger échangeur de chaleur; échangeur de refroidissement; serpentin; ~ **gun** buse chauffante; chaufferette (chauffrette)

heating element résistance chauffante; élément de chauffage; ~ **plate** plaque de chauffe

heat loss dissipation de chaleur; perte thermique

heatproof *adj* calorifuge

heat-protective visor visière anti-chaleur

heat sensor vigitherme; ~ **shield** bouclier thermique; écran thermique

heat-shrinkable thermo-rétrécissant; ~ **PTFE sheath** gaine en téflon rétractable; ~ **sleeve** cordon de frettage; ~ **tube/sheath(ing)** gaine thermorétractable

heat-shrinking frettage

heat sink radiateur de chaleur; refroidisseur; ailette de refroidissement; collecteur de dissipation; dissipateur (thermique); drain thermique; puits de chaleur; source froide

heat-transfer agent agent réfrigérant; ~ **link** frein thermique

heavily-doped buried layer couche enterrée fortement dopée

Heaviside layer couche E

heavy current courant fort

heavy-duty *adj* service continu; fort calibre; fort régime grande puissance; renforcé; série lourde; service sévère; ~ **fuse (high rating)** fusible de fort calibre; fusible classe gI; ~ **machine** machine grosses consommatrices; ~ **motor** moteur à service intensif; ~ **relay** relais à fort pouvoir de coupure; contacteur

heavy-gauge *adj* de grande section; ~ **sheet steel** tôle forte

heavy loading pupinisation lourde; ~ **telephone traffic** trafic intense de téléphonie; ~ **traffic** fort trafic

hectometric wave onde hectométrique

heel *n* (of angle iron) carre

height change-over switch commutateur d'altitude

heightened contrast contraste accentué

height finder radar mesureur d'altitude

height-finding radar radar d'altimétrie

height-position indicator (HPI) indicateur de hauteur et de distance

heiligtag effect erreur de trajets multiples

helical groove rainure hélicoïdale; ~ **groove cable** câble à jonc rainuré; ~ **resonator** cavité hélicoïdale; ~ **waveguide** guide d'ondes hélicoïdal

heliotropic solar generator générateur solaire héliotrope

helipot *n* potentiomètre hélicoïdal

helix *n* hélice d'inscription

Hell (mosaic telegraphy) **printer system** système Hell; ~ **receiver** (mosaic telegraphy) récepteur de Hell

Hellschreiber system système Hell

Helmholtz' theorem théorème de Thévenin

HELP (key) AIDE

help command commande aide; ~ **file** fichier guide (opérateur)

HELP function aide à l'opérateur; guide opérateur

hertz (Hz) (= cycles/second: c.p.s.) Hz (Hertz) (~)

heterochronous *adj* hétérochrone

heterodyne (beat-frequency) **oscillator (BFO)** oscillateur hétérodyne; ~ **frequency** fréquence hétérodyne; ~ **interference** interférence hétérodyne; ~ **receiver** récepteur hétérodyne; ~ **signal generator** hétérodyne; ~ **wavemeter** ondemètre hétérodyne;

~ **whistles** sifflement hétérodyne

heterodyning n hétérodynation

heterogeneous multiplex multiplex hétérogène

hetero-junction transistor transistor à couches d'arrêt

heteropolar alternator alternateur hétéropolaire

heuristic adj heuristique; provisoire

hexadecimal notation numération hexadécimale

hexagon key clé mâle (six pans)

hexagon-recess pan head screw vis à tête cylindrique bombée large à six lobes internes (CBLX); vis à six pans creux (SPC = vis CHc)

hexagon voltage tension en triangle

hex code code 16; ~ **inverter** inverseur sextuple; ~ **socket wrench** clé mâle (six pans)

HF (s. high frequency); ~ **carrier** (current) **telegraphy** télégraphie par courants porteurs; ~ **carrier current telephone channel** voie de communication par porteuse de haute fréquence; ~ **coaxial cable** câblage coaxial HF; ~ **equalization** compensation des hautes fréquences; ~ **feeder** câble haute fréquence; ~ **repeater distribution frame** répartiteur à haute fréquence

hidden flange charnière montée en feuillure; ~ **loss** affaiblissement secret

hierarchical (mutually-synchronized) **network** réseau hiérarchisé; ~ **set of processing routines** ensemble hiérarchisé de programmes de traitement

hi-fi telephone téléphone haute fidélité

high-altitude satellite circuit circuit par satellite à haute altitude

high-carbon steel acier dur

high channel separation faible diaphonie entre amplis

high-definition display écran haute résolution

high-density adj compact; de faible encombrement; ~ **assembly** compactage

high-directional aerial antenne projecteur

high-efficiency Cassegrain aerial antenne Cassegrain à haut rendement

high electron-velocity camera tube tube analyseur à électrons rapides

higher-ranking adj supérieur

high fibre-packing density grande densité de fibres

high-fidelity system chaîne haute fidélité

high-field emission arc arc à effet de champ

high frequency (HF) haute fréquence

high-frequency absorption absorption des aigus; ~ **alternator** alternateur à haute fréquence; ~ **carrier system** système à courants porteurs à haute fréquence;

~ **circuit** circuit à haute fréquence; ~ **compensation** compensation des hautes fréquences; ~ **current** courant haute fréquence; ~ **emphasis** accentuation des hautes fréquences

high frequency radio link liaison radioélectrique sur ondes décamétriques

high-frequency transformer transformateur haute fréquence

high-gain aerial antenne à gain élevé

high-impedance relay relais à haute impédance

high-input impedance amplifier amplificateur à haute impédance d'entrée

high inverse-voltage rectifier redresseur à crête de tension inverse

high-key trace image brillante

high-level active actif à l'état haut; ~ **data link control procedure (HDLC)** procédure de commande à haut niveau; procédure de commande de chaînon (de données); ~ **language** langage évolué

high-lighted area zone surbrillante

high-lighting n surbrillance; vidéo inversée

high/low bias test essai aux limites (E/L)

highly reliable ultra-fiable

high-order adj gauche; ~ **address** adresse gauche; ~ **bit** bit de poids fort; bit de gauche

high-pass filter filtre de haute déviation; filtre passe-haut

high-performance adj performant; puissant; ~ **asynchronous line controller** ligne asynchrone - haute performance (LAS.HP)

high-pitched adj aigu

high polarization discrimination aerial antenne à haute pureté de polarisation; ~ **power amplifier (HPA)** amplificateur de puissance

high-Q cell cellule émission-réception à bande étroite; ~ **coil** self à grande surtension

high-recombination rate contact contact à vitesse élevée de recombinaison

high-reliability electric lines lignes électriques à grande sécurité de service

high-resistance joint (HR) soudure à résistance élevée; ~ **loop** boucle forte

high-resolution TV (over 100 scanning lines/frame) télévision à haute définition

high-rupture capacity fuse (HRC) fusible à haut pouvoir de coupure (HPC)

high-speed addressing adressage rapide; ~ **backing store** mémoire de masse rapide; ~ **bus** bus rapide; registre mémoire; ~ **carry** report accéléré; accélération de la retenue; report simultané; retenue propagée; ~ **channel** canal rapide; ~ **format** forme interne; ~ **highway** voie rapide; ~ **logic gate** porte logique rapide; ~ **mem-**

ory mémoire à accès rapide; ~ **morse receiver/recorder** récepteur morse rapide; ~ **multiplex link** liaison multiplex à haute vitesse; ~ **printer** imprimante rapide (IR); ~ **relay** relais rapide; ~ **scanning aerial** antenne rotative de radar à grande vitesse; ~ **selector/switch** sélecteur rapide; ~ **switching diode** diode rapide; ~ **teleprinter** téléimprimeur rapide

high state état H

high-temperature aging vieillissement à la chaleur

high traffic capacity station grande station

high-usage circuit group faisceau débordant; faisceau de circuits à utilisation élevée; faisceau de premier choix; ~ **route** artère à fort trafic; faisceau à utilisation élevée; ~ **trunk** circuit à fort trafic; circuit à utilisation élevée; ~ **trunk group** faisceau transversal

high-voltage line ligne haute tension; ~ **supply** alimentation en haute tension; ~ **switch** interrupteur haute tension

highway n canal d'une voie; artère; bus; distributeur; liaison; ligne; trolley; voie; ~ **junction** étage T

hike n augmentation

hill-and-dale recording gravure en profondeur enregistrement vertical

hinge n charnière; ~ **bar** biellette

hinged adj pivotant; rabattable; ~ **stay** compas d'ouverture

hinge-pin axe d'articulation

hire n location

hiring n (of employees) embauche

hiss n bruit; souffle; bruit de grenaille; bruit de microphone; bruit erratique

histogram n histogramme

history file historique; fiche de suivi; fiche suiveuse; ~ **sheet** passé

hit n variation brusque; réponse pertinente

hitch n incident

hit-on-the-line perturbation

hit rate taux de rappel

hitting n (of key) appui

Hittorf dark space espace sombre cathodique

hiving off scission

H-network réseau en I

hobbyist n bricoleur

hog-horn n cornet parabolique

hoisting gear appareil de levage

hold v maintenir (se); mettre en garde; coller; ~ (in abeyance) retenir; ~ **a circuit** rester à l'appareil

hold-back current courant de rabattement; courant de maintien; courant de repliage

hold consulted party garde de rétro-appel; ~ **current** courant de non retombée

holder n support; douille

hold for enquiry double appel courtier (va-et-vient); ~ **in abeyance** mise en attente

hold-in contact contact d'auto-alimentation

holding beacon radiophare d'attente; ~ **beam** faisceau de régénération; ~ **circuit** circuit à maintien; bloqueur; ~ **(coil) circuit** circuit de collage

holding-code signal signe d'occupation

holding current courant de maintien; courant hypostatique; ~ **earth potential** terre de maintien; ~ **pulse** impulsion de garde; ~ **time** durée d'occupation; délai de maintien; durée de prise; temps d'occupation; ~ **voltage** tension de maintien

holding-wire current courant de mesure

hold-in range (of PLL) plage de maintien; zone d'enclenchement

hold-off n récurrence de balayage; ~ **voltage** tension maximale de blocage

hold-over n maintien; blocage de chaîne; ~ **key** clé d'arrêt

hold-the-line veuillez patienter; rester à l'appareil; ~ **message** message de patience

hold time-out pointe de temporisation de garde; ~ **tone** tonalité de garde

hold-up n blocage

hole n trou; ajour; alvéole; bouchet; lacune; lumière; zone morte; ~ **current** courant lacunaire

hole-electron pair paire électron-trou

hole layout (diagram) gabarit de perçage; plan de perçage; chemin de perçage

Hollerith code code Hollerith; code H

hollow conductor câble creux; ~ **shaft** arbre creux; ~ **square** carré vide

holographic storage mémoire holographique

holster n étui

home (position) n origine; position repos; début; début de page; début feuille; ~ adj direct; intérieur; local; national; ~ **address** adresse de base; adresse (de) début; adresse de rangement; adresse directe; adresse domiciliaire; ~ **amateur** amateur de radio; sans filiste; ~ **area** zone de rattachement; ~ **base station** relais nominal; ~ **distributed data processing** télétravail; ~ **indicator** indicateur du numéro demandé

homelanding n retour au repos

home-made système D (débrouillez-vous)

home market marché intérieur; ~ **office** centre de rattachement nominal; ~ **Office switch** interrupteur de mise à la terre; ~ **(position)** position initiale; adresse de début; repos; ~ **record** premier article de chaîne; ~ **telephone** téléphone domestique

homing n autoguidage; radioralliement; approche d'un radiophare; retour au repos;

route d'approche; ~ **aerial** antenne de radio-guidage; antenne autoguidage; ~ **aid** dispositif auxiliaire de radioralliement; ~ **band** fuseau de radioguidage; ~ **beacon** radiophare d'approche; ~ **range** fuseau de radioguidage; ~ **receiver** récepteur d'approche; ~ **target finding** direction d'un projectile radioguidé sur le but

homochronous *adj* homochrone

homodyne reception réception homodyne; réception synchrone

homogeneous *adj* cohérent; ~ **multiplex** multiplex homogène; ~ **section** section homogène

homopolar alternator alternateur homopolaire; ~ **relay** relais homopolaire

hone *v* rôder

honeycomb *adj* cellulaire; ~ **coil** bobine en nid d'abeille

honeycomb winding enroulement en nid d'abeille

hood *n* calotte; capot; capuchon; hotte

hooded lens cabochon

hook *n* crochet; berceau; collerette; ~ **spanner** clé à ergot

hook-switch crochet commutateur; pédale; ~ **flash** rappel d'enregistreur; ~ **mounting** support pédale

hook-up *n* interconnexion; établissement d'une communication; raccordement (racct.)

hoot stop avertisseur sonore; alarme sonore; boucle d'alarme; signal sonore

hop *n* bond; saut; trajet; écart; réflexion; section

hopper *n* trémie; magasin; case; casier; chargeur; bac

horizon elevation angle angle de site de l'horizon

horizontal and vertical absolute position (HVP) positionnement absolu du curseur; ~ **and vertical blanking** effacement ligne et trame; ~ **busbar** barre d'alimentation horizontale; ~ **channel** canal; ~ **distribution frame (HDF)** répartiteur à sorties horizontales; ~ **hold** (control) commande horizontale de synchronisation

horizontally-polarized aerial antenne à polarisation horizontale; ~ **wave** onde à polarisation horizontale

horizontal oscillator relaxateur horizontal; ~ **parity** parité longitudinale; ~ **tabulation (HT)** tabulation horizontale; tabulation avant; ~ **tabulation set (HTS)** pose de tabulation

horizontal-wire aerial antenne en fil horizontal

horn *n* pavillon acoustique; ~ **aerial** antenne en cornet; antenne en pyramide renversée

horn-break switch interrupteur à cornes

horn-gap switch interrupteur à cornes

horn-reflector aerial antenne à réflecteur en cornet

horn speaker chambre de compression

host *n* support; centralisateur; ~ **computer** ordinateur principal; ordinateur central; ordinateur hôte; structure d'accueil; ~ **computer centre** serveur

hostile circuit circuit perturbé; ~ **environment** milieu agressif

host node nœud principal; ~ **processor** ordinateur principal; ~ **terminal** console d'accueil

hot-air blower buse chauffante; chaufferette (chaufrette); générateur air chaud

hot-carrier diode diode Schottky de puissance

hot cathode cathode à chauffage direct; cathode à chauffage ionique; cathode chaude; cathode incandescente

hot-cathode gas-filled triode thyratron; ~ **stepping tube** trochotron; ~ **tube** tube à cathode chaude

hot-dipped *adj* galvanisé

Hoth noise bruit à spectre de Hoth

hot line appel au décrocher/décroché; ligne à accès direct; acheminement immédiat; ligne directe; ligne sans numérotation; ~ **line** (USA-USSR) téléphone rouge; ~ **line** (France-USSR) téléphone vert

hot-line call appel sans numérotation; appel enregistré; ~ **connection** connexion directe; ~ **station** poste à correspondant unique (PCU); ~ **subscriber** (extension) correspondant préenregistré; ~ **telephone** poste à sélection directe

hot load (of satellite) charge chaude

hot-plate *n* banc de mise en chauffe; réchaud électrique

hot-potato network réseau à commutation par paquets (RCP)

hot slide-in insertion en activité; ~ **spot** point d'alarme; ~ **standby** attente active; secours automatique; ~ **tinning** étamage à chaud; ~ **well** source chaude; milieu chaud

hot-wire ammeter ampèremètre thermique

hot-wire anemometer anémomètre à fil chaud

hot-wire voltmeter voltmètre thermique

hot working formage à chaud

hour-glass effect effet de sablier

hourly percentage paid time rendement horaire

house cable câble d'immeuble

housekeeping *n* opération de servitude; opération annexe; gestion; aménagement; ~ *adj* de service; ~ **bit** bit de service; élément numérique de service; ~ **information** information d'aménagement; ~ **instruction** instruction de service

housekeeping/overhead operation opération de service; opération d'aménagement

housekeeping routine tâche de gestion; ~ **stuffing bit** élément numérique de service de justification; ~ **task** phase systématique; ~ **word** mot de service

housing *n* logement; abri; boîtier; caisse; caisson; carter; coffret; corps; couvercle; cuvette; meuble; montage; ~ (for PCBs, disks and PSU) servante

howl *n* microphonicité

howler *n* hurleur; tonalité cadencée; tonalité de faux appel

howling *n* bruit de cornemuse

h.p. (horsepower) ch (cheval-vapeur = CV)

HPA (s. high power amplifier)

HPI (s. height-position indicator)

H-plane lens lentille à lames parallèles dans le plan H; ~ **sectoral horn** cornet sectoriel H

HR (s. high-resistance joint)

HRC (s. high-rupture capacity fuse)

HT (s. horizontal tabulation)

HTS (s. horizontal tabulation set)

HT supply alimentation en haute tension

hub cross-connect unit multiplexeur-aiguilleur de transit; ~ **polling** sollicitation des entrées en progression binaire

hum *n* ronflement; bourdonnement; bruit d'alimentation; bruit de fond; ~ **balancer** égalisateur de ronflement; ~ **displacement** décalage du ronflement; ~ **voltage** tension de ronflement

hundred O/G lines centaine de directions

hundreds-group centaine

hundredth of an hour (0.6 sec) centième d'heure (ch)

hunt *n* recherche

hunter *n* chercheur

hunt group groupement de lignes

hunting *n* recherche d'une ligne (libre); sélection automatique; ~ (of control system) pompage; oscillation pendulaire; ~ **selector** commutateur auxiliaire d'abonné; ~ **switch** commutateur auxiliaire d'abonné

hunt method loi de recherche

husband *v* économiser

HVP (s. horizontal and vertical absolute position)

H wave onde H

hybrid *n* passage deux fils-quatre fils; ~ (terminal) terminal à quatre fils; ~ *adj* mixte; différentiel; ~ (terminal) terminal de circuit à quatre fils; ~ **balance network** équilibrage des termineurs; ~ **card** (magnetic stripe with microprocessor) carte mixte; ~ **circuit** circuit hybride; ~ **coil** termineur équilibreur; transformateur différentiel; ~ **computer** calculateur hybride; ~ **coupler** coupleur différentiel; ~ **disconnection** effacement du termineur; ~ **integrated circuit** circuit semi-intégré; circuit intégré hybride; ~ **junction** jonction différentielle; ~ **microwave system** système microondes hybride; ~ **ring** anneau hybride; ~ **separation** annulation de la réflexion; ~ **set** équilibreur; termineur; ~ **termination** transformateur différentiel à équilibreur

hybrid-T junction té hybride; té magique; T hybride; T magique

hybrid transformer transformateur différentiel équilibré

hydraulic engineering hydraulique mécanique

hydrogen ion concentration (pH value) ions OH

hydrometeor fading affaiblissement dû aux hydrométéores

hydrometer *n* aréomètre; densimètre

hyperbolic continuous radar system système radar continu hyperbolique; ~ **navigation system** radionavigation hyperbolique; ~ **quantizing law** loi de quantification hyperbolique

hyphenation *n* coupure de mot

hypothetical exchange bureau téléphonique en projet; ~ **reference circuit** circuit fictif de référence; circuit hypothétique de référence; ~ **reference connection** communication fictive de référence; ~ **reference digital path** circuit numérique fictif de référence; conduit numérique de référence; ~ **(reference) point** point fictif

hypsogram *n* hypsogramme

hypsometer *n* hypsomètre; népermètre; décibelmètre; ~ **card** carte hypso

hysteresis *n* hystérésis (= hystérèse); ~ **comparator** comparateur à hystérésis; ~ **loop** boucle d'hystérésis; cycle d'hystérésis; ~ **loss** perte par hystérésis

I

IAM (s. initial address message)
IAR (s. instruction address register)
IBG (s. inter-block gap)
IC (s. integrated circuit)
I/C (s. incoming)
IC container (s. stick)
icing *n* givrage
ICM (s. inference crunching machine)
icon *n* icône
iconoscope *n* iconoscope
ICS (s. interphone control system)
I/C status bit état incident
IC stick (dispenser) réglette à profil U; distributeur de circuits intégrés
I/C terminal exchange translateur
IC tester maquette d'essais
ID (s. identification)
IDC (s. insulation displacement connection)
ideal *adj* nominal; optimal; parfait; théorique; ~ aerial antenne théorique; ~ articulation netteté idéale; articulation idéale; ~ crystal cristal idéal; ~ instants of a modulation (or of a restitution) instants idéals d'une modulation (ou d'une restitution); ~ receiver récepteur parfait; ~ transducer transducteur idéal; ~ transformer transformateur parfait
identification (ID) *n* reconnaissance; repérage; identité; dépistage; désignation; récupération; nom; ~ beacon radiophare d'identification; ~ circuit circuit d'identification; ~ code request demande d'indicatif; ~ group groupe d'identification; ~ mark repère; ~ of position indication de position par impulsion d'émetteur; ~ signal signal d'identification; ~ sleeve collier à plaquette; ~ thread filin de reconnaissance
identified as symptomatic (of fault condition) mise en accusation
identifier *n* identificateur; descripteur; identité; indication; nom symbolique; circuit d'identification; libellé
identifying pulse impulsion de discrimination
identify primary source of fault mettre en cause
identity *n* équivalence (logique)
ideogram *n* pictogramme
IDF (s. intermediate distribution frame)
IDH (s. input digital highway)

idle *adj* au repos; désarmé; déwatté; disponible; mort; tranquille; inactif; libre; ~ channel voie disponible
idle-channel noise bruit de la voie au repos; ~ weighted noise bruit pondéré d'une voie au repos
idle character caractère nul; caractère blanc; caractère non imprimable; ~ circuit circuit disponible; ~ condition état de repos; ~ current courant déwatté; ~ indicator lamp lampe de disponibilité; ~ jack jack libre; ~ junction ligne de jonction libre; ~ line ligne libre
idle-line indication signalisation de ligne libre
idle loop boucle inactive; ~ message message de repos; ~ period temps de repos; ~ position position de repos
idler *n* galet
idle ratio taux de silence
idler pulley poulie folle; ~ wheel galopin
idle state repos; ~ time temps d'entretien; temps mort; ~ trunk jonction disponible; ligne de jonction libre; ~ turn spire morte
idling *n* marche à vide; ~ cycle cycle blanc; ~ position point mort
IDN (s. integrated digital network)
IDT (s. isolated data transmitter)
I.E.C. mains plug embase mâle; ~ mains plug socket (s. straight cable socket)
ier multiplieur
IF (s. intermediate frequency)
IF-and-only-IF équivalence (logique)
IF circuit circuit moyenne fréquence; circuit MF
IFF (identification friend or foe) radar d'identification
IF rejection pénétration de la moyenne fréquence
if required s'il y a lieu
IF-THEN operation implication; inclusion
ignition *n* allumage; amorçage; démarrage; ~ coil bobine d'allumage; ~ lead câble d'allumage
ignitor *n* électrode pilote
ignitron rectifier redresseur ignitron
ignore character caractère d'effacement; caractère de rejet; caractère d'oblitération
ikon (of graphics) icône
IL (s. insert line)
I^2L (s. integrated injection logic)

illegal *adj* interdit; illégal; non utilisé; ~ **character** caractère interdit

illicit transmitter émetteur clandestin

illuminated indicator bank rampe lumineuse; ~ **pushbutton** bouton éclairé

illumination *n* éclairage; allumage; ~ (of a target) irradiation (d'un objet); illumination; ~ **angle** angle d'illumination

illustrate *v* montrer

illustration *n* représentation graphique; figurine; graphique; tableau

image analyser analyseur optique; ~ **attenuation constant** affaiblissement sur image; ~ **contrast** contraste d'image; ~ **converter** convertisseur d'images; tube transformateur d'image; ~ **digitizer** numériseur d'images; ~ **dissector** dissecteur d'image; ~ **file** fichier vidéo; ~ **frequency** fréquence image; fréquence conjuguée; ~ **frequency interference** perturbation par la fréquence image; ~ **frequency rejection** réjection de la fréquence image; élimination de la fréquence image; ~ **iconoscope** supericonoscope; ~ **impedance** impédance image; ~ **interpretation** évaluation de l'image radar; ~ **message** message vidéo; ~ **mode** mode image; ~ **phase(-change)** constant déphasage sur image(s); ~ **potential** tension d'image; ~ **processing** imagerie; traitement des images; ~ **processor** serveur d'images; ~ **reject filter** filtre image; filtre BLU (de réjection image)

imagery (remote terrain sensing) imagerie; prise de vue

image sensor dispositif à couplage de charges (DCC)

imaginary *adj* fictif; faux

imbalance *n* déséquilibre; dissymétrie; asymétrie; désaccord; balourd

immaterial *adj* sans signification

immediate access accès direct; accès instantané; ~ **action alarm** alarme intervention immédiate; ~ **address** adresse immédiate; adresse directe; adresse virtuelle; ~ **addressing** adressage direct; ~ **appreciation percentage** taux de compréhension immédiate; ~ **hot-line station** correspondant unique immédiat (PCUI); ~ **operand** opérande immédiat; ~ **response** action instantanée; ~ **ring-back tone** retour d'appel immédiat; ~ **ringing** appel immédiat

immersion *n* trempe; ~ **heater** chauffe-eau; ~ **heater** (portable) thermoplongeur

immobilization *n* indesserrabilité

immune *adj* insensible; ~ (to) non influencé par

immunity to conducted interference susceptibi-

lité en conduction; ~ **to interference** insensibilité aux brouillages

impact *n* choc; ~ **avalanche transit device** élément semiconducteur Impatt; ~ **drill** perceuse tamponette percussion; ~ **test** essai de résilience; essai de percussion

impair *v* altérer; dégrader; mettre en cause; nuire; perturber

impairment *n* dégradation; gêne; réduction de qualité; incohérence

IMPATT diode (impact ionization avalanche transit time) diode Impatt; élément semiconducteur Impatt

impedance *n* impédance; résistance apparente; composante Z; ~ **bridge** pont d'impédance; ~ **drop** perte en charge; ~ **loss** perte en charge; ~ **matching** adaptation d'impédance; équilibrage d'impédance

impedance-matching transformer adaptateur d'impédance

impedance mismatch déséquilibrage des impédances; ~ **relay** relais d'impédance; ~ **transformation characteristic** caractéristique de transformation de l'impédance; ~ **unbalance** déséquilibrage des impédances; dissymétrie; ~ **unbalance measuring set** équilibromètre; ~ **unbalance to earth** déséquilibre d'impédance par rapport à la terre

impeller *n* roue à ailettes; turbine; rotor

impenetrability *n* hermétisme

imperative qualité absolue

impermeability *n* hermétisme

impermeable *adj* étanche

impervious *adj* insensible; étanche

implement *v* réaliser; matérialiser; assurer; effectuer

implementation *n* mise en œuvre; réalisation

implicate *v* mettre en faute

implicit address adresse implicite

implied addressing adressage implicite

import (of files) archivage

impregnated *adj* humecté; ~ **fibre-glass** verre époxy (époxyde)

imprint *n* empreinte; filigrane; impression en creux; repère

impromptu spontanément

improper instruction contrôle d'existence

improvement factor coefficient d'amélioration

impulse *n* impulsion; ~ (noise) **generator** générateur de bruits impulsifs; ~ (flashover) **voltage** tension fugitive (d'impulsion); ~ **current peak value** valeur de crête de choc du courant; ~ **excitation** excitation par choc; excitation par impulsion; ~ **generator** générateur d'impulsions; générateur de chocs; ~ **machine** impulsographe;

~ **noise** bruit impulsif; ~ **ratio** rapport d'impulsion; ~ **sender** émetteur d'impulsions; ~ **sparkover voltage** courbe de tension d'amorçage au choc en fonction du temps d'un parafoudre; ~ **suppressor** suppresseur d'impulsions

impure adj non vierge

impurity activation energy énergie d'activation des impuretés

in. (s. inch)

IN (s. interconnecting network)

inaccessible indisponible; interdit

inactivity ratio taux de silence

inadvertent adj prématuré; intempestif; à tort

in-band attenuation affaiblissement dans la bande; ~ **signalling** signalisation dans la bande

in batch mode dans un contexte de traitement par lots; en environnement batch

inbound adj arrivée; ~ **lead** fil RON (réception)

in-building adj d'immeuble

in byte mode octet par octet

in-call facility code suffixe

incandescent lamp lampe à incandescence

in cascade en série

inch v progresser (faire -); ~ **(in.)** n pouce (po.)

inching n avance pas à pas; progression; réglage fin; à coup (accoup); ~ **control system** commande de coup par coup

incident angle angle d'attaque; angle d'incidence; ~ **beam** faisceau incident; ~ **current** courant initial; ~ **energy** (of UV lamp, in mW/cm2) puissance délivrée; intensité; rayonnement; ~ **optical power** puissance optique incidente; ~ **(transmitted) power** puissance directe; ~ **ray** rayon direct; rayon incident; ~ **signal** signal utile; ~ **wave** onde incidente

incipient adj amorce de; début de; infantile; ~ **defect** défaut de jeunesse; déchet infantile

in-circuit adj connecté; présent

incised marking gravure en creux

inclement adj adverse

inclination n orientation

incline n pente

inclined V-aerial antenne en V incliné

including (Y out of X) dont (X dont Y)

inclusion n (logic function) implication

inclusive OR opération OU; base de numération 2

inclusive-OR circuit circuit à anticoïncidence; mélangeur OU; réunion (circuit-)

income bénéfices

incoming (I/C) entrant; d'arrivée; incident; ~ **call** appel entrant; appel extérieur; communication d'entrée; ~ **circuit** circuit d'arrivée; circuit d'entrée; ~ **connection** connexion d'arrivée; ~ **end** extrémité d'arrivée; amont; ~ **goods** réception; ~ **goods inspection** contrôle d'entrée; recette; ~ **goods inspection requirements** conditions de réception; ~ **goods quality inspection** contrôle de qualité à la réception; ~ **hypsometer** hypsomètre arrivée; ~ **international exchange** centre international d'arrivée; ~ **international terminating exchange** centre tête de ligne internationale d'arrivée; ~ **junction** ligne urbaine entrante; ~ **junctor** joncteur entrant; circuit entrant; ~ **local centre** centre de raccordement à l'arrivée; ~ **national exchange** centre national d'arrivée; ~ **one-way circuit** ligne pour le trafic entrant

incoming-only line ligne SPB (spécialisée en arrivée)

incoming operator opératrice d'arrivée; opératrice translatrice; ~ **position** position d'arrivée; ~ **queue** file d'attente de commutation; ~ **response delay** délai d'attente en présélection; attente de tonalité; délai de réponse en présélection; durée de présélection; ~ **R2 register** enregistreur R2 arrivée; ~ **selector** sélecteur d'arrivée; ~ **side** amont (en -); ~ **signal** signal d'entrée; ~ **signal level** intensité du champ de réception; ~ **terminal exchange** (in the international service) centre translateur (dans le service international); ~ **test call responder** robot d'arrivée (RAV); ~ **time switch** commutateur temporel carré; ~ **traffic** trafic entrant; trafic d'arrivée; ~ **trunk** ligne jonction entrante (LJE); jonction entrante; jonction arrivée; ligne urbaine entrante; ~ **trunk call** communication urbaine entrante; arrivée extérieure; ~ **trunk group** faisceau de lignes entrantes; ~ **trunk junctor (ITJ)** joncteur d'arrivée (JA)

incomplete call appel incomplet; ~ **number** numéro incomplet

inconclusive adj controversé

in ... configuration en guise de

incongruity n incohérence

inconsistency n incohérence

in contact (with) engagé

inconvenience n gêne

in conversational mode sous dialogue

incorporated adj intégral; solidaire; encastré

incorrect adj erroné; infidèle; déréglé; non conforme (KO); ~ **keying** mauvaise manipulation; ~ **restitution** restitution erronée

increase n augmentation; accroissement; gain

increased power gain en puissance; ~ **tenfold**

(by a factor of 10) décuplé

increase in (number of) main subscriber lines accroissement du parc de lignes principales; ~ **the severity of** (test) resserrer

increment n pas de progression; accoup; accroissement; augmentation; bond; cran; gain en puissance; intervalle; palier

incremental adj croissant; ~ **computer** calculateur incrémentiel; calculateur à incréments; calculateur par accroissements; ~ **duplex** circuit duplex à courant de repos; duplex par addition

incrementally adj pas à pas (PAP)

incremental representation représentation par accroissements; ~ **resistance** résistance en courant alternatif; résistance interne différentielle

incrementing message register (subscriber's private meter) imputation sur le compte de l'abonné

increments, in 50g ~ cinquante grammes par cinquante grammes

incriminate v mettre en faute

incrimination piloting mise en faute

incubator n étuve

inculcation of skills transfert de connaissances

in daisy-chain configuration chaîné

indent n alinéa; cascade (dans une arborescence); flèche; saut de colonne

indentation n défonçage

indented adj échancré

indent(-ion) n aplomb

independent keyboard clavier mobile; clavier séparé; ~ **power supply** excitation séparée; ~ **sideband transmitter** émetteur à bandes latérales indépendantes; ~ **variable** variable indépendante

in-depth examination étude approfondie; ~ **visual examination** contrôle visuel renforcé

indeterminate band zone d'incertitude

index n indice; aiguille; barillet; bilan; caractéristique(s); édition; (éd.); exposant; index; liste; module; page-guide; rang; tableau; ~ **area** zone indicatif; ~ **card** fiche

indexed adj répertorié; ~ **address** adresse indexée; ~ **address constant** constante d'adresse indexée; ~ **field** champ répétitif; ~ **item** occurrence; ~ **sequential** séquentiel indexé

index file fichier de recherche; fichier indexé

indexing n indexation; permutation; enregistrement; ~ **table** plateau rotatif; ~ **template** gabarit d'indexage

index-linking n majoration (MAJ); valorisation

index mark repère; ~ **marking** indiçage

index-matching liquid (material) liquide adaptateur d'indice

index of cooperation module de coopération; ~ **profile** profil d'indice; ~ **register** registre d'index; registre d'adresses; registre de base; registre de cumul; ~ **word** mot d'index

indicate v indiquer; afficher; caractériser; désigner; déterminer; visualiser; ~ (of fault) incriminer

indicating instrument appareil à aiguille

indicator n aiguille; alternat; balise; diode de contrôle; herse; index; lampe de visualisation; mot d'état d'organe; d'organe; indicateur; avertisseur; voyant; ~ **circuit** circuit d'annonce; ~ **lamp** lampe de signalisation; lampe indicatrice; ~ **on** afficheur monté; ~ **panel** panneau de lampes; cadran; ~ **switch** culbuteur

indirect (space) **wave** onde spatiale; ~ **address** adresse indirecte; adresse différée; adresse complémentaire; ~ **addressing** adressage indirect; adressage par indirection; ~ **control** commande indirecte; ~ **drive** commande indirecte

indirectly-addressed file fichier indirect

indirectly-heated cathode cathode à chauffage indirect; cathode équipotentielle; ~ **tube** tube à chauffage indirect

indirect power puissance réfléchie; ~ **radiation** rayonnement indirect; ~ **ray** rayon indirect; ~ **wave** onde indirecte; onde d'espace; onde réfléchie

individual adj particulier; caractéristique; différent; distinct; indépendant; ponctuel; propre; spécifique; unitaire; ~ **inspection** contrôle unitaire; ~ **or legal entities** personnes physiques ou morales; ~ **packaging** emballage particulier; ~ **subscriber** abonné simple; ~ **trunk** (direct exchange line) ligne individuelle (d'abonné)

indoor temperature température interne

induced charge signal imprimé (par aimantation); ~ **coil** induit; ~ **current** courant induit; consommation d'appel; ~ **noise** bruit induit

inducing vacuum mise sous vide

inductance n bobinage; inertie magnétique; réactance inductive; self; inductance

inductance-capacitance coupling couplage L-C

inductance coil bobine d'inductance; inducteur; ~ **factor (A$_L$)** inductance spécifique

induction ammeter ampèremètre d'induction; ~ **coil** bobine d'induction; transformateur différentiel; ~ **current** (of solenoid) courant d'appel; ~ **field** champ d'induction; ~ **generator** machine électrique à induction; ~ **loudspeaker** haut-parleur à induc-

tion; ~ **machine** générateur électrostatique; éliminateur; ~ **motor-generator** convertisseur asynchrone; ~ **regulator** régulateur d'induction; ~ **relay** relais à induction
induction-type voltmeter voltmètre à induction
induction zone zone d'induction
inductive circuit circuit inductif; ~ **coupling** couplage inductif; ~ **load** charge inductive; ~ **loop** boucle selfique; ~ **reactance** réactance inductive
inductivity n pouvoir inducteur spécifique
inductor n inductance; bobine d'inductance; inducteur; self
industrial adj professionnel; ~ **application(s)** industrialisation; ~ **design** esthétique; ~ **environment** milieu industriel; ~ **estate** zone industrielle; ~ **feasibility** faisabilité industrielle; ~ **fuse** fusible classe g1; ~ **plant** ensemble industriel; ~ **workload** charges industrielles
industry-standard adj industriel
inert atmosphere atmosphère neutre; ~ **filling gas** gaz de remplissage inerte
infant mortality (of components) défaut de jeunesse
inference crunching machine (ICM) coprocesseur séquentiel
infinitely variable réglable à l'infini
infinite periodic array réseau infini d'antennes accordées
infinitesimal dipole doublet électrique; dipôle électrique
influence factor facteur de forme; ~ **machine** générateur électrostatique; éliminateur
information n renseignement(s); information(s); ~ **bearer channel** voie support d'information; ~ **bus** faisceau connecteur; ~ **card** fiche de renseignements; ~ **channel** voie de transfert des informations; voie utile; ~ **content per symbol** contenu en information par symbole; ~ **cycle** cycle d'information; ~ **feedback system** système correcteur d'erreurs par retour de l'information; ~ **field** zone d'information; ~ **flow** débit d'information; ~ **management software** logiciel informationnel; ~ **message** message d'information; ~ **network** réseau d'information; ~ **operator** opératrice de renseignements; ~ **provider** producteur de données; serveur; ~ **rate** contenu total en information; ~ **retrieval** recherche d'informations; exploitation des renseignements; ~ **system** tableau de bord; ~ **technology** télématique; ~ **theory** théorie de l'information; ~ **transfer** transfert d'information; ~ **unit** unité d'information; ~ **value** valeur de l'information; ~ **volume** volume d'information

infra-red lamp lampe d'infrarouge; ~ **range and direction-finding equipment** radar à rayons infrarouges; ~ **telephony** téléphonie à rayons infrarouges; ~ **tracker** appareil de poursuite infrarouge
infrasonic frequency fréquence infra-acoustique
infringement of patents contrefaçon de brevets
in gear en service (ES)
ingress n pénétration; entrée
in head-to-tail configuration (of diodes) montées tête-bêche; montées en opposition
inherent (hardware) addressing adressage inhérent; ~ **distortion** distorsion inhérente
inherent-noise bandwidth largeur de bande du bruit propre
inherited error erreur accumulée; erreur héritée; erreur propagée; erreur propre; erreur répercutée
inhibit v bloquer; arrêter; inhiber; mettre en faute; protéger; ~ **gate** porte interdiction; inhibiteur
inhibiting signal signal d'interdiction
inhibition control commande d'inhibition
inhibitor n frein
inhibit pulse impulsion de blocage
in-house adj intérieur; interne
initial adj de départ; ~ **address** adresse d'origine; ~ **address block** bloc d'adresse initiale; ~ **address message (IAM)** message d'adressage initial; ~ **alignment** alignement initial; ~ **charge** taxe de mise en présence; taxe de mise en relation; ~ **clip** mutilation initiale; ~ **current flow** courant initial; ~ **deposit on account** dépôt de garantie initial; ~ **draft** première frappe
initialization n initialisation; démarrage à froid; armement; mise en œuvre; RZG (remise à zéro générale)
initial menu dialogue initial; ~ **page** page de mise en service; ~ **permeability** perméabilité initiale; ~ **program load** réinitialisation à froid; ~ **signal unit (ISU)** unité de signalisation initiale; ~ **translation** traduction de départ; ~ **voltage** tension initiale
initiating relay relais primaire
initiator n préparateur
in-jack jack d'entrée
inked pad tampon encreur
inker n enregistreur à stylet
inking n encrage
ink-jet printer imprimante à jet d'encre
ink pen stylo-marqueur; ~ **recorder** enregistreur à stylet; ~ **writer** enregistreur à stylet
inlet n entrée; amenée; accès; admission; point d'accès; point d'entrée; voie entrante; ~ **side** amont (en -)
in-line adj séquentiel; simultané; ouvert

in linear progression linéairement
in-line processing traitement immédiat; ~ **receptacle** clip de connexion
in mid-position à mi-place
innate *adj* interne; propre
inner conductor conducteur intérieur; ~ **layer** couche interne; ~ **loop** boucle auxiliaire; boucle secondaire
inner-shell electron électron interne
inner work function travail interne
inoperative hors service (h.s.); inopérant; hors fonctionnement
in phase en phase; isochrone; synchronisé
in-phase amplification amplification en phase; ~ **loss** perte ohmique
in phase opposition (180° out of phase) opposition de phase
in-phase position line ligne isochrone en phase
in-plant *adj* interne; ~ **system** système interne; ~ **testing** plate-forme d'intégration
input *v* écrire; charger (en); ~ *n* entrée; saisie; acquisition; affichage; attaque; lecture; réception; ~ **(power)** énergie d'entrée; ~ **amplifier** amplificateur d'entrée; ~ **and output ports** bornes d'entrée et de sortie; ~ **attenuator** atténuateur d'entrée; ~ **bias** polarisation d'entrée; ~ **bit** donnée d'entrée; ~ **block** bloc d'entrée; ~ **buffer** mémoire tampon d'entrée; ~ **capacitance** capacité d'entrée; ~ **capacitance (output open-circuited to AC)** capacité d'entrée, sortie en circuit ouvert; ~ **capacitance (output short-circuited to AC)** capacité d'entrée, sortie en court-circuit; ~ **capacitance in common-base configuration** capacité d'entrée en base commune; ~ **capacitance in common-emitter configuration** capacité d'entrée en émetteur commun; ~ **circuit** circuit d'entrée
input-controlled commandé par l'amont
input current courant d'entrée; ~ **data** données d'entrée immédiate; ~ **digital highway (IDH)** liaison numérique entrante (LNE); ~ **electrode** électrode d'entrée; ~ **file** fichier d'entrée; fichier de réception; ~ **filtering** filtrage des entrées; ~ **gap** espace d'interaction; résonateur d'entrée; ~ **impedance** impédance d'entrée; ~ **job queue** file d'attente d'ordre (FAO); file d'attente de réception; ~ **job stream** flot (de commande) d'entrée; file d'attente réception; ~ **level** niveau d'entrée; ~ **load** charge d'entrée; ~ **load factor** facteur de charge d'entrée (en entrée); ~ **mixer** mélangeur d'entrée; ~ **offset voltage** tension de décalage en entrée
input/output (I/O) entrée/sortie (E/S); ~ **controller** contrôleur d'entrée/sortie;

contrôleur E/S; ~ **device** périphérique d'entrée/de sortie; ~ **isolation** résistance d'isolement; ~ **library** bibliothèque d'entrée/sortie; ~ **peripheral handler** handler de périphérie informatique; ~ **switch** commutateur d'unités; ~ **terminal** organe de sortie/d'entrée; organe de service; support de travail; ~ **time-switch control memory** mémoire de commande temporelle d'entrée/de sortie; ~ **unit** unité d'échange (UE)
input port accès d'entrée; ~ **power** puissance d'entrée; ~ **program** programme d'introduction; ~ **resonator** résonateur d'entrée; ~ **side** amont (en -); ~ **signal** signal d'entrée; signal incident; ~ **signal check** contrôle des signaux d'entrée; ~ **terminal** poste de saisie; borne d'entrée; terminal de saisie; ~ **time stage** étage de commutation temporelle d'entrée; ~ **time switch** commutateur d'entrée; commutateur temporel carré; ~ **to memory** emmagasinage; ~ **transformer** transformateur d'entrée; ~ **voltage** tension d'entrée; ~ **winding** enroulement primaire; ~ **work queue** file d'attente d'ordre (FAO)
in quadrature décalés en phase de 90°; en quadrature
inquirer *n* demandeur
inquiry *n* interrogation; demande; requête; question
in range en gabarit; ~ **real time** en temps réel; ~ **response** to en réaction à
inrush *n* avalanche; ~ **consumption** consommation d'appel; ~ **current** appel de courant d'entrée; consommation; courant d'appel; courant d'enclenchement; courant d'entrée; point d'intensité
inscriber *n* marqueur
inscription *n* repère
insensitive time temps mort
in series en série
insert *n* cosse à insérer (picot); cavalier; douille; embout; intercalaire; ~ **(of PCB)** platine d'insertion; ~ **earphone** écouteur interne
insertion *n* enfichage
insertion/extraction tool pince de préhension
insertion gain gain d'insertion; ~ **gauge** calibre; ~ **grid** implantation; ~ **head** tête d'insertion; ~ **loss** affaiblissement d'insertion; équivalent de traversée; perte d'insertion; ~ **loss data** caractéristique d'insertion; ~ **phase change** déphasage d'insertion; ~ **pitch** pas d'implantation; ~ **test** contrôle insertion; ~ **tool** pince insertion; poussoir; ~ **transfer function** coefficient d'insertion

insert jumper ponter; ~ **line (IL)** insertion de ligne

in-service en service (ES); engagé

inset *n* capsule; ~ *adj* encadré; encastré; noyé; représenté en médaillon; affleurant; ~ **etching** gravure en creux; ~ **nut** écrou cage

inside *adj* intérieur; interne; ~ **information** informations internes; ~ **vapour phase oxidation (IVPO)** oxydation intérieure à l'état vapeur

in-slot signalling signalisation et intervalle de temps

inspection *n* contrôle; vérification; ~ **by attributes** contrôle par attributs; ~ **hatch** porte de visite; ~ **of mechanical components** contrôle des pièces mécaniques; ~ **plan** gamme de contrôle

install *v* implanter; ~ **a (power) line** tirer une ligne

installation *n* installation; chantier; constitution; ensemble; équipement; groupe; implantation; mise en œuvre; montage; pose; réalisation; site; ~ **quality group** groupe contrôle qualité sur site; ~ **tape number** numéro de bande de site

installed *adj* équipé; présent; implanté; inclus; en place; prévu; ~ **base** équipement d'infrastructure; parc

installer/wireman monteur-câbleur

installing *n* mise en place

instalment *n* acompte

instance *n* cas

instant *adj* instantané

instantaneous acoustical power (sound energy flux) **per unit area** puissance surfacique acoustique instantanée; ~ **acoustical speech power** puissance vocale instantanée; ~ **bandwidth** largeur de bande instantanée; ~ **characteristic** caractéristique instantanée; ~ **companding** compression-extension instantanée; ~ **connection** connexion instantanée; ~ **current** courant instantané; ~ **cut-out** disjoncteur instantané; ~ **frequency** fréquence instantanée; ~ **frequency deviation** écart de fréquence instantané; ~ **load** charge instantanée; ~ **power** puissance instantanée; ~ **power output** puissance de sortie instantanée; ~ **relay** relais instantané; ~ **sound-energy density** énergie volumique acoustique totale instantanée; ~ **sound pressure** pression acoustique instantanée; ~ **traffic load** intensité du trafic instantanée; ~ **voltage** tension instantanée

instant blocking (forced call release) blocage brutal

in step à la cadence; en phase

instigate *v* mettre en oeuvre; provoquer; lancer; ~ **a loop** actionner une boucle

instruction *n* instruction; commande (cde); consigne; formation; indication; mot programme; ordre; phase; stage; ~ (addressed) phase préparée; ~ **address** adresse de phase; adresse d'instruction; phase; ~ **address register (IAR)** registre de phases; registre d'adresse d'instruction; registre d'opérations échelonnées

instructional *adj* didactique; pédagogique

instruction card fiche d'instruction; ~ **character** caractère de commande; ~ **code** code instruction; ~ **counter** registre d'adresse d'instruction; ~ **decoding** décodage des mots programme; ~ **generator** générateur d'ordres; ~ **handler** gestion mot programme; ~ **manual** fiche technique; ~ **op-code indicator** indicateur d'ordres de phase; ~ **pointer (IP)** pointeur d'instructions; ~ **processing** traitement des phases; ~ **(address) register** compteur d'instructions; compteur d'assemblage; ~ **repertoire** jeu d'instructions

instructions *n pl* mode opératoire; indications

instruction set répertoire; jeu d'instructions; code d'ordre

instructions for use notice d'emploi; mode d'emploi

instruction sheet fiche (de) consigne; ~ **step** saut de phase; ~ **steps** succession d'ordre des phases; ~ **time** phase

instructor *n* formateur

instrument *n* appareil

instrumentation amplifier amplificateur de mesure

instrument display panneau; ~ **error** erreur instrumentale; ~ **panel** pupitre de commande; planche de bord; tableau de commande; tableau de bord

instruments *n pl* appareillage

insufficient modulation sous-modulation

insulance *n* résistance d'isolement

insulate *n* isoler

insulated *adj* étanche; isolé; ~ **base** (of PCB) support isolant; ~ **enclosure** coffret isolant; ~ **single-core wire** fil simple isolé; ~ **sleeving** souplisseau; ~ **tubing** gaine isolante; ~ **wire** fil gainé; conducteur isolé

insulating *adj* diélectrique; ~ (material) isolant; ~ **barrier** cloison isolant; ~ **base** matériau isolant; ~ **bush** entretoise; ~ **mat** tapis isolant; ~ **material** matière de l'isolant; ~ **pad** (for IC) *n* isolant électrique; ~ **panel** cloisonnement; ~ **screw joint** sucre; ~ **staple** cavalier; ~ **tape** ruban isolant; ~ **varnish** vernis isolant; ~ **wafer** corps isolant; ~ **wall**

caisson d'isolement (diélectrique)

insulation *n* isolant; enveloppe; isolation; isolement; ~ **breakdown** claquage; ~ **breakdown test** essai de claquage; ~ **displacement connection (IDC)** connexion auto-dénudante (CAD); ~ **displacement connector (IDC)** prise vampire; ~ **displacement tool** canon; ~ **fault** défaut d'isolement; ~ **resistance** résistance d'isolement; ~ **resistance test** essai d'isolement; ~ **tester** diélectrimètre

insulator *n* isolant; isolateur; ~ **set** chaîne d'isolateurs

in sync en phase; en synchronisme

intake *n* entrée; aspiration

integer *n* nombre entier; ~ **value** valeur entière

integral *adj* intégré; solidaire; incorporé; entier; autonome; cohérent; encastré; global; indivisible; intérieur; interne; isolé; ~ **counter** compteur intégré

integrate *v* totaliser; intercaler; intégrer (à)

integrated cohérent; complet; harmonieux; homogène; synthétique; ~ **circuit (IC)** circuit intégré; microstructure; boîtier; ~ **circuit handler** chargeur de circuit intégré; ~ **circuit package** boîtier de circuit intégré; ~ **communications system** système intégré de communications; ~ **data processing** traitement intégré de données; ~ **digital network (IDN)** réseau numérique intégré (RNI); ~ **injection logic (I²L)** logique intégrée à injection; ~ **network** réseau intégré; ~ **numbering plan** plan de numérotage integré; ~ **package** (of solutions) offre; ~ **product** solution; ~ **services digital network (ISDN)** réseau numérique à services intégrés (RNIS); réseau numérique avec intégration des services; réseau multi-services

integrating capacitor condensateur d'intégration; ~ **circuit/network** montage intégrateur; ~ **frequency divider** diviseur de fréquence à intégration; ~ **meter** compteur totalisateur; ~ **network** réseau intégrateur; ~ **relay** relais totalisateur

integration count moyennage; ~ **tests** mise au point (MAP)

integrator *n* totalisateur; montage intégrateur

integrity *n* sûreté; cohérence

intelligence signal signal désiré

intelligent subscriber interface régisseur d'abonné; régie intelligente

intelligibility *n* articulation des mots; intelligibilité; netteté

intelligible crosstalk diaphonie intelligible

intensification *n* concentration

intensified *adj* renforcé

intensifier *n* multiplicateur; ~ **electrode** électrode de post-accélération

intensify *v* améliorer

intensity *n* intensité; luminosité; puissance (Pce); ~ **modulated display** indicateur à modulation d'intensité

intensive *adj* approfondi

intentionally *adv* volontairement

interaction factor coefficient d'interaction; ~ **impedance** impédance de couplage; ~ **loss** affaiblissement d'interaction

interactive *adj* interactif; bavard; communicant; de dialogue; ~ (public) **broadcast terminal** terminal grande diffusion; ~ **cursor** curseur mobile; ~ **electronic office automation** télébureautique

interactively *adj* sous dialogue

interactive mode mode dialogué; en mode connecté; mode conversationnel; mode interactif; ~ **operator terminal** organe périphérique; ~ **terminal** console de dialogue; terminal conversationnel; terminal d'échange; ~ **working** relations homme-machine (RHM)

inter-aid relay relais d'entraide; ~ **vertical** (path) verticale d'entraide

inter-band telegraphy télégraphie inter-bandes

inter-block gap (IBG) espace arrêt-marche; espace interbloc; entre-bloc

inter-carrier *n* interporteuse

intercept *v* capter; intercepter; mettre en écoute; ~ *n* captage de données; interception; ~ **circuit** circuit capteur; circuit de blocage temporaire

intercepting trap intercepteur; ~ **trunk** ligne de renvoi

interception *n* filtrage; interception; saisie

intercept method méthode d'écoute; ~ **operator** opératrice d'interception

interceptor fighter intercepteur

intercept/predicted target (objective) but/ point futur

intercept receiver appareil d'interception; ~ **relay** relais d'écoute; ~ **routine** captation; ~ **service** service d'écoute; ~ **station** poste d'écoute

interchange *n* échange; commutation; conversation; dialogue; permutation

interchangeability *n* mariabilité; transportabilité; ~ **index** indice d'exploitation; ~ **list** plan d'équivalence composant

interchangeable *adj* interchangeable; commutable; ~ **earth** terre commutable; ~ **pair** paire combinable; ~ **stocks** fongibles

interchange circuit circuit de jonction; circuit de liaison; jonction; ~ **fault** faute échange; ~ **module** module d'échange; ~ **signalling sender** émetteur auxiliaire de signalisation;

~ **trunk** jonction; ~ **unit** bloc échangeur; échangeur; unité d'échange (UE)
inter-channel crosstalk diaphonie entre voies; ~ **spacing** distance entre canaux
intercom *n* interphone; téléphone de bord; dispositif d'intercommunication; ~ **call** appel en interphonie
intercommunication equipment interphone
intercom switch commutateur parole-écoute
interconnect *v* interconnecter; relier
interconnected *adj* couplé
interconnect glue connectique
interconnecting network (IN) réseau interconnexion (RI)
interconnection *n* interconnexion; cheminement; enchaînement; ~ **circuit** circuit d'interconnexion; ~ **diagram** diagramme d'interconnexion
interconnect point point d'interconnexion
intercontinental service service intercontinental
intercorporate *adj* interentreprise
intercrystalline disintegration désagrégation intercristalline
interdependent *adj* solidaire
interdialling *n* intersélection
inter-digit pause durée de l'interchiffre; inter-MOM; intervalle entre les chiffres; temporisation interchiffre; temps mort entre chiffres; intertrain
interdisciplinary *adj* polyvalent
inter-exchange *n* entre centraux; ~ **links** entraide(s); ~ **signalling** signalisation entre autocommutateurs; signalisation inter-centraux; ~ **transmission** transmission interurbaine; ~ **transmission** (plant) la transmission; ~ **trunk position** position de communication inter-réseaux; ~ **trunks** jonctions intercentraux; circuits de transit
interface *n* jonction; accès; adaptateur; bloc d'adaptation; bride; canal; entrée/sortie (E/S); interconnexion; interface; joncteur; liaison; organe de raccordement; passerelle; raccordement (racct.); régie d'abonnés; surface de séparation; circuit de connexion
interfaceability *n* compatibilité; souplesse d'adaptation
interfaceable *adj* adaptable (à); accessible; connectable; opposable
interface adaptor adaptateur de jonction; compliance; ~ **circuit** circuit d'interface; ~ **connector** connecteur d'interface; ~ **controller** coupleur de raccordement
interfaced *adj* connecté
interface equipment organes d'utilisation; ~ **functions** entrefaces d'entrée/sortie; ~ **kit** pieuvre; ~ **module** module de

couplage; terminal de jonction; accesseur; ~ **routine** programme d'adaptation; ~ **switching point** point de commutation de jonction; ~ **unit** tiroir d'éclatement; ~ **zone** zone de couplage
interfacing *n* adaptation; connexion; couplage; jonctionnement
interference *n* parasite(s); brouillage; bruit; interaction; interférence; parasites atmosphériques; perturbation; troubles; ~ **coupling** couplage parasite; ~ **current** courant perturbateur; ~ **factor** facteur d'interférence; ~ **fading** évanouissement par interférence; ~ **field strength** champ perturbateur; ~ **filter** filtre anti-parasites; ~ **fit** ajustement immobile
interference-free *adj* déparasité
interference from power lines interférence due aux courants du secteur électrique; ~ **level** niveau d'interférence; ~ **limiting** limitation d'interférence; ~ **pattern** moirage (en télévision); ~ **power** puissance perturbatrice; ~ **region** zone d'interférence; ~ **source** perturbateur; source d'interférence; ~ **suppression** antiparasitage; élimination de parasites; ~ **suppression equipment** équipement de parasitage; ~ **suppressor** circuit bouchon; ~ **wave** onde d'interférence
interfering transmitter brouilleur; émetteur brouilleur
intergranular corrosion corrosion intercristalline
interior *adj* intérieur; interne; ~ **label** label de bande
interlaced *adj* imbriqué; ~ **scanning** balayage cathodique entrelacé; analyse (ligne par ligne) entrelacé; séquence d'entrelacement
interlacing *n* imbrication; étalage; imbriquage
interleaved calling sequence chaîne d'appels imbriqués; ~ **scan** balayage intercalaire
interleaving *n* imbrication; accès mémoire simultané; imbriquage
interlink *v* interconnecter
interlinked phase voltage tension entre phases
interlock *v* bloquer; épouser; ~ *n* verrou; bloquer; enclenchement; interruption; sécurité protecteur; verrue d'opératrice; blocage; ~ **code** code de verrouillage
interlocked *adj* solidaire; solidarisé
interlocking *n* articulation; couplage; ~ **equisignal system** radioalignement à enchevêtrement; ~ **relay** relais d'accouplement; relais d'enclenchement; ~ **roller** galet récepteur
interlock switch clé de sécurité; commutateur de verrouillage
intermediate distribution frame (IDF) répartiteur intermédiaire (RI); répartiteur de

croisement (RC); ~ **echo suppressor** suppresseur d'écho intermédiaire; ~ **equipment** équipement intermédiaire; ~ **exchange** central intermédiaire; ~ **frequency (IF)** fréquence intermédiaire (FI); fréquence moyenne; moyenne fréquence (MF)

intermediate-frequency breakthrough induction parasite de fréquence intermédiaire; ~ **circuit** circuit moyenne fréquence; circuit MF; ~ **stage** étage de fréquence intermédiaire

intermediate handling retransmission; réexpédition; transit manuel; ~ **selection unit (ISU)** élément de sélection intermédiaire (ESI); ~ **tone override** franchissement des tonalités intermédiaires; numérotation intégrée

intermesh v engrener

intermeshed adj confondu; homogène

intermittent adj périodique; ~ **current** courant intermittent; ~ **interference** bruit périodique; ~ **noise** bruit récurrent; ~ **service** fonctionnement intermittent

inter-mode interference interférence inter-mode

inter-modulation distortion bruit d'intermodulation; ~ **distortion ratio** coefficient d'intermodulation; ~ **frequency** fréquence différentielle; fréquence d'intermodulation; ~ **meter** intermodulomètre; ~ **noise** bruit d'intermodulation; diaphonie; distorsion d'intermodulation; ~ **products** produits d'intermodulation

internal (resident) **staff** personnel direct; ~ **blocking probability** taux de blocage interne; ~ **capacitance** capacité propre; ~ **characteristic** caractéristique intérieure; ~ **layer** couche interne; ~ **rate of return (IRR)** taux interne de récupération (TIR); ~ **resistance** résistance interne; ~ **retaining ring** (circlip) anneau intérieur; ~ **roll-off** circuit de compensation interne; ~ **slaving** asservissement intérieur

international access code préfixe international; ~ **accounting** comptabilité internationale; ~ **call** communication internationale; ~ **calling frequency** fréquence internationale d'appel; ~ **code** indicatif international; ~ **control station** position de contrôle du trafic téléphonique international; ~ **demand service** service international rapide; ~ **exchange** central international; centre international automatique; ~ **maintenance centre** centre international de maintenance; ~ **network** réseau international; ~ **numbering plan** plan de numérotation international; ~ **service** service international; ~ **switching and test centre** centre

de commutation et d'essais internationaux (CCEI); ~ **switching maintenance centre (ISMC)** centre international de maintenance de la commutation (CIMC); ⌁ **Telecommunications Union (ITU)** Union Internationale des Télécommunications (UIT); ~ **telegraph alphabet** alphabet télégraphique international; ⌁ **Telegraph and Telephone Consultative Committee (CCITT)** Comité Consultatif International Télégraphique et Téléphonique (CCITT); ~ **telegraph code** code télégraphique international; ~ **telephone circuit** circuit téléphonique international; ~ **telephone line** ligne téléphonique internationale; ~ **terminating exchange** centre de tête de ligne international; ~ **traffic** trafic international; ~ **transit call** communication internationale de transit; ~ **transit centre** centre de transit international; ~ **transmission maintenance centre (ITMC)** centre international de maintenance de la transmission (CIMT)

inter-office adj entre centraux; ~ **trunk** ligne urbaine de jonction

interphase reactor self interphase; transformateur équilibreur

interphase control system (ICS) interphone

interpolate v intercaler

interpolation n interpolation

interposition circuit ligne d'appel entre positions interurbaines

interpreter n programme interpréteur; traducteur; traductrice; ~ **program** interpréteur

interpretive processor processeur de dépouillement; ~ **trace program** programme d'analyse; ~ **trace routine** interpréteur

inter-processor data link liaison série doublée; réseau d'information temporelle; ~ **link** liaison intercalculateur; ~ **link access** automate central; ~ **mailbox** boîte aux lettres inter-processeur (BIP)

inter-record gap (IRG) espace arrêt-marche; entre-enregistrement; espace arrêt-marche; pas d'enregistrement; entre-bloc

inter-regional network réseau interrégional; ~ **trunk** circuit interrégional

inter-register signalling signalisation d'enregistreur; ~ **signalling code** code enregistreur

interrogate clock consultation horloge

interrogating pulse impulsion de test

interrogation n consultation; interpellation; invitation à émettre; ~ **frame** séquence d'invitation à émettre; ~ **frequency** fréquence d'interrogation

interrogator n émetteur pilote; interrogateur

interrupt v cadencer; interrompre; ~ n

interruption; arrêt; blocage; microcoup; rupture; ~ **cam** cadenceur; ~ **clock** périphérique horloge générale; ~ **code** code d'arrêt; ~ **controller/handler** contrôleur d'interruptions

interrupted call appel coupé; ~ **ring-back tone** retour d'appel cadencé; ~ **ringing** sonnerie cadencée; ~ **ringing current** courant d'appel cadencé; ~ **task consistency checking program** terminateur; ~ **tone** tonalité cadencée

interrupt handling traitement des interruptions

interrupt-handling program programme de gestion des interruptions

interrupt hierarchy hiérarchie des interruptions

interruptible adj (of inverter) avec coupure

interruption n sollicitation extérieure; coupure; microcoup; ouverture; ~ **key** clé de rupture

interrupt level niveau d'interruption; ~ **logic** logique d'arrêt; ~ **memory** mémoire microcoup; ~ **point** point interruptible; ~ **rate** cadence de base; cadencement; fréquence des interruptions; ~ **servicing** traitement des interruptions; ~ **source** origine de l'interruption; ~ **system** système d'interruption; ~ **timed-out** acquittement d'interruption; interruption claquée

inter-satellite service service de radiocommunication entre satellites

intersect n (logic function) opération ET

inter-shelf connecting cable cordon inter-alvéoles; ~ **wiring** câblage inter-alvéoles

inter-site coupling loss affaiblissement par couplage entre sites; ~ **error** erreur régionale

interspersed adj alterné

inter-stage coupling couplage cathodique; couplage entre étages

inter-stellar noise bruit cosmique; bruit extra-terrestre

inter-suite adj intertravée

inter-switchboard line ligne interstandard (LIS); ligne privée

inter-symbol interference interférence par symboles

inter-toll trunk liaison interurbain

inter-turns insulation isolation entre spires

interval n intervalle; délai; écart; pas; période; temps; périodicité; ~ **selector** circuit discriminateur de temps; ~ **signal** signal de repos; signal d'intervalle; ~ **timer** intervallomètre; compteur de périodes; compteur d'intervalles de temps; compteur temporisateur; programmateur; rythmeur; séquentiel

interval-timer oscilloscope oscilloscope de mesure d'intervalle de temps; oscilloscope-intervallomètre

inter-winding capacitance capacité entre enroulements; capacité entre spires; ~ **insulation** isolation entre spires

interworking n interfonctionnement; association; coopération; enchaînement; entraide(s); synergie; ~ **network** réseau à entraide

in-test measurement mesure en cours d'épreuve

in the calling phase en conversation; ~ **the call set-up phase** en phase d'établissement; ~ **the field** sur site; ~ **the open** (air) àl'extérieur; ~ **the open sea** au large; ~ **the opposite direction** dans les trois symétries; ~ **the 'ready use' position** en état de marche; ~ **the ringing phase** en sonnerie; ~ **the speech phase** en conversation; ~ **the vicinity of** vers

into (of power delivered into load) sous

intolerable noise parasites intolérables

intra-band telegraphy télégraphie intrabande; télégraphie et téléphonie simultanées

intra-city call communication locale; ~ **exchange** central urbain

intra-exchange intra-central

intra-office call appel local; appel interne

intrinsic absorption absorption intrinsèque

intrinsically safe sécurité intrinsèque

intrinsic resistance résistance pure; ~ **semiconductor** semiconducteur intrinsèque; ~ **temperature** température intrinsèque

introduction ("hello") **page** grille d'accueil

intruder alarm alarme effraction

intrusion n entrée en tiers; intervention opératrice; entrée en ligne; ~ **suffix** (dialling code) suffixe d'intrusion; ~ **tone** tonalité d'intervention; tonalité d'avertissement d'entrée

in uniform increments sans à-coups

invalid call appel non valable

inventory n bilan; dotation; état de gestion; nomenclature; parc; répertoire; stock; ~ **check** contrôle d'inventaire; dénombrement; ~ **control** approvisionnement; ~ **position/status report** état de stock

inverse (reciprocal) **of turns ratio** pont de rapport de transformation; ~ **function** opération inverse; ~ **impedance** impédance réciproque

inverse/reciprocal amplification factor transparence de grille

inverted commas guillemets; ~ **cone aerial** antenne en cône renversé; ~ **crosstalk** diaphonie d'écho; diaphonie inintelligible; ~ **file** fichier inverse; ~ **solidus** barre inversée; ~ **V-aerial** antenne en V renversé

inverter *n* onduleur; convertisseur continu-alternatif; circuit inverseur; commutatrice; changeur; ~ (logic switching circuit) inverseur (circuit i.); ~ **cable** câble croisé
inverting amplifier amplificateur inverseur; ~ **gate** inverseur; ~ **input** entrée inverseuse; entrée inversée
invert mode mode inverse
invigilator *n* contrôleur de séquence; mouchard
invitation to tender appel d'offres
invitation-to-transmit signal ('K' in morse code) invitation à transmettre (IT)
invocation *n* sollicitation
invoice *n* facture
invoicing *n* facturation
invoke *v* appeler; mettre en oeuvre
inward *adj* d'arrivée; entrant
I/O (s. input/output); ~ **adaptor** adaptateur d'entrée-sortie; ~ **channels** canaux d'E/S; ~ **controller** contrôleur d'échanges; contrôleur d'entrée/sortie; précoupleur; ~ **device** support de travail; ~ **(data) handler** superviseur d'entrée-sortie
ion burn tache ionique; ~ **burning** brûlure ionique; ~ **conduction** conduction ionique; ~ **density** densité ionique; ~ **deposition printer** imprimante à dépôt ionique; ~ **gun** canal ionique
ionization anomaly anomalie de l'ionisation; ~ **current** courant d'ionisation; ~ **energy** énergie d'ionisation; ~ **potential** potentiel d'ionisation; ~ **probability** probabilité d'ionisation; ~ **rate** vitesse spécifique d'ionisation; ~ **time** temps d'ionisation; ~ **voltage** tension d'ionisation
ionized atmosphere atmosphère ionisée; ~ **layer** couche E
ion-magnetic component composante magnéto-ionique
ionogram *n* ionogramme
ionosphere *n* ionosphère
ionospheric absorption absorption ionosphérique; ~ **cross-modulation** transmodulation ionosphérique; effet Luxembourg; ~ **defocussing** défocalisation ionosphérique; dérive de trajet ionosphérique; ~ **disturbance** perturbation ionosphérique; ~ **fading** évanouissement ionosphérique; ~ **focussing** focalisation ionosphérique; ~ **layer** couche ionosphérique
ionospheric-path error erreur de propagation ionosphérique
ionospheric prediction prévision ionosphérique; ~ **ray** rayon ionosphérique; ~ **recorder** sondeur ionosphérique; ~ **sounding** sondage ionosphérique; ~ **storm** orage ionosphérique; tempête ionosphérique

ion semiconductor semiconducteur ionique; ~ **trap** piège d'ions
I/O port accès; organe de sortie/d'entrée; organe de service; ~ **supervision** supervision des accès; ~ **terminal** périphérique d'entrée/de sortie
IP (s. instruction pointer)
IRG (s. inter-record gap)
iris *n* (of waveguide) diaphragme
iron-clad *adj* cuirassé
iron-core coil bobine à noyau de fer
ironwork *n* ossature; serrurerie
IRR (s. internal rate of return)
irradiated (electron bombardment) irradié
irregular *adj* intermittent; ~ **distortion** distorsion fortuite; distorsion irrégulière
irregularity reflection coefficient facteur de réflexion sur les irrégularités
irreparable damage dégâts irréversibles; destruction
irretrievable *adj* irrécupérable; ~ **loss** perte irrémédiable; panne mortelle
irreversible magnetic process perte irrémédiable
ISDN (s. integrated services digital network); ~ **optical fibre network** réseau optique multiservices
island effect effet d'îlot
ISMC (s. international switching maintenance centre)
isochronous distortion distorsion isochrone; ~ **line** ligne isochrone; ~ **restitution** restitution isochrone; ~ **signal** signal isochrone
isolate *v* isoler; couper; découpler; neutraliser; séparer
isolated *adj* autonome; bloqué; en blocage; séparé; ~ **data transmitter (IDT)** découpleur galvanique/galvanométrique; ~ **phase** régime isolé; ~ **region** zone isolante
isolating block plot élastique; ~ **circuit** *n* séparateur; ~ **link** broche de sectionnement; tube de sectionnement; ~ **plug** fiche d'isolement; ~ **relay** relais d'isolement; relais de sectionnement; ~ **screen** écran; ~ **strip** barrette de sectionnement; ~ **switch label** étiquette de blocage d'organe; ~ **tube** tube isolant
isolation *n* mise hors service (HS); découplage; dépistage; isolement; mise en blocage; mise en faux-appel; sectionnement; suppression; ~ (of PCM highways) mise en indisponible; ~ **amplifier** amplificateur d'isolement; amplificateur tampon stabilisé; ~ **transformer** transformateur d'isolement; ~ **voltage** tension d'isolement; isolation galvanique; tension de

I

tenue
isolator *n* coupe-circuit; affaiblisseur non réciproque; isolateur; clivage; sectionneur
isometric projection perspective cavalière; ~ **tube** tube cavalier
isotope *n* isotope (d'un élément)
isotropic *adj* dans l'axe; équidirective; omnidirective; simple
isotropic/equiradial aerial antenne sans effet directif
isotropic radiated power puissance émise isotropiquement; ~ **radiator** antenne équidirective; antenne omnidirectionnelle; antenne isotrope; ~ **target** cible simple
issue *v* émettre; diffuser; éditer; lancer; ~ *n* édition; (éd.); parution; sortie; ~ **date** date de parution; ~ **of standard** enregistrement de norme
issuing bank code code émetteur
ISU (s. intermediate' selection unit); ≃ (s. initial signal unit)
italic *adj* (of print) penché
italics (font) attribut italisé

item *n* article; chapelet; élément; entité; pièce (pce); poste; rubrique; repère; ~ **delimiter** séparateur d'article
itemized bill facture détaillée; ~ **billing** facturation détaillée; ~ **billing entitlement** droit aux justifications
item size longueur d'article
iteration *n* bouclage; boucle; itération; occurrence; répétition; reprise
iterative attenuation coefficient affaiblissement itératif; ~ **impedance** impédance itérative; ~ **loop** boucle d'itération; ~ **phase-change constant** déphasage itératif; ~ **procedure** procédé itératif; ~ **transfer coefficient** exposant itératif de transfert
ith ime
ITJ (s. incoming trunk junctor)
ITMC (s. international transmission maintenance centre)
ITU (s. International Telecommunications Union)
IVPO (s. inside vapour phase oxidation)

J

jack *n* conjoncteur; douille; jack; ~ **bush** douille de jack

jacket *n* enveloppe; chemise; manchon; microdossier; support; ~ (of fibre cable) enrobage; ~ (of film) farde

jack field massif de jacks; panneau de jacks; tableau de jacks; ~ **guide** guide pour jacks; ~ **panel** panneau de jacks; tableau de jacks; ~ **plug** fiche de jack; cavalier

jack-plugging *n* connexion

jack sleeve corps de jack; ~ **socket** douille de jack; ~ **strip** réglette de jacks; bande de jacks

J-aerial antenne en J

jag *n* dent de scie (DDS)

jam *v* brouiller (intentionellement); coincer; ~ *n* embouteillage; **(card)** ~ enrayage

jammed active bloqué à l'état actif; ~ **inactive** bloqué à l'état inactif

jammer *n* brouilleur; perturbateur; ~ **modulator** modulateur de brouillage

jamming *n* brouillage; blocage; bourrage; calage; embouteillage

jam nut receptacle embase à fixation par écrou

janitor *n* portier électronique

jargon *n* terme de métier

jaw clamp pince à mors

jet test essai de dissolution à la goutte

jettisoning *n* délestage

Jiffy bag [T.N.] étui piqué

jig *n* gabarit; bâti; dispositif

jigger *n* bobine de couplage

jig saw scie sauteuse

jingle *n* mélodie

jitter *n* gigue; bruit; décrochage (D); distorsion accidentelle; distorsion de ligne; distorsion fortuite; distorsion irrégulière; instabilité d'image; sautillement; scintillement; vacillement

jitterbug *n* générateur d'impulsions arythmiques

jitter effect effet papillon; ~ **suppressor** suppresseur de gigue

j.n.d. (s. just-noticeable difference)

job *n* tâche; travail; passe; emploi; ~ **batches** trains de travaux

jobber's drill foret mécanicien

job breakdown décomposition du travail en éléments; ~ **card** carte paramètre; ~ **controller** contrôleur de tâches; ~ **description** description de la tâche; ~ **description schedule** gamme de fabrication; ~ **estimate** devis; ~ **flow** cheminement du travail; ordonnancement; ~ **handler** contrôleur de tâches; ~ **handling** répartition des tâches; ~ **order** ordre de travail (OT); fiche de travaux

job-oriented terminal terminal habilité; terminal spécifique

job queue file de travail (informatique); ~ **request** demande de travail; ~ **satisfaction** travail gratifiant; ~ **scheduler** programmateur de travaux; ~ **scheduling** répartition des tâches; ~ **sheet** bordereau; ordre de travail (OT); ~ **step** unité de traitement (UT); ~ **streams** trains de travaux; ~ **string** chaîne de traitement

Joe took father's shoe bench out (test sentence) PARIS - BORDEAUX - LE MANS - SAINT-LEU - LEON - LOUDUN

jog *v* progresser (faire -)

jogging *n* réglage fin

joggle *v* battre; ~ **plate** plaque anti-bourrage

joggler *n* batteur de cartes

joggling *n* soyage; battage

Johnson noise bruit d'agitation thermique; effet de grêle; effet de grenaille

join *v* raccorder

joint *adj* commun; mixte; solidaire; ~ **access** accès commun; ~ **denial** NON OU (= NI)

jointing *n* jonctionnement

joint services (of military specifications) interarmées; ~ **trunk position** position de communication inter-réseaux; ~ **venture** affaire en participation; collaboration; coopération; ~ **venture group** groupement d'intérêt économique (GIE)

joist *n* sous-poutre

jolt *n* à coup (accoup)

jotter *n* mémoire bloc-notes

journal *n* fichier gazette; journal

joystick *n* levier de commande

JSC (s. junction scanner)

jth jme

jubilee clip collier PC

judder *n* broutage; soubresaut

jumbo group groupe quinaire

jump *n* saut; aiguillage; branchement; rupture

jumper *n* cavalier; agrafe; barrette; connexion en U; connexion volante; étrier de court circuit; fil volant; jarretière; pont; raccordement (racct.); strap; ~ **and switch settings** programmation technique

jumper-connected daughter board module à agrafes

jumper field construction(s); tableau de brassage; brasseur

jumpering mutations; ~ **wire** fil jarretière

jumper layout brassage; ~ **lead** cavalier

jumper-selectable modifiable par cavalier

jumper-selected câblé

jumper wire fil volant; fil jarretière

jump grading discrimination; ~ **instruction** instruction de branchement; ~ **to last cursor position** saut dernière position curseur; ~ **to next column** saut de colonne forcé; ~ **to start address** branchement adresse démarrage

junction *n* jonction; connexion; couple; dérivation; interface; jonc; ligne auxiliaire; raccordement; ~ **(of transistor)** couche; ~ **(data transmission)** croisement; ~ **barrier** barrière de potentiel; ~ **box** boîte de raccordement; boîte de branchement; boîte d'éclatement; boîte de dérivation; boîte de distribution; boîte de jonction; rosace; ~ **capacitance** capacité de jonction; capacité de transition

junction-case thermal resistance ($R_{th(j-c)}$) résistance thermique jonction-boîtier

junction frequency fréquence maximale utilisable; ~ **group** faisceau de jonctions communes; ~ **scanner (JSC)** explorateur de jonction (EXJ); ~ **temperature** température de jonction; ~ **traffic** trafic suburbain; ~ **transistor** transistor à jonction; ~ **wire** conducteur de jonction; conducteur de raccordement

junctor *n* joncteur; maille; circuit de connexion

jury aerial antenne provisoire; antenne de secours; antenne de fortune

just-discernible signal signal perceptible minimal

justifiable digit time slot intervalle de temps pour élément numérique justifiable

justification *n* bourrage d'impulsions; cadrage; ~ **ratio** taux de justification

justified text texte justifié

justifying digit élément numérique de justification

just noticeable peu apparent

just-noticeable difference (j.n.d.) différence juste perceptible

just-perceptible noise parasites à peine perceptibles

K

Karnaugh map table de Karnaugh
K-band power source source d'énergie en bande K
keep-alive electrode anode d'entretien; électrode d'entretien; électrode pilote; anode d'excitation
keeper n armature; arrêtoir; gestionnaire; maître
keeping n mémorisation temporaire
keep up-to-date mettre au courant
Kelvin bridge pont Kelvin; ~ effect effet de peau; effet pelliculaire
Kelvin-Varley slide diviseur de tension
kenetron n kénétron
Kennelly-Heaviside layer couche E
kernel n noyau; cœur
kerosene n pétrole (lampant)
Kerr effect effet électro-optique
key v émettre; dactylographier; frapper; moduler; pianoter; numéroter; ~ n clé; touche; adhérence; bouton; conjoncteur; critère; indicatif (IF); interprétation; légende; maître; repère; signification; clef; ~ (pushbutton) telephone set poste téléphonique à clavier
keyboard n clavier; ~ code code clavier; code interne; ~ perforator clavier perforateur; perforateur à clavier; ~ sender-receiver (KSR) clavier émetteur-récepteur; ~ switch interrupteur fugitif; ~ transmitter émetteur à clavier
key cap pavé; ~ click bruitage; claquement (de manipulation)
keyed automatic gain control commande automatique de gain par impulsions; ~ clamping circuit circuit de calage manipulé; ~ continuous wave onde continue manipulée; ~ CW jamming perturbation par onde continue manipulée; ~ random access accès aléatoire par clé; ~ sequential access accès séquentiel par clé
keyer n émetteur; générateur d'impulsions de radar; ~ adaptor démodulateur fac-similé
key field n massif des clés; zone indicatif
keying n manipulation; modulation; numérotation; calage; ~ chirps signaux instables; ~ circuit circuit de manipulation; ~ error erreur de manipulation; ~ error rate taux d'erreur d'une manipulation; ~ filter filtre de manipulation; filtre de cliquetis; filtre

télégraphique; ~ in composition; ~ pulse intervalle de manipulation; ~ signal signal commutateur; signal déclencheur; ~ speed vitesse de manipulation; ~ unit appareil de manipulation
keyless ringing appel automatique
key letter in context (KLIC) permulettre
keylock switch commutateur de verrouillage
key-out v composer au clavier; numéroter
keypad n clavier; bloc de touches; tablette graphique; émetteur d'impulsions; ~ telephone set poste à clavier
key pulsing envoi des signaux au clavier; télésélection de nombres téléphoniques avec un clavier
keypunch n perforateur à clavier
keypunching n dactylocodage
key selection télésélection de nombres téléphoniques avec un clavier
keysender n clavier d'appel; clé-pilote; émetteur clavier; émetteur d'impulsions
keysending n envoi des signaux au clavier; émission au clavier; télésélection de nombres téléphoniques avec un clavier
keyset n clavier
key sort tri par dichotomie
keystone distortion distorsion en trapèze; distorsion trapézoïdale
key-stroke n frappe; pression de touche; tabulation
key switchboard tableau commutateur à clés
keytape n appareil d'enregistrement direct; clavier-bande
key telephone system (KTS) poste d'intercommunication; système téléphonique à poussoirs
key-tone selection numérotation au clavier multifréquences
keyway n rainure
keyword n mot clé; abréviation mnémotechnique
kHz (s. kilohertz)
kicksorter analyseur multicanaux; ~ analyser discriminateur
kill v désactiver; effacer
killer, (echo) ~ suppresseur d'écho
kilohertz (kHz) kilohertz (kHz)
kiloline n kiloligne (KL)
kilometric wave (LF band) onde kilométrique
kilovolt n kilovolt

kilovolt-ampere kilovoltampère
kilowatt *n* kilowatt
kilowatt-hour kilowattheure
kinematic viscosity viscosité cinématique
kinescope *n* tube cathodique à image; tube cinéscope
kinetic energy énergie cinétique
kink *v* tortiller; ~ *n* cloque; ondulation
kinked *adj* tordu
kiosk *n* cabine
Kipp relay bascule monostable
kiss-of-life insufflation pulmonaire
kit *n* lot; boîte; ensemble; jeu; maquette
klaxon *n* alarme sonore
KLIC (s. key letter in context)
kludge *n* raccord; rustine
klystron *n* klystron; ~ **power amplifier** amplificateur de puissance à klystron; ~ **reflector** réflecteur de klystron; ~ **repeller** réflecteur de klystron; ~ **tube** klystron
kneck *n* épaulement
knee *n* coude
knife *n* couteau
knife(-blade) fuse fusible à couteau
knife-blade *n* lame
knife edge *n* arête en lame de couteau;

couteau (d'une balance); ~ **switch** commutateur à couteaux; interrupteur à couteau
knife-switch tag board réglette à couteau
knob *n* bouton; flèche; poignée
knock-off *n* (of armature) blocage
knock-on effect effet d'entraînement; répercussion; ~ **electron** électron de recul
knock-out (of plastic/metal housing) pastille prédéfoncée; ~ **pin** (of injection moulding) éjecteur
know-how *n* savoir-faire
known error faute propre
known-good board carte étalon
knurled screw vis à tête moletée; ~ **thumbscrew** bouton moleté
knurling tool porte-molette
Kooman's aerial antenne colinéaire; ~ **array** antenne en arête de poisson; antenne en sapin; rideau multiple de doublets
kraft *n* (paper) papier kraft
K-rating coefficient de distorsion harmonique
KSR (s. keyboard sender-receiver)
KTS (s. key telephone system)
Kynar [T.N.] polyfluorure de vinylidène (PVF2)

L

LA (s. local area)

label *v* désigner; ~ *n* étiquette; habillage; libellé; marque; nom; pastille; plaque; référence nominative; repère; rubrique

label-holder *n* porte-étiquette (PE)

labelled *adj* prémarqué

labelling *n* étiquetage

label record article-label

labile oscillator oscillateur à télécommande

laboratory *n* salle blanche; ~ ambient temperature ambiance du laboratoire; ~ dish cuvette labo; ~ technician agent technique; ~ test essai inopérant; essai en laboratoire; essai statique

labour *n* main d'œuvre; ~ catchment bassin d'emploi

labourer *n* ouvrier non spécialisé

lacing *n* grille

lacquer *n* vernis épargne (VE)

ladder *adj* itératif; ~ network réseau en échelle

ladle *n* louche

L-aerial antenne en L

lag *n* décalage en arrière; écart de temps; retard; traînée; ~ angle angle de décalage en arrière

lagging *n* calorifugeage; ~ *adj* déphasé en arrière; différé; ~ current courant déphasé en arrière; ~ distortion distorsion de retard; ~ load charge inductive

lag/lead *n* déphasage

LAMA (local automatic message accounting) comptabilité automatique locale des appels (CALA)

Lambert's law (surface illumination) loi de Lambert

laminar navigation and anti-collision system (LANAC) système de radar LANAC

laminate *n* stratifié

laminated *adj* pelliculé; ~ aerial antenne en pelure d'orange; ~ base board plaque stratifiée; ~ (magnetic) circuit circuit feuilleté; ~ core noyau feuilleté

lamination(s) *n pl* empilage; emboutissage

lamp cap cabochon; ~ field bandeau lumineux; panneau de lampes; rampe lumineuse; signalisation; tableau indicateur optique

lamp-holder *n* douille de lampe

lamp housing corps de voyant; ~ oil pétrole (lampant); ~ panel afficheur; bandeau lumineux; ~ test essai lampe

LAN (s. local area network)

LANAC (s. laminar navigation and anti-collision system)

land *n* bourrelet; dépôt conducteur; impression conductrice; pastille; îlot; ~ gap (of PCB) épargne

landing beacon radiophare d'atterrissage

land line liaison terrestre; ligne terrestre; ~ pattern (PCB track layout) modèle de circuit imprimé

lands *n pl* recouvrement; ~ (of micrometer) entre-touches

landscape printing impression à l'italienne

land-station charge(s) taxe terrestre

lane *n* couloir; phase; zone

language digit chiffre de langue

lanyard *n* tirette de largage

lanyard-release plug prise largable

lap *v* guiper; rôder; ~ *n* spire jointive; spire morte; faux tour

lapel microphone microphone de boutonnière

lap joint soudure par recouvrement

Laplace transform transformation de Laplace

lapped wire fil guipé

lap winding guipage

LAR (s. low-altitude bombing radar)

large-aperture aerial antenne à grande ouverture

large-scale integrated circuit circuit intégré à grande échelle; ~ integration (LSI) intégration à forte densité; intégration à grande échelle; technologie à haute intégration

Larsen effect (s. acoustic feedback)

LASCR (s. light-activated silicon-controlled rectifier)

laser beam scanning balayage à faisceau laser; ~ communications transmission par laser; ~ diode diode laser; ~ printer imprimante à laser

lash *v* ficeler

lashing *n* ligature; lien

last-choice *adj* de dernier choix; ~ circuit group faisceau de dernier choix; ~ route voie de dernier choix; faisceau de dernier choix

last-digits file fichier numéro d'annuaire

last-in/first-out (LIFO) *n* mémoire à liste inversée; mémoire à liste refoulée

last-number redial mémorisation du dernier numéro; bis (fonction -); appel enregistré

last number repetition button touche de relance du dernier numéro composé; ~ **party release** libération par le dernier abonné (à raccrocher); ~ **radio contact** dernier contact par radio; ~ **stored number redial** mémorisation du dernier numéro

last-stored state état sauvegardé

last subscriber release libération par le dernier abonné (à raccrocher)

latch v coller; bloquer; basculer; ~ n bascule de retenue; mémoire unitaire; mot mémoire; multivibrateur bistable; registre de retenue; cliquet; crochet; fermeture; levier; loquet; ~ (of connector) accrocheur; ~ (one-bit storage device) point-mémoire

latched adj verrouillé

latching n accrochage; blocage; collage; maintien; verrouillage; ~ adj sans rappel; sans retour; ~ (of relay contact) maintien au collage; ~ **current** courant d'accrochage; ~ **current** (of relay) courant de rémanence; ~ **mechanism** sauterelle; ~ **pushbutton** poussoir à enclenchement; ~ **relay** relais à accrochage; relais à adhérence; relais à blocage; relais à enclenchement; relais à mémoire; relais d'accouplement; relais de verrouillage

latch-up n remontée à vide; ~ (phenomenon) (of op. amp.) verrouillage haut

latency (time) temps d'attente; ~ **code** code à accès mimimum

latent image image latente

lateral axis axe de l'ordonnée; ~ **deviation error** erreur de déviation latérale; ~ **parity bit** bit de contrôle transversal; ~ **shift** angle de déviation; ~ **thinking** détour productif

lath n tasseau

lattice n grille; maille; pont; réseau; réticule; treillis; ~ **coil** bobine en nid d'abeille; ~ **filter** filtre en treillis; ~ **network** réseau en treillis; connexion de pont; montage en pont; réseau maillé; ~ **parameter** maille du réseau

launch n lancement; ~ (of light signal) injection; ~ **conditions** conditions d'injection; ~ **date** date de mise en service; ~ **loss** perte à l'injection; ~ **peak** pic d'entrée; ~ **service** service de lancement

lay n orientation; pose; sens; ~ adj non adapté; non qualifié; non spécialisé

layer n couche; enduit

lay of binder pas de filin

layout n implantation; agencement; aménagement; arrangement; circuit; cliché; configuration; découpage; dispositif; disposi-

tion; mise en page; pistage; plan; présentation; réseau; schéma; tracé (de carte); ~ adj découpe fonctionnelle; ~ **character** caractère de mise en page; ~ **sheet** gamme

lay ratio pas de toronnage

lay-up n pas de torsade; composition du conducteur; confection; pas de toronnage

lay user non informaticien; profane

"Lazy Susan" (component mounting stand) plateau rotatif

LB (s. local battery system)

L-band phase array réseau d'antennes phasé pour bande L

LBO (s. line build-out network)

lc (s. lower case)

LC (s. tuned circuit)

LCD (s. liquid crystal display); ~ **driver** circuit d'attaque de cristaux liquides

LCL (s. longitudinal conversion loss)

LC network (inductance-capacitance) cellule LC

LDA (s. local data adaptor)

LDN (s. long-distance network)

LE (s. local exchange)

lead n fil volant; amenée; artère; câble; avance; conducteur; connexion; cordon de liaison; ligne; passage; sortie; toron; décalage en avant; écart; pas (de filetage); pas (de vis); pas (d'hélice); branche; queue; patte; picot

lead-acid battery batterie à plomb

lead angle angle de décalage en avant; ~ **contractor** maître d'oeuvre

lead-covered cable câble nu

leader n (of tape) début; amorce; ~ **cable** câble de radioguidage; ~ **dot** point de conduite

lead feed changement de ligne

lead-forming tool outil de clipsage

lead-in n avant-trou; accès; arrivée; chanfrein; entrée d'antenne; entrée de poste

leading adj déphasé en avant; de poids fort; gauche; ~ **blanks** espaces vierges de gauche; ~ **current** courant vagabond; courant déphasé en avant; ~ **distortion** distorsion en avance; ~ **edge** n or adj front avant; bord d'attaque; de pointe; ~ **load** charge capacitive

lead-out n brochage; départ; dépassement; sortie

lead pitch écartement; ~ **screw** vis sans fin

lead-sheathed cable câble sous plomb

lead temperature échauffement des broches

lead-through wire fil de gué

lead time délai de livraison; délai d'attente; délai de montage; délai de satisfaction (de la demande); mise en service

lead-to-lead distance entr'axe des pattes

lead wire descente
leaflet n notice
leaf spring lame ressort
leak n fuite; dérive; déperdition; onde résiduelle
leakage n fuite; décharge; déperdition; dispersion; isolement; perditance; perte; ~ coefficient coefficient de dispersion; ~ current courant de fuite; courant dérivé; ~ factor coefficient de dispersion; ~ field champ de dispersion; champ de fuite; ~ indicator (earth fault detector) détecteur d'isolement terre; ~ inductance inductance de fuite; inductance de dispersion; ~ resistance résistance de fuite; résistance à l'isolement
leakance n perditance
leak-proof welded joint soudure étanche
leaky bucket panier percé
leap n bond; saut; ~ forward essor
leapfrog test test saute-mouton; test sélectif
learning n assimilation
leased adj loué; privé; spécialisé; ~ circuit circuit loué; ~ circuits service service de location de circuits; ~ common carrier ligne louée; ~ line liaison spécialisée; ligne à quatre fils; ligne louée; ligne spéciale; circuit permanent; ~ transponder répéteur loué
leasing agreement contrat de location
least-busy method équirépartition de charge
least-cost network design conception de réseau au moindre coût; ~ routing acheminement avec débordement; acheminement de secours; acheminement détourné; acheminement sur voie de débordement; acheminement sur voie secondaire; ~ routing station poste de débordement
least-significant adj faible; de droite
least significant bit (LSB) bit de poids faible; chiffre de poids faible
lecture call service de communication conférence unilatérale
LED (s. light-emitting diode); ∴ display affichage à diodes (électroluminescentes); afficheur
ledge n tasseau de surélévation; trottoir
left arrow flèche horizontale gauche
left-hand circular polarization polarisation circulaire gauche; ~ counter cutter contre-couteau gauche; ~ polarized wave onde polarisée elliptiquement/(circulairement sinistrorsum)
left-justified adj cadré à gauche
leftmost adj de poids fort; gauche
left-truncated adj troncature à gauche
leg n branche; contrefort; dérivation; phase
legacy n patrimoine

legend n inscription; interprétation; légende; signification; bâton
legibility n lisibilité
length n (of data block) longueur; ~ (in bytes) nombre d'octets; ~ (of storage area/element) taille (de zone/secteur); ~ of lay pas de câblage; ~ of oblique exposure longueur d'une section de rapprochement oblique; ~ of parallelism longueur de parallélisme; ~ of time on waiting list ancienneté de la demande; ~ of travel course acquittée
lengthwise adj longitudinal; ~ member longrine
lens n lentille; cabochon; ~ aerial antenne lentille
Lenz's law (direction of current) loi de Lenz
lesser adj inférieur
less-relay starter discontacteur sans relais
less than full complement incomplet
let-down approach système standard d'approche à radiophare
lettergram n lettergramme
lettering n écriture
letter-out v effacer
letter quality (LQ) qualité courrier; qualité correspondance
letters blank blanc de lettres
letters-case série lettres
letters-shift signal signal d'inversion lettres
level n niveau; banc de broches; cascade (dans une arborescence); échelon; élément; étage; moment (MOM); palier; ~ (of tape) canal; ~ (of signalling code) couche; ~ (of data) hiérarchie; ~ adj plan; ~ adjustment ajustage de niveau; ~ bar ruban de niveau; ~ breakdown perte de niveau; ~ characteristic caractéristique de niveau; ~ compensator compensateur de niveau; ~ contact contact de décade; ~ control contrôle du niveau; ~ converter translateur de niveau
level-dependent phase phase dépendant du niveau
level diagram hypsogramme; diagramme des niveaux; ~ difference différence de niveau; ~ distortion distorsion de niveau; ~ equalization égalisation du niveau; ~ equalizer égalisateur de niveau
level/gain measurement circuit montage de mesure hypso-kerdo
level generator voltmètre sélectif; ~ hunting sélection libre à plusieurs niveaux; ~ instability instabilité du niveau
levelled off affleuré
levelling n nivelage; ~ time temps de pointage
level measuring set hypsomètre; appareil de mesure de niveau; voltmètre sélectif; ~ monitoring contrôle de niveau; ~ of drive charge de cristal; ~ overflow motion

L

rotation jusqu'au bout de course; ~ **record-er** hypsographe; enregistreur de niveau; ~ **recorder chart** graphique enregistré

levels n pl décuples (déc.)

level shift variation de niveau

level-triggering n déclenchement sur front

level-two busy tone tonalité d'occupation interdictive

level variation variation de niveau

lever n levier; commande (cde); manche; manette

lever-action DIL switch bouton à levier

lever key clé à levier; ~ **press** outil de sertissage; ~ **roller** (of microswitch) levier à galet; ~ **switch** commutateur à levier

levy v prélever; comptabiliser; imputer; ~ n imputation

levying charges taxant

LF (s. line feed); ≏ (s. low frequency)

L.H. (lefthand) **slide/runner** glissière gauche

liable susceptible; ~ **to change** évolutif; ~ **to impair operation** nuisant au bon fonctionnement

librarian n bibliothécaire

library n mémorisation de phrase; ~ **program** programme de bibliothèque; ~ **(sub-)routine** sous-programme de bibliothèque; ~ **tape** bande bibliothèque

licence n agrément; homologation; permis; redevance annuelle; ~ **plate** plaque d'agrément; ~ **transfer** cession de licence

license v homologuer

licensed adj agréé; ~ **components** composants sous licence

licensee n licencié; cessionnaire du transfert

licensing n cession de licence

lid n couvercle

LIDAR (s. light-detection and ranging)

life n robustesse; durée; endurance; ~ **expectancy** durée de vie; ~ **span** durée de vie; ~ **test** vieillissement

LIFO (s. last-in/first-out); ≏ **stack** (pushdown stack) LIFO (pile refoulée)

lift handset décrocher

lifting tackle appareil de levage; étrier

light n balise; jour; lumière; ~ **(up)** allumer

light-activated silicon-controlled rectifier (LASCR) photothyristor

light beam aigrette; rayon optique; ~ **box** planchette lumineuse; table à lumière; table de données; table éclairante; ~ **cell** cellule photoconductive/-trice

light-detection and ranging (LIDAR) système LIDAR

light detector photodétecteur; photorécepteur; récepteur de lumière; récepteur optique

light-duty adj série légère; ~ **lock nut** écrou

Pal

light emitter (laser source) émetteur de lumière

light-emitting cell cellule photoémettrice; ~ **diode (LED)** diode électroluminescente (DEL); afficheur électroluminescent

light entertainment divertissements

light-fastness adj résistance à la lumière; solidité à la lumière

light fixtures luminaire

lighthouse tube tube phare

lighting and power plant installations d'éclairage et de force motrice; ~ **circuit** réseau d'éclairage

light load charge partielle; ~ **loss** perte de lumière

lightly dipped humecté

light modulator modulateur de lumière

lightning n foudre; ~ **arrester** parafoudre; paratonnerre; ~ **conductor** paratonnerre; terre parafoudre; ~ **protection** protection contre la foudre; ~ **rod** parafoudre

light pen crayon lumineux; photostyle; ~ **pulse** impulsion lumineuse; ~ **ray** rayon optique; ~ **reader** lecteur optique

light-reflecting surface miroir

light-sensitive adj photosensible

light sensor photostyle; ~ **source** émetteur optique; ~ **traffic period** période de faible trafic

light-wave communications communications optiques; optronique; photonique

lightweight adj léger; ~ **headphones** microcasque

limb n membre

limbo position (column 81 of data line) position fantôme

limit n seuil

limited access porte fermée

limited-access satellite satellite à accès limité

limited availability accès imparfait; accessibilité partielle; accessibilité restreinte; réduction d'accessibilité; ~ **demand** faible besoin; ~ **extent** laconisme; ~ **production run** petite série

limiter n limitateur; écrêteur; ~ **attack time** temps de transition d'un limiteur; ~ **diode** diode limitatrice

limit frequency fréquence limite; ~ **gauge** (GO/NO-GO) pige

limiting coil bobine de limitation; ~ **condition** contrainte; ~ **conditions of use** (absolute maximum ratings) caractéristiques de gabarit; applications des valeurs limites; ~ **device** limiteur; ~ **frequency** fréquence limite; ~ **value** butée

limit of interference valeur limite d'une perturbation

limits *n* fourchette

limit switch fin de course (FC); disjoncteur de sécurité; ~ test essai aux limites (E/L); ~ values for electrical parameters (of subscriber line) gabarit de ligne d'abonné

line *n* ligne; circuit; fil; file; secteur; tension de secteur; tracé; ~ (control) procedure procédure de ligne; ~ (side) amont (en -); ~ (of graphics image) filet; ~ (of radiation in KeV) raie; ~ access point point d'accès à une ligne; ~ adaptor unit adaptateur de ligne; ~ amplifier amplificateur de ligne

linear active network réseau actif linéaire; ~ amplifier amplificateur linéaire; ~ atmosphere atmosphère linéaire; ~ compensating circuit circuit linéariseur; ~ correction compensation linéaire; ~ detection détection à réponse linéaire; ~ detector détecteur linéaire; ~ distortion distorsion linéaire; ~ filament lamp ampoule à filament rectiligne; ~ file fichier direct; ~ gain amplification linéaire; ~ gain distortion défaut de linéarité de gain; ~ integrated circuit circuit intégré linéaire; circuit analogique

linearity control dispositif de réglage de la linéarité; ~ correction ajustage de la linéarité; ~ error erreur de linéarité; précision relative

linearizer linéariseur; circuit compensateur

linear list liste linéaire

linear/logarithmic (tracking of potentiometer) loi de variation A/B

linearly-dispersive delay line filtre dispersif linéaire

linear motion mouvement dirigé; ~ phase distortion distorsion linéaire de phase; ~ polarization polarisation rectiligne; ~ potentiometer potentiomètre rectiligne; ~ programming programmation linéaire; ~ propagation propagation rectiligne; ~ regression analysis analyse par régression linéaire; ~ regulation régulation linéaire; ~ resistor résistance ohmique; résistance linéaire; résistance en continu; ~ section partie linéaire; ~ tracking variation linéaire; ~ transducer transducteur linéaire

line attenuation affaiblissement de ligne; ~ balance équilibreur; ~ bend (correction) signal de correction parabolique de ligne; ~ bit rate débit en ligne

line-blanking interval intervalle de suppression de ligne

line break coupure de ligne; rupture de ligne; ~ broadcasting télédiffusion par fil; ~ build-out network (LBO) complément de longueur

line-by-line scanning analyse ligne par ligne

line category discrimination d'abonné; ~ circuit circuit de ligne; équipement d'abonné; équipement de ligne; joncteur

line-circuit pack carte d'équipement de ligne

line coding codage en ligne; ~ communication communication par fil; ~ concentrator concentrateur; sous-répartiteur automatique (SRA); ~ (contact) bank banc de contacts de lignes; ~ control block bloc de gestion de lignes; ~ creation création; ~ current courant en ligne

line-driven *adj* mode ligne

line driver amplificateur de ligne; boîtier d'adaptation réseau (BAR); émetteur de ligne; transmetteur de ligne; ~ envelope gabarit de ligne; ~ equalization égalisation de ligne; ~ equalizer correcteur de ligne; égaliseur automatique; filtre correcteur; ~ equipment status memory mémoire de discrimination d'abonnés; mémoire d'état d'équipement; ~ fault analyser (of time-domain reflectometry)) contrôleur de circuit; ~ feed (LF) avance de ligne; changement de ligne; saut de ligne; à la ligne suivant; ~ filter filtre anti-parasites; ~ finder chercheur de lignes; identificateur de jonction; ~ finder with allotter chercheur distributeur

line-finding recherche de ligne appelante

line-free circuit circuit de déblocage

line frequency fréquence de balayage horizontal; fréquence de ligne; fréquence (de) secteur; ~ graph graphe courbe; ~ group groupement de lignes; lignes groupées

line-hunting group faisceau de lignes groupées

line impedance équilibreur; impédance de ligne; ~ inductance self de ligne; ~ insulation tenue aux fuites de ligne; ~ intensity intensité des raies; ~ interface interface de ligne

line-jump scanning balayage entrelacé

line lamp lampe d'appel; ~ load charge d'une ligne; pourcentage d'utilisation

line/local connexion/fin

line lockout mise en faux-appel; ~ lock-out renvoi en faux appel; ~ loop boucle; ligne de renvoi; ~ loss perte en ligne; ~ manager cadre professionnel

lineman's climber griffe de monteur

line monitor moniteur de ligne; ~ noise bruit de ligne; ~ non-linearity distorsion de balayage horizontal; ~ occupancy occupation des lignes

line-of-sight *adj* à portée optique; à visibilité directe; ~ radio link faisceau hertzien à visibilité directe; ~ repeater relais à portée optique; ~ transmission transmission en

L

vue directe

line on hold ligne en attente; ligne en garde; ~ **oscillator** oscillateur taux d'erreur(s); ~ **out-of-service** abonnement suspendu; ~ **out-of-service signal** signal de ligne hors service; ~ **preference** présélection; ~ **printer** imprimante; imprimante par ligne; ~ **processing unit** unité d'adaptation des lignes

liner *n* intercalaire; chemise

line receiver récepteur de ligne; ~ **reference parameter** gabarit de ligne; ~ **regulating section** section de régulation de ligne; ~ **regulation** régulation amont; régulation en entrée/d'entrée; ~ **regulator** régulateur de tension; ~ **relay** relais d'appel; relais d'annonciateur; relais de ligne; ~ **repeater** répéteur de ligne; ~ **repeating coil** transformateur de ligne; ~ **residual equalizer** compensateur d'affaiblissement

lines busy occupation des lignes

line-scan generator générateur de signaux de balayage ligne

line scanner explorateur de lignes; ~ **scan start** instant de départ de la dent de scie; ~ **section** section de ligne; ~ **seizure pulse** impulsion de prise (de la ligne); ~ **selector** connecteur final; ~ **set** coupleur acoustique

line-shortening facility repliement de lignes

line-side *adj* en provenance des circuits amonts

line signal (supervisory signal) signal de ligne; ~ **signal code** code de signaux de ligne; ~ **signalling controller** unité d'extraction de la signalisation de ligne; ~ **(signal power density) spectrum** spectre d'énergie (émis en ligne); ~ **simulator** ligne artificielle; complément de ligne

lines installed parc

line slip glissement (défilement) horizontal de l'image; ~ **spacing** interligne; ~ **speed** vitesse en ligne

lines per inch (LPI) lignes par pouce (LPP)

line split tester contrôleur coupure de ligne

line-stabilized oscillator drive pilote à ligne résonnante

line sweep balayage horizontal; balayage de ligne; ~ **switch** interrupteur de ligne; ~ **switchboard** bâti de présélecteurs; ~ **switching** commutation de lignes; commutation de circuits; ~ **switching unit (LSU)** élément de sélection de ligne (ESL); ~ **synchronization pulse** top de ligne; ~ **synchronizing signal** signal de synchronisation ligne; ~ **temporarily out of service** ligne suspendue; ~ **terminal** terminal de ligne; ~ **terminating network** réseau de

connexion (CX/RCX); ~ **test board** panneau d'essai des lignes; ~ **test curve** gabarit d'essai de ligne

line-to-neutral neutre sorti

line transfer renvoi de lignes; mutation; ~ **transformer** translateur; ~ **transient response** réponse impulsionnelle à un échelon de tension d'entrée; ~ **unit** coffret de manœuvre; coffret de commande; ~ **unit with magnetic biasing** équipement de ligne à pot compensé; ~ **up** *v* régler

line-up *n* alignement; réglage; égalisation; ~ **period** période de réglage; ~ **record** feuille de référence

line-usage factor facteur d'utilisation de lignes

line visibility visibilité des lignes; visibilité de la trame; ~ **voltage** tension du secteur; tension de ligne; tension composée; ~ **winding** enroulement primaire; ~ **wire** fil de ligne; fil secteur; ~ **with directory number assigned** ligne désignable; ~ **withdrawal** retrait de lignes; ~ **with isolating transformer** ligne translatée

lining *n* garniture; revêtement

link *v* relier; assembler; chaîner; connecter; mailler; raccorder; ~ *n* liaison; adresse de chaînage; arête; artère; barrette; bielle; biellette; broche; canal; chaînon; circuit de conversation; connexion; faisceau; lien; maillon; pont; relation; section de ligne; tronçon; tube; cavalier; ~ (of satellite) trajet; ~ **address** adresse de retour; pointeur

linkage *n* enchaînement; chaînage; couplage; liaison; raccordement (racct.); ~ **data** état d'avancement; articulation aval; ~ **editor** éditeur de liens (EL); chaîne de production de logiciel

link/bridge circuit pont local

link budget bilan de liaison

link-by-link connections exploitation tandem; ~ **selection/pathfinding** sélection pas à pas (étage par étage); ~ **signalling** signalisation section par section; ~ **signalling call** appel tandem

link circuit circuit de connexion; circuit de liaison; pont de conversation; ~ **connection terminal** terminal de prise de liaison; ~ **control** fin de contrôle de ligne; ~ **control procedure** procédure de liaison; procédure de transmission

linked *adj* articulé; engagé; ~ **exchanges** bureaux connectés; ~ **field** champ couplé

link editor éditeur de liens (EL)

linked-list data structure structure de données liées

linked numbering scheme/plan plan de numérotage coordonné; ~ **subroutine** sous-programme fermé

linking *n* maillage; chaînage; enchaînement; ~ **dots** points de conduite; ~ **module** module d'enchaînement; ~ **statement** connecteur

link isolation blocage de liaison; ~ **library** bibliothèque de liaison; ~ **line extension** circuit de prolongement; ~ **list** anneau

link-loader *n* chargeur éditeur de liens

link loading édition des liens (EL); ~ **matrix** matrice de brassage

link-pack area (LPA) zone de couplage

link pointer pointeur de chaînage; ~ **program** accesseur; ~ **protocol** procédure de liaison; procédure de ligne; ~ **seizure** prise de liaison; ~ **sequencer** automate

link-sharing *n* partage de maille

link signalling communication en chaîne; ~ **status memory** mémoire de maille; ~ **status signal unit** trame sémaphore d'état canal; ~ **strap** jarretière; ~ **transmitter** émetteur relais; émetteur relayeur; ~ **unit** conveyor convoyeur élément de liaison

lint-free cloth chiffon non pelucheux

lip angle angle de coupe; ~ **ring** anneau de garde

liquid assets marge brute d'autofinancement; ~ **core fibre** fibre optique à cœur liquide; ~ **crystal display (LCD)** afficheur à cristaux liquides; ~ **epitaxy** épitaxie liquide

list *n* liste; barème; état; index

list(ing) chain chaîne de listes

listed *adj* répertorié; ~ **directory number** numéro principal

listen *v* écouter

listener *n* instrument écouteur; auditeur

listen-in mettre en écoute

listening-in relay relais d'écoute; ~ **tone** tonalité de présence

listening jack jack d'écoute; ~ **key** clé d'écoute; ~ **position** position d'écoute; ~ **tone** bruit d'écoute; ~ **zone** zone d'écoute; zone auditeur

list heading bannière

listing *n* listage; inscription; listing; homologation

literal *n* littéral; libellé; ~ **constant** constante littérale; ~ **pool** pool des libellés

literature *n* documentation

lithium cell pile au lithium

lithography *n* gravure

litmus paper papier de tournesol; papier réactif

little used peu répandu

live *adj* sous tension; à chaud; actif; ~ **(of broadcast)** en direct; ~ **broadcast** radiodiffusion directe; ~ **lock-out circuit** circuit de

faute d'abonné (parking); ~ **part** pièce sous tension; point chaud; ~ **pictures** images animées en temps réel; ~ **recording** enregistrement direct

livery *n* coloris; couleurs

live TV transmission émission de télévision en direct

liveware *n* ressources humaines; effectif; personnel

live wire conducteur de phase; fil sensible; fil sous tension

living expenses frais de séjour; ~ **language** langue naturelle

LL (s. long-life memory)

LNA (s. low-noise amplifier)

L-network circuit en L

LO (s. local oscillator)

load *v* charger; afficher; alimenter; armer; consigner; garnir; rapatrier; transférer; ~ *n* charge; chargement; consigne; courant de sortie; régime; transfert; utilisation; ~ *adj* exécutable; ~ **(carrying) capacity** capacité de charge; ~ **(of disk, tape)** monter

load-and-go chargement et exécution

load and traffic data mesures de charge; ~ **box** pondeuse; ~ **circuit** circuit de charge; courant de sortie; impédance de charge; ~ **coil** bobine de charge; ~ **counter** compteur de charge; ~ **current** courant de charge; courant de blocage; ~ **diagram** diagramme de charge; ~ **direction** sens d'utilisation

loaded *adj* chargé; pupinisée; ~ **aerial** antenne chargée; ~ **cable** câble pupinisé; câble chargé; ~ **impedance** impédance en charge normale; ~ **line** ligne pupinisée

loader *n* chargeur

load factor capacité de charge; caractéristique en charge; coefficient de sécurité; coefficient de surcharge; facteur d'utilisation; ~ **impedance** impédance de charge; résistance ballast; résistance de charge; ~ **impedance diagram** diagramme d'impédance de charge

loading *n* chargement; affichage; approvisionnement; charge d'une ligne; entrée; occupation; préaffichage; rapatriement; ~ **(to known address)** pointage; ~ **address** adresse d'implantation; ~ **arm** bras de chargement; ~ **circuit** circuit de charge; ~ **coil** bobine pupin; bobine de charge; bobine de pupinisation

loading-coil section section de pupinisation

loading paper (in printer) approvisionnement en papier; ~ **program** chargeur; ~ **rate** vitesse de régénération; ~ **routine** programme chargeur

load into memory graver en mémoire; ~ **inverter** inverseur à charge

load-limiting resistor résistance chutrice

load line droit de charge

load-matching resistor résistance d'adaptation

load module module chargeable; module exécutable

load-module library bibliothèque image-mémoire

load point adresse; capacité de charge; ~ **pull-down** charge interne de tirage; ~ **regulation** régulation aval; régulation en charge; ~ **relief busbar** barre délestable; ~ **resistor** résistance de terminaison

load-sharing partage de charge; partage de trafic

load-shedding n délestage; régulation de charge; ~ **busbar** barre délestable

load shift désencombrement; ~ **side** aval (en)

load-splitting n fractionnement de la charge

load test épreuve de charge; ~ **transient response** réponse impulsionnelle à un échelon de courant de sortie; ~ **variation** variation de charge

lobe n lobe; pétale; enveloppe

lobed adj hélicoïdal

lobe switching/swinging radiodécction à basculement de diagramme

local alarm rack herse; ~ **area (LA)** zone de numérotage; zone de rattachement; zone urbaine (ZU); zone locale (ZL); ~ **area call** appel de zone; appel urbain; ~ **area network (LAN)** réseau de communication d'entreprise (RCE); réseau local d'entreprise (RLE); réseau local d'établissement (RLE); ~ **automatic message accounting (LAMA)** comptabilité automatique locale des appels; enregistrement des justificatifs de taxe; ~ **automatic trunk testing device** hypsomètre urbain; ~ **battery (LB)** batterie locale (BL)

local-battery switchboard tableau commutateur à batterie locale; ~ **system (LB)** système téléphonique à batterie locale; ~ **telephone set** appareil téléphonique à batterie locale

local call appel local; appel intérieur; appel interne; conversation urbaine; ~ **carrier demodulation** réception avec restitution de la porteuse; ~ **carrier reception** réception avec porteuse locale; ~ **central office** bureau urbain; ~ **centre** centre local (CL); ~ **check** contrôle local; ~ **circuit** circuit local; ~ **clock** horloge locale; ~ **communication** trafic local; ~ **concentrator** concentrateur électronique d'abonnés locaux; ~ **connection** connexion locale; ~ **copy** visualisation locale; ~ **(polarity) correction**

correction de signes à la réception; ~ **data adaptor (LDA)** adaptateur de données local (ADL); ~ **demand-traffic circuit** ligne locale pour service immédiat; ~ **digital concentrator** concentrateur numérique local; ~ **digital satellite exchange** centre satellite numérique local; ~ **direct trunk access** prise directe urbaine; ~ **electronic subscriber connection unit** concentrateur électronique d'abonnés locaux; ~ **electronic subscriber line concentrator** concentrateur satellite électronique local; ~ **exchange (LE)** centre urbain; centre local (CL); autocommutateur de rattachement; bureau téléphonique local; central local; central urbain; ~ **exchange network** réseau téléphonique local; ~ **exchange with no multi-routing capability** centre satellite sans autonomie d'acheminement; ~ **extension circuit** ligne d'extension locale; ~ **fading** fading rapproché; ~ **group switch** commutateur de groupes locaux

localized adj ponctuel

localizer beacon émetteur de radioguidage à signaux équilibrés; radioalignement de piste

local jack jack local; ~ **junctor** jonncteur local; ~ **line** raccordement (racct.); ~ **loop** ligne d'abonné; ~ **loopback** bouclage local

locally-unrestricted extension poste à prise directe restreinte

local mode mode local; mode autonome; ~ **network** réseau local; réseau urbain; ~ **operator** opératrice de départ; opératrice locale; ~ **oscillation** oscillation hétérodyne; ~ **oscillator (LO)** oscillateur de battement; oscillateur local (OL); ~ **record line** ligne local d'enregistrement; ~ **satellite exchange** centre local satellite; ~ **security-call module** module de communication locale de sécurité; ~ **service area** zone de taxation locale; zone de taxation urbaine; ~ **subscriber** usager interne; ~ **subscriber connection unit** unité de raccordement local; ~ **subscriber exchange** autocommutateur d'abonnés

local/tandem switch unité mixte abonnés/transit

local television line ligne locale pour télévision; ~ **terminal exchange line** ligne locale de bureau rural; ~ **time base** (independent of exchange time base) base de temps mobile; ~ **traffic** trafic local; ~ **transfer line** ligne locale de renvoi; ~ **trunk circuit** ligne de jonction locale

locating n recherche; dépistage; détrompage; ~ **(to centre)** centrage; ~ **a transmitter** localisation d'un émetteur; ~ **hole** trou de régistration; ~ **key** détrompeur mâle; cimblot (simbleau); ~ **pattern** mire de géométrie; ~ **pin** pion de centrage; pion détrompeur; ~ **stud** téton de positionnement

location n adresse; implantation; logement; position; rang; emplacement; ~ **counter** compteur de positionnement; compteur ordinal; localisateur; registre d'adresse d'instruction; registre d'instruction; ~ **identifier** descripteur d'emplacement

locator n positionneur; repère

locked field champ protégé; ~ **loop** circuit de liaison entre opérateurs; circuit de ligne; circuit de suivi; circuit d'opératrice; ~ **oscillator** oscillateur bloqué

locked-out frequency divider diviseur de fréquence (d'un oscillateur synchronisé)

locked pulse jammer brouilleur intentionnel à impulsions retardées

lock-in n enclenchement; verrouillage; ~ **amplifier** amplificateur synchronisé

locking n asservissement; blocage; réglage de fréquence; verrouillage; ~ **adj** sans rappel; ~ **button** bouton à enclenchement; ~ **contact** contact d'automaintien; ~ **dial telephone** téléphone avec bloque-cadran; ~ **frequency** fréquence de verrouillage; ~ **key** clé à enclenchement; clavette; ~ **lever** accrocheur; ~ **pin** doigt de blocage; doigt de verrouillage; ~ **pliers** pince de blocage; pince étau; ~ **pulse** impulsion d'asservissement; ~ **relay** relais à accrochage; relais à adhérence; relais àmémoire; relais à point nul; relais de verrouillage; ~ **winding** (of relay) enroulement de maintien; ~ **wrench** pince de blocage

lock nut contre-écrou; écrou frein

lock-out v renvoyer; ~ n blocage; bloqueur; interdiction; perte de synchronisation; refus; renvoi en faute; verrouillage; ~ (of operator) exclusion; ~ (of line) neutralisation; ~ **relay** relais de mise en faute; relais de renvoi en faux-appel; ~ **switch** interrupteur de blocage

lock-over circuit bistable

lock washer rondelle de sécurité à crans

"Loctite" [T.N.] liquide frein

locus n lieu; site

lodge v (of order) passer (une commande)

log v enregistrer; consigner; étalonner; inscrire (sur); noter; stocker; ~ n cahier de suivi; diagraphie; état; historique; journal

logarithmic n (of potentiometer track) courbe logarithmique (loi de variation B); ~ **amplifier** amplificateur logarithmique; ~ **compression** loi de transformation

logarithmique; ~ **converter** convertisseur logarithmique; ~ **decrement** décrément logarithmique; ~ **quantizing law** loi de quantification logarithmique; ~ **reception** réception logarithmique

logatom articulation netteté pour les logatomes

log book cahier; ~ **file** fichier d'erreurs

logged-on adj connecté

logger n enregistreur automatique; inscripteur; marqueur

logging n enregistrement; acquisition de données; aiguillage; collecte de(s) données; consignation; diagraphie; émission; étalonnage; étalonnement; inscription; emmagasinage; ~ **device** enregistreur (enr.); ~ **load** charge inductive

logging-off n déconnexion

logging-on connexion

logging unit unité témoin; unité de marche

logic n calcul; ~ adj logique

logical-add opération OU

logical and procedural interface protocole; ~ **code number** numéro de compte; ~ **comparison** comparaison logique; ~ **connective** opérateur relationnel; opérateur logique; ~ **design** conception logique; ~ **error** erreur logique; ~ **machine** machine logique; ~ **operation** calcul; ~ **output number** numéro logique d'édition; ~ **product** multiplication logique; opération ET; ~ **record** enregistrement logique; article logique; ~ **sum** opération OU; addition; ~ **unit** unité symbolique

logic amplifier amplificateur logique; ~ **analyser** maquette d'essais; testeur; ~ **circuitry** la logique; ~ **diagram** ordinogramme; diagramme logique; ~ **driver** décodeur DCB décimal à collecteur ouvert; ~ **earth** masse logique; ~ **gate** porte logique; ~ **input** charge logique; ~ **line counter** compteur de lignes (de la logique); ~ **pin** broche logique; ~ **signal (input) isolation** découplage de signaux logiques; ~ **state** (0 or 1) variable logique binaire; ~ **swing** excursion d'amplitude; ~ **unit fault** faute de la logique (FLOG)

log-in n appel; accès; accueil; ~ **directory** répertoire d'accès; ~ **file** fichier d'inscription; ~ **point** point d'accès

log listing liste de messages

log-normal logarithmo-normal

logo(-type) sigle

log-off v clore; quitter; ~ n clôture; fermeture

log-on v appeler; ~ n appel; ~ (password) contrôle d'identité; ~ **form** grille d'accueil

log-out maintenir l'historique

log-periodic aerial antenne périodique à accord logarithmique

log-roll printing journalisation

lone electron électron célibataire; **~ signal unit (LSU)** unité de liaison solitaire; unité de signalisation solitaire

long break interruption longue; séparatif

long-delay echo écho retardé

long-distance backscatter rétrodiffusion indirecte; **~ cable** câble à grande distance; **~ call** appel longue-distance; **~ circuit** circuit interurbain; **~ communication** trafic interurbain; **~ connection** communication à grande portée; connexion à grande distance; connexion interurbaine; **~ dialling** appel interurbain; **~ loop** ligne d'abonné pour l'interurbain; **~ network (LDN)** réseau interurbain (RI); **~ traffic** trafic à grande distance; **~ xerography** téléxérographie

long format format long

long-format shift register ligne mémoire

long-haul adj à grande distance; **~ circuit** circuit à grande distance; **~ communications** communication à grande portée; **~ link** liaison à grande distance; artère à grande distance; **~ radio network** réseau radioélectrique pour communications à grande distance; **~ television circuit** ligne de télévision à grande distance; **~ trunk** circuit à grande distance

longitudinal check contrôle par bloc; **~ circuit** circuit unifilaire; **~ conversion loss (LCL)** affaiblissement de symétrie; **~ electromotive force** composante transversale d'une force électromotrice; **~ judder** broutage longitudinal

longitudinally non-uniform dielectric diélectrique non uniforme dans le sens longitudinal

longitudinal magnetization enregistrement magnétique longitudinal; **~ redundancy check (LRC)** contrôle longitudinal par blocs; contrôle de parité longitudinale

long-life memory (LL) mémoire longue durée

long line ligne longue

long-line adaptor adaptateur pour ligne longue

long load convoi exceptionnel

long-nose pliers pince télévision

long-path bearing azimut du grand arc

long-persistence CRT tube cathodique à persistance; **~ screen** écran à longue persistance

long pointed-tip shears ciseaux à becs longs pointus

long-range accuracy radar system (LORAC) système LORAC; **~ navigational system (LORAN)** système LORAN

long-reach probe (with spring-loaded hook) grip-test grand modèle; **~ test prod** pointe longue

long real key (eight-byte real number) clé réel long

long-shift register registre à décalage long

long-tailed pair montage différentiel; déphaseur à deux tubes

long-term adj longue durée; pluri-annuel

long-wave (LW) grandes ondes (GO); onde longue (OL); **~ transmitter** émetteur à ondes longues

long weekend pont

long-wire aerial antenne à long fil

look-ahead n anticipation; préalable; prédiction

look-up table table d'équivalence; table d'accusation; **~ terminal** terminal de consultation

loom n (of cables) peigne; faisceau; harnais

loop v boucler; **~** n boucle; bande; circuit fermé; circuit téléphonique à deux fils; cycle; itération; ligne; paire métallique; ventre

loop(ing) n bouclage

loop (circuit) circuit métallique; (directional) **~ aerial** cadre radiocompas; cadre radio-goniométrique; **~ aerial** antenne à cadre; antenne en boucle

loop-alignment error erreur de calage

loop-around circuit circuit bouclé

loop attenuation affaiblissement de boucle

loop-back n rebouclage; rappel; reprise; **~ link** cavalier de rebouclage; **~ test** test en rebouclage

loop body corps de boucle

loop-break rupture de boucle

loop-break button bouton de terre; bouton calibré; bouton de manœuvre; bouton de reprise

loop-break dialling numérotation par rupture de boucle; numérotation en boucle; numérotation par ouverture de boucle; **~ distortion** distorsion de numérotation; **~ switch** clé de rappel

loop checking contrôle par comparaison; contrôle par retour de l'information; **~ current** courant de boucle; **~ dialling** numérotation par rupture de boucle; numérotation en boucle; numérotation par ouverture de boucle

loop-disconnect v déboucler; **~ dialler** circuit de numérotation par interruption de boucle

loop disconnection débouclage

loop-disconnect key clé de boucle; **~ pulsing** numérotation en boucle; numérotation par ouverture de boucle; **~ pushbutton** clavier décimal loop echo path loss affaiblissement aller-retour; ~ extender adaptateur pour ligne longue; dispositif de suralimentation

loop-feeder circuit bouclé

loop frequency fréquence de boucle; ~ iteration n rebouclage; répétition de boucle; ~ measurement mesure en boucle

loop-opening rupture de boucle

loop parameters image bande pilote; ~ plant réseau de distribution; ~ propagation time temps de propagation en boucle; ~ pulsing numérotation à circuit de retour par la terre; ~ range radiophare à quatre voies et antenne en boucle; ~ reporting télémesure de ligne d'abonné; ~ resistance résistance de boucle; résistance en boucle; ~ ringing système à boucle; ~ start prise par établissement d'un boucle; ~ state état de boucle

loop-state transition changement d'état

loop status état de boucle

loop-status information information d'état de boucle

loopstick antenne à noyau magnétique; ~ aerial antenne à ferrites

loop testing contrôle par boucle; ~ topology interconnexion en boucles; ~ transmission transmission en boucle; trame

loose adj lâche; ~ components composants en vrac; ~ coupling couplage lâche; ~ fibre fibre libre

loosen v desserrer

loose tube fibre cable câble à fibre libre

LORAC (s. long-range accuracy radar system)

LORAN (s. long-range navigational system)

lose contact perdre le contact

loss n perte; affaiblissement; atténuation; dissipation; fuite; manque; ~ angle angle de perte; ~ dispersion dispersion de l'affaiblissement; ~ factor facteur de pertes

loss-less adj sans perte; non dissipatif; ~ feed network réseau d'alimentation sans pertes

loss of accuracy dérive; ~ of bit timing perte du signal de rythme; ~ of compatibility régression; ~ of control raté de blocage; ~ of definition aberration sphérique; ~ of frame alignment perte de verrouillage; ~ of multiframe alignment perte de verrouillage de multitrame; ~ of power (of transponder) déchet; ~ of residual magnetism perte magnétique résiduelle; ~ of revenue pertes de taxation; ~ of sync asynchronisme; ~ probability taux de perte(s); ~ system système avèc perte

lossy adj dissipatif

lost call appel perdu

lost-call probability probabilité d'échec; pro-

babilité de perte; ~ request demande desservie avec perte

lot size effectif du lot

loudness n intensité sonore; force du son; intensité; intensité acoustique; volume acoustique; ~ rating indice de force des sons

loud ringing bell sonnerie forte

loudspeaker n haut-parleur; porte-voix; ~ horn pavillon de haut-parleur; ~ telephone set poste téléphonique à haut-parleur; poste à réception amplifiée

louvre n lumière; ouie d'aération; persienne(s)

louvred adj ajouré

low-/(high-)level output niveau logique 0/(1)

low air pressure basse pression atmosphérique

low-altitude bombing radar (LAR) radar pour bombardement à faible altitude

low-capacity oil break à volume d'huile réduit

low core mémoire basse

low-cost adj à faible coût

low-density print impression pâle

low-disparity code code à disparité restreinte

low-distortion modulator modulateur à basse distorsion

lower v abaisser; débasculer; rabattre

lower-case (lc) bas de casse (bdc); minuscule

lowering n abaissement

lower order ordre inférieur

lower-ranking inférieur

lower sideband bande latérale inférieure

lower-sideband television channel canal inversé

lower specification boundary limite inférieure de la spécification (LIS)

lowest usable frequency (LUF) fréquence minimale utilisable

low frequency (LF) basse fréquence (BF)

low-frequency current courant basse fréquence; ~ transformer transformateur basse fréquence; ~ waveform generator générateur TBF

low-level active actif (en) état bas; ~ flowchart organigramme détaillé

lowlight n intensité réduite

low loss faible dissipation; ~ loss (of capacitor) très bonne tenue aux impulsions

low memory (LOWMEM) mémoire basse

low-noise amplifier (LNA) amplificateur à faible bruit; ~ frequency converter convertisseur de fréquence à faible bruit

low-order adj de droite; ~ bit bit de poids faible; bit de droite; ~ bit bit de rang inférieur

low-pass filter filtre passe-bas

low-power modulation modulation à bas niveau; ~ radio beacon radiophare à basse puissance

L

low priority priorité lente
low-profile *adj* bas; discret; plat; ~ **independent keyboard** clavier mobile plat
low-Q diode diode en basse Q
low-resistence loop boucle faible
low side-lobe faible lobe latéral; ~ **side-lobe aerial** antenne à rayonnement latéral; ~ **speed** basse vitesse; faible vitesse
low-speed terminal terminal léger
low standby current drain faible courant de repos; ~ **state** état L; ~ **tension (LT)** basse tension; ~ **tone** son grave; ~ **traffic** (level) faible trafic; ~ **voltage** basse tension
lozenge *n* pastille
LPA (s. link-pack area)
LPI (s. lines per inch)
LQ (s. letter quality)
LRC (s. longitudinal redundancy check)
LSB (s. least significant bit)
L-section circuit en L
LSI (s. large-scale integration)
LSU (s. lone signal unit); ~ (s. line switching unit)
LT (s. low tension); ~ **distribution board** tableau basse tension
LTX line ligne locale de bureau rural
lubricator *n* graisseur

Lucite *n* Plexiglas
LUF (s. lowest usable frequency)
lug *n* cosse; boucle; broche; étrier; fourche; languette; patte; talon; becquet (béquet); ~ **connection strip** plaquette à cosses
lull *n* abaissement; faible trafic
luminance compression compression des luminances; ~ **flicker** distorsion de luminance horizontale
luminescence *n* luminescence
luminescent centre centre luminogène
luminescent-screen tube tube cathodique à écran luminescente
luminous efficiency coefficient d'efficacité de la luminescence; ~ **flux variation** variation de flux lumineux; ~ **intensity** intensité lumineuse; ~ **sensitivity** sensibilité lumineuse; ~ **signal** signal lumineux
lumped *adj* composé; concentré; ~ **capacitance** capacité concentrée; ~ **capacitive loading** charge capacitive concentrée; ~ **constants** constantes localisées
lump-sum *adj* forfaitaire
lunar bug punaise
Luxembourg effect effet Luxembourg; transmodulation ionosphérique
LW (s. long wave)

M

MA (s. metropolitan (urban) **area**)
machine *n* machine; bécane (vern.); ~ **address** adresse absolue
machine-aided programming programmation automatique
machine code binaire exécutable; code absolu; code machine
machined nozzle bec usiné; ~ **washer** rondelle précise
machine entry inscription machine; ~ **language** langage machine; ~ **(language) instruction** instruction machine; ~ **language op code** ordre machine; ~ **learning** apprentissage automatique; ~ **positioning shim** cale position machine
machine-readable *adj* assimilable; interprétable; ~ **code** code interprétable
machine ringing appel semi-automatique; sonnerie continue; sonnerie monocoup; ~ **run** passage en machine; ~ **screw** vis à métaux; vis d'assemblage; vis pour métaux
machine-spoilt work time temps de reprise
machine time temps machine
machining *n* usinage; ajustage; façonnage; façonnement; rectification; ~ **allowance** surépaisseur d'usinage; écart d'usinage; ~ **error** défaut erratique
mackle plate plaque antimaculage
macro-assembler *n* macroassembleur
macro-assembly language macroassembleur
macro call appel de macro(-programme)
macro-element *n* macroélément
macro-instruction *n* instruction macroprogramme; mot macroprogramme; macroinstruction; ordre macroprogramme
macro-logic function macrofonction
macroprogram *n* macroprogramme; programme principal enregistreur; ~ **subsystem** macromachine
made-to-measure *adj* spécifique; personnalisable
magazine *n* cartouche; case; casier; chargeur; magasin; panier; bac
magic-eye tube œil magique
magic-T junction té hybride; T hybride; té magique; T magique
magnet *n* aimant; ~ **coil** bobine magnétique
magnetic amplifier Amplistat [A.C.]; ~ **balance** balance magnétique; ~ **bearing** azimut magnétique; ~ **biasing** pot compensé; ~ **blow-out** (circuit) soufflage magnétique; ~ **bridge** pont magnétique; ~ **bubble memory** mémoire à bulles; ~ **character reader** lecteur magnétique; ~ **charge** (impulse/signal) signal magnétique; ~ **circuit** circuit magnétique; ~ **deflection** déviation magnétique; ~ **dipole aerial** antenne dipôle magnétique; ~ **disk** disque magnétique; ~ **dispersion coefficient** coefficient de dispersion magnétique; ~ **doublet radiator** dipôle magnétique; doublet magnétique; ~ **field** champ magnétique; ~ **field intensity** énergie magnétisante; intensité d'aimantation; ~ **field strength** énergie magnétisante; intensité d'aimantation; ~ **flux** flux magnétique; ~ **flux density** inductance magnétique (uniforme); induction; ~ **focussing** concentration magnétique; focalisation électromagnétique; ~ **head** tête magnétique; ~ **induction** induction magnétique; ~ **ink character recognition (MICR)** reconnaissance magnétique de caractères; ~ **intensity** puissance magnétisante; ~ **latching** maintien magnétique; maintien mécanique; ~ **leaf** feuillet; ~ **leakage** dispersion magnétique
magnetic-loop memory mémoire à boucle magnétique
magnetic lug tambour magnétique; ~ **permeability** perméabilité magnétique (absolue); ~ **pole** pôle magnétique; ~ **potential** force magnétomotrice; potentiel magnétique; ~ **reading** magnétolecture; ~ **recorder** enregistreur magnétique; ~ **resistance** magnétorésistance; ~ **rod aerial** antenne à noyau magnétique; ~ **saturation** saturation magnétique; ~ **screen** blindage magnétique; ~ **shield** écran magnétique; ~ **signalogram** signalogramme magnétique; ~ **storage** mémoire magnétique; ~ **storm** orage magnétique; ~ **strength** puissance magnétisante; ~ **tape** bande magnétique; ruban magnétique; ~ **tape cartridge** cartouche de bande magnétique; ~ **tape cassette** cassette de bande magnétique; ~ **tape drive (unit)/handler** dérouleur de bande magnétique; ~ **tape editor** éditeur de bande magnétique; ~ **tape file** fichier sur bande magnétique; ~ **tape unit** unité à bande

magnétique; unité de bande magnétique

magnetization *n* aimantation; ~ **curve** courbe d'aimantation

magnetizer *n* excitateur

magnetizing current courant magnétisant; ~ **force** énergie magnétisante; intensité d'aimantation; puissance magnétique; puissance magnétisante

magneto *n* machine d'appel; ~ **crank** manivelle de magnéto

magnetometer *n* magnétomètre

magnetomotive force (m.m.f.) force magnétomotrice; potentiel magnétique

magneto-optic(al) effect effet magnéto-optique

magneto party line (hand ringer) ligne partagée à magnéto

magnetostriction loudspeaker haut-parleur à magnétostriction; ~ **microphone** microphone à magnétostriction

magnetostrictive delay line ligne à retard à magnétostriction; ~ **memory** mémoire à magnétostriction

magneto system système à magnéto; ~ **telephone set** téléphone à magnéto; poste téléphonique à appel magnétique; système téléphonique à appel magnétique

magnetron moding variation du champ de fréquences d'un magnétron

magnet rotor inducteur; ~ **wheel** inducteur

magnification factor facteur de qualité; facteur de surtension

magnifier *n* loupe; amplificateur; ~ (of oscilloscope) commutateur de gammes

magnitude *n* grandeur; valeur absolue; importance

magslip *n* transformateur rotatif; selsyn; synchro

magtape *n* bande magnétique

mail *n* courrier

mailbox *n* boîte à lettres; ~ **management** gestion de boîte aux lettres

mailing *n* postage; publipostage

mail order supplies vente par correspondance; ~ **shots** publipostage; édition des courriers

main quantum number nombre quantique principal; ~ **aspects** généralités; ~ **beam** faisceau principal; ferme; ~ **cable** transport; câble principal; ~ **carrier** porteuse principale; ~ **characteristic** rendement; ~ **control unit** bloc de commande générale; ~ **distribution frame (MDF)** répartiteur général (RG); répartiteur principal; répartiteur d'entrée (RE); ~ **exchange** central principal

mainframe *n* ordinateur central; centralisateur d'informations; ordinateur hôte; ordinateur lourd; ordinateur principal

mainland France la France métropolitaine

main line ligne principale

main-line program module exécutable

main lobe lobe principal; ~ **memory** mémoire centrale; mémoire principale; ~ **monitor** noyau; ~ **operating centre** centre principal d'exploitation (CPE); ~ **path** chemin suivi; ~ **power switch** interrupteur général; ~ **processor** processeur central; processeur principal; ~ **repeater station** station principale de répéteurs

mains *n* secteur électrique; réseau de distribution public; ~ **control switch** interrupteur de service; ~ **distribution board** distributeur secteur; ~ **end** en provenance des circuits amonts; ~ **extension lead** nourrice; ~ **failure** panne du secteur; coupure secteur; ~ **filter** filtre secteur; ~ **frequency** fréquence (de) secteur

main shaft arbre de couche

mains hum ronflement de secteur; bruit de secteur

main sideband bande principale

mains lead fil secteur; ~ **outlet** prise secteur; prise de courant (PC)

mains-powered *adj* alimentation par le secteur

mains power point prise de courant

main spring ressort de commande

mains pulsatance pulsation du secteur; ~ **receiver** récepteur secteur; ~ **setting** position alternatif; ~ **(power) supply** alimentation secteur; ~ **supply connection** connexion de réseau (électrique); ~ **supply socket** prise secteur; ~ **supply spur** sectionnement

main station poste téléphonique principal

mains transformer transformateur d'alimentation

main subscriber line ligne principale d'abonné; ~ **subscriber station** poste principal d'abonné; ~ **(power) supply circuit** circuit de puissance

mains voltage tension de secteur

main switching centre centre de commutation principal

maintainability *n* maintenabilité; capacité d'entretien

maintenance *n* maintenance; entretien; gestion; intervention; tenue à jour; ~ **centre** centre de maintenance; ~ **console** banc de maintenance; pupitre de maintenance; valise de réglage; ~ **data sheet** fiche technique; ~ **device** organe de maintenance; ~ **file** fichier de mouvement; fichier détail; ~ **handbook** notice de réglage; ~ **kit** lot de maintenance; ~ **register** infoduc; ~ **service (engineer)** dérangements; ~ **sheet** fiche de mouvement; ~ **signal** signal de maintenance; ~ **tele-**

printer téléimprimeur de maintenance
main terminal station station principale maîtresse (SPM); **~ transit centre (MTC)** centre de transit principal (CTP); **~ (trunk) exchange** centre principal; **~ trunk exchange** centre nodal (CN); **~ trunk route** arête
major alarm alarme urgente
majority (voting) **logic** logique majoritaire; **~ carrier** porteur majoritaire; **~ element** élément majoritaire
major loop boucle principale; **~ refit** (of ship) carénage grand; **~ third** tierce majeure
make (contact) travail ('T')
make-and-break *n* coupleur; branchement-débranchement; conjoncteur-disjoncteur
make-before-break contact (MBB) contact travail-repos (TR)
make-break tout ou rien (TOR); **~ contact** contact inverseur; **~ ratio** rapport cyclique; rapport d'impulsions
make contact contact de travail; contact de fermeture
make-contact unit dispositif de contact de fermeture
make pulse impulsion de fermeture
makeshift rig antenne de fortune; antenne provisoire
make time (of dial pulses) temps de fermeture
make-type circuit layout schéma à mise de tension; **~ connection** liaison à mise de tension
making good reprise; réparation
maladjustment *n* déréglage; déséquilibre
malfunction *n* aléa de fonctionnement; anomalie (de fonctionnement); défaut; dérangement; faute; incident; panne; avarie; **~ indicator** centralographe; **~ routine** sous-programme de traitement d'anomalies
malicious call appel malveillant; **~ call tracing** dépistage des appels malveillants; identification des appels malveillants
mallet *n* maillet
management and control system (MCS) centre d'exploitation et de maintenance (CEM); **~ centre** centre de gestion; **~ forecasting** gestion prévisionnelle; **~ information systems (MIS)** information et communication d'entreprise (ICE); tableau de bord; **~ official** cadre supérieur; **~ routine** programme de gestion; **~ signalling** signalisation de gestion; **~ training** formation des cadres
manager *n* responsable; gestionnaire; directeur
manager-and-secretary station poste directeur-secrétaire
manager extension poste d'abonné filtré

manager-secretary station poste de filtrage; **~ telephone system** installation de filtrage
manager station poste filtré
mandate *n* mission
mandatory *adj* obligatoire; impératif
mandrel *n* mandrin; arbre
manhole *n* chambre souterraine
manilla *adj* (colour) havane
man-machine communication digigraphie; **~ dialogue terminal** terminal de dialogue; **~ language (MML)** relations homme-machine (RHM); langage homme-machine; dialogue
man-made *adj* artificiel; synthétique; **~ noise** parasite industriel; perturbation industrielle
manned orbiting laboratory laboratoire orbital habité
manoeuvrability *n* facilités de manœuvre
manpower *n* main d'œuvre; effectif; ressources humaines
mantissa *n* mantisse
mantle *n* enveloppe
manual *n* notice; documentation; **~** *adj* manuel; **~ call** appel manuel; **~ changeover** mutation manuelle; **~ circuit** circuit à exploitation manuelle; **~ coil winder** bobineuse; **~ console I/O port** accès pupitre manuel; **~ exchange** bureau central manuel; **~ hold** maintien manuel

manually-operated à commande musculaire
manual patching interconnexion manuelle; **~ position** position manuelle (PM); **~ ringer** magnéto; **~ ringing** appel manuel par clé; **~ switchboard** standard manuel; tableau commutateur manuel; **~ switching system** système de commutation manuelle; **~ tape relay** transit manuel par bande perforée; **~ telephone system** système téléphonique manuel; **~ testing** essai manuel; **~ tie line** ligne interstandard (LIS); **~ trunk** intermanuel; **~ wiring** câblage manuel; **~ working** exploitation manuelle
manufacture *n* fabrication; réalisation matérielle
manufacturer *n* fabricant; fournisseur; réalisateur; constructeur
manufacturer's instructions gamme; **~ nameplate** étiquette de constructeur; plaque de constructeur; sigle de constructeur
manufacturing overheads frais de fabrication; **~ process sheet** feuillet de procédé de fabrication; **~ technology** art de fabrication
many-valued *adj* polyvalent
many-wire *adj* multifilaire
map *v* rapatrier; affecter; afficher; appliquer; relever; **~** *n* table de correspondance;

configuration; implantation; mémoire; relevé; carte; topologie; ~ **of network dynamic status** connexité topologique; ~ **partition onto window (MPW)** affectation des fenêtres aux partitions

mapping *n* rapatriement; topographie; affectation; constitution; transformation; ~ **file** carte de rapatriement

marching bit bit baladeur; ~ **one** un galopeur/baladeur/migrant; ~ **ones and zeros** alternance des 0 et 1

marching-ones load chargement un baladeur

marching zero zéro migrant

margin *n* bordure; marge; tolérance

marginal occupancy occupation marginale; ~ **test** essai aux limites (E/L); ~ **testing** contrôle par marges; contrôle des tolérances

margin of a telegraphic apparatus marge d'un appareil télégraphique; ~ **of service** marge de service; ~ **stop** taquet de marge; curseur de stop

marine radar radar maritime

maritime satellite communications communication maritime par satellite

mark *v* appliquer le courant de signe; annoter; signaler; ~ *n* tache; amorce; condition un (1); créneau; drapeau; état Z; insigne; marque; un; ~ (of dial plate) plein

marker *n* marqueur; aiguille; balise; créneau; drapeau; étiquette; impulsion de synchronisation; impulsion d'étalonnage; index; indicateur; ~ **aerial** antenne de balise; ~ **beacon** radioborne; ~ **channel** voie balise; ~ **pulse** créneau; ~ **signal** signal de marquage; ~ **switch** sélecteur marqueur; ~ **system** système avec marqueur

market, on the open ~ de la concurrence

marketed *adj* commercialisé

market forces nécessité conjoncturelle

marketing configuration configurateur commercial; ~ **engineer** ingénieur technico-commercial (ITC)

market research analyse de marché; étude de marché; ~ **survey** étude de marché; analyse de marché

mark-hold *n* maintien au repos

marking/(keying) wave marqueur

marking bias prédomination vers le côté négatif; ~ **bus** bus de marquage; ~ **current** courant actif; courant de signalisation; courant de travail; ~ **logic** logique de marquage; ~ **machine** machine tampographique; ~ **out** traçage; ~ **path** voie de marquage; ~ **path interference** connexion aux voies de marquage; ~ **percentage** pourcentage de signe; taux de travail; ~ **report link** liaison compte-rendu de

marquage; ~ **subsystem** chaîne de marquage; ~ **wave** signal de travail

mark off cocher

Markov chain séquence de Markov

mark-sense card carte à lecture graphique; carte à graphiter; carte à pistes magnétiques; carte magnéto-lecture

mark-sensing *n* magnétolecture; graphitage; lecture graphique

mark-space tout ou rien (TOR); ~ **ratio** rapport cyclique; rapport d'impulsions; taux de remplissage

marshal *v* regrouper; centraliser; rassembler

marshalling unit module de regroupement

mask *n* cache; caractère variable; filtre; gabarit; masquage; obturateur; protection; vernis éepargne (VE); vernis isolant

maskable *adj* masquable

masked (of metal electropotential) passivé; ~ **state** état masqué

mask extractor masque

masking *n* masquage; découpage électronique; effet de masque; extraction; filtrage; inhibition; obturation; pose d'épargne; ~ **tape** ruban cache; Chatterton [A.C.]; ruban isolant; ~ **word** mot de masques

mask microphone microphone de masque; ~ **register** registre de masquage

mass *n* masse; base volumique; ~ **market** le grand public; ~ **production** fabrication en série; grande série; ~ **rate of flow** débit de masse; débit massique; ~ **ratio** charge spécifique d'un porteur électrisé; ~ **resistivity** résistivité transversale; ~ **splicing** épissurage de masse; raccordement de masse; épissure multifibres; ~ **storage** saisie de masse

mast *n* pylône d'antenne

master *v* maîtriser; ~ *n* maître; directeur; étalon; maîtresse; mère; partie noble; père; pilote; principal; typon; ~ **card** carte maîtresse; ~ **clock** horloge pilote; horloge maîtresse; horloge mère; horloge principale; rythmeur; ~ **copy** archivage; ~ **drawing** plan directeur; ~ **file** fichier principal; données pilotes; fiche principal; fichier de base; fichier maître; fichier permanent; fichier pilote; ~ **frequency** fréquence principale

mastergroup *n* groupe tertiaire

master library tape bande programme d'exploitation; ~ **line** ligne de tête; ~ **mode** mode pilote; ~ **mode instruction** instruction privilégiée; ~ **oscillator** oscillateur pilote; maître-oscillateur; pilote d'émetteur; ~ **oscillator power amplifier (MOPA)** amplificateur de puissance de l'oscillateur pilote; ~ **plan** plan directeur; ~ **program**

file bande programme d'exploitation; ~ re-cord article du fichier permanent; ~ set poste principal

master-slave maître-esclave

master/slave system système d'asservissement

master station station maîtresse; ~ switch coupe-tout; ~ telephone transmission reference system système de référence; ~ transmitter émetteur pilote; ~ workstation serveuse

matability n mariabilité

match n appairage; assortiment; concordance; égalisation; égalité; équivalence (logique)

matched adj apparié; symétrique; ~ filter filtre adapté; ~ junction jonction adapté; ~ load charge adaptée; résistance de terminaison; terminaison adaptée; ~ termination terminaison adaptée; charge adaptée; ~ transformer transformateur double

matching n adaptation; accord; comparaison; correspondance; équilibrage; pairage; centrage; ~ adj symétrique; homologue; ~ and tuning devices organes d'adaptation et d'accord; ~ cores noyaux appairés; ~ equipment joncteur; ~ error erreur d'adaptation; ~ half-cores demi-pots appairés; . ~ key clé égale; ~ memory mémoire de correspondance; ~ network réseau d'adaptation; ~ of television aerial cable impédance terminale d'un câble de télévision; ~ pillar pilier d'adaptation; ~ plate plaque d'adaptation; ~ post tige d'adaptation; ~ screw vis d'adaptation; ~ section section d'adaptation; ~ stub adaptateur de ligne; ~ transformer transformateur d'adaptation; ~ unit bloc d'adaptation

match mode en microsynchronisme

material n matériau

material/chromatic dispersion dispersion matériau/chromatique

material process procédé physique

materials handling gestion physique

mathematical model modèle mathématique

mating adj conjugué; complémentaire; ~ area (of contact) partie utile; ~ device (spigot/cavity) détrompeur; ~ face face d'appui; côté broches à raccorder; ~ hole trou d'ancrage; ~ spigot détrompeur mâle; ~ strength force de rétention

matrix n matrice; grille; implantation; ~ printer imprimante par points; ~ store mémoire matricielle

matt adj mat

mavar (mixed/modulated amplification by variable reactance) amplificateur paramé-trique

maximize v accroître

maximum access programming programmation optimum; ~ available power puissance maximum disponible; ~ average power output puissance maximale moyenne de sortie; ~ carrier level niveau maximal de porteuse; ~ cut-out disjoncteur protecteur; ~ line usage factor facteur maximum d'utilisation de lignes; ~ oscillation frequency fréquence maximale d'oscillation; ~ output level niveau maximal de sortie; ~ permissible noise level niveau maximal de bruit admissible; ~ pre-travel grande vitesse d'attaque; ~ rating charge maximale; ~ recurrent reverse voltage tension inverse de pointe répétitive; ~ tolerance tolérance maximum (TM); ~ usable frequency (MUF) fréquence maximale utilisable; onde limite; ~ writing speed vitesse maximale d'exploration à la réception

Maxwell-Boltzmann velocity distribution law loi de distribution des vitesses de Maxwell-Boltzmann

Mazak [T.N.] Zamak

MBB (s. make-before-break contact)

MC (s. media copy)

MCS (s. management and control system)

MCW (s. modulated continuous wave)

MDC (s. message distribution circuit)

MDF (s. main distribution frame)

mean absolute power level niveau absolu de puissance moyenne; ~ activity factor coefficient d'activité moyen; ~ axial plane of terminal fibre moyenne de la borne; ~ (call) holding time durée moyenne de communication; durée moyenne de la tentative d'appel; ~ carrier frequency fréquence moyenne de la porteuse; ~ cathode loading charge cathodique moyenne; ~ connection time délai moyen de raccordement (DMR)

meander-line transformer translateur de ligne à méandre

mean free path (of a charged particle) parcours moyen libre (PML) (d'un porteur électrisé)

meaning n motif; interprétation; signification

mean occupancy taux moyen d'occupation; ~ power puissance moyenne; ~ time heure centrale; ~ time between failures (MTBF) moyenne des temps de bon fonctionnement (MTBF); délai d'intervention; temps moyen de bon fonctionnement; temps moyen entre défaillances; ~ time to repair (MTTR) moyenne technique des temps de réparation (MTTR); délai de réparation;

temps moyen de réparation; temps moyen d'intervention; ~ **time to repair indicator** maintenabilité; ~ **traffic intensity** intensité moyenne de trafic; ~ **value** valeur moyenne
measling *n* tache d'imprégnation; filigrane
measurand *n* valeur à mesurer
measured operation times (of work study) temps gamme; ~ **value** valeur lue; ~ **variable** valeur à mesurer
measurement *n* mesure; ~ **adaptor** pied de mesure; ~ **coordinator** mesureur; ~ **panel** tête de mesure; ~ **position** point de mesure; ~ **system module** coffret chaîne de mesure
measuring apparatus appareil de mesure; ~ **bridge** pont de mesure; ~ **circuit** circuit de mesure; ~ **current** courant de mesure; ~ **instrument** vérificateur; calibre; instrument de mesure; ~ **microscope** microscope de mesure; ~ **point** point de mesure; ~ **rod** pige; ~ **scale** échelle de mesure; ~ **sensor** capteur de mesure; ~ **set** appareil de mesure; mesureur; ~ **signal** signal de mesure; ~ **transducer** convertisseur de mesure; ~ **transformer** transformateur de mesure
mechanical admittance admittance mécanique; ~ **class** classe mécanique; ~ **drawing** dessin industriel; ~ **impedance** impédance mécanique; ~ **latching** maintien mécanique
mechanically-despun aerial antenne stabilisée par contre-rotation mécanique
mechanically-latched mini-crossbar switch minisélecteur à maintien électromécanique
mechanically-latching contact contact à air libre
mechanical reactance réactance mécanique; ~ **recorder** enregistreur mécanique; ~ **resistance** résistance mécanique; ~ **restrictions** contraintes mécaniques; ~ **rotation** (sweep of potentiometer) angle de rotation électrique; angle de rotation totale; ~ **specifications label** étiquette de constructeur; ~ **strength** résistance mécanique
mechanic's toolbox coffret mécanicien
mechanism *n* mécanisme; dispositif; machine
media conversion conversion de support; ~ **copy (MC)** copie support; transmission ligne ou page
media-oriented *adj* médiatisé
medium *n* milieu; support
medium-altitude satellite circuit circuit par satellite à altitude moyenne
medium frequency (MF) fréquence moyenne; ~ **frequency band** bande de fréquences moyennes
medium-frequency field champ d'ondes moyennes; ~ **telegraphy** télégraphie à

fréquence moyenne; ~ **wave** onde à moyenne fréquence
medium-haul à moyenne distance
medium pitch (of screw thread) qualité moyenne
medium-range radar radar à portée moyenne
medium-scale integration (MSI) intégration à densité moyenne
medium-sized aerial antenne moyenne
medium speed vitesse moyenne
medium-term *adj* intérimaire
medium wave (MW) petites ondes (PO); onde moyenne (OM)
meet (logic function) opération ET
meet-me call forwarding renvoi temporaire (commandé); renvoi variable; renvoi temporaire variable; ~ **conference** conférence rendez-vous
megger *n* (megohmmeter) mégohmmètre; ohmmètre à magnéto; méganomètre (vern.); magnéto
megohmmeter *n* mégohmmètre; ohmmètre à magnéto; magnéto
melograph *n* (intonation emulator) mélographe
melting temperature température de fusion
member *n* article détail; abonné; détail; ~ (of indexed data set) membre
membership *n* appartenance; composition
membrane *n* diaphragme; ~ **keypad** clavier à nappe élastomère
memo quality qualité courrier approché
memorandum *n* message de service; mémento; note de service; récapitulatif; ~ (NB) pour mémoire (PM)
memory access interface automate mémoire; ~ **address** adresse-mémoire; adresse d'implantation; ~ **address register** compteur d'adresse de la mémoire; ~ **bank** banc de mémoire; banc (mémoire) d'octets; ~ **board** support
memory-bound *adj* subordonné à la capacité de mémoire
memory capacity capacité d'une mémoire; ~ **chip** boîtier mémoire; ~ **core** image; ~ **field** zone mémoire; ~ **flip-flop** bascule de retenue; ~ **interface** adaptation mémoire; ~ **location** adresse d'implantation; cellule mémoire; emplacement (de) mémoire; endroit; ~ **management** gestion mémoire; ~ **management card** gestion informations mémoire; ~ **management unit (MMU)** unité de gestion mémoire; ~ **map** topogramme; carte mémoire; géographie de la mémoire; implantation mémoire; relevé de la mémoire
memory-mapped *adj* en configuration mémoire; ~ **I/O ports** E/S banalisées

memory mapping affectation de mémoire; ~ **occupancy** taille mémoire; ~ **page lock** verrou de page; ~ **plane** plan mémoire; ~ **processing card** gestion informations mémoire; ~ **register** (distributor) registre mémoire; ~ **search exclusion** exclusion de recherche en mémoire; ~ **size** encombrement mémoire; ~ **start address** début image; ~ **switch** registre d'aiguillage de données

menu *n* liste d'options; écran; option(s); panneau; possibilité(s); sommaire; ~ **display** affichage d'un menu; affichage écran; écran choix de fonctions

menu-driven mode menu

mercury arc converter convertisseur à vapeur de mercure; ~ **delay line** ligne à retard à mercure; ~ **pool cathode** cathode à bain de mercure; ~ **switch** interrupteur à mercure

mercury-vapour lamp lampe à mercure; ~ **rectifier** redresseur à mercure; redresseur à vapeur de mercure

mercury-wetted contact contact mouillé; ~ **relay** relais à contact mouillé au mercure; relais à mercure

merge *v* fusionner; intégrer (à); interclasser; mixer; triturer

merger *n* fusion

merge sort tri par fusion (équilibrée); tri par interclassement

merging *n* fusion; intégration; interclassement; panachage; ordonnancement

mesh *n* grille; boucle; filet; filtre à fils; tissu métallique; ~ *adj* (of network topology) maillé; ~ **connection** couplage polygonal; ~ **current** courant cyclique; courant périodique

meshed *adj* maillé; non hiérarchisé; ~ **network** réseau en mailles

mesh link maille; ~ **topology** interconnexion en matrice; ~ **voltage** tension en triangle; tension polygonale

mesochronous *adj* mésochrone

meson *n* méson

message *n* message; communication; échange; envoi; information(s); mention; radiogramme; signal; télégramme; texte; courrier; argumentaire; ~ **alignment** alignement de message; ~ **analysis** analyse de message; ~ **calls** messagerie vocale; ~ **concentrator** concentrateur de messages

message-distribution circuit (MDC) circuit distributeur de message

message distributor marqueur

message-ending character signe final

message feedback contrôle par retour de l'information; ~ **field** argument; ~ **file** fichier de texte; ~ **format** structure de message; corps du message; disposition de message

message-forwarding centre centre de retransmission de messages

message handling gestion de messages; ~ **label** libellé; ~ **lamp** lampe de message; ~ **link** liaison d'information; ~ **numbering** numérotation de message; ~ **packet** paquet; ~ **preamble** tête de message; ~ **prefix** préfixe de message; ~ **present** (bit) présence message (PM); ~ **processing** acquittement (des messages); ~ **queue** file des échanges; sémaphore; ~ **queuing** mise en attente de messages; ~ **rate** tarif unitaire; ~ **register** compteur d'abonné; compteur d'appels

message-register facility compteur de taxe à domicile; ~ **pulse** télétaxe (TLT)

message retrieval recherche de message; récupération de messages

message-sending routine programme de service

message-sequence control transmission au coup par coup

message signal unit trame sémaphore de message; ~ **source** source de messages; ~ **structure** syntaxe; structure de message; ~ **switching** commutation de messages

message-switching centre centre de commutation de messages; ~ **network** réseau de commutation de messages

message-taking service service de communications téléphoniques

message terminal load (MTL) caractère de fin de message

message-transfer control circuit informateur; ~ **delay** temps de transfert de messages; ~ **part (MTP)** sous-système de transport de messages (SSTM)

message unloading start point tête de vidage; ~ **waiting (MW)** message en attente

message-waiting lamp lampe de message

messaging *n* messagerie de l'écrit; messagerie; télé-écriture; télémessagerie

messenger call communication personnelle avec messager

messenger-call fee surtaxe d'avis d'appel

messenger charge taxe d'envoi de messager; ~ **wire** câble porteur

metacharacter *n* métacaractère

metacompiler *n* métacompilateur

metal bubble key coupelle métallique; ~ **film resistor** résistance à couche métallique; ~ **former** mandrin métallique

metal-glaze (thick film) **resistor** résistance à couche métallique

metallic *adj* métallique; ~ **(through-)connection** passage en métallique; ~ **circuit** circuit bifilaire; ～ **line** ligne métallique; ～ **loop** liaison métallique

metallization *n* métallisation

metallized *adj* métallisé; ～ **polyester film capacitor** condensateur polyester métallisé; ～ **screen** écran métallisé

metal oxide (of rectifier) oxymétal; ～ **package** boîtier rond; ～ **plating** métallisation; ～ **rectifier** redresseur sec; ～ **screw** vis à tôle; ～ **square with beam** équerre métallique à chapeau; ～ **strength member** porteur métallique

metal-stripping agent démétallisant

metal valve tube en métal; ～ **weight** masse métallique (Mm)

metameric matching adaptation métamérique

metastable state état métastable

meteorological broadcast radiodiffusion météorologique

meter *n* compteur; cadran; contrôleur; indicateur; instrument(s) de mesure; mesureur; ～ **display** présentation par instruments de mesure

metered unit taxation de base facturée (TBF)

meter fee zone zone de taxation

metering *n* comptage; mesure(s); taxation; ～ **circuit** circuit de comptage; circuit de mesure; ～ **clock** horloge de taxation; ～ **coupler** coupleur de taxation; ～ **digit** signe indiquant les taxes; ～ **docket/ticket** ticket d'appel; ～ **over junction** taxation en arrière; ～ **panel** panneau d'appareils de mesure; ～ **pulse** impulsion de taxe; impulsion de comptage; ～ **pulses to subscriber's premises** télétaxe (TLT); ～ **pulse transmission** émission du signal de télétaxe; ～ **pulse transmitter** dispositif d'émission de la télétaxe; ～ **rate** cadence de taxation; ～ **rate period** période de taxation; ～ **time schedule** horaires de taxation; ～ **unit** dispositif de taxation; ～ **zone** zone de taxation

meter pulse impulsion de taxe; ～ **wire** (M-wire) fil de comptage; fil compteur

methanol dioxane alcool méthylique dioxane

methyl alcohol alcool méthylique

methylated spirits alcool méthylique; alcool dénaturé

methyl bromide bromure de méthyle

meticulous finish finition soignée

metre-amperes produit mètre x ampères

metre tape mètre ruban

metric wave (VHF band) onde métrique

metronome *n* tronc synchro

metropolitan France l'hexagone; ～ **network** réseau de grande ville; ～ **subscriber exchange** centre urbain

MEW (s. microwave early warning)

MF (s. medium frequency); ～ (s. multifrequency code); ～ **pushbutton dialling** signalisation du type clavier à multifréquences; ～ **signalling** signalisation multifréquence; code MF à impulsions; ～ **signalling circuit** circuit à signalisation multifréquence

mho (s. reciprocal ohm)

mica capacitor condensateur à mica

MICR (s. magnetic ink character recognition)

microammeter *n* microampèremètre

micro-assembly *n* microstructure

micro-bending *n* (of fibre optics) microcourbure

microcard *n* microcarte

microcircuit *n* microstructure; circuit miniaturisé; microcircuit

microcomputer *n* micro-ordinateur; microcalculateur

microcomputing *n* micro-informatique

microcopy *n* microvue

micro-electronics *n* microélectronique

micro-etching machine machine de microgravure

micro-exchange *n* microcentral

micro-exposure *n* microvue

microfiche *n* microfiche

microfilm *n* microfilm

microfilming *n* microscopie

microfilm reader lecteur optique

microgroove *n* microsillon; sillon fin

micro-instruction *n* micro-instruction; microcommande

micromedium *n* microforme

micrometer dial gauge comparateur Zivy

micromicrofarad (uuF) *n* picofarad

micromodule *n* circuit monolithique; micromodule

microphone *n* microphone; ～ **circuit** circuit microphonique; ～ **current** courant d'alimentation du microphone; intensité micro; alimentation microphonique; ～ **directivity** directivité microphone; ～ **effect** effet microphonique; microphonicité; ～ **insert** capsule microphonique; ～ **noise** bruit de microphone; ～ **output** puissance de sortie d'un microphone; ～ **stand** support de microphone; pied de microphone

micro-potting *n* microenrobage

microprint *n* microvue

microprocessor *n* microprocesseur; ～ **card** carte futée

microprogram *n* microprogramme; automate

microprogrammed computer calculateur microprogrammé

microprogram subsystem micromachine (MR)

microsection *n* coupe micrographique; coupe métallographique

microstrip *n* ruban plat

microswitch *n* minirupteur; microcontact; micro-interrupteur; microrupteur

microtelephone *n* combiné

microtext *n* microforme; ~ **reader** passe-vue

microtransparency *n* microvue

microwave *n* micro-onde; onde hyperfréquence (HF); ~ **aerial** antenne à hyperfréquences; ~ **beam** faisceau hertzien (FH); ~ **channel** voie hertzienne; canal hertzien; ~ **early warning (MEW)** alerte avancée à microondes; ~ **lens aerial** antenne microondes lenticulaire; ~ **line-of-sight** trajet; ~ **link** artère hertzienne; liaison à microondes; liaison hertzienne; relais hertzien; voie microondes; ~ **resonance spectrum** spectres de résonance pour micro-ondes; ~ **system** système hertzien; système à microondes; ~ **tower** tour hertzienne

middle management maîtrise; sous-commandiers; ~ **marker beacon** radioborne intermédiaire

middleware *n* logiciel adapté à l'utilisateur

middle wire fil froid

midget lamp lampe Liliput; ~ **valve** tube miniature

midnight-line service abonnement de nuit

mid-position mi-course

mid-travel à mi-place; mi-course

mid-way milieu; à mi-place

migration *n* déplacement; transfert; évolution; remontée

mil *n* (10^{-3} in./0.0254 mm) millième de pouce

mild steel acier doux

militate against défavoriser

milled knob bouton moleté; ~ **nut** écrou moleté

Miller circuit circuit de Miller; ~ **integrator** intégrateur de Miller

millimetric (dwarf) wave (EHF band) onde millimétrique

milling channel dégagement de fraise; dégagement d'angle

millivoltammeter *n* millivoltampèremètre

mimetic diagram tableau synoptique; tableau indicateur optique; tableau de bord

mimic *v* refléter; ~ **diagram** tableau synoptique; tableau indicateur optique; tableau de bord; ~ **display card** carte synoptique

mingling *n* panachage

miniature circuit circuit miniaturisé; ~ **core** microtore; ~ **crossbar switch** minirépartiteur; microsélecteur; ~ **overlay** minibandeau; ~ **relay** relais miniature; ~ **solid-state buzzer** vibreur électronique miniature; ~ **switch** micro-interrupteur; ~ **valve** tube miniature; ~ **wire-wrap connection** connexion enroulée miniature (W)

minicomputer *n* mini-ordinateur; mini-calculateur

mini-crossbar switch minisélecteur électromécanique

mini-disk *n* disquette

minimal tree arbre optimum

minimum access code code à accès mimimum; ~ **carrier level** niveau minimal de porteuse; ~ **clearing** amélioration du minimum; amélioration du zéro; ~ **interval** intervalle minimum; ~ **operate current** courant minimal de fonctionnement; courant minimal de commande; ~ **perceptible noise** parasites à peine perceptibles; ~ **period of service** durée minimale d'abonnement

minimum-phase frequency characteristic caractéristique à déphasage minimal; ~ **network** réseau à déphasage minimal

minimum range portée mininale; ~ **rating** charge minimale

mini-PCB cartelette

miniprocessor *n* miniprocesseur

mini-selector *n* minisélecteur

mini-strip *n* minibandeau

miniswitch *n* minisélecteur électromécanique; sélecteur crossbar miniaturisé; ~ **(programming) card** carte de programmation

minor carrier alarm alarme de groupe; ~ **control** (sorting) mineur; ~ **discrepancy** écart faible; ~ **exchange** centre local primaire; central de secteur; centre de secteur

minority carrier porteur minoritaire

minor lobe lobe latéral; lobe secondaire; ~ **loop** boucle auxiliaire; boucle secondaire; ~ **part** pièce de détail

minuend *n* diminuende

minutes *n pl* procès-verbal (PV)

minute switch minuterie

mirror reflection echo écho indirect

MIS (s. management information systems)

misaligned *adj* désaxé; de côté; déréglé; excentré

misalignment *n* déréglage; décadrage; défaut de parallélisme; désalignement; dissymétrie; écart; déverrouillage

miscellaneous interference interférences variées

mischief call appel malveillant; appel importun; appel abusif

misdial(ling) *n* fausse manœuvre

misfiling *n* erreur de classement

misfire *n* raté d'allumage

mis-keying *n* mauvaise manipulation; erreur de manipulation

mismatch *n* déséquilibre; asymétrie; changement d'état; déport; déréglage; désaccord; erreur d'adaptation; erreur d'assortiment;

M

~ factor coefficient de pertes due aux réflexions; **~ loss** perte due aux réflexions; affaiblissement par défaut d'adaptation

misoperation n fausse manœuvre

mispocket n erreur de case

misregistered adj excentré

misregistration n erreur de cadrage

mis-routing n acheminement erroné; mauvais acheminement

missile n engin

missile-tracking radar radar de poursuite d'engins

missing page interruption besoin de page

mis-sort n erreur de tri

mis-tabulation n mauvais cadrage

mistake n manœuvre intempestive; faute; erreur

mitigate v pallier

mitre n angle oblique

mix n assortiment; mélange

mixed adj hétérogène; **~ number** valeur mixte; **~ radix notation** numération à base multiple

mixer n mélangeur; changeur de fréquence; **~ panel** tableau de brassage

mixing n panachage; brassage; confection; **~ console** pupitre de mélange; **~ network** réseau de brassage; **~ stage** étage de brassage

m.m.f. (s. magnetomotive force)

MML (s. man-machine language)

mnemonic n mot sigle; nom symbolique; abréviation mnémotechnique; **~ code** code mnémonique

mobile (cellular R/T) mobile; **~ aerial** antenne transportable; **~ base early warning equipment** installation de l'alerte avancée transportable; **~ exchange** central mobile; **~ frame** cadre roulant; **~ radar control post** poste mobile de contrôle de radar; **~ radio station** radiostation transportable; **~ radiotelephone** radiotéléphone mobile; **~ station** station mobile; **~ television station** émetteur de télévision portatif; **~ terminal** terminal mobile; **~ transmission equipment** équipement d'émission mobile; **~ transmitter** émetteur mobile

mock-up n maquette

mode n mode; contexte; état; fonctionnement; régime; **~ behaviour** comportement du mode; **~ change** changement de mode

mode-change key touche de passage

mode changer transformateur de mode; **~ coupling** (of propagation) couplage de modes; **~ dispersion** dispersion intermodale; **~ filter** filtre de mode; **~ format** mode grille

model n gabarit

mode-locked laser laser à modes verrouillés

modem n modem (modulateur-démodulateur); convertisseur; **~ turnaround** délai d'inversion

mode pattern oscillogramme du mode; **~ protection** sauvegarde (contexte s.); **~ reset** restauration des modes; **~ separation** différence de fréquence de mode; **~ switch** sélection technique; **~ transformer** transformateur de mode

modification file fichier détail; **~ sequence** suivi

modified alternate mark inversion signal bipolaire modifié; **~ refractive index** indice de réfraction modifié

modifier n modificateur; mot d'index; compensateur de phase; indice; **~ register** registre index

modular adj modulaire; extensible; sectionnable; **~ expansion** modularité d'extension; **~ folding** repliage de mise en boîte; **~ fuse-carrier** coupe-circuit sectionnable

modularity n extensibilité

modularization n fractionnement; cloisonnement

modularizing n mise en boîte

modular (telephone) jack fiche gigogne

modulate v moduler

modulated amplifier amplificateur modulé; **~ carrier** porteuse modulée; **~ continuous wave (MCW)** onde entretenue modulée; **~ continuous wave keying** modulation à trait permanent; **~ CW jammer** brouilleur à modulation par courant; **~ stage** étage modulé; **~ wave** onde modulée; modulat

modulating choke bobine de modulation; **~ voltage** tension modulatrice; **~ wave** onde modulante; signal modulant

modulation n modulation; **~ bridge** modulateur en pont; pont de modulation; **~ carrier** porteuse de modulation; **~ coherence** cohérence d'une modulation; **~ current** courant de modulation; **~ depth/percentage** taux de modulation; **~ electrode** électrode de modulation; électrode de commande; grille de modulation; **~ element** élément de modulation; **~ envelope** enveloppe de la modulation; **~ factor** taux de modulation; coefficient de modulation; profondeur de modulation; **~ frequency** fréquence de modulation; **~ frequency harmonic distortion** distorsion de modulation; **~ frequency intermodulation distortion** distorsion d'intermodulation par la fréquence de modulation; **~ grid** grille de modulation; **~ hum** ronflement de la modulation; **~ index** facteur de modulation; indice de modulation; **~ level meter**

appareil de mesure du niveau de modulation; ~ **meter** modulomètre; contrôleur de modulation; ~ **noise** bruit de modulation; ~ **phase angle** angle de phase de la modulation; ~ **product** produit de modulation; ~ **range** plage d'admission; ~ **rate** rapidité de modulation; vitesse télégraphique; ~ **rate measuring set** mesureur de vitesse; ~ **signal** signal de modulation; signal modulant; ~ **standard** norme de modulation; ~ **suppression** effacement; ~ **suppression rate** taux de suppression de la modulation; ~ **transfer function** fonction de transfert de modulation; ~ **(stage) transformer** transformateur de modulation; ~ **triangle** triangle de modulation; ~ **voltage** tension de modulation

modulator *n* modulateur; ~ **driver** étage excitateur du modulateur; ~ **load** appareil d'essai du modulateur; ~ **tube** tube modulateur; ~ **voltage** tension de modulateur

module *n* module; bloc; boîtier; carte; cellule; élément; maquette; version

modulo K sum somme modulo K (SMK); ~ **N check** contrôle modulo N; ~ **2 sum** base de numération 2; OU exclusif

modulus (absolute value norm) *n* module; valeur absolue; valeur réelle; coefficient; ~ **of elasticity** module d'élasticité

moiré *n* (effect) moirage (en télévision)

moisture *n* humidité; ~ **content** état anhydre

molecular weight masse moléculaire; poids moléculaire

mole grips pince de blocage; pince étau

momentary action (of switch) à rappel automatique

momentary-action pushbutton touche fugitive; bouton poussoir (à tête) à impulsion; ~ **switch** interrupteur fugitif

moment of force couple; ~ **of inertia** moment d'inertie

momentum *n* moment (linéaire) cinétique

monadic operation opération unaire

monitor *v* contrôler; analyser; écouter; mettre en écoute; passer en revue; ~ *n* appareil de surveillance; contrôleur; écran; jack d'écoute; programme directeur; programme exécutif; programme moniteur; visionneuse; ~ **card** carte moniteur

monitored *adj* surveillé; ~ **memory** circuit mémoire commandée

monitor function fonction moniteur

monitoring *n* contrôle; écoute; observation; prise en compte; suivi; surveillance; ~ **aerial** antenne de contrôle; antenne du moniteur de réception; ~ **amplifier** amplificateur d'écoute; ~ **circuit** circuit de contrôle; ~ **device** contrôleur; ~ **equipment** équipement de contrôle; dispositif d'écoute; ~ **key** clé d'écoute; clé de surveillance; ~ **of transmission level** contrôle de modulation; ~ **post** poste d'écoute; ~ **report link** liaison de compte-rendu de contrôle; ~ **subsystem** chaîne de contrôle; ~ **unit** organe de contrôle

monitor micro-jack jack micro-monitrice

monkey wrench clé à crémaillère; clé anglaise

monochord *n* sonomètre (objective)

monochromatic *adj* monochromatique

monochrome *adj* monochrome; noir et blanc

monocoaxial *adj* monocoaxial

monodyne reception réception synchrone

monogram (inlaid in PCB) filigrane

monolithic *adj* globalisé; monolithique; ~ **integrated circuit** circuit intégré monolithique

monomode fibre fibre monomode

monophase current courant monophasé

monopole beacon aerial antenne unipolaire de radiophare

monopulse coupler coupleur monopulse; ~ **radar system** système radar à monoimpulsion; ~ **tracking** poursuite monopulse

monostable *adj* monocoup; ~ **trigger circuit** bascule monostable

Monte Carlo simulation simulation discrète

MOPA (s. master oscillator power amplifier)

Morse (or 5-unit) printer traducteur imprimeur; ⁓ **alphabet** code morse; ⁓ **character** signe morse; ⁓ **code** code morse; ⁓ **dash** trait morse; ⁓ **dot** point morse; ⁓ **key** couineur; ⁓ **sender** émetteur morse; ⁓ **telegraph** télégraphe morse

mortar-locating radar radar localisateur de mortiers

mosaic telegraphy télégraphie à mosaïque; télégraphie par décomposition des signes

most-busy method remplissage au fur et à mesure

most significant bit (MSB) bit de gauche; bit de poids fort

mothballing *n* mise sous cocon

mother board carte mère; carte support; fond de panier (FdP/FdeP/FDP); panier d'alimentation; platine

motional impedance impédance cinétique

motive (driving) power force motrice

motor *n* moteur (MOT); machine de travail; machine motrice

motorboating *n* amorçage basse fréquence; choc de basse fréquence; oscillation BF parasite

motor control card carte régulation moteur; ~ **control circuit board** carte commande moteur; ~ **converter** convertisseur à cascade; ~ **current** intensité absorbée par

moteur

motor-driven actuator vérin motorisé; ~ **pump** motopompe

motor fuel essence; ~ **gearbox assembly** ensemble moto-réducteur; ~ **generator set** groupe convertisseur; groupe moteur-générateur

motorized keyboard clavier (à entraînement) mécanique; ~ **uniselector** sélecteur rotatif à moteur

motor-protection fuse fusible classe aM (accompagnement moteur)

motor spirit essence

motor-ventilator bank groupe moto-ventilateur

mottled *adj* chiné

moulded capacitor condensateur enrobé; ~ **spool** carcasse moulée

moulded-track potentiometer potentiomètre à piste moulée

mould growth (test) moisissure

moulding flash toile; ~ **stalk** carotte

mount *n* monture; support

mounted *adj* fixé

mounting *n* montage; berceau; calage; fixation; implantation; massif; piget de montage; réglette (rg.); ~ **bar** barrette de fixation; barreau support; ~ **base** embase (connecteur fixe); ~ **bracket** patte support; pontet; ~ **details** collage; ~ **direction** sens de montage; axe de fixation; ~ **frame** étiré support; ~ **pad** (for resistor) coussinet de montage; ~ **panel** panneau d'assemblage; ~ **pitch** (in subrack) pas d'implantation; ~ **plate** plaque support; platine de fixation; patte; ~ **rail/track** support profilé; profilé traverse; ~ **stud** pied de fixation; pavé; ~ **tab** pavé de fixation; ~ **track** Oméga [A.C.]

mount reverse assemblage symétrique

mouthpiece *n* embouchure; pavillon; cornet

mouth-to-mouth resuscitation insufflation pulmonaire

M out of N code code N dont M

MOVE key déplacement (DEP)

movement *n* défilement; activité; déplacement; mouvement; avance; ~ **file** fichier d'activités; ~ **window** fenêtre de déplacement

move ticket fiche de suivi; fiche suiveuse

moving charge charge mobile; ~ **coil** bobine mobile; équipage mobile

moving-coil ammeter ampèremètre à cadre mobile; ~ **galvanometer** galvanomètre à câble mobile; ~ **instrument** instrument à cadre mobile; ~ **loudspeaker** haut-parleur à bobine mobile; ~ **meter** appareil de mesure à aiguille; ~ **microphone** micro-

phone à bobine mobile; ~ **receiver** récepteur à bobine mobile

moving-conductor microphone microphone à conducteur mobile; microphone à ruban

moving contact (of relay) lame mobile; contact mobile; ~ **cursor** curseur mobile; ~ **display** affichage dynamique; ~ **echo** écho mobile

moving-head disk (unit) disque magnétique à tête mobile

moving-iron loudspeaker haut-parleur à induction; ~ **microphone** microphone à fer mobile

moving tailstock poupée mobile

moving-target indication radar (MTI) radiodétection à effet Doppler-Fizeau; radiodétection à élimination des échos fixes

MPW (s. map partition onto window)

MSB (s. most significant bit)

MSI (s. medium-scale integration)

MTBF (s. mean time between failures); ~ **indicator** fiabilité

MTC (s. main transit centre)

MTI (s. moving-target indication radar)

MTL (s. message terminal load)

MTP (s. message transfer part)

MTTR (s. mean time to repair)

MUF (s. maximum usable frequency factor)

mu-factor *n* facteur d'amplification de tension

muffled *adj* amorti

mu-law encoding codage non uniforme

muldem *n* multiplexage-démultiplexage

muldex (digital multiplexer plus demultiplexer) multiplexeur-démultiplexeur

multi-address call appel multi-adresses; ~ **calling** adresses multiples; ~ **message** communication télégraphique circulaire; message collectif

multi-aperture core transfluxeur

multi-aspect search recherche multicritères

multi-band aerial antenne multibande

multi-beam aerial antenne à faisceaux multiples; ~ **satellite link** connexion de satellite à plusieurs faisceaux

multi-bus system réseaux parallèles

multi-carrier operation exploitation multiporteuse; ~ **transmitter** émetteur à plusieurs porteuses; ~ **transponder operation** opération de répondeur à porteuses multiples

multi-cellular loudspeaker haut-parleur multicellulaire

multi-channel communications line ligne de télécommunication multiplex; ~ **connector** connecteur multivoie; ~ **decentralized system** système à canaux multiples décentralisé; ~ **multi-carrier system** système à plusieurs porteuses sur voies multiples; ~ **radio teletype** système à plusieurs voies de radio-téléimpression; ~ **radio transmitter** émetteur radioélectrique à plusieurs canaux; ~ **straight receiver** récepteur à amplification directe avec plusieurs canaux; ~ **system** faisceau; ~ **telegraphy** télégraphie à plusieurs canaux; ~ **television** télévision à plusieurs canaux; ~ **VF telegraphy** télégraphie harmonique à plusieurs voies

multi-component signal signal composé

multi-conference circuit circuit multiconférence

multi-core multibrins; ~ **cable** câble multiple; câble à plusieurs conducteurs

multi-coupler n amplificateur séparateur

multi-criterion search recherche multicritères

multi-disciplinary polytechnique

multi-drop (line) à dérivation multiple; liaison multipoint; ~ **network** réseau multipoint

multi-electrode valve polyode; ~ **voltage stabilizer** tube à cathode froide à plusieurs électrodes; tube stabilisateur à plusieurs électrodes

multi-fibre splicing (mass splicing) épissure collective

multi-file volume volume multi-fichier

multiframe n multitrame; ~ **alignment pattern** verrouillage multitrames; ~ **loss** perte de multitrame; ~ **signal** signal de multitrame; ~ **structure** composition de la multitrame

multifrequency adj multifréquence (MF); à fréquences multiples; ~ bifréquence; toutes-ondes; ~ **circuit** circuit à signalisation multifréquence; ~ **code (MF)** code bifréquence; code multifréquence; ~ **transmitter** émetteur à fréquences préréglées

multi-function multi-tasking monitor moniteur multifonctions multitâches (MMT)

multigraph n multigraphe

multi-hop transmission transmission par réflexions successives

multilayer circuit circuit multicouche; ~ **coil** bobine à couches multiples; ~ **diode** diode multijonctions; ~ **printed circuit board** circuit imprimé multicouche; ~ **winding** enroulement à plusiers couches

multi-leaving n multi-émission

multi-level adj hiérarchisé; multiniveau; ~ **addressing** adressage indirect; ~ **code** code à plusieurs niveaux; ~ **coding** codage multiniveau; ~ **discrimination** sélection sur plusieurs niveaux; ~ **exchange** centre multibrique; ~ **fax** télécopie nuancée; ~ **pulse code** code de modulation d'impulsions à plusieurs niveaux; ~ **sort** tri à plusieurs niveaux

multi-line extension poste multiligne (sym-

bole); ~ **hunting group** groupement; ~ **transmission circuit** dispositif de diffusion

multimeter n contrôleur universel

multimetering n taxation par impulsions périodiques

multi-modal transient excitation excitation transitoire à modes différents

multi-mode distortion distorsion multimode; ~ **fibre** fibre multimode

multi-national adj transnational

multipactor gap loading charge de l'espace d'interaction

multi-party call appel collectif; ~ **line** ligne collective; ligne multipartie

multi-path fading évanouissement sous plusieurs angles; ~ **propagation** propagation par trajets multiples; transmission par trajets multiples; ~ **reflection** réflexion par plusieurs voies; ~ **return** retour par trajets multiples; ~ **signals** signaux à plusieurs voies; ~ **transmission** émission sous plusieurs angles

multi-pin adj multibroche

multiple n banc de contacts de lignes; multiplage décalé; ~ **access** accès multiple

multiple-access satellite satellite à plusieurs accès

multiple-address multi-adresse

multiple addressing adressage multiple

multiple-address instruction instruction à plusieurs adresses

multiple-answering equipment équipement de réponse multiple

multiple-beam aerial antenne à faisceaux multiples

multiple-bit adj multivalent

multiple cards cartes multiples

multiple-channel analyser analyseur multicanaux; ~ **connector** connecteur multivoie

multiple-coil relay relais multiple (RM)

multiple conductor conducteur multiple; ~ **connection** connexion multiple; ~ **connector** connecteur multiple

multiple-contact switch combinateur; combineur

multiple conversion multiconversion; ~ **crosstalk** diaphonie multiple; ~ **ferroresonance** ferrorésonance multiple; ~ **folded dipole** doublet replié multiple

multiple-gun CRT tube cathodique à plusieurs canons

multiple image image fantôme; écho; ~ **jack** jack multiple; ~ **modulation** modulation multiple

multiple-mount assembly implantation multiposes; multipose

multiple plug connecteur multiple; ~ **relay**

relais multiple (RM); ~ **signal** signe multiple; ~ **switch** contacteur multipolaire; ~ **switchboard** tableau commutateur multiple; ~ **transmitter** émetteur radioélectrique multiple

multiple-twin (quad) cable quarte Dieselhorst-Martin (DM); câble à quartes DM (Dieselhorst-Martin); câble à paires combinables

multiple-unit steerable aerial (MUSA) antenne musa; antenne orientable

multiplex v multiplexer; aiguiller; ~ n concentration; ~ (carrier) multiplex; ~ **aggregate bit rate** débit binaire cumulé d'un multiplex; ~ **aggregate bit stream** train de bits composite multiplexé; ~ **channel** voie composite; canal multiple; ~ **connection unit** unité de raccordement multiplex

multiplex-demultiplex circuit opérateur de transformation orthogonale

multiplexed data paquet; ~ **homing radar** radar d'approche à multiplexage; ~ **information** information paquetée

multiplexer (MUX) n multiplexeur; multiplicateur; polyplexeur; combinateur; combineur

multiplex hierarchy hiérarchie de multiplexage

multiplexing n multiplexage; aiguillage; répartition; panachage; ~ **equipment** équipement de multiplexage; ~ **with flying capacitor** multiplexage à transfert capacitif

multiplex interface jonction électronique numérique

multiplexor n multiplexeur

multiplex system téléphonie par courants porteurs; ~ **telegraphy** télégraphie multiplex; ~ **telephony** téléphonie multiplex; ~ **transmitter** émetteur multiplex

multiplication factor facteur de multiplication

multiplier n diviseur; multiplicateur; multiplieur

multipling over/to multiplage (sur)

multi-ply (of paper roll) multicopie

multiplying punch calculatrice perforatrice

multi-point adj multibroche; ~ **circuit** circuit multipoint; ~ **link** liaison multipoint; ~ **network** réseau multipoint; réseau à points multiples; ~ **selector** sélecteur à plusieurs étages; ~ **TDM telegraphy** télégraphie numérique multipoint

multi-pole switch contacteur à touches; contacteur multipolaire

multi-position switchboard standard

multiprocessing n multitraitement

multiprogramming n multiprogrammation

multi-purpose language langage universel; ~ **tester** machine de contrôle polyvalent

multi-rate meter compteur à tarifs multiples

multiregister multi-enregistreur

multi-routing n multiroutage; ~ **capability** autonomie d'acheminement; ~ **time switch** unité de commutation temporelle à autonomie d'acheminement

multi-signaller n multisignaleur

multi-slot connection connexion semi-permanente (par groupes de voies temporelles)

multi-source adj hétérogène

multi-spectral imagery prise de vue multispectrale; ~ **scanner** analyseur multispectre

multi-stage amplifier amplificateur en cascade; ~ **call holding** multigarde; ~ **index table** table à tiroir; ~ **network** réseau àétages

multi-switch (thumbwheel switch) n présélecteur; contacteur multipolaire

multi-tasking adj multitâche

multi-tuned aerial antenne à accord multiple

multi-turn wire-wound potentiometer potentiomètre bobine multitours

multi-unit message (MUM) message multiple

multi-up layout implantation multiposes

multivibrator n bascule instable; multivibrateur; oscillateur; basculeur bistable

multi-way adj multicontact; multipoint; ~ **connector** connecteur multibroches; connecteur multicontacts; ~ **switch** contacteur multipolaire; ~ **terminal** borne multipolaire

multi-wire circuit circuit plurifilaire

MUM (s. multi-unit message)

"**Mumetal**" [T.N.] (high permeability magnetic zinc alloy) mumétal

MUSA (s. multiple-unit steerable aerial)

mush n brouillage; distorsion

mushroom-head joint soudure bouton; ~ **rivet** rivet goutte de suif; ~ **screw** vis Poêlier

mushy signal signal brouillé

music circuit circuit radiophonique; ~ **line** ligne de modulation

music-on-hold n attente musicale; musique d'attente; ~ **signal** commande d'attente musicale

mute n arrêt bip; ~ **button** touche secret; ~ **function** fonction secret; inhibition microphone; ~ **key** clé de coupure de sonnerie

mutilate v altérer

mutilated adj incohérent; erroné; incomplet; ~ (of message packet) mutilé

mutilation n altération; détérioration; pollution

muting n affaiblissement; atténuation; blocage; inhibition; ~ **circuit** blocage (d'un récepteur); ~ **control** réglage silencieux

mutual aid entraide(s)

mutual-aid network réseau à entraide
mutual assistance collaboration; coopération; ~ **back-up** secours croisé; ~ **broadcasting system** radiodiffusion à ondes communes; ~ **capacitance** capacité effective; capacité de sonde; ~ **characteristic** caractéristique mutuelle; ~ **conductance** pente; transconductance; ~ **consent** accord commun; ~ **coupling** couplage mutuel; couplage par transformateur; ~ **impedance** impédance de transfert; transimpédance; ~ **inductance** inductance électrique; inductance mutuelle
mutual-inductance coefficient coefficient d'induction mutuelle; ~ **coupling** couplage par inductance mutuelle
mutual- inductance coupling transformer transformateur à induction
mutual induction induction mutuelle; effet de couplage; ~ **interaction** interaction mutuelle; ~ **interference** perturbation réciproque
mutually exclusive s'excluent
mutually-synchronized network réseau à synchronisation mutuelle
mu-tube (variable) lampe à pente variable
MUX (s. multiplexer)
MW (s. medium wave); ~ (s. message waiting)
M-wire *n* fil TRON (transmission)
myriametric wave (VLF band) onde myriamétrique

N

NA (s. numerical aperture); ∼ (s. not applicable)

NAK (s. negative acknowledgement)

name plate plaque d'identification

naming and invocation of geometric codes désignation et appel des codes géométriques; ∼ **rules** règles et tables d'échantillonnage

NAND (= NOT AND) NON-ET; ET-NON; ON; ∼ **function** interdiction alternative; ∼ **gate** circuit NON-ET; circuit de Sheffer; porte NON-ET

nanosecond n nanoseconde

narrative n commentaire

narrow-band n fréquence fixe; ∼ adj à bande étroite; infratéléphonique; ∼ **amplifier** amplificateur à bande étroite; ∼ **channel** voie infratéléphonique; ∼ **circuit** circuit à bande étroite; ∼ **frequency modulation** modulation de fréquence à bande étroite

narrow-bandpass filter filtre à bande étroite

narrow-beam aerial antenne à faisceau étroit

narrow-casting n radiodiffusion spécialisée

narrow pulse impulsion fine

N-**ary digit** chiffre N-aire; ∼ **symbol** symbole N-aire

national call communication nationale; ∼ **exchange** central national; ∼ **extension (trunk) circuit** circuit national de prolongement; ∼ **management centre** centre national de gestion; ∼ **number** numéro national; ∼ **numbering plan** plan de numérotation national; plan de numérotage national; ∼ **traffic** trafic national; ∼ **trunk circuit** circuit interurbain national; ∼ **videotex centre** centre national vidéotex

natural disaster cas de force majeure; ∼ **draught** tirage naturel; ∼ **frequency** fréquence propre; ∼ **interference** parasite naturel; bruit naturel; ∼ **logarithm** logarithme népérien; logarithme en base 10; ∼ **magnet** aimant naturel; ∼ **mode** condition d'oscillation propre; ∼ **noise** bruit naturel; ∼ **period** période propre; ∼ **wave** onde propre; ∼ **wavelength** longueur d'onde propre

navigation aid aide à la navigation

navigational radar radiodétecteur de navigation

navigator chain chaîne de radionavigation

NC (s. normally-closed contact); ∼ (s. not connected); ∼ **push-button** (break) bouton repos (R)

NCR **paper** (non-carbon ribbon) papier autocopiant; liasse dupli-autocopiant

NCTE (s. network circuit terminating equipment)

NDB (s. non-directional radio beacon)

near adj proche; adjacent; ∼ **echo** écho rapproché

near-end crosstalk (NEXT) paradiaphonie; ∼ **crosstalk attenuation** affaiblissement paradiaphonique

nearest approach distance critique d'approche; ∼ **preferred value** valeur normalisée la plus proche

near-field region région d'induction

near-infrared adj proche infrarouge

near-letter quality (NLQ) qualité courrier approché

nearly-logarithmic quasi-logarithmique

near-singing condition tendance à l'amorçage; ∼ **distortion** distorsion au voisinage du point d'amorçage

near zone zone d'induction

neck n (of tube) col

necking adj rétrécissant

neck region zone du col; ∼ **shadow** ombre du col

needle counter tube tube compteur à aiguille

negation logic logique d'inversion

negative acknowledgement (NAK) accusé de réception négatif (NAK); non bien reçu; ∼ **bias** polarisation négative; ∼ **booster** dévolteur; ∼ **edge-triggered latch** bascule (type) SR

negative-feedback condition dégénérescence

negative glow lumière négative

negative-going pulse impulsion négative; ∼ **transition** front descendant; front de descente; transition négative

negative-impedance converter convertisseur d'impédance négative; ∼ **repeater** répéteur à impédance négative

negative justification justification négative; ∼ **kilo-calorie** frigorie; ∼ **line feed** saut de ligne arrière; ∼ **logic** actif à l'état bas; ∼ **modulation** modulation negative; ∼ **pole** pôle négatif

negative-temperature coefficient (NTC) thermistor résistance CTN

negative terminal borne négative; ~ **transmission** transmission à modulation négative; ~ **two-wire repeater** répéteur négatif téléphonique pour circuit à deux fils; ~ **wire** fil négatif

negentropy *n* contenu moyen de l'information

NEITHER-NOR NON OU (= NI)

neon indicator tube tube indicateur à néon; ~ **lamp** lampe à néon

Neoprene [T.N.] polychloroprène

neper néper

nest *v* imbriquer; emboîter; ~ *n* alvéole; faisceau de tubes; nid

nested (sub-routines) sous-programmes imbriqués; ~ **loop** boucle imbriquée; boucle emboîtée

nesting *n* emboîtement; imbrication; imbriquage

net control station station de contrôle du réseau; ~ **loss** affaiblissement net; équivalent

net-loss measurement mesure d'équivalent

net margin marge nette; ~ **present value (NPV)** valeur actualisée nette (VAN); ~ **switching loss (NSL)** affaiblissement net de commutation

nett (after tax) toutes taxes compris (TTC); net

net transmission equivalent équivalent de transmission

network *n* réseau; appareil; chaîne; circuit; dispositif; pont; ~ **access device** organe d'accès au réseau; ~ **analyser** analyseur de réseaux; ~ **analysis point** centre d'analyse du réseau; ~ **circuit terminating equipment (NCTE)** équipement de raccordement d'abonné; ~ **cluster** faisceau de faisceaux; réseau partiel; ~ **controller** exploitation; ~ **control signalling unit** unité de commande de réseau; ~ **development** développement du réseau; ~ **digitization** numérisation des réseaux

networked *adj* communicant; communiquant; coopérant; ~ **services** téléservice

network equipped with arc-suppression coils réseau équipé au moyen de bobines d'extinction; ~ **gateway** frontal d'accès

networking *adj* fédérateur

network interface module (NIM) boîtier d'adaptation réseau (BAR); dispositif de raccordement (au réseau); ~ **layer** (ISO protocol) couche acheminement; ~ **management** gestion du réseau; ~ **management point** centre de gestion du réseau; ~ **management signal** signal de gestion du réseau; ~ **parameter** caractéristique du réseau; ~ **planning** planification des réseaux; études de réseaux; prévision du réseau;

~ **planning group** groupe d'études réseaux; ~ **protocol** procédure réseau; ~ **supervision centre** centre d'exploitation; ~ **termination** régie d'installation d'abonnés; ~ **utility field** champ des services inter-réseau; ~ **with earth-connected neutral** réseau neutre relié à la terre; ~ **with isolated neutral** réseau à neutre isolé

net worth situation nette

neutral *n* point neutre; masse; point mort; zéro; ~ *adj* neutre; au repos; mort; non polarisé; sans importance; sans influence; stable; ~ **conductor** régime du neutre; fil froid

neutral-current generator générateur de courant simple; ~ **telegraphy** télégraphie à courant simple

neutral direct-current system transmission par simple courant; ~ **(isolating) link** (sectionnement du) tube de neutre

neutralization *n* équilibrage

neutralizing bridge neutralisation en pont; ~ **capacitor** condensateur d'équilibrage; condensateur neutrodyne; ~ **circuit** circuit de neutrodynage (en croix)

neutral keying modulation à simple courant; ~ **lead** conducteur de neutre; ~ **line** ligne neutre; ~ **link** tube du neutre; ~ **point** régime du neutre; ~ **relay** relais non polarisé; relais à l'indifférence; ~ **square-wave voltage** tension simple d'onde carrée; ~ **wire** conducteur de neutre

neutrodyning *n* neutrodynage; ~ **capacitor** condensateur d'équilibrage; ~ **circuit** circuit de neutrodynage (en croix)

new-call event signalling nouvel appel (NA); ~ **message** message de nouvel appel (NA)

new line (NL) retour à la ligne

new-line mapping mode topographie d'interligne

news (bulletin) information(s)

newscast *n* journal parlé

newsflash *n* dépêche

news media moyens d'information

newspaper column colonne journalistique; ~ **transmission** transmission de journaux

news service service du journal parlé

new subscriber service service supplémentaire

next forcé

NEXT (key) SUITE; ~ (s. near-end crosstalk)

next-function stringing enchaînement

next generation horizon 2000; ~ **instruction** passage en séquence

next-instruction address phase suivant; phase préparée; ~ **code** code d'enchaînement

next page (instruction) page suivante; saut de page; ~ **phase** forçage avance; ~ **transmitted bit** bit suivant transmis

N

nibble *n* (nybble) quartet; demi-octet; groupe de quatre bits (= tétrade)

nibbler *n* grignoteuse

nickel-cadmium battery accumulateur cadmium-nickel

nickel-silver maillechort

night (trunk) **answer** renvoi de nuit; ~ **alarm** sonnerie de nuit

night-alarm switch commutateur de nuit

night-answer service services simplifiés

night bell sonnerie de nuit; ~ **call** communication nocturne

night-call number numéro d'appel de nuit

night console pupitre de nuit; ~ **effect** effet de nuit

night-effect-free radio beacon radiophare protégé des erreurs de nuit

night error erreur de nuit; ~ **kiosk** cabine de nuit; ~ **light** veilleuse; ~ **position** position de nuit; ~ **rate** tarif de nuit

night-reception zone zone de nuit

night service (general ringer) appel général; ~ **service** mise de l'installation en renvoi

night-service connection renvoi des lignes pour le service de nuit; ~ **key** clé de renvoi de nuit

nightwatchman service contrôle de ronde

NIM (s. network interface module)

ninety-degree double tongue connector connecteur chantourné

nip *n* enfoncement; pincement

nippers *n pl* pince flanc

nipple *n* embout

Nixie tube [T.N.] tube indicateur; tube Nixie

NL (s. new line)

N-level address adresse indirecte

NLQ (s. near-letter quality)

NO (s. normally-open contact)

no-address instruction instruction sans adresse

no-answer call appel sans réponse

no-bell station abonné non sonné

noble metal métal précieux

no-current pulse moment d'absence de courant

nodal exchange centre nodal (CN); ~ **sorting centre** centre nodal de triage

node *n* aboutissement; nœud; point nodal; pôle; sommet; ~ **of grid store** nœud du maillage

no-dialling call appel sans numérotation

nodular cast iron graphite sphéroïdal

no flutter sans scintillement

no-free-path circuit circuit d'occupation totale

no-free-trunk condition refus de prise

no-go *n* refus

noise *n* bruit; parasites radio; ~ (QRN) distorsion; ~ **allocation** attribution du bruit; ~ **allotment** attribution du bruit;

~ **amplifier** amplificateur à bruit; ~ **band** bande de fréquence du bruit; ~ **blanking** suppression des parasites; ~ **current** courant perturbateur; courant du bruit; ~ **eliminator** dispositif antiparasite; ~ **field** champ perturbateur; ~ **figure** figure de bruit; facteur de bruit; niveau de bruit; ~ **filter** filtre anti-parasites; ~ **generator** perturbateur; générateur de bruit; ~ **induction** induction de bruit; ~ **intensity** intensité du bruit; ~ **inverter** inverseur de parasites; limiteur de parasites; ~ **jamming** perturbation; ~ **limiter** limiteur de bruit; inverseur de parasites; ~ **margin** marge de protection contre les perturbations; ~ **measurement** mesure du bruit; ~ **measuring apparatus** appareil de mesure de bruit; ~ **meter** psophomètre; sonomètre (objective); mesureur de la tension de bruit; ~ **output** puissance du bruit; ~ **peak** crête de bruit; ~ **power** puissance de bruit; ~ **prevention** prévention de bruit; ~ **reduction** réduction du bruit; ~ **resistance** résistance de bruit; ~ **signal** signal de bruit; ~ **source** perturbateur; source de bruit; source d'interférence; ~ **spectrum** spectre de bruit; ~ **spike** parasite(s); ~ **suppression** limitation des parasites; ~ **suppressor** limiteur de parasites; inverseur de parasites; ~ **temperature** température de bruit; ~ **voltage** tension perturbatrice; tension de bruit

noisy *n* bruyant; ~ **blacks** noir perturbé; ~ **circuit** circuit bruyant; circuit friteureux

NOK (non-compliant) KO (non conforme)

no-load *adj* à vide; ~ **current** courant à vide; ~ **operation** marche à vide; ~ **test** essai à vide; ~ **voltage** tension à vide

nomenclature *n* nomen(clature) (Nre.); désignation

nominal *adj* idéal; nominal; théorique; ~ **black** noir artificiel; ~ **black signal** signal de noir nominal; ~ **frequency** fréquence de travail; ~ **margin** marge nominale; ~ **maximum circuit** circuit fictif de référence; ~ **operating time** (of relays) temps de réponse à U_n; ~ **polarization** polarisation principale; ~ **pulse** impulsion idéale; ~ **range** portée nominale; ~ **reference equivalent** équivalent de référence nominal; ~ **transmission loss of the four-wire circuit between virtual switching points** affaiblissement nominal entre extrémités virtuelles du circuit à quatre fils; ~ **white** blanc artificiel

nominated direct circuit circuit direct spécialement désigné

nomogram *n* abaque

non-ambiguous univoque

non-associated mode (of signalling) code (de signalisation) non-associé; ~ **signalling mode** exploitation en mode non asssocié; mode non associé

non-axial ray rayon non axial

non-blocking *n* absence de blocage; ~ **network** réseau sans blocage; ~ **switching network** réseau de connexion à blocage nul

non-centralized control dispersion de la commande

non-chargeable *adj* sans taxation; ~ **call** appel non taxé

non-combustible *adj* incombustible

non-compelled message message spontané; ~ **multifrequency code** code multifréquence non asservi

non-compensated length longueur non compensée

non-completion code code d'échec; ~ **rate** (of calls) taux d'échec

non-compliance *n* intolérance

non-conductive diélectrique

non-conjunction *n* NON ET (= ON/ET-NON); incompatibilité

non-contiguous *adj* disjoint

non-cumulative (tolerance) non cumulatif (NC)

non-dedicated area zone banalisée; ~ **distributed core** architecture à cœur réparti universel; ~ **storage** mémoire utilisable; ~ **terminal** terminal au repos

non-delayed action action instantanée

non-destructive read lecture sans effacement; lecture non destructive

non-deviation absorption absorption ionosphérique sans déviation de vitesse de groupe

non-directional aerial antenne omnidirectionnelle; antenne non directionnelle; antenne non directive; antenne sans effet directif; antenne omnidirective; ~ **microphone** microphone omnidirectionnel; ~ **radio beacon (NDB)** radiophare à diagramme circulaire

non-disjunction *n* NON OU (= NI)

non-dissipative stub bras de réactance

non-duplicated *adj* non doublé; ~ **logic circuit** logique simple

non-electrical hole trou mécanique; ~ **noise** bruit mécanique

non-entry (ex-directory subscriber) non inscription dans l'annuaire (liste rouge)

non-equivalence *n* circuit à anticoïncidence; OU exclusif

non-equivalent line ligne non groupée

non-erasable storage mémoire inaltérable; mémoire non effaçable

non-exclusive grant concession non exclusive

non-execution *n* inexécution

non-existent code check contrôle d'existence

non-fatal error erreur récupérable

non-fired *adj* non vitrifié

non-flammable *adj* ininflammable; ignifuge

non-folded network réseau droit

non-fulfilment *n* non satisfaction

non-fusing factor courant de non fusion

non-identity operation opération OU

non-inductive *adj* aselfique; ohmique; ~ **capacitor** condensateur non selfique; ~ **resistance** résistance non inductive

non-intelligible crosstalk diaphonie inintelligible

non-interactive output sortie hors dialogue

non-inverting amplifier amplificateur non inverseur; amplificateur suiveur; ~ **input** entrée non inverseuse

non-ionizing radiation level niveau du rayonnement non ionisant

non-linear distortion distorsion non linéaire; distorsion de non linéarité; distorsion de temps de propagation; distorsion harmonique; ~ **distortion factor** facteur de distorsion non linéaire; ~ **frequency multiplier** multiplicateur de fréquence non linéaire; ~ **network** réseau non linéaire; ~ **susceptibility** susceptibilité non linéaire; ~ **transformation** transformation non linéaire

non-loaded cable câble non pupinisé

non-locking (of key) fugitive (clé f.); ~ **button** bouton à retour

non-lossy *adj* non dissipatif; sans perte

non-metric *adj* en pouces

non-modulated frequency fréquence au repos

non-null *adj* différent de zéro; ~ **list** liste non vide; ~ **value** valeur quelconque

non-operate current courant inactif

non-operation *n* non fonctionnement

non-operational *adj* statique

non-oriented graph graphe non orienté

non-party line ligne non partagée

non-phantom circuit circuit non combinable

non-polarized *adj* non polarisé; ~ **relay** relais non polarisé

non-porous *adj* étanche

non-printing character caractère non imprimable; ~ **service signal** signal de service sans impression

non-quad cable câble à paires

non-quantized system système non quantifié

non-reactive *adj* ohmique; ~ **load** charge résistive; ~ **loop** boucle selfique; boucle franche; ~ **resistance** résistance réactive

non-recoverable failure panne mortelle

non-reflective *adj* antireflet

non-repeatered circuit ligne sans répéteurs

non-repetitive peak reverse voltage tension inverse de pointe non répétitive

non-resident *adj* amovible; ~ **program** programme amovible

non-resonant aerial antenne apériodique; antenne de Beverage; ~ **(Beverage) aerial** antenne en losange; ~ **circuit** circuit apériodique

non-retriggerable *adj* non redéclenchable

non-return *adj* sans retour

non-returnable *adj* jetable; ~ **deposit** forfait; ~ **packaging** emballage perdu

non-return-to-zero (NRZ) non retour à zero; ~ **code** code sans retour à zéro

non-reversing motor moteur à un sens de marche

non-saturated NOR circuit circuit NI sans capacité

non-selective attenuation affaiblissement non sélectif

non-self-cancelling sans rappel

non-(self-)locking key clé à retour; ~ **pushbutton** bouton poussoir à retour

non-shorting switch commutateur à plots isolées

non-shrink *adj* sans retour

non-specialization *n* polyvalence

non-specular *adj* diffusant

non-spill battery accumulateur inversible

non-standard *adj* spécifique; exceptionnel; hors gabarit; hors tolérance(s)

non-stationary interference interférence non stationnaire

non-stop *adj* permanent

non-system *adj* extérieur; externe

non-telephone services services paratéléphoniques

non-temporary (of data set) semipermanent

non-toggling flip-flop bascule antirebond

non-transient fault anomalie permanente

non-transparency *n* discontinuité

non-trigger current courant de non amorçage; ~ **voltage** tension de non amorçage

non-tropical *adj* métropolitain

non-uniform (continuous) quantization codage non uniforme

non-urgent alarm alarme différée; alarme intervention différée; alarme sans intervention

non-vacant *adj* non vide

non-volatile *adj* non volatile; rémanent; ~ **memory** mémoire sauvegardable; mémoire fixe; mémoire inaltérable; mémoire non volatile; mémoire permanente; mémoire rémanente; mémoire statique

non-volatility *n* sauvegarde par batteries; rémanence

non-weekday *n* jour non ouvrable

non-wetting *n* non mouillage

non-working day jour férié; jour non ouvrable; ~ **period** (holiday) congé(s)

non-zero *adj* non nul(le) (d'une valeur); différent de zéro

no-op *adj* ignoré

no-operation (NO-OP) opération ineffective; passage en séquence

no-op instruction (NOP) instruction fictive

NOP (s. no-op instruction)

NOR (= NOT OR) NI (= NON-OU); ~ **gate** circuit NI; circuit NON-OU; porte NI

norm *n* étalon; régime

normal DC restoration restauration normale de la composante continue; ~ **distribution curve** courbe de Gauss; ~ **distribution fuse** fusible classe gF; ~ **energy level** état normal (énergétique); niveau (énergétique) normal; ~ **glow discharge** décharge luminescente normale

normalized impedance facteur d'impédance d'onde

normal load circuit de charge réel

normally-closed contact (NC) contact de repos; contact à ouverture

normally-open contact (NO) contact de travail; contact à fermeture

normal/net margin of start-stop apparatus marge nette des appareils arythmiques

normal route voie d'acheminement normale; ~ **routing** acheminement normal; ~ **running torque** couple résistant en marche normal; ~ **starting duty** coupure moteur lancé; ~ **state** état normal (énergétique); ~ **transit** transit normal

Norton's theorem (equivalent to Thévenin's theorem = Helmholtz' theorem) théorème de Norton

nose cone ogive

nosing *n* nez de marche

no-such *adj* inexistant

no-such-number tone signal d'information

not différent de

NOT (element) NON (organe)

not-accepted fault défaut non accepté (DNa)

NOT-AND (NAND) operation incompatibilité; ~ **gate** circuit intersection-négation

not applicable (NA) sans objet; inutile; néant; ~ **assigned** inutilisé

notation *n* numération

NOT-BOTH NON ET (= ON/ET-NON)

not busy channel voie disponible

notch *n* encoche; cran; découpe; échancrure

notched belt courroie crantée; ~ **(cable) clip** collier cranté; ~ **plate for wiring board** peigne de quadrillage; ~ **washer** rondelle Z

notch filter filtre de réjection à flancs raides

notching *n* connexion en cascade; ~ **relay**

relais intégrateur d'impulsions
notch-tracer/-follower *n* palpeur
not-cleared fault défaut non effacé (DNe)
not connected (NC) non équipé; non câblé; sorties non connectées
notes *n* mémento
NOT gate circuit inverseur; circuit NON
notice file fichier gazette; fichier notice
notification avis
NOT-IF-THEN *n* exclusion; sauf
not implemented non exécutable
not-in-service hors service
not installed non équipé; hors meuble; ~ **in use** hors d'usage; hors service (h.s.); ~ **known** indéterminé; ~ **less than** au moins égale; ~ **optional** obligatoire; ~ **permitted** impossible; ~ **ready** non prêt
not-ready signal generator élaboration du "pas prêt"
not recognized inconnu; ~ **recommended** déconseillé; à proscrire; ~ **serviced** ignoré; ~ **set** non armé; ~ **shown** non dessiné; ~ **to be brought into contact with** craint; ~ **to scale** selon les cotes (s.l.c.); ~ **to standard** non conforme; ~ **upright** penché; ~ **used** inutilisé; non utilisé; ~ **working** hors service (h.s.)
novenary *adj* (to the base nine) novénaire
no-voltage trip déclencheur à manque de tension
nozzle *n* buse; nez; tuyère; ~ (of wave-soldering machine) fontaine céramique; carter céramique
n-p-i-n transistor transistor n-p-i-n
n-plus-one instruction instruction à adresse n-plus-une
N-port network réseau à paires de bornes; réseau à pôles
NPV (s. net present value)
NRZ (s. non-return to zero); ~ **code** code sans retour à zéro
NSL (s. net switching loss)
N-terminal network réseau à paires de bornes; réseau à pôles
nth n^e. (n-ième)
N-type coaxial connector fiche N; ~ **(p-type) conductivity** conductivité type n; ~ **semiconductor** semiconducteur par excès d'électrons
nuclear engineering génie nucléaire; ~ **particle** particule nucléaire; nucléon
nucleon *n* nucléon; particule nucléaire
nucleus *n* noyau
nuisance *n* gêne; ~ **call** appel malveillant; appel abusif; appel importun
null *n* zéro; caractère nul; caractère blanc; ~ *adj* nul; vide; ~ **adjustment** réglage du zéro; ~ **adjust pin** excentrique; ~ **character**

caractère non imprimable; ~ **circuit** amplificateur de boucle; ~ **device** périphérique nul; ~ **error** erreur de zéro; ~ **instruction** instruction fictive; instruction ineffective; instruction insignifiante; ~ **list** liste vide; ~ **message** message vide; ~ **modem cable** câble croisé; ~ **point** point d'équilibre
null-point detection équilibrage zéro; ~ **detector** signalisation de positionnement zéro
null shift dérive du zéro; ~ **signal** signal zéro; ~ **string** chaîne vide
number *v* numéroter; ~ *n* nombre (nb., nbre); chiffre (ch.); rang; numéro (N^o.); ~ **change** dénumérotage
number-crunching power puissance de calcul
number disk (of dial) couronne
numbering *n* numérotation; numérotage; ~ **area** zone de numérotage; ~ **machine** numérateur; ~ **plan** plan de numérotation; plan de numérotage; ~ **plan area (NPA)** zone de numérotage; ~ **plan area code** indicatif régional (IR); ~ **scheme** plan de numérotation; plan de numérotage; ~ **system** système de numération
number not-in-use signal de numéro non utilisé; ~ **of channels** parc de voies; ~ **of reported faults** taux de signalisation (SI); ~ **of signification conditions** (of a modulation or a restitution) valence; ~ **plate** (of rotary dial) disque numéroté
number-received signal signal de fin de sélection; signal de numéro reçu
number receiver annotateur; ~ **selection** numérotation; ~ **sign** (#) signe dièse
number-stamping device numéroteur à molettes
number-unobtainable tone (NU) tonalité d'abonné inaccessible; tonalité d'intervention interdictive; signal d'occupation de ligne
numeral *n* chiffre (ch.); ~ **ring** cadran numéroté
numerator *n* numéroteur à molettes; numérateur
numerical *adj* numérique; ~ **aperture (NA)** ouverture numérique (ON); ~ **code** code numérique; indicatif numérique; ~ **control** commande numérique
numeric data données numériques
numerical digits signes en chiffres; ~ **display** présentation numérique; ~ **selection** sélection numérique
numeric keypad clavier numérique; bloc numérique
nut *n* écrou; ~ **driver** clé à tube; clé emmanchée
NU tone tonalité de numéro inaccessible
nuts and bolts visserie

nut spinner clé à tube; clé emmanchée
nybble *n* demi-octet

Nyquist demodulator démodulateur à talon; ∼ **interval** bande Nyquist; ∼ **interval bandwidth** talon

O

OB (s. outside broadcast)
obeying *n* prise en compte
OBI (s. omnibearing indicator)
object code code exécutable; binaire exécutable; code résultant; ~ file fichier image
objective *n* but; visée; zone utile; ~ lens objectif
object language langage objet; langage d'exécution; langage machine; langage résultant; ~ module module résultant; module objet; unité de traduction objet; ~ procedure procédure objet
oblique exposure rapprochement oblique
oblique-incidence ionospheric recorder sondeur ionosphérique oblique; ~ ionospheric sounding sondage ionosphérique à incidence oblique; ~ transmission transmission sous incidence oblique
oblique projection perspective cavalière; ~ stroke barre; oblique
obliterate *v* effacer
obliteration *n* effacement
oblong *adj* rectangulaire
oboe (radar distance measuring system) système hautbois
observation post poste de contrôle (pc)
observed bearing angle de relèvement; ~ subscriber line abonné observé
obsolescent en extinction
obsolete *adj* désuet; périmé
obstruct *v* boucher
obstruction *n* engorgement
OB van car de reportage
obverse/reverse recto-verso
obviate *v* éviter
occasional *adj* fortuite; accidentel; éventuel; ~ fixed-time call conversation fortuite à heure fixe
occluder *n* obturateur
occupancy *n* facteur d'utilisation; durée de l'occupation de ligne; occupation; rendement; taux d'occupation; volume d'encombrement; ~ time durée d'occupation
occupant *n* propriétaire
occupied *adj* occupé; ~ bandwidth largeur de bande occupée; ~ position position occupée
occurrence *n* événement
oceanic satellite system système océanique de satellites

OCR (s. optical character recognition)
octal code code octal; ~ D-type flip-flop with clear octuple bascule type D avec RAZ; ~ tri-state buffer/latches amplificateur à trois états, huit bascules
octantal component of error composante sinusoïdale octantale de l'erreur; ~ error erreur d'espacement; erreur octantale
octave *n* bande d'octave
octode *n* octode
octothorpe carré (symbole: #); dièse
octupler *n* octuplicateur de fréquence
octuplex telegraphy télégraphie par superfantôme
odd *adj* impair
odd(-number) frame trame impaire
odd-even recto-verso; ~ check contrôle de parité; contrôle de parité impa -paire
odd harmonic harmonique d'ordre impair; ~ harmonic distortion distorsion de l'harmonique impair; ~ parity imparité; ~ parity bit élément binaire d'imparité; ~ parity check contrôle d'imparité; ~ translator gestion impair
ODH (s. output digital highway)
OE (s. original equipment)
OEM products (original equipment manufacturer) produits de départ
off *adj* l'arrêt; coupé; coupure; éteint; hors d'usage; hors service (h.s.); au repos; ouvert
off-air *adj* hors conversation; ~ call set-up établissement d'appel hors canal de conversation
off-axis angle angle par rapport à l'axe; ~ gain gain hors axe
off-boresight angle angle par rapport à l'axe de visée
off-centre *adj* désaxé; excentré; ~ plan display indicateur panoramique à excentration; ~ voltage tension d'excentrement
off-centring *n* décentrage de l'image
off-circuit *adj* hors circuit; ~ test essai à vide
off condition état ouvert
off-cuts *n* déchets
offending *adj* incriminé
offering *n* présentation; ~ call appel d'offre; ~ signal signal d'offre; signal d'appel
off-hook *n* (condition) décrochage (D); ~ *adj* décroché; déconnecté; ~ condition état

décroché; nouvel appel (NA); ~ **signal** signal de réponse

off-host adj semi-autonome

office n bureau; ~ adj administratif; ~ **automation** bureautique; ~ **cable** câble de service; ~ **code** code de bureau; indicatif (IF); liste d'indicateurs; ~ **code table** table de codes de bureau; ~ **of destination** bureau de destination; ~ **of origin** bureau d'origine; ~ **software** logiciel adapté aux sites; ~ **terminal** équipement terminal du centre

official n agent; ~ **call** conversation de service; ~ **communication** trafic de service; ~ **endorsement** visa pour application

off-line adj hors ligne; autonome; déconnecté; en différé; en local; hors fonctionnement; hors trafic; mode non connecté; non branché; ~ **printing** impression déportée; impression locale; impression spoulée

off-load v décharger; ~ adj à vide; au repos; à vide; hors tension; ~ **voltage** tension à vide

off-location working (of telematics) travail à distance; télétravail

off-net station station sans connexion au réseau

off-normal contact contact de tête; ~ **rest position** position de repos anormale

off-peak adj service restreint; réduit; ~ **load** charge moyenne; ~ **period** période creuse; heure creuse; ~ **rate** tarif hors pointe; ~ **tariff** tarif hors pointe; ~ **times** heures de faible trafic

off period temps de blocage du courant; ~ **position** position de repos

off-premises hors lieux; ~ **line** ligne longue

off-punching n décadrage

off-registration n décadrage

offset n écart; action différée; compensation; crantage; décrochement; dégagement; déplacement; déport; déréglage; dérive; désalignement; déséquilibre; excentrage; pente; ~ (blur) maculage; ~ adj déréglé; avancé; coudé; cranté; décalé; de côté; déporté; désaffleurant; désaxé; écarté; ~ (left margin) marge gauche

offset aerial antenne excentrée; ~ **(base) address** adresse de décalage; ~ **box wrench** clé en tube coudée; ~ **carrier** porteuse décalée; ~ **carrier system** système à ondes porteuses décalées; ~ **current** courant de décalage; ~ **deviation** dérive de pente; déformation; déviation d'inclinaison; écart en échelon

offset-fed alimentation excentrée

offset feed source primaire décalée; ~ **hole** (of PCB pad) mouche excentrée; ~ **null**

annulation de la tension de décalage; équilibrage; ~ **null voltage** dérive de la tension de décalage; ~ **plate/film** typon; ~ **PPI** (plan position indicator) image excentrique; ~ **printing** impression par report

offset-reflector aerial antenne à réflecteur excentré

offset register registre à décalage; ~ **screwdriver** tournevis coudé; ~ **signal method** système à signal décalé; ~ **socket wrench** clé à pipe

off-setting n décalage; réglage du zéro

offset variation variation d'offset; ~ **voltage** tension de déport; tension de décalage; ~ **voltage drift** gamme d'ajustement de la tension de décalage

off-shoot n dérivé

off-shore radio radiostation maritime

off-site adj déporté; base arrière; extérieur

off-state adj en blocage; ~ **aging** vieillissement en blocage; ~ **current** courant au blocage; ~ **recovery time** temps de recouvrement à l'état bloqué; ~ **voltage** tension à l'état bloqué

off-the-peg adj prêt à lemploi

off-the-shelf shipment livraison à lettre lue

off time temps de fermeture

off-white blanc cassé

O/G (s. outgoing)

ohmic contact contact ohmique; ~ **loss** perte ohmique; ~ **resistance** résistance en continu; résistance ohmique; ~ **resistor** résistance linéaire

ohmmeter n ohmmètre

Ohm's law loi d'Ohm

oil-break relay relais huilé; ~ **switch** disjoncteur à huile

oil exploration platform barge de forage

oil-filled relay relais huilé

oil-insulated relay relais huilé

oil-switch connection connexion d'interrupteur à huile

OK adj bon; ~ (prompt) tout va bien

oligarchic (synchronized) **network** réseau oligarchique

OMC (s. operation and maintenance centre); ~ **console** télépupitre

omnibearing indicator (OBI) indicateur d'azimut automatique

omnibus circuit ligne collective; ~ **(telegraph) system** système à postes embrochés

omnidirectional adj omnidirective; tous azimuts; ~ **aerial** antenne omnidirectionnelle; antenne à plan de sol; antenne à polarisation horizontale; antenne équidirective; antenne isotrope; antenne sans effet directif; antenne omnidirective

ON marche (MA); sous tension; passant; conducteur; distribué

on (of tones) émission; ~ (of switch) fermé

on-board *adj* de bord; embarqué; interne; ~ switching commutation embarquée

on call en astreinte

on-call channel canal de réserve

on-chip *adj* incorporé; interne; propre; ~ clock horloge intégrée; ~ microprocessor microprocesseur intégré; ~ oscillator horloge interne

on-demand *adj* à la demande; en temps réel; ~ call forwarding renvoi temporaire (commandé); renvoi temporaire variable

one, two, ...n-address instruction instruction à 1, 2, ... n adresses

one-ahead addressing adressage à progression automatique

one degree of freedom (of phase rule) monovariant

one-digit adder additionneur élémentaire à deux entrées; additionneur sans retenue

one digit out of ten un chiffre parmi dix; ~ duplex voice channel liaison duplex euphonie; ~ gate OU (cf. union, réunion)

one-level address adresse absolue; adresse directe; ~ code code absolu

one-pass compiler compilateur monopasse

one-piece case monobloc

one-plus-one address à une plus une adresses

one-port network accès d'un réseau

ones complement complément (binaire) à un; complément (binaire) restreint

one-shot *adj* à coup unique; monostable; ~ identification identification unique; ~ trigger circuit bascule monostable

one-step relay relais pas à pas

one-switch connection communication de transit simple

one-time *adj* non répétitive

one-to-n (connection) memory mémoire de diffusion

one-to-one (correspondence) bi-univoque; bijection; isomorphe

one-unit message message isolé; message simple

one-way *adj* unidirectionnel; à sens unique; unilatéral; ~ circuit circuit unidirectionnel; ~ network réseau unidirectionnel; ~ operation exploitation unidirectionnelle; ~ repeater répéteur unidirectionnel; répéteur dans un seul sens; ~ simplex communication à sens unique; ~ teletext vidéodiffusion

one-wire *adj* monofilaire

on full load à pleine charge

ongoing *adj* permanent; en cours

on-hold en garde; en instance

on-hook *adj* raccroché; connecté; ~ condition raccrochage; état raccroché; ~ dialling prise de ligne sans déchrochage (PLSD); numérotation sans décrocher; numérotation combiné raccroché; ~ message message de raccrochage (RAC)

on-hook/off-hook condition état du crochet commutateur

on-hook signal signal de raccrochage; signal de fin

on-line *adj* en ligne; connecté; en connexion; en direct; en fonctionnement; en mode connecté; en temps réel; immédiat; mode dialogué; ~ (application) en temps réel; ~ printing impression directe; impression immédiate; ~ TV programme library télévidéothèque; ~ user assistance convivialité (en temps réel)

only-route trunk group faisceau direct non débordant; faisceau d'acheminement unique; faisceau totalement fourni

on-net *adj* connecté; ~ station station connectée au réseau

on-off *adj* tout ou rien (TOR); ~ action action tout ou rien; ~ keying manipulation par tout ou rien; modulation par tout ou rien; ~ ratio rapport cyclique; rapport d'impulsions; ~ relay relais tout ou rien; ~ signalling modulation d'amplitude

ON/OFF switch commutateur marche-arrêt (MA); interrupteur de service

on-off telegraphy télégraphie entretenue pure; entrée tout ou rien

on opposite sides vis à vis; ~ or around au niveau de; ~ period temps d'ouverture

on-position position de travail

on-roll program block recording sauvegarde des pavés

on-screen distortion distorsion d'image

on-shore *adj* à terre

on stand-by activable; à puissance réduite

on-state aging vieillissement en fonctionnement; ~ channel canal conducteur; ~ resistance (R_{on}) résistance dans l'état passant; ~ slope resistance résistance apparente à l'état passant; ~ threshold voltage tension de seuil à l'état passant; ~ voltage tension à l'état passant

on-station à poste

'on' steady (lamp) allumé fixe

on-the-air en émission; en ondes

on-the-job training formation sur le tas

on the open market courant; du commerce; de la concurrence

on-the-spot *adj* instantané

on the verge of oscillation à la limite d'accrochage; ~ trial à l'essai; en expérimentation

OP (s. operator position); ~ **code (operation code)** code d'ordre; code d'opération; code opération
op-code DO bouclage
open (of system architecture) hétérogène; ~ **address** adresse ouverte; ~ **aerial** antenne libre; ~ **circuit** circuit ouvert
open-circuit admittance admittance en circuit ouvert; ~ **impedance** impédance en circuit ouvert; ~ **transfer impedance** impédance de transfert en circuit ouvert; ~ **voltage** tension à vide; ~ **working** transmission par envoi de courant
opened-out *adj* évasé
open end extrémité ouverte
open-ended *adj* évolutif; adaptable; dimensionnable; dynamique; extensible; ~ **spanner** clé à fourche; clé plate
open field champ de sécurisation; ~ **ground** terre franche
opening *n* ouverture; échancrure; fenêtre; lumière; ~ (of file) accès (à un fichier); ~ (of verticals) rupture
open-length numbering numérotation ouverte
open-loop line ligne en boucle ouverte
open market marché mondial; ~ **numbering plan** plan de numérotation ouverte
open-numbering plan short-code dialling numérotation abrégée ouverte
open routine sous-programme ouvert
open-shop *adj* porte ouverte
open-shut *adj* tout ou rien (TOR)
open-systems interconnection (OSI) (ISO) interconnexion des réseaux hétérogènes; interconnexion des systèmes ouverts; ~ **network** réseau banalisé
open wire fil en l'air; fil nu aérien; ligne aérienne
open-wire balancing network équilibreur de ligne aérienne; ~ **circuit** circuit aérien; ~ **line** ligne aérienne; ligne en fils nus aériens
open(-wire) loop boucle ouverte
open-wire telegraphy télégraphie sur ligne aérienne; ~ **telephone line** ligne aérienne pour la téléphonie
operand *n* facteur; ~ **field** (of instruction) partie opérande
operate *v* fonctionner; mettre en oeuvre; opérer; piloter; solliciter; ~ (of relay) enclencher; ~ **current** courant d'attraction (I$_A$); ~ **level** niveau de fonctionnement; ~ **time** temps de collage; temps de fonctionnement; ~ **time of a rectifier type echo suppressor** temps de fonctionnement d'un suppresseur d'écho à action continue
operating *adj* en service (ES); marche (MA); sous tension; distribué; ~ **a transmitter of**

high modulation percentage opération à modulation complète d'un émetteur; ~ **authority** exploitant; Administration (PTT); ~ **characteristics** caractéristiques de gabarit; ~ **company** compagnie exploitante; ~ **conditions** *n* régime; ~ **cost** coût d'exploitation; ~ **current** courant de travail; courant de déclenchement (I$_D$); ~ **cycle** cycle d'exploitation; ~ **error** erreur de manœuvre; ~ **frequency** fréquence de fonctionnement; ~ **frequency characteristic** caractéristique puissance de sortie/fréquence de travail; ~ **instructions** consignes d'exploitation; ~ **lever** levier de commande; ~ **limit** puissance limite admissible; ~ **memory** mémoire de travail
operating/output status memory mémoire d'occupation
operating point point de fonctionnement; point de détection; ~ **procedure** mode d'emploi; ~ **program** programme d'exploitation; ~ **schedule** calendrier d'exploitation; ~ **sequence** déroulement; ~ **system** système d'exploitation; ~ **temperature** température de service; température de basculement; température de fonctionnenent; température de régime; ~ **threshold** seuil de réponse; ~ **time** temps de réponse; ~ **transmitter** émetteur en service; ~ **voltage** tension de fonctionnement; tension de polarisation; tension de régime
operation *n* exploitation; action; activité; attaque; battement; collage; fonctionnement; instruction; manœuvre; mise en marche (MM); opération
operational amplifier amplificateur fonctionnel; ~ **diagram** schéma cinématique; chaîne cinématique; ~ **program** programme opérationnel; ~ **program binary** image mémoire rééditable; ~ **reasons** raisons d'exploitation; ~ **security** sécurité de fonctionnement; ~ **software** logiciel opérationnel; ~ **software development program** programme de support; ~ **software magnetic tape** bande système; ~ **versatility** souplesse de mise en œuvre
operation and maintenance (O & M) gestion; exploitation et maintenance; ~ **and maintenance centre (OMC)** centre d'exploitation et de maintenance (CEM); centre de traitement des informations (CTI); centre de gestion; ~ **and maintenance centre console** télépupitre; ~ **and maintenance message** message d'exploitation et de maintenance; ~ **and maintenance signal** signal d'exploitation; ~ **and maintenance terminal** organe d'exploitation; ~ **code** code d'opération; ~ **function** charge d'exploitation

operative *n* agent

operator assistance assistance d'un opérateur; intervention manuelle

operator-assisted conference call appel en conférence établi par l'opérateur; ~ test essai manuel

operator circuit circuit d'opératrice; ~ commands relations homme-machine (RHM); ~ command sheet fiche opérateur; ~ connection indicator indicateur de connexion opérateur (ICO); ~ console poste opérateur (PO); poste d'opératrice; pupitre activateur; pupitre de service; pupitre d'opératrice; ~ control intervention manuelle

operator-controlled exchange bureau manuel

operator data sheet fiche opérateur; ~ desk table d'opératrice; ~ group common circuit (GCC) circuit commun du groupement d'opérateur (CCG); ~ identification circuit circuit d'identification d'opérateur; ~ override intervention opératrice; ~ position manuel; meuble; position dirigeuse; position d'opératrice; position manuelle (PM); poste d'agent; table d'opératrice; ~ position (OP) poste opérateur (PO); ~ position coupling key clé à groupement; ~ recall rappel de l'opératrice; assistance; ~ release retrait

operator-selected *adj* paramétrable

operator set groupe opérateur; ~ station poste de service; poste central; poste d'agent; poste dirigeur

operator's telephone set poste d'opératrice; ~ time to answer délai de réponse (d'opératrice)

operator terminal poste de travail; terminal activateur

operator-to-operator intra-central

opposite-handed *adj* symétrique

opposite-phase en opposition de phase

opposition duplex système de téléimpression duplex; duplex par opposition

optal decoupler découpleur optique

optic(s) optique

optical *adj* optique; photosensible; ~ aberration aberration optique; ~ absorption absorption optique; ~ acceptance acceptance optique; ~ aerial antenne optique; ~ ammeter photocoupleur; ~ axis axe optique; ~ bus ligne bus optique; ~ carrier wave porteuse optique; ~ character reader lecteur optique; ~ character recognition (OCR) reconnaissance optique de caractères; lecture optique; ~ communications photonique; ~ communications research centre centre d'études de communications optiques; ~ comparator machine de pro-

jection; projecteur de profil; ~ conductor conducteur optique; ~ coupler coupleur optique; ~ emitter émetteur optique; ~ entrance unit prise optique d'appartement (PA); ~ fibre fibre optique; ~ fibre cable câble optique; jonc; ~ fibre link liaison optique; déport hertzien; ~ fibre pigtail fibre intermédiaire (de couplage); ~ fibre video cheveux de lumière; ~ fibre waveguide fibre guide de lumière; ~ horizon distance distance optique de l'horizon; ~ image (in a television camera) image optique (sur un tube analyseur); ~ imagery resources moyens optiques de l'imagerie

optically-aligned emitter émetteur linéaire

optical mark reader lecteur optique de marques; ~ modulator modulateur optique; ~ receiver capteur optique; ~ resonance résonance optique; ~ sound reproducer lecteur optique de son; ~ switch commutateur optique; ~ taper fibre fibre conique; ~ termination unit tête optique; ~ transmission transmission optique; ~ twinning hémitropie optique; ~ wattmeter wattmètre optique; ~ waveguide guide d'ondes optique

optimal merge tree arbre de fusion optimum; ~ (merge) tree computation calcul d'arbre minimal

optimization *n* optimalisation

optimizer *n* optimiseur

optimum *adj* meilleur; optimal; nominal; parfait; ~ addressing adressage optimal; ~ bunching groupement optimal; ~ code code à accès mimimum; ~ load impedance charge optimale; ~ traffic frequency fréquence optimale de trafic (FOT); ~ working frequency fréquence optimale de trafic (FOT); fréquence optimale de fonctionnement

option *n* possibilité(s)

optional *adj* facultatif; sur option; s'il y a lieu; à titre d'information; à titre indicatif; éventuel; ~ assignment affectation facultative; ~ extras option(s); ~ halt instruction instruction d'arrêt facultatif

opto-acoustic deflection déviation opto-acoustique

optocoupler *n* photocoupleur; coupleur optique; coupleur opto-électronique

opto-electronic component composant opto-électronique; ~ generator générateur électro-optique; ~ receiver récepteur électro-optique

opto-electronics *n* optoélectronique; optique électronique

opto-isolator *n* opto-seuil

optronics *n* optronique

orbit *n* orbite

orbital (second) **quantum number** nombre quantique secondaire; ~ (earth) **satellite** satellite; ~ **altitude** altitude d'orbite; ~ **arc** arc d'orbite; ~ **height** altitude d'orbite

orbit **assignment** attribution d'orbite; ~ **pollution** pollution d'orbite

orbit-sharing *n* partage d'orbite

OR **circuit** OU (cf. union, réunion)

order *n* ordre; commande (cde); consigne; rang; ~ **book** carnet de commandes; commandes enregistrées; ~ **booking** prise de commandes; ~ **checking** conformité des commandes

ordered **tree** arbre ordonné

order **hopper** file d'attente d'ordre (FAO)

ordering *n* classement; ~ **bias** écart d'ordre; ~ **code** codification commerciale; ~ **details** libellé d'une commande; ~ **schedule** commande programme

orderly **closedown** arrêt normal

order **of arrival** (of messages) priorité d'arrivée; ~ **of magnitude** ordre de grandeur; ~ **register** registre d'information; ~ **signal** (of radio broadcasting) signal d'ordre; ~ **turret** poste opérateur (PO); pupitre d'opératrice; position; ~ **wire** ligne d'ordre; ligne de renvoi; ligne de service; voie de service

order-wire **call** appel d'ordres; ~ **circuit** circuit de liaison entre opérateurs; circuit de renvoi; circuit de service; circuit d'ordres; ~ **pair** paire de service

ordinal **counter** compteur ordinal; ~ **number** nombre ordinal

ordinary **and multi-line extension** PABX autocommutateur mixte; ~ **call** conversation normale; ~ **line** ligne simple; ~ **private call** (in the international service) conversation privée ordinaire; ~ **subscriber line** abonné simple; ~ **subscriber line equipment** joncteur ordinaire

ordinate *n* axe des Y

ordinator *n* ordonnanceur

ORE (s. overall reference equivalent)

OR **element** OU (cf. union, réunion)

organ-console **model** type mobile; type piano

organizational **diagram** organigramme

OR **gate** circuit OU; mélangeur OU; porte OU

orientation *n* sens; sens de montage; visée; ~ **angle** angle d'orientation; ~ **range** plage d'orientation

oriented *adj* adapté (à); asservi; à vocation; lié (à); subordonné à; ~ **graph** graphe orienté

orifice *n* lumière; ouverture; trou; ajour

origin *n* origine; adresse primitive; source

original *n* historique; ~ *adj* novateur; brut; primitif; ~ **drawing** maquette; ~ **equipment (OE)** pièce montée (PM); ~ **packaging** conditionnement

originating (outgoing) **call** appel départ; communication de départ; ~ **class-of-service** discrimination départ; ~ **country** pays de départ; ~ **exchange** autocommutateur de départ; bureau de départ; ~ **mobile** mobile demandeur; ~ **number display** identification de la ligne appelante; ~ **register** enregistreur de départ; ~ **traffic** trafic de départ

originator *n* créateur; émetteur; initiateur

O-ring *n* joint torique; segment; garniture

OR **only** OU exclusif; ~ **operation** union; réunion

orphan *n* ligne orpheline

oscillating **current** courant d'oscillation

oscillation *n* oscillation; accrochage; balancement; battement; branle; ~ **characteristic** caractéristique d'oscillation; ~ **error** erreur d'oscillation; ~ **generator** générateur d'oscillations; ~ **peak** crête d'oscillation

oscillator *n* circuit oscillateur; oscillateur; pilote; ~ **crystal** cristal oscillateur; ~ **stage** stade oscillateur; ~ **tube** tube oscillateur

oscillogram *n* oscillogramme

oscillograph *n* oscillographe

oscilloscope *n* oscilloscope; ~ **carriage** chariot pour oscilloscope; ~ **channel** voie d'oscilloscope

OSI (s. open-systems interconnection)

other **than** différent de

O & M (s. operation and maintenance)

out *adj* (of lamp) éteint; ~ (end of communication) terminé

outage *n* indisponibilité; coupure; défaillance; panne; rupture de liaison; rupture de ligne; isolement

outance *n* coupure; défaillance

out-band (out-of-band) **signalling** signalisation hors bande

outbound *adj* (de) départ

out-dial *v* numéroter vers le réseau public

outdoor **aerial** antenne extérieure

outer **conductor** conducteur extérieur; ~ **layer** couche externe; ~ **loop** boucle principale; ~ **marker site** position de la radioborne extérieure; ~ **packaging** emballage global

outer-shell **electron** électron de valence; électron optique; électron périphérique

outfit *n* lot

outflow *n* sortie

out-gassing *n* dégazage

outgoing (O/G) *adj* sortant; de départ; ~ **call** conversation de départ; appel sortant; ~ **call restriction** droit au verrouillage de poste; ~ **circuit** circuit de départ; circuit de sortie; ~ **connection** connexion de départ; ~ **end** extrémité de départ; ~ **feeder** départ vers baie; ~ **formatter** convertisseur parallèle-série; ~ **hypsometer** hypsomètre départ; ~ **international exchange** centre international de départ; ~ **international terminating exchange** centre tête de ligne internationale de départ; ~ **junction** ligne de jonction de départ; ~ **junctor** joncteur sortante; circuit sortant; ~ **line** ligne de départ; direction

outgoing-only line ligne SPA (spécialisée en départ)

outgoing operator opératrice de départ; ~ **position** position de départ; ~ **queue** file d'attente de lignes; ~ **routing** acheminement départ; ~ **selector** sélecteur de départ; sortant; ~ **side** aval (en); ~ **signal** signal de sortie; ~ **traffic** trafic de départ; ~ **trunk** ligne jonction sortante (LJS); jonction départ; ~ **trunk group** faisceau de lignes sortantes; faisceau départ; ~ **trunk multiple** sectionnement général

out-jack n jack de sortie

outlet n sortie; créneau; évacuateur; point d'accès; prise de courant murale; ~ (mains distribution supply) départ

outline n tracé squelettique; aperçu; circuit; contour; diagramme; rappel; schéma; sous-schéma; traçage; canevas; ~ **specifications** présentation générale

outlying adj distant; décentralisé; ~ **computer centre** centre de calcul décentralisé

out-of-action immobilisé; hors service (h.s.)

out-of-band adj hors bande; ~ **radiation** rayonnement hors de bande

out-of-calibration adj décalibré

out-of-commission indisponible

out-of-frame alignment time durée de perte du verrouillage de trame; ~ **sync** perte de verrouillage de (multi-)trame

out-of-level désaffleurant

out-of-limits hors gabarit; hors norme; hors tolérance(s); ~ **alarm condition** seuil d'alarme; ~ **condition** franchissement de seuil; dépassement de seuil; ~ **parameter** anomalie

out-of-operation hors exploitation; hors trafic

out-of-order en dérangement; en panne

out-of-phase déphasé

out-of-print épuisé

out-of-range hors gabarit

out-of-register excentré

out-of-sequence déclassé

out-of-service hors service (h.s.); isolé; ~ **state** état hors service

out-of-sight plant réseau dissimulé

out-of-step (dial) déréglé

out-of-stock épuisé

out-of-sync n décrochage (D)

out-of-traffic mode état autonome; autonomie; ~ **time** temps à trafic nul

out-of-true adj désaxé; excentré; voilé

out-phasing n déphasage

out-pulse v envoyer des impulsions

out-pulsing n envoi; réémission

output v sortir; délivrer; éditer; imprimer; ~ n sortie; débit; édition; (éd.); émission; extraction; puissance (Pce); refoulement; rendement; restitution; signal; ~ (write memory) écriture; ~ **amplifier** amplificateur de sortie; amplificateur final; ~ **attenuator** affaiblisseur de sortie; ~ **back-off** recul de sortie; ~ **beam mirror** miroir de sortie; ~ **bit** donnée de sortie; ~ **buffer** tampon de sortie; ~ **capacitance** capacité de sortie; ~ **capacitance** (input open-circuited to AC) capacité de sortie, entrée en circuit ouvert; ~ **capacitance** (input short-circuited to AC) capacité de sortie, entrée en court-circuit; ~ **capacitance in common-base configuration** capacité de sortie, en base commune; ~ **capacitance in common-emitter configuration** capacité de sortie, en émetteur commun; ~ **carry** retenue de sortie; ~ **circuit** circuit de sortie; circuit de charge; ~ **control** commande aval (commutateur temporel)

output-controlled commandé par l'aval

output coupler coupleur de sortie; ~ **current** courant de sortie; ~ **digital highway (ODH)** liaison numérique sortante (LNS); ~ **electrode** électrode de sortie; ~ **file** fichier de sortie; ~ **filter** filtre de sortie; ~ **frequency** (of crystal oscillator) plage d'asservissement; ~ **gap** espace d'interaction de sortie; résonateur de sortie; ~ **impedance** impédance de sortie; ~ **(job) file** fichier d'émission; ~ **job queue** file d'attente de sortie; file d'attente d'émission; file d'attente des réponses (FAR); ~ **level** niveau de sortie; ~ **load factor** facteur de charge de sortie (en sortie); ~ **meter** indicateur de sortie; ~ **pentode** pentode de sortie; ~ **point** point de sortie; ~ **port** accès de sortie; ~ **power** caractéristique puissance de sortie/fréquence à accord fixe; caractéristique puissance de sortie/fréquence de travail; puissance de sortie (W sous ohms); ~ **program** programme d'édition; ~ **register** registre de sortie; ~ **resonator** résonateur de sortie; ~ **ripple** (noise) (in mV p-p) réinjection sur la source

outputs floating sorties en l'air; sorties non connectées

output side aval (en); ~ **signal** signal de sortie; ~ **spectrum** spectre d'émission; ~ **stage** étage final; ~ **terminal** borne de sortie; ~ **time stage** étage temporel de sortie; ~ **time switch** commutateur de sortie; ~ **transformer** transformateur de sortie; ~ **voltage** tension de sortie; ~ **voltage swing** dynamique de sortie; excursion de la tension de sortie; ~ **work queue** file d'attente des réponses (FAR); ~ **writer** éditeur de sortie

outrigger n prolongateur de carte

outscriber n convertisseur de sortie; éditeur de sortie

out-sender n envoyeur

out-servicing n mise hors service (HS)

outside adj extérieur; externe; ~ **broadcast (OB)** reportage extérieur; ~ **broadcast van** car de reportage; ~ **call** appel extérieur; ~ **plant** installations extérieures; équipement terminal; ~ **staff** (non-resident) personnel indirect; ~ **suppliers** hors parc; ~ **temperature** température extérieure; ~ **vapour phase oxidation (OVPO)** oxydation extérieure à l'état vapeur

out-slot signalling signalisation hors bande; signalisation hors intervalle de temps

out-station n poste supplémentaire (PS); poste extérieur; terminal; poste d'abonné

out-trunk switch sélecteur de départ

outward line départ; ~ **toll board** position interurbaine de départ

out-working (with IT resources) télétravail

oval-head screw vis à tête fraisée bombée (FB/90˚)

OVD (s. optical video disk)

oven n étuve; chambre; enceinte (régulée en T˚); four; ~ **conditioning** étuvage

oven-fired adj cuite au four (peinture)

oven with conveyor four à passage

"over" (cue) à vous; à l'écoute; invitation à transmettre (IT)

overall attenuation équivalent de transmission; ~ **attenuation curve** caractéristique de l'équivalent; ~ **check** contrôle global; ~ **circuit routine test** essai rapide de circuit; ~ **dimensions** encombrement; ~ **efficiency** rendement global; ~ **gain** gain composite; ~ **harmonic distortion** distorsion harmonique totale; ~ **length** hauteur hors tout; ~ **loss** affaiblissement net; affaiblissement composite; affaiblissement effectif; ~ **(net) loss** affaiblissement résultant; ~ **reference equivalent (ORE)** équivalent de référence global (ERG); ~ **tolerance in gain variation** tolérance totale de la variation de gain; ~ **view** vue d'ensemble

overbunching groupement excessif; ~ **klys-** tron klystron fonctionnant en sustension

over-current n surintensité de courant; ~ **protection** protection en courant; ~ **release** discontacteur; ~ **trip** déclencheur à surintensité

over-damped oscillation oscillation apériodique

overdimensioning surdimensionnement (du réseau)

overdrive n surcharge

over-estimated (with error margin) majoré (avec garde)

over-excitation n surexcitation

overflow n débordement; dépassement de capacité supérieur; refoulement; saturation; surcharge; ~ **area** pas de débordement; ~ **load** charge de débordement; ~ **meter** compteur de débordement; enregistreur d'appels infructueux; ~ **position** position de rotation jusqu'au bout de course; ~ **route** voie détournée; ~ **routing** acheminement avec débordement; ~ **tape** bande utilisée en alternance; ~ **traffic** trafic de débordement; ~ **trunk group** faisceau de débordement

overhang n dépassement; décalage; saillie

overhaul v mettre en état; ~ n remise en état; reprise; révision; ~ **life** durée entre révisions

overhead n servitude(s); charge à vide; déperdition; période hors service; ~ (machine time with zero traffic) temps à trafic nul; ~ **bit** bit supplémentaire; ~ **block** bloc supplémentaire; ~ **cable** câble aérien; ~ **circuit** circuit aérien; ~ **conductor** conducteur aérien; ~ **duct** conduit élevé; ~ **light** plafonnier; ~ **lighting** lumière tombante; ~ **line** ligne aérienne; ligne en fils nus aériens; ~ **operation** opération de servitude; ~ **projector** rétroprojecteur

overheads npl charges financières; frais généraux; charges; coût d'exploitation; fonctions annexes; intrants

overhead wire fil aérien

overkill n surdimensionnement (du réseau); ~ **capacity** surpuissance

overlaid adj superposé

overlap n chevauchement; simultanéité; recouvrement; ~ **angle** angle d'empiètement; angle de recouvrement

overlap-compelled asservi avec chevauchement

overlap out-pulsing envoi avec chevauchement

overlapping adj confondu; ~ **channels** canaux partiellement superposés; ~ **of turns** chevauchement des spires

overlap signalling signalisation avec chevauchement; ~ **transmission** transmission avec chevauchement

overlay *n* recouvrement; cache; aire de transit; fond de page; segment actif; segmentation; ~ *adj* amovible; ~ (of keyboard) bandeau; ~ **area** zone amovible; zone de recouvrement; ~ **area zone** aire de transit; ~ **check** contrôle des superpositions; ~ **program** programme amovible; ~ **segment** segment de recouvrement; ~ **tree** arbre de recouvrement

overline service service de lignes groupées

overload *n* surcharge; franchissement de seuil; surintensité; ~ **capacity** surcharge admissible

overloaded *adj* encombré

overload factor réserve de linéarité; ~ (direct) **forward current** courant de surcharge prévisible à l'état passant; ~ **level** puissance limite admissible; niveau de saturation; ~ **relay** relais de surcharge; ~ **release** discontacteur; ~ **switch** disjoncteur protecteur; ~ **test** essai de surcharge

over-modulation *n* surmodulation; dépassement; supermodulation

over-modulation limiter limiteur de surmodulation

overprint surimpression

over-pulsing *n* surnumérotation

overpunch *n* zone de perforation; perforation hors texte

override *n* entrée en tiers prioritaire; blocage; dérogation; effacement; interception d'appel; mise hors service (HS); offre d'appel; offre d'appels interurbaine; shunt; suppression; (timing) ~ clé de suppression; ~ **device** dispositif d'exclusion; ~ **feature** possibilité d'entrer en tiers; ~ **function** entrée d'inhibition; ~ **security facility** protégé contre les intrusions; protégé contre l'offre; ~ **warning tone** tonalité d'intervention

over-run *n* engorgement; dépassement du temps d'émission; ~ (of data channel capacity) erreur de rythme

overs and shorts excédants et manquants

overscoring *n* surlignement

overseas relay émission de l'étranger; ~ **telegram service** gentex

overshoot *n* dépassement; rebondissement; suroscillation; ~ (factor) facteur de rebondissement; ~ (logic) surmodulation; ~ **distortion** distorsion de suroscillation; ~ **factor** taux de surmodulation; ~ **ratio** rapport de suroscillation

overstrike text (to show deletions) texte rayé

overswing *n* rebondissement; surdéviation; ~ **ratio** rapport de suroscillation

over-the-horizon aerial antenne transhorizon; ~ **communications** communication transhorizon; ~ **microwave transmission** transmission par microondes dépassant l'horizon; ~ **propagation** propagation transhorizon; ~ **radio link** faisceau hertzien transhorizon; ~ **scatter propagation** propagation transhorizon troposphérique

overthrow distortion distorsion de suroscillation

overtone *n* oscillation harmonique; ~ **crystal** cristal à harmoniques

overtravel *n* surcourse; ~ (of limit switch) débattement (grande surcourse)

overtype *n* surimpression

overview *n* présentation générale; synoptique; généralités

over-voltage protection protection contre les surtensions

overwrite *v* détruire; surcharger en écriture; surécrire; surinscrire

overwritten *adj* (of data) écrasé

OVPO (s. outside vapour phase oxidation)

owner *n* propriétaire; maître

own exchange centre de rattachement

own-exchange *adj* local; ~ **junctor** circuit de connexion local

own-premises meter émetteur de télétaxe; compteur de taxe à domicile; ~ **metering** taxation à domicile; ~ **metering bit** bit de télétaxe

oxide-coated cathode cathode à oxyde

oxide coating couche d'oxyde

oxidizing agent oxydant

oxy-acetylene welding soudure à l'autogène; soudage à la flamme

oxygen index (of combustion) indice d'oxygène

P

PABX (s. private automatic branch exchange); ∻ **inter-working** exploitation derrière autocommutateur; ∻ **network line** ligne réseau privée; ∻ **station** poste supplémentaire (PS); ∻ **subscriber trunk line** ligne d'abonné spécialisée pour l'interurbain

PAC (s. pacing (function))

pacemaker *n* stimulateur (électrique de cœur); tronc synchro

pacing (function) (PAC) délai d'attente entre caractères

pack *v* comprimer; condenser; garnir; ~ *n* paquet; bloc; boîtier; cartouche; groupe; pochette

package *n* ensemble; jeu; livraison; lot; programme-produit; **(software)** ~ *n* progiciel; ~ **earthed** boîtier à la masse; ~ **group** groupe de boîtiers; ~ **of products and services** solution

packaging *n* mise en boîte; emballage; ~ **and storage** conditionnement

pack-carrier television station émetteur de télévision portatif

packed array tableau comprimé; ~ **decimal** nombre décimal condensé

packet assembler assembleur de paquets; ~ **assembly-disassembly (PAD)** assemblage-désassemblage des paquets; ~ **binding machine** cercleuse de colis; ~ **data transmission** transmission de données par paquets; ~ **disassembler** désassembleur de paquets; ~ **format** format de paquet; ~ **mode terminal** terminal en mode paquet

packet-switched data transmission service service de transmission de données à commutation par paquets

packet switching commutation par paquets

packet-switching centre centre de commutation de paquets; ~ **network** réseau à commutation par paquets (RCP)

packet transmission transmission par paquets

packing *n* compression; condensation; tassement; ~ **(of data)** retassement; ~ **case** boîte d'emballage; ~ **density** densité d'enregistrement; compacité; volume d'encombrement; ~ **effect** effet de tassement; ~ **list** état de colisage

packing(-piece) *n* garniture; cale (c. d'épaisseur)

pack programme (of cable TV) programme prêt-à-porter

pad *v* garnir; ~ *n* affaiblisseur; atténuateur; bloc de touches; caractère tampon; cellule d'affaiblissement; complément de ligne; embout; galette; gamme; grain; ligne d'affaiblissement; pastille; patin; pavé; plot; tampon; ~ **(air-gap)** lamelle; ~ **(of PCB)** rondelle

PAD (s. packet assembly-disassembly)

padded *adj* matelassé; piqué; ~ **case** étui piqué; ~ **with blanks** garni (d'espaces/de zéros); complément à blanc

padder *n* condensateur série d'équilibrage

padding *n* bourrage; remplissage; ~ **capacitor** condensateur série d'équilibrage

padlock *n* cadenas

pad shunting effacement cellule

pad-to-track separation/clearance échappement

page *v* appeler; ~ **copy** copie (sur) papier; imprimé; ~ **eject** saut de papier; ~ **fault** besoin de page; ~ **frame** cadre de page

page-in *v* charger

page-out *n* transfert

page overflow (PO) dépassement de (capacité de) page (DP); ~ **pointer** pointeur de pages; ~ **printer** imprimante par page

page-printing receiver traducteur imprimeur en page; ~ **telegraph** télégraphe imprimeur de page

page receiver récepteur sur page

page-skip margin marge basse

page teleprinter traducteur imprimeur en page; ~ **translation exeption** besoin de page

paging *n* défilement des pages; appel de pages; diffusion; message d'appel; mise en page; pagination; ~ **area** zone d'appel de mobile; zone de recherche de mobile; ~ **call** appel en diffusion; ~ **device** téléavertisseur

paid minutes minutes taxées

paid-out aerial antenne déroulée

paid-time ratio rendement horaire

paid words mots taxés

pair *n* paire; couple; bifilaire; ~ **cable** câble à deux conducteurs; ~ **count** nombre de paires

paired *adj* apparié; ~ **cable** câble à paires torsadées; ~ **comparison** comparaison par paires; ~ **disparity code** code à disparité compensée; code à disparité restreinte; ~ **operator connection** bride

pairing n pairage

pair of modulation currents couple de modulation

pair-wound wires fils en main

PAL (s. programmable array logic)

pallet n palette; plate-forme; ~ **handler** transpalette

PAMA (s. pulse-address multiple access)

PAM bit stream train MIA

pamphlet n plaquette

pan n bac

PANAR (s. panorama radar)

panchromatic photography prise de vue panchromatique

panel n panneau; boîtier; cadre; capot; case; face; meuble; plaque; platine; pupitre; table; tableau; volet; ~ **cut-out** découpe; perçage cloison; ~ **office** central à sélecteurs plans; ~ **of full-wave dipoles** panneau de doublets; ~ **of slot radiators** panneau à fentes; ~ **selector** sélecteur plan

panel-ware n instrument(s) de mesure

pan head screw vis à tête cylindrique (C); vis à tête cylindrique bombée large (CBL)

panoply n kyrielle

panorama radar (PANAR) radiodétecteur panoramique

paper bail (of printer) barre presse-papier; barre antimaculage; ~ **exit sensor** détection sortie papier; ~ **feed** avance papier

paper-feed sprocket entraîneur papier

paper-insulated cable câble sous papier

paper insulation isolement au papier; ~ **out** fin de papier

paper-slew saut de papier; ~ **rate** (in inches per second) vitesse d'avance papier

paper tape ruban du papier; bande de papier

paper-tape loop boucle d'asservissement; ~ **punch** perforateur de bande; ~ **reader** lecteur de bandes perforées; ~ **splicer** colleuse; ~ **transmitter** notificateur d'information

paper-throw n saut de papier; éjection du papier; ~ **character** caractère de saut de papier

paperwork n documentation

PAR (s. precision approach radar)

parabolic (dish) aerial antenne à cylindre parabolique

parabolic-index profile fibre fibre à gradient d'indice parabolique; fibre à répartition parabolique d'indice

parabolic (reflector) microphone microphone en réflecteur; ~ **reflector** réflecteur parabolique

paraffin n pétrole (lampant)

paragraph n alinéa; ~ (16-kbyte division of segment) paragraphe

parallel access accès en parallèle; ~ **circuit** connexion en parallèle; ~ **computer** calculateur parallèle; ~ **connection** connexion en parallèle; montage en parallèle; ~ **controller** coupleur parallèle; ~ **exposure** parallélisme; ~ **feed** alimentation en parallèle

paralleling n connexion en parallèle

parallel interface interface parallèle

parallelism n parallélisme

parallel-plate lens lentille à lames parallèles; ~ **oscillator** oscillateur à plaques parallèles

parallel printer imprimante parallèle; ~ **processing** parallélisme; ~ **register** registre parallèle; ~ **resistance** résistance parallèle; ~ **resistor** shunt; ~ **resonance** résonance shuntée

parallel-resonant circuit circuit antirésonnant; ~ **frequency** fréquence de résonance en parallèle

parallel-rod oscillator oscillateur à barres parallèles

parallel-running (of pilot program) multipériodique

parallel-search storage mémoire rapprochée

parallel-serial converter convertisseur parallèle-série; sérialisateur (sérialiseur); ~ **full adder** additionneur parallèle/série

parallel-to-serial conversion conversion parallèle-série

parallel transmission transmission en parallèle; ~ **winding** enroulement parallèle

parameter n paramètre; caractéristique(s); critère; grandeur; information(s); mesure(s); objet; rubrique; valeur; ~ **assignment** paramétrage; ~ **block** bloc de paramètres; ~ **card** carte paramètre

parameterization n paramétrage; paramétrisation

parameter sheet fiche de régie; ~ **value** item

parametric amplifier (paramp) amplificateur paramétrique; ~ **gain** gain paramétrique; ~ **oscillator** oscillateur paramétrique; ~ **radiation** rayonnement paramétrique

paramp (s. parametric amplifier)

parapet n allège

paraphase amplifier inverseur de polarité

parasitic aerial élément passif; élément secondaire; ~ **echo** écho interne; ~ **radiator** élément passif; ~ **stopper** impédance d'étouffement

parcel of traffic flux (de trafic)

parent code code créateur; ~ **exchange** centre de rattachement nominal; ~ **station** émetteur pilote

parity parité; ~ **bit** bit de parité; élément de

P

parité; ~ **check** contrôle de parité; contrôle par imparité; ~ **error** erreur de parité; faute d'imparité; ~ **function** fonction de parité

park v mettre en garde

parking area aire de réception; ~ **circuit** circuit de garde pour le parcage; ~ **file** fichier de suivi; fichier d'attente; fichier de relance; ~ **orbit** parcage; renvoi sur garde

parse (of syntax) v décomposer; analyser

parsing n découpage; analyse; décomposition

part n pièce (pce); élément; partie

part(s) per million (p.p.m. = $1,10^{-6}$) millionième(s)

partial frequency fréquence partielle

partially-restricted extension poste supplémentaire avec prise contrôlée du réseau (public)

partially-suppressed carrier porteuse à suppression partielle

partial monitoring contrôle partiel; ~ **monitoring sampling board** opérateur de prélèvement des échantillons pour contrôle partiel; ~ **multiple** sectionnement particulier; ~ **reset** remise à zéro partielle (RZP); ~ **restoring time** temps de fermeture partielle; ~ **secondary working** sélection conjuguée avec entraide; ~ **test** test unitaire; ~ **tone reversal** inversion partielle des nuances

particle n particule

particle-size n (analysis) granulométrie

partition v découper; décomposer; ~ n partition; alvéole; case; cloison; cloisonnement; compartiment; segment; tranche

partitioned adj cloisonné; mixte; ~ **file** fichier partitionné

partition hardware montage cloison

partitioning n décomposition; découpage; dédoublement; quadrillage

partition insulator isolateur de traversée

parts and labour pièces détachées et main d'œuvre (PD et MO); ~ **list** nomen(clature) (Nre.)

part-time leased circuit circuit téléphonique loué à temps partiel; ~ **private telephone wire** circuit téléphonique loué à temps partiel

party n correspondant; abonné; abonné utilisateur; intervenant; ~ **connector unit** (PCU) mise en présence (MP); ~ **line** ligne partagée; ligne banalisée; ligne commune (dans un multiplage partiel); ~ **line extension** poste de ligne partagée

Paschen's law (breakdown voltage) loi de Paschen

pass n passe; phase de travail

passageway n couloir; dégagement

pass-band n bande passante; passe bande; bande utile

pass/generate a current circuler un courant

passim adv au fil de la réduction; et suivant

passivated adj passivé; noirci; monolithique

passivating film couche de conversion; ~ **layer** film de conversion

passivation n métallisation; noircissement chimique; oxygénation

passive adj au repos; passif; ~ **aerial** élément passif; élément secondaire; ~ **(idle) character** caractère inactive; ~ **continuity check** contrôle passif de continuité (CP); ~ **discriminator** discriminateur passif; ~ **jamming** brouillage accidentel; ~ **network** réseau passif; ~ **reflector** réflecteur déviateur; ~ **retransmission** réémission passive; ~ **(balance) return loss** affaiblissement passif d'équilibrage; ~ **satellite transponder** répéteur de satellite passif; ~ **singing point** point d'amorçage passif; ~ **synchrodyne receiver** récepteur synchrodyne passif; ~ **transducer** transducteur passif

pass transistor transistor ballast

password n mot de passe; mot de contrôle; clé d'accès

paste n pâte

pasted plate (of battery) plaque à oxyde rapporté; plaque Faure

PA system porte-voix à amplification électrique

patch v enficher; raccorder; rapiécer; ~ n modification; lien; raccord; retouche; rustine; sous-programme; module; ~ **area** zone rapiécée; zone de retouche; ~ **board** répartiteur

patch-board reconfiguration déplacement répartiteur

patch card carte de correction; ~ **cord** cordon de renvoi; fiche; ~ **editor** éditeur de liens (EL); ~ **field** zone de pièces; ~ **file** fichier de pièces

patching n correction par pièces; brassage; enfichage; interconnexion; mutation; raccordement (racct.); renvoi; répartition; ~ **cord** câble de raccord; fiche de connexion; cavalier; ~ **lead** fil jarretière; ~ **of swapped-in overlay** modification sur segment de recouvrement transféré; ~ **rate** taux de rapiéçage

patch panel brasseur; miniréseau de connexion; panneau de mutation (PM); panneau de raccordement; répartiteur

patent n brevet; ~ **counsellor** avocat de brevets d'invention; ~ **licence** concession de brevet

path n chemin; accès; branche; canal; conduit; enchaînement; grain; itinéraire;

liaison; ligne; maille; parcours; route; sens; trajectoire; voie; support; trajet; ~ (microwave line-of-sight) trajectoire visuelle; ~ **analysis** calcul d'itinéraire; ~ **attenuation** affaiblissement de propagation; ~ **command** commande voie; ~ **difference** différence de phase; ~ **diversity routing** multiroutage

path-finding *n* recherche d'itinéraire; recherche de chemin; sélection; exploration des voies; recherche de voies

path-holding wire fil de maintien

path-length microwave lens lentille à retard pour microondes; lame à retard pour microondes

path loss affaiblissement sur le trajet; ~ **mixing stage** brassage de maille; ~ **of moving contact** grain de contact mobile; ~ **search** recherche de chemin

path-tracing process remontée par le chemin de propagation

pattern *n* configuration; carte; circuit; combinaison(s); dessin; diagramme; format; forme; gabarit; implantation; maquette; modèle (mle); motif; réseau; schéma; série; structure; tracé; ~ (scope) oscillogramme; ~ **density** taux de remplissage; ~ **generator** mire électronique; générateur de séquences; ~ **interference** interférence de mire

pattress *n* boîte d'encastrement; plaque d'assise; plaque de base; plaque de fond; plaque support (= platine)

Pauli Fermi principle principe d'exclusion de Pauli Fermi

pause *n* arrêt momentané; interruption; intervalle; pause; repos; ~ (of video recorder) arrêt sur image

pawl *n* doigt d'arrêt; cliquet; crochet d'arrêt; gâchette; toc; ~ **conveyor** convoyeur à doigts

Pawsey stub symétriseur à ligne symétrique

PAX (s. private automatic exchange)

payload *n* charge utile

payment *n* règlement; ~ **card** support paiement

payout drum dévidoir; ~ **reel** détendeur; ~ **stand** table desserte

pay-phone *n* appareil téléphonique à prépaiement; cabine publique à prépaiement; publiphone

payroll *n* paie

pay-station *n* cabine publique; poste téléphonique public

pay-television télévision à péage; télévision à accès conditionnel

pay tones signalisation de prépaiement

PBX (s. private branch exchange); ∻ **group**

lignes groupées

PC (s. personal computer)

PCB (s. printed circuit board); ∻ **assembly** circuit imprimé équipé (CIE); carte équipée; ensemble constitué; ∻ **auto-router** routeur; ∻ **cleaner** gomme détersive; ∻ **conveyor** convoyeur de CI; ∻ **drafting sheet** grille inactinique; ∻ **eraser** gomme détersive

PCB-mounting edge plug fichier encartable; ∻ **keyboard rocker switch** inverseur fugitif unipolaire CI; ∻ **plug** socle; ∻ **socket** embase à piquer (sur CI)

PCB profile détourage; ∻ **selector plug** shunt; ∻ **track detour/offset** oméga

PCH (s. firmware processor communications handler for bus control)

PCM (s. pulse-code modulation); ∻ **binary code** code binaire MIC; ∻ **bit stream** train MIC; ∻ **channel bank** équipement d'extrémité MIC; ∻ **code converter** extrémité MIC; ∻ **data channel** canal sémaphore; ∻ **frame format** constitution de la trame MIC; ∻ **highway** multiplex MIC; autoroute électronique; ligne de réseau (LR); ligne PTT; ∻ **line terminal** terminal MIC; ∻ **link** liaison MIC; jonction; rattachement en MIC; ∻ **link loop-back** rebouclage de MIC; ∻ **link with CCS and CAS signalling** MIC actif; ∻ **link with channel-associated signalling only** MIC passif

PCM/LTX (local terminal exchange) link liaison MIC/LTX

PCM module tiroir MIC; ∻ **multiplex** ligne de réseau (LR); terminal numérique d'extrémité; ∻ **multiplex equipment** équipement de multiplexage MIC; ∻ **serial/parallel conversion** MIC/SPA; ∻ **subscriber line** abonné réclamant

PCM-TDM multiplexer (MUX) multiplex numérique à modulation MIC; jonction temporelle

PCM trunk jonction MIC; circuit MIC; ∻ **trunk distribution frame** répartiteur de jonctions MIC; ∻ **word** signal de caractère

P-counter compteur d'instructions

PCU (s. party connector unit)

p.d. (s. potential difference)

PDM (s. power-down mode); ∻ (s. pulse density modulator)

peak *n* crête (c); bosse; sommet; pic; pointe; ~ **alternating gap voltage** tension de crête de l'espace d'interaction; ~ **amplitude** amplitude de crête; ~ **amplitude of an elementary echo** amplitude de crête d'un écho élémentaire; ~ **busy hour** heure de pointe; ~ **current** courant de crête; courant de pic; courant maximal; ~ **current at onset**

of increase in resistance courant maximal de résistance/basculement; ~ distortion distorsion de la crête de l'amplitude

peakedness factor facteur d'irrégularité

peak emission wavelength longueur d'onde au pic d'émission; ~ envelope power (PEP) puissance nominale de crête; puissance de crête; puissance en crête de modulation; ~ excursion excursion maximale; ~ factor facteur de crête; facteur d'amplitude; facteur de pointe; ~ forward current courant direct de crête; ~ forward gate voltage tension directe de pointe de gâchette; ~ forward voltage tension directe transitoire de pointe; tension de crête en sens conducteur

peak-hour traffic trafic ponctuel

peaking n alignement de crête; accentuation; écrêtage; ~ circuit circuit d'augmentation de la pente; circuit écrêteur; circuit linéaire; circuit dérivateur; ~ coil inductance de relèvement; ~ network circuit de différentiation; différentiateur

peak limiter limitateur d'amplitude; ~ limiting limitation de crête; limitation de la dynamique

peak-limiting amplifier amplificateur limiteur de crêtes

peak-limiting voltage tension d'écrêtage; ~ load charge de crête; charge de pointe; pointe de charge; ~ load period heure chargée; ~ noise meter appareil de mesure de la tension de crête de bruit; ~ non-operate current courant maximal de non opération; ~ off-state voltage tension de crête à l'état bloqué; ~ off-state working voltage tension de crête de fonctionnement à l'état bloqué; ~ (overload) detector détecteur de crête; ~ period période de pointe

peak-power output puissance de sortie de crête

peak programme meter voltmètre de crête; ~ pulse power puissance maximale d'une impulsion; ~ rectifier circuit circuit redresseur de crêtes; ~ reduction réduction de la pointe; ~ reverse anode voltage crête de tension anodique inverse; ~ reverse current courant inverse de crête; ~ reverse gate voltage tension inverse de pointe de gâchette; ~ reverse off-state voltage tension inverse de crête à l'état bloqué; ~ reverse voltage tension inverse de crête; ~ sensor écrêteur; ~ side-band power (PSP) puissance de crête de bande latérale; ~ (signal) level niveau de crête du signal; ~ speech power pointe de puissance vocale; ~ times heures rouges

peak-to-peak (p-p; pk-pk) crête à crête (c/c);

~ amplitude amplitude crête-à-crête; ~ displacement déplacement crête-à-crête; ~ value valeur crête à crête

peak transient reverse voltage tension inverse de pointe non répétitive; ~ undershoot pointe de dépassement inférieur; ~ value valeur de crête; intensité; pointe; ~ value (of power) intensité de puissance; ~ value of forward recovery voltage tension directe de pointe répétitive; ~ voltage tension de crête; tension de pointe; tension de pic; ~ voltmeter voltmètre de crête; ~ wavelength (of LED) couleur (lambda p); ~ white (level) niveau de crête du blanc; blanc maximum; blanc parfait; ~ withstand(ing) voltage tension de tenue

pearl adj dépoli

pecker n (of computer) palpeur

pedestal n coffret; console; décollement du niveau du noir; palier; patte; pied support; plateau; socle

peek n recherche sélective; lecture

peel v décoller

peeling n (of PCB track) décollement

peg n cheville; clou; doigt; fiche; picot; tige; ~ board planche à clous; ~ count comptage d'appels; comptage de prises; ~ counter compteur totalisateur; compteur de nombre d'appels; compteur d'observation; ~ counting comptage de prises

peg-count meter compteur de trafic; compteur manuel de communications

peg insertion gauge calibre de pointage

pel n (pixel) point d'image

pellet n (of transistor) pastille

Peltier effect effet thermoélectrique; ~ element module à effet Peltier

pencil beam faisceau crayon; faisceau filiforme

pencil-beam aerial antenne à faisceau très étroit

pending adj en instance

pen-down mode mode plume baissée

pendular adj curviligne

pendulum start-stop telegraphy télégraphie pendulaire

penetration factor coefficient de pénétration

pen-plotter n traceur

pen stall (of graph recorder) porte-stylo

pentode n pentode

PEP (s. peak envelope power)

PER (s. program event recording)

percent(age) n pourcent(age); taux

percentage modulation pourcentage de modulation; ~ occupied time coefficient d'occupation d'un circuit; ~ of effective-to-booked calls pourcentage des demandes satisfaites; ~ overflow pourcentage de débordement

percent completion pourcentage des demandes satisfaites; ~ **denial** taux de refus

per-channel codec codec monovoie voie par voie; codeur monovoie; codec par voie

percolation n suintement

percussion power drill perceuse tamponette percussion

perfect modulation manipulation parfaite; ~ **restitution** reproduction parfaite

perforate v percer

perforated adj ajouré; cranté; ~ **angle-iron** cornière perforée

perforations pl prédécoupage

perforator n perforateur

performance n comportement; efficacité; qualité de fonctionnement; rendement; tenue; ~ adj fonctionnel; ~ **characteristic** caractéristique de qualité; ~ **chart** diagramme de fonctionnement; ~ **data** caractéristique(s); contraintes; ~ **details** limites d'utilisation; ~ **rating** caractéristiques fonctionnelles; ~ **test** essai fonctionnel

period n période; délai; intervalle; point; vacation; récurrence; durée

periodic dump sauvegarde incrémentielle; ~ **duty** fonctionnement en périodique régulier

periodicity n fréquence

periodic noise bruit périodique; bruit récurrent

periodic-pulse time switch minuterie (impulsions pour régime) périodique

periodic pulse train groupe d'ondes périodiques; ~ **time** temps de période; ~ **waveform** forme d'onde périodique

peripheral n (device) organe; unité d'échange (UE); support; unité périphérique; ~ **address selector switch** sélecteur d'adresse (SAD); ~ **controller** coupleur de périphérique; ~ **controller board** carte coupleur de périphériques; ~ **equipment** équipement périphérique; ~ **interface channel** adaptateur d'entrée-sortie; canal d'adaptation; ~ **unit** appareil périphérique; ~ **unit controller system (PUCS)** contrôleur de périphériques

periphery n pourtour

periscope aerial antenne périscope

perishable items fongibles

per-line codec équipement de codage par ligne d'abonné analogique; ~ **codecs** (system) codage individuel

permanent assignment assignation permanente; ~ **data file** fichier commun; ~ **echo** écho permanent; ~ **echo cancellation** suppression d'écho fixe; ~ **file** fiche permanent; fiche principal; fichier de base; fichier maître; fichier pilote

permanent-line condition ligne en faux appel; ~ **relay** relais de mise en faux appel; relais de renvoi en faux-appel; ~ **signal** impulsion permanente; ~ **status** passage en faux appel; ~ **tone** tonalité de faux appel

permanent loop boucle permanente

permanently-locked envelope enveloppe verrouillée en permanence

permanent magnet aimant permanent; ~ **magnet twistor** mémoire à fil; ~ **memory** mémoire fixe; ~ **record** trace; ~ **storage** archivage; ~ **virtual circuit** circuit virtuel permanent (CVP)

permeability n perméabilité; ~ **of vacuum** perméabilité du vide; ~ **tuning** accord par réluctance

permeameter n perméamètre

permeance n perméance

permissible noise level niveau de bruit admissible; ~ **threshold** seuil toléré

permission n autorisation

permit n permis

permitted defectives unités défectueuses tolérées; nombre de défauts tolérés; défauts admissibles

permittivity n constante diélectrique absolue; permittivité; pouvoir inducteur spécifique; ~ **of vacuum** permittivité du vide

perm signal tonalité de faux appel

permutation code numérotation au clavier

per route basis sur les directions

persistence n persistance (d'écran)

persistent adj rémanent

personal access code clé d'accès; ~ **call** appel avec préavis (PAV); ~ **computer (PC)** ordinateur individuel (OI)

personalized billing (ABC - auto bill calling service) facturation personnalisée

personnel n effectif; ~ **complement** personnel

person-to-person call appel avec préavis (PAV); appel personne à personne

perspective diagram descriptif

Perspex [T.N.] n Plexiglas

Pertheric code code réfléchi à excédent trois

per whole or part (thereof) indivisible

petal n (of print-wheel) pétale

PETP (s. polyethylene terephthalate)

Petri network machine de Pétri

petrol n essence

petty cash (file) frais

p.f. (s. power factor)

PF (s. pulse frequency); ~ (s. picofarad)

PFM (s. pulse-frequency modulation)

PF meter phimètre

PFN (s. pulse-forming network)

PGOF (s. page overflow)

phanotron n phanotron

phantastron *n* phantastron; transitron intégrateur; ~ **(delayed-pulse) circuit** circuit phantastron

phantom *n* fantôme; ~ *adj* artificiel; faux; fictif; superposé; ~ **aerial** antenne artificielle; antenne fictive; antenne sans charge; ~ **capacity** capacité entre paires; ~ **circuit** circuit approprié; circuit combinable; circuit fantôme; ~ **loading** charge du circuit fantôme; ~ **loading coil** bobine de charge de circuit fantôme; ~ **radar target** cible fausse de radar; cible fantôme; ~ **repeating coil** bobine translatrice de circuit; ~ **telegraph circuit** circuit télégraphique fantôme; ~ **telegraphy** télégraphie en fantôme; ~ **telephone connection** circuit téléphonique double; ~ **view** représentation en transparence

phase *n* étape; palier; tranche

phase adjustment ajustage de phase

phase-amplitude distortion distorsion phase/amplitude

phase angle angle de phase; angle électrique

phase-balance relay relais polyphasé

phase(-balance) voltage tension d'équilibrage; tension entre phase et neutre

phase bandwidth largeur de bande de phase; ~ **black** signal de mise en phase sur noir; ~ **change** changement de phase

phase-change coefficient déphasage linéique; fonction de phase

phase changer convertisseur de phase; décaleur; déphaseur; ~ **check** contrôle de phase; ~ **coincidence** coïncidence de phase; ~ **comparator** comparateur de phase; ~ **constant** constante de phase; constante de déphasage; ~ **converter** convertisseur de phase; décaleur; déphaseur

phase-corrected horn cornet à correction de phase

phase current courant de phase

phased array radar system système de radiolocation à réseau à éléments en phase

phase delay temps de propagation de phase; ~ **detector** démodulateur amplitude-phase; discriminateur de phase; ~ **difference** signe de la phase; différence de phase; facteur de déphasage (cos phi); ~ **difference** (leading) cos phi avant; ~ **discriminator** discriminateur de phase; ~ **displacement angle** angle de décalage de phase; ~ **(displacement) angle** angle de déphasage; ~ **distortion** distorsion de phase; ~ **equalizer** compensateur de phase; compensateur du temps de propagation; correcteur de distorsion de phase; self interphase; transformateur équilibreur; ~ **error** déphasage; erreur

statique de phase; ~ **error correction** correction d'erreur de phase; ~ **failure** coupure de phase; ~ **fluctuation** fluctuation de phase; ~ **frequency** fréquence de phase

phase-front distortion distorsion du front de phase

phase hit variation brusque de phase; ~ **integrator** intégrateur de phase; ~ **interlinking** raccordement des phases; ~ **inversion** renversement des phases; opposition de phase

phase-inversion modulation modulation par inversion de phase

phase inverter changeur de phases; déphaseuse; montage inverseur de phase; ~ **jitter** gigue de phase; bruit de phase; ~ **lag** déphasage en arrière; retard de phase; ~ **lead** déphasage en avant; avance de phase; conducteur de phase

phase-less boost récupération d'énergie sans distorsion

phase-locked *adj* à asservissement de phase; ~ **loop (PLL)** boucle de phase; boucle à asservissement de phase; boucle à verrouillage de phase; boucle de réaction à accrochage de phase; ~ **oscillator** oscillateur asservi en phase; oscillateur verrouillé en phase

phase locking accrochage de phase; ~ **matching** adaptation de phase; ~ **meter** phasemètre; phimètre; ~ **modulation** modulation de phase; ~ **modulation by inductance variation** modulation de phase par inductance à noyau magnétique; ~ **modulation with reference phase** modulation de phase avec phase de référence; ~ **modulator** modulateur de phase; ~ **opposition** opposition de phase; ~ **oscillation** oscillation pendulaire; ~ **pre-compensation** précorrection de phase

phaser *n* déphaseur; synchronisateur; cadreur

phase regulator régulateur de phase; ~ **relationship** relation de phase

phase(-frequency) response characteristic rapport phase/fréquence vidéo

phase reversal inversion de phase; renversement des phases

phase-sensitive detection détection sensible à la phase

phase sequence succession d'ordre des phases; ~ **shield** écran; ~ **shift** décalage angulaire électrique; changement de phase; décalage de phase; déphasage; éphasage; variation de phase; ~ **shifter** déphaseur

phase-shifting transformer synchronisateur

phase-shift keying modulation par saut de phase; modulation par inversion de phase; ~ **keying (PSK)** modulation par déplacement de phase; ~ **oscillator** oscillateur taux d'erreur(s)

phase-space cell cellule de l'espace de phase

phase splitter séparateur de phases; déphaseur multiple; ~ **splitting** découpage de phase; déphasage en arrière; ~ **stability** stabilité de phase; ~ **sync** accrochage de phase; ~ **synchronization** mise en phase; ~ **velocity** vitesse de phase; ~ **voltage** tension de phase; ~ **white** signal de mise en phase sur blanc

phase-wound rotor rotor à enroulement

phasing *n* mise en phase; cadrage; ~ **line** ligne de cadrage; ~ **signal** signal de cadrage; ~ **transformer** synchronisateur

phasor *n* nombre complexe; vecteur représentatif

phenolic resin résine phénolique

Phillips screw [T.N.] vis cruciforme

phoneme *n* phonème

phonetic/syllabic speech power puissance vocale phonétique syllabique

phonic wheel roue phonique

phonogram (service) service des télégrammes téléphonés

phonograph *n* électrophone

phosphor *n* substance luminescente

phosphorescence *n* phosphorescence

phosphoroscope *n* phosphoroscope

photicon *n* iconoscope-image à dimensions réduites

photocathode *n* photocathode

photocell *n* pile photovoltaïque; photopile

photochemical cell élément photochimique

photoconductive cell cellule photorésistante; ~ **effect** photoconduction

photocopy copie diazoïque

photodetector *n* photodétecteur; capteur optique; photorécepteur

photodiode *n* photodiode

photo-electric *adj* photosensible; ~ **(PE) cell** cellule photoélectrique; cellule photoconductive/-trice; ~ **cathode** cathode photoélectronique; ~ **controlled switch** interrupteur à commande photoélectrique

photo(-electric) current courant photoélectrique

photo-electric effect effet photoélectrique; ~ **emission** photoémission; ~ **relay** relais photosensible

photo-electrolytic cell élément photochimique

photo-electromotive force force photoélectromotrice

photo-electron *n* photoélectron

photo-engraved *adj* photogravé

photofacsimile telegraphy phototélégraphie

photographic mask cliché

photography *n* prise de vue

photo-luminescence *n* photoluminescence

photon *n* photon

photoplotter *n* table optique

photoplotting technique tracé optique

photo-resist *n* résine photosensible (photogravure à r.); ~ **copper-clad** (epoxy glass) **board** plaque présensibilisée

photosensor *n* cellule photoélectrique

phototelegram *n* phototélégramme; bélinogramme

phototelegraph call communication phototélégraphique

phototelegraphic apparatus appareil phototélégraphique

phototelegraph station poste phototélégraphique

phototelegraphy *n* phototélégraphie; téléphotographie

phototypesetter *n* photocomposeuse

photovalve *n* tube photoélectronique

photovoltaic cell cellule photovoltaïque; cellule à couche d'arrêt; couple photoélectrique; photopile; ~ **effect** effet photovoltaïque

physical address adresse géographique; ~ **connection** connexion métallique; ~ **item** objet; ~ **line** liaison métallique

PIC (s. programmable interrupt controller)

pick *n* fil

picker *n* aiguille de tri; galet d'alimentation; ~ **belt** courroie d'alimentation

pickling *n* décapage; avivage

pick-off *n* capteur; ~ **brush** balai d'exploration

pick up (of relay) *v* monter

pick-up *n* capteur; acquisition; lecture; lecteur de son; mise en travail; prélèvement; prise d'appel; reprise; ~ (of relay) excitation; remontée; ~ **arm** bras de lecture; ~ **cartridge** cartouche de lecteur; ~ **circuit** circuit capteur; ~ **current** courant d'attraction (I_A); ~ **ratio** rapport des hauteurs d'entrée; ~ **stylus** pointe de lecture; ~ **time** temps de réponse

picofarad (pF) *n* picofarad

pictogram *n* pictogramme

pictorial representation figurine

picture *n* image; ~ **bank** banque d'images; ~ **black** niveau du noir; noir d'une image; ~ **bounce** tremblement de l'image; ~ **communication** vidéocommunication; ~ **distortion** distorsion d'image; ~ **editor** éditeur d'images; ~ **element** (pixel) point d'image; point graphique; élément d'image; ~ **element matrix** matrice d'éléments d'image; ~ **facsimile telegraphy** télécopie nuancée; ~ **frequency** fréquence d'image; fréquence de trame; ~ **monitor** moniteur d'image;

P

~ **ratio** rapport d'amplitude de synchronisation; ~ **receiver** récepteur d'images; ~ **resolution** définition d'image; ~ **signal** signal d'image; ~ **slip** glissement (défilement) vertical de l'image; ~ **synchronizing pulse** top d'image; ~ **telegraphy terminal** terminal téléautographique; ~ **tone** fréquence porteuse d'image; ~ **transmission** téléphotographie; phototélégraphie; transmission d'images; ~ **transmission frequency** vidéofréquence; ~ **tube** cinéscope; kinéscope; tube cathodique à image; ~ **white** niveau du blanc; blanc d'image
PID (proportional integral and derivative action) PID
pie chart graphe sectoriel ("camembert"); courbe sectoriel; graphe secteurs
pierced *adj* ajouré
Pierce function NON OU (= NI); ⏦ **ring** trame vide
pie winding bobinage en galette
piezoelectric quartz-crystal microphone microphone à quartz piézoélectrique
piezo-electric crystal microphone microphone à cristal
pigeon-hole *n* casier
piggyback board carte mère; carte de passage; ~ **connections** connexions superposées
pigtail *n* fibre amorce; fibre intermédiaire (de couplage); cordon monofibre; jarretière; ~ **connector** connecteur monofibre; connexion tressée
pilcrow *n* signe nouveau paragraphe (alinéa)
pile-up (of relay contacts) empilage; banc; pile
pillar *n* colonnette; chandelle; montant; tuteur; ~ **graph** histogramme
pill-box aerial antenne en D
pillow distortion distorsion en coussinet
pilot *n* pilote; ~ **card** carte pilote; ~ **carrier** porteuse pilote; onde pilote; signal de commande; ~ **(wire) circuit** circuit de commande; circuit directeur; circuit pilote; ~ **device** appareil de commande; auxiliaire de commande; ~ **exciter** excitatrice pilote; ~ **frequency** fréquence pilote; ~ **hole** avant-trou
piloting *n* pilotage
pilot lamp lampe témoin; lampe de surveillance; ~ **light** veilleuse; diode de contrôle; unité de signalisation; voyant; ~ **line** ligne tête de groupement; ~ **loss** perte de pilote; ~ **radio service** radio du service de pilotage; ~ **receiver** récepteur de la fréquence pilote; ~ **scheme** petite série; ~ **signal** signal de commande; signal pilote; ~ **tone** signal se surveillance; ~ **wave** onde pilote; ~ **wire** fil pilote; ligne pilote; fil d'épreuve

PIM (s. pulse-interval modulation)
pi-mode mode pi
pin *n* aiguille; borne; broche; contact; doigt; ergot; fiche; languette; passage; patte; picot; point; point de connexion (PCX); pointe; sortie; tige; axe; pinoche; pôle; ~ **assignment** brochage
pincers *pl* pince
pinch *n* pincement; ~ **bar** pied-de-biche
pinchbeck alloy (red brass) chrysocal; chrysocolle
pinch effect effet de pincement; effet de rupture
pinch-off voltage tension de coude; tension de pincement
pin configuration brochage
pincushion distortion equalizing correction de la distorsion en coussinet
pin drift chasse-goupilles
pine-tree (aerial) array rideau de doublets; rideau de dipôles horizontaux à réflecteurs; ~ **aerial** antenne en sapin; antenne colinéaire; antenne en arête de poisson
pi-network cellule en pi; réseau en pi
pin feed entraînement par ergots
pin-feed tractor chenille(tte) à ergots
ping-pong *n* mode continu; alternance; exploitation à l'alternat
pinhole *n* piqûre
pin identification brochage
pink noise bruit rose
pin-out(s) *n* brochage
p-i-n photodiode diode linéaire
pin-point *adj* ponctuel; capillaire
pin readout lecture d'une broche
pin-setting tool outil de clipsage
pin spanner clé à ergot
pin-tester machine à pointes
pintle *n* axe
pin-to-pin *adj* point à point; ~ **compatible with** brochage compatible avec
pinwheel *n* marguerite
pip *n* impulsion; top
pipe *n* artère; buse; conduit; retassure; tube; tuyère
pipe-bending machine cintreuse
pipe-diaphragm waveguide guide d'ondes à diaphragme tubulaire
pipeline (architecture) mode cascadable; ~ **register** registre de microinstruction; infoduc
piston *n* piston; ~ **attenuator** affaiblisseur à piston
pistonphone *n* pistonphone
pit *n* cratère; enfoncement; puits
PIT (s. programmable interval timer)
pitch *n* pas (de filetage); caractères par pouce (CPP); densité de caractères; densité

d'impression; échappement; entr'axe; en-tre-axe; espacement (pas); hauteur de son; inclinaison; intervalle; pas; pente; pente d'accord; ~ (of thread) pas axial; ~ **angle** angle de tangage; ~ **attitude** angle d'inclinaison longitudinale; ~ **axis** axe de tangage; ~ **setting** (of tape or disk speed) réglage fin de vitesse

pitting *n* piquage (sur CI)

pit-to-pit crête à crête (c/c)

pivot *n* point d'appui; axe

pixel *n* point d'image; ~ (pel) point graphique; ~ **grid** matrice d'éléments d'image

P/L (s. plain language text)

place in parallel shunter

placement *n* passation

place on stand-by mettre au repos

plain *adj* naturel; ~ **cable** câble nu; ~ **coupling** bride lisse

plain-language text (P/L) document en clair; copie en clair

plain work-piece pièce lisse

plait *n* fuseau; tresse

plan *n* plan; dessin; gamme

planar epitaxial structure structure plane épitaxiée; ~ **graph** graphe planaire; ~ **network** réseau plan

plane angle (in radians) angle plan; ~ **of polarization** plan de polarisation

plane-polarized wave onde polarisée rectilignement

plane-reflector aerial antenne à réflecteur plan

plane-strain fracture facteur d'intensité de contrainte critique

planned *adj* prévu; éventuel; prévisionnel; théorique; ~ **obsolescence** désuétude calculée

planner *n* ingénieur de projet; planificateur

planning *n* étude; ordonnancement; organisation; planification; programmation; ~ **office** bureau d'études

plan position indicator (PPI) indicateur panoramique

plant *n* installation technique; équipement d'infrastructure; ensemble; groupe; infrastructure matérielle; local technique

Planté plate plaque Planté

plant room local technique

plan view vue en plan

"plastic" coating peinture par poudrage

plastic effect plastique; ~ **enclosure** plasturgie

plastic-faced mallet massette plastique

plastic money support paiement

plastic(s) matière plastique

plastic sheath gaine plastique; ~ **support element** support plastique

plate *v* revêtir (de); ~ *n* plaque; anode; armature; disque; galette; gousset; plaquette

plateau *n* (of graph) palier

plate battery (B) batterie d'anode; batterie de plaque

plate-cathode capacitance capacité plaque-cathode

plate characteristic caractéristique de plaque; ~ **circuit** circuit anodique; circuit de plaque

plated *adj* chemisé; ~ **caps** (of fuse) embouts protégés; ~ **crystal** cristal à électrodes en couches métalliques

plated-through bush canon de métallisation; ~ **hole** trou métallisé; trou métallique

plated-wire memory mémoire à boucle inductive; mémoire à fil

plate effect facteur d'utilisation; ~ **efficiency** rendement anodique; rendement de conversion

platen *n* cylindre

platform *n* estrade; palette; palier; plénum; quai; ~ **truck** plateau roulant

plating *n* plaquage; chemise

platinum *n* platine

platter (of disk pack) disque; plateau

play *n* jeu

playback *n* lecture; audition; contrôle d'enregistrement; ~ **characteristic** caractéristique de lecture; ~ **head** tête de lecture; ~ **loss** perte du lecture

PLC (s. power line carrier)

please-hold-on message message de patience; veuillez patienter

plesiochronous network réseau plésiochrone

pliability *n* souplesse

pliers *n pl* pince

plinth *n* semelle; bâti; embase; pied support; piètement; plaque d'assise; plaque de base; plaque de fond; plinthe; socle; support; élément de surélévation

PLL (s. phase-locked loop)

PLM (s. pulse-length modulation)

plot *v* tracer; dresser; ~ *n* tracé; courbe; graphique

plotter *n* table traçante; marqueur

plotting *n* pointage; relevé; ~ **interval** intervalle de pointage; ~ **table** traceur de courbes

plucker *n* ensemble prise billets

plug *v* relier; ~ *n* alvéole; bouchon; cheville; conjoncteur; connecteur mâle; couvercle; prise mobile; tampon; fiche

plug-board *n* panneau de raccordement; tableau de connexions; panneau de mutation (PM); carte à pointes

plug connection connexion par fiches; ~ **cord**

P

cordon

plug-ended cable cordon enfichable; câble équipé; prise mobile

plug gauge (GO/NO-GO) tampon

plugged-in *adj* enfiché

plugged-out *adj* défiché

plug-in *adj* enfichable; amovible; embrochable; mobile; débrochable

plug-in-and-play taux de PIP

plug-in cable câble enfichable; ~ **circuit pack** carte enfichable; ~ **connector** connecteur enfichable; ~ **module** tiroir; élément enfichable; ~ **relay** relais enfichable; relais à fiches; ~ **unit** bloc amovible

plug socket fiche femelle

plug-to-plug compatibility mariabilité

plug-to-plug-compatible *adj* connectable

plumb line fil à plomb

plunger *n* pousseur; ~ (of head load) palette; ~ (of fuse) percuteur; ~ **attenuator** affaiblisseur à piston; ~ **key** piston; bouton poussoir (BP); ~ **relay** relais à bobine plongeante

plurivalent term polysème

plus-minus rule règle de bipolarité

plus sign (+) croix

ply *n* couche; toron

plywood *n* contre-plaqué; multiplis

PMBX (s. private manual branch exchange)

PMX (s. private manual exchange)

p-n boundary couche d'arrêt p-n

pneumo-oil (of circuit-breaker) oléopneumatique

p-n junction jonction p-n

PO (s. page overflow)

POA (s. private operating agency)

pocket *n* case; clapet; îlot; ~ **receiver** récepteur de poche; récepteur portable

pod *n* pied

point *n* point; contact; sommet; tête; ~ (of contact) grain; ~ **contact** contact de pointe

point-contact diode diode à pointe; ~ **rectifier** redresseur à contact par pointe

pointed to by indiqué par

pointer *n* pointeur; adresse de chaînage; adresse logique; aiguille; connecteur; doigt; flèche; index; indicateur

pointing *n* visée; ~ **angle** angle de pointage

point-junction transistor transistor à contacts de pointe et à jonction

point of convergence jonction; ~ **of sale (POS)** point de vente

point-of-sale polling télécollecte; ~ **terminal (POST)** terminal point de vente (TPV)

point-to-group graph graphe point-à-groupe

point-to-multipoint telegraph multiplexer multiplexeur télégraphique point-multipoint

point-to-point circuit circuit point-à-point;

circuit de poste à poste; ~ **communication** connexion de sections; ~ **link** liaison point à point; ~ **multiplexing** point-to-multipoint multiplexing; ~ **traffic** flux (de trafic)

Poisson distribution loi de Poisson; distribution de Poisson

poke *v* charger (en); ~ *n* écriture

poking *n* pointage

polar direct current system transmission par courant double; ~ **drive** commande polarisation

polarity *n* polarité; signe; sens; ~ **detector** détecteur de polarités; ~ **diversity reception** réception à polarisation multiple; ~ **reversal** inversion de polarités; renversement de la polarité

polarization analyser analyseur de polarisation

polarization-coupling loss affaiblissement par couplage de polarisation

polarization error effet de nuit; erreur de nuit; erreur de polarisation

polarized aerial antenne polarisée; ~ **capacitor** condensateur polarisé; ~ **electric drainage** drainage électrique polarisé; ~ **electromagnet** électro-aimant polarisé; ~ **relay** relais polarisé

polarizing *n* détrompage; codage; ~ **cavity/receptacle** détrompeur femelle; ~ **key** pion de centrage; pièce d'indexation; ~ **recess** encoche

polar keying modulation à double courant

polarograph *n* couloscope

polar radiation pattern diagramme polaire de rayonnement

pole *n* pôle; poteau; ~ (of magnetron segment) dent

pole-piece *n* armure; pièce polaire

police and ambulance services police-secours (code 17 en France)

policy guideline directive

poling *n* interversion de conducteurs

Polish notation notation polonaise

polling *n* accès sélectif; interrogation systématique; appel sélectif; appel systématique; balayage; chaînage; collecte de(s) données; consultation; exploration temporelle (d'une ligne); interrogation sélective; invitation à émettre; recherche; scrutation; sondage; sollicitation; ~ **command** commande d'invitation à transmettre; ~ **interval** délai d'appel; ~ **signal** signal d'appel

polyacetal *n* polyoxyméthylène (POM)

poly-core cable câble multiple

polyethylene *n* polyéthylène; ~ **sheath** gaine PE; ~ **terephthalate (PETP)** polytéréphtalate d'éthylène

polyformaldehyde polyoxyméthylène (POM)

polygraph *n* (P-graph) multigraphe
polymethyl methacrylate Altuglas [A.C.]; Plexiglas
polyphase generator génératrice polyphasée; ~ motor moteur polyphasé; ~ winding enroulement polyphasé
polyphenylene oxide phénylène polyoxide (NORYL); PPO
polyrod antenne pylône diélectrique; antenne en cierge
polytetrafluoroethylene (PTFE) Téflon [A.C.]
polythene *n* polyéthylène
polyvalent *adj* hétéropolaire; multivalent
polyvinyl alcohol rhodoviol; ~ chloride (PVC) polychlorure de vinyle (PCV)
polyvinylidene fluoride polyfluorure de vinylidène (PVF2)
pool (of machines) banc; ~ abbreviated dialling numérotation abrégée collective; ~ cathode cathode liquide
pooled *adj* collectif; coopérant; en commun avec
pooler *n* concentrateur; compteur
pooling *n* regroupement
pool rectifier redresseur à cathode liquide; soupape à cathode liquide
pop *n* (from stack) retrait de la pile
popcorn noise bruit en créneau
populated *adj* équipé
population, (statistical) ~ grandeur; ~ counting dénombrement
porcelain insulator isolateur en porcelaine
porch *n* palier
porous anode anode poreuse; ~ cathode cathode poreuse; ~ stone (of foam fluxer) bougie poreuse; diffuseur; pierre de diffusion
port *n* point d'accès; borne; canal; circuit d'accès; chambre; fenêtre; point d'entrée; porte; portier; sortie; terminaison; voie; ~ (constant) constante de porte
portability *n* portabilité (d'un programme)
portable *adj* amovible; portatif; ~ maintenance console valise de maintenance; ~ maintenance kit banc de maintenance; ~ radar radar portatif; ~ routine tester maquette de maintenance; ~ television receiver (walkie-lookie) téléviseur portatif
porterage *n* manutention
porthole *n* hublot
porting *n* transfert; passage (en); portage
portion *n* partie
port operations service service radio de port; ~ radar radar de port
POS (s. point of sale)
position *n* position; état; pas; point; poste; rang; emplacement; ~ (jump) forward/backward saut avant/arrière

positional notation numérotation pondérée; ~ response réponse d'identification de position; ~ signal signal d'identification de la position
position and homing indicator indicateur de position et de cours d'approche; ~ grouping key clé de liaison
positioning *n* positionnement; ~ and fault-handing subsystem chaîne(s) de positionnement(s) et de faute(s); ~ block cimblot (simbleau); ~ board opérateur de réception des positonnements; ~ function fonction de positionnement
position of maximum signal position d'intensité maximale; ~ pulse impulsion de commutation; impulsion de positionnement; ~ selector sélecteur de position
positive and negative en différentielle; ~ column colonne positive; ~ control commande desmodromique; ~ correlation corrélation à caractère réciproque; ~ edge-triggered synchronisé DT$_{RS}$; ~ edge-triggered D-type flip-flop bascule type DT$_{RS}$; ~ edge-triggered latch bascule à commande dissymétrique; ~ electron positon; ~ feedback réaction positive; rétrocouplage
positive-feedback system système asservi
positive-going edge front positif; ~ transition transition active; front de montée; front montant; transition positive
positive justification justification positive; ~ key presssure bruitage; ~ logic actif à l'état haut; ~ magnetic return keypad clavier à rappel magnétique; ~ (amplitude) modulation modulation positive; ~ polarity connected to chassis masse du bâti; ~ pole pôle positif; ~ pulse signal utile; ~ stop butée; déclic; ~ temperature coefficient (PTC) thermistor résistance à coefficient de température positif (CTP); ~ terminal borne positive; ~ value valeur réelle; ~ voltage amplitude positive
positron *n* positon
post *v* afficher; annoter; consigner; enregistrer; signaler; ~ *n* poteau; borne; doigt; tige
POST (s. point-of-sale terminal)
postal coding desk poste d'indexation
postamble *n* postambule
post-deflection accelerating electrode électrode de post-accélération
post-dialling delay délai d'attente après numérotation; temporisation avant transmission
post-emphasis circuit circuit de désaccentuation
post-indexing *n* postindexation
posting *n* enregistrement; attribution; indexa-

P

tion; passage; signalement; inscription; remontée

postings file fichier de signalement

post-mortem (routine) autopsie

postpone *v* ajourner; renvoyer; report

postponed *adj* différé

postprocessor *n* programme d'adaptation

post-selected busy hour heure de pointe

post-selection time délai de postsélection

post-slew *n* saut après impression

post-sync field-blanking interval intervalle de suppression de trame après synchronisation

post-test end-point (PTE) sanction; critère de défaillance; ~ **end-point measurements** mesures finales

pot core pot pour inductance; ~ **core with trimmed air-gap** pot (de ferrite) taillé

potency *n* puissance (Pce)

potential *n* tension; niveau; pouvoir; potentiel; ~ **barrier** barrière de potentiel; ~ **difference (p.d.)** différence de potentiel (d.d.p.); ~ **divider** diviseur de tension; ~ **drop** chute de potentiel; ~ **energy curve** courbe d'énergie potentielle; ~ **malfunction** accusation; ~ **plateau** plateau de potentiel; ~ **trough** cuvette de potentiel; puits de potentiel

potentiometer *n* potentiomètre; ~ **measurement** mesure potentiométrique

pot life temps de gélification

potting *n* enrobage; ~ **compound** résine

pouch *n* étui

Poulsen arc converter émetteur Poulsen

pound sign (#) dièse

powder coating enrobage par fluidisation; peinture par poudrage; poudrage

powdered molybdenum-permalloy poudre d'alliage molybdène-permalloy

power (up) *v* alimenter en énergie; ~ *n* puissance; énergie; exposant; pouvoir; régime; ~ **addition** addition en puissance; ~ **amplification** amplification de puissance; ~ **budget** bilan de consommation; ~ **cable** câble d'énergie; câble d'alimentation; ~ **component** (in VA) consommation; ~ **connection** liaison d'énergie; ~ **consumption** puissance consommée; consommation d'énergie; ~ **conversion** commutation de puissance; ~ **cord** cordon d'alimentation; ~ **density** puissance volumique; ~ **distribution** alimentation; ~ **distribution cabinet** grille d'énergie; ~ **distribution interface** grille d'alimentation; ~ **distribution network** réseau de transport d'énergie électrique; ~ **divider** répartiteur de puissance

power-down *n* coupure secteur; ~ **mode (PDN)** mode réduction de consommation

power drawn puissance absorbée; consommation; puissance consommée; ~ **drawn in speech mode** consommation en phonie; ~ **drill** perceuse

power-driven system système à entraînement mécanique

power driver visseuse

powered-down *adj* hors tension

power factor (p.f.) cosinus phi (cos φ); cos phi; facteur de puissance; ~ **fail** chute d'alimentation; ~ **failure** panne d'alimentation; ~ **feed** alimentation en énergie; ~ **feed** (group) sectionnement

power-feed bridge circuit de connexion; pont local; ~ **circuit** circuit d'alimentation; ~ **junctor** joncteur alimentateur

power-flux density densité de puissance

powerful *adj* performant; puissant

power gain gain en puissance; ~ **gain** (referred to isotropic radiator) gain absolu d'une antenne; gain isotrope d'une antenne; ~ **heat sink** radiateur de puissance; ~ **induction** bruit induit

powering-down *n* mise hors tension

powering-up *n* mise sous tension (MST)

power level niveau de puissance; énergie (en dBm); ~ **level difference** différence de niveau de puissance; ~ **line** ligne d'énergie; ligne de transport; ligne industrielle; ~ **line carrier (PLC)** courant porteur sur ligne à haute tension; onde porteuse sur ligne de transport; ~ **loss** perte dissipative; perte de puissance; ~ **miser** économiseur d'énergie; ~ **network** réseau de force motrice; ~ **oscillator** oscillateur de puissance; ~ **outlet** prise; ~ **output** puissance de sortie (W sous ohms); ~ **pack** bloc de puissance; bloc d'alimentation; pont d'alimentation; pont de puissance; ~ **plant** atelier d'énergie; centrale d'énergie; groupe moteur; installation d'énergie; installation motrice; matériel d'énergie; station d'énergie; ~ **point** organe de puissance; ~ **rail** barre d'alimentation (BA); bande d'alimentation; ~ **rating** puissance (Pce); capacité de charge; dissipation; puissance d'emploi; ~ **rating of a transmitter** indice de puissance d'un émetteur; ~ **ratio** rapport de puissance; ~ **relay** relais de puissance; ~ **requirements** consommation; ~ **resistor** résistance de puissance; ~ **ringing** appel par courant alternatif; ~ **room** salle d'énergie; ~ **separation filter** filtre d'aiguillage; ~ **socket** prise de courant; ~ **source** source d'alimentation; station d'énergie; ~ **spectrum** spectre de puissance

power-spectrum deformation distorsion du

spectre de la puissance
power stage stade de puissance; ~ **supplies** énergie de servitude; ~ **supply** alimentation en énergie; bloc d'alimentation; fourniture (de courant); source d'énergie; ~ **supply connection** connexion de réseau (électrique); ~ **supply grid** gri/réseau d'alimentation; gri; ~ **supply plane** plan d'alimentation; ~ **transformer** transformateur de puissance; ~ **traverse** à translation électrique; ~ **tube** tube de puissance; ~ **vibrator** mutateur de puissance
P-PH-M (s. pulse-phase modulation)
PPI (s. plan position indicator)
PPM (s. pulse-position modulation)
p-p; pk-pk (s. peak-to-peak)
p-pulse impulsion de commutation; impulsion de positionnement
practical skill connaissance pratique
practice factor coefficient de pratique expérimentale
practised *adj* confirmé
preamble *n* préambule; généralités; libellé; mot d'en-tête
pre-amplification *n* préamplification; ~ **transformer** transformateur de préamplificateur
pre-amplifier *n* préamplificateur (PA)
pre-analysis *n* préanalyse
pre-arranged call conversation avec préavis
pre-assigned station night answering service renvoi de nuit
pre-bias current courant de prépolarisation
pre-built block IC CI précaractérisé
precedence call conversation avec priorité
precious metal métal précieux
precipitate *adj* intempestif
precipitation *n* coulure; migration; remontée
precision *n* justesse; ~ **adjustment** réglage fin; ~ **approach radar (PAR)** radiodétecteur d'approche de précision; ~ **sweep** instrument de mesure de précision
pre-concentrator *n* préconcentrateur
pre-correction *n* précorrection
pre-cut grain-oriented silicon iron coupé en fer silicium orienté
predetermined counter compteur électromécanique d'impulsions
predetermined night answer renvoi général (RG)
predict *v* prévoir
pre-distortion *n* prédistortion
pre-drilled plate support perforé; ~ **upright** montant perforé
pre-emphasis *n* préaccentuation; précorrection; ~ **filter** filtre de préaccentuation
pre-emption *n* présélection; prise initiale
pre-emptive *adj* intempestif; prématuré;

~ **fault** faute prématurée
pre-equalization *n* pré-égalisation
prefabricated wiring filerie préfabriquée
pre-fade listening écoute préalable
preference facility possibilité d'entrer en tiers
preferred voltage tension préférentielle
prefix *n* indicatif (IF); préfixe; présignal; ~ **code** liste d'indicateurs
preform drawing process étirage des préformes
pre-formed cable peigne de câble; ~ **(standard) fixing rail** support profilé
pre-group *n* prégroupe; sous-groupe; ~ **decoupler** découpleur de prégroupes; ~ **translator** traducteur de prégroupes
pre-heating time temps de chauffage
pre-knock pulse préimpulsion
preliminary adjustments mise en œuvre; ~ **schedule** préprogrammé; ~ **stages** période de mise au point
pre-load time temps de précharge
premature *adj* intempestif; infantile; ~ **release** libération anticipée
premature-release rate taux de relâchement
premature stoppage arrêt intempestif
premises *n* local; lieux; locaux
pre-modulation clipping écrêtage avant la modulation
pre-oscillation current courant au démarrage
preparatory period période préparatoire
pre-payment *n* prépaiement; acompte
pre-payment kiosk cabine publique; cabine (à) paiement
pre-preg *adj* pré-enrobé
pre-processing *n* prétraitement
pre-production (advance prototype) présérie
pre-punched card carte pré-perforée
pre-recorded *adj* différé; ~ **list** répertoire
pre-scaling *n* prédivision
pre-scored lines trait de découpe au ciseau
pre-scoring *n* demi-cisaillage
pre-selection *n* présélection; accès automatique au réseau; préconditionnement
pre-selection (line) stage étage de présélection
pre-selector *n* présélecteur
presentation control function fonction de commande pour la présentation
present value cost (pvc) coût actualisé
preset *v* programmer; afficher; présélectionner; ~ *adj* préréglé; fixe; forcé; paramétrable; prédéfini; prédéterminé; présélectionné; taré; ~ **equalizer** compensateur préréglé; ~ **frequency** fréquence préréglée; ~ **jammer** brouilleur préréglé; ~ **potentiometer** potentiomètre d'ajustage
presettable *adj* à prédétermination
presetting *n* présélection; préaffichage; programmation
preset trim potentiometer potentiomètre ajus-

table à couche de carbone

pre-slew *n* saut avant impression

press *v* appuyer; actionner; enfoncer; ~ **ahead** continuer

pressboard *n* carton isolant; carte de Lyon; carton comprimé

press-cutting agency pige publicitaire

pressel switch pédale d'alternat

press-fit *adj* à insertion sans soudure (ISS); ~ **contact** contact à insertion forcée (CIF)

press-fit pin broche à insertion sans soudure

pressing *n* emboutissage; ~ **deadline** délai réduit

presspahn *n* carton comprimé; carton isolant

press-to-talk switch (PTT) bouton d'alternat

pressure-cast *adj* moulé sous pression

pressure connector prise de pression; ~ **controller** pressostat; ~ **drop** chute de pression; ~ **gauge** manomètre

pressure-gradient (velocity) **microphone** microphone à gradient de pression

pressure level niveau de pression; ~ **plate** poussoir; ~ **regulator** appareil de détente; ~ **seal** presse-étoupe; traversée étanche; ~ **switch** manocontact

pressure-tight window fenêtre étanche (de guide d'ondes)

pressurization *n* pressurisation

pressurized *adj* pressurisé; ~ **connection** connexion par pression

pre-stored *adj* précalculé (message)

pre-stress *n* précontrainte

presumptive address adresse de base; adresse d'origine; adresse primitive; ~ **instruction** instruction primitive

pre-tax *adj* hors taxe (HT)

pre-trigger pulse préimpulsion

prevailing condition condition en vigueur; ~ **standards** règles de l'art

preventive maintenance maintenance préventive (MP); entretien préventif

previous page page précédente

pre-wired *adj* précâblé; câblage prévu pour; ~ **circuit board** carte câblée

PRF (s. pulse repetition frequency)

priced *adj* valorisé

price list tarif

price/performance trade-off rapport prix/performance

price quotation cotation

primary block bloc primaire; ~ **cable feeder** câble de transport primaire; ~ **cell** pile; ~ **centre** centre d'autonomie d'acheminement; centre de groupement; centre primaire; ~ **channel** voie aller; ~ **circuit** circuit primaire; ~ **coating** (extramural cladding) revêtement primaire (RP); ~ **coil** bobine primaire; ~ **electron** électron

primaire; électron incident; ~ **emission** (characteristic) caractéristique d'émission; ~ **fault** faute déterministe; ~ **group** groupe à douze canaux; groupe primaire; ~ **half-winding** demi-primaire; ~ **high-usage trunk group** faisceau direct à débordement; ~ **instruction** instruction élémentaire; ~ **keying** manipulation dans le circuit primaire d'alimentation; ~ **radar** radiodétection primaire; ~ **radiation** rayonnement primaire; ~ **radiation pattern** diagramme de rayonnement primaire; ~ **radiator** élément actif; élément rayonnant primaire; ~ **resistance** résistance statorique; ~ **resistance starter** démarreur statorique; ~ **route** voie primaire; voie normale; ~ **service area** zone couverte primaire; zone de service primaire; ~ **side/winding** côté basse fréquence; ~ **signal** signal primaire; ~ **skip zone** zone primaire de silence; ~ **source** (origin) **of fault** primitive d'activation; ~ **switching centre** centre primaire; ~ **voltage** tension primaire; ~ **winding** enroulement primaire; bobinage primaire

prime *v* amorcer; apprêter; armer; ~ **contractor** maître d'oeuvre; chef de file; ~ **contractor status** maîtrise d'œuvre; ~ **cost** prix de revient; ~ **data** donnée primaire

prime-line preference présélection automatique

prime mover machine motrice; machine de travail; ~ **number** premier nombre

primer *n* base d'accrochage; couche de conversion; film de conversion; peinture d'impression; peinture primaire

prime time heure de pointe

primitive polynomial polynôme de base; ~ **routine** primitive

principal frequency fréquence fondamentale; ~ **(main) group** groupement principal

print *v* imprimer; éditer; lister

print *n* édition; (éd.); sortie

printable *adj* affichable

printed circuit circuit imprimé; ~ **circuit assembly** carte équipée; ~ **circuit board (PCB)** carte équipée; carte imprimée usinée; carte imprimée nue; plaque de circuit imprimé; plaquette imprimée; bloc de circuit imprimé; ~ **component** composant imprimé; ~ **wiring** câblage imprimé; ~ **wiring backplane** fond de panier imprimé

printer *n* imprimante; récepteur imprimeur

printergram télex; ~ **service** service de transmission des télégrammes par téléimprimeur

printer keyboard bloc machine à écrire;

~ **magnet** électro-aimant imprimeur; ~ **perforator** récepteur-perforateur imprimeur; ~ **port** canal desservant une imprimante; ~ **ribbon** ruban encreur; ~ **select** choix de l'imprimante; ~ **spacing chart** grille d'imprimante; ~ **tape** bande d'impression; bobineau; ~ **terminal** terminal d'impression; ~ **thimble** (print drum) tulipe

print file fichier impression; ~ **head** tête d'impression

printing code converter transcodeur imprimeur; ~ **keyboard perforator** clavier perforateur avec impression; perforateur imprimeur à clavier; ~ **reception** réception à impression; ~ **reperforator** récepteur-perforateur imprimeur; ~ **speed** vitesse d'impression; ~ **telegraph** téléimprimeur; télégraphe imprimeur; ~ **telegraphy** télégraphie par appareils imprimeurs; typotélégraphie

print margins sortie page; ~ **master** calque

printout n édition sur imprimante; copie (sur) papier; extraction; ~ **file** fichier logique d'édition

print page recopie d'écran; ~ **roll** cylindre d'impression

printwheel n roue d'impression

prior adj préalable

priority extension/station poste prioritaire; ~ **group** groupement préférentiel; ~ **level** niveau prioritaire; ~ **line** ligne essentielle; ~ **routine** programme d'avant-plan; ~ **subscriber line** abonné privilégié; abonné essentiel

prism aerial antenne pyramidale

privacy n confidentialité; masquage; le secret; ~ **code** code de masquage; indice préservation; ~ **key** touche secret; ~ **switch** pédale de secret

private attachment matériel d'abonné; ~ **automatic branch exchange (PABX)** autocommutateur privé à prise directe du réseau; central automatique privé avec accès au réseau; installation automatique d'abonné avec postes supplémentaires; ~ **automatic exchange (PAX)** commutateur automatique privé; central automatique privé sans accès au réseau; autocommutateur privé; central privé automatique; ~ **branch exchange (PBX)** central manuel privé avec opérateur ayant accès au réseau; central privé relié au réseau public; commutateur privé (à postes supplémentaires); installation privée (IP); standard d'abonné; ~ **(branch) exchange (PBX)** installation privée (IP); ~ **call** conversation privée; ~ **charge metering** télétaxe (TLT); ~ **circuit** circuit spécialisé;

circuit privé; ~ **common carrier** ligne privée; ~ **connection** connexion privée; ~ **exchange (PX)** central privé; ~ **line (local loop)** ligne spécialisée; liaison spécialisée; ligne directe; ligne privée; ~ **manual branch exchange (PMBX)** installation d'abonné avec postes supplémentaires à exploitation manuelle; ~ **manual exchange (PMX)** central manuel privé; ~ **meter** compteur de taxe à domicile; compteur télétaxe; ~ **number** numéro privé; ~ **operating agency (POA)** exploitation privée; ~ **service** service privé; ~ **switching system** système de commutation privé; ~ **telegram** télégramme privé; ~ **telegraph network** réseau télégraphique privé; réseau privé à téléimprimeurs; ~ **telegraph wire** ligne télégraphique privée; ~ **telephone network** réseau téléphonique privé; ~ **transit exchange** commutateur de transit privé; ~ **wire** circuit privé; circuit spécialisé; fil de maintien; ~ **wire circuit** circuit téléphonique loué en permanence

privatization n concession de service public

privileged adj privilégié

probability density densité de probabilité; ~ **of collision** probabilité de choc

probe n sonde; canne; grip-fil; grip-test; pointe; touche; engin; ~ **coil** bobine exploratrice; ~ **hatch** passe-perches; ~ **transformer** transformateur-sonde

probe-tube microphone microphone à sonde

problem-oriented language langage d'application; langage orienté-problème

problems pl troubles

problem-solving n dépannage

procedural adj algorithmique; ~ **language** langage adapté aux procédures

procedure, (operating) ~ mode opératoire

procedure-oriented input entrée de procédure (EN); ~ **language** langage adapté aux procédures; langage procédurier

proceedings n compte-rendu (CR)

proceed I/O (input/output) branchement E/S

proceed-to-dial tone tonalité d'invitation à numéroter; tonalité d'invitation à transmettre

proceed-to-select signal signal d'invitation à numéroter; signal d'invitation à transmettre

proceed-to-send signal (PTS) commande d'invitation à transmettre; signal de demande de chiffres

process n traitement; processus; ~ **chart** ordinogramme; ~ **control** automatisme industriel; commande de processus; gestion automatisée; l'automatique

process-control computer calculateur industriel; ~ **equipment** équipements d'automatisme

processed call appel traité

processing n traitement; calcul; dépouillement; gestion; ~ **action** unité de traitement (UT); ~ **centre** centre de traitement; ~ **hierarchy** hiérarchie des traitements; ~ **logic** logique de traitement; ~ **manager** contrôleur du système (de base de données); ~ **mode** mode d'exécution; ~ **subsystem** ensemble logique; ~ **unit** unité de traitement (UT)

process inspection label fiche suiveuse

processor n calculateur; coffret; logique; machine; organe de calcul; processeur; programme de traitement; unité de traitement (UT); bloc de calcul; ~ **control** commande par processeurs; ~ **crash** arrêt calculateur; ~ **data interchange memory** mémoire d'échanges entre processeurs; ~ **interchange card** carte d'échange interprocesseurs; ~ **interface macro-instruction** primitive; ~ **overhead** temps à vide; ~ **test routine** examineur

process register registre de processus; ~ **status** état d'un traitement; ~ **utility** utilitaire des traitements

procurement n approvisionnement

prod n poignard de test; sonde; bâtonnet

producer n fournisseur; ~ **goods** équipement d'infrastructure; moyens de production

product data sheet fiche produit; ~ **design** conception du produit; ~ **design consistency** suivi; ~ **despatching group** groupe de gestion physique; ~ **development** élaboration du produit; ~ **engineering** définition de produit; ~ **family** famille

production batch lot de production; ~ **centre** centre de production; ~ **control** contrôle de production; contrôle de fabrication; ~ **cycle** cycle de production; ~ **engineering** productique; préindustrialisation; ordonnancement; ~ **line** chaîne de production; ~ **lot** lot de production; ~ **master** gamme de fabrication

productive hours heures productives

product line gamme; offre; ~ **marketing group** groupe produits; ~ **mix** différentiation des produits; gamme

product specification fiche de produits; ~ **status sheet** fiche d'évolution

professional and executive personnel (P&E) cadre(s)

professional-grade adj à usage professionnel; de type professionnel

proficiency n maîtrise; savoir-faire

profile code code cliché

profiled adj épaulé

profile projector projecteur de profil; coordi-

natographe

profiling n détourage

profitability n rentabilité

profit-sharing n participation des salariés

pro forma modèle (mle)

program n programme (pg); ~ **access key** clé programme; ~ **address** adresse logique; ~ **binary image** mémoire; ~ **booking centre** service centralisateur; ~ **bug** erreur de programmation; ~ **connector** bouchon

program-controlled adj programmé

program counter compteur ordinal; compteur d'adresse; compteur d'assemblage; compteur de phase; compteur d'instructions; registre de phase; registre programme

program-detected error faute programmée

program event recording (PER) contrôleur d'événements de programme

program-generated fault message faute programmée

program generator configurateur; ~ **halt** blocage programme; ~ **instruction** instruction de programme; ~ **library** programmathèque; ~ **loader task** tâche de chargement des programmes

programmable adj paramétrable; ~ **array logic (PAL)** réseau logique programmable; ~ **connector** bouchon résistif; ~ **counter** compteur programmable; ~ **interrupt controller (PIC)** contrôleur programmable d'interruptions; ~ **interval timer (PIT)** temporisateur programmable; boîtier temporisateur; ~ **key** touche programmée; ~ **logic (unit)** unité de gestion programmée; ~ **memory** mémoire utilisable; ~ **read-only memory (PROM)** mémoire morte programmable (MMP); mémoire morte; mémoire non inscriptible par le logiciel; ~ **ROM (EPROM)** mémoire semi-permanente; ~ **voltmeter** voltmètre programmable

programme n émission; contenu de stage; ~ **circuit** circuit téléphonique de radiodiffusion; circuit radiophonique

programmed algorithm automate; ~ **call** placement rappel rendez-vous; ~ **halt** arrêt programmé; ~ **off-line control** commande autonome programmé (CAP); ~ **selective dump** sauvegarde incrémentielle

programme line ligne de modulation

program memory mémoire (de) programme

programmer n programm(at)eur informaticien; réalisateur

programme schedule (of TV) grille de programmation

programme-switching centre centre de commutation radiophonique

programming n programmation; positionnement; réalisation des programmes; réalisation logicielle; ~ **language** langage de programmation; ~ **sheet** bordereau

program origin adresse d'origine; ~ **relocation table** table d'affectation des sections; ~ **section** tranche programme; ~ **segment** partie programme

program-sensitive fault pseudo-défaut

program sequence évolution de programme; ~ **signal** signal de modulation; signal modulant; ~ **status register** registre d'état programme; ~ **status word (PSW)** mot d'état de programme; ~ **subset** bloc programme; ~ **switching data** paramètre d'aiguillage; ~ **trace** trace du chemin suivi; ~ **word servicing** gestion mot programme

progress chaser sheet fiche de suivi; ~ **check** suivi

progression n pas; ~ adj pas à pas (PAP)

progressively adj au fil de l'eau

progress record card fiche de suivi; ~ **report** état d'avancement; cahier de suivi

prohibited area zone interdite

project coordinator maître d'oeuvre; ~ **engineer** ingénieur d'affaires; ~ **guide** guide d'affaire

projectile n engin

projecting/rough connection connexion agressive

projection n bossage; dépassement; galbe; ~ **CRT** tube cathodique de projection; ~ **TV receiver** récepteur à projection

project management ingénierie; maîtrise d'œuvre

PROM (s. programmable read-only memory); ~ **card** carte programmable

promote v favoriser; animer; contribuer à; faciliter; plaider en faveur (de); promouvoir; impulser

promotional circulars publipostage

prompt n caractère indicateur; attente de l'entrée; guide opérateur; indication; message de guidage; message d'état; message guide; mire; rappel; intitulé; ~ (message) sollicitation; ~ **alarm** alarme intervention immédiate; ~ **character** guide

prone adj sensible; susceptible

prong n griffe; lyre; pince

proof load charge d'épreuve; ~ **machine** classeuse totalisatrice; ~ **stress** limite élastique; limite d'élasticité; ~ **total** total de contrôle

prop n appui; chandelle; tuteur

propagated error erreur répercutée; erreur propagée; erreur propre

propagation axis axe de propagation; ~ **characteristic** caractéristique de propagation; ~ **coefficient** exposant linéique de propa-

gation; ~ **constant** constante de propagation; ~ **delay** temps de propagation; ~ **error** erreur de propagation; ~ **loss** affaiblissement de propagation; perte de propagation; ~ **mode** mode de propagation; ~ **path** parcours des ondes; ~ **path-tracing method** trace du chemin suivi; ~ **time** temps de propagation; ~ **velocity** vitesse de propagation

property n bien

proportional band bande proportionnelle; ~ **spacing** échappement proportionnel; ~ **spacing printer** imprimante à espacement proportionnel; ~ **to the square root of** en racine carrée de

proportion of lost calls proportion d'appels perdus

proprietary adj du commerce; ~ **mark** désignation commerciale

pros and cons points forts et points faibles

proscribed adj interdit

prosign (precedence indicator) préfixe de message

prospect n perspective

protect v protéger; sauvegarder

protected adj inséparable; privilégié; ~ (of data) verrouillé; ~ **area** zone protégée; ~ **expression** expression insécable; ~ **field** champ protégé; zone insécable; ~ **space** espace insécable

protection cap capot de protection; ~ **channel** canal de protection; ~ **code** indice de préservation; ~ **key** clé de validité; ~ **line** liaison de secours; ~ **ratio** rapport de protection; ~ **relay** relais de protection; ~ **switch** interrupteur de protection; ~ **switching** commutation de voies

protective casing plastron; ~ **circuit** circuit de protection; ~ **earth(ing)** mise à terre de protection; ~ **ground** terre de protection; ~ **measures** sécurités; ~ **overlay** vernis; ~ **screen** écran protecteur; ~ **tape** ruban de protection

protocol conversion conversion de protocole; ~ **identifier** identificateur de procédure; ~ **wire** fil de procédure

proton n proton; ~ **microscope** microscope protonique

prototype n avant-projet; maquette; ~ **test** essai d'homologation

prototyping maquettage

protractor n rapporteur d'angle

protruding adj en saillie

proud adj désaffleurant

provide back-up (fail-safe) **facilities** sécuriser

proving n épreuve; vérification

provision for future splices (of optic cable) réserve d'atténuation

proximity effect effet de proximité; ~ **fuse** fusée de proximité; ~ **switch** stati-contact; capteur; ~ **zone** zone d'induction

PRR (s. pulse repetition rate)

pseudo *adj* fictif; factice

pseudo-code *n* pseudo-code; code symbolique; langage symbolique; pseudo-instruction

pseudo-data *n* données fictives

pseudo-instruction *n* directive; pseudo-instruction

pseudo-noise carrier porteuse modulée par le pseudo-bruit

pseudo-offlining impression en différé

pseudo-random *adj* pseudo-aleatoire; ~ **generator** générateur pseudo-aléatoire; ~ **noise** bruit quasi-impulsif; bruit pseudo-aléatoire

pseudo-register pseudo-enregistreur

pseudo-ternary code code pseudo-ternaire

PSK (s. phase-shift keying)

PSN (s. public switched network); ∻ **line** ligne de réseau (LR); ligne commutée par numérotation

psophometer *n* psophomètre; mesureur de la tension de bruit

psophometric e.m.f. force électromotrice psophométrique; ~ **noise** bruit psophométrique; bruit pondéré; ~ **power** puissance psophométrique; ~ **voltage** tension psophométrique; ~ **weight** poids psophométrique

PSP (s. peak side-band power)

PSW (s. program status word)

PTE (s. post-test end-point)

PTFE (s. polytetrafluoroethylene); ∻ **sheathing** gaine téflon

PTM (s. pulse-time modulation)

PTS (s. proceed-to-send signal)

PTT (s. press-to-talk switch); ∻ **approval plate** plaque d'agrément

p-type semiconductor semiconducteur par défaut d'électrons

public address télédiffusion; porte-voix à amplification électrique

public-address amplifier amplificateur de sonorisation; ~ **call** appel en diffusion; ~ **system** sonorisation

publication date date de parution

public building and works génie civil; ~ **callbox** appareil téléphonique à prépaiement; cabine publique; poste à prépaiement; ~ **call office** poste téléphonique public; ~ **concentrator/message-switching unit** concentrateur-aiguilleur public (CAPU); ~ **data network** réseau public de transmission de données; ~ **data service** service public de données; ~ **exchange** central

public; ~ **pay station** poste à prépaiement; ~ **radio service** service public de radiocommunications; ~ **switched network (PSN)** réseau téléphonique commuté (RTC); ~ **switched network line** ligne PTT; ~ **symbol** symbole commun; ~ **telegraph network** réseau télégraphique public; ~ **telephone** poste téléphone public; ~ **telephone coin counting** précomptage; ~ **telephone network** réseau téléphonique public; ~ **telephone station** poste téléphonique public

puckering *n* (of paper) gaufrage

PUCS (s. peripheral unit controller system)

P&E (s. professional and executive personnel)

pull-down resistor résistance de rappel; résistance de tirage

pulling figure indice de glissement aval; ~ **range** plage d'entrainement; ~ **station** relais de tirage; ~ **wire** câblette

pull-in range (of PLL) plage de capture; ~ **voltage** tension d'enclenchement

pull-off strength résistance à l'arrachement; effort d'arrachement; ~ **test** essai de résistance à la traction

pull-out knob tirette

pull-up current courant d'excitation; ~ **resistor** résistance de rappel

pulsatance *n* fréquence angulaire

pulsating current courant pulsé; courant modulé; courant pulsatoire; ~ **siren** sirène modulée; ~ **voltage** tension pulsatoire; ~ **waveform** forme d'onde pulsatoire

pulse *v* cadencer; moduler; ~ *n* impulsion; impulsation; signal; top; ~ **action** sélection par impulsions

pulse-address multiple access (PAMA) accès multiple avec adresse par impulsions (AMAI)

pulse amplifier amplificateur d'impulsions

pulse-amplitude modulation (PAM) modulation d'impulsions en amplitude (MIA); modulation (d'amplitude) par variation de charge; impulsions modulées en amplitude

pulse analyser analyseur d'impulsions; ~ **and bar test signal** signal comportant une impulsion et une barre; ~ **average time (tpav)** largeur d'impulsion; ~ **bandwidth** largeur de bande d'impulsion; ~ **carrier** train porteur; ~ **characteristics** mesure en impulsions; ~ **clipper** écrêteur d'impulsions

pulse-code modulation (PCM) modulation par impulsions codées (MIC); modulation par impulsions codées (MIC)

pulse coding codage d'impulsions

pulse-controlled avance pas à pas; ~ **selector** sélecteur pas à pas

pulse corrector régénérateur d'impulsions; correcteur d'impulsions; ~ **counter** compteur d'impulsions; ~ **counting** comptage d'impulsions

pulsed *adj* impulsionnel; alternatif; clignotant; en impulsions; pulsé; sinusoïdal; ~ **automatic gain control** commande automatique de gain par impulsions; ~ **beacon** radiophare à impulsions

pulse decay affaiblissement d'une impulsion; ~ **density modulator (PDM)** modulateur de densité d'impulsion; ~ **dialling** numérotation décimale; ~ **direction-finding** relèvement par impulsions; ~ **dissipation** puissance dissipée d'une impulsion; ~ **distortion** distorsion d'impulsion; ~ **distributor** distributeur d'impulsions

pulsed signalling signalisation par impulsions; signalisation impulsionnelle

pulse duration durée d'impulsion

pulse-duration modulation modulation d'impulsions en durée

pulse duty cycle taux d'impulsions; ~ **echo attenuation** affaiblissement d'écho de l'impulsion de mesure; ~ **echometer** échomètre à impulsions; appareil de mesure du retour d'impulsions; ~ **edge** flanc d'impulsion; ~ **emitter** émetteur d'impulsions

pulse-excited aerial antenne à excitation par choc

pulse filter filtre de télétaxe

pulse-forming network (PFN) réseau conformateur d'impulsions

pulse frequency (PF) fréquence d'impulsion

pulse-frequency modulation (PFM) modulation d'impulsions en fréquence

pulse generator générateur d'impulsions; ~ **group** train d'impulsions

pulse-height analyser discriminateur d'amplitude; ~ **analysis** analyse d'amplitude; ~ **selector** détecteur à double seuil; détecteur à deux limites

pulse interrogation interrogation par impulsions

pulse-interval modulation (PIM) modulation d'impulsions en espacement

pulse jitter instabilité de l'impulsion; ~ **length** (t_d) durée d'impulsion

pulse-length modulation (PLM) modulation d'impulsions en durée

pulse-limiting curves gabarit de l'impulsion

pulse-limiting rate taux d'écrêtage d'impulsions

pulse marker top; ~ **meter** compteur d'impulsions

pulse-modulated hyperbolic system système hyperbolique à modulation par impulsions

pulse modulation modulation par impulsions;

~ **noise** bruit d'impulsion; ~ **period** durée d'impulsion; ~ **period meter** intervallomètre

pulse-phase modulation (P-PH-M) modulation d'impulsions en position

pulse-position modulation (PPM); modulation d'impulsions en position; modulation d'impulsions à variation de temps; modulation d'espacement des impulsions

pulse radar radar à impulsions; ~ **rate** (reciprocal of pulse period) fréquence de récurrence; ~ **ratio** rapport d'impulsions; ~ **regeneration** régénération d'impulsions; ~ **repeater** régénérateur d'impulsions; répéteur d'impulsions; ~ **repetition frequency (PRF)** fréquence de répétition des impulsions; ~ **repetition rate (PRR)** taux de répétitéon d'impulsions; ~ **(re-)shaping** restitution (de l'impulsion); ~ **response** réponse impulsionnelle; ~ **response curve** caractéristique de réponse aux impulsions; ~ **shape** forme d'une impulsion; ~ **shaper** amplificateur normaliseur; circuit configurateur d'impulsions; correcteur d'impulsions

pulse-shaping circuit circuit de mise en forme; circuit configurateur d'impulsions

pulse shaping line ligne formatrice d'impulsions

pulse-shaping network réseau conformateur d'impulsions

pulse signals signaux de type à impulsions; ~ **spacing** largeur d'impulsion; espacement entre impulsions; ~ **spectrum** spectre d'une impulsion; ~ **spike** impulsion parasite; ~ **spreading** élargisssement des impulsions

pulses to subscriber's private meter impulsions de télétaxation

pulse stretcher circuit élargisseur; correcteur de forme d'onde; correcteur d'impulsions; ~ **stuffing** compression d'impulsions; ~ **tail** traîne de l'impulsion; ~ **tilt** palier incliné; ~ **time** durée d'impulsion

pulse-time modulation (PTM) modulation d'impulsions dans le temps

pulse top palier; ~ **trailing edge** flanc arrière de l'impulsion; ~ **train** train d'impulsions; série d'impulsions; ~ **transformer** transformateur d'impulsion; ~ **transmitter** émetteur de télétaxe; ~ **triggering** déclenchement par impulsion; ~ **width** (t_w) durée d'impulsion; largeur d'impulsion

pulse-width coding codage en durée d'impulsions; ~ **modulating comparator** comparateur modulateur de largeur; ~ **modulation (PWM)** modulation d'impulsions en durée; ~ **modulator** modulateur de largeur

pulse(-width) recorder impulsographe

P

pulsing *n* cadencement; battement; modulation; numérotation; ~ **signal** signal de manœuvre

pump frequency (of paramp/maser) fréquence pompe; ~ **power** puissance de pompage

punch *n* perforateur; composteur; perforation

punched *adj* ajouré; ~ **card** carte perforée; carte mécanographique (perforée)

punched-card reader lecteur de cartes perforées; ~ **scraps** débouchure

punched tape bande de papier perforée

punched-tape reader lecteur de bandes perforées

punched tape transmission transmission de bande perforée

punching *n* poinçonnage; emboutissage

punching-error rate gâche

punching pin poinçonneuse

punchings *n* débris de perforation

punch knife poinçonneuse

punch-through perforation électrique; ~ **voltage** (V_{pt}) tension de perçage; tension de pénétration

puncture (impulse) **voltage** tension de percement

pupinized *adj* pupinisée

purchase *n* ancrage

purchaser *n* acquéreur

purchasing *n* approvisionnement; ~ **lead time** délai d'approvisionnement

pure binary code binaire naturel; ~ **chance traffic** trafic de pur hasard; ~ **continuous wave** onde continue non modulée; ~ **resistance** résistance pure; ~ **sound** son pur; ~ **substance** corps pur; ~ **tone** fréquence pure

purge *v* effacer; supprimer; ~ **date** date de péremption; date limite de validité

purging *n* nettoyage

purification *n* (of data) nettoyage

purple plague peste pourpre

purpose *n* but; objet

purpose-built *adj* spécifique

pursuant to en application

pushbutton *n* bouton poussoir (BP); clé; touche; ~ **calling** numérotation au clavier; ~ **dial** clavier de numérotation; clavier multifréquence; ~ **dialling** numérotation au clavier; télésélection de nombres téléphoniques avec un clavier; ~ **set** poste à clavier; ~ **switch** interrupteur à poussoir; ~ **telephone** poste à clavier bidirectionnelle; téléphone à poussoirs; ~ **telephone set** appareil téléphonique à clavier

push-down list liste inverse; liste refoulée; ~ **stack** (LIFO) pile refoulée; ~ **store** mémoire à liste inversée; mémoire à liste refoulée

pushing into the stack mise en pile

push-in test essai de poussée

push in the stack sauvegarder dans la pile

push-on terminal blade languette de connexion; ~ **amplifier** amplificateur symétrique; amplificateur compensé; amplificateur push-pull; amplificateur symétriseur; ~ **circuit** montage symétrique; circuit de neutrodynage (en croix); montage en push-pull; ~ **oscillator** oscillateur symétrique; ~ **sound track** trace acoustique symétrique; ~ **transformer** transformateur asymétrique-symétrique

push-pull configuration montés en symétrie

push-rod *n* poussoir

push-to-test button bouton test

push-up *adj* empilement; ~ **list** liste directe; file; récepteur FIFO; ~ **stack** (FIFO) pile directe (file); ~ **store** mémoire à liste directe

put (aside) écrire

put-aside *v* écarter; ranger; recopier; ~ **function** mémorisation; ~ **register** registre de retenue; ~ **storage** mémorisation temporaire; ~ **vocabulary** phrase préenregistrée

put-back *n* reprise de transmission

PVC (s. polyvinyl chloride)

pvc (s. present value cost)

p.v. of a.c. (present value of annual charges) valeur actuelle des charges annuelles (VACA)

P-wire *n* fil de maintien; fil de test

PWM (s. pulse-width modulation); ≏ **comparator** comparateur modulateur de largeur

pyramidal horn cornet pyramidal

Q

Q-aerial antenne à adaptateur d'impédance; antenne Q
QAM (s. quadrature amplitude modulation)
QAVC (s. quiet automatic volume control)
Q-band rejection réjection de la bande Q
Q-code code télégraphique Q
Q-factor *n* facteur de surtension; facteur de qualité; facteur Q; coefficient de qualité; coefficient de surtension
Q-meter *n* acuimètre
Q-multiplier *n* multiplicateur Q
QOS (s. quality-of-service supervisory)
QPSK (s. quadrature phase-shift keying); ∼ **encoder** codeur quadriphase
QRN (s. atmospherics)
quad (cable) *n* quarte; ∼ étoile; ∼ **bistable latch** registre à quatre éléments binaire; ∼ **bit** quadribit; ∼ **cable** câble à quartes; ∼ **helix aerial** antenne à quatre hélices
quad-pair cable câble à paires en étoile; câble à plusieurs quartes
quadrant aerial antenne quadrant
quadrantal component of error composante sinusoïdale quadrantale de l'erreur; ∼ **elevation** angle de tir; ∼ **error clearing loop** boucle de compensation de l'erreur quadrantale; ∼ **error correction** compensation de l'erreur quadrantale
quadrature *n* (reactance) (à) réaction; ∼ (second-order) **distortion** distorsion quadratique; ∼ **amplitude modulation (QAM)** modulation d'amplitude en quadrature de phase; ∼ **component** (of voltage/current) composante active/réactive; ∼ **detector** détecteur en quadrature de phase; ∼ **oscillator** oscillateur à déphasage; ∼ **phase-shift keying (QPSK)** déplacement de phase à quatre états
quadriphase modulator modulateur à phase rectangulaire
quadripole *n* quadripôle; circuit équivalent
quadruple *n* quarte
quadruplex service/operation opération quadruplex; ∼ **system** système quadruplex; ∼ **telegraphy** télégraphie en quadruplex
quad tri-state bus transceiver quadruple coupleur de bus bidirectionnel à trois états
qualification and dimensional inspection contrôle qualificatif et dimensionnel
qualification-approval test essai de qualification (industrielle)
qualification attribute attribut de définition
qualified service engineer personnel compétent
qualifier probe sonde de qualification
qualifying *n* majoration (MAJ); coefficient de majoration
qualitative maintenance maintenance qualitative
quality assurance surveillance qualité; assurance (de la) qualité; contrôle entrée; ∼ **conformance** assurance (de la) qualité; ∼ **control** contrôle de la qualité; ∼ **control plan** plan qualité; ∼ **control sheet** fiche de qualité; ∼ **factor** facteur de mérite; caractéristique de qualité; coefficient de qualité; coefficient de surtension; facteur de qualité; ∼ **inspection** contrôle d'entrée; ∼ **monitoring** surveillance qualité; ∼ **monitoring report** fiche fiabilité; ∼ **of service** qualité de service
quality-of-service supervisory (QOS) qualificateur-scripteur (QS)
quantal response réaction tout ou rien
quantify *v* chiffrer; dimensionner; valoriser
quantity (qty) *n* nombre (nb., nbre); grandeur; quantité (qté); valeur; ∼ **of electricity** quantité d'électricité
quantization *n* quantification; conversion en numérique; numérisation
quantize *v* quantifier; codifier en numérique; numériser
quantized system système quantifié
quantizer *n* quantificateur; codeur numérique; numériseur
quantizing *n* discrétisation; échantillonnage; ∼ **distortion** distorsion de quantification; bruit de quantification; ∼ **distortion power** puissance de distorsion de quantification; ∼ **error** erreur de quantification; ∼ **interval** intervalle de quantification; ∼ **noise** bruit de quantification; ∼ **step** échelon de quantification; niveau de quantification; pas de quantification; ∼ **step bit** bit de pas
quantum *n* quantum; niveau de quantification; ∼ **efficiency** rendement quantique; ∼ **number** nombre quantique; ∼ **yield** rendement quantique
quarter-plane (of switching matrix) quarte de plan
quarter-turn catch verrouillage quart de tour;

Q

~ **device** dispositif de quart de tour

quarter-wave aerial transformateur en quart d'onde

quarter-(wave) bar symétriseur

quarter-wave(length) coaxial line symétriseur à ligne symétrique

quarter-wavelength line ligne en quart d'onde

quarter-wave (-length) stub/aerial (QWA) antenne quart d'onde; ~ **line** symétriseur; transformateur en quart d'onde; ~ **skirt dipole** antenne à jupe; ~ **sleeve** symétriseur à écran coaxial; symétriseur à manchon; ~ **stub** antenne à impédance élevée; ~ **transmission line** ligne de transmission à quart d'onde

quartet n quartet; groupe de quatre bits (= tétrade)

quartz-controlled generator quartz de base; ~ **resonator** résonateur à quartz

quartz-crystal controlled oscillator oscillateur à quartz; ~ **microphone** microphone piézoélectrique; ~ **unit** quartz

quartz lamp lampe de quartz

quasi-associated mode (of signalling) code (de signalisation) quasi-associé; ~ **signalling link** liaison de signalisation quasi-associé; ~ **signalling mode** exploitation en mode quasi-associé

quasi-impulsive noise perturbation quasi-impulsive

quasi-instruction pseudo-instruction

quasi-omnidirectional aerial antenne quasi-équidirective

quasi-peak detector détecteur de quasi-crête; ~ **voltmeter** voltmètre de quasi-crête

quaternary centre centre quaternaire

quench v étouffer; ~ (of laser printer) décharger

quench(ing) capacitor condensateur à soufflage

quenched adj amorti; ~ **and hardened** trempe et revenu (TRR); ~ **spark gap** éclateur à étincelles amorties

quencher n extincteur (de luminescence); oscillateur à extinctions

quench frequency fréquence de découpage

quenching n amortissement; ~ **lamp** réglette de décharge

quench oscillator oscillateur de découpage

query n contestation de taxe

question-and-answer dialogue dialogue interactif; interrogation

queue n file; file d'attente; pile directe (file)

queued adj en attente; ~ **access method** méthode d'accès avec file d'attente

queued-call request demande desservie avec attente

queue discipline ordre de passage

queued task terminal terminal de transaction

queue handler gestionnaire de file d'attente

queueing n mise en file d'attente; ~ **theory** théorie des files d'attente; ~ **time** temps d'attente

queue-loading pointer pointeur de remplissage

queue place position de file

queue-unloading pointer pointeur de vidage

quibinary code code quibinaire

quick-break automatic switch disjoncteur rapide; ~ **fuse** fusible instantané

quick-chip n réseau rapide

quick-connect insertion sans soudure (ISS)

quick cut-out disjoncteur instantané

quick-drying ink encre siccative

quick-release pin goupille rapide

quick start redémarrage à chaud

quick-trip circuit-breaker disjoncteur différentiel

quiescent adj au repos; indisponible occupé; tranquille; ~ **anode current** courant permanent d'anode; ~ **bias point** point de détection; point de fonctionnement; ~ **carrier** porteuse interrompue dans les silences

quiescent-carrier modulation modulation à interruption de porteuse

quiescent current courant de repos; courant de veille; ~ **period** temps de repos; ~ **point** point de repos; ~ **state** état de repos; veille; ~ **value** valeur de repos

quiet automatic volume control (QAVC) antifading à réglage silencieux

quintet n groupe de cinq bits

quintuple n quinte

quintuplet (five-coil) relay brochette

quire n (25 sheets of paper) main

quit v abandonner; se débrancher (dans)

quotation marks guillemets

quotient n module

QWA (s. quarter-wave (-length) **stub/aerial)**

R

RA (s. relative address); ⁓ (s. routing area)
RAAC (s. radar aircraft altitude calculator)
raceway *n* chemin de câbles (CdC); caniveau; conduit; goulotte; ⁓ **floor** faux plancher
rack *n* armoire; baie; bâti; berceau; cadre; case; châssis; étagère; meuble; poutre; support; ⁓ **alarm indicator** voyant de synthèse; ⁓ **alarm indicator panel** herse de synthèse d'alarmes
rack-and-pinion *adj* à crémaillère
rack assembly mise en bâtis; ⁓ **buffer** tampon de baie; ⁓ **configuration** organigramme du bâti; ⁓ **console** pupitre d'exploitation; pupitre organe; ⁓ **equipment label** plaque de constitution de baie; ⁓ **feeder** départ vers baie; ⁓ **identification label** étiquette de baie
racking *n* mise en bâtis
rack inverter retourneur de baie; inverseur de baie
rack-mounted *adj* intégré dans le bâti
rack-mounting unit bloc individuel
rack spacing pas d'installation en travée
rack-top (amplifier shelf) cadre haut de serrurerie; ⁓ **test panel** pupitre
rack transporter chariot porte-bâti; chariot support de bâti
rack-up (of VDU display) rouleau
radar (R) **band** bande de fréquence pour le radar; ⁓ **aircraft altitude calculator (RA-AC)** calculateur intégrateur de la hauteur d'avions; ⁓ **approach control centre** centre de réglage par radar d'approche; ⁓ **array** rideau de radar; ⁓ **beacon** balise de radiodétection; ⁓ **beam** faisceau de rayons de radar; ⁓ **(reflector) buoy** bouée de radar; ⁓ **calibration** calage par radar; ⁓ **camouflage** camouflage (contre la radiodétection); ⁓ **cell** élément dans l'espace radar; ⁓ **chain** chaîne de radar; ⁓ **cross-section** surface de diffusion; ⁓ **decoy** piège de radar; ⁓ **detector** récepteur radar d'alarme; ⁓ **evasion** évasion du radar; ⁓ **frequency** fréquence de radar; ⁓ **gap** zone morte; ⁓ **glider positioning system** système de radar pour planeurs; ⁓ **head** tête de radiodétecteur; ⁓ **jammer** brouilleur de radar; ⁓ **link** réseau de transmission de l'image; ⁓ **optics** optique de radar; ⁓ **pulse** top de radiodétection; ⁓ **receiver** récepteur radar; ⁓ **reconnaissance** reconnaissance par radar; ⁓ **reflector buoy** bouée à balise passive; ⁓ **relay** relais de radiodétection; ⁓ **station** station radar; ⁓ **target** cible de radar; ⁓ **tracking station** station de poursuite radar; ⁓ **trap** piège de radar; ⁓ **warning net** réseau de surveillance par radar
radial *adj* étoilé; en parallèle; ⁓ **truss** ferme radiale
radian angular frequency fréquence angulaire; ⁓ **frequency** pulsation du secteur
radiant energy énergie rayonnante; énergie radiante; ⁓ **flux** flux énergétique; ⁓ **flux density** densité du flux énergétique; densité de l'énergie radiante; ⁓ **intensity** intensité radiante
radiated power puissance émise; puissance rayonnée; ⁓ **power per unit in a given direction** puissance rayonnée dans une direction
radiating aerial antenne d'émission; ⁓ **circuit** circuit de rayonnement; ⁓ **curtain** rideau rayonnant; ⁓ **double dipole** doublet électrique; ⁓ **doublet** dipôle électrique; ⁓ **waveguide** guide d'ondes rayonnant
radiation *n* insolation; radiation; rayonnement; ⁓ **angle** angle de rayonnement
radiation/beam pattern (of antenna) diagramme de rayonnement
radiation-coupled reflector élément passif
radiation coupling couplage par rayonnement; ⁓ **diagram** diagramme de directivité; ⁓ **effect** effet d'antenne; ⁓ **efficiency** coefficient de rayonnement; effet d'antenne; ⁓ **excitation** (of gas) excitation par rayonnement; ⁓ **field** champ de rayonnement; ⁓ **lobe** pétale de rayonnement; ⁓ **loss** perte par rayonnement; ⁓ **pattern** diagramme de directivité; ⁓ **potential** potentiel d'ionisation; ⁓ **resistance** résistance de rayonnement
radiator *n* émetteur; antenne
radio advertising publicité radiophonique; ⁓ **aiming device** appareil de pointage radioélectrique; ⁓ **altimeter** radioaltimètre; ⁓ **amateur** ("ham") radioamateur
radio-amateur traffic trafic d'amateur
radio atmosphere atmosphère radioélectrique;

~ **beacon service** service de radiophares;
~ **beacon with double modulation** radiophare à deux modulations différentes;
~ **beam** faisceau de radioguidage; axe balisé; faisceau dirigé; ~ **broadcasting** diffusion par voie radioélectrique; ~ **broadcasting service** radiodiffusion
radio-carrier frequency fréquence de porteuse radio
radio channel canal de radio; voie de radiocommunication; voie radioélectrique; ~ **circuit** circuit radioélectrique; ~ **communication link** liaison radio; ~ **communications** radiocommunication
radio-controlled adj radiocommandé
radio control station station de contrôle du réseau; ~ **control transmitter** émetteur d'ordres; ~ **conversation** conversation radiophonique; conversation sans fils; ~ **deception** tromperie par radio; ~ **determination** radiolocalisation; ~ **direction finder** radiogoniomètre; chercheur (radiogoniométrique); ~ **direction-finding (RDF)** radiogoniométrie; localisation radio-électrique; radiorepérage; relèvement radiogoniométrique; ~ **disturbance** perturbation radioélectrique; parasites radio; ~ **echo** écho radioélectrique; ~ **engineering** radiotechnique; ~ **facsimile** radio fac-similé; ~ **fade-out** évanouissement brusque; effet Dellinger; ~ **fan marker** radiophare à faisceau en éventail; ~ **frequency (RF)** fréquence radioélectrique; hyperfréquence (HF)
radio-frequency amplifier amplificateur à haute fréquence; ~ **channel** canal radioélectrique; ~ **oscillator** oscillateur à haute fréquence
radiogram n radio(graphie); radiogramme; radiotélégramme
radiograph n radio(graphie)
radio guidance radioguidage; ~ **ham** amateur de radio; sans filiste; ~ **horizon** horizon radioélectrique
radio-horizon distance distance de l'horizon (radioélectrique)
radio interference brouillage radioélectrique; friture; ~ **link** faisceau hertzien (FH); chaîne de stations radio; liaison harmonique (deux fils et retour commun); liaison hertzienne; liaison radioélectrique; liaison radiophonique; voie de radiocommunication
radiolocation n radiolocalisation; radiorepérage
radio mast tour hertzienne
radiometer n radiomètre
radionavigation n radionavigation; radiorepérage

radio network réseau de radiodiffusion; ~ **news** journal parlé; ~ **noise** bruit radioélectrique; ~ **operator** radiotélégraphiste; télégraphiste
radiopaging n radiorecherche de personnes
radiophone n radiotéléphone
radio range radiophare d'alignement quadrantal; ~ **range-finding** radiotélémétrie; ~ **receiver** radiorécepteur; récepteur radioélectrique; ~ **reconnaissance** reconnaissance radioélectrique; ~ **relay** rediffusion; relais hertzien; répéteur
radio-relay communications ligne de télécommunication à station; ~ **link** liaison station-relais; ~ **route** artère hertzienne; ~ **station** station hertzienne; station de relais électronique; ~ **system** système hertzien
radio remote control télécommande de radio; ~ **set** récepteur radioélectrique; ~ **silence** discrétion
radiosonde (meteorological sounding balloon) radiosonde
radio station station radioélectrique; radiostation; ~ **talk** causerie pour la radio
radiotelegraphy radiotélégraphie; télégraphie sans fil (TSF); ~ **station** station de radiotélégraphie
radiotelemetering n radiomesure
radiotelemetry n radiomesure
radiotelephone n radiotéléphone; ~ **aerial** antenne de radiotéléphone; ~ **call** conversation sans fils; ~ **circuit** circuit radiotéléphonique; ~ **link** liaison radio(télé-)phonique; ~ **service** service de radiotéléphonie; ~ **system** système radiotéléphonique
radiotelephony n radiotéléphonie
radio teleprinter radiotéléimprimeur; ~ **teletype** télex sans fil; ~ **traffic** trafic radioélectrique; ~ **transmission** émission radioélectrique; ~ **transmitter** émetteur radioélectrique; émetteur HF (à hyperfréquence); radioémetteur; ~ **tube** tube radio; ~ **valve** lampe radiotechnique; ~ **warning** avertissement radioélectrique
radio-wave adj hertzien; ~ **propagation** propagation d'ondes radioélectriques
radius n rayon; arrondi
radiused adj mouché; ~ **tip** extrémité avec rayon
radius of action autonomie; ~ **of curvature** rayon de courbure; ~ **of the earth** rayon terrestre
radix n racine; base de numération; ~ **base** indice; ~ **component** complément à la base; ~ **notation** numération de base; ~ **point** séparation fractionnaire; virgule

radome *n* radôme (= radome)
rail *n* barre; bande; conducteur; glissière; guide; Oméga [A.C.]; piste; pontet; rampe; rebord (de manchon); trolley; ~ (Omega) profilé en U; ~ **fixing nut** écrou à agrafe
rain-barrel effect effet tonneau
rain clutter écho de pluie; fouillis par la pluie
rainfall attenuation affaiblissement dû à la pluie
raised *adj* en saillie; ~ **cosine energy spectrum** spectre d'énergie en cosinus élevé; ~ **floor** faux plancher; ~ **platform** cheminée
rake *n* inclinaison; pente; ~ **angle** angle d'attaque; angle de dégagement
RAM (s. random-access memory)
Raman effect effet Raman
ramjet *n* statoréacteur
RAM loader (mode) configuration usine
ramp *n* échelon; forme d'onde en dents de scie; rampe; ~ (voltage) **generator** générateur de rampe; ~ (waveform) dent de scie (DDS); ~ **function** échelon de vitesse; fonction rampe; ~ **generator** générateur de dents de scie
ramping time temps total d'établissement
ramp response time temps total d'établissement; ~ **voltage** tension de rampe; rampe de tension; tension de déviation; tension en dents de scie
ram spigot (of press) pigeonneau; ~ **stroke gap** butée de descente
random *adj* aléatoire; accidentel; intempestif; ~ **access** accès aléatoire; accès direct; accès instantané; accès sélectif
random-access memory (RAM) mémoire vive; mémoire à accès aléatoire
random back-off temporisation aléatoire; ~ **circuit noise** bruit de circuit erratique; ~ **distribution** distribution aléatoire; ~ **error** erreur aléatoire; erreur intermittente
random-function signal signal de fonction aléatoire
randomization *n* transformation aléatoire
random noise bruit d'allure erratique; bruit aléatoire; bruit de fond; bruit rose; ~ **noise weighting network** filtre de pondération de bruit; filtre vidéométrique; ~ **number** nombre aléatoire; ~ **sampling** échantillonnage au hasard; ~ **selection** non désignation; ~ **sequential file** fichier direct séquentiel
random-setting *adj* infiniment variable; réglable à l'infini
random signal signal aléatoire; ~ **test** essai statistique; ~ **traffic** trafic aléatoire; ~ **variable** variable aléatoire
range *n* gamme; assortiment; calibre; distance franchissable; domaine; échelle (éch.); étendue; fourchette; gabarit; plage; portée; référence de distance; régime; sensibilité; zone
range-amplitude display indicateur d'amplitude et de distance
range-bearing display indicateur de distance et de gisement (d'azimut)
range calibration calibrage de la distance; ~ **circle** cercle de distance; ~ **discrimination/resolution** pouvoir séparateur radial; ~ **finder** télémètre
range-finding télémétrie; mesure de distance
range frequency fréquence du faisceau directionnel
range-height indicator indicateur de hauteur et de distance
range marker marqueur de distance; ~ **match** corrosion intergranulaire; ~ **of bearings** étendue des relèvements; ~ **operator** opérateur d'étendue; ~ **rings** repère de distance; ~ **search** recherche en distance; ~ **select** commande d'échelle; sélection de portée; ~ **switch** sélecteur de gamme
ranging, echo ~ échométrie; ~ **accuracy** précision télémétrique; ~ **error** erreur télémétrique
rank *n* rang; échelon; ordre
ranking *n* classement; classification; coefficient hiérarchique; hiérarchisation
rapid-access loop boucle à accès rapide
rapid change of temperature choc thermique; ~ **service** service international rapide; ~ **sweep** exploration rapide
raster *n* trame; canevas; mire; réseau
ratchet *n* cliquet; crochet d'arrêt; ~ **time base** balayage dent de scie
rate *n* allure; barème; cadence; facteur; fréquence; intensité; niveau; régime; tarif; taux; vitesse; ~ **centre** centre tarifaire; ~ **change** translation de débit; translation de vitesse
rated *adj* admissible; nominal; ~ **breaking capacity** (of fuse) pouvoir de coupure (d'un fusible); ~ **capacitance** capacité nominale; ~ **current** intensité nominale (I_n); courant d'emploi; ~ **inductance factor** inductance spécifique nominale; ~ **(insulation) voltage** tension nominale d'isolement; ~ **operating conditions** conditions nominales de fonctionnement; ~ **output power** puissance de sortie nominale; ~ **power** puissance nominale; consommation; puissance théorique; ~ **range** étendue de mesure; ~ **ripple current** courant ondulé nominal; ~ **(thermal) current** courant nominal (thermique); ~ **voltage** tension nominale (U_n); tension admissible; tension d'isolement; ~ **voltage pick-up time** temps de réponse à U_n

rate fixing tarification; ~ **increase** hausse tarifaire; ~ **of rise** gradient; ~ **regulator** cadenceur

rating *n* calibrage; calibre; caractéristique(s); classement; indice; indice de performance; indice de qualité de transmission; intensité; pouvoir; puissance délivrée; régime; valeur; ~ (of motor) régime moteur (RM); ~ **plate** plaque signalétique; calibrage

ratio *n* rapport; facteur; indice; taux; ~ **amplifier** amplificateur de rapport; ~ **detector** détecteur de rapport

ratio-less circuit (of MOS logic) circuit à précharge; logique non proportionnel

rationalize *v* optimiser

rationalized *adj* harmonieux

rat-race *n* anneau hybride

raw *adj* brut; naturel; ~ **data** données brutes; ~ **material(s)** matière première

RAX (s. rural automatic exchange)

ray *n* rayon

Rayleigh disk disque de Rayleigh; ∻ **scattering** diffusion de Rayleigh

RBM (s. receive buffer memory)

R-C (s. resistance-capacitance coupling)

RCA (s. read cursor address)

RCG (s. remote concentration group)

R-C oscillator oscillateur R-C

RD (s. read instruction)

RDF (s. radio direction-finding); ∻ (s. repeater distribution frame)

reach *n* portée

reach-through voltage tension de pénétration; tension de perçage

reactance *n* réactance; ~ **circuit** circuit de réactance; ~ **coil** self de blocage; bobine de réactance; ~ **tube oscillator** oscillateur à tube de réactance

reaction *n* réponse; ~ **coil** bobine de réaction

re-activate *v* débloquer; désinhiber; relancer

re-activation *n* réenclenchement

reactive *adj* déwatté; ~ **attenuator** affaiblisseur réactif; ~ **component** composant réactif; ~ **current** courant réactif; ~ **load** charge réactive; ~ **load compensation** compensation de la charge réactive; ~ **power** puissance réactive; ~ **voltage** tension réactive

reactor *n* bobine; inductance

read *v* lire; consulter; prélever; ~ (off) relever; ~ **address bus** ligne d'adresse de lecture; ~ **amplifier** amplificateur de lecture

read-back *n* relecture; ~ **check** contrôle par écho; prélecture (de vérification)

read backward lecture arrière; ~ **circuit board** carte lecture; ~ **cursor address (RCA)** lecture adresse curseur; ~ **enable** autorisation de lecture

reader *n* lecteur

read forward lecture avant; ~ **head** tête de lecture

read-in *v* envoyer; stocker

reading *n* relevé; accès; consigne; ~ (of message relay system) émission; ~ **band** aire de lecture; ~ **direction** sens de lecture; ~ **error** lecture incorrecte; ~ **in (of data)** emmagasinage; mémorisation; ~ **range/band** plage de lecture

read instruction (RD) instruction de lecture

re-adjustment *n* recalage

read mode (of file records) déblocage

read-modify-write (function) sémaphore

read-mostly memory mémoire à lecture majoritaire

read-only *adj* à interdiction d'écriture; ~ **access** consultation seule; ~ **memory (ROM)** mémoire morte; mémoire à lecture seule; mémoire fixe; mémoire inaltérable; mémoire permanente

read-out *n* lecture; affichage; extraction; sortie

read strobe output échantillonnage lecture

read-write access consultation de mise à jour

ready *v* apprêter; ~ *adj* prêt; activable; à l'écoute; disponible; paré; ~ (queue) exécutable; ~ **cue** à vous; ~ **for data** poste prêt pour données

readying time durée d'échauffement

ready queue file d'attente d'exécution; file de tâches en exécution; ~ **software task queue** file de tâches logicielles prêtes; ~ **state** état prêt (paré); ~ **task** tâche exécutable

ready-wired *adj* précâblé

real *adj* réel; effectif; propre; vrai; ~ **component of voltage** composante active de la tension; ~ **constant** constante en virgule flottante; constante réelle

realign reprendre

realignment *n* recadrage; reprise

re-allocation *n* nouvel abonnement/changement de titulaire

real power puissance active

real-time address adresse virtuelle; ~ **clock (RTC)** horloge en temps réel; ~ **communication** trafic direct; ~ **computer** calculateur en temps réel; ~ **input** introduction en temps réel; ~ **I/O system** impression immédiate; ~ **monitor** superviseur temps réel; ~ **operation** fonctionnement en temps réel; ~ **processing** traitement immédiat; traitement momentané

real/virtual address mapping table mémoire topographique

ream *n* (500 sheets = 20 quires) rame (= 20 mains)

re-answer *n* redécrochage

rear *n* fond; ~ *adj* arrière (AR); ~ **connection** connexion arrière

rear-fed *adj* à alimentation traversière

rear mirror rétroviseur; ~ **panel** panneau arrière

reasonableness check table tableau de contrôle de vraisemblance

re-boot *n* réinitialisation

re-broadcasting rediffusion

re-broadcast receiver récepteur de réémission; ~ **transmitter** émetteur relais; émetteur relayeur

recalculation recalcul de feuille

recalibration *n* vérification de l'étalonnage

recall *n* rappel; récupération; reprise d'appel; ~ **distant-end subscriber** rappel du distant; ~ **key** bouton de rappel; clé de rappel

recapitulation *n* rappel

re-categorization *n* reclassement

recce (s. reconnaissance)

receipt *n* réception

receive amplifier amplificateur de réception; ~ **amplifier card** module d'amplification en réception; ~ **buffer memory (RBM)** mémoire tampon réception (MTR); ~ **channel** canal de réception

receive-data (signal) information(s) de sortie

received character timing base de temps pour les caractères reçus; ~ **digits zone** zone de réception du numéro demandé; ~ **frame** trame incidente

receive filter filtre de réception; ~ **frequency** fréquence de réception; ~ **interruption** rupture de réception; ~ **loss** affaiblissement à la réception; ~ **margin measuring set** mesureur de marge; ~ **memory** mémoire de réception

receive-only (RO) terminal équipement terminal de réception; ~ **non-typing reperforator** récepteur-perforateur non imprimeur; ~ **teleprinter** téléimprimeur specialisé pour la réception; ~ **typing reperforator** récepteur-perforateur imprimeur (= reperforateur-imprimeur)

receiver *n* récepteur; combiné; écouteur; ~ (as opposed to driver) sortie; ~ **aerial** antenne de réception; ~ **attenuation** affaiblissement du récepteur

receive reference equivalent (RRE) équivalent à la réception

receiver inset capsule réceptrice; ~ **noise** bruit propre; ~ **off-hook (ROH)** faux appel; ~ **output** puissance de sortie d'un récepteur; ~ **pick-up** décrochage (D); ~ **ready (RR)** présence porteuse; ~ **rest** crochet du récepteur; ~ **signal element timing** éléments de signalisation à la réception;

~ **transfer characteristic** caractéristique de transfert du récepteur; ~ **VF modulator/ translator** traducteur de réception

receiving *n* (section of tape store) écriture; ~ **aerial** antenne de réception; ~ **amplifier** amplificateur de réception; ~ **area** zone réceptrice; ~ **direction** direction de réception; ~ **end** extrémité de réception; ~ **fibre** fibre réceptrice; ~ **frequency** fréquence de réception; ~ **office** bureau récepteur; ~ **perforator** récepteur-perforateur; ~ **reference equivalent** équivalent de référence à la réception (ERR); ~ **sensitivity** efficacité à réception; ~ **station** station de réception; station réceptrice; ~ **terminal** terminal de réception

receptacle *n* caisse; alvéole; embase; prise; support

reception *n* accueil; ~ **(RX)** réception; ~ **quality** indice de qualité de réception (IQR)

recess *n* alvéole; cavité; logement; puits; bac; évidement

recessed *adj* affleuré; encastré; ~ **hole** trou borgne

recession *n* retassure; éloignement; retrait

recipient *n* receveur; destinataire

reciprocal *n* pont; ~ *adj* complémentaire; inverse; ~ **bearing** azimut inverse; ~ **circuit** circuit dual; ~ **ohm (mho)** siemens

reciprocating *adj* alternatif; aller-retour; va-et-vient; ~ **motion** mouvement alternatif; mouvement de va-et-vient

reciprocity *n* correspondance; ~ **coefficient** coefficient de réciprocité; ~ **principle** principe de réciprocité

recirculating ball screw vis à billes

reckoning *n* calcul

recognition time durée de reconnaissance; durée d'identification

recognized private operating agency (RPOA) exploitation privée reconnue

recoil *n* rebondissement; ~ **electron** électron de recul

recombination *n* recombinaison

recommendation *n* conseil(s); avis

recommended *adj* conseillé; préconisé; recommandé; ~ **conditions of use and associated characteristics** caractéristiques de gabarit

recondition *v* mettre en état

reconditioned as new récupération état neuf; ~ **carrier reception** réception avec régéneration de la porteuse

reconditioning *n* remise en état; réparation

reconnaissance (recce) *n* reconnaissance

re-connection *n* réenclenchement; reprise d'abonnement

reconnect to (another party) reconsulter

R

reconstitution *n* reprise
reconstructed sample échantillon reconstitué
re-copy *n* retranscription
record *v* enregistrer; consigner; imprimer; inscrire (sur); mémoriser; prélever; relever; ~ *n* enregistrement; article; bilan; bloc; cliché; historique; livret; rapport; relevé; répertoire; rubrique; ~ **blocking** verrouillage des articles; ~ **circuit** ligne d'annotatrice
recorded *adj* prélevé; ~ (of program) instrumenté; ~ **announcement** film parlant; annonce parlée; film de dissuasion; film de parole; film sonore; ~ **announcement equipment** machine parlante; ~ **announcement junctor** joncteur de films; ~ **announcement tone** indication audible donnée par une machine parlante; ~ **announcement unit** dispositif de diffusion; ~ **announcement unit interface controller** coupleur de machines parlantes; ~ **audio signal** image; ~ **broadcast** radiodiffusion différée; ~ **delay announcement** annonce de patience; avis d'attente enregistré
recorded-delivery registered letter lettre recommandée avec accusé de réception
recorded number call appel enregistré; ~ **programme** enregistrement
recorder *n* enregistreur (enr.); compteur; inscripteur
record form fiche; ~ **head** tête d'enregistrement; tête d'inscription
recording *n* enregistrement; annotation; consignation; emmagasinage; inscription; marquage; saisie; ~ **ammeter** ampèremètre enregistreur; ~ **characteristic** caractéristique d'enregistrement; ~ **completing trunk** ligne d'appel de l'opératrice d'inscription et de départ; ~ **density** densité d'enregistrement; ~ **head** tête d'écriture; tête d'enregistrement; ~ **loss** perte d'enregistrement; ~ **room** cellule d'enregistrement; ~ **surface** couronne d'enregistrement; ~ **tape** bande d'enregistrement; ~ **trunk** ligne d'annotatrice; ~ **unit** détecteur de signaux (télégraphiques)
record length longueur d'enregistrement; ~ **player** électrophone; tourne-disque; ~ **position** ligne d'annotatrice; ~ **separator** séparateur d'article
recoup investment(s) rentabiliser; amortir les investissements
recover *v* récuperer; régénérer; reprendre; restituer
recoverable error erreur récupérable
recovered charge charge recouvrée; ~ **clock** (signal) horloge régénérée
recovery *n* récupération; redressement; réem-

ploi; reprise; ~ **current** courant de recouvrement; ~ **of distant end signal element** extraction de l'horloge distante; ~ **time** temps de rétablissement; durée de reprise; temps de désionisation; temps de fermeture; ~ **time** (of expander) temps de retour au repos; ~ **vehicle** char de dépannage; ~ **voltage** tension de recouvrement
rectangular horn cornet rectangulaire; ~ **network folded using an additional stage** réseau droit replié par un étage supplémentaire; ~ **network with folded outlets** réseau droit replié par ses sorties; ~ **network with outlets folded back to inlets** réseau droit replié sorties vers entrées; ~ **pulse** impulsion rectangulaire; ~ **wave** onde rectangulaire; ~ **waveform** forme d'onde rectangulaire; ~ **waveguide** guide d'ondes rectangulaire
rectified current courant redressé
rectifier *n* redresseur; clapet; diode; mutateur; soupape; transformateur; ~ **bridge** pont redresseur; ~ **relay** relais à redresseurs secs; ~ **tube** tube redresseur (à gaz)
rectifying effect effet redresseur; effet Edison
recuperation *n* reprise; dépistage
recurrent *adj* répétitif; clignotant; itératif; périodique; ~ **noise** parasites de récurrence; ~ **task** tâche périodique; ~ **wave** onde récurrente
recursion *n* boucle; bouclage; récurrence; récursivité; ~ **check** contrôle de récurrence
recursive *adj* récursif; récurrent; ~ **call** appel récursif; ~ **subroutine** sous-programme bouclé
recursivity *n* récursivité; récurrence
re-cycle *v* régénérer; reprendre
re-cycling *n* reprise; récupération; réemploi
re-deploy *v* désaffecter
re-dial *v* reprise de présélection; reprendre; ~ *n* réémission
re-direct *v* réaiguiller; rapatrier; renvoyer
re-directed message message détourné
re-direction address adresse de réacheminement
re-do feature fonction répétition
re-draw screen (display) régénérer l'écran
redress *v* compenser
red-tape *n* servitude(s)
reduce *v* diminuer; dégrader; ramener
reduced *adj* allégé; écourté; ~ **bandwidth** (of quad PSK) encombrement spectral réduit
reduced-carrier transmission émission à porteuse réduite
reduced charge taxe réduite
reduced-level carrier porteuse à niveau réduit
reduced rate tarif réduit; ~ **test** contrôle

R

réduit

reduction/expansion cascading arborescence

reduction gear démultiplicateur; ~ **gear motor** moto-réducteur

redundancy n doublement; parité; redoublement; ~ **bit** bit de redondance; ~ **check** contrôle par redondance

redundant bit eb superflu; bit de contrôle; ~ **character** caractère inutile; caractère redondant; ~ **code** code redondant

reed n lame; peigne; tige; ~ (of relay) barre; languette; ~ **contact** contact à tige; ~ **crosspoint** point de croisement scellé; ~ **relay** relais à ampoule scellée; relais à contacts scellés; relais à lames souples; relais à tige; relais scellé sous ampoule; ~ **switch** interrupteur à lame souple (ILS); commutateur à tige; contact en ampoule; contact en ampoule scellée; contact hermétique; contact sec

reel n bobine; bobineau; dévidoir; roquette; touret

reeled-out aerial antenne déroulée

reeling n enchainement

re-enable revalider; débloquer; désinhiber; réarmer

re-enabling n remise en service

re-enter v réintroduire; boucler; reprendre

re-enterable adj invariant; réinscriptible; ~ **program** programme invariable

re-entrant procedure call appel récursif; ~ **program** programme invariable; ~ **technique** technique de bouclage

re-entry document document navette; document aller-retour; document tournant; ~ **point** point de reprise; point de retour

reference address adresse de base; adresse primitive; ~ **atmosphere** atmosphère de référence; ~ **circuit** circuit de référence; ~ **clock** horloge de référence; ~ **coupler** coupleur de référence; ~ **display panel** (of PCB components) panoplie; ~ **earth potential** niveau 0 (zéro); ~ **edge** bord de référence; liseret (liseré); ~ **electrode** électrode de zéro; ~ **equivalent** équivalent de référence; ~ **equivalent** (quality) téléphonométrie; ~ **frequency** fréquence de référence; ~ **grid** graticule; ~ **input signal** signal d'entrée de référence; ~ **level** niveau de référence; ~ **line** ligne de référence; ligne de cadrage; ~ **loss** affaiblissement de référence; ~ **mark** marque de repère; ~ **monitor** moniteur de référence; ~ (**parameters**) gabarit; ~ **period** talon; ~ **pilot** onde pilote; ~ **potential** masse; 0B (barre zéro); potentiel de comparaison; ~ **signal** signal étalon; ~ **signal generator** générateur de signal-standard; ~ **speech power** puissance vocale de référence; ~ **supply** alimentation de référence; polarisation; ~ **system for the determination of the articulation reference equivalents** appareil de référence pour la détermination des affaiblissements équivalents de référence; ~ **tape** bande étalon; ~ **value** valeur de consigne; ~ **voltage** tension de référence; niveau zéro; potentiel de comparaison; tension de synchronisation

reference-voltage busbar barre zéro (0B); ~ **generator** générateur de seuils

reference volume volume de référence

referred to par rapport à; référencé à; ~ **to earth** mise à la masse

refined adj affiné; élaboré

refinement n perfectionnement; enrichissement; évolution; mise au point (MAP); modification

refining n nettoyage; rôdage

reflect v refléter; répercuter; répéter

reflectance n facteur de réflexion; pouvoir réfléchissant

reflected binary (Gray) code code binaire réfléchi; code cyclique; code de Gray; ~ **impedance** impédance réfléchie; réflexion; ~ **power** puissance réfléchie; ~ **radiation** rayonnement indirect; ~ **wave** onde indirecte; onde récurrente; onde réfléchie

reflecting aerial antenne à réflecteur; ~ **curtain** rideau réfléchissant

reflection n réflexion; écho; image; mirage; réinjection; réverbération; ~ **angle** angle de réflexion; ~ **coefficient** coefficient de courants réfléchis; coefficient de réflexion relatif à l'intensité; ~ **factor** coefficient de pertes due aux réflexions; facteur de réflexion; ~ **lobe** lobe réfléchissant; ~ **loss** perte due aux réflexions; ~ **mode filter** filtre de mode à réflexion

reflective network réseau réfléchissant

reflectometer n réflectomètre; échomètre-réflectomètre; appareil de rétrodiffusion

reflector n réflecteur; balise; élément réfléchissant; (**hooded**) ~ cabochon; ~ **aerial** antenne à réflecteur; ~ **space** espace de réflexion

reflex n réponse; ~ **action** rebondissement; ~ **circuit** circuit dual; ~ **klystron** klystron réflexe

reflow oven four de refusion; ~ **soldering** refusion par flux d'air chaud; étamage à chaud; refusion étain-plomb; soudage à flux d'air chaud; brasage par flux d'air chaud

re-format v reformer

re-formatting *n* recomposition; redressement
refraction angle angle de réfraction
refractive index indice de réfraction; milieu d'indice; ~ **index of core** indice du cœur; ~ **modulus** module de réfraction
reframing *n* reprise de verrouillage de trame
refresh *v* raviver; ~ *n* rafraîchissement (d'écran); régénération; restauration; ~ **rate** vitesse de régénération
refrigerant *n* fluide frigorigène
refurbishment *n* reprise; aménagement; échange; remplacement
refused call communication refusée
refute *v* infirmer
regenerate *v* raviver
regeneration *n* régénération; restauration; rétrocouplage; rafraîchissement (d'écran)
regenerative feedback réaction positive; ~ **memory** mémoire à régénération; ~ **pulse repeater** répéteur régénérateur d'impulsions; ~ **reception** réception à réaction; ~ **repeater** translateur rectificateur; répéteur correcteur de la distorsion; répéteur régénérateur; ~ **store** mémoire de rafraîchissement
region *n* zone; champ; compartiment; domaine; plage; région
regional *adj* de province; régional; ~ **call** communication régionale; ~ **centre** centre régional; centre de compartiment; ~ **code** indicatif régional (IR); ~ **concentrator** concentrateur régional; ~ **exchange** central régional; ~ **management centre** centre régional de gestion; ~ **traffic** trafic régional; ~ **transit exchange** centre de transit régional; ~ **transmission centre** centre régional transmission; ~ **videotex centre** centre régional vidéotex
register *v* enregistrer; ~ *n* enregistreur (enr.); accumulateur; compteur d'adresse; compteur de trafic; mot mémoire; page enregistreur; registre; transducteur; ~ **assignment** (to a call) prise d'enregistreur; ~ **clock** horloge enregistreur; ~ **control** commande par enregistreurs
register-control device combinateur; combineur
register-controlled exchange central à commande par enregistreurs
registered trade mark marque déposée
register finder chercheur enregistreur (CE); ~ **processing system** système spatiale; ~ **recall** rappel d'enregistreur; ~ **recall button** bouton flashing; ~ **recall signal** signal de rappel; signal d'appel d'enregistreur; ~ **sender** distributeur d'enregistreur; ~ **signal** signal d'adresse; signal d'enregistreur; ~ **size** format d'enregistreur;

~ **transfer system** système temporel
register-translator *n* enregistreur-traducteur; annotateur ordonnanceur
register word (page of 1 Kbit) mot enregistreur
registration *n* alignement; cadrage; centrage; inscription; indexage; ~ **sensor** détection début de feuille; ~ **stud** pion de centrage
registry *n* archive
reglet *n* réglet
re-grading *n* reclassement
regularity return loss affaiblissement de régularité; affaiblissement de l'onde réfléchie sur les irrégularités
regulated power supply alimentation stabilisée
regulating pilot onde pilote de régulation; pilote régulateur; ~ **transistor** ballast
regulations *n pl* réglementation
regulator *n* régulateur; soupape; variateur de vitesse
reheating *n* échauffement
reinforced concrete béton armé (BA); ~ **concrete mesh** radier
reinforcement *n* armature; entretoise
reinforcing panel contre-plaque
re-initialization *n* démarrage à chaud
re-initialize *v* réinitialiser
re-insertion of carrier réintroduction de la porteuse
re-inspection *n* contrôle reprise
re-instatement *n* remise en état; déblocage; réarmement; remise en service; reprise
re-issue *v* relancer
reject *n* rebut
rejection band bande de réjection; ~ **criterion** critère de refus; ~ **filter** filtre de réjection; ~ **frequency** fréquence de réjection; ~ **rate due to inadequate provision of plant** taux de rejet d'infrastructure des lignes (TRIL)
rejector circuit circuit réjecteur; circuit éliminateur; circuit bouchon
reject pocket case rebut
rejuvenator *n* régénérateur
related *adj* apparentés; connexe; ~ **model** modèle associable
relational condition condition relationnelle; ~ **operator** opérateur de relation; opérateur relationnel
relationship *n* relation; correspondance; lien; rapport
relative address (RA) adresse relative; adresse symbolique; adresse d'espacement; adresse flottante; déplacement; ~ **bearing** gisement; ~ **current level** niveau relatif d'intensité de courant; ~ **density** masse volumique; densité relative; ~ **equivalent** équivalent relatif; ~ **humidity** (in %) humidité relative (HR); taux hygrométrique; hygrométrie; ~ **level** niveau relatif de

R

puissance; ~ **permeability** perméabilité relative; ~ **power level** niveau relatif de puissance réelle; ~ **response** efficacité relative; ~ **sensitivity** efficacité relative; ~ **status** coefficient hiérarchique; ~ **voltage level** niveau relatif de tension

relaxation circuit circuit de relaxation; ~ **oscillation** oscillation BF parasite; ~ **oscillator** oscillateur à relaxation; multivibrateur; oscillateur R-C

relay v réémettre; renvoyer; répéter; retransmettre; relayer; ~ n relais; déviation; réémission; réexpédition; renvoi; soupape; transit; déport; ~ **armature** armature de relais; ~ **automatic system** système automatique tout à relais; ~ **cabinet** armoire de relayage; ~ **channel** canal du signal relais; ~ **coil** bobine de relais; ~ **connection** connexion de relais; ~ **facility** installation de commutation; ~ **from abroad** émission de l'étranger

relaying n retransmission; translation

relay output circuit circuit de sortie à relais; ~ **rack** baie de relais; ~ **receiver** récepteur de réémission; ~ **satellite** satellite relais; ~ **set** groupe de relais; relais interchangeable; ~ **socket** support relais; ~ **station** station relais; centre de retransmission de messages; émetteur de relais; station amplificatrice; ~ **strip** plaque de relais; ~ **transmitter** réémetteur; ~ **type echo suppressor** suppresseur d'écho à action discontinue

release v libérer; déclencher; décourt-circuiter; dégager; démasquer; désinhiber; dessaisir; desserrer; diffuser; franchir; raccrocher; relâcher; retomber; ~ n libération; coupure; décollage; déconnexion; détente; fin; lancement; mise en disponibilité; palier technique; parution; relâchement; remise au repos; rupture; traction (d'un bouton); ~ (rel.) édition (éd.); ~ **button** bouton de libération; ~ **current** courant de déclenchement (ID); courant de relâchement; ~ **date** date de création; date d'enregistrement; date de parution

released call appel relâché

release forms (RLF) libération de l'état grille; ~ **guard** libération de garde

release-guard signal signal de libération de garde

release mechanism détendeur; déclencheur; ~ **message** message deconnexion; ~ **pulse** impulsion de mise au repos; ~ **relay** relais de déclenchement; relais de libération; ~ **signal** signal de fin; signal de libération; ~ **time** temps de relâchement; temps de libération; temps de retombée; ~ **valve** (of

gas cylinder) tube plongeur; ~ **version** édition de lancement; ~ **wire** fil de libération

releasing n déclenchement; déblocage; déconnexion; déverrouillage; ~ **a line** libération d'une ligne

relevance tree arbre d'implication

reliability forecast fiabilité prévisionnelle

reliable adj fiable

relief n détente; allègement; bossage; délestage; ~ adj auxiliaire; de secours; ~ **angle** angle d'incidence; ~ **cable** câble auxiliaire; ~ **relay** relais auxiliaire; ~ **valve** détendeur

relieve v pallier; soulager

relinquish control rendre la main; remettre au contrôle

relinquishment n cession

reload v recharger; regarnir; régénérer; réinitialiser; ~ n réaffichage; restauration; régénération; réaffichage

relocatable adj amovible; ~ **address** adresse translatable; ~ **binary** binaire translatable (BT); ~ **binary object code** langage mémoire rééditable; code binaire objet translatable; ~ **loader** chargeur-translateur; ~ **object code** code objet translatable; ~ **program** programme translatable; programme relogeable

relocation n rapatriement; déplacement; réimplantation; délocalisation

reluctance n réluctance; ~ **tuning** accord par réluctance

remedial action intervention; ~ **maintenance** maintenance curative; entretien correctif; ~ **maintenance sheet** fiche réflexe (dépannage)

reminder (letter) lettre de relance

remission n détaxe

remnant n solde

remodulation n remodulation

remote adj distant; à grande distance; asservi; (en) aval; décentralisé; déporté; éclaté; éloigné; séparé; tributaire; ~ **alarm** téléalarme; ~ **batch processing** télétraitement par lots; ~ **(batch) terminal** terminal lourd; ~ **billing centre** centre d'enregistrement distant; ~ **charging** télétaxe (TLT); ~ **clock** horloge distante; horloge incidente; ~ **concentration group (RCG)** groupe éclaté de concentration (GEC); ~ **concentrator** concentrateur électronique d'abonnés distants; ~ **console** télépupitre; ~ **control** télécommande; commande à distance; téléréglage

remote-control circuit ligne de télécommande; ~ **encoder** codeur d'ordres de télécommande

remote controller télémate; ~ **cut-off valve**

R

tube à pente réglable; ~ **diagnostics** télédiagnostic; ~ **digital concentrator** concentrateur numérique éloigné; ~ **digital satellite exchange** centre satellite numérique distant; ~ **display** téléaffichage; ~ **electronic subscriber connection unit** concentrateur électronique d'abonnés distants; ~ **electronic subscriber line concentrator** concentrateur satellite électronique distant; ~ **exchange** central distant; ~ **fault tracing** télélocalisation des fautes; ~ **functions** téléactions; ~ **gain control** téléréglage du gain; ~ **indicating instrument** téléindicateur; ~ **indication** téléaffichage; télésignalisation; ~ **job entry (RJE)** télésoumission de travaux; soumission des travaux à distance; téléchargement; télétraitement; ~ **line identification** identification des correspondants; ~ **line unit (RLU)** concentrateur; centre satellite; ~ **loop-back** télébouclage

remotely-controlled oscillator oscillateur à télécommande

remote maintenance télémaintenance; maintenance à distance; ~ **management** télégestion; ~ **management centre** centre distant de gestion (CDG); ~ **metering pulses** télétaxation; signalisation de télétaxe; ~ **monitoring** télécontrôle; ~ **monitoring circuit** circuit de télésurveillance; ~ **operation and maintenance** téléexploitation et télémaintenance; ~ **peripheral equipment (RPE)** équipement périphérique distant (EPD); ~ **power feed (RPF)** téléalimentation; entraide(s); ~ **processing** télétraitement; télégestion; ~ **receiver** récepteur séparé; ~ **regulation** téléréglage; ~ **sensing** télédétection; télémesure; ~ **station** station asservie; ~ **subscriber** abonné lointain; ~ **subscriber connection unit** unité de raccordement distant; ~ **subscriber terminal group** groupe d'abonnés temporel éclaté; ~ **supervision** télésurveillance; ~ **surveillance** télésécurité; ~ **switch** interrupteur déportable; ~ **switching system** unité de raccordement distante; ~ **teleprinter** téléimprimeur à distance; ~ **terminal identification** identification du terminal distant; ~ **terminal station** station principale asservie (SPA); ~ **terrain sensing** prise de vue; ~ **tester** robot (d'appels); ~ **testing** essai à distance; ~ **transmission** télétransmission; ~ **trunk arrangement (RTA)** raccordement distant

removable *adj* amovible; démontable; mobile; ~ **cartridge disk** disque à cartouche amovible; ~ **disk unit** unité disque amovible; ~ **magnetic disk** disque magnéti-

que amovible

removal *n* suppression; élimination; démontage; ~ **of plug** défichage

remove *v* démonter; enlever

remreed *n* relais à tiges à maintien magnétique; relais à rémanence; tige rémanente

renaming *n* (of files) rebaptisation

render transparent masquer

rental *n* location; redevance; ~ **period** période d'abonnement

renumbered *adj* dénuméroté

re-order (of supplies) relancer

re-ordering *n* réapprovisionnement

re-order tone tonalité d'encombrement

REP (s. repeat)

repair *n* réparation; dépannage; intervention; rectification; remise en état; reprise

repairability *n* réparabilité

repair centre centre de réparation; ~ **inspection** contrôle reprise

repairman *n* réparateur

repair shop atelier de dépannage

repeat *v* répéter; réémettre; régénérer; retransmettre; ~ **(REP)** *n* répétition de caractères; ~ **accuracy** reproductibilité; fidélité de répétition; le bon aiguillage; ~ **call attempt** reprise de présélection; ~ **circuit** circuit de répétition

repeated identification identification cyclique; ~ **signal** signal répété

repeated-until-acknowledged signal signal répété jusqu'à accusé de réception

repeater *n* répéteur; amplificateur; bobine translatrice; circuit amplificateur; émetteur; régénérateur; relais; répétiteur; transmetteur de ligne; dipôle à impédance négative; retransmetteur; ~ **distribution frame (RDF)** répartiteur basse fréquence (RBF)

repeatered circuit circuit amplifié; ~ **line** ligne avec répéteurs; ligne translatée

repeater gain gain d'un répéteur; ~ **housing** pot de répéteur

repeaterless system structure passive

repeater overloading surcharge des répéteurs; ~ **point** point de répétition; ~ **rack** baie de répéteurs; ~ **section** section de régénération; section de répéteurs; ~ **selector** sélecteur répéteur; ~ **spacing** pas d'amplification; pas de régénération; ~ **station** station de répéteurs; centre d'amplification; émetteur de relais; poste relais; station amplificatrice; poste répétiteur

repeating *n* amplification; réémission; ~ **coil** bobine translatrice; relais translateur; transformateur; translateur; ~ **relay** relais à action répétée

repeat interval temps de reprise; périodicité;

~ **transmission** retransmission
repellent n frein
repeller n réflecteur
reperforation n reperforation
reperforator n récepteur-perforateur; retransmetteur à bande perforée; ~ **switching** commutation avec retransmission par bande perforée
reperforator-transmitter récepteur-perforateur transmetteur
repertoire n ensemble; jeu
repertory n répertoire; jeu; stock; ~ **dialler** composeur automatique de numéros; agenda; ~ **dialling** numérotation abrégée
repetition n répétition; ~ **frequency** fréquence de répétition; fréquence de récurrence; ~ **rate** cadencement; fréquence de répétition; taux de répétition; ~ **station** station d'évaluation
repetitive addressing adressage répétitif; ~ **peak on-state current** courant direct de pointe répétitif à l'état passant; ~ **peak reverse current** courant inverse de pointe répétitif; ~ **peak reverse voltage** tension inverse de pointe répétitive
re-phasing n recadrage; ~ **pulse** impulsion de blocage
replacement part élément de rechange
replacing receiver raccrochage
replenisher n rechargeur
replenishment n réapprovisionnement; approvisionnement; lancement en atelier; remplissage
replica n copie; homologue
replicate v sécuriser; replier
replicated adj double
replication n sécurisation; doublement; redondance
reply n réponse
report n état; état d'impression; historique; procès-verbal (PV); rapport; tableau; ~ **charge** taxe de préparation; ~ **generator** éditeur; générateur de compte-rendus; générateur d'état; programme d'édition
reporting n signalisation; ~ **station** (of nightwatchman service) poste de pointage
report program generator (RPG) générateur de programme d'édition
repository n magasin
representative n agent; délégué; représentant
reprocessing n recyclage
reproduce v recopier; répercuter; reprendre; reproduire
reproducer n magnétophone
reproducibility n reproductibilité; fidélité de répétition
reproducible copy contre-calque
reproduction characteristic caractéristique de

lecture; ~ **head** tête de lecture; ~ **ratio** rapport de reproduction
reprotect n modification de protection
request n demande; ordre; requête
request-driven system recherche de dénombrement et de sélection
request for information demande de renseignements; ~ **for proposal** appel d'offres
request-repeat system système détecteur d'erreurs avec demande de répétition; RQ automatique
request-to-send (signal) (RTS) demande d'émission; prêt
required join espace insécable
requisition n procurer
requisitioning n approvisionnement
re-radiation error erreur de réflexion locale
re-recording réenregistrement
re-route v réaguiller; débrancher; renvoyer
re-routed adj détourné
re-routing n réacheminement; circuit de détournement; déroutement; détournement; déviation; filtrage; réaiguillage; renvoi
re-run n reprise
re-rung adj remis en sonnerie
rescinded adj résilié
rescue dump table des reprises en secours; sauvegarde; ~ **point** point de reprise; point de retour
research n étude; analyse; recherche; ~ **and development (R & D)** recherche; ~ **department** bureau d'études; ~ **design** schéma conceptuel
reservation callback top d'annotation (de rappel automatique); ~ **charging** tarification sur réservation
reserve adj de secours
reserved adj privilégié
reserve tape (at end of roll) réserve de bande; ~ **time** autonomie de batterie
reset v initialiser; mettre à zéro; ramener; réarmer; réinitialiser; reprendre le réglage; rétablir; ~ n remise à zéro (RZ/RAZ); déblocage; démarrage à chaud; effacement; réarmement; recalage; redémarrage lent; réemploi; retour à zéro; ~ adj à rappel au zéro; à temps de réemploi écourté; dépositionné; désarmé; hors signal; ~ **contact** contact repos; ~ **facility** dispositif de RAZ (remise à zéro); ~ **input** entrée initialisation; ~ **signal** signal de remise à zéro; ~ **time** temps de retour; ~ **to initial value** revalorisé
re-shaping n restitution
residency n implantation
resident adj résidant; implanté; interne; présent; propre

R

residential building cable câble d'immeuble; ~ **charge metering** télétaxe (TLT); ~ **line** ligne d'abonné; ~ **metering** taxation à domicile; ~ **subscriber** abonné ordinaire; abonné résidentiel; abonné simple

resident kernel noyau résident; ~ **module** module interne; ~ **program** programme résident

residual air gap entrefer (d'un relais); ~ **capacitance** capacité résiduelle; ~ **carrier** composante résiduelle de courant porteur; ~ **current** courant résiduel

residual-current state régime de courant résiduel

residual deflection erreur de zéro; ~ **(undetected) error rate** taux d'erreurs résiduelles; ~ **excitation** excitation rémanente; ~ **hum** ronflement résiduel; ~ **magnetism** rémanence; ~ **noise** bruit propre; ~ **relay** relais à point nul; ~ **screw** (of relay) butée; ~ **spacing** (octantal) **error** erreur d'espacement résiduelle; ~ **voltage** (of power line) tension résiduelle (d'une ligne industrielle)

residue n reliquat; dépôt

resilience n souplesse

resilient adj élastique; insensible (aux chocs); résistant; ~ **material** matière tendre; ~ **mounting** amortisseur; bloc amortisseur; isolateur de vibration; montage à résilience; silentbloc; suspension élastique

resin n résine; colophane

resin-bonded adj pré-enrobé; ~ **plywood** bois résinifié

resin-core solder soudure à âme de résine

resin-flow barrier frein de fluage

resistance n résistance; tenue; ~ **attenuation** affaiblissement de résistance; ~ **balancing** équilibrage de résistance; ~ **bridge** pont de résistance

resistance-capacitance coupling (R-C) couplage par résistance-capacité; ~ **network** circuit résistance capacitance (RC); cellule RC; ~ **oscillator** oscillateur R-C

resistance coupling couplage par résistance; ~ **decade box** boîte de résistance; ~ **loss** perte ohmique; ~ **matching** équilibrage de résistance; ~ **network** boîtier de résistances; ~ **noise** bruit d'agitation thermique; ~ **per unit length** résistance linéique; ~ **plug** bouchon résistif; ~ **thermometer** sonde Pt100; ~ **to solder heat** (thermal shock) résistance à la soudure (choc thermique); ~ **to solvents** tenue aux solvants; ~ **unbalance** déséquilibre de résistance; ~ **welding** soudure électrique

resistive attenuator affaiblisseur à absorption; affaiblisseur résistif; ~ **circuit** circuit résistant; ~ **load** charge résistante; ~ **pho-**tocell** cellule photorésistante; ~ **torque** couple résistant (moteur à cage)

resistor n résistance; ~ **bulb** résistance de charge; ~ **network** réseau résistif; ~ **network module** module de résistance

re-site v réimplanter

resolution n définition; espacement (pas); pouvoir séparateur; précision; sensibilité; ~ **grid** mire de définition

resolver n séparateur

resolving dilemma/ambiguity lever de doute

resonance n résonance; accord; harmonie; ~ **peak** crête de résonance; ~ **scattering** absorption de résonance; ~ **state** niveau de résonance; ~ **wave-meter** ondemètre à résonance

resonant (cavity) frequency meter fréquencemètre à résonance; ~ **aerial** antenne accordée; ~ **cavity** cavité résonnante; ~ **chamber** cavité résonnante; ~ **circuit** circuit résonnant

resonant-circuit drive pilote à circuit oscillant

resonant frequency fréquence de résonance; fréquence d'accord; ~ **impedance** impédance à la résonance; ~ **mode filter** filtre de mode résonnant

resonant-transfer technique technique du transfert résonnant

resonant/tuned circuit circuit oscillant

resonator n résonateur; cavité; circuit de résonance parallèle; ~ **crystal** cristal résonateur

resource allocation nivellement; structure logique; ~ **chaining** chaînage de ressources; ~ **management** gestion physique

resources n pl moyens

response n sensibilité; accord; action; caractéristique(s); champ d'action; coefficient de sensibilité; efficacité; fidélité; marquage; prise en compte; réaction; réponse; ~ **curve** courbe de réponse; ~ **delay** délai de réponse; ~ **pattern** courbe; ~ **range** échelle de sélectivité; ~ **time** temps de réponse; constante de temps; temps de réaction; ~ **time alignment** cadrage du temps de réponse; ~ **to current** réponse au courant; ~ **to interference** réponse parasite

rest n crochet; appui; berceau; repos

restart v recommencer; n recyclage; reprise sur erreur; redémarrage; régénération; réinitialisation; reprise sur incident; remise en marche; ~ **bit** bit de reprise; ~ **point** point de reprise; ~ **procedure** procédure de reprise

restitution n modulation arythmique; reproduction; restitution; ~ **delay** délai de restitution; ~ **element** élément de modulation

re-stocking n lancement en atelier; réapprovisionnement

restoration n régénération; récupération; reprise; ~ **control point** centre de commande de rétablissement du service (CCR)

restore v restituer; décourt-circuiter; ramener; rapatrier; réactiver; récuperer; reprendre; rétablir; ~ **default** (options) configuration usine

re-storing n rapatriement

restraining voltage tension retardatrice

restricted adj limitatif; borné; ~ **access** accès imparfait; accessibilité partielle

restricted-access station poste discriminé

restricted access subscriber abonné discriminé; ~ **mode** mode restreint; ~ **service** service restreint

restriction n filtrage

re-striking voltage tension de rallumage

result analysis exploitation des résultats; ~ **processing** exploitation des résultats

results hopper file d'attente des réponses (FAR); file d'attente de sortie

resume v reprendre; relancer

résumé n récapitulatif; rappel; synthèse

resumption of load-sharing reprise du trafic

resynchronisation memory mémoire de resynchronisation

retailer n revendeur

retained earnings bénéfices non distribués

retaining band jonc; ~ **bar/rod** fer de garde; ~ **clamp** crochet d'arrêt; ~ **clip** harpon; ~ **clip** (of pot core) bride-ressort; ~ **ring** anneau Truarc; cadre

retardant n frein

retarding-field oscillator oscillateur de freinage

retention date date de péremption; ~ **(grandfather) cycle** cycle de rétention

retentive adj rémanent

retentivity n persistance (d'écran)

reticule n graticule

re-timing n recalage; réajustement du rythme

re-touch n retouche

retrace n retour du spot

retractable adj escamotable; ~ **button** tirette

retracted adj rentré

retraction n dégagement

re-training n reconversion

retransmission n déport; réémission; réexpédition; répétition; retransmission; transit; translation

retrievable (transmission) error erreur de transmission bénigne

retrieval n récupération; extraction; lecture; obtention; rapatriement; recherche; saisie; mise à disposition; reprise

retrieve v récuperer; acquérir; appeler; consulter; obtenir; rapatrier; réavaler; reprendre; restituer

retro-fit v postfixer

retrofit n adaptation; évolution; mise à jour (MAJ); mise à niveau; mise à palier; modification; post-transformation; rattrapage; reprise

retro-fitted adj greffé

retrogressive adj en arrière

return (current) réflexion; **(PCM)** ~ **multiplex** ligne réseau sortante (LRS); ~ **address** adresse de retour; adresse de chaînage; phase de renvoi; phase de retour; pointeur de chaînage; ~ **band** bande retour; ~ **channel** canal retour; ~ **code** code de renvoi; code retour; ~ **control to console** repasser le contrôle au pupitre; ~ **(reflected) current** courant de retour; ~ **current** courant réfléchi

return-current coefficient coefficient de courants réfléchis; coefficient d'adaptation; coefficient d'équilibrage; coefficient de réflexion

return direction sens retour; ~ **information available** information de retour disponible (IRD); ~ **instruction** instruction de retour; phase de retour; ~ **light** (of radio broadcasting) signal de réponse; ~ **line** ligne de retour; ~ **loss (RL)** affaiblissement d'adaptation; affaiblissement des courants réfléchis; coefficient de réflexion; perte due aux réflexions; perte par réflexion; affaiblissement d'équilibrage; ~ **loss measuring set** équilibromètre; ~ **message** réponse; ~ **multiplex** ligne réseau sortante (LRS); ~ **on investment** rentabilité; ~ **path** voie de retour; canal auxiliaire; canal de retour; chemin réception; support réception; voie retour; ~ **point** point de reprise; ~ **power** puissance réfléchie; ~ **side** aval (en); ~ **spring** ressort d'appel/de rappel; ~ **terminal** borne de reprise; ~ **to call on hold** reprise d'appel; reprise d'une ligne en garde; ~ **tone** (of level measuring set) onde en retour; ~ **to zero** retour à zéro; ~ **voltage** tension réfléchie

re-type v retaper

reverberation n réverbération; ~ **time** durée de réverbération

reversal n inversion; renversement

reverse n marche arrière; sens inverse (bloqué); ~ **bias** polarisation inverse; tension inverse

reverse-blocking state état bloqué inverse; ~ **triode thyristor** redresseur à silice

reverse channel voie de retour

reverse-charge call PCV (payable à l'arrivée = percevoir) (code 10 en France)

R

reverse charging (collect) taxation à l'arrivée; taxation du demandé; taxation à l'arrière; ~ **continuous (direct) voltage** tension inverse (continue); ~ **coupling** contre-réaction; ~ **crosstalk** paradiaphonie; ~ **current** courant inverse

reverse-current relay relais directionnel; ~ **trip** contacteur à courant inverse

reversed connector connecteur inversé

reverse electrode current courant inverse d'électrode

reverse-frequency operation exploitation avec permutation des fréquences

reverse gate continuous (direct) voltage tension inverse (continue) de gâchette; ~ **gate-source (DC) voltage** tension inverse (continue) grille-source

reverser/contactor block bloc de puissance; unité de puissance

reverse recovery current courant inverse de recouvrement; ~ **recovery time** temps de recouvrement inverse; ~ **tape transport mode** marche arrière du dérouleur; ~ **transfer capacitance** capacité de réaction; ~ **transfer capacitance** (input short-circuited to AC) capacité de transfert inverse, entrée en court-circuit; ~ **transfer capacitance in common-base configuration** capacité de transfert inverse, en base commune; ~ **transfer capacitance in common-emitter configuration** capacité de transfert inverse, en émetteur commun; ~ **video** vidéo inversée; contraste inversé; ~ **voltage** tension inverse; ~ **voltage surge** surtension inverse

reversible *adj* mixte; symétrique; ~ (serial-parallel) orthogonal; ~ **assembly** pièce symétrique; ~ **counter** (accumulator/scaler) compteur-décompteur; ~ **(deformation)** zone de réversibilité; ~ **modem** modem retournable; ~ **ratchet** cliquet réversible; ~ **switch** interrupteur à bascule

reversing *adj* à deux sens de marche; ~ **charges** virement des frais; ~ **starter** discontacteur inverseur

reverting switch clé de rappel du demandeur

revertive *adj* en arrière; ~ **metering** taxation avec renvoi des impulsions de taxe; ~ **pulse circuit** circuit d'impulsions inverses; ~ **pulse system** système à impulsions en arrière

review (function) rebobinage rapide

revision *n* refonte; révision; mise à jour (MAJ); modification; reprise; ~ (rev.) édition (éd.); ~ **notes** rappel; ~ **status** indice d'exploitation; indice d'interchangeabilité

revoked *adj* résilié

revolution *n* cycle tour/rotation; circonvolution; pan

revolver *n* boucle à accès rapide

revolving radio beacon radiophare tournant

rewinding *n* rebobinage; rembobinage

RF (s. radio frequency); ⸰ **channel** canal RF; ⸰ **choke** self inductance HF; ⸰ **conductor** conducteur hyperfréquence; ⸰ **coupler** coupleur UHF; ⸰ **gate** vanne HF (hyperfréquence); ⸰ **head** tête à radiofréquence

RFI (radio-frequency interference) assembly filtre secteur

RFI-EMI control combat d'interférences radio-électriques

RF inductor ferrite hyperfréquence

RFI survey (radio-frequency interference) étude d'interférences radio-électriques

RF preselection filter filtre présélecteur HF; ⸰ **preselection stage** étage présélecteur HF; ⸰ **receiver unit** coffret hyper de réception

R.H. (righthand) slide/runner glissière droite

rheostat *n* rhéostat

rhombic aerial antenne apériodique; antenne de Beverage; antenne en lasange

rhombus *n* (decision box) losange

rib *n* épaulement; côte; voile

ribbed insulator impédance à ailettes; isolateur à nervures

ribbon *n* bande; ruban; ~ **(of optical fibre cable)** rubanage; ~ **cable** câble à ruban; câble en nappe; câble méplat; câble nappé; câble plat; cordon plat; limande; nappe de fils

ribbon-cable wiring câblage en nappe

ribbon microphone microphone à ruban; microphone à conducteur mobile; ~ **structure** structure à ruban

Richardson-Dushmann equation (emission of electrons) loi de Richardson-Dushmann

rider *n* en dérogation

ridged *adj* épaulé

ridge waveguide guide d'ondes à moulures

Rieke diagram diagramme de Rieke

riffle *v* (of paper) déramer

rig *v* monter; ~ *n* antenne; construction(s)

rigging *n* construction(s)

right angle angle droit

right-angled *adj* orthogonal; coudé; ~ **pull-off strength** tenue transversale; ~ **wiring** câblage orthogonal

right arrow flèche horizontale droite

right-hand circular polarization polarisation circulaire droite; ~ **counter cutter** contre-couteau droit

right-hand/left-hand page recto-verso

right-hand polarized wave onde polarisée elliptiquement/(circulairement dextrorsum)

rightmost *adj* de droite; poids faible (pf)

right-of-way *n* accès; droit; priorité; ~ **station** poste prioritaire

right shift décaler à droite

rigid *adj* rigide; compact; ~ **disk** disque rigide

rigour *n* sévérité

rim *n* joue; flasque; périphérie; tasseau de surélévation

rimless *adj* débridé

ring *v* téléphoner; appeler; signaler; retentir; sonner; ~ *n* bague; anneau; collerette; boucle; nuque (de jack); ~ **aerial** antenne en anneau; ~ **armature** anneau de Gramme; armature en anneau

ring(s), (coloured) ~ guirlandage

ring-around-the-rosy boucle permanente

ring-back facility test de sonnerie; ~ **key** clé de rappel du demandeur; ~ **signal** signal de rappel du demandeur; ~ **tone** tonalité de retour d'appel

ring core tore (de ferrite); ~ **counter** compteur annulaire; compteur circulaire; compteur en anneau; ~ **demodulator** démodulateur annulaire

ring-down circuit circuit à signalisation manuelle; circuit de courant d'appel; circuit de/en garde; circuit manuel; ~ **operation** exploitation avec appel sur le circuit

ringer *n* dispositif d'appel; machine d'appel; organe d'appel; signaleur; sonnerie; unité d'appel

ring-forward signal signal de rappel; signal d'appel en avant

ringing *n* appel; mise en sonnerie; oscillation transitoire; scintillement; sonnerie d'appel; suroscillation; ~ *adj* sonnant; ~ **change-over switch** commutateur de sonnerie; ~ **code** code d'appel; ~ **current** courant d'appel; courant de sonnerie

ringing-current circuit circuit de courant d'appel; ~ **connect relay** relais de commande de sonnerie; ~ **connect signal** signal d'appel; ~ **conversion** conversion du signal d'appel; ~ **generator** générateur d'appel; ~ **transformer** transformateur d'appel; ~ **transmission** sonnerie

ringing current transmitter envoyeur d'appel; ~ **current trip** arrêt du courant d'appel; arrêt du courant de sonnerie; ~ **extension** poste en sonnerie; ~ **frequency** fréquence du courant d'appel; ~ **generator** générateur de courant d'appel; ~ **interval** périodicité d'appel; phase d'appel; ~ **inverter** onduleur d'appel; ~ **key** clé d'appel; bouton d'appel; ~ **lead** fil de sonnerie d'appel; ~ **level** niveau d'appel; ~ **line** ligne appelante; ~ **machine** machine

d'appel

ringing-off *n* raccrochage

ringing relay relais d'appel; ~ **repeater** circuit de déviation d'appel; signaleur à fréquence basse; ~ **signal** retour d'appel; signal d'appel; ~ **time** durée de réponse; ~ **tone** tonalité de retour d'appel; mélodie de sonnerie; signal de retour d'appel; signe d'appel; sonnerie; ~ **tone reactivated** relance de sonnerie

ringing-tone signal signal de retour d'appel

ringing voltage tension d'appel

ring-main *n* couronne; serpentin

ring mode filter filtre de mode à anneaux; ~ **modulator** modulateur annulaire; modulateur en anneau

ring-off *n* libération; ~ **indicator** indicateur de fin d'appel; indicateur de fin à volet; ~ **signal** signal d'appel de fin

ring-out point central d'alarme

ring priority networks réseaux hiérarchisés en anneau; ~ **shift** décalage cyclique; décalage circulaire; décalage de cycle; ~ **source** source annulaire; ~ **spanner** clé polygonale; ~ **switch** commutateur à anneau; ~ **tip** gabarit d'arrêt d'appel

ring-trip arrêt d'appel; inhibition sonnerie

ring-when-free mise en attente

ring wire fil de nuque

ripple *n* tension résiduelle; bruit; coefficient d'ondulation; ondulation résiduelle; tension de réinjection; ~ (of solder mask) frisure; ~ (noise) ronflement résiduel; ~ **component** composante ondulatoire; ~ **counter** compteur décimal; ~ **current** courant résiduel; courant d'ondulation résiduelle; courant ondulé; intensité résiduelle

rippled-wall amplifier amplificateur à paroi ondulée

ripple factor ondulation relative; ~ **filter** filtre redresseur; ensemble de filtrage; ~ **ratio** taux d'ondulation; ~ **rejection** taux de filtrage

ripple-through-carry retenue propagée; report accéléré; report simultané

ripple time temps d'ondulation; ~ **voltage** tension de ronflement

rippling *n* traitement par priorité

rise *n* élévation à une puissance; ~ **time** (t_r) temps de montée; temps des fronts; temps de croissance; temps de transition

rise-time correction correction du temps de montée; ~ **distortion** distorsion du temps de montée; ~ **optimization** optimalisation du temps de montée

rising *adj* ascendant; croissant; ~ **edge** front de montée; front montant

R

rivet clincher poussoir rivet
riveter n outil de sertissage
rivet gun jaw mâchoire pistolet; ~ **snap** bouterolle
rivetting bar bouterolle
RJE (s. remote job entry)
RL (s. return loss)
RLF (s. release forms)
RLU (s. remote line unit)
r.m.s. (s. root mean square); ~ **amplitude** amplitude efficace; amplitude quadratique moyenne; ~ **current** courant efficace
r.m.s.-to-DC converter extracteur de valeur efficace
r.m.s. value valeur efficace; valeur moyenne quadratique; ~ **voltage** tension efficace; ~ **voltmeter** voltmètre efficace
RO (s. receive-only)
roamer n abonné itinérant; abonné mobile; station mobile
roaming subscriber abonné itinérant; abonné mobile
robber bar piste voleur (= voleur de courant)
robot n automate
robotics n robotique; automatisme
robot transponder (exchange automatic answering service) robot (d'appels)
robust adj insensible aux chocs; résistant; solide
robustness of terminations robustesse des sorties
rocker n couronne; ~ **arm** balancier
rocket n fusée; engin
rod n tige; aiguille; barre; barrette; bielle; baguette; jonc; ~ **aerial** antenne en tige; ~ **insulator** isolateur à tige
rod-in-tube (method) barreau tube
rod mirror réflecteur à tiges; miroir grille; ~ **reflector** réflecteur à tiges; miroir grille
ROH (s. receiver off-hook)
roll axis axe de roulis
roll-back v répéter; ~ n reprise sur incident; reprise sur erreur; ~ **routine** programme de reprise
roller switch interrupteur à galets
roll-in n recyclage
rolling (mode) rouleau; ~ **average** moyenne cumulative; ~ **stock** matériel roulant; ~ **test** test défilant
rolling-vane motor moteur hydraulique
roll mode mode rouleau
roll-off n taux de coupure progressive; circuit de compensation; circuit éliminateur; compensation interne; pente; circuit bouchon; courbe de pondération; pente de diminution; pente d'une courbe
roll-out v recopier; transférer en mémoire auxiliaire

rollover frappe anticipée; ~ **function** mémoire tampon du clavier (SUR IMP)
ROM (s. read-only memory)
roman character caractère romain
ROM software logiciel figé
Ron (s. on-state resistance)
roof aerial antenne de toit
room n (in memory) place; **at ~ temperature** en ambiance; ~ **noise** bruit de salle; ~ **temperature** température ambiante
root n racine; base; ~ **mean square (r.m.s.)** valeur efficace; moyenne quadratique; ~ **mean square value** valeur moyenne quadratique; ~ **segment** racine
rope n drisse
roster n liste; tableau
rostrum n estrade
rotary attenuator affaiblisseur rotatif; atténuateur rotatif; ~ **beam aerial** antenne à faisceau rotatif; ~ **converter** convertisseur rotatif à induit unique; commutatrice; ~ **dial** cadran; cadran de numérotation; ~ **dial set** poste à cadran (CAD); ~ **dial telephone** poste décimal; ~ **drum sander** touret à abrasion; ~ **group selector** sélecteur rotatif de groupe; ~ **indexing table** ("Lazy Susan") carrousel; ~ **phase changer/phase-shifter** déphaseur rotatif; ~ **potentiometer** (with switch) potentiomètre rotatif (avec interrupteur); ~ **spark gap** éclateur tournant; ~ **step** pas de rotation; ~ **switch** commutateur sélectif; rotacteur; sélecteur rotatif; ~ **switching** commutation à sélection rotative; ~ **system** système automatique à commutateurs rotatifs
rotatable adj manœuvrable en rotation; orientable
rotate in step tourner en coïncidence
rotating direction-finder radiogoniomètre à chercheur
rotating-field aerial antenne à champ tournant; ~ **detector** détecteur de champ tournant; ~ **magnet** électro-aimant de rotation
rotating-frame aerial cadre rotatif
rotating joint joint tournant
rotating-loop direction finder radiogoniomètre à cadre
rotation n giration; permutation; ~ **axis** orientation error erreur d'inclinaison
rotor n induit; rotor; roue polaire; ~ **loss** perte rotorique; ~ **resistance** résistance rotorique; ~ **resistance starter** démarreur rotorique
rough-cast adj brute de fonderie
rough edge bavure; ~ **handling** choc
roughness n rugosité; aspérité

R

rough treatment choc

round v (off) arrondir; ~ (of exchange nightwatchman service) parcours de ronde; ~ down arrondir par défaut

rounded edge angle abattu

rounded-off adj mouché

rounded tip angle abattu; épaulement

round-headed wood screw vis BTR

rounding-off error erreur d'arrondi

round-nose pliers pince bec rond

round-off v compléter (par)

round-robin hunting interrogation sélective; interrogation séquentielle; multiplexage cyclique; permutation circulaire; permutation cyclique; recherche cyclique; recherche par décalage

round-the-clock adj continu; permanent; ~ service service permanent; ~ watch-keeping veille permanente

round-the-world echo écho tour de terre

round-trip document document aller-retour; document navette; document tournant; ~ end delay retard aller-retour en extrémité

round up arrondir par excès

route v acheminer; aiguiller; orienter; relier; ~ n chemin; artère; direction; faisceau; itinéraire; parcours; route; voie; ~ administration gestion des acheminements; ~ analysis calcul d'itinéraire; ~ analysis completed appel traité; ~ card (tag) fiche de suivi; fiche suiveuse

routed call appel offert

route monitoring surveillance de l'acheminement; ~ monitoring access code préfixe de surveillance de l'acheminement

routine n programme (pg); module; office; routine; segment; sous-bloc; tâche; traitement; ~ adj périodique; courant; de service; habituel; systématique; ordinaire; ~ adjustment réglage systématique; ~ maintenance maintenance périodique; entretien courant; ~ operations opérations d'exploitation

routiner n maquette de maintenance; module d'essais (= robot d'essais); robot (d'appels); banc de mesure d'abonnés; équipement d'essais systématiques; simulateur d'appels

routine servicing entretien en cours d'usage; ~ task tâche périodique; ~ task file fichier agenda; ~ test essai systématique; essai périodique

routing n acheminement; aiguillage; branchement; cheminement; façonnage; sélection; orientation (sur un poste); ~ area (RA) secteur de routage (SR); ~ code indicatif d'acheminement (IA); code indicateur;

indicatif (IF); ~ code number numéro de code d'indicatif; ~ data données d'acheminement; ~ digit chiffre d'acheminement; ~ distributor notificateur (nr.); ~ form feuille d'acheminement; ~ indicator indicateur d'acheminement (IA); ~ information information d'acheminement; ~ label étiquette d'acheminement; ~ office section d'acheminement; ~ path voie d'acheminement; ~ plan plan d'acheminement; ~ relay relais d'itinéraire; ~ section section d'acheminement; ~ selector sélecteur discriminateur; identificateur de jonction; ~ table table d'acheminement; ~ tone tonalité d'acheminement; ~ unit unité de sélection

roving adj mobile; stratifil

row n ligne; file; rang; rangée; ~ binary card carte binaire par ligne; ~ pitch interligne; ~ scanning balayage de rangées

royalty n redevance

RPE (s. remote peripheral equipment)

RPG (s. report program generator)

r.p.m. vitesse de révolution

RPOA (s. recognized private operating agency)

RR (s. receiver ready)

RRE (s. receive reference equivalent)

RS (reset-set) flip-flop bascule à commande dissymétrique

R$_T$ (s. zero power resistance)

RTA (s. remote trunk arrangement)

RTC (s. real time clock)

R$_{th(j-c)}$ (s. junction-case thermal resistance)

R$_{th}$ (s. thermal resistance)

RTS (s. request to send)

R/T voice transmission phonie (radio-)

rubber-band store mémoire à liste directe; file circulaire

rubber boot capuchon en caoutchouc

rubber-insulated cable câble sous caoutchouc; ~ wire fil à isolement caoutchouc

rub out v effacer

rub-out n (mode) gomme; ~ character (DEL)caractère d'effacement; caractère d'oblitération

R & D (s. research and development)

rugged adj solide

ruggedness n robustesse

rule n contrainte; loi

rule-of-thumb adj par approximation; heuristique

ruler line réglette (rg.)

rules of the art règles de l'art

run n déroulement; chemin; course; entraînement; exploitation (EXPL); passage; passe; phase; phase de travail; suite; vacation

R

runaway *n* paramètre défectueux; catastrophe; ~ *adj* aberré; aberrant; défectueux; discret
run book dossier d'exploitation
run-down battery accumulateur déchargé; ~ **state** mode dégénéré
run file fichier exécutable; ~ **file library** bibliothèque exécutable
rung *adj* mis en sonnerie; appelé
run-length coding codification de la longueur de trajet
runner *n* coulisseau; glissière
running *adj* en cours; en service (ES); exécutable; lancé; marche (MA); ~ **column** (of bit pattern) colonne galopante; ~ **newspaper column** colonne serpentine forcée; ~ **numeric sum** somme numérique courante; ~ **one** (of memory array) un galopeur; ~ **order** état de fonctionnement; ~ **task** tâche en cours; tâche en exécution; ~ **torque** couple de rotation; couple utile; ~ **total counter** compteur totalisateur
run-off *adj* débobiné
run-out *n* coulure; ~ **time** temps écoulé; ~ **timer** décompteur programmable

run queue file d'attente d'exécution; file de tâches en exécution; ~ **time** temps d'exploitation; durée de fonctionnement; temps de passage
run-up *n* période préparatoire; mise en route; ~ **time** durée d'échauffement
rupture *n* coupure
rural automatic exchange (RAX) autocommutateur rural; central automatique rural; bureau téléphonique automatique rural; ~ **carrier circuit** circuit rural à courants porteurs; ~ **electronic subscriber line concentrator** concentrateur satellite électronique rural; ~ **exchange** central rural; ~ **metallic (loop) circuit** circuit rural métallique; ~ **network** réseau rural; ~ **party line** ligne partagée; ~ **subscriber** abonné rural
ruthless pre-emption intervention en tiers; intervention prioritaire
R-wire *n* (connected to subscriber line B-wire) fil de nuque; réception
RX (s. reception)
R-Y, test loop and repeated ~ (5-unit) **code transmission** roulement RY

R

S

SAC (s. storage access channel)
sacrificial anode anode enterrée; anode active; ~ **protection** protection galvanique
saddle *n* étrier; berceau; chape; jonc; serre-fils
safeguard copy copie de déchargement
safe load charge admissible; ~ **operating area (S.O.A.)** aire de fonctionnement de sécurité; domaine d'utilisation
safety *n* sécurité; sûreté; ~ **call** appel de sécurité; ~ **connection** liaison de sécurité; ~ **factor** coefficient de sécurité; ~ **features** sécurités; ~ **fuse** coupe-circuit à fusible; ~ **margin** marge de securité; ~ **wire** fil de freinage
safe workstation poste de travail protégé
sag *n* flèche
saleable *adj* vendable
sales, (telephone) ~ agence commerciale; ~ **back-up** service après-vente (SAV); ~ **engineering department** service technico-commercial
salesman *n* agent commercial; représentant
sales pattern configurateur commercial
salient pole pôle saillant
salt-laden environment climat salin
salt-mist test essai au brouillard salin
salts (in wave soldering pot) cristaux intermétalliques
salt spray brouillard salin; pluie saline
salvage *v* récuperer
salvaging *n* (of files) restitution
SAM (s. subsequent address message)
sample *v* prélever; ~ *n* échantillon; modèle (mle)
sample-and-hold *n* (circuit) échantillonneur-bloqueur; ~ (function) échantillonnage et mémorisation
sampled *adj* prélevé; ~ **data** données échantillonnées
sample file fiche d'essais; ~ **intelligence** échantillon de signal; ~ **mean** moyenne mobile
sampler *n* circuit discriminateur; aiguilleur
sample size amplitude d'échantillon; ~ **voltage** tension de modulation
sampling *n* prélèvement; échantillonnage; exploration; sondage; ~ **and acceptance conditions** conditions de prélèvement et d'acceptation; ~ **circuit** circuit discrimina-

teur; ~ **frequency** fréquence d'échantillonnage; cadence d'échantillonnage; ~ **gate** porte d'échantillonnage; ~ **inspection** contrôle par prélèvements; ~ **interval** intervalle d'échantillonnage; ~ **level (SL)** taux de prélèvement; ~ **period** période d'échantillonnage; ~ **plan** plan d'échantillonnage; ~ **pulse** impulsion d'échantillonnage; ~ **rate** taux d'échantillonnage; cadence d'échantillonnage; fréquence d'échantillonnage; taux de prélèvement
sand blasting sablage; ~ **storm** vent de sable
sandwiching *n* empilement
sash *n* cadre; enjoliveur
s/assy (s. subassembly)
SATCOM (s. satellite communication)
satellite *adj* décentralisé; **(earth)** ~ **relay station** station terrienne; ~ **acquisition** acquisition de satellite; ~ **aerial** antenne de satellite; ~ **automatic picture reception** réception automatique d'une image transmise par satellite; ~ **centre** centre satellite; ~ **circuit** circuit par satellite; circuit spatial; ~ **communications (SATCOM)** télécommunications spatiales; communication par satellite; ~ **communications service** service de communication par satellite; ~ **exchange** centre satellite; ~ **link** circuit spatial; liaison par satellite; ~ **navigation system** système de navigation par satellites; ~ **operation** exploitation par satellite; ~ **orbit** orbite de satellite; ~ **relay station** terrienne; ~ **relay microwave link** liaison hertzienne par satellite; ~ **repeater** répéteur de satellite
satellite-shore link liaison satellite-côte
satellite tracking acquisition de satellite; ~ **transmission** transmission par satellite
satin-anodized aluminium aluminium satinisé; aluminium brossé
satisfactory *adj* bon
saturable reactor (= transductor) inductance saturable
saturated logic (transistors) commutation tout ou rien
saturation *n* coude de saturation; ~ **current** courant de saturation; ~ **noise** bruit de saturation; ~ **state** régime de saturation; ~ **voltage** tension de saturation
sausage aerial antenne pyramidale

S

save v sauvegarder; économiser; protéger; ~ **dialled number key** touche de mise en mémoire temporaire d'un numéro

SAW (s. surface acoustic wave)

sawtooth n dent de scie (DDS); forme d'onde triangulaire; ~ **coupling** couplage en dents de scie; ~ **current** courant à dents de scie; ~ **generator** générateur de rampe; générateur de dents de scie; ~ **keyboard** clavier à action directe; ~ **oscillator** oscillateur de dents de scie; ~ **pulse** impulsion triangulaire; impulsion en dent de scie; impulsion en triangle; ~ **voltage** tension en dents de scie; ~ **wave** onde en dents de scie; ~ **waveform** forme d'onde en dents de scie

SB (s. simultaneous broadcast)

SBA (s. standard beam approach)

SBM (s. send buffer memory)

SBO (s. sideband only)

scalar group agrégat de scalaires

scale v cadrer (à droite/à gauche); dimensionner; étalonner; proportionner; ~ n échelle (éch.); barème; étendue; gamme; grandeur; importance; plage; taux; **not to** ~ selon les cotes (s.l.c.); ~ **down** réduire; ~ **expander** expanseur d'échelle; ~ **model** maquette; ~ **of charges** tarif

scale-of-two circuit circuit bistable; ~ **counter** bascule dédoubleuse

scaler n démultiplicateur; compteur d'impulsions; diviseur

scaling n cadrage; dilatation; dimensionnement; division; étalonnement; homothétie; exfoliation; décapage; écaillement; ~ **factor** facteur d'échelle

scalloped adj échancré

scalpel with interchangeable blades couteau scalpel à lame interchangeable

scan area secteur d'exploration; ~ **frequency** (in Hz) images par seconde; ~ **line** ligne d'exploration; ~ **matrix** grille codée

scanned area aire exploré

scanner n explorateur; analyseur; lecteur; scrutateur; ~ (of facsimile) tête de lecture; ~ **and driver** explorateur-distributeur

scanner-distributor n explorateur-distributeur

scanner tube tube analyseur

scanning n balayage; analyse; broutage; exploration; interpellation; scrutation; synthèse; ~ **address** adresse de distribution; ~ **aerial** antenne rotative; antenne à balayage; ~ **amplifier** amplificateur d'exploration; ~ **beam** faisceau explorateur; ~ **coil** aimant de cadrage; ~ **density** finesse de la trame; ~ **disk** disque analyseur; ~ **field** champ exploré; ~ **interval** intervalle d'exploration; ~ **line** ligne d'exploration; ligne d'analyse; ligne de synthèse;

~ **line frequency** fréquence de ligne; ~ **loop** boucle de scrutation; ~ **pitch** pas d'exploration; ~ **raster** trame d'exploration; ~ **signalling frame** trame de signalisation en exploration; ~ **speed** vitesse de balayage; vitesse d'exploration; ~ **spot** spot analyseur; tache d'exploration; ~ **strip** bande d'exploration; ~ **test bit** bit baladeur; ~ **traverse** translation d'exploration

scan point electrical characteristic caractéristique électrique des points de test; ~ **table** (mnemonics) exploration table; ~ **time** temps d'exploration

SCART (single-channel asynchronous receiver/transmitter) **TV peripheral connector** prise péritélévision SCART

scatter v diffuser; disséminer; éclater; ~ n diffusion; dispersion; écart; éclatement

scattered adj décentralisé; éclaté; ~ **radiation** rayonnement diffusé

scattering n déchaînage; éclatement; ~ **angle** angle de diffusion; ~ **centre** centre diffusant; ~ **cross-section** surface de diffusion; aire de rerayonnement

scatter propagation propagation troposphérique; ~ **read** lecture avec éclatement

schedule n calendrier; agenda; barème; bilan; bon; bordereau; durée; état de gestion; horaire; planning; programme (pg); tableau

scheduled adj ordonné; prévu; programmé

scheduler n planificateur; répartiteur; superviseur; ~ **and despatcher** explorateur-distributeur; ~ **utility** utilitaire de moniteur

scheduling n ordonnancement; enchaînement; gestion; planification; programmation; répartition; découpage du temps; ~ **group** file d'attente de planification

schematic adj découpe fonctionnelle; ~ **diagram** représentation graphique

scheme n plan; barème; dessin; programme (pg); projet; schéma

Schmitt trigger double trigger de Schmitt

schools broadcast émission didactique

Schottky barrier rectifier diode Schottky de puissance; ~ **effect** effet de grenaille; effet de grêle; ~ **noise** effet de bruit Schottky

scintillation fading affaiblissement dû aux scintillations

scooping n écrasement; défaut d'accouplement

scope n portée; domaine d'application; fourchette

scorched adj brûlé

scored text texte rayé

score mark rayure

scoring n prédécoupe

scouring n décapage

S

SCP (s. select current partition)
SCPC (s. single channel per carrier)
SCR (s. silicon-controlled rectifier)
scramble *v* embrouiller; altérer; brouiller (intentionellement)
scrambled *adj* mutilé; ~ telephony téléphonie à inversion de fréquence
scrambler *n* embrouilleur; circuit brouilleur
scrambling *n* paroles brouillées; altération; brouillage; embrouillage
scrap *v* démonter; ~ *n* déchets; bocage; dépouille; mise au rebut
scraping pliers pince à décaper
scrapping *n* démontage
scraps *n* pavé
scratch *n* rayure; ~ date date de péremption; ~ device appareil de manœuvre; ~ disk disque banalisé; disque de manœuvre; ~ file fichier de manœuvre; fichier de travail; support banalisé
scratching *n* effacement; suppression
scratch-pad *n* bloc-notes; brouillon; mémoire de travail; ~ area zone de travail; ~ memory mémoire banale; antémémoire; mémoire bloc-notes; mémoire de boucle intermédiaire; ~ register registre de travail
scratch resistance résistance à l'abrasion; ~ tape bande de manœuvre
screen *n* cloison; écran; page; trame; visionneuse; ~ attribute rendu visuel; ~ burn brûlure d'écran; ~ characteristic caractéristique d'écran; ~ clear effacement automatique d'écran; ~ display affichage écran; ~ dump printer imprimante de recopie d'écran; ~ echo recopie d'écran; impression en écho; réfléchi (sur écran)
screened *adj* blindé; abrité à ventilation forcée; déverminé; ~ cable câble sous écran; câble à tresse métallique; ~ line ligne blindée; ~ loop aerial cadran blindé; ~ pair paire blindée; paire sous écran; ~ wire fil sous écran
screen efficiency rendement d'écran
screen-grid valve tube à grille-écran
screening *n* blindage; déverminage; filtrage; mise sous écran; nettoyage; ~ braid tresse de blindage; ~ factor coefficient de protection électrique; ~ inspection contrôle intégral
screen link continuité de blindage; ~ management gestion de l'écran; ~ monitor console de visualisation (CV); ~ page page-écran; image; ~ painting dessin d'écran; ~ process printing sérigraphie
screw *n* vis; ~ cutting décolletage
screwdriver finder douille de guidage
screw home visser à fond
screw-machined contact contact (en) tulipe

screw-retaining screwdriver tournevis fixe-vis
screw shackle tendeur; ~ tightly visser à fond
screw-type terminal réglette à bornes
scriber *n* pointe à tracer; éditeur
scribing *n* prédécoupe; ~ block trusquin; ~ laser laser de découpe
script *n* scénario vidéo
scroll down ligne précédente
scrolling *n* défilement de texte; exploration
scroll up ligne suivante
scrub *v* annuler; effacer
scrutiny *n* analyse; contrôle; dépouillement
SCU (s. switching control unit)
SD (s. slow driver)
S + D (s. speech-plus-duplex equipment)
SDF (s. supergroup distribution frame)
SDR (s. slow driver)
sea clutter écho de mer; écho de vagues
seal *n* étanchéité; fenêtre étanche (de guide d'ondes); clôture; fermeture; garniture; repère
sealant *n* mastic; frein
sealed *adj* étanche; hermétique; ~ consumption consommation au maintien; ~ contact contact scellé
sealed-contact relay relais à contacts scellés; relais à contact en ampoule hermétique
sealed current courant de rabattement; courant de maintien; ~ multicontact matrix matrice scellée multicontacts (à maintien magnétique)
sealed-off tube/valve tube scellé
sealed relay relais étanche
sealing *n* herméticité; colmatage; scellement; ~ (test) étanchéité; ~ compound pâte de scellement; ~ current courant d'excitation; ~ gasket joint torique; ~ glaze verre de scellement; ~ kit dispositif de plombage; ~ ring joint torique; segment; ~ voltage tension d'excitation
seam *n* bavure
seamless *adj* sans soudure
seam welding soudure continue
searchable *adj* adressable
search and replace (S & R) recherche et substitution; ~ coil bobine exploratrice; rotor inductif; ~ condition état de veille
searcher *n* chercheur
search file fichier de recherche; ~ frequency fréquence de veille
searching storage mémoire associative
search key critère de recherche
searchlight *n* projecteur
search-lighting (of aerial) direction constante
search table table chaînée; ~ time temps de recherche; temps d'exploration
season cracking crique saisonnière
seat *n* (of fire) foyer

S

seated *adj* plaqué

seating *n* logement; carlingage; placage; planéité; portée; siège; ~ **plane** plan de pose

secondary carrier porteuse secondaire; ~ **cell** accumulateur; ~ **channel** voie de retour; ~ **coil** bobine secondaire

secondary-emission coefficient coefficient d'émission secondaire; ~ **factor** facteur d'émission secondaire; ~ **rate** (of a surface) taux d'émission secondaire

secondary half-winding demi-secondaire; ~ **line** ligne secondaire; ~ **line switch** chercheur secondaire; ~ **network** réseau secondaire; ~ **pattern** diagramme secondaire; ~ **radar** radiodétection secondaire; ~ **radiation** rayonnement secondaire; ~ **radiation pattern** diagramme polaire secondaire; ~ **radiator** élément secondaire; élément passif; ~ **route** voie secondaire; ~ **service area** zone de service secondaire; ~ **storage** saisie de masse; archivage; ~ **surveillance radar (SSR)** radar secondaire de surveillance; ~ **(switching) centre** centre secondaire; ~ **transit centre (STC)** centre de transit secondaire (CIS); ~ **voltage** tension (au) secondaire; ~ **winding** enroulement secondaire

second-channel frequency fréquence image; fréquence conjuguée

second-choice route voie de deuxième choix; ~ **trunk route** faisceau de deuxième choix

second harmonic deuxième harmonique

second-level address adresse indirecte; adresse complémentaire

second line finder chercheur secondaire

second-sourced *adj* en deuxième source

second Townsend discharge deuxième décharge de Townsend

secrecy *n* le secret; invisibilité; isolement

secretarial call pick-up service filtrage

secretary station poste filtrant; poste filtreur

section *n* section; bloc; bond; branche; cadre; domaine; galette; partie; pont diviseur; rubrique; segment; titre; tranche; tronçon; zone; ~ (of overhead cable) canton; ~ (of filter of delay line) cellule; ~ (of assembly) baie

sectionalize *v* tronçonner

sectional representation dessin de coupe; ~ **view** vue en coupe

section of circuit section de ligne; ~ **sign** signe paragraphe

sector *n* secteur; adresse physique; palier; zone; ~ **display** indicateur sectoriel

sectored *adj* (of disk) sectorisé

sector exchange central de secteur; ~ **interleaving** saut inter-secteurs; ~ **scanning** exploration sectorielle

sector-scanning beacon radiophare à diagramme oscillant

secure *adj* encastré

securing *n* calage; blocage; raccrochage; ~ **components** (nuts and bolts) pièces de fixation; visserie; boulonnerie; ~ **fluid** liquide frein; ~ **staple** harpon; ~ **strip** barrette de fixation

security *n* sécurité; défense; ~ **and fault-handling software** logiciel de défense et localisation d'avaries; ~ **fuse** (to protect proprietary logic) fusible de protection; ~ **module** module de sécurité (défense); ~ **procedure** mesures de défense; ~ **task** tâche de défense

sediment *n* dépôt

Seebeck effect effet thermoélectrique

seek address adresse de recherche; ~ **area** cylindre; ~ **error** erreur de recherche; ~ **time** temps de recherche

seepage *n* coulure

see-saw *n* bascule; va-et-vient; ~ **amplifier** amplificateur déphaseur; inverseur de polarité

S-effect (s. surface-charge effect)

segment *v* fractionner; décomposer; découper; scinder; tronçonner; ~ *n* tranche; découpe; demi-mot; partie; partition; segment; tronçon; zone; ~ (of display character) bâtonnet; ~ (of commutator) lame radiale; secteur; ~ (of pie chart) part; ~ (of program) section

segmentation *n* fractionnement; décomposition; découpage; segmentation

segmented *adj* sectorisé; sécable; ~ **encoding law** loi de codage à segments; ~ **quantization** codage à segments

segment register registre de segment; ~ **size** taille d'un segment

segregate *v* séparer; isoler

segregation *n* aiguillage; isolement

seising signal signal de déclenchement

seize *v* coincer; piéger; ~ (of line) occuper; ~ **area** zone prise

seized *adj* engagé; ~ **trunk circuit** circuit interurbain pris

seize signal signal de prise

seizing *n* blocage; grippage; prise; ~ **signal** occupation; signal de prise

seizure *n* (of line) prise; ~ **acknowledgement** contrôle de prise; ~ **attempt** tentative de prise; ~ **request** appel présenté; ~ **signal** signal d'appel; ~ **time** temps de prise

select *v* sélectionner; accorder; adresser; chercher; choisir; commuter; composer au clavier; désigner; déterminer; numéroter; prendre; programmer; ~ **bar** ruban de sélection; ~ **code** code sélectionné; ~ **current partition (SCP)** activation d'une partition

selected *adj* spécifique; demandé; pointé; ~ **data** données particulières; ~ **from** pris dans; ~ **pin** broche affichée

select graphics rendition (SGR) sélection rendu graphique

selecting finger doigt de sélection; embrayeur; ~ **menu option** pointage d'une case du segment menu

selection *n* choix; adressage; affichage; constitution; demande; désignation; discrimination; instauration; invitation à recevoir; mise en fonction; programmation

selection-finder *n* orienteur

selection (group) stage étage de sélection; ~ **module** module de choix; ~ **pawl** doigt de sélection; ~ **subsystem** chaîne sélective; ~ **time** temps de sélection

selective (contention) test essai d'arbitrage; ~ **attenuation** affaiblissement sélectif; ~ **calling** interrogation séquentielle; invitation à recevoir; ~ **circuit** circuit sélectif; ~ **digit emitter** distributeur; ~ **dump** sauvegarde sélective; ~ **fading** évanouissement sélectif; affaiblissement sélectif; fading sélectif; ~ **level meter synthesizer** voltmètre sélectif; ~ **level synthesizer** analyseur voltmètre sélectif; ~ **protection** protection sélective; ~ **ringing** appel sélectif

selectivity control réglage de sélectivité

select mode mise en fonction

selector *n* sélecteur; aiguilleur; chercheur; connecteur; curseur; sélecteur rotatif; ~ **bank** banc de sélecteurs; ~ **channel** canal sélecteur; ~ **drive** entraînement du sélecteur; ~ **relay** relais progresseur; ~ **switch** commutateur; combinateur

select zone rendition (SZR) sélection rendu de zone

selenium (rectifier) cell cellule à sélenium; ~ **rectifier** redresseur à sélénium

self-adapting *adj* auto-adaptatif

self-adhesive label étiquette auto-collante

self-analysis *n* autoscopie

self-biased *adj* autopolarisé

self-cancelling *adj* à rappel au zéro

self-capacitance capacité répartie; capacité propre

self-checking code code détecteur d'erreur(s)

self-clocked read lecture autorythmeuse

self-colouring (of insulation) coloration dans la masse de l'enveloppe

self-compensating *adj* complémenté

self-complementing *adj* autocomplémenteur

self-contained *adj* autonome; isolé; ~ **test**

program programme autonome de test

self-correcting *adj* autocorrecteur

self-destruct *v* autodégrader (s')

self-excitation *n* auto-excitation

self-excited transmitter émetteur auto-oscillateur

self-fluxing solder soudage autodécapante; soudure autodécapante

self-focussing fibre fibre selfoc

self-grip wrench pince de blocage; pince étau

self-healing *n* autocicatrisation; autorégénération; ~ **layer capacitor** condensateur multicouches auto-cicatrisant

self-holding contact contact d'automaintien

self-inductance inductance propre

self-induction *n* auto-induction; ~ **coefficient** coefficient de self-induction; ~ **coil** bobine self-induction

self-inductive *adj* selfique

self-inking paper (for dot matrix printer) papier autorévélateur

self-jamming *n* autobrouillage

self-latching *adj* (à) automaintien; (à) autoverrouillage

self-learning *adj* autodidacte

self-locking barb crantage; ~ **button** bouton à enclenchement; ~ **function** indesserrabilité

self-maintained discharge décharge autonome

self-modulation *n* automodulation

selfoc fibre fibre selfoc

self-organizing program programme auto-organisateur

self-oscillating system système auto-oscillant

self-oscillation *n* oscillation interne spontanée

self-oscillator *adj* auto-oscillateur

self-quenched counter tube tube compteur autocoupeur

self-quenching oscillator oscillateur commandé par oscillations de relaxation

self-relative addressing adressage auto-relatif

self-relocating *adj* autotranslatable

self-reset *v* autoconfigurer (s')

self-resetting loop boucle auto-restaurée

self-return button bouton à retour

self-starting *adj* auto-excité

self-sufficient *adj* autonome; alimentation séparée

self-supporting *adj* autoporteur; ~ **tower** pylône autostable

self-tapping screw vis autotaradeuse; vis à tôle; vis Parker

self-taught *adj* autodidacte

self-teaching *n* apprentissage proprioceptif

self-test(ing) *n* autocontrôle; autotest; test interne

self-test program programme de test de bon fonctionnement; programme spécifique de

S

test

self-whistling n autosifflement

self-wiping contact contact auto-nettoyant

selsyn n arbre électrique; selsyn; synchro

semantic content valeur sémantique

semi-attended station station semi-surveillée

semi-automatic call appel semi-dirigé; ~ **exchange** central semi-automatique; ~ **key** touche semi-automatique; ~ **operation** exploitation semi-automatique; ~ **service** service semi-automatique; ~ **switching system** système de commutation semi-automatique; ~ **traffic** trafic semi-automatique; ~ **wiring** câblage semi-automatique

semi-compelled multifrequency code code multifréquence semi asservi; ~ **signalling** (pulse) signalisation à impulsion

semiconductor n semiconducteur; ~ **source** (diode laser) source semiconductrice

semi-continuous signalling signalisation semicontinue

semi-custom adj prédiffusé; précaractérisé; ~ **circuit** circuit prédiffusé; réseau prédiffusé

semi-electronic switching commutation semiélectronique

semi-fault condition état de demi-faute

semi-finished product demi-produit

semi-restricted extension/station poste surveillé; poste supplémentaire contrôlé

semi-self-maintained discharge décharge semiautonome

semi-skilled worker/operative ouvrier spécialisé (OS)

senary (six-base) sénaire

send v émettre; envoyer; livrer; ~ **amplifier card** module d'amplification en émission; ~ **back** réémettre; ~ **buffer memory (SBM)** mémoire tampon émission (MTE); ~ **distortion** distorsion dans l'émission

sendee n destinataire

sender n envoyeur; distributeur; émetteur; transmetteur; enregistreur de départ; ~ **selector** chercheur enregistreur (CE); chercheur d'enregistrement

send filter filtre d'émission

sending n émission; envoi; ~ **end** extrémité d'émission; ~ **office** bureau émetteur; ~ **sensitivity** efficacité à émission; ~ **task** tâche émettrice; ~ **terminal** expéditeur

send last but one digit envoyez précédent; ~ **last but three digit** envoyez précédent l'antépénultime; ~ **last but two digit** envoyez antépénultime; ~ **level** niveau d'entrée; ~ **morse** (code) couiner; ~ **next digit** envoyez le chiffre suivant

send/receive émission-réception (E/R); ~ **switch** commutateur émission-réception

send reference equivalent équivalent à l'émission; ~ **register** registre d'émission

send-tone message message «émission de tonalités»

send transformer transformateur de sortie

send(ing)/transmitting amplifier amplificateur d'émission

seniority n ancienneté

senior staff cadre(s)

sense v analyser; capter; détecter; lire; ~ **finder** indicateur de lever de doute

sense-finding n lever de doute

sense input entrée logique; ~ **switch** aiguilleur; élément de contact; inverseur; ~ **voltage** tension de lever de doute; ~ **wire** fil de lecture

sensing n lecture; analyse; captage de données; détection; lever de doute; ~ **device** capteur; ~ **element** élément détecteur; ~ **element** (of strain gauge) élément transmetteur; ~ **relay** relais détecteur

sensitiser n sensibilisateur

sensitive component composant sensible

sensitivity n sensibilité; efficacité; champ d'action; ~ **analysis** analyse de sensibilité; ~ **coefficient** coefficient de sensibilité; ~ **control** commande de sensibilité

sensitivity-frequency characteristic caractéristique efficacité-fréquence

sensitivity of the artificial ear efficacité de l'oreille artificielle; ~ **test** épreuve de sensibilité; ~ **threshold** seuil de sensibilité; ~ **time control** régulateur de sensibilité temporisé

sensitized adj présensibilisé; ~ **paper** papier sensible

sensor n capteur; détecteur; palpeur; senseur; sonde; tête de lecture

sentence articulation netteté pour les phrases

sentinel n délimiteur; drapeau; indicateur; sentinelle; caractère fin de bloc

separately-excited adj (of DC motor) à excitation séparée

separately supplied alimentation séparée

separating character caractère de séparation

separation n écartement; dispersion; écart; isolement; rupture; sélection; triage; tri; ~ **circuit** circuit de triage de signaux; circuit écrêteur; ~ **filter** filtre séparateur; ~ **point** coupure; ~ **thread** filin

separator n délimiteur; banane; caractère de liaison; caractère de séparation; drapeau; écarteur; écran isolant; entretoise; intercalaire; sémaphore; sentinelle; séparateur

septenary (seven-base) septénaire

sequence n séquence; chaîne; filière; ordre; progression; rang; session; suite; ~ (of execution) ordre de passage; ~ **break**

rupture de séquence; ~ **call** conversation en série; ~ **controller** séquenceur; séquentiel; ~ **counter** compteur de séquence; ~ **error** erreur de classement; ~ **of signals** succession de signaux

sequencer *n* séquentiel; ordonnanceur

sequence switch séquentiel; combinateur; ~ **system** système d'ordonnance; ~ **timer** programmateur

sequencing *n* enchaînement; classement; ordonnancement; rangement; séquencement; mise en séquence; ~ **logic** logique de déroulement; ~ **program** programme d'enchaînement; ~ **zone** zone de chaînage

sequential *adj* séquentiel; combinatoire; progressif; ~ **file** fichier séquentiel; ~ **logic** logique séquentielle; ~ **memory test** test baladeur; ~ **monitoring** contrôle cyclique d'un émetteur; ~ **scanning** analyse non entrelacée; synthèse ligne par ligne non entrelacée

serial *adj* séquentiel; en série; ~ **access** accès séquentiel; accès en série; ~ **adder** additionneur en série; ~ **call** appel en chaîne; appel en série; chaînage; conversation en série; ~ **call forwarding** renvoi en cascade; ~ **computer** calculateur série; ~ **controller** coupleur série; ~ **data communications controller** sérialisateur de données; ~ **feed** alimentation colonne par colonne; ~ **interface** (RS 232) adaptation de liaison série R 232; ~ **interface adaptor** sérialisateur (sérialiseur); ~ **interface controller** coupleur V24; ~ **I/O controller** sérialisateur (sérialiseur); ~ **number** numéro d'ordre; nombre ordinal; numéro (N⁰.); numéro d'individualisation; ~ **output interface** sortie IEEE/RS 232

serial-parallel conversion transposition; transformation série/parallèle; ~ **converter** convertisseur série-parallèle; désérialiseur

serial-parallel/parallel-serial conversion transformation orthogonale

serial poll appel en série; appels en chaîne; ~ **printer** imprimante série; ~ **programmable interface** interface série programmable

serial-to-parallel conversion conversion série-parallèle

serial transmission transmission en série

series *n* série (en -); chaîne; chapelet; classe; séquence; suite; train; ~ (regulating) **transistor** transistor ballast; ~ **ballast** ballast; ~ **characteristic** caractéristique série; ~ **circuit** circuit échelonné; ~ **connection** montage en série; connexion en série; ~ **excitation** excitation en série

series-fed vertical aerial antenne verticale

isolée à la base

series index indice d'exploitation

series-loaded aerial antenne à charge série

series mounting embrochage

series-multiplex telegraph télégraphe multiplex en circuit échelonné

series-regulating device régulateur série

series regulation régulation linéaire; ~ **resistor** résistance série; ~ **resonance** résonance série

series-resonant circuit circuit à résonance en série; ~ **frequency** fréquence de résonance en série

series-T té série; T plan E

series winding enroulement en série; ~ **working** opération en circuit série

serif *n* empattement

seriousness *n* gravité

serrated *adj* cranté; cannelé; en dent de scie; strié; ~ **pulse** impulsion à crête fractionnée; top fractionné

server network réseau serveur; ~ **workstation** poste serveur

service *v* entretenir; ~ (information) **provider** fournisseur (d'information); prestataire; ~ (of interrupt) prendre en charge; **in** ~ en service (ES)

serviceability *n* aptitude au service; état de bon fonctionnement

serviceable *adj* utilisable

service aisle doigts gris; ~ **and equipment supplier** prestataire; ~ **arc** arc de service; ~ **area** zone desservie; zone de service; ~ **area diagram** carte de la zone de service; ~ **band** bande attribuée; ~ **bit** bit de service; chiffre de service; élément numérique de service; ~ **button** bouton de terre; ~ **call** communication de service; ~ **capacity** (of motor) puissance de sortie (W sous ohms); ~ **channel** canal de service; voie de service; ~ **circuit** ligne de service; chercheur d'auxiliaire; ~ **digit** élément numérique de service; ~ **earth** bouton de terre; ~ **exchange** échange standard; ~ **extension** poste de service; ~ **factor** facteur d'utilisation; ~ **flag** drapeau d'intervention; ~ **instruction** instruction de service; ~ **intercept** renvoi sur position de renseignements; ~ **language** langage de service; ~ **life** durée de vie; ~ **line** voie de service; ~ **observation** observation de service; ~ **provider** prestataire; serveur; ~ **request** demande de service; ~ **routine** utilitaire; ~ **selector** sélecteur de central; ~ **signal** signal de service

services rendered prestation(s)

service telegram télégramme de service; ~ **terminal** terminal de service; ~ **traffic**

S

trafic de service; ~ **TTY** machine à écrire (MAE); ~ **voltage** tension de service; ~ **wire** ligne de service; ~ **word** mot de service

servicing n prise en compte; entretien; gestion; intervention; prise en charge; traitement

serving area interface répartiteur de distribution

servo-amplifier circuit amplificateur d'asservissement

servo-control servodyne

servo-mechanism n appareil d'asservissement

session n vacation; échange

set v régler; afficher; armer; consigner; durcir; figer; mettre à un; porter; poser; positionner; prépositionner; provoquer; ~ (of memory partition) dimensionner; ~ (of flip-flop) enclencher; ~ (of bit) forcer (à); ~ (of event) positionner (un événement); ~ n ensemble; appareil; écriture; fourchette; groupe; jeu; lot; maquette; ~ adj activable; chargé; en signal; figé; fixe; ~ (of bit) présent; ~ **a currently-selected task** sélectionner une tâche; ~ **contact** contact travail; ~ **down** (of switch) baisser; ~ **file prefix** positionnement du préfixe fichier; ~ **highlight** n réglage intensité normale; ~ **log** aiguillage des messages système; ~ **low** porter au niveau bas; ~ **lowlight** réglage intensité réduite; ~ **mode (SM)** instauration de mode; ~ **noise** bruit propre; ~ **of consecutive subscriber numbers** fourchette d'abonnés; ~ **of two parameters** (pair) doublet; ~ **point** point de consigne (PC); valeur désirée; index; ~ **priority** établissement des priorités

set/reset bit forçage de bit à 1/0; ~ **latch** bascule (type) SR

set screw vis sans tête; vis à déformation; vis pointeau; ~ **status** mise à l'état; ~ **time** mise à jour date et heure

setting n réglage; affichage; ajustement; armement; calage; consigne; contexte; durcissement; écriture; enregistrement; figeage; forçage; mise à l'heure; point; pose; position; positionnement; ~ (of mode) instauration; ~ (of bit) **to** (state) **1 or 0** positionnement en 1/0; ~ **an interrupt** activation d'une interruption; ~ **compound** durcisseur; ~ **potentiometer** potentiomètre d'affichage; ~ **time** temps de basculement

setting-up n mise en place; établissement; tarage; (on keyboard) composition

setting-up signal signal de positionnement

settling n stabilisation; colmatage; ~ **period** durée de reprise; ~ **time** temps de reprise; temps de rétablissement

set to idle mettre au repos; ~ **to limiting value** réglé en butée; ~ **transmit state (STS)** transmission du message au lecteur de badge; ~ **up** v établir; apprêter; construire; créer

set-up time temps de prépositionnement; temps de préparation

set value point de consigne (PC); réglage du seuil; ~ **value adjuster** afficheur de consigne

seventeen-pin/seventeen-way connector connecteur dix-sept points

seven-unit code/alphabet alphabet à sept moments

sever v couper; casser; rompre

severance n coupure; rupture

severe adj grave; sévère

severely errored second seconde gravement erronée

severity n gravité

sextet n groupe de six bits (= hexet)

SF (s. shift forward); ~ (s. signal frequency)

SFERT speech level meter indicateur de volume du SFERT

SGR (s. select graphics rendition)

shackle n douille; étrier

shaded adj hachuré; grisé

shades of grey niveaux de gris

shading n teinte; ~ **correction** correction d'ombrage; ~ **scale** échelle de nuances

shadow cursor curseur (de suivi/de contrôle); ~ **factor** facteur de diffraction; facteur d'ombre

shadowgraph n projecteur de profil

shadow grid grille alignée; ~ **mask tricolour kinescope** tube trichrome à pénétration; ~ **printing** texte ombré; ~ **region** zone d'ombre; ~ **variable** variable fictive

shaft n arbre; bobine; broche; axe; ~ (of rotary switch) sabre; ~ **encoder** codeur de rotation

shake down n rôdage; (cruise) croisière d'essais

shallow adj peu profond; plat

shank n (of bolt) corps

shape v cambrer; mettre en forme; ~ n forme; ~ **analyser** analyseur de formes en relief

shaped-beam aerial antenne à diagramme directionnel spécifique; antenne à faisceau (con)formé

shaped loss affaiblissement non uniforme

shaper n conformateur d'impulsions; formateur; configurateur

shaping (of pulses, signals) mise en forme; ~ **rule** règle de formage

shared adj partagé; banalisé; en commun avec; partageable; ~ **access** accès commun; ~ **band** bande commune; ~ **channel**

S

onde commune; ~ **codecs** (system) codage par groupe; ~ **line** ligne partagée; ~ **logic** multiposte; ~ **memory** mémoire commune; ~ **network** réseau banalisé; ~ **private line service** service de voies de transmission louées et partagées par plusieurs entreprises; ~ **service line** ligne partagée à deux directions; ~ **storage** espace partageable
sharing n partage; répartition
sharp adj aigu; brutal; précis; ~ **cut-off filter** filtre coupure forte; ~ **edge** angle vif; coude brusque; ~ **edges to be rounded off** angles vifs abattus
sharpening of the minimum affûtage du minimum du relèvement
sharp resonance résonance aiguë; ~ **S** (German ß) signe allemand; ~ **tuning** accord aigu; accord pointu
shatter-proof incassable
shaving, (metal) ~ paille
shear n cisaillement
shearing n cisaillage
shear mode mode transversal
shears n pl ciseaux
shear test essai de cisaillement
sheath n gaine; armature; étui; fourreau
sheathed (direct strand) cable câble à fibre gainée
sheathing n enveloppe; souplisseau; gaine extérieure
shedding of traffic mise hors trafic
sheen n brillance
sheet n feuille; page; planche; ~ **metal enclosure** coffret métallique; ~ **metal screw** vis Parker
Sheffer stroke (function) NON ET (= ON/ET-NON)
shelf n alvéole; cadre; châssis; étagère; niveau; clayette; ~ **buffer** tampon d'alvéole
shelf-life durée de vie; durée de conservation; stockage; durée limite de stockage
shelf positioning frame cadre de positionnement des alvéoles
shelf-wiring n raccordement intra-alvéoles
shell n boîtier; chape; corps; enveloppe; module; ~ (of switch) plastron; ~ (of operating system) interpréteur de commandes; ~ (of lamp) verrine; ~ **size** diamètre; module; calibre
shelter n abri; cabine
shield v masquer; ~ n écran isolant; armature; blindage; gaine; grille; visière anti-chaleur
shielded cable câble armé; câble blindé; ~ **loop aerial** cadran blindé; ~ **pair** paire sous écran; ~ **wire** fil blindé
shield factor coefficient de protection électri-

que
shielding n mise sous écran
shift n déplacement; décalage; dérive; déviation; équipe; faction; glissement; inversion; migration; oscillation; passage; permutation; recalage; saut; vacation; variation; ~ (function) majuscule(s)
shifted adj décalé
shift forward (SF) précompensation d'écriture
shift-in (SI) n entrée; passer en code; accès aux caractères; ~ **code (SI)** code normal
shift key manipulateur de commutation
shift-lock n (upper case) corbeille haute; fonction haute permanente; ~ (mechanism) garde d'inversion; ~ **key** verrouillage corbeille haute; touche fugitive; ~ **keyboard** clavier avec garde d'inversion
shift network réseau de décalage; ~ **out** v passer hors code
shift-out (SO) n accès aux symboles graphiques; hors code; ~ **character** caractère de code spécial
shift register registre à décalage; accumulateur à décalage; enregistreur à décalage; registre à glissement; registre de décalage (cyclique); ~ **signal** signe de change
shim n cale (d'épaisseur); entretoise
shin n éclisse
ship-air guided missile engin radioguidé bord-air
shipborne adj embarqué; de bord; ~ **radar** radar de bord; ~ **radio** radio maritime; ~ **radio station** radiostation maritime; ~ **satellite communications system** système embarqué de communication avec un satellite
shipment n lot; lot de livraison; envoi
shipping company transitaire; ~ **costs** coûts de transport; ~ **note** bordereau de livraison (BL)
ship radar scanner antenne tournant embarquée
ship's company équipage; ~ **emergency transmitter** émetteur de détresse maritime
ship-ship inter-bâtiment; ~ **communication** radiocommunication bateau-bateau
ship-shore communications liaison maritime; ~ **radio service** service de radio côtier; ~ **working frequency** fréquence de travail bateau-côte
ship's radar radar de bord
ship-to-ship adj inter-bâtiment; ~ **channel** canal vocal vaisseau-vaisseau; ~ **signalling** échange entre bâtiments
shipyard n chantier naval
shock n choc
shock-proof adj insensible (aux chocs)
shock-resistant insensible aux chocs

S

shock wave onde de choc
shoe n sabot
shoebutton tube tube bouton
shooting n prise de vue
SHORAN (s. short-range navigation system)
shore-based radar radar côtier
shore station station terrienne côtière
short(-circuit) v mettre en court circuit; court-circuiter
short adj abrégé; allégé; réduit
shortage n manquant
short break interruption courte; ~ burst paquet bref; ~ callsign indicatif d'appel abrégé
short-circuit admittance admittance en court-circuit; ~ brake frein à court-circuit; ~ current courant de court-circuit
short-circuited rotor rotor en court-circuit
short-circuit impedance impédance en court circuit; ~ input capacitance in common source configuration capacité d'entrée, sortie en court-circuit, en source commune
short-circuit/open-circuit faults défauts inopérants électriques
short-circuit output capacitance in common-source configuration (drain-source short-circuited to AC) capacité de sortie, entrée en court-circuit, en source commune; ~ resistance résistance en court-circuit; ~ voltage tension de court-circuit
short-code dialling sélection abrégée; ~ dialling (central repertory) numérotation abrégée collective; ~ dialling (individual repertory) numérotation abrégée individuelle; ~ number numéro abrégé (NA); numéro simplifié
short cross-border circuit circuit de voisinage; ~ cycle bouclette
short-distance backscatter rétrodiffusion directe
short-duration pulse impulsion de courte durée
shorted turns court-circuit entre spires
shortened adj écourté; réduit
short-form (of catalogue) adj condensé; minimum
short format format court
short(-format) register registre réduit
short-haul adj à courte distance; local; ~ receiver récepteur de faible portée; ~ transmitter émetteur de faible portée
shorting n isolement; ~ link cavalier d'isolement; strap; ~ strip barrette de continuité
short-life memory (SL) mémoire courte durée
short-lived adj passager; court
short number numéro simplifié
short-path bearing azimut du petit arc
short-persistence screen écran à courte persistance

short pointed-tip shears ciseaux à becs courts pointus
short-profile adj à encombrement réduit
short-range adj local; ~ fading fading local; ~ field champ à courte distance; ~ navigation system (SHORAN) système de radionavigation SHORAN; ~ radar radar à courte distance; ~ receiver récepteur de faible portée
short real key (four byte real number) clé réel court; ~ wave (SW) ondes courtes (OC)
short-wave receiver récepteur à ondes courtes; ~ telegraphy télégraphie à ondes courtes; ~ transmitter émetteur à ondes courtes
shot blasting grenaillage; ~ effect effet de grenaille; effet de grêle; bruit de grenaille; ~ noise bruit de grenaille; bruit erratique; bruit gaussien
shoulder n bourrelet; ~ (of IDC terminal) bossage; ~ tap (to standby processor) prise de relais
show v montrer; afficher; indiquer; représenter
shredder n (of documents) destructeur
shrewd adj astucieux
shrinkage n retrait; ~ hole retassure
shrink fit ajustage serré; ajustement serré
shrinking n frettage
shroud n jupe; calotte; capot; capuchon; chemise; enveloppe; habillage; hauban
shrouded adj chemisé; surmoulé (enrobé de plastique); ~ chassis plug embase mâle; ~ plug fiche femelle
shunt v mettre une ligne en dérivation; court-circuiter; shunter; ~ n dérivation; cavalier; découplage; pontage; shunt; strap; ~ capacitor decoupling capacitor; by-pass capacitor condensateur d'isolement; ~ connection branchement en dérivation; connexion en parallèle; ~ current courant dérivé
shunted adj dérivé; doublé; en parallèle; ~ derivation excitation en dérivation
shunt-fed aerial antenne à alimentation en parallèle
shunt feed alimentation en parallèle
shunt-field adj à dérivation magnétique; ~ relay relais à dérivation magnétique; relais à champ de shunt; relais de dérivation
shunt generator génératrice shunt; ~ inductance self transversale
shunting n court-circuitage; dédoublement; effacement; shuntage
shunt motor moteur shunt; ~ ratio rapport du shunt; ~ resonance résonance shuntée; ~ switch commutateur de shuntage

S

shunt-T té parallèle; T plan E
shunt winding enroulement parallèle
shutdown n panne; arrêt; indisponibilité; interruption; protection
shut-down adj immobilisé
shutter n obturateur électrique; vantail
shutter(s) n persienne(s)
shuttle n navette
SI (s. speech interpolation); ⁓ (s. shift-in)
siccative sachet déshydratant
side n côté; bord; face
sideband n bande latérale; raie latérale; ⁓ attenuation affaiblissement de la bande latérale; ⁓ interference brouillage dû à une bande latérale; ⁓ only (SBO) bande latérale unique (BLU); ⁓ reduction réduction de la bande latérale; ⁓ splash diaphonie entre les bandes latérales; ⁓ suppression suppression de la bande latérale
side-brazed IC circuit intégré brasé
side-by-phantom far-end crosstalk télédiaphonie entre réel et fantôme
side circuit circuit combiné (double); circuit combinant; circuit composant; circuit fantôme double; circuit réel; circuit superfantôme
side-circuit capacitance capacité du circuit combinant
side cladding habillage latéral; ⁓ cutters pince coupante diagonale; pince flanc; ⁓ echo écho latéral
side-fed adj alimentation latérale
side frequency fréquence latérale; ⁓ lobe lobe latéral; lobe secondaire
side-lobe reduction réduction du lobe latéral
side-looking airborne radar radar à exploration latérale
side member longeron
side-panel n flasque
side plate joue; ⁓ screen écran latéral (sur borne)
side-stable relay relais bistable; relais à deux positions stables
side-tone n bruit parasite d'ambiance; effet local; friture; ⁓ reference equivalent équivalent de référence de l'effet local
side-to-side capacitance capacité entre deux paires; ⁓ crosstalk paradiaphonie; ⁓ far-end crosstalk télédiaphonie entre circuits combinants
side-track v (of traffic) dérouter
side view vue de profil
side-viewing angle angle de vision latérale
sidewall n flanc cloison
sideways adj sur chant
sifting n dépouillement
sight n visée

signal n signal; commande (cde); communication; donnée; impulsion; indication; information(s); mot; mot somme; signe
signal(ing) n signal(-isation)
signal (name) nom de l'information; ⁓ amplifier amplificateur de signal; régénérateur; ⁓ amplitude amplitude de signal; ⁓ analyser maquette d'essais; testeur; ⁓ analysis analyse de signaux; ⁓ attenuation affaiblissement du signal; ⁓ balance ratio rapport d'équilibre des signaux; ⁓ busy gestion occupé; ⁓ channel canal de signal; voie de signal; ⁓ clipping mutilation de signaux; ⁓ comparison tracking radioalignement à comparaison; ⁓ component composante d'un signal; élément de signal; ⁓ connection liaison logique; ⁓ content contenu de signal; ⁓ current courant de signal
signal-distance code (= Hamming distance) code cyclique
signal-distortion rate degré de distorsion d'un signal
signal duration durée de signal; ⁓ electrode plaque collectrice; ⁓ element élément de signal; ⁓ envelope enveloppe du signal; ⁓ field champ du signal; ⁓ frequency (SF) fréquence de signal; ⁓ generator générateur basse fréquence (BF); générateur de signaux; émetteur; ⁓ ground terre de signalisation; zéro logique; OBs; ⁓ ID nom de l'information; ⁓ imitation signalisation intempestive par imitation de signaux; ⁓ indicator contrôleur de signal; ⁓ information field domaine d'information de signalisation; ⁓ interpolation error erreur d'interpolation de signaux; ⁓ inversion inversion de signal; ⁓ lamp lampe témoin; indicateur lumineux; ⁓ lamp panel herse
signalled adj (station) appelé
signaller n signaleur
signal level niveau de signal
signalling n signalisation; appelant; envoi; numérotation au clavier; relation; ⁓ adaptor group groupe adaptateur de signalisation; ⁓ battery batterie de signalisation; ⁓ button bouton de signalisation; ⁓ byte octet de signalisation; ⁓ capacity capacité de signalisation; ⁓ channel voie de gestion; ⁓ circuit circuit de sortie; ⁓ code code de signalisation; ⁓ converter signaleur; ⁓ current courant de signalisation; courant de travail; ⁓ earth terre de signalisation; ⁓ equipment signaleur à basse fréquence; ⁓ fault appel de dérangement; ⁓ frequency fréquence de signalisation; ⁓ lamp lampe de signalisation; ⁓ limit limite de signalisation; ⁓ link liaison de signalisa-

S

tion; ~ **link blocking** (common channel) blocage d'un canal sémaphore; ~ **message** message de signalisation; ~ **module** signaleur; ~ **multiplex** multiplex de signalisation; ~ **over subscriber loop** signalisation sur la ligne d'abonné; ~ **path** trajet de signalisation; ~ **point (SP)** point sémaphore (PS); ~ **pre-processor** préprocesseur de signalisation; ~ **processor** gestion de la signalisation; ~ **pulse** impulsion de commutation; ~ **receiver** récepteur auxiliaire de signalisation; ~ **relay set** signaleur; ~ **security unit** unité de défense de signalisation; ~ **sender monitor** unité de gestion des distributeurs; ~ **speed/rate** vitesse d'émission télégraphique; ~ **subsystem** chaîne de signalisation; chaîne(s) de positionnement(s) et de faute(s); ~ **system** système de signalisation; ~ **time slot** intervalle de temps de signalisation; ~ **transfer point (STP)** point de transfert sémaphore (PTS); ~ **unit** coffret de commande; signaleur; unité de commande; ~ **wire** fil de signalisation

signal loss affaiblissement du signal; ~ **message** message de signalisation; ~ **mixer unit** unité de distribution de signaux; ~ **noise** bruit de signal; ~ **output current** valeur absolue du courant de sortie du signal; ~ **phase** phase de signal; ~ **plate** anode collectrice; plaque collectrice; ~ **potential** tension d'information; ~ **probability** probabilité de signal; ~ **processing** traitement des signaux; ~ **processing subsystem** logique d'acquisition; ~ **processing unit** logique d'acquisition; ~ **receiver** récepteur de signaux

signal-recording telegraphy télégraphie par enregistrement des signaux

signal relay relais de signalisation; ~ **repeater** répétiteur de signal; ~ **repertoire** richesse sémantique; ~ **return** réflexion du signal; ~ **routing** acheminement du signal; ~ **sender** émetteur de signalisation; ~ **separator** séparateur de signaux; ~ **shaper** conformateur de signaux

signal-shaping amplifier amplificateur conformateur de signaux

signal source générateur; ~ **space diagram** diagramme vectoriel; ~ **spill-over** débordement de signal; ~ **splitter** répartiteur de signaux; ~ **spread** distribution de signaux

signal-strength meter S-mètre

signal-structure diagram constellation

signal tail queue de signal

signal-to-crosstalk ratio écart diaphonique

signal to far-end crosstalk ratio écart télédiaphonique

signal-to-hum ratio rapport signal sur ronflement

signal-to-near-end crosstalk écart paradiaphonique

signal-to-noise ratio (S/N) rapport signal-bruit; écart entre signal et bruit; rapport B (bruit); S + B/B (signal + bruit/bruit)

signal-to-quantizing noise ratio rapport signal à distorsion totale; rapport signal à bruit de quantification

signal train sématème; ~ **transfer point (STP)** point de transfert de signaux; ~ **transfer time** temps de transfert des signaux; ~ **transition** transition de signal; ~ **transmission area** zone d'envoi; ~ **transmission medium** liaison d'information; ~ **transmission path** voie de signal; ~ **unit** trame sémaphore; ~ **unit alignment** alignement des trames sémaphores; ~ **voltage** tension de signal; tension d'information; ~ **wave** code de travail; ~ **waveform** gabarit; diagramme; ~ **waveform element** élément de forme d'onde du signal; ~ **winding(s)** enroulement de commande

signature *n* visa; empreinte (de fonction)

sign bit bit de signe; ~ **character** caractère de signe

signed field zone algébrique

significance *n* poids

significant condition (mark/space) état significatif; ~ **condition of a modulation** état significatif d'une modulation; ~ **condition of a restitution** état significatif d'une restitution; ~ **figure** chiffre significatif; ~ **instant** instant significatif; ~ **interval** intervalle significatif; ~ **national number** numéro national significatif; ~ **number** numéro significatif

sign-off *v* clore; quitter; ~ *n* fin du travail; fermeture; rupture de contact

sign-on *n* appel d'une application; prise de contact; accueil; bannière; procédure d'échange; connexion; ~ **file** fichier d'inscription; ~ **form** grille d'accueil; grille d'émargement; ~ **procedure** procédure d'appel-réponse

sign selection sélection de signes

silent fuse cartouche fusible sans percuteur; ~ **period** intervalle de silence; période de silence; ~ **zone** zone de silence

silica *n* silice

silicon *n* silicium; ~ **compound** silane; ~ **conductive keypad** clavier à nappe élastomère

silicon-controlled rectifier (SCR) diode redresseur au silicium; redresseur à gâchette

silicone rubber élastomère

silicon gate grille au silicium; ~ **rectifier**

redresseur à silice
silk binder filin en soie
silkscreened pad pavé sérigraphié
SIL package boîtier plat (à sorties unilatérales)
silver-plated *adj* argenté
simple tone fréquence pure
simplex *adj* à l'alternat; simplex; unidirectionnel; communication alternée dans les deux sens; ~ (operation) alternat unidirectionnel; ~ **call** communication unidirectionnelle; ~ **channel** voie unidirectionnelle; ~ **circuit** circuit approprié; circuit simplex; ligne de transmission unidirectionnelle; ~ **communication** (link) liaison simplex; ~ **connection** connexion unidirectionnelle; ~ **line** ligne unidirectionnelle; ~ **operation** exploitation simplex; ~ **repeater** répéteur unidirectionnel
simulated *adj* fictif; ~ **fault measurement** pseudo-tarage; ~ **line** complément de ligne
simulator *n* simulateur; (cable) ~ complément de cable
simultaneous broadcast (SB) radiodiffusion par réseau d'émetteurs; ~ **broadcasting transmitters** émetteurs sur ondes égales; ~ **facsimile transmission** transmission multiple d'images; ~ **frequency and amplitude modulation (FAM)** modulation de fréquence et d'amplitude simultanée; ~ **operation** opération en simultané; traitement parallèle
sine *n* sinus; ~ *adj* sinusoïdal; ~ **bar** barre de sinus; ~ **galvonometer** boussole de sinus
sine-squared pulse impulsion en sinus carré
sine wave sinusoïde
sine-wave generator générateur d'ondes sinusoïdales; ~ **input** entrée d'onde sinusoïdale
singing *n* amorçage d'oscillations; oscillation interne spontanée; oscillation parasite; ~ **current** courant inverse; ~ **margin** marge d'amorçage; ~ **path** parcours d'écho; voie des courants de réaction; ~ **point** point d'amorçage des oscillations; ~ **suppressor** suppresseur de réaction
single access accès simple
single-access satellite satellite à simple accès
single-acting *adj* à simple effet
single-address instruction instruction à une adresse
single-armature converter convertisseur rotatif à induit unique
single-board computer automate de gestion
single-card guide guide carte simple
single-channel analyser analyseur monocanal; ~ **connector** connecteur monovoie
single-channel-per-carrier (SCPC) équipement de transmission par porteuse mono-

voie
single-channel transmission transmission à monocanal
single chip puce seule
single-coil relay relais simple
single-component signal signal à un élément
single conductor (of wire pair) fil unitaire
single-conductor cable câble monofilaire; câble monoconducteur
single contact contact simple
single-control bistable trigger circuit bascule bistable à une entrée
single-copy shot autocopie
single-core conductor conducteur monobrin; ~ **wire** fil simple
single crystal monocristal
single-current mark élément unitaire de signal télégraphique; ~ **message channels of a quadruplex telegraph circuit** canaux de communications à courant simple d'un circuit télégraphique quadruplex; ~ **telegraphy** télégraphie à courant simple; ~ **transmission** transmission par courant simple
single-density (of disk) simple densité
single digital signal signal numérique unique
single-ended amplifier amplificateur asymétrique; amplificateur symétrique série; ~ **control** commande locale; ~ **cord** circuit monocorde
single-entry book-keeping unigraphie
single-fee metering comptage simple
single-fibre connector monoconnecteur
single-frequency *adj* fréquence singulaire; monochromatique; ~ **noise** bruit sur une seule fréquence; ~ **operation** exploitation sur une fréquence; ~ **signalling** signalisation monofréquence; signalisation à une fréquence
single housing monobloc
single-in-line package (SIP) boîtier plat (à sorties unilatérales)
single-layer *adj* monocouche; ~ **coil** bobine à une couche
single-line diagram plan unifilaire; ~ **spacing** simple interligne
single-mode fibre fibre monomode
single-needle system galvanomètre
single-pass compiler compilateur monopasse
single-phase *adj* monophase; ~ **current** courant monophasé
single ply (of cable wires) tordon
single-pole *adj* monopolaire; ~ **double-throw switch (SPDT)** va-et-vient; commutateur unipolaire à deux directions; ~ **plug** fiche monopolaire
single power supply monotension
single-processor mode simplex; ~ **system**

S

système monoprocesseur

single programming monoprogrammation

single-pulse circuit monocoup réglable

single shift 2 (SS2) accès aux accents et aux symboles spéciaux

single-shot *adj* monocoup; pas à pas (PAP); à coup unique; ~ **trigger circuit** circuit de déclenchement à coup unique; circuit de déclenchement à cycle simple

single sideband (SSB) bande latérale unique (BLU)

single-sideband adaptor adaptateur à bande latérale unique; ~ **modulation** modulation à bande latérale unique; ~ **reception** réception à bande latérale unique; ~ **suppression** suppression de bande latérale unique; ~ **transmission** émission à bande latérale unique

single-sided *adj* simple face; unilatéral

single-speaker system monolocuteur

single square-wave voltage tension simple d'onde carrée

single-stage index table table à accès direct

single-step relay relais pas à pas; relais progresseur

single-stranded wire fil de câblage monobrin

single-stream processor processeur file

single-stroke bell sonnerie à coups espacés

single-switch call communication de transit

single target objectif simple

single-terminal *adj* monoposte

single-throw switch commutateur à une direction

single trace (of oscilloscope) monocourbe

single-tube *adj* monocoaxial

single-valued *adj* univoque

single-wire *adj* monofilaire; ~ **aerial** antenne unifilaire; antenne à fil unique; ~ **cable** câble monofilaire

sink *n* bloc récepteur; destinataire; circuit absorbant; ~ **current** courant absorbé; intensité absorbée

sinking *n* réception

sink voltage tension de drain

sinter *v* (of lamp filament) concrétionner

sintered anode anode frittée

sintering *n* frittage

sinusoid *n* sinusoïde

sinusoidal current courant sinusoïdal; ~ **oscillation** infléchissement continu

SIP (s. single-in-line package)

siphon recorder enregistreur à siphon

site *n* chantier; emplacement; implantation; site; ~ **documentation** guide d'affaire; ~ **management department** service chantier

sitrep (s. situation report)

situated on full-word boundaries situés sur des frontières de mots

situation report (sitrep) tableau de bord; compte-rendu (CR); ~ **vacant** poste à pourvoir

six-bit byte groupe de six bits; hexet

six-level (wire) **multiple** sixte

six-sided case parallélépipède

sixteen-state quadrature-amplitude modulation modulation seize QAM (16 QAM)

size *v* dimensionner; ~ *n* grandeur; calibre; contenance; encombrement; format; jauge; jaugeur; module; taille; capacité; ~ **of disk storage block** (in sectors) granulé (grandeur du bloc transféré entre disque et mémoire centrale)

sizing *n* ensimage; ~ **parameter** paramètre de dimensionnement

sizzling *n* grésillement; friture

skeletal code code paramétrable

skeleton *adj* réduit; ~ **diagram** synoptique

sketch *n* croquis; ébauche; canevas; ~ **pad** feuille de dessin

skew *v* biaiser; ~ *n* décalage; défaut de parallélisme; déréglage; désalignement; distorsion asymétrique; distorsion biaise; distorsion de déviation; distorsion d'image; distorsion dissymétrique; distorsion en parallélogramme; distorsion oblique; obliquité; retard; ~ (of character) inclinaison; ~ (of tape) mise en travers; ~ (of disk tracks) vissage inter-pistes; vissement inter-pistes; ~ **(adjustment)** correction de dentelures

skewed *adj* détourné; excentré; penché

skiatron *n* skiatron; tube à trace sombre; tube cathodique à écran absorbant

skid *n* sabot

skill *n* compétence; connaissance; maîtrise

skill(s) savoir-faire

skilled *adj* expérimenté; qualifié; ~ **operative** ouvrier professionnel (OP); ~ **technician** personnel compétent

skillet *n* creuset

skin effect effet de peau; effet pelliculaire; ~ **hardness** dureté superficielle

skinning pliers pince à dénuder

skip *n* (of page) saut; ~ **area** zone de silence; zone sautée; ~ **distance** étendue de la zone de silence radio; distance de saut; ~ **keying** sous-division de la fréquence de répétition d'impulsions; ~ **routing** acheminement hors hiérarchie; ~ **zone** zone de silence

skirt *n* collerette; jupe

skirting board plinthe

skull-and-crossbones (danger symbol) tête de mort

sky wave onde spatiale; onde d'espace; onde ionosphérique

SL (s. sampling level); ~ (s. short-life

memory)

slab *n* groupe de douze bits; galette

slack *adj* mou; lâche

slacken off desserrer

slack period période creuse

slant *n* barre oblique; ~ *adj* oblique

slanted *adj* penché

slash *n* barre oblique

slashed zero (∅) zéro barré

slave card carte fille; ~ **clock** horloge asservie (HA)

slaved *adj* asservi

slave ground station station terrestre asservie; ~ **mode** mode asservi

slave/satellite transmitter transpondeur

slave station station asservie; ~ **tube** tube cathodique asservi

sleeve *n* chemise; enveloppe; gaine; jaquette; manche; manchon; symétriseur; ~ (of jack) corps; ~ (of disk) pochette; ~ **conductor** troisième fil

sleeve-control cord circuit cordon de connexion avec troisième fil; ~ **switchboard** commutateur manuel à supervision par troisième fil

sleeve dipole antenne à jupe; ~ **dispenser** distributeur de manchons

sleeveless *adj* nu

sleeve wire (S-wire) troisième fil; fil de blocage; fil de corps; fil de douille; fil de maintien; fil d'état

sleeving *n* manchonnage; dégraissage; ~ **pliers** pince à manchonner

slenderness (ratio) élancement

slew *n* déséquilibre; pente; saut

slewed *adj* déréglé; ~ **aerial** antenne décalée; ~ **printing** impression de travers

slew rate (SVOAV) pente moyenne du signal de sortie; vitesse de variation de la tension de sortie; temps de montée; taux de balayage; pente maximale du signal de sortie

SLIC (s. subscriber line interface circuit)

slice *n* tranche; lame; plaquette; rondelle; segment; secteur

slide(r) *n* coulisseau; glissière

slide attenuator atténuateur rectiligne

slide-back voltmeter voltmètre à lampe

slide bar guide

slide contact connector connecteur à contacts glissants

slide-on (of terminal) soyage

slider *n* curseur; ~ **pot** potentiomètre rectiligne

slide valve tiroir

slideway *n* coulisseau; glissière

sliding *n* glissement; ~ *adj* descendant; ~ **clamp** écrou coulissant; ~ **contact** prise

sabot; contact glissant; curseur; frotteur; ~ **fit** ajustement glissant; ~ **fixture** brancard

sliding-scale *adj* dégressif

slim-line *adj* étroit

slip *n* glissement; dérive; saut

slip-delete saut en écriture

slip-joint wire cutters pince coupante articulée

slip knot nœud coulant

slip-on filter filtre interchangeable

slippage *n* décalage

slipped band multiplage décalé; ~ **bank** banc décalé

slip regulator rhéostat de glissement (rotorique)

slip-repeat doublement en écriture

slip ring bague collectrice

slip-ring motor moteur à bague

slit *adj* fendu

slitting cord cordonnet

SLM (s. sound-level meter)

slope *n* pente; angle; côte; courbe; gradient; inclinaison; orientation; ~ **conductance** pente

sloped *adj* oblique

slope resistance résistance en courant alternatif; résistance interne différentielle

sloping *adj* penché

sloping-wire aerial antenne à fils inclinés

slot *n* fente; ajour; créneau; découpe; dégagement; emplacement; encoche; évidement; fenêtre; grille; intervalle; lumière; rainure; trame; ~ (in PCB frame) case; ~ **aerial** antenne à fente(s); ~ **aligner** dispositif de verrouillage de trame; ~ **array** réseau d'antennes à fentes; réseau de fentes rayonnantes

slot-fed dipole doublet symétrisé par coaxial fendu

slot radiator fente rayonnante

slot-ripple frequency fréquence de denture

slotted *adj* cannelé; ~ (corrugated) **waveguide** jonc rainuré; ~ **cheesehead drive screw** vis C/P fendue

slotted-core cable câble à jonc rainuré

slotted cylinder cylindre à fentes

slotted-cylinder aerial antenne à cylindre fendu

slotted-guide aerial antenne guide à fente

slotted-head screw vis à tête fendue

slotted light-shield bonnet à trèfle; ~ **line** banc de mesure; ligne fendue de mesure; ~ **measuring section** ligne fendue de mesure; banc de mesure; ~ **opto-switch** fourche opto(-électronique); ~ (V-grooved) **cylindrical former** câble à structure cylindrique rainurée

slow-acting relay relais temporisé; relais à

S

action différée; relais à action lente; relais à attraction retardée

slow blinking clignotant lent

slow-blow fuse fusible temporisé; fusible retardé

slow-down *n* croissance en ralentissement

slow drift glissement graduel de la fréquence; ~ **driver (SDR)** distributeur lent (DL); ~ **interrupted ringing** sonnerie lente; ~ **release** relâchement différé; relâchement retardé; rupture retardée; ~ **restart** redémarrage lent; ~ **time constant** constante d'intégration lente

SLS (s. subsriber line scanner)

sludge *n* salissure; calamine

slug *n* noyau plongeur; manchon; noyau; bague

slugged *adj* chemisé; ~ **coil** bobine à noyau mobile; ~ **relay** relais chemisé; relais bagué

slurred speech paroles brouillées

SM (s. set mode)

small-object detector appareil de détection de petits objets

small-scale mechanical engineering petite mécanique; ~ **model** modèle réduit

small-signal capacitance capacité différentielle; ~ **coupling coefficient** facteur de couplage pour signaux faibles; ~ **depth of velocity modulation** taux de modulation de vitesse pour signal faible; ~ **value of the short-circuit input impedance** impédance d'entrée (sortie en court circuit)

small wedge lamp Liliput courte

smart card carte à mémoire; carte futée; ~ **card PIN code authenticator** (personal identification number) certificateur; ~ **terminal** terminal (inter)actif; ~ **terminal supervisor** régie intelligente

smear *n* distorsion d'image

smearing *n* usure

S-meter *n* S-mètre

smooth-bodied conductor câble lisse (clos)

smoothed bar barre adoucie; ~ **current** courant filtré

smoother *n* filtre de redresseur

smoothing *n* calcul approché; filtrage; lissage; ~ **capacitor** condensateur de filtrage; condensateur de filtration; condensateur de recalage; ~ **choke** self de filtrage; bobine de filtrage; inductance de filtrage; ~ **circuit** circuit de filtrage; filtre; ~ **current** courant de filtrage; ~ **factor** taux de modulation; ~ **filter** filtre électrique

smooth jacket enveloppe lisse; ~ **off** araser; ~ **the way for** faciliter; ~ **traffic** trafic régularisé; ~ **transition** passage délicat

smudge *n* salissure

smudge-proof *n* antimaculage

smudging *n* maculage

S/N (s. signal-to-noise ratio)

snake *n* câble de traction; ~ **column** colonne journalistique; colonne serpentine

snap *n* (action of contacts) rupture brusque

snap(-head) rivet rivet goutte de suif

SNAP (s. standard network access protocol)

snap-back diode diode de commutation rapide

snap fastener attache rapide; vis à baïonette

snap-fitting *n* encliquetage

snap-in card carte clic

snap-off diode diode de commutation rapide

snap-on connector sucette

snap ring clips

snapshot *n* cliché de faute; prise de vue; trace; ~ *adj* instantané; sélectif

snap(-shot condition) état instantané

snapshot dump sauvegarde sélective; vidage par instant; ~ **printout** impression sélective; ~ **(trace) program** programme d'analyse sélective

snap switch interrupteur à action brusque; contact à commande mécanique (rupture brusque); microrupteur; minirupteur

sneak *adj* intempestif; ~ **current** courant de fuite

SNF (s. system noise figure)

sniffer *n* (nitrous explosive detector) renifleur; reniflard

snipe-nose pliers pince à becs demi-ronds

snipping *n* cisaillage

snips *n pl* ciseaux; pince

snooper *n* mouchard

snoop file fichier mouchard

snowfall attenuation affaiblissement dû à la chute de neige

snubber circuit réseau d'aide à la commutation (RDC); réseau de protection (RDC)

SO (s. shift out)

S.O.A. (s. safe operating area)

soak *n* saturation magnétique; ~ (of dielectric) polarisation

soakage *n* polarisation diélectrique

soaked *adj* humecté

soak test essai de vieillissement; rôdage; ~ **testing** déverminage; vieillissement accéléré

socket *n* baïonette; alvéole; culot; douille; embase (connecteur fixe); fiche femelle; monture; prise fixe; prise mâle; support; prise de courant (PC)

socket-head cap screw vis CHc (cylindrique à six pans creux)

socket strip barre

sodium hydroxide soude

soft copy affichage écran; copie fugitive; image fugitive; inscription fugitive; ~ **error**

S

faute logicielle; erreur de programmation; erreur de transmission bénigne; faute programmée; ~ **fail** blocage doux; ~ **hyphen** tiret de coupure de mot; ~ **solder** soudure étain-plomb; ~ **start-up** démarrage progressif; ~ **ticket** ticket de facturation

software *n* logiciel; aides de programmation; programmerie; ~ **address** adresse logicielle; ~ **clock** horloge logicielle; ~ **control** commande par logiciel

software-controlled programmé; calibré à partir du logiciel

software-defined reconfigurable

software design ingénierie informatique; ~ **engineeering workshop** atelier de génie logiciel (AGL); ~ **error** erreur logique; ~ **file** dossier des programmes; ~ **interrupt** interruption logique; ~ **library** bibliothèque de programmes; ~ **module** brique de logiciel; ~ **package** ensemble logiciel; ~ **partitioning** structure du logiciel; ~ **routine** automate détaillé; moulinette; ~ **status code** indice de fabrication; ~ **table** table logiciel

SOH (s. start of heading)

solder (joint) soudure

solderability *n* brasabilité; soudabilité

solderable lacquer vernis soudable; ~ **wire** fil soudable

soldered *adj* soudé; posé au soudage; ~ **wire** fil soudé

solder flux colophane

soldering *n* soudage; ~ **frame** cadre de soudage; ~ **iron** fer à souder; chane; ~ **iron rest** support fer à souder; ~ **pot** picot; ~ **tag** patte à souder

solderless connection connexion sans soudure; ~ **insertion** insertion sans soudure (ISS); ~ **pin** broche à insertion sans soudure

solder mask vernis épargne (VE); ~ **pot** pot de soudure; ~ **resist** vernis épargne (VE); ~ **shroud** cône de soudure; ~ **side** (of PCB) face soudure (FS); côté soudure; côté verso; ~ **spill** (of connector) languette à souder; picot à souder; ~ **stick** baguette de soudure; ~ **tail** patte à souder; ~ **wire** fil de soudure

sole agency représentation exclusive; ~ **agent** concessionnaire exclusif; ~ **discretion** entière discrétion

solenoid *n* électro-aimant; solenoïde

sole plate plaque d'assise; plaque de base; socle

solid *adj* massif (massive); plein; rigide; ~ **angle** angle solide

solid-conductor cable câble monobrin

solid earth terre franche; ~ **line** ligne en trait plein; ~ **printing** impression trait; ~ **radiation pattern** diagramme solide de rayonnement; ~ **shaft** arbre sorti

solid-state (of relay) hermétique; ~ **circuit** circuit statique; circuit solide; ~ **circuitry** miniaturisation; ~ **components** composants solides; ~ **device** dispositif transistorisé; dispositif à semiconducteurs; ~ **relay** relais statique

solidus *n* barre oblique

solid wire fil plein; conducteur rigide

solvent cleaning nettoyage au solvant; ~ **still** distilleuse

SOM (s. start of message)

sone (unit of loudness) sonie (sone)·

sonic boom détonation balistique; ~ **delay line** ligne à retard (LAR); ligne acoustique (LA)

sophisticated *adj* évolué; complexe; confirmé; élaboré; performant; poussé

sort *n* tri

sorter *n* trieuse; aiguille de tri; ~ **pocket** case de sélection

sorter-reader trieuse-liseuse

sort generator générateur de tri

sorting machine trieuse

sort key critère de tri; clé de tri; indicatif de tri

SOS team SAMU (service d'aide médicale d'urgence) (code 15 en France)

sound *n* son; ~ **analyser** analyseur de son; ~ **articulation** netteté pour les sons; ~ **barrier** mur du son; ~ **box** lecteur acoustique

sound-carrier frequency fréquence porteuse (de) son

sound effect effet sonore

sound-energy density densité d'énergie acoustique; ~ **flux** puissance vocale instantanée

sounder *n* parleur

sound field champ acoustique; ~ **head** lecteur de son; ~ **intensity** intensité acoustique; ~ **level** volume acoustique; niveau du son

sound-level meter (SLM) sonomètre (objective)

sound locator appareil de repérage acoustique; ~ **management** (structures) moyens d'exploitation rigoureuse; ~ **operator** opérateur de son; ~ **particle velocity** vitesse acoustique; vitesse d'une particule; ~ **power** puissance acoustique

sound-powered telephone téléphone autogénérateur

sound-pressure level niveau de pression acoustique

sound programme circuit circuit pour transmission radiophonique

sound-proof booth niche insonorisée; studio sourd

S

sound-proofing *n* insonorisation; isolation phonique

sound quality qualité du son; ~ **reception** réception à l'écoute; ~ **recorder** enregistreur sonore; appareil d'enregistrement; enregistreur de son; ~ **recording** enregistrement du son

sound-recording cubicle cabine technique (de prise de son)

sound reproduction reproduction de son; ~ **spectrum** spectre acoustique; ~ **track** trace acoustique; ~ **transmission** transmission sonore; ~ **wave** onde acoustique

source *v* fournir; ~ *n* source; amenée; appelant; demandeur; d'origine; émetteur; origine; tributaire; ~ **address** adresse source; ~ **current** courant fourni (par les alimentations); courant (continu) de source; ~ **document** bordereau de perforation; document de base; feuille de programmation; feuille mécanographique; ~ **error** erreur d'émetteur; ~ **file** fichier origine; ~ **impedance** impédance d'entrée; ~ **language** langage d'origine; ~ **line** ligne de code; ~ **module** module source; ~ **of fault** incriminé; ~ **resistance** résistance interne

source-sink relationship relation source-collecteur

source voltage (V$_{SS}$) tension de source

SP (s. signalling point)

space *n* espace; caractère blanc; caractère inactive; condition zéro (0); emplacement; état A; place; repos; zéro; zone; ~ (of dial code) creux; ~ (void) un blanc; ~ **bar** barre d'espacement; ~ **character** caractère espace; ~ **charge** charge spatiale; charge d'espace

space-charge density densité de charge d'espace; ~ **region** zone de charge spatiale; zone de charge d'espace; ~ **wave** onde de charge d'espace

space communications service service de communication en espace; ~ **condition** (à l')état fermé; ~ **current** courant d'espace

spaced-aerial direction finder radiogoniomètre à antennes espacées

spaced aerials combinaison d'antennes antifading

spaced-carrier operation exploitation à porteuses distinctes

spaced-frame aerial cadran sans effet de nuit

space-division concentration concentration spatiale

space(-division) stage étage de commutation spatiale multiplex

space-division switching commutation électronique spatiale; aiguillage spatial; commu-

tation par répartition dans l'espace; commutation spatiale

spaced-loop aerial cadran sans effet de nuit; ~ **direction finder** radiogoniomètre à cadres espacés

space-domain *adj* spatial

space-erectable aerial antenne déployable dans l'espace

space-multiplex switching commutation spatiale multiplexée

space occupied encombrement; ~ **out** *v* aérer

spacer *n* entretoise; bague; butée; cale (c. d'épaisseur); rondelle d'éloignement; ~ **key** bouton d'espacement

space segment (for telegraph transmission) secteur spatial (en télégraphie); ~ **shuttle** navette spatiale; ~ **signal** signal d'espace; ~ **station** station orbitale; ~ **suit** scaphandre

space-switch control memory mémoire de commande spatiale

space switching commutation spatiale

space-switching card opérateur double aiguillage spatiale

space-time concentrator concentrateur spatio-temporel; ~ **junction (S-T)** jonction multiplex de sortie (JMS)

space wave onde d'espace

spacing *n* espacement; écart d'isolement; écartement; entr'axe; entre-axe; intervalle; isolement; pas; pas d'implantation; ~ **between transmitters** distance entre émetteurs; ~ **current** courant de repos; ~ **error** erreur d'espacement; erreur octantale; ~ **key** bouton d'espacement; ~ **signal** signal d'espacement; ~ **washer** canon; ~ **wave** onde de repos; onde stationnaire; signal de repos

spade lug plot à fourches; ~ **terminal** cosse à fourches; plot à fourches; cosse à visser

spaghetti-sheathed *adj* sous souplisseau (s/s)

span *n* plage; distance; étendue; fourchette; pont; portée

spanner *n* clé; clef; ~ **wrench** clé à ergot

spanning tree arbre

spar *n* longeron; couple

spare *n* élément de rechange; pièce (pce); ~ *adj* de réserve; de secours; inutilisé; libre; non utilisé; de rechange; ~ **bit** bit de réserve; ~ **line** ligne non affectée; ~ **order-wire channel** voie de service de réserve; ~ **part** pièce détachée; pièce de rechange; ~ **parts** lot de maintenance

spares catalogue catalogue de pièces détachées

spark *n* étincelle; ~ **arrester** pare-étincelles; ~ **discharge** décharge par étincelles; ~ **gap** éclateur à étincelles

sparkle *v* scintiller
spark-over *n* amorçage
spark-over of a lightning conductor amorçage d'un parafoudre
spark quench pare-étincelles
spark-quench (circuit) circuit anti-étincelles; circuit éliminateur d'étincelles; étouffeur d'étincelles
spatter *n* éclaboussure; projection
SPC (s. stored program control)
SPDT (s. single-pole double-throw switch)
speak *v* parler
speak-back circuit émetteur d'ordres
speaker cabinet enceinte acoustique; ~ **circuit** circuit de service
speaker-phone facility écoute amplifiée (EA); mains libres
speaking and ringing key clé d'appel et de conversation; ~ **circuit** circuit téléphonique; ~ **clock** horloge parlante; service de l'heure; ~ **distance** distance de conversation; ~ **key** clé de conversation; ~ **pair** fils de conversation; ~ **wire** fil de conversation
special (pictorial) **symbol** pictogramme; ~ **case** dérogation; ~ **character** caractère additionnel; ~ **code selector** sélecteur auxiliaire; ~ **concession** dérogation; ~ **feature** service supplémentaire
special-purpose *adj* débanalisé
special service service spécial; ~ **subscriber line** abonné discriminé; ~ **subscriber line equipment** joncteur discriminé; ~ **symbol** graphisme spécial
specific acoustic impedance impédance acoustique intrinsèque; ~ **acoustic reactance** réactance acoustique intrinsèque; ~ **address** adresse absolue
specification data information par attributs
specifications *n pl* cahier de charges (CdC)
specific code code absolu; ~ **conductivity** conductivité; ~ **emissivity** pouvoir émissif spécifique d'une surface; ~ **gravity** densité relative; ~ **humidity** rapport de mélange; ~ **inductive capacity** pouvoir inducteur spécifique; ~ **ionization coefficient** coefficient spécifique d'ionisation; ~ **resistance** résistance spécifique
specified lower limit limite inférieure de la spécification (LIS); ~ **upper limit** limite supérieure de la spécification (LSS)
specifier *n* descripteur
specify *v* préciser; désigner; déterminer; prévoir
specimen *n* échantillon; éprouvette; exemplaire; génératrice; jalon; maquette; modèle (mle); pièce (pce); unité d'inspection; vignette
speck *n* trace

spectral amplitude amplitude spectrale; ~ **band** bande de spectre; ~ **response** (characteristic) sélectivité spectrale; caractéristique spectrale
spectral-response range largeur de bande spectrale
spectral sensitivity largeur de bande spectrale
spectrum *n* spectre; courbe spectrale; gamme; panoplie; ~ **analyser** analyseur de spectre; ~ **analysis** analyse spectrale; ~ **pressure level** niveau spectral élémentaire; ~ **shaping** mise en forme du spectre
specular reflectance réflexion plane
speech *n* parole; phonie; voix; conversation; ~ (signal) **processing** traitement du signal de parole; ~ **amplifier** amplificateur de modulation; ~ **analyser** analyseur de parole; ~ **band** bande vocale; bande de conversation; ~ **circuit** circuit de parole; circuit de conversation d'un poste téléphonique; circuit microphonique; ~ **circuit muting** inhibition partie transmission; ~ **communication** liaison téléphonique; ~ **crosstalk** diaphonie causée par la voix; ~ **current** courant vocal; ~ **detector** détecteur de parole; ~ **generator** générateur de parole; ~ **input** entrée vocale; entrée son; ~ **interpolation (SI)** concentration des conversations; ~ **inverter** démodulateur; ~ **junction** paire conversation; ~ **link** liaison de parole; ~ **mode** mode dialogué; mode conversationnel; mode interactif; mode phonique
speech-modulated wave onde à modulation vocale
speech modulation modulation vocale; ~ **network** circuit de conversation d'un poste téléphonique; ~ **path** voie de parole; chemin de parole; circuit de conversation; circuit de parole; voie de conversation; voie téléphonique; ~ **path asymmetry** asymétrie de la voie de conversation
speech-path marking marquage des connexions; ~ **subsystem** chaîne de parole; chaîne de conversation téléphonique; chaîne de transmission; réseau de conversation; réseau de parole
speech period durée de conversation; ~ **phase** conversation
speech-plus-duplex equipment (S + D) équipement bivocal
speech-plus-simplex (S + S) equipment équipement univocal
speech position position de conversation; ~ **power** puissance phonétique de parole; ~ **processing** traitement du signal de conversation; ~ **recognition** module de reconnaissance de parole; ~ **sam-**

S

ple échantillon de signal de parole; échantillon de conversation; échantillon vocal; ~ **scrambler** modulateur multiple; ~ **signal power** énergie des signaux vocaux; ~ **synthesis module** module de synthèse vocale; ~ **time** durée de conversation; ~ **transmission quality** qualité de transmission de la parole

speech-unit charge metering taxation par unités de conversation

speech voltage pression acoustique de la voix; ~ **voltmeter** voltmètre de parole; ~ **wave** onde acoustique; ~ **wires** fils de conversation

speed *n* vitesse; allure; cadence; régime; ~ **calling** numérotation abrégée; ~ **dialling** numérotation abrégée; appel direct (de l'opératrice); sélection abrégée; ~ **of answer** délai de réponse (d'opératrice); ~ **of revolution** vitesse de révolution; ~ **of service** rapidité de service; ~ **of telegraph transmission** vitesse d'émission télégraphique

spent *adj* usé

sphere *n* (printer element) boule; ~ **of influence** mission; ~ **of interest** domaine d'activité

spherical aberration aberration sphérique; ~ **waveguide** guide d'ondes sphérique

spider *n* cimblot (simbleau); diaphragme de centrage; ~ **bonding** soudage en pattes d'araignée

spigot *n* ergot; broche; doigt; pion de centrage; pion détrompeur

spike *n* picot; impulsion de courte durée; impulsion parasite; pic; pointe transitoire; top; ~ **bar** pied-de-biche

spikeless oscillation oscillation sans pointe

spill *n* contact à picot; ~ (of edge connector) palette

spillage *n* débordement

spill-forward *n* (feature) détournement; débordement

spill office central intermédiaire

spill-over loss facteur de débordement; facteur d'utilisation; ~ **traffic** trafic de débordement

spin axis axe de rotation propre

spindle *n* axe; arbre; broche; fuseau; sabre

spin drier essoreuse; sécheuse centrifuge

spinning *n* (of metal) repoussage; ~ **space station** station spatiale tournante

spin-off *n* retombée; rayonnement

spin printer imprimante à aiguilles

spin-stabilized *adj* (à) stabilisation dans les trois axes

spiral aerial antenne en spirale; ~ **array** réseau en spirale; ~ **cylinder printer**

imprimante à cylindre hélicoïdal; ~ **lead** guirlande; ~ **scanning** analyse en spirale

spirit *n* alcool

splash *n* (vern.) diaphonie

splashing *n* projection

splayed side of soldering pot sifflet de fût

splice *n* épissure; raccord; raccordement (racct.); ~ **piece** éclisse

splicing *n* épissurage; découpage; jonctionnement; ~ **chamber** boîte de jonction; ~ **station** banc d'épissurage; ~ **tape** bande adhésive

spline *n* clavette; pion de centrage; pion détrompeur

splined *adj* cannelé

split *v* fractionner; découper; ~ *n* fêlure; éclatement; lacune; ~ *adj* éclaté; double; séparé; ~ (of broker's call) va-et-vient; ~ **aerial switching** radiodéction à basculement de diagramme; ~ **anode** anode fendue; anode divisée

split-anode magnetron magnétron à anode fendue

split-beam CRT tube à rayons cathodiques à deux faisceaux

split call double appel courtier (va-et-vient); ~ **control** structure à deux niveaux; ~ **duplex circuit** circuit duplex à branchement; ~ **frame** partage de fenêtre; ~ **groups** aiguillage sur groupements; ~ **key** clé de séparation; ~ **keyboard** clé fractionnable; ~ **(locking) washer** rondelle Grower [A.C.]; ~ **multiplex** télégraphie multiplex à branchement

split-phase *n* division des positions de temps

split pin goupille fendue; ~ **platen** plateau partagé; ~ **point** point de division; ~ **power supply** alimentation siamoise; alimentation double; alimentation symétrique; ~ **response** signal double; ~ **screen** écran partagé; écran séparé; ~ **table** table éclatée

splitter *n* boîte de branchement; boîte de dérivation; boîte de distribution; boîte de jonction; coupleur de réception; diviseur; séparateur; répartiteur; ~ **switch** coffret de distribution

splitting *n* fractionnement; aiguillage; coupure; découpage; dédoublement; partage; répartition; segmentation; séparation; ~ **arrangement** dispositif de coupure; ~ **electrode** électrode diviseuse; ~ **terminal block** réglette à coupure; tête de coupure; ~ **time** temps de coupure

split washer rondelle Supergrower [A.C.]

split-winding rectification redressement à enroulement fractionné

spoke (of print-wheel) pétale

spoking n effet de roue
spontaneous emission émission spontanée
spool n bobine; carcasse; galette; roquette; touret
spooled adj différé
spooler n réenrouleur
spooling n impression spoulée; enregistrement en différé; impression déportée; partage des imprimantes
sporadic adj intermittent; intempestif; irrégulier; ~ **E layer** couche E sporadique; ~ **ionization** ionisation sporadique
spot n point; spot; tache
spot-beam aerial antenne à faisceau en pinceau; antenne à faisceau étroit; antenne à faisceau ponctuel
spot check contrôle forcé
spot-facing n lamage
spot frequency fréquence fixe; raie
spot-frequency RT receiver récepteur radiotéléphonique à fréquence fixe
spot jammer brouilleur à bande étroite
spotlight n projecteur
spot-retrace time temps de retour image
spot-size aperture diamètre du spot
spot welding soudure par points
spout n tuyère; ~ (of waveguide) buse
spraying n pulvérisation; projection
spray shield brise jet
spread v diffuser; distribuer; ~ n dispersion; distribution; écartement; élargissement; empiètement; étendue; zone d'empiètement; ~ **in transmission performance** dispersion de la qualité de transmission; ~ **sheet** tableur
spreadsheet n feuille de calcul; feuille de planification (et de modélisation) financière
spread-spectrum modulation modulation type spectre étalé; ~ **multiple access (SSMA)** accès multiple par étalement du spectre (AMES)
spring n ressort; lame; réseau; ~ adj élastique; ~ **balance** dynamomètre; tensiomètre; ~ **clip** bride-ressort; ~ **contact** contact élastique
spring-loaded connector block prise rapide
spring pin goupille élastique; goupille cylindrique; goupille Mécanidus [A.C.]; ~ **return to neutral** à rappel au zéro; ~ **shaft** (of relay) contre-lame; ~ **strip** connecteur de bord; ~ **washer** rondelle Grower [A.C.]; rondelle Onduflex [A.C.]; rondelle Supergrower [A.C.]
sprocket n denture d'accouplement; ~ **drive** tracteur; ~ **feed** entraînement par ergots; entraînement par roues à picots; ~ **holes** (of continuous form stationery) bande

Caroll
sprue (of moulding) n point d'injection; carotte
spun aluminium aluminium satiné; aluminium brossé; ~ **concrete pole** (cable mast) poteau centrifuge; ~ **glass** soie de verre
spur n ligne dérivée; branche; branchement; bras; butée; contrefort; épaulement; griffe; partie noble; ~ **band** bande de fréquences pour ligne dérivée
spurious adj parasite; aberrant; défectueux; étranger; fugitif; ~ **condition** brouillage; ~ **coupling** couplage parasite; ~ **effects** influences parasites; ~ **emission** rayonnement non essentiel; ~ **interference** bruit parasite; ~ **oscillation** oscillation interne spontanée; ~ **out-band signals at output** signaux parasites hors bande à la sortie; ~ **parameter** paramètre défectueux; ~ **radiation** émission sur bande interdite; ~ **response** accord parasite; ~ **sideband** bande latérale parasite; ~ **signal** signal parasite; ~ **wave** onde vagabonde; onde transitoire
sputtering n pulvérisation; métallisation
squared paper papier cadrié (quadrillé)
square flange collerette carrée
square-law adj quadratique; parabolique; ~ **detection** détection à réponse quadratique; détection parabolique; ~ **detector** voltmètre quadratique; détecteur quadratique
square pot-core assembly pot carré; ~ **pulse** créneau
squarer n circuit conformateur d'onde carrée
square-root cosine racine carrée de cosinus
square-wave n (generator) équarriseur
square wave onde carrée; signal rectangulaire
square-wave analyser analyseur d'onde carrée
square waveform forme d'onde carrée; forme d'onde rectangulaire
square-wave frequency fréquence d'ondes carrées; ~ **generator** générateur d'ondes carrées; générateur de signaux carrés; ~ **pulse** impulsion rectangulaire; ~ **response** caractéristique de réponse d'onde carrée; ~ **voltage** tension crénelée; créneau de tension; tension d'onde carrée
squaring circuit circuit conformateur d'onde carrée
squawker n haut-parleur pour fréquences moyennes; haut-parleur médium
squeeze v comprimer; condenser
squeezing n compression; retassement
squegger n coupleur continu-continu; oscillateur à extinctions; oscillateur de découpage
squegging n suroscillation; pompage; ~ **oscillator** oscillateur à extinctions; oscillateur

S

commandé par oscillations de relaxation

squelch *n* accord silencieux; blocage automatique; porte silencieux; réglage silencieux; antifading à réglage silencieux; ~ **circuit** circuit éliminateur de bruit de fond

squid *n* (on control panel) fiche double

squint angle erreur de directivité; angle de strabisme

squirrel-cage motor moteur à cage; ~ **rotor** rotor à cage; ~ **winding** enroulement à cage d'écureuil

squitter *n* production d'oscillations propres non désirées

SRE (s. surveillance radar element)

SRL (s. stability return loss); ± (s. structural return loss)

SS2 (s. single shift 2)

S + S (s. speech-plus-simplex)

SSB (s. single sideband)

SSD (s. static-sensitive device)

SSMA (s. spread-spectrum multiple access)

SSR (s. secondary surveillance radar)

SST (s. step-by-step test)

SSU (s. subsequent signal unit)

S-T (s. space-time junction)

stability return loss (SRL) affaiblissement d'adaptation pour la stabilité

stabilized aerial platform plate-forme d'antenne stabilisée; ~ **amplifier** amplificateur à amplification constante

stabilized-feedback amplifier amplificateur à réaction

stabilized local oscillator oscillateur local stabilisé; ~ **reference potential** OBs; ~ **supply voltage** tension d'alimentation stabilisée

stabilizer *n* durcisseur

stabilizing amplifier amplificateur stabilisateur

stable *adj* statique; ~ **mode simulator** simulateur d'équilibre de mode; ~ **monochromatic source** source monochromatique stable; ~ **sort** tri stable; ~ **trigger circuit** basculeur bistable

stack *n* pile; assemblage; banc; colonne; empilage; galette; montage; pont

stackable *adj* gerbable; ~ **test lead** prolongateur à reprise arrière

stack control gestion de pile

stacked *adj* étagé; superposé; ~ **array** rideau d'antennes; antenne réseau; ~ **beam** faisceau étagé

stacker *n* casier de réception; case; magasin; rampe; récepteur

stacking *n* empilement; gerbage; réception; ~ **height for storage and transit** gerbage statique et dynamique

stack pointer pointeur de piles; ~ **register**

registre à empilement

staff *n* personnel; collaborateur(s); effectif

stage *n* étage; appareil; cellule; étape; niveau; phase; platine; ~ (of shift register) bascule; ~ (of circuit) élément; ~ (of microscope) porte-objet; ~ **plate** (of microscope) platine porte-objet

stagger *n* (ratio) taux de décalage

stagger-damped amplifier amplificateur à atténuation décalée

staggered *adj* échelonné; alterné; décalé; en quinconce; étagé; ~ **circuit** circuit décalé; ~ **concentric tracks** pistes concentriques décalées; ~ **frequency** fréquence décalée; ~ **pair** deux circuits décalés; ~ **pulse repetition frequency** fréquence de répétition d'impulsions échelonnée

stagger-tuned amplifier amplificateur à accords décalés; ~ **circuit** circuit accordé décalé

stagger tuning accord décalé

stain *n* tache; salissure

stainless steel acier inoxydable (inox)

stalk *n* barrette; pied

stall(ing) *n* plantage

stall current courant de blocage

stalled program programme figé

stalling *n* figeage; blocage; calage; ~ (of motor) décrochage (D); ~ **angle** angle critique; angle de décrochage

stamp *n* tampon; composteur; empreinte; repère; visa

stamped circuit circuit imprimé découpé à la presse

stamping (with matching fixed dies) emboutissage à flans bloqués

stanchion *n* colonnette; poteau métallique; potelet

stand *n* pied; meuble; piètement; socle; ~ (of microscope) statif

stand-alone *adj* autonome; isolé; monoposte; unique; ~ **centre** centre autonome; ~ **unit** bloc isolé; ~ **workstation** poste unique; poste individuel

standard *n* norme; étalon; niveau; outil; palier; régime; ~ *adj* normalisé; banalisé; classique; courant; de base; généralisé; minimum; nominal; simple; ~ **beam approach (SBA)** système standard d'approche à radiophare; ~ **calibration oscillator** oscillateur de calibrage; étalonneur; ~ **cartridge** cartouche étalon; ~ **deviation** écart type; ~ **device protocol** protocole standard d'appareil; ~ **enquiry** profil; ~ **functions** fonctionnalités; ~ **inter-exchange telephone circuit** circuit standard; ~ **interface** jonc nominal

standardization *n* harmonisation; banalisation

standardized *adj* banalisé; homogène; normalisé

standard letter lettre type

standard/limiting curves(s) gabarit

standard line (of printed text) pige; ~ **microphone** microphone étalon; ~ **network access protocol (SNAP)** protocole standard d'accès; ~ **oscillator** oscillateur à autoexcitation; ~ **profile selection** choix du profil normalisé; ~ **propagation** propagation normale; ~ **radio atmosphere** atmosphère radioélectrique normale; ~ **reference telephone circuit** circuit téléphonique étalonné de référence; ~ **refraction** réfraction normale

standards converter (of TV) convertisseur de normes

standard sentence phrase-type; ~ **shim** cale étalon; ~ **television signal** signal étalon de télévision (SET); ~ **tone** fréquence sonore étalon; ~ **trunk dialling (STD)** interurbain automatique (IA); accès à interurbain; numérotation directe (DND); ~ **value** valeur implicite

standard-wave error erreur type de polarisation

stand-by *adj* de réserve; annexe; auxiliaire; de secours; en attente; homologue; passif; ~ **battery bar** barre de sécurité; ~ **channel** canal de réserve; ~ **circuit** circuit de réserve; circuit de recours; ~ **consumption** consommation en veille; ~ **equipment** équipement de secours; ~ **facility** utilisable en entraide; ~ **for answer** veille réponse; ~ **function** fonction attente; ~ **logic unit software** logiciel réserve; ~ **mode** à consommation réduite; mode de secours; mode non adressé; mode réduction de consommation; ~ **position** position auxiliaire; ~ **processor** calculateur de réserve; logique auxiliaire; ~ **ready acknowledgement** accusé de réception de liaison de réserve prête; ~ **recording unit** dispositif de secours; ~ **service** service réduit; ~ **state** état de veille; ~ **system** sécurisation; ~ **transmitter** émetteur de réserve

standing by à l'écoute; ~ **charge** abonnement; forfait; ~ **current** courant de repos; ~ **DC component** composante continue inutile

standing-on-nines (carry) report simultané; report bloqué à neuf

standing proud en saillie; ~ **wave** onde stationnaire; onde de repos

standing-wave aerial antenne à ondes stationnaires; ~ **meter** instrument de mesure du taux d'ondes stationnaires; ~ **ratio (SWR)** rapport d'onde stationnaire (ROS)

stand-off *n* surélévation; butée; décrochement; épaulement; montage vertical; rehausse; retard; tasseau de surélévation; trottoir; ~ **rim** pied de lavage; ~ **spur** cale de surélévation

standstill *n* arrêt

staple *n* agrafe; gâche

star aerial antenne en étoile; ~ **button** (digit) chiffre étoile; ~ **connection** connexion en étoile

star-connection transformer transformateur à primaire étoile

star-delta connection connexion étoile-triangle; ~ **starter** démarreur étoile-triangle; ~ **switch** commutateur étoile-triangle

star network réseau en étoile; réseau centralisé; ~ **program** programme vedette; ~ **quad** quarte étoile

star-quad cable câble à quartes en étoile

start *v* allumer; amorcer; commander; enclencher; lancer; mettre en marche; provoquer; ~ *n* début; départ; origine

start(-up) *n* mise en marche (MM)

start address adresse de base; adresse (de) début; adresse de lancement; phase de départ; ~ **bit** bit de départ; signal de début; ~ **box** début de cases; ~ **code** code de déclenchement; ~ **defining** début de sélection

start-dialling signal signal d'invitation à numéroter; signal d'invitation à transmettre

starter *n* allumeur; discontacteur de puissance; électrode pilote; ~ (of fluorescent tube) ballast; ~ **battery** batterie de démarrage; ~ **circuit** circuit de démarrage; ~ **current** courant de l'électrode d'amorçage; ~ **gap** intervalle d'amorçage d'allumage

starting current courant de démarrage; intensité au démarrage; ~ **peak** pointe de démarrage; ~ **relay** relais de mise en marche; ~ **resistor** résistance de démarrage; ~ **rheostat** rhéostat de démarrage; ~ **voltage** tension d'amorçage; tension de démarrage

start instruction phase de départ

start-of-block signal signal de début de bloc

start of heading (SOH) début d'en-tête; ~ **of message (SOM)** début de message

start-of-message character signe initial

start of pulsing début de numérotation; ~ **of text (STX)** début de texte

star topology interconnexion en étoile

start polarity polarité de départ

start-pulsing signal signal d'invitation à numéroter; signal d'invitation à transmettre

start signal (of start-stop system) signal de mise en marche

S

start-stop *adj* arythmique; asynchrone; tout ou rien (TOR); ~ **apparatus** appareil arythmique; ~ **distortion** distorsion arythmique; ~ **distortion measuring set** distorsiomètre arythmique; ~ **mode** mode arythmique; ~ **modulation** modulation arythmique; ~ **signalling system** système de signalisation asynchrone; ~ **system** système arythmique; ~ **telegraphy** télégraphie arythmique; ~ **transmission** transmission arythmique; ~ **transmitter** émetteur arythmique

start time temps d'accélération; temps de mise en marche; ~ **timing** début de renforcement

start-up *n* démarrage; lancement
start wire fil de démarrage
star voltage tension entre phase et neutre; ~ **washer** rondelle éventail
state *n* état; allure; condition; niveau; phase; positionnement; régime; ~ **change** changement d'état; ~ **forcing** nettoyage; ~ **immaterial** état indifférent
statement *n* état; carte de contrôle; commentaire; déclaration; énoncé; exposé; expression (logiciel); instruction; ordre; relevé; ~ **number** numéro d'instruction
state-of-the-art *adj* de pointe; moderne; ~ **architecture** architecture moderne
state point point figuratif; ~ **transition diagram** diagramme de transition des états; diagramme de transition du statut
static *n* parasites atmosphériques; ~ *adj* inopérant; statique; au repos; perturbation atmosphérique; ~ **capacitance** capacité statique; ~ **characteristic** caractéristique statique; ~ **column break** coupure de colonne statique; ~ **discharger** déperditeur de potentiel; ~ **dump** vidage à l'arrêt; mémoire statique; ~ **electricity** électricité statique; ~ **firing** amorçage statique; ~ **inverter** convertisseur statique; microréseau de génération
staticizer *n* convertisseur série-parallèle; bascule
static level niveau de bruit; ~ **luminous sensitivity** sensibilité lumineuse statique; ~ **machine** générateur électrostatique; ~ **memory** mémoire morte; ~ **modulator** bloqueur; modulateur statique; ~ **page break** coupure de page statique; ~ **parameters** caractéristiques statiques; ~ **pool** (of molten solder) bain mort; ~ **power converter** convertisseur de courant; ~ **relay/modulator** bloqueur; relais statique
static-sensitive device (SSD) circuit sensible à l'électricité statique
static split radiodétection à goniométrie

instantanée d'amplitude; ~ **test** essai inopérant; essai statique; ~ **threshold** (servo-system) seuil statique; ~ **value of the forward current transfer ratio** (in common-emitter configuration) valeur statique du rapport de transfert direct du courant en émetteur; gain statique (h$_{FE}$)
station *n* position; abonné; banc; centre; émetteur; poste; station; ~ **address** adresse d'appel
stationary stationnaire; figé; fixe; statique; ~ **echo** écho fixe; ~ **field winding** enroulement champ fixe (ECF); ~ **(lead acid) battery** accumulateur stationnaire (au plomb); ~ **orbit satellite circuit** circuit par satellite sur orbite stationnaire; ~ **source** source stationnaire; ~ **wave** onde de repos
station call identification identification de la ligne appelante; ~ **camped-on** poste en attente
stationery *n* papeterie; support
station forced busy mise en veilleuse; ~ **group** groupement de postes; ~ **identification** indicatif (IF)
station-keeping (of satellite) stabilité en orbite; ~ **satellite** satellite télécommandé
station line ligne d'usager; ligne de poste supplémentaire; ligne intérieure; raccordement (racct.); rattachement; ~ **line circuit** (of telex system) jonction; ~ **number display** identification de la ligne appelante; ~ **override security** protection contre les interventions
station-to-station *adj* poste à poste; ~ **call** appel interne; appel local
station user poste d'usager
statistical analysis dénombrement; ~ **delay** retard statistique; ~ **distribution** loi statistique
stator *n* stator; inducteur
status bit bit d'état; indicateur; ~ **channel** voie d'état; ~ **code** code d'état; ~ **indication image**; ~ **indicator** indicateur d'état; ~ **light** voyant; ~ **map** table de correspondance; ~ **message** message d'état; message de contrôle
'status now' report état
status panel tableau de bord; ~ **portion** partie états; ~ **register** registre de contrôle; ~ **report** état d'avancement; compte-rendu (CR); journal de bord; message d'état; rapport d'état; tableau de bord; ~ **transition** changement d'état; ~ **word** mot d'état; mot qualificatif; ~ **word string (SWS)** chaîne de mots d'état
statutory hedge haie; ~ **instrument** arrêté ministériel
stay *n* appui; chandelle; tasseau

staying n haubanage (haubannage)

stay-put position (limit switch) à position maintenue

stay rope hauban

STC (s. switching and test centre); $\doteqdot$ (s. secondary transit centre)

STD (s. standard trunk dialling); $\doteqdot$ (s. subscriber trunk dialling)

steady adj régulier; permanent; stationnaire; ~ **anode current** courant permanent d'anode; ~ **carrier** porteuse constante; ~ **glow** feu fixe (allumage); ~ **noise** bruit permanent; bruit soutenu

steady-state amplitude amplitude en régime permanent; ~ **circuit** circuit statique; ~ **operation** régime statique; ~ **oscillation** oscillation stationnaire; ~ **temperature resistance** tenue en température en régime permanent

stealing n prélèvement

steam n vapeur d'eau; ~ **bath** bain marie; ~ **trap** captation des vapeurs

steel wire armoured cable câble en fils d'acier

steeply-rising wave onde à front raide

steer v orienter; diriger; manœuvrer; piloter

steerability n facilité de manœuvre

steerable adj orientable

steering n orientation; manœuvre; pointage; ~ **accuracy** précision de pointage; ~ **angle** angle d'orientation; ~ **committee** comité d'organisation; comité d'orientation

stem n queusot; pied; poignée

stems from provient de

stencil n typon; ~ (of typing) frappe non encrée

step v progresser (faire -); basculer; ~ n pas; action; avance; bond; cran; cycle; échelon; étape; jalon; marche; mesure; niveau; phase; pied; séquence; ~ **and repeat** image par image

step-and-repeat process procédé photomultiplication

step bit bit de pas

step-by-step adj pas à pas (PAP); progressif; ~ **automatic system** système automatique pas à pas; ~ **exchange** commutateur pas-à-pas; ~ **problem-solving** algorithmique; ~ **selection** sélection pas à pas (étage par étage); ~ **switching** commutation à commande successive; commutation pas-à-pas; ~ **system** système pas à pas; ~ **telegraph** télégraphe pas à pas; ~ **test** (SST) essai par paliers

step change variation discrète; ~ **counter** compteur de phase; ~ **deviation/swing** écart en échelon

step-down (inverted) amplifier amplificateur de seuil; ~ **converter** convertisseur abais-

seur; ~ **station** poste abaisseur; ~ **transformer** transformateur réducteur; dévolteur; transformateur abaisseur

step function fonction échelon

step-function response réponse à l'échelon

step-in déplacement avant

step-index fibre fibre à échelon d'indice; fibre à saut d'indice

step length longueur de pas

stepless adj continu

step load change variation de charge

step-mode execution avance

step-out n déplacement (en) arrière

step outside the range/limits franchir le seuil

stepped adj échelonné; ~ (of keyboard layout) en gradin; ~ **index** discontinuité d'indice

stepped-reflector aerial antenne à réflecteur échelonné

stepped start-stop system système arythmique cadencé

stepper motor moteur fractionnaire

stepping control commande d'avance; ~ **down** détalonnage; ~ **lines** lignes d'impulsions; ~ **magnet** aimant de progression; ~ **mechanism** mécanisme de progression; ~ **motor** moto-réducteur; ~ **relay** relais à action échelonnée; relais à cascade; relais d'avance; relais de coupure; commutateur pas-à-pas; ~ **resistor** (rheostat) résistance à plots

step-recovery diode diode de commutation rapide

step response réponse transitoire

steps, in (X-second) ~ par bonds (de X secondes)

step-stool n marchepied

step switch commutateur à plots; combinateur; interrupteur à gradin; ~ **termination code** code de fin d'étape; ~ **track** poursuite pas à pas; ~ **trim** nez de marche; ~ **twist** guide en torsade binomial

step-up station poste élévateur; ~ **transformer** transformateur élévateur; autotransformateur élévateur; transformateur survolteur

step wedge échelle des teintes; échelle de nuances

stereo adj (of microscope) binoculaire; ~ **amplifier** amplificateur stéréophonique

stereography n stéréoscopie

stereophonic sound system système acoustique stéréophonique

stereoscopic photography stéréoscopie; ~ **television** télévision en relief

stick n chapelet; étui; manche; ~ (of ICs) distributeur; ~ **(IC container)** fourreau

sticker n décalcomanie; étiquette; marque; réflecteur de bande; étiquette de début de

S

bande
sticking at zero (of bit) collage à 0; ~ **potential** tension de blocage; ~ **voltage** tension limite
stick insulator isolateur à tige
stick-off voltage tension de lever de doute
stiffener *n* raidisseur
stiffnut *n* écrou Nylstop [A.C.]
stifle *v* étouffer
still *adj* statique
stillage *n* chariot sans roulette; plate-forme
still bath bain mort
still-picture transmitter émetteur d'images fixes
stimulation (carrier-photon) recouvrement
stimulus *n* excitation; affichage
stipulation *n* disposition; provision
stirrup *n* étrier; ~ (of fuse-carrier) plaquette
stitch wiring câblage par points de soudure
stochastic noise bruit aléatoire; ~ **process** procédé stochastique
stock *n* matériel
stock(s) *n* dotation
stock and die set coffret filière; ~ **control theory** gestion des stocks; ~ **depletion** rupture de stocks; ~ **endurance** couverture des stocks; ~ **number** numéro de dotation
stocks *pl* souche
stocktaking *n* contrôle d'inventaire; contrôle de stocks
stock (up) *n* approvisionnement
stoichiometric composition composition stoichiométrique
Stokes law (particles in a fluid) loi de Stokes
stop at address blocage sur une phase
stop-band attenuation affaiblissement de blocage; affaiblissement d'élimination de bande
stop bit bit d'arrêt; signal de fin (de communication); ~ **code** code d'arrêt; code de remplissage; ~ **defining** fin de sélection (FIN SEL); ~ **logic** logique d'arrêt; ~ **mark** marque d'arrêt (MA); ~ **measure** cale étalon; ~ **on address** arrêt sur adresse
stop-on-fail arrêt refus
stop on fault arrêt sur faute
stoppage *n* blocage; interruption; suppression
stopped *adj* à l'arrêt; bloqué; coupé; immobilisé
stopper *n* bouchon; arrêtoir; circuit bouchon; embout; bouchée; ~ **circuit** circuit anterésonant; circuit éliminateur; circuit réjecteur; ~ **ring** anneau stoppeur
stop polarity polarité d'arrêt
stop-sending-tone message message «arrêt de l'émission de la tonalité»
stop-send signal signal d'arrêt d'émission

stop state état d'arrêt; ~ **time** temps d'arrêt; ~ **washer** rondelle de sécurité à crans
stopwatch *n* chronomètre
stop-words list antidictionnaire
storage *n* mise en mémoire; archivage; archive; emmagasinage; enregistrement; entrée; mémoire; mémorisation; paramétrage; paramétrisation; rangement; stockage; ~ **access channel (SAC)** canal sac; ~ **allocation** affectation de mémoire; gestion mémoire; ~ **area/block** zone de mémoire; ~ **bank** banc de mémoire; ~ **battery** batterie d'accumulateurs; ~ **bin** bac; ~ **block** bloc mémoire; ~ **block** (chained record) pavé (bloc d'informations chaîné); ~ **camera tube** tube analyseur à accumulation; ~ **capacity** capacité mémoire; ~ **cell** cellule mémoire; ~ **data image**; ~ **device** module mémoire; ~ **factor** facteur de qualité; facteur de surtension; ~ **keyboard** clavier à transfert; ~ **location** mot mémoire; ~ **oscilloscope** oscilloscope à mémoire; ~ **protection** protection mémoire; ~ **ramp** sabot de rangement; ~ **register** registre mémoire; ~ **ring** anneau de stockage; ~ **space** place mémoire; ~ **temperature** température de stockage; ~ **tube** tube à mémoire; ~ **vault** local à archive
store *v* charger; consigner; emmagasiner; enregistrer; mémoriser; ranger; stocker
store(s) *n* magasin
store (screen display) photographier (l'écran); ~ **address** adresse-mémoire
store-and-forward *n* enregistrement en différé; mémorisation et retransmission; mode différé; ~ **network** réseau de commutation de messages; ~ **switching** commutation de messages
store-back restockage en mémoire; réenregistrement; ~ **bit** déchargement de bit
stored call facility appel enregistré; ~ **charge** charge stockée; ~ **order** chaine cataloguée; ~ **(physical) record** enregistrement numérique; ~ **program** programme enregistré; ~ **program** (control) **network** réseau à programme enregistré; ~ **program computer** calculateur à programme enregistré; ~ **program control** commande par calculateurs; ~ **program control (SPC)** commande par programme enregistré (CPE); ~ **program (control) system** automate programmé; ~ **record** enregistrement physique; ~ **states of hardware devices** images des organes
storekeeper *n* magasinier
store level niveau mémoire; ~ **spillage** débordement de mémoire; ~ **zero (STZ)** *v*

remettre à zéro; ~ **zero (STZ)** remise à zéro (RZ/RAZ)

storing *n* enregistrement; rangement

stove *n* étuve

stoved *adj* cuite au four (peinture); martelé

stowage *n* rangement

STP (s. signal transfer point)

straggler message message détourné

straight bank banc aligné; ~ **binary** binaire naturel; ~ **cable socket (IEC mains plug socket)** fiche femelle; ~ **circuit** récepteur à amplification directe; ~ **connector** connecteur droit; ~ **jack (plug)** fiche droite

straight-line sans boucle; ~ **coding** programmation sans boucle; ~ **frequency** variation linéaire de fréquence

straight section (of waveguide) élément droit; ~ **signals** signaux normaux; ~ **terminal tag** plage droite

straight-wire probe sonde capacitive; antenne de couplage

strain *n* contrainte

strainer *n* crépine

strain gauge jauge de contrainte; capteur de compression; ~ **relief** retenue mécanique

strain-relief bushing passe-fil(s)

strand *n* brin; toron; tresse; ~ (of wire) monofilament

stranded *adj* multibrins; ~ **cable** câble torsadé; ~ **conductor** conducteur toronné; ~ **wire** cordon d'antenne

stranding *n* toronnage; ~ **angle** angle de tressage

strand setting relaxation de câblage

strap *n* cavalier; bande; barrette; bride; estrope; fil jarretière; liaison; pont; pontet; strap; combinaison

strap configuration brassage; ~ **key** contacteur à lame ressort

strapping *n* jarretiérage; brassage; cerclage; construction(s); pontage; rebouclage; mutations; ~ **block** bloc de combinaisons; bloc de construction; ~ **connector module** panier de brassage; ~ **panel reconfiguration** déplacement répartiteur

strap-selected modifiable par cavalier

stratagem astuce

strategic development plan plan directeur

stratum *n* couche

stray *adj* parasite(s); étranger; ~ **capacitance** capacité parasite; ~ **coupling** couplage parasite; ~ **current** courant de terre; ~ **feedback** réaction parasite; ~ **field** champ parasite; ~ **inductance** inductance de fuite

straying *n* migration

stray oscillations oscillation parasite; ~ **radiation** rayonnement parasite; raies parasites;

~ **resonance** accord parasite; ~ **signals** influences parasites

streaking *n* traînage

stream *n* flot; suite; train; file

streamer (tape) cartridge cartouche de sauvegarde

stream-oriented *adj* en continu

street alarm box avertisseur public

strength *n* pouvoir; grandeur; ~ (of magnetic field) **load** intensité; ~ **puissance** (Pce); résistance; robustesse; tenue

strengthened visual inspection contrôle visuel renforcé

stress *n* contrainte; charge; gêne; pression uniforme; ~ **analysis** calcul de résistance; ~ **measurement system** chaîne de mesure d'effort; ~ **relief** (of metal) détente

stress-relief annealing recuit de détente

stretch *n* allongement à la traction; ~ (of memory) extensibilité

stretcher extenseur; circuit compensateur

stretching *n* allongement; extension

stride *n* bond

strikeover *n* surfrappe

striker *n* percuteur; ~ **plate** plaque de percussion

strike-through (screen attribute) barré

striking current courant d'amorçage; ~ **voltage** tension d'amorçage

string *v* concaténer; chaîner; enchaîner; ~ *n* chaîne; chapelet; monotonie; série (en -); train; ~ **break** rupture de monotonie

string-building *n* constitution de monotonie

stringent *adj* sévère; rigoureux

stringing *n* chaînage; concaténation; enfilage

string of spaces suite de zéros; ~ **parameter** paramètre chaîné

strip *n* barrette; bande; barre; cosse; languette; piste; plaque; plaquette; platine; réglette (rg.); ~ **attenuator** affaiblisseur à lamelle

strip-board ("Veroboard": T.N.) plaque d'étude

stripe *n* piste magnétique; ~ (of ribbon cable) liseret (liséré)

strip label étiquette de bandeau; ~ **light** bandeau lumineux

strip-light holder applique

strip-line *n* conducteur triplaque; guide d'ondes à ruban; ruban plat

strip packaging conditionnement en bande

stripped *adj* dénudé; nu; séparé; ~ (side) dépouille

strippers (of wire insulation) pince américaine

stripping *n* décapage; ~ (of wire) dénudage; ~ déshabillage; élimination; ~ **and scraping pliers** pince à gratter à mors; ~ **force/ effort** force de dénudage; ~ **length**

S

longueur de dégainage; ~ **machine** machine à dénuder; ~ **pliers** pince à dénuder; pince américaine

strobe *n* impulsion d'échantillonnage; trace repère; ~ (marker pulse) rythme; ~ **marker** créneau; marqueur stroboscopique; ~ **output** signal d'échantillonnage; ~ **pulse** créneau; impulsion de rythme; impulsion de strobage

stroboscopic (reflector) disk disque sectorisé; ~ **tube** tube stroboscopique

stroke *n* coup; barre oblique; branche; course; frappe; ligne; segment; temps; top

strong brown paper papier kraft

strongly deprecated fortement déconseillé

Strowger selector sélecteur à double mouvement; ~ **switching** commutation Strowger

structural breakdown synoptique

structurally dual networks réseaux réciproques

structurally-similar device modèle associable

structural return loss (SRL) affaiblissement de régularité

structure *n* structure; arrangement; articulation; charpente; composition; configuration; constitution; décomposition; découpage; découpe; disposition; facture; forme; implantation; schéma

strut *n* bielle; entretoise; étai

STS (s. set transmit state)

stub *n* symétriseur; ~ **(of waveguide)** adaptateur; ~ antenne; barrette; dérivation; embout; pied; talon; toc; tronçon; ~ **aerial** antenne courte

stubbing *n* (of contacts) écrasement

stubby screwdriver boule courte

stub card carte à talon

stub-matched aerial antenne accordée à impédance élevée; antenne à adaptateur d'impédance; antenne Q

stuck *adj* figé; bloqué

stud *n* goujon; axe; borne; broche; capsule; cavalier; clou; cosse; doigt; œillet; picot; pied; plot; pointe; tige

studio *n* cellule d'enregistrement; ~ **operation** prise de son

study *n* étude; analyse; recherche; ~ **programme** programme d'études

stuffing bit élément binaire de bourrage; élément numérique de justification; ~ **bit(s)** bourrage; ~ **box** presse-étoupe; ~ **byte** octet de bourrage; ~ **character** caractère de bourrage; ~ **rate** coefficient de cadrage; ~ **ratio** taux de justification

stunt box (of teleprinter) coffret codeur; ~ **box** bloc de fonctions; coffret de commande

sturdiness *n* robustesse

sturdy *adj* résistant; compact; solide

STX (s. start of text)

styling *n* usinage

stylish *adj* esthétique

stylo *n* bâtonnet

stylus *n* aiguille; pointe; ~ **printer** imprimante à aiguilles; imprimante par points

STZ (s. store zero)

subassembly (s/assy) élément; sous-ensemble (ssens); soustranche; ~ **inspection instructions** fiche d'instruction de contrôle

sub-audio telegraphy télégraphie infra-acoustique

sub-burst *n* sous-paquet

sub-carrier *n* sous-porteuse; onde porteuse intermédiaire; ~ **frequency** fréquence de sousporteuse; ~ **frequency modulation** modulation en fréquence d'une sousporteuse; ~ **sideband** bande latérale de la sousporteuse

sub-centre *n* centre local primaire; sous-centre; satellite

sub-channel *n* canal secondaire; sous-canal

sub-clutter visibility taux de refus d'échos fixes; visibilité d'objets malgré les échos de sol

sub-code *n* sous-indicatif

subcontractor *n* sous-traitant

sub-control station station sous-directrice

subdivide *v* décomposer; éclater; ~ scinder

subdivision *n* décomposition; découpage; dédoublement

subdued background fond sous-brillant; ~ **brightness** intensité réduite; ~ **lighting** veilleuse

sub-feeder *n* conduite secondaire

sub-field *n* sous-domaine

sub-frame *n* sous-trame; secteur de trame

sub-function *n* sous-fonction

sub-group *n* sous-groupe; groupe de lignes (dans un multiplage partiel)

sub-harmonic *n* harmonique inférieur; ~ **component** composante sous-harmonique; ~ **frequency** fréquence sous-harmonique

subject *n* motif; étude; objet

subjective noise bruit subjectif; ~ **noise meter** appareil de mesure subjective du bruit

subliminal technique (psychological induction in advertising) subfascination

submarine cable câble sous-marin de grand fond

submerged aerial antenne sousmarine; ~ **repeater** répéteur immergé

submission *n* mise à disposition (MAD)

submit *v* présenter; fournir

sub-multiple *n* sous-multiple

subordinate inférieur; ~ **computer** centre antéserveur; ~ **station** station tributaire

sub-parameter sous-paramètre

sub-position sous-position(nement)
subrack *n* châssis; alvéole; panier; bac à cartes; ~ **level label** étiquette de repérage de niveaux
sub-rate *adj* à bas débit
sub-refraction *n* infraréfraction
subroutine *n* sous-programme; procédure; section
subscriber (line) *n* abonné; ~ correspondant; usager; utilisateur; **A-~** abonné demandeur (DR); abonné appelant; **B-~** abonné demandé (DE); abonné appelé; **temporarily-disconnected** ~ abonné suspendu; ~ **access subsystem** collecte d'abonnés; ~ **account** abonnement
subscriber-busy signal signal d'abonné occupé
subscriber carrier equipment équipement à courant porteur pour lignes d'abonnés; ~ **carrier system** synthétiseur évolutif; ~ **carrier technique** multiplexage; ~ **category** catégorie d'abonné; ~ **class-of-service** discrimination d'abonné; ~ **directory number** numéro d'abonné; ~ **drop** (wire) chevelure; ~ **exchange** centre d'abonnés; autocommutateur de rattachement; ~ **extension station** poste téléphonique supplémentaire; ~ **free** abonné libre; ~ **group** groupe d'abonnés; ~ **jack** fiche de réponse; ~ **line** ligne d'abonné; ligne terminale; raccordement (racct.); rattachement; ~ **line administration** gestion d'abonnés; ~ **line and final selector unit** baie des lignes d'abonnés et des sélecteurs; ~ **line connection** gestion des abonnés; ~ **line connection unit** unité de raccordement d'abonnés (URA); ~ **line equipment** subrack châssis d'éléments d'abonnés; ~ **line free** signal d'abonné libre; ~ **line interface** jonction d'abonné; ~ **line interface circuit (SLIC)** interface d'abonné; joncteur d'abonné (JAN); carte d'abonnés; ~ **(line) observed by sampling** abonné observé par sondage (OBS); ~ **line scanner (SLS)** explorateur d'abonnés (EXA); ~ **(line) transformer** pot d'abonné; ~ **(line) without priority** abonné sans priorité; ~ **line with permanent line condition** abonné en faux appel; ~ **(line) with priority** abonné avec priorité; ~ **loop** ligne d'abonné
subscriber-loop equipment équipement d'abonné; équipement de ligne
subscriber loop plant la distribution; ~ **loop tester** banc de mesure d'abonnés; ~ **main station** poste téléphonique principal; ~ **meter** compteur d'abonné; compteur d'appels; compteur de taxes d'abonné; ~ **multi-ser-**

vice régie d'abonnés; ~ **register** compteur d'appels; ~ **selector** identificateur d'abonnés
subscriber's number numéro d'appel
subscriber stage étage d'abonnés; ~ **station** poste téléphonique d'abonné; ~ **station protector** boîte d'entrée de poste d'abonné à protection; ~ **station/set** poste d'abonné; ~ **terminal concentrator** concentrateur de terminaux annuaire; ~ **trunk dialling (STD)** exploitation automatique interurbaine; sélection à distance de l'abonné demandé; service interurbain automatique; ~ **uniselector** présélecteur; ~ **with private meter** abonné télétaxé; ~ **with special class of service** abonné discriminé
subscript *n* indice inférieur; suffixe
subscription *n* abonnement; redevance annuelle; ~ **call** conversation par abonnement
subsection *n* alinéa; ~ (of clause) point
subsequent address message (SAM) message d'adresse subséquent; ~ **counter** compteur auxiliaire; ~ **signal unit (SSU)** unité de signalisation subséquente
subset *n* sous-ensemble; bloc; jeu partiel (de caractères); morceau; poste
subsidiary *n* société filiale
subsidy *n* subvention
subsistence expenses frais de séjour
sub-sonic frequency fréquence infra-acoustique
substance *n* (unit: g/m^2) grammage
sub-standard *adj* seconde qualité
substation *n* poste asservi; sous-station
sub-status *n* état secondaire
substrate *n* substrat; stratifié; base; ~ **current** courant de substrat
sub-structure *n* infrastructure; corps
sub-surface *adj* sous-jacent
sub-switch *n* commutateur
subsystem *n* sous-système; bloc; chaîne; élément; ensemble fonctionel; équipement
sub-table *n* sous-schéma
sub-telephone frequency fréquence infra-téléphonique
sub-titling *n* télésous-titrage
subtract *v* retrancher
subtracter soustracteur
subtrahend *n* diminuteur
sub-voice *adj* à bande étroite; infratéléphonique; ~ **channel** voie infratéléphonique
sub-zonal centre centre de transit
successful *adj* efficace; ~ **call** communication efficace; ~ **tendering party** adjudicataire
succession *n* suite; train
successive-approximation register registre à approximations successives

S

suction accumulator bouteille anticoup de liquide; ~ **hood** hotte aspirante; ~ **screen** crépine

sudden *adj* brutal; brusque; inopiné; ~ **blow** choc; ~ **ionospheric disturbance** perturbation ionosphérique à début brusque; ~ **phase anomaly** déviation brusque de phase

suffix *n* suffixe; indice

suitability *n* aptitude

suitable for use in tropical conditions tropicalisé

suite *n* rangée; batterie; travée; ~ (of programs) ensemble; enchaînement (de programmes); ~ **of configuration programs** (for exchanges of the same class) générique; ~ **tests** contrôle des travées

sulphur hexafluoride hexafluorure de soufre

sum(mation) frequency fréquence résultante

summary *n* synthèse; bordereau; état récapitulatif; rappel; résumé; ~ **card** carte récapitulative; ~ **sheet** feuille récapitulative

summation *n* synthèse; ~ **check** test de totalisation; ~ **word** (checksum) mot de totalisation

summit *n* sommet

summons *n* sollicitation

sump *n* carter

sundry *adj* divers

super-audio (AC telegraphy, above 3.4 kHz) supraphonique; ~ **frequency** fréquence supra-acoustique; fréquence ultra acoustique; fréquence ultra sonore; ~ **telegraphy** télégraphie supra-acoustique

supercharger *n* suralimenteur

supercode *n* surindicatif

superframe alignment pattern verrouillage multitrames

supergroup *n* groupe secondaire (de voies téléphoniques à courants porteurs); ~ **allocation** position de transmission de groupes secondaires; ~ **carrier** porteuse de groupe secondaire; ~ **distribution frame (SDF)** répartiteur de groupes secondaires (RGS); ~ **frequency** fréquence de groupe secondaire; ~ **link** liaison en groupe secondaire; ~ **reference pilot** onde pilote de groupe secondaire; ~ **section** section de groupe secondaire

superheterodyne receiver récepteur à superhétérodyne

superhighway *n* supermultiplex

superimposed DC field champ continu superposé; courant continu superposé; ~ **ringing** signalisation multiple; ~ **telegraphy** télégraphie supra-acoustique

supermastergroup *n* groupe quaternaire (GQ)

superposed AC voltage tension alternative superposée; ~ **circuit** fantôme; circuit approprié; circuit superposé; ~ **ringing** appel par courant superposé; ~ **ringing current** appel bi-courants; courant d'appel superposé; ~ **telegraph circuit** ligne de télégraphie simultanée

super-refraction *n* superréfraction

super-regenerative receiver récepteur à super-réaction

superscript *n* exposant; indice supérieur

superseded *adj* périmé; dépassé

supersedes annule et remplace; tient lieu et place de

supersonic frequency fréquence supra-acoustique; ~ **threshold** mur du son

superswitch *n* diode ultrarapide

super-telephone frequency fréquence supratéléphonique

super-turnstile aerial antenne en supertourniquet

supervision *n* surveillance; contrôle; maîtrise; supervision

supervisor *n* responsable; centralisateur; maître d'oeuvre; moniteur; programme exécutif; pupitreur; surveillant(e); ~ **call** appel du superviseur (SVC); ~ **position** position de surveillance

supervisory lamp lampe de clôture; lampe de fin de conversation; lampe de supervision (SUPER); ~ **message** message de surveillance; ~ **program** programme superviseur; ~ **program director** programme directeur; ~ **relay** relais de coupure; relais de supervision; ~ **routine** programme moniteur; ~ **signal** signal de supervision; signal se surveillance; ~ **staff** encadrement; ~ **unit** joncteur

supplant *v* remplacer

supplementary service service supplémentaire

supplier *n* fournisseur

supply *v* fournir; alimenter; livrer; ~ *n* approvisionnement; amenée; ~ **and demand** l'offre et la demande; ~ **bridge** pont d'alimentation; ~ **busbar** barre d'alimentation (BA); ~ **cabinet** armoire alimentation; ~ **cables** câbles d'adduction; ~ **current** (IOL) courant fourni (par les alimentations); ~ **point** prise; ~ **tolerance control** marginal; ~ **voltage** tension d'alimentation

support *n* aide; appui; berceau; chevalet; contrefort; gaine; socle; tasseau; tuteur; (cable) ~ **structure** cobrette; ~ **card** fiche d'accompagnement; ~ **chip** organe d'appui

supported hole trou métallisé

supporting details complément; ~ **document** annexe; ~ **member** flasque

support plane plan d'appui; ~ **software**

logiciel de support

suppress v étouffer

suppressed aerial antenne encastrée; antenne plaquée

suppressed-carrier transmission émission à porteuse supprimée

suppressed carrier transmitter émetteur à suppression de porteuse; ~ **frequency band** bande de fréquence supprimée; ~ **sideband** bande latérale supprimée

suppression capacitor condensateur d'antiparasitage; ~ **filter** filtre d'arrêt; ~ **hangover time** temps de maintien pour la suppression; ~ **loss** affaiblissement de blocage; ~ **trap** filtre éliminateur (de bande); ~ **wave** filtre éliminateur (de bande)

suppressor n éliminateur; épurateur; self; ~ **circuit** circuit anterésonant; circuit antiparasité; ~ **grid** grille d'arrêt

supra-national adj transnational

S & R (s. search and replace)

surcharge n surtaxe; charge supplémentaire

surety n cautionnement

surface n face; couche; ~ **acoustic wave (SAW)** onde de surface acoustique

surface-barrier transistor transistor à barrière superficielle

surface-charge effect (S-effect) effet de charge superficielle

surface-coating (process) traitement de surface; revêtement; traitement

surface-coating adhesion adhérence du revêtement; ~ **colouring** coloration superficielle

surface-contact rectifier redresseur à contact par surface

surface discharge décharge superficielle; ~ **duct** conduit de surface; ~ **finish** rugosité; état de surface; ~ **gauge** trusquin; ~ **irregularity** éclat

surface-mounted adj en saillie

surface mounting n report en surface

surface-mounting adj embrochable

surface pattern quadrillage; ~ **plate** marbre; marbrier

surface-recombination velocity vitesse de recombinaison superficielle

surface resistivity résistivité superficielle; ~ **tension (SI unit)** rugosité; tension superficielle; ~ **texture** état de surface; ~ **vessel** bâtiment; ~ **wave** onde directe; onde de surface

surge (of current) n afflux; ~ **battement**; choc; pointe; surcharge passagère; saut de tension; surtension; ~ adj transitoire; ~ (non-repetitive) **voltage** tension de surcharge (accidentelle/non-répétitive); ~ **absorber** parasurtenseur amortisseur d'ondes; absorbeur d'ondes; ~ **admittance**

admittance caractéristique; ~ **arrester** parasurtenseur amortisseur d'ondes; parafoudre; ~ **characteristic** caractéristique du saut; ~ **current** courant de surcharge (non répétitif); courant de choc; ~ **diverter** parasurtenseur; ~ **forward current** courant direct (de pointe) de surcharge; ~ **generator** générateur de bruits impulsifs; générateur de chocs; générateur d'impulsions; ~ **impedance** impédance d'onde caractéristique; ~ **modifier** absorbeur d'ondes; ~ **(non-repetitive) on-state current** courant de pointe accidentelle non répétitif à l'état passant; ~ **protection** protection contre les surtensions; ~ **relay** relais à maximum; ~ **voltage** tension de choc; énergie transitoire

surplus n excédent

surround n cache; capot; drageoir; entourage; collerette frontale

surrounded by cadré par

surrounding adj environnant

surveillance n contrôle; ~ **radar element (SRE)** radiodétecteur de surveillance d'approche

survey n étude; aspect; contrôle; récapitulatif; rappel

survival wind vent de survie

susceptance n (imaginary part of admittance) susceptance

suspect adj incriminé; en cause; ~ **card** carte mise en cause; ~ **period** période d'accusation

suspended cage balancelle; ~ **ceiling** faux plafond; ~ **line** ligne résiliée

suspense file fichier de suivi; fichier d'attente; fichier de relance

sustained adj continu; ~ **fault** défaut permanent; ~ **noise** bruit continu; bruit soutenu

sustaining voltage tension d'entretien; tension de maintien

SW (s. short wave)

swaged lead fil embouti; ~ **metal** métal embouti

swaging n matriçage; emboutissage

swamped circuit circuit bruyant

swamping n embouteillage; saturation

swap v échanger; extraire; recouvrir; remplacer

swap-in n (of overlay) transfert

swap-out n (of overlay) extraction

swappable adj permutable

swapping n recouvrement; remplacement; substitution; ~ **disk** disque d'évacuation; ~ **operating system** système d'exploitation échangé

swapping-out n extraction de partie d'un

S

programme
swap time temps de transfert
swarf *n* copeaux; bavure; cambouis
sweating *n* ressuage; refusion étain-plomb; suintement
sweep angle angle de flèche; ~ **frequency** fréquence de wobulation; ~ **generator** vobulateur; générateur de balayage; générateur de dents de scie; générateur de rampe; oscillateur à relaxation
sweeping *n* balayage; exploration
sweep lock-out pontet; ~ **modulation** ululation; vobulation; ~ **oscillator** oscillateur en dents de scie; ~ **range** bande d'exploration; ~ **rate** cadence de balayage; ~ **(relaxation) oscillator** oscillateur de relaxation; ~ **speed** base de temps (BT)
sweep-through jammer brouilleur wobulateur
sweep velocity vitesse de balayage; ~ **voltage** tension de balayage; tension de décharge; tension de déviation; tension de rampe; tension en dents de scie
swell *n* bombement
swelling *n* écaillement; boursoufflure
swept-frequency vibration vibrations à fréquence balayée; vibrations à fréquence variable; vibrations sinusoïdales
swept gain gain variable dans le temps (GVT); régulateur de sensibilité temporisé
swing *v* basculer; ~ *n* déflection; déplacement; déviation; dynamique; plage de relèvement; plage d'orientation; surmodulation; variation; excursion
swinging *n* oscillation; balancement du chercheur; ~ **cable link** balancier d'accompagnement
swing-out *adj* pivotant
S-wire *n* troisième fil; fil de corps; fil de douille; fil de maintien; fil de test; ~ (s. sleeve wire)
Swiss exchange commutateur universel
switch *v* aiguiller; basculer; orienter; commuter; ~ *n* bascule; clé; commutateur; contact; coupe-circuit; relais; interrupteur; inverseur; passage; ~ (of packet switching system) aiguillage (de paquets); ~ (floating cable pushbutton type) poire
switchable *adj* déconnectable; ~ **pad** complément de ligne escamotable
switch blade couteau d'interrupteur
switchboard *n* panneau de mutation (PM); commutateur manuel; panneau de distribution; panneau de raccordement; standard téléphonique; tableau de commutation; tableau électrique; tableau de distribution; ~ **connection** connexion de tableau; ~ **incoming trunk junctor** (SWIJ) ligne interstandard (LIS); ~ **indicator** lampe de tableau;

~ **operator** standardiste
switch clicks bruit de commutation; ~ **connection** connexion de l'interrupteur; ~ **core** noyau de commutation
switched access accès commuté
switched-beam direction finder radiogoniomètre à basculement du diagramme
switched capacitance capacité commutée
switched-capacitance bandpass filter filtre passe-bande à capacités commutées
switched circuit circuit commuté; ~ **connection** communication par commutation; ~ **line** ligne de réseau (LR); ligne commutée; ~ **loop** courant de trafic (CT); flux (de trafic)
switched-loop operation spécialisation de trafic; exploitation de classe B
switched network réseau commuté; ~ **on** (à l')état fermé; ~ **transit country** pays de transit en commutation; ~ **virtual circuit** circuit virtuel commuté (CVC)
switch fuse fusible à couteau
switchgear *n* autocommutateur; l'automatique; organes de commutation
switch hook crochet commutateur; ~ **house** coffret extérieur
switching *n* commutation; aiguillage; découpage; permutation; orientation (sur un poste); paramètres d'aiguillage; ~ **algebra** algèbre des circuits; ~ **and control** commutation et commande; ~ **and test centre** (STC) centre de commutation et d'essais (CCE); ~ **array** matrice de commutation; ~ **centre** centre de commutation (CDC); ~ **circuit board** carte de commutation; ~ **comb** échelle mobile; ~ **control pilot** onde pilote de commutation; ~ **control unit** (SCU) mise en présence (MP); ~ **current** courant commuté; ~ **equipment** organes centraux; matériel de commutation; ~ **equipment room** salle de l'autocommutateur; ~ **gate** porte logique
switching-in *n* enclenchement
switching interface répartiteur de jonctions MIC; ~ **maintenance** maintenance de la commutation; ~ **matrix** maille; matrice de commutation; ~ **network** réseau de connexion (CX/RCX); réseau de commutation; réseau de conversation; réseau de parole; ~ **network control unit** unité de gestion du réseau de connexion; ~ **network input line** ligne réseau entrante (LRE); ~ **network link** ligne réseau (LR); ~ **network output line** ligne réseau sortante (LRS); ~ **node** autocommutateur; nœud de commutation; ~ **noise** bruit de commutation et de friture; bruit sonore de commutation

switching-on *n* mise sous tension (MST); mise en circuit; mise en route

switching parameters paramètres de commutation; ~ **pilot** onde pilote de commutation; ~ **plane** sous-réseau; commutateur élémentaire; matrice; ~ **point** point de commutation; extrémité; ~ **pulse** impulsion de commutation; ~ **regulator** régulateur à découpage; ~ **spike** pointe de commutation; pic de commutation; surtension de commutation; ~ **stage** étage de commutation; ~ **subrack** panier de commutation; ~ **system** système de commutation; ~ **threshold** seuil de basculement; ~ **time** temps de commutation; durée de commutation; ~ **time waveforms** diagramme des temps; ~ **to** passage (en); ~ **to test circuits** renvoi aux essais; ~ **transistor** transistor de commutation; ~ **tube** tube de commutation; ~ **unit** commutateur; autocommutateur; discontacteur; ~ **voltage** tension de basculement

switch key clé de contact; ~ **module** commutateur; commutateur élémentaire; ~ **multiple** groupement; ~ **off** mettre hors tension; couper; débrancher; découper; ~ **on** allumer; brancher (sur); mettre le contact; mettre sous tension

switch-over *n* basculement; oscillation; permutation; ~ **time** temps de basculement; ~ **voltage** tension de basculement

switch panel tableau de distribution; ~ **path** maille d'accès; barre; chaîne de connexion; itinéraire; traversée de commutateur

switch-path map mémoire d'itinéraire

switch-point *n* aiguillage

switchroom *n* salle de l'autocommutateur

switch-selectable *adj* configurable par commutateur

switch unit coffret

swivel-arm lamp lampe articulée

swivel base patte orientable

swivelling *adj* pivotant

swivel stand plaque tournante

SW/LW selector (short-wave/long-wave) commutateur OC/OL (ondes courtes/ ondes longues)

sworn translation traduction jurée

SWR (s. standing-wave ratio)

SWS (s. status word string)

SxS switching commutation pas-à-pas

syllabic compander compresseur-extenseur syllabique

syllable articulation netteté pour les logatomes; articulation de syllabes

syllabus *n* contenu de stage; programme (pg)

symbol *n* symbole; sigle

symbolic address adresse symbolique; adresse flottante; ~ **coding** codage symbolique; programmation symbolique; ~ **language** langage symbolique; ~ **machine language** assembleur; ~ **name** nom symbolique; ~ **representation** diagramme; ~ **text updating facility** metteur à jour de textes symboliques

symbolize *v* caractériser

symbol rate débit de symboles; ~ **string** chaîne de symboles

symmetrical aerial input entrée d'antenne symétrique; ~ **binary code** code binaire symétrique; ~ **clipper** écrêteur symétrique; ~ **deflection** déviation symétrique; ~ **diode** diode symétrique; ~ **grading** multiplage partiel symétrique; ~ **power supply** alimentation siamoise; alimentation symétrique; ~ **star connection** montage symétrique en étoile; ~ **time-division matrix** matrice temporelle symétrique; ~ **triangular waveform** signal triangulaire symétrique

symmetric cable pair paire symétrique; ~ **difference** OU exclusif; addition sans retenue; exclusion réciproque

symptomatic *adj* déterministe

synchro (generator/transmitter) *n* arbre électrique; selsyn

synchronism *n* synchronisme

synchronization *n* synchronisation; accrochage; cadrage; concordance; recalage; verrouillage; ~ **byte** multiplet de synchronisation; ~ **equipment group** groupe d'équipement de synchronisation; ~ **failure** perte de synchronisation; ~ **module** module de synchronisation; ~ **of received signals** mise en phase du train incident; ~ **pattern** schéma de synchronisation; ~ **signal unit** unité de signalisation de synchronisation; ~ **with local clock** reprise en horloge locale

synchronized *adj* en synchronisme; asservi; cohérent

synchronizer *n* synchronisateur

synchronizing *n* topage; ~ **counter** compteur synchronisable; ~ **pilot** onde pilote de synchronisation; ~ **pulse** impulsion de synchronisation; ~ **pulse repeater** régénérateur de synchronisation; ~ **ratio** rapport d'amplitude de synchronisation; ~ **relay control scan point** commande du relais de signalisation; ~ **signal** signal de synchronisation

synchronous alternator alternateur synchrone; ~ **character** caractère de synchronisation; ~ **converter** convertisseur rotatif à induit unique; ~ **correction** correction de synchronisme; ~ **data network** réseau synchrone de transmission de données; ~ **decade counter** compteur binaire décimal

S

synchrone; ~ **duplex mode** en microsynchronisme; ~ **duplex operation** système au synchronisme; ~ **machine** synchronoscope; ~ **margin of start-stop apparatus** marge au synchronisme des appareils arythmiques; ~ **motor** moteur de synchronisation; ~ **network** réseau synchrone; ~ **serial** série synchrone; ~ **signalling system** système de signalisation synchrone; ~ **system** système synchrone; ~ **vibrator** mutateur de puissance; vibreur synchrone; ~ **voltage** tension synchrone; ~ **working** fonctionnement synchrone

synchroscope *n* synchronisateur
sync pulse top; créneau; signal de synchronisation; ~ **regenerator** régénérateur de synchronisation; ~ **separator** séparateur de synchronisation; ~ **signal** top de synchronisation
synergistic relationship synergie; association
syntax *n* (of message) forme; ~ **rules** règles de syntaxe
synthesized message message synthétisé
synthesizer filter filtre de synthèse
synthetic *adj* artificiel; composé; ~ **address** adresse calculée
synthetic-aperture radar radar à ouverture synthétique
synthetic language langage artificiel; ~ **material** matériau composé
syntony *n* accord; résonance de tension
SYSEND clôture
system *n* système; chaîne; dispositif; ensemble; régime; réseau; vacation; ~ **architecture** architecture du système
systematic *adj* systématique
system back-up sécurisation; ~ **blocking** blocage système; ~ **build** configuration; ~ **building** génération de système; ~ **communications interface** canal de communication système; ~ **configuration display** icône; ~ **context** contexte système; ~ **control signal unit** unité de signalisation pour la commande du système de signalisation; ~ **control station** station de contrôle (d'un faisceau); ~ **core storage** image système; ~ **crash** arrêt involontaire; écrasement système; incident système; ~ **data generator** configurateur; ~ **deviation** écart de régulation; ~ **disk** disque d'exploitation; ~ **file** fichier interne; ~ **(flow-)chart** organigramme d'analyse; ~ **handler** contrôleur du système (de base de données); ~ **information message** message de guidage; ~ **library** ordinothèque; ~ **(loading) tape** bande système; ~ **log** pupitre; ~ **monitoring/checkout** espionnage système; ~ **noise figure (SNF)** figure de bruit d'un système
systems analysis analyse fonctionelle de systèmes; expertise; ~ **analyst** analyste de systèmes; informaticien
system scheduler programme explorateur; moniteur
systems design conception de système
system security sécurisation
systems engineer ingénieur technico-commercial (ITC)
system simulation utility décors; ~ **software** logiciel de base; logiciel d'exploitation; ~ **tape generator** générateur de la bande système; ~ **time restriction** contrainte de temps (d'un système)
SZR (s. select zone rendition)

S

T

tab *n* languette; ailette; becquet (béquet); cosse; étiquette; onglet de protection; patte; pavé; pied; talon; ~ **card** carte mécanographique (perforée); ~ **collar** collier à plaquette; ~ **key** tabulateur

table *n* table; barème; matrice; tableau; ~ **interrogation** consultation de table; ~ **look-up** consultation de table; ~ **model telephone set** poste à socle; ~ **of differentials** table des écarts; ~ **packing** compactage des tables

tab stop taquet de tabulation

tabular entry frappe de texte en colonnes

tabulating *adj* électro-comptable; ~ **stop** taquet de tabulation

tabulation *n* cadrage; saut de colonne; ~ **clear (TBC)** suppression de tabulation; ~ **key** tabulateur

TACAN (s. tactical air navigation system)

tachogenerator *n* dynamo tachymétrique; alternateur tachymétrique; tachy

tachometer *n* tachymètre

tactical air navigation system (TACAN) système de radionavigation TACAN; ~ **communication satellite** satellite tactique de communication

tactile *adj* dactyle (dactylique)

tag *n* cosse; barre; borne; broche; délimiteur; descripteur; étiquette; indicateur; patte; point; repère; ~ **bit** bit drapeau; ~ **strip** bornier; plaquette à cosses; réglette (rg.)

tail *n* section locale; ~ **(of comet)** chevelure

tail-eating switching commutation à travers les enroulements des transformateurs

tailing *n* traînage

tailored *adj* à la demande; sur mesure; ~ **radiation pattern** diagramme proportionné de rayonnement

tailoring *n* adaptation; ajustage

tailstock *n* contre-point

take *v* (of map) construire; ~ (checkpoint) créer; ~ **a trap** prendre un déroutement

take-down *n* démontage

take-off *n* décollage

take-over facilities entraide(s)

take-up factor facteur de câblage; ~ **spool** bobine de réception; bobine enrouleuse; bobine réceptrice; enrouleur de bande

taking *n* (of checkpoint) constitution

talk-back circuit émetteur d'ordres; circuit d'intercommunication; circuit d'ordres; ~ **range** portée du poste mobile

talking key clé de conversation; ~ **pair** fils de conversation; paire conversation; ~ **wire** fil de conversation

talk-out range portée du poste fixe

talk-through facility dispositif d'intercommunication

tally *n* bilan; ~ **counter** compteur comptable; ~ **down** comptage régressif; décomptage

tallying *n* comptage

tally register registre accumulateur; ~ **roll** bande d'impression; ~ **system** système de compteur; ~ **up** comptage progressif

tamper-proof *adj* inviolable

tandem *adj* itératif; ~ **area** zone d'un centre nodal; ~ **call** appel en transit; appel transit; ~ **call forwarding** renvoi en cascade; ~ **completing trunk group** faisceau de transit local d'arrivée; ~ **connection of items** éléments en cascade; ~ **exchange** centre nodal (CN); centre de transit régional; centre nodal de transit; centre principal de transit; ~ **operation** exploitation en tandem; ~ **originating trunk group** faisceau de transit local de départ; ~ **(processor) system** biprocesseur; ~ **selector** sélecteur final; ~ **switch** centre de transit; ~ **switched circuit** circuit commuté en tandem; ~ **switching** commutation de transit; commutation (en) tandem; ~ **switching centre** centre de commutation en transit; ~ **tie trunk** ligne de jonction de transit; ~ **tie trunk network (TTTN)** réseau tandem de lignes de jonction; ~ **traffic** trafic de transit; ~ **trunk** circuit de transit; ~ **trunking (of PABX)** transit de lignes; acheminement de transit; ~ **working** exploitation en tandem

tangent galvanometer boussole de tangentes

tangential wave path rayon tangent

tangent of loss angle tangente de l'angle de pertes; ~ **ray** rayon tangent

tangle *n* enchevêtrement

tank *n* ligne à retard à mercure; réservoir; ~ **circuit** résonateur; circuit à bouchon; circuit de résonance parallèle; circuit oscillant final

tank-circuit capacitance capacité d'un circuit oscillant

T

tantalum-bead capacitor condensateur au tantale goutte

tantalum capacitor condensateur tantale

tap v écouter; prélever; ~ n mettre en dérivation; prise; taraud; ~ (of delay line) prise intermédiaire

tape n bande; ruban; enrubanage; ~ **change** fiche de mouvement; ~ **chronograph** chronographe électrique; ~ **copy** copie sur bande; ~ **deck** dérouleur de bande; ~ **drive** unité de bande magnétique; ~ **feed** avancement de la bande; ~ **file** volume; ~ **footage counter** compteur de défilement de bande; ~ **generator** configurateur; ~ **handler** dérouleur de bande magnétique; ~ **library** bandothèque; sonothèque; ~ **mark** marque de bande; réflecteur; ~ **marker** label de bande; ~ **punch** perforatrice de bande

taper n (of waveguide) raccord progressif

tape reader lecteur de bande; ~ **reader-punch** lecteur-perforateur de bande

tape-reading head tête de lecture de bande

tape recorder magnétophone; ~ **recording** enregistrement sur bande

tapered adj tronçonique; ~ **coaxial line** ligne coaxiale à résidence ondulaire à chargement continu; ~ **distribution** répartition en cloche; ~ **radome** radôme conique

tape reel bobine à ruban; volume bande; ~ **relay** transit par bande perforée; ~ **roll** bande porteuse

tape-roll packaging conditionnement en bande

taper pin goupille conique; pointe conique; ~ **washer** cale biaise

tape sensing device appareil explorateur de bande; ~ **switch** commutateur de bande; ~ **transmitter** émetteur télégraphique à bande perforée; ~ **transport** dérouleur de bande magnétique; ~ **winder** enrouleur de bande

taping n rubanage

tapped adj fileté; prélevé; ~ (through) **hole** trou (débouchant) taraudé (TT); ~ **transformer** transformateur à prises

tapper n mouchard; (cadence) ~ émetteur de cadence

tappet n cavalier; ~ **switch** interrupteur à bascule

tapping n prise; dérivation; écoute clandestine; écoute discrète; picot; piquage (sur CI); plot; point; prélèvement; branchement; ~ **key** contacteur à lame ressort; ~ **loss** perte en puissance apparente due à une dérivation

tap switch commutateur à prises; ~ **wrench** tourne-à-gauche

target n cible; but; objectif; objet; visée; ~ adj destinataire; ~ **acquisition** acquisition de la cible; ~ **acquisition and fire control** appareil d'acquisition de la cible et de contrôle du tir; ~ **area** zone utile; ~ **bearing** relèvement de la cible; ~ **blip** réponse de la cible; ~ **byte** octet cible; ~ **computer** calculateur d'exécution; ~ **discrimination** discrimination de cibles; ~ **distance** distance de la cible; ~ **identification** identification de la cible; ~ **language** langage objet; langage résultant; ~ **locating set** appareil de localisation de cibles; ~ **machine** machine cible; ~ **voltage** tension de coupure

tariff n tarif; ~ **rate** palier de taxe; ~ **standard** norme tarifaire; ~ **unit** unité de charge

task n tâche; mission; travail ('T'); ~ **activation calendar** gestion d'agenda; ~ **despatcher** distributeur de tâches (DDT); ~ **image** image tâche; ~ **in progress** tâche en cours; ~ **queue management** gestion des files d'attente des tâches; ~ **scheduling** enchaînement de tâches; gestion des tâches

TB (s. terminal block)

TBC (s. tabulation clear)

TC (s. transit centre)

TCM (s. trellis-coded modulation); ∼ (s. time-compression multiplex)

TCXO (s. temperature-compensated crystal oscillator)

TD (s. translator-distributor); ∼ (s. transmitter distributor)

TDM (s. time-division multiplexing)

TDMA (s. time-division multiple access); **(satellite)** ∼ **terminal** logique d'accès partagé au satellite (LAPS)

TDMS (s. telegraph distortion measuring set)

TD multiplex (transmission) télégraphie multiple

tearing n distorsion en drapeau; déchirure

technical assistance assistance technique; ~ **data sheet** cahier de charges (CdC); ~ **hitch** aléa de fonctionnement; ~ **operator** preneur de son; ~ **sales representative** ingénieur technico-commercial (ITC); ~ **sheet** fiche technique; ~ **source** origine technique; ~ **term** terme de métier; ~ **training** formation technique

technological cooperation coopération technologique; ~ **infrastructure** (mainframe, microcomputers, etc.) plate-forme technologique; ~ **spin-off** retombée technologique

TED (s. threshold extension demodulator)

tee junction jonction en té

teething trouble faute de jeunesse

Tefzel [T.N.] fluorure d'éthylène; copolymère d'éthylène tetrafluoroéthylène (ETFE)

telco *n* (telephone company) exploitant

tele-alarm *n* transmetteur d'alarme

telearchics télécommande; télécollecte

tele-autograph *m* téléautographe

telecast *n* émission de télévision; émission télévisée

telecine (equipment) télécinématique

telecommunications channel voie de télécommunication; ~ **network** réseau de télécommunication; ~ **service** service de télécommunication; ~ **tower** tour de télécommunication

telecommuting *n* télétravail

teleconference *n* téléconférence; téléréunion

teleconferencing *n* réunion téléphone; réunion à distance

telecontrol *n* télécommande; téléconduite; télécollecte

telegram *n* télégramme; ~ **tranmsission by telephone** transmission des télégrammes par téléphone

telegraph *n* télégraphe; ~ **alphabet/code** code de données; alphabet télégraphique; ~ **apparatus** appareil télégraphique; ~ **by-pass set** appareil de déviation télégraphique; ~ **cable** câble télégraphique; ~ **centre** centre télégraphique; ~ **channel** voie télégraphique; ~ **circuit/line** voie de communication télégraphique; ~ **connection** connexion télégraphique; ~ **conversation** échange télégraphique d'informations; ~ **crosstalk** diaphonie télégraphique; ~ **current** courant de télégraphie; ~ **demodulator** démodulateur télégraphique; ~ **distortion** (of a modulation or a restitution) distorsion télégraphique (d'une modulation ou d'une restitution); ~ **distortion measuring set (TDMS)** appareil de mesure de la distorsion télégraphique; distorsiomètre; ~ **electromagnet** électroaimant télégraphique; ~ **exchange** commutateur automatique télégraphique

telegraphist *n* télégraphiste

telegraph key manipulateur (télégraphique); ~ **line** ligne de télégraphie; ~ **magnifier** amplificateur télégraphique; ~ **modulation** modulation télégraphique; ~ **network** réseau télégraphique; ~ **noise** bruit télégraphique; ~ **office** bureau télégraphique; ~ **pole** poteau téléphonique; poteau électrique; ~ **position** position télégraphique; ~ **relation** relation télégraphique; ~ **relay** relais miniature (polarisé); ~ **repeater** translateur télégraphique; répéteur télégraphique; translation télégraphique; ~ **route** voie d'émission télégraphique;

~ **service** service télégraphique; ~ **signal element** élément de signal télégraphique; ~ **speed** rapidité de modulation; vitesse télégraphique; ~ **station** poste télégraphique; ~ **switch** commutateur automatique télégraphique; ~ **traffic** relation télégraphique

telegraph-transmission coefficient facteur d'émission télégraphique

telegraph transmitter émetteur télégraphique; ~ **word** mot télégraphique

telegraphy by the on-off keying of a modulating audio frequency or frequencies télégraphie par manipulation par tout ou rien d'une ou de plusieurs fréquences audibles de modulation; ~ **on pure continuous waves** télégraphie non modulée

telematics *n* télématique

telemessage service transmission des télégrammes par téléphone; service de téléphonogrammes; télégramme téléphoné

telemetering télémesure

telemetry *n* télémesure; ~ **tracking and command (TTC)** sous-système de télémesure trajectographie et télécommande

telepayment *n* télécollecte

telephone accessories matériel de péritéléphonie; ~ **amplifier** répéteur

telephone-answering machine alibiphone

telephone area zone téléphonique; ~ **bill** facture téléphonique; ~ **booth/box** cabine téléphonique; ~ **breakdown** dérangement du téléphone; ~ **cable** câble téléphonique; ~ **call** conversation téléphonique; communication téléphonique; ~ **carrier current** courant porteur téléphonique; ~ **central office** central téléphonique; ~ **channel** voie téléphonique; ~ **code** code téléphonique; ~ **company** (telco) compagnie téléphonique; ~ **connection** communication téléphonique; connexion téléphonique; ~ **conversation** conversation téléphonique; entretien téléphonique; ~ **data acquisition handbook** guide de recueil de données; ~ **earth** terre téléphonique; ~ **engineer** (repair service) dérangements; ~ **equipment** matériel téléphonique; ~ **exchange** bureau téléphonique; standard téléphonique; ~ **frequency** fréquence téléphonique; fréquence vocale (FV); ~ **influence factor (TIF)** facteur téléphonique de forme; ~ **junction box** (jack socket) conjoncteur; ~ **layout** (of numeric keypad) configuration téléphonique; ~ **line** ligne téléphonique; ~ **line concentrator** concentrateur de lignes; ~ **loop** circuit téléphonique bifilaire; ~ **number** numéro de téléphone; ~ **operator** standardiste; téléphoniste; ~ **peripheral**

accessory appareil de péritéléphonie; ~ plant équipements téléphoniques
'telephone' pliers pince téléphone
telephone receiver récepteur téléphonique; ~ relation relation téléphonique; ~ relay relais téléphonique; ~ repeater répéteur téléphonique; ~ ringer sonnerie de poste téléphonique; ~ sales office agence commerciale; téléboutique; ~ service service téléphonique; ~ set appareil téléphonique; poste téléphonique; ~ showroom téléboutique; ~ station poste téléphonique d'abonné; ~ support facilities péritéléphonie; ~ switchboard tableau commutateur téléphonique; ~ switching commutation téléphonique; ~ system système téléphonique; ~ traffic relation téléphonique; ~ transmission quality qualité de transmission téléphonique; ~ transmission rating évaluation d'une transmission téléphonique; ~ transmission reference circuit circuit de référence pour la transmission téléphonique; ~ user part (TUP) sous-système utilisateur téléphonique (SSUT)
telephonist n téléphoniste
telephonometry n téléphonométrie
telephony n téléphonie
telephotometer n téléphotomètre
teleprinter n téléimprimeur; télétype de dialogue; téléimprimeur arythmique; téléscripteur; ~ code code télex; code de téléimprimeur; ~ conference circuit circuit de conférence par téléimprimeurs; ~ exchange central télex; ~ keyboard selection numérotation au clavier (télégraphique); ~ message communication téléimprimée; ~ signal signal de téléimprimeur; ~ (start-stop) appareil télégraphique arythmique
teleprinter/telex perforator perforateur pour téléimprimeur; perforateur pour télex
teleprinter/TTY télétype en dialogue
teleprinting apparatus téléimprimeur
teleprocessing n télétraitement
telerecording n téléenregistrement
telescopic aerial antenne téléscopique; ~ mast mât télescopique
telescoping n focalisation
teleservices n pl téléactions
teletypewriter (TTY) n téléscripteur; périphérique léger; téléimprimeur arythmique; machine à écrire (MAE)
television (TV) n télévision; ~ accessories péritélévision; ~ aerial antenne de télévision; ~ band bande de télévision; ~ bandwidth restrictions limitations de la largeur de bande de télévision; ~ broadcast émission télévisée; ~ broadcasting radiodiffusion visuelle; ~ cable câble de

télévision; ~ camera caméra de télévision; ~ centre station de télévision; ~ channel canal de télévision; chaîne; ~ channel using upper sideband canal direct; ~ direct pick-up link liaison par reprise directe de la télévision; ~ frequency converter unit convertisseur de canal de télévision; ~ image image de télévision; ~ interference (TVI) interférence en télévision; ~ licence redevance de télévision; ~ line ligne de télévision à grande distance; ~ link liaison par lignes de télévision; ~ network switching centre centre de commutation du réseau de télévision; ~ picture image de télévision; ~ picture tube tube cinéscope; ~ programme switching centre centre de modulation de télévision; ~ receive-only (TVRO) télévision-réception seule; ~ receiver récepteur de télévision; téléviseur; ~ reconnaissance reconnaissance par télévision; ~ satellite satellite de télévision; ~ set téléviseur; ~ signal level niveau du signal de télévision; ~ sound transmitter émetteur radioélectrique de son de télévision; ~ standards normes de télévision; ~ station link chaîne de stations émettrices de télévision; ~ system système de télévision; ~ system converter convertisseur de définition; ~ test pattern mire; ~ transmission transmission télévisuelle; ~ tube tube cathodique à image; cinéscope; tube de télévision; ~ waveform forme d'onde de télévision
telewatch n télécontrôle
telewattmeter n téléwattmètre
teleworking n télétravail
telewriter (= teleautograph machine) téléautographe; téléscripteur
telewriting n messagerie de l'écrit; écriture électronique; téléautographie; télé-écriture
telex n télex; ~ code code télex; code de téléimprimeur; ~ conference circuit circuit de conférence par téléimprimeurs; ~ exchange central télex; ~ message communication téléimprimée; ~ network réseau télex; ~ service service télex; ~ signal signal de télex; signal de téléimprimeur; ~ subscriber abonné télex
teller terminal terminal de guichet
tell-tale n mouchard; ~ lamp voyant
teltouch dialling numérotation au clavier multifréquences
temper n dureté
temperature coefficient coefficient de température; ~ coefficient (of resistance, measured in p.p.m.) dérive en température (des valeurs de résistances); ~ coefficient of working voltage coefficient de température

de la tension de fonctionnement

temperature-compensated crystal oscillator (TCXO) oscillateur pilote thermostaté; oscillateur à quartz thermostaté; ~ **oscillator** oscillateur à compensation de température

temperature-compensating diode thermistance

temperature-compensation equalizer correcteur d'effet de température; ~ **network** réseau à compensation de température

temperature-controlled *adj* thermo-régulé; ~ **environment** étuve

temperature deviation dérive en température; ~ **drift** dérive en température; ~ **error offset** compensation de variations de température; ~ **inversion** inversion de température; ~ **lag** inertie thermique; ~ **reference conductor** conducteur de repérage de la température

tempered steel bar barre adoucie

template *n* gabarit; calibre; ~ **file** fichier modèle

tempo *n* allure; cadence; vitesse

temporal coherence (of fibre optics) cohérence temporelle

temporarily-disconnected subscriber abonné suspendu

temporarily out of service suspendu

temporary *adj* provisoire; passager; ~ **call forwarding - follow me** renvoi temporaire; ~ **connection** connexion temporaire; ~ **hyphen** tiret de coupure de mot; ~ **stop** arrêt momentané; ~ **storage area** (of register) garage; ~ **work queue** file d'attente (fichier)

ten-fibre element élément à dix encoches

ten-point selector sélecteur à dix sorties

tens-group *n* dizaine

tensile strength résistance à la traction; résistance mécanique; ~ **test** essai de résistance à la traction; ~ **tester** maquette de traction

tensimeter *n* tensiomètre

tension *n* (of spring) rigidité; ~ **arm** bras amortisseur

tension/compression scale (tester) tensiomètre

tensioner *n* tendeur

tension pulley tenseur

ten storage locations décade

tentative *adj* provisoire; évolutif; ~ **address** adresse provisoire

tenting *n* galbage

ten-wire connector liaison décimale

terminal *n* accès; borne; connexion; cosse; jonction; languette; organe; périphérique; plot; point; support; terminal; tête de réception; ~ **apparatus** appareil terminal; ~ **assignment list** liste de bornage; ~ **blank** espace à droite; ~ **block (TB)** barrette; bloc de raccordement; connecteur; domino; planchette de bornes bornier; réglette (rg.); ~ **board** bornier; plaquette de connexion; ~ **box** boîte de distribution; boîte d'extrémité; ~ **capacity** capacité de raccordement; ~ **charge** taxe terminale; ~ **circuit** joncteur; circuit terminal; équipement terminal; ~ **circuit connections** brassages et interconnections; ~ **clamp** étrier; serre-bornes; ~ **echo suppressor** suppresseur d'écho terminal; ~ **equipment** matériel d'extrémité; poste terminal; ~ **exchange** central terminal; ~ **exchange group selector** sélecteur de groupe du centre terminal; ~ **exchange line** ligne de central terminal; ~ **group** groupe terminal; ~ **half-echo suppressor** demi-suppresseur d'écho terminal; ~ **identification** repère; ~ **impedance** impédance de terminaison; ~ **interface** interface de terminal; ~ **pad/land** lamelle; ~ **post** tige polaire; ~ **printer** imprimante de sortie; ~ **rack** bâti étroit; ~ **repeater** répéteur terminal; ~ **seizing signal** signal de prise terminal; ~ **station** station terminale; ~ **strip** barrette de raccordement; planchette de bornes; réglette de connexion(s); réglette à broches; ~ **traffic** trafic terminal; ~ **trunk exchange** bureau interurbain extrême; ~ **unit tester (TUT)** coffret TUT

terminate *v* arrêter; désactiver; ~ (at) aboutir (à); déboucher

terminated level niveau composite adapté

terminate in a load boucler sur une charge

terminating *adj* d'arrivée; de droite; ~ **(incoming) call** communication d'arrivée; ~ **circuit** circuit d'arrêt; ~ **class-of-service** discrimination arrivée; ~ **country** pays d'arrivée; pays terminal; ~ **exchange** central d'arrivée; autocommutateur d'arrivée; bureau d'arrivée; ~ **impedance** impédance de terminaison; cellule de bouclage; ~ **mobile** mobile demandé; ~ **observed subscriber** (line) abonné observé à l'arrivée (OBA); ~ **register** enregistreur d'arrivée; ~ **set** termineur; circuit hybride; ~ **traffic** trafic d'arrivée

termination *n* aboutissement; arrêt; bout; branchement; fin; patte; picot; queue; résiliation; résistance de terminaison; sortie; terminaison; charge adaptée; tête

terminator *n* caractère d'arrêt

termipoint soldering thermi-point; ~ **wiring** connexion point à point par clips

term set circuit hybride; réseau de connexion (CX/RCX)

term-set attenuation affaiblissement d'un termineur

terms of reference précision de l'objet

ternary alphabet code ternaire; ~ code code ternaire

terrain clearance indicator altimètre radioélectrique; ~ clearance warning indicator avertisseur de hauteur

terrestrial aerial antenne terrestre; ~ connecting network réseau de connexion terrestre; ~ line ligne terrestre; ~ link liaison terrestre; ~ MUX multiplex terrestre; ~ network interface switching equipment centre de raccordement au réseau terrestre; ~ station station terrienne; ~ telephone circuit circuit téléphonique de terre

tertiary centre centre tertiaire; ~ power supplies (of converters) énergie tertiaire; ~ sector (offices, shops, services and research organisations) secteur tertiaire

test v contrôler; éprouver; essayer; ~ n essai; contrôle; épreuve; interrogation; test

test(ing) bench banc d'essai

test aerial antenne d'essai; ~ alphabetic contrôle alphabétique; ~ and diagnostic data stimulis; ~ apparatus appareil d'essai; ~ at design stage essai à l'étude; ~ bed plate-forme d'intégration; banc d'essais; ~ board table d'essais et de mesure; panneau d'essai; table d'essais; ~ brush frotteur d'essai; ~ bus ligne de best; liaison de test; ~ bush prise de test

test-busy signal signal de blocage

test call appel d'essai; communication d'essai; connexion d'essai; conversation de test; ~ call generator simulateur d'appel téléphonique; ~ call indicator indicateur d'appel de maintenance; ~ card carte de contrôle; ~ centre centre d'essais; ~ chart logigramme de test; ~ circuit pont de mesure; circuit de contrôle; ~ circuit transfer renvoi aux essais; ~ clip (of IC) pince d'essai; ~ conditions sanctions; ~ configuration configuration du test; ~ connection connexion de mesure; ~ connector connecteur d'essai; ~ console coffret de contrôle; banc d'essai; pupitre d'essai; ~ continuity sonner (un circuit); ~ coupon (of PCB) éprouvette; ~ data information par mesures; ~ date date d'épreuve; ~ deck jeu d'essai(s); ~ desk table d'essais et de mesure; position d'essais; ~ enclosure chambre d'essai; ~ equipment équipement d'essai

tester n appareil de mesure; banc de maintenance; contrôleur; machine de test; mesureur; testeur; valise

test frequency fréquence de mesure; fréquence de contrôle; fréquence d'essai

testimonial n référence

testing n mesure(s)

test instrument appareil d'essai; ~ interface canal de test; ~ jack jack d'essai; ~ jig bâti de test; ~ lead cordon de mesure; cordon pointe de touche; ~ level niveau de mesure; ~ line ligne de test; ~ load charge d'essai; ~ loop and repeated R-Y (5-unit) code transmission roulement RY; ~ matrix tête de mesure; ~ module boîtier de test; ~ OK bon aux essais; ~ panel tableau d'essai; panneau de coupure; ~ parameters gabarit d'essai; ~ pattern vidéo mire; cible; image utile; ~ piece éprouvette; ~ pin point de contrôle; ~ point prise d'essai; point de contrôle; ~ position poste de contrôle (pc); banc d'essai; ~ probe poignard de test; ~ procedure conduite d'essai; ~ prod grip-test; pointe de touche; ~ program programme d'essai; ~ rack table de coupure; ~ rate cadence de test; ~ receptacle prise de test; ~ recess puits de test; ~ relay relais de test; ~ rig banc d'essai; ~ section section d'essais; ~ set testeur; ~ sheet fiche de mesure; ~ signal signal de mesure; ~ signals stimulis; ~ station poste de test; ~ terminal prise de test; ~ tone tonalité de contrôle; signal d'essai; ~ traffic trafic d'essai; ~ transformer transformateur d'essai; ~ tube éprouvette; ~ under consideration essai à l'étude; ~ unit organe de maintenance; ~ voltage tension d'essai; ~ wire fil de blocage; fil de maintien; fil de test

tetrad n groupe de quatre bits (= tétrade)

tetrode n tetrode

TE wave onde H

text n libellé; corps du message; motif; texte; ~ constant constante de texte; ~ editor éditeur de textes; ~ format format de texte; ~ messaging courrier électronique; ~ put-aside mémorisation de phrase

T flip-flop bascule à commande symétrique

TGF (s. through-group filter)

thaw n démasquage

thawing n (interrupt enable) déblocage

theme n motif

the neutral (side) le négatif

theoretical cut-off frequency fréquence de coupure; ~ duration of a significant interval (of modulation or restitution) durée théorique d'un intervalle significatif (de modulation ou de restitution); ~ graph courbe théorique; ~ timing diagram diagramme séquentiel théorique

theory n calcul; hypothèse; philosophie

the outside world le monde extérieur; ~ quick brown fox jumps over the lazy dog (test sentence) Voyez la brique géante que je

jette auprès du wharf
thermal agitation (voltage) effet thermique;
~ **compensation** compensation de température; ~ **conductivity** conductivité thermique; ~ **effect** effet thermique; ~ **imaging** thermographie; ~ **inertia** inertie thermique; inertie calorifique; ~ **infra-red mapping** thermographie; ~ **loss** perte thermique
thermally-insulated *adj* calorifugé
thermal microphone microphone thermique;
~ **noise** bruit d'agitation thermique; bruit blanc; bruit gaussien; parasites d'agitation thermique; ~ **padding** matelas thermique; ~ **printer** imprimante thermique; ~ **rating** courant thermique; ~ **relay** relais magnétothermique (Rmt); relais électro-thermique; relais thermique (Rt); ~ **resistance (R$_{th}$)** résistance thermique; ~ **resistor** thermistance; ~ **runaway** emballement thermique; ~ **shock** choc thermique; ~ **shutdown** sécurité thermique; limitation thermique; protection thermique; ~ **shutdown device** dispositif magnétothermique; ~ **switch** interrupteur thermique; bilame; ~ **time constant** constant de temps thermique; ~ **tuning rate** vitesse d'accord thermique; ~ **unit rating** puissance calorifique unitaire
thermionic arc arc thermoélectronique;
~ **emission** émission thermoélectronique; effet Edison; effet redresseur; émission thermionique; ~ **relay** relais thermionique
thermistor *n* thermistance; sonde; thermorésistance; résistance themométrique
thermocouple *n* couple; couple thermoélectrique; thermocouple; ~ **ammeter** ampèremètre à thermocouple
thermodynamic temperature température thermodynamique
thermo-electric effect effet thermoélectrique;
~ **module** module à effet Peltier; ~ **power station** centrale thermoélectrique/thermique
thermo-electronic cathode cathode thermoélectronique
thermo-fit sleeve cordon de frettage
thermo-forming *n* thermoformage
thermography *n* thermographie
thermojunction *n* couple thermoélectrique
thermomagnetic device dispositif magnétothermique
thermophone *n* thermophone
thermoplastic acrylic resin Plexiglas
thermo-setting *adj* thermodurcissable
thermostat *n* thermostat
thermostatically-controlled crystal oscillator (TCXO) oscillateur à quartz thermostaté
Thévenin's theorem théorème de Thévenin

thickening agent durcisseur
thick film couche épaisse (CE)
thief track voleur de courant; piste voleur
thin film couche mince (CM)
thin-film memory mémoire à films minces;
~ **storage** mémoire à films minces (magnétiques)
"think tank" réservoir à pensée
thinner *n* diluant
thin-route telephony téléphonie à trafic dispersé
third-generation *adj* bisaëul
third-order distortion distorsion cubique;
~ **high-density bipolar coding (HDB3)** haute densité bipolaire d'ordre trois; ~ **intermodulation** intermodulation du troisième ordre
third-party entry entrée en tiers
third party on hold tiers en garde
third-party vendors hors parc; réseau de distribution tiers; concurrence
third wire fil de corps; fil de douille; fil de maintien; fil de test et blocage
third-wire control commande du troisième fil
thirteen-group treiz. (treizaine)
Thomson effect effet redresseur; effet Edison
thousand lines kiloligne (KL)
thousands-group *n* millier
thrashing *n* emballement; affolement
thread *v* (of flux) traverser; ~ *n* brin; fil; filet
thread-cutting screw vis autotaraudeuse
threaded cotter pin axe fileté; ~ **file** fichier enchaîné; ~ **rod** tige filetée; ~ **stud** goujon fileté
threading *n* enchaînement; enfilage; mise en place; ~ (of flux) passage
thread insert (wire type) douille filetée intervis
three-bit byte groupe de trois bits (= triade)
three-condition cable code code trivalent pour câble; ~ **telegraph code** code télégraphique trivalent
three-conductor cable cordon trifilaire; cordon à trois fils
three-digit thumbwheel Contrave à 3 chiffres [A.C.]
three-dimensional direction-finding relèvement tridimensionnel; ~ **radar** radar tridimensionnel
three-input adder additionneur à trois entrées
three-link international call communication internationale de transit double
three-party conference conférence tripartite
three-phase counter compteur triphasé; ~ **current** courant triphasé; ~ **line** ligne triphasée; ~ **mesh connection** couplage en triangle; ~ **rectifier** montage en étoile; ~ **to DC converter** commutatrice triphasée continue

three-point connection montage Hartley
three-pole starter discontacteur tripolaire
three-slot winding bobinage à trois encoches
three-state line unit ligne à signalisation par changement d'état; ~ port porte tri-état
three-term control (proportional-integral-derivative PID) régulation PID; ~ controller (PID) régulateur à trois actions
three-terminal circuit (hybrid) tripôle (d'aiguillage)
three-way call appel à trois; ~ calling conférence additive; conférence programmée; ~ conference conférence à trois; ~ conference call circuit joncteur de conférence; ~ switch interrupteur va-et-vient
three-wire gauge gabarit à trois joncs
threshold n seuil; marge; quota; ~ current courant de seuil; ~ data données de sensibilité; ~ effect effet de seuil; ~ element critère de décision; ~ extension demodulator (TED) démodulateur à extension du seuil; ~ frequency fréquence critique; ~ generator générateur de rampe; ~ level niveau de seuil; ~ of luminescence seuil de luminescence; ~ performance performance de seuil; ~ setting réglage du seuil; ~ voltage tension de seuil; ~ wavelength seuil de longueur d'onde photo-électronique
throat n cou de cornet; ~ microphone laryngophone
through-connection n transit; passage; ~ delay durée d'établissement (d'un autocommutateur); ~ filter filtre de transfert
through-dialling sélection directe à l'arrivée (SDA); prise directe contrôlée; sélection automatique à distance
through group groupe primaire non démodulé
through-group filter (TGF) filtre de transfert de groupe primaire
through-hole plated plaqué; métallisé; ~ plating métallisation
through-level n niveau absolu de tension; dénivellement; niveau d'essai non adapté
through line circuit de transit; ligne de transfert
through-line repeater répéteur embroché
throughput n rendement; cadence; capacité; débit; défilement
"through" signal mise en présence (MP)
through supergroup groupe secondaire non démodulé; ~ 15-supergroup assembly connection point assemblage de 15 groupes secondaires point de transfert d'assemblage
through-switching n passage en métallique; passage en conversation

through traffic trafic de transit
through-trunk exchange centre principal de transit
throw v actionner; baisser; basculer; enclencher; manœuvrer; ~ n saut; transfert
throwing n basculement
throw-over switch commutateur à bascule
thrust n poussée; ~ arm pousseur
thumbnail description canevas; généralités
thumb nut écrou O
thumbwheel n roue codeuse; ~ switch afficheur
thump n (vern.) bruit de télégraphie; interférence
thyristor communicating circuit alternistor; ~ stack pont de puissance
tick n battement
ticker tape bande télégraphique
ticket n ticket; étiquette; relevé
ticketing n justification de taxe; établissement de fiches; taxation
tickler file fichier d'attente; fichier de relance; fichier de suivi
TICOSS (s. time-compressed single-sideband system)
tie v ficeler; attacher; ~ n bride; collier; jonc; liaison; lien; ligature
TIE (s. time interval error)
tied letters (diphtong) ligature
tie-down point fréquence d'alignement
tie-line n inter-auto (IA); ligne de branchement; ligne de jonction; ligne entre centraux privés; ligne interautomatique; ligne interinstallations; ligne privée; ligne spécialisée
tier n empilage
tiered array antenne réseau; antenne rideau; rideau d'antennes
tie-trunk n interurbain automatique (IA); connexion transversale; jonction interautomatique; ligne de jonction; ligne interautomatique; ligne interinstallations; ligne privée
tie wire fil d'attache; ligature
TIF (s. telephone influence factor)
tight adj serré; étanche; ~ coupling couplage serré; couplage fort
tighten (-up) resserrer
tightened-up adj sévérisé
tighten (screws) alternately at opposite corners serrer en croix
tighter tolerance limits resserrement des tolérances
tight fibre (of cable) fibre enrobée; ruban serré; ~ fit ajustement serré
tilt v basculer; orienter; ~ n pente; angle; bascule; inclinaison; orientation; ~ (angle) angle d'inclinaison

tilted *adj* penché

tilting *adj* basculant; ~ **arm** béquille de réglage d'inclinaison

time-and-date coding horodatage; ~ **signals** signaux horodateurs; ~ **stamp** horodateur

time-and-distance metering taxation périodique; comptage à la distance et à la durée; impulsions périodiques; ~ **metering rate** palier de taxe

time-and-motion study étude chronométrique

time-and-zone metering taxation par zone et la durée

time band tranche horaire

time-base *n* base de temps (BT); dent de scie (DDS); cadencement; ~ **circuit** circuit de base de temps; ~ **error correction** correcteur d'erreur de base de temps; ~ **frequency** fréquence de la base de temps; ~ **generator** générateur de base de temps; générateur de dents de scie; générateur de rampe; générateur de rythme; oscillateur de base de temps; ~ **sync** (phase difference) différentiel

time between pulses intervalle de manipulation; ~ **channel** voie temporelle (VT); ~ **check** contrôle du temps

time-compressed single-sideband system (TI-COSS) système de bande latérale unique comprimée dans le temps

time-compression multiplex (TCM) mode continu

time-consistent busy hour heure chargée moyenne

time constant of resonant amplification constante de temps d'amplification à résonance

time-consuming *adj* fastidieux

timed call communication taxée à la durée; ~ **changeover switch** contact OF (ouvert/fermé) temporisé

time-delay circuit circuit temporisation; ~ **disable** blocage cames; ~ **initiation** armement temporisation; ~ **memory** mémoire de temporisation; ~ **relay** relais temporisé; relais à action différée; relais à action lente; relais à attraction retardée; relais retardé; ~ **unit** temporisateur; ~ **zone** zone de temporisation

time demodulation démodulation dans le temps

time-dependent *adj* à la durée; en fonction de l'heure

time-derived channel sous-voie; voie dérivée en temps

time-division electronic switching commutation électronique temporelle; ~ **exchange** autocommutateur temporel; ~ **multiple access (TDMA)** accès multiple par réparti-

tion dans le temps (AMRT); multiplexage temporel; ~ **multiplexing (TDM)** multiplexage temporel; transmission par secteurs; transmission multiplex à répartition temporelle; multiplexage par partage du temps; multiplexage dans le temps; ~ **multiplex telegraphy** télégraphie par répartition dans le temps; ~ **multiplex transmitter** émetteur multiplex à répartition dans le temps; ~ **stage** étage de commutation temporelle

time division switching *time switching; digital switching* commutation temporelle; commutation numérique; commutation par répartition dans le temps; connexion temporelle

time-division switching network réseau de connexion temporel

timed loop-break coupure calibrée

time-domain *adj* temporel; ~ **synthesis** synthèse de la gamme supérieure

timed-out *adj* échéancé; temporisé; la temporisation physique est tombée; ~ **call forwarding** renvoi temporisé; renvoi sur non réponse

timed reminder rappel temporisé

time equalizer correcteur d'écho; ~ **function** fonction du temps; ~ **instant** moment (MOM); ~ **interval** durée

time-interval error (TIE) erreur sur la durée

time-invariant *adj* asynchrone; indépendant du temps

time-keeper *n* tronc synchro

time lag action différée; arrêt différé; temporisation; décalage de temps; décalage temporel

time-lag fuse fusible temporisé; ~ **relay** relais retardé

time management gestion du temps; ~ **of day** heure

time-of-day clock horloge temps réel; horloge interne

time on-line durée en ligne

time-out *n* débordement de la temporisation; acquittement; durée d'activation; échéance; épuisement; intervention de cames; temporisation d'arrêt; temporisation écoulée

time overlap recouvrement du temps; ~ **per unit** durée d'une unité; ~ **pre-assignment** préassignation variable dans le temps

time-quantized control commande à quantification temporelle

timer *n* compteur horaire; chronomètre; générateur de rythme; horloge; minuterie; temporisateur; sablier; ~ **unit** bloc temporisé

time scale barème de temps; ~ **selector** circuit

T

discriminateur de temps

time-sharing *n* partage de temps; ~ *adj* différé; à utilisation collective; ~ **I/O system** impression différée

time signal signal horaire; came; top; ~ **slice** vacation; ~ **slicing** allocation de temps; ~ **slot** tranche horaire; canal; créneau; élément de trame; fenêtre temporelle; voie numérique; ~ **slot interchange** changement de position temporelle

time-space junction (T-S) jonction multiplex d'entrée (JME)

time switch commutateur temporel; interrupteur à temps; interrupteur horaire

time-switch buffer memory board opérateur de mémoire temporelle

time-switching stage étage de commutation numérique; étage de commutation temporelle

time switch with backward control commutateur temporel à commande amont; ~ **switch with forward control** commutateur temporel à commande aval

timetable *n* calendrier; échéance; planning; horaire

time-time network (TT) réseau temporel-temporel

time-transparent *adj* temporellement transparent

time-uncoordinated *adj* asynchrone

time zone fuseau horaire

timing *n* cadencement; calage; calibrage; chronométrage; rythme; synchronisation; temps; temporisation; ~ **chain** chaîne de distribution; ~ **circuit** rythmeur; ~ **circuitry** circuit de génération d'horloge; ~ **control** génération d'horloge (GH); ~ **device** minuterie; ~ **diagram** chronogramme; diagramme de fonctionnement; diagramme des temps; diagramme temporel; gabarit; séquentiel; ~ **error** erreur de cadence; ~ **gear** engrenage de synchronisation; ~ **hardware** oscillateur incorporé; ~ **logic** logique de basculement; logique d'horloge; ~ **mark** marque de synchronisation; ~ **memory** mémoire de temporisation; ~ **module** module de synchronisation; ~ **oscillator** oscillateur de synchronisation; ~ **pulse** créneau; impulsion de marquage; impulsion de rythme; ~ **recovery circuit** circuit de reconstitution du rythme

timing-signal signal de rythme; cadence; créneau; horloge; ~ **card** opérateur des signaux de temps; ~ **circuit board** carte de base de temps; ~ **distribution** logique majoritaire; ~ **extraction** récupération du rythme; récupération d'horloge; ~ **generation** production des cames; ~ **generator**

générateur de rythme; ~ **recovery** récupération du rythme; reconstitution du signal de rythme

timing signals temps d'aiguillage; ~ **track** code temporel; ~ **unit** temporisateur

timistor *n* timistor

tin *n* étain

tin(-plate) fer blanc

tin-cry *n* cri

tine (of IDC connector) lyre

tinkle *n* tintement

tin-lead alloy plating dépot d'alliage étain-plomb; ~ **plating** étamage

tinman's solder soudure étain-plomb; soudure étain-plomb 60/40

tinned wire conducteur étamé

tinning *n* étamage

tin-plated brass laiton étamé

tinsmith's solder soudure étain-plomb 60/40

tinted acrylic Plexiglas fumé

tiny air bubble microbulle

tip *n* bout; buse; embout; grain; point; pointe; sommet; ~ (of jack) pointe de fiche; ~ **jack** douille femelle; ~ **of soldering iron** panne de fer

tip-side conducteur relié à l'extrémité d'une fiche bipolaire

tip-wire fil de pointe; conducteur relié à l'extrémité d'une fiche bipolaire

tissue paper papier de soie

title *n* intitulé; caractérisation; désignation; libellé; titre; ~ **block** cartouche (c. de plan); ~ **page** page de garde

titration *n* dosage

T-junction jonction en té

to a greater or lesser degree plus ou moins; sensiblement; ~ **be defined** à l'étude; ~ **CCITT standards** normalisé CCITT

toggle *v* basculer; faire passer; ~ **circuit** circuit bistable; ~ **clamp** étau instantané; ~ **fastener** genouillère; ~ **switch** basculeur; commutateur; interrupteur à bascule; interrupteur à genouillère; interrupteur à levier; inverseur

toggling *n* alternance; basculement; passage; rebonissement

token-passing protocol protocole à jeton

tolerable delay délai d'attente acceptable

tolerance *n* marge; sensibilité; ~ **limit(s)** sanction; gabarit

toll board position interurbaine; meuble interurbain; table d'opérateur; table interurbaine; ~ **cable** câble interurbain; ~ **call** appel interurbain; ~ **circuit** circuit téléphonique interurbain; circuit local; ~ **collection** péage; ~ **denial** interdiction d'appels longue distance; ~ **desk** meuble interurbain; ~ **dialling** sélection interurbaine automatique; numérotation interurbaine; ~ **discriminator** discriminateur

toll-free call appel libre; ~ **number** numéro vert

toll line ligne interurbaine; ~ **network** réseau interurbain (RI); ~ **office** centre interurbain; ~ **operator** annotatrice; ~ **readout** relevé de taxes; ~ **restricted station** poste à prise directe restreinte; ~ **switch** centre de transit interurbain; ~ **switchboard** tableau commutateur interurbain; ~ **switching trunk** ligne intermédiaire; ~ **ticket** relevé de communication

tonal *adj* sonore

tone *n* tonalité; fréquence; intensité; mélodie; signal; signe; son; ~ **alert** (of pager) bip

tone-and-pulse distribution courants spéciaux

tone-buffer memory mémoire tampon de tonalités

tone burst train de sonnerie; alarme sonore; impulsions sonores; top sonore; ~ **buzzing** avertissement par ronfleur; ~ **code** code de tonalité; ~ **control** réglage de tonalité; ~ **control aperture** diaphragme des teintes; ~ **detector** détecteur de tonalité; ~ **dialler** numéroteur à fréquence vocale; ~ **dialling** numérotation à fréquences vocales; numérotation au clavier multifréquence

tone-dialling keypad clavier multifréquence (MF)

tone disabler neutralisateur de tonalité; ~ **feed** alimentation en tonalités; ~ **feeder** dispositif d'émission de tonalités

tone-feeder control memory mémoire de commande des tonalités; mémoire de commande des voies sources

tone generator générateur de tonalités (GT); générateur de fréquences; machine d'appel; ~ **indicators** signalisation acoustique; ~ **keyer** ondulateur; ~ **level** niveau de tonalité; niveau de fréquence; ~ **off** onde absente; ~ **on** onde présente

tone-on condition ligne d'abonné libre

tone-on-idle signalling out of band signalisation hors bande par changement d'état à bas niveau

tone-on signal onde de signalisation

tone pitch hauteur de son; ~ **presence scan point** détection de tonalité; ~ **present** présence de tonalité

toner *n* encre

tone reversal inversion des nuances

toner fleck tache noire

tones and announcements system tonalités et annonces parlées; auxiliaire

tone scale échelle de nuances; ~ **select memory** mémoire de sélection de tonalités

tongs *pl* pince

tongue *n* palette

tonic-train signalling signalisation par ondes musicales

tool *n* outil; aide; machine

tooling *n* outillage; façonnement; ~ **feature** mire de géométrie

tool kit *n* valise

tools *n pl* outillage; ~ **and equipment** outillage

toothed belt courroie crantée; ~ **wheel** roue dentée

top (of memory) sommet; **(rack)** ~ haut (de baie); ~ **coat** (of paint) peinture finition; ~ **cut** coupure des aiguës

top-down *adj* décroissant; descendant; ~ **method** approche descendante

top-fed aerial antenne à alimentation terminale

topical programme émission actuelle

top load charge maximale

top-loaded aerial antenne à capacité terminale

top margin *n* marge haute

top-mounted *adj* suspendu

topocentric angle angle topocentrique

top of form haut de page; ~ **of memory** début de la mémoire; ~ **of stack** sommet de la pile

top-of-the-range product produit haut de gamme

topology *n* interconnexion; implantation; **loop** ~ interconnexion en boucles; **star** ~ interconnexion en étoile

TOPS (s. traffic operator position system)

top section fronton

top-up additif; recharge

top view vue de dessus

torch *n* chalumeau

torn tape relay transit manuel par bande perforée

toroid *n* tore (de ferrite); chambre à vide; transformateur torique; aimant torique

toroidal core tore; ~ **transformer** transformateur torique

torque *n* couple de serrage

torque(-limiting) screwdriver tournevis dynamométrique

torque band (of galvanometer) cadre simple; ~ **meter** dynamomètre; ~ **rating** caractéristique couple; ~ **wrench** clé dynamométrique; clé à cadran

torsion-resistant rigide

torsion spring ressort cylindrique (à action angulaire); ressort à épingle; ~ **tester** dynamomètre

torus (doughnut/donut) tore (de ferrite)

to scale grandeur réelle; en vraie grandeur; grandeur nature

total angular momentum quantum number nombre quantique interne; ~ **anode power**

T

input puissance totale anodique d'entrée;
~ **attenuation** équivalent de transmission;
~ **continuous spectrum noise** souffle;
~ **electrode capacitance** capacité d'électrode; ~ **electrode dissipation** dissipation totale des électrodes; ~ **harmonic ratio** affaiblissement de distorsion harmonique totale
totalizer n totalisateur
totalizing check test de totalisation
totally enclosed abrité à ventilation forcée
total monitoring contrôle global; ~ **number** parc; ~ **polarization error** erreur de polarisation maximale; ~ **quiescent leakage current** courant de fuite total au repos; ~ **reflection** réflexion totale; ~ **sales** chiffre d'affaire; ~ **system error** erreur d'installation
tote bin casier; ~ **box** bac
touch calling numérotation au clavier multifréquences
touch-sensitive mat tapis de présence
touch-tone (pushbutton) **telephone** téléphone à clavier; ~ **dialling** appel au clavier; numérotation à clavier; ~ **telephone** poste à clavier multifréquence
touch-typing (of tape punch) perforation à la touche
toughness n dureté; facteur d'intensité de contrainte critique
tough steel acier dur
tournament (sorting algorithm) tournoi (tournoiement)
tower aerial antenne pylône
tpav (s. pulse average time)
T-pulse impulsion de durée T
trace n analyse; identification; ~ (program) dépistage; ~ (recording) tracé; ~ **a path through** (of circuit) emprunter (un circuit); ~ **mode** traceur; ~ **off** fin de jalon; ~ **on** jalon
tracer n outil de trace; filin de reconnaissance; marqueur
trace utility command ordre d'instrumentation
tracing (of faults) n localisation; dépistage; identification; ~ **line** cordeau à tracer; ~ **paper** papier calque
track n piste; bande; canal; chemin; couloir; fil; grain; impression conductrice; sillon; trolley; voie; ~ (of disk) adresse physique; ~ **beacon** radiophare d'alignement; ~ **circuit** circuit d'occupation; ~ **cutting** coupure de piste; ~ **diagram** tableau de voies; ~ **guidance system** radioalignement
tracking n pointage; affichage; balayage; cheminement; distorsion; entraînement; poursuite; recherche; suivi; trajectographie; ~ **aerial** antenne de poursuite;

~ **device** aligneur; dispositif d'accord décalé; ~ **down** dépistage; ~ **radar** radar de poursuite; ~ **receiver** récepteur de poursuite; ~ **station** station terrienne; ~ **system** chaîne de poursuite
track layout tracé; ~ **load** câble porteur; ~ **record** acquis
tractor feed tracteur; entraînement
tractor-feed printer imprimante à papier
trade v échanger; ~ adj professionnel; commercial; de la concurrence; ~ **mark** n sigle; ~ **name** marque déposée; appellation commerciale
trade-off n compromis
trade surplus balance commerciale excédentaire
trading year n exercice
traditional adj classique
traffic n trafic; circulation; exploitation; ~ **balancing** équilibrage de trafic; ~ **capacity** capacité de trafic; ~ **carried** trafic écoulé; ~ **channel** voie du trafic; ~ **code** numéro de route; ~ **converter** convertisseur d'exploitation; ~ **distributor** distributeur d'appels
traffic-engineering n dimensionnement
traffic flow capacité d'écoulement de trafic; courant de trafic; intensité de trafic acheminé; ~ **handled** trafic écoulé; ~ **handling capacity** capacité d'écoulement de trafic; ~ **item** flux (de trafic); ~ **load imbalance** déséquilibre du trafic; ~ **matrix** matrice de trafic; ~ **measurement** mesure de trafic; observation; ~ **meter** compteur de trafic; ~ **metering** comptage du trafic; ~ **observation** observation de trafic; mesures de trafic; ~ **offered** trafic offert; ~ **on hand** trafic en instance; ~ **operator** opératrice de trafic; ~ **operator position system** (TOPS) position automatisée de téléphoniste; ~ **position** position de trafic; ~ **record** enregistrement de trafic; ~ **recorder** enregistreur de trafic; compteur de nombre d'appels; calculographe; ~ **recording** enregistrement du trafic; ~ **relations** courant de trafic; flux de trafic; ~ **routing** (logical path) acheminement (chemin logique); ~ **routing rules** règles d'acheminement; ~ **routing strategy** politique d'acheminement; ~ **scanner** analyseur de débordement
traffic-sharing n partage de trafic; partage de charge
traffic stream flux (de trafic); ~ **surge** point brusque de trafic; ~ **transfer** basculement du trafic; ~ **unit** unité de trafic; ~ **usage recorder** (TUR) compteur de trafic; ~ **volume analysis** analyse du volume de trafic;

~ **waiting** trafic en instance; ~ **wave** onde de service

trailer *n* fin; ~ **block** bloc fin; ~ **card** carte de fin de groupe; ~ **label** label-fin; ~ **record** article complémentaire de fin; ~ **socket** nourrice

trailing *n* traînage; ~ *adj* descendant; de droite; poids faible (pf); ~ **aerial** antenne traînante; ~ **edge** flanc arrière; bord arrière; durée d'affaiblissement d'impulsion; flanc descendant; front arrière; ~ **end** fin de bande; ~ **socket** nourrice; prise mobile roulante; traînard

train *n* suite; série (en -); train

trainee *n* stagiaire

training *n* formation; conditionnement; entraînement; pointage; ~ **course** stage; ~ **generator** générateur de conditionnement; ~ **manual** présentation de l'instruction; ~ **pattern** procédure de réapprentissage; ~ **scheme** filière; ~ **scheme information sheet** fiche de formation

trajectory *n* trajectoire; rayon

transact *v* opérer

transaction *n* mouvement; échange; opération; passe; saisie de l'information; ~ **card** carte mouvement; carte détail; ~ **code** code mouvement; ~ **data** données variables; ~ **date** date du mouvement; ~ **file** fichier détail; fichier de manœuvre; fichier de mouvement; fichier de travail; ~ **record** article mouvement; enregistrement de détail; enregistrement de mouvement; ~ **tape** bande mouvement(s)

transadmittance compression ratio taux de compression de la transadmittance

transatlantic cable câble transatlantique

transceiver *n* émetteur-récepteur; accès bidirectionnel; transcepteur; coupleur; ~ **container** caisson émetteur-récepteur

transcoding *n* transcodage

transconductance *n* transconductance; pente

transcribe *v* recopier; transcrire

transcription *n* transcription

transducer *n* capteur; convertisseur; traducteur; ~ **gain** gain transductique; ~ **loss** affaiblissement transductique

transfer *v* transférer; basculer; charger (en); déplacer; muter; orienter; répercuter; ~ *n* transfert; basculement; décalcomanie; déplacement; échange; extraction; passage; remise; renvoi; report; ~ **abort command** commande d'abandon du transfert; ~ **address** phase de renvoi; ~ **admittance** admittance de transfert; ~ **allowed** autorisation de transfert; ~ **back** rapatrier; ~ **call(ing)** communication en chaîne; ~ **characteristic** caractéristique de trans-

fert; caractéristique mutuelle (de deux électrodes)

transfer-charge (collect) **calls** taxation du demandé; communication payable à l'arrivée (PCV); appel en PCV; PCV (payable à l'arrivée = percevoir) (code 10 en France)

transfer circuit circuit de renvoi; circuit de transfert; ~ **coefficient** facteur de transfert; ~ **constant** constante de transfert; ~ **current** courant de transfert; courant d'échange; ~ **cycle** cycle d'échange

transfer-decay current courant de déclin; courant de traînage

transfer-enable unit dispositif d'acceptation de basculement

transfer exchange centre téléphonique de transfert; ~ **extension** poste prédéterminé; ~ **function** gain isomorphe; gain en tension; transmittance isomorphe; ~ **impedance** impédance de transfert; ~ **interpreter** traductrice reporteuse; ~ **jack** jack de renvoi; ~ **key** clé de renvoi; ~ **line** ligne de renvoi; ~ **link** maille; instant de transfert; ~ **mechanical impedance** impédance mécanique de transfert; ~ **of control** appel; ~ **panel** panneau de renvoi; ~ **rate** débit d'information; cadence de transfert; vitesse de transfert

transferred subscriber abonné transféré

transfer register registre espion; ~ **relay** relais intermédiaire; ~ **request** demande de basculement

transfer-request unit dispositif de demande de basculement

transferring back rapatriement

transfer signal signal de renvoi; signal de basculement; ~ **station** station de transfert (Sdt); ~ **switch** commutateur; ~ **time** temps de transfert; temps de passage; ~ **time-slot** instant de transfert; ~ **voltage** tension de basculement; ~ **wire** cordon de renvoi

Transfluxor [T.N.] transfluxeur

transform *v* convertir

transformation (process) évolution

transformer *n* transformateur; ~ **casing** carcasse transformateur; habillage transformateur

transformer-coupled amplifier amplificateur à transformateur

transformer coupling couplage mutuel; couplage par transformateur; ~ **coupling bush** bague; ~ **point** point de transformation; ~ **primary** primaire de transformateur

transformer-rectifier transformateur redresseur (TR)

transformer station station de transformation

transforming section section d'adaptation

T

transient *n* pointe; clic; microcoupure; phénomène transitoire; ~ *adj* transitoire; apériodique; de transfert; épisodique; fugitif; intermittent; ~ **charge** variation fugitive; ~ **current** courant transitoire; ~ **decay current** traînage; ~ **distortion** distorsion due aux phénomènes transitoires; ~ **effect** effet transitoire; ~ **oscillation** oscillation apériodique; ~ **overload** surcharge passagère; ~ **response** réponse aux phénomènes transitoires; caractéristique du saut; ~ **state** régime transitoire; ~ **suppressor** résistance VDR; ~ **surge** variation accidentelle; ~ **undervoltage** manque fugitif du réseau

transinformation content contenu de la transinformation

transistor *n* transistor; triode à cristal; triode au germanium; ~ **array** groupement de transistors

transistor-mounting pad isolateur; entretoise transistor

transistor-to-transistor logic (TTL) logique TTL

transit call appel transit; communication de transit; ~ **call indicator** indicateur d'appel de transit; ~ **centre (TC)** centre de transit (CT); centre nodal (CN); ~ **charge** taxe de transit; ~ **connection** connexion de transit; ~ **country** pays de transit; ~ **dialling** sélection automatique à distance; ~ **exchange** centre de transit; centre interurbain; ~ **indicator** indicateur de transit

transition *n* passage; transition; traversée

transitional aid migration; ~ **link** passerelle

transition connector connecteur de transition; ~ **fit** emmanchement juste; ~ **frequency** fréquence de transition; ~ **radius** rayon de raccordement

transit level niveau d'essai non adapté

transit-line repeater répéteur embroché

transit loop boucle en transit; ~ **network** réseau de transit

transitory *adj* passager; ~ **closure** fermeture transitive

transit pad complément de ligne à affaiblissement fixe; ~ **phase angle** angle de transit; ~ **point** point de transit; ~ **position** position de transit; ~ **register** enregistreur de transit

transitron oscillator oscillateur à transitron

transit route voie de transit; ~ **routing** acheminement de transit; ~ **seizure signal** signal de prise pour transit; ~ **telegram** télégramme de transit; ~ **(test) call** appel en transit; ~ **time** temps de parcours; temps de passage; temps de transit; ~ **traffic** trafic de transit

translating equipment équipement de modulation

translation *n* modulation; traduction; ~ **authenticated under oath** traduction jurée; ~ **digit** chiffre de traduction; ~ **look-aside buffer** répertoire des pages actives; ~ **oscillator** oscillateur de transposition; ~ **table** table de traduction; ~ **zone** zone de traduction

translator *n* traducteur; compilateur; convertisseur; émetteur de relais; transformateur; ~ **(station)** réémetteur

translator-distributor (TD) *n* notificateur d'information

translator-register interface circuit d'appel des traducteurs

transmission *n* émission; communication; envoi; transmission; transport; ~ **band** bande de transmission; ~ **block** (X-block) bloc de transmission; ~ **bridge** pont de transmission; joncteur; pont d'alimentation; ~ **cable** câble de radiodiffusion; ~ **centre** centre de démodulation et modulation (CDM); ~ **channel** voie de transmission; ~ **control character** caractère de commande de transmission; ~ **controller** contrôleur de transmission; ~ **diagram** diagramme d'émission; ~ **direction** sens de transmission; ~ **distortion** distorsion de la transmission; ~ **envelope** gabarit; enveloppe de transmission; ~ **error rate** taux d'erreurs sur une modulation; ~ **facility** moyen de transmission; ~ **failure** échec de la transmission; ~ **filter** filtre de transmission; ~ **gain** gain de transmission; ~ **impairment** dégradation de la qualité de l'émission; ~ **level** niveau de transmission; énergie (en dBm); niveau relatif de puissance; ~ **limit** limite de transmission; ~ **line** ligne de transmission

transmission-line amplifier amplificateur à répartition

transmission line monitor moniteur de ligne de transmission

transmission-link artère de transmission

transmission log journal de transmission; ~ **loss** affaiblissement de transmission; perte de transmission; ~ **loss adjustment** réglage de l'équivalent; ~ **maintenance** maintenance de la transmission; ~ **maintenance work** entretien du réseau de transmission; ~ **(level-)measuring set** appareil de mesure de transmission; hypsomètre (= népermètre/décibelmètre); ~ **medium** support de transmission; ~ **network** réseau de transport; réseau de transfert; réseau de transmission; ~ **of ringing current** envoi de sonnerie; ~ **path** voie de transmission;

chaîne de transmission; trajet de transmission; ~ **performance** indice de qualité de
transmission; ~ **plan** plan de transmission;
~ **quality** qualité de transmission
'**transmission ready' indication** signalisation
émission parée
transmission reference equivalent affaiblissement relatif en émission; ~ **reference point**
point de référence pour la transmission;
~ **reference system** système de référence
pour la transmission; ~ **standards** normes
de transmission; ~ **system** système de
transmission; ~ **test** essai de transmission;
~ **time** délai de transmission; ~ **unit** unité
de transmission; arbre; ~ **zero** zéro de
transmission
transmit v émettre; donner l'image; envoyer;
lire; ~ **at rate zero** cadencer en 0;
~ **cross-polarization isolation contours**
contours de découplage (de polarisation) à
l'émission; ~ **flow control** contrôle de flux
transmit-receive (T-R) **switch** inverseur émission-réception; ~ **aerial** antenne d'émission-réception; ~ **switching** commutation
émission-réception
transmittance n coefficient de transmission;
transmittance
transmitted band bande transmise
transmitted-data (signal) information(s) d'entrée
transmitted power puissance de l'émetteur;
~ **sideband** bande principale; ~ **signal
level** niveau de signal transmis
transmitter n émetteur; microphone; transmetteur
transmitter-blocker (T-B) **cell** verrou d'émetteur
~ **distortion** distorsion à l'émission; ~ **distributor** (TD) lecteur de bande; ~ **feed
current** courant d'alimentation du microphone; ~ **monitor** moniteur de l'émetteur;
~ **mute** inhibition du microphone; ~ **noise**
bruit de microphone; ~ **off** (X-OFF) arrêt
de la transmission; ~ **on** (X-ON) caractère
de repris; ~ **outage** panne de l'émetteur
transmitter/receiver signal element timing
(DTE/DCE) base de temps pour les
éléments de signal à l'émission/réception
transmitter signal element timing horloge
émission; éléments de signalisation à
l'émission; ~ **site** situation radiogéographique de l'émetteur; ~ **site error** erreur
d'émetteur; ~ **tuning** accord d'émetteur
transmit time durée de parcours
transmitting n (of section of tape store)
lecture; ~ **aerial** antenne d'émission;
antenne émettrice; ~ **direction** direction

d'émission; ~ **power** puissance d'émission;
~ **station** station d'émission; poste émetteur; station émettrice
transmultiplexer n transmultiplexeur
transparency n invisibilité; transparence; ~
(cellulose acetate) rhodoïd; calque
transparent background fond transparent;
~ **label cover** écran d'étiquette
transponder n répéteur de satellite; émetteur-
récepteur asservi par impulsions; répondeur; transpondeur
transport n défilement; acheminement; amenage; entraînement
transporter n chariot
transport factor/ratio taux de transit
transposed telephone line ligne téléphonique
croisée; ~ **transmission line** ligne de
transmission avec transpositions
transposition n croisement; ~ **of subscribers'
numbers** interversion des numéros d'appel
trans-put process transfert radial
trans-shipped adj transbordable
transverse check contrôle par caractère(s);
~ **cross-section** section droite; ~ **electrical
confinement** confinement transverse électrique; ~ **electric wave** onde H; ~ **filter** filtre
transversal; ~ **gyro frequency** gyrofréquence transversale
transversely unhomogeneous coaxial line ligne
coaxiale non homogène dans le sens
transversal
transverse magnetic (TM) **mode** mode magnétique transversal; ~ **optical confinement**
confinement transverse optique; ~ **route**
voie transversale; ~ **strength** tenue transversale; ~ **voltage** tension transversale;
~ **wave** onde transversale
transverter n commutatrice
trap (to) v brancher (sur); ~ coincer; piéger;
~ n déroutement; débranchement; instruction de branchement; interruption; séparateur; ~ **circuit** piège électrique; trappe
trapezium distortion (of CRT) distorsion
trapézoïdale; distorsion en trapèze; ~ **effect** effet trapezoïdal
trapezoidal deflection déviation trapézoïdale
trap handling gestion du fichier
trapped mode mode de propagation guidé
trap(ping) centre piège
trap to an address brancher sur une adresse
travel n déplacement; course
traveller n (card) fiche de suivi; carte
suiveuse; fiche suiveuse
travelling expenses frais de voyage; frais de
déplacement; ~ **(overhead) crane** pont
roulant; ~ **wave** onde progressive
travelling-wave aerial antenne à onde progressive; ~ **amplifier** amplificateur à ondes

T

progressives; ~ **magnetron** magnétron à ondes progressives; ~ **tube (TWT)** tube à ondes progressives (TOP); ~ **tube amplifier (TWTA)** amplificateur tube à ondes progressives(ATOP)

traverse *n* croisement; longrine; pont; ~ **mounting** chariot baladeur

traversing *n* défilement; ~ **bed** table X-Y; ~ **table** table X-Y

tray *n* bac; tiroir; clayette

T-R cell verrou de récepteur; tube alternat

treble *adj* aigu; ~ **control** réglage des aiguës; réglage des fréquences élevées; ~ **correction** correction des aiguës; ~ **damping** coupure des aiguës; ~ **tone** fréquence élevée

tree *n* (of data base) arbre

trellis-coded modulation (TCM) codage en treillis à huit états

trembler *n* sonnerie trembleuse

trench *n* chemin de câbles (CdC); conduit; fossé; goulotte; gouttière

trend *n* allure; courbe; direction; évolution; orientation; perspective; sens; trajectoire; tendance

tress *n* tresse

trestle *n* chevalet

triac thyristor bidirectionnel; ~ **gate** gâchette de triac

triad *n* groupe de trois bits (= triade)

trial *n* épreuve; test; ~ **(run)** manœuvre à vide

trial-and-error *adj* (problem-solving) heuristique; à approximations successives; de synthèse

trial connection connexion d'essai; ~ **installation** montage à blanc; ~ **model** avant-projet; modèle (mle)

triangle aerial antenne en triangle

triangular dipole dipôle en triangle; ~ **noise** bruit triangulaire; ~ **pulse** impulsion triangulaire; impulsion en triangle; ~ **random noise** bruit erratique triangulaire; ~ **waveform** forme d'onde triangulaire; dent de scie (DDS); tension à rampe symétrique

triaxially stabilized stabilisation dans les trois axes

tributary *n* jonction affluente; ~ **digital signal** signal numérique affluent

trickle charge charge d'entretien; charge en tampon

trickling *n* coulure; ruissellement

trigatron *n* éclateur à étincelle pilote

trigger *v* déclencher; actionner; basculer; enclencher; lancer; provoquer; solliciter; ~ *n* gâchette; bascule; détendeur

triggerable ramp generator générateur de rampe synchronisable

trigger circuit circuit de déclenchement; circuit à détente; circuit d'amorçage; circuit déclencheur; ~ **current** courant de gâchette; courant d'amorçage; ~ **delay** décalage du déclenchement; ~ **device** déclencheur

triggered blocking oscillator oscillateur à blocage déclenché; ~ **mode** mode déclenché; ~ **spark-gap** éclateur déclenché

trigger electrode électrode pilote; électrode de déclenchement; ~ **gap** intervalle de déclenchement

triggering *n* amorçage; basculement; déclenchement; démarrage; détente; sollicitation; synchronisation; ~ **level** point de basculement

trigger level tension du seuil; ~ **pair circuit** basculeur bistable; ~ **pulse** impulsion de déclenchement; déclencheur; impulsion d'attaque; ~ **signal** signal de synchronisation; ~ **slope** déclenchement; ~ **voltage** tension d'amorçage; ~ **word** (of logic state analyser) mot de déclenchement

trigonal reflector aerial antenne de réflexion à trois angles

trigonometrical calculation cercle trigonométrique

trihedral aerial antenne en triangle; antenne de réflexion à trois angles

trim *v* araser; casser les angles (vifs); équilibrer; ~ *n* bordure; collerette frontale; drageoir; encadrement; enjoliveur; habillage; ~ **down** (of memory) dégraisser

trimmed *adj* équilibré; mouché; ~ **cable sheath** dégraissage

trimmer *n* condensateur shunt d'équilibrage; condensateur d'appoint; potentiomètre de réglage; résistance ajustable; **(PCB-mounting)** ~ capacité sur picot

trimming *n* ajustage; décolletage; découpage; lissage; réglage d'accord; ~ **capacitor** condensateur d'appoint; ~ **laser** laser de réglage; ~ **pliers** pince à ébarber; ~ **screw** vis de réglage; ~ **tape** galon; ~ **tool** lame de redressement; outil de rangement

trim-pot *n* potentiomètre d'ajustage; résistance ajustable

trim potentiometer potentiomètre d'ajustage

triode electron gun canal électronique à trois anodes; ~ **pentode** triode-pentode

trip *v* déclencher; actionner; basculer; solliciter; ~ **coil** bobine de relais

triple input triple entrée statique; ~ **jack** jack triple; ~ **outlet** distributeur trois socles

tripler *n* triplicateur de fréquence

triple redundancy tridondance

triplet *n* groupe de trois bits (= triade)

tripod mount monture tripode

tripping *n* disjonction; déclenchement; sollicitation; ~ **current** courant de déclenchement (ID); ~ **device** déclencheur à surintensité; ~ **relay** relais de déclenchement; relais de libération; relais instantané; ~ **time** délai de déclenchement

trip point seuil; ~ **setting** point de contrôle; ~ **signal** signal de déclenchement; ~ **switch** contacteur disjoncteur; ~ **temperature** index

tri-state port sortie trois états; porte tri-état

trolley *n* desserte; chariot

tromboning *n* (of calls) bouclage

tropicalized *adj* tropicalisé

tropopause *n* tropopause

troposphere *n* troposphère

tropospheric absorption absorption troposphérique; ~ **reflection** réflexion troposphérique; ~ **scatter** diffusion troposphérique; propagation transhorizon; ~ **scatter radio link** liaison hertzienne transhorizon

trouble *n* incident; dérangement; panne

troubleshooting *n* dépannage; maintenance curative; mise au point (MAP); mise en accusation; recherche de dérangements; relève des défauts; ~ **chart** arbre de dépannage

trough *n* goulotte; bac; conduit; gouttière; puits

truck *n* chariot

true *adj* vrai; affirme; efficace; réel; ~ **attenuation** affaiblissement réel; ~ **bearing** azimut (direct); ~ **bearing ground-to-ground** relèvement vrai station-station

true-false qualifier fonctionnement vrai-faux

true-motion radar radar de route vraie

true plot pointage vrai

true-plot radar radar de route vraie

true resistance résistance ohmique; résistance en continu; ~ **watt** watt efficace

truncated *adj* tronqué

truncation *n* suppression d'éléments (binaires); coupure; ~ **error** erreur de troncature; erreur de chute; ~ **noise** bruit de troncature

trunk *n* faisceau; bus; canal; circuit; distributeur; inter-auto (IA); joncteur; jonction; liaison; ligne; maille; trolley; voie commune; (**inter-position**) ~ circuit de renvoi; ~ **access** accès au faisceau réseau; ~ **access code** préfixe interurbain; préfixe de prise; ~ **and local** mixte; ~ **board** position interurbaine; ~ **cable** câble de jonction; câble interurbain; ~ **call** appel interurbain; communication à grande portée; conversation interurbaine; ~ **call held** réseau mis en garde

trunk-call signal signal d'appel interurbain

trunk camp-on cord circuit monocorde de mise en attente des circuits interurbains; ~ **circuit** circuit interurbain; circuit de prolongement; circuit télégraphique de jonction; circuit téléphonique interurbain; ~ **(circuit) subscriber** abonné sur circuit; ~ **circuit with dialling facility** circuit interurbain avec sélection à distance; ~ **code** indicatif interurbain; ~ **connection** connexion à grande distance; connexion interurbaine; ~ **connection unit** unité de raccordement des circuits ou jonctions BF; ~ **connector** connecteur interurbain; ~ **desk** meuble interurbain; ~ **dialling** appel interurbain; numérotation extérieure; ~ **distribution frame** répartiteur interurbain; ~ **exchange** centre interurbain; bureau central interurbain; ~ **group** faisceau de lignes; faisceau de circuits; groupement de lignes réseau; ~ **group down** coupure de faisceau; ~ **group file** fichier des faisceaux

trunking *n* élément de filerie; élément de goulotte; gouttière; ~ **diagram** diagramme de jonctions; diagramme de liaisons; plan de groupe

trunk junction circuit local; ligne intermédiaire; ~ **junctor** joncteur local; ~ **line** ligne interurbaine; ~ **network** réseau interurbain (RI); ~ **offering** offre d'appels interurbaine; offre en tiers; ~ **offering final selector** connecteur local interurbain; ~ **operator** annotatrice; ~ **operator dialling** sélection à distance de l'abonné demandé (en exploitation semi-automatique); ~ **position** table interurbaine

trunk-record circuit circuit d'annotation; ~ **position** position d'annotatrice; position d'inscription

trunk re-dial renouvellement d'appel extérieur; ~ **reservation** accès au réseau controlé (par l'opérateur)

trunk-routed call appel écoulé

trunk seizure signal signal de prise; ~ **selection unit (TSU)** élément de sélection de joncteurs (ESJ); ~ **selector** connecteur interurbain; ~ **switchboard** commutateur interurbain; ~ **system** chaîne interurbaine; ~ **tandem exchange** centre de transit interurbain; ~ **test rack** table d'essais et de mesure; ~ **tie line** circuit interurbain; ~ **traffic** trafic interurbain; trafic interzone; ~ **zone** zone interurbaine

trunnion axis axe d'articulation

truss *n* bielle; ~ **wire** hauban

truth table table de vérité; matrice des phases; table de correspondance; table de définition; table de fonctions; vérification de la

T

fonction logique

trying-to-connect-you (message) message de patience; veuillez patienter

T-S (s. time-space junction)

TS (s. time slot)

T-section filter (Butterworth/Chebyshev filter) filtre en T

T-span *n* liaison numérique

TSU (s. trunk selection unit)

TT (s. time-time network)

TTC (s. telemetry tracking and command)

TTL (s. transistor-to-transistor logic)

TTM (s. two-tone modulation)

TTTN (s. tandem tie trunk network)

TTY (s. teletypewriter)

tub *n* bac

tube *n* tube; ~ **socket** douille de lampe

tubing *n* souplisseau

tubular filter filtre tubulaire

'Tufnol' (laminated board) [T.N.] Céleron [A.C.]

tufted fabric moquette aiguillé

tumble card tête-bêche (carte)

tumble-mode (printing) tête-pied (impression)

tumbler *n* gâchette; ~ **switch** interrupteur à bascule; interrupteur à culbuteur

tune *v* accorder; régler

tuned aerial antenne accordée; ~ **amplifier** amplificateur syntoniseur; amplificateur accordable

tuned-anode oscillator oscillateur à circuit anodique accordé

tuned cavity cavité accordable; ~ **circuit (LC)** circuit LC (inductance/capacitance); circuit résonnant; circuit syntonisé; circuit d'accord; ~ **dipole** dipôle accordé; ~ **filter** filtre de résonance; filtre accordable; ~ **frequency** fréquence d'accord

tuned-grid oscillator oscillateur à circuit de grille accordé

tuned relay relais à résonance; ~ **RF** (straight) **reception** réception à amplification directe

tuner *n* bloc d'accord; accordeur; sintonisateur; syntonisateur

tungsten sensitivity sensibilité au tungstène

tuning *n* syntonisation; accord; adaptation; réglage; résonance de tension; ~ **capacitor** condensateur d'accord; ~ **coil** bobine d'accord; ~ **error** erreur d'accord; désaccord; ~ **fork contact** lyre

tuning-fork oscillator drive pilote à diapason

tuning indicator (meter) indicateur d'accord; œil magique; ~ **knob** bouton d'accord; ~ **losses** perte à l'accord; ~ **note** note d'accord; ~ **out** (of load reactance) équilibrage; ~ **range** plage d'accord; gamme d'accord; ~ **screw** vis d'accord; ~ **set** dispositif d'accord; ~ **time** durée

d'accord

tunnel *n* goulotte; ~ **effect** effet tunnel

TUP (s. telephone user part)

tuple (= row) ligne

TUR (s. traffic usage recorder)

turbulence *n* perturbation

Turing machine automate

turn *n* spire

turnaround (of modem) retournement; ~ **document** document aller-retour; document navette; document tournant; ~ **time** délai de réponse; délai de basculement; délai de mise en œuvre; délai de restitution; délai d'exécution; délai d'exploitation; délai d'inversion; temps de renversement; temps de rotation

turnbuckle *n* tendeur; douille

turned-pin contact contact (en) tulipe

turned/rotated through 180° permutation cyclique; permutation circulaire

turning *n* décolletage

turning-on *n* basculement

turning the part à la retourne

turnkey delivery fourniture clés en main

turn off *v* couper

turn-off *n* mise en blocage; temps de coupure; temps de fermeture; ~ **current** courant de désamorçage; ~ **time** temps de déstockage; temps d'établissement en inhibition; ~ **time** ($t_{off} = t_s + t_f$) temps total de coupure; retard à la décroissance; temps de désaturation; temps de mise en blocage; temps total de décroissance; ~ **voltage** tension de désamorçage

turn on *v* allumer; mettre en marche

turn-on time ($t_{on} = t_d + t_r$) temps d'ouverture; retard à la croissance; retard à la mise en conduction; temps de mise en conduction; temps d'établissement en conduction; temps total de croissance; temps total d'établissement; ~ **voltage** tension d'amorçage; tension directe

turnover *n* retournement; ~ **frequency** fréquence de transition; ~ **point** point d'inflexion

turns counter compte-tours; ~ **ratio** rapport de transformation

turnstile aerial antenne à cadres croisés; antenne à champ tournant; antenne Bellini-Tosi; antenne croisée; antenne en tourniquet; ~ **jammer** brouilleur à antenne en tourniquet

turntable *n* plaque tournante; électrophone; étoile

turret *n* tourelle; affût; meuble; position dirigeuse

turtle tortue

TUT (s. terminal unit tester)

TV (s. television); ～ **broadcast** émission de télévision; ～ **broadcasting to schools** télévision scolaire
TVI (s. television interference)
TVRO (s. television receive-only)
tweeter *n* haut-parleur d'aiguës; haut-parleur pour fréquences élevées
tweezers *n pl* brucelles; pince; précelles
twelve-channel group (of carrier current system) groupe primaire; groupe à douze canaux; ～ **telephone system** système téléphonique à douze voies; ～ **term set** termineur à douze voies
twelve-group *n* douzaine
twelve-level multiple duodécuple
twelve-way plug and socket connection connexion à fiches et prises de 12 voies
twenty-first century horizon 2000
twice-yearly *adj* biannuel
twin-armature relay relais à armature double
twin blade bilame; ～ **cable** câble à paires torsadées; ～ **check** contrôle par duplication; ～ **contacts** contacts doublés; contacts jumelés
twin-core cable câble à deux conducteurs
twin-engined *adj* bimoteur
twin feeder circuit d'alimentation double
twin-ganged capacitor condensateurs jumelés
twin-line matching section section d'équilibrage à câble à deux conducteurs
twin loop cadres jumelés
twinning *n* pairage
twin pair (tip and sleeve) dicorde
twinplex *n* télégraphie diplex à quatre fréquences; télégraphie duplex
twin plug fiche bipolaire
twin-T network réseau en double T
twin wafers (of switch) galettes jumelées
twin-wire *adj* bifilaire
T-wire *n* (connected to subscriber line A-wire) fil de pointe
twist *n* vrillage; voile; ～ (of tone dialling frequencies) différence de niveau de fréquence de signalisation
twisted *adj* tordu; torsadé; assemblés en hélice; ～ **pair** paire torsadée; ～ **strand** brin toronné; ～ **wire** fil torsadé
twisting moment moment de torsion; ～ **of strands** toronnage des brins
twistor *n* (memory) mémoire à fil
twist transposition system transposition par rotation
two-bit byte doublet
two-channel *adj* bi-canal; ～ **amplifier** amplificateur à deux voies
two-condition cable code code bivalent pour câble
two-control-point method méthode de deux points directeurs
two-core cable câblage bifilaire
two-dimensional array table à double entrée
two-/(four-) wire transit centre centre de transit deux/(quatre) fils
two-frequency channel voie à deux fréquences vocales
two-group combining circuit circuit de deux groupes
two-input adder additionneur à deux entrées
two-letter code (digraph) bigramme
two-level facsimile télécopie contrastée
two-link international call communication internationale de transit simple
two-mode waveguide guide d'ondes à deux modes
two-monthly *adj* bimestriel
two-motion selector sélecteur à deux mouvements
two-out-of-five code code quinaire; code deux parmi cinq/sur cinq (2/5)
two-out-of-six multifrequency code code à deux fréquences parmi six
two pair-wound wires deux fils en main
two-part *n* binôme
two-party call conversation à deux
two-phase *adj* biphase; diphasé; ～ **current** courant biphasé
two-pin plug fiche bipolaire
two-plus-one address à deux plus une adresses
two-port input to deux entrées sur
twos complement complément vrai; ～ **complemented** affiché en complément à deux
two-spot display indicateur à double spot
two-stage amplifier amplificateur à deux étages
two-state device bascule
two-step relay relais bistable; relais à action échelonnée; relais à deux seuils; relais à deux temps
two-switch connection communication internationale de transit double
two-to-four wire term set (terminating set) transformateur différentiel
two-tone fax télécopie contrastée; ～ **keying** télégraphie par multivoie à deux fréquences porteuses; ～ **modulation (TTM)** modulation sur deux fréquences audibles; ～ **telegraph system** télégraphie par multivoie à deux fréquences porteuses
two-valued variable variable binaire
two-way bus bus bidirectionnel; ～ **line** ligne banalisée; ～ **long-haul link** relation bilatérale à grande distance; ～ **network** réseau bidirectionnel; ～ **simplex** communication bilatérale; ～ **simplex system** exploitation par voies conjuguées; ～ **split** consultation séparée; ～ **splitting** écoute avec sépara-

T

tion; ~ **switch** commutateur va-et-vient; ~ **television** télévision bilatérale; télévision dans les deux sens; ~ **trunk** circuit mixte; ligne de jonction utilisée dans les deux sens; ~ **working** trafic bilatéral

two-wire circuit ligne bifilaire; circuit à deux fils; ~ **cluster link** câblage sub-local B (CSL-B); ~ **connection** connexion à deux fils

two-wire/four-wire term set circuit hybride; passage deux fils-quatre fils

two-wire intermediate repeater répéteur intermédiaire pour circuit à deux fils; ~ **(loop) circuit** ligne à deux fils; circuit bifilaire; ~ **repeater** répéteur pour circuit à deux fils; ~ **side circuit** circuit réel bifilaire; ~ **switched trunk junction** circuit de jonction connecté en deux fils; ~ **switching** commutation à deux fils; ~ **telephone circuit** circuit téléphonique à deux fils; ~ **termination** terminaison à deux fils; ~ **winding** enroulement bifilaire

TWT (s. travelling wave tube)

TWTA (s. travelling-wave tube amplifier)

TWT **power amplifier** amplificateur de puissance à TOP

TX/RX émission-réception (E/R)

type v frapper; dactylographier; pianoter

type-ahead feature frappe anticipée; mémoire tampon du clavier (SUR IMP)

type bar barre à caractères; ~ **B display** indicateur de distance et de gisement (d'azimut); ~ **code** désignation; ~ **printer** appareil imprimeur; ~ **printing** télégraphie par appareils imprimeurs; typotélégraphie

typesetting n composition

type specifications clauses techniques

typewriter n machine à écrire (MAE); ~ **keyboard** clavier dactylographique; ~ **pad** bloc machine à écrire

typical adj caractéristique; à titre indicatif; classique; nominal; normal; pour mémoire (PM); recommandé; ~ **applications data** caractéristiques; ~ **voltages** gabarit de tension

typing n frappe; ~ adj dactylographique; ~ **element** boule

typology caractérisation

U

UAX (s. unit automatic exchange)
u.c. (s. upper case)
U/C (s. up-converter)
UFO (s. unidentified flying object)
UHF (s. ultra-high frequency)
UJ (s. universal joint)
U-link *n* cavalier; étrier de court circuit; connexion en U
UL-listed (Underwriters' Laboratories) homologué UL
ultimate tensile strength résistance à la rupture; ~ tensile stress charge de rupture
ultradyne *n* ultradyne
ultra-fast high-density IC technology filière submicronique
ultra-high frequency (UHF) ultrahaute fréquence (UHF)
ultra-short wave (VHF band) onde ultra-courte (OUC)
ultrasonic electrode sonotrode; ~ frequency fréquence ultra sonore; fréquence supra-acoustique; fréquence ultra-acoustique; ultrason
ultrasound *n* ultrason
ultra-violet (UV) *adj* actinique; ~ aging vieillissement aux radiations UV; ~ eraser effaceur ultra-violet; ~ screen écran luminescent; ~ tube tube actinique
umbrella *n* réseau étoile
umbrella-loaded aerial antenne en parapluie
umlaut *n* (') tréma
UNA (s. universal/unassigned night answer service)
unabsorbed field strength champ en l'absence d'absorption
unacceptable *adj* inadmissible
unadjusted *adj* non pondéré; ~ values valeurs brutes
unaffected level niveau inchangé
unallocated number numéro non utilisé; numéro libre
unallowable digits contrôle d'existence
unanswered call appel sans réponse
unarmoured cable câble non armé; câble non blindé
unassigned *adj* en réserve; disponible; libre; non désigné
unattended exchange bureau central non surveillé; ~ operation exploitation télésurveillée; fonctionnement non surveillé; télésurveillance; ~ station station non surveillée; station télésurveillée
unauthorized access accès intempestif; ~ channel canal interdit
unavailability *n* indisponibilité
unavailable *adj* indisponible; inadmissible; ~ busy indisponible occupé; ~ idle indisponible libre
unbalance *n* dissymétrie; balourd; déséquilibre; ~ about earth *unbalance to earth* déséquilibre par rapport à la terre
unbalanced *adj* dissymétrique; asymétrique; désaxé; ~ wire circuit circuit dissymétrique
unbalance to earth dissymétrie par rapport à la terre
unbalancing voltage tension de déséquilibre
unbiased *adj* (address) non relative
unbind *v* défretter
unblock *v* décomprimer; décomposer; décondenser; décourt-circuiter
unblocking *n* décompression; dégroupement; ~ acknowledgement accusé de réception de liaison de déblocage
unbreakable *adj* incassable
unbundling *n* dégroupage (tarifaire); débottelage; décompression; dégroupement; dissociation; facturation séparée; tarifs dissociés
unclad cable câble non armé
uncladding *n* déshabillage
unclamp *v* défretter; déclamper
uncoded *adj* clair (texte etc.); en toutes lettres
uncoil *v* défretter
uncommitted *adj* (of gate array cell) libre; non désigné
uncompleted call appel infructueux; appel inefficace; appel instable; appel non établi; appel sans aboutissement; communication non établie
unconditional fault panne franche; ~ jump branchement inconditionnel; saut systématique
unconnect *v* débrancher; déboîter
unconnected call appel non desservi
uncontrolled experiment expérience à caractère subjectif
uncorrected *adj* non pondéré; ~ values valeurs brutes
uncorrupted *adj* sain
uncouple *v* désaccoupler; déboîter; débran-

cher
undamped wave onde continue non modulée; onde non amortie
undemountable disk disque non démontable
under-beam height hauteur sous poutre
under-bunching n groupement inférieur
under-burn n terminaison du programme en moins de temps prévu
undercoat n peinture primaire; peinture d'impression
under consideration à l'étude; pour ordre
undercurrent/undervoltage relay relais à minimum
undercut n contre-dépouille; ~ **and overhang** gravure sous-jacente et saillie
undercutting n détalonnage
under development à l'étude
under-excitation n sous-excitation
underflow n dépassement de capacité inférieur; dépassement négatif; poids faible (pf); sous-dépassement
undergoing field tests en expérimentation
underground adj enterré; souterrain; ~ **aerial** antenne souterraine; ~ **cable** câble souterrain; ~ **circuit** ligne souterraine; ~ **vault** caisson enterrable
under intermittent/transient load en transitoire de charge
underlap n interlignage; non juxtaposition
underline symbol tiret
underlining n soulignement
underlying adj sous-jacent
under-modulation n sous-modulation
under-populated area zone à habitat dispersé
under review à l'étude
underscoring n soulignement
undersea cable câble sous-marin
undershoot n dépassement de capacité inférieur
underside n fond
under test à l'essai; en test
undervoltage n sous-tension; ~ **condition(s)** régime accidentel
underwater communications communication sous-marine
undirected graph graphe non orienté
undistinguished adj indifférencié
undo (function) annulation
undulation n onde
unencumbered adj accessible
unequal-letter telegraph télégraphe à signes de longueur inégale
unequipped adj nu
unevenly trimmed mal sectionné
unevenness n aspérité
un-exposed (of film) vierge
unfaceted crystal cristal non-facetté
unfired adj non vitrifié

unforeseeable adj imprévisible
unforeseen circumstances (hostilities/embargo, etc) force majeure
unformatted adj hors gabarit
unfurlable aerial antenne déployable
unguarded area zone non gardée; ~ **interval** intervalle non protégé
unhooking n décrochage (D)
unidentified flying object (UFO) objet volant non identifié (OVNI)
unidirectional aerial antenne unidirectionnelle; ~ **magnetic field** champ magnétique unidirectionnel; ~ **pulse** impulsion unidirectionnelle; ~ **transmission line** ligne de transmission unidirectionnelle
uniform adj homogène; régulier; cohérent; associé (à); ~ **encoding** codage uniforme; ~ **grading** reproductibilité dans les gradients
uniformity n identité; homogénéité; suivi
uniform random noise bruit à spectre continu et uniforme; ~ **response curve** courbe de réponse uniforme; ~ **(spectrum) random noise** bruit blanc; ~ **waveguide** guide d'ondes homogène
unifying adj fédérateur; ~ **architecture** (network) mécanisme d'assemblage
unimpaired adj sain
uninterrupted adj permanent; sans interruption; ~ **tone** tonalité superposée
uninterruptible adj (of inverter) sans coupure; ~ **power supply (UPS)** alimentation secourue
union n addition; réunion (circuit-)
unipolar adj monopolaire
unipolar-to-bipolar conversion conversion unipolaire-bipolaire
unipole aerial antenne unipolaire
uniprogramming n monoprogrammation
unique adj propre; spécifique; ~ **abbreviated dialling** numérotation abrégée individuelle
uniqueness n unicité
uniselector n sélecteur à mouvement unique; commutateur sélectif; rotacteur; sélecteur rotatif; ~ **guide** guide d'unisélection
unit n organe; appareil; bloc; boîte; boîtier; centre; dispositif; élément; ensemble; étage; exemplaire; groupe; maquette; pièce (pce); platine; signe; ~ **area acoustic reactance** réactance acoustique intrinsèque; ~ **automatic exchange (UAX)** central de structure simplifiée; ~ **charge** (of international service) unité de taxe; ~ **code** code à éléments; code à moments; ~ **element** moment (MOM); élément unitaire; ~ **function response** caractéristique du saut; ~ **interval** intervalle unitaire; ~ **load** unité de charge; ~ **pulse response** réponse à une

action impulsive de Dirac; ~ **record** enregistrement logique; ~ **separator** (data delimiter) séparateur de sous article; mono-séparateur

units group/digit unité

unit-status signalling functions gestion de positionnements

unit status word mot d'état d'organe; ~ **string** chaîne unitaire

unity gain gain unitaire

universal *adj* polyvalent; diversifié; global; ~ **amplifier** amplificateur universel; ~ **frequency counter** compteur universel; ~ **joint** (UJ) cardan (joint c.); ~ **keyboard** clavier standard; ~ **language** langage universel; ~ **night answer** (UNA) **mode** en service réduit; ~ **product code** code à barres (CAB); ~ **repeater** répéteur universel

universal/unassigned night answer service (UNA) service réduit

unjustified *adj* mauvais cadrage

unknown *adj* inconnu; ignoré

unlatching *n* déloquetage

unless otherwise specified/indicated sauf dérogation; sauf indication au contraire

unlimited *adj* infini; ~ **access** porte ouverte

unload *v* (of tape, disk) démonter

unloaded cable câble non pupinisé; câble non chargé; ~ **line** circuit non chargé; ligne non chargée; ligne non pupinisée

unloading *n* délestage; démontage

unlocked cell cellule non protégée

unlocking *n* déverrouillage; déblocage; décrochage (D); déloquetage

unmachined *adj* nu; naturel

unmanned *adj* autonome; ~ **exchange** bureau central non surveillé; ~ **operation** exploitation sans personnel

unmarked *adj* non gravé

unmasking *n* démasquage

unmodified *adj* en mode natif; ~ **instruction** instruction primitive

unmodulated carrier porteuse non modulée

unobtainable *adj* inaccessible; ~ **number** numéro inaccessible

unpack *v* décomprimer; décondenser; détasser; éclater

unpacked *adj* éclaté

unpacking *n* éclatement; décompression; dégroupement

unpatching *n* nettoyage du logiciel

unperforated *adj* vierge; plein

unpigmented *adj* incolore

unplug *v* désenficher

unplugged *adj* déconnecté; défiché

unpopulated *adj* nu; non équipé

unpredictable *adj* imprévisible

unprocessed *adj* brut

unprogrammed *adj* implicite; vierge; ~ **branch** déroutement; ~ **memory** mémoire nue; ~ **status** virginité

unprotected area zone non protégée; zone sécable; ~ **cell** cellule non protégée

unreasonable message message irrationnel

unrecoverable *adj* irrécupérable

unrefined *adj* brut

unrelated *adj* indépendant

unreliability *n* défiabilité

unrestricted access accès parfait; accessibilité totale; ~ **direct-dialling extension** poste à prise directe intégrale; ~ **extension** poste à prise directe libre; ~ **local network dialling** sans contrôle de la numérotation (émise)

unrig *v* démonter

unsampled form forme intégrale

unscheduled *adj* non programmé

unscrambling *n* déchiffrage (déchiffrement)

unscrew *v* desserrer

unserviceability *n* défaillance

unserviceable *adj* hors service (h.s.); hors d'usage; hors fonctionnement; en panne; inopérant; inutilisable

unshaded *adj* clair (texte etc.)

unshielded cable câble non armé

unshift-on-space blanc des lettres (automatique)

unshipping *n* délestage

unsigned integer entier non signé

unskilled worker ouvrier non spécialisé; manœuvre

unsmoothed *adj* non filtré

unsolder *v* dessouder

unsophisticated *adj* artisanal; fruste

unsound contact mauvais contact

unspecified *adj* implicite

unsuccessful attempt échec; ~ **call** appel infructueux; tentative infructueuse; ~ **seizure** prise inefficace; ~ **(uncompleted) call** appel n'ayant pas abouti

unsupported hole trou mécanique; trou non métallisé

unsymmetrical grading multiplage partiel asymétrique

untapped hole trou lisse (TL)

untimed call communication non taxée à la durée

untimely *adj* intempestif

untuned aerial antenne apériodique

unused *adj* inutilisé; ~ **command/code** contrôle d'existence; ~ **number** numéro libre; numéro non utilisé

unwanted *adj* intempestif; parasite; ~ **current** flux (de trafic); ~ **echo** écho parasite; ~ **output power** puissance de sortie non essentielle; ~ **signal** signal brouilleur

unweighted *adj* non pondéré

unwinding *n* dévidage; déroulement

unwired subrack alvéole nu

unwrapping tool dérouleur; outil à déwrapper

unwritten space espace invisible

up-and-down circuit circuit mixte; voie unidirectionnelle; ~ **converters** équipement de transposition de fréquence; ~ **station** (of satellite) stations émettrice/réceptrice; ~ **working** exploitation à l'alternat

up arrow flèche verticale haute

up-chirp filter filtre à compression

up-converter (U/C) *n* étaleur de bande; transposition émission

up-counting *n* comptage

update *v* mettre à jour; actualiser; ~ *n* rafraîchissement (d'écran)

up-dating *n* mise à jour (MAJ); régularisation

up/down émission-réception (E/R); ~ **counter** compteur-décompteur; compteur réversible

upgradable *adj* extensible

upgrade *v* évoluer; actualiser; améliorer; développer; valoriser

upgrading *n* évolution; développement; enrichissement; extension; migration; mise à niveau; mise à palier; modification; nettoyage du logiciel; régularisation; ~ (of alarm condition) aggravation

upkeep *n* entretien; maintenance

up-line exchange centre amont

up-link *n* réception; trajet ascendant; trajet ascendant; montant; ~ **power control** commande de puissance à l'émission

up-loading *n* remontée; transfert de fichiers

up-locking *n* accrochage rentré

up-market *adj* haut de gamme

upper boundary majorant

upper-case (u.c.) majuscule(s); haut de casse (hdc)

upper/lower thresholds gabarit

upper pole-piece pièce polaire supérieure; ~ **sideband** bande latérale supérieure; ~ **specification boundary** limite supérieure de la spécification (LSS)

up-posting *n* indexation générique; autopostage générique

upright *n* ferme; montant

UPS (s. uninterruptible power supply)

upset distance (of welding) distance d'écrasement; ~ **pressure** (of welding) pression de refoulement

upside *n* amont

upstanding *adj* (of component on PCB) non plaqué

upstream *n* amont

up-time disponibilité; temps en service; temps exploitable

upward-compatible *adj* compatible dans le sens croissant; à compatibilité ascendante

urgency signal signal d'urgence

urgent alarm alarme immédiate; alarme intervention immédiate; alarme urgente; ~ **call** communication urgente; ~ **private call** conversation privée urgente; ~ **telegram** télégramme urgent

U/S (s. unserviceable)

usable display area écran utilisable

usage *n* emploi

usage/allocation demand factor taux de remplissage

use *n* emploi

U-section *n* profilé en U

used *adj* (of tape) non vierge

useful line ligne libre; ~ **output power** puissance utile de sortie

use of phantom circuits utilisation des circuits fantômes

user *n* utilisateur; usager; ~ **code** code utilisateur; ~ **context** contexte usager

user-defined *adj* personnalisable; choix libre; particulier; spécifique

user error fausse manœuvre; ~ **facility** installation d'abonné

user-friendliness *n* convivialité; maniabilité; souplesse extrême

user-friendly *adj* souple; orienté opérateur; personnalisé

user group groupe d'usagers; ~ **ID** (identifier) nom utilisateur; ~ **manual** notice d'exploitation; manuel d'utilisation; notice d'emploi; ~ **memory space** espace mémoire utilisateur; ~ **programs** application

user-selectable option sélection technique

user's handbook notice d'emploi

UT (universal time) **chart** carte ionosphérique TU

utility *n* outil; servitude(s); ~ **function** fonction de service; ~ **hardware** matériel de servitude; ~ **program** utilitaire; programme de service

uuF (s. micromicrofarad)

UV (s. ultra-violet); ⌁ **eraser** (drawer) tiroir d'effacement; ⌁ **exposure unit** (of PCB etching) machine à insoler; ⌁ **fluorescent tube** tube actinique

V

V(BO) (s. breakover voltage)
vacant *adj* disponible; inutilisé; libre; ~ **number** numéro non attribué; numéro inutilisé; ~ **number signal** signal de numéro non utilisé
vacuum drier étuve à vide; aspirateur; ~ **gauge** vacuomètre; ~ **photocell** cellule à vide; ~ **rectifier** kénétron; ~ **tube** lampe
vacuum-tube amplifier amplificateur à tube
vacuum-tube/thermionic-valve oscillator oscillateur à tube à vide
vacuum-tube voltmeter (VTVM) voltmètre à lampe; voltmètre électronique
vacuum valve tube à vide
VAD (s. vapour (phase) **axial deposition**)
V-aerial antenne en V
valence band bande de valence; ~ **electron** électron de valence; électron optique; électron périphérique
valid *adj* valable; signifiant
validate *v* prendre en compte; valider
validity *n* correspondance; ~ **check** contrôle de vraisemblance; contrôle d'appartenance
valid signal element élément de signal utile
valley (point) current courant de vallée
value *n* valeur; grandeur
value-added tax (VAT) threshold base TVA
valve *n* lampe; clapet; soupape; tube; ~ **base** socle de lampe (= culot)
valve-holder support de lampe; support de tube
valve tester analyseur de lampes; ~ **tube** kénétron; ~ **voltmeter** voltmètre à lampetmètre électronique
VA meter voltampèremètre
Van Allen (radiation) **belt** ceinture de Van Allen
vane *n* armature (d'un condensateur); lame; palette; ~ **attenuator** affaiblisseur à cloison longitudinale
vaned *adj* hélicoïdal
vapour (phase) axial deposition (VAD) dépôt chimique en phase vapeur
VAR (s. volt-ampere reactive); ~ (s. visual/ aural range)
varactor *n* diode à capacité variable
variable *n* variable; grandeur; ~ *adj* paramétrable; commutable; pour mémoire (PM)
variable(-frequency) oscillator (VFO) oscillateur variable

variable address adresse indexée; ~ **area track** trace à amplitude variable; ~ **attenuator** affaiblisseur réglable; affaiblisseur variable; ~ **autotransformer** alternostat
variable-block format disposition à bloc variable
variable call-forwarding renvoi commandé
variable-capacitance diode diode à capacité variable
variable capacitor condensateur réglable; condensateur variable (CV)
variable-capacity *adj* dimensionnable
variable-density track trace à densité variable
variable earth terre commutable
variable(-length) field champ variable; zone variable
variable gain préamplification variable; ~ **gain device** dispositif à amplification variable; ~ **indicator** (i,j) rang; ~ **(word) length** longueur variable
variable-length cavity cavité à longeur variable; ~ **field** zone de longueur variable; ~ **numbering plan** plan de numérotation ouverte
variable mutual-conductance valve tube à pente réglable; ~ **range ring** anneau de mesure de distance; ~ **reactance amplifier** amplificateur paramétrique; ~ **reluctance microphone** microphone à réluctance variable; ~ **resistance** rhéostat; ~ **resistor (rheostat)** résistance variable; ~ **speed** (transmission) **controller** variateur de vitesse; ~ **voltage** tension variable
variance *n* désaccord
variant card carte à variante
variation *n* écart; ~ **of attenuation with amplitude** variation d'affaiblissement en fonction de l'amplitude
variety *n* assortiment
variocoupler *n* variocoupleur
varioplex varioplex
various *adj* divers
varistor (non-linear resistor) *n* varistance; résistance VDR
varnish *n* vernis épargne (VE)
varying direct current courant continu pulsé
vault *n* (of cables) chambre souterraine
V-beam system radiodétecteur à diagramme en V
V-belt courroie trapézoïdale; courroie crantée

VCC (s. voice-controlled carrier)
V$_{cc}$ (s. component side)
VCXO (s. phase-locked oscillator); ∻ (s. voltage-controlled (crystal) oscillator)
VDR (s. voltage-dependent resistor)
VDU (s. visual display unit)
vectograph n image stéréoscopique
vector v (of interrupt) démasquer; ∼ n vecteur
vectored interrupt interruption vectorisée
vector shift décalage vectoriel
VEDAR (s. visible energy detection and ranging)
vee groove rainure en vé
vehicular adj mobile
veined adj marbré
Veitch diagram diagramme de Veitch
velocity n vitesse
velocity-modulated tube (VM) tube à modulation de vitesse
velocity-modulation television system système de télévision à modulation de vitesse du faisceau
velocity of light vitesse de lumière dans le vide
vendee n acquéreur; acheteur
vendor n fournisseur
Venetian blind effect effet de persiennes
Venn diagram diagramme de Venn
vent v décharger; purger
ventilate v aérer
ventilation panel ventouse
venting (of air valves) mise à l'échappement
Verdan system système Verdan bande pilote
verification projector machine de projection
vernacular n nom courant; terme de métier
vernier n (arrangement) démultiplicateur de vitesse; ∼ (scale) vernier; ∼ caliper pied à coulisse (PC); vérificateur; ∼ control réglage de précision
versatile adj polyvalent; souple
versatility n souplesse d'emploi
version card carte à version; ∼ code édition; (éd.)
vertex n sommet; ∼ feed alimentation axiale; ∼ plate (of aerial reflector) cache sommet
vertical bar (of distribution frame) ferme; ∼ channel (of oscilloscope) voie verticale; ∼ clearance hauteur libre; ∼ coverage zone de couverture verticale; ∼ deflection balayage vertical; ∼ deflection coefficient amplitude; ∼ directivity pattern diagramme de directivité verticale; ∼ effect effet d'antenne; ∼ format unit bande pilote; ∼ format unit load (VFL) chargement bande pilote; ∼ hold linéarité verticale; commande verticale de synchronisation
vertical-incidence ionospheric recorder son-

deur ionosphérique vertical
vertically-polarized aerial antenne polarisée verticalement; ∼ wave onde à polarisation verticale
vertical movement déplacement vertical; ∼ parity parité transversale; ∼ recording gravure en profondeur; enregistrement vertical; ∼ redundancy check (VRC) contrôle de parité transversale; parité impair transversale; ∼ reference unit centrale de verticale; ∼ registration réglage haut de page; ∼ scan (of oscilloscope) amplitude verticale; ∼ tabulation tabulation verticale; ∼ terminal block tête verticale; ∼ unipole aerial antenne verticale au sol
vertical-wire aerial antenne à fil vertical
very high frequency (VHF) très haute fréquence; ∼ lightly-loaded coil ligne à charge très légère; ∼ long range (VLR) très grande portée; ∼ long wave (VLF band) onde très longue; ∼ low frequency (VLF) très basse fréquence (TBF); ∼ low voltage très basse tension (TBT); ∼ short-range radar radar pour faible portée
vessel n récipient; bâtiment
vestigial sideband bande résiduelle; bande latérale résiduelle (BLR); bande latérale restante
vestigial-sideband transmission émission à bande latérale résiduelle
vetting n nettoyage
VF (multi-channel) telegraphy (VFT3) télégraphie à fréquences vocales; ∻ (s. voice frequency); ∻ band bande à fréquences vocales; bande téléphonique; ∻ dialling télésélection par fréquences vocales
VFL (s. vertical format unit load)
VF link liaison harmonique (deux fils et retour commun)
VFO (s. variable oscillator)
VF receiver signaleur à fréquence vocale (FV); ∻ ringing appel à fréquence vocale; ∻ signalling signalisation par ondes musicales; ∻ signalling relay set signaleur à fréquence vocale (FV); ∻ signal(ling) transformer convertisseur de courant d'appel à fréquence vocale; ∻ subscriber line abonné analogique
VFT (s. voice frequency telegraph)
VF telegraph system système harmonique; ∻ telegraphy télégraphie harmonique; ∻ telephony téléphonie à fréquence vocale; ∻ trunk jonction BF
VG (s. voice-grade); ∻ channel voie à fréquences vocales
V-groove rainure en vé
V-grooved cylinder cable câble cylindrique de

rainure; jonc cylindrique; ⌁ **cylinder structure** structure cylindrique rainurée
VHF (s. very high frequency); ⌁ **choke** self d'arrêt et de découplage
via hole trou de passage; trou de pilotage; ~ **net loss** équivalent en transit
vibrating reed lame vibrante
vibrating-reed amplifier mutateur de puissance; amplificateur à condensateur vibrant
vibrating relay relais vibrateur
vibration meter vibromètre
vibration-resistant adj antivibratile
vibration test essai de vibration
vibrator n vibreur; ~ **rectifier** redresseur vibratoire; ~ **unit** trembleur
vice n étau
vicenary (twenty-base) vicésimal
vice versa réciproquement; inversement
vicissitude n péripétie
video amplifier amplificateur vidéo; ~ **attribute** rendu visuel
videobanking télématique bancaire
video (cassette) recorder magnétoscope; ~ **clamp** alignement vidéo
videoconference n visioconférence; vidéoconférence; ~ **studio** salle de visioconférence
video current courant de vidéofréquence; ~ **detection** détection vidéo; ~ **disk** vidéodisque; ~ **display** écran vidéo; visionneuse; ~ **frame** image
video-frequency adj vidéofréquence; ~ **band** bande de vidéofréquences
video image image télévisée; ~ **library** vidéothèque; ~ **network** réseau d'images; ~ **page** page-écran
videophone n vidéophone; vidiophone; ~ **conference** vidéoconférence
videophony, (still-picture) ~ visiophonie
video picture image télévisée; ~ **pulse** impulsion vidéo; ~ **recorder** magnétoscope; vidéo-enregistreur sur film; vidigraphe; vidéo-enregistreur magnétique; ~ **recording** magnétographie; ~ **relay link** retour-image; ~ **signal** signal vidéo; image; signal de vision; signal d'image à radiofréquence; signal d'image complet; ~ **terminal** console de visualisation (CV); visu; visualisateur
videotex vidéotex; télématique; vidéographie; ~ **buying facility** téléachat; ~ **centre serveur**; ~ **enquiry** consultation de vidéotex
Videotext (interactive videography system) [T.N.] vidéotexte
video transmission bélinogramme; ~ **transmitter** émetteur vidéo; ~ **voltage** tension vidéo
view v visualiser; ~ (of file index) lister

Viewdata vidéotex; vidéographie
viewer n visionneuse; lecteur; (TV) ~ téléspectateur
view-finding n visée
viewing angle (of LED) angle de distribution; angle de vision; ~ **hood** visière; parasoleil
vinculum n surlignement
vindicate v justifier
V24 interface liaison V24
violation n viol; dépassement; violation
VIP (s. voice information processing); ⌁ **executive station** poste à appel individuel; poste superprivilégié
virgin (blank) adj vierge; ~ **blanc**; primitif; ~ **memory check** virginité
virtual (r.m.s.) value efficace; ~ **address** adresse virtuelle; ~ **address lock** verrou virtuel; ~ **address space** espace adresse; ~ **call** communication virtuelle; message virtuel; ~ **carrier frequency** fréquence porteuse virtuelle; ~ **cathode** (potential minimum surface) cathode virtuelle; ~ **circuit** circuit virtuel (CV); circuit de liaison secondaire; circuit superposé; ~ **circuit mode** mode circuit virtuel; ~ **circuit packet switching** commutation de circuits virtuels; ~ **data** données virtuelles; ~ **decision value** amplitude virtuelle de décision; ~ **junction temperature** température virtuelle de jonction
virtually immune peu sensible
virtual machine machine logique; ~ **machine environment (VME)** milieu virtuel; ~ **memory** mémoire fictive; ~ **storage** mémoire virtuelle; ~ **switching point** extrémité virtuelle; ~ **value** valeur efficace; valeur moyenne quadratique; tension alternative superposée
viscosity n traînage
Vise-Grip [T.N.] pince étau; pince de blocage
visibility factor facteur de visibilité
visible adj apparent; ~ **and invisible spectrum** lumières visibles ou invisibles; ~ **energy detection and ranging (VEDAR)** système de détection et de mesure de distance par énergie visible
vision signal signal d'image à radiofréquence
visited base station relais de passage
visual alarm alarme visuelle
visual/aural range (VAR) radiophare à quatre voies et indication optique et acoustique
visual busy signal lampe d'occupation (LO); ~ **direction-finding** relèvement visuel; ~ **display** visualisation; ~ **display console** console de visu télévidéo; ~ **display unit (VDU)** écran de visualisation; terminal cathodique; visu; visualisateur; visuel; console de visualisation (CV); ~ **examina-**

tion aspect; contrôle visuel; ~ **reception** réception enregistrée; ~ **telephony** vidéophonie

vitreous (wire-wound) **resistor** résistance vitrifiée; ~ **coating** verre de scellement

VLF (s. very low frequency)

VLR (s. very long range)

VM (s. velocity-modulated tube)

VME (s. virtual machine environment)

vocabulary n mémorisation de phrase

vocal level puissance vocale

vocational guidance orientation professionnelle; ~ **training** formation professionnelle

voice n parole; voix

voice-activated carrier activation de la porteuse par la parole

voice-actuated dialling composition vocale

voice answer-back réponse vocale

voice-band n bande à fréquences vocales; bande téléphonique; bande vocale

voice communications communication vocale; ~ **control** contrôle par la voix

voice-controlled carrier (VCC) porteuse à modulation par la parole

voice-frequency adj harmonique; ~ (VF) **transmission** transmission basse fréquence (BF)

voice frequency (VF) fréquence téléphonique; fréquence vocale (FV); basse fréquence (BF)

voice-frequency circuit circuit basse fréquence; ~ **equipment** équipement à fréquences vocales; ~ **link** liaison à fréquences vocales; ~ **multi-channel system** faisceau de télégraphie harmonique; ~ **signal** échantillon vocal; ~ **signalling** signalisation à fréquence vocale; ~ **telegraph (VFT) system** faisceau de système de télégraphie harmonique; ~ **telegraphy** télégraphie à bande vocale; télégraphie à fréquence acoustique

voice-grade (VG) adj téléphonique; ~ **channel** voie de qualité téléphonique; canal téléphonique; canal vocal; voie à fréquences vocales; ~ **circuit** circuit téléphonique; ~ **line** ligne téléphonique

voice information processing (VIP) système de reconnaissance vocale; ~ **level** niveau vocal; ~ **messaging** messagerie vocale

voice-modulated carrier porteuse modulée par une fréquence vocale

voice-operated device (anti-singing) Vodas; ~ **device for automatic transmission** Vodat; ~ **gain-adjusting device** Vogad; ~ **switching** commande par courants vocaux

voice recognition and voice synthesis board carte de reconnaissance et de synthèse vocale; ~ **signal** signal vocal; ~ **storage**

system (VSS) système de mémoire vocale; ~ **synthesizer** synthétiseur de voix

void n manque de revêtement; blanc; caractère inutile; retassure; capacité inutilisé; discontinuité de dépôt; manque de produit d'enrobage; non encrage; ~ **date** date de péremption; ~ **list** liste noire

volatile adj altérable; dynamique; non rémanent; rapide; mobile; ~ **display** affichage non rémanent; image non rémanente

voltage n tension; niveau; potentiel; ~ **adaptor** sélecteur de tension; ~ **addition** addition en tension; ~ **balance** symétrie de la tension; ~ **balancer** balance voltmétrique; ~ **between lines** différence de potentiel (d.d.p.); tension de ligne; ~ **between phases** tension de ligne; ~ **boosting** suralimentation; ~ **clamp** diode de limitation

voltage-controlled (crystal) oscillator (VCXO) oscillateur asservi en phase; oscillateur commandé en tension; oscillateur à commande par tension

voltage-dependent resistor (VDR) résistance VDR

voltage divider diviseur de tension; chaîne potentiométrique; ~ **divider bridge** pont diviseur; ~ **doubler** doubleur de tension; ~ **drop** chute de tension; conjonction; pertes de charge; tension de conjonction; ~ **factor** facteur d'amplification de tension

voltage-failure detector détecteur de défaut de tension

voltage feedback réaction de tension; ~ **follower** suiveur de tension; ~ **gain** facteur d'amplification de tension; ~ **generator** générateur de tension; ~ **level difference** différence de niveau de tension; ~ **loop** ventre de tension; ~ **offset transistor** translateur de niveau continu; ~ **plane** plan de tension; ~ **proof** rigidité diélectrique; tension de tenue

voltage-proof tester appareil de rigidité

voltage range gabarit de tension; ~ **ratio** rapport de transformation

voltage-reference tube tube étalon de tension

voltage-reflection coefficient coefficient de réflexion de la tension

voltage-regulator valve tube régulateur de tension

voltage resonance résonance de tension; ~ **response** réponse en tension; ~ **sensing** ballast

voltage-stabilizing tube tube régulateur de tension; tube stabilisateur de tension

voltage standing-wave ratio (VSWR) rapport d'amplitude de tension; taux de réflexions; ~ **surge** choc de tension; ~ **swing** excursion de la tension; ~ **to neutral** neutre

sorti; tension entre phase et neutre; ~ **transducer** traducteur de tension; ~ **transformer** transformateur de tension
voltameter *n* voltampèremètre; coulomb-mètre; ~ **test** méthode voltampèremétrique
volt-ampere reactive (VAR) voltampère réactif
volt box diviseur de tension
voltmeter *n* voltmètre; **(DC) valve** ~ voltmètre à lampe
voltohmmeter *n* voltohmmètre
volt-ohm-milliammeter (VOM) contrôleur universel
volume *n* volume; intensité; masse; profondeur; ~ (audio level) niveau d'écoute BF; ~ (of data) quantité (qté); ~ (bulk direct access store) volume; ~ **compressor** compresseur de volume; ~ **control** régulateur d'intensité; réglage de puissance
volume-control telephone appareil téléphonique à amplificateur du son
volume home block bloc de base de volume; ~ **index** répertoire de volume; ~ **indicator** indicateur de niveau sonore; volumètre; ~ **level** niveau sonore; ~ **level meter (VU-meter)** volumètre; ~ **lifetime** vie moyenne du porteur minoritaire; ~ **loss per unit length** affaiblissement de référence par

unité de longueur; ~ **of traffic** trafic écoulé; ~ **range** dynamique; ~ **range control** réglage de la dynamique; ~ **range distortion** distorsion de dynamique; ~ **rate of flow** débit volumique; ~ **recombination rate** vitesse de recombinaison volumique; ~ **resistivity** résistivité (en volume ohmique) transversale
volumetric coverage volume de couverture
volume-unit (VU) unité américaine de volume; ~ **meter** décibelmètre; indicateur de volume; ~ **of sound (VU)** décibel (dB)
volume/volumetric coverage couverture
VOM (s. volt-ohm-milliammeter); ⩰ (s. Avometer)
voucher *n* bon; papillon; volet
vowelized *adj* vocalisé
VRC (s. vertical redundancy check)
V_{ss} (s. solder side)
VSS (s. voice storage system)
VSWR (s. voltage standing-wave ratio)
VTVM (s. vacuum-tube voltmeter)
VU (volume-unit) **meter** vumètre; ⩰ (s. volume-unit)
VU-meter *n* décibelmètre; indicateur de volume; ⩰ (s. volume level meter)

W

wadding *n* bourre

wafer *n* plaquette; galette; microplaquette; plaquette gaufrée; puce; tranche; plaquette micro-élément

wages fund masse salariale

wailing *n* bruit de cornemuse

waist *n* (of lattice tower) corset

wait *n* attente

wait delay temporisation d'attente

waiting-allowed facility service complémentaire d'attente autorisée

waiting for time-out en attente temporisée

waiting-in-progress signal signal de mise en attente

waiting probability probabilité d'attente; ~ signal signal d'attente; ~ state état d'attente; ~ time délai d'attente; battement; délai de satisfaction (de la demande); durée d'attente; temps d'attente; ~ tone tonalité de garde

wait state état attente

waive *v* renoncer

waiver *n* dérogation

wake-me call service réveil automatique; ~ call time heure du réveil; ~ facility service réveil

wake-up call réveil automatique

walk-down *n* perte d'information; perte irrémédiable

walkie-talkie *n* émetteur-récepteur portatif; talkie walkie

walking *adj* progressif; ~ one un galopeur/baladeur/migrant; ~ strobe pulse impulsion de strobage progressive

walk-through *n* contrôle visuel renforcé; point de passage; passage

wall *n* cloison; cloisonnement; ~ anode anode sur la paroi; ~ chart affiche murale; ~ light hublot

wall-mounted type mural

wall socket prise de courant murale; ~ telephone téléphone mural

wall-telephone booth niche téléphonique

wall telephone set poste mural; ~ thickness surépaisseur

wand *n* baguette

wander *n* dérapage; aberration; migration; ~ lamp baladeuse (lampe b.)

wanted number numéro demandé; ~ party abonné appelé; abonné demandé (DE);

~ signal signal utile; signal désiré

warble tone mélodie; ululation; tonalité modulée; son ululé

warehouse *n* magasin

warehousing *n* stockage

warhead *n* charge militaire

warming-up period temps de mise en route

warm restart redémarrage à chaud; ~ standby secours semi-automatique; ~ start reprise partielle; démarrage à chaud; réinitialisation

warm-up *n* échauffement; période préparatoire; mise en route; ~ time préchauffage; temps de chauffage; durée d'échauffement; temps de mise en route

warn *v* signaler

warning *n* détection; ~ (system) signalisation; ~ circuit circuit d'annonce; ~ device avertisseur; ~ lamp lampe d'avertissement; ~ notice mise en garde; ~ signal signal d'alarme; ~ tone tonalité d'avertissement

warp *n* flèche; gauchissement; sabre; voilage; voile; vrillage

warped *adj* infléchi

warranty against material defects garantie pièces et main d'œuvre

washer *n* rondelle; cale (c. d'épaisseur)

washing bottle pissette

waste *n* déchets; perte; ~ instruction instruction fictive; instruction ineffective; instruction insignifiante

watch *n* veille; surveillance

watchdog (timer) *n* chien de garde; contrôleur de séquence; mouchard; surveillant(e); ~ time-out débordement du dispositif chien de garde; ~ timer dispositif de temporisation chien de garde

watch receiver récepteur de veille

water bath bain marie; ~ content état anhydre; ~ load charge à eau; charge liquide

waterproof *adj* étanche

water-repellent *adj* hydrofuge

watertight enclosure caisson étanche; ~ installation poste étanche

WATS (s. wide-area telephone service)

wattage *n* capacité de charge

wattful loss perte ohmique

wattless *adj* déwatté

wave *n* onde; ~ aerial antenne apériodique;

antenne de Beverage; ~ **analyser** analyseur d'ondes

waveband *n* bande d'ondes; ~ **switch** commutateur de gammes d'ondes

wave filter filtre d'ondes

waveform *n* forme d'onde; oscillogramme; ~ **component** composante du signal de télévision; ~ **distortion** distorsion de forme d'onde; distorsion harmonique; distorsion non linéaire; ~ **monitor** oscilloscope de contrôle de télévision; ~ **response** courbe de réponse à une action; régime transitoire; ~ **synthesis** synthèse de la forme d'onde

wave front front de l'onde; onde enveloppe; ~ **generator** générateur d'ondes

waveguide *n* guide d'onde(s); ~ **bend** guide d'ondes coudé; ~ **characteristic** impédance d'onde caractéristique; ~ **conditions** conditions de guidage; ~ **excitation** excitation d'un guide d'ondes

waveguide-fed aerial antenne alimenté par un guide d'ondes

waveguide filter filtre de guide d'ondes; ~ **gasket** joint d'étanchéité

waveguide impedance impédance d'onde

waveguide shim joint plein; ~ **switch** commutateur de guide d'ondes

wave-interference error erreur de trajets multiples

wavelength *n* longueur d'onde; ~ **constant** constante de déphasage; ~ **of light** (lightwave) onde lumineuse; ~ **shortening** raccourcissement de la longueur d'onde; ~ **switching** commutation fréquentielle

wave meter cymomètre; fréquencemètre; ondemètre; ondomètre; ~ **motion** mouvement ondulatoire; ~ **peak** crête d'onde; ~ **range selector** commutateur de gammes d'ondes

wave-soldering machine machine à souder à la vague

wave surge front raide; ~ **tilt** inclinaison de l'onde de sol

wave-train frequency fréquence de train d'ondes

wave transposition croisement d'onde; ~ **trap** circuit bouchon; circuit anterésonant; ~ **washer** rondelle Onduflex [A.C.]; ~ **winding** enroulement ondulé

wax impregnated imprégnation cire

way *n* (of multicore cable) point; pôle

waybill feuille de route

way circuit système à postes embrochés; ~ **station** relais ·

WD (s. write instruction)

weak coupling couplage lâche; ~ **current** courant faible; ~ **signal** signal faible

wear *n* usure

wearing connector connecteur d'usure; ~ **part** *adj* pièce d'usure

wear-out *n* dégradation progressive

weatherproof telephone poste étanche

weather report radiodiffusion météorologique

weather-reporting station station de diffusion de renseignements météorologiques

weather-resistant *adj* inaltérable

weather satellite service service par satellite météorologique

web *n* toile; bande; ~ **offset** (of screen printing) décalage de trame

wedge *n* cale (c. d'épaisseur); coin; entretoise; ~ **lamp** lampe Liliput

weekday *n* jour ouvrable

weekly log état hebdomadaire

weeping *n* ressuage; suintement

weighing machine pont bascule

weight *n* poids; masse; ~ (coefficient) pondérateur

weighted code code pondéré; ~ **noise** bruit pondéré; ~ **sum** sommation pondérée; ~ **value of a current** valeur pondérée d'un courant; ~ **value of a voltage** valeur pondérée d'une tension

weighting *n* pondération; facteur de correction; ~ (factor) majoration (MAJ); coefficient de pondération; ~ **network** réseau pondérateur; réseau filtrant

weight per unit length (of conductor) poids linéaire d'un câble

weld *n* bourrelet

welded *adj* soudé

welded-contact rectifier redresseur à contact par pointe soudé

welded on posé au soudage; ~ **rack** bâti mécano-soudé; châssis; ~ **steel** acier mécano-soudé

welding *n* soudage; soudure; ~ (of contacts) collage; ~ **bulge** point de soudure; ~ **frame** cadre de soudage; ~ **rod** baguette de soudure; ~ **set** poste de soudure; soudeuse; ~ **tongs** pince à souder

well *n* puits; alvéole; fossé; réservoir; bac; ~ **strobe** créneau

welter *n* enchevêtrement

west spot faisceau ouest

wet-bulb temperature température humide

wet cell pile liquide

wetting *n* mouillage; ~ **capacity** mouillabilité; ~ **current** courant de mouillage

Wheatstone automatic transmission system système Wheatstone; ~ **bridge** pont de Wheatstone

wheel-and-track mount (of aerial) monture type carrousel

where applicable éventuellement; s'il y a lieu

where-used (information, file, etc.) cas d'em-

ploi; ~ **list** liste des besoins
whine n jappement
whip aerial antenne-fouet
whirly-bird n chargeur de disques
whistle v (of circuit) amorcer
white adj blanc; opale; ~ (cast) **iron** fer blanc;
~ **level** niveau du blanc; ~ **noise** bruit
blanc; bruit à spectre continu et uniforme
whiter-than-white ultra-blanc; dépassement
d'amplitude; surblanc
white-space tabulation saut d'espaces à haute
vitesse
white spot carré blanc; ~ **spot inverter**
inverseur de parasites
white-star indicator indicateur optique en
étoile
who-are-you ? (WRU) qui est là? demande
d'indicatif
whole n ensemble; ~ adj entier; global;
~ **number** nombre entier
wholesale price prix brut
wicking n remontée de soudure
wide-aperture aerial antenne à large ouverture; ~ **direction finder** radiogoniomètre à
grande ouverture
wide-area telephone service (WATS) service
interurbain planifié; service à plein temps
wide-band adj (sweep) à fréquence variable
wideband aerial antenne à large bande;
~ **amplifier** amplificateur à bande large;
~ **channel** canal à large bande; ~ **circuit**
circuit à large bande; ~ **dipole** dipôle à
large bande; ~ **filter** filtre à large bande;
~ **noise** bruit large bande; ~ **signal** signal à
large bande; ~ **sweep transmitter** émetteur
à fréquence variable; ~ **system** système à
large bande
wide load convoi exceptionnel; charge encombrante
widespread adj répandu; courant; dispersé;
généralisé
wide-sweep radar radiodétecteur panoramique
widow n ligne isolée; ligne veuve; ~ **adjust**
élimination des lignes isolées
width control (of TV) commande de largeur
d'image
Wien bridge oscillator oscillateur à pont de
Wien
wild-card character caractère de substitution;
métacaractère
winch n treuil
winchester disk disque dur; disque rigide
winch line (of cable laying) filin de tirage
winding n enroulement; bobinage; spire
morte; ~ **bench** banc à bobiner; ~ **drum**
(for film) spire; ~ **machine** machine à
bobiner; ~ **resistance** résistance des enroulements

window n fenêtre; circuit à déclenchement
périodique; enveloppe; hublot; évidement;
~ (of pulse height selector) fenêtre
d'anticipation
"window" (of ECM foil strips) nuage de
bandelettes
window detector détecteur à double seuil;
détecteur à deux limites
windowing n fénétrage
wing n aile; bras; branche; ~ **nut** écrou à
oreilles; écrou O
wipe n commutation par volet; ~ **area** zone de
contact (utile); partie utile
wiper n balai collecteur; brosse de lecture;
frotteur
wire v brancher (sur); raccorder; ~ n fil;
artère; câble; câblogramme; conducteur;
cordon; fil métallique; ligne; télégramme;
~ adj métallique; ~ **bonding** montage
thermosonique de fil; ~ **broadcast** radiodistribution; ~ **brush** brosse métallique;
~ **bundle** nappe de fils; ~ **bush** passe-fil(s);
~ **clinch** pique-fil; ~ **communication**
communication par fil
wire-connected lamp présence de fils
wire connection liaison métallique; ~ **crimping** sertissage; ~ **cutter** coupe-fil
wired backplane cadre arrière câblé; ~ **broadcasting** câblodistribution; ~ **city** ville
câblée
wired-in (type) à souder; ~ **check** contrôle
câblé; ~ **software** logiciel câblé
wired logic logique statique; automate câblé;
~ **logic circuit** logique
wired-OR circuit montage à OU câblé
wired program programme câblé; ~ **program
computer** calculateur à programme câblé
wired(-up) for câblage prévu pour
wired wireless télégraphie à bande vocale;
système harmonique; télégraphie harmonique
wire grating filtre à fils; ~ **group** nappe;
~ **guide** passage de fil
wireless n télégraphie sans fil (TSF); ~ **operator** télégraphiste; ~ **telegraphy** radiotélégraphie; ~ **telephony** téléphonie sans fils
wireman n câbleur
wire-mounted crystal cristal monté sur fil
métallique
wire pair paire de fils; paire métallique;
~ **printer** imprimante à aiguilles; imprimante matricielle; imprimante par points
wire-pulling device tréfileuse
wire rod fil machine; ~ **routing** tracé (de
carte); ~ **soldering** thermi-point
wire-tap n écoute téléphonique
wire-tapping espionnage téléphonique
wire-twisting tool touret moteur; torsadeur

wire-wound *adj* bobiné; ~ **potentiometer** potentiomètre bobiné; ~ **resistor** résistance bobinée; ~ **rheostat** rhéostat bobiné
wire-wrap connection connexion enroulée; connexion à enroulement; ~ **lug** patte à wrapper
wire-wrapper *n* (person) câbleuse
wire wrapping connexion de fils par enroulement
wire-wrap remover outil à déwrapper; ~ **tool** pistolet à wrapper
wiring *n* câblage; acheminement; branchement; canalisations électriques; connexion; embrochage; filerie; raccordement; ~ **bench** cadre de travail; ~ **board** planche à câbler; ~ **diagram** schéma de câblage; schéma des connexions; ~ **duct** pavé; ~ **error** erreur de câblage; ~ **fault** erreur de câblage; ~ **harness** peigne de câblage; ~ **layout** cheminement; ~ **machine** câbleuse; ~ **magazine** magasin à fils; ~ **panel** bac à fils; panier; panneau de câblage (PC); ~ **plane** plan de câblage; ~ **scissors** ciseaux de câbleur; ~ **side** (of PCB) côté soudure; ~ **tool** peigne de quadrillage
with back-up AC source secouru par le secteur; ~ **camp-on facility** à attente
withdraw *v* résilier; supprimer
withdrawn line abonnement résilié
withdraw - serial call retrait avec chaînage
with drop-and-insert capability dérivable; ~ **full complement** chargé
within tolerance dans les limites des tolérances
with min./max. output en mini-maxi
without a break sans interruption; ~ **boosting** non entretenu; ~ **caption** (keys) non gravé; ~ **flange** débridé; ~ **handshaking** non asservi; ~ **resistance** retour libre
with vowels vocalisé
wobblestick *n* rupteur à tige
woofer *n* haut-parleur de graves; haut-parleur pour basses fréquences
word *n* mot; parole; ~ **articulation** netteté pour les mots; articulation des mots; ~ **chaining** articulation des mots
wording *n* libellé; parole
word intelligibility netteté des mots; ~ **interval** intervalle de mots; ~ **length** longueur de mot; ~ **processing** traitement automatique de textes
word-processing *adj* dactylographique
word processor machine à traitement de texte
word-processor networking télétraitement de texte (télétex)
word processor operator bureauticienne; ~ **slice** tranche de mot
words per minute (w.p.m.) mots par minute

work *n* (energy, heat) énergie mécanique; ~ **area** partition
workbench *n* banc de montage; ~ **shears** cisaille d'établi
worker logic unit pilote logique
worker-standby system système actif-réserve
work file fichier de travail
workforce *n* main d'œuvre; effectif; ressources humaines
work function travail de sortie
working *n* exploitation; fonctionnement; ~ *adj* actif; ~ **area** zone de manœuvre; zone de travail; ~ **current** courant de commande; ~ **day** jour ouvrable; ~ **document** dossier de travail; ~ **drawing** dessin d'atelier; dessin d'exécution; ~ **example(s)** cas d'exploitation; ~ **file** fichier de manœuvre; ~ **frequency** fréquence de fonctionnement; ~ **life** autonomie de fonctionnement; ~ **line** liaison normale; ~ **load** charge de service; ~ **order** état de fonctionnement; ~ **party** groupe de travail; ~ **range** plage de fonctionnement; ~ **reference telephone circuit (WRTC)** circuit téléphonique étalon de travail; ~ **standard** système étalon de travail; ~ **storage** mémoire de travail; mémoire banale; ~ **surface** tablette de travail; ~ **tape** bande de manœuvre; ~ **temperature** température de fonctionnenent; température de régime; température de service; ~ **time** temps d'exploitation; ~ **voltage** tension de service; tension de fonctionnement; tension d'emploi; tension de polarisation; tension d'utilisation
work-in-progress queue file d'attente d'exécution; file de tâches en exécution
workload *n* charge
work queue file de travail (informatique)
worksheet *n* page mémoire de travail
workshift *n* équipe
workshop manual livre technique; notice de réglage; ~ **procurement** lancement en atelier
workstation *n* poste de travail; ~ **cluster** grappe de stations; ~ **instruction sheet** fiche de poste; ~ **layout sheet** fiche de configuration
work study étude chronométrique
world numbering zone zone de numérotage mondial
worm (gear) vis sans fin
worst-case *adj* le cas le plus défavorable; dans le cas pire; le plus défavorisé
wound spirally enroulé en hélice
wow *n* pleurage; papillotement
w.p.m. (s. words per minute)
wraparound *n* renouement; bouclage; boucle;

rebouclage; report circulaire; rouleau; ~ **list** liste en anneau

wrapper *n* enveloppe

wrapping *n* emballage; connexion par enroulement

wreck *n* bourrage de cartes

wrecked *adj* épavé

wrench *n* clé; clef

write *v* écrire; désigner; enregistrer; inscrire (sur); mémoriser; prendre en charge; introduire; ~ (to address) incriminer; ~ **address** adresse d'écriture; ~ **address bus** ligne d'adresse d'écriture; ~ **back** reporter; ~ **buffer** amplificateur d'écriture; ~ **cycle** cycle écriture; ~ **date** date d'écriture

write-enable validation de l'écriture; ~ **ring** anneau d'autorisation d'écriture; bague d'autorisation d'écriture

write forward *n* écriture avant; ~ **head** tête d'écriture; tête d'inscription

write-in *n* inscription

write-inhibit ring bague d'interdiction d'écriture

write instant instant d'écriture; ~ **instruction (WD)** instruction d'écriture

write-permit ring anneau d'autorisation d'écriture; bague d'autorisation d'écriture

write-protect notch encoche de protection en écriture; ~ **sticker** onglet de protection

writer *n* éditeur

write strobe output échantillonnage écriture

write-then-read relecture

write-through cache antémémoire d'écriture

write time slot instant d'écriture; ~ **to disk** écriture disque

writing *n* écriture; désignation; enregistrement; mémorisation; prise en charge; rédaction; ~ (section of tape store) réception; ~ **bar** couteau d'impression; ~ **edge** couteau d'impression; ~ **speed** vitesse d'exploration à la réception

written space point de conduite

wrong *adj* faux; erroné; invalide; ~ **connection** fausse connexion; ~ **number** faux numéro; numéro erroné

wrought alloy alliage corroyé; alliage de transformation; ~ **article** pièce ouevrée

WRTC (s. working reference telephone circuit)

WRU (s. who-are-you signal)

wye (Y) connection étoile

X

X-axis axe des X
X-band amplifier amplificateur en bande X;
∼ **oscillator** oscillateur en bande X
XCVR (s. transceiver)
xenon flash tube tube à éclat
X-OFF caractère d'arrêt
X-ON (transmitter on) reprise de transmission
XPOL (s. cross-polarization)
XPOLAR (s. cross-polarization)
X-ray *n* radio(graphie); ∼ **photography**
radioscopie
XS3 (s. excess-three code)
X-Y addressing adressage en XY; ∼ **axis
cross-slide** table mobile en X-Y; ∼ **plane** (of
numerical control) axe de cotation; ∼
plotter enregistreur X-Y; pointeur à coordonnées; ∼ **plotting table** table X-Y;
traceur de courbes; ∼ **recorder** variplotter;
∼ **selector** sélecteur X-Y; ∼ **traversing
table** table mobile en X-Y

Y

Y (s. wye)
Yagi aerial antenne Yagi; antenne à rayonnement longitudinal
yardstick *n* référence
yaw angle angle de lacet; ~ **axis** axe de lacet
Y-axis *n* axe des Y; axe de l'ordonnée
Y-circulator circulateur Y
Y-connection connexion en étoile
Y-coupler coupleur en Y

year (of manufacture) millésime
yes/no test essai par tout ou rien
yield point limite élastique; limite d'élasticité; ~ **strength** charge à la rupture
yoke *n* bobine de déviation; butée; carcasse; chape; déviateur; étrier; ~ (of printer) bloc; ~ (of transformer) gorge; ~ **assembly** (of CRT) collier de déviation

Z

Zamak [T.N.] special high-grade low melting-point zinc alloy Zamak

zap v purger

Z component composante Z

Zener diode diode de Zener

zenithal angle angle zénithal

zero (relative level) point point de niveau relatif zéro; point de passage par zéro

zero-access store mémoire à accès rapide

zero-address instruction instruction sans adresse

zero beat battement nul; battement zéro

zero-beat frequency fréquence identique à battement nul; ~ reception réception synchrone

zero-bias tube tube à polarisation nulle

zero-blocking n blocage nul

zero capacity capacité résiduelle; ~ carrier porteuse zéro; ~ catcher radar récepteur d'avion de guet; ~ clearing amélioration du minimum; amélioration du zéro; ~ conductor conducteur neutre; ~ detector régulateur suiveur

zero-filled adj garni (d'espaces/de zéros)

zero-frequency component composante de la fréquence zéro; ~ signalling signalisation à fréquence zéro

zeroizing n remise à zéro (RZ/RAZ)

zero level niveau zéro

zero-level address adresse directe; ~ sensitivity sensibilité rapportée au niveau zéro

zero line ligne zéro

zero-loss circuit circuit sans perte

zero modulation condition non modulée

zero-phase modulation modulation de phase nulle

zero plan (null attenuation) plan zéro

zero-point energy énergie au zéro absolu

zero power resistance (R_T) résistance normale à dissipation nulle; ~ print key (jargon) binoquet

zero-range approximation approximation de portée zéro; ~ origin origine de portée zéro

zero relative level niveau relatif zéro; ~ setting (of amplifier) réglage du zéro; ~ shift glissement du zéro; ~ signal signal zéro; ~ signal current courant permanent d'anode; ~ signal screen current courant d'écran en absence de signaux

zero-skip frequency (ZSF) fréquence critique de saut

zero stability stabilité de point zéro; ~ suppression suppression des blancs

zero-time reference référence de temps zéro

zero transmission level point point de niveau relatif zéro

zig-zag aerial antenne en dents de scie; ~ reflection réflexions multiples

zinc-electroplated steel acier galvanisé

Zobel (electric-wave) filter filtre de Zobel

zonal blocking verrouillage par zone

zone bit bit hors texte; ~ blanking suppression d'un secteur

zoned lens lentille à échelons

zoned-lens aerial antenne lentille à zones

zone levelling/splitting nivellement en zones; ~ position indicator (ZPI) radar auxiliaire à faisceau mince; ~ punch zone de perforation

zone-punching perforation hors texte

zone selector sélecteur de zone

zoning n découpage

zoom n (of CRT display) loupe

zooming n (of satellite photography) sectorisation

Z-parameter n paramètre de résistance

ZPI (s. zone position indicator)

Z polarity polarité Z

ZSF (s. zero-skip frequency)

Z transfer function transfert en Z

Z transform transformée en Z